NEW TESTAMENT EPISTLES

PAUL'S PRISON EPISTLES

A CRITICAL & EXEGETICAL COMMENTARY ON EPHESIANS, COLOSSIANS, PHILEMON, & PHILIPPIANS

_____ *by* _____

GARETH L. REESE

HEAD OF NEW TESTAMENT DEPARTMENT
CENTRAL CHRISTIAN COLLEGE OF THE BIBLE
MOBERLY, MISSOURI

Scripture Exposition Books, LLC
803 McKINSEY PLACE
MOBERLY, MISSOURI
65270

The information in this book is intended for personal study as well as classroom and pulpit use by Bible students and teachers. Therefore, readers who wish to produce any of the comments or Special Studies in the form of free handouts to students or listeners, or in sermon outlines as they are being preached, are encouraged to do so with no need to seek prior permission. We ask that you simply include a line giving credit to the source you have copied.

ACKNOWLEDGMENT

The Scripture quotations contained herein, unless otherwise noted, are from the New American Standard Bible®, copyrighted© 1960, 1962, 1963, 1968, 1971, 1972, 1973, 1975, 1977, 1995 by the Lockman Foundation. Used by permission. www.Lockman.org

ISBN: 978-0-9984518-0-0

Dedication

This book is dedicated to all the faithful Christians who for three generations have supported Central Christian College of the Bible.   They were responsible for the College's beginning, and they have then helped keep it going through their prayers for God's help and their own faithful stewardship of God's blessings to them.

FORWARD by Lloyd M. Pelfrey

Intense! That's the word that best describes Gareth L. Reese in any task that he undertakes, including the writing of this commentary on the books of the New Testament that are designated as the Prison Epistles.

If Professor Reese writes a new commentary, one thing is certain: you do not have to examine 10-12 others so as to consider the varying views. He has already done that for you, and the reader benefits from the intense research that he has invested for the benefit of anyone who wants to learn more.

I first became aware of Gareth in his freshman year of college in 1950. His intensity soon became known to the other students. If he were outside engaged in a pickup game on campus – stick ball, softball, or whatever the game – for him it was not just a game to be played, but a game to be won.

That same attitude was with him in the classroom as well. He intended to do his best and to excel. An illustration is the writing of term papers. On one occasion, most of the other students were submitting papers with the minimum number of pages, and on subjects that were helpful, but somewhat routine. That was not Gareth Reese. He chose a topic on which there was (and still is) disagreement among the scholars. It seemed that his real goal was to resolve the issue. He went to work, burned the proverbial midnight oil, and turned in a paper of 29 pages that represented more hours of work than there were pages in what he wrote. That was in the day when the hours of research and writing were followed by typing with manual typewriters.

The same patterns continued in his work for his first two graduate degrees. There was a difference, however, for now the numbers of the pages reached as many as 500 pages. That was Gareth Reese, the young scholar.

In the fall of 1957 the Reeses, Gareth and Kathy, came to Moberly for the beginning of a new Bible college: Central Christian College of the Bible. That same word, "intense," continued as Professor Reese situated himself on the other side of the desk. His classes became popular with the students, and they wanted to take any class which he taught.

The students loved his dynamic presentations in the classrooms. They soon learned, however, that he demanded much from them in return – just as he had always demanded much from himself. The good students knew that the types of tests that he gave required hours of preparation, and the tests themselves were lengthy.

In those early days the students also did something else: they took notes, copious notes! It soon became obvious that it would really be helpful to the professor and the students if there were detailed notes ready to distribute. The first forms of those projects were mimeographed notes. Kathy worked beside him in these efforts, and the two of them gave greatly of themselves for those who wanted to understand the Word of God. Only those people who have typed stencils for a mimeograph can understand the accuracy that is required in typing stencils.

Those notes became his first "commentary" for the first book he would produce. They were the prelude to what became a goal that was forming in his mind – perhaps writing commentaries on every book of the New Testament.

The first publication came off the presses in 1966. Professor Reese provided a commentary on the book of Acts. The result was a lengthy commentary, and it had several "special studies" on some of those knotty topics. This 690-page work was based on the American Standard Bible, which was the basic text for the college at that time.

Later, however, the New American Standard Bible was published, and it became the recommended text for the classes in Bible. The new translation combined with other factors to cause the professor to put forth the effort to use the NASB for the new edition of his commentary. That was a prodigious task, and he gave himself to it. The first copies of the revised edition were ready for distribution in 1976, and the number of pages had increased from 690 pages to almost 1,000 pages, and ... it had a detailed index.

The impact of Professor Reese's first commentaries became significant in several ways, as shown in these illustrations.

1. A professor of New Testament said that he had thought about writing a new commentary on the book of Acts. After he saw Reese's book, he abandoned his proposed project.

2. A former teacher in a Bible college was in California, and he was trying to win a space engineer to Christ. The teacher then loaned his volume of Reese's commentary on Acts, and the engineer read it. The accuracy and documentation in the commentary convinced him, and he became just a Christian.

3. A phone call came to the office of CCCB during the inter-semester break. The caller identified himself   as being with a non-instrumental church of Christ

school, and he wanted to know if this were the college where Professor Reese taught. He had called for this reason: the school where he taught was using Reese's commentary on Acts, and they had heard that Reese now had another commentary. If so, the school wanted to obtain copies of it also.

4. A great tribute to Professor Reese's commentaries is that missionaries have made the efforts to translate it into other languages. Acts was completed in Russian in 1996, and Romans in 2004. Lucma Adolphe in Haiti is working on a translation into French. Others have started such projects, and we trust that with the Lord's help they, too, will be completed.

Through the decades other commentaries have been printed. Each one began as teaching notes, and then developed into researched, documented commentaries. Following is a listing of these works, according to their order in English Bibles, with publication dates.

Romans, 1987
1 Corinthians, 2004
2 Corinthians and Galatians, 2004
Timothy and Titus, 1999 and 2007
Hebrews, 1992 and 2008
James and 1, 2 & 3 John, 2007
1 & 2 Peter and Jude, 2004

That 29-page term paper – it was just the beginning. The total number of pages for the exegetical comments and the indices in the previous works from Professor Reese is well over 5,000 pages. The work in your hands adds to that total.

The primary purpose of a *Foreword* is to show why a person should obtain and read the book at hand. Based on my knowing Gareth L. Reese (Professor Emeritus of New Testament) for many decades, and being aware of his thorough and intense preparations throughout those years, it is my pleasure to recommend this book if you want to know more about the Prison Epistles in the New Testament. If you have already made the purchase – congratulations! If you are considering a purchase, it is simply logical that you will "obtain and read" this book.

Lloyd M. Pelfrey, President Emeritus, and Professor Emeritus of Old Testament
December, 2016

TABLE OF CONTENTS

Note that each epistle is begun with a concise introduction followed by verse-by-verse comments. A Detailed Introductory Study for each of these Prison Epistles is included in the back of this book.

GENERAL INTRODUCTION TO THE PRISON EPISTLES

Page

A. The Prison Epistles Form Group Three of Paul's Letters 1
B. The Book of Acts Names Several Places Where Paul Was Imprisoned 4
C. The Place of Writing
    1. Was it Philippi? 7
    2. Was it Ephesus? 8
    3. Was it Caesarea? 15
    4. Rome is the place of writing 17
D. The Date of Writing and the Order of Composition of the Prison Epistles... 21
E. Authorship of the Prison Epistles 25

THE EPISTLE "TO THE EPHESIANS"

Concise Introduction 29
    Outline of Ephesians 31

Commentary
    Chapter 1 37
    Chapter 2 75
    Chapter 3 108
    Chapter 4 133
    Chapter 5 183
    Chapter 6 224

THE EPISTLE "TO THE COLOSSIANS"

Concise Introduction 261
    Outline of Colossians 262

Commentary
    Chapter 1 265
    Chapter 2 304
    Chapter 3 339
    Chapter 4 372

THE EPISTLE "TO PHILEMON"

Concise Introduction 399
    Outline of Philemon 401

Commentary
    Chapter 1 403

THE EPISTLE "TO THE PHILIPPIANS"

Concise Introduction 429
    Outline of Philippians 430

Commentary
    Chapter 1 433
    Chapter 2 470
    Chapter 3 510
    Chapter 4 543

DETAILED INTRODUCTIONS
TO THE PRISON EPISTLES

EPHESIANS
    Historical Allusions 578
    Destination 583
    Authorship and Attestation 593
        The importance of the study of authorship 593
        Internal and external evidence concerning the authorship 595
        An overview of higher criticism's denial of the Pauline authorship.... 598
        Conclusion: The evidence points to the Pauline authorship 602
    Time and Place of Writing 603
    Occasion and Purpose of Writing 604

(Continued on next page)

EPHESIANS, continued
Other Critical Issues
    1. The similarity of Ephesians and Colossians has proven difficult ... 605
    2. The relationship of Ephesians to the other Pauline epistles 607
    3. Concerning the relation between Ephesians and 1 Peter 608
    4. Which letter (Colossians or Ephesians) was written first? 609
Ephesians in the Hands of Contemporary Interpreters 612
    1. Genre 613
    2. Life-setting 614
    3. A proliferation of new methods and approaches 615
Contents 623

COLOSSIANS
Historical Allusions 627
The City of Colossae and the Founding of the Church There 631
    1. The city 631
    2. The church 636
Authorship and Attestation
    Internal evidence 640
    External evidence 640
    The Pauline authorship has been questioned/rejected
        mainly on internal grounds 644
    The Pauline authorship has been stoutly defended 648
    There is no irrefutable reason to question the Pauline authorship 653
The Colossian Crisis
    Allusions to the teachings and practices of the religious system 655
    Brief introduction to 2nd and 3rd century Gnosticism 660
    Compatibility with incipient Gnosticism 666
    The Christology of Colossians 672
Time and Place of Writing 673
Occasion and Purpose of Writing 674
Critical Matters
    1. The Epistle from Laodicea 675
    2. Early Christian hymns copied? 677
    3. How were these Prison Epistles sent out? 679

PHILEMON

Historical Allusions 681
Why is This Epistle Included in the New Testament? 687
Authorship and Attestation
    Internal evidence for the Pauline authorship 690
    External evidence for the Pauline authorship 691
Date and Destination
    Date and place of writing 693
    Destination 693
Occasion and Purpose of Writing 696
Critical Matters
    "Right of Sanctuary" 699
    Is this letter an allegory of the work of Christ? 700
    Location in the canon 700

PHILIPPIANS

Historical Allusions 703
History of Philippi and the Philippian Church
    1. The location of Philippi 708
    2. History of Philippi 709
    3. History of the Philippian church in the apostolic age 711
    4. Post-apostolic history of the church and town 712
Authorship and Attestation
    Internal evidence 713
    External evidence of the Pauline authorship 714
    Since the mid 1800s, some have tried to deny Pauline authorship 717
    Most modern scholars no longer attempt to deny Pauline authorship 719
Place of Writing 719
Date of Writing 719
Occasion of Writing 720
Critical Issues
    The integrity of the epistle 721
    The controversy over the interpretation of Philippians 2:5-11 724
        What title shall we use to designate these verses? 726
        The form and structure of Philippians 2:5-11 in modern research 727
        The authorship of Philippians 2:6-11 728
        The search for the source of the alleged ancient hymn 730
        The real issue modern critics are facing is the high Christology
          of these verses 732

(Continued on the next page)

PHILIPPIANS, continued
  Critical Issues, continued
      The controversy over the interpretation of Philippians 2:5-11, continued
        Was the concept that Jesus is God an idea that developed
          slowly?.. 751
        The place and purpose of these verses in the letter 753
        The views taken in this commentary 755
      The meaning of *pistis christou* in Philippians 3:9............................... 756
      Paul's opponents in chapter 3 760
      Purpose/genre 764

Index .... I-1 thru I-29

THE PRISON EPISTLES

General Introduction[1]

A. THE PRISON EPISTLES FORM GROUP THREE OF PAUL'S LETTERS.[2]

Numerous features tie together the New Testament letters known to us as Ephesians, Philippians, Colossians, and Philemon.

1. These letters are **all signed by Paul** (Ephesians 1:1, 3:1; Philippians 1:1; Colossians 1:1; Philemon 1,19), and the uniform testimony of early Christian literature is that these epistles were written by Paul[3] from Rome during his two-year imprisonment there as recorded in Acts 28:30-31. This is the position which our studies have also led us to adopt.

2. These letters have been called **the Prison Epistles** because in all of them the writer indicates that he is a prisoner at the time he writes the letters (Ephesians 3:1, 4:1, 6:20; Philippians 1:7,13; Colossians 4:3,18; Philemon 1,10,13,23). The reason he is now a prisoner is that he has been fulfilling his commission as apostle to the Gentiles (Philippians 1:13).[4] In Philippians 1:7 he speaks of his "imprisonment" (literally, "bonds") "in the defense and confirmation of the gospel." Again in 1:14 he refers to how his imprisonment has caused many brethren to have greater courage to speak the word of God without fear.

---

[1] Ordinarily, the first thing we do in the study of the epistles is to search each letter for any historical allusions that will help us determine the author, date, destination, place, and purpose of writing. However, in this case, as we begin with a general introduction to the Prison Epistles, it seems more appropriate to call attention to the similarities found in the Prison Epistles, and then later to search for the specific historical allusions as part of a special Detailed Introduction to each letter.

[2] The Thessalonian letters form Group #1. 1 & 2 Corinthians, Galatians and Romans form Group #2. The Pastoral Epistles (1 & 2 Timothy and Titus) form Group #4.

[3] Since some contemporary scholars have attempted to repudiate the Pauline authorship, especially of Ephesians and Colossians, these modern denials of the Pauline authorship will be examined and refuted in the Detailed Introductory Studies to the various letters.

[4] Paul, as he writes, feels that in suffering thus he may expect the sympathy and prayers of his readers. He expresses the hope that through the prayers of his friends he may be set at liberty.

In Philippians 1:13 Paul tells us the cause of his imprisonment has become "well-known throughout the whole praetorian guard and to everyone else."

In Colossians 4:18, as he concludes his letter, Paul exhorts the readers to "Remember my imprisonment."

In Ephesians 3:1 and 4:1, Paul calls himself the "prisoner of Christ Jesus for the sake of you Gentiles" and a "prisoner of the Lord."

In Ephesians 6:20, Paul characterizes himself as an "ambassador in chains" who nevertheless asks for their prayers that he may represent the gospel as he had been sent by Christ to do.

In verse 1 of Philemon, as he signs this letter, Paul speaks of himself as "a prisoner of Christ Jesus." In verse 9, Paul identifies himself as "the aged" person, and "now also a prisoner of Christ Jesus." In verse 10, Paul speaks of how Onesimus has become Paul's spiritual child by being begotten by Paul during what he calls "my imprisonment." Onesimus has been led to Christ by Paul while Paul was in prison.

These references to imprisonment imply that it has been of considerable duration, thus distinguishing it from those brief imprisonments which Paul had previously experienced before the close of the third missionary journey (2 Corinthians 11:23).

3. Ephesians, Philippians, Colossians, and Philemon are generally considered to have been **written at nearly the same time** in Paul's life, and have been called "Group Three of Paul's letters."[5]

   a. Several features indicate Colossians and Philemon were written together. Onesimus, the slave whom Paul is returning to his master Philemon, is mentioned as accompanying both the letters to the Colos-

---

[5] Paul's letters naturally fall into four different groups because of certain marked characteristics as to subject and time of writing. Group #1 includes the Thessalonian epistles, written from Paul's second missionary journey and emphasizing the subject of eschatology. Group #2 includes 1 and 2 Corinthians, Galatians, and Romans. They were written toward the close of Paul's third missionary journey and deal with soteriology. Group #3 consists of the Prison Epistles; they emphasize Christology. Group #4 consists of the Pastoral Epistles which come from a date after Paul's first Roman imprisonment, and emphasize ecclesiology.

sians (4:9) and to Philemon (10-11). Archippus receives messages in both letters (Colossians 4:17; Philemon 2). The same Pauline associates send greetings in both (Colossians 4:10-14; Philemon 23,24).

b. Ephesians and Colossians were sent out at the same time and carried to their destinations by the same carrier. That carrier/messenger is Tychicus, whose assignment to report orally about Paul's circumstances is given in almost identical words (Ephesians 6:21, 22; Colossians 4:7,8).[6]

"It is particularly the similarity of the contents, so that Ephesians and Colossians have been regarded as companion if not twin epistles, which links these two letters together and makes a parallel study desirable."[7]

c. The letter to Philemon was sent at the same time as Ephesians and Colossians (Colossians 4:7-9; Philemon 10-12,23,24; Ephesians 6:21,22).

d. Philippians, it is commonly assumed, was written either sometime before the other three, or sometime after the other three, and carried by a different messenger (Epaphroditus, Philippians 2:25-28).

4. **The people surrounding Paul** are the same in these letters, indicating the letters came from the same time period in Paul's life.

a. *Timothy* – Colossians 1:1; Philippians 1:1, 2:19; Philemon 1
(Timothy accompanied Paul on his journey to Jerusalem, Acts 20:4.)

b. *Luke* – Colossians 4:14; Philemon 24
(The "we-passages" indicate Luke accompanied Paul from Philippi to Jerusalem, Acts 20:4-6, and from Caesarea to Rome, 27:1ff.)

---

[6] When we compare Ephesians 6:21,22 and Colossians 4:7,8, we find there is verbatim correspondence between twenty-nine consecutive words (although *kai sundoulos* is omitted in Ephesians).

[7] Michael Weed, *The Letters of Paul; to the Ephesians, the Colossians, and Philemon* (Austin, TX: R.B. Sweet, 1971), p.7.

c.   *Aristarchus* of Thessalonica – Colossians 4:10; Philemon 24
(Like Timothy, this man also accompanied Paul to Jerusalem, Acts 20:4, and to Rome, 27:2. Earlier, on the occasion of the riot of the silversmiths in Ephesus, he temporarily was deprived of his freedom, Acts 19:29.)

d.   *Epaphras* – Colossians 1:6-8, 4:12; Philemon 23

e.   *Tychicus* – Ephesians 6:21,22; Colossians 4:7,8
(This man also accompanied Paul from Macedonia to Jerusalem with the offering, Acts 20:4.)

f.   *Demas* – Colossians 4:14; Philemon 24
(Perhaps he was a native of Thessalonica, 2 Timothy 4:10.)

g.   *Mark* – Colossians 4:10; Philemon 24

h.   *Jesus Justus* – Colossians 4:11

5.   These letters are marked by **a special emphasis on the person and work of Christ** and thus are characterized as being Christological in content.

In Ephesians, the church is the body of Christ (Ephesians 1:22.23).

In Colossians, Christ is the head of the church (Colossians 1:18).

In Philippians, Paul's joy in Christ is emphasized. "Rejoice in the Lord," Paul says (Philippians 3:1, 4:4,10).

In Philemon, what Christ has done for men should motivate Philemon in his behavior toward Onesimus, who is now a brother in Christ.

B. THE BOOK OF ACTS NAMES SEVERAL PLACES WHERE PAUL WAS IMPRISONED.

1.   On Paul's second missionary journey he was briefly imprisoned at Philippi (Acts 16:23-40).

2.   Imprisonments for Paul at Jerusalem, Caesarea, and finally Rome are recorded in Acts 20-28.

a. In the winter of AD 58, Paul was in Corinth when he wrote to the Romans. He is about to finish his third missionary journey by delivering an offering to the poor Christians in Jerusalem. After this trip to Jerusalem, he expected to go to Rome (Acts 19:21; Romans 1:10,11, 15:25-29.)

b. According to his stated plan (Romans 15:25,26), Paul went to Jerusalem with the offering for the poor saints there (Acts 20-21; 24:17).

c. While he was in Jerusalem in the temple area, a riot against Paul was initiated by unbelieving Jews from Asia (Acts 24:17-19), resulting in Paul's being arrested and imprisoned there for a short time.

d. When a plot to kill Paul was discovered, Paul was taken to Caesarea (Acts 23:12-24).

    1) Paul was kept in custody at Caesarea for two years.
        (He was on trial, or awaiting trial during this time.)

    2) Felix, the Roman governor, wanted a bribe, so he kept Paul in bonds.
        (Felix was later taken to Rome and tried for being the type of judge who would accept bribes.)

    3) Festus became governor in AD 60 (Acts 25:1).
        (He was convinced of Paul's innocence, but because of a desire to please the Jews, he did not release Paul.)

    4) Paul appealed to Caesar (Nero) so that he could get justice (Acts 25:11).
        (When a man appealed to Caesar, he had to be sent to Caesar.)

e. So, in the spring of AD 61 Paul comes to Rome (Acts 28:11-14).
    (But not in the manner he anticipated when writing to the Romans.)

f. Of Paul's first imprisonment at Rome we are aware of these things:
    1) He was there for two years, Acts 28:30.
    2) He lived in his own hired dwelling. (Prisoners at Rome had to rent their own places to stay. The Romans furnished a "round-the-clock" guard to make sure the prisoner did not escape. Often, the prisoner even had to provide for the feeding of the soldier who was his guard.)

3) People had free access to Paul, even though he was chained to a Roman soldier at all times.

4) From the silence, we assume Paul's accusers did not appear to accuse him before Caesar; so he was probably freed (according to the custom in Roman courts.) (See Dio Cassius, LX.28.)

5) Concerning Roman jurisprudence:

   a) The only reason a person was held in custody under the Roman system was to await trial. A prison term was not a method of punishment under the Romans.

   b) Under the Romans, the sentence a man might receive were these:

      i. Set free (often "beaten and set free")

      ii. Exiled

      iii. Executed

         (Torture was used for punishment, amusement, or to gain information.)

3. So, according to Acts, Paul was in prison in several cities. Do the Prison Epistles themselves offer any clues about which imprisonment it was during which these four letters were written?

The most definite indications as to the place of composition are found in Philippians 1:13 ("praetorian guard") and Philippians 4:22 ("Caesar's household"). However, the purport of both terms has been disputed.

The Greek word translated "praetorian guard" can also be translated as simply "praetorium" (the governor's palace).

"Praetorium" may be used of any building that served as a governor's house or an army headquarters, whether in Jerusalem (Mark 15:16; Matthew 27:27; John 18:28,33) or in Caesarea (Acts 23:35). If Philippians 1:13 were translated "praetorium" (rather than "praetorian guard") then the imprisonment could have been in Rome or in any of the places where the Roman army had a headquarters or a governor's palace. Modern contemporary higher critics opt for the translation "praetorium" at Philippians 1:13 in order to have the Prison Epistles written from a place other than Rome.

However, in Philippians, the language "the whole praetorian guard and to everyone else" (1:13) certainly refers to people, not buildings. If we translate Philippians 1:13 (as does the NASB) as "praetorian guard" to reflect the fact this verse is talking about people,   the case is strengthened for Rome as the place of imprisonment when this letter was written.[8] It is unlikely that Paul would be imprisoned in Caesar's "palace" in Rome; it is more reasonable to understand that he was guarded by members of the praetorian guard (Acts 28:16 [KJV] reads "the centurion delivered the prisoners to the captain of the guard"). It would be following the Roman custom for prisoners awaiting trial before Caesar if Paul was guarded by the praetorian guard.

In Philippians 4:22 there is reference to "Caesar's household." This fits only if Rome is the place from which Philippians is written. The term "household" would include the praetorian guard, but it could include much more.

In addition there is Paul's anticipation that his case will soon be settled, resulting in his release (Philippians 2:23-24). This reference has commonly been understood as pointing definitely to Rome as the place of writing for Philippians.

4. The uniform tradition in the early church that the Prison Epistles were written from Rome has been questioned in modern times by writers advancing views that the place of writing for one or all of these epistles was Philippi, or Caesarea, or Ephesus, not Rome. It is appropriate to now investigate these matters further at this place in our introductory studies.

C. THE PLACE OF WRITING

Some who accept the view that Philippians was written from Rome hold that the other three Prison Epistles were written from Caesarea. Others have advanced the hypothesis that one or more of these epistles were written during an Ephesian imprisonment, or even from a Philippian imprisonment. We will need to sort through each of these hypotheses.

1. Was it **PHILIPPI** from which these letters were written?

   a. Evidence for this opinion: 1) Paul was in prison in Philippi, Acts

---

[8] In the commentary section of this book, at Philippians 1:13 are further notes on "praetorian guard" and "Caesar's household," which will indicate these terms rather require Rome as the place of writing for Philippians.

16:23-34. 2) The date for this imprisonment would be about AD 51, at the beginning of Paul's second missionary journey.

b. Objections to this opinion: 1) The churches to which two of these epistles (Colossians and Ephesians) are addressed had not yet been founded when Paul was in prison in Philippi. 2) Further, would Paul write a letter to the Philippians when he was in Philippi?

c. Clearly, Philippi must be ruled out as the imprisonment from which the Prison Epistles were written.

2. Was it **EPHESUS** from which these letters were written?[9]

a. Attempts were made in the early years of the 20th century to make a case (even though Acts says nothing about such an imprisonment) that Paul was imprisoned at Ephesus,[10] and that it was from Ephesus that one or more of the Prison Epistles were written.[11] Such an alleged imprisonment is supposed to have occurred between AD 54 and AD 57, during the time of Paul's great Ephesian ministry. Acts 19:1-20:1 and 20:31 tell us that Paul was a long time in Ephesus during his third missionary journey.

b. Though Acts is silent about any such imprisonment in Ephesus, could such have happened?

---

[9] For a concise presentation of this position, see the introduction to J.H. Michael's *The Epistle of Paul to the Philippians* in *The Moffatt New Testament Commentary* (New York: Harper, 1927), p.1319; T.W. Manson, "St. Paul in Ephesus. The Date of the Epistle to the Philippians," *BJRL* 23 (1930), p.182-200; J. Peter Bercovitz, "Paul at Ephesus and the Composition of Philippians," *Proceedings: Eastern Great Lakes and Midwest Biblical Societies* 8, (Grand Rapids, Mich: 1988), pp. 61-76.

[10] See A. Deissmann (*Light From the Ancient East,* p.229n), W. Michaelis, "The Trial of St. Paul at Ephesus," (*JTS* 29 [1928], p.368-375]), and G.S. Duncan (*St. Paul's Ephesian Ministry*, [1929], p.66-161); *idem.*, "The Epistles of the Imprisonment in Recent Discussion," *ExT* xlvi (1934-5), pp. 263ff.; *idem.*, "Were Paul's Imprisonment Epistles Written From Ephesus?" *ExT* lxvii (1955-6), pp.163ff; James Moffatt, *An Introduction to the Literature of the New Testament*, 3rd ed. (Edinburgh: T&T Clark, 1933), p.622.

[11] Some would have only Philippians written from Ephesus. Some hold that the three Asian epistles were written from Ephesus. Others have attempted to have all four of the Prison Epistles written from Ephesus.

The arguments which have been marshaled to support this hypothetical Ephesian imprisonment include the following:

1) In 1 Corinthians 15:32, Paul says that he had "fought with wild beasts at Ephesus."

1 Corinthians was written from Ephesus in the spring of AD 57. It is said you would have to be in jail and then cast into the arena in order to have to fight with wild animals. But it is very possible that Paul is talking about two-legged beasts, not four.[12] If so, the case for an Ephesian imprisonment is seriously weakened.

A tradition, dating back to the early part of the third century in the apocryphal *Acts of Paul*, relates that Paul was thrown to a lion in the arena at Ephesus and that the lion licked his feet.[13] "This story sounds like an apocryphal invention to give a literal meaning to 1 Corinthians 15:32, 'I fought with beasts at Ephesus'."[14]

Concerning the tower in Ephesus which is pointed out to tourists as being Paul's prison, Ramsay wrote "Though the tower certainly was in existence at the time of St. Paul's residence in the city, there is no reason to think he was ever imprisoned in Ephesus."[15]

---

[12] The context in 1 Corinthians 15:32 is metaphorical as it describes Paul as saying "I die daily" (1 Corinthians 15:31) at a time when he is writing as a free man. For a Roman citizen to be condemned to the lions was very rare. In another place, Paul tells the Ephesian elders that "savage wolves" would soon come among them (Acts 20:29), language which no one has suggested should be taken literally. The same Greek word for "wild beasts" found in 1 Corinthians 15:32 is used by Ignatius (*Ad Rom.* v.1) in a clearly metaphorical sense (i.e., of a detachment of soldiers). See Arndt and Gingrich, *A Greek-English Lexicon of the New Testament*, 1957, p.361.

[13] Duncan (*op. cit.*) also cites the *Acts of Titus*, Hippolytus' commentary on Daniel, and the fourteenth-century historian Nicephorus Callisti who speak of this encounter. This is very slender evidence, for it has been affirmed that the *Acts of Titus* is not an independent witness but rather is copied from the *Acts of Paul* (M.R. James, *The Apocryphal New Testament* [London: Oxford, 1924], p.271ff, 291). Furthermore, the author of the *Acts of Paul* seems to place the alleged event after Paul's release from his first Roman imprisonment, a date too late for the writing of the Prison Epistles.

[14] D. Edmond Hiebert, *Introduction to the New Testament: Vol.2 – The Pauline Epistles* (Chicago: Moody Press, 1978), p.210.

[15] William Ramsay, *The Letters to the Seven Churches of Asia* (Grand Rapids: Baker, 1963, reprint of 1904 edition), p.213.

2) 2 Corinthians 1:8-10 speaks of serious trouble "in Asia" (Ephesus was the Roman capital of the province of Asia) which was so severe Paul thought he would not live through it. We do not know precisely what the affliction was to which he refers.

Acts records the riot and contention stirred up by the silversmiths of Ephesus. Was the mob's two hours of shouting "Great is Artemis of the Ephesus" also a cry for Paul's life? Some have attempted to make a connection between the riot and what Paul writes in 2 Corinthians 1:9,10.[16]

In Romans 16:3,4, written shortly after Paul left Ephesus, Paul tells how Priscilla and Aquila had recently risked their lives to save him. Does that point to an imprisonment in Ephesus from which those two somehow managed to rescue him? On what evidence do we connect the events told about in 2 Corinthians 1:8-10 with Romans 16:3,4, save a proximity in time?

Paul's words in 2 Corinthians do speak of a serious crisis in which he and others were involved (he uses the plural "we" in 2 Corinthians 1:8), but imprisonment is not the only possible explanation of what the crisis was.

3) In 2 Corinthians 11:23 Paul speaks of being in "far more imprisonments" than others who claim to be servants of Christ, and 6:5 reads "imprisonments" (plural). Yet at the time 2 Corinthians was written, the only imprisonment recorded in Acts is the one in Philippi.

An early tradition (the prologue to Colossians in the Marcionite canon[17]) which ascribes an Ephesian imprisonment to the apostle

---

[16] In this writer's commentary *New Testament Epistles: 2 Corinthians and Galatians*, he suggests the serious trouble at Ephesus was not the riot of the silversmiths.

[17] See footnote #20 below.

is thought to be plausible because of what Paul wrote in 2 Corinthians 11:23 about being in prison often. (We date 2 Corinthians in AD 57, so whatever imprisonments are alluded to would all have to have occurred prior to that date. Acts 20-28 records imprisonments Paul suffered after 2 Corinthians was written.)

Those who hold to an Ephesian imprisonment urge that we know through Acts of no other imprisonments except at Philippi, and his trial at Corinth. Therefore, there must also have been an imprisonment at Ephesus for Paul to speak as he does in 2 Corinthians 11:23.

But there are many things that we do not know about Paul about which he writes in 2 Corinthians 11:23-33. He must have been imprisoned in several different towns. If so, verse 23 does not *have* to refer to Ephesus.

4) Evidence for an imprisonment in Ephesus has also been mistakenly derived from Romans 16:7 which names some to whom greetings are being sent by Paul as having been at some time Paul's "fellow-prisoners."

However, to make Romans 16:7 a proof text for an Ephesian imprisonment, as some attempt to do, first requires a rejection of the integrity of Romans by making Romans 16 a fragment of some letter addressed to Ephesus.

When Romans 16 is said to enjoy integrity, it is viewed as being an original and integral part of one single letter (now divided into 16 chapters) written by Paul from Corinth to people who are in Rome. Since a denial of the integrity of Romans is not warranted by the manuscript evidence, any argument which first requires a mutilation of Romans is seriously flawed and is to be rejected. Thus, Romans 16 cannot be used as a proof text for an Ephesian imprisonment of the apostle Paul.

c. Other arguments have been used to support Ephesus as the probable place of writing:

1) It has also been conjectured that Onesimus, the runaway slave, would go to a city like Ephesus to get lost in the crowd. It is also suggested that when Paul asks Philemon to prepare a guest room for him (Philemon 22) for when he was released, is not a journey from nearby Ephesus more plausible than a journey from Rome?[18]

2) Ephesus, it is urged, would make a natural center from which to distribute the Prison Epistles to the Lycus River valley and to Philippi.

3) Ephesus would be a place where Paul would have been surrounded by a substantial number of helpers, such as Colossians 4:10-14 suggests he was.

4) Supporters of the case for Ephesus insist that Paul's desire to visit Philippi and the churches of Asia Minor after his release is easier to fit into an Ephesian imprisonment than a Roman one, inasmuch as Paul had expressed his wish to visit Spain after going to Rome (Romans 15:24).[19]

5) Clement of Rome (*ad Cor.* V.6) mentions that Paul was imprisoned seven times, so there were more than just the imprisonments described in Acts and 2 Timothy. But we do not know where the ones not named in the New Testament were, be it Ephesus or wherever.

6) The prologue to Colossians in the Marcionite canon reads "therefore the apostle already in bonds writes to them from Ephesus."[20]

7) Philippians seems to tell of several journeys back and forth between Paul in prison and Philippi. A journey between Rome and Philippi usually took four to five weeks. The journeys indicated in Philippians would demand a long time interval if Rome

---

[18] See this view defended by David DeSilva, *An Introduction to the New Testament* (Downers Grove: Inter-Varsity, 2004), p.668.

[19] The response to this is that the Roman imprisonment caused Paul to change his plans about going to Spain.

[20] Donald Guthrie, *New Testament Introduction: The Pauline Epistles* (Chicago: Inter-Varsity, 1963), p.93. This statement of Marcion is mitigated when he has both Philippians and Philemon written from Rome.

were the place of writing. Much less time would be involved if Paul were in Ephesus when he wrote Philippians, since it was only a six or seven day journey between Philippi and Ephesus.

d. Objections to the idea that an Ephesian imprisonment was the time and place of the writing of the Prison Epistles:

1) No mention is made of any Ephesian imprisonment in the book of Acts.

2) If Paul were in prison in Ephesus when these letters were written, why should he write a letter to Ephesus?[21]

3) The mention of the "praetorium" (praetorian guard) and "Caesar's household" are hardly compatible with the view that Philippians was written from Ephesus. The ordinary meaning of these terms would point to Rome.[22]

4) Onesimus, the runaway slave, would have been more likely to go to Rome than to Ephesus. Colossae, where Philemon lived, and Ephesus were only 100 miles apart. Businessmen from Colossae might easily see Onesimus in Ephesus and report back to Philemon, his owner.

It is helpful to have an idea of the lay of the land in this part of the ancient world. Toward the eastern side of the Roman province of Asia was the Lycus River valley. The Lycus is a tributary running into the Maeander River. Situated on the Lycus River, about 100 miles east of Ephesus, there were three cities. Laodicea was the largest, the capital of the area. Colossae, 15 miles distance, was the smallest of the cities. Hierapolis, probably so called because it was the "sacred city" (Gr. *hierapolis*) of the tribe of the Hydrelitae, lay about 12 miles north-

---

[21] Some would answer that the letter we call Ephesians was originally addressed to the Laodiceans. See notes at Colossians 4:16.

[22] Attempts to appeal to inscriptions to show that *praetoriani* ("praetorian guard") were stationed in Asia, or that persons belonging to the *familia Caesaris* ("Caesar's household") were in Asia, are mistaken. See notes at Philippians 1:13.

west of Colossae and some 6 miles north of Laodicea.[23] See the map of the area of Asia where Ephesus, Colossae, and the other cities were located.

5) It is hardly possible that the letter to the Philippians was written from Ephesus.[24]

a) Philippians is a thank-you note for an offering just received from the church at Philippi. It is unlikely that the Philippians would send an offering *to Ephesus* since Paul was there surrounded by a large circle of friends (cf. 1 Corinthians 16:19,20). Further, it was probably at Ephesus that Aquila and Priscilla risked their lives for Paul (Romans 16:3,4). It is much more likely that an offering was needed by Paul when he was *in Rome* since, as Colossians 4:11 intimates, he had fewer friends in that city on whom to rely.

---

[23] See Ramsay, *Cities*, v.1, p.184ff.

[24] See P.N. Harrison, "The Pastoral Epistles and Duncan's Ephesian Theory," *NTS* ii (1955-6), pp.250-261, in which it is argued from Duncan's own premises that "Paul cannot have written Philippians from Ephesus, and must have done so at Rome."

b) The Philippians' hiatus in giving financial support to Paul before sending the contribution by Epaphroditus (Philippians 4:10) is not as easy to explain if the money were being sent to Ephesus, as it is if the money were being sent to Rome.

c) If Philippians was written from Ephesus, it must be placed either shortly before or shortly after the writing of 1 Corinthians.   At the time 1 Corinthians was written the offering for the poor saints at Jerusalem was the matter uppermost in Paul's agenda.   On the supposition that Philippians was written at Ephesus, the silence in Philippians concerning that offering is inexplicable.

6) Luke and Mark were with Paul when Colossians (Colossians 4:10,14) and Philemon (Philemon 24) were written.   "Luke was with Paul in Rome; we have no evidence that Luke was with him at Ephesus.   Mark is traditionally associated with Rome, not with Ephesus."[25]

7) The greatest weakness of the case for an imprisonment in Ephesus is that it is unsupported by any solid documentary evidence.

3. Was it **CAESAREA** from which at least some of these letters were written?

a. While holding that Philippians was written from Rome, H.A.W. Meyer (*Critical and Exegetical Handbook to the Epistle to the Ephesians*) and others have maintained that the three other prison epistles were written at Caesarea.[26]

---

[25] F.F. Bruce, *BJRL* 48 (1965), p.87f.

[26] This theory was first advanced about 1804 by Heinrich Paulus and restated more recently by Ernst Lohmeyer in *Die Briefe an die Philipper, an die Kolosser und an Philemon* (1964), p.3;   L. Johnson, "The Pauline Letters from Caesarea," *ExT* lxviii (1956-7), pp.24ff.; and Bo Reicke, "Caesarea, Rome, and the Captivity Epistles," *Apostolic History and the Gospel*, W.W. Gasque and R.P. Martin, editors, (1970), pp.277-286.   Johnson not only has the Prison Epistles written from Caesarea, but also 2 Timothy.   To arrive at his conclusion, Johnson first argues that Acts 28:30,31 does not belong after Acts 28:29 but after Acts 24:26.   His textual emendation rests on the doubtful argument that both Luke and Acts originally had ninety columns.   To make Acts have ninety columns, he not only must move 28:30,31, but he also must argue that our present ending is incomplete and merely patched up.   He also eliminates the reference to Rome in 2 Timothy 1:17. The absence of any supporting evidence for his textual emendation or his excising of the text renders Johnson's conclusions as improbable.   Gerald F. Hawthorne, *Philippians*, *WBC* 43 (Dallas: Word, 1983), p. xli-xliv, is one of a very few modern authors to defend the Caesarean imprisonment as the time and place of writing for Philippians.

b. Evidence marshaled to support this hypothesis that Caesarea was the place of writing:

   1) Paul was a prisoner in Jerusalem and Caesarea for about 2 years (Acts 21-27), from Pentecost AD 58 to autumn of AD 60. The record in Acts is unambiguous in this point.

   2) The "praetorium" ("palace," Philippians 1:13 KJV), it is claimed, could be understood of Herod's palace at Caesarea (Acts 23:35), for Caesarea was the seat of the Roman governor of Palestine and Syria. Or, others claim, the soldiers stationed there might well be called a "praetorian guard" (Philippians 1:13 NASB).[27]

   3) At Caesarea, Paul's friends did have access to him (Acts 24:23,27).

   4) The fugitive slave Onesimus could have fled to Caesarea (on the assumption that the epistles to the Colossians and Philemon came out of the same imprisonment as Ephesians).

   5) Further, the polemic against Jewish teachers (Colossians 3:1-16) fits well the period of Jewish antagonism toward Paul that led to his arrest and imprisonment.

   6) If the Prison Epistles were written from Caesarea, their route overland would bring them first to Colossae in the Lycus valley where Onesimus would be returned to Philemon; Colossians would be delivered to the church there; and then Tychicus could proceed on toward Ephesus.

c. Objections to this suggestion that Caesarea is the place of writing:

   1) A fugitive slave like Onesimus would be more likely to go to a great city like Rome where he would have a much better chance to lose himself among the multitudes, even as fugitives today seek refuge in our large cities. Caesarea would offer comparatively fewer chances of avoiding detection and apprehension by the slave-catchers. It is more likely that Onesimus would want to put more miles between himself and his former master than just the distance from Colossae to Caesarea.

---

[27] This claim concerning "praetorian guard" meaning either a government building or praetorian soldiers being in Caesarea is refuted in notes at Philippians 1:13.

2) Philip the evangelist dwelt in Caesarea; Paul and his companions had lodged with Philip shortly before Paul's arrest (Acts 21:8-14). If the Prison Epistles were written from Caesarea, how do we explain that this worthy preacher is not named in these epistles (Colossians 4:10,11)? Has Paul forgotten Philip the evangelist? Or does the failure to mention him silently imply that Philip has become hostile toward Paul?

3) Philippians 1:13 makes it clear that folk nearby where Paul was imprisoned became aware he was a prisoner in the cause of Christ. We have no information about folk nearby to Caesarea who become aware that Paul was a prisoner because he has been fulfilling his mandate to take the gospel of Christ to the Gentiles. Such a thing did happen at Rome.

4) Philippians 1:14 makes it clear that Paul's imprisonment had caused many people to become courageous in preaching the gospel. This presupposes a place possessing a church of some size, a requirement that Caesarea does not easily fit.

5) Did Paul expect to be released from Caesarea as the Prison Epistles imply?

The obvious expectation of the writer (Philippians 2:24; Philemon 22) of a speedy release from captivity, which would enable him to visit, not Rome and Spain as was his intention at the time he was taken prisoner in Jerusalem (Acts 19:21; Romans 15:24,25), but Macedonia and the eastern churches, is another evidence that the Caesarean imprisonment is not the captivity from which these epistles are written.

There was no hope for Paul's release through Felix except by paying a bribe (Acts 24:26), a thing Paul would not do.

4. **ROME** is the place of the imprisonment from whence these letters were written.

This, the traditional view which identifies Paul's imprisonment with the one at Rome described in Acts 28:16-31, was unchallenged for 18 centuries. Nor have the other recently proposed places for the writing of the Prison Epistles gained much of a following.   The arguments in favor of Paul's writing the epistles from any place other than Rome have too many problems inherent in them to supplant the traditional view.   After studying all the conjectures that Philippi or Ephesus or Caesarea was the place of writing, the traditional view that Rome was the place of writing still has the best chance of being right.

A review of Paul's life as recorded in Acts 20-28 shows the signature on the epistles and the references to imprisonment in these epistles can be taken at face value.

There are multiple reasons to hold that the evidence confirms the traditional view that all four epistles were written by Paul during his first Roman imprisonment (Acts 28:30,31):

- Paul was a prisoner in Rome (Acts 28:11ff).
- This view best accounts for the measure of freedom which the Prison Epistles (Ephesians 6:18-20; Philippians 1:12-18; Colossians 4:2-4) indicate Paul enjoyed during his imprisonment and the preaching ministry he was able to carry forward afterwards (cf. Acts 28:16, 30,31).   During his imprisonment in Caesarea, it does not appear Paul had the kind of freedom that the Prison Epistles imply.   In Caesarea, only Paul's friends were admitted to see him (Acts 24:23).   However, in Rome, Paul lived in his own rented house where already on the third day the leading men of the Jews had a session with him, followed a few days later by an all-day session with a still greater representation of Jewish leaders (Acts 28:17,23)
- The prayers Paul requests in Ephesians 6:19 and Colossians 4:3,4 fit his captivity in Rome, but not that in Caesarea.   His plans at the time he was in custody in Caesarea were to go to Rome, not to Asia.
- The "praetorian guard" and "Caesar's household" (Philippians 1:13, 4:22) can be given their natural and unstrained significance if Rome is the place of composition.
- Having the letters written from Rome accounts for the silence about Philip the evangelist and gives the story of Onesimus its most natural setting.
- Onesimus would be most likely to go to Rome since he was a runaway slave.   (a) In Rome it would be easier than any place else in the empire for a man to get lost among the crowd of slaves and freedmen. Slaves had the Greek letter Delta, Δ, for *doulos*, branded on their forehead and arm.   A man with such a brand in Rome would attract less attention to himself.   (b) The presence of numerous freedmen in

Rome would make it more difficult for the *fugitivarii* (slave catchers) to find him, even after receiving the description of the fugitive.

- Paul hoped to visit Philippi soon (Philippians 2:24). That would fit his first Roman imprisonment, but not the one at Caesarea, where his aim was next to go to Rome (Romans 15:24-28), and his appeal to Caesar made a trip to Philippi out of the question.
- The Marcionite Prologue (c. AD 170) states that Philippians and Philemon were sent from Rome. While Philippians offers the strongest evidence that the place of writing was Rome, there is nothing in Ephesians, Colossians, or Philemon which points to a different place than Rome as the place of writing for those letters.
- Paul's companions named in the letters can be connected with Rome: Aristarchus (Colossians 4:10, Acts 27:2) and Luke (Colossians 4:14, Acts 28:14-16).
- "The Roman imprisonment provides the indicated conditions for the work of Paul's co-laborers in preaching during his imprisonment and explains the implication as to the decisive nature of the issue of his trial (Philippians 1:14-17,20)."[28]

Upon leaving Rome, Tychicus and Onesimus would have been anxious to get to Colossae as quickly as possible, once they landed in Asia. Landing at Miletus, the quickest route would be to travel up the Maeander River valley directly to Colossae, where Onesimus would be returned to Philemon, and the letter to the church in Colossae delivered. Then Tychicus could travel toward Ephesus delivering the letter known to us as "To the Ephesians." A copy, which was intended to circulate among the local churches (Colossians 4:16), seems also to have been left with the church at Laodicea.

5. Why do some commentators wish to have the Prison Epistles written from some place other than Rome? The chief reason seems to be that these commentators do not want to acknowledge the possibility of the Pauline authorship of the Pastoral Epistles.

   a. Some higher critics wish to argue that Paul was killed at the end of his two year imprisonment at Rome (Acts 28:30). Since the historical occasion for the Pastorals cannot be found in the book of Acts, and since, in the thinking of the negative critics, Paul was killed at the end

---

[28] D. Edmond Hiebert, *An Introduction to the New Testament: Volume Two – The Pauline Epistles* (Chicago: Moody, 1977), p. 211.

of the two years in Rome, they insist that Paul could not have written the Pastoral Epistles.

b.   However, if the Prison Epistles were written in Rome, and if Paul was released from the Roman imprisonment (as is implied by the prison epistles), it undermines their argument against the genuineness of the Pastorals.

c.   The reason, then, that some want these epistles written from else-where than Rome is because the Prison Epistles show Paul's expectation of being released shortly.

  1)   The critics wish to say Paul was expecting to be released from Ephesus or Caesarea, but not from the custody at Rome.

  2)   But to use the critics' own arguments against them: according to their interpretation, Paul was not expecting to be released even from Ephesus, but fully expected to be killed there (2 Corinthians 1:8-11).

d.   Of course, a denial that the Prison Epistles were written from Rome does not prove, *ipso facto*, that Paul could not have written the Pastoral Epistles, even if these four Prison Epistles were written before Paul's first Roman imprisonment.   If the Prison Epistles were written before the Roman imprisonment recorded in Acts 28, it is still possible that Paul wrote the Pastorals during that Roman imprisonment.

It is our studied conclusion that the Pastorals came from a time after Paul's release from his first Roman imprisonment with one letter (2 Timothy) coming from a second Roman imprisonment.   However, the higher critics say that the Pastorals depict a later period in the church than AD 60-70, and were not written by Paul.   These critics often admit that Paul wrote some fragments at Rome; but they assert that a Paulinist, about the beginning of the second century, wrote the Pastorals as we have them now.   Such a denial that letters which carry Paul's signature were actually written by him is the result of mistaken speculation which in turn has its roots in a misguided attempt to make the Scriptures match the current popular philosophy of the age.

D. THE DATE OF THE WRITING AND THE ORDER OF THE COMPOSITION OF THE PRISON EPISTLES

1. The **date of writing**. Paul's first Roman imprisonment is dated from AD 61-63. Having opted for the traditional view that these letters were written during Paul's first Roman imprisonment, we are led to assign a date in the early AD 60's for the writing of these letters. Whether the letters come from early or late in that imprisonment is a more complicated determination.

2. The **order of the composition** of the Prison Epistles

That Ephesians, Colossians, and Philemon were written at about the same time is evident from the fact that all three were dispatched at the same time. This leaves us to attempt to determine whether Philippians was written before or after the other three were sent.

What we find in the literature is that scholars have advocated both views. Lightfoot held strongly to the priority of Philippians.[29] His major reason for assigning priority to Philippians was similarity of subject matter in Romans and Philippians. He placed Colossians later to allow time for the new themes and peculiar expressions to develop. Sanday and Hort likewise have Philippians written first. However, this commentator declines to agree with the idea Philippians was written early in the first Roman imprisonment, though attempts categorically to decide the issue seem to overreach the available evidence. For example, Timothy is included in the salutations to Philippians, Colossians, and Philemon, but he is not included in the letter "to the Ephesians." Arguments about the order of composition have been based on this fact, and exactly opposite conclusions have been advocated. Some argue that Ephesians was first, being written before Timothy joined Paul; others argue that Ephesians was written last, after Timothy had left Paul on some mission for the apostle. Or, perhaps the correct view is that Timothy was present when Ephesians was written, but his name was omitted from the epistolary opening because he did not serve as the scribe who penned that letter as Paul dictated it.

That Philippians comes from near the end of Paul's first Roman imprisonment seems to be indicated from the following considerations:

    a. It is implied in Philippians that before the letter to Philippi is written,

---

[29] J.B. Lightfoot, *St. Paul's Epistle to the Philippians* (Grand Rapids: Zondervan, 1953 reprint of the 1913 edition), pp.30-46.

the imprisonment has already been of some duration (Philippians 1:12-17).

b. To place Philippians in the earlier part of the Roman imprisonment does not seem to allow sufficient time for the events to have taken place about which we read in Philippians 2:25-28. In those verses, we learn the reason why Epaphroditus has been sent back to Philippi. Once the Philippians learned Paul was a prisoner in Rome, they had sent an offering to him. It was carried by Epaphroditus (Philippians 4:18). 2:26 tells about Epaphroditus becoming critically ill and nearly dying, though it does not tell us exactly when he became sick. The Philippians have heard about the illness and were concerned. News had come to Rome that the Philippians were concerned. Now, by the grace of God, Epaphroditus has recovered and is being sent back to Philippi in order to relieve the people there of their concern. Considerable time, perhaps a month each way, is needed for messages to travel back and forth the 800 miles that separate Rome and Philippi. To place the writing of the letter to Philippi in the early part of Paul's imprisonment does not allow sufficient time for these things to transpire.[30]

---

[30] Those who advocate an early date for Philippians argue that the number of trips can be reduced, thus shortening the time required to satisfy the communications back and forth. It is said to be conceivable that the offering from Philippi had been timed to reach Paul shortly after his arrival in Rome. Somehow the Philippians heard of his impending imprisonment at Rome and tried to anticipate his needs. It is then conjectured that Aristarchus, who started with Paul on his voyage to Rome (Acts 27:2), is the one who brought news to Philippi of Paul's whereabouts. This scenario says that early in the voyage to Rome, when Paul's party changed ships at Myra, Aristarchus did not change ships, but went on toward his home (Thessalonica), perhaps traveling through Philippi. It is then supposed that Aristarchus told the Philippian church (as he passed through Philippi on his way to Thessalonica) that Paul would now be in the Roman prison, and to pray for him. The next time we hear of Aristarchus, he is in Rome (Colossians 4:10). It is supposed that Epaphroditus, bearing the offering for Paul, could have followed Aristarchus to Rome almost immediately. It is also conjectured that Epaphroditus became ill as he was on his way to Rome, and that someone immediately returned to Philippi with the report. In this way, the amount of time inferred by the trips back and forth is reduced, and thus makes it possible for Philippians to have been written early in Paul's first Roman imprisonment.

There are several problems with this scenario. (1) Rather than the hypothesis that he became ill while he was traveling to Rome, the language of Philippians 2:25-28 should more likely be understood to say that it is while Epaphroditus was in Rome ministering to Paul's needs that he became critically ill. (2) Can "now at last" (Philippians 4:10) fit an offering being received right at the beginning of the Roman imprisonment? Does that expression not imply a longer interval than the beginning of his Roman imprisonment would allow? Once he arrived in Rome, Paul (guarded by a soldier) stayed in temporary quarters (Acts 28:16 and 23). It is not until later that he moved to "rented quarters" (Acts 28:30), the money to pay for which could well have come from his friends there as well as from Philippi. (3) The conjecture about Aristarchus traveling overland to Rome via Philippi and Thessalonica has certain problems. The Christians at Rome knew Paul was coming, for they came out 70 miles to meet him (Acts 28:15). How did they come to know Paul was coming? Did Aristarchus arrive in Rome before Paul did? Is he the one who told the Roman church Paul was

c. Luke and Aristarchus, both of whom accompanied Paul to Rome (Acts 27:2) and who sent greetings to the Colossians (Colossians 4:14) and to Philemon (verse 24), are not mentioned in Philippians. Does the absence of their names indicate they had been sent on a missionary journey since Colossians and Philemon were written? If Luke was with Paul when Philippians was written, would it be strange if one who was so well known at Philippi is not named in the letter? Or could it be said he was included with the "brethren" who send greetings (4:21)?

d. The progress of Christianity among the soldiers is said to indicate a date late in the first Roman imprisonment. The whole praetorian guard had heard the gospel. The good news had a foothold in Caesar's household. It is probable that such a spread of the gospel indicates that some time has passed since Paul came to Rome.

e. Paul's language in Philemon 22, when compared with Philippians 2:24, seems to show a later date for Philippians. Philemon reads, "I hope thru your prayers to be set free," but in Philippians he writes, "I trust that I shall come *shortly*."

f. The Philippian letter indicates that a crisis has been reached in the apostle's case. Perhaps the two years of imprisonment are about over and the imperial court soon will have to rule on Paul's case (Philippians 2:23). "He promises to send Timothy as soon as he knows the verdict (2:19, 23), and he hopes that he himself will soon be able to come (2:24). While he expects to be set free (1:25, 2:24), he yet realizes that the nature of the verdict is uncertain. He is ready for death if that should be the issue and even desirous of it on his own account (1:23). Whatever the result, the outcome is to be known before long. This definitely points to the last part of the Roman im-

---

coming? This conjecture is hard to accept, since the time element is hard to conceive. After leaving Myra, Paul spent 14 days drifting in the storm, and three months on Malta, and yet when he finally came up the road toward Rome, there were the Roman Christians ready to meet him. How did they know what week or month Paul was arriving? Aristarchus could not have known that. We must presume the news of Paul's impending arrival proceeded him from Malta?

There seems to be little way to further reduce the amount of time required to exchange messages back and forth between Rome and Philippi. Even if we accept an early arrival of Epaphroditus, we have not noticeably reduced the time span needed for the journeys to be made. Rather than having Philippians written early in Paul's imprisonment, if we date the writing toward the end of his imprisonment, these journeys no longer pose a problem to the suggested date of writing.

prisonment. We conclude that Philippians was the last of the prison epistles."[31]

A still more complicated problem is encountered when one attempts to find a solution to the question of whether Ephesians was written before Colossians, or whether Colossians was written before Ephesians. The endeavor to find a solution to the order in which these two epistles were written is based on a study of the inner relationship between the two letters and has likewise led to opposite conclusions. In the words of Shaw, "The grounds on which priority is usually based are mainly of a subjective kind, according as individual writers think that a general or a special treatment is the more likely to have come first."[32] One wonders whether or not the early views that defended the priority of Colossians to Ephesians were based on an evolutionary model, where the simple becomes more complex as time passes.

Nevertheless, the question as to the exact order in which the three epistles addressed to Asia were written has elicited differing scenarios:

- One scenario has Colossians written first, followed by Ephesians and Philemon.[33] Colossians was occasioned by the visit of Epaphras to Rome with news about a new problem facing the church at Colossae. Once Paul has composed a letter to meet their specific needs, he decides to write a letter to other area churches about Christ and the church in order to warn them about and insulate them from that same perilous heresy. Onesimus, having come to Rome and having come into contact with Paul, has been led to become a Christian. That Tychicus was going to Colossae gave Paul an opportunity to write a letter of sanctuary ("right of sanctuary") for Onesimus.

- Another scenario has Paul writing Ephesians, Colossians, and Philemon

---

[31] Hiebert, *op. cit.*, p.213.

[32] R.D. Shaw, *The Pauline Epistles* (Edinburgh: T & T Clark, 4th ed., 1924 reprint), p. 277.

[33] For the moment we are not considering internal arguments, which are made by contemporary scholars, about the order of composition to the effect that Paul wrote neither of these two letters that carry his name, but that whoever wrote Ephesians made a verbose copy Colossians, or whoever wrote Colossians abbreviated Ephesians.

in this order.[34]   During his absence from Asia Minor, Paul has been thinking about the needs of those churches.   He has composed Ephesians (a circular letter, we judge) as a general letter intended to meet the needs of a number of churches.   Then Epaphras (Colossians 1:7,8; 4:12) comes to Rome with news about a new problem facing the church at Colossae. This calls forth a letter addressed specially to their needs.   Tychicus will carry the letter to Colossae.   In the meantime, Onesimus, having fled from his Colossian slave master Philemon, has come to Rome, found Paul, and has been led to become a Christian.   That Tychicus was going to Colossae gave Paul an opportunity to write a letter of sanctuary ("right of sanctuary") for Onesimus.

E. AUTHORSHIP OF THE PRISON EPISTLES

All four letters are signed by Paul, and internal and external evidence of authorship both support the traditional view that Paul wrote all four letters.   This detailed evidence may be examined in the Detailed Introductions to each epistle which are included at the back of this commentary.   The traditional view of Pauline authorship is the one presented in this book.

Over the last couple of hundred years several writers have written denials of the traditional view.   The arguments advanced by these writers are also surveyed and answered in the Detailed Introductions included at the back of this commentary.   What must be realized is that when the Pauline authorship is denied, and the letters attributed to some forger or some pseudonymous writer, the net result is a denial of the inspiration and apostolic authority of the Prison Epistles, a result that is totally unacceptable.

---

[34] This second scenario is the one adopted in this commentary.   In the Detailed Introduction to Ephesians included at the back of this commentary, the arguments for the priority of Ephesians as well as the arguments for the priority of Colossians will be given in detail.

Commentary On

Ephesians

Concise Introduction to Ephesians[1]

As it comes to us, the letter identifies its writer, the apostle Paul, and its intended readers, "the saints who are at Ephesus." It also indicates a wider audience of those "who are faithful in Christ Jesus" (Ephesians 1:1).

The letter "to the Ephesians" is thought by many Bible students to have been a circular letter – i.e., that it was addressed to a group of churches rather than to one specific congregation. Two reasons are often given for this conclusion. (1) The first is the lack of personal information and references included in the letter. Paul had been closely associated with the Ephesian church – he spent three years in Ephesus (Acts 20:31) – yet this letter does not contain the kind of warm, personal language that one would expect to see. (2) The second piece of evidence for believing that Ephesians was a circular letter is that the earliest copies of the book do not have the words "at Ephesus" in the opening verse. Why, then, did the letter come to be called the book of Ephesians? The church in Ephesus may have been the largest or most prominent among the group of churches to which the letter was sent. Perhaps it was the church that took custody of the autograph copy of the letter.

On the other hand, the letter is not completely without personal language. Paul mentions his prayers for the recipients (1:15-23; 3:14-19) and asks for theirs (6:18-20). He also notes that Tychicus would bring them personal information about him (6:21,22). And, of course, we do not have the original copy of the letter, so we do not know whether the words "at Ephesus" were part of the original or not. Nor were the words necessary since the letter was probably carried directly to its destination(s) by Tychicus, one of Paul's friends (6:21).

The idea of a circular letter is not foreign to the New Testament. Paul told the Colossians, "When this letter is read among you, have it also read to the church of the Laodiceans; and you, for your part read my letter that is coming from Laodicea" (Colossians 4:16). The message included in each of the letters to the seven churches of Revelation (Revelation 2 and 3) is intended for all the churches ("He who has an ear, let him hear what the Spirit says to the churches").

---

[1] A Detailed Introduction to Ephesians is included later in this commentary. Readers of this commentary will find explanations there for many of the statements made in this concise introduction.

The address still carries a strong and tender feeling of family. From God, the Father of the writer and all his readers, and from Jesus, who is Messiah and Lord of all alike, it bespeaks grace and peace (verse 2). Those who belong to God in Christ are not strangers and foreigners to one another no matter where and when they may live.

It is impossible to apply a yardstick or a calendar to the grand themes of Ephesians. As a general letter, taken up with the glory of Christ and the grandeur of His church, and without references to persons or circumstances in any one place, it could have been copied and sent alike to churches in several cities.

"One name, Tychicus (Ephesians 6:21 and Colossians 4:7), ties this epistle in time and circumstance to the writing to Colossians and Philemon. All three came from Paul, for delivery to the same general area in Asia Minor. Note the wide range of subjects and circumstances in these letters. Philemon deals with a matter of personal concern. Colossians speaks to a local situation in which one church in one city faced a special problem of doctrinal issues. Ephesians knows no bounds of time or space."[2]

The book of Ephesians falls naturally into two parts.

"The first three chapters present all-inclusive doctrine of the church. Christ is the head of His body, the church; Christ is the foundation of His spiritual building, the church. The teaching is interlaced, however, with practical implications. The body is to glorify its Head; the building is to grow into a suitable dwelling for God's Spirit. In chapter 3 Paul describes his commission as apostle to the Gentiles which accounts for his care and his prayer for the readers of this letter.

Chapters 4-6 deal mainly with the saints' suitable response to their calling as God's people. They may now be fellow citizens with the saints and members of the household of God (2:15) but they still lived in pagan surroundings. They needed continuing Christian instruction, motivation, and encouragement."[3]

---

[2] Ed Hayden, *Standard Lesson Commentary* (Cincinnati: Standard Publishing, 1988), p.298-299)

[3] *Op. cit.*, p.314.

Outline of Ephesians

Epistolary Opening.   1:1,2

PART ONE: DOCTRINAL PORTION.
The Church is Chosen, Redeemed, and United in Christ.   1:3-3:23

A. Thanksgiving and Praise to God for the Spiritual Blessings Which the Church Enjoys in Christ Jesus.   1:3-14
1. *Blessing #1* – The church is chosen by the Father.   1:4
2. *Blessing #2* – The church is predestined to adoption as sons.   1:5,6
3. *Blessing #3* – In the Beloved, God richly demonstrated His grace toward us.   1:7,8a
4. *Blessing #4* – God has made known the mystery of His will.   1:8b-10b
5. *Blessing #5* – In Christ, God made (the Jews) a heritage.   1:10c-12
6. *Blessing #6* – In Christ, Gentiles also were sealed with the Holy Spirit of promise.   1:13,14

B. Paul's Prayer that the Readers of this Letter May Grow in Spiritual Knowledge.   1:15-23
1. The content of the prayer.   1:17-19a
2. A lengthy meditation on the power of God manifested in Christ.   1:19b-23

C. The Unity of All (Jewish Believers and Gentile Believers) in Christ.   2:1-22
1. Reminder of their previous condition of death and of their present condition, that of being a glorious new creation.   2:1-10
    a. What the readers were in the past.   2:1-3
    b. What we are in the present.   2:4-6
    c. What we shall be in the future.   2:7-10

2. Redemption (deliverance from death in the new creation) produces a reconciliation of the Jews and Gentiles to God, uniting each other into one new body.   2:11-22
    a. What Gentiles were without Christ.   2:11,12
    b. What Jews and Gentiles are when united with Christ – they are one new body.   2:13-18
    c. What Jews and Gentiles are when united with Christ – one city (or country), one family, one building, one growing body (temple). 2:19-22

D. The Apostle's Office and Prayer in View of the Mystery of the Universal Church. 3:1-21

    1. The beginning of Paul's prayer for their strengthening. 3:1a

    2. Digression -- Paul's ministry as an apostle of the mystery of Christ. 3:1b-13
      a. His present situation in Rome. 3:1b
      b. The mystery was made known to Paul by revelation. 3:2,3
      c. The mystery can be known by reading Paul's writings. 3:4
      d. The mystery was unknown in previous ages. 3:5
      e. The mystery concerns the Gentiles' equal privileges. 3:6
      f. Paul, though undeserving, was appointed to preach the mystery. 3:7-9
      g. It is the church's privilege to make known the wisdom of God. 3:10-12
      h. Paul's request that they not let his sufferings be a cause of discouragement. 3:13

    3. Paul's prayer for the readers completed – by three requests. 3:14-19
      a. That they would be powerfully strengthened in the inner man, so that (as a result) Christ may settle down once and for all in their hearts. 3:16,17
      b. That they may never forget the fact that God and Christ love them. 3:18-19a
      c. That they may begin to love as God loves. 3:19b

    4. Doxology suggested by the thought of the glorious things just prayed for. 3:20,21

PART TWO: PRACTICAL EXHORTATIONS
Exhortations Concerning the Believer's Conduct in the World. 4:1 - 6:20

A. Exhortation to Preserve the Unity of the Spirit in the Bond of Peace. 4:1-16
    1. Introduction to the second part of the epistle and statement of the first exhortation. 4:1-3

    2. The fundamental reasons why there is an initial unity which Christians should endeavor to preserve. 4:4-6
      a. There is one body. 4:4

      b.   There is one Spirit. 4:4
      c.   There is one hope. 4:4
      d.   There is one Lord.   4:5
      e.   There is one faith. 4:5
      f.   There is one baptism. 4:5
      g.   There is one God and Father of all. 4:6

3. Preserving the unity is aided/facilitated by the diversity of gifts given to the church. 4:7-11

4. The objectives in mind as the gifts are used. 4:12-16
    a.   The saints are equipped for service to build up the body. 4:12
    b.   Goals to be reached in our ministry/service. 4:13
      1) Unity of the faith and knowledge of the Son of God. 4:13
      2) Spiritual maturity. 4:13
      3) Christlikeness in spiritual stature. 4:13
    c.   Results when the goals are reached. 4:14,15
      1) No longer children tossed here and there
      2) We grow up into Christ
    d.   How the body is designed to function. 4:16

B. An Exhortation to Live a Holy Life (Because They Have Put off the Old Man, and Put on the New). 4:17-24
   1. No longer live as the pagans do. 4:17-19
   2. Live as the gospel prescribes. 4:20-24

C. Some Rules for the New Life so that Christians do not Wrong Their Neighbors. 4:25-32
   1. Tell the truth instead of lying. 4:25
   2. Control yourself. 4:26,27
   3. Work hard and be generous. 4:28
   4. Be clean in speech. 4:29
   5. Be led by the Spirit. 4:30
   6. Be free from ill-will. 4:31
   7. Be full of goodwill. 4:32

D. Exhortation to Imitate God and Walk in Love. 5:1-14
   (4 areas where we can walk in love)
   1. In purity of life. 5:3
   2. In purity of speech. 5:4-6
   3. In separation from sin. 5:7-10
   4. In reproving evil. 5:11-14

E. An Exhortation to Walk in Christian Wisdom.   5:15-20
   1. A careful walk depends on wisdom, which can come only from knowing the Lord's will.   5:15-17
   2. A careful walk involves letting the Holy Spirit fill you.   5:18-20

F. The New Life in Christ: Submission to One Another in Family Relationships.   5:21-6:9
   1. The relationship of wives and husbands.   5:22-33
      a. Wives are to be submissive to their husbands.   5:22-24, 33b
      b. Husbands are to love their wives.   5:25-33a

   2. The relationship of parents and children.   6:1-4
      a. Children are to be submissive (obey).   6:1-3
      b. Fathers are to nurture their children.   6:4

   3. The relationship of slaves and masters.   6:5-9
      a. Slaves are to be submissive (obedient).   6:5-8
         1) With fear and trembling.   6:5
         2) In singleness of heart.   6:5
         3) As unto Christ.   6:5
         4) Not in the way of eye-service.   6:6
         5) As slaves of Christ.   6:6
         6) Doing service with good will.   6:7
         7) Knowing that we shall receive from the Lord that which we do.   6:8
      b. Masters obey the golden rule.   6:9
         1) Treat slaves as they are to treat you.   6:9
         2) Forbear threatening.   6:9

G. Closing Exhortation for All to Stand Against the Great Spiritual Enemies of the Body of Christ.   6:10-20
   1. Exhortation to put on the whole armor of God.   6:10-13
      a. Be strong in the Lord.   6:10
      b. Put on the whole armor of God.   6:11
      c. Why the whole armor of God is needed – because our enemies are spiritual.   6:12
      d. Anticipated outcome of the battle.   6:13

   2. The armor described. 6:14-17
      a. Girdle of truth. 6:14
      b. Breastplate of righteousness. 6:14
      c. Feet shod with preparation. 6:15
      d. Shield of faith. 6:16
      e. Helmet of salvation. 6:17
      f. Sword of the Spirit. 6:17

   3. Exhortation to prayer. 6:18-20
      a. At all seasons for all saints. 6:18
      b. For Paul. 6:19,20
         1) That he may speak the right words. 6:19
         2) That he might speak with boldness. 6:19,20

CONCLUSION AND FINAL SALUTATION.   6:21-24
   1. Commendation of Tychicus. 6:21-22
   2. Closing Benediction. 6:23,24
      a. Peace – unity between Jew and Gentile. 6:23a
      b. Love. 6:23b
      c. Grace. 6:24

Epistle to the Ephesians

Epistolary Opening.   1:1,2

1:1 -- *Paul, an apostle of Christ Jesus by the will of God, to the saints* who are at *Ephesus and* who are *faithful in Christ Jesus:*

Paul – As was the usual way to begin a letter in the ancient world (signature, destination, greeting), the author of this letter first signs his name. "Paul" is the name by which the apostle to the Gentiles was known during the most active and eventful part of his life.

An apostle of Christ Jesus – The word "apostle" means a commissioned messenger, one dispatched or sent out on a mission. Any power or authority an apostle possessed was delegated power. There were two kinds of apostles in the New Testament – those sent by Jesus, and those sent by churches (2 Corinthians 8:23; Philippians 2:25). Paul here claims to be an apostle who had been sent by Jesus Himself. This allusion to his apostleship gives this letter an official character, 'I represent Jesus!' "Christ" is the transliteration of *Christos,* which was "anointed," and this Greek word is the translation of the Hebrew for "Messiah," which also means "anointed one". Jesus of Nazareth, the Son of God, is of course the long-promised Messiah. Compare Acts 2:36.

By the will of God – Paul says, 'I am an apostle of Jesus Christ because God wanted me to be such.'[1] He thus justifies undertaking in this letter to instruct congregations, to some of whom he was a stranger. Paul's special call to apostleship (i.e., the Lord's appearance to him on the Damascus road, Acts 26:16-18) is emphatically expanded in Galatians 1:1.[2]

---

[1] The Greek word here is *thelema*. On the distinction, if any, between *thelema* and *boule*, see notes on "the counsel of His will" (Ephesians 1:11). "When Paul says that he was an apostle 'through the will of God,' the accent in his voice was not the accent of pride, it was the accent of sheer amazement. To the end of the day Paul stood amazed that God could have chosen a man like him to do His work." (William Barclay, *Letters to the Galatians and Ephesians* [Philadelphia: Westminster Press, 1957], p.86.)

[2] At times, these words "by the will of God" point to a depreciation of Paul's apostolic authority by Judaizers and other false preachers. Whether it so implies here, this writer does not know. (Compare 1 Corinthians 1:1; 2 Corinthians 1:1; Colossians 1:1; 2 Timothy 1:1.)

To the saints who are at Ephesus – Concerning the words "at Ephesus" being absent from some manuscripts, see the Detailed Introduction to Ephesians where there is a full discussion of the destination of this letter. A "saint" is a living person who is set apart (i.e., separated, dedicated) to the service of God. In the New Testament, the word implies "no special degree of moral or doctrinal perfection beyond what is expected of every Christian."[3]

And *who are* faithful in Christ Jesus – The persons who are called "saints" are further identified. To address the readers simply as "saints" would not adequately identify them as Christians. *Pistois* may mean either "believing *ones*" or "faithful, steadfast *ones*."[4] Many Jews were dedicated to God. There were "saints" in the Old Testament. Many folk in Ephesus were dedicated to pagan gods and goddesses. This letter is addressed specifically to those saints who are "in Christ."

This is the first time we meet the expression "in Christ" in this epistle. "In Christ," which occurs 164 times in Paul's writings, is an expression that deserves our special attention and study. "A key concept in Ephesians is that it is 'in Christ' that God's blessings are conferred. Paul uses phrases like 'in Christ,' 'in Him,' 'in the Beloved,' about a twenty times in chapters one and two. To be 'in Christ' is not to arrive at a geographical location, but to respond to a spiritual vocation (call). It is more than a position to be occupied; it is a life to be lived."[5]

1:2 – *Grace to you and peace from God our Father and the Lord Jesus Christ.*

Grace to you – The salutation (verse 2) is actually a prayer for the readers – and is stated in similar words in most of Paul's letters. Paul's prayer is that the readers may continue to enjoy God's favor and blessing. The usual Greek greeting was *charein* (Acts 15:23, 23:26) but Paul uses *charis*, a word which sounds similar but has a richer meaning. Scripturally, the word speaks of unmerited favor, bestowed upon man by God. "It refers to God's offer of salvation, with all which that offer implies. [It takes in] Calvary's cross with all the personal sacrifice which that included. [It takes in the forgiveness of sins,

---

[3] S. Edward Tesh, *Adult Lesson Commentary 1973-74* (Cincinnati: Standard, 1972), p.378.

[4] T.K. Abbott, *A Critical and Exegetical Commentary on the Epistles to the Ephesians and to the Colossians* (Edinburgh: T and T Clark, 1956), p.3.

[5] Tesh, *ibid.*

even to those who deserved nothing but punishment], a forgiveness given out of the bounty and free heartedness of the Giver."[6]

And peace – Paul's prayer for his readers is that they may continue to enjoy untroubled and undisturbed well-being. "Peace is the tranquil state of a soul assured of its salvation through Christ, and so fearing nothing from God and content with its earthly lot, of whatever sort that is."[7]

From God our Father and the Lord Jesus Christ – Both members of the Godhead are the source of grace and peace. God and Jesus are of the same rank, the same essence, that of Deity. The distinction between them is in respect of relation to believers. To the receivers of grace and peace, God stands in the relation of FATHER; to the same subjects Jesus stands in relation of LORD. God is FATHER, having made them children through adoption. Jesus Christ is LORD, being constituted head of the church, and having won the right to their loving obedience and honor.

PART ONE: DOCTRINAL PORTION.   The Church is Chosen, Redeemed, and United in Christ.   1:3-3:23

A. Thanksgiving and Praise to God for the Spiritual Blessings Which the Church Enjoys in Christ Jesus. 1:3-14

> *Summary*: Verses 3-14 are one long sentence in the Greek. Six blessings appear to be emphasized, all of which are intended to redound in praise being given back to God, the giver of the blessings. In nearly the same words (verses 6,12,14), this idea of praise is highlighted three times.

1:3 -- *Blessed* **be** *the God and Father of our Lord Jesus Christ, who has blessed us with every spiritual blessing in the heavenly* **places** *in Christ,*

Blessed *be* -- Verse 3 begins with a call for men to speak well of (praise) God for

---

[6] Kenneth S, Wuest, *Ephesians and Colossians in the Greek New Testament* (Grand Rapids: Eerdmans, 1953), p.23. Words in brackets added by this writer.

[7] Joseph H. Thayer, *A Greek-English Lexicon of the New Testament* (Chicago: American Book Co., 1889), p.182.

the spiritual blessings granted.[8]   The verb must be supplied.   "Let God be well spoken of."   We have the same words in 2 Corinthians 1:3.

The God and Father of our Lord Jesus Christ – To speak of God as "Father of our Lord Jesus" is how the relationship of the members of the Godhead is viewed from the standpoint of Jesus' humanity.   There is a kinship between us and Christ – God is "our Father" (verse 2) and He is the "Father ... of Jesus" (verse 3).   "The expression 'God ... of our Lord Jesus' refers to our Lord in His humanity as worshiping and being obedient to God the Father."[9]   Jesus became temporarily subordinate to the Father during His incarnation.   Jesus is still subordinate to the Father, and will be until the second coming (1 Corinthians 15:23-28).   The designation "Father of our Lord Jesus," though misunderstood and misapplied by the Arians and their successors in modern times, is entirely consistent with Christ's own words (Matthew 27:46; John 20:17), and with the highest view of His Person.   We call Jesus the Son of God because of the incarnation (Luke 1:35).

Who has blessed us – "Blessed" (here it is the verb form of *eulogeo*) literally means (1) "to speak well of," (2) "to request good for," or (3) "to do good to." This verse uses the word in the first and third ways.   "We are called on to speak well of God; in fact, we are to praise Him with all we are and have, because He has done good to us in ways that only He could do."[10]   The verb "blessed" is in the aorist tense, speaking of a completed act in the past time.   The answer to the question of when did this blessing take place will depend on what spiritual blessing is in view.   What does Paul mean by "us"?   While some would limit "us" to the apostles, or others like Paul, we judge the reference is evidently to the Christians, the *saints* addressed in verse 1, all Christians, all the believers who are in Christ.

With every spiritual blessing – "These blessings   are spiritual because of their

---

[8] There are two words translated "blessed" in the New Testament.   (1) There is *makarion*, which means happy, spiritually prosperous (see Mathew 5:3-11 where it might be translated as "O the blessedness of the one who ....").   (2) There is the verbal adjective *eulogetos*, the word used here, which is made up of *lego*, "to speak", and *eu*, "good," thus, "to speak well of."   Verbal adjectives ending in *-tos* signify that what the word suggests is capable or possible.   Since such praise is possible, it is appropriate to express it.   The word "praise" repeated in verses 6,12 & 14 conveys the same idea as *eulogetos*.

[9] Wuest, *op. cit.*, p.52.

[10] Edwin Hayden, *Adult Lesson Commentary 1988-89* (Cincinnati: Standard, 1987), p.299.

Spiritual origin.[11]   Also, they are spiritual because they deal with spiritual, rather than physical, matters.   God does, of course, shower many physical blessings upon us, but here Paul is concerned with spiritual blessings.   Several of these are mentioned in the verses that follow."[12]   Here, in outline form, are the spiritual blessings Paul has in mind:

(1) God chose us in Christ,
      That we should be holy and blameless.

(2) In love God predestined us to adoption as sons,
      According to the kind intention of His will,
      To the praise of the glory of His grace bestowed on us in the Beloved.

(3) In the Beloved, God richly demonstrated His grace toward us.
      In Christ we have redemption,
      The forgiveness of our sins.

(4) God made known to us the mystery of His will
      According to His kind intention which He purposed in Christ,
      With a view to an administration suitable to the fullness of the times,
      To sum up all things in Christ.

(5) In Christ, God made us a heritage,
      Having been predestined according to His purpose,
      Who works all things after the counsel of His will.
      To the end that we who were the first to hope in Christ should be to
        the praise of His glory.

(6) In Christ, we also ... were sealed with the Holy Spirit of promise,
      Who is a pledge of our inheritance
      With a view to the redemption of God's own possession,
      To the praise of His glory.

---

[11] Alford, Vincent, and Wuest all affirm *pneumatikos* ("spiritual") always in the New Testament implies the working of the Holy Spirit.   Thus, the blessings are produced and given by the Holy Spirit.

[12] John William Wade, *Adult Lesson Commentary 1992-93* (Cincinnati: Standard, 1991), p.124.

In the heavenly *places* (literally, "in the heavenlies"[13]) – We treat the Greek word as being neuter rather than masculine. This expression occurs five times in Ephesians (1:3,20, 2:6, 3:10, 6:12). The Bible knows of three heavens (2 Corinthians 12:2), either the atmosphere, the starry heavens, or the place where God sits. One of the three fits each reference in Ephesians. For instance, 6:12 likely refers to the lower heavens or the heaven of the clouds (Thayer). Which one is it here? Likely it references the place where God dwells. This expression also occurs at Hebrews 8:1, describing where the glorified Christ now sits. It seems best to connect the words "in the heavenlies" with "chose" (verse 4), and say that the divine election or choosing took place in heaven.

In Christ – "Only when we are 'in Christ' (having become one with Christ) do we receive all the spiritual blessings."[14] "God is the source of the blessings, but it is only 'in Christ' that his blessings are given and must be received."[15]

1. *Blessing #1* -- The church is chosen by the Father.   1:4

1:4 -- *just as He chose us in Him before the foundation of the world, that we would be holy and blameless before Him in love. (ASV)*

Just as – "Just as" introduces the explanation of the spiritual blessings.

He [God] chose us in Him before the foundation of the world – "Chose" means to pick out, to select. The verb is in the middle voice, indicating that God was acting for His own benefit. The *ek* on *eklego* ("chose") means He has chosen us out of the world. The doctrine of "divine election" is here presented.[16]   God has

---

[13] The original has *en tois epouranois*, which can be either masculine or neuter, dative plural. Literally it means "in the heavenlies." It is an adjective and we must supply the noun. Wuest *(Ephesians and Colossians in the Greek New Testament*, p.28) suggests "in the heavenly regions." R. Martin Pope has argued that *"in the heavenlies"* is used uniformly in Ephesians with reference to the unseen world *(ExpT* 23 [1912]: p. 365-368).

[14] Orrin Root, *Adult Lesson Commentary 1985-86* (Cincinnati: Standard, 1984), p.27.

[15] Tesh, *op. cit.*, p.379.

[16] This is one of the places where Paul presents the doctrine of divine election (the words "chose" and "elect" come from the same Greek word). Care must be exercised here. Some who use the term "divine election" mean thereby that back in eternity God chose some to be lost and some to be saved, no matter what they might do in life. This doctrine of double predestination is also called unconditional election. Neither of these ideas is being presented in this present text. The doctrine of election and predestination do not impinge upon the freedom of man's will. ("God so loved the world ... that *whoever* believes ..." [John 3:16].)

elected or chosen that all those who were *in Christ* would be saved.   Whether or not a person is "in Christ" is that person's choice, not the product of naked divine predestination.   God elected to salvation those who believe in Christ and accept the redemption offered in Him.[17]   The spiritual blessings are inseparably connected with the eternal election of God.   "Us in Him" indicates that God decided that those who were in Christ would be saved.   "God's people are chosen and predestined, not by name as individuals, but generally as a class of people."[18] "Before the foundation of the world" reminds us that before He ever started creating,[19] God made a plan.   (Both Romans 8:28-30 and Jude 24,25 talk about this plan or purpose of God.)   He made a choice as He made His plan.   The general sense of the passage is this – the spiritual blessings are bestowed upon Christians in accordance with an eternal purpose in the mind and heart of God.[20]

That we should be holy and blameless before Him in love – Paul now states what God's intentions were when He made His plan back in eternity.   God did not choose some because He foresaw their holiness, but "in order that" they might

---

[17] On the basis of an interpretation of 1 Peter 1:1,2 ("chosen [elect] according to the foreknowledge of God the Father") some have affirmed that God's election has an individual nature as well as a corporate nature.   The word "foreknowledge" is interpreted to mean "to know ahead of time" (rather than to approve ahead of time), and then the explanation is that God "chooses or elects certain individuals to be saved or to enjoy the blessings of salvation on the basis of His advance knowledge of the choice they will make concerning Jesus Christ.   Thus, God does not cause (predestine) some to be saved and some to be lost, but rather He knows in advance who will accept His gracious offer of salvation."   (Michael Shannon, *Adult Lesson Commentary 1999-2000* [Cincinnati: Standard, 1998], p.380.)

[18] Hayden, *ibid.*

[19] The phrase (*katabole kosmou*, from *ballo*, "to throw," and *kata*, down) used here, and in ten other New Testament passages, is understandable and denotes the creation of the universe. The attempt is misguided which tries to make the phrase mean "the downfall of the world" and to link it up with an alleged catastrophic interpretation of Genesis 1:2.   We deny the theory of creation-ruination-recreation sometimes imposed on that passage.

[20] "Let us note that God's plan for human redemption was not drawn up in some haphazard, spur-of-the-moment fashion."   (Wade, *ibid.*)

become "holy and blameless in love."[21]   It appears to this commentator that the punctuation of the ASV, which has the words "in love" connected to the words "holy and blameless before Him," is to be preferred to the punctuation of the verses found in the NASB.   The NASB puts a period after "blameless before Him" and begins a new sentence (verses 5 and 6) with the words "In love." Connecting the words "in love" with verse 5, rather than verse 4, results in the verse saying that God's predestination of some to adoption was an act motivated by God's love.[22]   If a man's love for God is characterized as being holy and blameless, what does that love look like?   "Holy" means "separated to God." The heavenly Father as the sole object of our affections is what God was looking for.   The Greek word *amomos*, translated "blameless," is a word that is a sacrificial word.   Under Jewish law, before an animal could be offered as a sacrifice, it must be examined and inspected; if any blemish was found, it must be rejected as unfit for an offering to God.   Only the best was fit to offer to God. God wants the love His family members have for Him to be free from blemish, the kind of love that is a fit offering to God. [23]   "Before Him" pictures God as He looks down upon us.

According to what we read in Ephesians 1:4ff, back in eternity, God wanted a family of folk who would love Him, not because they had to, but because they wanted to.   So He set about to create a world and a man to inhabit it.   The man was given freedom of the will so he could choose to love God.   As He made His plans for man, God considered the option that man might choose to rebel. God thus also included in His plan a means of saving man (all sinners) in Christ. Before the foundation of the world, it was determined that if a savior were needed, Jesus would be the One who would come to be that savior.   As He made His plan, God also determined that all of those who were "in Christ" would be part of that family which He wanted.   Whether or not a man is in Christ is his own choice, not God's.   God still wants folk in His family who love Him with a holy and blameless love, not because they have to, but because they want to.

---

[21] The two adjectives "holy" and "blameless" occur together also in Ephesians 5:27, and the whole clause here is closely related to Colossians 1:22, "to present us as holy, blameless, and faultless before Him."   (Robert Bratcher, *Translator's Handbook on Paul's Letter to the Ephesians* [United Bible Society, 1982], p.12.)

[22] Calvinists have often been stung by an accusation that their doctrine of absolute double predestination looks arbitrary, cruel, etc.   To counter that charge, some use this verse (as punctuated in the NASB) in an attempt to show that God's predestination was a loving thing.   Since this verse later speaks of the kind intention of His will, we are not sure that "in love" is intended to speak of God's loving nature also.   If the verses are punctuated as the ASV did, the "love" of verse 4 is man's love for God.

[23] "When 'holy' and 'blameless (without blemish)' occur together, they describe a suitable sacrifice." *(Tesh, ibid.)*

2. *Blessing #2* – **The church is predestined to adoption as sons. 1:5-6**

1:5 -- *He predestined us to adoption as sons through Jesus Christ to Himself, according to the kind intention of His will,*

He predestined us to – To "predestine" means to determine something ahead of time. Before the world began, in His mind and plan, God established a destiny for those who, by their own free choice, are "in Christ." He determined that they would be adopted as His children through Jesus (John 1:12; Galatians 4:4,5). "Us" speaks of the same individuals as the "us" introduced in verse 3. Paul quite properly said, "He has chosen *us*," and "predestined *us*," because Paul and his readers were among those who had believed and been baptized into Christ, so were "in Christ."[24]

Adoption as sons – The metaphor of "adoption" is used five times in the New Testament – Romans 8:15,23; 9:4; Galatians 4:5, and here. Paul is the only New Testament writer to use the adoption metaphor, though the concept is consistent with other New Testament images (see, for example, John 1:12). It appears to be taken from "the Roman practice of legally adopting a child, and thus not only bequeathing to him the material possessions of the one adopting, but also giving the adopted his civil status."[25] Under Roman law, an adopted son enjoyed the same status and privileges as a real son. Christ is God's son "by nature." Believers are God's sons only by adoption. So we believers in Jesus become of the same status in God's sight that Jesus has. A nobody becomes a somebody, just as in a Roman adoption.[26] We are fellow-heirs with Christ (Romans 8:17).

Through Jesus Christ – God's plan was that Jesus Christ would make such adop-

---

[24] This verse brings us face to face with one of the theological problems that Christians have struggled with through the centuries, namely, predestination and free will. Jesus said, "He who has believed and has been baptized shall be saved; but he who has disbelieved shall be condemned" (Mark 16:16). Then are we to suppose that God compels some of us to believe regardless of our choice, and compels some others to disbelieve regardless of their choice? No, we cannot conclude that. God loved the whole world; He sent Jesus so that the whole world might be saved (John 3:16,17). God's invitation is to "whosoever will" (Revelation 22:17 KJV)." (Root, *op. cit.*, p.27) We add that if a man chooses to accept the terms, he is foreordained to adoption as a son. If he chooses to reject the terms, he is foreordained to damnation.

[25] Wuest, *op. cit.*, p.36.

[26] But we will not become deity – little gods – as we are elevated to be "some-bodies." One day we will get a body just like the one Jesus now has.

tions possible. It is through Christ's incarnation and mediation (Galatians 3:26-4:7) that adoption is possible. Our adoption is not yet complete; we are still looking forward to its completion (Romans 8:23), namely, our glorified resurrection bodies.

To Himself – The words "to Himself" refer to the subject of the verb "predestined," namely, God the Father. We have said that God wanted a family, and He determined, even before the creation of the world, that those who were "in Christ" were to be adopted into His family. "He predestined us through Jesus Christ unto Himself."

According to the kind intention of His will – He planned and did all this because it pleased Him to do it this way. "Will" in this place translates the Greek word *thelema.*[27] God did things the way He did because it pleased Him to do it that way; this is the way One with kind intentions would want to do it. Lipscomb wrote, "God foreordained the provisions of salvation, the characters that should be saved, and the conditions and tests by which they would be saved. He left every man free to choose or to reject the terms and provisions of salvation ...."[28] It might be added that if man chooses to accept the terms, he is foreordained to adoption as a son of God. It he chooses to reject the terms, he is foreordained to damnation.

1:6 -- to the praise of the glory of His grace, which He freely bestowed on us in the Beloved.

To the praise of the glory of His grace – This verse tells us the purpose behind God's choosing of people who are in Christ, and then predestining them to adoption as His sons. He wanted those sons to praise and honor Him for His grace.[29] Grace (see notes on "grace" at 1:2) in this verse seems to be equal to "kind intention" in the previous verse.[30] The multiplication of genitive phrases in "of the glory of His grace" has been explained in different ways. Some suppose "glory" attempts to express the remarkable richness, fullness, and abun-

---

[27] On the meaning of *thelema*, see notes on "will" at 1:1 and 1:11 "the counsel of His will."

[28] David Lipscomb, "Ephesians, Philippians and Colossians" in *New Testament Commentary Series* (Nashville: Gospel Advocate, 1960), p.19.

[29] Note this phrase, "to the praise of His glory," also occurs in verses 12 and 14.

[30] When singing of God's amazing grace, we must remember that it is God, and not grace itself, that we must praise. Without God, there is no grace. (Hayden, *op. cit.*, p.300).

dance of God's grace.   Since "glory" is used in the Bible to describe the manifestation of God's presence with His people, some suppose we should think about how God's presence has been made visible in God's gracious acts.

Which He freely bestowed on us in the Beloved – The antecedent of "which" is "grace."   It is grace that was bestowed on us.   We understand that Jesus Christ is "the Beloved," since God, on occasion, spoke of Jesus as being "My beloved Son."[31]   The words "in the Beloved" are a dative of sphere.[32]   That is, it is in virtue of our unity with His Beloved Son that we are recipients of God's freely bestowed grace.   "Freely bestowed" speaks of the abundance of the gift.[33]   "Us" refers to us who have become Christians, i.e., the chosen individuals introduced in verse 4.   If we are not "in Christ," we receive none of these spiritual blessings.

3.   *Blessing #3* – **In the Beloved, God richly demonstrated His grace toward us.   1:7,8a**

1:7 – *In Him we have redemption through His blood, the forgiveness of our trespasses, according to the riches of His grace*

In Him – The antecedent of "Him" is "the Beloved" (Jesus Christ, verse 6) who here is described as the One in whom we have redemption.   In verses 7-10, we come face to face with several of the great concepts of the Christian faith – redemption (deliverance), forgiveness, mystery, and dispensation (management).

We have – The verb is a present tense verb.   We Christians already have redemption.[34]   John 3:16,36 and 6:47 indicate that eternal life is a present posses-

---

[31] Matthew 3:17 (parallel Mark 1:11), 12:18, 17:5; Colossians 1:13.

[32] "Beloved" is a translation of a perfect participle.   The perfect tense speaks of an action completed in the past time having present, and in a context like this one, permanent results. (Wuest, *op. cit.*, p.39.)   Only here is this participle used of Christ in the New Testament.

[33] "He freely bestowed" (or, 'He gave') translates a verb (*charitoō*) which is used only here and in Luke 1:28 (where the angel told Mary she was "highly favored," ASV) in the New Testament. The word means "to give generously."

[34] It may also mean that our redemption is a process, so far as our individual lives are concerned.   It is something we have right now.   "We have and are still having." (A. Skevington Wood, "Ephesians" in EBC [Grand Rapids: Zondervan, 1978], p.25.)

sion for the Christian. The present tense also reminds us that redemption only in Christ is an abiding fact.[35]

Redemption – The Greek is not *agorazo* (purchase in a market place) but *apolutrosis*, the word used of freeing of slaves or prisoners by payment of a ransom price.[36] Commentators have argued at length whether the word *lutroō* (the root of *apolutrosis*), when speaking of the redemption accomplished in Christ, always includes the idea of the "price" paid to ransom or redeem. In the New Testament, there are times that the "price" is included in the idea of ransom (redemption). See 1 Peter 1:18-19, where we are told that the ransom price is the shed blood of Christ. See also Titus 2:14. And it seems evident that here in Ephesians 1:7, the word redeem includes the price, for the very next words "through His blood" speak of the price. The chief difficulty arising when we think of the word "redeem" as including the price of the redemption, is the question of "to whom was the price given?" The Patristic idea that the ransom was paid to the devil is hardly found in the Bible. It is best not to try to determine to whom the ransom might have been paid, but simply to emphasize the idea of the freedom that is now experienced.

Through His blood – This is the price for freeing the slaves of sin. "Jesus shed His blood to secure for men the remission of sins. 'For this is My blood of the covenant, which is poured out for many for forgiveness of sins,' Matt 26:28."[37] "The Scriptures uniformly present the blood of Christ as the purchase price of our redemption (Acts 20:28; 1 Corinthians 6:20; 1 Peter 1:18-20; Hebrews 9:12). Colossians 1:14 parallels this verse."[38] "In speaking of the 'blood' of Jesus Christ there is something more than merely 'death,' since in this type of context 'blood' reflects the sacrificial system of the Old Testament to which Christ's death

---

[35] One prominent feature of Paul's usage of the word "redemption" is the double reference in the word: it has a *present* application to the forgiveness of sins based on the ransom price of the shed blood of Christ (Ephesians 1:7; 1 Peter 1:18-19); and it has a *future* application to the deliverance of the body from its present debility and liability to corruption (Romans 8:23). This latter event is associated with the day of redemption (Ephesians 4:30).

[36] For more details in "redemption" see notes at Romans 3:24 in Reese, *New Testament Epistles: Romans.*

[37] Lipscomb, *op. cit.*, p.20.

[38] Ralph Martin, "Ephesians" in *Wycliffe Bible Commentary* (Chicago: Moody, 1962), p.1304.

is constantly related in New Testament passages."[39]

The forgiveness of our trespasses – The "redemption" we have is here defined as the forgiveness of sins. Freedom from our slavery to sin was purchased for us. "Forgiveness (*aphesis*) is loosing someone from what binds him."[40] It may also speak of the release from the consequences of our trespasses (*paraptoma* is to fall aside, to deviate from truth and uprightness). The Greek word used for "trespass" pictures taking the wrong road, when we could have and should have taken the right one; it is missing the truth that we might have known and should have known; and therefore "trespass" is the failure to reach the goal and the journey's end that we ought to have reached. The forgiveness of sins is what makes the gospel "good news."[41] "Forgiveness is the great and needed blessing for which we are taught to pray, along with daily bread (Matthew 6:11,12)."[42]

According to the riches of His grace – "According to" translates *kata*, a preposition which denotes relationship, or proportion, and has reference to agreement or conformity to a standard.[43] God's forgiveness is in harmony with or in agreement with the riches (*ploutos*, wealth, abundance, plenitude) of His grace. His grace is not limited. In fact, the first phrase of verse 8 says His grace was lavished on us.

1:8a – *which He lavished upon us.*

Which He lavished upon us – "Which" points back to "grace" (verse 7). "Lavished" translates the Greek word *perissueo*, an adjective which means more than enough, "beyond the usual (amount or size), to exceed beyond a fixed num-

---

[39] Bratcher, *op. cit.*, p.16.

[40] Wood, *ibid*.

[41] "The forgiveness of sins is what makes the gospel 'good news.' Good news is a call from your stockbroker that your stock has hit a new high. It is your doctor's report that your cancer operation was a complete success. Good news is a telegram saying that your son who was missing in action is safe and will be home soon. But the greatest 'good news' of all is the news that God has forgiven our sins and redeemed our soul through the blood of His Son." (Tesh, *op. cit.*, p.380.)

[42] Hayden, *op. cit.*, p.300.

[43] Thayer, *Lexicon*, p.328.

ber or measure."[44]   God has with open-handed generosity lavished the riches of His grace upon those who will receive the redemption (the forgiveness of their trespasses) which He offers.

4. *Blessing #4* – God has made known to us the mystery of His will.   1:8b-10b

1:8b – *In all wisdom and insight*

In all wisdom and insight – This phrase should be treated as the beginning of the sentence which continues on in verse 9.[45]   "Wisdom" (*sophia*) includes "striving after the best ends as well as using the best means."[46]   It also includes the ideas of "skill in handicraft and art, skill in matters of common life, sound judgment, intelligence."[47]   "Insight" (*phronesis*) means understanding.   Moulton and Milligan say *phronesis* leads to right action, as compared with the more theoretical *sophia*.[48]   God was striving after the best ends (wisdom) and using all the best actions (insight) as "He made known to us the mystery of His will" (verse 9).

1:9 – *He made known to us the mystery of His will, according to His kind intention which He purposed in Him*

He made known to us the mystery of His will – In New Testament terminology, a "mystery" is something which was not clearly revealed in Old Testament times, but which has now been revealed through Jesus and His apostles.   "Will" (as in verses 1 and 5) translates *thelema,* which comes from the verb *thelo*.   The verb

---

[44] Thayer, *Lexicon*, p.595.

[45] In Greek the last clause of verse 8 is the prepositional phrase "in all wisdom and insight." There are two questions: Does this phrase go (1) with what precedes or (2) with what follows? Does it refer (a) to God or (b) to believers? In this commentator's judgment, the NASB does right by connecting the phrase to what follows. It is God's insight and wisdom that are emphasized.

[46] R.C. Trench, *Synonyms of the New Testament* (Grand Rapids: Eerdmans, 1966), p.283.

[47] Henry G. Liddell and Robert Scott, *A Greek-English Lexicon* (New York: Harper & Brothers, 1846), p.1368.

[48] James Hope Moulton and George Milligan, *The Vocabulary of the New Testament* (London: Hodder & Stoughton, 1963), p.676.

thelo means "to resolve, determine, purpose, to desire or wish." So the noun *thelema*, "will," refers to what one objectively wishes or desires to be done; it is the thing willed.[49] From the previous verses in Ephesians, it might be said that it is God's will for us to be redeemed by Christ's death and become God's adopted children. In this context, the particular thing God willed is that at a time suitable to God, the summing up of all things in Christ would transpire (verse 10). The aorist participle "made known" indicates that before Paul wrote Ephesians the making known had already happened.[50] "Us" to whom the mystery has been made known could be the apostles and prophets of Jesus (Ephesians 3:5), or it could be to all of us Christians (Colossians 1:26) who have learned it from the holy apostles and prophets of Jesus. Men become believers through the words of the apostles (Romans 10:17; Ephesians 3:2-4).

According to His kind intention – "Kind intention" translates *eudokia*, a word that speaks of "what seems good or well." The making known of the mystery was done as it seemed best to God to do it. "God shaped his plan or purpose in Himself without consulting us. It was His plan. He shaped it as He wished, according to His good pleasure. We know about it because He made it known to us through the gospel."[51]

Which He purposed in Him - "Which" is feminine and refers back to the feminine word translated "kind intention." Christ is the means by which God's kind intentions were put into operation.[52] "From all eternity the Father cherished in His own mind a plan that was to be carried out in Christ."[53]

---

[49] Thayer, *Lexicon*, p.285, 286. "The word 'will' here is a translation, not of *boule*, a desire based upon reason and deliberation, but *thelema*, a desire based on the emotions. God's will or desire here comes from His heart of love" (Wuest, *op. cit.*, p.44).

[50] Is this statement intended to counteract incipient Gnosticism which just now was beginning to appear in Asia Minor? It certainly implies that folk do not need to go to the Gnostics to learn about the mystery of God's will. By the time Jude 3 was written, the faith had already been delivered once and for all to the saints. God is not making known additional truths to anyone.

[51] Root, *op. cit.*, p.28.

[52] The KJV translated *en auto* as "in himself." Perhaps the NASB has a better translation. "This makes it clear that it is in Christ that God will bring to fruition His divine plan for His creation" (Tesh, *op. cit.*, p.381).

[53] Wood, *op. cit.*, p.26.

1:10 – *with a view to an administration suitable to the fullness of the times,* **that is,** *the summing up of all things in Christ, things in the heavens and things upon the earth.*

With a view to an administration suitable to the fullness of the times – "With a view to" tells us that verse 10 expresses the end, the design which God had in view, as He kept His plans a "mystery" through the long ages of the Old Testament times. God had His reason for the long delay in the revelation of the "mystery." That reason lay in the fact that the world was not ripe for the dispensation of grace which formed the contents of the mystery (cp. Galatians 4:1-11). The Greek word *oikonomia*, translated "administration" in the NASB and "dispensation" in the ASV, literally means the "management of a house." The word is often translated as "stewardship," for a steward is one who manages the house or affairs of another. A "dispensation" is a certain period of time marked by a certain method in which God administers the affairs of mankind, such as the Patriarchal or Mosaic dispensation. But this is not quite the idea in this passage. Here it refers to God's own management or administration of the fullness of times. Paul says that God has been planning and thinking and administering and arranging history, so that it comes out where He wants it to. "Fullness of the times" tells us that God set His own schedule. "Times" expresses the idea that there are certain periods of time, such as the Patriarchal, Mosaic, and Christian periods, included in God's plan. God is managing things so that when the time is ripe (in His sight) He will unify everything in heaven and earth, with Christ as head over all.

***That is,* the summing up of all things in Christ** – "That is" (in italics in the NASB) indicates that the infinitive translated "summing up" is an explanatory infinitive, "supplying at once the content of the mystery, the object of the kind intention, and the object reserved for the administration."[54] "Summing up" is the opposite of the disharmony so obvious in our world, a disharmony that has resulted from sin. "Summing up" translates the compound Greek verb *anakephalaioō*. The *ana-* signifies "again," thus pointing back to a previous condition where no separation existed; and *kephalaioō* means "to collect under one head." The full meaning of the word is "to gather again under one head the things that had originally been one, but had since been separated."[55] The Greek

---

[54] Abbott, *op. cit.*, p.18.

[55] Lipscomb, *op. cit.*, p.25. "The Greek word translated 'summing up' is a mathematical term and describes how numbers were totaled in New Testament times. Whenever a column of figures was added, the total was placed at the top (not at the bottom as most of us are accustomed to doing). Paul is saying that at the end, everything will 'add up' to Christ" (Shannon, *op. cit.*, p.381).

verb is middle voice, meaning God did it this way for His own benefit. "It is remarkable that Paul has here used a word ("all things") which is in the neuter gender. It is not just all persons, or all angels, or all men, or all the elect, but all things are to be gathered together in Christ."[56] We remember that even the physical universe was affected by sin, and is to be restored to its former state. The following phrases explain what is included in all things. It is the totality of creation – all created objects, men, and things. "In Christ" shows that Christ is the "head" around whom all things are to be gathered. "In Christ" (the Greek reads "in the Christ" – the article "the" showing that a special point is being emphasized) shows that Jesus the Christ is God's agent, instrument, and sphere of operation in carrying out His plan to fulfillment. "Since Christ is pre-eminent in God's purpose in the universe and in the church, the individual who does not have Christ pre-eminent in his life is entirely out of harmony with the purpose of the Father."[57]

Things in the heavens and things upon the earth -- This phrase is a concept that is unfolded in Romans 8:20-22 and Colossians 1:16-20. "In the heavens" (*epi tois ouranois*) is not quite the same expression as "in the heavenlies" (verse 3, *en tois epouranois*). Thus, this phrase is one of great doctrinal importance, being one of the select class of passages that refer to the cosmic significance of Christ's person and work. Christ's blood was needed to cleanse the heavenly tabernacle after there was war in heaven and the devil and his angels sinned (Hebrews 9:23,24). When Christ returns, all of creation is to be restored to its former state (Romans 8:20-22). According to His good pleasure, it is God's will to have gathered together all things in Christ when the succession of ages closes. "To unite a divided world is both incredible and impossible, on human terms. Restoring man to fellowship with God, or even with his fellow man, seems equally unlikely. The idea of a plan or purpose in the seemingly disordered and discordant complexity of life and events is rejected by some. But God knows what He is doing, and, in Christ, he will tie up all the loose ends and bring order and good out of chaos and evil in a world gone wrong."[58]

---

[56] Albert Barnes, "Ephesians" in *Barnes' Notes* (Grand Rapids: Baker, 1953), p.25. "This is not to be taken as some form of syrupy universalism that says that everyone will go to heaven. That would make this passage contradict other passages in Ephesians as well as countless other Scriptures. It simply means that all of history is pointing to the second coming of Jesus and will be consummated when He returns (1 Corinthians 15:14-28)." (Shannon, *op. cit.*, p.381)

[57] Martin, *op. cit.*, p.1304.

[58] Tesh, *op. cit.*, p.381.

5. *Blessing #5* – In Him (Christ), God made the Jews a heritage. 1:10c-12

1:10c,11 – *In Him also we have obtained an inheritance, having been predestined according to His purpose who works all things after the counsel of His will,*

In Him – "In Him" is an emphatic resumption of the "in the Christ" in whom all things are summed up. Verse 13 will also begin with "In Him." As the NASB has punctuated this passage, "in Him" (at the end of verse 10) introduces the new sentence that continues on in verse 11. What the whole sentence says is that "in Christ" we have been made an inheritance (a heritage).

Also we have obtained an inheritance – The Greek is passive, and the ASV rightly translated it as "we were made a heritage." A heritage is something God gets, not something we inherit.[59] In the church God gets a family of people who love Him because they want to. "Also" says that in addition to summing up all things in Christ, another thing God willed was that we Christians might be designated as His heritage. "We" in this verse refers to Jewish Christians, as contrasted with "you" (Gentile Christians) in verse 13.[60] In Old Testament times, Israel (i.e., the true Israel within Israel) was God's heritage; now His heritage is much more inclusive. All that Israel of old was to God, the church is now. (Of course, since Calvary and Pentecost, the physical descendants of "Israel" are not excluded – what is required for them is to come to be "in Christ" as Romans 11:23 indicates. Then they too will be part of God's heritage.)

Having been predestined according to His purpose – That those who are in Christ would be part of God's heritage was something that was part of the plan ("purpose," cf. Romans 8:28-30) God made back in eternity. God's workings are not the result of chance or impulse. Before time began, God laid out in His own mind a program (*prothesis*, or purpose) for the ages. In verse 5, it will be remembered, believers are said to have been predestined "to adoption as sons."

---

[59] The NASB/KJV which both read "inheritance" here state that we who are in Christ have come into possession of what God had planned for His chosen people. When translated "inheritance" and then when the combination of "predestined" (*prooristhentes*), "purpose" (*prothesis*, plan), "counsel" (*boule*) and "will" (*thelema*) which follow is figured in, Calvinists find here a proof text for God's sovereignty and the unconditional predestination of certain souls to be saved. The ASV rightly says that we are made God's inheritance. God Himself gets something in the saints.

[60] "In verses 11-14 Paul compares and contrasts the status of both Jews (verses 11,12) and Gentiles (verse 13) in their (Jew and Gentile united, verse 14) inheritance in Christ" (Tesh, *op. cit.*, p.381).

Now this verse tells us something else God planned, namely, that He would receive a heritage.

Who works all things after the counsel of His will – God not only has a plan that He made back in eternity, but He works at carrying out His plans. Everything in the plan is the result of reason and intelligent deliberation ("counsel") on His part, and everything is in harmony with the way a loving God willed to act as He goes about providing redemption.[61]   In theological language, this working of all things in harmony with the counsel of His will is called God's providence.

1:12 – *to the end that we who were the first to hope in Christ should be to the praise of His glory.*

To the end – This clause states the ultimate end God had in view in foreordaining some Jews to be His heritage.

That we who were the first to hope in Christ – "We" refers to "we Jews" (i.e., we Jews who are now Christians[62]) as the rest of the verse shows,   for they were

---

[61] See footnote #49 above.   In the phrase "the counsel of His will," the word translated "counsel" (*boule*) has in it the idea of intelligence and deliberation.   The word translated "will" is *thelema* (see verse 5) which speaks of God's desire based on His emotion of love.   The distinction between *boule* and *thelema* is very much debated (especially among Calvinists), with scholars taking precisely opposite views on the implications of these two synonyms.   (One may consult Thayer's *Lexicon* at page 286 to see how even the lexicographers cannot agree on the meaning of the terms.) To Calvinists, if the sovereign God "wills" something (whether the word be *boule* or *thelema*), that thing was predestined and would have to happen.   There must be something faulty in that doctrine, for in Luke 7:30 we are told the Pharisees rejected God's purpose (*boule*), so God's "purpose" or will (*boule*) is not bound to happen.   In 2 Peter 3:9, we read that God is "not wishing (*boulomenos*) for any to perish."   This verse hardly means that all men are predestined to be saved.   If Calvinists cannot use *boule* to show something has to happen, the attempt is then made to show that God's *thelema* ("will") means the thing is predestined to happen.   Yet 1 Thessalonians 5:18 uses *thelema* ("will") in a verse that reads "in everything give thanks; for this is God's will for you in Christ Jesus." Such prayers are not predestined to happen, it would appear.   Also in Matthew 7:21 the doing of the will (*thelema*) of the Father in heaven is something that a man can reject to do.   1 John 2:17 likewise indicates that the will of God is something a man may or may not choose to do.   God's *thelema*, as far as men's behavior is concerned, is not always something that is absolutely predestined to occur.   What God Himself wills and plans to do, however, is the way things will happen.

[62] One of the issues commentators face as they work through Ephesians is the change of pronouns from first person plural ("we" and "our") to second person plural ("you" and "your").   What, if anything, is signified by this change?   "We" in 1:11 and "our" in 1:14 clearly refer to all Christians. However, how shall we understand "we" in verse 12 and "you also" in verse 13?   Nearly all modern commentators accept the distinction that in verse 12 "we" refers to Jewish Christians, while "you also" in verse 13 refers to Gentile Christians.   This explanation harmonizes well with the idea that Ephesians is concerned with the relationship between Jewish Christians and Gentile Christians.   It gives the word *pro* ("before") its proper meaning.

the first to anticipate the coming of the Messiah.[63]   "In Christ" should be "in the Christ" (there is an article in the Greek, *en to christo*), as the subject of Messianic expectation and not as "Jesus," for whom "Christ" had passed into a proper name. It is equivalent to "in the Messiah."[64]   The Jews had fixed their hope on the coming Messiah (Christ) long before any other nations came to know Him.   It was fitting then, that they should rejoice and praise God for the fulfillment of their long expectation.   By writing "we" Paul included himself among those Jews who had accepted Jesus as the promised Messiah.   In verse 13 Paul will turn to the Gentiles.

Should be to the praise of His glory – "Glory" is a hard term to explain, but how wonderful God is may begin to catch the idea.   Verse 6 has already spoken about praising the glory of His grace.   "Praise" being given to God is the final purpose which God had in mind for believers in Christ who are admitted to the family of God (cp. Isaiah 43:21).   God's plan was always to include Jewish believers in His family.

6. *Blessing #6* – In Him (Christ), Gentiles also were sealed with the Holy Spirit of promise.   1:13,14

1:13 – *In Him, you also, after listening to the message of truth, the gospel of your salvation – having also believed, you were sealed in Him with the Holy Spirit of promise,*

In Him, you also – "In Him" (literally "in whom" in the Greek) refers to the Christ.   "You" refers to Gentile Christians (as contrasted with "we" [in verses 11,12] which spoke of Jewish Christians).   "Paul now directs his thoughts to Gen-

---

[63] In place of the NASB's translation "first," the older English versions read "before" ("we had before hoped in Christ").   Some think the "before" speaks of the times prior to the conversion of the Gentiles, but after Pentecost.   Others (with whom we agree) think the "before" speaks simply of the time before the advent of Christ.

[64] M.R. Vincent, *Word Studies in the New Testament* (Wilmington, DE: Associated Publishers and Authors, 1972), p.847.

tile Christians, among whom the readers of this letter were numbered."[65]   The "dash" in the middle of verse 13 in the NASB indicates we have a broken sentence in the Greek.   The main verb in this sentence is "you were sealed."   It is preceded by two participles, listening and believed.   You listened, you believed, and then you were sealed.[66]   "Also" says that this sealing is just as true for Gentile Christians as it was for Jewish Christians.

After listening to the message of truth, the gospel of your salvation – The process of the Gentiles' inclusion is the same as the process as that by which Jewish folk come to be included in the body of Christ.

> The Jews first heard the truth of the gospel as preached by the apostle Peter on the day of Pentecost after Christ's resurrection and ascension into heaven (Acts 2:22-36).   They believed and were baptized into Christ, receiving the promised gift of the Holy Spirit (Acts 2:37-41).   Gentiles had the gospel preached to them first by the same apostle Peter in the house of Cornelius at Caesarea (Acts 10:34-43); their belief was attested by a special manifestation of the Holy Spirit, and they were baptized into Christ (Acts 10:44-48).[67]

The second of these two clauses ("the gospel of your salvation") explains what Paul meant when he said "the message of truth."   Romans 10:17 makes it plain that faith comes from hearing the word of Christ.   The Word is influential in the new birth (John 17:17; Colossians 1:5; James 1:18).   To characterize the gospel as "the message of truth" may be a contrast to Old Testament types and shadows (Hebrews 8:5), and/or it may be a contrast to heathenism's errors.

[In whom] having also believed – It is an obedient faith if they believed "in Christ."   They became converts to Christ.   They believed in Him.[68]   The emphasis upon "in Christ" which occurs throughout this whole section (verses 3-14) is, via the phrase "in whom," forcefully brought forward once more.

---

[65] Hayden, *op. cit.*, p.301.   Perhaps Paul's handling of this subject reflects what verses like Romans 1:16 say, "to the Jew first, and also to the Greek."

[66] Paul indicates there are several stages in the administration of the Gentiles' affairs.   1) They heard the gospel.   2) They believed.   3) They were sealed.   4) They will be glorified.

[67] Hayden, *op. cit.*, p.302.

[68] This second "in whom" (so the Greek of this verse reads, being translated by "in Him" in the NASB, but with a marginal note explaining it is literally "in whom") is a resumption of the first "in whom" found in verse 13.

You were sealed in Him with the Holy Spirit of promise – The sealing and the believing in Him are simultaneous. The KJV at this place (which reads "in whom also *after* you believed you were sealed") leaves the reader with a mis-understanding. The sealing did not take place as something subsequent to salvation, but was simultaneous with salvation.[69] The translation found in TEV, "God put His stamp of ownership on you by giving the Holy Spirit He had promised," helps us understand the figure of speech in "sealed." A seal indicated possession or ownership.[70] "Of promise" reminds us that God had promised in the Old Testament prophecy the coming of the Holy Spirit (Joel 2:28-32; 3:1-5; Isaiah 32:15, 44:3; Ezekiel 36:26, 39:29; Zechariah 12:10). The sealing action of the Holy Spirit is mentioned elsewhere in the New Testament (cf. 2 Corinthians 1:22; Ephesians 4:30). The Holy Spirit Himself is the seal. His presence indicates that we are "in Christ" (Romans 8:9-11). What is here called a seal is elsewhere referred to as the gift (Acts 2:38,39) and indwelling (Romans 8:9-11) of the Holy Spirit.[71]

That the receiving of the Holy Spirit is to accompany baptism is evident also in Paul's inquiries of several disciples at Ephesus (Acts 19:2,3). When he asked whether they

---

[69] The doctrine of subsequence is the idea that after one has become a Christian, another operation of the Holy Spirit is needed, either to conquer an alleged old sinful nature, or to empower the Christian with miraculous powers. This commentator rejects both of these ideas because "believed" and "sealed" are both in the aorist tense, and grammarians call the construction a "co-incident aorist." The "sealing" and the "believing in Him" are co-incident. The sealing does not follow the believing; it is not a second work being talked about. (See Moulton, *Grammar of New Testament Greek*, p.131 note; and F.F. Bruce, *Ephesians, in loc*.) Other examples in the New Testament of this "co-incident aorist" construction are Acts 19:2, "Did you receive the Holy Spirit when you believed?" and Ephesians 1:20,22, where "raised, seated, gave" and "put in subjection" are all aorist tense.

[70] In ancient times, it was a practice for animals and other property to be marked with a seal ("branded") as a means of identification. The mark denoted ownership and carried with it the protection by the owner. Thus, those who enter the Christian fellowship are sealed by the Holy Spirit – a mark of identification and a pledge of protection by the owner, God Himself. If it be asked, to whom does the presence of the Holy Spirit make this attestation, perhaps the answer is twofold: to others, to show them we belong to God; and to ourselves, an attestation to our own consciousness that we belong to God (Romans 8:16).

[71] The indwelling Spirit helps Christians to live the Christian life by strengthening when difficulties and temptations are faced (Romans 8). "The Spirit's presence does not provide complete protection against ourselves, however. If we choose to go with the devil, we can take ourselves out of the Savior's hand. Thus it is possible to fall away even after being a partaker of the Holy Spirit (Hebrews 6:4-6). The Holy Spirit does not destroy our will, but He guides it if we are willing to accept His guidance" (Woodrow Phillips, *Adult Lesson Commentary 1979-80* [Cincinnati, OH: Standard, 1979], p.83).

received the Holy Spirit when they believed, they replied in the negative. Paul's next question, "Into what then were you baptized?" reveals his understanding that the immersion of penitent believers is attended by the reception of the gift of the Holy Spirit.[72]

1:14 – *who is given as a pledge of our inheritance, with a view to the redemption of* God's own *possession, to the praise of His glory.*

Who is given as a pledge of our inheritance – "Who"[73] refers back to the "Spirit of promise" (verse 13). The indwelling Holy Spirit is described as being both the seal (verse 13) and the "pledge of our inheritance." A "pledge" is a down payment, a promise which binds the purchaser to pay in full.[74] "The Holy Spirit is the first of God's gifts to the obedient believer in Christ, and so becomes the assurance of all promised blessings to come."[75] The word "inheritance" (*kleronomias*) is not the same as "inheritance" in verse 11. Verse 11 spoke of a heritage which God gets in the church. This verse speaks of an inheritance which Christians will get. The next clause of this verse identifies exactly what Paul has in mind. Paul calls it "*our* inheritance" because he has in view the combined body of Jewish and Gentile believers, reconciled to God and to each other in Christ.

With a view to the redemption of *God's own* **possession** – We object to inserting words in italics (as the ASV and NASB do) as though the idea here is the same as in 1 Peter 2:9 ("a people for *God's* own possession"). The Greek here simply reads the "redemption of the purchased possession" (see the KJV). This phrase refers to the fact that we Christians have a glorified body coming, and the indwelling Holy Spirit is a pledge of this (cp. Romans 8:23). "Redemption" – 'a deliverance or release' – from the guilt and power of sin has already been enjoy-

---

[72] Tesh, *op. cit.*, p.381.

[73] There is a manuscript difference here. There is a masculine reading *hos* ("who") and a neuter reading *ho* ("which") found in the Chester Beatty Papyrus P[46] and some important uncials like Codex Alexandrinus (A) and Codex Vaticanus (B). Normally, relative pronouns agree in gender with their antecedent. Since the Greek word "Spirit" is a neuter word, the relative pronoun (*ho*) is also in the neuter. Perhaps the scribal change to masculine (*hos*, "who") was done to make sure the personality of the Holy Spirit is not jeopardized by either usage.

[74] The "pledge" (*arrabon*) was a part of the purchase price of anything paid in advance as a guarantee that the rest of the price would in due time be paid. Moulton and Milligan (*Vocabulary of the Greek New Testament*, p.79) show there are many Greek commercial documents (papyri) still extant in which the word occurs.

[75] Hayden, *op. cit.*, p.302.

ed by those who are in Christ, but not until He comes in glory and judgment will they be finally redeemed from physical corruption and death."[76]

To the praise of His glory – See verses 6,12.   The final redemption of the body, which will complete the process of redemption which began with the redemption of the soul, will result in the praise of God's glory.

B.   Paul's Prayer that the Readers of this Letter May Grow in Spiritual Knowledge.   1:15-23

> *Summary*:   Verses 15-23 are one long sentence in the Greek, with a minor break at verse 22.   The main verb comes in verse 16 ("[I] do not cease giving thanks").   Verses 17-19a give the content of the prayer, and the prayer closes with a lengthy meditation on the power of God manifested in Christ (verses 19b-23).

1:15 – *For this reason I too, having heard of the faith in the Lord Jesus which* **exists** *among you and your love for all the saints,*

For this reason – "For this reason" (*dia touto*) means on account of what has been said before.   It is because the spiritual blessings (verses 3-14) in which we share are so tremendous that Paul begins a long sentence (verses 15-23) in which his main thought is "I pray for you."   Since many church members actually appreciate material blessings (such as money) more than they do their spiritual blessings, in this section (1:15-23) we find Paul praying that his readers might know and appreciate their spiritual blessings.

I, too – Who is included besides Paul?   Is someone else also praying a similar prayer?   Is it his informant, from whom Paul had heard about the readers?   Is it the readers themselves, supposing they had been taught to offer such prayers at an earlier occasion?   If they have not already been offering such prayers, the readers certainly can learn about the content of prayers a Christian might offer by studying Paul's prayers for them.

Having heard of the faith in the Lord Jesus which *exists* **among you** – "Having

---

[76] *Ibid.*

heard" means that Paul has been informed about the readers. What he had been told is stated in the phrases following in this verse. In the Detailed Introduction to Ephesians, the possible bearing this verse has on the identification of the intended recipients of this letter has been alluded to. The conclusion this commentator has reached includes several ideas. "Paul was in prison at Rome when he wrote this letter. Many people, including Christians, traveled freely at that time, so the apostle, with the liberty given him as a 'trusty' prisoner, had ample opportunity to receive reports from the fields in which he had successfully labored."[77] It had been 3 years or more since Paul had been in the area to which this letter is addressed. "Having heard" indicates that there were going to be readers of this letter whom Paul did not know personally, and others whom he had not seen for several years. But at some time previous to this writing, he had heard about them from someone. This interpretation of "having heard" appears to be confirmed by the similar expression ("heard of your faith") in Colossians 1:4 which is addressed to a church Paul had never visited.[78] In the words "the faith in the Lord Jesus which *exists* among you" Paul is referring to their loyalty to the Lord Jesus, their personal steadfastness in the faith.[79] Perhaps the Greek *ten kath' humas pistin*, translated "which *exists* among you," implies that some of the readers did not have this faith. If so, this fact would add weight to the prayer which follows.

And your love for all the saints – Notice that Paul has heard (perhaps from Tychicus?) about two things concerning the first readers of this epistle: their faith

---

[77] Guy Leavitt, *Standard Bible Teacher and Leader 1958*, (Cincinnati, OH: Standard, 1957), p.122.

[78] Those who hold a strictly Ephesian destination for this letter will write about how what Paul is talking about is their progress in the Christian faith since he last saw them, about 3 years previous. He was concerned about them. When at last he heard about them again, he heard the glad news that their faith in Christ was unshaken and their love of other Christians was strong. This brought joy to Paul which is reflected in this letter. Appeal is also made to a similar expression which occurs in Philemon 5, addressed to Paul's beloved fellow worker. That language must say that Philemon was known personally to Paul. Philemon 5 reads, "I hear (a present tense verb, 'I am hearing') of your love and of the faith which you have toward the Lord Jesus." The verb form at Ephesians 1:15 for "heard" is an aorist participle, and could well be translated "after I heard ...." Abbott (*op. cit.*, p.25) argues that the change of tense between Ephesians 1:15 and Philemon 5 makes all the difference in how these similar expressions are interpreted.

[79] Such an explanation can be harmonized either with a strictly Ephesian destination for the letter, or it can be harmonized with the idea Ephesians was a circular letter which would reach some churches which Paul had never visited.

and their love.[80]   If the words "your love" are genuine, it is the readers' love for the brethren, as expressed in actions helpful to them (cp. 1 John 3:17,18), that has been reported to Paul.   Jesus had taught the need for love for the brethren (cf. Matthew 25:31-46).   About thirty years later, the apostle John will address a letter to the same audience as this letter "to the Ephesians" is addressed, and in three different places in that letter which we call 1 John he will emphasize the necessity of love for the brothers as being part and parcel of being a child of God. (Gnostics, against whom John was warning, made no such emphasis.)   The two things which must characterize any true church are *loyalty to Christ* and *love for the saints*.   The faith and love of the readers to whom this letter was addressed was an incentive to Paul to pray for their continued spiritual growth.

1:16 – *do not cease giving thanks for you, while making mention* of you *in my prayers;*

[I] do not cease giving thanks for you – This clause expresses the continuation of an action that was going on before Paul recently "heard" of their faith and love. "I am always giving thanks" is a good way to render the kind of double negative in the Greek "do not cease."   "Paul's joy over what he has heard about the readers was expressed immediately in thanksgiving to God.   That did not have to wait until he could write a letter and find some traveler to carry it."[81]

While making mention *of you* in my prayers – *Mneian poioumenos* ("making mention") implies that when Paul prayed he named the ones for whom he was praying.[82]   2 Corinthians 11:28 speaks of Paul's constant concern for all the churches.

1:17 – *that the God of our Lord Jesus Christ, the Father of glory, may give to you a spirit of wisdom and of revelation in the knowledge of Him.*

---

[80] Several manuscripts (P[46], Aleph, B) omit "your love," making the text read "your faith in the Lord Jesus and toward all the saints."   With the words omitted, Paul is saying he has heard of both their loyalty to Christ and to His people.   This variant closely links Christ and the church, an emphasis very much in harmony with what is written later in this letter about the church being the body of Christ and the need for oneness in the body.   The longer reading which includes the words "your love" here is similar to Colossians 1:4.

[81] Phillips, *op. cit.*, p.84.

[82] The Greek is hard to translate so that an implication is not left that Paul forgot all about them except when he was praying.

That the God of our Lord Jesus Christ – Beginning with "that" (*hina*), verses 17-19a tell us for what Paul had been praying when he made mention of the readers in his prayers.   Along with his new joyous thanksgiving went urgent requests for the Ephesians, with the specific things he was requesting being detailed in the verses following.   Paul's prayers were addressed to the One who was capable of answering them, "the God of our Lord Jesus Christ."[83]

The Father of glory – Since the expression "Father of glory" is not found elsewhere in the New Testament (though see James 1:17, "the Father of lights"), it has occasioned some uncertainty regarding the writer's intent.[84]   Among the suggestions offered are these: (1) "Glory" might (for example) indicate God's uniqueness and majesty, and the phrase could be translated "glorious Father." (2) God dwells in unapproachable light (1 Timothy 6:16), and that may be why He is designated as the "Father of glory."   (3) Some see a reference in the word "glory" to the Shekinah, the glorious visible symbol of God's manifested presence.   (4) The word "glory" here might pick up the phrase "to the praise of His glory" in Ephesians 1:6,12,14.   He who is the Father of all those adopted children is the One to whom glory (praise) belongs.   (5) F.F. Bruce suggested that Paul here may be introducing the idea of "the archetypal Fatherhood of God" – which is further elaborated in Ephesians 3:15 where we learn that "all fatherhood in heaven or on earth is in one way or another derived from His Fatherhood"[85] – and so there is a certain glory connected with the fact that He is a Father.

May give to you a spirit of wisdom and of revelation – This is the first of the specific requests for which Paul prayed for his readers.   There are several issues which require comment.

(1) One has to do with the Greek verb translated "may give."   The best supported reading is an optative mood,[86] and it is unusual to have an optative mood in a *hina*

---

[83] For an explanation of the phrase "the God of our Lord Jesus Christ," see comments in verse 3.

[84] There was a rather strange interpretation of the word "glory" during the exigencies of the Arian controversy, where "Father of our Lord Jesus Christ" was made to refer to His humanity, and "Father of glory" to His divinity.   Jesus has always existed, so it is not correct to think of Him being generated by the Father.

[85] F.F. Bruce, *The Epistle to the Ephesians* (New York: Fleming H. Revell, 1961), p.39.

[86] "The verb translated "may give" should be read as the optative, δῴη, but Blass and Moulton view it as an Ionic subjunctive, δώῃ, thus preserving the customary sequence of moods. Codex B reads the Attic subjunctive, δῷ." (E.K. Simpson and F.F. Bruce, *Commentary on the Epistles to the Ephesians and Colossians*, in the NICNT [Grand Rapids: Eerdmans, 1957],   p.37).

clause with a present tense introducing that clause. Perhaps Paul wrote this unusual expression because he expected the gift to be given to his readers at a different time than at the very moment he was praying.

(2) A second issue concerns the question, Did Paul pray that God would reveal His truth *directly* to the Ephesians? The correct answer to this question is, No. Such a prayer would contradict both Ephesians 3:3,4 and the very next phrase of this verse which speaks about the full knowledge of God as being the source of the wisdom and knowledge.[87]

(3) A third issue is whether "spirit" should be written with a small "s" (as the ASV and NASB read) or a capital "S" (like TEV and NIV read). (a) Capital "S" makes this a reference to the Holy Spirit,[88] and the comments to explain such a reading would be in this fashion: since they already have the indwelling Spirit (they have been "sealed"), Paul is not asking God to give them that measure of the Holy Spirit. He might be asking that the indwelling Spirit will continue to be at work in them. See Luke 11:13 where the Holy Spirit is given to those who ask Him, and see Ephesians 5:18 where the "filling" of the Holy Spirit is a constant thing. What Paul perhaps has in mind is that the Spirit will help them to understand and will disclose to them more and more of the knowledge of Him (cp. 1 Corinthians 2:14). (b) With a small "s" the reference is to man's spirit (man being composed of body, soul, and spirit). When a person becomes a Christian, and that person's spirit has become alive again because of the new birth (John 3:6), that spirit is what gives guidance to the soul, which in turn animates the body. Perhaps verse 18 helps us decide in favor of "spirit" (man's spirit) when it speaks of the "eyes of your heart," for it looks like "heart" and "spirit" are interchangeable terms. (c) Alford says, "Certainly it would not be right to take *pneuma* (spirit) here as solely the Holy Spirit, nor as solely the spirit of man: rather as a complex idea, of the spirit of man influenced by the indwelling Spirit of God."[89]

---

[87] 1 John 2:20,27 speak of an "anointing of the Holy Spirit," but they do *not* speak of direct illumination of the human spirit. 1 John 2 rather speaks of the result of an anointing (the suffix on the Greek word translated "anointing" is -*ma*, which emphasizes result), namely, the inspiration of the apostles. 1 John 2 says the inspired words of the apostles are the source from which Christians learn truth about God. 1 Corinthians 2:14,15 do speak of an illumination of the Holy Spirit to help hearers of the apostles to understand what was being taught.

[88] Salmond's arguments that the reference is to the Holy Spirit are impressive. (S. D. F. Salmond, *The Epistle to the Ephesians* in Expositor's Greek Testament, [Grand Rapids: Eerdmans, 1967], Vol.3, p.274.)

[89] Henry Alford, "Ephesians" in *Alford's Greek Testament* (London: Rivingtons, 1871), Vol.3, p.81.

(4) A fourth issue concerns the explanation of the words "wisdom and revelation." How these terms are explained depends on how we understand "spirit/Spirit," which introduces these terms. (a) If we translate it "Spirit," then we have here another of the forty some names by which the Holy Spirit is identified in Scripture. (b) If we translate it "spirit," then "wisdom" is "discernment to choose between good and evil in the ordering of conduct, or discernment of the divine plan for man (cf. 1 Corinthians 2:5-14),"[90] while "revelation" speaks of the capacity of apprehending or understanding the things revealed "in the knowledge of Him," as the verse goes on to say.[91]

In the knowledge of Him – The phrase "in the knowledge of Him" goes with both "wisdom and revelation"[92] and indicates where Paul's readers will find the wisdom and revelation for which he prays. "Knowledge" translates *epignosei* and means full knowledge, thorough knowledge.[93] Only in the sphere of the full knowledge of God will men find the "wisdom and revelation" which Paul is anxious for them to experience. Such a full knowledge of God is found in Jesus Christ, who said, "He who has seen Me has seen the Father" (John 14:9) and "I and the Father are one" (John 10:30).

---

[90] Michael R. Weed, *The Letters of Paul to the Ephesians, the Colossians, and Philemon* (Austin, TX: R. B. Sweet, 1971), p.130.

[91] Salmond (*ibid.*) argues that *apokalupsis* ("revelation") refers not to understanding something, but is actually a reference to "disclosing" something to others. Taking "Spirit" as a reference to the Holy Spirit, Salmond has Paul praying that a gift will be given to them to help them disclose the mysteries to others.

[92] The NIV's dynamic equivalent handling of this phrase, resulting in the reading "so that you may know Him better," is difficult to defend. It would be easier to defend the idea that we should connect this phrase "in the knowledge of Him" with the verse that follows, making full knowledge of God the sphere in which the eyes of their hearts have been enlightened. The connection of this phrase to the context is disputed, and in this commentator's judgment it should be connected with what precedes, rather than what follows.

[93] Later in the writings of Timothy, Peter, and John, *epignosis* will be a key term in the controversy against Gnosticism. Whether or not it is so here in Ephesians is problematical. Is the writing of Colossians the first inkling of incipient Gnosticism beginning to affect the churches? Later books and letters in the New Testament take up the theme in earnest. Perhaps this great letter "To the Ephesians" was likewise intended to be a preventive. If Christians already have full knowledge (*epignosis*) available through the words of the apostles (i.e., through them the faith has been once for all delivered), when the Gnostics do come along, no one should give a ready ear to their claim "join us to learn knowledge (*gnosis*) you can not get from the apostles." They already have access to the "full knowledge" of God.

1:18 – I pray that *the eyes of your heart may be enlightened, so that you may know what is the hope of His calling, what are the riches of the glory of His inheritance in the saints,*

I pray that **the eyes of your heart may be enlightened** – This is the second of the specific requests (see verse 17) for which Paul prayed for his readers. If the eyes of their hearts are enlightened, there are blessings which they will come to appreciate. These blessings (i.e., the hope of His calling, the riches of glory, and the surpassing greatness of His power) are unfolded in the three phrases that follow in this verse and the next. As in the previous verse, so here, some extended comments are needed.

(1) "Eyes of your heart" refers to the Christian's spiritual powers of sight, what might also be called the eyes of your mind.[94] Jesus spoke of this inner "eye" in Matthew 6:22,23.

(2) "May be enlightened" is a perfect tense participle, referring to an act in the past time with present completed results. "Having been enlightened" (as it could be translated) means back when they heard the gospel and became believers.[95]

(3) The gist of the sentence is this: 'Since you have made a beginning in the Christian life (your eyes were enlightened in the past), you now need to grow in spiritual knowledge, until you understand the following three blessings (as given in the next phrases).'

So that you may know what is the hope of His calling – This is the first of three blessings for which Paul prays. "Know" is *oida*, which speaks of knowledge gained by perception, learning, or study. "The word 'what' is *tis*, not 'how great,' nor 'of what kind,' but simply 'what' – what the hope really and essentially is."[96] "Hope" here means the thing hoped for. He wants them to know and contemplate the thing they have hoped for – heaven, with all its joys and blessings. Compare Colossians 1:5, "the hope (that is) laid up for you in heaven," and recall Peter's exhortation, "fix your hope completely on the grace to be brought to you

---

[94] *Kardias* ("heart") – This reading rests on decisive authority. It is that of Aleph, A, B, D, G, K, L, P, Vulg, Syr, Orig, Chrym, etc. The *dianoias*, "mind," of the Textus Receptus, is supported only by a few cursives, Theodoret and Oecumenius (Abbott, *op. cit.*, p.29). Yet it is very likely the "mind" that *kardias* refers to at this place.

[95] The word "enlightened" here is used as it was in early Christian literature as a synonym for baptism. That seems to be the point back to which the perfect tense verb points.

[96] Wuest, *op. cit.*, p.53.

..." (1 Peter 1:13). Such a hope will change men's behavior, as it did in the case of Abraham (Hebrews 11:9,10).[97] God calls men (invites men to become Christians) through the word of the gospel (2 Thessalonians 2:14).

What are the riches of the glory of His inheritance in the saints – This is the second of three blessings Paul wants them to know. On "riches" see notes at verse 7-8a where it was explained as expressing a lavish, open-handed, abundance. Ephesians 3:16 also speaks of "the riches of His glory." Who is thought of as receiving the inheritance this verse speaks of? Is it the inheritance which God gives to the saints (similar to verse 14)? Is it the inheritance which God Himself has in the saints (similar to "inheritance" in verse 11)? We judge Lipscomb is correct when he wrote, "It should be noted that the inheritance is spoken of as HIS and that it is an inheritance IN the saints and not FOR the saints."[98] "Paul prays that we might know how precious the saints are in God's eyes as His inheritance."[99] We can scarcely imagine what it means to God to see His purpose come to completion. In the church, God inherits: (a) An institution that is the fulfillment of His plans, the fruit of His labors, and the realization of His fondest desires. (b) A family of children who all bear His features and characteristics – His image. (c) These upon whom He can rightly lavish His deepest emotions. God cannot take His eyes off of us – because He loves us. (d) Workers who labor for Him. (e) What He feels when love, adoration, thanksgiving, and praise are offered to Him by His beings.

1:19 – *and what is the surpassing greatness of His power toward us who believe. These are in accordance with the working of the strength of His might*

And what is the surpassing greatness of His power toward us who believe – This is the third blessing Paul wanted his readers to know as a result of their hearts being enlightened. He prays that they may know the enormous power of God; actually, it is a whole series of acts of power which are exerted in the salvation of

---

[97] In recent decades a new way of interpreting the thrust of Christianity was introduced by Jurgen Moltmann and others. It has been called the Theology of Hope. This passage in Ephesians should not be pressed into service as a Biblical precedent for that very questionable approach to explaining the Christian's mission in the world. For a good introduction to this matter, see S.M. Smith, "Hope, Theology of" in Walter Elwell's *Evangelical Dictionary of Theology* (Grand Rapids: Baker, 1984), p.532-34.

[98] Lipscomb, *op. cit.*, p.34.

[99] Wuest, *op. cit.*, p.53.

men.   There is power (the Greek is *dunamis*) exerted in their conversion (Romans 1:16).   There would be power exerted in keeping them (1 Peter 1:5).   There would be power in raising them up from the dead (1 Corinthians 6:14; Philippians 3:21), and exalting them with Christ to heaven (Ephesians 2:6).   The idea almost staggers the imagination,[100] but it is true.   The same power that was used in raising Jesus from the dead is used in saving people.   Study the notes on verses 20-22 to see how God used His power in the life of Jesus and remember that this is an illustration of the power He uses to deliver us from evil, rule providentially in our lives, and to raise us from the dead.   "Enormous power" is how Wood translated it.[101]   The souls toward whom the divine power will go forth are, namely, those who are believers, i.e., believers in Jesus Christ, whether they be Jewish believers or Gentile believers.

***These are* in accordance with the working of the strength of His might** – The Greek leaves open the question of what it is that is said to be according with the working of God.   Probably it means that the "power" promised to Christians (verse 19a) is the same working of God that worked in Jesus' case.[102]

"From here on (verses 19b-23), the prayer on behalf of the readers is left behind, and the writer reflects on the nature of the power which is at work in those who believe in Christ."[103]   Paul collects all the synonyms he can lay his hands on as he attempts to describe the surpassing greatness of the power of God.   The word "working" is *energeia*, from which we get our word "energy."   It speaks of energy put forth, energy in operation,[104] and in the New Testament it always refers to superhuman power.   "Strength (*kratos*) denotes strength or power as shown in action in overcoming resistance and in exercising control (6:10).   "Might" (*ischus*) is used of bodily strength and muscular force, and refers to an inherent power that God has.   Verses 20-23 are a statement of some of the places where God's surpassing power can be seen at work.

---

[100] "Surpassing greatness" translates *huperballon*, the same word that is used at 2:7.

[101] Wood, *op. cit.*, p.30.

[102] "These are," added in italics by the NASB translators, shows those translators believed that knowledge of the three things for which Paul has just prayed are what is said to be in accordance with the working of God.

[103] Bratcher, *op. cit.*, p.34.

[104] Wuest, *op. cit.*, p.54.

1:20 – *which He brought about in Christ, when He raised Him from the dead, and seated Him at His right hand in the heavenly* **places,**

Which He brought about in Christ - All through the centuries the unlimited power of God had been demonstrated. The Old Testament is filled with many instances (e.g., the miracles in Egypt and the crossing of the Red Sea on dry land) where God's power saved Israel from powerful enemies. Christians do not have any reason to merely wish for God to demonstrate His power now like He did in Old Testament times. In fact, He does (see verse 19a). The greatest demonstration of God's power was when He raised Jesus Christ from the dead and seated Him in the heavenly places. Paul wants his readers to be aware that the same power is available to Christians. We are made new creatures by that same power, and our bodies shall be raised and changed as was Christ's by that same power.

When He raised Him from the dead – Two participial phrases now describe two ways God used His power in Christ's case. The highest example of the power of God that is revealed to man is the power used in the resurrection of Jesus from the dead.

And seated Him at His right hand in the heavenly *places* – The exaltation of Jesus to the place of honor and authority that followed His resurrection is a further witness to what the working power of God can effect.[105] Because the description in Revelation 4-8, a description of heaven as it now is, has the Lamb before the throne in heaven,[106] we understand "the heavenly *places*" in this verse to be a reference to heaven as it now is.[107] The visions accorded to John of the glorified Christ (in the book of Revelation) represent the Christ as glorified, robed in splen-

---

[105] From the earliest days of the apostolic preaching, the resurrection and enthronement of Christ were proclaimed side by side as integral to the good news, and both were presented as the fulfillment of prophecy (see Acts 2:25-36, where both Psalm16:10 and Psalm 110:1 are quoted as being fulfilled).

[106] There is a manuscript variation here, some manuscripts reading an aorist tense *energesen* (so Aleph, D, G, E, L, F) which speaks of a completed act in the past, and some reading a perfect tense *energeken* (A, B, Cyr.) which implies not only completed action in the past, but present continuing results.. Westcott & Hort and Nestle prefer the perfect tense. UBS has the aorist and no note in apparatus indicating there is a variation. "The neighboring aorist might readily lead to the substitution of the aorist for the perfect. The counter change would not be so easily accounted for. The perfect is properly employed, because the effect (Christ being raised and enthroned) continues while the separate acts in which this 'working' realized itself follow in aorist." (Abbott, *op. cit.,* p.31)

[107] For "in the heavenly *places*," see notes at Ephesians 1:3

dor, with many diadems upon His head (Revelation 19:12). Christ's mediatorial reign is alluded to here. Christ is now sitting on David's throne as the Old Testament indicated He would (see Acts 2:33-35). Psalm 110:1 ("Sit at My right hand until I make Thine enemies a footstool for Thy feet") is highlighted in Hebrews. Christ's presently being seated at God's right hand and reigning as king is a clear doctrine of Scripture.[108]

1:21 – *far above all rule and authority and power and dominion, and every name that is named, not only in this age, but also in the one to come.*

Far above all rule and authority and power and dominion – The thread of thought continues without a break from verse 20. Christ has been seated far above all rule and authority, power and dominion. The word rendered "far above" (*huperano*) is a compound, meaning *high above*, or greatly exalted. Christ was not merely *above* the ranks of beings, as head; but he was *infinitely exalted* over them.[109] Four synonyms indicate the powers over whom Jesus is infinitely exalted. It is not easy to decide whether earthly or heavenly powers are intended by these words. Some think it refers to powerful men who exercise religious or governmental authority on earth. However, the fact that the immediate place of reference here is the "heavenly places" and the subject is Christ's position at the right hand of the Majesty on high, seems at once to suggest we should not limit these "powers" to earthly powers. It is more than likely that Paul is referring to angelic beings in this phrase, and is saying that no matter what rank angels may have, Christ is exalted far above all. Paul takes the existence of ranks of angels for granted. He gives a similar list of angels in Colossians 1:16. Different orders of angels around the throne in heaven are described in Revelation 4-8. There are cherubim, seraphim, archangels, and other orders or

---

[108] "Scripture presents the risen Christ as now being in heaven and sitting at the right hand of God (Mark 16:19; Hebrews 8:1, 10:12, 12:2; Colossians 3:1), and this representation not only indicates His majesty, but also teaches us that His work of reconciliation has been fully accomplished by His one sacrifice offered once and for all upon the cross, after which He took His seat (Hebrews 10:12) on God's right hand" (F. Meyrick, "Ephesians" in *The Bible Commentary* edited by F.C. Cook [New York: Scribners, 1886], New Testament Vol.3, p.547).

[109] Albert Barnes, "Ephesians, Philippians and Colossians" in *Barnes' Notes on the New Testament* (Grand Rapids: Baker, 1955), p.33.

ranks of angels.[110] Christ is exalted above them. As Hebrews 1:4 says, Christ has "Become as much better than the angels, as He has inherited a more excellent name than they," or as Hebrews 2:9 says, Christ, while He was on earth "was made a little lower than the angels," but now He is "crowned with glory and honor," far above the good angels.[111] For another Pauline statement about this exaltation of Christ, see Philippians 2:8-11.

And every name that is named – There is apparently an advance in the statement of Christ's supreme rank, over what was said of His being over all the angels. He is supreme over all created objects of whatsoever name or title of authority they are called.

Not only in this age, but also in the one to come. – "This age" is the one we call the Christian age. The age "to come" is likely heaven.[112] Christ's exaltation is not temporary, but eternal.

1:22 – *And He put all things in subjection under His feet, and gave Him as head over all things to the church,*

And He put all things in subjection under His feet – Verse 22 continues the thought of verse 20. Paul is still speaking about how God's power was exerted in Jesus' case. Using two participial phrases, verses 20 and 21 have indicated two ways in which God used His power to exalt Jesus. Now, verse 22 indicates two more facets in the exaltation of Christ. One facet deals with His headship over all creation. Though the NASB did not include the words of this first phrase of verse 22 in small caps, nevertheless what we have here is similar to Hebrews

---

[110] Abbott, *op. cit.*, p.33, has a useful note concerning the angelology of various Jewish and Christian theologians. For example, Origen (*De princip*. I.5.3), writing in Latin, enumerates 5 classes of angels in ascending order: "*Sancti angeli* (holy angels), *principatus* (= Greek *archai*, rule), *potentes* (= *exousias*, authority), *sedes* or *throni* (= *thronoi*, thrones), and *dominationes* (= *kuriotetes*, dominions)."

[111] This passage says that Christ now rules above all powers inhabiting the heavens (heavenly places). Since the demons (fallen angels) also have a hierarchy, perhaps they, too, are in Paul's view.

[112] The translation of the KJV, "in this world," would leave the English reader to think the Greek word is *kosmos*. However, the word here is *aion*, which speaks of duration. So, the New Testament writers designate the period before the second coming of Christ as "this age" (*ho aiōn houtos*; or *ho nun aiōn*, 1 Timothy 6:17; or *ho enestos aiōn*, Galatians 1:4; or simply *ho aiōn*, Matthew 13:22) – and the period beginning with the second coming as "the age to come" (*ho aiōn ho mellon*, or *ho aiōn ekeinos*, Luke 20:34; or *ho aiōn ho erchomenos*, Mark 10:30).

2:6-8, where the words of Psalm 8:6 are applied to Christ. Psalm 8 was David's reflection on Genesis 1 and how the dominion given to Adam had been lost because of Adam's sin. The thrust of the passage in Hebrews is that one reason Jesus became a man was in order to win back man's lost dominion. As pointed out in 1 Corinthians 15:25-27 and Hebrews 2:8,9, the complete fulfillment of these (Psalm 8:6) words in Christ will not come to be completed until death itself is destroyed and God is all in all. But Christ's present enthronement at God's right hand is assurance enough that this blessed consummation will come without fail.[113] He will deliver creation from its present subjection to futility (Romans 8:20,21).

And gave Him as head over all things to the church – The crown rights of the Redeemer are twofold. Not only is He head over all creation, He is also head over the church. "[God] gave Him ... to the church" indicates that Christ is God's gift to the church. The temporary subordination of Christ to the Father is recognized throughout this remarkable passage.[114] This is the first time "church" appears in Ephesians. The Greek word for "church" is *ekklesia*, "a body of called out individuals."[115] He is head over the universal church as well as the local church.[116] This is the first time that the idea that Christ is head of the church is introduced here in Ephesians. It is a truth that is unfolded in Colossians. In this context the principal suggestion is that Christ is the *ruler* (or "head") over the church. He directs the church as a human head directs the body beneath it. Ephesians 5:24 makes it very plain that the relationship of the body to the head is that of *subjection*. The church is subject to Christ who is the head

---

[113] Human language is not adequate to describe the exaltation, power, and authority of Christ. Paul struggles to give us some idea of it. He tells us where Christ is (verse 20), that He is far above all other beings (verse 21). Now he makes it more emphatic by saying the same thing with another figure of speech derived from how a conquering king treated his defeated enemy, making him to lie down on the floor in front of the throne and using his body for a foot stool.

[114] The voluntary subordination of Jesus (in function, not in Deity) to God the Father is part of what was involved in Christ's emptying of Himself to become a human (Philippians 2:6,7). Jesus will be subordinate to the Father until the second advent (1 Corinthians 15:27-29).

[115] Wuest, *op. cit.*, p.56.

[116] *Ekklesia* can be used for any type of assembly in ancient Greek: the "church in the wilderness" (Acts 7:38 ASV), or an "assembly" to conduct the civil affairs of a town (Acts 19:41). When *ekklesia* is used in a Christian sense in the New Testament, it most usually denotes the company of believers in Christ in some particular geographical place, what we call a "local church." But there are a few passages (and this is one of them) where the term is used without any local restriction, and is what we call the church universal, which is exactly how our Lord used the term in Matthew 16:18. Other passages that speak of the church universal are 1 Corinthians 12:28; Philippians 3:6; Colossians 1:18,24.

in everything, and the church does not exercise authority like she were the head. The church cannot make laws for Christ. "He is the head over *all things* to the church: her worship, her laws, her plan of salvation, her moral standards, etc. The body doesn't make rules for the Head (Christ). No pope, bishop, church council, convention, synod, prophet, preacher, or anyone else dares to rob Christ of any of the authority God gave to Him."[117] Just consider what the surpassing power of God did for Jesus. God raised from the dead (verse 20) and exalted Him to His right hand (verse 20). God put all things under His feet (verse 22), and God made Him to be head over all things to the church (verse 22).

1:23 – *which is His body, the fullness of Him who fills all in all.*

Which is His body – Verse 23 begins by defining the church as the body of Christ. "This comparison of the church with a person or body, of which the Lord Jesus is the head, is not uncommon in the New Testament (cp. 1 Corinthians 11:3, 12:27; and Ephesians 4:15,16)."[118] Abbott tells us that the word translated "which" (*hetis*) is rather forceful, and might be translated "which is in fact His body." The reason for the forceful word seems to be this – Paul wants us to think of more than just the idea of rule and authority when we hear the word "head." He wants us to think of the organic connection between the head and the body, that the life of the church springs from its union with Christ as its head.[119]

The fullness of Him who fills all in all – The church is not only the body, it is further described as "the fullness of Him ...." "Fullness" translates *pleroma* and this is a difficult passage. (1) Perhaps it means the church is the complement (fullness) of Christ's power and glory. This is the explanation given by Barnes. Of the church he wrote, "It is that without which His dominion would not be complete. He has control over the angels and over distant worlds, but His dominion would not be complete without the control over His church, and that is so glorious it *fills up* the honor of universal dominion, and makes His empire complete."[120] Abbot's explanation follows the same interpretation. "When Christ

---

[117] Wilbur Fields, *The Glorious Church: A Study of Ephesians,* in the Bible Study Textbook Series (Joplin, MO: College Press, 1960), p.51.

[118] Barnes, *op. cit.,* p.34.

[119] Abbott, *op. cit.,* p.34.

[120] Barnes, *ibid.*

is called head, the figure implies that however complete He is in Himself, yet *as head* He is not complete without His body."[121]   Our glorified Lord's mission to earth is incomplete without His church.   (2) Perhaps it means that Christ's fullness is communicated to the church.   The idea seems to be that "the fullness of the Christ's Divine powers and qualities are imparted by Him to His church, so that the latter is pervaded by His presence, animated by His life, filled with His gifts and energies and graces."[122]   "Fills" is likely to be understood as a middle voice verb[123] which implies that Jesus fills the church for His own benefit.   What is written in Ephesians 4:9-11 would be an elaboration of this idea.   The church may indeed be the body without which Christ would not be complete.   If so, then Christ nourishes and cherishes His body, the church, so that it will become all the Head wants her to be.   In these last verses of chapter 1, Paul has called the church by her greatest title – *the body of Christ.*

---

[121] Abbott, op. cit., p.37.

[122] Salmond, *op. cit.*, p.282.

[123] Actually the Greek verb "fills," *pleroumenou,* can be either middle or passive voice.   In such cases the context must decide.   The passive would be translated "is being filled" (with the idea of His own benefit being unspoken).   Thayer (*op. cit.*, p.518) gives the following for *pleroma* ("fullness"): "that which fills, or with which a thing is filled.   It was used of a ship, inasmuch as it is filled (i.e., manned) with sailors, rowers, and soldiers; in the New Testament [it is used of] the body of believers, as that which is filled with the presence, power, agency, and riches of God and of Christ."

C. The Unity of all (Jews and Gentiles) in Christ.   2:1-22

1. Reminder of their previous condition of death and of their present condition, that of being a glorious new creation.   2:1-10

a. What the readers were in the past.   1-3

2:1 – *And you were dead in your trespasses and sins,*

And you were dead – Verses 1-7 form one long sentence in the Greek.   In the Greek the first main verb ("made ...   alive") in this long sentence is found in verse 5,[1] but the 1901 ASV inserted the verb from verse 5 at this place in verse 1.   The ASV reads "And you *did he make alive* ..." with words printed in italics to indicate the insertion.   This repeating of the main verb is a great help for English readers who would grasp the idea emphasized in this long section.   The updated NASB breaks it up into shorter sentences and if readers are not careful we will miss the overall thrust of the paragraph.

"You" probably speaks of Gentile readers who have become Christians.   While "you" is the main topic of the first two verses, verse 3 with its "we" and verse 5 with its "us" shows the same was true for Jewish Christians as is here claimed for Gentile Christians.[2]   This chapter is closely connected in sense with the closing verses of chapter one, and should not have been separated from it.   The great object of these verses is to illustrate that the same power - by which God raised Jesus from the dead (1:20), and exalted Him far above all other authority and power, and gave Him as head of the church (1:21,22) - has been in operation as He made spiritually alive those who had been dead in trespasses and sins.[3]   Chapter 2 begins by telling how the readers of this letter who were Chris-

---

[1] The NASB text reads "And you *were* dead ..." but has a marginal note indicating that the Greek translated "were" is not really a verb but is the participle "being."   In the paragraph that includes verses 1-10, the first sentence which ends at verse seven has three main verbs in the Greek ("made alive" [verse 5], "raised" [verse 6], and "might show" [verse 7]), all of which are part of a compound sentence connected by "and."   Later there are two more main verbs in this paragraph, "have been saved" (verse 8), and "are" (verse 10).

[2] The closing words of verse 3, "even as the rest," seems to decide in favor of verses 1-4 making a distinction between Jews and Gentiles – and not just between Christians and non-Christians.

[3] This chapter contains some of the most significant doctrinal themes found in the letter to the Ephesians.   In certain respects this text reminds us of the themes found in Paul's letter to the Romans, though they are considered here in a much more concise manner.

tians came to be part of that church over which Christ is head. "Dead"[4] refers to the fact that they were spiritually dead. Their spirits were dead.[5] Upon reaching the age of accountability, personal sin results in man's spirit dying; that is, it becomes suppressed, dormant, unable to function as God intended the spirit to function. Of course, if a man's spirit remains dead, the time will come when he will suffer another kind of death, eternal death.[6]

In your trespasses and sins – The NASB margin reads, "by reason of ...." There is no preposition in the Greek. What we have are dative plurals. We treat them as a dative of means or a dative of instrument. Sin was the cause why men were spiritually dead.[7] "Trespasses" here, as at 1:7, translates the word *paraptoma*, which means to fall aside, to deviate from the truth. What "truth" did the Gentiles have? They had truth that could be learned from both special and general revelation (Romans 1:18-32). The Greek for "sins" is *hamartano*, which means to miss the mark,[8] a failure to be what we ought to be, and could be. It speaks of the time when men were not Christians. Both words for sin are deliberate acts of disobedience, a failure to measure up to God's standards.

2:2 – *in which you formerly walked according to the course of this world, according to the prince of the power of the air, of the spirit that is now working in the sons of disobedience.*

In which you formerly walked – The dative plural "in which" refers back to the "trespasses and sins." Before Paul completed the idea he began in verse 1, we

---

[4] The word translated "dead" is a present participle in the Greek. NASB treats it as a finite verb. If the participle had been translated "being dead," we English readers could grasp the idea that the phrase "expresses the condition they were in when God's power first wrought in them" (Salmond, *op. cit.*, p.283).

[5] This comment assumes man's make-up as including spirit, soul, and body (1 Thessalonians 5:23).

[6] There is another way a man can die. We die *physically* when our soul and spirit leave our physical body. That will happen to all of us if Jesus delays His coming for another hundred years. We die in a different way (we die *spiritually*) when we habitually sin. Our spirit ceases to be able to help direct our souls and bodies with the result that we walk according to the course of this world.

[7] It is a man's own personal sins that result in his spiritual death, not inherited depravity (as some mistakenly affirm).

[8] This Greek word *hamartano* "was used in the Greek classics of a spearman missing the target at which he aimed his spear" (Wuest, *op. cit.*, p.60).

have what has been called a typical Pauline digression suggested by the words "trespasses and sins." The interrupted thought of verse 1 is not resumed until verse 5. The words "walk" or "walked" are used figuratively in Scripture to refer to behavior, daily conduct, or manner of life.[9] "You" still has the Gentiles in view. "Formerly" speaks of the time before they became Christians.

According to the course of this world – "According to" in this clause and the next gives the standard to which the Gentiles' lifestyles conformed when they were walking in trespasses and sins. It pictures living by the world's styles and the world's values.[10] The Gentiles lived in conformity with the customs and manners of the unregenerate world at large. "There is a paradox here in that the dead people ('dead through trespasses and sins') are represented as walking. Everyone apart from Christ is dead and is walking according to the course of this world and according to the prince of the power of the air."[11]

According to the prince of the power of the air – This is a second way the unconverted Gentiles' behavior is characterized. They were living in harmony with ("according to") how the devil wanted them to live. "The prince" is the devil.[12] It seems obvious that this language is equivalent to "the god of this world" (2 Corinthians 4:4). This general idea is clear, but the exact explanation of the other words in this clause and the next is much debated. First, let it be noted that "power" is singular in the Greek and in the NASB, not plural as the ASV has it, "the powers of the air."[13] Three different shades of meaning are suggested for *exousia* ("power") here: (a) since the word "power," both in the

---

[9] Here is a sermon idea. For its title, use "A Walk Through Ephesians" or "The Christian Walk." Look for the word "walk" in Ephesians. There were ways we walked in the past, and ways we should be walking now. See Ephesians 2:2, 2:10, 4:1, 4:17, 5:2, 5:8,15.

[10] The combination of words in this phrase causes some difficulty. It is unusual to find the word "age" (*aiōn*, here rendered "course") and the word "world" (*kosmos*) together in one passage. "Both of these words have come to have an ethical sense as is seen from their usage in the New Testament" (Martin, *op. cit.*, p.1306). It is similar to Galatians 1:4, "this present evil age." The Germans have a word for it, *zeitgeist*, "the spirit of the age" (Wuest, *op. cit.*, p.61).

[11] Martin, *ibid.*

[12] "Prince" (*archonta*, "ruler") is applied to the devil in Matthew 9:34, 12:24; Mark 3:22; Luke 11:15; and John 16:11.

[13] The ASV translators evidently were thinking the reference is to the demons, whose sphere of operation is the "air." The devil, of course, is their ruler (prince).

singular and the plural, is used in this epistle almost technically to mean superhuman power, there is a reference to the devil's superhuman power;   (b) the word "power" should be treated as a collective noun, referring to the totality of evil powers, all that is known as evil authority;   (c) the word "power" refers to the *domain* or sphere of authority where the devil holds sway, as possibly the same word means in Colossians 1:13.   What does Paul's word "air" (*aeros*) mean?   In all the other cases in the New Testament where "air" appears,[14] it has its literal sense, what we call the atmosphere.   Since "power" (or domain) is singular, and the phrase is talking about the devil, "of the air" likely should be treated as giving the region where[15] the devil exerts his power.[16]

Of the spirit that is now working in the sons of disobedience – Issues that are debated continue.   (a) "Of the power of the air" was a phrase in the genitive case, used to describe the prince/ruler.   "Of the spirit that is now working" is also in the genitive case.   Is it another phrase used to describe the devil?   Or should we agree with those who say the Greek grammar has "spirit" in apposition to "power,"[17] not to "prince"?   (b) To call the devil "the prince of the spirit that now works" is an unexpected expression.   It apparently alerts us to the fact that "spirit" in this place refers to the rebellious attitude that pervades the "sons of disobedience."   (c) "Sons of disobedience" is a Hebraism meaning characterized

---

[14] Acts 22:23; 1 Corinthians 9:26, 14:9; 1 Thessalonians 4:17; Revelation 9:2, 16:17.

[15] The genitive "of the air" is treated as a genitive of the place where.

[16] Those who treat "power" as a plural ("powers," i.e. demons) suggest that "they inhabit the air about men and exercise an evil influence upon them" (Enos Dowling, *Standard Lesson Commentary 1962* [Cincinnati: Standard Publishing, 1961], p.393).   Abbott, *op. cit.*, p.42, has references showing that Jewish Rabbinic sources taught demons had their abode in the air.   Care must be exercised here.   (a) William Hendriksen ("Ephesians" in the *New Testament Commentary* series [Grand Rapids: Baker, 1967], p.114) has strongly and correctly argued that the literal meaning of "air" is basic, without assuming that Paul simply has accommodated his thinking to the "grotesque and highly speculative notions of rabbinical literature."   (b) From this verse some of the Early Church Fathers believed that storms and disturbances of the atmosphere were caused by the "power" or "authority," *exousia*, of the demons.   Such an idea is probably unscriptural.   See Psalm 148:8 and Revelation 7:1-4.

[17] Some affirm that the Greek here shows that the word "spirit" must be understood as being in apposition to "power" – not to "prince," since "prince" is in the accusative case; "spirit" is in the genitive case, as is "power."   Others affirm that the Greek here is genitive case, rather than accusative because of attraction to the previous genitive case.   Missing this matter of grammar, many commentaries write about how the devil (the prince) is a spirit being.   That is true, but this is not the verse to prove it.

by disobedience. The devil refuses to listen to or obey God, and Gentiles (before their conversion) are likewise characterized by disobedience. The devil is the prince/ruler who instigates this attitude of rebellion. "Now working" says that the devil's operations were going on at the time Paul was writing. The fact that this rebellious attitude/spirit is still working in others makes the escape of the readers from it even more striking.

2:3 – *Among them we too all formerly lived in the lusts of our flesh, indulging the desires of the flesh and of the mind, and were by nature children of wrath, even as the rest.*

Among them – i.e., the sons of disobedience. We lived, says Paul, just like other sons of disobedience.

We too – "We" refers to Jewish people. It is an important distinction to observe that the "we" of verse 3 is contrasted with the "you" in verse 1. By using "you" in the preceding verses, Paul indicates he was speaking specially of the Gentiles. By writing "we," the apostle now passes to the Jews. Before they became Christians, Jewish folk were in no better situation than were the Gentiles. They were all guilty of sin (cp. Romans 3:9-18). By using "we" Paul includes himself in this general indictment that men were spiritually dead because of their own trespasses and sins.

All formerly lived – "Lived" is *anestraphemen*, a different verb from the one used in verse 2, though the meaning is similar. When used figuratively of human conduct, this verb means "to behave or act" in accordance with "certain principles."[18] Paul will identify those principles in the following phrases of this letter.

In the lusts of our flesh – We allowed the feelings and desires[19] (stirred up by the devil) to carry us beyond the limits God has set. In Romans 7 Paul describes how things were for the Jew. Romans 7:14-24 shows that the unconverted Jew was a slave to sin, and was led around by his "body" (as it was influenced by the devil).

---

[18] William F. Arndt and F. Wilbur Gingrich, *A Greek-English Lexicon of the New Testament and Other Early Christian Literature* (Chicago: University of Chicago Press, 1957), p.60.

[19] "Desires" (*epithumia* in the Greek) is used in its bad sense here, so the NASB uses "lusts" to translate it. Literally, the word "flesh" speaks of the physical body, or one of the parts of the physical body. In our comments at this place, it should be noted that we are carefully avoiding any idea that "flesh" equals an alleged old sinful nature inherited from Adam.

Indulging the desires of the flesh and of the mind – They yielded to the physical desires and wicked thoughts and purposes which the devil stirred up. "Desires" here translates *thelema*, "wishes," the thing willed. "Here is the apostolic explanation of the preceding phrase, 'formerly lived.' They yielded completely to the appetites and desires of the flesh and the mind."[20] F.F. Bruce substitutes "our thoughts" to convey the idea that *dianoia* ("mind") is plural in the Greek.[21] "Indulging" translates the Greek word for "do." This phrase speaks of doing as the body and mind suggest and lead us to do.

And were by nature children of wrath – "By nature," in this context, means because of the long practice of sin and disobedience. It does not mean we were born that way.[22] "Children of wrath" is a Hebraism denoting those who deserve wrath, or who are exposed to wrath. "Wrath" (*orge*) is God's settled displeasure with sin. It expresses itself both in temporal punishments (Romans 1:18) and future punishments (Romans 2:8). See also John 3:36 and Hebrews 10:26,27 on God's wrath.

Even as the rest -- "Even as" means just as the Gentiles were children of wrath, so were the Jews. The Jews stood on the same ground as the Gentiles. Jews and Gentiles alike, if they are without Christ, were all children of wrath because of a long practice of sin. (Everyone needs the salvation offered in the gospel is the gist of Romans 1-3.)

   b. **What we are in the present.**   **4-6**   *(We have been made alive.)*

2:4 – *But God, being rich in mercy, because of His great love with which He loved us,*

---

[20] Dowling, *op. cit.*, p.393.

[21] Bruce, *op. cit.*, p.49.

[22] "By nature" is used of Gentiles in Romans 2:14,27 and speaks of their being without a written revelation. "By nature" here, used of Jews, speaks of the time before their conversion. By nature may be contrasted to "adoption," that is, the Jews [by their sins] had broken their covenant position as the people of God (cp. Romans 11:16,21). From the time of Augustine the words "by nature" have been supposed by many to contain a direct assertion of original sin. Abbott (*op. cit.*, p.45) gives several objections to such an interpretation, including: (1) Such an interpretation would be out of harmony with the context since both verse 1 and 5 teach that we were dead spiritually because of our own personal acts of sin; and (2) The doctrine of original sin evidently originated with Augustine, since Chrysostom and others who antedate Augustine regarded these words as guarding against such a doctrine.

But God – "God" is the subject of the long sentence which began with verse 1. The main verb of this long sentence ("made us alive") is found in verse 5 in the Greek. "But" contrasts how things are now as compared with how things were when we were rushing toward inevitable ruin. God stepped in.

Being rich in mercy – This participial phrase ("being rich") introduces the qualities or motives which led God to make us alive. In this verse and the next three such qualities are identified – mercy, love, grace. On the use of this word "rich" as an adjective to describe the generosity and lavishness of God's mercy, see notes at 1:7,18. His mercy was not handed out parsimoniously. "Mercy" is kindness, beneficence (bringing about or doing good), providing relief to those in misery, or the act of treating an offender with less severity than he deserves.

Because of His great love – This gives a reason for the lavishness of God's mercy. God was merciful to us because of the totally unselfish love (*agape*) He had for us, this verse says. "Love" (*agape*) is deliberately doing what is spiritually best for the other person.[23]

With which He loved us – The addition of this phrase, when it is "not necessary to the sense of the verse, gives great emphasis to the expression of the Divine love."[24] The expression "love with which He loved us" is a Hebrew way of describing the greatness of His love. We marvel that it could be that God was not just merciful to us, but *loving*. "Us" now includes both the "you" of verse 1 and the "we" of verse 3, and therefore includes both Jews and Gentiles.

2:5 – *even when we were dead in our transgressions, made us alive together with Christ (by grace you have been saved),*

Even when we were dead in our transgressions – "Dead" speaks of being spiritually dead. Our spirits had died when we committed our first sins (the NASB margin reads, "by reason of"). The Greek is in the dative case. Recall

---

[23] Here are some things such a love does and does not do: (1) It sees a need. (2) It moves to meet that need. (3) It does not count the cost. (4) It does not consider whether or not the person deserves to have that need met. (5) It does not calculate what the person who loves will get out of it for himself. (6) It makes decisions for the well-being of the other person. No wonder such love is called "great love." It is great in the kind of love it is. It is great in the things it does. It is great in the results it brings. (Knofel Staton, *Adult Bible Teacher 1992-93* [Cincinnati, OH: Standard, 1992], p.411.)

[24] Abbott, *op. cit.*, p.47.

what was written in verse 1 of this chapter.[25]   Men become spiritually dead by reason of their own trespasses and sins.

Made us alive together with Christ – "God made us alive" the sentence reads. In "made alive" we have come to one of the main verbs of this long sentence (2:1-7).   Actually, there are three main verbs (all prefixed with "with," *sun-* in the Greek), one here in verse 5, and two more in verse 6.   All of the verbs describe what God has done in Christ for every Christian.   The *sun* ("with") means that all three verbs are true only if we are united to Christ.   "Made us alive" reverses all that is implied in the words "dead by reason of our transgressions" (NASB margin).   It is our spirits that God has made alive (John 3:6), the very spirits that were dead because of the sins we committed.[26]   "Made us alive..." has an exact parallel in Colossians 2:12,13, which is speaking about what happens when a penitent believer is immersed.[27]   Parallel ideas are expressed in Romans 6:4, "raised from the dead ... so we too might walk in newness of life," and in Romans 8:10, where we read that a man's spirit is alive because of righteousness (God's way of saving man).   "Together with Christ" reminds us that "everywhere in the New Testament, the close connection of the believer with Christ is affirmed.   We are crucified with Him.   We die with Him.   We rise with Him.   We live with Him.   We reign with Him.   We are joint heirs with Him.   We share His sufferings on earth (1 Peter 4:13), and we share His glory with Him on his throne (Revelation 3:21)."[28]   His resurrection from the grave involves our resurrection to spiritual life (recall Ephesians 1:20,21, which spoke of the same power being exercised in His case and ours).

(By grace you have been saved) – This parenthetical note seems to give another quality that led God to provide salvation for us who were dead in trespasses and sins.   It is because of God's grace (His goodwill exhibited in kindness) that folk who are dead in trespasses and sins have an opportunity to be made alive.   Grace

---

[25] The article in the Greek at this place, "*the* trespasses," is an example of the article of previous reference, the trespasses already mentioned in verse 1.

[26] The meaning one gives to "dead" (2:1, 5) affects the meaning one gives to the verb "made alive."

[27] Ephesians 2:5, "we were made alive," does not teach monergism, which is the doctrine that those who are dead by reason of their trespasses and sins were made alive apart from any exercise of their own free will, i.e., that God does it all.   The following context shows that the extension of His grace to us is conditioned on faith.

[28] Barnes, *op. cit.*, p.41.

is an attribute of God, His divine, generous loving-kindness that extends mercy and forgiveness to men whose sins have caused them to become spiritually dead. "You have been saved" is a perfect tense verb which indicates past completed action with present continuing results. You were saved and continue to be so.[29] "Saved" in this context refers to salvation from sins, man's spirit being made alive, but it should be remembered that God's grace – His kind efforts to save a man – is not limited to the time of his regeneration. There is help given all through the Christian life. The doctrine of salvation by grace (because God is so kind) is further explained and amplified in verses 8-10.

The Bible uses several different verb tenses as it describes men's salvation. (1) "Saved" appears in the aorist tense in 2 Timothy 1:9. (2) It appears in the present tense in 1 Corinthians 1:18 and 2 Corinthians 2:15. (3) It appears in the future tense in Romans 5:10. (4) Here and in Romans 8:24 it appears in the perfect tense. We must be careful to emphasize all equally, and not emphasize one idea to the exclusion of the others.

2:6 – *and raised us up with Him, and seated us with Him in the heavenly* **places** *in Christ Jesus,*

And raised us up with Him – "Made us alive" (verse 5) has already occurred. Is "raised" something that has already occurred, or is it potential? Those who picture it as having already occurred point to Romans 6:4 ("walk in newness of life" as a result of being united with Him in the likeness of His resurrection) as being synonymous. Those who understand it as potential, the reference being to the future resurrection of the body, find a similar idea in Romans 8:29,30 – when God made His plans before He created, there were certain things He planned to do for people who were united with Christ. When He raised Christ from the dead, He did in effect raise up all believers together with him. "In Christ shall all be made alive" (1 Corinthians 15:22 ASV).

And seated us with Him in the heavenly *places* – This is the third time (see 1:3,20) this expression "the heavenly *places*" has been used in this epistle with apparently the same meaning. "Seated" is the third verb in the sentence which began at verse 1 – "made alive," "raised," now "seated." Christ is already seated

---

[29] NOTE: We must be careful, in our notes in the rest of this paragraph, to walk the fine line between the two extremes: (1) That man is wholly passive in salvation. (God made you alive; by grace you are saved. Both could be taken as though man were passive, with God being the agent who does it all.) and (2) That man's response to God's invitation is somehow meritorious. (Man's obedience puts God in debt – God owes him salvation because he has earned it.) Neither should the perfect tense be pressed to prove the doctrine of unconditional eternal security.

in the heavenly places; Ephesians 1:20 has indicated that Jesus is seated at the Father's right hand in the heavenly places. Christ is entered into heaven as the forerunner (Hebrews 6:20). Jesus is already seated, but how can it be said that Christians are seated with Him? Thus, the same question that was asked about "raised" (has it already occurred or is it potential) is also asked concerning "seated." Those who picture Christians as having already been seated with Christ point to Philippians 3:20 ("our citizenship is in heaven") as perhaps conveying a similar idea. Others point to the expression that calls the church the "kingdom of heaven." Those who understand it as potential point to Revelation 3:21 where the promise is made to those who overcome that they shall share His throne.[30] They are not yet, indeed, present in heaven in the body,[31] but they are so in point of right (Colossians 3:1-4), for that is what God determined He would do for all those who are in Christ. To so honor those who are in Christ was part of His eternal plan.

In Christ Jesus – "It seems best to understand 'in Christ' as completing and defining with more precision what was intended by 'with Him' in the previous phrase, for it is not simply together with Christ that this vivification and exaltation take place, but also *in* Him, by virtue of union with Him as the Head."[32]

c. What we shall be in the future. 7-10

2:7 – in order that in the ages to come He might show the surpassing riches of His grace in kindness toward us in Christ Jesus.

In order that – All that God has done (i.e., made us alive, raised us, seated us) had one single purpose in view. God had a publicity program in mind – He was giving evidence for all to see exactly how gracious He is.

In the ages to come – It may be that this   language speaks of the future ages of

---

[30] Some eschatological theories have Christ seated on His throne and ruling during a coming millennium following His second coming. In notes at Ephesians 1:20 we showed from Scripture that Christ is already seated on His throne. Therefore, we reject the view that the seating of Christians with Him awaits the beginning of a millennium.

[31] Revelation 6:9 and 15:1,2, describing how things are now in the intermediate state, picture the souls of the redeemed on the sea of glass before the throne in heaven. The redeemed will not receive their resurrection bodies until the second coming of Christ (1 Corinthians 15:20-23).

[32] Abbott, *op. cit.*, p.50.

both time and eternity.[33]   If so, this verse tells us that God has made us alive in order that He might show kindness toward us both in time and eternity.   "God exhibits the richness of His grace by His kind and gracious dealing with His church on earth, generation after generation, as well as by glorifying it hereafter."[34]

He might show the surpassing riches of His grace – "Show" is a middle voice verb which implies that God is acting for His own benefit.   God exhibits His abundant and lavish grace in kindness to the saints for His own glory, in order that He may be glorified (see Ephesians 1:6).   "Surpassing riches" being used to describe grace denotes the valuableness of it, as well as its plenty and abundance.[35]

In kindness toward us in Christ Jesus – "*En* ('in') indicates *by what* God will manifest the exceeding great riches of His grace in the ages to come, namely, *by kindness toward us in Christ Jesus*."[36]   God's grace (His favorable attitude) is displayed or exhibited in benefits toward us.[37]   Examples of such benefits are providing a Savior for us, and then making us alive, raising us, and seating us with Christ in the heavenly places.   It is by being kind to us that God shows how rich His grace is.   That kindness is extended to those who are in Christ Jesus.   That God's surpassing grace is exhibited in kindness toward sinners in all the ages to come is an encouragement to sinners to keep coming to Christ for they will find forgiveness.   They, too, may experience the extraordinary greatness of God's grace.

2:8 – *For by grace you have been saved through faith; and that not of yourselves,* it is *the gift of God;*

---

[33] "Ages to come" is another way of saying "unto the ages of the ages" (the ancient Greek way of saying the eternal future).

[34] Meyrick, *op. cit.*, p.551.   This expression "ages to come" may tip the scales in favor of taking "raised" and "seated" (in verse 6) as potential.

[35] See notes at Ephesians 1:7-8 for the "riches of His grace" and at 1:19 for the adjective "surpassing."

[36] H.A.W. Meyer, *Critical and Exegetical Handbook to the Epistle to the Ephesians* (Winona Lake, IN: Alpha Productions, 1979) p.372.

[37] "Kindness" is not *agathos* ("good") but *chrestos* ("an effort to be helpful, generous").   It is noteworthy that the LXX used "grace" to translate the Hebrew *hesed* ("loving-kindness").

For by grace you have been saved through faith – "For" tells us this verse is intended to be an illustration of the kindness that results from God's grace. "Grace" is an attribute of God,[38] the same loving favor that was spoken about in verses 5 and 7.[39] "By grace" says that God's grace (His loving-kindness, favor) is the cause of salvation being provided.[40] "You" includes Gentile Christians as well as Jewish Christians. As Peter said (Acts 15:11), God puts no difference between Jew and Gentile when it comes to His loving-kindness. As was the verb "saved" in verse 5, the verb "saved" here in verse 8 is a perfect tense verb, indicating a past completed action with present continuing results. "Saved" from first to last, from the time one was made alive (Ephesians 2:5) until the time of one's glorification (Ephesians 2:6). "Through faith" indicates that participation in the salvation provided because of God's grace is conditional. To be recipients of His salvation, we must meet the condition, and that condition is "faith." The same condition is given in Romans 1:17 and 4:16. In all these passages "faith" (or "faithfulness"[41]) is habitually doing what God says. Faithfulness is what God looks for, whether at the time we were made alive, or in the days following until our final glorification. Whereas Ephesians 1:6 told us that because of His grace God provided the plan by which sinners are saved, this verse tells us that because of His grace He discloses to us the conditions by which we may be recipients of that salvation.[42]

---

[38] This statement (that grace is an attribute of God) is in harmony with how the word "grace" has been explained earlier in Ephesians (see Ephesians 1:2,7, 2:5,7).

[39] In this context, verses 5 and 7 have spoken of God's grace. Since in the Greek there is an article before "grace" in this verse, and there was no article in verse 5, it is probably correct to treat the article before "grace" in both verses 7 and 8 as the article of previous reference.

[40] We judge that "by grace" here in verse 8 is a dative of cause and this verse basically is saying the same thing that Paul wrote at Ephesians 1:7, namely, that it is because of the riches of God's grace that redemption and forgiveness have been provided.

[41] That the Greek word can be translated either "faith" or "faithfulness" can be seen from a comparison of the KJV and NASB at Matthew 23:23. In that place the KJV reads "faith" and the NASB reads "faithfulness." That these two words are both possible translations of the Greek should indicate to us that the faith which is a condition of salvation is more than mental assent or trust. It also includes action on our part. For example, Galatians 3:26,27 tell us that baptism is included in the faith on which a man is justified.

[42] Because it is faithfulness that God looks for, not a one-time faith or belief, it is not correct to affirm, as some theologians have, that "we have been saved" means a person could never lose his or her salvation.

And that not of yourselves, *it is* **the gift of God** – Greek grammar shows that "you have been saved" is what is here called the gift of God.[43] The NASB marginal note on "that" – "i.e., that salvation" – points us in the right direction. Since "by grace" spoke of the source of our salvation, we interpret the phrase "not of ourselves" as likewise speaking of the source of our salvation. We recall that Ephesians 1:9 alluded to the plan God made by which we are saved. If we are going to be saved, it will be by the way He has planned and worked out, not by any plans we have made. "It is by God's mercy that He sent His Son to proclaim and demonstrate the way of life and to die on the cross to open the door of heaven for us. It is not even of ourselves that we know about the gospel. The inspired writers of the New Testament and the kind Christians who preached to us and taught us have placed us forever in their debt. We are not in any position to say that we have produced the salvation we enjoy. God produced it."[44] The Greek reads "God's is the gift" with "God's" being placed first by way of emphatic contrast with "of yourselves." Romans 6:23 also refers to salvation as being a free gift from God. It is not something that men can earn; it is something that God freely gives when men meet the conditions he has set forth.

As we move on to verse 9, the former part ("not of ourselves") will be explained by the words "not of works," the latter ("God's gift") by the declaration of verse 10, "we (and all that is in us) are His workmanship."

2:9 – *not as a result of works, that no one should boast.*

---

[43] A rule of Greek grammar says that a pronoun (such as the demonstrative pronoun "that," Greek *touto*) must agree with its antecedent in gender and number. The word "that" ("it") is neuter. The antecedent cannot be "faith" for that word is feminine in gender. The antecedent cannot be "grace" because "grace" is feminine. Commentators who mistakenly say that it is faith that is the gift of God are likely to maintain that those who respond to God were first given the gift of faith by the Holy Spirit so that they would believe. Not only this, but it is affirmed that it is impossible for them not to believe. Then Hebrews 11:1 is brought into play, especially the KJV translation which reads "faith is the evidence of things not seen." If a person has faith it is treated as evidence or proof that he is one of the elect whom God has chosen to save. This is an erroneous use of Hebrews 11:1. In addition, this interpretation that faith is the gift of God "diminishes the factor of man's free will, which is emphasized in 'whosoever' passages, such as John 3:16 and Revelation 22:17" (Shannon, *op. cit.*, p.387).

[44] R.C. Foster, *1966 Standard Bible Teacher* (Cincinnati, OH.: Standard, 1965) p.75. Foster goes on to make this point: The New Testament indicates there are two parts to our salvation, God's part and man's part. If man has a part, how can we still say "it is not of yourself"? Foster's response was in this vein: Even though it reads "through faith," the emphasis in this passage is not on man's response (we men must decide whether or not we will accept Christ and give Him our lives) but rather with the fact that the opportunity to enter into heaven has been planned and prepared by God. God's grace is the source of our salvation.

Not a result of works – "Through faith" (verse 8) tells us that a God-given condition for salvation is to habitually do what God says. "Works" here in verse 9, therefore, must be something in contrast to faith (i.e., a contrast to habitually doing what God says). Therefore, we conclude that "works" that are here excluded are man-made religious rules and rites.[45] Specifically, it is a mistaken notion to say 'I do not need Christ and His way of salvation; I can do it myself.' Paul does not say "works of the Law" (as he did in Romans 3:20,28 and Galatians 2:16) because he is not writing to Jewish believers. "Works of the Law" (as we have learned from 4QMMT) referred to man-made rules based on certain verses in the Law of Moses – religious rules like those of the Pharisees, rules that voided the Law of Moses (as Jesus plainly declared in Mark 7 and Matthew 15). We conclude that "works" here in Ephesians 2:8 equals man-made religious rules based on some other plan than what God has revealed as He made known the mystery of His will (Ephesians 1:9,10).[46] Recall the previous phrase "and that not of yourselves" (verse 8). Salvation is done God's way, not man's way. We are not free to make up our own way, and then claim it is just as good as what God has done.[47]

That no one should boast – The word *kauchesetai* ("boast") is an everyday Greek word designating an excessive or undue evaluation of one's self or one's accomplishments. If salvation were something that man had invented or devised, he could brag (boast) about what he had done. But instead of bragging about what men have done, we are instructed in the Word to boast in the Lord (1 Corinthians 1:31; 2 Corinthians 10:17,18). "The Old Testament protest against boasting in any but the Lord and the prophet's jealousy for the honor of God (Jeremiah 9:23,24; Isaiah 52:8,14) burn with a yet intenser flame in Paul, most of all

---

[45] The term "works" is used in two senses in the New Testament. (1) It is used to denote the inventions or devices of men. (2) It is also used to speak of things appointed by God to be done. This latter concept is often called "works of faith" (cp. James 2:14-26). Such works of faith are not excluded by Paul's "not of works."

[46] Might not Gentiles be tempted to rely on man-made religious rules just as the Pharisees did? Gentiles surely did have a host of man-made religions, idols, and spiritism practices. None of these save. They only enmesh a man deeper and deeper into his slavery to sin.

[47] We have deliberately chosen to avoid making a comment like "you can't earn your salvation" as we have explained "not a result of works." In many commentaries these "works" which are excluded are characterized as being "meritorious works," works by which salvation is hoped to be merited or earned (in opposition to the Roman Catholic dogma of "works of supererogation."). Now, of a surety, the old Roman Catholic idea of earning days out of purgatory is not a biblical idea, and needs to be refuted by Bible teachers. In their attempt to refute those erroneous ideas, the Protestants jumped on the verses that had salvation by faith, not by works. In so doing, they have infected the theological world with a meaning for "works" that was not true in New Testament times.

when he touches the great theme of man's salvation. The glory of that salvation belongs wholly to God!"[48]

2:10 – *For we are His workmanship, created in Christ Jesus for good works, which God prepared beforehand that we should walk in them.*

For – Here in verse 10 is the reason why salvation is designated as God's gift, and why we cannot boast as though we invented or produced the way of salvation.

We are His workmanship – HIS (emphatic) workmanship are we. The Greek word is *poiema,* which is used of the product of an artist's labor, of the chair which is the workmanship of the carpenter, of the jar which is the handiwork of the potter.[49] We Christians are something God has made – remember all the *sun-*verbs in 2:5,6; Christians are all part of God's "work of art." Here is proof that our salvation is not by our works. If our being made alive, being raised up, and being seated are all God's workmanship (handiwork), our salvation is not a work (a production) planned and executed by man.[50] It was God who made the plan. It was God who predestined from all eternity those in Christ for adoption (1:5). It was God who formed the Christian family (1:10). It was God who gave them spiritual life when they were dead in their trespasses and sins (2:1,5). God did all these things because grace (loving-kindness) is one of his attributes (1:6,7).

Created in Christ Jesus for good works – It is not the original creation of the heavens and earth that is in view; rather, "created" refers to what took place at conversion (if anyone is in Christ, he is a new creature, 2 Corinthians 5:17), when those who were dead in their trespasses and sins were "made alive" (Ephesians 2:5). The original creation and the new creation are both works of art (God's handiwork). Perhaps "in Christ Jesus" speaks of more than being in union with Christ; recall we are made alive with Christ, raised with Christ, and seated with Christ (verses 5,6). Perhaps the long-term plan of God that a Messiah would be needed is also in the background. Perhaps "in Christ Jesus" speaks of all Jesus

---

[48] Salmond, *op. cit.*, p.289.

[49] Meyrick, *op. cit.*, p.552.

[50] Note again: this passage does not affirm that "faith" is the work of God. It does not say that men become believers because God creates faith in them. Nor is this passage to be forced into being a proof text for "total depravity." The *Pulpit Commentary* so interprets the passage. "We have to be fashioned anew by God before we can do anything aright... So little inward capacity had we for such works, that we required to be created in Christ Jesus in order that we might do them" (p. 64).

the Messiah went through during His incarnation. Think of Him being a baby needing care from Joseph and Mary; think of Him contemplating what will happen to Him as He is being tempted; think about the agony in the Garden, the scourging and the mockery and the nails. Think of Him having to be shown to be the Messiah by His resurrection and exaltation (Acts 2:33-36). This was part of God's handiwork to bring about redemption. "For good works" says that folks who are beneficiaries of God's way of saving man ("by grace you have been saved through faith") have some "good works" to do. These are deeds, these are actions, which God Himself has determined He wants saved men to do.[51] "The inventor knows the purpose of his creation. If it does not serve his purpose, it is of no value, no matter how attractive it may appear. But when it works, a celebration is in order. What marvelous things God can do, and frequently does, through willing lives."[52] In Ephesians 4-6, we can find specific examples of the kind of thing Paul has in mind when he speaks of the "good works" God expects of His new creation. Another very clear passage is the sheep and goat judgment scene depicted in Matthew 25:31-46. According to one of the faithful sayings in Titus, Christians are to be careful to maintain good works (Titus 3:8).

Which God prepared beforehand, that we should walk in them – "Which" refers to "good works" and this verse emphasizes the significance of the "good works" God wants people to do. "Prepared beforehand" indicates that the new lifestyle and behavior of the believer is also an essential part of God's eternal plan, purposed "before the foundation of the world" (1:4), and also further emphasizes that good works are not the believer's own doing or invention. "Walk (*peripateo*) in them" means "to regulate one's life, to conduct one's self, to order one's behavior,"[53] and the verb tense indicates habitual, continuous action. God's plan was that believers should actually and habitually be doing the kind of good works He wants done. "God has not predetermined any course of action,

---

[51] "Works" here in verse 10 are not the same as the "works" in verse 9. In verse 9 Paul was speaking of the kind of "works" (man-made rules) that some might think are the way of salvation. In verse 10 Paul speaks of doing the kind of things God has always wanted His people to excel in. Special care must be exercised lest we repeat the typical Protestant explanations of this verse, which, because of an imperfect definition of faith, go like this – "Works play no part at all in securing salvation. Initial salvation is by grace alone, and by faith alone. But afterwards Christians will prove their faith by works." What is imperfect about this is the expression "by faith alone," as though this passage taught that the faith that initially saves requires no acts of obedience to what God has commanded as conditions of salvation.

[52] Hayden, *op. cit.*, p.307.

[53] Wuest, *op. cit.*, p.71.

but He has ordained (decreed) that the life of every one of His children must be filled with good works in order to meet His approval (Matthew 5:16, 7:21; Revelation 20:11-13)."[54] Romans 2:6-10 also shows that God's judgment will be "according to deeds." Orrin Root wrote a paragraph entitled "The Church is Christ's Body."

> What would you do without a body? You wouldn't earn a living as you do now. You wouldn't play golf on Saturday, or load up the car and go on a picnic. You wouldn't put on your Sunday clothes and go to church. You wouldn't shake hands with your friends or even smile at them. Jesus did fantastic things in His body, marvelous things, beautiful things. He took children in His arms and blessed them. He laid His hands on the sick and made them well. He opened His mouth and taught the truth. He broke a boy's lunch into so many pieces that five thousand people ate and were filled. But finally He went back to heaven and took His body with Him. Still, Jesus has a body in the world, and in it He is doing wonderful things. He is feeding the hungry when you carry a casserole to the family whose homemaker is sick, or when you join in sending food to brethren in India or Africa. He is healing the sick when Christians build a hospital or medical school. He is preaching the gospel of the kingdom through all His servants. This helps us understand the "good works" God has in mind that we do.[55]

2. **Redemption (the deliverance from death that is part of the new creation) produces a reconciliation of the Jews and Gentiles to God, uniting each other into one new body.   2:11-22**

   a. **What Gentiles were without Christ.   11,12**

2:11 – *Therefore remember, that formerly you, the Gentiles in the flesh, who are called "Uncircumcision" by the so-called "Circumcision," which is performed in the flesh by human hands –*

Therefore – "As *dio* ("wherefore" ASV) indicates, what follows is a personal, ethical application of what has been said;   and the application is drawn not from

---

[54] Dowling, *op. cit.*, p.395.

[55] Root, *op. cit.*, p.26.

the immediate preceding sentence, but from the contents of the prior paragraph as a whole."[56]

Remember – In the first paragraph of chapter 2 Paul has reminded the Ephesians that they had been "made alive" (verse 5). To help them appreciate what a change has been made in their lives when they were made alive in Christ, the Ephesians are called on to remember what they formerly were, before they came to Christ. Several particulars follow (verses 11,12) which spell out the outward condition and lack of privilege that accompanied being a Gentile.

That formerly you, the Gentiles in the flesh – "Formerly" refers to the time before they became Christians. Most of the Christians in and around Ephesus by birth or physical descent were Gentiles, not descendants of Israel.

Who are called "Uncircumcision" by the so-called "Circumcision," *which is* **performed in the flesh by human hands** – These words are a reminder that the Gentiles were treated with scorn by their Jewish neighbors. In the ancient world, Jews were quick to let Gentiles know they were not God's people. Jews expressed their disdain for the Gentiles as they contemptuously labeled them "uncircumcised"[57] while proudly calling themselves "the circumcision." Barclay tells us of some of the things Rabbinic Jews thought and said about Gentiles.

> The Gentiles, said the Jews, were created by God to be fuel for the fires of Hell. God, they said, loves only Israel of all the nations that He had made. A good snake you would crush, they said, and the best of the Gentiles you would kill. It was not even lawful to render help to a Gentile mother in the hour of her sorest need, for that would simply be to bring another Gentile into the world. Until Christ came, the Gentiles were an object of contempt to the Jews. The barrier between them was almost absolute. If a Jewish boy married a Gentile girl, or if a Jewish girl married a Gentile boy, the funeral of that Jewish boy or girl was carried out.[58]

It is not a pleasant place to live where there is such racial disparagement, where your neighbors and townspeople are hostile in attitude and unsociable in actions. As Paul describes how things were, he uses language to show he is not in agree-

---

[56] Salmond, *op. cit.,* p.291.

[57] David's disdainful reference to Goliath as an "uncircumcised Philistine" (1 Samuel 17:26,36) illustrates the traditional use of the term. (Hayden, *op. cit.,* p.308). Peter was accused of going "to men uncircumcised" and eating with them following his visit to Cornelius (Acts 11:1-3).

[58] Barclay, *op. cit.,* p.125.

ment with the reproachful behavior of the Jews. Circumcision was the sign and seal of the covenant first made by God with Abraham (Genesis 17:10-27) and later incorporated in the Law of Moses (Leviticus 12:3). "Which is performed in the flesh, by human hands" refers to the fact that the Jews religiously circumcised their baby boys when the boys were 8 days old. Paul is far from depreciating circumcision, in its true significance, as the sign of membership in the commonwealth of the people of God. But Jews whose attitudes toward Gentiles led them to be disrespectful and disdainful were not what God intended when he made a special people out of Israel. The words "performed ... by human hands" are clearly depreciatory, 'a merely external and artificial thing.' Paul uses the word "so called" which suggests that for many Jewish people, their circumcision had no corresponding spiritual significance. Paul elsewhere speaks of a circumcision that was not really circumcision (Romans 2:28-29; Philippians 3:4,5; Colossians 2:11).

2:12 – remember *that you were at that time separate from Christ, excluded from the commonwealth of Israel, and strangers to the covenants of promise, having no hope and without God in the world.*

Remember – The thought begun in verse 11 is continued. There was more to be remembered by the Gentiles than the racial animosity they experienced. Five more descriptive phrases detail the spiritual situation of the readers before they knew Christ.

That you were at that time separate from Christ – "At that time" refers to the time in their lives before they became Christians. One of the deplorable things about their condition is that they were "separate from Christ," that is, they never expected a coming Messiah. They knew of no Savior, they knew of no atonement for sin. They had no assurance of pardon. They had no well-founded hope of eternal life. They had no reason to be optimistic about the future.

Excluded from the commonwealth of Israel – The second thing true of the Gentiles is that they were "excluded," "shut out from fellowship and intimacy with."[59] "Excluded" is the opposite of feeling at home with a person or object. The thing from which the Gentiles were excluded was citizenship in the kingdom over which God was the ruler. The word translated "commonwealth" is *politeuma*, a word that speaks of citizenship. Folk who make up the Israel of God

---

[59] Thayer, *op. cit.*, p.54.

have special privileges. Gentiles had no rights of citizenship in the community of Israel. The people of Israel were different from other peoples. They were God's chosen people. God was using them for a job He wanted done in the world (Romans 9). Gentiles, before their conversion, had no such purpose in the world.

And strangers to the covenants of promise – "Promise" is singular; the particular blessing promised was the coming of the Messiah. God made numerous covenants with individuals and groups in Old Testament times that contained the promise of the Messiah.[60] Examples include (1) the covenant with Abraham (Genesis 22:15-18; Galatians 3:15-16); (2) with David (2 Samuel 7:12-16); (3) with Joshua, the high priest (Zechariah 3:6-8); (4) with all who hunger and thirst (Isaiah 55:3-5). But the Gentiles knew nothing of these gracious, glowing covenants of the promise. They were strangers to them, they did not belong to the community where the covenants were enjoyed.

Having no hope – The fourth thing true of the Gentiles was they had no hope – no hope, that is, for a better future in this world or in the life to come (see 1 Thessalonians 4:13). The conjectures of heathen philosophers concerning a future life were at best vague and utterly unsatisfactory. Gentiles lived without anything good to look forward to. Gentiles lived without being able to imagine that any good would come to them.

And without God – The fifth thing true of the Gentiles was that though they had many idols, and gods many and lords many, they had no knowledge of or relation with the one true God.[61] The most tragic words in the Bible are "having no hope and without God." "It is little wonder, then, that heathen Gentiles sank into the appalling sins listed in Romans 1:18-32."[62]

In the world – This phrase should perhaps be joined to both "having no hope and without God." Two ideas come to mind when we think about "the world." "The world" often has a bad connotation in Scripture (1 John 2:15). This world

---

[60] On the meaning of the word "covenant" (an agreement among unequals, in which one party with plenary power makes all the rules; the other can only accept or reject the rules, but cannot change them), see Galatians 3:15; 1 Corinthians 11:25; Hebrews 7:22, 9:15-17; Acts 3:25.

[61] Compare what Paul said to a Gentile audience at Lystra, "You should turn from these vain things to a living God who made heaven, and earth, and the sea, and all that is in them" (Acts 14:15).

[62] Hayden, *op. cit.,* p.308.

has many troubles and evils (Galatians 1:4; 2 Corinthians 4:4), and it is a bad place to be without hope and without God.   On the other hand, this is my Father's world.   He made it, and He providentially governs what He has made.   To live in the world He has made, and yet have no evidence of His favor, no assurance of His love, no hope of dwelling with Him, is a sad thing, indeed.   Verses 11 and12 have described what it means to be lost.   However, such a situation does not have to be terminal.   It can be changed.

b.   What Jews and Gentiles are when united with Christ – they are one new body.   13-18

> *Summary*:   Jew and Gentile have been united in Christ, and the latter is now as near to God as the former.   They have been reconciled man to man, verses 13-15; they have been reconciled man to God, verses 16-18.

2:13 – *But now in Christ Jesus you who formerly were far off have been brought near by the blood of Christ.*

But now in Christ Jesus – By using "now," Paul is giving the readers a picture of "before" and "after" in their spiritual lives.   He has pictured the desperate situation of the Gentiles before Christ.   But now this situation has been radically altered by the cross.   The long-promised Messiah in the person of Jesus has visited our world.   A new stage has now been reached in the unfolding of God's redemptive plan.   This new situation is described in the following verses.   "In Christ" is contrasted to "without God" (verse 12).   They may still physically be "in the world" (verse 12), but if they are "in Christ" (in union with Christ) things have changed radically.   After all, they are with Christ in the heavenly places.

You who formerly were far off – Compare Isaiah 57:19 which will be quoted below at verse 17.   Isaiah had heard God say, "Peace, peace to him that is afar off, and to him that is near" (ASV).   "Far off" and "near" were Hebrew expressions to describe the position of Gentiles and Jews.   Before the coming of Christ, faithful Jews were nearer to God and to heavenly Jerusalem than were the Gentiles.   The Gentiles were those who were "far off" (Acts 2:39); that is, away from God.

Have been brought near by the blood of Christ – "Near" equals near to God, and near to each other.   "Brought near" is in contrast with the whole previous condition of separation from Christ, with all that meant with regard to the commonwealth of Israel, the covenants, hope, and God.   "By the blood of Christ" likely is intended as a reference to Calvary.[63]   The blood of Christ has made it possible for them to be cleansed from sin, have a covenant relationship with God, and to no longer be aliens and strangers.

2:14 – *For He Himself is our peace, who made both* **groups** into *one and broke down the barrier of the dividing wall,*

For -- Beginning with "for" shows that verse 14 is intended to be an explanation of how the Gentiles have been brought near.   "From here through verse 18 the writer concentrates on what Christ has done in bringing about the reconciliation of Jews and Gentiles and making them one new people, united in Christ."[64]

He Himself is our peace – "He" is an emphatic pronoun in the Greek; that is why the NASB translates "He Himself," which means "*He and no one else*" is our peace.   Jesus the Christ and no other has solved the problem of our relationships with God and man.   The word translated "peace" is *eirene*, which comes from the verb *eiro* and means "to join together that which is separated."[65]   "The word describes that which is friendly and free from anger and quarrelsomeness.   It denotes harmonious relations, whether between persons, or between nations, or between a man and God."[66]   The context shows that what is primarily intended by "*our* peace" is the union of Jews and Gentiles.   "There is clearly allusion ... to the many promises in the Old Testament of the 'Prince of Peace' (Isaiah 9:5-6, et al.), [and] still more to the 'Peace of Earth' of the angelic song of Bethlehem, and to the repeated declarations of our Lord, such as, 'Peace I leave with you: My peace I give unto you'."[67]

Who made both *groups into* **one** – "Both" translates the adjective *amphotera*. Since in the Greek there is no noun stated, we must supply some word agreeing with the adjective, such as the two *parties*, the two *classes,* or the two *groups*.   In

---

[63] It is not possible to draw any satisfactory distinction between "by the blood" [Greek, *en to haimati*] as here, and "through His blood" [Greek, *dia tou haimatos autou*] in Ephesians 1:7 and Colossians 1:20 (Abbott, *op. cit.*, p.60).

[64] Bratcher, *op. cit.*, p.55.

[65] Wuest, *op. cit.*, p.75.

[66] Hayden, *op. cit.*, p.308.

[67] Alfred Barry, "The Epistles to the Ephesians, Philippians, and Colossians" in *Ellicott's Commentary* (Grand Rapids: Zondervan, 1981), Vol.8, p.27.

this verse, it seems to refer to what might be called "groups" of people, namely, the Jews and Gentiles. "One" is also an adjective with no noun stated. "One new group" might catch the idea. Chrysostom, long ago, had an apt explanation: "Not," says Chrysostom, "that He has brought the Gentiles up to the nobility of the Jews; but that He brought both of them up to a greater nobility. It is as if one should melt down a statue of silver and one of lead, and the two should come out gold."[68]

And broke down the barrier of the dividing wall – Exegetically, the "and" with which this phrase begins probably means "inasmuch as." Christ made Jew and Gentile one, inasmuch as He broke down the barrier that heretofore divided them. It is not easy to decide what might be the figure of speech behind "barrier" (*phragmon*) and behind the rare word (*mesotoichon*, "dividing wall") which Paul uses here. (1) Not a few writers make allusion to the wall in the temple area at Jerusalem that separated the court of the Gentiles (the area where the Gentiles were to assemble for worship) from the court of Israel (the area where Jews were to assemble for worship). At intervals along the wall signs were posted which threatened Gentiles with death if they crossed the barricade into the Jewish area.[69] (2) "Perhaps the explanation of Paul's words may be found in the verses which follow, where he writes about the abolition of the Law of Moses which stood as a wall between Jew and Gentile."[70] (3) Others suggest that "enmity" between the races was the barrier, since it is possible that this is what the next phrase (verse 15) talks about.

2:15 – *by abolishing in His flesh the enmity,* **which is** *the Law of commandments* **contained** *in ordinances, that in Himself He might make the two into one new man,* **thus** *establishing peace,*

By abolishing in His flesh the enmity – This verse explains how the barrier was broken down. "In His flesh" is a reference to the sacrifice of His body on the

---

[68] Cited in Abbott, *op. cit.*, p.61.

[69] Josephus tells about these "marble walls" in his *Wars* 5.5.2 and *Antiq.* 15.11.5. In 1871, a French archaeologist named Clermont-Ganneau discovered at Jerusalem one of these inscriptions chiseled in stone. If the objection is raised that when Ephesians was written that wall had not yet been taken down (since it was not until AD 70 that the barrier was literally taken down), it has been replied that if Christ did not actually take down that wall of stone, He did end the separation it symbolized.

[70] Leavitt, *op. cit.*, p.291. The next verse makes it clear that the barrier that divided folk was the Law. In Divine intention the Law was a "hedge" (Isaiah 5:2; Matthew 21:33) around the Old Israel.

cross.[71] "Abolishing" means to render inoperative, to supersede by something better than itself.[72] "Enmity" (*echthran*) speaks of hostility that existed between these deeply divided groups. Jesus, at Calvary, removed the cause of the hostility between the groups, and between man and God.

***Which is* the Law of commandments *contained* in ordinances** – This part of the passage is recognized as being especially difficult by both translators and commentators. It was the view of the translators of the KJV, ASV and the NASB, as shown by the insertion of "even" or "which is," that the "Law" was the cause of the enmity. To many, this view is objectionable, because it is hard to explain how the Law of Moses could be called "enmity" or be thought of as the cause for the enmity.[73] If we do not add any words in italics, our translation would match what the Greek can also say; namely, that Christ abolished two things by His death: one, the enmity, and two, the Law. Thus the verse says, "All that stood between Gentile and Jew, including the Jewish commandments or ordinances, was removed through the death of Jesus and the inauguration of a new covenant. See 2 Corinthians 3."[74]

Careful thought needs yet to be given to the words "Law of commandments *contained* in ordinances." An "ordinance" is an authoritative decree, edict, or law. In Luke 2:1 and Acts 17:7 the word refers to an edict issued by Caesar; in Acts 16:4 and Colossians 2:14 it is an authoritative decree given by God. "Commandments" call to mind the "thou shalts" and the "thou shalt nots" of the Law of Moses.   The NASB translators were probably   correct to add the word

---

[71] Some who have Ephesians written after Colossians think that "in His flesh" is an implicit refutation of heretical views that denied Jesus had a physical body (cf. Colossians 1:21,22, 2:9,14; John 1:14; 2 John 7).

[72] The word "abolishing" is the word often used by Paul when he wants to express the idea "to supersede by something better than itself" (see Romans 3:31; I Corinthians 1:26, 13:8-10).

[73] Barclay calls attention to the hundreds of rules and regulations the Pharisees had developed from their study of the Law, and thinks that these rules (which he thinks are here designated as "ordinances") were the cause of the enmity between Jews and Gentiles. Others appeal to the ceremonial rules found in the Law of Moses as being the cause of the alienation between Jews and Gentiles. Their religious practices were fundamentally different. In this commentator's judgment, it is not helpful to treat "ordinances" as being a reference solely to ceremonial rules in the Law of Moses.

[74] Enos Dowling, *1964 Standard Lesson Commentary* (Cincinnati: Standard, 1963), p.218.

"contained" in italics.[75]   Thus, "commandments ... ordinances" reminds us that the Mosaic Law consisted of commandments, and the form in which these commandments were expressed was that of authoritative decrees (ordinances). The whole Mosaic covenant, not just the ceremonial and judicial parts, has been set aside (abrogated) and replaced by something better (Hebrews 7:12,18, 10:9,10).[76]   God's covenant with Abraham includes "all nations" being blessed in the seed, which is Christ (Galatians 3:16).   Christians live under the new covenant (Jeremiah 31:31-34 and Hebrews 8-10).[77]

That in Himself He might make the two into one new man – "That" introduces a purpose clause.   The purpose of Christ's reconciling work is (1) to create the two in Himself into one new man, verse 15b; and (2) to reconcile both in one body to God, verse 16a.   The "two" are Jew and Gentile.   The "new man" is a new humanity, the Christian.   "New" is *kainos*, which means new in point of quality, a new quality that did not exist before.   The Gentile is not turned into a Jew, nor is the Jew turned into a Gentile, but both are turned into one new man.   Christ produces a new kind of person out of both, although they remain Gentiles and Jews.   This is what removes all grounds of hostility/enmity, and Christ is the head of this new man.[78]

***Thus* establishing peace** – The verse in Greek   ends with the   participial phrase

---

[75] The Greek is dative plural, and some (treating it as a dative of means) have tried to say the Law was abolished by means of the doctrines (decrees, ordinances) taught by Christ.   This explanation seems to ignore the expression that it was "in His flesh" that Christ abolished the Law.

[76] The Mosaic Law as such, not merely in certain aspects of it, has come to an end in Christ.   He is the "end of the law" (Romans 10:4).   Now that faith has come, we are no longer under the schoolmaster (Galatians 3:24,25).

[77] Some, at first, have thought Paul's statement here, that Christ abolished the Law, is contrary to Jesus' declaration that He did not come "to destroy the law, or the prophets ... but to fulfil" (Matthew 5:17).   However, since the Law pointed to its own abrogation (Deuteronomy 18:15), it cannot be said that Jesus destroyed it.   He fulfilled it.   He did exactly what the Law and prophets said the coming Messiah would do.

[78] It may well be that we have something here to learn.   The tendency has always been that when we send missionaries abroad we tend to produce people who wear American clothes and speak the English language, and have an education like one gets in America.   There are indeed some missionary Churches who would have all their congregations worship with the same "liturgy" which is used in the churches at home.   But it was not Jesus' purpose that we should turn all men into Americans -- but that there should be Christian Indians and Christian Africans, whose unity lies in their Christianity.   The oneness in Christ is in Christ, and not in any external change.

"establishing peace." It is a present tense participle indicating not that He made or established peace once, but rather that by this new creation He continually is making peace. In this verse the peace is between formerly estranged Jew and Gentile. Jesus continually makes peace by removing every barrier to union and peace. "Peace is the result of the oneness that obtains through Jesus Christ. As members of the one body, Christians cannot make war on one another. They are dependent one upon the other, even as the members of the human body are interrelated and dependent upon each other."[79] "'There is neither Jew nor Greek, there is neither bond nor free, there is neither male nor female; for ye are all one in Christ Jesus' (Galatians 3:28). This does not mean there are no differences among us; it means those differences make no difference in our fellowship, love, and care. We belong to the same family as brothers and sisters, because we are children of the same eternal father."[80]

2:16 -- *and might reconcile them both in one body to God through the cross, by it having put to death the enmity.*

And might reconcile them both in one body to God – "And" likely indicates a logical sequence of thought. We find the subject of this verb "reconcile," and indeed of the whole sentence, back in verse 14, "He Himself." Verse 15 gave one purpose behind Christ's death, namely to do away with the Law in order to make Jew and Gentile into one new man. Now verse 16 continues with a second purpose, indeed, the main purpose behind Christ's death. 2 Corinthians 5:18-21 is a famous passage in Paul's writings where reconciliation to God is the topic. However, there the Greek verb is *katallasso*, not the compound form *apokatallasso* which occurs only here and at Colossians 1:20,21. Commentators cannot agree whether the *apo-* simply intensifies the notion of reconciliation, or whether it means "again" so that here the word "reconcile" involves the idea of restoration of that primeval unity of men and God that had been marred and broken by sin. Since the context deals with reconciliation with God, perhaps the idea of a restoration of a condition which had been lost is in view. "Both" (*amphoterous*, the same word used in verse 14) is a masculine plural; both great groups, Jewish and Gentile believers. Several interpretations have been proposed for "in one body." One is that the one fleshly body of Jesus is contrasted to the numerous animal sacrifices of Old Testament times.[81] Several

---

[79] Dowling, *1962 Standard Lesson Commentary*, p.410.

[80] Staton, *op. cit.*, p.420.

[81] This view has against it (1) the fact that it anticipates Paul's own words "through the cross," and (2) the fact that "in one body" immediately follows "both" in the Greek, showing that a contrast with both is intended by "one body."

see a reference to the church which elsewhere (Ephesians 1:23, 3:6) is described as the body of Christ.   Others think of the new man (of verse 15) formed by the combination of Jewish and Gentile believers.   Still others think Paul's custom of likening the church to a human body with its many members (see 1 Corinthians 12:14-27) is the figure behind "one body."   "To God" is the indirect object of the verb "reconcile."   This passage emphasizes that man is reconciled to God.   Men can be at peace with each other when they are at peace with God.

Through the cross, by it having put to death the enmity – If we take "through the cross" with the preceding, the prepositional phrase "through the cross" indicates the means by which the action of reconciliation is accomplished.   Or, if we take "through the cross" with the following, it indicates the means by which the enmity was slain.   It looks as if the enmity talked about in this verse is a different enmity from that which verse 15 talked about.[82]   If so, this enmity is that between God and man resulting from man's sin.   That this is the meaning here seems plain from Romans 5:10, "If, while we were enemies, we were reconciled to God through the death of His Son."   By His death Christ has removed all the obstacles to reconciliation between men and God.

2:17 – *AND HE CAME AND PREACHED PEACE TO YOU WHO WERE FAR AWAY, AND PEACE TO THOSE WHO WERE NEAR;*

AND HE CAME AND PREACHED PEACE -- The proceeding verses have shown how Christ secured peace with God; this verse shows how He proclaimed it.   The NASB has printed this verse in small caps because it may be a quotation of Isaiah 57:19.   Literally the Greek reads, "having come, he announced the glad tidings: peace to you who were far off and to those near."   We have earlier noted (verse 14) that at the very beginning of His days on earth, the announcement that Christ's advent was intended to bring peace was made by Zachariah (Luke 1:78,79); and the angelic choir at the time of Jesus' birth said "Peace among men with whom He is pleased" (Luke 2:14).   But when did Christ announce such glad tidings?   Does the context require us to make this coming something which followed His crucifixion and death, or can we refer it to His whole incarnation?   In the upper room   the night He was betrayed,   Jesus spoke about   peace to the

---

[82] Those who interpret "enmity" in verses 15 and 16 as being the same thing, namely, something caused by the "Law," now appeal to Colossians 1:14 and Galatians 2:19-20, 3:13, to show that in other passages, as well as here, the truth is taught that the Law was abolished at the cross.

assembled apostles (John 14:27, 16:33). Jesus surely insisted that He had come as a light unto the Gentiles (Matthew 4:12-16). Perhaps the word "came" recalls to our thoughts the Lord's own preaching, when, after the resurrection, He came "and stood in the midst of them, and said, 'Peace be unto you'" (Luke 24:36; John 20:19; John 20:21 ASV). Or, perhaps, we should affirm that the reference is to Christ's message being spread by the apostles after Pentecost. Abbott defends this view by stating that the verb "preached" means "caused to be preached," and then he affirms that "what is done by His commissioned apostles is properly said to be done by Christ."[83]

TO YOU WHO WERE FAR AWAY, AND PEACE TO THOSE WHO WERE NEAR -- In verse 13 it has already been explained that "those who were far off" or "far away" are the Gentiles. The Jews are characterized as being "those who were near," because, as a rule, the Jews were closer to God than the Gentiles, for they had known the true God for centuries, while God had allowed the Gentiles to walk in their own ways. Paul writes "you who were far away" because this letter is addressed to readers who were mostly Gentiles. Jesus proclaimed the same terms of peace[84] both to the Gentiles who were far off and to the Jews who were nigh. Both groups needed to have reconciliation with God ("peace") preached to them. The one way of salvation offered in the gospel gives the same terms of peace for all men.

2:18 – *for through Him we both have our access in one Spirit to the Father.*

For – Beginning with "for" (*hoti,* "because"), this verse is a confirmation of the previous statement.[85] If we have access to God, the enmity must have been removed. There is but one way to peace for Gentile and Jew alike. There is salvation in none other than Jesus Christ.

Through Him we both have our access – It is solely through Christ ("Him" is emphatic) that both Jews and Gentiles now (present tense) have their "access" to God the Father. "Through Him" (*di' autou*) might mean "because of what He has done" or it might speak of His mediatorship ("He ... lives to make intercession

---

[83] Abbott, *op. cit.*, p.67.

[84] The repetition of *eirene* ("peace") is supported by good textual authority (P[46], Aleph, A, B, D).

[85] In the Greek text verses 17-18 are one sentence, with a minor break (semicolon) at the end of verse 17.

for us," Romans 5:12). The word translated "access" (*prosagoge*) is a technical word for being presented to a king in an oriental court.[86] The official in an oriental court who conducted visitors into the king's presence and introduced them to the king was called a *prosagogeus*. Jesus is the one who introduces us to His Father. "Both" is masculine plural, as in Ephesians 2:16. Both the great groups, in all their individual members, have this access, this privilege of admission to the throne room of the Almighty. This access is something that occurs in this life, perhaps in prayer and worship (Ephesians 3:12). It is not speaking of entering His presence in heaven when we die physically. Without Jesus, there is no way of access to the Father. Until our sins are covered, men have no right of access to God (Isaiah 59:2). Christ's death was a propitiatory sacrifice. He lives to make intercession for us. Both are needed for access to the Father.

In one Spirit – It is difficult to decide whether or not to capitalize the word "spirit" at this place. If we use small "s," the reference in "spirit" is to a common disposition that now characterizes the formerly separate groups. If we use a capital "S," the verse says the Holy Spirit has something to do with our access to the Father.[87] Perhaps the Holy Spirit is understood to have had something to do with the preaching of verse 17. Perhaps the Holy Spirit had something to do with encouraging all to be baptized into the one body (1 Corinthians 12:13.)

To the Father – "Access ... to the Father" is the thing being talked about. To those who have access to God through Christ, God is known as *Father,* a relationship particularly stressed throughout the letter (1:17; 3:12, 14, 15). "The Holy Spirit, promised and given to believers at their baptism into Christ (Acts 2:38), enables each one to know and address the Creator as 'Abba, Father' (Romans 8:15,16)."[88]

> ### c. What Jews and Gentiles are when united with Christ – one city (or country), one family, one building, one growing body (temple). 19-22

Summary: The figure of the church as a human body now shades into the

---

[86] The corresponding verb is found in 1 Peter 3:18, "Christ also suffered for sins ... the just for the unjust, that He might bring us to God." Romans 5:2 also refers to this introduction into the grace in which we stand.

[87] If we capitalize "S," there results a reference to the Father, Son, and Holy Spirit in this text.

[88] Hayden, *op. cit.*, p.309.

> figure of the church as a great building (temple). The Holy Spirit lives in the temple (as a whole) or in each individual stone.

2:19 – *So then you are no longer strangers and aliens, but you are fellow-citizens with the saints, and are of God's household,*

So then – "So then" (*ara oun*, "consequently," "as a result") introduces the logical conclusion from what has just been written in verses 14-18. In Greek, this verse begins a sentence which continues to the end of verse 22. In it we have various figures to describe the new humanity that has been created by the reconciling work of Christ.

You are no longer strangers and aliens – That from which the Gentiles once were excluded (verse 12) has all been changed. This *first metaphor* pictures the new humanity as one city or one country. "Strangers" (*xenoi*) are transients, foreigners, those who have no rights of citizenship. Life for a stranger was not easy. "Stranger" denotes inferiority when contrasted to the status of a "fellow-citizen." Transients were often regarded with suspicion and dislike. That sorry state has now been reversed. "Aliens" (*paroikoi*) were temporary residents, who might stay in a certain place, work there, and pay a tax for the privilege of living in a land that was not their own. They were still foreigners as far as the local populace was concerned. Both "strangers and aliens" were on the outside -- they were on the fringe. So Paul says to the Gentiles, 'You are no longer on the fringes. You are real citizens of the society of God. You are full members of the family of God.'

But you are fellow-citizens with the saints – There were faithful Jews (here called "saints") who never were cut off from the olive tree (Romans 11:24). Gentile believers have been grafted in among those saints. In Christ, Jews and Gentiles together have a new citizenship (cf. Philippians 3:20,21). "Fellow-citizens" reverses the condition expressed by "strangers" and "aliens." "The Ephesian Christians were no longer strangers; they held citizenship in the kingdom of God, with all its rights, privileges, and responsibilities that were involved in this citizenship."[89]

And are of God's household – The *second metaphor* used to describe the new humanity is that of family or household. "Household" (or family) implies that all Christians are children of the same Father. "They may have been adopted from many different backgrounds, but in the family relationship they are equals,

---

[89] Dowling, *1964 Standard Lesson Commentary*, p.219.

brothers and sisters, not by their choice of one another, but by their common parentage."[90]

2:20 – *having been built upon the foundation of the apostles and prophets, Christ Jesus Himself being the corner* stone,

Having been built upon the foundation of the apostles and prophets – The *third metaphor* to describe the new humanity is that of a building, a great temple. This metaphor is developed in verses 20-22. The aorist tense verb, "having been built," refers to the time when they became Christians. It is a passive voice verb, with the implied agent being God. God added them to the building/temple. The apostles of Jesus and the New Testament prophets are the ones here in view.[91] While several explanations have been offered to explain the figure "foundation of the apostles and prophets,"[92] we opt for the idea that the church is built on the foundation of the apostles and prophets in the sense that it is through them that we know Jesus and His will. They were instrumental in delivering the first inspired messages that led to the faith that produced the first building stones in this spiritual building. The point of this metaphor is that Jewish believers and Gentile believers are stones in the same building.

Christ Jesus Himself being the corner *stone* – In ancient building construction, the cornerstone was a massive stone placed where two walls of the building came together,   forming a part of the wall and determining the direction the walls will

---

[90] Hayden, op. cit., p.309.

[91] In the notes at Ephesians 4:11 are detailed explanations about apostles and prophets. The same phrase occurs in Ephesians 3:5, where the prophets are, undeniably, Christian prophets. In Acts 15:32 it is two "prophets" who "encouraged and strengthened" (the Greek word suggests precisely settlement on a foundation) the Gentile believers at Antioch.

[92] This genitive phrase ("of the apostles and prophets") has been understood in three different ways: (1) as a genitive of possession: the apostles' and prophets' foundation, i.e., the foundation upon which the apostles and prophets (as well as yourselves) are built;   (2) as a genitive *auctoris*, the foundation which they laid as they preached the gospel;   and (3) as a genitive of apposition, the foundation which consists of the apostles and prophets, they themselves are the foundation.   View #3 is the view of the majority of modern commentators and English versions. In this commentator's judgment, the second explanation is best: the apostles and prophets laid the foundation as they preached.   The third explanation is harder to justify.   While one might envision the apostles being the first building stones in this spiritual building, it is hard to see how the New Testament prophets could also be thought of as being among the first building stones, for before there were New Testament prophets on the scene there were folk who became Christians who likewise can be pictured as being living stones in this great spiritual temple.

run. Christ is the One who joins Jew and Gentile together. The metaphor seems to be drawn from Psalm 118:22 or Isaiah 28:16, and is also used at Acts 4:10,11.[93]

2:21 – *in whom the whole building, being fitted together is growing into a holy temple in the Lord,*

In whom the whole building – Two "in whom" clauses (verses 21,22) give us the *fourth metaphor.* The first "in whom" clause (verse 21) focuses on the building as a growing organism, while the second one (verse 22) focuses on the part the Gentiles have in it. "In whom" refers back to Jesus Christ, the cornerstone. "The whole building" refers not to the completed building itself, but the process of construction (the building, the erection) of the structure.[94] Individual believers are being added to the ever-growing structure.

Being fitted together – The present tense participle pictures the process of harmonious framing as still going on. It is a house that God is in the process of building – not a house that He has already built. The temple is in the process of being built. Each new Christian finds a place in the building, and it will not be completed until the last "living stone" (1 Peter 2:5) has been added to it. Truly the enmity between Jews and Gentiles, the enmity between all men and God, is broken down in the church, and thus every part is fitly framed together into one structure.

Is growing into a holy temple in the Lord – "Growing" (*auxei*, rises) is present tense, giving us the picture of a building constantly growing bigger and higher. The building is not completed. It continues to grow as additional stones (Christians) are added to it. Peter speaks of it in these words: "You also, as living stones, are being built up as a spiritual house ..." (1 Peter 2:5). "In the Lord" seems to mean dedicated or consecrated to the Lord Jesus. A temple (*naos*, sanctuary) is a place where a deity dwells. The church is a temple just for the Lord, a temple infinitely superior to the one in Jerusalem or the one in Ephesus dedicated to Artemis.

---

[93] The Greek word *akrogoniaios* can be translated as corner stone, capstone, or keystone, depending on the context. Here "corner stone" seems to be the correct word.

[94] There is a manuscript variation at this place, some reading *pasa he oikodome* as does the NASB ("the whole building") and others reading *pasa oikodome* as does the ASV ("each several building"). The NASB pictures one vast building. The ASV pictures individual Christians being worked into the ever growing structure of the church. The balance of manuscript evidence is strongly against the insertion of the article. The mental image given by the ASV is the correct image to keep in mind.

2:22 – *in whom you also are being built together into a dwelling of God in the Spirit.*

In whom you also are being built together – The fourth metaphor begun in verse 21 is now completed by emphasizing the part the Gentile Christians have in the temple. Gentile believers have a full share in this high privilege of being part of the growing temple dedicated to the Lord. "You are built" is a present tense verb.[95] The process of building is still going on. The final end has not yet been reached. "Together" seems primarily intended simply to emphasize the truth already enunciated in verse 20, that the readers of this letter themselves are now being made part of the Church of Christ – they "are being built together" (along with the Jewish believers in Christ).

Into a dwelling of God in the Spirit – "In the Spirit" may refer to the agency of the building process, the Holy Spirit, who is at work in leading believers to be baptized (1 Corinthians 12:13) and is the source of the cohesion in the church. Or it may designate the mode of God's dwelling in the body now – in the person of the Holy Spirit. Formerly, God dwelt in the temple at Jerusalem. Now, in the person of the Holy Spirit, He dwells in the church (1 Corinthians 3:16; 1 Peter 2:9). God's Spirit dwells in the temple (the church); His presence hallows it.

---

[95] The Greek verb may be either an indicative or imperative. We should treat it as indicative. The apostle is describing what the readers are (cp. verses 19-20), not what they ought to be.

D. The Apostle's Office and Prayer in view of the Mystery of the Universal Church in Christ.   3:1-21

Summary: In a lengthy digression concerning his apostolic commission, Paul "explains how his knowledge of the mystery of Christ (verse 4) was given to him (verses 2-3) and what the mystery is (verse 6). Three times he speaks of the grace of God which was given to him (verses 2, 7, 8), which he defines specifically as his commission to proclaim the Good News to the Gentiles (verses 8-9). The purpose of all this is to make the wisdom of God known to the angelic rulers and powers in the heavenly world (verse 10), in keeping with God's eternal purpose (verse 11).   The section concludes with an exhortation to the readers that they not become discouraged because of the writer's sufferings (verse 13)."[1]

1.   Beginning of Paul's prayer for their strengthening.   3:1a

3:1 –*For this reason I, Paul, the prisoner of Christ Jesus for the sake of you Gentiles —*

For this reason – "For this reason" refers back to the whole preceding statement in the letter, God's grace to the Gentiles.   "Having finished his portrait of the church (consisting of Jews and Gentiles, founded upon Christ, built up harmoniously in Christ, and constituting the habitation of the Holy Spirit), Paul begins a prayer that his readers may rise to a full apprehension of the blessed privileges of which they have been made partakers."[2]

I, Paul – "I, Paul" is the subject of the sentence.   "The writer's repetition of his name here shows that he attached seriousness and importance to what he was about to write."[3]   Where are the verb and object?   The nominative "I, Paul" is left suspended without a verb; the NASB has a dash at the end of verse 1 to show it is a broken sentence.   Perhaps the verb is finally supplied in verse 14,   since

---

[1] Bratcher, *op. cit.*, p.67.

[2] Meyrick, *op. cit.*, p.555.

[3] Martin, *op. cit.*, p.1308.

"for this reason" is repeated in 3:14 and seems to pick up the thread of the prayer once more.[4]

2. Paul's ministry as an apostle of the mystery of Christ.   3:1b-13[5]

a.   His present situation in Rome.   1b

The prisoner of Christ Jesus for the sake of you Gentiles – We are accustomed to Paul's describing himself as "the apostle of Christ Jesus," but here he substitutes the word "prisoner," descriptive of his present situation in Rome.   At the time he writes this letter he is a prisoner in Rome, not for a crime or an unpaid debt or as a captive in a war, but as a direct consequence of his activity for Christ as an apostle to the Gentiles.   It is true that during his first Roman imprisonment, while he was waiting for his Jewish accusers to come, Paul had certain privileges (Acts 28:16-31).   He was allowed to stay in his own hired house, and his friends were allowed access to him.   But, even then, night and day he was a prisoner; night and day he was chained to the wrist of the Roman soldier who was his guard, and whose duty it was to see that Paul would never escape.   An ordinary person, looking at Paul in prison, would have said Paul was the prisoner of the Roman government, and in one sense he was.   But Paul never thought of himself as the prisoner of Rome; he always thought of himself as the prisoner of Christ.[6]   No sooner does he write "for the sake of you Gentiles" than he digresses into a lengthy discussion of his apostolic commission as apostle to the Gentiles.   At verse 14 the digression is completed and he returns to the prayer which he had begun as he wrote verse 1.[7]

b.   The mystery was made known to Paul by revelation.   2,3

3:2 – *if indeed you have heard of the stewardship of God's grace which was given to me for you;*

---

[4] Other attempts to locate a verb to complete this sentence include the verb in verse 13, "I ... ask you not to lose heart," or the verb in 4:1, "I ... entreat you."

[5] These verses constitute a lengthy digression or parenthesis in Paul's prayer for his readers.

[6] Because of this language this letter is grouped with Paul's other letters written from prison, namely, Philippians (Philippians 1:13), Colossians (Colossians 4:3) and Philemon (verses 1 and 17).

[7] This digression is one of the longest ones found in Paul's writings.

If indeed you have heard -- This verse begins a sentence which, in the Greek, goes to the end of verse 7. "If indeed" here is not an expression of uncertainty, but is an assumption that what is said is true. We could also translate it, "For you must have heard...," or "Assuming that you have heard ...."[8] What is uncertain is from whom the readers have heard. This verse has some bearing on the question whether the Epistle was an encyclical letter, or one addressed to the Ephesian Church. It is not easy to explain this language if the letter were addressed solely to a church like Ephesus which had been personally instructed by the writer for nearly three years. But if this letter was addressed to a circle of churches, many of them would not have had Paul as their preacher, and their knowledge of him and his ministry to the Gentiles would have been heard from others.

Of the stewardship of God's grace – This profound expression is Paul's way of saying that because of God's grace he had been given a job to carry out. "Grace" may have a more restricted meaning here than it did at 2:5,8. In 3:2,7,8, "grace" is related to Paul's commission to preach the good news to the Gentiles,[9] and in 3:2,3 grace is identified as resulting in a revelation being made known to Paul.[10] "Stewardship" translates the Greek noun *oikonomia*; this word appears also in Ephesians 1:10, where it was translated "administration" in the NASB. It suggests that as God managed history, He made this arrangement that Paul should be the apostle to the Gentiles and be given a revelation of the mystery, about which verse 3 will speak.

Which was given to me for you – The Greek shows it was "grace" (not "stewardship") that was given to Paul. "For you" in this case means specifically to you who are Gentiles. That the Lord had called Paul to preach the gospel to the Gentiles (Acts 26:16-18) is the thing being spoken of in the letter part of this verse.

3:3 – *that by revelation there was made known to me the mystery, as I wrote before in brief.*

That by revelation – Verse 3 identifies in more   detail what Paul assumes they

---

[8] The Greek expression *ei ge* is presumptive rather than suppositional. When Paul uses the same formula in Ephesians 4:21 he is not suggesting for a moment that his readers have never heard of Christ (Wood, *op. cit.*, p.44). BAG (p.152) translates "inasmuch as."

[9] At Romans 1:5 "grace" and "apostleship" are virtually synonymous.

[10] As he explains the "grace" that was given to Paul, Wood (*op. cit.*, p.45) writes about "the equipment that enabled him to fulfill his calling as a missionary to the Gentiles (cf. Ephesians 3:7,8, 4:7-13)."

had heard (verse 2) about the grace that was given to him.   "By revelation" is in the emphatic position in the Greek, and thus calls special attention to *the way* in which the "mystery" was made known to Paul.   In comments on 1 Corinthians 2:10-12, we have defined revelation as "the act of the Holy Spirit making known to God-chosen messengers truths they were incapable of discovering by unaided human research."[11]   We suppose the best option is to affirm that Paul received this revelation during the three years he spent in Arabia (Galatians 1:11,12,17,18) just shortly after Jesus called him to be an apostle.

There was made known to me the mystery – In notes at Ephesians 1:9, we learned that a "mystery" is something not clearly revealed in Old Testament times, but now is.   God's plan, long kept hidden from men, included His determination to incorporate Gentile believers into the one body of the church (Ephesians 2:16) as equal partners with believing Israel (Ephesians 3:6).[12]   God had revealed His hidden plan to Paul – and to other apostles and prophets (Ephesians 3:5) – and it was Paul's responsibility to explain it to the Gentiles.

As I wrote before in brief – "Wrote" is an epistolary aorist, referring to what has just been written in this epistle at 1:9-14 and 2:11-22, which describes the oneness of Jews and Gentiles in the church.   A few writers have proposed that Paul makes reference to an earlier letter he had written, rather than to this very letter.   However, the next verse seems to imply he has reference to something he had just written, not a previous letter.   "In brief" means in a few words or in a short space.

c.   The mystery can be known by reading Paul's writings.   4

3:4 – *And by referring to this, when you read you can understand my insight into the mystery of Christ,*

---

[11] See Gareth L. Reese, *New Testament History: Acts* (Moberly, MO: Scripture Exposition Books, 2002), p.127.   Compare Galatians 1:11,12, 1 Corinthians 2:7-16, and Romans 16:25 for Paul's insistence of a direct reception of the gospel from the Lord Jesus Christ Himself, without any human intermediaries.   Paul preached a message that had been revealed directly to him by Christ.   Paul had no contact with the other apostles for several years after his conversion.   He never did have much contact with them (see Galatians 1), but he preached the same message that they did, for Christ revealed the same gospel to all.

[12] Before, at 1:9, "mystery" was used regarding the whole spectrum of God's redemptive plan for the universe.   Here in 3:3-6, Paul has in mind one particular aspect of that all-inclusive mystery, namely, the incorporation of the Gentiles into God's elect people.   Later in Ephesians we shall learn of other aspects included in the "mystery."

And by referring to this, when you read – "Read" is a present tense verb in the Greek. It is "while you are reading" or "as you read" that perception of Paul's understanding would come. The epistles were read aloud in the public assembly of the church,[13] and by reading and re-reading what he has written, they could gain an understanding of his insight into the mystery of Christ. "When Paul wrote that men should study his writings, it was not vainglory or egotism on his part, but the mere statement of the basic obligation of every Christian to study divine revelation in the Scriptures."[14]

You can understand my insight into the mystery of Christ – Intellectual understanding will come to the Christian from reading what Paul has written.[15] "Understand" is *noesai,* which means to grasp with the mind. "My insight" (*sunesis,* a word which occurs repeatedly in the New Testament in the sense of mental apprehension, a critical understanding of the bearings of things: Luke 2:47; 1 Corinthians 1:19; Colossians 1:9, 2:2; 2 Timothy 2:7) speaks of a profound comprehension of the mystery that results from the revelation granted to Paul.[16] "The mystery of Christ" likely means the mystery relating to Christ in that it was bound up with His work.[17] "God's message concerning the coming of Christ as it was revealed in the Old Testament was accurate but incomplete. It was given in limited ways and for particular circumstances. God had to prepare Himself a people and arrange the circumstances for the full revelation of Himself and His plan. That complete and perfect revelation came in Christ, for He 'has in these last days spoken unto us by His Son ... the express image of his person ...' (Hebrews 1:2,3 KJV)."[18]

---

[13] Quite often the Greek verb "to read" in the New Testament means "to read aloud in public," for example, Colossians 4:16; 1 Thessalonians. 5:27; Revelation 1:3 (see also Mark 13:14).

[14] James B. Coffman, *Commentary on Galatians Ephesians, Philippians, and Colossians* (Austin, TX: Firm Foundation Publishing House, 1977), p.181.

[15] We Christians do not expect to get revelation directly from God into our minds and speech, as Paul did.

[16] Critics who question the genuineness of this epistle regard this verse as an expression of a boastfulness not in accordance with the dignity of an apostle. On the contrary, when Paul is speaking to folk who may or may not know him personally, a reminder that apostles could speak with authority on subjects was perfectly proper.

[17] "This does not refer to anything mysterious in the person of Christ; or the union of the divine and human nature in Him; or to anything difficult of apprehension in the work of the atonement" (Barnes, *op. cit.*, p.56). The next verse here in Ephesians sheds much light on the New Testament usage of the word "mystery."

[18] Tesh, *op. cit.*, p.387.

d. The mystery was unknown in previous ages. 5

3:5 – *which in other generations was not made known to the sons of men, as it has now been revealed to His holy apostles and prophets in the Spirit;*

Which in other generations was not made known to the sons of men – "Which" points to the mystery relating to the inclusion of the Gentiles in the body of Christ (verse 6). "Other generations" are those before the time of Christ. In those ages before Christ, God's plan was concealed from men; it was a "mystery". "Sons of men," if we compare its use in Mark 3:28, is apparently a comprehensive term for mankind in general. He does not say "was not revealed," but rather "was not made known." Old Testament prophets did receive revelations which they dutifully handed on, but often they did not themselves know the import of what they spoke by inspiration.[19] However much Adam, Abraham and David knew about the coming of Messiah, they did not know the full extent of God's grace to the Gentiles. That God intended to bless the Gentiles was alluded to by God from time to time,[20] but it was not as clearly revealed then as it is being revealed now to Christ's holy apostles and prophets.

As it has now been revealed to His holy apostles and prophets – "As" is comparative, meaning with such clearness as it has now been revealed. "Now" refers to these days since Jesus ministered here on earth. Paul will not claim he is the only one to receive a revelation [21] of the mystery, but he does insist that the

---

[19] 1 Peter 1:10-12 gives us a glimpse into Old Testament prophetic consciousness. Peter tells us that after making a prophecy, the Old Testament prophets searched what time or what person the Spirit within them was pointing to. They had a revelation, yes, but complete understanding, no. The same thing happened to Peter on Pentecost when he declared that the promise was to you and your children and for all who are far off (Acts 2:39), and yet, years later, was hesitant to offer an invitation to the Gentile Cornelius. By inspiration, Peter had said it right, but he did not understand all that he had said.

[20] That God's blessing was to extend to the Gentiles was taught in the Old Testament. See the promise to Abraham in Genesis 12:3 and as repeated until we come to Genesis 22:18. See the string of Old Testament passages quoted by Paul in Romans 15:9-12. See the quotation of Isaiah 49:6 at Acts 13:47. See also Isaiah 66:18ff.

[21] See notes above at verse 3 for a definition of "revelation."

revelation he received is no different than what the other apostles of Jesus and New Testament prophets had received.[22] Paul likely received his revelation during his time in Arabia (Galatians 1:15-17). We do not know when such a revelation was made to the twelve, though before His ascension, Jesus even told His apostles that repentance and forgiveness of sins should be proclaimed in His name "to all nations" (Luke 24:47). Peter, on Pentecost, quoted an Old Testament prophecy as he preached the first recorded Gospel sermon (Acts 2:21). Perhaps the apostles did not, at first, clearly perceive the full meaning of what they were preaching by inspiration. If Old Testament prophets could be called "holy,"[23] there is nothing incongruous with calling the apostles and prophets "holy."[24] "Holy" indicates that these men were dedicated or consecrated to God, set apart to a sacred service. They were especially appointed by God to serve Him.

In the Spirit – It was the Holy Spirit who revealed the mystery of Christ to the apostles and prophets. We are told in Revelation 1:10 that John was "in the Spirit" when he received a command to write what he saw in a book and send it to the seven churches. We understand that something similar happened to the apostles and prophets when they received their revelation of the mystery. Just as holy men were inspired by the Holy Spirit in Old Testament times (2 Peter 1:20,21), so were the New Testament apostles and prophets. It is a fulfillment of what Jesus promised when He said He would send the Spirit to guide the apostles into all truth (John 16:13).

e. The mystery concerns the Gentiles' equal privileges. 6

3:6 – to be specific, *that the Gentiles are fellow-heirs and fellow-members of the body, and fellow-partakers of the promise in Christ Jesus through the gospel,*

---

[22] "Apostles" and "prophets" are discussed in great detail at Ephesians 4:11.

[23] The epithet is applied to the Old Testament prophets in Luke 1:70; Acts 3:21; 2 Peter 3:2.

[24] Some critics have alleged that it is incredible that an apostle would call other apostles and prophets "holy," and they have insisted that this expression betrays the fact that this letter was forged at a later date by someone who was not an apostle. While at a later date "holy" may have been used to express the personal character of "sinless perfection," the word does not carry that connotation in apostolic times. If individual Christians can be characterized as "saints" (a translation of the same word that is translated "holy"), then certainly, it is appropriate *a fortiori* to style the apostles and prophets as "holy," i.e., set apart for the special task of proclaiming Christ.

***To be specific*, that the Gentiles are fellow-heirs** – This is the content of the mystery about which he has been speaking in this immediate context.   This statement summarizes the idea already unfolded in Ephesians 2:11-22.[25]   Though it was a "mystery," there were in the Old Testament faint predictions and intimations that Gentiles would be included in the body of Christ.[26]   Gentiles are "fellow-heirs" (not with Christ, but) with believing Jews.   The term implies the closeness between the heirs, and a lack of superiority on the part of either Jews or Gentiles.   At Paul's call to be an apostle, he was commissioned to go to the Gentiles, "that they may receive forgiveness of sins *and an inheritance* among those who have been sanctified by faith in Me" (Acts 26:18).

And fellow-members of the body – Gentiles are co-members of the same body (the term *susoma* may have been coined by Paul); they are incorporated into the same new body of which Christ is the head as were Jewish believers.   Gentile Christians are constituent portions of the body, the church, as are Jewish believers; they are as closely related to Christ, and as much partakers of His life as their Jewish brethren.[27]   The mystery was not that Gentiles should be saved – there is much in the Old Testament concerning the salvation of the Gentiles, particularly in Isaiah – but that they should be joined with the Jews in one new body is the mystery.

And fellow-partakers of the promise in Christ Jesus through the gospel – "Fellow-partakers" is the third of three Greek words which are prefixed by the preposition *sun-* ("with" or "together with" or "co-"), all of which express the sharing and opening of previously closed avenues of fellowship: fellow-heirs, fellow-members, fellow-partakers.   To be a "fellow-partaker" (*summetocha*, a

---

[25] The NASB has rightly added "to be specific" because the infinitive (*einai*) with which this verse begins in Greek is epexegetical.

[26] The footnotes in the old Scofield Reference Bible make the affirmation that the church was not predicted in the Old Testament.   This passage in Ephesians is but one of many which shows that such an affirmation is flatly wrong.   It was dimly taught in the Old Testament that Gentiles would be included in the glorious church, the body of Christ.   Acts 3:24 asserts that Samuel and all of the prophets spoke of these days (i.e., the church).

[27] Most Jews felt that if the Gentiles were ever accepted to God, it would be only when they became subject to the Law of Moses.   The revelation that both Jews and Gentiles stand on equal footing with God through Jesus Christ was more than many zealous Hebrew Christians could easily at first accept (Acts 15:5).

co-partner, a co-sharer, an equal participant) of the promise is to be joined with others who were included as recipients of the same promise. "This statement of religious equality between Jews and Gentiles is strong, clear, complete; the more remarkable when we remember that Paul himself once had such strong Jewish prejudices; obviously, only one who now had the clearest insight and the highest courage could proclaim the truth so emphatically."[28] "The promise in Christ" is perhaps an allusion to the promise made to Abraham that in his seed all the nations of the earth would be blessed (Genesis 22:18). "In Christ" may say that the promised seed was Christ (Galatians 3:16), or "in Christ Jesus" may be shorthand for the body of Christ. They do not get this blessing by becoming Jews, but by becoming Christians; this is how Gentiles "become fellow-heirs, fellow-members, and fellow-partakers in Christ Jesus, enjoying all privileges in Him, in a state of union and fellowship with Him."[29] "Through the gospel" is how men are invited or admitted to the new body. Men are called (invited) to become Christians through the gospel (2 Thessalonians 2:14).

f. Paul, though undeserving, was appointed to preach the mystery. 7-9

3:7 – *of which I was made a minister, according to the gift of God's grace which was given to me according to the working of His power.*

Of which I was made a minister – "Which" can point to either "Christ" or the "gospel"; "gospel" is the nearest antecedent. Paul did not train for the job over a period of time, but he became a minister at a given time and place, namely, when Christ called him on the Damascus road (Acts 26:16-18). The Greek word (*diakonos*) translated "minister" speaks of one who serves.[30] Preaching the gospel is how Paul served Christ.

According to the gift of God's grace – Paul viewed his selection as a servant/minister as a gift of God's grace (loving-kindness).

---

[28] W.G. Blaikie, "Ephesians" in *The Pulpit Commentary* (Grand Rapids: Eerdmans, 1962 reprint), p.105.

[29] Lipscomb, *op. cit.*, p.58.

[30] "The Greek term used here for minister is the ordinary word for servant. Our word deacon is derived from it. The term has two meanings: one is the name for a class of church officers, the other is a general word to express high-class service of any type. It is in this latter sense that Paul used it here" (Leavitt, *op. cit.*, p.58).

Which was given to me according to the working of His power – It has been said, "Whom God calls He qualifies." Not only was Paul given the ministry to the Gentiles, he was also accorded "the working of His power;" that is, he was given divine power from God to carry out his ministry. In 1 Timothy 1:12 ("strengthened" translates the same Greek word for "power" that was used at Acts 1:8) Paul claims the same power that was given to the twelve on Pentecost. This divine power was manifested in the miracles, the inspiration, and the spiritual insight that resulted from the special measure of the Holy Spirit given to the apostles.

3:8 – *To me, the very least of all saints, this grace was given, to preach to the Gentiles the unfathomable riches of Christ,*

To me, the very least of all saints – Paul here describes himself in contrast to the greatness of God's power. "In 2 Corinthians 12:11 he acknowledges that in himself he is a nobody while at the same time recognizing that God has made him a somebody."[31] "Paul always looked back upon his days of bitter persecution of the church with humility, regret, and thanksgiving to God for forgiveness."[32] He thought of himself as undeserving of the honor of being a minister of the gospel.[33]

This grace was given – "This" points to what follows, namely, the evangelization of the Gentiles. "The special commission to preach to the Gentiles is here called grace. (See also Acts 9:15; 22:15; 26:16,17)."[34] This is the third time in this chapter that Paul speaks of his office as apostle to the Gentiles as being a consequence of God's grace.

---

[31] Wuest, *op. cit.*, p. 47. The word here (*elachistoteros,* "the least of the least," NEB) is a comparative adjective formed from a superlative adjective. The form identifies Paul, in his own mind, as being someone who is least important.

[32] Foster, *op. cit.*, p.123.

[33] Though some modern commentaries (e.g., Mitton, *The Epistle to the Ephesians*, p.15,136; E.J. Goodspeed, *Introduction to the New Testament*, p.231; Beare, "Ephesians" in *The Interpreter's Bible*, p.660) actually teach the very opposite, this language in 3:8 excludes the possibility that this epistle was written by some admiring disciple of Paul (such as Onesimus), rather than by Paul himself. "No disciple of Paul would have dreamed of giving the apostle so low a place" (Bruce, *op. cit.*, p.63). "Is it conceivable that an admirer of Paul, writing in his name to enhance his reputation in the late-first-century church, would ascribe such a self-demoting confession of him?" (Wood, *op. cit.*, p.47).

[34] Foster, *ibid.*

To preach to the Gentiles – This is the result of "the grace" that was given to Paul. The meaning of "preach" (*euangelidzesthai*) is to evangelize, to proclaim good tidings to others. When Paul received his commission as an apostle, he was told that he was a chosen instrument to carry Christ's name before the Gentiles (Acts 9:15, 26:16-18).

The unfathomable riches of Christ – This is the message Paul preached. The "riches" that Christ has made available is the whole wealth of salvation He bestows. The figurative use of "riches" has no biblical parallel outside Paul's writings; however, he uses it 14 times.[35] The riches of Christ are called "unfathomable" because they are so vast that no human can trace out all the priceless aspects and phrases of them.[36] No man can completely comprehend the boundless wealth available in Christ.

3:9 – *and to bring to light what is the administration of the mystery which for ages has been hidden in God, who created all things;*

And to bring to light – In addition to preaching the unfathomable riches of Christ to the Gentiles, this verse gives another specific task that was assigned to Paul. In teacher training class, we learned to shine a light on a small chart to make it visible to more folk in the room. Paul had the job of throwing light on the subject of how God has been managing the mystery.

What is the administration of the mystery – See 1:9 and 3:3 where this language has already been explained.[37] God's redemptive program, designed before creation (Ephesians 1:4), has been unfolding in history just as God arranged it. God has chosen to wait until after Jesus was incarnate to fully make known to men what His program was. It was Paul's job to explain to men how God has been managing history. He is to help men to see how God's redemptive program has been unfolding in history, just as God planned it would be.

---

[35] Compare what was written at Ephesians 1:7.

[36] The only other time the word "unfathomable" is used in the New Testament is Romans 11:33. The idea was also taught in the Old Testament, esp. in Job 5:9 and 9:10.

[37] The KJV at this place reads "to make all see what is the fellowship of the mystery." The words "all" and "fellowship" are not well supported in the better manuscripts. If "all" is retained, the idea will be that of the enlightenment of all as to what the administration is. Instead of *koinonia* ("fellowship") the better supported reading is *oikonomia* ("administration").

Which for ages has been hidden in God – "For ages" covers all the time since the world began up until the time when men like Paul were commissioned to be apostles of Jesus. This verse, along with verses 4-6, helps us to understand the sense in which Paul uses the word "mystery." As has been explained, the word speaks of something not clearly revealed in ages past, but now is being clearly revealed through the preaching of the apostles. "Hidden in God" tells us that God formed the plan in His mind, but kept it to Himself in ages past. We might ask, "Why did God wait so long to reveal His mystery, when the world needed it so greatly?" We cannot know God's reasons for doing things. But it is evident to everyone that by the time that God revealed His mystery, the world had fully discovered that it could not save itself by philosophy, law, military might, or any other human means. Hence, the world should have been fully ready to receive Christ.

Who created all things – What is the point of these words? "The simplest explanation is that God who is creator was free to make whatever arrangement He pleased as to the concealment and revelation of His plan/purpose."[38]

> ## g. It is the church's privilege to make known the wisdom of God. 10-12

3:10 – *In order that the manifold wisdom of God might now be made known through the church to the rulers and the authorities in the heavenly* **places.**

In order that ... now – The ASV's translation "to the intent that" helps us see that God had the following intent as He kept His plans pretty much to Himself in Old Testament ages. In God's plan, there would come the day when it was the right time to make His plans known. Paul is about to make an astounding assertion of the greatness of the church's role in the divine plan of redemption. It is through the church that God intended His plan be developed and unfolded. "Now" equals now that the time for the revelation of the mystery has arrived. The very existence of the church is a visible exhibit of God's unifying plan and purpose at work in history.

---

[38] Abbott, *op. cit.*, p.88. The KJV adds the words "through Jesus Christ" so that the verse reads "who created all things through Jesus Christ." The Textus Receptus alone carries the addition, and it does not therefore enjoy integrity. Perhaps it is an interpolation from Colossians 1:15,16. R.C. Foster, who was commenting on the text in the KJV, wrote, "God was not taken by surprise when Eve and Adam succumbed to the devil's wiles in the Garden of Eden. He knew what could happen. He had a plan before the world was created. The fact that Christ was the active agent of God in creation is introduced to underscore the Deity of Christ and prepare for the glorious tributes to Christ that follow in the next verses" (Foster, *op. cit.*, p.123).

The manifold wisdom of God – In 1 Corinthians 1:30 Paul tells us that the wisdom of God includes righteousness, sanctification, and redemption. "Manifold" translates *polupoikilos*, which literally means "many colored," wrought in many details. The word probably refers to the variety of God's dealings with Jews and Gentiles in former times, which are now seen to have worked to one end.

Might ... be made known through the church – The angels are represented to us not only as ministering to the church (Hebrews 1:14), but as learning from the existence and fortunes of the church more and more about the wisdom of God. Peter has told us that angels desired to look into the things that were being prophesied by the Old Testament prophets (1 Peter 1:12).

To the rulers and the authorities – At Ephesians 1:21 we learned that these names refer to different orders or ranks of angels. "Not only are human beings unable to fathom the depths of God's wisdom, but angels likewise are limited in their understanding. They too had to await God's good pleasure in making known to them His plan in Christ. Through the church they are witnessing the gradual unfolding of plans that were made before God created the heavens and the earth."[39]

In the heavenly *places* – This is the dwelling place of the angels (rulers and authorities) who are learning as they watch what God does through the church.[40]

3:11 – This was *in accordance with the eternal purpose which He carried out in Christ Jesus our Lord,*

This was **in accordance with the eternal purpose** – The action expressed in verse 10 was in harmony with the plan God formed before He ever created. That angels might learn about the wisdom of God by looking at the church is what is in harmony with God's plan from the beginning. On God's eternal purpose, i.e., the plan that He made before He created, see Ephesians 1:11 and Romans 8:29.[41]

---

[39] Tesh, *op. cit.*, p.389.

[40] At Ephesians 1:3,20 and 2:6 we have already studied what region is indicated in the expression "heavenly places." Since Ephesians 6:12 has evil angels dwelling in the "heavenly places" we probably should understand that all the angels, both good and bad, are learning as they watch what God is doing in the church.

[41] Literally, the Greek reads "the purpose of the ages." It probably means "the purpose that runs through the ages." In the classical writers *prothesis* ("purpose") frequently denotes a deliberate plan or scheme (*BAG*, p.713). "Eternal" may be a reasonably accurate rendering of the Greek in light of 2 Timothy 1:9, "from all eternity."

Which He carried out in Christ Jesus our Lord – The Greek can mean either that the plan was "formed" or "executed" in Christ Jesus. F.F. Bruce combines both ideas when he writes, "God's purpose was conceived in Christ, and it attains its fulfillment in Christ."[42] Earlier in Ephesians (1:4) we learned that God planned or determined that all those who were in Christ would be part of His adopted family.

3:12 – *in whom we have boldness and confident access through faith in Him.*

In whom we have boldness – In Christ we (Jews and Gentiles) have boldness (an absence of fear and shame, a contrast with Adam who hid himself among the trees of the garden, and a contrast with the lost who cry for the rocks and mountains to cover them). While the word "boldness" designated the freedom of a citizen in a Greek democracy to speak openly in public meetings, and is therefore often limited to being a reference to prayer where we come boldly to the throne of grace, as Hebrews 4:16 talks about, perhaps here the word denotes not a rashness but a cheerful boldness, "the joyful mood of those reconciled to God."[43]

And confident access – "Confident" (*pepoithesis*) is a rare word, used in the New Testament only 6 times, and all by Paul.[44] It speaks of the assurance of being welcomed and accepted when we go into God's presence. For the word "access" see 2:18. It speaks of our being presented to God by Christ Jesus. Apart from Christ we could not draw near (chapter 2).

> In Jesus we have confidence to freely approach God. It sometimes happens that some friend of ours knows some very distinguished person. We ourselves would never have any right to enter into that person's presence; but our friend takes us in, and in our friend's company we have the right of entry. That is what Jesus does for us with God. In His presence and in His company there is an open door to the presence of God which no man can ever shut.[45]

---

[42] Bruce, *op. cit.,* p. 65.

[43] Meyer, *op. cit.,* p.417.

[44] 2 Corinthians 1:15, 3:4, 8:22, 10:2; Philippians 3:4, and here. There is a manuscript difference, but "confidence" (according to the better reading) seems to go only with "access," not with both "boldness and access" as the KJV has it.

[45] Tesh, *op. cit.,* p.389.

Through faith in Him – The Greek is a genitive construction, literally, "through the faith of Him." We take it as being an objective genitive meaning our faith in Him[46] (i.e., Christ is the object of our faith). The confidence of being welcomed and accepted when we go into God's presence springs from our faith in Christ. Our access is conditioned on our faithfulness.

h. Paul's request that they not let his sufferings be a cause of discouragement. 13

3:13 – *Therefore I ask you not to lose heart at my tribulations on your behalf, for they are your glory*.

Therefore I ask you not to lose heart – "Therefore" might be connected with the whole preceding paragraph (verses 2-12) – "Since I am the appointed apostle to you Gentiles, I ask ...," or it might pick up the "I, Paul, the prisoner of Christ Jesus for the sake of you Gentiles – " (verse 1). The main verb in Greek (*aiteo*) can mean (1) "I pray" or (2) "I ask," or "I request. " As the marginal note in the NASB shows, the words following the verb can be interpreted two different ways: either "I pray that I may not lose heart" or "I pray that you may not lose heart."[47] To "lose heart" means to become discouraged, so as to want to quit. Perhaps Paul is thinking they could lose heart out of fear that they would soon be enduring the same miseries that Paul was enduring. Or perhaps there was danger that the Christians (of Gentile background) might think the Christian religion was vain and false because Paul was suffering so much from his countrymen (the Jews) on account of it. Paul counters this possibility by writing a sentence that says that just because he is suffering should not lead them to believe that the Christian religion is false.

At my tribulations on your behalf – The "tribulations" to which Paul alludes refer to what has happened to him since the last time he was in Asia Minor (Acts 20) and bade the Ephesian elders farewell. There have been sufferings, trials, and persecutions, and four years of imprisonment, all of which came upon him because he was the apostle to the Gentiles.

---

[46] While we have indicated our preference for interpreting this genitive as objective, it must be observed that it is becoming acceptable among many modern commentators (including Barth and Coffman, p.188) to treat the genitive as a subjective genitive, as though it refers to Christ's faithfulness, that is, He faithfully carried out the plan that God had made back in eternity.

[47] The Greek infinitive "to lose heart" has no subject indicated in the Greek, so the various possibilities have been proposed.

For they are your glory – Paul's tribulations (sufferings) turned out for the furtherance of the gospel. They will result in his readers being glorified, sharing in the glory of God. Paul bids the readers of this letter to find in his sufferings, not a cause of discouragement, but a cause for taking courage.

3. Paul's prayer for the readers is resumed and completed. 3:14-19

> *Summary:* Paul prays that they may be filled with all the spiritual blessings which God has for them.

3:14 – *For this reason I bow my knees before the Father,*

For this reason – With the same words found at the beginning of 3:1, Paul's interrupted prayer is now resumed. What is said about "for this reason" in verse 1 applies here.[48] If the church is ever to be the instrument whereby men are brought into one, the people within it must be a certain kind of people. That is why Paul is praying; he is praying that the people within the church may be such that the whole church will be in truth the body and the complement of Christ. Verses 14-19 are one sentence in the Greek. The main verb is "I bow (my knees)" in verse 14. Verse 15 is a parenthetical comment on the "Father" of verse14; verses 16-19 (if we let the three *hina* clauses guide us) seem to state three requests Paul makes to God in this prayer.

I bow my knees – "Bow my knees" is a present tense verb. It indicates Paul kneels now and again to offer the following prayer. Bowing on the knees – literally, bending both knees rather than just one, dropping to one's knees – was so universally a posture when praying that to bow the knees meant to pray.[49]

Before the Father – "'Before' (*pros*) is a face-to-face preposition applicable to

---

[48] It is because we understand Ephesians 3:2-13 as being a parenthetical discussion of his apostolic ministry that we look back to what preceded 3:1 as the reason for the prayer.

[49] Concerning posture in prayer, the Scripture does not indicate that any one bodily posture is necessary in prayer. (Coffman, *op. cit.*, has a good paragraph on the topic, p.190.) The usual posture in praying was standing (Mark 11:25; Luke 18:11,13). But kneeling is mentioned (1 Kings 8:54; Daniel 6:10; Luke 22:41; Acts 7:60, 20:36, 21:5). David prayed on his bed at night (Psalm 63:6). The ordinary Jewish posture when praying was standing, with the hands stretched out with the palms upward, and eyes toward heaven (cp. John 11:41). Paul's prayer for the church is so intense that he drops to his knees before God as he makes his entreaties.

an intimate relationship."[50]   Paul was conscious that, when he was praying, he was directing his prayer to God, who was listening while he prayed.   To call God the "Father" indicates that not only can we speak about accessibility to God (verse 12), but we find that God is like a Father to us.[51]   Holy, yes.   But also like a father.   He is the father of His adopted family.   His spiritual sons and daughters have been born again.   He has a personal interest in His children.

3:15 – *from whom every family in heaven and on earth derives its name,*

From whom – This verse seems to explain why we can address the Father in prayer, and expect results.   It is because of His adoptive love in Christ.   However, the rest of the verse is not easily explained.

Every family in heaven and on earth – A "family" (*patria*) is a group united by descent from a common ancestor, a family lineage going back to a common father.   So Joseph was both of the house (*oikou*) and family (*patrias*, lineage) of David (Luke 2:4).[52]   Since "every family" is an unexpected expression (we usually think of only one family of God), the commentators debate whether the Greek can be translated "the whole family" (as the KJV has it) rather than "every family."[53]   The answer is that "the whole family" apparently is a justifiable translation of the New Testament Greek.[54]   The "whole family" would include all of the redeemed

---

[50] Wood, *op. cit.,* p.50.

[51] The KJV has an extra phrase in this verse, "unto the Father of our Lord Jesus Christ." That changes the meaning of the verse considerably.   The manuscript evidence is against the insertion of this phrase in this verse (it is absent in Aleph, A, B, C, P, 17, 67[2]).   This additional phrase was first made in the Latin Codices, and evidently was originally an interpolation from Ephesians 1:3.

[52] The Israelites were divided into tribes (*phulai*), and then into families (*patriai*), each deriving its descent from one of Jacob's grandsons; and these again into houses (*oikoi*).   "Family" is perhaps the nearest equivalent we have in English for the Greek word *patria*.

[53] Attempts to explain who might be included in "every family" are several.   Perhaps Paul uses *pasa patria* ("every family") to refer to local congregations considered as groups within the total family of God.   This would cover the families on earth.   The families in heaven include the spirits of righteous men made perfect (Hebrews 12:23) and could perhaps also include the holy angels (angels are called "sons of God," Job 1:6, 38:7).   Each of these families has the same father, God.

[54] We meet here with a perplexity similar to that in Ephesians 2:21 where the debate was over "the whole building" or "every building."   At that place there is a manuscript variation, with one reading actually saying "the whole building."   Here in 3:15 there is no manuscript variation.   There is no manuscript that has a "the" in the phrase so that it reads *pasa he patria*, which would mean "the whole family"; all manuscripts simply read *pasa patria*, "every family."   In classical Greek, the absence of the article would require the translation "every family," but New Testament Greek apparently is not so exact.   Acts 2:36, where the article is similarly omitted, and yet the translation is, "all the house of Israel," shows that in New Testament Greek the translation "all the family" or "the whole family" is justifiable at this place.

– those saints of God who have died and are now with the Father in heaven and those saints who are still alive here on earth. These all together are considered to be but one family, of which God is the Father. To opt for the translation "whole family" seems more in accord with the scope of the passage, for here Paul has been emphasizing not separate groups but the gathering into one of all believers (see 2:14-20).

Derives its name – The Greek verb is either middle or passive in form and literally means "is named." God Himself is the one who calls believers "family."[55] The words suggest a motive for prayer. The One being addressed by members of the family is a "Father," a personal, intelligent being. He may be expected, when appealed to, to make full and corresponding provision for the wants of the members of the family.

3:16 – *that He would grant you, according to the riches of His glory, to be strengthened with power through His Spirit in the inner man,*

That He would grant you – This and the following verses express the content of Paul's prayer for his readers. In the Greek there are three clauses that begin with *hina* ("that"), and if we let the *hina* clauses guide us, we have three things prayed for: (1) that (*hina*) they would be powerfully strengthened in the inner man, so that as a result Christ may settle down once and for all in their hearts (verses 16,17); (2) that (*hina*) they may never forget the fact that God and Christ love them (verses 18-19a); and (3) that (*hina*) they may begin to love as God loves (verse 19b).

According to the riches of His glory – This speaks of the measure or the limit up to which God is being asked to grant Paul's requests for the readers. We had "riches of the glory" at Ephesians 1:18. Paul requests God to be bountiful and lavish as He grants the requests.[56]

---

[55] There is a play on words (a paronomasia) in the Greek. The word translated "Father" (*pater*) in 3:14 and the word translated "family" (*patria*) in 3:15 have the same root.

[56] The phrase "riches of His glory" is a favorite expression of Paul (Ephesians 1:18; Philippians 4:19; Romans 9:23; Colossians 1:27). The fact that it is used here in Ephesians is a further proof that Paul actually wrote Ephesians, and that the epistle is not a forgery under Paul's name, as some have dared to suggest.

To be strengthened with power– This is an infinitive phrase which serves as the object of the verb "that He would *grant* you." The first of the three things which Paul wants God to give to the readers of this letter is strengthening with power through His Spirit in the inner man. "With power" might be treated as adverbial ("powerfully strengthened").[57] "Strengthened" is the opposite of "lose heart" (verse 13). In Ephesians 1:19 Paul used three terms (*dunamis, kratos,* and *ischus*) to signify aspects of God's power toward us who believe. Now he uses two of the same terms to describe what he prays will be made available to the believers.

Through His Spirit in the inner man – "Through His Spirit" indicates the Holy Spirit is the agent who will do the strengthening. Paul's prayer is addressed to the Father requesting that He would use the indwelling Holy Spirit to strengthen the inner man of each of the readers of this letter. Since this is the first time we have encountered this expression, "the inner man," in this letter, we need to spend a moment to become familiar with what this language means. It appears that the New Testament pictures man being made up of body, soul, and spirit (1 Thessalonians 5:23). The "inner man" is the man's spirit, as contrasted to his outer man (2 Corinthians 4:16), which refers to the physical body. Paul talks about the inner man in Romans 7:22, when he says, "I joyfully concur with the law ... in the inner man." "Inner man" here in Ephesians 3:16 is virtually the same in meaning as "in your hearts" in the next verse (3:17). Recall too that Ephesians 1:18 referred to "the eyes of your heart." When any man who has become spiritually dead because of his own trespasses and sins (Ephesians 2:1,5) is born again, it is the spirit part of man which becomes alive again when the new birth occurs (John 3:6). Once a man's spirit is alive because of righteousness (Romans 8:10), it is the "spirit" or the "inner man" who gives directions to the soul and body. If a man were strengthened in the inner man (i.e., if the indwelling Holy Spirit is allowed to prompt and direct the human spirit), since God intended for the spirit to give directions to the soul which in turn animates the body, the

---

[57] The dative case word translated "with power" *(dunamei)* has been taken several ways. Some take it as an instrumental dative (or a dative of means), and translate, "that you may be strengthened by means of the power given you by the Holy Spirit." So translated it has become for some a prayer for a second work of grace (a doctrine demanded by certain theologies, but one difficult to find in the New Testament). Others treat it is a dative of manner, which has the force of an adverb, and translate "that you might be powerfully strengthened."

man's activities (his whole life) would be those which are becoming for a Christian. How does the Spirit do this strengthening? We understand that the Spirit can work through the Word to instruct our spirits (see Revelation 2-3 where the letters to the churches are explained as being "what the Spirit says to the churches"), and also can work apart from the Word but in harmony with it as He can plant thoughts in our minds in answer to prayer (Luke 11:13).

3:17 – *so that Christ may dwell in your hearts through faith;* **and** *that you, being rooted and grounded in love,*

So that – This is not a *hina* clause, but an infinitive; the clause thus introduced likely expresses the result of being strengthened in the inner man. The strengthening of the inner man by the Spirit is a prerequisite to the dwelling of Christ in the heart.

Christ may dwell in your hearts through faith – "Heart" in this verse seems to be synonymous with "inner man" of verse 16. If not synonymous, then it appears that the heart is an important component of the inner man.[58] The Greek infinitive translated "dwell" is not just *oikeo* (to dwell) but *katoikeo*, to settle down, a verb which may be contrasted to a related verb (*paroikeo*) which means to sojourn or dwell temporarily in a place. This infinitive is an aorist infinitive which suggests finality. We might paraphrase Paul's prayer thus, 'That Christ might be allowed (He never forces His way in) to finally settle down and feel completely at home in your hearts.' As to what it is for Christ to dwell within, the commentators are not agreed.[59] Some of the more valuable suggestions include: (1) Paul is praying that the principles and teachings of Christ may actuate them all the time. The name of Christ is sometimes used to denote His teachings (e.g., Romans 13:14). If this suggestion is correct, Paul is praying that the Ephesians may wholly and entirely embrace the doctrines of Christ, and be controlled by them. (2) Perhaps as was true in Romans 8:9-11, where "Christ" and "Spirit" were used interchangeably, so here Holy Spirit and Christ may be used interchangeably. If it is possible to resist, to grieve, and to quench the Holy Spirit, then on the other

---

[58] "The *kardia* ("heart") is the center of feeling, thinking, willing" (cf. Keil M. Delitzsch, *A System of Biblical Psychology* [Grand Rapids: Baker, 1966 reprint], p.295).

[59] The verse should not be used for a proof text that a person may be a Christian for a period of time before he receives the Holy Spirit. The indwelling gift of the Spirit accompanies conversion, rather than being something subsequent to conversion (Acts 2:38; Ephesians 1:13). Nor should this verse be explained as being a prayer for a mystical experience of Christ Himself. Mysticism is not something taught or encouraged by New Testament Christianity (see Colossians 2:18,19).

end of the scale would be permitting Him to settle down in the heart. "Through faith" says faithfulness on the part of the Christian is the condition necessary if Christ is ever to settle down in our hearts.

And **that you** – Our translators have transported the *hina* ("that") from verse 18 (where it appears in the Greek) to this place in the translation, thus making this the beginning of Paul's second petition for the readers.

Being rooted and grounded in love – Our translators have, correctly in this commentator's judgment, treated this clause as introducing what follows in verse 18, rather than connecting with what had already been written in verse 17.[60] The word picture is that love (likely, God's love for man, see 1:4) is the soil in which they are rooted, the foundation on which they rest. Paul mixes metaphors here. "Rooted" pictures a tree striking its roots down deeper and spreading wider in the soil. "Grounded" speaks of a building which rests on a firm foundation. Both "rooted" and "grounded" are perfect tense participles, indicating past completed action with present continuing results. Paul is not praying that they may become rooted and grounded in love for the first time. They already are so rooted and grounded. The sentence begun in the middle of verse 17 continues in verse 18.

3:18 – *may be able to comprehend with all the saints what is the breadth and length and height and depth,*

(That you) may be able to comprehend – This verse continues the second petition for which Paul prays. As a result of their being rooted and grounded in love, Paul prays that his readers may be able to comprehend the dimensions of the love in which they are rooted and grounded. The Greek word translated "may be able" is the compound verb *exischusete* (the word occurs only here in the New Testament and is rare in ordinary Greek), which means "to be eminently able, to have full capacity, to be fully able." The Greek word translated "comprehend" literally means to grasp or to hold (something) as one's own. Here it means to grasp or take hold of something mentally. The subject Paul wants them to try to comprehend is a subject beyond man's natural capacity, but not beyond one's spiritual capacity to grasp or understand. Saints can get it!

---

[60] If we were to take this phrase with the preceding, we must understand that it is a construction called a nominative absolute. If we were to treat it as a nominative absolute the phrase means that being "rooted and grounded" is the result of the indwelling of Christ, which is how Luther, Eadie, Ellicott, Alford, and others interpret it.

With all the saints – What Paul asks for is not a matter of private experience, an isolated experience unique to the readers of this letter. It is not just for a select few. This is a knowledge available to every Christian.[61]

What is the breadth and length and height and depth – These four dimensions indicate the vastness of the thing to be comprehended. What is it of which the readers are to learn the dimensions? Paul leaves the object unnamed; he does not write anything in the genitive case. As a result, many answers have been given to the question.[62] Of all answers to this question that have been suggested, the best is the love of God in which they are rooted and grounded. The four dimensions of this love cause us to ponder the magnitude of God's love. We suppose that Frederick M. Lehman tried to catch the idea when he wrote, "The love of God is greater far than tongue or pen can ever tell ...."

3:19 – and to know the love of Christ which surpasses knowledge, that you may be filled up to all the fullness of God.

And to know the love of Christ – Not only does Paul want them to come to understand the dimensions of God's love for them, he also wants them to experience Christ's love for them.[63] The "love of Christ" speaks of Christ's love for us, who "loved the church, and gave Himself up for her" (Ephesians 5:25); "Who loved me, and delivered Himself up for me" (Galatians 2:20). "Comprehend" (*katalambano*, verse 18) was a conceptual knowledge. "Know" here is *ginosko*, a knowledge gained by personal experience. By long experience with Christ, study of His word, and prayer, more and more we come to know the surpassing nature of His love for us.

---

[61] At Ephesians 1:1 we learned that a "saint" is someone who is dedicated to God, separated for sacred service.

[62] The early fathers delighted to refer it to the cross and they came up with imaginative spiritual meanings for each of the dimensions. Another suggestion is that these are the dimensions of the mystery that was once hid but is now revealed (Ephesians 3:6,9). Another suggestion is that the reference is to the Christian church, the body of Christ, which was introduced at 2:21. Some think the reference is the wisdom of God spoken of at Ephesians 3:10. Many commentaries take "the love of Christ" (verse 19) as the subject being described by these four words of measure.

[63] There is an "and" (*te*) in the Greek that seems to make this phrase distinct from what was written in verse 18. When used in a series of words that are related, *te* indicates the harmony or symmetry of the terms being connected by it. (Meyer, *in loc.*) Christ's love and God's love are very much alike.

Which surpasses knowledge – This phrase helps us decide that "the love of Christ" is Christ's love for us, rather than our love for Christ.   It is not our love for Christ – that would hardly be described as one which "surpasses knowledge." The language about knowing something that surpasses knowledge is paradoxical. We are attempting to understand that which is beyond understanding.   "No matter how much the saint experiences of the love of Christ, yet there are oceans of love in the great heart of Christ that have not been touched by his experience."[64] His love surpasses (*huperballousan*) knowledge; still, we can know enough of Christ's love to rejoice in it.

That you may be filled up to all the fullness of God – If we let the *hina* clauses determine, this is the third petition Paul asks God to grant to the readers of this letter.   It is this commentator's judgment that our interpretation of this prayer should be based on the use of the words "filled" (*plerothete*) and "fullness" (*pleroma*).   Ephesians 1:23 has already introduced the idea that Christ fills the church with divine powers so that the believers are pervaded by His presence, animated by His life, filled with His gifts and energies and graces.   The preposition "to" (*eis*) suggests their being filled progressively "up to the measure of" God's fullness, just as Ephesians 4:13 speaks of their ultimately reaching the "measure of the stature of the fullness of Christ" (ASV).   With these words Paul ends his prayer.

4. Doxology suggested by the thought of the glorious things just prayed for. 3:20,21

> *Summary*: Let praise be given to God who answers our prayers in ways exceedingly greater than we anticipated.

3:20 – *Now to Him who is able to do exceeding abundantly beyond all that we ask or think, according to the power that works within us,*

Now to Him – "Him" is God, the Father.   Paul ends this portion of his letter with a doxology, a word of praise to God, the One to whom he bends the knee (verse 14).

Who is able to do exceeding abundantly beyond all that we ask or think – Paul has been praying for great things.   He is confident God will grant them because they are not too much for God to give.   So confident is Paul that God can and will grant his petitions that he offers this doxology to God before the pray-

---

[64] Wuest, *op. cit.*, p.90.

er is ever answered. The compound word ("exceeding abundantly beyond," *huperperissou*) is a superlative of superlatives in force. It speaks of the ability of God to do something, that ability having more than enough potential power, this power being exhaustless, and then some on top of that. "God's capacity to meet people's spiritual needs far exceeds anything they can either request in prayer or conceive by way of anticipation (Philippians 4:7)."[65]

According to the power that works within us – God's answers to prayer are actualized through His power (*dunamis*) which continually operates (*energoumenen*) within the lives of believers. What specifically is indicated by the word "power"? Is it a reference to the indwelling Holy Spirit (Romans 8:26)? If so, this verse seems to say the indwelling Holy Spirit has something to do with answers to prayer. He plants thoughts in our minds in answer to prayer (see Luke 11:13 where we are told God gives the Holy Spirit to those who ask Him).[66]

3:21 – *to Him* **be** *the glory in the church and in Christ Jesus to all generations forever and ever. Amen.*

To Him - The pronoun "Him" which began verse 20 is repeated for emphasis.

Be **the glory in the church and in Christ Jesus** – "*Be* glory" means let God be praised.[67] The Greek has an article, "*the* glory," and calls attention to the glory that is due Him and befits Him. "In the church" refers to all congregations of the people of God, wherever the glad tidings are preached. The church, whose splendors have been now brought to light by the admission of both Jewish believers and Gentile believers within its bounds, is the body from whom glory is given to God (Ephesians 1:12,14). Instead of "*and* in Christ Jesus" the KJV reads simply "by Christ Jesus" because there is a manuscript variation at this place which omits the word "and."[68]   With the "and" omitted, the verse means Christ

---

[65] Wood, *op. cit.*, p.53.

[66] Another answer to the question "What specifically is indicated by the word 'power'?" is that it is the same power referred to in 1:20 (i.e., the same power it took to raise Jesus is available to the Christian). The change which the Ephesians had already experienced (as they were made alive, Ephesians 2:5) through the mighty working of the power of God in them, was a sufficient foundation on which to build their hope of receiving answers to their prayers that were beyond their imagination.

[67] As far as the Greek is concerned, this may be an indicative verb ("to Him *is* the glory") or an imperative verb ("to Him *be* the glory"). We take it to be an imperative.

[68] "And" is omitted by D[b], K, L, P, as well as the Syr., Eth., Arm., and Goth. versions.

is the medium through Whom praises are given to God by the church. With the "and"[69] included, the phrase means that it is only in Christ (in union with Him) that the believer or church can really praise God.[70]

To all generations forever and ever – The original expression is emphatic: "to all the generations of the age of ages." It pictures each generation, one after another, adding its own voice in the ever-swelling chorus of praise and thanksgiving to God all through not only this age but eternity.[71]

Amen – The word means "So be it!" "So let it be!" This "Amen" may be the writer (Paul) adding his "amen" to what the Spirit has led him to say. In some cases the "amen" was added by later scribes as a signal to the worshiping congregation when to say "amen" as the letter is read out loud in the public assembly.

"The doxology (some call it a benediction) brings the first great division of this epistle to a close. We have been told what God has done for us, and about our position in Christ."[72]

---

[69] "And" is included in *Aleph*, A, B, C, 17, and is the better supported reading.

[70] The Western text reverses the order, so as to read "in Christ and in the church." But the best authenticated reading presents an ascending order of worth: in the church, which is the body of Christ, and in Christ Jesus, who is Head of His church, let God be glorified.

[71] We are accustomed to reading "for ever," or "for ever and ever," which represent the "unto the age," or "unto the ages," or "unto the ages of the ages" in the Greek. What is unusual here is the addition of the words "all generations."

[72] Martin, *op. cit.*, p. 1309.

II. PART TWO: PRACTICAL EXHORTATIONS –
Concerning the Believers' Conduct in the World.   4:1-6:20

A. Exhortation to Preserve the Unity of the Spirit in the Bond of Peace.   4:1-16

Summary: "The writer urges his readers to put into practice those Christian virtues which will help preserve the unity of the body, the church (verses 1-3). This unity results originally from the fundamental oneness that is the heart of the Christian faith (verses 4-6). The unity of the body is not weakened, but rather affirmed and strengthened, by the variety of gifts bestowed on individual Christians by the one Lord of the church (verses 7-12). These various gifts promote the health and growth of the body of Christ, in conformity with His nature and His will for the church (verses 13-16)."[1]

1. Introduction to the second part of the epistle and a statement of the first exhortation.   4:1-3

4:1 – *I therefore, the prisoner of the Lord, entreat you to walk in a manner worthy of the calling with which you have been called,*

I therefore – "Therefore" serves to connect the exhortations which are about to be written in chapters 4-6 to all that has been written in the first three chapters of this letter. Since God has done all He has for the readers, lavishly bestowing on them spiritual privileges and revealing to them the great mystery of redemption, here is how they, as redeemed men, ought to live (4:1-6:20).

The prisoner of the Lord – This is more than a reminder of his condition (cf. 3:1).[2] It suggests that, 'If I (while being a prisoner) can do what the Lord wills regarding Christian behavior, so can you readers (who are free men).'

Entreat you to walk in a manner worthy of the calling with which you have

---

[1] Bratcher, *op. cit.*, p.92.

[2] At Ephesians 3:1 the Greek was "prisoner OF the Lord."   Here, the Greek reads "prisoner IN the Lord."   Perhaps this slightly different expression means Paul sees himself imprisoned "in the Lord's cause," or because he is in union with Christ, or because the Lord so willed it.

been called – Paul begins his exhortation to unity and harmony with a sense of urgency. *Parakaleo* ("entreat" or "exhort") is an appeal to the readers' wills. What Paul wants is a willing response on their part. He wants them to make a deliberate determination to behave as he here is about to ask. If Ephesians is a circular letter, "you" (plural) has more than local interest. What Paul is asking of his readers is part of the universal gospel which is intended for all who have named the name of Christ. "Walk" is often used in a figurative sense to denote our conduct, our behavior, our manner of life (see 2:2,10). "The calling with which you have been called" refers to a divine invitation to salvation which God makes to the sinner through the gospel (2 Thessalonians 2:14).[3] The church (*ekklesia*, the "called out") results from folks' positive response to the calling (*kaleo*) or invitation. "A manner worthy" translates a Greek adverb which means "having the same weight."[4] In the balances of life, our walk (our daily manner of life) should be "of the same weight" as our calling. Christians have an exalted position in Christ. If our lives are to measure up to our position in Christ there are some attitudes and behaviors that must be cultivated.

4:2 – *with all humility and gentleness, with patience, showing forbearance to one another in love,*

With all humility – In this verse and the next Paul identifies four temperaments, or attitudes, that each Christian must nurture and develop if we are to walk in a worthy manner. "Unity and growth in the body (the church) depend on proper relationships – proper attitudes – among the members."[5] If Christians are careless and fail to cultivate these dispositions, the result will be a rupturing of the unity and harmony that Christ desires in His church. Thayer defines *tapeino-*

---

[3] See also Ephesians 1:13. "Invitations" extended by human beings to each other are often looked upon merely as being a polite request. Whether or not a person responds is of no great moment. An invitation from God is more of a summons, a word which conveys notions of urgency in the voice and the authority of the voice. To refuse God's invitation has eternal consequences that are dreadful. The parable of the sower indicates it is the soil (the heart) of the one hearing the invitation, not a difference in the kind of invitation offered, that leads to a reception or rejection of the invitation. The statement expressed in the *Westminster Shorter Catechism* is greatly flawed in this matter when it makes a difference in the kinds of calling God gives to men -- be it an effectual call or a general call. It reads that an "effectual calling is the work of God's Spirit, whereby convincing us of our sin and misery, enlightening our minds in the knowledge of Christ, and renewing our wills, he doth persuade and enable us to embrace Jesus Christ freely offered to us in the gospel."

[4] Wuest, *op. cit.*, p.93

[5] Hayden, *op. cit.*, p.315.

phrosune ("humility") as "having a humble opinion of one's self."[6]   The opposite of this grace is pride or haughtiness. If we have "humility," we will not be the kind of person who always asserts himself, always insisting that his way is right, thus tending to rupture the unity possible between brethren.   There is no boisterous self-assertion or rude striving with others.[7]

And gentleness – *Praütēs* describes an attitude that is the opposite of self-assertion.   It describes that unresisting, uncomplaining disposition of mind which enables us to bear without irritation or resentment the faults and injuries of others. Sometimes the word is best translated "meekness," a controlled strength or temperament in the face of adversity and persecution.[8] Meekness relates to the manner in which we receive injuries. We are to bear them patiently, and not retaliate or seek revenge.   To prevent party bickering between Jew and Gentile, both must make conscious effort to give no offense to others nor respond to provocation with resentment.

With patience – *Makrothumia* (here translated "patience") is a word that speaks of a long temper, especially when putting up with people. Trench, using the KJV's "longsuffering" and "patience" to translate, differentiates between the two different Greek words in this fashion. "*Makrothumia* [longsuffering, the word used here in verse 2] will be found to express patience with respect of persons, while *hupomone* [patience, as at 2 Corinthians 1:6 and 6:4] expresses endurance in respect of things.   The man who is longsuffering, is he who, having to do with injurious persons, does not suffer himself easily to be provoked by them, or to blaze up in anger.   The man who is patient (*hupomone*) is he who under a great siege of trials, bears up and does not lose courage."[9] Ephesians 4 indicates that when people do things that provoke us, the patient person suffers a long time, patiently bearing some things he or she does not like.

Showing forbearance to one another in love – Forbearance is holding back the

---

[6] Thayer, *op. cit.*, p.614.

[7] "In classical Greek, *tapeinos* is a derogatory term suggesting low-mindedness and groveling servility.   The adjective was redeemed by the gospel to represent a distinctively Christian virtue, and this euphonious noun was coined to stand over against the admired high-mindedness of the heathen" (Wood, *op. cit.*, p.55).

[8] A good way to illustrate "meekness" or "gentleness" is "to consider, for example, a horse brought under control for the purpose of plowing or riding.   He has not lost any of his strength, but his strength has been channeled toward a useful and beneficial purpose" (Shannon, *op. cit.*, p.395).

[9] Trench, *op. cit.*, p.195.

arm or word of retaliation. "People will inevitably disappoint us and will tax our patience at times. What we must never forget is how much we need people to be patient with *us*."[10] Toleration of some unpleasantness is a small price to pay for the privilege of unity with God's people. We may teach, reprove, or correct those who have sinned, but at the same time we do it, we must hold them up, sustain them, support them. "One another" is a reciprocal pronoun. It is a mutual forbearance that is to be practiced. "In love" means we make allowances for faults in those we love. Our goal is to do what is spiritually best for the other person.

4:3 – *being diligent to preserve the unity of the Spirit in the bond of peace.*

Being diligent – This is what the humility, gentleness, patience, and forbearance (of verse 2) are all about. They are absolutely essential if Paul's readers are to be diligent to preserve the unity between brethren intact. "Being diligent" (*spoudazontes*) speaks of careful and earnest efforts. "The word suggests difficulty and a resolute determination to overcome it."[11] Unity is something that must be worked at. Part of the effort to preserve the unity (after we have become Christians) is by being humble, gentle, patient, and showing forbearance with one another. A lack of effort by any one of us in developing the four qualities just named in verse 2 will jeopardize Christian unity.

To preserve – The Greek verb means to guard something by exercising a watchful concern. Both "being diligent" and "to preserve" are present tense verb forms, indicating constant action. It is assumed that a unity between Christians already exists. The job of Christians is to preserve it, not create it.

The unity of the Spirit – "Unity" is *henotes*, a special Greek word for unity, unanimity, harmony, or agreement.[12] The old enmity between Jew and Gentile has been broken. This new agreement, this harmony among Christians is the

---

[10] Shannon, *ibid.*

[11] Wood, *op. cit.*, p.55.

[12] The special Greek word for unity used here "appears only twice in the New Testament (at Ephesians 4:3 and 13). This does not mean, of course, that Ephesians 4 is the only place in the New Testament that addresses the concept of *unity*. Other texts use various other words to project the idea of *unity* or *oneness* (examples: Acts 1:14; John 17:11,21,22)." Krause, *2012-13 Adult Lesson Commentary* (Cincinnati, OH: Standard, 2012), p.138.

product of the work of the Holy Spirit.[13]   Ephesians 2:18 says "Through [Christ] we both [Jewish believers and Gentile believers] have access by one Spirit unto the Father" (KJV).   This Spirit-produced unity must never be allowed to slip away.   If we allow it to slip, we are not walking in a worthy manner.

In the bond of peace – A "bond" (*sundesmos*) is something which binds together. The root meaning of "peace" is 'to be joined together.'   Peace is the bond that ties Christians together.   The way we preserve the unity of the Spirit is by working to maintain the peace that holds us together and by trying to live at peace with one another.[14]   "If we demand our own way, if we are furious at every slight, if we seek revenge for every wrong, we shatter the peace that is the bond of unity. Such a way is unworthy of our calling."[15]

2. Seven fundamental reasons why there is an initial unity which Christians should endeavor to preserve.[16]   4:4-6

a.   There is one body.   4

4:4 – There is *one body and one Spirit, just as also you were called in one hope of your calling;*

***There is* one body** – All through these 7 phrases, "one" emphasizes the idea that there is but *one* for both Jew and Gentile.   It will be remembered that Ephesians 2:16 reads, "that he might reconcile them both to God in one body," and Ephesians 2:14-16,21, 22 speak of "one new body" and "one new man."   The "one body"

---

[13] "Unity of the Spirit" is equivalent to "the unity of which the Holy Spirit is the author."   It is a genitive of originating cause.   It seems fairly certain that *pneuma* here is not the human spirit but God's Spirit.   Compare 1 Corinthians 12:13 which speaks of the Spirit's work in leading men to be baptized.   See the Special Study "The Person and Work of the Holy Spirit" in the author's *New Testament History: Acts*, p.89-101.

[14] Of course, it is not peace at any price.   Jesus was first king of righteousness, then king of peace (Hebrews 7:2).   So must we be.

[15] Root, *1985-86 Adult Lesson Commentary*, p.35.

[16] A number of sermons entitled "How to Have Religious Unity in Our Community" have been preached, in which these seven items in verses 4-6 are treated as doctrinal matters to which erring Christians are summoned to agree so that we may achieve the unity for which Jesus prayed (John 17:20,21), a unity that is now sadly lacking.   However, verses 4-6 of Ephesians 4 do not deal with how we are to go about *creating* a unity.   Rather, it is because of these seven things that there *already is* a unity among believers – a God-made unity which the believers are then to endeavor to preserve.

speaks of the church, an organism composed of the Lord Jesus Christ as the head and all true believers in Him as the body mentioned earlier in this letter (1:22,23).[17]   In the pagan world there were many religious cults to choose from. Christianity is not like that.   God never intended that there be one body for the Jew and another body for the Gentile.   He intended there be one body that included both.   1 Corinthians 12:25 indicates there should be no friction or division between members of the body.   The one body, the church, is designed to work smoothly in coordination without friction.   If one member fails to follow Jesus perfectly, the other members respond with forgiveness, not fury.   "The hand is not angry with the foot, even if the foot stumbles.   The foot is not furious with the hand, not even if the hand accidentally drops something on the foot."[18]

b.   There is one Spirit.   4

And one Spirit – If we have become a Christian, the Holy Spirit had something to do with convicting us of our sin (John 16:7-9), with leading us to want to be baptized into the body (1 Corinthians 12:13), and He lives in each Christian (Romans 8:9-11) to motivate and guide us through the Word of God.   Ephesians 2:18,22 have already introduced us to the Spirit's work in the body.   His work is the same whether the believer be of Jewish or of Gentile background.   That is why there is an initial unity of the Spirit which we must then endeavor to maintain.

c.   There is one hope.   4

Just as also you were called in one hope of your calling – "Just as" (*kathōs*) indicates the unity of the Spirit is something entirely in accordance with their calling, with their initial invitation through the gospel to become Christians.[19] "You" is plural and includes all the readers, all the members of the body. Whenever they heard the gospel and through it received their invitation to become Christians, they all alike, whatever their nationality, heard the same promise of eternal life based on the resurrection of Jesus ("Because I live, you shall live also,"

---

[17] In the Greek there is no connective (*gar* or something else), and no verb (*eimi* or *ginomai*). All we have are several items simply set down as such for the readers, and thus made the more striking.

[18] Root, *ibid.*

[19] "Calling," an invitation through the gospel to become a Christian, was explained in notes at Ephesians 4:1.   "Call" and "hope" were both explained at Ephesians 1:18.

John 14:19) and based on the promise of His second coming with all the blessings of the future life (Titus 2:13; 1 Peter 1:13).[20] "*One* hope" highlights the fact that there is no difference between Jewish and Gentile Christians when it comes to that which is hoped for, their eschatological expectations.   There are not different glorified bodies, one for the Jews and another for the Gentiles.   There are not different heavens, one for the Jews and another for the Gentiles.   The same hope was held out for all who heard and believed the gospel.   The fact that there was but one hope is another reason there is a unity of the Spirit which the readers must endeavor to maintain.

d.   There is one Lord.   5

4:5 – one Lord, one faith, one baptism,

One Lord – There are not several Lords, but one Lord for both Jews and Gentiles alike (Acts 10:36, Matthew 28:19).   That one Lord obviously is Jesus Christ.   If there were two Lords, then there might not be unity.   But Jesus is Lord of all. The term "Lord," as it is used of Jesus in the New Testament, may call attention to His authority as ruler of men, or it may call attention to His Deity.[21]   There is a unity of the Spirit to be maintained precisely because there is but One Lord to whom they all have pledged their allegiance.

e.   There is one faith.   5

One faith – Sometimes in the New Testament "faith" is a body of doctrine,[22] and other times it refers to what a person believes in his heart (Romans 10:8-10). Both ideas have been advocated here as being the reason why there is a unity of the Spirit that believers are to be diligent to preserve.   If we treat "faith" as a body of doctrine, we are being told that Jesus and His apostles have taught but one body of doctrine to men, whether they be Jew or Gentile.   Because there is but one body of doctrine, there is a unity of the Spirit which we must endeavor to

---

[20] The genitive "of your calling" may either be a genitive of possession ("the hope belonging to your calling") or a genitive of origin ("the hope that originated or was caused by your calling").

[21] The word used for "Lord" in the Greek is *kurios*.   This word can have an idea of Deity in it since *kurios* was regularly used to translate the sacred name YHWH.

[22] Some of the verses where "faith" is doubtless a body of doctrine are Acts 6:7; Galatians 1:23; Philippians 1:27; 1 Timothy 2:7, 4:1,6, 5:8, 6:10,21, and Jude 3.

maintain.[23]   If we treat "faith" as the act of believing, then the verse affirms that as men became converts they all expressed the same faith, namely, "I believe that Jesus is the Christ, the Son of the living God."[24]

f.   There is one baptism.   5

One baptism – There is not one baptism for the Jew and another for the Gentile, but one uniform ordinance of Christ that is obeyed by both.   Since the passage speaks of how unity was initially created, baptism here must be the baptism of the Great Commission, a baptism which is described as "into Christ" (Romans 6:3; Galatians 3:27), into (Greek) the name of the Lord Jesus (Acts 19:5), in (Greek, *en*) the name of Jesus Christ (Acts 2:38, 10:48), and "into (Greek, *eis*) the name of the Father and of the Son and of the Holy Spirit" (Matthew 28:19).[25]   When we consider the meaning of the Greek word *baptizo* (the verb form means "to dip or plunge") and the evidence provided in the book of Acts (Acts 8:38,39, for example, where Philip and the eunuch "both went down into the water" and "they came up out of the water"), along with the evidence of Romans 6:4 ("we have been buried with Him through baptism"), it is clear that originally baptism was done by immersion.   The immersion commanded in the Great Commission is the one ordinance of Christ by which all, Jew or Gentile, enter the body of Christ.[26]   Since all have submitted to the same ordinance, there is a resulting unity.   This one baptism is another reason why,   between Jewish and Gentile believers, there

---

[23] Since the Bible speaks of "one faith," it is not scriptural to speak of "many faiths" or "interfaith activities," as many do.

[24] Those who have treated "faith" at this place as being personal faith rather than one universal body of doctrine have used Romans 3:30 (since "God is one, and he shall justify the circumcision by faith, and the uncircumcision through faith" [ASV]) to explain what Ephesians 4:5 might mean.

[25] Whenever "baptism" is spoken of without qualification or explanation, it is always the common baptism practiced in all cases (Acts 2:41, 18:8), i.e., the baptism commanded in the Great Commission, an immersion of the penitent believer in water.   Whenever the baptism of the Holy Spirit or the baptism of suffering is meant it is always specifically so designated.

[26] If "one faith" is treated as personal belief, then this passage which also speaks of "one baptism" reminds us of Mark 16:16 and Colossians 2:12.

is a unity that every effort must be made to maintain.[27]

g.   There is one God and Father of all.   6

4:6 – one God and Father of all who is over all and through all and in all.

One God and Father of all – If there were one God for the Jews, and another God for the Gentiles, there could never be unity.   People who worship different gods (such as pagan cultures did, 1 Corinthians 8:5,6) cannot hope to be united. But that is not how things are in Christianity.   There is but one God.   Jewish Christians and Gentile Christians have the same God.   That's why there is a unity of the Spirit which requires diligence to maintain.   In the identification of God as being the "Father of all," "all" speaks of those Jews and Gentiles who have now become believers, and thus are adopted sons of God.[28]   It was the same Father who adopted them all.   It is one big family.   That is why there is unity.   Perhaps as Paul characterized God as "Father," he was calling attention to His love for mankind that led Him to set about to redeem those who would respond to His overtures of love.

It has been rightly observed that in these verses the members of the Godhead have been named in reverse order – Spirit, Lord, God.   The Christian believes as firmly as does the Jew or Mohammedan that there is *one* God. However, the Christian accepts the profound revelation that one God has given about Himself; namely, that although He is one God, yet there is a pluralistic unity in the Godhead – three perfectly harmonious identities within that one God – Father, Lord Jesus Christ, and Holy Spirit.

---

[27] In the New Testament church there were no unbaptized members.   There was one baptism required of all.   Because of the tragic distortions which have arisen in the practice of baptism, and, even more significantly, in the understanding of the meaning of baptism, it is difficult for modern readers to grasp the force of Paul's appeal to the "one baptism" as being a reason why unity existed, a unity that baptized believers are to endeavor to preserve.   "Substitutes (such as pouring or sprinkling) for the burial in water of a repentant believer in Christ for the forgiveness of sin had not been introduced when the apostle wrote of one baptism" (Hayden, *op. cit.*, p.316).   While both points are true, it probably is beyond the scope of this passage to use it to prove   (1) that "one baptism" means there was but one mode/form of baptism (immersion, not pouring or sprinkling) or (2) that the convert was immersed only one time (rather than trine immersion, three times in the names of the Father, the Son, and the Holy Spirit).

[28] Those who believe that this verse speaks of the "fatherhood of God," i.e., God's fatherhood over all men by virtue of creation, are evidently mistaken.   The context here, which speaks of Christian unity, is against it.   And, of course, God is not the spiritual father of sinners, nor can sinners (unrepentant, and unjustified) claim His blessings (John 8:44).   Passages that speak of adoption into God's family include Ephesians 1:5; Romans 8:15; Galatians 3:26 and 4:5.

Who is over all and through all and in all – "Who" says that the three prepositional statements refer to God the Father.[29] These statements which speak of "all" are evidently soteriological, that is, they are limited to believers, the ones who are being exhorted to walk in a manner worthy of their calling (Ephesians 4:1). The three prepositions evidently cover all of the Father's relationships to the redeemed. But the exact thing intended is not easy to determine. Perhaps "over all" speaks of the Father's location above in the heavenly places. "Through all" might refer to His providential care especially to those in the household of faith. "In all" might allude to the indwelling of the Spirit of God that pervades the family members, since all the persons of the triune Godhead are said in various passages of Scripture to indwell the believer.

What we have learned from these first six verses of Ephesians 4 is that Christians must work at certain positive attitudes if the unity of the Spirit, which is based on the seven-fold fundamental oneness that undergirds the Christian religion, is to be maintained.

3.　Preserving the unity is aided/facilitated by the diversity of gifts given to the church by Christ.　4:7-11

4:7 – *But to each one of us grace was given according to the measure of Christ's gift.*

But – This verse begins a new section in the discussion about endeavoring to maintain the unity of the Spirit. It still deals with unity (see verse 13), but takes up a new phase of the subject; namely, the fact that unity is served, not hindered, by a diversity of individual gifts. There are seven different items (verses 4-6) upon which the Holy Spirit has united all the members of the church. Although we are united upon these seven matters, each of us is different because we have received different gifts. Unity in the church is not maintained or preserved by making all the members exactly alike. "The church is a body, and the body needs different members that are designed to do different things. A hand, a lung, a thymus gland are not alike, but the body needs them all. So it is with the members of the church."[30] In Romans 12:4-8 and 1 Corinthians 12:4-11 this conception of

---

[29] Since the passage has referred to one Spirit, one Lord, and one God, some have tried to align these prepositional phrases with the members of the Godhead. Some try to say it is Christ who is over all, the Spirit who is through all, and God who is in all – or God is over all, Christ through all, and the Spirit in all.

[30] Root, *op. cit.,* p.36.

diversity in the church body is written about in detail.

To each one of us – It seems likely that "each one of us" in this verse refers to the same Christians as were designated by "all" in the previous verse.[31]   Indeed, verse 11 will speak of certain leadership functions, but the rest of the paragraph speaks of those individual members who are trained for ministry by the leaders.

Grace was given – "Grace" here is something given to Christians.[32]   Perhaps we might call it "equipping grace."[33]   Since His ascension (verse 10) Christ has been filling all things.   He is the agent who bestows grace on each individual Christian so he or she may contribute to maintaining the unity of the Spirit in the bond of peace.

According to the measure of Christ's gift – The *grace* that each Christian receives is determined by Christ's generosity.   One may get a larger measure – another may get a smaller measure – as Christ sees best to give it.   The word "gift" here (*dorea*) signifies a gratuity or an expression of favor.   Christ always gives bountifully and graciously.

> Christ in His grace gives a gift to every one of us, but not the same gift to all. One can sing gloriously; another can cheerfully direct traffic in the parking lot. One can preach eloquently in the pulpit;   another can sit on the floor and guide

---

[31] "Up to this point the apostle has spoken chiefly of the whole body and its total unity. Now he turns to the individual members – each one of us" (Hayden, *op. cit.*, p.316).

[32] Some theologians have created a host of distinctions when they speak of God's grace: they may refer to actual grace, common grace, prevenient grace, saving grace, justifying grace, pardoning grace, sufficient grace, efficacious grace, sanctifying grace, persevering grace, and subsequent grace.   To such theologians this passage tells them that such measures of grace have been bestowed upon each Christian, freely and liberally.   See the Special Study "Grace" in the author's *New Testament Epistles: Romans* (Moberly, MO: Scripture Exposition Books, 1996), pp.52-64.

[33] Here the Greek reads "the grace" just as it did at Ephesians 3:2,7,8).   In those instances "grace" has a concrete sense of a special gift.   It likely does in this instance, too.   Since the word here is *charis* ("grace"), not the *charisma* ("spiritual gifts"), this commentator is hesitant to make an appeal to 1 Corinthians 12:4-31 in an attempt to explain what the grace was which Paul here says each of the readers of Ephesians had received.   While 1 Corinthians 12-14 do emphasize the miraculous spiritual gifts that some in the early church received by the laying on of an apostle's hands, still 1 Corinthians 12:7 does speak of "different manifestations of the Spirit" received by "each one" -- of which the miraculous gifts were but one example.   Romans 12:3-8 also refers both to miraculous and non-miraculous gifts as it speaks of how members of the body (the church) have "gifts that differ according to the grace given" to them.

the Beginners class. Unity comes as each member uses his gift gladly and unselfishly for the good of the whole body. Verse 11 gives excellent examples of some of the different tasks for which people were fitted by the abilities given to them.[34]

4:8 – *Therefore it says, "WHEN HE ASCENDED ON HIGH, HE LED CAPTIVE A HOST OF CAPTIVES, AND HE GAVE GIFTS TO MEN."*

Therefore it says -- "Therefore" (*dio* in the Greek) introduces the words which follow as being a substantiation of what has just been said about Christ giving gifts. Since the quotation which follows (printed in small capital letters in the NASB) is obviously taken from Psalm 68:18, the third singular verb *legei* can be translated "He says" (making it a reference to God's inspiration of the Psalm) or "it says" (meaning either Scripture says, or the Psalm says).[35] Paul is saying that the passage from Psalms was a Scriptural prediction that Messiah would give gifts.[36]

---

[34] Root, *ibid.*

[35] Several matters connected with the Psalm have caused some consternation among the commentators. (1) Paul's words match neither the Masoretic Text nor the LXX (Paul has "*gave* gifts" whereas the Old Testament reads "*received* gifts"). This has proven to be a problem for many commentators. Perhaps the most satisfactory explanation is to recall there was a version of the Old Testament in use in the first century that differed from both the MT and LXX, and on occasion Paul seems to quote this version. (E.g., at Romans 12:19 and Hebrews 10:30 there is a word-for-word allusion to Deuteronomy 32:36 which follows neither the MT nor LXX.) Here at Ephesians 4:8 the Syriac Peshitta reads "thou hast given gifts to men" (Wood, *op. cit.*, p.57). Thus, we should be very hesitant to accuse Paul of a deliberate mishandling of an Old Testament text. (2) What Psalm 68 refers to in its original setting is greatly disputed and this has consequently led to doubts about the appropriateness of its use here in Ephesians as a reference to Christ. For example, the author who comments on Ephesians in the *Interpreter's Bible* accuses Paul of twisting the Psalm, of misapplying the Psalm to Christ, and of reverting to Rabbinical methods of interpretation (all of which impinge on Paul's inspiration). *The Bible Commentary* on Psalms gives a good summary of the arguments pro and con concerning the dating of the Psalm. "On what particular historic occasion this highly poetic song was composed, is for our passage a matter of indifference. According to the traditional view, it was composed by David on the occasion of the removal of the ark of the covenant from the house of Obed-edom to Jerusalem (2 Samuel 6:12 ff.; 1 Chronicles 15,16)" (Meyer, *op. cit.*, p.443). What we have here in Ephesians 4:8 is another case where the New Testament affirms that Old Testament Scriptures contained forecasts of coming Messianic events.

[36]Lange's commentary on the Psalms shows clearly that it is not an exaggeration to see Psalm 68 as Messianic. He points out that the Psalm is divided up into several strophes, and he makes note that there is an abrupt break at verse 15. He identifies the main theme of the Psalm as being "the proclamation of the spreading of the Divine kingdom among the heathen by means of the victorious deeds of the God of historical revelation, who is enthroned upon Zion as in heaven" (J.P. Lange, "Psalms," in *Lange's Commentary on the Holy Scriptures* [Grand Rapids: Zondervan, nd], p.383). The early parts of the Psalm are pictured as glorifying God for His power and victories in battle, for His wonders at Sinai and in the wilderness. By the time we come to verses 18 and 19, we have pictured the ascent of God into Heaven after He had made Himself known on earth in deeds of omnipotence and love. He continues to dwell in Zion enthroned as Jah Elohim.

WHEN HE ASCENDED ON HIGH – In Paul's citation of Psalm 68:18, Christ is the One who is pictured as ascending on high.[37]   That Jesus ascended to the Father between His first two post-resurrection appearances can be learned from a comparison of John 20:17 with Matthew 28:9.   He also ascended to heaven from the Mount of Olives at the close of His 40-day post-resurrection ministry (Acts 1:9-11).   In either case, Christ's ascension took place before He distributed the gifts.

HE LED CAPTIVE A HOST OF CAPTIVES – If we let similar language at Judges 5:12 guide us, the captives are friends of Christ whom He has rescued from their captor.[38]   We suppose it was on the day He arose from the dead that Jesus took the souls of the Old Testament redeemed with Him from Hades to heaven.[39]

AND HE GAVE GIFTS TO MEN – Included in these gifts (verse 11 will explain) are the workers known as apostles, prophets, evangelists, and pastoring-teachers, whose job is the equipping of the saints for their work of service.   Peter said something similar on Pentecost.   Peter said (Acts 2:33) that since Christ had received from the Father what had been promised (namely, to sit on David's throne at the Father's right hand),   Christ "poured forth   this which you see and

---

[37] Perhaps what we have here is another place where the New Testament applies to Christ what the Old Testament has said of Jehovah.   The subject of the Psalm was Jehovah.   Paul speaks of Christ.   As elsewhere in the New Testament, the Jehovah of the prophets and Psalms is identified with the Christ of the apostles; and what is affirmed of the former in the Old Testament is ascribed to the latter in the New Testament.   That can be done because Jesus is one of the self-existent members of the Godhead, all of whom are called "Jehovah" in the Scriptures.   Jesus is Lord (*kurios* was the translation of the LXX for YHWH) and Jesus claimed to be "I AM" (Jehovah or Yahweh) in John 8:58.   Other places where what is said of God in the Old Testament is applied to Christ in the New Testament are Exodus 13:21 compared with 1 Corinthians 10:4 and Psalm 102:25-27 compared with Hebrews 1:10-12.

[38] Two other interpretations of the captives are: (1) men still living on earth who, once enemies of Christ and prisoners of Satan, have now become servants of Christ, and are thus given by Christ to the church.   Paul, once an enemy, now an apostle, is given as a good example of what is here spoken of (see the two-part article by Owen Crouch in the *Christian Standard* [February 12, 1955 p. 99; and February 19, 1955, p.117]); and (2) the demonic rulers and authorities which Colossians 2:15 speaks about.   In the Colossians passage, however, it was at the cross that Jesus triumphed over them, rather than at the time of His ascension.

[39] See the Special Study #7, "Hades and the Intermediate Place of the Dead" in the author's commentary *New Testament History: Acts*, p.135-144, esp. p.142.

hear" (the coming of the baptism of the Spirit on the apostles to empower them for their ministry, Acts 1:8). "Psalm 68, significantly enough, was associated in the synagogue calendar with Pentecost."[40]   The point is, since Christ has ascended, He has given gifts to men just as it was predicted in the Old Testament that He would do.

4:9 – (*Now this* **expression,** *"He ascended," what does it mean except that He also had descended into the lower parts of the earth?*

(**Now this** *expression* – Ephesians 4:9 and 4:10, treated as being parenthetical, show what the ascension of Christ (alluded to in Psalm 68:18) presupposes and explains why Christ is therefore qualified to give the gifts He has to the church.[41] As he makes these points in the phrases following, Paul first quotes the salient words of the Psalm, and then applies them to Jesus.

"He ascended" – The Psalm (68:18) affirms that the Christ was to ascend, and give gifts to men. Now Paul shows that there was more to being qualified to give such gifts than just ascending to heaven.

What does it mean except that He also had descended – This is a rhetorical question to get the readers to think. Since it was the belief of those whom Paul addressed that Jehovah God's proper abode was in heaven, any statement that says He ascended presupposes a prior descent.[42]   Acts 1:9 and Mark 16:19 tell us how Jesus returned to heaven. He could not have ascended thus if He had not first descended from heaven to earth (John 1:1,14).

---

[40] Bruce, *op. cit*, p.82.

[41] This commentator has not been impressed with the suggestion that Ephesians 4:9 is nothing but a Rabbinical argument intended to show that the subject of Psalm 68:18 is none other than Christ, because only of Him alone could be predicated that descending which "he ascended" presumes to have gone before.   Such an argument would have been aimless, since (1) the Psalm pictures Jehovah, after the Exodus, as marching through the wilderness ahead of His people and His presence as causing Mt. Sinai to quake (Psalm 68:7,8), and (2) Paul did not have to prove to his readers that 68:18 was Messianic since the latter part of Psalm 68 was recognized even by the Jews as being Messianic.

[42] There is a manuscript variation at this place, with some manuscripts reading "he also descended *first*."   The weight of the authority is on the side of the omission of the word "first," even though the thought added by "first" is apparently correct.

Into the lower parts of the earth – To what Paul makes reference in the words "He descended" depends on the meaning we give to this phrase "the lower parts of the earth." (1) If we take "lower parts of the earth" to refer to "Hades" (i.e., a partitive genitive), then the descent took place between Christ's death and resurrection (cp.1 Peter 3:18-22). While His body was in the tomb ("in the heart of the earth," Matthew 12:40) after He died on the cross, Christ's soul was temporarily in Hades (Acts 2:27). (2) If we take the genitive "of the earth" to be appositional, then the "lower parts" are or constitute the earth (as compared to heaven above). If "lower parts of the earth" is equal to "earth," then the descent was the incarnation. John 3:13, where Jesus speaks to Nicodemus about His descent from heaven, would be similar. Psalm 139:13,15 uses the expression "lowest parts of the earth" (ASV) to refer to the womb. If this is how Paul uses the words here, then the descent has reference to Christ's incarnation. The second of these two options may be the better idea. His incarnation, and all that is connected with that momentous event, is one thing that qualifies Jesus to give gifts to His church.

4:10 – *He who descended is Himself also He who ascended far above all the heavens, that He might fill all things.)*

He who descended is Himself also He who ascended far above all the heavens – When the days of His incarnation and earthly ministry were completed, the same Christ who had descended also ascended. The Greek construction is an emphatic assertion of the identity of Him who ascended with Him who descended. The Son of God did not by His incarnation (His descent) become other than what He was; He never gave up His Deity. Nor did the assumption of the human nature add any thing to His person, any more than a man is made another person by the clothes he puts on. Christ descended without emptying Himself of His being as God, and His ascension in a glorified human body did not make any change in who He is, Deity. What was called "on high" in Ephesians 4:8 is here more precisely described as the region highest of all. "Far above all the heavens" reminds us that Scriptures speak of three heavens. The atmosphere is spoken of as "heaven" in such phrases as "the birds of the heavens" (Jeremiah 4:25). Outer space is spoken of as "heaven" in such phrases as "the stars of heaven" (Deuteronomy 28:62). The "third heaven" where God dwells is mentioned in 2 Corinthians 12:2 and 2 Chronicles 6:18. This passage in Ephesians is very similar to Hebrews 4:14 which tells us that, on the day of His resurrection, Christ "passed through the heavens" (the heaven of the clouds, and the heaven of the planets, into the heaven of heavens, into the presence of God). One of the purposes of His ascension into heaven is explained at Hebrews 9:11-28. Another purpose is identified in the words immediately following which speak of what He was now qualified to do.

That He might fill all things) – No one else is qualified to "fill all things." Christ ascended, not to abandon His church as orphans (John 14:18), but to provide her with rich gifts of "grace" (Ephesians 4:7), thus filling all things.[43] The language here reminds us of Ephesians 1:23 which tells us that Jesus fills the church.   The gifts were to facilitate the preserving of the unity of the Spirit.

4:11 – *And He gave some* **as** *apostles, and some* **as** *prophets, and some* **as** *evangelists, and some* **as** *pastors and teachers,*

And He gave some – Having finished his parenthetical thought (verses 9-10 were in parentheses in the NASB), Paul now resumes the train of thought which he began in verses 7 and 8.   The sentence that begins here at verse 11 in the Greek continues through verse 16.   The pronoun "He" with which the sentence begins is emphatic in the Greek.   He, the One who ascended, He and no one else, gave the gifts about to be enumerated.   Among His other gifts (4:7) there were some leadership gifts given to the church by the ascended Christ.[44]   The verb "gave" is an aorist tense, a completed act in past time.   The act of giving these gifts/ functions to the church was completed before Paul wrote; that is, all were in existence and functioning at the time Paul wrote this letter.   There is another listing of gifts found in 1 Corinthians 12:28.   Both listings (at least the first two or three gifts named) seem to be in order of descending authority, and also, perhaps, in the chronological order of their appearance in the church.   The higher office likely includes many of the functions of the lower offices.[45]

(Some) *as* apostles – It is not surprising that "apostle" heads the list.   It has been well said that, in the church, the apostles of Jesus were first in rank,   first in time,

---

[43] While what Christ does for the church is certainly in view in the immediate context here in Ephesians, there is a strong possibility that "all things" includes more than the Christian community. King Jesus can now wield His kingly sway as He sustains and governs over the whole universe and moves history to its goal.   He will continue to exercise this sway until the consummation as indicated at 1 Corinthians 15:28.

[44] When it is remembered that Christ Himself bestowed these gifts about to be named, it becomes obvious that the organization of the church is not a mere human arrangement; its offices are of divine appointment.   "The positions named are sometimes called 'offices.'   More accurately, they are 'functions.'   Each term specifies a work to be done, even more than an office to be held. They are distinct, complementary, and most essential" (Tesh, *op. cit.*, p.388).

[45] Christ Himself was an apostle, prophet, evangelist, shepherd, and teacher.   Paul the apostle was also a teacher.   And Timothy, who did the work of an evangelist, was also a teacher.

and first in dignity.   The apostles of Jesus were a special class of servants chosen by the Lord Himself.[46]   In order to be qualified to be an apostle, a man must have seen the risen Lord so he could be a witness of His resurrection (Acts 1:21,22). They were chosen and commissioned by Christ, and were endowed through a special impartation of the Holy Spirit for the work of establishing the church (John 14:26, 16:12-15; Acts 1:5,8).   This impartation of the Spirit included the power to work miracles (Acts 2:43) and the ability to speak by inspiration as the Spirit gave them utterance (Acts 2:4; 1 Corinthians 2:13).   In order to impart spiritual gifts on others, the apostles could also lay hands on others whom they might choose to assist in that work (Acts 8:18, 19:6; 2 Timothy 1:6).   Apostles were the specially chosen messengers to bear witness of what they knew of Jesus (Acts 1:8, 26:16), to reveal the truths they had learned from Jesus (John 16:13; Luke 24:49), and to demonstrate His Deity by the miracles they worked (Acts 3:11-13, 5:12,13, 9:32-35, 14:8-18).   Apostles of Jesus have no personal successors in the church, but their witness and work continue through the books of Scripture authored by them.   We still have apostles in the church in the sense that we have their writings to guide us.

And some *as* prophets – New Testament prophets were an order of teachers/ messengers distinct from the apostles, and next to them in order of authority or rank.   Agabus (Acts 11:27,28; 21:10,11), the daughters of Philip (Acts 21:8-11), Judas and Silas (Acts 15:32) are some specifically so identified in the New Testament.   A prophet by definition is a person who spoke the words and thoughts of God by inspiration, no matter what the content of the message, whether the content related to past, present or future.   In other words, to prophesy does not mean merely to predict the future, though there were times when they did predict the future (Acts 11:27,28, 21:10,11).   A prophet spoke to edify, to exhort, to comfort (1 Corinthians 14:3; Acts 15:32).   One important function of prophecy was edification (1 Corinthians 14:1-26).   At Ephesians 3:5 we were told that prophets had the privilege of explaining the mystery just as did

---

[46] See comments at Ephesians 1:1 where it was explained that there are two kinds of apostles in the New Testament, depending on who chose the person to be a commissioned messenger, whether it was Jesus or a local congregation.   Apostles chosen by Jesus include the eleven, plus Matthias, and Paul, and several others, including Barnabas (Acts 14:4,14); James, the Lord's brother (1 Corinthians 15:7; Galatians 1:19); and perhaps Andronicus and Junias (Romans 16:7).   (That Andronicus and Junias are here called apostles is but one of two possible interpretations of Romans 16:7).

the apostles. Prophets evidently received their commission by the laying on of an apostle's hands (Acts 19:6).[47] Though we do not have prophets present in person today (1 Corinthians 13:9,10), we do have prophets in the church today in the sense that we have their words preserved in some of the books in the New Testament canon.[48]

And some *as* evangelists – The nature of this office is known only from the meaning of the term[49] and the work of those who bore the designation. Philip (one of the ones selected to minister to the widows who were being neglected, Acts 6:2-6) became an evangelist (Acts 21:8). He was a herald of Christ to the unconverted in Samaria, on the road to Gaza, and in the cities of the plain of Sharon (Acts 8:5-40). He eventually settled in Caesarea where he served for upwards of 20 years (he is still there at Acts 21:8). Luke served as evangelist with the church at Philippi for a period of 5 years or so (as indicated by the absence of "we" passages between Acts 16:16 and 20:6). Titus, who labored with the churches on the island of Crete, is pictured as being an evangelist, as are Artemis and Tychicus, one of whom would relieve Titus of his responsibilities (Titus 3:12). Timothy served the church at Ephesus for a period of years (as is indicated by the New Testament letters written to him by Paul), a congregation that already had elders (Acts 20:17-38) before Timothy ever came to town to do the work of an evangelist there.[50] Some evangelists were itinerant (as was Philip early in his ministry), and some worked with a local congregation as they preached the gospel (Luke, Timothy). Thus, it appears, that "evangelist" in the

---

[47] The office of prophet (like that of the apostles of Jesus) was temporary in the church, designed for the settlement and establishment of the church, and then, like the apostolic office, having accomplished its purpose, was to cease (1 Corinthians 13:9-10). They were part of the foundation, just as were the apostles (Ephesians 2:20).

[48] Mark, Luke, and Jude (who were authors of several New Testament books) were close associates of apostles and likely received the ability to speak and write by inspiration by the laying on of an apostle's hands. Silas also was a prophet (Acts 15:32) and he had some responsibility in the penning of 1 Peter (see 1 Peter 5:12, Silas being a shortened form of Silvanus).

[49] Liddell and Scott (*op. cit.*, p.279) tell us that in addition to being a bringer of good tidings, a preacher of the gospel, the word evangelist is used in Ecclesiastical writers of those who were writers of the Gospels.

[50] Since Timothy is also called a "good minister of Jesus Christ" (1 Timothy 3:2, 4:6, KJV; 2 Timothy 4:5) we suppose that others designated as being "ministers" (e.g., Epaphras in Colossians 1:7 KJV, and Tychicus in Ephesians 6:21 and Colossians 4:7 KJV) also held the position of evangelist.

New Testament and "preacher" in our day and age are analogous functions in the church.[51]   Evangelists received their commission from churches (Acts 14:1-3; Timothy in 1 Timothy 4:14; 2 Timothy 2:2),[52] and not directly from Christ as did the apostles. We have evangelists in the church, still. This office, by its very nature, must be permanent in the church. Evangelists will be needed as long as any person on earth has not heard the good news – for the word means "a bringer of good news."[53]

And some *as* pastors and teachers – The first issue which must be decided is whether these two words express two distinct offices, or are two descriptive titles for the same office/function. Sharp's rule of grammar[54] and the fact that "and some" is not repeated before "teachers" should help us see that we do not have two different offices, but two titles for the same office/function. The reference is to the office/function elsewhere in the New Testament known as "elder" or "bishop" (overseer). The words "elder" and "bishop" are two more words for the same office (Acts 20:17,28; Titus 1:5,7). The word "pastor" (a Latin word meaning "shepherd"[55]) is applied in the New Testament to the office of elder, not the office of evangelist.   It is to be regretted that in modern usage, the word *pastor* is frequently used to refer to the preacher rather than to the elders. To a people who are accustomed to call Bible things by Bible names, such a usage of

---

[51] See Gareth L. Reese, "Special Study #4: Evangelist," in *New Testament Epistles: 1 and 2 Timothy and Titus* (Moberly, MO: Scripture Exposition Books, 1999), p.192-208; and Weldon Bennett, "J.W. McGarvey's Concept of the Ministry," *Restoration Quarterly* (Third Quarter 1981), p.167ff.

[52] Concerning the qualifications of an evangelist see Don DeWelt, *The Church in the Bible* (Joplin, MO: College Press, 1958), p.94-95.

[53] Thayer, *op. cit.*, p.257.

[54] Granville Sharp's rule of grammar is this: When two nouns in the same case are connected by the Greek word "and," and the first noun is preceded by the article "the," and the second noun is not preceded by the article, the second noun refers to the same person or thing to which the first noun refers, and is a further description of it (Wuest, *Practical Use of Greek New Testament*, p.22; Dana and Mantey, *Manual Grammar of Greek New Testament*, p.147). In this instance in Ephesians 4:11, the words "pastors" and "teachers" are in the same case, and are connected by the word "and." In the Greek, the word "pastors" is preceded by the article "the," whereas the word "teachers" is not. This construction requires us to understand that the words "pastors" and "teachers" refer to the same individual, and that the word "teacher" is a further explanation or description of the individual called a "pastor."

[55] See Luke 2:8,15,18,20; John 10:2,11-12,14,16, where the Greek word here translated "pastors" is rendered "shepherd" and "shepherds." See also Hebrews 13:20; 1 Peter 2:25.

"pastor" for the preacher/evangelist can only lead to a confusion in people's minds about Bible things. "While the preacher may perform a variety of pastoral duties, such duties are usually associated in the New Testament with the office of elder (also called "overseer" or "bishop"). The word *pastor* literally means "shepherd," and it is the elders who are exhorted to shepherd the flock of God (Acts 20:17,18; 1 Peter 5:1,2)."[56] Likewise, the word "teacher" is often applied to the office of elder (1 Timothy 3:2, 5:17; Titus 1:9). The description "pastors and teachers" (or pastoring-teacher) practically outlines two distinct duties of this leadership function in the local church – shepherd and teach. "They were to feed the flock, which is the church, to protect it from ravenous human wolves attempting to destroy it, visit the sick, and exercise sympathetic care for those entrusted to their oversight."[57] The office/function of "pastoring teacher" or "shepherding teacher" was intended by God to be a permanent office in the church, just as is evangelist.[58]

4. The objectives in mind as the gifts are used.   4:12-16

a. The saints are equipped for service to build up the body.   12

4:12 – *for the equipping of the saints for the work of service, to the building up of the body of Christ;*

For – "For" *(pros)* marks the aim or purpose behind the ministries Christ has given to the church. What are the leaders named in verse 11 to accomplish? This verse continues the sentence begun in verse 11 and gives the answer to that question. Leaders have one task – the equipping of the saints.

---

[56] Shannon, *op. cit.*, p.397.

[57] Leavitt, *op. cit.*, p.75.

[58] Perhaps there needs to be a reflection on the position or rank of evangelist, who in this passage is named before elders ("pastoring-teachers"). Likewise, in 1 Timothy 5:19,20 the evangelist has disciplinary functions over elders who sin, yet the elders are called the "rulers, overseers." In addition, even Titus, who was to appoint elders in every congregation, apparently did so by giving the individual congregations a voice in the choice, even as the church at Jerusalem had a voice in the choice of those who would minister to the widows (Acts 6:3). It would appear that the evangelist is not authoritarian over elders, but rather an outside advisor to the elders as together they lead and shepherd the congregation.

The equipping of the saints – In the language of the New Testament, all Christians are saints. *Katartizo* ("equipping") is an interesting and picturesque word. It is used of setting broken bones, or of putting a joint that is out of place back into its place. In the New Testament it is used of mending nets (Mark 1:19) and of disciplining an offender until he is fit to take his place again within the fellowship of the church ("restore," Galatians 6:1), of a teacher training a pupil (Luke 6:40), and of completing what is lacking in someone's faith (1 Thessalonians 3:10). Training the saints for service is the idea. Think of the rounds of endless drills an army goes through in preparation for battle. Soldiers learn how to use their weapons, how to defend each other, etc. It is the job of the church leaders to train the rest of us soldiers for Christ. Not many local churches follow this New Testament idea. Rather than encouraging him to train workers to do the ministering, "it is a common practice to let the preacher do all the ministering. Sometimes the preacher temporarily may find it easier to do the work himself than to train others to do it. But his job is to train workers, and in the long run his ministry will be more effective if he does so."[59] There are two jobs which all the saints are to be trained to do: (1) the work of service, and (2) the building up of the body of Christ (both clauses begin with *eis* in the Greek).[60]

For the work of service – "For" *(eis)* marks one of the jobs for which the saints should become equipped. The ASV reads "unto the work of ministering." The gifts enumerated in verse 11 do not monopolize the church's ministry; their function rather is to so help and direct the church that each and all the members may perform their several ministries for the good of the whole, helping each other to grow to the spiritual maturity ("the unity of the faith") that verse 13 talks about.[61] When the saints are trained/equipped, one of the things they will do is

---

[59] Martin, *op. cit.*, p.1311.

[60] "As it appears in the KJV, this passage appears to mean that the apostles, prophets, evangelists and pastoring-teachers are given to do three things: (1) perfect the saints, (2) do the work of the ministry, and (3) edify the body of Christ. However, the Greek prepositions seem to suggest that the apostles, prophets, evangelists and pastoring-teachers are given to do one thing: to equip/train the saints so that the saints will do two things: (1) do the work of the ministry and (2) edify the body of Christ. The last two responsibilities are not the work of the leaders alone" (Root, *op. cit.*, p.36).

[61] "Here we see a misrepresentation of the meaning of the Spirit, in the use of the term 'ministering.' Preaching is the prominent idea connected with the work of the ministry at the present day. Today the preacher is 'the minister.' Originally the minister was the individual who performed the most menial and laborious work in the congregation – physical labor for the congregation – who waited upon the sick, fed the hungry, and labored for the relief of sorrow, distress, and the physical ills of the outcasts of earth" (Lipscomb, *op. cit.*, p.78).

devote themselves to meeting peoples' needs in the name of Christ. "The needs may be material and physical (James 1:27), emotional and social (Romans 12:15), or spiritual (Galatians 6:1,2)."[62] Every Christian household should imitate the example of the house of Stephanas, who devoted themselves for ministry to the saints (1 Corinthians 16:15).   That would be a wonderful type of devotion.

To the building up of the body of Christ – "To" (*eis*) introduces a second job all saints are to be equipped (trained) to do.   All of us are trained to build the church (the body of Christ, Ephesians 1:23), to help it grow bigger and better. We are to be saving souls and helping babes in Christ to grow to spiritual maturity. These are the tasks of the saints.

b.   The goal of the ministry/service of the saints.   13

4:13 – *until we all attain to the unity of the faith, and of the knowledge of the Son of God, to a mature man, to the measure of the stature which belongs to the fullness of Christ.*

Until we all attain – The sentence begun in verse 11 and carried into verse 12 continues on.   "We all" refers to the saints alluded to in verse 12.[63]   The verb translated "attain to" means to arrive at.   This verse says that each saint is in need of making progress in spiritual growth.   What a high goal this presents for all us saints.   We work together to help each other arrive at the goal.   Three times in verse 13 we have the preposition *eis* ("to") to identify the goal toward which progress is to be made.   "The three clauses following (each introduced by *eis*) do not seem to be three different goals, but three ways of describing the same goal."[64]

1)   Unity of the faith and knowledge of the Son of God.   13

To the unity of the faith, and of the knowledge of the Son of God – This is the first of three ways of describing the goal of the ministry/service of the saints to one another.   At first, it is unexpected to read there is a unity to be attained since, according to Ephesians 4:3, we already have a unity which needs to be preserved.

---

[62] Hayden, *op. cit.*, p.317.

[63] Clearly "we all" is limited to all believers.   It does not include all men, even those who are not believers, for that would make the verse teach universal salvation, an idea clearly at odds with the New Testament elsewhere (e.g., Matthew 7:13,14).

[64] Root, *op. cit.*, p.36.

But the areas of unity are not the same. The area of *unity to be guarded* is the things that strained that unity. The area of the *unity to which we all must attain* is a unity of faith and of knowledge of the Son of God.[65] Since the following verses speak of avoidance of false doctrine, we think "the faith" here is a body of doctrine about Jesus, the Son of God. Such a unity as it relates to the Son of God is reached only by a careful study of the Word of God, allowing it to form and frame our beliefs (our doctrine). Christians must be taught to observe all that Jesus has commanded (Matthew 28:20), and this is done by continuing steadfastly in the apostles' teaching/doctrine (Acts 2:42). There is also a necessary growth in knowledge about Jesus, the Son of God. When we first become Christians we know enough about Jesus to confess Him as the Christ, the Son of the living God. But there is more to be learned about Jesus as we grow as Christians. Such a unity of knowledge about the Son of God would come from a careful study of the Gospels, Hebrews, and the great Christological passages of Scripture.[66]

2) Spiritual maturity.   13

To a mature man – This is a second way of describing the goal we are trying to reach. "Mature" (*teleios*, "full grown," ASV) is the opposite of *nepios* ("children") in verse14. When Paul uses this word (often translated "perfect" in the KJV), he does not refer to the doctrine of sinless perfection, but to spiritual adulthood as compared with that of spiritual childhood. Just as a child's physical well-being often is measured by his growth, so it is with spiritual life. Growing to full-grown spiritual maturity is the thing pictured. Paul has in mind the spiritual maturity of each individual saint. He spoke of "we all" (verse 13a).

3) Christlikeness in spiritual stature.   13

To the measure of the stature which belongs to the fullness of Christ – This is a third way of describing the goal of the saint's ministry/service to one another. This gives the standard by which one determines or measures what is spiritual maturity. Each saint's maturity is measured by comparison with the "fullness of

---

[65] In this commentator's judgment, we should let the preposition *eis* ("to") guide us so that all the words following the first "to" here in verse 13 form one goal. In addition, the genitive phrase "of the Son of God" is to be connected to both "faith" and "knowledge."

[66] The church in this commentator's lifetime has not done well in helping all its members to a unity of knowledge (full knowledge – *epignosis*) concerning the Son of God – His Deity, His teachings, the ethics He expects of us.

Christ."[67] To explain what is "the fullness of Christ" think of Luke 2:52. He grew in wisdom and stature and in favor with God and men. "The simple words of the song, 'I Would Be Like Jesus' capture in essence Paul's final goal: to be like Jesus 'all day long,' says everything. Here is a goal to test our very best, a goal that is valid for all men for all time."[68] "Is being like Jesus an impossible goal for Christians today? Well, yes and no.[69] Certainly we have not reached it yet, but all of us who have been trying are closer than we were."[70]

c. The result of reaching for the goal. 14,15

4:14 – *As a result, we are no longer to be children, tossed here and there by waves and carried about by every wind of doctrine, by the trickery of men, by craftiness in deceitful scheming;*

As a result -- The sentence that began in verse 11 continues. The Greek is *hina* which suggests this verse is intended to state the purpose or the result of the equipping and the subsequent ministry of the saints (verse 12). The result is stated first negatively (verse 14), and then positively (verse 15).

We are no longer to be children – The word *nepios,* here translated "children," is used of minors (Galatians 4:1) and of the immature and untaught (Matthew 11:25; Romans 2:20; Hebrews 5:13). New converts are like little children; they are babes in Christ (see 1 Peter 1:22,23; 2:1,2). "No longer" suggests that such new converts need to grow out of their spiritual childhood as quickly as possible. Indeed, Jesus did call attention to some traits that children have which are helpful to becoming a disciple of Jesus (Matthew 18:1-6; Mark 10:15; Luke 18:17), but likewise there are childish traits that leave a newborn Christian vulnerable. For example, until they grow older and learn better, little children will believe almost

---

[67] The Greek word *helikia*, translated "stature" here, may be used either of height (as in Luke 19:3, where Zacchaeus is "little of stature") or of age (as in John 9:21, where "he is of age" is literally "he has *helikia*"). It is saying that Christ is the standard against which we compare ourselves to determine if our spiritual growth is what it should be.

[68] Tesh, *op. cit.,* p.389.

[69] Whether this goal is reached in this life or the next is determined by the meaning given to "faith" and "knowledge." It appears, from the following verse, that this is a goal reachable in this life, for the individual Christian.

[70] Root, *op. cit.,* p.37.

anything they may be told, even if it is a lie. Since false teachers often go after new converts, trying to proselyte them to false religions (2 Peter 2:14,18-20), new converts to Christ need to be protected, nurtured, taught. As he describes the equipping of the saints for ministry, Paul is giving the divine method to help such spiritual children to maturity and a vital involvement in the church.

Tossed here and there by waves, and carried about by every wind of doctrine – Paul mixes metaphors as he vividly describes how a spiritually immature person will find himself being harmed and deceived and taken advantage of. His first metaphor pictures a small boat in a storm, unable to hold a steady course. It is being tossed to and fro like a cork on the surging sea, and spinning around while being driven off her true course by strong winds. In its spiritual application, the rough waves and strong winds (as the context shows) are applied to wrong teachings which carry immature Christians away from the truth of the gospel and get them off their true course. That is the danger if new Christians fail to grow. "Christians are to be equipped so that they become strong in faith and knowledge with the result that they would cease to be troubled by erroneous and false teachings."[71] "The doctrine here taught is that Christians are to have settled religious beliefs. When they have carefully examined what is truth, and have found it, they should adhere to it. They do not yield to the coming of every new teacher, but instead are willing to follow the truth wherever it leads."[72]

By the trickery of men, by craftiness in deceitful scheming – This second metaphor is drawn from the world of the con artist who uses deception and clever words to deceive others. "Trickery" (*kubeia*) is a word that meant sleight of hand, cheating at dice. The false doctrines that are taught are sometimes presented by dishonest means, even as dice players sometimes use dishonesty. Like a naive young man who finds himself the victim of card sharks, so is the untrained soul before the winds of false doctrine. "Of men" is in contrast with "the faith and ... knowledge of the Son of God" (4:13). The metaphorical language is dropped and the evil influences to which childish instability is a prey are described in clear terms. "Craftiness" (*panourgeia*) describes the treacher-

---

[71] Tesh, *op. cit.*, p.389. "Doctrine" translates *didaskalia*, which speaks of the thing taught. The word also occurs at 1 Timothy 1:10, 4:6, 6:1,3; 2 Timothy 4:3; Titus 1:9, 2:1,10.

[72] Barnes, *op. cit.*, p.81.

ous deceitfulness and unscrupulous words and actions of those who deliberately try to deceive and destroy.[73]   "Craftiness" is translated by Goodspeed as "ingenuity in inventing error."   "Deceitful scheming" suggests the trickery and craftiness behind the false teaching is the result of the work of the devil. "Scheming" translates *methodeian,* "a deliberate plan, or system."[74]   "Deceitful" translates a Greek word which means to wander hither and thither.   The whole phrase, which is difficult to translate, may suggest that the schemes are intended to get immature Christians to err in thought or in practice, to go down the wrong road, to believe what is not true.[75]

4:15 – *but speaking the truth in love, we are to grow up in all* **aspects** *into Him who is the head,* **even** *Christ,*

But – Here is stated the positive result when the proper equipping (verse 12) of the saints is done by the leaders.[76]   We grow up into Christ.

Speaking the truth in love – When properly equipped (verse 12) each one of us saints does this – we are faithful to the truth of the gospel.   The Greek verb (*aletheuontes*), which occurs only one other time in the New Testament (Galatians 4:16), expresses more than just speaking the truth; it includes the thought of living and loving truth.   Alford renders "being followers of truth."[77]   The NASB mar-

---

[73] This Greek word was used of the sneaky cunning of the snake in the Garden of Eden (2 Corinthians 11:3).   See also Luke 20:23, where its use is well illustrated.

[74] The noun form *methodeia* is found only here and at Ephesians 6:11 (where the devil is the author of the schemes), and does not occur in non-Biblical Greek.   A verb form *methodeuo* is known.   It means primarily to pursue a plan, whether honest (Diod. Sic., i., 81) or dishonest (Polyb., xxxiv., 4, 10), and it came to have the sense of being tricky, cunning, treacherous, practicing deceitful devices (Diod., vii., 16; 2 Samuel 19:27).

[75] This reference is so definite in the Greek that many are tempted to believe that Paul had in view some particular scheme of erroneous teaching which had already put down roots in the soil of Asia Minor.   The Epistle to the Colossians shows that such false teaching had already appeared at Colossae, and was the germ of Gnosticism, (See the Detailed Introduction to Colossians, "The Colossian Heresy").

[76] Verse 14 stated a negative result -- we are no longer children tossed to and fro by every wind of doctrine.

[77] Alford, *op. cit.,* p.119.

ginal note reads, "holding to, or walking in" the truth.[78] Paul's readers had
learned the saving truth of Christ from the apostles, prophets, and evangelists
whom Christ had given them.[79]   In verses 14 and 15, after they have been
cautioned about avoiding false teaching, they are here pictured as continually
embracing the truth in which they had been instructed and so grow to maturity in
the Christian life. "In love" can be taken with "speaking the truth" or with "we
are to grow up." Perhaps Paul has in mind love for God, perhaps love for one
another, or perhaps both.[80]

We are to grow up in all *aspects* **into Him, who is the head,** *even* **Christ** – The
aorist subjunctive verb "grow up" is still part of the clause introduced by "as a
result" at verse 13. The nominative plural participle "speaking (walking in) the
truth," which agrees with the first-person plural verb "we grow up," tells how all
of us grow up. Such growing comes between the state of children (4:14) and
full-grown men (4:13). The extent or scope of this growing into Christ is
expressed by *ta panta*, "all aspects" or "all things." "In every area of life –
mentally, morally, and spiritually – the Christian must reach toward full maturity
as it is found in Christ."[81]   On Christ being the "head" of the body, see Ephesians
1:22.[82] R.A. Knox pointed out that a baby's head is very large in relation to his
body, and that his body, as it develops, is really growing up more and more into
a due proportion with the head.[83] Whether this sort of analogy was in Paul's
mind or not, it serves as a pleasing illustration of his teaching here. It is by
growing up to match the Head (Christ) that the body of Christ, made up of each

---

[78] "Truth" here is contrasted with the deception, trickery, unscrupulousness, and deceitful scheming (verse 14) which endangers babes in Christ.

[79] "Truth" here likely embraces "the faith and knowledge of the Son of God" about which verse 13 spoke. Jesus Christ is "the way, and the truth, and the life" (John 14:6); His word is the truth that makes men free (John 8:32,36).

[80] Wood (*op. cit.*, p.59) takes it as love for one another when he comments, "the church cannot allow falsehood to go uncorrected, yet the truth must always be vindicated in the accents of love." Likewise, Bratcher (*op. cit.*, p.106) whose comment is "it is the Christians' love for one another in the body of Christ which guarantees growth and health (see also Ephesians 5:2)."

[81] Dowling, *op. cit.*, p.442.

[82] A note about Greek grammar may be in order. "The use of the nominative *Christos* in apposition with 'him,' where we might have expected the accusative in apposition to 'head,' is a usual Greek construction" (Abbott, *op. cit.*, p.124).

[83] R. A. Knox, *St. Paul's Gospel* (London: Sheed and Ward, 1953), p.84.

and every saint, attains "the measure of the stature of the fullness of Christ" (verse 13).

d. How the body is designed to function.   16

4:16 – *from whom the whole body, being fitted and held together by that which every joint supplies, according to the proper working of each individual part, causes the growth of the body for the building up of itself in love.*

From whom the whole body – Verse 16 is the conclusion of the sentence begun in verse 11.   Stripped of its many qualifying phrases, the gist of verse 16 is this: under the direction of the Head, the whole body helps the whole body to grow. In other words, all the members of the church must work together if it is to be a body that is healthy and fully functioning.   "Every part is important to the whole. Love enables the parts to work together for the edifying of all."[84]   "From whom" (Christ, the head) recalls the fact that Christ has given a measure of grace to each member of the body (Ephesians 4:7) and that the members of the body have been equipped by the leaders given to the church by Christ (Ephesians 4:12).

Being fitted and held together – These two present tense participles describe a process still going on, still continuing.   The whole body, whether the members be Jewish Christians or Gentile Christians, is fitted together perfectly to form the whole.   "Fitted ... together" speaks of *inter-adaptation*.   As ball-and-socket joints fit together in the human body, so all the members of the body of Christ are here pictured as closely joined together/integrated.   "Held together" pictures the body as being an *aggregate* of component parts.   The word picture is of stones bonded together by cement.   The members of the church are not just placed side by side, but are to become coalesced into one living body.   These two words picture a growth in harmony between the members ("fitted") and a growth in solidity and strength ("held together").

By that which every joint supplies – This conclusion to the sentence begun in verse 11 seems to indicate how the growth of the body takes place.[85]   Christ, of

---

[84] Shannon, *op. cit.,* p.398.

[85] This whole phrase presents the interpreter with some difficult decisions. Precisely what is meant by the Greek word translated "joint" is not absolutely clear.   And whether this whole phrase should be connected with the preceding verbs "fitted and held together," or whether it should be connected with the following verb "causes growth," is uncertain.   In these notes we have opted for the latter.   Had we chosen the former option, the "joints" would be the points of union where the Head passes needed nourishment to the different members of the body.

course, is the source of the supply, the source of nourishment of the spiritual body. Each member of the body is pictured as being generous as it passes on needed nourishment to its neighbor.[86]   It is as the members touch each other, get involved in each other's lives, that the nourishment is passed from one part of the body to the next.[87]

According to the proper working of each individual part – The church is the body of Christ.   Just as every member of the human body must function properly in its relation to every other member if the body as a whole is to do its work, so it is in the church.   Each member must perform his or her own work if the body as a whole is to function effectively (Romans12:4-8). A failure anywhere handicaps all.   Every saint must minister if the body of Christ is to be built up (Ephesians 4:12).   "Like a fine watch or a complex machine, a slight misadjustment in a part can hinder the performance of the whole.   Among the members of the body of our Lord, a relationship exists that requires a wonderful interdependency. Anything that interrupts the relationship is serious or may even be fatal."[88]

Causes the growth of the body – Here the active participation of the body as a living organism in promoting its own growth is brought out.   The Greek verb is in the middle voice, indicating that the body acts for its own benefit as it promotes its own growth.   One area of growth this very passage has emphasized is found in verse 13, "until we all attain to the unity of the faith, and of the knowledge of the Son of God, to a mature man."

---

[86] The Greek word *epichoregia* ("supplies") originally meant to lead a choir, or to defray the expenses of a choir, to render a public service. It denoted a lavish contribution to cover the expenditures. The *choregos* was the man who met the cost of staging a Greek play with its chorus. Each Christian is to meet the cost of furnishing the body with what is needed.

[87] The English word "joint" here is an attempt to translate *haphe* (from *hapto*, to touch). As it occurs in Colossians 2:19 the word has its common physiological meaning, namely, as denoting where two parts of a limb or finger touch (i.e., elbow, hip, or knee).   Barnes (*op. cit.*, p. 83) thinks the word denotes the blood vessels, cords, tendons, muscles, and nerves, which bring every part of the body, even the remotest, into contact with the head.   More likely the word refers to the place where two members of the body touch or contact each other.

[88] Tesh, *op. cit.*, p.389.

For the building up of itself in love – The several parts go about their mutual work in an atmosphere of love. Because each member of the body loves the other members, each member works to make increase of the other parts of the body. With these words we have concluded the first exhortation, the exhortation to preserve the unity of the Spirit in the bond of peace.

B. An Exhortation to Live a Holy Life (Because They Have Put off the Old Man, and Put on the New). 4:17-24

1. No longer live as the pagans do. 4:17-19

4:17 – *This I say, therefore, and affirm together with the Lord, that you walk no longer just as the Gentiles also walk, in the futility of their mind,*

This I say, therefore – "Therefore" picks up the thought of 4:1 where Paul encouraged his readers to walk in a worthy manner. The first thing involved in such a worthy walk is to endeavor to maintain the unity of the Spirit in the bond of peace (4:3-16). The second thing involved in a worthy walk, to live a holy life, begins with this verse.

And affirm together with the Lord – "Affirm" translates *martureo*, to testify, to make a solemn declaration. "Together with the Lord" is equivalent to claiming to speak with the Lord's authority as Paul gives this next exhortation. As he writes about living a holy life, these are Christ's words, not just his own.

That you walk no longer just as the Gentiles also walk – At Ephesians 2:2 and 4:1 we had this verb "walk" used to describe a person's behavior. "No longer" may suggest that some of Paul's readers were not living as Christians ought to live. Ethnically, many of the readers had a Gentile background, and though there would have been a lot of pressure to continue to live like their unconverted neighbors, the new converts to Christianity did not have to live and act and talk like unconverted Gentiles do. Four particulars now follow which describe how those unconverted Gentiles live.

In the futility of their mind – This is the *first* of the ways the Gentiles walk, a walk to be avoided by Christians. "Futility" (*mataios*) indicates purposelessness; they had no reason for living. Think of the vanity of which the Preacher (Ecclesiastes 1:2) and the Psalmist (Psalm 39:5, 144:4) speak. This is how men live if they do not have the reality of a revelation from God to rest upon and guide their thoughts. "What they did and said was directed by thinking that was without God, and therefore it was vain, worthless, unable to produce right conduct."[89]

4:18 – *being darkened in their understanding, excluded from the life of God because of the ignorance that is in them, because of the hardness of their heart;*

Being darkened in their understanding – This is the *second* of the ways the Gentiles walk. Such darkening is the result of sin.[90] Sin cuts the optic nerve of the spirit. They don't think right. Their intellect is clouded; their thinking is not clear. Satan has blinded the minds of the unbelieving (2 Corinthians 4:4).

Excluded from the life of God – The rest of verse 18 gives the *third* of the ways the Gentiles walk. "Excluded" says they are alienated, estranged, shut out from fellowship or intimacy,[91] and at Colossians 1:21 the word is used of those who alienated themselves. "The life of God" is a phrase that occurs nowhere else in the New Testament. Perhaps it speaks of the kind of life that God offers to mankind. The Gentiles "don't see the beauty and goodness and value of such a life. They can see the pleasure in a life of sin, but not the value of a life of goodness."[92] Perhaps in this letter, which speaks of how God has made us alive (Ephesians 2:5), there is reference to a man's spirit becoming dead because of his trespasses and sins. That is the "life" from which men become excluded. In the following phrases, both of which begin with "because," Paul gives two explicit reasons why unconverted Gentiles are excluded from the life of God.

Because of the ignorance that is in them – In this first reason for being excluded from the life of God, "the Greek word for 'lack of understanding, ignorance' contains an element of willfulness; it describes an unwillingness to learn, a refusal to admit the truth."[93] According to Romans 1:28 (and 1:21-23), their ignorance was not because they could not know, but because they ignored or refused to

---

[89] Root, *op. cit.,* p.42.

[90] The darkening was not inborn. Compare notes at Ephesians 2:1.

[91] "Excluded" translates the perfect passive participle of the Greek verb meaning "to be an alien, a stranger" (see notes at Ephesians 2:12, "separate from Christ"). As for the life of God, they are strangers. As was true of the participle "darkened," so the participle "excluded" indicates there was a time when they were not excluded.

[92] Root, *ibid.,* p.43.

[93] Bratcher, *op. cit.,* p.111.

acknowledge available truth.   Their ignorance was an inexcusable lack of knowledge about divine things.

Because of the hardness of their heart – This clause seems to give a second reason for the exclusion/alienation from the life of God.[94]   Their hearts (minds) have become so petrified that they have lost power to feel at all.[95]   "Hardening of the heart" (ASV) is likely a Semitic phrase for stubbornness.[96]   "Their hearts (minds) were calloused and insensitive to the subtle influence of God's Spirit."[97]

4:19 – *and they, having become callous, have given themselves over to sensuality, for the practice of every kind of impurity with greediness.*

And they, having become callous – This introduces the *fourth* of the ways the Gentiles walk.   "Having become callous" ("past feeling"[98]) explains why they give themselves over to sensuality.   They have lost any sense of pain, the pain that results from temporal punishment for their sins.[99]

---

[94] It is also possible to treat this clause as giving a reason for the ignorance that is in them, i.e., it is a thing caused by the hardening of their hearts.

[95] The Greek word used here is derived from *poros*, "hardening," not *peros*, "blindness." The KJV wrongly has "blindness" for "hardening" in 4:18. The Greek *poros* originally meant a stone that was harder than marble. It came to have certain medical connotations. It was used for the chalk stone which can form in the joints and completely paralyze action. It is used of the callous that forms where a bone has been broken and has been re-set, a callous which is harder than the bone itself. It is the word for "callous," a hardening of the skin. Where there is a callous, there is not as much feeling as in other parts of the hand.

[96] On hardening of the heart, see the case of Pharaoh as recorded in Exodus 8 where we are told that Pharaoh hardened his own heart, God hardened Pharaoh's heart, and Pharaoh's heart was hard. See notes at Mark 3:5 and Acts 19:9 on "becoming hardened," and see "their minds were hardened" in 2 Corinthians 3:14.

[97] Tesh, *op. cit.,* p.395.

[98] *Apelgekotes* is a medical expression denoting deadness to pain. "Pain urges us to seek the means of a cure; and when the pain is removed, not only hope, but also the desire and thought of good things are lost, so that a man becomes senseless, shameless, hopeless" (J.A. Bengel, *Gnomon of the New Testament* [Edinburgh: T & T Clark, 1860], Vol.4, p.95).

[99] Sin is like an anesthesia. At first, sin is offensive, and our conscience revolts against it. However, if we do not get away from it, it soon becomes less offensive to us, and then finally overpowering. We could also compare sin to the cold of the great North, which can benumb its victims until they are doomed, but feel no cold. Being "past feeling" is the last stage before destruction. If a man's conscience never bothers him any more, he is in terrible peril!

Have given themselves over to sensuality – At Romans 1:21-24 we are told that, when men do not honor God and become futile in their speculations, God gives men over. He withdraws His gracious preventive aid, with the result that one of the things men begin to practice is sensuality. Their sin is thus made their punishment. "Sensuality" (*aselgeia*) is a term that covers "every kind of uncleanness, drunkenness, drug abuse, and immoral sex. Being beyond any feeling of remorse, they do these things without restraint, with greediness."[100] The man who once had a sense of decency and shame becomes a soul who does not care how much he shocks public opinion, or how much he defies and insults all decency so long as he can gratify his desires.

For the practice of every kind of impurity with greediness – "Practice" here denotes total preoccupation with, being absorbed in, filthy practices. The Gentiles do not do iniquity hesitantly, but with greediness or eagerness. The term "greediness" refers to a greedy desire to have more. They desire the pleasures of sin, and go greedily after them. There is no longer any restraint in their desires to have more of the pleasures of sin.[101]

2. Live as the gospel prescribes. 4:20-24

4:20 – *But you did not learn Christ in this way,*

But you – "But" introduces a contrast to the insensitive, passion-dominated pagans who exist only to satisfy their lusts and physical desires. "You" is emphatic, which points to a contrast; the Christian life is a stark contrast when

---

[100] Root, *op. cit.*, p.43.

[101] "Paul drew a frightening picture of the brazen and unrestrained pagan indulgence in lust and filth, but it was not exaggerated or overdrawn. The abominable practices of prostitution and homosexuality were not only fully accepted in pagan society, they were elevated to the level of religious ritual. The ancient vices are again (or still) popular. Many people are demanding the legalizing of homosexual 'marriages' and repeal of all laws prohibiting sexual activity between consenting adults. The argument that no one is harmed by these activities is the devil's own lie. The 'consenting adults' are themselves harmed immeasurably, and the damage and pain inflicted radiate to parents, children, and friends and weaken the institution of marriage, which is the foundation of the family and the moral fiber of the whole social structure. Sin seldom looks sinful to those who indulge in it; but to God it is 'exceedingly sinful' (Romans 7:13)." Tesh, *ibid.*

compared with the behavior of the unconverted Gentiles. The songwriter Rufus H. McDaniel has caught the idea when he penned, "What a wonderful change in my life has been wrought since Jesus came into my heart."

Did not learn Christ in this way – The Greek reads "not thus," which suggests something quite otherwise than the sensual lifestyle of the unconverted Gentiles. "Did learn" is an aorist tense and looks back at the time when they became Christians.[102] There were taught certain Christian truths as part of preparation for becoming a Christian. The verb translated "learn" is the verb from which is derived the noun "disciple" (or pupil, apprentice, student).[103] "'Christ' is here considered as neither teacher nor example, but as the lesson to be learned.[104] Parallels may be seen in Acts 8:5,35. Philip went to Samaria and 'preached Christ unto them'; later he spoke to the Ethiopian eunuch and 'preached unto him Jesus'."[105] How the readers of Ephesians learned Christ is explained in the next verse where we have the verbs "heard" and "taught." Christ's way is different. He taught just the opposite of an immoral life. There is a content to the gospel. If the readers had listened to the gospel, they would have repented and quit those old Gentile behaviors. "Some Gentiles have been restored. Ignorance and blindness of heart are not necessarily permanent. Darkened understanding can be enlightened by the gospel, if one will listen. So it was that some of the Gentile readers of Ephesians had become Christians, and so it is that some 21st century heathen become Christians."[106]

4:21 – *if indeed you have heard Him and have been taught in Him, just as truth is in Jesus,*

If indeed you have heard Him – The "if indeed" with which the Greek begins does not put in doubt what follows; it is a way of reminding the readers about the

---

[102] This aorist tense verb is one of what has been called Paul's "baptismal aorists."

[103] "The expression implies more than receiving catechetical instruction, though that is included. It is to learn in such a way as to become a devotee or disciple (*mathetes*)." Wood, *op. cit.*, p.62.

[104] "Learn Christ" involves a most unusual use of the Greek verb "to learn," for it is followed with a direct object of a person.

[105] Tesh, *op. cit.*, p.395.

[106] Root, *op. cit.*, p.43.

facts of their Christian experience.[107]   The Ephesians had heard "Him," Christ.[108] What a striking way to put it.   Christ Himself had not evangelized the readers in person, but when gospel preachers spoke to them they heard Jesus speaking to them (cp. Hebrews 12:25).   This is the "hearing" that precedes faith and conversion.

And have been taught in Him – After they had become Christians, there were instructions they had been taught.   Those who have become Christians are said to be "in Christ" and here they are said to have been taught in Him, i.e., after they became Christians and were in fellowship with Him.   Matthew 28:20 indicates that immersed believers are to be taught to observe all things that Jesus has commanded.

Just as truth is in Jesus – If you were taught the truth in your training classes, you have been taught to put off the old way of life and put on the new.   The use of the name "Jesus," by itself, is so rare in Pauline letters that, when it occurs, we look for some special significance in it, some emphasis on our Lord's historic incarnation and earthly life.   Here the idea likely is that the very words of the historical Jesus were given during the pre- and post-baptismal instruction of converts.   In the verses following three things are identified as being included in the "truth" which they had heard and been taught.

4:22 – *that, in reference to your former manner of life, you lay aside the old self, which is being corrupted in accordance with the lusts of deceit,*

That, in reference to your former manner of life – "That" introduces three infinitive phrases (verses 22-24) which are a repetition and reminder of the truth they had heard and been taught, namely,   (1) to lay aside the old self;   (2) to be renewed in the spirit of your mind; and   (3) to put on the new self.   The "former manner of life" is the way (verses 17-19) Gentiles lived before becoming Christians.

You lay aside the old self – This is the *first point* they had been taught.   It is a metaphor of taking off and casting away outworn and filth-encrusted garments. "Lay aside" (*apothesthai*) is an aorist infinitive.   It is another of Paul's baptismal

---

[107]   "If indeed" is *ei ge* which means "assuming that."   (Cp. 3:2 where we had the same words.)

[108] Here, as in verse 20, Jesus Himself is the object of the verb.

aorists (cp. Romans 6:6; Colossians 3:9).[109] This is what happened when you were immersed. The "old self" (the NASB marginal note tells us the Greek is literally "the old man") is the unsaved person, dominated, like the Gentiles, by sin (verses 18-19).[110] That was to be laid aside.

Which is being corrupted – The present tense ("being corrupted") indicates a process that was going on continuously before they laid aside the old man.[111] The unsaved person (and the Christian who continues to walk as the Gentiles do, verse 17) is subject to a continuous process of corruption which grows worse and worse as time goes on, ultimately ending up in eternal punishment (Galatians 6:8).

In accordance with the lusts of deceit – "In accordance with" tells us that the corruption the old man experienced was the result of desires that were deceitful. "Lusts" *(epithumia)*, the same word used in Ephesians 2:3, are cravings, passionate desires.[112] "Deceit" reminds us the devil has the ability to stir up desires in our bodies, desires that promise thrills and satisfaction. Instead, they bring only disappointment, shame, disgrace, misery, and degradation. They are deceitful. The more the old man followed his lusts, the more he found himself corrupted, because the lusts are deceitful.

4:23 – *and that you be renewed in the spirit of your mind,*

And that you be renewed – This is the *second point* he reminds them they had been taught; namely, that in their Christian experience (since they put on the new man) they are being continually, day by day, renewed in the spirit of their mind. The present passive infinitive *(ananeousthai,* "be renewed") indicates the renewing is a continuing process, whereas "lay aside" (verse 22) and "put on"

---

[109] Verses 21-24 do not contain an exhortation to put off the old man. Instead, these verses are a reminder of the teaching they had received on the occasion of their conversion, when they were adopted into Christ and first came to be "in Jesus." At that time, they are reminded, they had put off the old man and put on the new man. That is why they no longer are to continue to walk like the unconverted Gentiles walk.

[110] It is an anachronism to speak of an old Adamic nature as being the old self. Verses 18-19 show the corruption was not inherited by accident of birth.

[111] Since the present tense participle ("being corrupted") is introduced by a past tense infinitive ("lay aside"), the corruption "was" taking place continually before immersion. The unconverted Gentiles were rotting away.

[112] Romans 7:8-11 tell of the power of sin to deceive.

(verse 24) are decisive acts.[113]   The passive verb "be renewed" has the Holy Spirit as the implied agent (as also is implied in Romans 12:2) but is specifically stated in Titus 3:5.[114]

In the spirit of your mind – The "spirit of the mind" is the place or area where the renewing takes place.   However, this expression occurs nowhere else in the New Testament and so has proven difficult to explain.   Three options for "spirit" are available – "spirit" is a reference to the Holy Spirit, the human spirit, or an attitude.   (1) It is doubtful that "spirit" here refers to the Holy Spirit since, though He is called the Spirit "of holiness," "of adoption", "of Christ," "of God," He is never elsewhere in the Bible called "of us" or "of you" or "of your mind."   (2) A stronger case can be made for "spirit" referring to our human spirit.   Appeal can be made to Romans 7:6 (KJV) where Christians are said to serve "in newness of spirit"; or Romans 8:5 where Christians are described as living "according to the spirit" because they set their minds on "the things of the Spirit"; or 2 Corinthians 4:16 where we read "though our outer man is decaying, yet our inner man is being renewed day by day."   Though "spirit of the mind" might mean the spirit (having been born again, John 3:6) by which our mind is governed, it is hard to conceive how our human spirit must be continually renewed, yet this is what the present tense infinitive "renewed" calls for.   (3) The best explanation thus interprets "spirit" to mean an attitude or sentiment[115] that constantly needs renewing.   This would be more in harmony with Romans 12:2 which has the "mind" being the recipient of the renewing.   The idea thus expressed would mirror verses such as Matthew 16:23 which speaks about "setting your mind on God's interests"; or Colossians 3:2 ("set your mind on the things above, not on the things that are on the earth"); or Philippians 4:8 ("Let your mind dwell on these things," namely, whatever is true, honorable, right, pure, lovely, of good repute);   or Colossians

---

[113] In the parallel passage in Colossians 3:10, the putting off of the old man and the putting on of the new man are, as here, represented as things past, and the renewing as a thing still going on.   "The inward man is renewed day by day" (2 Corinthians 4:16).

[114] There are two Greek words translated "renew":   *ananoeo* which occurs only here at Ephesians 4:23, and *anakaineo* which is used at 2 Corinthians 4:16 and Colossians 3:10.   In Ephesians 4:24 the adjective rendered "new" (in the phrase "new self") is *kainos* (as at 2:15) whereas in Colossians 3:10 it is *neos.*   We probably are not to press the literal meanings of *kainos* (new in quality) and *neos* (new in time), either in the verb form or the adjective form, since in parallel passages both words for "new" are used.   The verb forms are both compounded with *ana-,* a preposition which sometimes carries the idea of restoring something to its former state.   However, many compounds with *ana-* express nothing more than change, while implying nothing concerning a possible restoration.   This much is certain, the readers and all Christians are constantly to be changed for the better in the spirit of their minds.

[115] The NIV has "made new in the attitude of your minds."

3:8-12 (where old attitudes such as anger, wrath, malice, slander, and abusive speech are to be laid aside and replaced with a heart of compassion, kindness, humility, gentleness and patience); or Romans 6:11 which speaks about how a man is to think now that he has become a Christian ("consider yourselves to be dead to sin"). It would be an attitude that says, 'I'm done living as the old man wants me to live; I'll live as the new self wants me to live.' "This new attitude and thought pattern – the mind 'in you which also was in Christ' (Philippians 2:5-8) – becomes the source of all words and actions."[116] After conversion, the spirit of the mind is continually renewed and thus the man lives differently from the way Gentiles live.[117]

4:24 – *and put on the new self, which in* the likeness of *God has been created in righteousness and holiness of the truth.*

And put on the new self – This is the *third point* he reminds his readers that they had been taught (verse 21). Just as did the aorist infinitive used of laying aside of the old self did (verse 22), here the aorist tense infinitive ("put on") looks back to the time of their baptism. Both took place at the same time. The new self (*kainon anthropon*, "new man," ASV) is put on at the beginning of the process of renewal.[118]

Which in *the likeness of* God – The Greek reads *kata theon*, "according to God," so the NASB has added "the likeness of" since *kata* is also used elsewhere to express likeness (Galatians 4:28; Hebrews 8:9; 1 Peter 1:15, 4:6). The following words in this verse explain wherein the likeness consists.

Has been created in righteousness and holiness of the truth – "Of the truth" modifies both righteousness and holiness and refers to "the truth" par excellence, the evangelical message, the objective truth given in the gospel (Galatians 2:5,14).[119] "Has been created" recalls Ephesians 2:10 which indicated that when

---

[116] Hayden, *op. cit.,* p.323.

[117] The creation of the new man does not at once stop all our sinning (verse 23), but it does place the new man in control of his life and conduct (verses 25-32). Self-control produces the end to sinning.

[118] Since the new man is put on at the beginning of the process of renewal, rather than at its end, the new man is not a reference to the glorified body which redeemed persons will receive at the second coming of Christ.

[119] In these words "of the truth" there is a contrast to "of deceit" in verse 22.

a person becomes a Christian he is the product of God's creative workmanship.[xx]
2 Corinthians 5:17 says that "if any man is in Christ, he is a new creature ...."
The use of the verb "created" suggests that "the change in people that comes
through faith and the incoming of the Holy Spirit is as great as the act that God
wrought when He created the material universe."[120] This clause describes the
new man as being created like God[121] in two of God's attributes: righteousness
and holiness. Righteousness might speak of God's unchanging love of right, of
how He always is and does right in His relationships to men, or perhaps the point
is that the quality of "righteousness" (*dikaiosune*) belongs to the new man because
God has reckoned righteousness to the one who has faith in Jesus (Romans 4:3,5).
The quality of "holiness" (*hosiotes*) belongs to the new man because God's
creative activity in the new birth has brought the man into harmony with the God
of the universe.[122] The word emphasizes religious conduct, a right relationship
with our Creator God. The only other place in the Scriptures where the words
holiness and righteousness occur together is Luke 1:75 where men are pictured as
serving God "in holiness and righteousness before Him all our days." So, if these
qualities are produced in the lives of Christians, they will have ceased to live like
the unconverted Gentiles do. As Paul continues writing, he becomes specific in
describing the Christian way that arises out of a renewed mind as one responds to
the truth of the gospel and makes Jesus his Lord.

C. Some Rules for the New Life So That Christians Do Not Wrong Their Neighbors.   4:25-32

1. Tell the truth instead of lying.   4:25

**4:25 – *Therefore, laying aside falsehood, SPEAK TRUTH EACH ONE* of you,
*WITH HIS NEIGHBOR, for we are members of one another.***

Therefore – As it did at 4:1 and 17, "therefore" (*dio*) makes a connection between

---

[xx] "Created does not say that man is wholly passive as God does all the creating work.
Spiritual creation is due to God's power in the gospel (Romans 1:16). The power to make the
change in people is as great as was used when God created the universe.

[120] Fields, *op. cit.*, p.139.

[121] Colossians 3:10, a parallel passage, says the new self is being renewed according to
the image of the One who created the new man.

[122] The word translated "holiness" is not the usual word *hagiosune,* which means set apart
for sacred service. The only other place in the New Testament where *hosiotes* occurs is Luke
1:75. See the meaning of these two words discussed in Trench, *Synonyms* ii. §§38.

doctrine (chapters 1-3) and the life a Christian is expected to practice. At this verse Paul introduces a third emphasis involved in walking in a manner worthy of the calling with which Christians have been called. Or perhaps the connection is this: Paul has been contrasting the old life with the new without giving any particulars. Now he will give several specific exhortations to provide us with some particulars.

Laying aside falsehood – The Greek is, literally, "having laid aside falsehood, speak the truth ...," or "since you laid aside falsehood." "Laying aside" (the same verb used at verse 22) is an aorist participle referring back to the time they were baptized. When the old man had been laid aside, so were the evil things, such as falsehood, the old man used to do.[123] The new man they have put on requires that positive virtues be put in their place. The word "falsehood" (*to pseudos*) is broader than lying and speaks of falsehood in all its forms, including concealing the truth or by acting in such a way as to mislead others. It is easy to embroider the details of a story. It is easy to make up some sort of story when a person is making an excuse for not doing, or for not having done, something. "Lying is common among the heathen. Without the guidance of God, unconverted men see no reason to tell the truth when it would be unpleasant or embarrassing to do so. They see no reason to tell the truth when a lie suits their convenience. They see no reason to avoid a lie if it is profitable to lie."[124]

SPEAK TRUTH, EACH ONE *of you*, WITH HIS NEIGHBOR – The words printed in small caps are a quotation from Zechariah 8:16 (LXX). This imperative verb is a present tense in the Greek, which demands that one continually, customarily be speaking truth. "Neighbor," as the rest of the verse indicates, has the meaning of fellow Christian. "With" (*meta*) gives the picture of personal association *with* other Christians, and stresses the need for mutual frankness, candor, and spotless integrity in all our dealings with each other. "It is thought by some that it is strange that Paul should admonish Christians long after their conversion to quit lying and be truthful. The Holy Spirit recognizes things just as they are. But few children of Adam ever attain the divine model of truthfulness, and it requires constant admonition from God and watchfulness on the part of man to be truthful as he should be."[125] God cannot lie (Titus 1:2); the Christian is to be like God (verse 24). It is expected that as God's children we are to be truthful. This first rule for the new life shows that it is in honesty that Christians live the new life.

---

[123] The same regulation against lying is given in Colossians 3:9,10.

[124] Root, *op. cit.*, p.44.

[125] Lipscomb, *op. cit.*, p.88,89.

For we are members of one another – This is the reason why we should not lie but speak truth with each other. Individual Christians are members of a body (Romans 12:5; 1 Corinthians 12:15-27). What would happen if members of a human body sent false signals to other members? "Shall the carpenter's nail-holding hand send false signals to his hammer-swinging hand concerning the location of the nail?"[126] The underlying idea is this: lying (falsehood) loosens the bonds of brotherhood. We are all members of the same spiritual body, and should seek the good of and serve one another.

2. Control yourself.   4:26,27

4:26 – BE ANGRY, AND yet DO NOT SIN; do not let the sun go down on your anger,

BE ANGRY, AND yet DO NOT SIN – The new topic in verses 26 and 27 is self-control. "Paul recommends self-control in two ways: (1) Do not sin. Do not do anything wrong, no matter how furious you are. (2) Do not stay angry: so do not let the sun go down on your wrath."[127] The words printed in small caps indicate these words are a verbatim quotation of the LXX of Psalm 4:4.[128] Three different words for "anger" are used in the New Testament. (1) *Thumos*, boiling anger, selfish anger is forbidden at Ephesians 4:31. (2) *Parorgismos* is exasperation, irritation, bitterness resulting from being provoked, and is not to be allowed to become a settled attitude (4:26b), nor is it something to be provoked in others per Ephesians 6:4. (3) *Orge* is anger aroused under certain conditions, and can be a settled habit of mind. *Orge* ("anger") can be good or bad depending on the cause.[129] Here in Ephesians 4:26a, the present imperative verb *orgizesthe*

---

[126] Hayden, *op. cit.*, p.323.

[127] Root, *ibid.*

[128] The KJV and ERV, following the Masoretic Text, render Psalm 4:4 as "Stand in awe, and sin not" (i.e., let wholesome fear keep you from sinning). The NASB at Psalm 4:4 has "Tremble, and do not sin" (with a marginal note that the trembling may be from anger or fear). The Hebrew verb *ragaz* may denote a variety of emotional disturbances, including trembling with fear or anger (Brown, Driver, Briggs, *Lexicon*, p.919). In the RSV the opening words of Psalm 4:4 are rendered, "Be angry, but sin not," probably to make it match this verse in Ephesians.

[129] Anger that is a response to personal offense because of slights or hurts imposed by others is bad. Anger that is an expression of opposition and indignation to wrong in loyalty to God is sinless.

("be angry") commands a continuous action, a righteous indignation against sin and sinful things.　Anger is not necessarily sinful.　Psalm 7:11 says that God is angry with the wicked every day.　There are times when a Christian should be angry, as was Jesus, on occasion (Mark 3:5).　However, because anger can stir one to vigorous action, care must be exercised so that anger does not lead to wrong actions.　That is what is warned about in the imperative "do not sin;" the Greek forbids the continuance of an action already going on (i.e., "stop sinning").

Do not let the sun go down on your anger – These words are not printed in small caps, though they may reflect the rest of Psalm 4:4 in the LXX which speaks of contrition for what was wrongly said as one lies on his bed at the close of the day. The word is *parorgismos,* "exasperation, irritation, bitterness."　Righteous anger can turn into bitterness, and should this occur, self-control is called for.　The feeling of bitterness must be quenched.　"Forgive us of our sins, as we forgive those who have sinned against us," Jesus taught.　Of course, we take the apostle's meaning as being with all possible speed to depose our embitterment and exasperation to others, not understanding him so literally that we may permit ourselves to be angry until sunset, and, say if you lived in Alaska, you could be bitter for 6 months because of their long day.

4:27 – *and do not give the devil an opportunity.*

And do not give the devil an opportunity – This construction in Greek again is the one which forbids the continuance of an action already going on.[130]　It is literally, "stop giving the devil opportunity."　The devil, who is also known as Satan (Revelation 20:2),[131] is the "tempter" of the brethren.[132]　When we nurse bitterness he is ready with his suggestions that we express that anger by hurting someone.　"An unreconciled quarrel provides the devil opportunity to drive the wedge deeper.　The devil is a powerful enemy,　and we dare not underestimate

---

[130] *Me* ("not") with a present imperative commands a cessation of an action already commenced.　(*Me* with an aorist subjunctive is a prohibition of an action not yet begun.)

[131] In his first recorded sermon (Acts 13:10), as in his later epistles (Ephesians 4:27, 6:11; 1 Timothy 3:6-7; 6:9; 2 Timothy 2:26; Titus 2:3), Paul used "devil" to identify the evil one.　In his earlier epistles, and less frequently in his later epistles (1Timothy 1:20, 5:15), Paul used the name "Satan" (Romans 16:20; 1 Corinthians 5:5, 7:5; 2 Corinthians 2:11, 11:14, 12:7; 1 Thessalonians 2:18; 2 Thessalonians 2:9).

[132] In the New Testament the noun *diabolos* regularly identifies the devil, not some man who may be a slanderer of Christians.

him.   Given even the slightest opportunity, the devil will enter and may take full possession as the proverbial camel who got his nose in the tent.   A Christian should never supply such an opening."[133]   We must be in control of ourselves. Verses 26 and 27 indicate the practice of self-control is one of the characteristic features of the new life that Christians live.

3.   Work hard and be generous.   4:28

*4:28 – Let him who steals steal no longer; but rather let him labor, performing with his own hands what is good, in order that he may have **something** to share with him who has need.*

Let him who steals steal no longer – The topic is helpfulness.   It looks like some of the habits of the "old man" were still being practiced by the Christians to whom this letter was addressed.   The Greek is "the one who is stealing, let him no longer be stealing."   Stealing was a common vice in the ancient world.[134]   It was common at the docks, and it was common in the public baths where clothing and personal effects were often the objects of theft.   There are other forms of theft that are just as wrong.   The tradesman who deals in short weights and measures, and overcharges for his wares, is a thief.   The servant who does not occupy faithfully in his master's service the hours and faculties for which he is paid is a thief.   The physician who prolongs his visits to his patient beyond what is necessary in order to get gain is a thief.   "It may seem strange that Christians should have to be taught not to steal.   But stealing is not uncommon.   Nowadays there are many sophisticated forms of stealing – embezzlement, cheating on tax reports, driving hard bargains, misrepresenting goods, loafing on the employer's time, shortening an employee's time, cheating on examinations, etc.   Let him that stole – regardless of how he did it, or what he stole – steal no more."[135]

But rather let him labor, performing with his own hands – Instead of making a living by stealth or dishonesty, the new man gets a permanent job, and works at it each day.   "Every Christian should have some calling, business, or profession,

---

[133] Tesh, *op. cit.*, p.397.

[134] The Greek verb "to steal" is the one used in the Septuagint to translate the commandment "You shall not steal" (Exodus 20:15), quoted in Matthew 19:18; Mark 10:19; Luke 18:20; Romans 13:9.

[135] Fields, *op. cit.*, p.143.

by which he may support himself.   The Savior was carpenter; Paul a tentmaker; and no man is disgraced by being able to build a house or to construct a tent."[136] The word "labor" here is the synonym for work which denotes the weariness which results from exhausting toil.[137]   "The new man is not selfish.   He wants to give full value for all that he receives.   So he works instead of stealing.[138]

What is good – "Good" (*agathos*) means useful or helpful.   "Earning a living is not the only thing to be considered.   Paul tells us to work at the thing which is good.   A farmer or grocer provides good food; a dentist or plumber gives good service.   But what is good about publishing pornography, pushing dope, or bottling booze?"[139]

In order that he may have *something* to share with him who has need – The Christian is a new man.   "The old man stole from others to satisfy his own need; the new man gives to others to supply their need."[140]   The motive for laboring given here is not the only true object of all Christian labor, for subsistence is an object of labor, and providing for one's own family is another.   In addition to this one at Ephesians 4:28, another verse dealing with the Christian work ethic is Titus 3:14.   "Him who has need" is anyone who is poorer than yourself.   "'To share' (*metadidonai*) means to distribute personally rather than by remote control through some agent or official."[141]   The new life is a life of generosity.   It takes the drudgery out of labor if, while working, we are contemplating how we can use the money we earn to help others.

4. Be clean in speech.   4:29

4:29 – *Let no unwholesome word proceed from your mouth, but only such* a word *as is good for edification according to the need* of the moment, *that it may give grace to those who hear.*

---

[136] Barnes, *op. cit.*, p.91.

[137] Geo. R. Berry, *New Testament Synonyms* (Chicago: Wilcox and Follett, 1948), §53, p. 135.   Thayer, *op. cit.*, p. 355.

[138] Root, *op. cit.*, p.45.

[139] Phillips, *op. cit.*, p.100.

[140] Root, *ibid.*

[141] Wood, *op. cit.*, p.65.

Let no unwholesome word proceed from your mouth – Here is the fourth in a series of specific exhortations about behaviors that will characterize the new way of life. This one (like James 1:26) calls for the practice of self-control over the words that come out of the mouth. "Unwholesome" translates *sapros*, which means "rotten, worn out, unfit for use, worthless, bad."[142] The Greek word is used literally of rotten fruit (Matthew 12:33) and spoiled fish (Matthew 13:48). When used figuratively for speech, it may carry the idea of foul language or words intended to harm another person's reputation. "We are too familiar with the corruptions of profanity and blaspheming, belittling God; or vulgarity and obscenity, besmirching man; or gossip and lying, tearing down another in a vain attempt to advance oneself. These are not for the mind or mouth of the follower of Christ."[143] "We find rotten talk increasing in TV programs, movies, printed material, and everyday conversation in homes and schools and in work places and market places. A Christian does not follow this popular trend. He keeps his own speech clean, specializing in talk that is good to the use of edifying."[144] If the rotten word is already on the tongue, self-control would lead to swallowing it rather than speaking it.

But only such *a word* as is good for edification according to the need *of the moment* – Self-control over our speech requires some forethought concerning the effect of our words on those who hear them. A Christian has not done all one is expected to do if only the wrong is avoided. Christians also have positive commands to obey. In the case of the words they permit themselves to speak, the words they permit to come out of their mouths are words that will make others spiritually better or will build up the church (Ephesians 2:21,22; 4:12,16). "Edification" seems to suggest a need in the hearer's spiritual condition. So words good for edification may be words of instruction, or exhortation to duty, or words of comfort, or words of rebuke with a call to repentance. "According to the need of the moment" says that the effort to build up must be adapted to the place and time and to the persons whose edification is sought.

That it may give grace to those who hear – "Grace" at this place probably has its broad meaning of "benefit," as it has at 2 Corinthians 1:15. As the Christian controls the words that come out of the mouth, the words which will be a spiritual blessing or a benefit to the hearer are especially what are desired. As Moffatt

---

[142] Thayer, *op. cit.*, p.568.

[143] Hayden, *op. cit.*, p.324.

[144] Root, *ibid.*

translates it, Eliphaz the Temanite paid Job a tremendous compliment. "Your words," he said, "have kept men on their feet" (Job 4:4). Such are the results that every Christian aims for as he or she speaks.

5. Be led by the Spirit.   4:30

4:30 – *And do not grieve the Holy Spirit of God, by whom you were sealed for the day of redemption.*

And do not grieve the Holy Spirit of God – As was true in verse 27, the Greek construction here is the one which forbids the continuance of an action already going on. It is literally, "stop grieving the Holy Spirit." These words are addressed to Christians, and are a plain warning that it is possible to grieve the Holy Spirit. "Grieve" means to afflict with sorrow, to make sad or sorrowful. "In some languages the equivalent of making someone sad is 'to cause them to cry'."[145] To grieve means to act in such a way as to produce pain in the heart of a friend who loves us.[146] When any Christian refuses to walk as a new man ought, he grieves the Holy Spirit. If we let the near context tell us how one may grieve the Holy Spirit, it would be by uttering unwholesome words. Rotten words would be repugnant to one who is Holy. The context also suggests the sins of falsehood, anger that is cherished and bitterness when provoked, dishonesty, and ill will (verse 31) are ways one may grieve the Spirit. The indwelling Spirit has been prompting our spirits about the kind of life to be lived (Romans 8:4,5). Refusal to listen breaks His heart. The Holy Spirit may be resisted (Acts 7:51), vexed (Isaiah 63:10), and quenched (1 Thessalonians 5:19), as well as grieved.

By whom you were sealed for the day of redemption – "The day of redemption" refers to the second coming of Christ, when He will redeem His people finally and completely, clothing them with their glorified bodies. Ephesians 1:13-14 introduced the topic of being sealed by the Spirit. The tense in the verb "sealed" points to the time of their baptism when they received the Holy Spirit. The indwelling Holy Spirit is God's seal of ownership, evidence that we are His adopted children. This clause furnishes the motive why one would not want to continue to grieve the Holy Spirit. Via the indwelling Holy Spirit, Christians have the security and assurance of realizing their complete redemption. It would

---

[145] Bratcher, *op. cit.*, p.119.

[146] If the Holy Spirit can be grieved, the Holy Spirit is a personality, and not just an impersonal influence.

be an eternal loss were they to grieve the Holy Spirit, and lose their security.[147]

6. Be free from ill will.   4:31

4:31 – *Let all bitterness and wrath and anger and clamor and slander be put away from you, along with all malice.*

Let all bitterness – The general topic in verse 31 is be free from ill will. Here in verse 31 the writer names six sins that result from ill will, all of which should have been put away when the old man was put away. "Bitterness" (*pikra*) is bitter feelings, long standing resentment, peevishness, spitefulness. It is a feeling or behavior that belongs to the old man, a feeling or temper or frame of mind which willfully retains and cherishes angry and resentful feelings. It broods over insults and slights received. It is ready to take offense and liable to break out in anger at any moment. It is a feeling that makes it hard to be reconciled. It harbors resentments and keeps scores of wrongs (something love does not do, 1 Corinthians 13:5).

And wrath – The Greek word is *thumos* which was explained above at verse 26. It is a temporary fury, a boiling over in anger that soon subsides, like the flame which comes from straw which quickly blazes up and just as quickly subsides. Such temporary outbursts of anger often arises from an imagination of an insult offered to us.

And anger – This Greek word is *orge* which was also explained above at verse 26. There is no real contradiction here to Ephesians 4:26 which spoke of legitimate anger, namely, righteous indignation. The anger that is to be put away is all anger that is not righteous anger. It might be long-lived anger as compared to wrath. Think of lasting anger as opposed to forgiving one another.

And clamor – The Greek word *krauge* denotes angry shouting, the raised and strident voice (cp. Acts 23:9). Clamor is the loud self-assertion and recrimination of a passionate and angry man who attempts to shout down his opponents. "Clamor is loud talk that often accompanies anger.   I do not like

---

[147] Writers in Calvinistic circles will comment after this fashion: "Although the Holy Spirit may be grieved, yet he will never leave the believer. He is our seal. We have been sealed unto the day of redemption (Ephesians 1:13)" (Martin, *op. cit.*, p.1312). This commentator's doubt about the doctrine of *unconditional* eternal security has been addressed in notes at Ephesians 1:13. He emphasizes that the New Testament teaches the security of those who continue to be faithful believers.

being yelled at, and other people probably do not appreciate it if I yell at them. Have I learned to keep my voice down? Better still, have I developed self-control to such a point that I do not even feel like yelling?"[148] Whenever we realize in any discussion or argument that our voice is raised, it is time to stop. It would save a great deal of heartbreak in the world if we simply learned to keep our voices down. "You must no longer yell at people or insult them."[149]

And slander -- The Greek word is *blasphemeia* which often refers to blasphemy against God and divine things. However, the context here seems to require it to be understood of speaking evil against man, or human things, as it sometimes is elsewhere in the New Testament (e.g., 1 Corinthians 4:13, 10:30; Colossians 3:8; Titus 3:2). The translation "slander" (or "railing, ASV) refers to the deliberate running down of another's character, the attacking of the reputation of those with whom one is angry, or exciting an evil feeling against them in the minds of others.

Be put away from you – The verb "put away" which means 'let it be removed and have no more to do with it,' covers all the sins named in this verse. The Christian is to get rid of each and every one of them. In the parallel passage, Colossians 3:8, the command is as decisive and as inclusive as here.

Along with all malice – Malice (*kakia*) is bad feelings, the intent to do harm or evil to others. It may be saying that if there are any other forms of malice besides the ones already specified, they are to be put away. It may be saying that all the sins listed in verse 31 are forms of malice which is something in the heart. Verse 31 provides a convenient checklist of attitudes the new man should no longer permit himself to have, and indicates that controlling our attitudes – so that ill will is stamped out – is another of the characteristic features of the new life the Christians live.

7. Be full of good will. 4:32

4:32 – Be kind to one another, tender-hearted, forgiving each other, just as God in Christ also has forgiven you.

And be kind to one another – Living the Christian life is not just observing a list of prohibitions (verse 31). It is also cultivating positive virtues (verse 32). The same list of virtues is found in Colossians 3:12,13. "Be" (*ginesthe*) probably is

---

[148] Root, *ibid.*

[149] Bratcher, *op. cit.*, p.121.

equal to "become" in this context. Christians have some growing to do. They have not yet attained "the measure of the stature which belongs to the fullness of Christ" (Ephesians 4:13). One virtue the new man works to develop is kindness. *Chrestos* ("kind") means to be benevolent, gracious, sweet, of amiable disposition, pleasant.[150] It is the desire to make others happy by doing good to them and by helping them to attain their goal of Christian living and being productive members of the body of Christ. "To one another" is a reciprocal pronoun. It pictures the subjects taking turns being kind to the other person.

Tender-hearted – The Greek word (*eusplangchnoi*) is a rare adjective used only here and in 1 Peter 3:8 in the New Testament.[151] "Tender-hearted" or "compassionate" are possible ways to translate the word here, since it seems to express the same idea that a similar expression is translated "a heart of compassion" at Colossians 3:12. The tender-hearted person yearns for the other's welfare, and "is especially disposed to show kindness to the faults of erring brethren."[152]

Forgiving each other – The Greek verb is *charizomai* (not *aphiemi*, the word usually used of God forgiving our sins); this word means "to do a favor to, do something agreeable or pleasant to, to forgive in the sense of treating the offending party graciously."[153] "Each other" in the Greek is literally "forgiving *yourselves*," which reminds us that since individual Christians are members of a body, what was done to another was really done to themselves.[154] Treating the offending party graciously "puts a time limit on anger and stops malice dead in its tracks. It is the practical answer to the irritations that are inevitable where

---

[150] We had a cognate word at Ephesians 2:7. Kindness is as concerned with the feelings of other people as it is with its own feelings. It is as concerned with the sorrows, the struggles, the problems of other people, as it is with its own.

[151] "The word in the original has been much misunderstood, as is shown by its frequent translation elsewhere as *bowels*. 'Heart' is correct. In the classical Greek this word referred to the organs of the upper body cavity; specifically the heart, lungs, and liver, as distinguished from the organs of the lower cavity (see the lexicons)." Martin, *op. cit.*, p.1312.

[152] Barnes, *op. cit.*, p.94.

[153] Wuest, *op. cit.*, p.117.

[154] At times the intensive pronoun *heautois* ("yourselves") is treated as though it were the reciprocal pronoun *allelois* ("one another"), both in classical Greek and in the New Testament (e.g., 1 Corinthians 6:7; Colossians 3:13,16). If that is the case here, this clause speaks of a reciprocal forgiveness (generous attitude).

people live in close association. Not every difference can be removed by even the most careful explanation, and not every hurt can be assuaged even by the assurance that it was not intended."[155]   But kind actions may help heal the wound.

Just as God in Christ also has forgiven you – "Just as," which could be expanded to "in the same way as" or "just like," shows that we are to take God's dealings with us as a model for our dealings with our neighbor.   The Greek verb here translated "forgiven" is the same verb (*charizomai*) just translated "forgiving."   Paul is saying that as God has forgiven us He was in fact treating the offending parties graciously.[156]   Though Paul uses a different word for "forgive" than did Jesus, Paul here seems to show acquaintance with Jesus' words which follow the Model Prayer (Matthew 6:14,15) or with the parable of the unmerciful servant (Matthew 18:23-35).   We realize how much of a debt God has graciously forgiven; we therefore graciously forgive the small offenses our neighbors commit against us.   The Greek translated "in Christ" does not seem to equal "for Christ's sake" (as the KJV translates), but rather calls attention to what Jesus did as being the supreme example of God's generous attitude toward us.[157]

> Verse 32 is a convenient checklist of three positive virtues the Christian wants to cherish and develop.   In the past week, have I really gone out of my way to help someone or to avoid hurting someone?   Am I sensitive?   Whose sorrow has really touched me in the past week?   Whose need have I seen and supplied?   Whose joy has made me genuinely glad?   Is there any offender whom I cannot or will not forgive as fully as God has forgiven me?   This is crucial.[158]

---

[155] Hayden, *op. cit.*, p.324.

[156] Many ancient authorities (including P[46]), as the ASV/NASB margin points out, have "us" instead of "you" at the end of the verse.   One reason why Greek manuscripts oscillate so much between *hemeis* ("we") and *humeis* ("you") is that the pronunciation of these two pronouns was practically identical in the first century AD and onward.   Hence, if a scribe was copying by dictation, he might well put the one for the other, especially in a context like this, where either pronoun makes good sense.

[157] "The KJV rendering, 'for Christ's sake,' is objectionable every way: it is not literal; it omits the characteristic feature of the Epistle, "in Christ," losing the force of the consideration that the forgiveness was dispensed by the Father, acting with or wholly one with the Son; and it gives a shade of countenance to the great error that the Father personally was not disposed to forgive until he was prevailed on to do so by the interposition of the Son."   Blaikie, *op. cit.*, p.154.

[158] Root, *ibid.*

D. An Exhortation to Imitate God and Walk in Love.   5:1-14

5:1 -- *Therefore be imitators of God, as beloved children;*

Therefore – As the word "therefore" has done at 4:1,17,25, it serves here to connect this new exhortation to all that was written in the first three chapters of this letter concerning all that God has done for the readers.[1]

Be imitators of God – As it did in 4:32, the present imperative "be" *(ginesthe)* probably is equal to "become." Now that you have put off the old man, become an imitator of God so that you are ever like Him. Perhaps the attribute of God that is to be imitated is His attribute of love (verse 2). Love is God's essential character (1 John 4:16). The Greek word for "imitators" is the one from which we get our word mimic.[2] "If we have ever seen a child mimic his father, imitating the father's walk, his mannerisms, his way of talking, we have an idea of how the Christian is to live. As children of God we are to mimic our heavenly Father, thinking His thoughts after Him, repeating His word to the world, imitating His truth and self-control and generosity and cleanness and good will (Ephesians 4:25-32)."[3]

As beloved children – This is the reason for the exhortation to become imitators of God. "Beloved" reminds the readers that they are loved by God (cp. Ephesians 1:4,5, "in love He predestined us to adoption as sons," and 1 John 3:1, "see how great a love the Father has bestowed upon us"). "Children" translates the Greek word that means "little born ones" and reflects the fact that the readers have been born again. Since they have experienced His love, they have a standard to uphold, a path to follow. Children should always strive to imitate what is good in a father who loves them.

5:2 – *and walk in love, just as Christ also loved you, and gave Himself up for us, an offering and a sacrifice to God as a fragrant aroma.*

And walk in love – The present imperative verb says   Christians are to be con-

---

[1] A less likely interpretation of "therefore" connects it with what was said in 4:32, making the idea this – just like God in Christ forgave you, you should forgive one another, and thus you will be imitators of God.

[2] This is the only place in the Bible where that bold word "imitate" is applied to the Christian's relation to God.   However, there are many passages that express the same idea (e.g., Matthew 5:48; Luke 6:36; 1 Peter 1:15).

[3] Phillips, *op. cit.*, p.101.

stantly walking in love.   It looks as though love for our brother/fellow man is the love intended (cf. the following context).   *Agape* (one of four Greek words for love[4]) is doing what is spiritually best for the other person.   It is a behavior that can be willed.

Just as Christ also loved you and gave Himself up for us -- "Just as" indicates there is a special example of love we are to copy.   The aorist tense ("loved") likely points to Calvary as the one supreme act of love on Christ's part.[5]   The phrase "for us" is *huper*, and here probably means "in behalf of us."   "Gave Himself" seems to refer to more than just Calvary (to which the previous verb "loved" seems to have reference).   Perhaps Lipscomb has best explained it:

> He who was the Lord (John 1:1) in heaven, with God, endowed with honors and glories with the Father that surpassed all other honors and glories of the universe, saw man had brought death and ruin, temporal and eternal upon himself, that he was helpless and hopeless in that ruin.   With man in this condition, heaven lost its charm to Him.   He gave it all up.   He came to earth, clothed Himself with human weakness to rescue man.   Jesus Christ, imbued with the true spirit of heroism, served and suffered for man.   He found more pleasure in the crown of thorns and the cross of Calvary, with the door open for man's return to His Father's house, than He found in heaven, with all its glories, with the door shut against man.[6]

"Gave himself" speaks of the voluntariness of what Christ did as He became incarnate; it was this that made His sacrifice on Calvary so pleasant in God's sight.

An offering and a sacrifice to God, as a fragrant aroma – The same words, "sacrifice and offering," are found in close connection in Hebrews 10:5 in a quotation from Psalm 40:6, a passage which goes on to indicate that it was in His fleshly body that Jesus would provide the kind of sacrifice that would take away the sins, something that the blood of bulls and goats could never do.   "Offerings" (*prosphera*) were of grain or cereal (an offering without blood) whereas "sacrifice" (*thusia*) was an offering made to God by killing an animal and burning

---

[4] There are four Greek words for "love" – *eros* is sexual love; *storge* is family love; *philia* is friendly love; *agape* is Christian love, doing what is spiritually best for the other person.   1 Corinthians 13 describes how *agape* acts.   Here Paul gives us the example of Christ to help us understand what it means to love.

[5] There is a manuscript variation in this verse, the pronouns varying between "you" and "us."   A number of manuscripts, including P[46], Aleph[3], D, G, and Textus Receptus, have "even as Christ loved *us*" in the first half of the phrase.   In the second half of the phrase, "gave Himself up for *us*" is supported by P[46], Aleph*, A, D, F, K, L and Textus Receptus.

[6] Lipscomb, *op. cit.*, p.97.

it on an altar, designed to make atonement for sin.   Perhaps those commentators are correct who have thought that in these two expressions are intended both the peace-offerings and the sin-offerings which were presented to God with a view to the restoration of broken fellowship.   The burning flesh of a sacrifice would give off an odor; the figure of speech translated "fragrant aroma" pictures the smell of that burning flesh as ascending to God and being pleasing to His nostrils.[7]   As is explained in Philippians 4:18 ("a sacrifice acceptable, well-pleasing to God"), to call the odor of a sacrifice a "fragrant aroma" was the Old Testament way of saying a sacrifice was pleasing and acceptable to God.   Offerings were acceptable to God when the worshiper's heart was in them.   Jesus' heart was certainly in His sacrifice and God was well-pleased with Christ's loving sacrifice. It was acceptable to Him.

1.   In purity of life.   5:3

5:3 -- *But immorality or any impurity or greed must not even be named among you, as is proper among saints;*

But – "But" means what is written in this verse is a contrast with "walk in love" with which the previous verse began.   "But" also suggests that all the sins about to be listed are not manifestations of love but of selfishness.   In fact, in verses 3-14, Paul identifies four areas where we exhibit love for our brother: by our moral purity, by purity in our speech, by walking as children of light rather than participating with them in their sins, and in exposing evil for what it is.   From the fact that catalogues of vices are found frequently in Paul's epistles (Romans 1:29-31; 1 Corinthians 5:11, 6:9ff; Galatians 5:19ff; Colossians 3:5ff), it has been inferred that in the earliest days of Christianity, a fairly uniform body of teaching about Christian behavior was communicated to the infant churches.

Immorality – Sexual misconduct and sexual relations outside of marriage are a violation of love for the other person.[8]   In the Bible, marriage is permanent, monogamous, heterosexual.

Or any impurity – The word "impurity" (*akarthasia*)   has already been used at

---

[7] Noah offered up his offering unto the Lord after the flood, and the Lord "smelled the soothing aroma" (Genesis 8:21).   The critics have had much sport out of belittling such descriptions of God as if He were in human form (anthropomorphisms).   But if the Scriptures say that God "smelled the soothing aroma," we are not so wise that we can describe what God did any more accurately.   The important thing is that the offering pleased the Lord and made the worshiper accepted.

[8] "Immorality" translates the Greek word *porneia*, which is the source of our English word "pornography."   "The Greek word is a general term for sexual misconduct" (Shannon, *op. cit.,* p.403).

Ephesians 4:19 as a characteristic of living as unconverted Gentiles live. The word is used of the "unnatural and perverted indulgence of the lusts as in Sodom (Genesis 19:5-8) as pictured in Romans 1:27-32."[9] Such behavior is primarily selfish, not loving.

Or greed – A greedy man is a man who, in pursuit of gold or sexual pleasures, neglects his soul, his intellect, his heart, and any love for the other person. "Greed" is only interested in "me" and "what I can get." See Ephesians 4:19, where the same Greek word *pleonexia* is translated "greediness." In Colossians 3:5 *pleonexia* is pictured as being idolatry, since it makes a god of what it seeks to possess.

Must not even be named among you – That is, do not let them exist. "Each Christian's conduct should be so spotless that there would not be a chance that any rumor or gossip about sexual misconduct would ever get started. The expression may be satisfactorily rendered as 'no one should ever have a reason to talk about any of you ever doing such things'."[10]

As is proper among saints – "The position of sainthood or separation to God, in which the gospel places the Christians, is so far apart from the license of the world as to make it utterly inappropriate for such sins to be found among Christians."[11]

2. In purity of speech. 5:4-6

5:4 -- *and* **there must be no** *filthiness and silly talk, or coarse jesting, which are not fitting, but rather giving of thanks.*

And *there must be no* **filthiness** – This is the only time the word *aischrotes* occurs in the New Testament, though a related noun, *aischrologian*, (rendered "abusive speech" in the NASB and "filthy language" in the NKJV) occurs at Colossians 3:8. When *aischrotes* occurs elsewhere in Greek literature it usually speaks of shameful, obscene, or immoral conduct. Since the rest of this verse refers to speech, perhaps *aischrotes* means that not only dirty deeds, but dirty jokes and dirty gestures have no place in the Christian's life.

And silly talk – The Greek word *morologia* is translated "foolish talking" in the ASV. The talk of fools describes the kind of talking which has ceased to distin-

---

[9] Lipscomb, *op. cit.*, p.98.

[10] Bratcher, *op. cit.*, p.126.

[11] Salmond, *op. cit.*, p.352.

guish what is right or wrong, wise or foolish, noble or base, and therefore is not intended to instruct, edify, or profit the hearer. Perhaps it includes jesting talk about sin, or joking about sin. The Christian will do well to remember the words of the Lord Jesus, "That every idle word that men shall speak, they shall give account thereof in the day of judgment" (Matthew 12:36).

Or coarse jesting – The Greek word here is *eutrapelia* which literally is "an easy turn of speech." So often the jesting of the world is based on double meanings of words. Jokes are formed using words that can be taken with two meanings, one harmless, the other shady. Some comedians think they are not funny unless they utter a few such jokes. The problem with such jests is that they are so easily remembered, which is the reason for controlling our speech so such words do not come out. We have harmed the other person, rather than extending love.

Which are not fitting – "Not fitting" says such words are "out of character" in a Christian. "They are not the proper engagement of the mind and tongue of the 'new man' who 'in the likeness of God has been created in righteousness and true holiness' (Ephesians 4:24)."[12] "They will soon be in heaven – and a man who has any impressive sense of that sober truth will habitually feel that he has much else to do than to make men laugh about sin."[13]

But rather giving of thanks – The sentence is incomplete; we must supply a suitable verb to complete the sense, something like "the giving of thanks *is fitting.*" While the Greek word *eucharistia* is understood by some to mean "gracious speech," i.e., words that are spiritually helpful (cp. Ephesians 4:29, words "for edification ... that it may give grace to those who hear"; Colossians 4:6, "let your speech always be with grace"), Paul elsewhere uses *eucharistia* to mean thanksgiving, gratitude (e.g., 2 Corinthians 9:11,12). There is a delightful play on sounds in Greek, *eucharistia* (which is fitting for the Christian) contrasted with *eutrapelia* (which is not fitting). It is much more in harmony with Christian character to use the tongue to speak of those temporal and spiritual blessings which we have received and for which we are grateful to God than to use it for the things Paul has just said are not fitting for the Christian. After all, our tongues are made to serve the Lord.

5:5 -- *For this you know with certainty, that no immoral or impure person or covetous man, who is an idolater, has an inheritance in the kingdom of Christ and God.*

---

[12] Hayden, *op. cit.,* p.325.

[13] Barnes, *op. cit.,* p.97.

For this you know with certainty – What follows in verses 5 and 6 is intended to be a reason to avoid the sins just named in verses 3 and 4. This passage warns about the serious consequences of continual sinning. The knowledge of the consequences comes from testimony, from revelation ("know" is *oida,* knowledge that comes from testimony). "Know with certainty" translates two different Greek words for "know": the verb *oida,* "to know," and the participle of *ginosko,* "to know."[14] The verb may be taken either as indicative or as imperative. The NEB ("for be very sure of this") treats the verb as being imperative, thus making the words which follow to be a solemn warning which accompanies the apostle's ban on impurity in deed, thought, or word. The NASB treats it as indicative, which makes the words express an ever-growing certainty based on what the Word of God says.

That no immoral or impure person – It appears that "immoral" summarizes verse 3,[15] and "impure" summarizes verse 4. While what this verse says is true of the immoral and impure pagan, it is also true of the immoral or impure Christian. In the Greek the negative particle negates the verb: thus it reads "every immoral or impure or covetous man, who is an idolater, does not have an inheritance in the kingdom ...."

Or covetous man, who is an idolater – On the term "covetous" see the word "greed" in verse 3.[16] Colossians 3:5 also stigmatizes covetousness as being idolatry. Whatever becomes the chief object of our desire, so as to claim our chief attention and love, is an idol. We are worshiping a false god, just as much as the man who bows down to a totem. Jesus Himself said, "You cannot serve God and wealth."

Has an inheritance in the kingdom of Christ and God – What is the "kingdom" here? It is the whole, glorified state, the goal of God's whole plan of salvation for believers (Matthew 25:34). It is the state of things after Christ turns all over to the Godhead (1 Corinthians 15:24,28). The verb in the Greek is a present tense ("has"), not a future tense ("shall have"). A man has salvation or condemnation now (John 3:36). Christians, in the indwelling of the Holy Spirit, do have a pledge of a future inheritance (Ephesians 1:14); however, this verse indicates they

---

[14] The Greek with its two words for "know" reflects the Hebrew way of expressing emphasis (e.g., "dying you shall die" = "you shall surely die").

[15] "Here the term 'immoral' is masculine, and speaks of a man who prostitutes his body to another's lust for hire, a male prostitute" (Wuest, *op. cit.*, p.122).

[16] Some manuscripts read *hos* (so A, D, K, P, Syr.[H], Syr.[P]), which makes the relative pronoun "who" refer to all three nouns (immoral, impure, covetous), and it says that any of these sins is tantamount to idolatry. The better reading is *ho* (see Aleph, B, 67, Jerome), so the relative pronoun "who" refers only to "covetous man."

forfeit that inheritance if they are immoral or impure or covetous. 1 Corinthians 6:9-11 teaches the same truth. So does Romans 6:12-23 and 8:4,5,13. Habitual and unrepented sin will result in a Christian's being lost. Unrepented sin will result in exclusion from the body of Christ now, and from heaven later. "One dare not treat the sins Paul has just listed as trivial, for too much is at stake. The person whose life is controlled by one of these evils has no inheritance in the kingdom of Him who is both [the] Christ and God."[17]

5:6 -- *Let no one deceive you with empty words, for because of these things the wrath of God comes upon the sons of disobedience.*

Let no one deceive you with empty words – The "empty words" (words without the substance of truth or reality) alluded to likely affirmed that the filthy behavior just condemned in verses 4 and 5 really does not exclude one from the kingdom of God. "Let no one deceive you" is an imperative in the Greek; this is a command the readers are to obey. Who might try to argue with the believers that such vices were after all harmless? The "one" who tries to deceive Christians could be anyone – an unbelieving friend of a Christian who might try to encourage the Christian to sin by using deceitful arguments that this will not hurt you, or a nominal Christian who downplays the evil of certain sins that are pleasant to them,[18] or a teacher of incipient Gnostic ideas (if we let a contemporary letter to the Colossians written to the same general area help us as we try to identify who the deceivers might be).

For because of these things – Paul here states the reason Christians must not let bad men deceive them into thinking they can sin without being hurt. "These things" are the sins just mentioned in verses 3-5. Scripture elsewhere contains similar warnings about the consequences of habitual sin. Romans 2:8,9 declare that habitual sin will bring wrath at the final judgment. 1 Corinthians 6:11, written to Christians, affirms that the sins listed in verses 8-10 of the same chapter will exclude their practitioners from the kingdom of God.

The wrath of God comes – At Ephesians 2:2,3 the wrath of God has already been introduced. In this verse, it evidently is a reference to the wrath of God at the

---

[17] Shannon, *op. cit.*, p.403. The Greek has one article before two nouns connected by "and." Sharp's rule of grammar makes both words "Christ" and "God" to be descriptions of the same person. This is an affirmation of Christ's deity (cp. 2 Thessalonians 1:12; 1 Timothy 5:21, 6:13).

[18] An interpretive issue difficult to decide is whether the "sons of disobedience" referred to later in this verse are the ones attempting to deceive the Christian, or whether it refers to Christians who, having been deceived, become disobedient to the Lord. The comments offered above reflect the rather common experience of Christians when it comes to folk who can be guilty of trying to deceive the Christian.

final judgment.[19]   "Comes" is a present tense verb indicating that divine retribution is so certain that it can be described as already on the way (see 2 Peter 2 and Jude).[20]

Upon the sons of disobedience – This expression is a Hebraism describing people who are characterized by disobedience (see Ephesians 2:2 where the same expression was a reference to the unregenerate).   The disobedience in view is doing the sins just enumerated that God has told men not to do.   So, the implication of the verse seems to be this: even though a person is a Christian, if he habitually disobeys God, he will experience God's wrath.

3. In walking as children of the light.   5:7-10

5:7 -- *Therefore do not be partakers with them;*

Therefore – This word points back to the wrath of God which is coming upon the sons of disobedience.   This verse introduces the third of four areas where we Christians are encouraged to exhibit love for our brothers by our pure behavior.

Do not be partakers – The Greek construction (the present imperative with *me*) prohibits the continuance of an action already going on.   "Stop being partakers with them" is the idea in the Greek.   Stop participating with them in their sins. Stop sharing in their punishment.

With them – "Them" may refer either to the "sons of disobedience" or to the folk who were trying to deceive the Christians (verse 6).   Don't get mixed up or involved with persons who are excluding themselves from the kingdom by their iniquity.

5:8 -- *for you were formerly darkness, but now you are light in the Lord; walk as children of light*

---

[19] "Note the reference to the *wrath of God* in verse 6. Some people have said that the God of the New Testament is a God of love, in contrast to the God of the Old Testament who is a God of wrath.   There is only one God, and He is the same in both the Old and New Testaments.   The *wrath of God* is as plainly taught in the New Testament, as it is in the Old.   Those who desire to reject Christ should carefully consider the terrors of God's wrath.   Let no clergyman, sociologist, professor, psychologist, or anyone else deceive you by saying that you can practice sin and not suffer God's wrath" (Fields, *op. cit.,* p.153).

[20] Another possible explanation of the present tense "comes" (rather than the future tense "shall come") is that this verse is one of those passages which tells us that "the wrath of God" is something that can be experienced in the present world (Romans 1:27) as well as in the world to come (Revelation 21:8).

For you were formerly darkness – The "for" with which this verse begins indicates it is a reason for no longer participating with the disobedient in their sins (e.g., the vices named in verses 3 and 4). "Formerly" refers to the time before their conversion to Christ. As he did in Ephesians 2:1-3 and 4:17-24, Paul reminds his readers of what they once were. He does not say "you were *in* darkness" (which of course was true[21]) but uses a stronger expression. He says they were themselves darkness, news sources, so to speak, of spiritual darkness in the society in which they lived.

But now you are light in the Lord – "Now," since their conversion as Christians, they are more than enlightened; they are light, new sources, so to speak, of light for the society in which they live (cp. "You are the light of the world," Matthew 5:14) as they live and teach the divine truth learned from Jesus. "In the Lord" says that it was a result of their fellowship with Christ that this new state of things had come to them, transforming their lives. Christ is the true light (John 1:4-9, 3:19, 8:12). Union with Him makes His servants to be light, just as the bit of carbon will glow as long as it is in contact with the electric force, and subsides again into darkness when that is switched off. So we become light as we are in contact with Christ.

Walk as children of light – Being a present imperative in form in the Greek, the verb "walk" commands habitual action: "be habitually conducting yourselves as children of light." Just as "children of disobedience" (Ephesians 5:6, KJV) was a Hebraism meaning characterized by disobedience, so "children of light" means to be characterized by light.[22] The word translated "children" is *teknon*, "born ones," which suggests the readers have become children of light by virtue of the new birth. To "walk as children of light" means to behave as Christians ought. Walking as children of the light and participating with the disobedient in their sins are incompatible behaviors.

5:9 – *(for the fruit of the light* consists *in all goodness and righteousness and truth),*

(For the fruit of the light *consists* – The whole verse is printed as a parenthesis, but the "for" with which it begins indicates it is a parenthesis with a purpose. Namely, this verse is intended to explain the command "walk as children of light"

---

[21] For "darkness" as a figure of life apart from God, see Ephesians 4:18 and Colossians 1:13.

[22] For some reason the NASB[95] has capitalized the word "Light" in verses 8 and 9. In none of these cases does "light" appear to be a reference to the Lord, so it does not appear to be correct to capitalize "Light." The older editions of NASB, correctly we believe, had the lowercase "l" ("light") in all these places.

with which verse 8 ended.[23]   With this parenthetical explanation before the readers, there can be no question what Paul had in mind when he commanded them to walk habitually as children of light.   Light is pictured as producing fruit, so "*consists*" is a good word to add after "fruit."   The metaphor is drawn from the world of botany.   In the spring, more hours of daylight trigger growth in plants that have been dormant through the winter when there is less daylight. Light is the necessary condition of that vegetative life which grows and yields fruit, while hours of darkness do not result in growth or fruit bearing.   Three cardinal virtues will be obvious when folk are walking as children who are characterized by light.   Anything else other than the virtues about to be listed would be out of keeping with what light properly produces.

In all goodness and righteousness and truth) – When the light of Christ shines in the lives of believers it produces goodness, righteousness, and truth.   Walking as children of the light will result in the growth of these qualities.[24]   "Goodness" *(agathosune)* has the idea of active goodness, benevolence, generosity of spirit. It is the disposition that leads to loving actions as described in Matthew 25:35,36. "Righteousness" (in this context which speaks about separation from sin) is a disposition that agrees with God's standards of right.   It is seeing eye-to-eye with the word of God, giving to God and men what is their due.   There is justice, and fair dealing toward all men, and freedom from the morally wrong, or anything that would be detrimental to men's eternal welfare.   Among the wide range of meanings for "truth" *(aletheia)*, the word "stands for genuineness, honesty, the absence of sham, pretense, falsehood, and hypocrisy.   It is not only something to be said but something to be done (see on Ephesians 4:25; 1 John 1:6, 3:18)."[25] These three qualities are ever the same.   The "light" never changes.   With these words the parenthetical explanation that is verse 9 has been finished.

5:10 -- *trying to learn what is pleasing to the Lord.*

Trying to learn what is pleasing to the Lord – The present tense nominative plural participle *dokimazontes* (translated "trying to learn") with which this verse begins is connected   grammatically to the plural "you" in the verb "walk" found

---

[23] There is a manuscript variation at this place.   The KJV has "fruit of the spirit" because the Textus Receptus (following P[46], D[c], K, L, Syr. Pes., Chrys.) has "fruit of the spirit."   The reading may have been influenced by Galatians 5:22.   "Light" is the reading of Aleph, A, B, D , G, P, 67[2], Vulg, Goth, Boh, Arm, Origen, Jerome.

[24] These three virtues are not exclusive.   We are reminded of Jesus' three-fold statement about "justice, mercy, and faithfulness" (Matthew 23:23).

[25] Wood, *op. cit.*, p.70.

in verse 8.   We do not have a word in English that exactly captures the twofold meaning of *dokimazo*.   The word means "(1) to test, to examine, to prove, to scrutinize (to see whether a thing be genuine or not) and (2) to recognize as genuine after examination, to approve, deem worthy."[26]   Since a good helping word to translate a present tense participle is "while" or "as," the sentence comprised of verses 8b and 10 has commanded "walk as children of light ... as you are trying to learn what is pleasing to the Lord."   Walking as "children of light" requires a constant searching to determine what the will of the Lord is, and approving it by letting what pleases Him be the rule that guides your behavior. We learn what pleases Him from the gospel (Philippians 1:27, "conduct yourselves in a manner worthy of the gospel") and our conscience (Romans 14:22,23) after our minds have been schooled and tutored in the Word of God. "Pleasing to the Lord" (a sacrificial term, Romans 12:2; Philippians 4:18; Hebrews 13:16) reminds us that the believer's life is an offering to God.   In this context, the thing that pleases the Lord is the opposite of hurting others. "Christian ethics is not a matter of legalistic little things, but of a positive ambition to be pleasing to God.   We do right out of respect to Him."[27]

4. In exposing deeds of darkness for what they are.   5:11-14

5:11 – *And do not participate in the unfruitful deeds of darkness, but instead even expose them;*

And do not participate in the unfruitful deeds of darkness – Because the earlier editions of the NASB have an "and" to begin the verse (as does Greek), we treat this verse as the beginning of the fourth subpoint in our list of ways we exhibit love for our brother (verse 2).   When it comes to "deeds of darkness" two things are commanded: stop participating in them[28] and expose them for what they are.   What are the "unfruitful deeds of darkness" that Christians are not to participate in?   Most likely Fields is correct when (1) he calls attention to the fact that the verb "participate in" (*sugkoinoneite*)   was an expression used by the

---

[26] Thayer, *op. cit.*, p.152. *Dokimazo* ("proving") is used with regard to testing metals as to whether they are genuine, of coins as to whether they are real metal and of full weight.   The word picks up the warning in verse 6, "Let no one deceive you."   Deception offers what is morally rotten as though it were perfectly sound.   Test every thought, word, and act.   NASB's translation "trying to learn" is a good attempt to capture the meaning in English.   The KJV reads "proving," a word which includes both finding out what is pleasing to the Lord, and then doing it.   The NEB reads, "Make sure what would have the Lord's approval."

[27] Staton, *op. cit.*, p.426.

[28] The prohibition is so written in the Greek that it demands the cessation of an action already going on.   So "stop participating" in them is a good translation.

Greeks to denote participation in religious rites, and (2) when he identified the "unfruitful deeds of darkness" as being a reference to the night-time ceremonies of the Eleusinian mystery religions[29] or the detestable iniquities of the Bacchanalia which were so bad that as early as 186 BC they were banished from Italy by the Roman senate.[30]   There may also be an indication in the word "darkness" that the deeds were inspired by the devil, the prince of darkness, and/or that they were the actions of men who were ignorant of God because their minds have been darkened.   Not only are the deeds described as being "of darkness," but the deeds of darkness are castigated as being "unfruitful"; they produce no goodness, give rise to no lasting satisfaction, to no moral results that are a joy forever; they produce no benefit to the body or the soul.   No wonder Paul wanted the Christians to have nothing in common with these deeds.[31]

But instead even expose them – More is commanded of the Christian than just non-participation in the unfruitful deeds of darkness.   Christians are also commanded to cause people to know their deeds are fruitless and are deeds of darkness.[32]   The KJV translation "reprove them" treats the verb as having a personal object.   This translation in turn has caused commentators to debate who is to be verbally rebuked for participating in such sins, whether they be erring Christians or unconverted pagans.   The NASB translation "expose them" does not require us to attempt to decide who is to be rebuked for being involved in deeds of darkness.   Whoever may be involved, the Christian is to expose the evil deeds for what they are.

5:12 – *for it is disgraceful even to speak of the things which are done by them in secret.*

For it is disgraceful even to speak – The "for" introduces this verse as giving a

---

[29] Fields, *op. cit.*, p.155.

[30]   Livy, *The History of Rome*, Vol 5, Book 39, IX.

[31] If Fields is right, then what we have here in Ephesians is similar to what Paul wrote in his letter to Corinth (1 Corinthians 10:21), where he prohibited the Christians from going to the idol's temple to participate in meals in honor of the gods.   In any case, it is the deeds (*ergoi*) that are to be shunned, not the doers.   Paul is not advocating Pharisaical separatism.   The follower of Jesus may go where his Master went and meet those whom his Master met, if he goes for the same purpose his Master had when He went and associated with the publicans and sinners.

[32] There is no word in the Greek for "them" after the verb *elengchete* ("expose").   When the object of this verb is a person, the verb (*elengcho*) means to convince or reprove so as to bring about conviction or confession of guilt.   But when the object of this verb is impersonal, the verb may signify to bring to light or expose so as to cause people to know about these things.   It is likely the unspoken object of the verb is "deeds."

reason for something just said, but commentators have had difficulty deciding what that something is. One problem is that verse 12 seems to be a contradiction to the command at the end of verse 11, since verse 11 insists upon the deeds being exposed while verse 12 suggests there is something shameful even to talk about such matters. Then there is the question for whom is it disgraceful? The audience, the speaker, or the ones engaged in deeds of darkness? Commentators working on the KJV text which called for *reproving* the doers of the deeds have offered differing explanations. Perhaps verse 12 gives the reason for not participating in deeds of darkness; they are disgraceful to talk about, much less do. Or, perhaps the phrase means that when rebuking the doers of deeds of darkness, one must be careful not to speak in detail of the actual things done in secret.[33] Some commentators who have seen verse 11 as calling for an *exposure* of the deeds of darkness have suggested that verse 12 is Paul's reason for speaking indefinitely about the vices done in secret, whereas he earlier specifically enumerated virtues.[34] Perhaps the best of the suggested explanations is this: just to state the things done by them, as we expose them, will cause a feeling of disgrace or shame for those who engaged in these deeds of darkness. It is "a shameful thing" (neuter) for them.[35] That is a good reason for exposing the deeds of darkness, for feelings of shame or disgrace often are the prelude to a change of lifestyle.

Of the things which are done by them in secret – If "things ... done ... in secret" is not synonymous with "deeds of darkness" (verse 11), then the things done "in secret" may well be a reference to the vile and immoral pagan religious rites performed in the worship of the heathen gods. Why do men try to hide the bad things they are doing? Why do they do them "in secret"? Because they know they are wrong and by trying to hide them they are admitting they are disgraceful.

5:13 -- *But all things become visible when they are exposed by the light, for everything that becomes visible is light.*

But all things become visible when they are exposed by the light – Both the thread of thought in verses 11-14 and the meaning of some of the words in these verses have been matters of running debate. The following is this commentator's

---

[33] As he comments on this verse, Blaikie (*op. cit.*, p.209) calls attention to the need for Christians to be careful to exclude from conversation even the faintest touch of what is unbecoming.

[34] It has been offered as an objection to this suggestion that Paul had no reticence naming deeds of darkness in Romans 1:26-31, or in 1 Corinthians 6:9,10, or in 1 Timothy 1:9,10.

[35] Lenski, *op. cit.*, p.609.

attempt to understand what Paul wrote. "All things" in Greek is *ta panta*. The article likely points back to "the things which are done in secret" or "the unfruitful deeds of darkness." "Are exposed" is a present tense, circumstantial participle meaning as they are exposed or when they are exposed. We propose to translate *de* as "and" (rather than "but") and thus verse 13 becomes a continuation of the thought about exposure of deeds of darkness by giving an explanation of how the exposure is accomplished. We would translate the passage this way, "all things as they are being exposed are made visible by the light."[36] "The light" that exposes the bad deeds is clearly a reference is to the Word of God (which is called "light" in Psalm 119:105 and 2 Corinthians 4:4). It is in the light of God's Word that all motives and actions must be tested. When Christians expose the deeds of darkness they do so by giving the word of God an opportunity to unmask the deeds for what they are.

For everything that becomes visible is light – The Greek participle *phaneroumenon* (translated as "becomes visible" in the NASB) is also passive. We would translate this clause as "everything which is being made visible is light." A question that naturally suggests itself is how can a "deed of darkness" now be called "light"? Rather than trying to explain how a deed of darkness can suddenly become light, perhaps the easiest way to explain this verse is by taking the word "light" in two different senses. We use the light (the revealing agent, the Word of God) as we expose the deeds of darkness (first part of verse 13), and thus every one of these deeds is "light," i.e., is seen for what it really is, an unfruitful deed of darkness (last part of verse 13).

5:14 -- *For this reason it says, "AWAKE, SLEEPER, AND ARISE FROM THE DEAD, AND CHRIST WILL SHINE ON YOU."*

For this reason it says – "For" indicates this verse gives a reason for something just said, but what in particular is debated. The quotation appears to be a further enforcement of the need for the readers to expose the deeds of darkness. "It says" (or "He says," NASB mg.) is regularly the formula that introduces a quotation from Scripture, but here there is a problem because the words quoted are not an exact quotation from any canonical Scripture.[37] Because of this, commentators

---

[36] The Greek *phaneroutai* (translated as "become visible" in the NASB) is a passive form. Vincent (*op. cit.*, p.863) says this verb "occurs nearly fifty times in the New Testament, and never as middle," yet the NASB has treated it as a middle voice form.

[37] The problem here is similar to the one we encountered at Ephesians 4:8 where we had a similar introductory phrase and a similar problem when trying to identify the source of the saying. The original edition of the NASB printed the words in small caps, which was their way of showing the passage came from the Old Testament Scriptures. The updated NASB prints the verses in small letters but puts them in lines like poetry is often printed, which leaves the readers with no intimation the words might be from the Old Testament.

have advanced numerous theories concerning the source of the statement which is about to be quoted.[38]   A note in the cross references in the margin of the NASB suggests the words quoted are a combination of several different references including Isaiah 26:19, 51:17, 52:1, and 60:1-3.[39]   Isaiah 60:1-3 bears a sufficiently close resemblance to this passage in Ephesians to vindicate the very commonly received opinion that the apostle is making an allusion to that prophecy by paraphrasing it.

AWAKE, SLEEPER, AND ARISE FROM THE DEAD – "Awake" and "arise" are imperative verbs, but who is the person being commanded to awake and arise?   If, as seems most likely, the appeal is to the readers of Ephesians, then the sleep and death alluded to would be a rebuke of their spiritual inactivity (there has been no exposing of the deeds of darkness, such as verse 11 called for).   The imperative verbs would be a call for the Christian readers to abandon their spiritual inactivity.[40]

AND CHRIST WILL SHINE ON YOU – Assuming the words are addressed to the readers of Ephesians, these words promise that if the deeds of darkness are exposed, Christ will add His power to the efforts of the person doing the exposing.

---

[38] As long ago as Jerome, the suggestion was advanced that the quotation was taken from some apocryphal source, though there was no agreement as to the actual source, though the *Apocalypse of Elijah*, the *Book of Enoch*, or a book written by Jeremiah were conjectures.   Another conjecture is that Paul cites some saying of Jesus that is not recorded in the Gospels, a saying similar to the one alluded to in Acts 20:35.   A number of contemporary writers postulate that Paul is quoting the words of some well-known hymn of the early church.   This much is sure – that we find the writers spending so much time in an attempt to find the source of this quotation, that many have ignored the meaning of the phrases.   So much time is spent trying to discern the source that we regularly find little help toward understanding what the words might mean.

[39] To speak of Ephesians 5:14 being a montage of several passages from Isaiah, all of which speak on the same subject, is a suitable explanation.   We have found a similar phenomenon in Hebrews and 1 Peter, where several verses that have the same word in them are woven together to make a point.

[40] Some, indeed, have argued that this verse is an appeal to the sinner to abandon his unfruitful deeds of darkness (verse 11).   The sleeper is said to be lying dead (spiritually dead) when he ought to be awake and arise.   Then, if the words "Christ will shine on you" are addressed to the sinner who is being rebuked, we have here a promise that Christ will shine upon the sinner with the saving light of His truth.

E. An Exhortation to Walk in Christian Wisdom.   5:15-20

Summary: Behavior that is guided by Christian wisdom involves (1) being careful to make the most of one's time and understanding what the will of the Lord is (verses 15-17), and   (2) living as does one who allows the Holy Spirit to fill him (verses 18-20).[41]

1. A careful walk depends on wisdom, which can come only from knowing the Lord's will.   5:15-17

5:15 -- *Therefore be careful how you walk, not as unwise men but as wise,*

Therefore – As it has done earlier in this letter (4:1, 17, 25, and 5:1), "therefore" marks the beginning of another section of exhortations, all of which are connected to what God has done for us (chapters 1-3 of Ephesians) and telling us how, as redeemed men, we ought to live.   The topic of this exhortation is an encouragement to pattern one's behavior just like Christian wisdom would direct a man to live.

Be careful – "Be careful" may be as close as an English translation can come to the Greek which is made up of the present tense imperative verb *blepete* ("see" or "take heed") and the adverb *akribos* ("accurately," "diligently," or "exactly"). The two words call for the readers to make sure their conduct is accurate with respect to the demands of God's Word.[42]

How you walk – This is the seventh time in Ephesians that the verb "walk" has been used figuratively for how one behaves, how one lives.   In the corresponding passage in Colossian 4:5, a similar admonition has especial reference to "outsiders," and bids Christians to conduct themselves with wisdom and to let their speech be with grace.   In the immediate context here in Ephesians such a walk would include exposing the deeds of darkness.

---

[41] A word of explanation is needed here to explain why we have chosen to insert a paragraph break at the close of verse 20, even though verse 21 uses the same participial construction found four other times in verses 19 and 20.   In more extended notes at verse 21, we shall learn that "being submissive" is indeed one of the results of allowing oneself to be filled with the Holy Spirit (verse 18), just as verses 19 and 20 have already listed some other results.   Yet we still choose to insert a paragraph break at verse 21 because of the length of this "being submissive" topic; all the verses between 5:22 and 6:9 give practical directives concerning how one lives if he or she is submissive (verse 21) as the Holy Spirit encourages the Christian to be.

[42] The idea suggested by the English "circumspectly" of the KJV, is not in the Greek.   The idea is not of looking around watching against dangers, but of "being careful" to find out the clear line of right, and then keeping to it strictly.

Not as unwise men, but as wise – These words unfold what Paul meant when he wrote "be careful." "The metaphorical contrast used earlier between light and darkness is now replaced by a contrast between wisdom and folly."[43] "Unwise men" are not being careful because they pay no attention to what the Lord wants them to do or where their way of living will terminate. What it means to be a wise man is explained in verses 16 through 20 which follow. Wise men pay strict attention to what the Lord wants them to do.

5:16 –– *making the most of your time, because the days are evil.*

Making the most of your time – "Making the most" translates a nominative participle (*exagorazomenoi*) which agrees with "wise" in the preceding verse, so verse 16 is saying that making the most of one's time is one thing a wise man habitually does. But what does "making the most of your time" mean? The marginal readings in the ASV ("buying up the opportunity") and NASB ("redeeming the time") are both attempts to translate the Greek participle which can mean either "redeem" or "buy." Translators have struggled to determine the intended meaning because the expression occurs in only one other place in the New Testament (Colossians 4:5) and there are but few proper parallels to it even in classical literature. To literally "redeem" or "buy" an item, something must be given up in exchange. This, in turn, has led commentators to conjecture what that something might be, since it is not specified in the text. Chrysostom, Theophylact, and Augustine spoke about "the sacrifice of earthly things" in order to use each moment rightly for the Lord.[44] Or again, "Seize every opportunity of wise dealing that is offered to you, whatever price you have to pay."[45] These conjectures may all be beside the point. The participle is in the middle voice which literally means "to buy up for one's own advantage"; so, instead of emphasizing what must be given up, think of how quickly a merchant, on seeing the value of an article and the good use to which he can put it, takes advantage of opportunities that present themselves. "Time" translates *kairos*, a special time that is adapted for a certain thing, a special opportunity which may soon pass. Every time you can do something good or every time you can expose a deed of darkness, take advantage of the opportunity.

Redeeming the time" (KJV) means grabbing all opportunities to "show and tell" the Christian way. Showing may be a small thing like declining too much change from a clerk who makes a mistake, or leaving a note when you scrape

---

[43] Wood, *op. cit.,* p.71.

[44] Meyer, *op. cit.,* p.504.

[45] Meyrick, *op. cit.,* p.571.

someone's fender. It may be reporting your income honestly, being faithful to your married partner, giving your employer a full day's work for a day's pay, treating your employee with kindness, writing to a television station or your political representative, or refusing to purchase products that sponsor immoral programs on TV.[46]

Because the days are evil – This is the reason for "making the most of your time." The word translated "evil" is not *kakos* (something bad in itself) but *poneros*, something that is not only bad but tries to get others to be bad. Because there is so much evil in the world is why the Christians have to behave a different way. They must try to set an example of good to encourage and influence others to be good.

5:17 -- *So then do not be foolish, but understand what the will of the Lord is.*

So then do not be foolish – "So then" (Greek, *dia*, "on account of this") may refer to the immediately preceding clause ("because the days are evil") or it may refer to the main idea "be careful" with which verse 15 began. "Foolish" (*aphron*, Greek) is a stronger word than "unwise" (*asophoi*) in verse 15. "Foolish" means to be "without reason, senseless, without reflection or intelligence, acting rashly."[47] As the rest of this verse will indicate, a person is "foolish" who pays no attention to what the will of the Lord is. The Greek prohibits the continuance of an action already going on. "Stop being foolish" Paul says, in a context where "foolish" means they have not exercised good judgment so as to make the most of the time.

But understand what the will of the Lord is – "Understand" translates *sunientes*, a verb that expresses intelligent, reflective thinking.[48] To be wise is to give the mind something to get a hold of and making an effort to grasp the sense. "Lord" here (as it was in Ephesians 5:10) is probably a reference to Christ,[49] and in this context "will of the Lord" speaks of what He wants us to do with each opportunity to make the most of the time as it comes along. The Greek verb "understand" is an imperative verb giving us a command to be obeyed. The most certain way to *understand* the Lord's will is to read His revealed Word and to reflect upon it.

---

[46] Staton, *op. cit.,* p.427.

[47] Wuest, *op. cit.*, p.127.

[48] As distinguished from *ginosko*, which means to be acquainted with a thing or merely knowing as a matter of fact, *suniemi* expresses intelligent, comprehending knowledge, knowing with understanding.

[49] A few ancient manuscripts and versions read "will of God" instead of "will of the Lord."

Perhaps Paul has in mind the same idea as Jesus expressed in His parable of the sower: "When anyone hears the word of the kingdom, and does not *understand* it" (does not consider or ponder it) "the evil one comes and snatches away what has been sewn in his heart."... "And the one on whom seed was sown on the good ground, this is the man who hears the word, and *understands* it; who indeed bears fruit, and brings forth, some a hundredfold, some sixty, some thirty" (Matthew 13:19,23). Then wisely seek to understand what the will of the Lord is, and then endeavor to do it.[50]

2. A careful walk involves living as does one who allows the Holy Spirit to fill him.   5:18-20

5:18 -- *And do not get drunk with wine, for that is dissipation, but be filled with the Spirit,*

And do not get drunk with wine – These words do not introduce an abrupt change of subject. The verse begins with "and," so what we have here in "get drunk" is another example of being "foolish." The Greek prohibits the continuance of an action already going on, "Stop getting drunk with wine!" This warning about not getting drunk with wine uses the same language as is used in the Septuagint at Proverbs 23:31.[51] There was a right use of wine for medicinal purposes (1 Timothy 5:23). It is an abuse of wine that is here forbidden.[52] Under the influence of too much wine we do not make good use of our minds, nor any effort to make the most of our time, buying up the opportunity for wise dealing. "In circumstances where safe drinking water was hard to find and where wine was a staple of daily fare, New Testament writers warned constantly against the dangers of drunkenness. This warning against drunkenness is easy for us to follow by total abstinence from alcohol, despite its wide acceptance and promotion."[53]

---

[50] Lipscomb, *op. cit.*, p.105.

[51] Barnes (*op. cit.,* p.104) calls attention to the fact that it is alcohol which is the cause of drunkenness, and that alcohol may be produced either by fermentation or by distillation.

[52] Many of the pagan religions (e.g., the cult of Dionysius) used wine, dancing, and music in wild rites designed to produce a frenzied intoxication which was believed to facilitate escape from the limitations of mortality, enabling communication with the deity. Paul's warning about not being drunk on wine should not be interpreted as being limited only to such pagan celebrations.

[53] Hayden, *op. cit.*, p.325.

For that is dissipation – "Dissipation" translates *asotia,* a word that means "no salvation." It is the root word used of the prodigal son who spent his wealth in "riotous" living. When one gets drunk,[54] he is scattering and wasting his resources.

But be filled with the Spirit – The verb translated "be filled" is a present tense imperative verb in the Greek, and possible translations that express the meaning are 'keep on being filled ...,' or 'go on being filled with the Spirit,' or 'let the Spirit keep on filling you ....'[55] "Be filled" is a plural verb meaning that this command is something for all Christians. Twice in Ephesians (Ephesians 1:13, 4:30) we have been told that Christians have already been sealed (aorist tense, one act in the past time) with the Holy Spirit. We are thus led to understand that this continual filling is an activity of the Spirit that is different from that sealing. Capitalizing the word "Spirit" so that it has reference to the Holy Spirit is probably correct since the verb "be filled" is a passive voice verb.[56] Since, as the command implies, the believer has some control over whether or not he is so filled, the verse seems to call on Christians to more and more allow the Holy Spirit to prompt their human spirit until the Holy Spirit has gained complete control of the life that is yielded to Him.[57] One way the Holy Spirit prompts is through the Word. This verse is closely similar to Colossians 3:16, "Let the word of Christ richly dwell within you ... teaching and admonishing one another with psalms ...."

---

[54] "The words 'for that is dissipation' are to be construed with the entire preceding clause (the habit of getting drunk), not with the word 'wine' alone" (Wuest, *op. cit.,* p.127).

[55] The present tense rules out any idea of a once-for-all filling, but rather points to a continuous replenishment (literally, "go on being filled"). Thus, Paul's teaching here cannot be harmonized with the Pentecostal/Charismatic doctrine of subsequence, namely, that there is a one-time filling of the Holy Spirit which follows conversion. Nor does this passage give any support to the Charismatic doctrine that the evidence of being filled by the Holy Spirit is speaking in tongues, for the command to be filled is followed here in Ephesians by five descriptive consequences of the Spirit's fullness, none of which is remotely related to the Pentecostal/Charismatic teaching about tongues being a prayer language for use when speaking to God.

[56] These comments treat the Greek "with the Spirit" as being a dative of agent. In Greek, the word *pleroō* ("be filled") is usually followed by a genitive of the thing that fills (Luke 2:40; Acts 13:52; 2 Timothy 1:4), or by the Hebraistic accusative (Philippians 1:11, Colossians 1:9) or dative (Romans 1:29; 2 Corinthians 7:4), but not by a prepositional phrase (like here, *en* and the dative). It is because of the unusual construction that some translate "spirit" (small "s") and treat the construction as a dative of sphere, with the man's "spirit" being the place where he is filled. The Holy Spirit is postulated as being the unnamed agent who does the filling, and the verse is then explained in this fashion: Be more concerned about your "spirit's" health than you are about satisfying a physical craving for alcohol.

[57] No believer in Christ is commanded to be indwelt by the Spirit, for His indwelling automatically accompanies conversion. Nor is a believer ever commanded to be baptized with the Spirit, for that was something to specially empower the apostles. Believers *are* commanded to be filled with the Spirit. Hence, we Christians have an individual responsibility to allow the Spirit to fill us.

Here in Ephesians, in the verses following in the Greek, we have five participles (speaking, singing, making melody, giving thanks, being subject) all of which are dependent on the imperative verb "be filled" and which therefore describe the behavior of a person who is constantly being filled by the Spirit.

5:19 – *speaking to one another in psalms and hymns and spiritual songs, singing and making melody with your heart to the Lord;*

Speaking to one another – This is the first of five participles describing how one who is being filled with the Spirit (verse 18) behaves. Our translators have not been able to decide how to translate the Greek word *heautois* here and at Colossians 3:16. Is it "speaking *to one another*" (as the text of the ASV and NASB read) or "speaking *to yourselves*" (as the RSV and the margin of the ASV and NASB read)?

- Technically, the Greek pronoun *heautois* is what is known as an intensive personal pronoun, whose translation would normally be "to yourselves" (as the marginal notes tell us). The Greek language also has a reciprocal pronoun, *allelous*, whose translation would be "to one another."[58]
- The reading offered in the ASV and NASB text ("to one another") implies that speaking in psalms, hymns, and spiritual songs is something taking place in the context of a public assembly of believers, whereas if the translation "to yourselves" offered in the marginal note is correct, the passage does not speak of the public assembly of Christians, but of something done in private.
- Commentators who think the marginal reading is correct will make comments like this one by Fields, "It is a very fine thing for people to be humming, or whistling, or singing some spiritual song to their daily activities."[59] Defenders of the translation "to yourselves" emphasize that the context does not speak of the worship, but of the every-day-of-life attitudes and acts. This being true, we would not expect this participle "speaking" to refer to singing in a congregational setting.
- Commentators who adopt the reading "to one another" will point to certain passages in early writings which describe Christians as singing songs to the congregation. Passages such as 1 Corinthians 14:15 (which requires songs whose words could be understood by others), or Pliny's letter to Trajan where-

---

[58] Further adding to the difficulty of choosing how to translate the intensive pronoun *heautois* here in 5:19 is the fact that this very pronoun was treated as reciprocal at Ephesians 4:32 ("be kind one to another," ASV or "forgiving each other," NASB). (Perhaps one reason the intensive pronoun is treated as reciprocal at Ephesians 4:32 is because the Greek text at that verse has both the reciprocal pronoun *allelous* ["be kind to one another," NASB] and the intensive personal pronoun *heautois* ["forgiving each other," NASB].)

[59] Fields, *op. cit.*, p.162.

in the Christians are described as being "accustomed to meet on a set day, before daylight, and to sing a song to Christ, as unto God, by turns among themselves."[60]   It is debated whether Pliny's "by turns" refers to antiphonal singing, or to solos such as Tertullian describes as occurring at the Christian love feast during which "each is invited to sing to God in the presence of the others from what he knows of the Holy Scripture or from his own heart."[61]

In the light of numerous places where the intensive personal pronoun is translated as if it were reciprocal ("one another"), we must allow for the possibility it has such a meaning at this place.   In the parallel passage in Colossians 3:16 we also have the intensive personal pronoun (*heautous*) in the Greek (which is also translated "one another" in the NASB), along with the words "teaching and admonishing," followed by "with psalms and hymns and spiritual songs."   Is that a congregational setting, or an every-day life-setting?   Staton's comments can be interpreted either way.   "In some of our songs we say words of teaching and encouragement to ourselves and to teach other – 'Stand Up For Jesus,' for example."[62]

In psalms and hymns and spiritual songs – At one time these three words for songs had distinctive meanings.[63]   "Psalms" are religious songs, especially those sung to a musical accompaniment (e.g., a harp), and in particular the Psalms of David, many of which were used by Christians since they were exactly suitable to express Christian sentiments (Acts 4:25ff; 1 Corinthians 14:26; James 5:13). "The leading idea in *psalmos* is accompaniment by the harp," says Lightfoot.[64] "Hymn" (*humnos*) suggests the idea of a song of vocal praise to God; often it was unaccompanied by instruments.   According to Acts 16:25, Paul and Silas, in the Philippian prison, were "hymning" (singing hymns) unto God.   An Old Testament psalm could be a "hymn" (Matthew 26:30; Mark 14:26); the "hymn" sung in the upper room would have come from Psalm 115-118.   "Hymns" could also be specifically Christian compositions in honor of Jesus as Lord and Savior. "Songs" (*odais*) refers to "all kinds of songs, secular or sacred, accompanied or

---

[60] Pliny, *Epistle to Trajan* x.76.   Pliny's words in Latin are *Carmenque Christo quasi Deo dicere secum invicem.*

[61] Tertullian, *Apology*, 389.

[62] Staton, *op. cit.*, p.428.

[63]   See the synonyms explained in Thayer's *Lexicon* under *humnos*.   Also see Trench, *New Testament Synonyms*, §lxxviii, p.279ff.

[64]   J.B. Lightfoot, *St. Paul's Epistles to the Colossians and to Philemon* (Grand Rapids: Zondervan, nd), p.225.

unaccompanied."[65]   *Ode* is a general name for lyrical poetry.[66]   For use by the Christians, especially if we are speaking of the public assembly, such poems should be limited to what can be described as "spiritual."   Songs may be designated as "spiritual" either "to differentiate them from secular compositions or because they represent spontaneous singing in the Spirit."[67]   "It was quite possible for the same song to be at once a psalm, hymn, and a spiritual song."[68]

Singing and making melody – These two participles give two further evidences of the filling of the Spirit (see verse 18).   The word "singing" and the word "songs" correspond; both having the same root.   "Singing" is done by means of the voice.   The word rendered "making melody" (*psallontes*) corresponds to "psalms" (*psalmos*) above.   It can mean playing a stringed instrument (literally, "to pluck") or singing praise to the accompaniment of a harp.   The two terms describe both vocal and instrumental music.

With your heart – Moule writes, "Both the voice and instrument (the singing and making melody) were literal and external to the heart, but the USE of them both was to be spiritual ...."[69]   So we see that "with your heart" means "heartily" or "spiritually.   It has no reference to the use or non use of an instrument.   It defines the attitude we should have while singing and making melody."[70]

To the Lord – Pliny's note about the early Christians singing songs "to Christ as unto God" reflects the same idea.   As we sing and make melody heartily, there is a solemnity and awe because we are aware that we are in the Lord's presence and every act of our life is related to Jesus who is Lord.[71]

---

[65] Salmond, *op. cit.*, p.363.   He cites Trench, *Synonyms*, p.279.

[66] Abbott, *op. cit.*, p.163.

[67] Wood, *op. cit.*, p.73.

[68] Lightfoot, *ibid.*

[69] H.C.G. Moule, *The Epistle To The Ephesians* in Cambridge Bible for Schools and Colleges (Cambridge: At the University Press, 1899), p. 137.

[70] The Greek preposition *en* (*en te kardia*) of the Textus Receptus is supported by K, L, most cursives.   It is omitted by Aleph, B, Origen, and the Nestle text.   If the preposition *en* is excluded, the phrase probably means "heartily."

[71] Perhaps a word should be added about the proper attitude and technique when singing or playing if the situation pictured is the public assembly; it is not to show off skill and ability but to cause glory to be given to Christ.

5:20 – *always giving thanks for all things in the name of our Lord Jesus Christ to God, even the Father;*

Always giving thanks – We take this participle as indicating a fourth way the Spirit-filled life is manifested.[72]   "Always" may show that this giving of thanks is not just a reference solely to the public assembly on the Lord's day.   "Always *(pantote)* speaks of a constant duty.[73]   A heart that appreciates its blessings gives thanks to the Giver of those blessings.[74]

For all things – The Greek word "all" can either be neuter (all things, i.e., according to the context, the spiritual blessings mentioned in this epistle) or masculine (all men, i.e., all the brethren who make up the one body, the church, whether they be Jew or Gentile).

In the name of our Lord Jesus Christ – In other passages, to do something in the name of another may mean either to do as representing him, or to do it by his authority, or to do it for his benefit.   Here, the phrase also may indicate that Jesus acts as our mediator when we give thanks to the Father.   In the light of what Jesus said to the apostles ("Whatever you ask in My name, that will I do, that the Father may be glorified in the Son," John 14:13), this phrase here in Ephesians may be best taken with a masculine "all," indicating that it is especially for men who bring honor to Jesus Christ that thanks are being given to God through Jesus.

To God, even the Father – This is the One to whom the prayers of thanksgiving are addressed.[75]

------

[72] We judge that the participle "giving thanks" (verse 20) is dependent on the main verb ("be filled," verse 18), rather than on the immediately preceding participle.   If it is dependent on the immediately preceding participle, this verse gives the content of the songs we are to sing.

[73] "Most definitely our thanksgiving should never be limited to one 'official' Thanksgiving Day each year" (Shannon, *op. cit.*, p.404).

[74] This man who, with his companions, sang hymns to God at midnight in the cramping discomfort of the Philippian stocks (Acts 16:25) has a right to recommend the same attitude of heart to others.

[75] Sharp's rule of grammar indicates that the two words "God" and "Father" are both describing the same person, the One who is both God and Father of the Christian.

F. The New Life in Christ: Submission to One Another in Family Relationships.   5:21-6:9

Summary: From Ephesians 5:21 to 6:9 the writer takes up the subject of submissive relationships in the Christian home: wives and husbands (5:22-33), children and parents (6:1-4), slaves and masters (6:5-9).   The same order of material is found in Colossians 3:18-4:1, but in Ephesians we find more space devoted to the subject, especially with regard to the duties of wives and husbands.

5:21 -- *and be subject to one another in the fear of Christ.*

And be subject to one another – We have hesitated concerning where to make our major paragraph break, whether after verse 20 or after verse 21.   There are several considerations that are part of the decision.   This participle "be subject" is the fifth in a series of participles dependent on the main verb "be filled" (verse 18), all of which give specific examples of how one demonstrates he is being filled with the Holy Spirit.   So, much could be said about including verse 21 with the previous paragraph.   However, "be subject" also serves as the umbrella statement under which the following verses are subsumed.   Since the following verses will give several concrete illustrations of what mutual submission looks like, we have chosen to begin the new paragraph in our outline with verse 21.

The verb "be subject" (*hupotasso*) denotes subordination or submission to those considered worthy of respect, either because of their inherent qualities or more often because of the position they hold.   Christians voluntarily are to submit to civil authorities (Romans 13:1-7; 1 Peter 2:13-17), to church leaders (Hebrews 13:17), to parents (Colossians 3:20), and to masters (1 Peter 2:18).   The whole structure of society as ordered by God depends on the readiness of its members to recognize such deference.   Without such respect and submission anarchy prevails.[76]   "To one another" is the reciprocal pronoun *allelous*.   Christian submission is not a one-way street; it is to one another.   Each submits to the other in areas indicated by one's ability, responsibility, and position.   There is to be one attitude for all, mutual submission.   Husbands and wives practice it.   Parents and children live by it.   Masters and slaves work at it.   The topic is mutual sub-

---

[76] "Christian submission does not abolish authority.   The king must rule, even if he is a Christian.   The Christian sheriff does not submit to lawbreakers.   The Christian foreman directs the workers; the Christian manager must manage; the Christian teacher does not submit to unruly pupils.   In the church, capable men are chosen to be overseers, and the rest of us are urged to submit to them (Hebrews 13:7).   We will be greatly helped if we recognize that the family also has its proper lines of authority, even though all its members are submissive rather than domineering" (Root, *op. cit.*, p.74).

mission.   Submission does not mean blind obedience, but it does mean the voluntary giving up of self-centered interests and agendas for the well-being of the other person.

In the fear of Christ-- A Christian has reverence for Christ.[77]   "In His ministry Jesus taught that each disciple should be willing to humble himself and serve others (Matthew 20:26-28).   Not only so, but He embodied the very spirit of willingness to humble self to meet the needs of others (see John 13:12-16).   As His disciples, we can do no less."[78]   Knowing that Jesus Himself modeled submission to God, the Christian follows Jesus' example of submission because he knows that is what Jesus wants him to do.   The following verses will give several concrete illustrations of what mutual submission looks like.

1.   The relationship of wives and husbands.   5:22-33

a.   Wives are to be submissive to their husbands.   22-24, 33b

> *Summary*:   Several points are emphasized: (1) as to the Lord (verse 22);   (2) the husband is head of the wife (verse 23);   (3) the wife is to be subject to the husband as the church is to Christ (verse 24); (4) the wife is to respect her husband (verse 33b).

5:22 -- ***Wives,* be subject *to your own husbands, as to the Lord.***

Wives, *be subject* to your own husbands – Our text assumes that both husband and wife are Christians.[79]   In the Greek, there is a manuscript variation here, some having a verb, some not having a verb.[80]   The absence of a written verb form here, however, presents no problem.   A person reading the Greek would mentally insert the participle ("be subject") from verse 21, or they would get the verb from verse 24.   It is not forced submission but voluntary submission that is

---

[77] There is a manuscript variation here, with some reading "fear of God."   The better reading, found in Aleph, A, B, L, P, is "fear of Christ."

[78] Hayden, *op. cit.*, p.331.

[79] 1 Peter 3:1,2 pictures a mixed marriage where the Christian wife's graceful submissive-ness may serve to convert the non-Christian husband.

[80] No verb appears in P[46], B, Clement, and Jerome.   But, Aleph, A, P, 17, Vulg, Goth, Boh, Clement, K., L, Syr, Chrysos, D, G, have some form of *hupotasso* ("be in subjection").   The testimony of Jerome, who knew of no Greek manuscript with the verb, is very important.

being called for here.[81]   Paul's instructions presume the divine hierarchy pictured in the Bible, which is God -- Christ -- husband -- wife (1 Corinthians 11:3).   "To your own husbands" indicates Paul is not subjecting all women to all men, but wives to their own husbands.   This is not a text on the inferiority of women to men, but it is a text on the Christian marriage relation.

> Some people meet this verse with hostility instead of understanding. They say Paul was a bigoted old woman hater; or if they believe he was inspired, they say God just made this concession to the customs of that benighted age. There seems to be an idea that submission is demeaning, that a wife who submits is accepting an inferior status. That is not necessarily true. When a policeman is directing traffic, the chief of police and the mayor submit to him just as everybody else does. They are his superiors in the political organization, but that is irrelevant. Their submission is to their advantage as well as to the advantage of others involved in the traffic jam. If a wife is more intelligent than her husband, if she is more sensitive, more perceptive, more intuitive, she senses nuances of a situation that may escape her husband. She is better equipped for adjusting to a submissive role. Her gracious submission may mark her as superior, not inferior.[82]

As to the Lord – The "as to" suggests a motive to help the wife be submissive. When there are defects in the husband's behavior, when he is hard and harsh, or fails to appreciate her kindness and love, or when she is discouraged and disheartened, it will help her to try to be as submissive as those defects will admit her to be, if she will act as she would if it were Jesus to whom she is submitting. It does not mean the wife should show her husband the same degree of submission shown to Christ. But it does mean that "as the church looks up to and obeys Christ, so in the ideal Christian family each Christian wife reverences and yields to her husband's will.   Where the ideal cannot be attained through the husband's defects, it is still the aim of the wife to realize it so far as those defects admit of it."[83]

5:23 -- *For the husband is the head of the wife, as Christ also is the head of the church, He Himself being the Savior of the body.*

For the husband is the head of the wife   –   This verse assigns a reason for the

---

[81] The verb used of children and servants is "obey" *(hupakouete)*. Since "be subject" *(hupotassomenoi)* is the verb supplied in the case of the wife, it may be said there is a greater equality in the case of husbands and wives.

[82] Root, *op. cit.,* p.75.

[83] Meyrick, *op. cit.,* p.572.

wife's submitting unto her husband.[84]   The relationship of husband to wife is found in the way God has ordained things.   "That the husband is the head of the family is accepted throughout the Scriptures (Colossians 3:18; 1 Peter 3:1; Titus 2:5)."[85]   When it is said the husband is the "head" (*kephale*) of the wife, it means that in God's arrangement of the home the wife takes her directions from the husband.[86]   Christ, who loves, gives commands for our own good.   Husbands who love never command so as to hurt.

As Christ also is the head of the church – At Ephesians 1:22 and 4:15 the headship of Christ over the church was introduced and explained.   "As" indicates that husbands have the same relationship to their wives that Christ has to the church, namely, headship.   Christ rules the church, and the church is subordinate to Him.   That is what is involved in the metaphor "head."   The married couple can have but one head, even as the church, the body, can have but one Head, Christ.   If it would be out of place for the church to expect Christ to submit to her, then it would be out of place for the wife to try to assume control of the marriage union.

He Himself *being* **the Savior of the body** – "He" refers to Christ (the nearest antecedent) and the "body" is the church as verse 24 goes on to show.   (See also Ephesians 1:23 and 4:16).   The word translated "Savior" may also be translated as "preserver."   If we were to translate it "preserver," then the analogy is continued

---

[84] The better Greek manuscripts read "a husband" (there is no "the" in the Greek before the word "husband"), so the idea is "any man belonging to the class of husbands" (Salmond, *op. cit.*, p. 366).

[85] Leavitt, *op. cit.*, p.249.

[86] Egalitarian interpreters have attempted to show that k*ephale* does not mean "head" but rather means "source," thus, in their view, eliminating this passage from being used as Biblical evidence of subordination of wives to husbands.   This attempted interpretation of *kephale* as "source" has, at best, a paucity of evidence in its favor.   Wayne Grudem has provided a survey of 2,336 instances of *kephale* in the writings of thirty-six Greek authors (based on *Thesaurae Linguae Graecae*) from the eighth century BC to the fourth century AD.   Of these, over 2,000 denote the "actual physical head of a man or animal," while "of the remaining 302 metaphorical uses, 49 apply to a person of superior authority or rank, or 'ruler', 'ruling part.'   No instances were discovered in which *kephale* had the meaning 'source' or 'origin'." (Wayne Grudem, "Does *Kephale* ('Head') Mean "Source" or "Authority Over" in Greek Literature?   A Survey of 2,336 Examples. [*TrinityJ* 6 (1983) p.38-59].   See also Grudem, "The Meaning of *kephale* ('Head'): A Response to Recent Studies," [*TrinityJ* 11 (1990), p.3-72].)

as it describes a way in which Christ and husbands are alike.[88]   This would give the wife a beautiful reason for submitting to her husband.   Staton words it on this fashion: "If a wife sees her husband as head in the way Christ is head of the church, she sees him as someone who will put his own interests second and her interests first, as someone who will provide for her, protect her, care for her, and serve her."[89]   However, since the next verse begins with "but" (marking a contrast), it appears the NASB is correct translating it "Savior," and we have departed from the analogy of how husbands and Christ are alike.   Instead, this clause describes one tremendous respect in which our divine Lord goes utterly beyond what any husband can do.[90]   The husband is head of the wife, and in that he is like Christ; but Christ is also that which the husband is not, namely, Savior of that whereof He is head.

5:24 – *But as the church is subject to Christ, so also the wives ought to be to their husbands in everything.*

But as the church is subject to Christ – "But" (*alla*, the strong adversative) indicates that even though the husband is not a savior in the sense that Christ is Savior, still there is truth in the analogy.   This difference does not affect the relation of headship which the husband holds to the wife.   "As" indicates that what is being stated is according to God's plan, both for the church and for wives. The Greek verb "is subject" is in the middle voice, which means that the church is acting for her own benefit when she submits herself to Christ.   "All authority" has been given unto the Lord, both in heaven and on earth (Matthew 28:18); therefore, the church must be subject to His authority.

So also the wives ought to be to their husbands – "So" means in a similar way is the wife to be in subjection to her husband.   The church subjects herself voluntarily, joyfully to Christ.   So the wife is to do to her husband.[91]

---

[88] The KJV reads "and he is the saviour of the body" but the better Greek manuscripts have neither an "and" nor an "is."   With those words omitted there is no formal connection with what precedes.

[89] Staton, *ibid.*

[90] The words "He Himself" are emphatic in the Greek and the whole clause is best translated "He, He Himself (i.e., = He alone as opposed to others) the Savior of the body."

[91] "In some languages and cultures there is a problem involved in the plurals that are found in the statement that wives must submit to their husbands.   In Greek and English one understands that each wife must submit herself to her own husband.   It does not countenance the idea of a plurality of wives for each husband.   So, in some languages it is necessary to use what is called a distributive singular so as to make clear that it is a matter of one wife and one husband, though applicable to all such individuals.   Therefore, the first part of verse 24 must be translated as 'and so each wife must submit herself completely to her husband'." (Bratcher, *op. cit.*, p.140).

In everything – "In everything," in this context, means everything in the marriage relationship where the husband may rightly exercise authority. "Paul does not mean that the husband is to be above God to the wife. Her personal responsibility to God is as great as that of her husband. God's authority is higher than the husband's, and should there be any conflict, the wife is under obligation to obey God."[92] Such submission is not degrading or dishonoring. As Christ was not dishonored by being submissive to the Father, and as the church is not dishonored by being subject to Christ, so neither is the wife dishonored by being in submission to her husband.

b. Husbands are to love their wives. 25-33a

Summary: Husbands are to love their wives, (1) as Christ loved the church, that love leading Him to give Himself up for her (verses 25-27), and to nourish and cherish her (verses 29b-30); and (2) as they love their own bodies (verses 28-29a, 33a). Holding out Christ's love for the church as an example to husbands is legitimate since the first marriage contained a mystery regarding Christ and the church (verses 31,32).

5:25 -- *Husbands, love your wives, just as Christ also loved the church and gave Himself up for her*

Husbands, love your wives – From here through verse 33a the writer dwells extensively on the Christian husband's relationship to his wife, comparing it to the relationship between Christ and the church.[93] The principal duty of husbands is to love their wives, for without love husbands are likely to abuse their position by tyranny and oppression. The verb "love" is in the imperative mood and calls for continuous action. It will require submission (see verse 21) on the part of the husband to carry out what Paul commands.[94] "The love (*agapao*) here recommended is not sexual, romantic love. It is the kind of intense, active, thoughtful

---

[92] Leavitt, *op. cit.,* p.250.

[93] "Following this are nine verses about the husband's role. Does this suggest that the Holy Spirit knew husbands would ignore or object to these guidelines and needed more instruction? On the wife's role we have only three verses, and all of them say the same thing" (Root, *op. cit.,* p.75).

[94] Again we must be careful. This verse does not so read that each husband (singular) has wives (plural).

goodwill that persuaded God the Father to give His Son for our salvation (John 3:16), and led Jesus to lay down His life for His flock (John 10:10-15)."[95]   It is subordination of one's own wishes and desires to the wishes and welfare of those about him.   The obligations in the marriage relationship, as taught in Christianity, are not one-sided, but mutual.   The husband's responsibility is as binding as that of the wife's.   This was a revolutionary rule in Greco-Roman society where it was recognized that wives had obligations to their husbands, but not vice-versa.[96]

Just as Christ also loved the church – Having put forward the church's subjection to Christ as an example to wives, now Paul presents the love of Christ for His church as a pattern for husbands to emulate.   He will show how that love led Christ to give Himself up for her, and also to nourish and cherish her.   The words "just as" tell us that what follows is "the measure of the love of a husband for his wife, the standard which has been set by the Lord.   If the husband lives up to this standard, then he is ever ready and willing to lay down his life for her, even as the Lord gave Himself for His church."[97]

And gave Himself up for her –To verbalize how much Christ loves the church, Paul calls attention to the degree with which Jesus loves the church and desires what is best for her.   Christ's love was expressed in self-sacrifice for her benefit.[98]   He gave up the glories of heaven, and went through suffering and death, for the church.   "You can search the world over and never find a woman happier than the wife who takes her guidelines literally and lives by them with a husband who lives by the guidelines laid down for him."[99]

5:26 -- *so that He might sanctify her, having cleansed her by the washing of water with the word,*

That He might sanctify her – The apostle apparently   leaves for a moment the

---

[95] Hayden, *op. cit.,* p.332.

[96] In this statement of the husband's and wife's mutual obligations, as in other respects, "Christianity introduced a revolutionary approach to marriage that equalized the rights of wives and husbands and established the institution on a much firmer foundation than ever before" (Wood, *op. cit.*, p.76).

[97] Leavitt, *ibid.*

[98] The preposition translated "for" is *huper,* the same preposition we had at Ephesians 5:2. It basically means "in behalf of" or "for the benefit of."

[99] Root, *ibid.*

analogy of the husband-wife relationship to comment further on Christ and the church. In verses 26 and 27 Paul explains more fully the aim of Christ's giving of Himself so far as the church is concerned. The immediate purpose for which He gave Himself for her (verse 25) was to sanctify her (verse 26), and the remote purpose was to present her to Himself a radiant church (verse 27). The basic idea in the verb "sanctify" is to make someone or something "holy," that is, set apart or dedicated to the service of God.[100] Ephesians 1:4 has told us that it was God's purpose "before the foundation of the world, that we should be holy and blameless before Him in love," and the mission of Jesus Christ in the world was also for that purpose. That was the object of His coming to earth to die on the cross.

Having cleansed her by the washing of water – The first matter that must be decided is whether "cleansed" and "sanctify" are contemporaneous events, or whether the cleansing precedes the sanctifying. Lenski has correctly argued in this case that since both the verb ("sanctify") and participle ("cleansed") are aorists, and since the two words are side by side (in the Greek) without any intervening word, that the two words ("cleansed" and "sanctified") speak of something simultaneous.[101] He thus makes this phrase about cleansing tell how the sanctifying was accomplished. 1 Corinthians 6:11, which speaks of being "washed ...sanctified ... justified," also has the one act of sanctifying taking place at the same time as one is washed and justified. "Cleansed" has reference to the forgiveness of sins, as it does at Titus 2:14, Hebrews 9:14, and 1 John 1:7,9. The "washing of water" is a reference to baptism in water, as is true at Titus 3:5 ("the washing of regeneration"), at Acts 22:16, and at Hebrews 10:22.[102] It is at the

---

[100] The verb form of "might sanctify" is aorist active subjunctive. The aorist tense indicates that this sanctification or dedication to sacred service is a one-time act. There is also a "sanctification" or growth in holiness that is a life-long process for the Christian (see Romans 6:19,22). The aorist verb tense at Ephesians 5:26 seems to indicate that this life-long process of sanctification is not the topic here.

[101] Lenski, *op. cit.*, p.632. Lenski is aware of the rule of Greek grammar which says the action indicated by an aorist participle usually precedes the action indicated by the main verb. If we follow that rule in this case, the aorist participle "cleansed" would indicate the action of cleansing is thought of as preceding the action of the main verb "might sanctify." This creates a theological problem, since the idea of a one-time act of sanctification (the verb "might sanctify" is an aorist tense) that follows a believer's initial cleansing is difficult to document elsewhere in the New Testament. See the Special Study on "Sanctification" in the author's *New Testament Epistles: Romans*, p. 277-288. H.E. Dana and Julius R. Mantey, *A Manual Grammar of the Greek New Testament* (New York: Macmillan, 1954), p.230 have stated "the aorist [participle] frequently expresses [action] contemporaneous [with the main verb]." That is the explanation Lenski follows here.

[102] In addition to these Scripture citations, early Christian literature also uses "washing" (*loutron*) with reference to baptism (Salmond, *op. cit.*, p.369). There is no reference to the ceremonial washings of the bride preceding an Eastern marriage, as some have thought. "The fact that the Subject here who cleanses by the bath of the water is Christ, while it was not the bridegroom who administered the pre-nuptial bath to the bride, makes an allusion to the bath taken by a bride before her wedding doubtful" (Salmond, *ibid.*).

time a person repents and is immersed that his sins are forgiven by God (Mark 16:16; Acts 2:38, 22:16; Romans 6:1-11; Galatians 3:26,27).

With the word – The Greek *en rhemati* means something spoken, an utterance. There is a debate among commentators concerning the grammatical connection of this phrase with the rest of the verse. Is *en rhemati* connected with "sanctify" or with "cleansed" or with "by the washing of water"?[103]

- Some writers who take *en rhemati* with "sanctify" appeal to John 17:17 ("sanctify them in the truth") as though it were an explanatory parallel passage. However, not only does that appear to be a misuse of John 17:17,[104] it also does not explain how *en rhemati* can be taken with "sanctify" when that verb is so remote from this phrase in question.
- To connect *en rhemati* with "cleansed" results in a clause that means "cleansed by means of the word." Against this idea are two things: (1) It is very difficult to find an analogy in Scripture for the idea of being cleansed "by the word." (2) Since the mode of cleansing is already given in the clause "by the washing of water," to treat "by the word" as another mode would be most irregular since there is no "and" connecting the two phrases.
- It is evidently best to understand *en rhemati* as being connected with "by the washing of water."

But exactly how to explain "with the word" (i.e., accompanied by a spoken word) is still strongly debated. The KJV translators who rendered *en rhemati* as "by the word" evidently thought the reference in "washing of water *by the word*" was to baptism done by the word (i.e., by the order) of Christ in the Great Commission. Another view is that *en rhemati* has a reference to the gospel which is preached and which leads a man to belief and repentance preliminary to baptism. By way of analogy, appeal is made to Romans 10:8 where the gospel is called the "word (*rhema*) of faith," and Romans 10:17 where we learn that faith comes by hearing "the word (*rhematos*) of Christ." *Rhema* ("word") is also used of the gospel at Ephesians 6:17 and Hebrews 6:5. Bruce suggests the rendering "the washing of

---

[103] If this third option is chosen, it would be a mistake to affirm that *en rhemati* means that "water" does not mean literal water, but instead is a figurative expression for the Word of God. For the Greek to mean this, there would need be an article in the Greek, something like either *to en rhemati* or *tou en rhemati*.

[104] John 17:17 and 17:19 are Jesus' words concerning the apostles. This passage in Ephesians is speaking about all believers.

water accompanied by a spoken word," with the spoken word referring either to the baptismal formula ("in the name of the Father and the Son and the Holy Spirit," Matthew 28:19), or to the word of confession of faith in Jesus spoken by the candidate in preparation to being immersed into Christ (Acts 8:37; Romans 10:9; Colossians 3:17).[105]

5:27 -- *that He might present to Himself the church in all her glory, having no spot or wrinkle or any such thing; but that she should be holy and blameless.*

That He might present to Himself the church – Whereas the sanctification of the church was the immediate purpose for which Christ gave Himself (verses 25,26), this verse gives the more remote purpose behind Christ's giving of Himself. Ultimately, He wants to present to Himself a spotless bride. "He" is emphatic in the Greek. Rather than the friend of the bridegroom presenting the bride, Jesus Himself is doing the presenting. The verb "present" is the regular verb for the presentation of the bride to the bridegroom.[106] It is an aorist tense, speaking of a one-time presentation. The church is here pictured as the bride of Christ, as it also is in 2 Corinthians 11:2 and Revelation 19:7. How can Christ present the church to Himself? 1 Corinthians 15:24-28 helps us with the answer to that question. He presents the church to Himself as a member of the Godhead.[107] This presentation here spoken of does not take place in this life. It takes place at the second coming, according to 1 Thessalonians 4:16,17 and Revelation 19:7-9.

In all her glory – The KJV reads "a glorious church" but the adjective "glory" is in the predicate position, not the attributive as the KJV has treated it. The predicate position adjective describes the church "as glorious" or as the NASB renders it, "in all her glory." What the "glory" involves is explained in the rest of the verse. The church "in all her glory" is probably analogous to the picture in Revelation 21:2, a bride "adorned for her husband."

Having no spot or wrinkle – "Without spot or wrinkle" may refer to the perfection of the bodies of the saints, as well as to their spirits. Mortal bodies cannot inherit the kingdom of God. But when we are caught up to meet the Lord, our bodies will have been transformed and glorified (1 Corinthians 15:51,52).

---

[105] Bruce, *op. cit.*, p.116,117.

[106] The verb "present" is also used (e.g., Romans 12:1) of the presentation of an offering to deity. However, it is incongruous to speak of a sacrificial offering in this context in Ephesians.

[107] This Ephesians 5:27 passage (in conjunction with 1 Corinthians 15:28) is a good one to read when talking with folk who deny the deity of Jesus. How can Christ present the church to Himself unless He is God?

Or any such thing – There will be nothing to mar the beauty of Christ's bride when she is presented to Him. Does this verse look back to our initially being sanctified (verse 26), or could it be said that the dedication to the service of God that began with their being cleansed has been followed by a lifetime of pursuing holiness?

But that she should be holy and blameless – The bride (the church) must have a character that conforms to her Lord. "Holy" says she is separate from evil. "Blameless" reminds us that "though the members of Jesus' bride cannot lay claim to a stainless past, He has provided them with His own purity through the washing with the word."[108]   All this is possible only because Christ is the Savior of His body (verse 23).

5:28 – *So husbands ought also to love their own wives as their own bodies.   He who loves his own wife loves himself*;

So husbands ought also to love their own wives – With "so" Paul returns from his digression (verses 26 and 27) to his analogy of the husband-wife relationship. "So" (*houtos*) refers back to what was written in verse 25; in fact, verse 28 repeats in substance the words with which verse 25 began, about husbands loving their wives.[109]   Verses 26 and 27 have indicated some wonderful things about Christ's love for the church, things which the husband cannot imitate in his love for his wife, but with "so" Paul again takes up a way in which husbands can be like Christ, namely, with a deep and unfailing love. The word "ought" (*opheilo*) indicates this love is a moral obligation that husbands have. Such a moral obligation is the plan and purpose of God.

As their own bodies – There is something more being said here than simply that the husband's love for his wife is to be like the love which he has for his own body. The word (*hōs*) translated "as" here does not mean simply "like"; it has a qualitative force that might be translated "as being." Just as the church is often called the body of Christ, there exists a similar relationship between husband and wife. A husband is to think of his wife as Christ thinks of the church, "as being" his own body. Just as the church, His body, is special to Christ, so the wife (as being his body) is to be something special to the husband. This verse may well be saying that "the wife is not to be treated as a piece of property, as was the custom in Paul's day. She is to be regarded as an extension of a man's own per-

---

[108] Hayden, *op. cit.*, p.332.

[109] Again, as in some preceding verses, because of the problem of polygamy in certain areas of the world, it may be important here in verse 28 to point out again that the Greek pictures each husband having but one wife.

sonality and so part of himself."[110]   With these words Paul gives a concluding summary to the sentence which began in verse 25.   This long sentence has as its theme that the husband is to love his wife with a sacrificial kind of love like that with which Christ loved the church.

He who loves his own wife loves himself – According to the punctuation adopted in the NASB, these words begin a new sentence in which Paul will make allusion to the Genesis account of Adam and Eve.   The thread of thought is not easy to follow, but the idea that these verses are intended to develop what Paul had in mind as he wrote "as (being) their own bodies" is appealing.   Ephesians 1:22,23 pictured the church as the body of Christ, "the fullness of Him who fills all in all."   Just as Christ promotes His own welfare by nourishing and cherishing the church, so does the husband who likewise treats his wife.

> Because she is one with him, their interests are identified.   By loving his wife as his own body, "he really promotes his own welfare when he takes care of her, as much as he does when he takes care of his own body.   A man's kindness to his wife will be more than repaid by the happiness which she imparts, and all the real solicitude which he shows to make her happy, will come to more than it costs.   If a man wishes to promote his own happiness in the most effectual way, he had better begin by showing kindness to his wife (Barnes)."[111]

5:29 – *for no one ever hated his own flesh, but nourishes and cherishes it, just as Christ also* **does** *the church*

For no one ever hated his own flesh – This verse gives an explanation of what Paul meant in the preceding verse.   In this context, we might have expected Paul to write "no one ever hated his own body."   "Flesh" is an unexpected change from the word "body" which Paul has been using, and, no doubt, was chosen with reference to the "one flesh" about to be quoted (verse 31) from Genesis 2:24.   The word "hated" does not refer to despising, but as the contrast following shows, to neglecting, the opposite of nourish and cherish.

But nourishes and cherishes it – The understood subject is "each one," the opposite ("but") of "no one" in the previous phrase.   A normal human being takes care of his body.   He provides for it in every way.   He "nourishes it" (*ektrephei* means to supply it with food to promote its development and maintain its health) and he "cherishes it" (*thalpei* literally means to keep it warm).   While the two ex-

---

[110] Wood, *op. cit.*, p.77.

[111] Leavitt, *op. cit.*, p.250.

pressions denote that a man provides food and raiment for the body, when it comes to applying these words to the relationship between husband and his wife, they likely speak of more than literal food and clothing. "The wife needs more than mere physical necessities. She needs a gentle hand, sweet talk, and loving looks. She needs more than someone who pays the bills, mows the lawn, and washes the car. She needs caring and tender compassion, not just a competent caretaker."[112]

Just as Christ also *does* the church – This phrase says that Christ's[113] treatment of the church is just like human beings nourish and cherish their own bodies. The glorified Christ nourishes and cherishes the church. If we were to attempt to identify specific ways in which Christ nourishes and cares for the church, it surely would be proper, at least, to point to His high priestly work in heaven, where He makes pleas on her behalf with the Father (Romans 8:34; Hebrews 7:25; 1 John 2:1,2). He is at work to make sure His bride is holy and spotless (verse 28).[114]

5:30 – *because we are members of His body.*

Because we are members of His body – With these words the sentence which began in the middle of verse 28 is completed, and this last clause gives the reason why Christ nourishes and cherishes (cares for) the church. The church is His body (Ephesians 1:23) and individual Christians are here being pictured as members (living parts) of Christ's body. He just as naturally takes care of the members of his body as men nourish and cherish their bodies.[115]

---

[112] Staton, *op. cit.*, p.436.

[113] The KJV reads "as the Lord (*kurios*) does the church," but the better manuscripts (Aleph, B, A, D, F, 17) read "Christ" (*Christos*).

[114] Even though the Lord's Supper is a participation in the body and blood of Christ (1 Corinthians 10:16), it may be questionable whether there is a reference to the Lord's Supper here in verse 29 (even though baptism was introduced at Ephesians 5:26). If one looks for passages that speak of nourishing, it might be more productive to recall how Christ called Himself the bread of life (John 6:48,51).

[115] A few manuscripts conclude verse 30 with the words found in the KJV, "of his flesh and of his bones." Though there is similar language at Genesis 2:23, both internal and external evidence seems to be in favor of the omission of these words here at Ephesians 5:30. If the words spoken by Adam found in Genesis 2:23 enjoy integrity here, they are intended to be a fuller explanation of what "members of His body" means. Just as Adam recognized that Eve was "out of (*ek*) his flesh, and out of (*ek*) his bones," so Paul seems to be asserting that we church members enjoy a similar relationship to Christ. We Christians are His body, because we have originated from Christ (*ek*, "out of"), analogous to the physical derivation of Eve from Adam and the consequent union subsequently between them.

5:31 -- FOR THIS CAUSE A MAN SHALL LEAVE HIS FATHER AND MOTHER, AND SHALL CLEAVE TO HIS WIFE, AND THE TWO SHALL BECOME ONE FLESH.

FOR THIS CAUSE – The Greek text of verse 31 is composed entirely of words taken (with a few changes) from the LXX of Genesis 2:24.[116]   One change has to do with the words that introduce the whole verse from Genesis.   Instead of the *heneken toutou* ("therefore") of Genesis 2:24, Paul wrote *anti toutou* ("for this reason").   In a moment Paul will say that Genesis 2:24 contains a great mystery. Perhaps Paul made this slight change in wording because he wanted to show the mystery, namely, that there is a proper parallel between Christ and the church, just as there is between a husband and his wife.   In other words, this citation is made in support of what was written in verse 28.[117]

A MAN SHALL LEAVE HIS FATHER AND MOTHER, AND SHALL CLEAVE TO HIS WIFE – It seems best to briefly comment on what these verses say about marriage between husband and wife, and wait until verse 32 to make any application to Christ and the church.   As recorded in Matthew 19:4,5, when Jesus appealed to this passage from Genesis 2, He said that the original cause for which a man was commanded to leave his father and mother and cleave to his wife is stated as since God "made them male and female."   That language says that the marriage bond is stronger than the bond between parent and child. "Leave" does not mean abandon, and it does not mean that a man will stop respecting his parents, but it does mean that he must not let attachment to his parents mar in any way his close, intimate relationship with his wife.   As recorded in Matthew 19:6, Jesus used these words about cleaving to one's wife as a Biblical rebuttal to the Pharisees who permitted divorce for any cause.   When He said "cleave to his wife," Jesus explained that God intended for husbands to have a commitment to an unbreakable union, not the nonchalant attitude toward marriage which the Pharisees encouraged.   What Paul here has been writing about the obligations of wives and husbands certainly helps us to understand what it means to "cleave" and "become one flesh."

---

[116] These words as they appear in Genesis 2:24 are Adam's words respecting the woman who had just been brought to him.   However, both Jesus (Matthew 19:5) and Paul (1 Corinthians 6:16) attribute these words to God.   Of course, the only way Adam could have known about a father and mother is if God had revealed such information to him before He made Eve.

[117] As the KJV reads, the words in verse 31 taken from Genesis 2:24 are intended to confirm what was just said in verse 30 about "out of his flesh, and out of his bones."   This immediately presents us with a problem when we try to explain verse 31.   Wherein is the great mystery?

AND THE TWO SHALL BECOME ONE FLESH – "This refers to both physical intimacy and to relational interdependence. The first can happen during the honeymoon; the second takes time to develop, for it is the opposite of independence. Husband and wife depend on each other emotionally, mentally, socially, and financially. Neither is complete without the other."[118]

5:32 -- *This mystery is great; but I am speaking with reference to Christ and the church.*

This mystery is great – A "mystery," in the Biblical definition of the term (as has been explained at Ephesians 1:9 and 3:4,5), refers to something that was not clearly revealed in the Old Testament, but now that Calvary and Pentecost have occurred the apostles and prophets of Jesus are clearly making known the truth that was somewhat hidden before.[119] "Mystery" says there is a hidden meaning in the Genesis text which can be understood only when the passage is interpreted in a typological or allegorical fashion. "Great" says the truth hidden in Genesis 2:24 has far reaching implications, only some of which he has revealed in this passage.

But I am speaking with reference to Christ and the church – The "I" is emphatic. Paul is explaining the mystery as it was given to the apostles to do. In other words, Genesis 2:24 contains a more profound truth than was realized until Christ came to win His bride, the church, by giving Himself for her on the cross. We can begin to apprehend the mystery when we think of Christ and His body the church, but this raises the difficult question concerning how many of the phrases in Genesis are to be interpreted as being a hidden reference to Christ and the church. Many of the early church writers assigned an allegorical meaning in each phrase. They made the leaving of father and mother to be a reference to Christ's first coming into the world (though they had difficulty trying to identify who Christ's mother was). They interpreted the cleaving to his wife to refer to Christ's gradual nourishing and cherishing the church during the present age.

---

[118] Staton, *ibid.*

[119] This verse is one of several places where the Latin Vulgate translates the Greek word "mystery" as "sacrament" (see also at Ephesians 1:9, 3:3-9; Colossians 1:27; 1 Timothy 3:16; Revelation 1:20). It is, no doubt, this mistaken rendering which led to marriage being designated as a sacrament. In an encyclical of 1832 occurs this statement, "Marriage is, according to Paul's expression, a great sacrament in Christ and in the church." It was from Augustine that the Catholic doctrine arose which makes marriage a sacrament ("sacrament" being defined by them as a means of grace, a condition for forgiveness of sins). In the Church of England a different definition is given to the word "sacrament." In that theological circle, a sacrament is defined as something instituted by Christ. Even with this definition, marriage should not be called a sacrament for it was not instituted by Christ, but by God in the Garden of Eden.

Then, the church and Christ become of one flesh in the future when the redeemed will receive resurrection bodies just like the one Christ now has.

In this commentator's judgment, just the last clause of verse 31 ("the two shall become one flesh") is where the great mystery is found.   In that phrase there was a temporarily hidden ("mystery") reference to the close relationship between Christ and the church, so close that the church can be thought of as "members of His body."

> It is interesting that God has chosen to refer to the church with the very same terms that we use to refer to our families.   He is the *Father*; we are His *children*; we are to one another *brothers* and *sisters*; we come into His family by *adoption* and by being *born again* (which happen at the same time); and the church is referred to as Christ's *bride*.   Elsewhere Paul said that when he brings people to conversion, he is the matchmaker who brings them together with the husband, Christ (2 Corinthians 11:2).   The church is a family, and Christ is our example of family love.[120]

5:33 -- *Nevertheless, let each individual among you also love his own wife even as himself; and let the wife* see to it *that she respect her husband.*

Nevertheless – "Nevertheless" means apart from what Paul has just affirmed about a mystery being contained in the words of Genesis 2:24.   Even though that is true, the application of Genesis 2:24 to human marriage remains unaffected.

Let each individual among you also love his own wife even as himself – The original edition of the NASB which reads "Let each individual among you also love his own wife" does a better job of conveying the meaning of the Greek present tense imperative verb, which commands each husband to keep on loving his own wife.   Each husband is addressed individually.   He is to go on loving his wife in the very manner just described.[121]   It is a command.[122]

---

[120] Staton, *ibid.*

[121] "As" again is *hōs*, the same comparative adverb used in verse 28.   It is used here with the same meaning it had in verse 28.   It does not say the husband is to love his wife *like* he loves himself, but he is to love *in this manner*, namely, just as Christ loves the church.

[122] Three times (in verses 25, 28, and 33) Paul commands Christian husbands to love their wives.   The first time, he appeals to the example of Christ's love.   The second and third times, he appeals to the "one body" and "one flesh" concept of marriage set forth in the Old Testament.

And let the wife *see to it* that she respect her husband – "Respect" is another present imperative.   The husband *must* love his wife.   The wife *must* be in subjection to her husband.   Wives are urged to have *respect* for their husbands' ordained authority, which is symbolic of the authority of Christ in the church. Verse 33 is a summary of the mutual submissiveness God expects in the family relationship as a normal result of the filling of the Holy Spirit (verse 18).

2. The Relationship of Parents and Children.   6:1-4

a. Children are to be submissive (obey).   1-3

6:1 -- *Children, obey your parents in the Lord, for this is right.*

Children – Notice that Paul addresses children directly. Since it was his expectation that this letter be read publicly in the assembly of the congregation, Paul assumes these children are both present and are old enough to be able to understand and heed the apostolic admonition concerning the necessity of obedience to parents.

Obey your parents in the Lord – In the line of authority, children are subordinate to parents and therefore are to be submissive to their parents. "Obey" is a present imperative, so the command is to be habitually obedient to your parents. The Greek word means to hear under authority. It pictures a readiness to listen to good advice given by the parents and be submissive.[1] Such behavior (or its opposite) can be willed. "Your parents" implies that father and mother are equal as objects of honor and obedience to their children.[2] Of course, the father is the head of the home and would have the last word, but both parents are objects of obedience for a child. Several meanings have been suggested for the words "in the Lord" depending on what the phrase is thought to modify. Perhaps it means the parents are Christians ("in the Lord"). Perhaps it modifies "obey" and thus children are to obey all commands that are not contrary to the Lord's will. Perhaps it is the children who are Christians ("in the Lord"), with the idea being that the life which even children lead when they are in fellowship with Christ makes such obedience more easy and more graceful even if the parents

---

[1] "Colossians 3:20 says, 'Children, be obedient to your parents in all things; for this is well-pleasing to the Lord.' If a child loves and respects God, he will seek to please Him by obeying his parents. That is no violation of a child's will or crippling of his personality. Instead, as the course chosen because of love, it becomes the flowering of the best and freest personality. Once again Jesus is our example (see Luke 2:51)." Hayden, *op. cit.*, p.333.

[2] "For Paul, disobedience to parents is one of several signs of alienation from God and of the consequent fragmentation of society (cf. Romans 1:30; 2 Timothy 3:2). Disobedience is a symptom of a disintegrating/decaying social structure. Christian families have a particular responsibility not to contribute to the collapse of an ordered community." Wood, *op. cit.*, p.80.

should not yet be Christians.[3]   Whether or not the parents are Christians, the parental commands that could be disobeyed because they were obviously sinful would be rare.

For this is right -- "Right" (*dikaios*) probably means that obeying one's parents is something that God says is right; such obedience is something that is ordained by God, one of God's eternal principles.   In Colossians 3:20, Paul says that such obedience "pleases the Lord."   "We people are not born with mature judgment. We attain it gradually through years of experience.   In our growing years we children desperately need the guidance of older people when their guidance is Godly, and we ought to accept it gladly and gratefully."[4]

6:2 – *HONOR YOUR FATHER AND MOTHER (which is the first commandment with a promise),*

HONOR YOUR FATHER AND MOTHER – The fifth commandment (Exodus 20:12 and Deuteronomy 5:16) is quoted verbatim from the LXX in confirmation of "this is right" in verse 1.   "Honor" (*timao*, "to estimate or fix the value," "to respect or esteem highly") is the disposition out of which obedience is born.[5]   The verb "honor" is a present imperative which makes this command say "be always honoring."   Such honoring of father and mother is something a child can do throughout his or her whole life.   "To honor father and mother is to discharge faithfully the duties the child owes them – obedience, in childhood; respect, reverence through life; tender care and support in old age (1 Timothy 5:3,4); and kindness and love at all times."[6]

---

[3] Such an expectation would be in harmony with other teachings of Scripture.   A woman whose husband is not a Christian was nevertheless to be in subjection to him, hoping to win him to Christ (1 Peter 3:1,2).   A Christian slave was to obey his master even if the master is "unreasonable," that is, unfair or surly (1 Peter 2:18).   A Christian is to be subject to the authorities in government (Romans 13:1,2), even if the head of them is the infamous Nero, later known for his wholesale murder of Christians.   (Root, *op. cit.,* p.77)

[4]   Root, *ibid.*

[5] "The Greek verb translated 'honor' is used of the attitude Christians should have toward the Roman Emperor (1 Peter 2:17) and toward Jesus Christ and His Father (John 5:23).   It means to consider worthy of honor, respect, obedience."   Bratcher, *op. cit.,* p.150.

[6] Lipscomb, *op. cit.,* p.119.

(Which is the first commandment with a promise) – This phrase gives a reason for honoring one's parents. Since the second command (Exodus 20:4-6) contains a declaration (something of a promise) and the third (Exodus 20:7) contains a threat, exactly what is intended by the description "first" is a topic of debate among commentators. Conjectures as to the intent include (1) this is a command of primary or foremost significance; (2) it is the first one on the second table of stones;[7] (3) it is the first command taught to children. The Greek translated "with a promise" is *en eppangelia*, and it is probably right to treat the preposition *en* as being equal to "accompanied with" a promise. The fifth of the Ten Commandments is the only one of the ten that names a benefit to be derived from obedience. Paul cites the promised benefit in the next verse (verse 3).

6:3 – *THAT IT MAY BE WELL WITH YOU, AND THAT YOU MAY LIVE LONG ON THE EARTH.*

THAT IT MAY BE WELL WITH YOU – This is the promise attached to the commandment just mentioned (Exodus 20:12). It can be easily seen that the promise was twofold: (a) that it may be well with you; (b) that your days on earth may be long. "It may be well with you," which holds out the idea that the children will prosper, certainly has reference to this world, and perhaps also to that which is to come.

> A positive relationship with a parent affects the spiritual, social, and physical health. Anger and temper tantrums increase the blood pressure, constrict the arteries, and cause an excessive flow of fluids to be dumped into the stomach. Want to feel better? Then relate better. And of course, children who obey their parents are much less likely to die in accidents, by murder, or by overdose of drugs.[8]

AND THAT YOU MAY LIVE LONG ON THE EARTH – In the Old Testament, this clause holds out the promise of Divine favor on those who honored their parents. This phrase continues the quotation from Exodus 20:12 and Deuteronomy 5:16; however, Paul omits the words "which the Lord your God has

---

[7] The commands were written on 2 tables of stone, but according to Philo and Josephus the Jews maintained that each table had 5 commandments on it. If "honor your father and mother" were the first command on the second tablet, that would make the second tablet have 6 commands.

[8] Staton, *op. cit.*, p.438.

given you."[9]   By this omission, Paul adapts the Old Testament promise, which was made to the Israelites with reference to living in the land of Canaan, to the children of the New Testament in whatever land they may be living.   The fact that this promise involves the opposite for children who do not honor their parents need scarcely be stated.

> Disobedient children usually do not realize how far-reaching the consequences of their disobedience can be.   In defiance of his parents, a ten-year-old takes up smoking – and fifty years later his life is cut short by emphysema or cancer.   A teen-age rebel illegally gets a supply of booze – and dies in a flaming crash on the highway.   Countless people who disregard the authority of parents and God will also disregard the rules of health.   We are told the average life span is inching upward because of the advances in medical science.   It might increase even more rapidly if everyone would just listen to Mom and Dad.[10]

b. Fathers are to nurture their children. 4

6:4 -- *And fathers, do not provoke your children to anger, but bring them up in the discipline and instruction of the Lord.*

And, fathers – "And" indicates that the obligation was not all on the side of the children.   Remember, these are examples of mutual submission (5:21).   If the child has obligations, so does the father.[11]   This is addressed to the father as the head of the home, which would imply that the mother should heed it, too.   In a society where the father's authority (*patria potestas*) was absolute, this precept about the father's responsibility toward his children represented a revolutionary concept.

Do not provoke your children to anger – "Stop provoking ..." is what the Greek construction signifies.   Fathers are cautioned against an excessive severity that

---

[9] The words about living long on the earth originally referred to the privilege of dwelling in the land of Canaan.   God warned Israel that if they were disobedient they would be driven out of the land (Deuteronomy 28:36).

[10] Root, *op. cit.*, p.77.

[11] In this place, the Jerusalem Bible and TEV translate the Greek plural *pateres* as "parents" (see Hebrews 11:23) even though the more common word for "parents" (*goneusin*) was just used in verse 1.   Thus, it is probably correct in the light of Colossians 3:21 to conclude that it is the fathers in particular who are being addressed.

provokes bitter, wrathful rebellion.[12]   Children should be corrected and restrained from self-will, and should be trained to be obedient to their parents from earliest childhood; but this should be done in love for the child. "Resentment or exasperation in children comes when parents fail to treat them with respect, making foolish and unreasonable demands just to show their authority. Disciplining is necessary, but generous praise and affection will reduce the tensions associated with it."[13]   "Parents are *not* to be provoking or irritating their children by constant nagging, by hostility, by verbal put-downs, by humiliating insults. Parents are not to yank them up, but to bring them up. This takes time, patience, and understanding. It is to be done in the nurture and admonition of the Lord."[14]

But bring them up in the discipline and instruction of the Lord – "But" indicates this is the alternative to provoking a child to anger and resentment. What is the father's responsibility? "It is definitely not a weak abandonment of responsibility, but is rather a firm, patient, and loving program of training and instruction."[15]   The phrase "of the Lord" obviously refers to Jesus Christ. The tense of the verb ("bring them up") speaks of a steady course of nourishing. "Bring them up" translates the same verb that appears in Ephesians 5:29 where it is translated "nourishes." Here it involves not merely food but also education, providing them with what they need. The Greek word *paideia* translated as "discipline" in the NASB is a general term for rearing children: it may be either punitive (in which case it is translated "chastening" as the ASV) or encouraging (in which case it is translated "nurturing" [as the KJV] or "training" or "upbringing"). It speaks both of appropriate rewards and punishments when necessary. "Instruction" (*nouthesia*) is instruction by word of mouth. The Greek word here means literally "to put (something) in the mind." Words of correction, words of encouragement, words of admonition, words of warning, words of direction, based on Scriptural principles,[16] are to be taught and repeated until they are firmly implanted in the child's mind. "Goodspeed saw in this pas-

---

[12] The command for children to obey does not give parents the right to be mean, overbearing, and cruel. (Staton, *ibid.*)

[13] Hayden, *op. cit.,* p.334.

[14] Staton, *ibid.*

[15] Hayden, *ibid.*

[16] "Of the Lord" might be treated as an objective genitive, which would mean that the teaching is about the Lord, or concerning the Lord. Or it may be treated as a subjective genitive, which would mean that parents are to teach what Jesus used to teach.

sage of Ephesians the beginnings of Christian education in the home."[17]   "When the Bible is not acceptable in public schools, the work of parents is the more crucial."[18]

3. The relationship of slaves and masters.   6:5-9

a. Slaves are to be obedient.   5-8

6:5 – *Slaves, be obedient to those who are your masters according to the flesh, with fear and trembling, in the sincerity of your heart, as to Christ;*

Slaves – That slaves are addressed directly indicates that they were expected to be present in the public assembly where this letter was read out loud.   Evidently, these were, for the most part, Christian slaves working for pagan masters.   We shall see in verse 9 that there were some Christians who were slave masters.

Be obedient – The Greek verb is a present imperative meaning "be constantly obedient" (or "submissive," which has been the topic since 5:21).   That slaves are to be obedient to their masters is the uniform direction in the New Testament.[19]

To those who are your masters according to the flesh – The Greek word "masters" here is *kurios* (often translated "Lord"), while *despotes* is used for "masters" in 1 Peter and the Pastoral Epistles.   This phrase at once implies the necessary limitation of all human slavery.   It can subjugate and even kill the body, but it cannot touch the soul; it belongs only to the visible life of this world, not to the world to come.   He is only a slave *kata sarka* ("according to the flesh").   In reality, the Christian slave is "the Lord's freedman" (1 Corinthians 7:22).   The Christian slave has a heavenly Lord to whom he owes supreme allegiance.   "Obedience" can be given grudgingly and with a surly attitude, or it can be given freely with a pleasant attitude. Paul goes on to use several expressions to indicate the kind of obedience he is teaching slaves to exhibit.

(1) With fear and trembling.   5

With fear and trembling – Paul's use of these same terms for himself (1 Corin-

---

[17] Wood, *op. cit.*, p.82.

[18] Root, *op. cit.*, p.78.

[19] See 1 Peter 2:15,25; 1 Timothy 6:1-3; Titus 2:9-10; Colossians 3:22, 4:1.

thians 2:3), for the Corinthians (2 Corinthians 7:15), and for the Philippians (Philippians 2:12) shows us that "fear" (*phobos*, respect) and "trembling" (*tromos*) are not to be confused with craven servility, or dread of human displeasure, or the master's whip or tongue. Rather they speak of a careful zeal in the discharge of duty, an anxious care not to come short.

(2) In singleness of heart.   5

In the sincerity of your heart – These words go with "be obedient" (not with "fear and trembling") and state the spirit in which the obedience was to be rendered. "Sincerity" (*haplotes*, "singleness") is the opposite of duplicity in thought or action. The Christian slave is not just to pretend to obey. Even if the job were irksome, the Christian slave was not to put on a facade or pretense of obedience, nor go about the service with a feeling of reluctance, but rather was to go about it with genuine heartiness and good will.

(3) As to Christ.   5

As to Christ – The Christian slave is determined to obey his human master as an expression of his commitment to the divine Lord. Paul says the Christian slave goes about his duties as though the services were rendered to Christ himself.[20] If a Christian slave had an unbelieving master, he would serve him the more faithfully now because the honor of Christ and the gospel was bound up with the quality of his service. If he had a Christian master, he would work all the harder, knowing that whatever benefit his work brought to the master was helping a Christian brother (1 Timothy 6:1,2).

(4) Not by way of eyeservice.   6

6:6 -- *not by way of eyeservice, as men-pleasers, but as slaves of Christ, doing the will of God from the heart.*

Not by way of eyeservice - This verse may be an amplification of the idea of "sincerity of your heart, as to Christ." "Eyeservice" is working hard only when their master is watching. The motive behind working hard when the master was watching was merely to gain undeserved favor. Such working hard only when the master was watching in actuality was a form of hypocrisy.

---

[20] See notes at Ephesians 5:22 and also at Colossians 3:22-25.

(5) As slaves of Christ.   6

As men-pleasers, but as slaves of Christ – "Men-pleasers" is the opposite of "as slaves of Christ." It equals "as if it were the main object to please man." The conviction of the Christian workman is that every single piece of work he produces must be good enough to show to Christ. A Christian slave in the first century (and much more a Christian employee in the twenty-first century) has the highest possible motive for doing his work well; it is primarily Christ, and not his earthly master, that he is endeavoring to please.

Doing the will of God from the heart – The marginal note tells us the Greek is literally "from the soul" (*ek psuches*), that is, with one's whole being. Thus "from the heart" is the opposite of listlessness. Taken with "doing the will of God" it tells us that God requires slaves to work so as to please Christ, and that involves "industry, fidelity, conscientiousness, submission, and obedience"[21] on their part.

(6) Doing service with good will.   7

6:7 -- *With good will render service, as to the Lord, and not to men*

With good will render service – "Good will" speaks of the servant's feeling toward his master, a regard for the master's interests. It is a "ready willingness which does not wait to be compelled."[22] With such an attitude of good will, "the Christian slave was in bold contrast with most non-Christian slaves of whom it was proverbially said that a man had as many enemies as he had slaves (Seneca, 'Ep.' 47)."[23]

As to the Lord, and not to men – The Christian slave who thinks of himself as serving his Lord will find it no problem to generate an attitude of good will as he

---

[21] Barnes, *op. cit.*, p.121.

[22] Robinson, J. Armitage, *St. Paul's Epistle to the Ephesians* (Cambridge: University Press, 1903), p.211.

[23] Meyrick, *op. cit.*, p.575. "Among the Oxyrhynchus Papryi there is a will dated AD 157 in which the testator freed five slaves 'because of their good-will and affection' (III. No. 494, lines 5,6). If even pagan slaves could display such qualities, how much more should Christians do so, without expecting manumission as a reward?" Wood, *op. cit.*, p.84.

serves.[24]   Who could be grudging when given an opportunity to do something for Jesus?

(7) Knowing that we shall receive from the Lord that which we do.   8

6:8 -- *knowing that whatever good thing each one does, this he will receive back from the Lord, whether slave or free.*

Knowing that whatever good thing each one does – "Knowing" is probably a causal participle; we do our work well and with good will *because* we know there is a reward for faithfulness in serving Christ.

This he will receive back from the Lord – It is Christ, and not one's earthly master, who is the final arbiter and rewarder of work well done.   The future tense "will receive" looks forward to the final judgment as the time when this compensation will be awarded.[25]

Whether slave or free – In the final judgment, slave and free will be treated alike by the Lord.   There is no discrimination.   A slave in the eye of Roman law may have had no rights, and therefore little hope.   What Paul does is to bid him, as a Christian, to lift his thoughts to the time of the final judgment in which all bond and free alike, may hear the welcome blessing, "well done, good and faithful servant."

b.   Masters (obey the Golden Rule).   9

(1) Treat slaves as they are to treat you.   9

6:9 -- *And, masters, do the same things to them, and give up threatening, knowing that both their Master and yours is in heaven, and there is no partiality with Him.*

And, masters – "And" introduces the reciprocal responsibilities of slave masters.

---

[24] Barnes (*ibid.*) offered a thought-provoking comment at this place.   "The slave should regard his lot in life as having been ordered by Divine Providence for some wise and good purpose, and he should perform his duties with fidelity, and feel that he was rendering acceptable service to the Lord."

[25] For the Christian's prospect of "reward," cp. Matthew 5:12, 6:1,4, 16:27; Luke 6:35, 14:14; Romans 2:6-10; 2 Corinthians 5:10; Hebrews 10:35; Revelation 22:12.

Masters, too, must be submissive, not to their slaves, but to the Lord. This exhortation is addressed to those slave owners who are Christians. It is Christians who are likely to be present in the public assembly when this letter was read out loud to the assembled worshipers. The instructions here given were contrary to prevailing law and custom in the first century.[26]

Do the same things to them – The words do not mean that the masters are to render service to the slaves as the slaves do to the masters, but if Christian masters are submissive to this command, they will treat their slaves with the same Christian principles and consideration that the slaves are to show to their masters. Paul's command is nearly synonymous with the command of Jesus, "Treat people the same way you want them to treat you" (Matthew 7:12).

(2) Forbear threatening. 9

Summary: Reasons to forbear threatening: (a) Christ, the Master of everyone, is in heaven; (b) Christ will have no respect of persons.

And give up threatening – The present tense imperative is a command to always refrain from the well-known habit (the Greek reads "*the* threatening") of masters threatening their slaves. By forbidding the threat, the execution of severe punishments was also equally excluded. What is prohibited is the disposition to govern by terror rather than by love.

Knowing that both their Master and yours is in heaven – "Knowing" here (as it was in verse 8) is also causal, "because you know." Christian slaves know they have a judgment to be faced where their deeds and attitudes will be taken into account by the Lord. Likewise, Christian masters know that God will reward the master with good or evil just as the master has treated his servants. "Their Master ... and yours" indicates the common fact that Jesus is Master (*kurios*, Lord) of both the slave and the slave master. Both alike are answerable to the Lord and therefore need to be submissive to His will.[27]

---

[26]   It is evident from this passage and others in the New Testament that there were in the church those who were slave-masters. Paul did not say that such could not be Christians. He did not say that they should be excluded at once from the communion of the local church. He did not hold them up to reproach, or use harsh and severe language in regard to them. He taught them their duty toward those who were under them, and laid down principles which, if followed, would make submission to such a master no more burdensome than that of a wife to her husband, or that of a child to his parent.

[27]   It follows then that a slave is not to be regarded as a "chattel," or a "thing," or as "property." He is a man; a redeemed man; an immortal man. He is one for whom Christ died. Christ did not die for "chattels" and "things." (Barnes, *op. cit.*, p.123)

And there is no partiality with Him – When He judges, the Lord does not show favoritism, especially on account of external advantages. "Slaves are as precious in His sight as masters, and more is expected from those who are entrusted with greater responsibilities."[28]

G. Closing Exhortation for All to Stand Against the Great Spiritual Enemies of the Body of Christ. 6:10-20

1. Exhortation to be strong in the Lord and put on the whole armor of God. 6:10-13

a. Be strong in the Lord. 10

6:10 -- *Finally, be strong in the Lord and in the strength of His might.*

Finally – "Finally" indicates this paragraph beginning in verse 10 is the culmination of the exhortations concerning the believer's conduct in the world.[29] Throughout this whole second part of this epistle, a great deal has been said about practical Christian living. Previous paragraphs have given directions concerning the Christian's relationships with other men. Now we learn there are spiritual beings (actually antagonistic spirits), too, that the Christian must be prepared to deal with as he lives the life Christians are to live.[30] Such spiritual enemies require each Christian to be diligent about being equipped with each of the pieces of spiritual armor which together make up the whole armor of God. This is the only protection against serious spiritual defeat.

---

[28] Wood, *ibid.*

[29] Some writers treat the Greek *tou loipou* as a genitive of time, meaning "from now on" or "from henceforth" or this is what remains for the readers to do in addition to all that has preceded it. The usual way "finally" is written in Greek is *to loipon* (as at Philippians 3:1 and 2 Thessalonians 3:1). BAG (p.481) tells us the phrases are substantially equivalent, meaning "with reference to the conclusion of the matter."

[30] Some manuscripts read "Finally, my brethren ...." If the words "my brethren" enjoy integrity (rather than being an interpolation from Philippians 3:1), Paul is reminding his readers that they are regenerate persons, who belong to the same family and household of God that he himself does. Whether or not Paul reminded his readers of the fact here, the people being addressed in this paragraph are Christians (see Ephesians 1:1).

Be strong in the Lord – The present tense verb translated "be strong," which can be either middle or passive voice in the Greek, is likely best treated as a middle voice, which would make the exhortation read "constantly be strengthening yourselves." The context (which commands "put on," verse 11; and "take up," verse 13) seems to imply that this is something for the Christian to do, not something done for the Christian. The verb is an imperative making this a command, and the fact that the verb is in the present tense is important; such strengthening is something that Christians need to do all the time, lest any time they should be caught by the enemy. Ephesians 3:16 has told us that such strengthening occurs in the "inner man." Ephesians has had much to say about Christians being "in Christ." It is taken for granted that if a close relationship with Jesus is maintained, the victory is already assured because of what Christ accomplished by His death and resurrection (Ephesians 1:22-23).

And in the strength of His might – If Christians try to depend upon their own might instead of the Lord's might, they will be defeated. "Did we in our own strength confide, our striving would be losing," says the old hymn. "All the resources the Christian needs to be victorious are drawn from Christ and 'His mighty power' (*en to kratei tes ischuos autou*). Three of the four synonyms for power noticed in Ephesians 1:19 are brought together again here."[31]

It will be recalled from Ephesians 1:19,20 and 2:1 that the same power that was exerted in raising Christ from the dead was at work when the readers of this letter were brought from being dead in trespasses and sins to new life in Christ. Now we see this same divine power is available to Christians when they are facing serious opposition from their spiritual enemies. At Ephesians 3:16, Paul has already prayed that his readers would be strengthened with power in the inner man by the work of the Spirit, and at 4:30 he cautioned against a course of life that would fritter away that provision. Christians can avail themselves of the strength of God's might, this context says, by putting on the pieces of the armor of God (6:14-17) and by prayer (6:18). To tap the power of God we need to put on all the pieces of armor He provides. When we do that, His power is available to us.[32]

---

[31] Wood, *op. cit.*, p.85.

[32] "If an army is to be successful in the battle, it must have supplies from head-quarters. No army can be victorious when its ammunition or fuel is gone. There is no excuse for the Christian to run out of fuel. God's supply line is unfailing. It never runs out or wears out. We are not to be strong in our own strength but in the Lord, using the strength and power He provides" (Staton, *op. cit.*, p.442).

b. Put on the full armor of God.   11

6:11 -- *Put on the full armor of God, that you may be able to stand firm against the schemes of the devil.*

Put on the full armor of God – The phrase "the full armor of God" probably means all the armor that God supplies, though some call attention to the fact that the armor the Christian is to put on is modeled on what God Himself wears (Isaiah 11:5; 59:17).   The Greek word translated "full armor" is *panoplia* (a word whose English spelling is "panoply") and is the technical term for the equipment worn by a heavy-armed Roman infantryman (a "hoplite") who was ready for battle.[33] Wherever Roman armies had marched, people would be familiar with their battle dress.   Paul wrote this letter while chained to a Roman soldier, and if such a custodian were in full battle dress, it would have been easy for him to see what the soldier was wearing and make the application to Christians in the church. The verb "put on" is a plural imperative form making this a command addressed to all the readers of this letter.   While God has provided this armor, the individual Christian has the responsibility of putting it on; that is, he must consciously appropriate the power the Lord Jesus Christ makes available to him.   He must put on the full armor – every last piece.   The individual pieces included in the armor are described in detail in verses 14-17.   First, though, the foes the Christian must face are detailed in verses 11,12.

That you may be able to stand firm against the schemes of the devil – This clause is a statement of the reason for putting on the full armor.   Without this full armor the Christian will not be able to stand.   "Stand firm" continues the military metaphor behind Paul's language here, and carries the idea of holding one's position against the enemy, rather than being routed and put to flight.   The word may also carry the idea of "to stand as victor, unvanquished."   The "devil" (who has already been introduced at Ephesians 4:27) is the commander-in-chief of the opposing forces, the sworn enemy of the church.   "Schemes" (*methodeia*), as we learned at 4:14, are the ingenious schemes, the insidious plans or systems of attack, the strategies, the "evil tricks" and deceitful tactics, the attempts to delude and destroy, used by the devil against the Christian.   "Wiles" (KJV) is a very appropriate English term.   "The devil will do anything to bring Christians down. He has a lot of friends, plans, weapons, and time to do it.   He knows he is helpless

---

[33] Polybius (vi. 23, 2), who has left us a detailed description of such armor, enumerates the parts of the soldier's armor as being shield, sword, greaves (leg shields), spear, breastplate, helmet. Paul omits spear and greaves, and adds girdle and shoes, which, though not armor, were an essential part of the soldiers' dress.

as long as we are wearing God's full armor.   His scheme is to get us to take it off. He wants us to distance ourselves from God, to neglect our prayer and worship, and not to equip one another."[34]

c. The whole armor of God is needed because our enemies are spiritual.   12

6:12 – *For our struggle is not against flesh and blood, but against the rulers, against the powers, against the world forces of this darkness, against the spiritual* **forces** *of wickedness in the heavenly* **places.**

For – The fact that the verse begins with "for" (Greek, *hoti*) shows that it is an explanation of what he meant by the "schemes of the devil" and thus underscores the reason why we need the full armor of God.   Our real enemies are diabolical powers in the spiritual realm, so we need spiritual resources.

Our struggle – The primary signification in the word "struggle" (*pale*) is a wrestling contest, where each wrestler tries to throw his adversary.[35]   The word also had a secondary sense where it was used to depict hand-to-hand combat between soldiers.   Infantrymen often found themselves engaged in fierce and mortal hand-to-hand combat.   Thus, we see no reason to suppose that Paul has momentarily changed his figure of speech from war to sports.   What Paul refers to is the personal, hand-to-hand conflict with the forces of the enemy.

Is not against flesh and blood – "Blood and flesh" (which is the word order in the Greek) probably stands for human beings, other people like us.[36]   In military strategy one must never underestimate the strength of the enemy.   The Christian's

---

[34] Staton, *op. cit.*, p.443.

[35]   Thayer (*op. cit.*, p.474) defines the word as follows: "A contest between two in which each endeavors to throw the other, and which is decided when the victor is able to press and hold down his prostrate antagonist, namely, hold him down with his hand upon his neck."

[36] Wood (*op. cit.*, p.86) suggests that perhaps blood is mentioned first lest flesh be regarded as inherently evil.   The peculiar transposition from the more usual "flesh and blood" to "blood and flesh" has been used to argue for a non-Pauline authorship of Ephesians.   However, Percy may be right when he suggested that Paul here wrote the unusual order to avoid the collision of two *sigmas*. Critics of this suggestion usually ignore Percy's own footnote, which is at pains to state that 1 Corinthians 6:16 and Ephesians 5:31 indeed admit the conjunction of two *sigmas*, but in citations from the LXX (p.184).   Cited by Danker, "Ephesians" in *New ISBE*, p.110.

struggle is not merely against human foes; it is a struggle to the death against supernatural foes. Once this is fully realized it is immediately obvious why the full armor of God is needed.

But against the rulers, against the powers, against the world forces of this darkness – The enemy the Christians are struggling with are members of Satan's army – rulers and powers of darkness. The reference is evidently to demons, the angels who fell when Satan rebelled (Revelation 12:7,8). The same terms are employed here to distinguish different classes of fallen angels as had been previously applied to the good angelic hosts (Ephesians 1:21, 2:2, 3:10). This suggests that the same ranks and gradations exist among the demons now as had existed before their fall. Demons of different rank have embarked upon rebellion against God and God's plans and people. Satan has spiritual beings that we cannot see with our physical eyes, just as God has spiritual beings that men cannot see unless their eyes are opened (as was the case with the servant of Elisha, 2 Kings 6:15-17).

Exactly what is intended by the word *kosmokratoras* (translated "world forces," NASB; or "world rulers," ASV) is debated by the commentators since the word appears neither in the LXX, Philo, nor anywhere else in the New Testament. The word has been found in Latin inscriptions and Rabbinical literature to designate human kings whose rule was world-wide,[37] while in the Orphic Hymns the word is used of the devil (iii., 3) and his angels (viii. 11, xi. 11).[38] "Darkness" has been interpreted to mean the heathen nations which are in spiritual darkness; it has been thought to be a deliberate contrast to the good angels who are called "angels of light" (2 Corinthians 11:14). "Darkness" has also been treated as an abbreviation for "the domain of darkness" (Colossians 1:13). Putting the terms all together, perhaps "world rulers of darkness" refers to an order of demons who have control over the spiritual darkness in whole countries (such as "the prince of the kingdom of Persia" in Daniel 10:13).[39]

---

[37] This word is used in the *Corpus Inscriptionum Latinarum* (5892) with reference to the emperor, and in *Bereshith Rabba* (fol.57.1) with reference to the four kings whom Abraham pursued whose rule was world-wide. In Rabbinical writings (Shir. R.3) it is also used of Nebuchadnezzar, Evil-merodach, and Belshazzar.

[38] Further references may be found under *kosmokratoras* in BAG, p.446.

[39] Perhaps it must also be considered that "world rulers of this darkness" means that Satan and the demons have control of certain politically powerful human beings in this world, people who are willing and eager soldiers of Satan.

Against the spiritual *forces* **of wickedness in the heavenly** *places* – Four times Paul has repeated the word "against" to stress the determined hostility confronting the Christian.[40] "Spiritual" is a neuter plural adjective for which we must supply a noun. Whether we supply "hosts" (ASV) or "forces" (NASB), the picture we get is of a large number of fallen angels under the devil's command. These demons are characterized by "wickedness" (*ponerias*, a word that means the evil ones try to get others to be evil, too). "In the heavenly places" seems to identify where this order of demons live and are active. We have had the term "heavenly *places*" before.[41] Perhaps here it corresponds to "air" of Ephesians 2:2, i.e., the atmospheric heavens. Paul's treatment here is a forcible testimony to the objective existence of the world of evil spirits. To an audience only a generation removed from Calvary, Paul warns Christians about the fact and reality of their tremendously powerful spiritual enemies, and he calls on his readers to put on the whole armor of God. This indicates that "until the end of the age these demonic forces, already defeated by Christ on the cross (Ephesians 4:9), exercise a certain limited authority in temporarily opposing the purposes of God."[42]

d. Anticipated outcome of the struggle.   13

6:13 -- *Therefore, take up the full armor of God, that you may be able to resist in the evil day, and having done everything, to stand firm.*

Therefore – "Therefore" looks back to the verse 12. Because we face demonic foes more formidable that mere human beings, we need the complete panoply (a full suit of armor); we need to be armed with all the help available.

Take up the full armor of God – This repetition of the command already given

---

[40] It is this commentator's judgment that four different classes or ranks of demons are indicated by the four times Paul uses the word "against."

[41] Scripture speaks of three heavens (2 Corinthians 12:2): the atmospheric heavens, the starry heavens, and the place where God dwells. The other four places where "in the heavenlies" appears in Ephesians are 1:3 (divine election took place in the heavenlies), 1:20 (Christ is in heaven), 2:6 (Christians are in heavenly places, potentially in heaven, or in a heavenly institution), and 3:10 (angels who live in heaven). Each of those times, the reference appears to be to the place where God dwells. However, here in Ephesians 6:12, since it is connected with demonic activity, the expression seems to have a different meaning than it did in the other four places where Paul used it. Perhaps here it denotes the atmospheric heavens as being the place where the demons are active. Jerome long ago suggested that this phrase should be treated like the phrase "the birds of heaven" (Matthew 6:26).

[42] Wood, *ibid.*

in verse 11 emphasizes its importance.[43] "Take up" means pick it up and put it on. Paul here uses words which would be used by the officer who commanded the soldiers to make ready for battle. The verb is an aorist imperative, which construction issues a command given with military snap and curtness, a command to be obeyed at once, and once for all. "Take it up now!" There won't be time to put it on once the evil day has begun. Again, the human responsibility for putting on the armor is emphasized. For the second time Paul emphasizes that it is the "full armor" that is needed. If we put on only five out of six pieces, we shall be vulnerable with an Achilles heel. We do not pick and choose what we like to wear. We need all that God offers us. Only with it all will we be able to stand in the evil day.[44] As it did in verse 11, "of God" says these pieces of armor are supplied or provided by God. They are the God-given ways by which God empowers Christians to meet the enemy and be victorious.

That you may be able to resist in the evil day – This clause indicates the purpose for the armor. Various malign influences are always loose in the atmosphere. No matter what we do or don't do, one day these forces may decide to focus on us, or our family.[45] Paul's language about an "evil day" (literally, "day of evil") means a day will come when we shall be attacked by the demons.[46] "Able to resist" means to stand against, to oppose the onslaught of the demons.

And having done everything, to stand firm – "Having done everything" (*hapanta katergasamenoi*) means having taken every precaution and made every

---

[43] The verb Paul uses here (*elabete*, take up, assume) differs from the one (*endusasthe*, "put on," literally, be clothed in) used in verse 11. Taken together the two verbs say. 'Get the weapons and put them on for combat.'

[44] "In WW II not every soldier liked wearing the heavy helmet, but it was necessary when the shrapnel flew. Not every soldier liked carrying the cumbersome shovel, but it was necessary to dig fox holes. Not every Christian likes to wear the total armor of God, but it is necessary. If we didn't have it all, Satan would find our weakness with one of his schemes" (Staton, *op. cit.*, p.443).

[45] Folk who get involved in witchcraft and other occult practices actually invite the attention of the demons. Christians do not consciously invite demonic attention, but nevertheless they may be attacked on occasion.

[46] Some writers, thinking an outbreak of Satanic or demonic power is expected to occur just before Christ's second coming (Revelation 20:7-9), depict that as being the evil day Paul warns about. This commentator's judgment is that Paul does *not* have in mind that day at the end of the world, since only Christians who are then living will see that battle. And in that battle it is not the panoply of God that will win the victory but "fire came down from heaven and devoured them" (the devil and his helpers).

preparation possible. It indicates leaving nothing undone that could contribute to the success of the struggle. The verb "stand firm" pictures what the situation is when the fight is finished, namely, the Christian is still standing. Having prepared for the conflict by putting on the whole armor of God, and having resisted when the evil day happens, the Christian is victorious. The Christian is not lying prostrate on the battlefield, but still standing and ready for another attack when it comes. These are reassuring words to all Christians and especially to folk living in an animistic culture like Ephesus and Asia Minor were in Paul's day.

2. The armor described. 6:14-17

a. Girdle of truth. 14a

6:14 -- *Stand firm therefore, HAVING GIRDED YOUR LOINS WITH TRUTH, and HAVING PUT ON THE BREASTPLATE OF RIGHTEOUSNESS,*

Stand firm therefore – The "stand firm" in the latter part of 13 denoted the end of the conflict. This "stand firm" is at the beginning of the conflict. This imperative repeats the call to arms for the third time (verses 11,13). The several items of the Roman soldier's armor about to be listed appear in the order in which they would be put on as the soldier prepared for battle. Together they comprise the *panoplia* worn before taking the field. Each of the pieces of armor is given a spiritual application or meaning. Since many of these pieces of armor are no longer used in modern warfare, an artist's picture of a Roman soldier has been included to help readers visualize the different pieces of armor.[47]

HAVING GIRDED YOUR LOINS WITH TRUTH – These words in the NASB are in small caps, reminding us the words come from the Old Testament, namely, the LXX of Isaiah 11:5, where the Messiah is depicted as wearing the belt of righteousness around His loins and faithfulness as the belt around His waist. The verb tense in "having girded" indicates the soldier put his armor on before he ever took the field to battle.[48] The verb is middle voice in the Greek, indicating this is something the soldier did for his own benefit. The "girdle"

---

[47] A color picture can be found in Logos Bible Infographics Software at Ephesians 6:14.

[48] The aorists (having girded, having put on, having shod, having taken up) are properly used, since the arming was complete before the "stand" was taken. If Paul had written present tense verbs here, that would mean that they were to be arming themselves as they were taking up their position, which would be rather a mark of unpreparedness.

worn by the Roman soldier was a belt made of leather and covered with metal plates. It encircled the soldier's waist and was not an ornament but served an essential purpose. It gathered in the short tunic and helped keep the breastplate in place when the latter was fitted on. The scabbard in which the sword was sheathed (verse17) was sometimes attached to the belt, and sometimes secured by

Another picture of a Roman Soldier in uniform can be viewed in Fields, *The Glorious Church*, p.175.

a baldric (leather strap) over the left shoulder. When Paul makes his spiritual application he says that "truth" (*aletheia*) serves as the belt in the Christian soldier's armor. "Truth" is best taken in its subjective sense as speaking of an element of personal character such as truthfulness or integrity.[49] The first piece of a Christian's spiritual armor is that he or she always tells the truth – no lies, no exaggeration, no deception is practiced.

b. Breastplate of righteousness. 14b

And HAVING PUT ON THE BREASTPLATE OF RIGHTEOUSNESS – Again, the printing of the phrase all in capital letters alerts us to the fact that it is a quotation from the Old Testament. In Isaiah 59:17 we are told that Yahweh Himself put on righteousness like a breastplate. The Roman breastplate, intended to protect the chest and the vital organs within, covered the body from the neck to the thighs, and covered the front, the sides, and the back. The common soldier's breastplate was made of overlapping hoops or rings of bronze or iron which curved so as to wrap around the body like ribs.[50] These overlapping metal pieces were actually supported by a leather tunic to which they were sewn. The hoops were hinged at the back and clasped or tied together in front. There were also shoulder pieces, each made of four curved strips of metal. Most breastplates were also fitted with heavy leather straps, some for a shield for the upper arms and others hanging from the bottom of the breastplate to protect the soldier's groin area. When Paul makes his spiritual application, he identifies "righteousness" as being the breastplate in the Christian's spiritual armor. "Righteousness" means always doing what is right, both to God and to man (Matthew 22:35-40; Romans 13:8-10).[51] Good soldiers always maintain a proper relationship with their commander and their fellow soldiers. Those in God's army must do no less. When a Christian consistently practices righteous living toward God and man, there is no weak place where the devil can successfully attack.

---

[49] While some commentators have taken it as referring to the objective truth of the gospel (and have offered comments about people who are girded with such "broad-mindedness" that they are indifferent to the truth and thus are of no value to the Lord), it seems to this commentator that the "sword" about to be named in verse 17 is a reference to the gospel, while "truth" in this verse is an element of personal character.

[50] Folk who have seen the movie "Ben Hur" will remember Messala's breastplate as being two molded pieces of bronze that fitted around the torso. It was officers such as tribunes who had such fine breastplates.

[51] If "righteousness" were taken in an objective sense, this piece of armor would refer to God's method of justifying sinners. However, just as "truth" in the previous clause was deemed to be a matter of personal character, so, in this commentator's judgment, "righteousness" should also be interpreted as being a character trait of the Christian.

c. Feet shod with preparation.   15

6:15 -- *and having shod YOUR FEET WITH THE PREPARATION OF THE GOSPEL OF PEACE;*

And having shod YOUR FEET – Once the breastplate has been fitted into position, the soldier next put on his strong army boots, or *caligae*.[52]   The Roman soldier wore heavy leather sandals which were bound by thongs over the instep and around the ankle, and the soles of the sandals were thickly studded with hob-nails.   The hob-nails, or cleats, gave the soldier confidence of having a firm footing in the case of attack, even on sloping or slippery surfaces.   One must have a firm footing for hand-to-hand combat.   The metaphor Paul wrote pictures the feet as having been shod or armed as with military sandals, and the sandal is the *hetoimasia*, or preparedness of, or caused by, the gospel of peace.[53]

WITH THE PREPARATION OF THE GOSPEL OF PEACE – "Preparation" may not be quite the exact English equivalent for the Greek expression *en hetoimasia*.   "Preparedness" or "readiness" would give readers a better idea of the Greek.   The word talks about the condition of a person who is prepared for some eventuality.   The expression thus seems to say that the gospel results in a peaceful, calm spirit.[54]   The Christian soldier knows no terror or hysteria in anticipation of the evil day and its struggle.   Our *peace with God* makes us confident about the outcome of our *battle with Satan*!   If God is for us, who can successfully be against us?   In the Christian's spiritual armor, a peaceful, calm spirit serves as the shoes that give him a firm footing.

---

[52] Josephus describes such boots, *Wars*, VI.1.8.

[53] The NASB has printed the major part of this verse in small caps, as though the language came from the Old Testament, but it is not easy to find a passage where these words all occur.   The NASB marginal note suggests that Paul had in mind Isaiah 52:7, which reads "How lovely on the mountains are the feet of him who brings good news, who announces peace."   However, making reference to that verse tends to send us off in the wrong direction as we look for an interpretation of the metaphor Paul here employed.   Since, of all the ideas found in Isaiah 52, only the word "peace" is found in Ephesians 6:15, that fact should tell us that Ephesians 6:15 is evidently not quite synonymous with Romans 10:15 where the words of Isaiah 52:7 are reproduced exactly.   In that passage the verse quoted from Isaiah carries the meaning of preparation to preach the gospel.   Though some commentators explain the words here in 6:15 to mean the same thing (readiness to go out at any moment to announce the Good News to others), perhaps the fact that of the words printed in capital letters here in Ephesians only the word "peace" actually is found in Isaiah 52:7 should cause us pause.   After all, in this passage (Ephesians 6:10-16) the Christian soldier is not pictured as advancing but as preparing to stand and fight.

[54] Animistic peoples live in constant fear of the spirits.   The gospel of peace gives us a reason to be done with such fear and hysteria, and to therefore be done acquiescing to what the spirits want because of our fear of them.

d. Shield of faith.   16

6:16 – *in addition to all, taking up the shield of faith with which you will be able to extinguish all the flaming missiles of the evil* **one.**

In addition to all – Perhaps *epi pasin* means "to cover all the rest."

Taking up the shield of faith – The shield (*thureon*, from *thura*, "door"), of the heavy-armed Roman soldier, to which reference is made, is described by Polybius as being 4' long and 2 ½' wide. It consisted of two or three layers of wood glued together, covered with linen and hide, and bound around the edges with iron or brass. It was held on the left arm and could be used to protect the entire body, and was very essential to the safety of the combatant. Soldiers standing side by side, some holding their shields about shoulder high, and others holding them overhead, could form a solid wall (*testudo*) of shields behind which and underneath which a whole body of troops could hide themselves from the rain of the enemies' missiles. In the Christian's spiritual armor, it is "faith" which serves as a shield. "Faith" is likely "faithfulness" to God so that no sin or disobedience tempts us. When Christians are determined to be faithful, the devil has no opening through which to successfully tempt us.

With which you will be able to extinguish all the flaming missiles of the evil one – "Flaming missiles" (*malleoli*) were wooden arrows tipped with tow (hemp or cotton fibers), dipped in pitch and set on fire.[55] Such flaming missiles were the most formidable and frightening offensive weapons the ancients had. "Arrows tipped with burning pitch can make a very painful and damaging wound, but not to an alert soldier equipped with a shield big enough to protect his whole body."[56] "The evil *one*" (Greek "the pernicious *one*"[57]) is a reference to the devil, "who is not content to perish in his own destruction, but seeks to drag everyone else down with him to the utter ruin that will be his in the future eternity."[58]   In Paul's metaphor, the flaming missiles seem to refer to demonic attacks launched

---

[55] The KJV reads "fiery darts."   Some of the older interpreters understood the word "fiery" to mean poisoned arrows that produced fever, but this is contrary to the grammatical meaning of the word.   Others see a reference in "fiery" to incitement of the passions, lusts, etc., but it is not likely that this is included, for the fire belongs to the enemy who shoots the darts.

[56] Phillips, *op. cit.*, p.108.

[57] The Greek word *ponerou* is singular, and undoubtedly is masculine rather than neuter – hence, "the evil *one*" is the proper translation.

[58] Wuest, *op. cit.*, p.144.

by the "evil one" on the "evil day" (verse 13) and employing the rulers, powers, world rulers, and spiritual hosts alluded to in verse 12. We are Satan's targets, and when those times occur, our long determination and habit of being faithful to God and Christ will serve as a shield to deflect the missiles.[59]

e. Helmet of salvation. 17a

6:17 -- *And take the helmet of salvation, and the sword of the Spirit, which is the word of God.*

And take the helmet of salvation – "Take" (*dexasthe*, an aorist imperative) may be translated "receive" or "accept" or "welcome" since the helmet and the sword were handed to the armed combatant by his aide or armor bearer. Appropriately, both salvation and the word of God are also given to the Christian. The Roman soldier's "helmet," as its name *perikephelaia* implies, covered the head (*kephale*). Made of thick leather or brass, and fitted to the head, with a visor to help protect the face, hinged cheek guards, plus a bill-shaped protrusion on the back to help protect the neck, its purpose was to guard the head from a swinging blow by a sword, a war club, or a battle-axe. "Salvation," that is, thoughts about our present and future salvation, along with a determination that that salvation must not be forfeited or missed, is part of a Christian's armor.[60] Since the topic here is not one's initial salvation, it is clearly implied that if Christians do not win the struggle on the evil day because they failed to put on the whole armor of God, their salvation is endangered. "It is fitting to think of our salvation as something that protects our minds. The battle for our souls is also in a very real sense a battle for our minds. It is the mind where evil takes hold, and it is the mind that God wants to transform (Romans 12:2; Ephesians 4:23)."[61] Satan is after the minds of us all since from our thoughts come our deeds. Our battle is to control our thoughts, and take the thoughts captive, bringing them to obey Christ (2 Corinthians 10:5).

---

[59] Revelation 9:4 also presents the comforting truth that demons cannot harm faithful Christians.

[60] The Greek word commonly used for the abstract idea of salvation is feminine (*soteria*). The word here translated "salvation" (*soterion*, the same word used in Luke 2:30; Luke 3:6; Acts 28:28) is either neuter or masculine. It is a general expression for something "which tends to salvation." In 1 Thessalonians 5:8, where Paul made another use of the metaphor of armor, the helmet is "the *hope* of salvation." The words "helmet of salvation" are printed in small caps in NASB[95] because they are found in the LXX at Isaiah 59:17.

[61] Shannon, *op. cit.*, p.413.

f. Sword of the Spirit. 17b

And the sword of the Spirit – Paul refers to the gladius sword (*machaira*), the short, two-edged, cut-and-thrust sword wielded by the heavily armed legionary, as distinct from the *rhomphaia*, or large Thracian broadsword. See Hebrews 4:12 for the only other New Testament passage where a "sword" appears in spiritual imagery. "Of the Spirit" likely means given by the Spirit.[62] It is called the sword "of the Spirit" because the Holy Spirit inspired the writers who set it down for us.

Which is the word of God – Since it is *rhema* that is translated "word" in the phrase "word of God," the expression refers to a spoken word, an utterance that comes from God.[63] As Peter calls the gospel which had been preached to his readers "THE WORD (*rhema*) OF THE LORD" which "ABIDES FOREVER" (1 Peter 1:25), we judge that in Paul's metaphor based on a Roman soldier's armor, the Scriptures serve as the Christian's spiritual sword.[64] Jesus, during His temptations in the wilderness (Matthew 4:1-11), has given us an example of how to use Scripture to meet various temptations offered by the devil. He countered the devil's temptations by quoting Scripture. It is significant that in Matthew's temptation narrative, Jesus Himself (quoting Deuteronomy 8:3) referred to "every word (*rhema*) that proceeds out of the mouth of God" (Matthew 4:4). He used Scripture with such good effect that the devil left Him. Luther's hymn reflects this use of Scripture against the devil in the words "the prince of darkness grim – we tremble not for him; His rage we can endure, for Lo! His doom is sure, One little word shall fell him." A realization that the word of God is such a powerful weapon should impress upon us how vital it is to make the diligent study and memorization of Scripture a priority in our own lives. That is how a Christian soldier takes up the sword of the Spirit.

---

[62] The suggested interpretation treats "of the Spirit" as a genitive of source or origin, just as the phrase "of God" was treated in the expression "the full armor of God," (verses 11,13).

[63] In the Bible, both *logos* and *rhema* are used of God's "word," the Scriptures (e.g., in Hebrews 4:12 *logos* is the Greek translated "word"). English readers who are accustomed to recall that at John 1:1-5 Jesus is called the "Word" should also be aware that the Greek word there is *logos*, not *rhema*. The use of *rhema* here in Ephesians points to a spoken word from God, not the personal word.

[64] Any of the sacred writings included in the Old and New Testaments would qualify as the "word of God." These writings are included in the canon because they were inspired by the Holy Spirit. Old Testament prophets, New Testament prophets and apostles, all spoke and wrote the utterances that came from God as the Spirit gave them utterance. Paul's expression "the sword of the Spirit" is very apropos.

3. Exhortation to prayer.   6:18-20

a.   For themselves and for all saints.   18

6:18 -- *With all prayer and petition pray at all times in the Spirit, and with this in view, be on the alert with all perseverance and petition for all the saints,*

With all prayer and petition – Since there is no comparison between prayer and some piece of a Roman soldier's armor, it would seem that prayer is not a seventh piece of armor.   It is best to treat the two participles in this verse ("praying" and "be[ing] on the alert") as being dependent on the main verb "stand" in verse 14. Thus, the connection is this: not only does the Christian soldier put on the whole armor of God as he prepares to make his stand, but he also spends time in prayer for his fellow soldiers.   "Prayer" and "petition" are two of the synonyms for prayer found in the New Testament.   The word "prayer" (*proseuche*) is a general word used of language addressed only to God, and can include requests, words of thanksgiving, words of praise and adoration.   "Petition" (*deēsis*) is a particular word which speaks of requests for something specific from God.   Might this be an allusion to one of the requests in the Model Prayer, "Do not permit us to be tempted, but deliver us from the evil one"?

Pray at all times in the Spirit – Praying "at all times" (*en panti kairo,* "on all occasions") reminds us of Jesus' parable to His disciples that they should pray at all times and not to lose heart (Luke 18:1), and Paul's exhortation to Christians to "pray without ceasing" (1 Thessalonians 5:17).   The Christian spends time in prayer at all seasons, [65] not just when putting on the pieces of armor.

What does it mean to "pray ... in the Spirit (*en pneumati*)"?[66]   Since the expression *en pneumati* has been made a reference to the Holy Spirit earlier in Ephesians (at 2:22, 3:5, 5:18), and since Jude 20 reads "praying in the Holy Spirit," the NASB translation "in the Spirit" appears to be the correct choice.   The

---

[65] "No period of life should be without prayer – youth, middle life, old age, all demand it. No condition of life – adversity, prosperity, sunshine, desolation, under sore temptation, under important duty, under heavy trial, under all the changing circumstances of life – should be without prayer" (Blaikie, *op. cit.,* p.260).

[66] This phrase has proven difficult for commentators to explain.   There is no agreement among the commentators whether to translate it "in the Spirit" or "in spirit," nor on what the verse may mean whichever way we treat *en pneumati*.

most likely explanation is the one that treats the dative *en pneumati* as a dative of sphere.[67] If we treat both this passage and Jude 20 as a dative of sphere, these parallel verses say that believers are to pray 'according to the Spirit's will (set forth in the written Word and made known by inner promptings)' as they offer their petitions and prepare to take their stand against the evil one. "The great requirement of standing ready for the combat (verse 14) can be made good only when prayer, constant, earnest, spiritual prayer is added to the careful equipping with all the parts of the panoply."[68]

And with this in view, be on the alert – "With this" (*eis auto*, "unto this") is neuter. It is difficult to determine precisely which idea in this paragraph is pointed to. Perhaps it continues the thought introduced by "stand firm" in verse 14. Perhaps it continues the thought introduced by "praying at all times in the Spirit." The explanation given for "be on the alert" *(agrupnountes*, "watching," ASV) will be influenced by our decision concerning "with this." Literally, the word *agrupnountes* means "keep awake" or "stay awake." But it does not seem probable that it is meant to be taken literally in this passage, so the NASB's "be ... alert" seems to be an apt choice of words to catch the figurative meaning. If the topic is being ready   to make one's stand in the evil day,   then Paul is urging

---

[67] Another option is to treat *en pneumati* as a dative of agent. If we treat *en pneumati* as a dative of agent, it says "the Spirit" (or "spirit") is the agent who motivates or prompts the Christian to pray. Having adopted the idea that it is a dative of agent, writers have then looked for parallel passages to help explain what Paul has written. Some appeal to Romans 8:26 while others appeal to 1 Corinthians 14:14-16. This commentator doubts that either of these passages is helpful. The passage in Romans does say the Holy Spirit helps our weaknesses, causing us to "yearn" or "sigh" (a feeling or expression which God can "read" and understand) when we do not know for what to pray, but the passage also specifically says there are no words spoken. All there is are sighs prompted by the Holy Spirit. Paul's words here in Ephesians 6:18 about prayers and petitions seem to be indicating more than "groaning" or "sighing" as one prays "at all times." So Romans 8 does not seem to be a parallel passage to Ephesians 6. In 1 Corinthians14, Paul is correcting the abuse of tongues (speaking in a foreign language in the public assembly when no one present can understand the language being spoken) by the Corinthian Christians. In the NASB, 1 Corinthians 14:14 is written (correctly we believe) with a small "s" – "I will pray with the spirit ...." So translated, the verse seems to refer, not to a prayer prompted by the Holy Spirit, but to a prayer in which the believer's "spirit" actively participates as he speaks words in a foreign language, words which were prompted by the Holy Spirit (1 Corinthians 12:10, Acts 2:4). When Paul continues (1 Corinthians 14:14) by writing "I will pray with the understanding (ASV)," he likely is saying he will offer a public prayer using a foreign language during the assembly only when the listeners who are present can understand what is being said, so that they know when to say the "amen" (1 Corinthians 14:16). Thus it seems that neither Romans 8:26 nor 1 Corinthians 14:14-16 are parallel passages to what Paul has written in Ephesians 6:18.

[68] Salmond, *op. cit.*, p.389.

the Christians to be constantly on guard ("alert") lest our enemies should surprise us.   If the topic is "praying in the Spirit," then what Paul is prompting the readers to do is to be alert for opportunities to pray; or be alert concerning all those things which would hinder prayer.[69]

With all perseverance and petition for all the saints – Not only do they persevere in prayer for themselves, but Christians are to pray for other saints. "Perseverance" means "to give constant attention to" a thing.   It implies that effort or exertion will be needed to accomplish this thing.   Jesus once taught a parable whose lesson was that men ought always to pray and not become discouraged so as to quit praying (Luke 18:1-8).   "Saints" is another name for Christians, indicating they are set apart, dedicated to sacred service.   We notice that not only are we to pray at all times, but we are to pray for all saints.   Such prayer acknowledges that all Christians have been targeted by the enemy and must therefore be undergirded with prayer.   Just as Satan is unrelenting in his efforts toward Christians, so Christians must pray with perseverance.   "We are not engaged in single combat with the power of evil, but are members of an army; we must be concerned with the welfare of all who fight alongside us."[70]

b. For Paul.   19,20

1) That he might speak the right words.   6:19a

6:19 -- *and* **pray** *on my behalf, that utterance may be given to me in the opening of my mouth, to make known with boldness the mystery of the gospel,*

And *pray* on my behalf – This verse continues the sentence which began with verse 17.   Paul has been exhorting his readers to be people of prayer, and as they offer their prayers for all the saints, he asks that they will specifically include him in their prayers.[71]   He directs them to include two specific requests in their prayers for him.

---

[69] This encouragement to alertness and prayer reminds us of Jesus' words to His apostles in Gethsemane (Matthew 26:38,41 and Mark 14:38).   Compare Colossians 4:2 and 1 Peter 4:7.

[70] Cited in Bratcher, *op. cit.*, p.165.

[71] "How often do we pray 'for all the sick' or 'all the missionaries' or 'all the Christians meeting in every place' or 'all the lost' without really thinking of anyone personally?   Our prayer will be more meaningful and powerful if we name names, if we ask God to supply specific needs of specific people whom we know, people who are in our hearts" (Phillips, *op. cit.*, p.110).

That utterance may be given to me in the opening of my mouth – The first thing Paul requests seems to be a prayer for inspiration from the Holy Spirit when he is about to speak.   Jesus made a promise to His apostles (recorded in Matthew 10:19,20) that when they were on trial before civil authorities, they themselves would not have to formulate defenses and make arguments.   Instead, Jesus said, "Do not become anxious about how or what you will speak; for it shall be given you in that hour what you are to speak.   For it is not you who speak, but it is the Spirit of your Father who speaks in you."   Since Paul is an apostle of Jesus, just as much as were the twelve, he could expect the same divine help when it came time to speak.   "In the opening of my mouth" equals "when I open my mouth." It is a common phrase for making a public address or a long defense.   Paul desired prayers that, with the Holy Spirit's help, the right words would come out when he opened his mouth to speak.

2) That he might speak with boldness.   6:19b-20

To make known with boldness the mystery of the gospel – This is the second thing Paul requests the readers to include in their prayers for him.   "Since he was a prisoner (verse 20), we might have expected Paul to ask for prayers for his freedom.   But something else was dearer to Paul's heart.   He asked the readers of this letter to pray that God would give him the courage to proclaim the gospel fearlessly."[72]   He wants to be bold, to speak freely regardless of who may be listening, or regardless of what might happen to him because he so spoke.   This request for boldness reflects the fact that "the spirits of the prophets are subject to the prophets" (1 Corinthians 14:32 ASV).   This means that when a revelation was made to a prophet, he could control whether or not he then spoke it in public. So, in Paul's case, even after the Spirit was ready to prompt his words (in answer to the first request he asks them to make to God), Paul could still refuse to utter them.

The term "ambassador" in verse 20 may indicate Paul has in mind that he envisions having to stand before imperial authorities – perhaps even before the emperor himself.   Paul anticipates he would be called on to give his testimony if and when his accusers should arrive.   Meanwhile, we read about Paul's day-to-day witnessing in Acts 28:30,31.   We are told he spoke to all who came to him while he was a prisoner in his own hired house in Rome.   Acts 28:31 says he spoke with "all boldness, none forbidding him" (ASV).   Thus we may conclude

---

[72] Phillips, *ibid.*

that this request for boldness and courage as he had opportunity to proclaim the gospel was answered. That Paul wanted to make known "the mystery of the gospel" (see Ephesians 1:9 and 3:4,5) reminds us that, as the apostles preached the gospel of Jesus Christ, they had the privilege of clearly and understandably presenting the truths which all along had been included in God's plan of redemption, but which had been only partially revealed in Old Testament times. What Paul requests his readers to pray about is in perfect harmony with Paul's special responsibility, which was to make known in no uncertain terms that God's redemptive plan was designed for Gentiles as well as for Jews. (See Ephesians 3:4-9. See also Romans 11:25; Colossians 1:26; 2 Timothy 1:9,10.)

6:20 -- *for which I am an ambassador in chains; that in* **proclaiming** *it I may speak boldly, as I ought to speak.*

For which I am an ambassador in chains – "For which" refers to the "mystery of the gospel." What Paul writes here is similar to what we read in Colossians 4:3,4. "Ambassador" points to a court. The emperor or the king receives the ambassador, nods, and thus permits him to deliver his message. Paul is thinking of the day he was so anxiously awaiting, when he would stand before the emperor to whom he had appealed his case. But see the vividness of Paul's mind. He sees himself in the most paradoxical light: presently a prisoner before a judge, and yet this role fades out into an ambassador sent by Christ, the King of kings, standing in the throne room of Nero, delivering the message of his King to the pagan imperial court. "In chains" translates *en halusei*. In the Greek, it is singular; literally, "in a chain."[73] It indicates a single short length of chain by which Paul's right wrist was fastened to his soldier guard's left wrist. "Ambassadors normally enjoyed diplomatic immunity, but Paul would be compelled to appear in the imperial court as a prisoner. Instead of wearing a gold chain of office, he would be shackled to his guard."[74] Paul describes himself as an ambassador of Christ (2 Corinthians 5:20). It was his mission to the Gentiles which had led to his being a prisoner.

---

[73] The singular "in a chain" occurs also in Mark 5:4 and Luke 8:29, where it is distinguished from a "fetter" properly so called, as binding the feet, and therefore obviously signifies a "manacle" binding the wrist.

[74] Wood, *op. cit.*, p.90.

That in *proclaiming* it I may speak boldly, as I ought to speak – By adding "proclaiming" in italics, the NASB has rightly shown that "in it" (Greek) refers to the mystery of the gospel, not his chain. As an ambassador of Christ he had an obligation to speak the message Christ wanted him to deliver. When Jesus called Paul to be an apostle, Paul was told the day would come when he would bear Christ's name before kings (Acts 9:15). When the day finally came that he would stand before the imperial court, then he must speak not as an intimidated prisoner but as a true ambassador. He asks for the prayers of the readers that he might have the courage to speak as he ought to speak. We do not know whether or not during this first Roman imprisonment Paul had the opportunity to speak before the emperor. However, 2 Timothy 4:16-18 seems to indicate that the day eventually did come, during Paul's second Roman imprisonment, when he did have a hearing before the emperor, and he did proclaim the gospel boldly on that occasion.

CONCLUSION AND FINAL SALUTATION.   6:21-24

1. Commendation of Tychicus.   6:21,22

6:21 -- *But that you also may know about my circumstances, how I am doing, Tychicus, the beloved brother and faithful minister in the Lord, will make everything known to you.*

But that you also may know about my circumstances, how I am doing – Having referred to his captivity, Paul knew it would be natural for his readers to desire more information about how he fared and his state of mind in captivity. Rather than giving such information in this letter, Tychicus would convey such news by word of mouth when he delivered the letter. The words "you also" may refer to each congregation to which Tychicus came with this circular letter. They may mean "you as well as the Christians here in Rome." Compare Colossians 4:7 which is almost a word-for-word parallel. Since Tychicus is to relate to the Colossians the same information he would to the readers of Ephesians, it is quite understandable that Paul employed the same terms.

Tychicus – On this one trip, Tychicus was to carry the three letters (Ephesians, Colossians, Philemon) to their respective destinations. He was also to deliver the slave Onesimus to Philemon, his master, in Colossae. Concerning Tychicus we know relatively little.[75]   We first meet him as he helps carry the offering from the Roman province of Asia to the saints in Jerusalem at the end of Paul's third missionary (Acts 20:4).   In the years that followed the journey to Asia spoken of here in 6:21, Tychicus is again alluded to as being one of Paul's companions in the interval between Paul's first and second Roman captivities; at that time, Paul proposed to send Tychicus to Crete to succeed Titus (Titus 3:12).   Later, during Paul's second Roman captivity, Tychicus is dispatched once more to Ephesus (2 Timothy 4:12) to free Timothy from the leadership responsibilities there so Timothy can make a journey to Rome.

The beloved brother and faithful minister in the Lord – "Brother" is probably to be taken in a spiritual sense – i.e., a brother in Christ, a brother dearly loved. We might also think of "minister" as being a designation for one who held the office of evangelist in the early church (cp. 1 Timothy 4:6).[76]

Will make everything known to you – Unlike most of his letters, this letter titled "to the Ephesians" gives us no personal information about Paul, except that he was in prison.   But Tychicus, as he went from congregation to congregation, would tell the Christians how Paul was faring, and would bring them a message of personal encouragement.

6:22 – *I have sent him to you for this very purpose, so that you may know about us, and that he may comfort your hearts.*

And I have sent him to you for this very purpose – "I have sent" is likely an example of the Greek construction called an epistolary aorist.   If so, it means that Paul is sending him right now (as soon as the letter is completed), but contemplated from the view-point of the readers,   at the time they read the letter,

---

[75] Early Christian literature offers little help.   It is not known when or where he became a Christian.   Hippolytus of Rome identified him as one of the seventy whom Jesus sent out two by two (Luke 10:1).   In addition, there are a few scattered references in Early Christian literature to places where he served as a church leader, places other than those named in the New Testament.

[76] The word "minister" is *diakonos*, but there is no reason to think that it is used technically to denote a holder of the office of deacon (as it is in Philippians 1:1; 1 Timothy 3:8,12).   Nor is it correct, in our judgment, to explain this term to mean that Tychicus was some kind of apostolic delegate.

the sending will have been a thing of the past.[77] "This very purpose" is, namely, to inform the brethren about Paul's circumstances, as he goes on to indicate.

So that you may know about us – "Us" reminds us that there were others with Paul (see Colossians 4:10-15), and he includes them. Paul wants his readers to know not only about himself but also about his co-workers and their circumstances.[78] As regards himself, Paul uses the verb which simply denotes knowing the facts (*oida*, verse 21); but here in verse 22, when he combines those others with himself, he writes the verb that indicates knowing with personal concern (*ginosko*).

And that he may comfort your hearts – To pagans, imprisonment was always dreadful; it was well for them to know how Christians could rejoice in tribulations (Romans 5:3). Tychicus, the beloved brother, was well qualified to relate this comforting view of Paul's situation.[79] It would encourage the readers to learn that Paul was being well treated and was free to preach to those who visited him (Acts 28:17-31).

2. Closing Benediction. 6:23,24

Summary: The benediction is a prayer in which Paul asks for three things for his readers.

a. Peace – unity between Jew and Gentile. 23a

6:23 – *Peace be to the brethren, and love with faith, from God the Father and the Lord Jesus Christ.*

Peace be to the brethren – The "brethren" are all the Christian brothers who are reading this letter.   Peace between Jewish and Gentile Christians (see 2:14-18,

---

[77] This verse corresponds word for word with Colossians 4:8 and serves as Paul's commendation of Tychicus to the readers. So Tychicus was sent to both the Colossians and the readers of Ephesians for a specific purpose.

[78] There are passages (see especially 1 Thessalonians 3:1-2) where Paul evidently uses "we" in the sense of "I"; but this is not likely here, in view of the "how I am doing," just before (Ephesians 6:21).

[79] The word translated "comfort" (*parakalese*) carries the idea of exhortation, encouraging, or strengthening, more than consolation. See notes at Ephesians 4:1 where it was translated "entreat."

4:3, 6:15), which has been a major theme of this letter, is the thing spoken of here. If they will just contemplate the fact they are brothers, that will go a long way toward ending the clashes and enmity that each had grown up with before they became Christians.

b. Love. 23b

And love with faith, from God the Father and the Lord Jesus Christ– Here, as in most of Paul's benedictions, we can find the major ideas of the epistle summed up. Not only were we told that in love God predestined us in Christ unto adoption as His sons (1:4), but earlier in this letter Paul has prayed that the readers may know both (1) the length, breadth, height, and depth of the love of God the Father and (2) the love of Christ which surpasses knowledge (3:17-19). As Paul pens this benediction the idea of the Father's and the Son's love resurfaces. "With faith" would say such love can continue to be experienced by those who are faithful.[80]

c. Grace. 24

6:24 – *Grace be with all those who love our Lord Jesus Christ with* **a** *love incorruptible.*

Grace be with all those who love our Lord Jesus Christ – "Those who love our Lord" is another way of saying "believers, Christians." The Greek reads "the grace," that is, the grace beside which there is no other.[81] In all Paul's earlier epistles (Romans 15:20; 1 Corinthians 16:23; 2 Corinthians 13:14; Galatians 6:18; 1 Thessalonians 5:28; 2 Thessalonians 3:18) and in the epistle to the Philippians, Paul specifies whose grace it is that he invokes, namely, that of our Lord Jesus Christ.   In his later epistles the expression has become so familiar that "the grace" can be used absolutely without any fear of misunderstanding whose grace is being invoked on the readers (see Colossians 4:18; 1 Timothy 6:21; 2 Timothy 4:22; Titus 3:15; Hebrews 13:25).

With *a love* **incorruptible** – Note that "love" is in italics, and a marginal note tells us the Greek (*en aphtharsia*) is literally "in incorruption."   There is some

---

[80] "The name of Christ the Son is associated with that of God the Father in perfect equality" (Wood, *op. cit.*, p.92).

[81] On the meaning of the word "grace" see 1:2.

difficulty regarding the final phrase, both as to its construction and its meaning.[82] The easiest explanation results from a straightforward translation of the Greek as "our Lord Jesus Christ in incorruption," with the idea being expressed that Jesus who is now in His glorified body (His body is incorruptible) is the One who is being loved. In these words of his benediction, Paul sums up another idea that was emphasized in the letter, for several times he has emphasized that Jesus has been raised and seated at the Father's right hand in the heavenly places. Thus, the surprise felt by so many regarding this closing phrase turns to admiration when Paul's meaning is understood. The epistle began with an ascription of praise to "the God and Father of our Lord Jesus Christ who has blessed us with every spiritual blessing in the heavenly *places* in Christ" (1:3). It closes with a prayer that God's grace will be on all those who love our glorified Lord Jesus Christ.[83]

---

[82] The KJV treats *en aphtharsia* as modifying love with its reading "love our Lord Jesus Christ in sincerity." That is an unexpected translation for *aphtharsia* which elsewhere in the KJV is translated as "incorruption" (1 Corinthians 15:42, 50, 53, 54; 2 Timothy 1:10). The ASV and NASB treat *en aphtharsia* as modifying love as is shown by the addition of "a love" in italics. But *en aphtharsia* is a strange way of expressing "undying love." Lenski prefers that we understand in the words *en aphtharsia* a fourth thing is being prayed for by Paul for his readers, namely, a glorified body, a new body in heaven, such as Paul speaks about in 1 Corinthians 15:50-54 (where the word *aphtharsia*, "incorruptible," appears several times).

[83] In the KJV the letter closes with an "Amen" and a subscription, neither of which are included in the NASB. The "Amen" is not found in Aleph, A, B, G, 17, while the subscription to this epistle (which reads, "Written from Rome unto the Ephesians by Tychicus"), like those affixed to the other epistles, is of no authority, and in this instance, like others, is perhaps only partly right.

Commentary On

Colossians

Concise Introduction to Colossians[1]

Colossians is one of four New Testament letters that the apostle Paul wrote during his imprisonment in Rome, about AD 62-63. Those letters (Ephesians, Colossians, Philemon, and Philippians) we collectively call the "Prison Epistles."

Colossians was written to the church in Colossae, a city in the Roman province of Asia (now western Turkey). The city was located about 100 miles inland from Ephesus, which was situated on the western coast of that land mass.

Tychicus, one of Paul's trusted helpers, was to deliver three of the Prison Epistles to their intended readers. Accompanying Tychicus was Onesimus, a runaway slave, whom Paul was sending back to Philemon in Colossae (Ephesians 6:21,22; Colossians 4;7-9).

Paul himself had not visited Colossae during his missionary journeys (Colossians 1:9, 2:1). The gospel had been carried there by Paul's associates (1:7).

While Paul had not been associated personally with the church in Colossae, he was greatly concerned about its welfare (Colossians 2:1,2). While in prison he had learned of the state of the Colossian Christians from Epaphras (Colossians 1:7,8). Epaphras had come to Rome from Colossae bringing word of the spiritual condition of the church in Colossae. He told Paul the faith of the Colossian Christians was being challenged by false teachings (which we designate as "the Colossian Heresy"). Epaphras wanted Paul's guidance concerning how to deal with the false teachings. Paul's "care of all the churches" (2 Corinthians 11:28 KJV) made him long to see their faith maintained and their spiritual strength remain unabated. Paul's approach to this problem was unequivocal, as we shall see as we study the four chapters in Colossians.

Several characteristics of these false teachings can be discerned from the content of Paul's letter. The heretics detracted from the divine nature and authority of Christ. They tried to blend the gospel with popular philosophies/religions of the day. They insisted on the observance of certain Jewish traditions. They taught the worship of angels. And they taught that the knowledge that leads to salvation is known only to a select few.

---

[1] A Detailed Introduction to Colossians is included later in this commentary. Readers of this commentary will find explanations there for many of the statements made in this Concise Introduction. Important discussions of matters such as the authorship of Colossians and the Colossian crisis are covered.

Outline of Colossians

I.   Introduction.   1:1-14

A. Signature, Address, and Greeting.   1:1,2

B. A Prayer of Thanksgiving.   1:3-8

Paul is thankful for their faith and prays that it may increase.

Prayer of thanks – for their faith and love, produced by the hope they had
learned in the gospel.   There is an emphatic reference to the "word of
truth, the gospel" as first preached unto them in all faithfulness by
Epaphras.

C. Prayer Requests for the Colossians.   1:9-14

Prayer requests made to God by Paul and his companions are (1) for their
knowledge of God's will to increase, (2) for them to walk worthily
(being encouraged by the hope of heaven, an inheritance for which
redemption in Christ has qualified them), and (3) for them to joyously
give thanks to the Father for the blessings of redemption.

II. DOCTRINAL FOUNDATION.   The Preeminence of Christ in All Relationships.   1:15-23

A. The Son's Preeminence in His Own Person.   1:15a

Christ is God.

B. The Son's Preeminence in the Universe.   1:15b-17

Christ is creator and sustainer of the universe.

C. The Son's Preeminence in the Church.   1:18-23

Christ is head of the church.

Application to the readers: Salvation in Christ is complete; the Gnostics
can add nothing!

III. CONTROVERSIAL SECTION.   Christ is Preeminent in Doctrine. 1:23-2:23

A. Paul's Work as a Servant of the Incomparable Christ. 1:24-2:7
   1. His ministry. 1:24,25
   2. His message. 1:26,27
   3. His motive.   1:28-2:3
   4. His mandate. 2:4-7

B. Elements of the "Colossian Heresy" to be Rejected. 2:8-23
   1. Its source is not divine, nor are its ideas in harmony with Christ. 2:8
   2. Its denial of some particular areas where Christ and His work excel. 2:9-15
   3. Its emphasis on obsolete Jewish ordinances. 2:16,17
   4. Its veneration of angels and its self-induced visions. 2:18,19
   5. Its asceticism. 2:20-23

IV. PRACTICAL SECTION.   Christ is Preeminent in Ethics.   3:1 - 4:6

A. The Foundation of True Christian Ethics. 3:1-4
   1. Seeking the things above. 3:1
   2. Setting the mind on things above. 3:2
   3. The motivations for these actions. 3:3,4

B. General Exhortations About the Christian Life. 3:5-17
   1. Vices to eliminate. 3:5-11
       a. Immoral behavior. 5-7
       b. Hostile attitudes. 8a
       c. Improper speech. 8b
       d. Lying. 9a
       e. Remember who you are. 9b-11

   2. Virtues to cultivate. 3:12-17
       a. A merciful spirit. 12
       b. A forgiving spirit. 13
       c. A loving spirit. 14
       d. A peaceful spirit. 15a
       e. A grateful/thankful spirit. 15b-17

C. Special Exhortations.   Family Relationships to be Strengthened.   3:18-4:1
  1. Wives and their husbands.   3:18,19
  2. Children and their parents.   3:20,21
  3. Slaves and their masters.   3:22-4:1

D. Religious Duties to be Faithfully Performed.   4:2-6
  1. Persistent prayer.   4:2-4
      Personal devotional life
  2. Behavior toward non-Christians.   4:5,6
      a. A winsome walk.   5   (Duty of witnessing)
      b. Gracious speech.   6

V. PERSONAL SECTION.   4:7-17

A. The Mission of Tychicus and Onesimus, 4:7-9

B. Salutations from Paul's Companions, 4:10-14

C. The Charge to Exchange Epistles with Laodicea, 4:15-17

Conclusion.   4:18
Autograph, salutation, exhortation, and benediction

Epistle to the Colossians

I. Introduction. 1:1-14

A. Signature, Address, and Greeting. 1:1,2

> *Summary:* Paul follows the standard form of letter writing in the first century, but in the greeting he adds a distinctly Christian emphasis.

1. Signature. 1:1

1:1 – *Paul, an apostle of Jesus Christ by the will of God, and Timothy our brother,*

Paul – As was the custom in ancient letters, the writer signs his name at the beginning. He identifies himself in the same words he used at the beginning of his letter "to the Ephesians." Paul is under a type of house arrest when he writes this letter. He had been falsely accused of crimes by the Jewish leaders at Jerusalem (see Acts 24:5,6). As a Roman citizen, Paul had exercised his right to appeal his case to Caesar (Acts 25:11). As a result, he had been taken from Judea to Rome in order that his appeal to the emperor might be heard. In his own hired house (Acts 28:16,20,30), he is chained to a soldier around the clock.

An apostle of Jesus Christ – By identifying himself as an apostle of Christ Jesus,[2] Paul is making it clear why he has a right to address a letter to folk who, for the most part, he has never met personally. He speaks as an authorized spokesman for Christ, duly commissioned as His representative, and empowered by the Holy Spirit so that the words contained in this letter are infallibly true. Christians are to give heed to the instructions of an apostle just as they would if the Lord Himself were speaking. The better attested word order is "Christ Jesus" (see ASV, RSV, NIV), and this puts a slight emphasis on the word "Christ," thus anticipating the high Christology that will be a feature of this letter. It suggests a special reference to His Messianic office and perhaps to His present glorification as Lord in glory.

By the will of God – It may be that this is a direct reference to the false teachers who are bringing deceptive doctrines to Colossae. They were not apostles of Christ Jesus and were self-willed, not sent by the will of God.

---

[2] See notes at Romans 1:1 or 1 Corinthians 1:1 or at Ephesians 1:1 for a detailed explanation of what it meant to be an apostle of Jesus Christ.

And Timothy our brother – There is every likelihood that Timothy served as the secretary who wrote this letter as Paul dictated it. Timothy was likely converted to Christ by Paul (1 Corinthians 4:17), and so is a brother in Christ. Timothy had traveled with Paul ever since the beginning of the second missionary tour (Acts 16:1ff) and is often associated with Paul as he is here in this letter (see 2 Corinthians 1:1; 1 Thessalonians 1:1; 2 Thessalonians 1:1; Philemon 1). Timothy was with Paul in a number of places, so that this is not a very good clue as to the time and place of writing. He was with Paul in Ephesus (cf. Acts 19:22) and in Macedonia (cf. 2 Corinthians 1:1). We must surely grant the possibility Timothy was with Paul in Rome at the time of Paul's first imprisonment there. Perhaps Timothy's name was omitted in the signature of Ephesians because in a circular letter to the churches the voice of the apostle alone needed to be heard.

2. Address. 1:2a

1:2 – *to the saints and faithful brethren in Christ who are at Colossae: Grace to you and peace from God our Father.*

To the saints and faithful brethren in Christ – The word *hagiois* ("saints") expresses their dedication to God.[3] "Brethren" expresses their union with their fellow-Christians. "In Christ," meaning in union with Christ, represents the formula frequently used by Paul to describe the intimate relationship which exists between Christians and their Lord. As is true in the opening verses of many of Paul's letters, here also he foreshadows his treatment of the problems besetting the church. Care must be exercised lest their dedication to God be compromised and their union be fractured.

Who are at Colossae – The history and geography of Colossae are covered in the Detailed Introduction to Colossians. Barclay has suggested that "in Christ" and "at Colossae" places two significant things side by side. He writes to the Christians who are in Colossae, and who are in Christ. "A Christian moves in two spheres. He is in the town, the place, the society where he happens to stay in this world; but he is also in Christ. ... We are all in our own Colossae, wherever that Colossae may be, but we are all in Christ, and it is Christ who sets the tone of our life and living."[4]

---

[3] The Greek word *hagiois* may be either an adjective ("holy") or a noun ("saints"). Elsewhere when the word occurs in the address of letters, it is treated as a noun (Romans 1:7; 1 Corinthians 1:2.; 2 Corinthians 1:1; Ephesians 1:1; Philippians 1:1).

[4] William Barclay, "The Letters to the Philippians, Colossians, and Thessalonians" in *The Daily Study Bible Series* (Philadelphia: Westminster Press, 1959), p.125.

3. Greeting.   1:2b

Grace to you and peace from God our Father – These words form a prayer for the Colossian Christians in which Paul prays that they may continue to be recipients of and enjoy God's grace and peace.   The same prayer formed the greeting of Ephesians where the terms were explained.[5]   If the Colossian Christians wish to continue to have God as their Father, and have His blessings, they must heed the warnings Paul is about to write.

B. A Prayer of Thanksgiving.   1:3-8

Summary: Paul thanks God for their faith and love, produced by or based on the hope they had learned in the gospel which had been faithfully preached to them by Epaphras.   Paul, out of apprehension that they might be beguiled from it, prays that their faith may increase.

1:3 – *We give thanks to God, the Father of our Lord Jesus Christ, praying always for you,*

We give thanks to God – In ancient letters, following the greeting, it was customary to include a word of thanksgiving for the readers.   Paul here writes "we give thanks."   This "we" may be an "epistolary" plural, that is, a conventional way of referring to the writer himself, or it may be a real plural including others besides himself.   The repetition of the "we" in verse nine causes us to believe that Paul and his associates often gathered together for prayer.[6]

---

[5] The words "and the Lord Jesus Christ" found here at the close of verse 2 in the KJV are present in the parallel passage Ephesians 1:2 but are probably to be omitted here, since the better manuscripts of Colossians do not carry the words.

[6] "In the light of (1) the singulars that occur (Colossians 1:23-27,29; 2:1-5; 4:3b-4; 4:7-10,18), and (2) the deliberate switch from the plural to singular (1:28-29; 4:3a, 3b), it seems probable that the plurals are real (1:3-14,28; 4:3a, 8b) and Paul intends to associate with himself not only Timothy (who is named in 1:1), but also the others of his immediate group."   Robert Bratcher and Eugene A. Nida, *A Translator's Handbook on Paul's Letters to the Colossians and Philemon* (Stuttgart: United Bible Societies, 1977), p.7.

The Father of our Lord Jesus Christ – "God" to whom the thanksgiving was addressed is here carefully identified as being "the Father of our Lord Jesus Christ." This identification may be a deliberate thrust against dualistic Gnostic ideas about God and about the Lord Jesus Christ's relationship to God.

Praying always for you – The preposition "for" in "praying for you" is *peri*, which means "concerning." It was concerning the needs and the circumstances of the Colossian saints that Paul and his co-workers were praying.[7] Other letters written by Paul also make note of his continual prayers on behalf of his readers (see Romans 1:8; 1 Corinthians 1:4; Ephesians 1:16; Philippians 1:3; 1Thessalonians 1:2; 2 Thessalonians 1:3; Philemon 4).

1:4 – *since we heard of your faith in Christ Jesus and the love which you have for all the saints;*

Since we heard of your faith in Christ Jesus – Verses 4-8 will highlight some of the things for which Paul gives thanks to God. The first thing Paul calls attention to is the report that has come to him about the faith and love of the Colossian Christians. It was from Epaphras (Colossians 1:7,8) that Paul and his companions[8] have heard of the spiritual condition of the Colossians. They evidently have not personally ever visited Colossae (cf. 1:9; 2:1).[9] "Faith in Christ Jesus" may be a faith that has Christ Jesus as its object, or He is the One on whom their faith rests or in whom it is anchored. Their faith (the content of what they believe about Jesus, and their corresponding lifestyle) is exactly right. For this Paul thanks God. Very likely there is a side glance at the deceptive teachers whose view of Christ Jesus was far from that revealed by the apostles.

And the love which you have for all the saints – The Colossian Christians have manifested caring love for their brethren. When they saw a brother in need, they supplied the need. The "saints" are the people of God, fellow Christians (see on verse 1; 2:1,2; 3:14). Here we have another side glance at the deceptive teachers, for it is well known that Gnostics did not exhibit a love for their brethren (1 John

---

[7] It makes little difference in meaning for the verse whether we construe "always" with the verb "give thanks" or with the verb "praying."

[8] We are treating the "we" as a real plural, rather than as an epistolary plural. See notes on verse 3, above.

[9] Compare Romans 1:8 where like language of thanksgiving is used of a church which Paul had not at the time visited.

3:10,11-18). The Colossian Christians have been doing just what Jesus taught. "This is His commandment, that we believe on the name of His Son Jesus Christ, and love one another" (1 John 3:23).

1:5 – *because of the hope laid up for you in heaven, of which you previously heard in the word of truth, the gospel,*

Because of the hope laid up for you in heaven – These words have been treated by some as a reason for the faith and love which verse 4 just named,[10] and by others (with whom we agree) as a second reason why Paul gives thanks. A heavenly home will be the outcome of a life of faith and love such as the apostle hears is true of the Colossian Christians.[11] "Hope" in this present passage is not the act of hoping but refers to the thing hoped for (cf. Galatians 5:5; 1 Peter 1:4). "Laid up" calls to mind the idea of a valuable and precious treasure. "In heaven" is the same Greek translated "in the heavenly *places*" in Ephesians 1:3 and 4:10. We suppose that by singling out this hope as the chief matter of his thanksgiving Paul intends to enhance its value in the eyes of his readers, while at the same time introducing an idea that will later be developed in this epistle. That idea is this – the Biblical doctrine of heaven stands in vivid contrast to the endless cycles of reincarnation which only lead to eventual absolution into the *pleroma* of Gnostic speculations.

Of which you previously heard in the word of truth, the gospel – When the gospel was first preached to them by Epaphras, they were told of the blessed heavenly rewards of a life of faith. When the Colossians first heard the gospel, that hearing resulted in their conversion (cp. Romans 10:17). Previous to the time when the Gnostic teachers came, they had already heard the pure gospel from Epaphras (Colossians 1:7,8). The word *euangellion*, translated "gospel," means "good news." It is implied that what the false teachers were teaching was not good news. Just the opposite: it imperils a man's hope.

Whereas Ephesians 1:13 described the gospel as "the gospel of your salvation," here in Colossians the gospel is described as "the word of truth." In

---

[10] Some writers connect verse 5 with "the love you have for all the saints" and suggest that thoughts of heaven ("hope laid up for you in heaven") are what motivates the believers to acts of love. This is thought to harmonize with "faith, hope, and love" which is the order found in 1 Corinthians 13:13.

[11] It is true that in most of his thanksgivings Paul thanks God for good things the readers are doing. However, in his thanksgiving for the Corinthians (1 Corinthians 1:4-9), Paul thanked God for what He has done for the Corinthians. So, if Paul is giving thanks for heaven that awaits the faithful Christian, it is not something unheard of for Paul to speak of what God has done in his thanksgiving.

this language "the word of truth" there is an implied warning against the new deceptive doctrines which are more fully identified in the doctrinal portions of Colossians. It is interesting to contemplate all that may be implied in these words that describe the gospel. One thinks of John 1:17 where we are told that the message of Jesus Christ surpasses the message in the Law of Moses. The Gospel is absolute truth which comes from the God of truth. It is spoken by men whose words are inspired by the Spirit of truth. It concerns Christ who is the truth and from Whom comes nothing but truth. The gospel is *truth*. Unrevealed religions and man-made philosophies and speculations are, at best, "guesses about God." The Christian gospel gives a man, not guesses, but certainties about God. Verses from John's epistles (1 John 2:27, 5:20; 2 John 1-4; 3 John 2,3) come to mind. Just as John expected his readers to stay the course, holding fast to the message that had been delivered to them from the beginning by the apostles of Jesus Christ, so did Paul expect from his readers.

1:6 – *which has come to you, just as in all the world also it is constantly bearing fruit and increasing, even as* **it has been doing** *in you also since the day you* **heard** **of** **it** *and understood the grace of God in truth;*

Which has come to you – This Greek participle *parontos* (a form of *pareimi*) which further describes "the word of truth, the gospel" could be translated "which is present among you." The newer teachings being heralded by the deceitful teachers at Colossae are not the true gospel. The true gospel they have had since the day they first heard it.

Just as in all the world also it is constantly bearing fruit and increasing – A third item in Paul's thankfulness is the progress of the gospel. The gospel that was preached at Colossae by Epaphras is no different from the gospel preached elsewhere in the empire. Two things about the gospel are emphasized in this verse. "In all the world" says that at the time when Colossians was being written, probably AD 62, the gospel of Christ had been preached and received in most of the countries within the Roman empire.[12] Unlike the local version of incipient Gnosticism which the false teachers were advocating, the gospel of Christ was a universal religion. Not only was it a universal message, but the true gospel produced a great and positive change in the lives of those who received it. In this, too, the gospel differed markedly from the message of the deceitful teachers who were troubling the church at Colossae.

---

[12] Before writing his letter to Rome about five years before he wrote Colossians, Paul had already preached the gospel fully from Jerusalem round about as far as Illyricum (Romans 15:19).

Two passive participles are employed by Paul to describe the continuing positive changes produced by the gospel. It produces spiritual fruit and causes growth.[13] Since the term "bearing fruit" occurs only here and in verse 10 in all of Paul's letters, it has been suggested that Paul here deliberately employed two terms found in the vocabulary of the deceitful teachers. In second-century Gnosticism the terms "grow" and "bear fruit" were used in the sense of advancing in the attainment of abstract knowledge and wisdom.[14] In direct opposition to such an idea, Paul affirms that true "fruit bearing" and "growth" are caused by the Christian gospel which demonstrates its power in the lives of men by bearing fruit "in every good work" and by helping men come to a better knowledge of God (Colossians 1:10).

Even as *it has been doing* in you also – Just as the gospel has been doing elsewhere in the world (bearing fruit and causing growth), it also had worked in Colossae.

Since the day you heard *of it* – Christians in Colossae had continued to grow in their knowledge of God and in spiritual character since the day they had first heard and obeyed the gospel.

And understood the grace of God in truth – God, the Father of Jesus Christ, is a God of grace. Calling attention to God's grace may be intended as a deliberate contrast to Gnostic teaching that the God of the Bible is an evil being. "Understood" translates the compound Greek verb (*epiginosko*) which means "to know thoroughly, completely." One did not have to embrace Gnostic ideas in order to know about God. The gospel already provides such knowledge. By "the grace of God" which is displayed in the gospel may be meant the love and favor of God who sent His only Son on a mission to be the Savior and Redeemer of lost sinners. "In truth" is the means Paul uses to extend his imprimatur to the message Epaphras had preached. If his gospel was "in truth," then it may be inferred that the Gnostic message was not truth from God.

1:7 – *just as you learned* it *from Epaphras, our beloved fellow bond-servant, who is a faithful servant of Christ on our behalf,*

Just as you learned *it* from Epaphras – A fourth item in Paul's expression of

---

[13] There is a manuscript variation here, with the result that the KJV does not carry the words *kai auxanomenon* ("and increasing"). The better attested reading which includes these words is represented by the ASV and NASB.

[14] Irenaeus, *Against Heresies* I.1.3; 4.4; 8.5; 14.5.

thankfulness is for the work of Epaphras (verses 7,8). Paul has been identifying the true gospel so the Colossians could differentiate it from the Gnostic message. He further identifies it by saying that it was the very message which they heard from Epaphras. All we know about Epaphras is what we can learn from Colossians 1:7,8, 4:12,13 and Philemon 23. He apparently was a native of Colossae (4:12,13), was the first evangelist to preach the gospel in his hometown,[15] and afterwards felt responsibility and concern not only for the Christians in Colossae, but also for the churches in the neighboring towns of Laodicea and Hierapolis (Colossians 4:13). That concern has caused him to make a trip to Rome to confer with Paul the apostle.

Our beloved fellow bond-servant – "Beloved" shows that Paul had developed a strong friendship and appreciation for Epaphras. "Fellow bond-servant" translates the Greek word *sundoulos*. When an apostle uses the term "bond-servant" (*doulos,* cp. Romans 1:1) of himself, he is claiming to be an inspired mouthpiece for God (just as was true of "My servants, the prophets" in the Old Testament). Was Epaphras so endowed as the result of the laying on of the apostle's hands to impart a spiritual gift? Or does the expression say that both Paul and Epaphras were alike serving Jesus Christ?[16]

Who is a faithful servant of Christ on our behalf – Have the false teachers at Colossae cast aspersions on Epaphras' message? If this were so, Paul's strong words of endorsement for him were intended to neutralize any negative effect which such statements of criticism were intended to arouse. The Greek word translated "servant" in this clause is *diakonos*, which is sometimes translated "minister" and sometimes "servant" and sometimes "deacon." It is perfectly in harmony with apostolic usage to give the designation "servant" or "minister" to the evangelist/preacher (see Ephesians 6:21 and 1 Timothy 4:6).[17] "Servant of Christ" says that Christ was the One whom Epaphras served faithfully. Since this is so, neither he nor his message is to be set aside for the new and erroneous teachers (Colossians 2:1-23) who are beginning to trouble the church.

---

[15] The KJV reads "just as you also learned it from Epaphras." The word "also" is omitted in the oldest manuscripts. The insertion of this word into the text implied that those inserting it thought that Paul had preached the Gospel to the Colossians before Epaphras did. The omission of the word in the oldest manuscripts of Colossians leaves the impression that Epaphras alone was the founder of the church at Colossae.

[16] In Philemon 23 Paul calls Epaphras "my fellow-prisoner." We do not know whether after Epaphras came to Rome he was arrested and imprisoned along with Paul, or whether he spent so much time with Paul the prisoner that Paul can speak of him as if he were a fellow prisoner.

[17] There was an office of evangelist in the apostolic churches. Philip filled such a place (Acts 21:8). Timothy fulfilled such a place while preaching in Ephesus (1 Timothy 4:6; 2 Timothy 4:5), as did Titus on the island of Crete. So did Epaphras as he preached the gospel in Colossae.

The manuscripts are nearly evenly divided on the question of whether Paul wrote "on our behalf" or "on your behalf."[18]   Each reading has provoked questions of interpretation and church polity.

- "On *your* behalf" has been interpreted to mean that Epaphras came to Rome to minister to Paul as a representative of the Colossian church, much as did Epaphroditus on behalf of the church at Philippi (Philippians 4:18).   But this does not seem to be correct since Epaphras is called a "servant of Christ," not a servant of the Colossian church.   If "on your behalf" was the original reading it means that when Epaphras made his trip to Rome, he was doing something for the benefit of the Colossian church.
- "On *our* behalf" has been interpreted to mean that Epaphras first went to Colossae to preach because Paul (during his stay in Ephesus, Acts 19:10) had sent him to do so.   If "our behalf" was the original reading, it means that Paul and Timothy could not personally go to all the places that needed the gospel. Young preachers like Epaphras went in their stead.

Indeed, there are other passages where Paul sent preachers to churches (Titus 3:12; 2 Timothy 4:12).   This, in turn, has been used to show that apostolic succession was the way the gospel was to be legitimated.   On the contrary, it is harmony with the word of God that makes a preacher's message legitimate, not the preacher's personal relationship to an apostle.

1:8 – *and he also informed us of your love in the Spirit.*

And He also informed us of your love – Perhaps it is their love for all the saints (verse 4) concerning which Epaphras has informed Paul, Timothy, and others at Rome.   If we read "on your behalf" in verse 7, perhaps it is the Colossian's love for Epaphras in return for his ministry to them.   If we read "on our behalf" in verse 7, perhaps it is the Colossian's love for the apostle Paul even though they had only heard of him.

In the Spirit – Translators have a difficult decision here, whether to write "spirit" or "Spirit."   There is no "the" in the Greek and this makes it uncertain whether the reference is to the Holy Spirit.   The only other use of *pneuma* in Colossians is a reference to the human spirit (Colossians 2:5).   On the other hand, when the

---

[18] The editors of the United Bible Societies Greek New Testament changed the reading from "our" (*hēmōn*) in the 2nd edition to "your" (*humōn*) in the 3rd edition.   The reading "our" has the better manuscript evidence (P[46] and Alexandrian and Western authorities), but widespread use of "your" in the versions and patristic witnesses led to the change, explained B.M. Metzger, *A Textual Commentary on the Greek New Testament* (New York: United Bible Societies, 1972ff).

next verse (verse 9) speaks of "spiritual wisdom and understanding" the work of the Holy Spirit is understood in the background.　If appeal is made to Galatians 5:22 ("the fruit of the Spirit is love"), even there it is uncertain whether "spirit" or "Spirit" is the proper way to translate *pneuma*.　When a man's spirit is born again (John 3:6), his spirit is now open to the influences of the Holy Spirit.　Thus, love may be said to be produced either by the Spirit or by the regenerated spirit of man.　Either way, love is not just a natural affection, but something that results from the fruit-bearing gospel (verse 6).

C. Prayer Requests for the Colossians.　1:9-14

Summary:　Prayer requests made to God by Paul and his companions are (1) for their knowledge of God's will to increase;　(2) for them to walk in a worthy manner pleasing the Lord in all respects;　(3) for them to be strengthened that they may be steadfast and patient;　and (4) for them to joyously give thanks to the Father for the blessings of redemption.

1.　A request that their knowledge of God's will would increase.　1:9

1:9 – *For this reason also, since the day we heard of it, we have not ceased to pray for you and to ask that you may be filled with the knowledge of His will in all spiritual wisdom and understanding,*

For this reason also – "For this reason" refers back to what the apostle and his companions have heard about the faith and love of the Colossians (verse 4).

Since the day we heard it – These words are an echo of verse 4.　Once they knew about the Colossian Christians, those Christians have been in the prayers of Paul and his companions.

We have not ceased to pray for you – "We" is understood here as it was in verse 3 as likely being a real plural, referring to Paul and his companions.　He has already spoken of their prayers for the Colossians (verse 3).　The expression does not mean that they prayed without ever stopping but that they regularly included them when they daily and regularly prayed (cf. Acts 20:31; Ephesians 1:16). "Pray" translates the word *proseuchomai*, which pictures the supplicant as facing the One to whom requests are being made.[19]　In the following phrases Paul will

---

[19] On the verbs used for praying, asking, and the like, in the Greek Scriptures, see Thayer, *op. cit.*, p.18; or R.C. Trench, *Synonyms of the Greek New Testament* (Grand Rapids: Eerdmans, 1966), p.143-146; or Geo. Ricker Berry, *New Testament Synonyms* (Chicago: Wilcox and Follett, 1947), p.130.

specify some of the particular requests they have been making to God.

And to ask that you may be filled with the knowledge of His will – "To ask" translates the Greek *aiteo*, the word for prayer that speaks of asking from God what is required and necessary for ourselves or for others.[20]   This is the first thing for which Paul and his comrades prayed, that the Colossians might "be filled with the knowledge of God's will," for such knowledge would safeguard them from the deceptive teachings which were threatening the Colossian church.   He offered a similar prayer in behalf of the Ephesians (Ephesians1:17-19), the Philippians (Philippians 1:9) and Philemon (verse 6).   The word translated "knowledge" is *epignosis,* a compound word which speaks of full knowledge. The Gnostics may claim to have knowledge (*gnosis*), but the knowledge for which Paul prays cannot be improved upon since it is full knowledge (*epignosis*).   In this context "God's will" perhaps has special reference to God's intention for the conduct of the Christian life.   With a full understanding of God's will the Colossian Christians will know whether or not ascetic practices (such as the deceptive teachers advocated) are required.   They will know whether or not the keeping of old Jewish rules are His will for this dispensation.   This may also reference God's eternal will whereby He purposed to reconcile men to Himself through Christ, and not through angels, as the false teachers in some degree taught (Colossians 2:18).   "Filled" (*plērōthēte*) is the first occurrence of a word used by the false teachers who claimed to offer something not found in the preaching of Epaphras.   They offered, they claimed, access to "fullness" (*plērōma*), a claim to which Paul responds by affirming that true fullness is found in Christ and His message of redemption.

In all spiritual wisdom and understanding – These two terms, which serve as boundary markers, tell us where full knowledge of God's will may be found.   It is not in the knowledge which the false teachers were trying to spread.   That was not spiritual, nor was the godless Sophia the deceivers spoke about.   The adjective *pneumatikos* ("spiritual," that is, proceeding from the Holy Spirit) shows that both genuine wisdom and understanding result from the inspiration of the Holy Spirit. In vivid contrast, what the Gnostics had to offer was fleshly wisdom (1 Corinthians 1:12) and the wisdom of men (Colossians 2:8).   If we were to look for a Biblical explanation of wisdom, there are verses in the Old Testament which tell us that true wisdom is found in the "fear of the Lord" and in the "keeping of His commandments" (Ecclesiastes 12:13; Job 28:28; Proverbs 1:7).   Or we might turn to 1 Corinthians 1:30 where we learn the wisdom of the Lord includes the profound matters of righteousness, sanctification, and redemption.   "Under-

---

[20] The word is translated "desire" in the KJV. In 16th century English, "desire" was sometimes used by Shakespeare and Spenser with the meaning of "ask."

standing" (*sunesei*, a word also used at Colossians 2:2) means an ability to clearly analyze a situation as one makes a decision what to do. The words of the Holy Spirit in Scripture give great principles by which the will of God can be known as decisions are being made. The word "all," qualifying "knowledge" and "understanding," is another thrust on the part of Paul against the claims of the Gnostics. If Christians already had access to *all* knowledge and understanding, what was there extra that the Gnostics might offer to folk who joined their movement?

2. A prayer for them to walk in a worthy manner, pleasing God in all respects. 1:10-12a

1:10 – *so that you may walk in a manner worthy of the Lord, to please* **Him** *in all respects, bearing fruit in every good work and increasing in the knowledge of God;*

So that you may walk in a manner worthy of the Lord – "So that" makes this phrase a statement of the practical results of a Christian gaining full knowledge of the will of God. "The Lord" refers, as is common in Paul's language, to the Lord Jesus Christ.[21] "Walk" is figurative language for a person's lifestyle (see Ephesians 4:1). "Worthy" translates *axios*, which means "of equal weight." It means to live a life that is commensurate with what the Lord has done for us and is to us. To walk "worthy of the Lord" is to live as the Lord Jesus Christ wants us to live. The songwriter Eliza Hewitt has well expressed the idea:

> Trying to walk in the steps of the Savior, trying to follow our Savior and King,
> Shaping our lives by His blessed example,
> Happy, how happy the praises we sing
> How beautiful to walk in the steps of the Savior, stepping in the light ....

To please *Him* in all respects – Involved in walking worthy of the Lord is a disposition to please Him in all respects. "Him" (referring to the Lord) has been correctly inserted by the NASB.[22] He is the One whom Christians try to please.

---

[21] The "worthy of God" of 1 Thessalonians 2:12 thus gives to the phrase here a deep significance in relation to the Godhead of Christ. Such alternative expressions indicate how truly for Paul the Father and the Son are Persons of the same Order of being.

[22] The way the KJV reads, "unto all pleasing," the verse speaks of attempting to please other men. But being a man-pleaser is a disposition which Paul elsewhere condemns (Galatians 1:10; Ephesians 6:6; Colossians 3:22; 1 Thessalonians 2:4).

The Greek word for "please" (*areskeian*) suggests an attitude of mind that anticipates and then moves to do His every wish in every aspect of life.[23] Four nominative plural participles found in verses 10-12 will identify what Paul specifically had in mind when he prayed the Colossians would please the Lord in "all respects."[24]

a. Bearing fruit. 10b

Bearing fruit in every good work – "Bearing fruit" (which translates a present tense participle, *karpophorountes*) means that the Christian life is to exhibit continual fruitfulness.[25] The fruit itself consists of deeds that are beneficial, practically good.[26] Matthew 25:34-40 gives a list of such good works.

b. Increasing in knowledge of God. 10c

And increasing in knowledge of God – The participle (*auxanomenoi*) is in the present tense, putting emphasis on habitual action, and is passive in voice.[27] This in turn suggests that the phrase should be translated "being increased *by* the knowledge of God."[28] When it is rendered like this, the text affirms that the

---

[23] The word is not found elsewhere in the New Testament, though a cognate verb is found in 1 Thessalonians 4:1. The word was used in Classical Greek where it had a bad connotation, denoting, as H.G.G. Moule observes, "a cringing and subservient habit ready to do anything to please a patron; not only to meet but to anticipate his most trivial wishes. But when transferred to ... the believer's relations to his Lord, the word at once rises by its associations. To do anything to meet, to anticipate, His wishes is not only the most absolutely right thing we could do. It is His eternal due; it is at the same time the surest path to our own highest development and gain." H.G. C. Moule, "Colossians" in the *Cambridge Bible for Schools and Colleges* (Cambridge: University Press, 1896), p.72.

[24] Many Gnostics did not have much to say about their speculative doctrines having any relationship to conduct. Christian knowledge, by contrast, does have a corresponding lifestyle.

[25] The participle is in the active voice because the subject doing the acting is personal.

[26] Paul lays stress on good works in several of his letters (cf. Galatians 5:5; Ephesians 2:10; Titus 1:16, 2;7,14, 3:8,15).

[27] See the same passive voice verb at Colossians 1:6. The verb appears in the active voice at Colossians 2:9 and 2 Peter 3:18. It occurs in the passive voice at 1 Peter 2:2.

[28] Unless we treat the dative as a dative of means, we will have difficulty explaining the passive participle translated "increasing."

knowledge of God is the means by which the Christian grows. As the knowledge of God's will (verse 9) increases the Christian grows. What rain and sunshine are to the nurture of plants, the knowledge of God is to the growth and maturing of the spiritual life, with a corresponding increase in good works.

c. Being strengthened. 11

1:11 – *strengthened with all power, according to His glorious might, for the attaining of all steadfastness and patience;*

Strengthened with all power – The Greek word translated "strengthened" (*dunamoumenoi*) is the third nominative plural participle in a row, each of which unfolds what it is to walk worthy of the Lord so as to please Him in all respects. Since the participle is passive in voice and present in tense (i.e., "being strengthened"), this verse speaks of a life that is constantly being fueled by God's power. "With all power" describes the means by which the strengthening takes place.[29] "Power" is *dunamis,* and "all power" designates its many-sided variety. Ephesians 3:16 gives fuller details about this strengthening as Paul prays for his readers "according to the riches of His glory, to be strengthened with power through His Spirit in the inner man." The indwelling Holy Spirit gives help to live the Christian life. Just as there must be a perpetual oxygenation of blood in the lungs, so an uninterrupted renewal of spiritual strength is necessary if one would be victorious in the wear and tear of life.

According to His glorious might – The Greek behind "His glorious might" (*to kratos tes doxes autou*) is better translated "the might of His glory."[30] "Might" represents *kratos,* a synonym for power that denotes strength, or dominion, or manifested power.[31] Concerning the emphasis on God's "glory" in these Prison

---

[29] The *en* is best treated as a dative of means, as it is in Colossians 1:9; Ephesians 6:10; 2 Timothy 2:1.

[30] The word "glorious" (in the NASB) represents similar Greek in the following passages: Romans 8:21; 2 Corinthians 4:4; Philippians 3:21; 1 Timothy 1:11; Titus 2:13. These all gain greatly in significance by the literal rendering.

[31] On *dunamis* and *kratos* and other synonyms for power, see notes at Ephesians 1:19 and 6:10. See Thayer, *op. cit.,* p.160.

Epistles, see Ephesians 1:6,12,14. Though "glory" (*doxa*) is used in various ways in the New Testament (see 1 Corinthians 11:7; 15:40,41; 2 Corinthians 6:8), the term is often shaped by its use in the LXX to translate the Hebrew *kabod*, a term closely associated with the mode of God's being as it is revealed in His mighty revelatory acts. John 1 says Jesus actually shares in the glory of God (John 1:14) and the apostles saw it while He was on earth. The apostles saw Jesus' "glory" not only at His transfiguration (Matthew 17:1,2) and in His glorified resurrection body as they saw a brilliant light such as the brilliant sphere of light in which God dwells (1 Timothy 6:16), but they also saw the evidence of His deity in such miracles as the turning of water to wine (John 2:11). In Romans 6:4 we read that Jesus was raised from the dead through the glory of the Father. In Ephesians 1:18-21 Paul prays that his readers may be able to know the surpassing greatness of the power that God puts at the disposal of those who believe.

For the attaining of all steadfastness and patience – In this case, Paul is not talking about a power that manifests itself in miraculous deeds, but of inner strength, strength of character. These two virtues will show themselves in the Christian's life as a result of the divine empowering. "Steadfastness" (*hupomone*, endurance, fortitude) is putting up with things. Steadfastness is illustrated by the example of Job (James 5:11) who experienced numerous physical trials (Job 1:21, 2:10). James 1:3,4 encourages Christians to pray for wisdom to know how to turn bad things into blessings. "Patience" (*makrothumia*) is an attitude manifested toward people who can, at times, be unpleasant, malicious, cruel, unteachable, foolish, irritable, and unlovely.[32] It is the patience of spirit which will not retaliate or blaze up in anger when provoked or insulted or injured.

d. Joyously giving thanks. 11d,12a

1:12 – *joyously giving thanks to the Father, who has qualified us to share in the inheritance of the saints in light.*

[Joyously] giving thanks to the Father – It is debated whether "joyously" should be construed with what precedes, "endurance and patience" (KJV, ASV, RSV, NEB), or with what follows, "giving thanks" (NIV, NASB). The fact that the two previous participles are preceded by a prepositional definition suggests that to continue the symmetry "joyously" should be connected with what follows.

---

[32] For help with the synonyms *hupomone* and *makrothumia*, see Trench, *op. cit.*, p.195-200; Geo. R. Berry, *Greek English New Testament Lexicon* (Chicago: Wilcox and Follett, 1948), p.10; and Thayer, *op. cit.*, p.387.

This fourth nominative participle in a row gives a final way in which Christians may please the Lord in all respects. Two reasons follow for expressing gratitude to the Father. Both are things no Gnostic would claim but are truths for which a Christian is delighted to give thanks to the Father. Perhaps, with a deliberate anti-Gnostic thrust, Paul chose the word "Father" to call attention to God's relationship to Jesus Christ (we call Jesus God's "Son" because of His incarnation, Luke 1:35) and to His Fatherly love which made arrangements for our adoption as His sons (Galatians 3:26, 4:4-6; Ephesians 1:5-7).

3. Two reasons for joyfully giving thanks to God the Father. 1:12b-14

Who has qualified us to share in the inheritance of the saints in light – One reason to joyfully give thanks to God is the fact that the Father has qualified believers to share in the inheritance of the saints.[33] The Greek word for qualified (*hikanosanti*) basically has in it the thought of making sufficient or competent,[34] and the aorist tense points back to the time of their conversion.[35] "To share in the inheritance" literally is "for the portion of the lot." Paul may draw this metaphor from the division of the promised land of the Jews by lot (see Joshua 15:1), and the share of the inheritance each Israelite had. "The saints" (*tōn hagiōn*) might refer to angels[36] or, more likely, to the redeemed of Old Testament times whose souls are now in God's presence (Hebrews 12:23). Christians ("the saints"), as the new people of God, have a far greater inheritance than mere land, and each believer is qualified to join the Old Testament redeemed without any of them having to go through a series of reincarnations (such as the Gnostics taught).

---

[33] The reading "us" is very doubtful. Tischendorf, Westcott and Hort, UBS[3], NA[21], NASB margin, and NIV prefer "you," as in the two oldest uncial manuscripts. If Paul wrote "us," he was including himself along with the believers at Colossae. If he wrote "you," he is particularly addressing the Gentile believers of Colossae and the "saints" would be those faithful Jewish folk who were Abraham's true spiritual descendants.

[34] It is the same word translated "adequate" in 2 Corinthians 2:16 and 3:6.

[35] Codex Vaticanus and the Old Latin version read "who called and qualified ...." This is one of the few readings in Vaticanus that Westcott and Hort rejected (see their 'Introduction,' §§ 320). Calvinists immediately speak of God's foreknowledge and effectual call, in virtue of which men are made Christians, and the past tense is even said to indicate such Christians cannot be separated from a share in the inheritance of the saints.

[36] Angels may be the ones intended by "holy ones" (*tōn hagiōn*) at 1 Thessalonians 3:13 (compared with 2 Thessalonians 1:7 and Matthew 25:31).

The connection of the words "in light" with the rest of the verse is debated. Some connect it with "the inheritance" as describing where the inheritance is.[37] Others connect it with "the saints" as describing the sphere in which the redeemed already live.[38] Still others connect it with the participle "qualified," treating the phrase as a dative of means which explains how God did the qualifying. This latter alternative is intriguing. If "light" is the means or power[39] God uses to qualify folk for heaven, then there is an anti-Gnostic thrust to the words. When we recall that Zoroastrianism had a God of light and a God of darkness, and when we recall that there are tinges of Eastern religious mysticism in the Colossian philosophy, to have Paul (in this and the next verse) affirming that the God of the Bible is the one who used the power of light to qualify folk for their inheritance, is very apropos to the reason behind his writing this letter to the Colossians.

1:13 – *For He delivered us from the domain of darkness, and transferred us to the kingdom of His beloved Son,*

For He delivered us from the domain of darkness – Technically, there is no word "for" in Greek. The Greek reads "who delivered ..." with the antecedent of "who" being the Father (verse 12) who qualified us to share in the inheritance. Thus, we have here in verses 13 and 14 a second reason to give Him thanks. "Delivered" translates *errusato*, a word that means to liberate, save, or rescue someone from adversity. Just as God delivered his Old Testament people from their enemies (Egypt, Assyrians, Babylonians), so Christians ("us") have been rescued from the domain of darkness. Jesus used the same phrase at the time of His arrest in Gethsemane (Luke 22:53). The devil is the tyrannical ruler of this kingdom. Men who live in his kingdom actually are stumbling and groping around in spiritual darkness. The principalities and powers to which the false teachers urged Christians to pay homage are designated as "the rulers of the darkness of this world" (Ephesians 6:12 KJV). Christians who are delivered from the power of darkness have no need to fear the spirits. In a letter written to

---

[37] Not only does God dwell in unapproachable light (1 Timothy 6:16), but the good angels are called "angels of light" (2 Corinthians 11:14), and heaven is represented as filled with light and glory (Isaiah 60:19; Revelation 4:3, 21:24, 22:5).

[38] This need not be limited to future glory. The children of God walk in light while still on the earth (Ephesians 5:8,9; 1 John 1:7, 2:10).

[39] There are verses that treat "light" as being a power: Jesus spoke of the "light of life" (John 8:12); Paul spoke of it as being armor (Romans 13:12); light produces its fruit (Ephesians 5:9), and reproves evil deeds (Ephesians 5:13).

an area that included Colossae, the Gnostic teachers about whom Peter warned in 2 Peter 2:1 were demonically inspired. 1 John, which is also an anti-Gnostic writing, uses the same terms "light" and "darkness" (1 John 1:5-7) to contrast Christianity with the spiritual sphere in which Gnosticism flourishes. Did Paul use this language about darkness and light because the Colossian heresy included some ideas that came from Zoroastrian belief, that there were two great kingdoms in the universe – that of light, and that of darkness?

And transferred us to the kingdom of His beloved Son – The "us" includes the Colossians, Paul, and other readers who have become Christians. "Transferred" translates *metestesen*, a word that was used in secular literature for the wholesale deportation of whole races of people by oriental potentates, and the settlement of those conquered peoples in a new home.[40] The aorist tense verb points to the time of their conversion as the time when this transferal took place. "Thus, baptism is at once 'for the remission of sins' and an 'entrance into the kingdom of God'."[41] "His beloved Son" is more striking and beautiful in the original – it is "the Son of His love." God's love (cp. John 3:16) is the reason behind His sending of His Son to be our redeemer (about which Colossians 1:14 will speak). The words are reminiscent of the words God the Father spoke of Jesus at the baptism and transfiguration (Matthew 3:17, 17:5). Jesus is not some distant emanation from God as the Gnostics taught; He was God's Son.[42] Years earlier, when Jesus had appeared to Paul on the Damascus road to call him to be an apostle, this was the task Paul was given to do – he was "to open their eyes, so that they may turn them from darkness to light and from the dominion of Satan to God, in order that they may receive forgiveness of sins and an inheritance among those who have been sanctified by faith in Me" (Acts 26:18).

1:14 – *in whom we have redemption, the forgiveness of sins.*

In whom we have redemption, the forgiveness of sins – Verse 14, with its state-

---

[40] Josephus (*Ant.* ix. 11.1) used it of the deportation of the Israelites by the Assyrian king.

[41] Barry, *op. cit.*, p.20. The same kingdom is intended by the expressions "kingdom of God," (Romans 14:17; Colossians 4:11), "kingdom of heaven" (Matthew 3:2), and "kingdom of Christ and God" (Ephesians 5:5).

[42] See notes above on verse 12 on what being God's "Son" means. Also consult the comments in the author's *New Testament Epistles: Romans* (Moberly, MO: Scripture Exposition Books, 1996) at Romans 1:4.

ment that in God's Son we have redemption and forgiveness of sins, is a powerful polemic against Gnosticism.   Since this verse corresponds verbally with Ephesians 1:7, the explanatory comments given at that place are apropos here, too.   The wonderful blessing contained in these words climaxes the reason to give thanks to God.

II. DOCTRINAL FOUNDATION – Christ is Preeminent in All Relationships. 1:15-23

Summary: In verses 15-23, Paul develops the core of his argument against the Colossian philosophy.   The most dangerous aspect of the deceptive religious system at Colossae was its depreciation of the person of Jesus Christ. To the errorists of Colossae, Christ was not the triumphant redeemer to whom all authority in heaven and earth had been committed.   At best He was only one of many spirit beings who bridged the space between God and men.   In refutation of this Paul lays stress on the preeminence of Jesus Christ: (1) the Son's preeminence in His own person (verse 15a);   (2) the Son's preeminence in the universe (verses 15b-17);   and (3) the Son's preeminence in the church (verses 18-23).

A. The Son's Preeminence in His Own Person. 1:15a

1:15a – *And He is the image of the invisible God,*

And – We have begun a new point in the outline at this place, following the paragraphing in the NASB.   So smoothly does Paul move from prayer to this presentation of who Christ is that it is difficult to know where one leaves off and the other begins.[43]   The Christology in this doctrinal section is the same high Christology as is found in the remarkable passage that opens the epistle to the Hebrews (Hebrews 1:2-14); the same is found in Ephesians 1:20-23; and the same high Christology as found in the great passage in Philippians 2:6-11 which speaks of Jesus as being "in the form of God," and having a name which is above every name.   Twelve times in Colossians 1:15-23 we read "He" or "Him," referring to Christ.   The affirmations of these passages were written about One who only 30 years earlier had died on a Roman cross.   That is hardly time for a myth to grow. Paul and John (John 1:1-14) did not originate   what they wrote about the Christ,

---

[43] Barry (*op. cit.,* p.20) began the discussion of Christ's preeminence back at verse 13 and calls verses 13,14 "Christ's preeminence in redemption."   The KJV treats verses 9-18 as one sentence.   The ASV has a period at the end of verse 17, thus beginning the new paragraph with verse 18.

now risen and glorified. They simply were writing what Jesus Himself had taught and shown them.

He is the image of the invisible God – The Greek word translated "image" (*eikon*) is used to describe an image on a coin or a person's reflection in a mirror. The word *eikon* is used for real and essential embodiment, as distinguished from mere likeness (Hebrews 10:1; Romans 1:23; 1 Corinthians 15:49; 2 Corinthians 3:18). The nature of God is perfectly represented in Jesus (Hebrews 1:3). Thus does Paul counter the false teaching that Jesus was simply one of many beings who came from God. Jesus was Immanuel – "God with us" (Isaiah 7:14; Matthew 1:23). Later Paul will affirm that in Christ "dwells all the fullness of the Godhead bodily" (Colossians 2:9). "Is" says that Christ always has been, is, and always will be the image of God.[44] God is not, and cannot be, seen otherwise. It is only in Christ, the image of the invisible God, that man can see God. John 1:18 expresses the same idea. "No man has seen God at any time; the only begotten God who is in the bosom of the Father, He (*ekeinos*, that One exclusively) has explained [revealed] Him (once and for all, *exegesato*)." As Jesus said, "anyone who has seen Me has seen the Father" (John 14:9 NIV).

B. The Son's Preeminence in the Universe.   1:15b-17

1:15b – *The first-born of all creation.*

The first-born of all creation – "Firstborn" (*prototokos*) is used of Christ here and in Colossians 1:18, Romans 8:29, Hebrews 1:6, and Revelation 1:15. It may denote either priority in time or supremacy in rank; in each place it is used, the context must decide. In this place the emphasis must be on His rank, His supremacy, His preeminence. "Firstborn" does not mean that Christ was created first and then other creatures were created.[45] In a context written against the errorists who taught that Christ is a created being, it will not do to have Paul using "firstborn" to mean the first one created.   Christ Himself made everything that

---

[44] Because God is invisible, some early church writers argued that if God is invisible, the image should be, too. They therefore applied this language to the pre-incarnate Jesus and appealed to the context which speaks of His relation to creation as proof of their view. However, it is difficult to reconcile Paul's present tense verb "is" with a limitation only to Christ's pre-existence.

[45] It is from this verse, translated "begotten before all creation," from whence came the "begotten before all worlds" of the Nicene creed. But Jesus is hardly a created being, nor was He an emanation.

was made (John 1:3).   Philippians 2 says He was always existing in the form of God.[46]   He is hardly a created being.   Hebrews 1:3 says Jesus is the exact representation of God's nature.   If God is eternal, Jesus also must be eternal, or He is not an exact representation.   The next two verses here in Colossians are introduced with "for," which shows they are giving a reason for calling Christ "firstborn," lest there be any possible confusion or mistaken understanding of what is being said.   When Paul wrote "all creation," He is portraying Christ's relation to the universe for he goes on to say that Christ is creator and sustainer of all things in the universe (heavens and earth).

1:16 – *For in Him all things were created,* **both** *in the heavens and on earth, visible and invisible, whether thrones or dominions or rulers or authorities – all things have been created by Him and for Him.*

For in Him all things were created – The causal particle *hoti* ("for" or "because") with which this verse begins shows Paul is now giving some reasons for designating Christ as "firstborn."   There are four of these reasons.   First, He is the Creator of all things.   Second, Christ is the owner and ruler of all things – all things were created for Him.   Third, Christ existed everlastingly before all things.   Fourth, Christ sustains all things.   Scholars have debated whether "in Him" is a dative of agent or a dative of sphere,[47] but either way, this verse counters the Gnostic notion of the world's creation by an evil demiurge.   "All things" (*ta panta*, the collective whole) occurs twice in this verse.   It includes the totality of things we call the universe.

Both **in the heavens and on earth** – "All things" is explained as including things both in the heavens and on earth, visible and invisible.   "In the heavens" is the same phrase translated "in the heavenly *places*" in Ephesians 1:3.   "Heavens" sometimes means the sky where we see the sun and moon and stars (Genesis 1:17), and sometimes it means God's abode beyond our sight (Ecclesiastes 5:2).   Here it probably includes both.

Visible and invisible – The series of expressions Paul has used, which effectively repudiates the dualism that undergirded the deceptive philosophy at Colossae, stress that everything, either in the physical world or in the spiritual world, whether visible to the human eye or not, are the result of Christ's creative activity.

---

[46] The Greek verb translated "existed" in the NASB is a present tense verb.

[47] Treating it as a dative of sphere, "in Him" means within the sphere of His personality resides the creative will and the creative energy, and in that sphere the creative act took place. Treating it as a dative of agent, the verse says Jesus was the agent who did the creating.

On earth there are tiny creatures such as microbes not visible to humans except through powerful microscopes. Distant galaxies are visible to humans only through powerful telescopes. Angels and spirits are included in the invisible things in the heavens.

Whether thrones or dominions or rulers or authorities – With special reference to the false teaching at Colossae, some of the "invisible" things in the heavens which were created by Christ are now more precisely specified. The same angelic hierarchy is given at Ephesians 1:21, save that here "thrones" introduces the list.[48] Because it occurs first in this list of terms it seems to indicate that, of the four orders here listed, the "thrones" occupy the highest place of dignity and nearness to the throne of God. Perhaps the 24 thrones of Revelation 4:4 are intended. If angels are created beings as Paul here affirms, and if it is wrong to worship and serve the creature rather than the Creator (Romans 1:25), then angels ought not to be worshiped as the false teachers at Colossae were encouraging men to do (cf. 2:15,18,20). Paul places Christ above all thrones, dominions, principalities, and powers.

All things have been created by Him and for Him – Meyer has proposed that the confirmatory sentence, which began with "for" at verse 16, is concluded with the last of the four orders of angels, and that a new sentence begins with this clause and continues through verse 17.[49] This may be a better suggestion for punctuation than the dash found at this place in the NASB. If the emphasis in verse 16 was on "created," the word order here places the emphasis on "all things." Earlier in verse 16, "created" was an aorist tense verb, indicating completed action in the past time. Now the verb is a perfect tense, indicating that what was created continues on. "By Him" (*di' autou*, "through him") says that Christ was the mediating agent through whom all the things just named actually came into being.[50] He was acting on behalf of the Father. The false teachers

---

[48] While not necessarily endorsing the angelic doctrine of the false teachers, Paul does indicate (both here and in Ephesians 1:21, 3:10) that there are orders of angels, and that Jesus is preeminent over them all. Some of the principalities and powers came to openly oppose their Creator and His people (Ephesians 6:10-12), just as do some people He created.

[49] H.A.W. Meyer, *Critical and Exegetical Handbook to the Epistles to the Philippians, Colossians, and Philemon* (Winona Lake, IN: Alpha Publications, 1980), p.230.

[50] "There is no contradiction with Genesis 1:1 which tells us that God created the heaven and the earth. Hebrews 1:2 tells us that God made the worlds by His Son, or through His Son, as some versions have it. This verse in Colossians tells us simply that all things were created by the Son" (Orrin Root, *Standard Lesson Commentary 1985-86* [Cincinnati, OH: Standard Publishing Co., 1985], p.12).

maintained that the universe proceeded from God indirectly, through a succession of emanations.   Christ, at best, was only an inferior emanation.   This speculation is flatly refuted by what Paul here writes.   "To Him" (*eis auton*) or "for Him" indicates that He is the end for which all things exist, the goal toward whom all things were intended to move.   They were meant "to serve His will, to contribute to His glory."[51]

1:17 – *And He is before all things, and in Him all things hold together.*

And He is before all things – The words "He is" (*autos estin*) are both emphatic. There is a personal pronoun ("He") in the Greek and it is used for emphasis.   He, and He only, is; all else is created.   The verb translated "is" may be pointed so it means "is" or "exists."[52]   Paul could have written "He was (*ēn*)" as John did at John 1:1.   He could have written "became" or "was made" (*egineto*).   He didn't. Paul used *estin*, a timeless present.   The Son is everlasting.   As it does the other times when Paul uses it, *pro* ("before") refers to time, not to rank.[53]   "All things" encompasses the universe including the orders of angels identified in the previous verse.   While earlier verses spoke of Christ's preeminence over all things, this verse refers to His pre-existence.   It is equivalent to saying He is eternal.

And in Him all things hold together – Exactly what is signified by *sunestēken* ("hold together") is debated.   One thinks it means that it is because of Jesus that all things which He created continue to exist; He preserves His universe in orderly fashion.   Another thinks it means that He causes His creation to come together in one system.   That is why it can be called a universe, a cosmos rather than a chaos. Still another thinks that Hebrews 1:3 ("He ... upholds all things by the word of His power"; He is moving history to its goal) is a good commentary on what Paul meant here in Colossians.   Either way, this description of the preeminence and pre-existence of the Son shows the folly of listening to the false teachers who were trying to seduce the Christians away from Christ, and instead to rely on angels (aeons) to help them with their salvation.

---

[51] Moule, *op. cit.*, p.78.

[52] *Esti* with an acute on the ultima means "is"; with an acute on the penult it means "exists." Lightfoot, Westcott and Hort, and Ellicott adopt the latter punctuation.

[53] Those who have tried to make Christ a created being will argue that *pro* refers to rank.

C. The Son's Preeminence in the Church. 1:18-23

Summary: Christ is head of the church, and is to be given first place in everything (verse 18). He is the One Who is reconciling all to God (verses 19-23). Salvation in Christ is complete – Gnostics can add nothing!

1:18 – *He is also head of the body, the church; and He is the beginning, the first-born from the dead; so that He Himself might come to have first place in everything.*

He is also head of the body, the church – Another emphatic "He" identifies He who is the image of God and the Lord of the universe (verses 15-17) as being the head of the church.   The word translated "church" *(ekklesia)* speaks of the assembly of God's called-out people, whether visible or invisible.   The significance of the church being "the body" of Christ has been explained in notes at Ephesians 1:22.[54]   If Christ is the One who as "head" governs and guides the church, folk who down-play the place of Christ, as the Gnostics did, are shown to be totally out of harmony with the actual preeminence of Christ.   Just as the life of a human body depends on continued union with its head, so every Christian must maintain the connection to his or her head, Jesus Christ.   We must accept orders from Him as the muscles of the body respond to the head.   We do this as we obey His word.

And He is the beginning – In the Greek the first word of this clause is a relative pronoun *(hos)* and in this context is almost equivalent to "because He is." "Beginning" translates *arche*, which refers to the cause or source.   Just as He originally created all things in the heavens and on earth (verse 16), so Christ (cp. Revelation 3:14 – "the beginning of the creation of God") is the source of the new humanity, a new creation (2 Corinthians 4:14 and Romans 8:21).

The first-born from the dead – It is by means of His resurrection from the dead that Christ became the source of the new creation.   It is not merely "of the dead," but "from the dead" – Christ not only died but He is no longer among the dead. He is risen.   In this context these are refutations of Gnostic ideas.   The same

---

[54] "'The body' is a very appropriate figure of speech for the church. A human body has hands, ears, a liver, and a multitude of other parts, each designed for one of the many tasks needed for the health and well-being of the whole body. So the members of the church have different abilities so they can contribute in different ways to the welfare of the whole congregation. One preaches eloquently from the pulpit, one speaks winsomely to a neighbor, one prepares a meal for a family whose homemaker is sick, one cleans the meeting house. With all their differences, these various parts work in harmony and mutual helpfulness because all of them are directed by the head, Jesus" (Root, *ibid.*).

title "first-born" is given to Christ in Revelation 1:5. There is no difference between the Christology of Paul and that of John. "First-born" means Christ was the first to rise from the dead, never to die again. "First-born" and "first fruits" (1 Corinthians 15:20) both imply more to come. Not only does Christ's resurrection make it possible for men to rise to walk in newness of life, it also makes it possible for their bodies to be raised from the dead, which will occur at Christ's second coming (1 Corinthians 15:22-23). Gnostics may claim there is no future resurrection (2 Timothy 2:18) and no second coming (cp. what the mockers of 2 Peter 3 claimed). Christ's resurrection as "first-born" means both these claims are false. There is a resurrection body in the future. The redeemed receive bodies just like the one Jesus now has (1 Corinthians 15:49).

So that He Himself might come to have first place in everything – There is a contrast in verbs here. Verse 15 said Christ "is" (*estin*, present tense) first in reference to all creation. Now we are told that His resurrection made it possible for Him to become (*genetai*, aorist tense) first in everything. By virtue of His resurrection He became head of the church, and thus is first in everything. Christ's exaltation after His incarnation is similarly gloriously described in Philippians 2:9-11. In this place there is a personal pronoun in the Greek for "He" (normally the personal ending of the verb gives all the pronoun that is needed). By adding the personal pronoun, Paul says that "He and He alone" ("He Himself," NASB) has this exclusive right to preeminence, to the first place.

1:19 – *For it was the* **Father's** *good pleasure for all the fullness to dwell in Him,*

For it was the *Father's* **good pleasure** – The *hoti* ("for") shows that verses 19-23 give the reasons why such preeminence (verses 15-18) is affirmed. Two reasons are given – one has to do with all the fullness dwelling in Him, the other calls attention to His reconciling work. The word "Father's" in italics is but one of three choices for translating this verse. The Greek has a third person singular verb (*eudokeo* - "he [or "it"] was well-pleased") followed by a neuter noun ("fullness") which can be either nominative (the subject of the verb) or accusative (the object of the verb). Three translations of the Greek are possible at this place:

(1) "For in Him all the fullness was pleased to dwell."[55]
(2) "For the Son was the Son was pleased that all the fullness should dwell in Him."[56]

---

[55] Moffatt, Goodspeed, RSV, and Philips are among those translators who treat "fullness" as the subject of the sentence.

[56] F.W. Conybeare, *The Life and Epistles of St. Paul* (Hartford, CT: S.S. Scranton Co., 1910), p.754, follows the Old Latin and Rhemish versions in adopting this reading.

(3) "For God the Father was pleased that all the fullness should dwell in the Son."[57]

Each view has had its defenders and detractors. The first is objected to on the grounds that "fullness" is neuter, yet the following participle "having made peace" is masculine. That looks like the third person singular verb should be translated as "he". The second is objected to on the grounds that it has Christ making a decision about "fullness" that might not be His alone to make. The third is objected to on the grounds it seems to say there was a time when "fullness" did not dwell in Christ. Nevertheless, a reading which supplies "the Father" or "God" as the subject is to be preferred, especially since it suits better with the following verse. So interpreted, this verse counteracts Gnostic speculation which separated Jesus from the Father by numerous supernatural aeons, each of them slightly inferior to his predecessor. Perhaps we should study the word "fullness," for once we have determined what this word means, the rest of the verse will be clearer.

For all the fullness to dwell in Him – Paul did not write a genitive in this verse (such as "fullness *of God*" [Ephesians 3:19] or "fullness *of Deity*" [Colossians 2:9]). He simply used the words "all fullness" (*pan pleroma*). The absence of a genitive allows this term "fullness" to gather up all that has been said about Christ in the previous statements – He is the image of God, the first-born of all creation, the Creator, the eternally pre-existent One, the Head of the Church, the victor over death, first in all things. If we must assign a point of time to this fullness, we would point to His incarnation. We would suggest there is an anti-Gnostic thrust to this verse when it says in the incarnate Christ there was a permanent residence[58] of the totality of the Divine powers and attributes. Nouns ending in *-ma* (like *pleroma* does) emphasize the result of the rest of the word. Note the word "all." If the incarnate Christ had only a partial imparting of this fullness, that would have been inadequate for the task He came to do, namely, reconciling the universe.

We naturally struggle to understand the concept of God and Christ that Paul presents in this passage. The Father and the Son are not rival deities, like the

---

[57] The translations that add "God" or "the Father" include the Douay, KJV, ERV, ASV, NASB, TEV, and NEB.

[58] The Greek word translated "dwell" is an aorist infinitive of the verb *katoikeo*. Two different Greek words mean "to dwell." *Paroikeo* is to dwell temporarily in a place, while *katoikeo* speaks of a permanent dwelling. Thus, in the LXX at Genesis 37:1 we are told that "Jacob dwelt (permanently, *katoikeo*) in the land where his father sojourned (*paroikeo*) as a stranger."

many fictitious pagan gods. The true God is one God, but existing as Father, Son, and Spirit. They share perfect love and unity of purpose. So God the Father's will is fulfilled in what God the Son has done, especially as the Son reveals the Father and accomplishes His plan to save and rule.[59]

1:20 – *and through Him to reconcile all things to Himself, having made peace through the blood of His cross; through Him, I say, whether things on earth or things in heaven.*

And through Him to reconcile all things to Himself – In the Greek, verse 20 continues without a break from verse 19, so the infinitive "to reconcile" is governed by the main verb "he was pleased" in verse 19, just as the infinitive "to dwell" in verse 19 was governed by the main verb. This verse calls attention to the purpose for which "fullness" dwelt in Jesus, namely, "to reconcile all things." The Greek verb translated "reconcile" is a double compound form (*apokatallasso*), which seems to emphasize that what is involved is the restoring of an originally harmonious relationship which has been lost.[60] "All things" which needed reconciliation are the same "all things" Paul has been writing about in verses 16-18.[61] Contrary to Gnostic doctrine, the Biblical teaching is that evil is not inherent in the creation. The Bible has God declaring that what He made was "good" (Genesis 1:10,12,21,25,31) and that what was originally a good thing was despoiled by sin, making the world a painful place for our existence. We have only a dim idea of the disasters resulting from the devil's rebellion and from

---

[59] Jon Weatherly, *Standard Lesson Commentary 2012-13*, (Cincinnati, OH: Standard Publishing, 2012), p.198.

[60] M.R. Vincent (*Word Studies in the New Testament* [Wilmington, DE: Associated Publishers and Authors, 1972], p.900) wrote that "the compounded preposition *apo* gives the force of *back*, hinting at restoration to a primal unity."

[61] A word of caution is needed concerning "all things" being reconciled. This verse has sometimes been used in isolation to substantiate the doctrine of universalism, i.e., that all men will ultimately be saved. "One must be careful not to interpret this in such a way as to make it contradict the clear teaching of other Scriptures. Admittedly, the statement might appear, on its surface, to indicate that eventually everything will be brought into a saving relationship with God. Such universalism, however, is contrary to those passages that affirm that apart from personal trust in Christ there is no salvation. Our Lord, in fact, spoke of the impenitent as going away into eternal punishment (Matthew 25:46). We should therefore understand this statement to be a reference to the cosmic significance of Christ's work, the thought being similar to, but not identical with, that of Romans 8:19-22. There the general sense is that the disorder that has characterized creation since the fall will be done away and divine harmony restored" (Vaughn, *op. cit.*, p.186).

human sin. The first word for sin (*ra*, "evil") in the Hebrew Bible (Genesis 2:9) speaks of a violent upheaval against order. Sin and death entered the world when Adam sinned (Romans 5:12). Adam soon found the ground producing thorns and thistles and demanding toil and sweat before it would supply his living (Genesis 3:17-19). We are appalled at the devastation of earthquake, tornado, and flood. We know from God's word that the whole creation is in turmoil, suffering while it waits for the work of redemption and reconciliation to be complete (Romans 8:19-23). The Father was pleased that all the fullness should dwell in Christ, and that He should fulfill God's eternal purpose by restoring the entire creation to harmony and submission to His authority. Ever since Calvary we live in the "period of the restoration of all things about which God spake by the mouth of His holy prophets" (Acts 3:21).

Having made peace through the blood of His cross – This whole clause describes the procedure by which the reconciliation was made. Gnostics taught that Calvary and the blood of Jesus had no salvific effects. Paul here pointedly calls attention to the blood of Christ to counter any Gnostic downplaying of what happened at Calvary. Men are described as being at enmity with God because of their transgressions. God Himself is the One who initiated the peace process whereby those who were at enmity might be at one with each other. This is why God is known as "the God of Peace" (Romans 15:33; 1 Thessalonians 5:23; Hebrews 13:20). This is how "we, having been justified by faith, have peace with God through our Lord Jesus Christ" (Romans 5:1). This is how Jews and Gentiles can have peace with one another (Ephesians 2:14).

Through Him, I say, whether things on earth or things in heaven – "Through Him, I say" is an emphatic way of resuming reference to the One in whom all the fullness dwells. He and He alone is equal to the task of reconciliation. "Things on earth or things in heaven" is explanatory of "all things" used earlier in this verse. "In heaven" is the same Greek as in verse 16 and that in Ephesians is translated "in the heavenly *places*." That things on earth needed reconciling is rather easy to see, but especially puzzling is the suggestion that even "things in heaven" need to be reconciled. We think of heaven (the place where God dwells) as a place of perfect harmony. Yet in Hebrews 9:25 we learn that heaven as it now is needed cleansing, likely because of the ravages that occurred there when there was war in heaven (Revelation 12:7-9). Perhaps the faithful folk in Old Testament times are included among the reconciled, since it was the blood of Jesus that was the propitiation for their sins (Romans 3:25; Hebrews 9:15). However, angels who sinned were thrown out of heaven long ago (2 Peter 2:4), and for them there seems to be no reconciliation, but only the horrible prospect of everlasting fire (Matthew 25:41). "Possibly 'heaven' in this case means the atmospheric heavens, and possibly, in some way we do not understand,   sin has thrown things out of adjustment so we have seasons too hot and too cold, too wet and too dry.   Perhaps all these will end, along with typhoons and tornadoes and floods, when 'things in heaven' are completely reconciled."[62]   What is written here in Colossians is, indeed, only a fuller exposition of the truth that "God was in Christ reconciling the world (the *kosmos*) to Himself" (2 Corinthians 5:19).

1:21 – *And although you were formerly alienated and hostile in mind,* **engaged in evil deeds,**

And although you were formerly alienated – Verses 21-23 make application of what is said about reconciliation to the special case of the Colossian readers in order to motivate them to steadfastness in the faith.   It appears that Paul began this new sentence with an intention to emphasize their previous condition before they heard the gospel.[63]   One feature of that condition was alienation. "Alienated" (a perfect passive participle in the Greek) denotes, not a subjective feeling on the part of the sinner, but an objective determination on the part of God.[64]   Sin results in man's relationship with God being severed.   The Colossians in their unsaved state were estranged, excluded from Divine favor ("without God in the world" as Ephesians 2:12 words it).

And hostile in mind – A second feature of their condition was hostility to God and to men in their minds.[65]   The word Paul uses for "mind" (*te dianoia*) is the word the LXX used to translate the Hebrew word "heart."   "Mind" denotes the faculty of thought, as opposed to powers of the body.

---

[62] Root, *op. cit.*, p.13.

[63] The word "you" is in the accusative and so functions as the object of the verb "reconciled" in verse 22, if the verb Paul wrote/dictated was in the active voice (*apokatellaxen*) as most manuscripts read.   However, two very important manuscripts (P[46] B) have a passive voice verb *apokatellagete* ("you have been reconciled").   If the passive was original, then Paul's grammar is broken, because it has an accusative as the subject of the verb, something one might do when dictating and especially when several words intervene.   The passive verb form was preferred by the editors of the UBS[2] text, but the editors of UBS[3] text preferred the active verb form. The notes in this commentary are based on the active voice reading.

[64] Such language implies the Colossians at one time were not estranged.   We would point to their relationship with God before they reached the age of accountability.   See also Romans 7:9.

[65] This explanation treats the dative word "mind" as a dative of reference, describing the part affected, and treats the Greek word translated "hostile" as being active, thus hostile to God in your mind.

Engaged **in evil deeds** – The hostility in mind was outwardly expressed by evil deeds. "Evil" is emphasized by its position in the Greek, and the word translated "evil" is the synonym that means not just bad or evil in itself, but it tries to get others to be bad.[66]

1:22 – *yet He has now reconciled you in His fleshly body through death, in order to present you before Him holy and blameless and beyond reproach* —

Yet He has now reconciled you in His fleshly body through death – By means of "yet ... now," Paul calls attention to the sharp contrast between their former state (verse 21) and their present reconciled state (verse 22). The verb translated "reconciled" is a double compound form which intensifies the meaning. The Colossian Christians have not been just partially reconciled, thus needing further reconciliation such as the Gnostics mistakenly supposed they could offer. "In His fleshly body" is literally "in the body of His flesh," a description which both distinguishes His earthly body from His body the church (Colossians 1:18), and at the same time is anti-Gnostic. Jesus had a real human body, something the docetic Gnostics denied. A physical body was a necessity if Jesus were to be able to die. "Through death" refers to Jesus' physical death at Calvary, a death which was a sin offering. Romans 8:3 (though not having Gnostics in view) states a similar truth, namely, that God sent His own Son in the likeness of flesh of sin, as a sin offering, and thereby condemned sin in the flesh. This, too, contradicts Gnostic doctrine which placed little or no value on what happened at Calvary.

In order to present you before Him – Ephesians 1:4 suggests that "before Him" is a reference to God. The "you" who are to be presented are the reconciled. Most likely the time when the presentation to God takes place is at the judgment day since verse 23 makes the presentation dependent on continuance in the faith.

Holy and blameless and beyond reproach – The three adjectives describe spiritual qualities that are the result of sins having been forgiven. "Holy" carries either the connotation of something set aside and dedicated to God, or something that is made free from sin. The word picture in "blameless" is of a sacrificial animal that was without flaw or blemish and therefore worthy of being offered to God. "Beyond reproach" or "free from accusation" calls to mind the language of Romans 8:33. Christians cannot be successfully accused before God ("who will bring a charge against God's elect?") because Christ died for them, rose again, and intercedes on their behalf.

---

[66] See Trench, *op. cit.*, p.315. Berry, *Synonyms*, p.128; Thayer, *op. cit.*, p.320.

1:23 – *if indeed you continue in the faith firmly established and steadfast, and not moved away from the hope of the gospel that you have heard, which was proclaimed in all creation under heaven, and of which I, Paul, was made a minister.*

If indeed you continue in the faith – "If indeed" (*ei ge* with the indicative) here is not an expression of uncertainty, but is an assumption that what is said is true. It gives a needful warning while at the same time refuses to admit failure. The verb (*epimenete*) translated "continue" is a compound form giving emphasis to the idea of persisting in or adhering to or staying with the faith. "The faith" here denotes a body of doctrine, namely, the message of the gospel which the Colossians had received from Epaphras (Colossians 1:7). "If you continue" indicates that the security of the believer is conditional.[67] Paul assures them they will be presented to God if they do not abandon Christianity.

Firmly established and steadfast – "Firmly established" is a perfect passive participle indicating continuing results based on past completed action. The word picture is of erecting a building on a solid foundation. Paul's wording reminds us of a familiar saying by Jesus (Luke 6:47-49), "Everyone who comes to Me, and hears My words, and acts upon them, I will show you whom he is like: he is like a man building a house, who dug deep and laid a foundation upon the rock; and when a flood rose, the torrent burst against that house and could not shake it, because it had been well built. But the one who has heard, and has not acted accordingly, is like a man who built a house on the ground without any foundation; and the torrent burst against it and immediately it collapsed, and the ruin of that house was great." "Steadfast" (or "settled"), referring to the stability of the building, is the result of being erected on the solid foundation. The same word occurs at 1 Corinthians 15:58 and in both places refers to a steady conviction that results from resting on eternal truth.

And not moved away from the hope of the gospel that you have heard – This phrase, too, is part of the condition that must be met if the Colossians would be presented by Christ to God. "The gospel that you have heard" refers to what Epaphras had preached when he established the church at Colossae. Their conversion had resulted from hearing the word of Christ. One of the things Epaphras emphasized as he preached was "hope."   The "hope" included in the

---

[67] Two helpful studies of this matter are Guy Duty, *If Ye Continue: A Study of the Conditional Aspects of Salvation* (Minneapolis, MN: Bethany Fellowship, 1966) and Robert Shank, *Life in the Son: A Study of the Doctrine of Perseverance* (Springfield, MO: Westcott Publishers, 1961).

gospel refers to the thing hoped for, namely, the future resurrection of the body when Jesus returns, and the future and immortal state of the redeemed in heaven. Such a "hope" would have to be abandoned if one is converted to Gnostic doctrines about the future. They taught that whatever resurrection there is was already past (2 Timothy 2:18), and their doctrine of reincarnation and aeon guards who control access to the Supreme Being is wholly different from what Christianity teaches about Jesus presenting the reconciled believers to the Father. "Not moved away" is a present participle picturing a continuous process. The teachings of the Gnostics would slowly but surely move their disciples away from the hope they had embraced when they heard Epaphras' gospel preaching. Paul is cautioning his readers that their promised inheritance (the hope of the gospel) would be jeopardized if they embrace what the false teachers want them to do and believe.

Which was proclaimed in all creation under heaven – Paul again sets his seal of approval on the form of the gospel which they had received from Epaphras. What the Colossians had heard is authentic, Paul is saying, the very gospel which Jesus commanded be preached by His messengers to all the world. "Proclaimed" is literally "heralded," "loudly and officially announced."[68] "In all creation under heaven" and "in all the world" (Colossians 1:6) say the same thing.[69] "Every nation under heaven" (Acts 2:5) included the whole Mediterranean world. Jesus Himself had said (Matthew 24:14) the gospel would be preached to all the world "for a witness to all the nations" before the destruction of Jerusalem (AD 70).

Of which I, Paul, was made a minister – Speaking of himself as a minister (see Ephesians 3:7), Paul assures the Colossians that the gospel which they heard from Epaphras, their "minister" (Colossians 1:7), is the same message of which Paul himself had been made a "minister." Paul closes his presentation about God reconciling all things to Himself through Jesus by warning his readers that if they are moved away from that gospel by the deceptive false teachings being presented by folk who were not ministers of the gospel, it will cause the loss of their reconciliation and of their presentation to God by Jesus.

---

[68] On the verb for "proclaimed" or "heralded" compare how Jesus worded His great commission, "Preach the gospel to all creation" (Mark 16:15) and how Paul calls himself a herald in 2 Timothy 1:11.

[69] The KJV reads "to every creature," and this would imply every individual had heard it. However, the better manuscripts read "in all creation" (NASB). This reading does not mean every individual, but every nation or every great population center of the Roman empire (cf. Romans 15:19-23).

III. CONTROVERSIAL SECTION – Christ is Preeminent in Doctrine.   1:24-2:23

A. Paul's Work as a Servant of the Incomparable Christ.   1:24-2:7

Summary: Having called himself "a minister of the gospel" (Colossians 1:23), Paul writes at greater length about himself and the message he preaches.

1. His ministry.   1:24,25

1:24 – *Now I rejoice in my sufferings for your sake, and in my flesh I do my share on behalf of His body (which is the church) in filling up that which is lacking in Christ's afflictions.*

Now I rejoice in my sufferings for your sake – "Now" is probably temporal meaning "now at this very moment."[70]   The verse affirms that both joy and suffering were realities at the time he was writing this letter.   "My sufferings" (*pathēmasin*) likely includes all the persecution and bodily harm and harassment he suffered as he went from place to place with the gospel.   There may also be an allusion to his situation as a prisoner (Colossians 4:8-10).   In three of the prison epistles Paul declares that in spite of the hardships of his ministry he is rejoicing, and in two of them he urges his readers to rejoice (Ephesians 3:13; Philippians 2:17).   Paul is not saying that he enjoys suffering, but rather that he can rejoice in the midst of his sufferings because he knows they were incurred in the line of duty.   "For your sake" indicates the Colossians were the beneficiaries of his ministry to the Gentiles.   Though at the moment he is suffering imprisonment, he can look back over his life with satisfaction of a job well done.

And in my flesh I do my share on behalf of His body (which is the church) – Paul further elaborates how he looks upon his physical sufferings.   In his fleshly body, he says, he is suffering for the sake of Christ's body, the church.[71]   His ministry, with its attendant sufferings, has benefits which extend to a larger audience than just the Colossians – indeed there are benefits for the whole body of Christ.

---

[70] The text behind the KJV has a relative pronoun at the beginning of verse 24, but the better attested text has no relative pronoun, but begins abruptly with "now."

[71] For the meaning of "body," and "the church," see on Colossians 1:18.

In filling up that which is lacking in Christ's afflictions – The words Paul wrote here are unique in some ways, and this has caused interpreters to draw different inferences from them.   The word translated "afflictions" (*thlipseōn*) means tribulations or troubles.   Since it is not the regular word for the sufferings of Christ on the cross it likely does not have reference to that, as though His death were not sufficient to atone for sins.[72]   Perhaps it means that Paul was suffering afflictions like those which Christ endured.[73]   Perhaps it alludes to the fact that Jesus suffers when Christians suffer.[74]   Most likely Paul is saying that he has been suffering just like Jesus promised he would.   Just after Jesus appeared to Paul on the Damascus road, in a vision Jesus told Ananias to go minister to Paul. When Ananias hesitated about going, Jesus said to him, "Go, for he is a chosen instrument of mine ... I will show him how much he must suffer for My name's sake" (Acts 9:15,16).   "Filling up" shows that Paul is aware that the suffering Jesus promised is not yet complete.

1:25 – *Of* **this church** *I was made a minister according to the stewardship from God bestowed on me for your benefit, that I might fully carry out the* **preaching of** *the word of God,*

Of *this church* **I was made a minister** – In the Greek this verse begins with a relative pronoun in the feminine case.   Since the noun "church" (verse 24) is the nearest feminine antecedent, our translators have rightly inserted "this church" in italics.   In verse 23 Paul described himself as a minister of the gospel.   Here he describes himself as a minister (or servant) of the church, which implies he thinks of himself as obligated to toil in whatever way the welfare of the church requires.

According to the stewardship from God – Paul here explains how he came to be a minister of the church.   "Stewardship" is an attempt to translate *oiknomian*, a word which has a wide range of meanings including plan, arrangement, steward- ship, management, administration.   The KJV and ASV read "according to the dispensation of God," a translation which suggests Paul's call to apostleship was part of the divine plan for the evangelization of the world   (cp. Ephesians 1:10).

---

[72] Catholic writers who quote this text in support of the doctrine of the merit of the saints are in error.   The sacrifice of Christ is the one sacrifice needed for the forgiveness of sins (Hebrews 10:10,18).

[73] The more common phrase, "the sufferings (*pathēmata*) of Christ" (2 Corinthians 1:5; Philippians 3:10) likewise means sufferings like He endured.

[74] Recall Jesus' words to Paul on the Damascus road, "Why are you persecuting Me?" (Acts 9:4,5).   Likewise, the *Letter from the Churches of Vienne and Lyon* speaks of Christ as suffering when the martyrs suffered (Eusebius, *H.E.*, v.1).

Goodspeed has "divine appointment," a translation which suggests God entrusted him with a special task.   Since a steward was a job of special responsibility in a household, and since the church is the household of God, Paul may be saying that God appointed him to a position of high privilege and sacred trust.   He may be a servant of the church, but in another sense he was a steward working for God.

Bestowed on me for your benefit – "To me," he says in the parallel passage in Ephesians 3:8, "... this grace was given to preach unto the Gentiles the unfathomable riches of Christ."   The Colossians were numbered among the Gentiles to whom Paul had been commissioned to preach.   The gospel benefits folk in that it results in their spiritual well-being.

That I might fully carry out the *preaching of* the word of God – This phrase begins to explain the particular task that was involved in the stewardship bestowed on Paul.   The infinitive translated "fully carry out" is literally "to fulfill" and here carries the idea that Paul was to "unfold God's message to the full."   The term speaks not so much of the geographical area covered, but rather how much he was entrusted to reveal.[75]   Paul will go on to explain that as an apostle of Christ it was his privilege to unfold what was previously a hidden "mystery."

2. His message.   1:26,27

1:26 – that is, *the mystery which has been hidden from the* past *ages and generations; but has now been manifested to His saints,*

That is – Verses 26 and 27 explain in terms of a "mystery" some of the contents of "the word of God" just identified as the message Paul was entrusted to preach.

The mystery which has been hidden from the *past* ages and generations – In this passage here in Colossians, a "mystery" is defined with perfect clearness as something long hidden, but which now has been revealed.   He explains how he is using the word "mystery," lest someone think he is speaking like a Gnostic.   He uses the word here just as he has used it in earlier writings such as 1 Corinthians (1 Corinthians 2:6,7; 15:51) Romans (Romans 16:25,26) and Ephesians.   Paul used the word "mystery" six times in Ephesians, and each time it spoke of some truth only dimly revealed in the Old Testament times,   but which is now clearly

---

[75] As the marginal reading at Romans 15:19 indicates, the similar expression "I have fully preached (lit., fulfilled) the gospel of Christ" may also refer to how much he was entrusted to reveal.

set forth by the apostles and New Testament prophets (Ephesians 3:4,5). By inspiration they communicated it to their audiences.[76] The particular thing that Paul has in mind in this passage that was but dimly revealed before Christ came is stated in the close of verse 27. "Past ages and generations" have been interpreted two different ways. One way treats the terms as referring to people living in former times. The Old Testament period was divided into Patriarchal and Mosaic ages, and each age was comprised of many generations. The other way pictures Paul as picking up some terms the Gnostics used to refer to angels[77] and has Paul refuting Gnostic teaching about angels by saying they did not know anything about the manifold wisdom of God until they learned it through the church (Ephesians 3:9,10). "Past ages and generations" underscores the fact that in Christ and the church God's redemptive purposes have reached a new stage in history, and until Christ the mystery was concealed from angels and men.

But has now been manifested to His saints – The mystery is no longer hidden from men. "Now" refers to the fullness of time, the coming of Christ (Galatians 4:4). "To His saints" is literally "to His holy ones," which might be the apostles and prophets (cf. Ephesians 3:5), or it might refer to Christians generally as the recipients, with the apostles and prophets being the understood organs whom God used as He made the revelation.

1:27 – *to whom God willed to make known what is the riches of the glory of this mystery among the Gentiles, which is Christ in you, the hope of glory.*

To whom God willed to make known – The antecedent of "to whom" is "to His saints." The sentence begun in verse 24 continues without a break. "God willed" is emphatic in the Greek. It was done the way it was done because that is the way God willed to do it. Likewise, in Ephesians 1:9 we read that God made known "the mystery of His will" just as His kind intention purposed to do it in Christ.

What is the riches of the glory of this mystery among the Gentiles – As he did in Ephesians 1:18 where we have the same phrase "the riches of the glory," Paul here piles up expression upon expression as he works to convey the breadth of the bountiful blessing which God has bestowed upon the Gentiles. "Riches" suggests

---

[76] The apostles were told by Jesus that to them it was given to know the mysteries of the kingdom (Matthew 13:11 = Luke 8:10).

[77] The word translated "ages" is also the word from which "aeons" is taken. The Gnostics did have endless genealogies (1 Timothy 1:4), though it is not certain this term was ever used of angels.

an inexhaustible treasure. "Glory" carries with it the idea of something divine.[78] "Mystery" says it always was God's intent to include the Gentiles among the objects of His mercy; it was there in the Old Testament, but it was a truth not as clearly revealed in the Old Testament times as it is in the gospel age. "Among the Gentiles" designates the sphere in which the riches of glory have been especially displayed.

Which is Christ in you, the hope of glory – The manuscripts differ on the word translated "which." Some have a masculine form referring to the riches; others have a neuter form referring to mystery. The similar passage in Ephesians 3:17 has Christ "dwelling in your hearts through faith." Christ dwelling in Gentile hearts is a wonder of wonders that is absolutely true. In Ephesians 3:6 Paul worded it this way, "that the Gentiles are fellow-heirs and fellow-members of the body, and fellow-partakers of the promise of Christ Jesus through the gospel." "Glory" connected with the word "hope" points to the heavenly future, and may even have allusion to the glorified body which the saints will receive.[79] The same offer of salvation and heaven was now opened for all, Gentiles included! Again, we note, as in Colossians 1:5 and 23, special emphasis is laid on the hope of heaven, something the Gnostics denied.

3. His motive.   1:28 - 2:3

1:28 – *And we proclaim Him, admonishing every man and teaching every man with all wisdom, that we may present every man complete in Christ.*

And we proclaim Him – From 1:28 through 2:3 Paul explains the driving motive behind his ministry. "We" is emphatic in the Greek and distinguishes Paul from the Colossian errorists.[80] Earlier (verse 23) Paul used the more common word for preach (*kerusso*). Here he uses "proclaim" (*katangello*), a word which suggests a public authoritative announcement. That, too, differed from the false teachers who did not publicly announce their deceptive ideas. "Him" refers to the Christ whom verse 27 just described in definite terms as "Christ in you [Gentiles], the hope of glory." This is not how the false teachers at Colossae, with their Jewish emphases and theosophic speculation, presented Christ.

---

[78] See notes at Colossians 1:11.

[79] See Bernard Ramm, *Them He Glorified: A Systematic Study of the Doctrine of Glorification* (Grand Rapids: Eerdmans, 1963).

[80] The plural may pick up Paul and Timothy and Epaphras (Colossians 1:7, 4:7,11,12), but in the context he has been dealing with his own special mission.

Admonishing every man and teaching every man with all wisdom – Two participles describe two things done as Christ is proclaimed. "Admonishing" or warning is reproof for the folly of sin (recall the Gnostic denial of personal sin, 1 John 1:8-10) and the consequences of rejecting the gospel. "Teaching" is instruction so that hearers will know the truth and be able to recognize falsehood when it appears. "With all wisdom" expresses either the content of the teaching or the way the teaching was done, and "every man" seems to be a deliberate contrast with the false teachers who reserved their higher teaching for the elite inner circle. God's "wisdom" as taught in Christianity includes righteousness, sanctification, and redemption (1 Corinthians 1:30).

That we may present every man complete in Christ – This is the clause that tells us what Paul's aim was as he proclaimed Christ. Paul's aim was the same as Christ's (Colossians 1:22), namely, that they may be able to present to God, at the return of Christ (1Thessalonians 5:23), souls redeemed and holy and spotless. The word "complete" is *teleios* which, when used of a believer as it is here, means "mature," spiritually mature and complete (cp. Ephesians 4:13). Such maturity is found only "in Christ." Vital union with Him is the *sine quâ non* of growth and maturity. Three times in this verse Paul writes "every man." In mystery cults "complete" or "perfect" was used to describe the few who had been initiated into the secrets and rituals (the "mystery") of the religion. Paul here makes a pointed comparison between the gospel and Gnosticism. The initiation available in Christ is available to "every man," not just some for the favored few.

1:29 – *And for this purpose also I labor, striving according to His power, which mightily works within me.*

And for this purpose also I labor – "For this purpose" points back to verse 28, namely, "to present every man complete in Christ." Perhaps in anticipation of the strong correction he is about to write (Colossians 2:8-23) Paul changes from the plural ("we") to singular ("I"). "Labor" (*kopiaō*) expresses hard, demanding work carried to the point of weariness.[81] Paul may be in prison when he writes this letter, with his activities somewhat curtailed. He still puts in long, wearisome hours on behalf of the churches.

Striving according to His power – The root word translated "striving" is used of Jesus praying in Gethsemane (Luke 22:44) and the same Greek word is used of Epaphras (Colossians 4:12), "laboring earnestly for you in his prayers." Paul here

---

[81] Berry, *Synonyms*, p.135., or Thayer, *op. cit.,* p.355.

likely makes reference to his prayers on behalf of his converts (see Colossians 1:3, 4:12; Romans 15:30; 1 Thessalonians 2:2; 1 Timothy 4:10).   In the words "according to His power," Paul affirms that the strength needed for such unremitting labor is not his own stamina.   Christ (the nearest antecedent of "His") is the One who empowers him to continue on (cp. Philippians 4:13, "I can do all things through Him who strengthens me").

Which mightily works within me – Perhaps, as in Galatians 2:8 ("He who effectually worked for Peter in his apostleship ... effectually worked for me also to the Gentiles"), Paul is making special allusion to the grace given him for his apostleship to the Gentiles. Using different words that speak of "power" and "energy," Paul seems to be saying that he was aware when the Holy Spirit was empowering him to speak or write – just as the Old Testament prophets knew when the Holy Spirit came upon them.

2:1 – *For I want you to know how great a struggle I have on your behalf, and for those who are at Laodicea, and for all those who have not personally seen my face,*

For I want you to know – "For" ties Colossians 2:1-3 to the closing verses of Colossians 1 by giving an explanation of how he was using the word "striving" in Colossians 1:29.[1] We are still in the midst of the paragraph, which began at 1:24, in which the apostle is describing his share in carrying out the work of the incomparable Christ. With his "I want you to know" Paul is imparting information he wants his readers to fully understand. All these words about his work as an apostle of Christ are introductory to the warning he is about to give, beginning in Colossians 2:8.

How great a struggle I have on your behalf – "On your behalf" (as the rest of the verse shows) means for the church at Colossae. "Struggle" translates the same root word translated "striving" in 1:29. It is *agōn*, the word used of athletes in the arena who are straining ("agonizing") both physically and mentally to defeat their opponents. How can Paul the prisoner carry on any "fight" on their behalf, when they are miles apart? Perhaps if we look at Colossians 4:12, we might refer it especially to "striving in prayer" for them. Paul has already described his ministry as an apostle to the Gentiles and the message with which he was entrusted. Now Paul wants the Colossians to know the great concern he has for them, especially regarding what might be their response to the error being propagated by the false teachers who lately have begun to trouble the churches.

And for those who are at Laodicea – Laodicea, we learned in the Detailed Introduction to Colossians, was a city just a few miles down river from Colossae. Paul informs them that the church at Laodicea also had been in his prayers. The mention of Laodicea indicates Paul was concerned that the dangerous deceptive teaching troubling Colossae might spread there, also.

And for all those who have not personally seen my face – This statement is a clear indication that Paul had not personally evangelized in the area. Someone else, likely Epaphras, had evangelized and started the churches in the Lycus valley, likely including the one at Hierapolis (Colossians 4:13), too. But the fact he had never been there does not mean that Paul is intruding into an area where he had no business, for an apostle of Jesus had responsibility and concern for all

---

[1] Paul wrote a letter, and it was not divided into chapters until years later. The chapter division here can cause English readers to fail to see that the thought begun in what is now numbered 1:28,29 is continued right on in what is numbered 2:1-3.

the churches (2 Corinthians 11:28). It was perfectly proper for Paul to be struggling not just for those whom he had met and knew personally but also for those who lived in places he had never been.

2:2 – *that their hearts may be encouraged, having been knit together in love, and* **attaining** *to all the wealth that comes from the full assurance of understanding, resulting in a true knowledge of God's mystery,* **that is,** *Christ* **Himself,**

That their hearts may be encouraged – If "struggle" speaks of struggling in prayer, then this clause indicates that for which he prays as he prays for the churches. Sometimes the word translated "encouraged" is a military metaphor, picturing soldiers not getting discouraged, breaking rank and retreating. Paul has just defined his goal as "presenting every man complete (mature) in Christ" (see 1:28). He returns to that idea here, stating that his prayer is that Christians (even those whom he has never met) may not retreat from Christ.

Having been knit together in love – "Knit together" is a circumstantial participle which tells the method by which Christians are strengthened or encouraged lest they retreat. In Colossians 3:14 Paul will write that love is the bond of unity. Soldiers will give their lives to defend their buddies. Paul wants the Colossians to be that concerned for their brethren. As Ephesians 3:17ff says, it is only as Christians are "rooted and grounded in love" that they can acquire the power to "comprehend *with all the saints*" the fullness of God's revelation.

And *attaining* **to all the wealth that comes from the full assurance of understanding** – The goal of their being united together in love (for which Paul prays) is that the Christians may arrive at a firm and settled conviction concerning the truth of the Christian doctrine. The accumulation of phrases ("wealth,"[2] "all the wealth," "full assurance"[3]) to describe the assurance to which he wants them all to come, may reflect His desire to impress upon them the momentous importance of the subject in hand. "Full assurance" will result in "understanding," i.e., the ability to analyze a situation as one makes a decision what to do (as at Colossians 1:9).

Resulting in a true knowledge of God's mystery – This clause explains what will result from their "understanding." He prays that they may more and more

---

[2] On the meaning of the word "wealth" as used by the apostle Paul, see the notes on "riches" at Colossians 1:27.

[3] "Full assurance" may stand in contrast to the doubts that persuasive false teachers can arouse.

enter into the "wealth" that is to be found in the "true (full) knowledge[4] of God's mystery."[5]   In this context that "true knowledge" will make them unsusceptible to Gnostic speculations.

***That is,* Christ** *Himself* – The word "Christ" is in the same case as "mystery," placing it in apposition to that word, so the NASB has added the right words in italics.[6]   The mystery Paul here has in mind is Christ.[7]   Who Christ would be and what He would do were foretold in the Old Testament Scriptures (though full understanding remained a mystery).   If we search them, and pay attention to them, the "day will dawn and the morning star" will arise in our hearts (says 2 Peter 1:19 which was also anti-Gnostic).   A careful study of Messianic prophecies will show Christ is preeminent, just as Paul has been affirming.

2:3 – *in whom are hidden all the treasures of wisdom and knowledge.*

In whom are hidden – Verse 3 tells the special emphasis one should look for as he or she studies the mystery concerning Christ.   The word order in the Greek causes a reader to pause and reflect; it is "in whom are all the treasures of wisdom and knowledge hidden."   "Hidden" is a plural adjective that modifies "treasures." "Hidden" (*apokruphoi*) can mean conceal, or it can have the connotation of being laid up or stored away, both of which were how treasures were treated in the ancient world.   Not only that, but since the word "hidden" was an almost technical word for Gnostic secret heretical teaching given only to the initiated, Lightfoot has suggested that Paul deliberately used a favorite word of the false teachers to reflect negatively on their pretense of having a special secret knowledge of spiritual matters.[8]

---

[4] The Greek is the compound form *(epignosis)* of "know" *(gnosis)*, thus "full knowledge."

[5] The Biblical meaning of "mystery" was explained at Colossians 1:26.

[6] There is considerable manuscript variation here.   The KJV reads "the mystery of God, and of the Father, and of Christ," but the words between "God" and "Christ" are not well supported. In addition to how the NASB has translated the accepted Greek text, two other ways the Greek could be translated are "The God of Christ" or "the God Christ."

[7] At Colossians 1:27 we recalled that several topics the apostles preached were once a mystery which it was now their privilege to unfold.

[8] Lightfoot, *op. cit.*, p.174.   Some years later, early Christian writers soon applied the term "apocryphal" *(apokruphoi)* to the false and spurious writings of the Gnostics.   It is, however, unlikely that any such Gnostic writings had already been produced at the time Paul writes Colossians.   The terms "apocryphal" along with "pseudepigraphical" are still applied to heretical writings.

All the treasures of wisdom and knowledge – Four words in this verse (wisdom, knowledge, treasures, hidden) were words the Gnostics used.   We suppose Paul borrowed their terminology in order to refer negatively to Gnostic ideas as he presents the preeminence of Christ.   In Christ (not in the Gnostic teachings) is where one finds wisdom (*sophia*) and knowledge *(gnosis)*.   God's "wisdom" is defined in 1 Corinthians 1:30 as including righteousness, sanctification, and redemption.[9]   "Knowledge" speaks of understanding what is requisite to guide us in the way to live.   When Paul says that all, and not merely some of, the treasures of wisdom and knowledge are stored up in Christ, he is implying that any search for them outside of Christ is doomed to failure.   Speaking of Christ, TEV has offered this translation for verse 3, "He is the key that opens all the hidden treasures of God's wisdom and knowledge."

4. His mandate. 2:4-7

2:4 – *I say this in order that no one may delude you with persuasive argument.*

I say this – Using the pronoun "this" (which may refer to what he wrote in verse 3, or to all that he has written in 2:1-3), Paul now begins to make clear the purpose of his preceding comments about his concern for them and especially about all the treasures of wisdom and knowledge being stored up in Christ.

In order that no one may delude you with persuasive argument – His purpose, he says, was that he might warn and fortify them against being deluded and led astray.   Now, for the first time, the danger threatening the church is brought clearly into focus.   The Greek word for "delude" (*paralogizomai*) implies being led astray by false reasoning or bad logic.   The word for "persuasive argument" (*pithanologia*) comes from the law court where the smooth-talking lawyer uses fine sounding arguments to make the bad look good, and thereby enable the criminal to escape his due punishment.   The reason for Paul's anxiety is the deceit and false reasoning used by the incipient Gnostic teachers.   Their tactics were so dangerous simply because they made it sound so good.   Paul was obviously thinking of the attempt of the errorists to lead the Colossians away from their convictions about Christ.

---

[9] See the notes on "wisdom" at Colossians 1:9,28.

2:5 – *For even though I am absent in body, nevertheless I am with you in spirit, rejoicing to see your good discipline and the stability of your faith in Christ.*

For even though I am absent in body – The reason Paul had to be physically absent from Colossae is because he was in prison in Rome as he wrote this letter.

Nevertheless I am with you in spirit – Though he was at a distance from them, nevertheless he was no indifferent spectator to their problems. He had a sincere interest in them. Some, following Jerome's lead, have argued we should use a capital "S" to translate "Spirit," and then have appealed to passages like 2 Kings 5:25-26 which speak of how the Holy Spirit gave information to Elisha about Gehazi's behavior, or to Ezekiel 8:12 which tells how the Holy Spirit helped Ezekiel to know about the secret actions of the Jews back in Jerusalem. In a similar way, it is suggested the Holy Spirit has helped Paul to see how the Colossians are responding to the gospel. If we use a small "s" to translate "spirit," as was done with the similar expression in 1 Corinthians 5:3, neither here nor in 1 Corinthians does the language imply that Paul's spirit could leave his body and travel to Colossae or Corinth simply to observe what was happening there. "I am with you in spirit" is a simple way of stating "his sense of close identification with his Colossian fellow Christians." Paul is saying, "Even though I am not there with you, I am still thinking about you constantly."[10]

Rejoicing to see your good discipline – The Greek words here translated "rejoicing to see" are two nominative singular participles in the present tense, a construction whose meaning commentators have found it difficult to decide. Peake observed that "if the object of his joy is the condition of the Church, we should have expected an inversion of the order, first seeing and then rejoicing at what he saw."[11] Meyer wrote that "rejoicing" means rejoicing to be present with them in spirit.[12] Lightfoot explained that the order indicates Paul was looking at them because it gave him joy to look.[13] Alford suggested that the word rejoicing should be connected to "with you" so that the verse says Paul is rejoicing with the

---

[10] Bratcher, *op. cit.,* p.47.

[11] Peake, *op. cit.,* p.520.

[12] Meyer, *op. cit.,* p.287.

[13]Lightfoot, *op. cit.,* p. 176.

Colossians over their relationship to Christ.[14] Perhaps Alford's explanation is the better one. "Good discipline" is a military metaphor. They are walking in step with the gospel which Epaphras delivered to them. This walking in step as well as their joy was threatened by the false teaching which tended to be very divisive.

And the stability of your faith in Christ – Perhaps the military metaphor is continued and "stability" pictures the situation at Colossae as being like that of an army under attack and affirms that their lines were unbroken. The implication would be that they should not let the Gnostics breach their lines. The Vulgate translators using *firmamentum* to translate the Greek word must have thought the figure was of a building that had a solid foundation. The gospel already preached to them by Epaphras had given them a solid basis for their faith. The implication is that the Gnostics had nothing useful or helpful to add. "Paul was doing more than just exposing false information; he is acting to preserve the eternal destiny of brothers and sisters in Christ."[15]

2:6 – As you therefore have received Christ Jesus the Lord, *so* walk in Him,

As you therefore have received Christ Jesus the Lord – "As" is *hōs*, "in the same manner as, like as." "As ... therefore" shows that Paul is making this appeal for loyalty to Christ Jesus the Lord in light of the warning given in verse 4 and the reason for it in verse 5. Looking back at their beginnings in Christianity, Paul speaks of them as having "received Christ Jesus the Lord." For many contemporary believers this language sounds like a commonly given invitation to become a Christian;[16] however, the expression Paul uses means more than that. Paul uses the verb "received" (*paralambano*), a word technically employed to denote the embracing of authoritative teaching which was delivered by oral tradition. Here it refers to hearing and believing the gospel message, as it does in 1 Thessalonians 2:13. This tradition began with the Lord giving it to Paul (1 Corinthians 15:1,2; Galatians 1:11,12), who then repeated it to Epaphras, who in

---

[14]Alford, *op. cit.*, p. 216.

[15] Robert Shannon, *Standard Lesson Commentary 1999-2000*, (Cincinnati, OH: Standard, 1999), p.426.

[16] To teach an unconverted person that all he or she needs to do is "receive Jesus into their heart" may not be quite Scriptural. The only place where the Bible has folk inviting Jesus in is Revelation 3:20, which is addressed not to folk who are potential converts, but to folk who are already Christians. John 1:12 does read "to as many as received Him, that is who believed in Him, to them He gave the power to become sons of God" (my translation). Since "believing in Him" is an obedient faith (as the Greek word "believe" followed by a prepositional phrase "in" or "on" shows), what is included in receiving Jesus in John 1:12 is an obedient faith, not just mental assent and trust.

turn taught it to the Colossians.   Paul is emphasizing the continuity of the transmission of Christian truth, something the false teachers cannot claim for their teachings.

The teachings the Colossians received and embraced included three ideas about Jesus:

- He is the Anointed of God ("Christ")
- He is the historic Savior ("Jesus")
- He is sovereign Deity ("Lord").

What they had been taught was exactly right.   Paul's word order places emphasis on the last word, "Lord."   This is significant, for the chief problem with the deceptive teaching at Colossae was that it was a subversion of the true idea of Christ – that He, and He alone, is Lord.   The preeminence of Christ was being repudiated.[17]   Cerinthian Gnostics, 30 years later,[18] distinguished between the *man* Jesus and the *aeon* Christ who (according to their theology) came upon Jesus at His baptism.   Paul anticipates and refutes this peculiar idea with his word order "Christ Jesus ...."

So **walk in Him** – The word "walk" is used metaphorically to denote the manner of life.   The Greek means "keep on walking in Him" ("just as you were taught ...," says verse 7).   The Colossians are not to give up any of the historic truths they were taught.   This is an exhortation to stand fast in the apostolic faith.   Four participles in the next verse describe how it is possible for them to continue to walk with confidence in what they had been taught.

2:7 – *having been firmly rooted* **and now** *being built up in Him and established in your faith, just as you were instructed,* **and** *overflowing with gratitude.*

Having been firmly rooted – Verses 6 and 7 are all one sentence in the Greek.   The four participles in this verse modify the main verb "walk" (in verse 6).   The perfect tense participle translated "firmly rooted" pictures something that happened in the past time with present continuing results.   Their faith was already long established, not merely beginning.   The metaphor is "of a big tree, with its roots deep in the soil.   The first stage in the growth of a plant is the establishment of roots.   All subsequent growth of the visible part of the plant de-

---

[17] "Lord" is used in the highest sense of the word, as at Philippians 2:11.   The mystic theosophy of the Gnostics put in peril the lordship of Christ at Colossae.   So it is in occult religions generally.

[18] Cerinthus is dated c. AD 100.   He was a contemporary of the apostle John.

pends on the nourishment it receives from the roots.   If the plant is severed from its roots it will die.   The first stage in the growth of a Christian is to be rooted in Christ."[19]

And now **being built up in Him** – "Built up" (*epoikodomoumenoi*) is a present tense participle, indicating a continual process.   Growing in the Lord is an ongoing process.   The metaphor is now of a building.   "'In Him' belongs to both participles, so that Christ is to be conceived doubtless as the soil for the roots striking downwards (Ephesians 3:17), and as the foundation (1 Corinthians 3:11) for the building extending upwards."[20]   "We build our lives block by block as we cement in our personal selection of beliefs, attitudes, character traits, priorities, goals, and actions.   Jesus' disciples must see that all these building blocks of life are derived from Him and harmonize with Him."[21]

And established in your faith – The third participle, "established" (*bebaioumenoi*, strengthened), is a present tense; it is a process going on.   Such strengthening or establishing is the result of being built up.   In this verse, the word "faith" probably refers, not to personal faith, but to a body of doctrine, that entire system of doctrinal truth that Christians believe, since faith is described in the next clause as something that the Colossians have been taught.   "He wanted them to have unwavering adherence to the gospel as it was originally proclaimed to them, not as it was modified by false teachers.   We obey this admonition today if we adhere to the gospel as it is revealed in the Bible."[22]

Just as you were instructed – This repeats the assurance that Epaphras had given them the truth.   This caution that they should not be listening to any novel doctrines reminds us of 1 John, where John urges folk who are being enticed by the Gnostics to stay the course in the teaching they had received from the beginning (from the apostles and Jesus).

And **overflowing with gratitude** – This is the fourth participle in this verse.   "Over-flowing" (*perisseuontes*) is a metaphor of a river overflowing its banks; it is a present tense participle,   meaning that the believer's giving of thanks ("grati-

---

[19] Wallace Worley, *Standard Lesson Commentary, 1988-89* (Cincinnati, OH: Standard, 1988), p.251.

[20] Meyer, *op. cit.*, p.289.

[21] Worley, ibid.

[22] *Ibid.*

tude") is to be a continual, habitual thing.[23]   If the believers are happy with the apostolic Christianity they have embraced, and keep giving God thanks for it, the teachings of the Gnostics will not be alluring.   A failure to give God thanks (Romans 1:21) can result in folk abandoning God for idolatry.

B. Elements of the "Colossian Heresy" to be Rejected.   2:8-23

Summary: All the elements of the deceptive philosophy are rivals of Jesus Christ – and if accepted they will dethrone Him from His rightful place.

1.   Its source is not divine, nor are its ideas in harmony with Christ.   2:8

2:8 – *See to it that no one takes you captive through philosophy and empty deception, according to the tradition of men, according to the elementary principles of the world, rather than according to Christ.*

See to it that no one takes you captive – "See to it" alerts the readers to serious danger; it means, "Be constantly alert, be constantly on your guard."   The way the warning is written in Greek[24] suggests that the danger is very real, though it has not happened as yet.   The singular "no one" has led some interpreters to conclude that Paul had in mind one particular false teacher who was taking the lead in introducing this deceptive philosophy.   Rather than pointing to one individual person, we would treat "no one" as a general reference to any one who might seek to win converts to the new system.   The word translated "takes captive" (*sulagogon*) which was regularly used of taking captives in war and leading them away as booty, depicts the false teachers as "men-stealers," wishing to entrap the Colossians and drag them away into spiritual enslavement.

Through philosophy and empty deception – These words express the means by which the false teachers attempted to trap and enslave the Colossians.   Sharp's rule of grammar (the use of a single article and a single preposition with two

---

[23] "The words ['thankful, give thanks, thanksgiving'] occur in St. Paul's writings alone of the apostolic Epistles.   In this Epistle especially the duty of thanksgiving assumes a peculiar prominence by being made a refrain, as here and in Colossians 3:15; 3:17, 4:2; see also Colossians 1:12" (Lightfoot, *op. cit.*, p.177).

[24] The Greek is written with a future indicative verb, rather than a subjunctive verb, after the negative particle *me* (lest, not).

nouns) indicates that the Greek construction here means the two words ("philosophy" and "empty deception") are intended to describe one thing – namely, a contemporary and very deceptive religious belief at Colossae. "Philosophy" is one of the words used in the first century to describe this religious belief. As Josephus has shown, any elaborate system of thought and/or moral discipline was, in those days, called a "philosophy" (*philosophiai*)."[25] "Empty deception" is a further description of the religious system. Paul categorized the philosophy as empty delusion. Like a mirage in the desert,[26] the heretic's religion promises big things but it cannot deliver on its promises. Deceit is a trick or cheat as opposed to the word of truth.

According to the tradition of men – This is the first of three descriptive phrases that Paul uses to characterize this deceptive philosophy, and each of the phrases is intended to be a reason why it should be rejected. "According to" (*kata* + the accusative) equals 'in harmony with.' "Tradition" is the word which refers to oral tradition, something handed down by word of mouth, perhaps even from generation to another.[27] Paul could be referring to either Jewish or pagan traditions, either of which were to be avoided if they led their followers away from Christ. Eastern religions such as Zoroastrianism were spread by oral tradition.[28] Zoroastrian Scriptures were called the *Avesta* ("tradition"). The *Avesta* circulated orally for centuries. Commentaries on the Avesta were composed in the 9th century AD and are known as the *Zend*. We have earlier stated that some

---

[25] Josephus, *Wars*, II.8.2;   *Ant.* XVIII.1.1ff.   He used the word of the sects of the Jews known as the Pharisees, the Sadducees, and the Essenes.   When we remember the fact that the Colossian philosophy had an affinity to Essenism, the term is seen to be very relevant.   The word "philosophy" has changed meanings as the years have passed.   Where the ancients spoke of "philosophy" we might speak of "moral philosophy."

[26] The old cowboy song about *Cool Water*, sung by the Sons of the Pioneers, speaks of a "mirage" – and the cowboy urges "Dan," his horse, not to go there because there is no water there.

"All day I face the barren waste without the taste of water, Cool water.   Old Dan and I with throats burned dry and souls that cry for water, Cool, clear water.

Keep a movin', Dan, don't you listen to him man.   He's a devil not a man, and he spreads the burning sand with water, cool, clear water."

[27] Paul and Peter both claim reverence for the traditions that had as their starting point a direct revelation from God (1 Corinthians 11:2; 2 Thessalonians 2:15, 3:6; 2 Peter 2:21), so it cannot be said that all oral tradition is necessarily wrong.   It is the traditions of men (not those which had the authority of Christ behind them) which Paul here castigates.

[28] See the article by Edwin M. Yamauchi about Zoroastrianism entitled "Did Persian Zoroastrianism Influence Judaism," in *Artifax* (Winter 2013), p.13-17).

of the elements of the Colossian philosophy were derived from eastern oriental mysticism.[29]   The traditions "of men" (Eastern religions) do not have their origin in either God or Christ.   Because of verses that speak of the traditions of the elders (e.g., Matthew 15:2,3,6; Mark 7:8,9), many older commentaries supposed Paul had reference here to ideas derived from Judaism that were incorporated into the deceptive philosophy.   However, it is this commentator's judgment that Paul does not take up *Jewish* "traditions of men" until verse 16.

According to the elementary principles of the world – A second characteristic of the "philosophy" that made it objectionable is that it was in harmony with (*kata* + the accusative) "the elementary principles (*stoicheia*) of the world (*kosmos*)." Commentaries will show that in the multiple passages where the expression "elementary principles" occurs, there were multiple meanings for *stoicheia* ("elementary principles").[30]   For this verse, the meaning that appeals to us, in light of 2:18 where we learn that the Colossian heresy made much of the veneration of angels, is that *stoicheia* here in 2:8 refers to the "elemental spirits" – the spirits or aeons which were thought by men to rule the elements.   If we rule out all reference to aeons at this place, verse 9 ("fullness") makes little sense. Therefore, in this commentator's judgment, Paul has in mind the animistic sense of *stoicheia,* namely, it is a reference to the spirits thought by pagans to operate behind the phenomena of the visible world controlling all that happens in a person's life.   "Paul's point is not to argue the existence or non-existence of such beings as taught by the heretics.   Certainly, he would affirm with the rest of the Bible that the unseen world of the spirit has many spirit beings, some angelic and some demonic.   But none of these has an authority that even begins to compare with Christ's authority."[31]   In fact the majority of the spirits reverenced in ani-

---

[29] The Jewish folk who, in the two centuries before Christ, were relocated from Babylon to Phrygia and the Lycus River valley likely brought these eastern ideas with them.

[30] The word *stoicheia,* translated "elemental principles," has a wide range of meanings. "Etymologically it means anything placed in a row [like stakes on which to hang fishing nets].   Then it came to be applied to the letters of the alphabet, the ABCs, or a file of soldiers.   Since Plato's time it was used to refer to the basic elements of which the world is composed [earth, air, fire, water].   In animistic religions, it was used to designate the elemental spirits [angels or demons] associated with the physical elements.   Metaphorically it designates any elementary teaching or knowledge" (R.C.H. Lenski, *Interpretation of St. Paul's Epistles to the Galatians, Ephesians, Philippians* [Columbus, OH: Wartburg Press, 1946], p.195).   The meaning of *stoicheia* ("elementary principles") here in Colossians seems not to be the same as the word had in Hebrews 5:12 or Galatians 4:3,9, where it was a reference to the Law of Moses.   In those passages, the Law of Moses is described as being like the ABC's of revealed religion, its elementary or first principles.

[31] Jon Weatherly, *Standard Lesson Commentary 2012-13* (Cincinnati, OH: Standard, 2013), p.204.

mistic cultures are demonic. If we accept the animistic sense for "elemental spirits" there are two possible interpretations: (1) the "philosophy" was a system instigated by the elemental spirits (the powers of evil), or (2) the "philosophy" had the elemental spirits as its subject matter (man's idea of the nature of the world as being ruled by spirits). How do men escape having their human lives controlled by these spirits? The Gnostics offered a password, a secret, learned only by being initiated into their religion. Christianity says Jesus has conquered whatever spirits there may be. In Him men escape having their lives controlled by the spirits.

Rather than according to Christ – A third factor that characterizes the "philosophy" and calls for its rejection is that it is not "according to (in agreement with) Christ." "This is Paul's most telling criticism of the Colossian heresy ... Christ is the standard by which all doctrine is to be measured, and any system, whatever its claims, must be rejected if it fails to conform to the revelation God has given to us in Him."[32]

2. Its denial of some particular areas where Christ and His work excel. 2:9-15

2:9 – For in Him all the fullness of Deity dwells in bodily form,

For – "For" shows that beginning with this verse and going on through verse 15, Paul is giving two reasons why he said the deceptive philosophy was not "according to Christ": (1) the false teachers did not recognize that the fullness of Deity dwells in Christ (verse 9), and (2) the readers have already "been made complete" in Christ (verses 10-15).

In Him all the fullness of Deity dwells in bodily form – By its position in the sentence, "in Him" is shown to be emphatic, the thought being that in Christ alone the fullness of Deity dwells.[33] "Dwells" is a present tense verb indicating that it is the exalted Christ, in the state of His heavenly glory, that is in view. Deity did not descend on Him for a time and then leave Him, as some Gnostics taught. He

---

[32] Vaughn, *op. cit.*, p.198.

[33] The emphatic "in Christ" (in Him, and in none else) does not contradict the idea that full Deity is found in the Father and the Holy Spirit as well. But it does deny the Gnostic idea that some (alleged) emanations from God had little or any deity at all.

still has all the fullness of Deity, just as He did in His incarnate state (Colossians 1:15,19). It dwells and remains forever "in bodily form," which means "clothed with a body."[34] Christ has a glorified human body now (Philippians 3:21), and in that glorified body dwells all the fullness of Deity. That which continues to dwell in Christ in its entire fullness – i.e., not, it may be, partially, but in its complete entirety – is specified here as "Deity" (*theotetos*). The word occurs only here in the New Testament, and is not quite synonymous with *theiotes* ("divine nature," divine qualities and attributes) used in Romans 1:20 (and there alone in the New Testament). What Paul here says is that "the whole glorious total of what God is, the supreme Nature in its infinite entirety"[35] is what dwells in Christ now. The false teacher's doctrine was not according to Christ, for "in Christ dwells the whole *plērōma* (fullness, plenitude)," the entire fullness of Deity, whereas they represented it as being dispersed among several spiritual agencies.

2:10 – *and in Him you have been made complete, and He is the head over all rule and authority;*

And in Him you have been made complete – This introduces the second reason why the "philosophy" was not in agreement with Christ. The context requires the emphasis to be thrown on the "in Him" (by virtue of union with Him). The Colossian Christians by virtue of their union with Christ have already been "made complete." In and from Christ the Colossians have everything necessary to their salvation. "Made complete" (*peplērōmenoi*) translates the same root word translated "fullness" (*plērōma*) in the previous verse. "Made complete" is a perfect tense which emphasizes past completed action with present continuing results. The Christian's fullness comes from His fulness.[36] The Colossians do not need to embrace the whole rigmarole of seven heavens each replete with its

---

[34] The suggestions that "bodily" is (1) a reference to the church which Paul has already called the body (1:18), or that it means (2) "essentially" or "actually," or (3) that it has in view the days past when Jesus was in the flesh here on earth, completely miss the point of this beautiful verse.

[35] Moule, *op. cit.*, p.144.

[36] "We must be careful to note that the fullness of God communicated to the saints does not consist of the divine essence which is alone possessed by Deity, but of such qualities as holiness, righteousness, and the like, as in Ephesians 3:19" (Kenneth S. Wuest, *Ephesians and Colossians in the Greek New Testament* [Grand Rapids: Eerdmans, 1960], p.204).

aeon guards (which the Gnostics called "fulness"[37]) and secret passwords in order to be complete. To participate in the divine *pleroma* is not a special privilege of the initiated few, as the Gnostics taught. Using the false teachers' own term ("fullness," *pleroma*), Paul asserts that all Christians, by virtue of being incorporated into Him in whom all the fullness dwells, have already come to fullness of life in Him. There is nothing the false teachers can add to the Colossians' lives. The idea that you are not complete in Christ is a Gnostic idea that is not "according to Christ."

And He is the head over all rule and authority – This phrase serves as a confirmation of the fact that they have their salvation filled or completed in Christ, and not otherwise, say by being dependent on angels. At Colossians 1:16 we learned that "rule" and "authority" are two different orders of angels. While there may not be any such beings as the "aeons" about whom the false teachers talked, there are angels, both good and bad ones. Since Christ is the head, the governing sovereign over every rule and authority, the Christian cannot have anything to expect from any angelic powers since all are subordinate to Christ. The Christian is in union with Him in whom all the fullness of Deity dwells. There is nothing angels can add. This statement about Christ's headship may be intended to be a refutation of spiritism/animism. There is no need to venerate or pay any respects to principalities and powers. Spirits may be involved in our world, but Jesus has shown Himself Lord and Master over all such beings.

2:11 – *and in Him you were also circumcised with a circumcision made without hands, in the removal of the body of the flesh by the circumcision of Christ;*

And in Him you were also circumcised with a circumcision made without hands – Paul is continuing to identify the places where the Colossian "philosophy" was not in agreement with Christ. This abrupt introduction of the idea of circumcision is understandable on the supposition that the deceptive teachers were urging circumcision on Gentile Christians. We are still in the beginning of a long section where Paul is saying that in Christ the believers have already been made complete; in order to be complete, they do not need the obsolete Judaistic ideas any more than they need the animistic or the Gnostic ideas which were included in that deceptive philosophy. "Made without hands" indicates Paul is not talking about physical circumcision such as God commanded Abraham to perform (Genesis 17:9-14), but rather is speaking of something spiri-

---

[37] See page 665 of the Detailed Introduction to Colossians where the idea of seven heavens each with aeon guards is explained.

tual, something that is not done with human hands.[38]   To obviate any need for physical circumcision, Paul wrote, "You were (aorist tense, once for all) circumcised" and, when he says the circumcision they had received was not made with human hands, he is saying the circumcision they had received far excelled the physical rite being recommended by the false teachers.   As Paul shows how this emphasis on physical circumcision is not according to Christ, he drives home the point that the circumcision of the heart (Romans 2:29, something not done by human hands) is what God is really interested in.   Since God no longer commands physical circumcision, the false teachers were in error to insist that the Colossian Christians needed to be circumcised.   That spiritual circumcision God is interested in had already occurred when the Colossians were immersed into Christ (as the verses following will show).

In the removal of the body of the flesh by the circumcision of Christ – The "circumcision of Christ" is the circumcision that Christ teaches (this does not refer to what was done to the baby Jesus at age 8 days, Luke 2:21).   This new kind of circumcision is not the removal of a piece of flesh, as is physical circumcision.   Rather, it is something that affects the whole body.   The body itself is not "put off" or "removed" for it is not evil[39]; it is a part of the true man, and becomes the temple of the Holy Spirit.[40]   It is the removal of the "flesh" from being the thing that controls a man.   When he becomes a Christian, a person's spirit is made alive again (John 3:6) and is able to prompt the Christian.   Just as he wrote in Romans 6:1-6 about how the body of sin is done away when a man is immersed into Christ, so here Paul will go on to say that the body of the flesh is removed when a man is immersed.

2:12 – *having been buried with Him in baptism, in which you were also raised up with Him through faith in the working of God, who raised Him from the dead.*

Having been buried with Him in baptism – It is at the moment a person is being baptized that the "true circumcision, the one not made by hands" occurs;   it is in

---

[38] Compare how "made without hands" is used in Mark 14:58; 2 Corinthians 5:1; Hebrews 9:11,24.

[39] Because the KJV reads "the body of the sins of the flesh" (a reading not well supported in the oldest manuscripts) not a few think "the body of the flesh" denotes an evil, fallen, sinful nature. Such a sinful nature is *not* inherited from Adam.   While not inborn, the Bible does suggest that a man's flesh, his body, can become a slave of sin because of personal transgressions and sins (see Colossians 2:13 and Ephesians 2:1).

[40] What the "body of the flesh" is, we see clearly by Colossians 3:9, "laid aside the old self."   It is very like the "body of sin" (in Romans 6:6) and the "body of ... death" (in Romans 7:24), the body so far as it is, in the literal sense of the word "flesh," fleshly.

baptism that the "removal of the body of the flesh" (verse 11) occurs.[41]   "Buried" is a term that nicely pictures what is done to people as they are lowered into the water as they are being "baptized."   "Buried" matches the idea that baptism is by immersion.   Religious washing ceremonies (*baptismos*, Greek[42]) were common in ancient Judaism, but these ceremonial cleansings were self-administered; a person dipped himself or herself in water.   The baptism (*baptisma*) commanded in the Great Commission differs in that it is administered by another.   Immersion is the time when a cleansing that one cannot do to oneself occurs, but which God provides (cp. Titus 3:5).   It is instructive to compare this passage with Romans 6:4, "Therefore we have been buried with Him through baptism into death, in order that as Christ was raised from the dead through the glory of the Father, so we too might walk in newness of life."

In which you were also raised up with Him – This phrase names another benefit that is part of their being made complete in Christ.   The Greek translated "in which" can be either masculine ("in whom" referring to Christ, as in the beginning of verse 11), or neuter ("in which" referring to baptism).   We judge the NASB translation to be correct which treats it as neuter.   Thus "raised" pictures the emergence from the water in which a person is immersed.   Because the baptized person is taken under the water and then brought out of it, the action resembles Christ's resurrection from the dead (Romans 6:4).   As the Colossian believers who were being immersed into Christ were brought up out of the water, they were "raised up with Him" as a result of the working of God.   Romans 6:5-7 explains what it means to be raised so as to "walk in newness of life."   Speaking of what happens at baptism, the passage reads, "For if we have become united with *Him* in the likeness of His death, certainly we shall be also *in the likeness* of His resurrection, knowing this, that our old self was crucified with *Him*, in order that our body of sin might be done away with, so that we should no longer be slaves to sin; for he who has died is freed from sin."   Christ was raised physically; "like-

---

[41] The aorist tense "buried" matches the aorist tense of "you were circumcised."   The two actions are simultaneous.   Bible students must be careful as they explain this passage!   This passage does not say that baptism in the new covenant is analogous to circumcision in the Mosaic covenant.   E.g., it is not a proof text for infant baptism.   Nor is it correct to say each was the entrance into a covenant with God – for Jewish babies were born into the covenant, and circumcision was a sign of the covenant already in existence.   Baptism is not the sign of the new covenant – the gift of the Holy Spirit is that sign (2 Corinthians 1:22; Ephesians 1:13, 4:30).

[42] There is a manuscript variation here, some (including P[46]and B) reading *baptismos*, and others reading *baptisma*.   The former is the regular word for Jewish ceremonial washings; the latter the regular word for the baptism commanded in the Great Commission.   Compare notes at Hebrews 6:3 in the author's commentary *New Testament Epistles: Hebrews*.

ness" says the immersed believer is raised spiritually. The old slavery to sin has been broken. It is part of being made complete in Christ.

Through faith in the working of God – It is not the simple dipping in water that effects the "circumcision made without hands" – but an immersion *dia tes pisteos* ("through the faith ..."), an action by which we demonstrate our belief in what God has done by raising Christ from the dead.[43]   In other words, baptism brings new life because of one's faith in the working of God.   Knowing that God broke the bonds of death and brought Jesus to life again, he is confident that God can break the bonds of sin and make him alive.   And because of his faith and repentance that is just what happens when he is baptized.   His spirit becomes alive again because of righteousness (God's way of saving man, Romans 8:10).

Who raised Him from the dead – Identifying one thing the working of God accomplished, this phrase says God was at work to cause Jesus to be raised from the dead.   Romans 4:24 also speaks of the need for belief in the resurrection if one is to be justified.   Compare Ephesians 1:19-23, which spoke in greater detail about the "working" and the energy of the mighty power of God.   The next verse will identify another thing the working of God accomplished.   The same God who raised Christ from the dead also had made the Colossians alive spiritually when they were immersed.

2:13 – *And when you were dead in your transgressions and the uncircumcision of your flesh, He made you alive together with Him, having forgiven us all our transgressions,*

And when you were dead in your transgressions and the uncircumcision of your flesh – "You" means "you Colossians" before you were immersed into Christ.   Ephesians 2:1 reads "you were dead in your trespasses and sins."   As it meant there, so here.   "Dead in your transgressions" indicates that each man's own personal sins had brought about spiritual death (the spirit of each sinner had died).[44]   They were physically alive,   while at the same time their spirits were

---

[43] The words "the working of God" are in the genitive case, which has led Luther and others to affirm that faith is the thing that is the result of the working of God.   However, Romans 10:17, which tells us that faith comes by hearing the word of Christ, is against the idea that God simply by fiat plants faith in some people's hearts.   It is better to treat the genitive "the working of God" as the object of faith, as the NASB has translated.

[44] "Transgressions" translates *paraptoma*, one of several Greek synonyms for sin.   It implies falling aside from God's mark when one should have stood upright.   (Berry, *Synonyms*, p.118).   That this passage speaks of spiritual death rather than physical is seen from the fact that physical death is the result of Adam's sin (Romans 5:12).

dead, unable to function. "Uncircumcision of your flesh" indicates not only that the Colossians were Gentiles by ethnicity, but more to the point, before their conversion, they were in the state that verse 11 talked about. They did not have the circumcision which Christ teaches. That is a second reason why they were "dead."[45]

He made you alive together with Him – Scholars debate whether God or Christ is to be thought of as the subject of "made alive." In this commentator's judgment, since Paul is talking about "the working of God" (verse 12), it is best to make "God" the subject of "made alive," "having forgiven" (verse 13), and "having canceled" (verse 14).[46] Just as God raised Jesus, so God has made the Colossians "alive." One of the blessed consequences of becoming a Christian is that the man's spirit is made alive (John 3:6). His live spirit can direct the man's behavior, and the new man can live in newness of life.

Having forgiven us all our transgressions – In this and the following verse Paul unfolds what is involved in the working of God as He makes people alive. Two participles dependent on the verb "he made you alive" tell what God has done: (1) He has forgiven us all our transgressions (verse 13), and (2) He canceled the certificate of debt (verse14). "Forgiven us all our transgressions" is one of the things God has done in the process of making alive; involved is the forgiveness of the transgressions (spoken of earlier in this verse) that had caused spiritual death. Paul includes himself in the "us." "Paul is eager to claim his share in the transgression, that he may claim it also in the forgiveness."[47] The Greek participle translated "forgave" (*charisamenos*), built on the root of the word for

---

[45] Both "in your transgressions" and "in the uncircumcision ..." are in the dative case, thus designating the reason or cause of their being spiritually dead.

[46] If we allow the parallel passage in Ephesians to guide us, we might argue for a change of subject when we come to verse 15. "God ... made us alive together with Christ" (Ephesians 2:5); "God in Christ also has forgiven" you/us (Ephesians 4:32); but Christ "abolished ... the Law (Ephesians 2:15)," and Christ "reconciled (us) to God through the cross" (Ephesians 2:16). This suggests a similar change of subject from God to Christ might also be possible here in Colossians, perhaps when we come to the phrase "He has taken" in verse 14 (since there is a change of verb tense at that spot).

[47] Lightfoot, *op. cit.*, p. 186. There is a manuscript variation here, with some reading "you" as does the KJV. The better attested reading is "us."

"grace," means literally "to grant as a favor."[48]   It is because of God's grace, His loving-kindness, that He grants forgiveness.   And note the fullness of His forgiveness. It covers "all the transgressions." This whole emphasis on sins being forgiven is anti-Gnostic (cp. 1 John 1:8-10).

2:14 – *having canceled out the certificate of debt consisting of decrees against us* **and** *which was hostile to us; and He has taken it out of the way, having nailed it to the cross.*

Having canceled out the certificate of debt consisting of decrees against us – This is the second participial phrase which explains the working of God as He "made us alive" (verse 13).   Exactly what is intended by this figure of speech and why it was used has long been a subject of debate.   The word translated "certificate" (*cheirographon*; literally, "handwriting") is a term used of any document written by hand.[49]   It is this written record that was "against us."[50]   A "decree" (Greek, *dogma*) is any ordinance or regulation publicly set forth by an authority.   The word is used of a decree from Caesar Augustus (Luke 2:1), of the ruling reached by the apostles and elders at Jerusalem (Acts 16:4), of the ordinances in the Law of Moses (Ephesians 2:15), and of an edict from Pharaoh (Hebrews 11:23).[51]   One intriguing suggestion concerning the meaning of this verse in Colossians is that God keeps a written record of man's sins, and "canceled" would say that the record was completely wiped clean as the man was

---

[48] Another Greek word (*aphiemi*) is often translated "forgive." To get a feeling for the meaning of *charizomai,* see Luke 7:42, 43; 2 Corinthians 2:7,10, 12:13; Ephesians 4:32; and Colossians 3:13.

[49] The NASB translators chose to translate it as "certificate of debt" on the belief that, since the Greek word was often used of what we would call an IOU (cp. Philemon 19, "I have *written it with mine own hand,* I will repay it"), somehow sinners had a debt to God that must be canceled. A case could be made that when the Law of Moses was given, the people said, "we will do it." Their failure to keep the Mosaic Law became a "debt" – an obligation which they had failed to keep. However, it becomes difficult to explain the words "against us" (which seems to include both Jews and Gentiles) if we assume *cheirographon* refers to the Law of Moses, since Gentiles did not have the Law. (It is a misuse of Romans 2:15 ["they show the work of the Law written in their hearts"] to use it in an attempt to explain this verse in Colossians concerning how the Law could be against the Gentiles.)

[50] The word order in the Greek is "the against us handwriting."

[51] The Greek behind "decrees" is *tois dogmasin,* in the dative case. This led the Greek early church writers to treat the expression as a dative of means which they then interpreted as meaning that the precepts of the gospel ("dogmas") had abrogated or set aside the Law ("the handwriting").

immersed and raised to walk in newness of life. No record of our past sins remains.[52]

***And* which was hostile to us** – Since the antecedent of "which" is *cheirographon*, it is the written record that was hostile to us. We understand that "us" includes either Jew or Gentile – both had a written record of sins that was hostile to them and both graciously had been forgiven (verse 13).

And He has taken it out of the way – Since verse 12 Paul has been explaining the working of God. "God" is clearly the subject of the verb "He made you alive" in verse 13, and grammatically there is no indication of a change of subject in verses 13,14, or 15.[53] "It" is the handwriting, the written record of man's sins.[54] "Has taken" is perfect tense verb, which denotes past completed action with present continuing results. God can cancel the record of sins against us because of Calvary. "Out of the way" translates Greek words which are literally "out of the midst." The word picture is of removing an obstruction so that it no longer intervenes between us and God. Unforgiven sins bar a man's access to God. God removed this obstruction at Calvary. The death of Jesus was the once and for all sacrifice for sins (Hebrews 10:14). Elsewhere we are told the death of Christ was a propitiation for sins (Romans 3:25). Isaiah 53:5,6 tell us that "He was pierced through for our transgressions, He was crushed for our iniquities; the chastening for our well-being fell upon Him, and by His scourging we are healed. All of us like sheep have gone astray, each of us has turned to his own way; but the LORD has caused the iniquity of us all to fall on Him." And 1 Peter 2:24 tells us "He Himself bore our sins in His body on the cross, that we might die to sin and live to righteousness; for by His wounds you were healed."

---

[52] Perhaps the existence of such a written record of deeds is implied in Revelation 20:12, "The books were opened, and the dead were judged out of things written in the books according to their deeds."

[53] Because it has proven difficult to explain how God could be the subject of the participle translated "disarmed" in verse 15, Lightfoot and others have argued for a change of subject somewhere in verses 14 or 15. He thought the best place to make the change was with the finite verb "he has taken" in verse 14. If a satisfactory explanation can be found for how God could be the subject of the participle, then "God" is the implied subject through the end of verse 15.

[54] The antecedent of "it" is *cheirographon* (certificate, handwriting). While it is true that the Law of Moses was abrogated at Calvary (Hebrews 7:12,18, 10:9), if we have explained Colossians 2:14 correctly, it is not a verse to be used as a proof text that the Law has been set aside. "On the supposed ancient custom of driving a nail through a document to cancel it, see F. Field, *Notes on the Translation of the New Testament* (Cambridge, 1899), pp.95ff, who could find no real authority for it" (Bruce, *op. cit.*, p.238).

Having nailed it to the cross – Many verses explain the real reason for Christ's death at Calvary, namely, Jesus was sent as a sin offering (Romans 8:3). "Now once at the consummation of the ages Jesus has been manifested to put away sin by the sacrifice of Himself" (Hebrews 9:26). Through His own blood Jesus has obtained eternal redemption (Hebrews 9:12). "God was in Christ reconciling the world to Himself, not counting their trespasses against them" (2 Corinthians 5:19). It is because of what happened at Calvary that God graciously can forgive our sins.

2:15 – *When He had disarmed the rulers and authorities, He made a public display of them, having triumphed over them through Him.*

When He had disarmed the rulers and authorities – In verse 15 the meaning of almost every word is disputed. The words "rulers and authorities" have occurred earlier in this very passage (verse 10), where Christ is exalted as "head over all rule and authority." In this verse, in the Greek there is an article ("the") before "rulers" and before "authorities," and it is hardly possible to avoid treating these articles as being articles of previous reference. In other words, Paul is talking about the same angels that verse 10 referred to. It is quite common to read in the commentaries that evil spirits were "disarmed" when Jesus died on the cross. At Ephesians 6:12, the context indicates that "rulers and authorities" there in view are evil spirits. However, the words "rulers and authorities" appear several times in this epistle to the Colossians, and in none of these verses do they indicate the <u>evil</u> angels.[55]

Now we must study this key word translated "disarmed."[56] "Disarmed" is an attempt to translate *apekdusamenos*, the middle voice participle of the verb *ekduo*. *Ekduo* in the active voice is used in the LXX and classical Greek of the victor "stripping" off the weapons, armor, and regalia of defeated enemies in war.[57] That meaning will hardly fit the needs of the context here since the "rulers and authorities" are not evil/enemies. Because the metaphor drawn from the

---

[55] Some have tried to show from "public display" and "triumphed over them" in the following clauses that the "rulers and authorities" are evil. We think this is a misunderstanding of both those metaphors.

[56] It must be remembered that the principal objection to taking "God" as the subject throughout verses 13-15 is the supposed difficulty or impossibility of interpreting this participle as being something God did.

[57] The KJV reads "having spoiled" which treats the participle in its metaphorical sense of plunder. It does not seem right to think that Paul is saying the rulers and authorities were plundered, especially if it is not *evil* angels in view. Are we to picture that the angels were clothed in armor that God stripped off?

battlefield where a defeated army is "disarmed" seems not to fit, it has been proposed that Paul's metaphor is drawn from a royal court in which public officials were demoted by being stripped of their office or power. But what are we to make of the middle voice?[58] One possible idea of the middle voice is that the subject of the verb is pictured as acting for his own benefit. The passage then says that at Calvary God, for His own benefit, stripped the rulers and authorities of either power or office they once had.[59] In Old Testament times, angels were rather prominent workers for God.[60] Colossians 2:15 seems to say that God stripped the angels of some of the powers they once had, and Jesus, who was made a little lower than the angels for the suffering of death, is now crowned with glory and honor (Hebrews 2:9).[61] He is greater than angels (Hebrews 1:4-14). Christ's superiority to even the good angels would be a powerful argument against the worship of angels (Colossians 2:18).

He made a public display of them, having triumphed over them through Him – The circumstantial participle (translated "having triumphed") tells how God made the public display that proclaimed that Christ is superior to angels. It is rather common to find the commentators appealing to the metaphor of a triumphal

---

[58] One connotation of the middle voice is that the subject acts upon himself. Thus, the Greek fathers who took Christ as the subject have Jesus, at Calvary, stripping Himself of hostile powers of evil. The Latin Fathers have Jesus stripping off His own body (drawing the object from Colossians 2:11). Neither of these ideas seems to fit the needs of this verse in Colossians.

[59] We arrive at the same interpretation if we follow O'Brien's conclusion concerning the meaning of this middle voice participle (P.T. O'Brien, "Colossians, Philemon" in *Word Biblical Commentary* Vol. 44 [Waco, TX: Word Books, 1982], p. 127). He says in effect that in New Testament Greek there was a tendency to substitute the middle voice for the active when using certain verbs, with *apekdouomai* being one of those verbs. (He cites BDF, para 316 and Robertson, *Grammar*, p.804,805). He concludes that perhaps the best way to resolve the exegetical difficulty is to regard *apekdusamenos* as a middle voice with an active sense ("strip") so indicating that God stripped the rulers and authorities of their dignity and might.

[60] Angels were present at creation (Job 38:7). Angels served as messengers for God (Genesis 18:2,16; Matthew 2:13; Luke 2:9; Hebrews 1:7 [which quotes Psalm 104:4]). Angels assisted, protected, and delivered God's people (Genesis 19:11; Psalm 91:11; 2 Kings 6:8-23; Daniel 3:28, 6:22). Sometimes they explained or interpreted God's will to men (Daniel 7:16, 10:5,11; Zechariah 1:9,13,14,19). They executed God's will toward men and nations (Genesis 19:12,13; 2 Samuel 24:16; Ezekiel 9:2,5,7). Angels had something to do with the giving of the Law (Acts 7:38,53; Galatians 3:19; Hebrews 2:2).

[61] Since *ekdusamenos* is a circumstantial participle, the "stripping" should be treated as an attendant circumstance at Calvary, not a cause of the removal of the "handwriting" that was against us.

procession to explain "having triumphed." However, it may be better to take the figure "from the festal procession of a Greek god who leads his worshipers along as witnesses of his power and celebrants of his glory."[62] Commenting on the Greek translated "through Him" in the NASB, James Dunn wrote, "this is the fifteenth 'in Him' in Colossians and the fifth since 2:9. It probably is simply Paul's attempt to retain the focus on what has been done 'in Christ' ...."[63] If we treat "in Him" as a reference to Christ, then the figure of a festal procession "fittingly describes the relation and the attitude of the angels to the Divine presence in Christ."[64]

Now we are ready to study the rare verb *deigmatizo* translated as "made a public display" in the NASB. The verb likely denotes simply to publicize or proclaim, rather than shameful exposure. For this latter idea the compound form *paradeigmatizo* is better suited (cf. Hebrews 6:6). With "them" referring back to angelic rulers and authorities of verses 15 and 10, if the verb *deigmatizo* is thought to denote a shameful exposure, we have the good angels being shamed. Such an idea will hardly do. But if the verb has the meaning of publicize or proclaim, it describes a public exhibition of the angels in their true character and position, a position which forbids them to be regarded as objects of worship (verse 18). God publicly exhibited the angels as the subordinates and servants of his Son (Colossians 2:10). Jesus Christ has been anointed with the oil of gladness above His angelic companions (Hebrews 1:9). On this note of celebration the list of places where Jesus and His work excel (Colossians 2:9-15) climaxes.

3. Its emphasis on obsolete Jewish ordinances. 2:16,17

2:16 – *Therefore let no one act as your judge in regard to food or drink or in respect to a festival or a new moon or a Sabbath day --*

Therefore – Perhaps the "therefore" points back to verse 10 – "you have been made complete in Christ." If we may assume the deceptive teachers emphasized the things (certain taboos and certain holy days) highlighted in this verse as a means of reaching "fullness," then the thrust of this verse is this: if you are already complete in Christ, then the claims made by the deceptive teachers that such practices are the means to "fullness" are false and misguided.

---

[62] Findlay, *op. cit.,* p.91.

[63] James D.G. Dunn, "The Epistles to the Colossians and Philemon" in the *New International Greek Testament Commentary* (Grand Rapids: Eerdmans, 1996), p. 169.

[64] Findlay, *ibid.*

Let no one act as your judge – "Let no one" is an imperative verb in the Greek. It is a command that prohibits the continuance of an action already going on. 'Stop letting anyone take you to task for your behavior in the matters about to be named.[65]   Do not let anyone condemn you because you do not observe certain holy days or certain taboos.'   Beginning with circumcision in verse 11, and continuing on in this verse, there is a Jewish flavor to the ideas emphasized by the false teachers.

In regard to food or drink – The words translated "food" and "drink" may refer to the act of eating and drinking more than to what was being consumed.[66] Commentaries are not agreed concerning to what Paul refers.   (1) It has been proposed that it is Jewish clean and unclean foods, since the context is Judaistic. However, Old Testament food laws did not extend to beverages, save in the case of priests or in the case of a Nazarite vow.[67]   (2) It has been advocated that the issue is between eating and drinking on the one hand, or abstinence on the other. I.e., asceticism rather than ritual uncleanness is the topic.[68]   (3) It is most likely that the deceptive teachers at Colossae were advocating the rigorous restrictions regarding both meat and drink like those prescribed by the Essenes who were vegetarians and abstained from wine.   Considerably more strict than the Pharisees and Sadducees, the Essenes found in the Nazarite life and the rules for the ministering Jewish priest (Numbers 6:3; Leviticus 10:8-11; Ezekiel 44:21) their ideal of holiness.

Or in respect to a festival or a new moon or a Sabbath day –   These are the

---

[65] It is correct to treat "no one" here as it was treated in Colossians 2:8, namely, a general reference to any one who might seek to win converts to the new system, rather than to one individual leader of the deceptive philosophy.

[66] "Food" translates *brōsis*, "the act of eating," not *broma*, the food itself; and "drink" translates *posis*, "the act of drinking," not *poma*.   Yet both nouns are also used in Scripture for that which was eaten and drunk (John 4:32, 6:27,55).

[67] The Mosaic food laws extended to beverages only in the case of a Nazarite vow (Numbers 6:3), for the period of priestly service (Leviticus 10:9), and the prohibition to drink liquid from an "unclean" vessel (Leviticus 11:34).

[68] There were four things all Christians are to abstain from (Acts 15:23-29).   That ruling at the Jerusalem Conference is not contradicted by what Paul here writes about food or drink.   Nor is Paul repealing his teaching about being concerned for a weak brother when it comes to matters of food and drink (Romans 14:1- 15:13; 1 Corinthians 8:1ff, 10:23ff).

annual, monthly, and weekly holy days on a Jewish calendar.[69]   The Dead Sea
Scrolls (*War Scroll* II,4) have the same three designations together as a listing of
holy days.   In this emphasis on certain Jewish calendar days we
see another parallel between the Colossian deceptive religious system and the
system known as Essenism.   The Essenes at Qumran attached great importance
to calendrical questions as 4QMMT indicates, but apparently they differed from
the Pharisees in their calculation of sacred seasons (perhaps following the
calendar enjoined in the Book of Jubilees).   It is plainly implied here in verse 16
that the Colossian Gentile Christians, disciples of Paul through their evangelist
Epaphras, had not been in the practice of observing such holy days.

2:17 – *things which are a mere shadow of what is to come; but the substance
belongs to Christ.*

Things which are a mere shadow of what is to come – "Which" embraces all
the things of the Law mentioned in verse 16.   The thrust of verses 16 and 17 is
the same argument that will be unfolded in detail in the epistle to the Hebrews.
"The Law ... has only a shadow of good things to come, not the very form (or
substance) of things" (Hebrews 8:5, 10:1).   The Law was a shadow (i.e., an
anticipation[70] from the Old Testament point of view) of things to come (Christ
and the Christian dispensation).   To accept the Mosaic food-laws, or to set aside
certain days for special observance because such is taught in the Mosaic
Scriptures, would be an acknowledgment of the continuing authority of those Old
Covenant Scriptures.   That would be a repudiation of the inauguration of the new
covenant by the blood of Christ.   It cannot be a correct doctrine.   It would be
elevating shadow over substance.   The reason Christians are not obligated to
keep the Law is that the Law has been abrogated.

But the substance belongs to Christ – The rituals and ceremonies in the Law of
Moses foreshadowed or typified or pointed to Christ.   "Christ is the goal of the

---

[69] We have here an exhaustive enumeration of the Jewish days of observance – *annual*
festivals (such as Passover, Pentecost, Tabernacles); *monthly* celebrations (Numbers 28:11); and
weekly observances, on the Sabbath day (Exodus 20:8-11, 31:14-16).   The Greek word translated
"Sabbath day" is plural, but the plural is regularly used in the New Testament in a singular sense.
The reference to the Sabbath day clearly points to a Jewish calendar, for only Jews kept the Sabbath.
The same enumeration of sacred seasons occurs several times in the Old Testament (1 Chronicles
23:31; 2 Chronicles 2:4, 31:3; Ezekiel 45:17; Hosea 2:11).

[70] "Shadow" was used of the outline which painters pencil onto the canvas before doing
the actual painting.

Law" (Romans 10:4 NASB mg.).[71]   The sacrifice of Christ is the reality which was foreshadowed by the Passover in Egypt (1 Corinthians 5:7,8).   The One foreshadowed by Israel's manna offered Himself as the Bread of Life (John 6:35,48).   How the Sabbath was a shadow of things to come is explained in Hebrews 4:1-11.

4.   Its veneration of angels and its self-induced visions.   2:18,19[72]

2:18 – *Let no one keep defrauding you of your prize by delighting in self-abasement and the worship of the angels, taking his stand on* **visions** *he has seen, inflated without cause by his fleshly mind,*

Let no one keep defrauding you of your prize – The metaphor behind "defrauding" is of an umpire or judge in the athletic games who unfairly, because of fraud or injustice, gave an adverse decision against a competitor.[73]   It is implied that the false teachers have been telling the Christians that, unless they adopt all the practices advocated by the deceptive religious system, their beliefs and practices are not adequate.   In the phrases following, Paul will go on to explain why such adverse decisions made by the false teachers against the Christians were not truthful decisions.   Using an imperative verb, Paul says (in language stronger than "let no one act as your judge," verse 16) that the Colossians are not to grant the status of umpire or judge to the false teachers in the first place.

By delighting in self-abasement and the worship of the angels – This is the first of four participial phrases which describe the persons who were attempting to act as judges of the Christians.   The phrases describe behaviors the false teachers themselves practiced, and which in turn they tried to impose on the Colossians.   However, exactly what is described is not entirely clear to us.   The meaning of each word in this clause has been the subject of endless discussion.

---

[71] See Victor E. Hoven, *Shadow and Substance* (St. Louis: Bethany Press, 1934).

[72] We are entering the topic of the deceptive teachers' emphasis on mysticism. Commentators acknowledge that some things written in these two verses are puzzling.

[73] Peake (*op. cit.,* p.531) says the Greek verb translated "defraud" had "apparently lost all reference to the prize, and meant simply 'to decide'."   If the thought is to let no one condemn you, the addition of "prize" to translate the verb is misleading, especially if folk then go on to try to identify the prize.

The participle translated "delighting" may mean something like voluntary, willing, delighting in, or insisting on.[74]   In Greek the word for "self-abasement" and the expression for "worship of angels" are governed by the same preposition, so there is a close connection between the "self -abasement"[75] and the "worship of angels."[76]   That is to say, the deceptive teachers are pictured as insisting that their worship of angels was an expression of humility and modesty on their part, as if personally they dared not come into the presence of the supreme God or address Him directly.   Since "worship" is *threskeia*, a word which denotes the external ceremonies and actions by which one demonstrates his beliefs,[77] it looks like Paul is alluding to actual ceremonies in which angels as a class were worshiped.   The angels who were worshiped by the false teachers are the "elemental spirits" (2:8), who also are identified as "rulers and authorities" (2:15). Rather than Arnold's view that Colossians 2:18 refers to the practice of invoking angels for protection, help, and deliverance,[78] it seems to be implied that the false teachers at Colossae, as did later Gnostics, taught that God was too high and that men were too insignificant to approach God directly, so they sought to contact deity through the mediation of angels (aeons).   In order that the angels might be obliged to pay attention to men, the men worshiped them.   Jesus is the one mediator between God and man (1 Timothy 2:5).   No saint or angel can take His place.   The worship/veneration of angels is strictly forbidden (Exodus 20:3-4; Revelation 22:8,9).   The self-appointed judges were greatly mistaken.

---

[74] Thayer, *op. cit.*, p.285,286. Alford, Moule and others connect this participle with the verb "keep defrauding" and make it read "willfully defrauding." The comments offered in our notes reflect the NASB which connects the participle with the words which follow.

[75] The word translated "self-abasement" is *tapeinophrosune*, which means modesty, humility, lowliness of mind. This is the only place in the New Testament where humility is spoken of in a condemnatory tone. In light of the words which follow, which picture the false teachers as "puffed up," Thayer (*op. cit.*, p.614) says the word is "used of an affected and ostentatious humility in Colossians 2:18,23."

[76] "Worship of angels" is a genitive construction. It may be a subjective genitive (i.e., worship offered by the angels) or an objective genitive (worship paid to angels). Luther, Zahn and others have advocated treating it as subjective. If so, the false teachers are pictured as attempting to emulate the devotion of angels as they worship. Behind this choice of subjective genitive was the belief that Judaism was too monotheistic to admit that anyone might actually worship angels. This assumption that it was Jews who taught the worship of angels may be a false assumption. Perhaps we should look for the behavior (the worship of angels) among the pagan Gentiles of Colossae. Angel worship was practiced by later Gnostics (the schools of Cerinthus and Valentinus).

[77] The same root word is used at James 1:26,27 where it is translated "religious." See Trench, *op. cit.*, p.175.

[78] C. Arnold, *The Colossian Syncretism: The Interface between Christianity and Folk Belief at Colossae* (Grand Rapids: Baker, 1996), p.230.

Taking his stand on *visions* he has seen – This is the second participial phrase which describes the behavior of the persons who were making themselves self-appointed judges of the Colossian Christians. The meaning of the Greek words here is also a matter of much debate. The Greek which reads simply "the things which he has seen"[79] is a phrase which can be interpreted either of the physical eyes or the eyes of the mind. The NASB translators, choosing the latter, have inserted the word "visions" in italics. This is likely the correct idea. In the Scriptures we read about genuine visions from the Lord (Genesis 15:1; Isaiah 1:1; Acts 9:10, 16:9,10) and of visions that result from self-induced altered states of consciousness (Zechariah 13:4; 2 Corinthians 12:1[80]). This passage in Colossians suggests the false teachers were relying on visions which were not from God since they preferred them over the apostolic Gospel. Even the meaning of the Greek word (*embateuon*) translated "taking his stand on" is debated.[81] Since the word can have the idea of "investigate, search into, examine, scrutinize minutely,"[82] it is likely the NASB's "taking his stand on" catches the idea. It means the self-appointed umpires were basing their negative decisions against the Colossian Christians on self-induced visions. The effect of the verb as used here by Paul, Ramsay suggested, "depends on the fact that it was a religious term familiar to his Phrygian readers,"[83] since it was the regular term

---

[79] The KJV has the negative particle "not" before the verb meaning "seen." The better manuscripts omit the "not," and even those which have it vary between the spellings *ouch* and *mē*, a variation which makes it likely the word "not" was originally an addition added by some copyist who was struggling to make the passage understandable.

[80] The language of 2 Corinthians 12:1 suggests that Paul's opponents claimed visions that were spurious compared to those which Paul himself had received from the Lord.

[81] Claiming the passage makes no sense the way it stands, some scholars (Lightfoot, Westcott and Hort, C. Taylor [*Journal of Philology*, vii., p. 130], and Zahn), have resorted to a conjectural emendation of the text. By omitting one letter the Greek can be made to read "treading on the air" (i.e., "indulging airily in vain speculations"). We doubt that emending the text is necessary to an understanding of what Paul here condemns.

[82] See Thayer, *op. cit.*, p.206; Wm. F. Arndt and F.W. Gingrich, *A Greek-English Lexicon of the New Testament and Other Early Christian Literature* (Chicago: University of Chicago Press, 1956), p.253; also J.H. Moulton and G. Milligan, *The Vocabulary of the Greek New Testament* (London: Hodder and Stoughton, 1963), pp.205,206. The latter two references give delightful details about the use of the word in the mystery religions.

[83] Wm. Ramsay, *The Teaching of Paul in Terms of the Present Day* (London: Hodder and Stoughton, 1914), p.300.

to describe the visions which initiates to the mystery religions experienced during the rites of initiation.   Those rites were designed to produce altered states of consciousness resulting in visions and mystical experiences.[84]

Inflated without cause by his fleshly mind – This is the third participial phrase characterizing the behavior of the persons who were making themselves judges of the Colossian Christians.   It accuses them, as they are passing judgment against the Christians, of being overly confident because they give too much value to thinking that is fleshly rather than spiritual.[85]   Minding the things of the flesh[86] is an attitude of a person who has not become a Christian, for Christians set their mind on things of the Spirit (Romans 8:5; Colossians 3:2; Philippians 3:19,20). "Inflated by his fleshly mind" seems to say that the visions seen by the deceptive teachers are not from God but are the result of a mind dominated by the flesh. "Without cause" says that, though the one presuming to judge is filled with a growing[87] exalted opinion of himself, he has no good reason to feel the way he does.

2:19 – *and not holding fast to the Head, from whom the entire body, being supplied and held together by the joints and ligaments, grows with a growth which is from God.*

And not holding fast to the Head – On Christ being Head, see 1:18 and Ephesians 1:22; 4:15. This fourth participial phrase, which characterizes the behavior of the persons   who were making themselves   judges of the Colossian

---

[84] A Jewish school of mystics flourished from about 100 BC to AD 1000. Its devotees claimed to have visions like those in Ezekiel 1, or in the *hekhalot* ("palaces") literature, concerning stories of ascents by means of a Chariot to the heavenly palaces and the throne of God.   Such mystical ideas were found in Judaism in the time of Paul, and we may have reflections of such ideas here in Colossians.   See "Heresies in the Colossian Church, Part 1," *Bib Sac.* 149 (Jan-Mar, 1992), p.45-59.

[85] Even in true visions of heavenly things, there was a danger lest the mind "should be exalted above measure" (2 Corinthians 12:7 KJV).

[86] "Fleshly mind" translates a Greek phrase which literally means "the mind of the flesh."

[87] "Inflated" ("puffed up," KJV) translates a present tense participle which indicates continuing action.

Christians, is even more devastating than the charge of being puffed up. It affirms that there was a fatal harm and damage connected to using their own private religious experiences as the basis of their authority, namely, they were in fact rejecting Christ as their Head. Seeking the mediation of angels repudiates the idea that Christ is the mediator between God and men. While he may claim that his mysticism brings him in touch with some "higher" reality, the truth is, the mystic actually deprives himself of any connection with the Head (Christ).

From whom the entire body ... grows – This passage is almost word for word the same as in Ephesians 4:15-16. In the Greek the word for "head" (*kephalē*) is feminine, while the relative pronoun "whom" is masculine. The Greek here violates a rule of grammar that the pronoun should agree with its antecedent in gender and number. This violation of grammar may have been done deliberately for the purpose of showing the personality of the Head (a thing which was specially indicated in Ephesians 4:15-16). It is under the direction of Christ, the Head, that the various parts of His body (the church[88]) function harmoniously together. If there is no connection to the Head, there is going to be no growth – whatever the false teachers may claim otherwise. The "entire body" indicates that no member of the body is excepted. "No member can expect from any other quarter what is destined for, and conveyed to, the whole body from the head."[89]

Being supplied and held together by the joints and ligaments – "Being supplied" and "held together" are present tense participles which pictures a continuing and developing process that stems from the body's connection to the Head. Each member of the body touches another member.[90] Any member that

---

[88] "It should not be necessary to defend the proposition that when the apostle, having just referred to Christ as the Head, now speaks of the entire body, he is thinking about the church. That, in such a connection, this is the only possible meaning is clearly implied in such passages as Colossians 1:18,24; 3:15; Ephesians 1:22,23; 4:16" (Hendriksen, *op. cit.*, p.128).

[89] Meyer, *op. cit.*, p.322.

[90] The English word "joints" denotes to us the places where two bones touch each other, while "ligaments" hold the bones together. The Greek words are not quite that specific. The Greek word translated "joints" indicates any point of contact between adjacent parts while the word translated "ligaments" expresses the actual connection. (Wuest, *op. cit.*, p. 213).

becomes detached from the body and its head soon dies.[91]   This is common knowledge, and should drive home to church members the importance of maintaining an unbroken fellowship with each other and our Lord.   The deceptive teacher who is without any contact with Christ, not only has cut himself off from the source of spiritual vitality for God's people, but he cannot possibly contribute to the growth of the church members.

Grows with a growth which is from God – "Grows as God wants it to grow" (TEV).   The growth envisioned may refer to numerical growth as new converts are added to the body or to personal growth in "grace and knowledge" (2 Peter 3:18).   Implied in this statement is the idea that any growth the deceptive teachers accomplish is diametrically opposite to the kind of growth which God wants.

5. Its asceticism. 2:20-23[92]

2:20 – *If you have died with Christ to the elementary principles of the world, why, as if you were living in the world, do you submit yourself to decrees, such as,*

If you have died with Christ – The "if-clause" does not express doubt or uncertainty.   Its force is argumentative – "since [because] you have died ...."   They died with Christ when they were buried with Him in baptism (Colossians 2:12; cp. Romans 6:3-9).   Becoming a Christian makes a difference when it comes to influences that are listened to.   Christians do not respond to the old stimuli they used to before they were immersed.

To the elementary principles of the world – Commentators will offer the same explanation for *stoicheia* ("elementary principles") here that they offered at 2:8.

---

[91] Lightfoot (*op. cit.,* p.200) gave a very full discussion of these terms and their use by medical writers.   He calls attention to the messages that go from the brain to extremities and the sensations that go back again from the extremities to the brain.   Hendriksen (*op. cit.*, p.128) called attention to the fact that it is the blood stream that carries nourishment to the various cells and tissues in the human body.   Of course, these workings of the nervous system and the blood steam are true only if the members of the body are connected to the body and the body to the head.

[92] A fifth element of the Colossian heresy which is to be repudiated is asceticism. Asceticism is the imposition of strict man-made rules concerning how one should deny all the physical body's desires, refuse its appetites, and cut its needs down to an irreducible minimum, all as a means (it is supposed) of gaining favor with God.   Asceticism is a mistaken belief.

If at 2:8 reference was seen to the multitude of spirits or emanations (aeons) which were thought by men to rule the elements and men's lives, the same explanation is used here. When the Colossians became Christians (i.e., when they died with Christ), they left the old religion (animism) which taught that men's lives were controlled by angels and spirits and deities who were supposed to live on the planets and stars. Since as this passage continues it speaks of ascetic practices, we may presume that these ideas were being taught by the elemental spirits.

Why, as if you were living in the world, do you submit yourself to decrees, such as – In this context, where there is a contrast with being buried with Christ to the principles of the world, "living in the world" must mean behavior influenced by pre-Christian ideas and types of religion. The deceptive teachers are still living in the world, and are influenced by the elementary spirits. Paul's question "why?" drives home the point that it is inconsistent for Christians to submit to such ungodly pagan rules. Verse 21 gives examples of the rules or decrees which the deceptive teachers were emphasizing. "Submit to decrees" translates a single Greek word (*dogmatizesthe*) which may either be middle or passive in voice. If it is taken as middle, Paul is asking why they are submitting themselves to such rules. If it is taken as passive, Paul is asking why be dictated to by the false teachers. The middle voice implies that some had submitted, while the passive voice implies that all the readers' resistance should be more energetic. We do not know precisely what the Gnostics had in view when they made certain ascetic rules, such as those about to be enumerated. If the visions of verse 18 are in the background, perhaps sensory deprivation was the way the worshiper arrived at self-induced altered states of consciousness.[93] If we allow verse 23 to guide, then the strict ascetic rules being advocated by the Gnostics were being made to keep men from indulging their physical appetites. Whether verse 18 or verse 23 guides us, Paul is asking the Colossians, why listen to deceptive teachers who are operating according to the elementary principles of the world? Christianity teaches a different means of self-control than severe ascetic practices (see Romans 6:12-19).

2:21 – *"Do not handle, do not taste, do not touch!"*

---

[93] The Greek word translated "ascetic" (*asketikos*, from *askeo*, meaning practice, training, exercise) spoke of the regimen which warriors and athletes followed to attain bodily fitness. Ascetic practices and regimens are found in all major religions. Strict asceticism is the way to enlightenment (altered states of consciousness). When in post-apostolic times Greek dualistic philosophy influenced the thinking of church men, one of the results was the introduction of ascetic practices into the life of the church. When Christians began to become interested, they supposed they found Scripture justification in the lives of John the Baptist, Jesus (40 days in the wilderness), and the apostles including Paul (3 years in Arabia). The deserts of the Middle East were at one time inhabited by thousands of hermits, all seeking enlightenment. The Eastern Orthodox Church's monastery at Mt. Athos is the center of asceticism for that religion.

Do not handle, do not taste, do not touch – Paul here quotes some of the rules set forth by the false teachers.[94]   Each prohibition is more strict than the one before it.   Do not obtain it, do not taste it, do not even touch it, with the underlying idea being that they would be defiled by any of the actions being prohibited.   "Touch" speaks of a slight, momentary contact with something. "Handle" speaks of deliberate contact with an intent to retain it.   (See its use at John 20:17 where it is translated "clings" or "detain").   It has been noted that "handle" translates the verb *hapto*, the verb used in 1 Corinthians 7:1.   In this passage in Colossians there is no reason to limit the meaning to a prohibition of sexual relations.   The next verse here in Colossians 2 seems to imply that all three verbs relate to matters of diet.   We do not know the milieu from which these taboos came.   We have indicated in the Detailed Introduction to Colossians that some of the elements of the Colossian "philosophy" came from Jewish people, and some from pagans.   Among the Jews both the Pharisees and Essenes had strict taboos.   Lightfoot thought the prohibitions reflect the influence of the Essenes in the Lycus River valley.[95]   But non-Jewish people had taboos also. Romans 14:2,5,21 reflect some of the taboos pagans held, and 1 Timothy 4:3 indicates that meat eating was forbidden by the Gnostic false teachers who required their followers to be vegetarians.

2:22 – *(which all* refer to *things destined to perish with the using)* – *in accordance with the commandments and teachings of men?*

(Which all *refer to* things destined to perish with the using) – By putting this clause in parentheses, the NASB treats these words as a comment by Paul in the middle of the question he is writing.[96]   This parenthetical statement is Paul's refutation of what the deceptive teachers have been claiming as the reason for their taboos.   "Which ... things" refers back to prohibitions just named in verse 21.   Paul is saying that foods and drinks are temporary so abstinence from them cannot be a condition of eternal bliss.   The last word "using" translates a Greek word which means not only using but using up, consumption.   Food, once eaten, ceases to be food.   If "perish" is used in the sense of physical decomposition, Paul's parenthetical statement is an   echo of the words of how the foods treated

---

[94] "The Latin commentators, Hilary and Pelagius, suppose these prohibitions to be the Apostle's own, thus making a complete shipwreck of the sense" (Lightfoot, *op. cit.*, p.202-03).

[95] *Ibid.*

[96] Commentators have long struggled with this passage.   Is the first part of the verse a continuation of the language of the false teachers, or is it Paul's refutation of their teaching?   What do the words translated "perish" and "using" really signify?   The explanations offered here have the advantage of making the flow of thought easiest to see.

as taboo by the Pharisees simply were eaten, and eliminated by the body (discharged into the latrine). It was not foods entering the body that defiled the body. The meats and drinks on which the deceptive teachers at Colossae place so much importance do not have any such importance. In the very nature of things they perish in their very use.

In accordance with the commandments and teachings of men? – Verse 8 indicated that the Colossian "philosophy and empty deception" had its origin in "the tradition of men" and in "the elementary principles of the world." Here, the same two sources have been cited again, first in verse 20 and now here in 22, as being the soil out of which the false teachers' ascetic ideas arose. Such regulative prohibitions as "Do not handle! Do not taste! Do not touch!" (verse 21) are man-made rules. They are not God's rules, not even in the Law of Moses. Asceticism is a man-made system of rules.

2:23 – *These are matters which have, to be sure, the appearance of wisdom in self-made religion and self-abasement and severe treatment of the body,* **but are** *of no value against fleshly indulgence.*

These are matters which have, to be sure, the appearance of wisdom – "These matters" (*hatina*) are a whole class of regulations like those listed in verse 21. Verse 23 is Paul's explanation why needless rules and regulations are accepted by so many people. They seem reasonable; they appear to be wise to men of the world. They make a false favorable impression, but the wisdom is not God's wisdom (1 Corinthians 1:30). By use of the particles *men* and *de,* the Greek can warn its readers that a contrast is coming. "To be sure" translates the *men,* warning that a contrast is coming, but there is no *de.* Nevertheless, the last part of the verse gives the contrast. This verse, too, has proven difficult for commentators. There are words that occur only once in the New Testament, and there are words that may not be used with their usual signification. For example, the word translated "appearance" (NASB) or "show" (KJV) is *logos.* Hendriksen tells us that "the meaning of *logos* depends on the context. Here it seems to have the connotation of *reputation,* which is akin to that which it frequently has, namely, *report.*"[97]

In self-made religion and self-abasement and severe treatment of the body – Paul may have coined the compound *ethelothreskia* (translated "self-made religion") since no examples of its use before Paul have been found. The two words which together make the compound were used in Colossians 2:18 where

---

they were translated "delighting" and "worship" (*threskeia*, the way one publicly demonstrates his religious beliefs). The choice of worshiping angels was a self-chosen method, a self-imposed ritual. It was not something commanded by God. "Self-abasement" was also used in 2:18 and has the same meaning here it carried there. "Severe treatment of the body" clearly points to asceticism. "Severe treatment" translates the word *apheidia* which is made up of *pheidomai*, "to spare," and an alpha privative which negates what the rest of the word says. Thus, the compound word means "unsparing treatment or severity." The ascetic taboos of verse 21 may be in view. In some circles flagellation of the body would be an example of severe treatment. This asceticism seems to have resulted from the Oriental theory that matter is the source of evil.

***But are* of no value against fleshly indulgence** – The translation of the Greek at this place offered in the NASB appears to be the correct one.[98] Paul is saying that the ascetic disciplines and taboos required by the false teachers do not really help a man as he tries to gain and practice self-control over desires of the flesh, desires which actually are stirred up or excited by the devil. Paul's final appraisal is that asceticism is a dismal failure.[99] Paul's repudiation of asceticism, of course, does not mean that once we are in Christ anything and everything is permissible; Christians are under law to Christ. But Christians are not subject to man-made rules like those the ascetics promulgated. Christians are expected to walk by the Spirit and not fulfill the lusts of the flesh (Galatians 5:16). In chapter 3 Paul will specifically set forth some expectations concerning Christian living.

---

[98] The Greek words which constitute this phrase have received very different explanations. The word translated "value" (or "honour," KJV) is *timē,* a word which ordinarily means price or honor. It is translated as "precious" at 1 Peter 1:19 and 2:4. The word translated "against" is *pros* which usually means "to" or "toward." "Fleshly indulgence" is a word used regularly with only a bad connotation, so the KJV "to the satisfying of the flesh" is a questionable rendering. Conybeare *(Life and Epistles of St. Paul* [London: Longmans and Green, 1873], p,695) offered the suggestion that the way to translate the Greek here is like the NASB does it. Conybeare's translation satisfies the context as no other does, supplying just such a counterpart as might be expected (from the use of the word "to be sure") to his admission that the asceticism had an "appearance of wisdom." Lightfoot (*op. cit.*, p.206,207) has a long note showing the Greek preposition (*pros*) may indeed have the meaning "against" in such a context as this.

[99] "These ascetic rules were supposedly made to keep men from indulging their physical appetites. Paul says they just do not do it. In fact, they may do the opposite. We may take a selfish and worldly pride in keeping a set of rules. If we discipline ourselves for show, we show a selfish craving for admiration and praise" (Orrin Root, *Standard Lesson Commentary 1979-80* [Cincinnati, OH: Standard, 1979], p.141).

IV. PRACTICAL SECTION – Christ is Preeminent in Ethics for Everyday Living. 3:1-4:6

> *Summary:* Paul has refuted both the doctrinal and practical errors of the false teachers. Their teaching, especially their ascetic emphases, pointed in the wrong direction as far as everyday living is concerned. To that topic of everyday living Paul now turns. If God really did enter the world in the person of Jesus, and we have been immersed into Christ, a different kind of life from how the world lives is expected from us.

A. The Foundation of True Christian Ethics. 3:1-4

1. Seeking the things above. 3:1

3:1 – *If then you have been raised up with Christ, keep seeking the things above, where Christ is, seated at the right hand of God.*

If then you have been raised up with Christ – The "if" construction here, as was true in 2:20, is not intended to cast doubt or uncertainty. It could as well be translated "since you have been raised up with Christ." The thought introduced in 2:12,13 is here continued. "Raised" refers to rising to walk in newness of life at baptism (Romans 6:4). The people to whom he was writing have been immersed and risen to walk in newness of life. Their spirits were made alive again.[1] Paul has been building his argument off of what happens to a man when he is baptized into Christ (2:12,20). He continues with the argument of what are the responsibilities of a man who has risen to walk in newness of life.

Keep seeking the things above – Since they have been raised up with Christ, instead of living like people do who have not died to the old way of life (3:3) and who were being encouraged to focus on taboos and severe ascetic practices (2:20-23), here is what they should focus on. What are "things above"? Before Paul has finished writing the verses that constitute chapter 3 in our letter, he will identify many of the things he has in mind – such things as tender-heartedness, kindness, humility, gentleness, patience, a forgiving spirit and above all love (3:12-14). Surely, if the hearts of believers are filled with such qualities there will be no room for fleshly indulgence (2:23). "Seek" is used with the sense of desiring and striving for these things, and the present tense imperative urges a continuous seeking.   When it comes to how one should live, Paul is giving the

---

[1] This language accords beautifully with baptism being the immersion of a penitent believer (an adult, not a baby; one who is conscious of what is involved, leading to new life).

same instructions Jesus gave when He encouraged men to seek first the Kingdom of God (Matthew 6:33) and to have the eye of the soul focused on a single thing (Luke 11:34). If we are risen with Christ, the things He likes are the things we like.

Where Christ is, seated at the right hand of God – What is meant by "above" (previous clause) is here defined as the place where Christ is. Christ is sitting at the right hand of God. "Christ" is repeated four times in the opening verses of chapter 3. In each case in the Greek there is an article prefixed. "*The* Christ" of Christianity (not some "Christ" of Gnosticism) is the One from whom Christians get their directions and the One on whom Christians focus. Christ's ascension to the right hand of God was predicted in Psalm 110:1, and His exaltation to that place of honor was a constant topic of apostolic preaching.[2] "To be at the right hand of a sovereign or king is to be stationed at the place of highest privilege. Even today a person may refer to a close friend or associate as his right-hand man."[3] We think it likely here that the description of Christ as "seated at the right hand of God" is an implied rejoinder to those deceptive teachers whose doctrines were diminishing Christ's role of preeminence.[4] If we are seeking the things above where Christ is, then our aim is to live in the same way we would live if we also were in the immediate and intimate presence of God the Father – as indeed we are.

2. Setting the mind on things above. 3:2

3:2 – *Set your mind on the things above, not on the things that are on earth.*

Set your mind on the things above – Another present imperative in the Greek, "set your mind" calls on the Colossians to control their thoughts, to constantly direct their thoughts, to keep thinking about the things above. Christians can control their thoughts. If we are risen with Christ, we are to train our affections to match His. We are reminded of the example of Abraham who kept seeking the

---

[2] Acts 2:33ff, 5:31, 7:55; Romans 8:34; Ephesians 1:20; Hebrews 1:3,13, 8:1, 10:12, 12:2; 1 Peter 3:22; Revelation 3:21.

[3] Shannon, *op. cit.*, p.434.

[4] How figurative or literal the language about sitting at God's right hand is intended to be, we are not able to say with certainty. God is pictured as sitting on a throne. Revelation 4:1ff pictures heaven as it now is. There is a throne there, and the lamb is also there, in the midst of the throne. The idea that Jesus is presently with the Father in heaven runs all through the book of Revelation.

heavenly city whose architect and builder is God (Hebrews 11:10). Christians have an inheritance reserved for them in heaven (1 Peter 1:4). Since the Christian's citizenship is in heaven (Philippians 3:20,21) his interests must be the same as Christ's interests.

Not on the things that are on earth – Does the context help us to identify what these things are? Such things as the heretics were emphasizing are certainly included. Perhaps, too, we might include temporal pleasures among the "things on earth." Things on the earth (sensual pleasure, money, luxury, comfort, praise) are easy to love without training. But, having risen with Christ, Christians will have to train their affections away from these. Not all things on earth are evil, but some of them are, and all are inferior to what is spiritual and heavenly. The verses which follow here in chapter 3 make it quite clear that Paul expected Christians to maintain normal relationships with the world. "But," as Barclay explains, "there will be this difference – from now on the Christian will see everything in the light of and against the background of eternity. He will no longer live as if this world was all that mattered; he will see this world against the background of the large world of eternity."[5]

3. The motivations for these actions.   3:3,4

3:3 – *For you have died and your life is hidden with Christ in God.*

For you have died – "For" indicates this verse gives one reason or motive why the Colossians should keep seeking those things which are above as verses 1 and 2 have suggested. "Died" is another of Paul's baptismal aorists (see 2:11,12,20). There is a profound meaning to baptism. They died to sin, and they died to this present visible world. They ought to live like that were true.

And your life is hidden with Christ in God – The Greek has two synonyms that are translated as "life" – *bios* and *zōē*. "*Bios* emphasizes the means of life, or livelihood, goods and property (see its use at Luke 15:12; 1 John 3:17). *Zōē*, the word used here, is life in its principle, and used for spiritual and immortal life."[6] "Hidden" may emphasize the idea that the spiritual life, the resurrection life (risen to walk in newness of life) which the saint enjoys is hidden from unbelievers who do not share it. It calls attention to the fact that the   world does not understand

---

[5] Barclay, *op. cit.,* p.177.

[6] Geo. R. Berry, *A New Greek-English Lexicon to the New Testament* (Chicago: Wilcox and Follett, 1948), p.19.

our new life. What "with (Greek, *sun*, 'in union with') Christ" means is that believers share His death, burial, and resurrection, His glorious position at God's right hand, and His final coming in power; that is, the Colossians' spiritual life and destiny[7] are determined by and are intimately tied to the whole of Christ's activity.   John 1:18, which tells us where Christ now is ("He is in [*eis*] the bosom of the Father"), may explain what "in (*en*) God" in this verse means.   Our Lord has ascended to where human eyes see Him no more (John 14:19) until His second coming.

3:4 – *When Christ, who is our life, is revealed, then you also will be revealed with Him in glory.*

When Christ, who is our life, is revealed – It is Christ's second coming that is alluded to in the words "is revealed." The time when Christ's *parousia* will occur is known only to the Father (Matthew 24:36).[8] In spite of the scoffers who repudiated the idea of a second coming, Jesus will come. Paul writes with the certainty that comes from Jesus' own words on the matter. When it is time for Him to return He will come forth from His concealment. Every eye shall see Him (Revelation 1:7). Christ is called "our life"[9] because He is the source of our life, spiritual and physical and eternal (John 14:19; 2 Corinthians 3:18, 4:10). Jesus said, "I am the resurrection and the life. Whosoever lives and believes in Me shall never die" (John 11:26 ASV).

Then you also will be revealed with Him in glory – This is a second motivation for seeking and setting the mind on things above.   It calls attention to the prospect of the believer's future manifestation with Christ in glory.   It describes the last stage of the life of the believer, our glorification with Christ in heaven.   1 Thessalonians 4:14 indicates that the souls of the redeemed will accompany Jesus as He returns.   When that occurs, the life once "hidden" from the world (Colossians 3:3) will be gloriously revealed, for Christ is our life.   Christians will receive glorified bodies just like the glorified body Jesus now has (1 Corinthians

---

[7] Christians confidently await their being "with Him" in the coming age (cf. 1 Thessalonians 4:14ff, 5:10; Philippians 1:23; 2 Corinthians 4:14ff, 5:6-10, 13:4).

[8] "Revealed" (Greek, *phaneroō*), although not as common as the word "coming" (Greek, *parousia*), is used in a number of passages to denote Christ's second coming (2 Thessalonians 2:8; 2 Corinthians 5:10; 1 Timothy 6:14; 2 Timothy 4:1,8; 1 Peter 5:4; 1 John 2:28; 3:2).

[9] The weight of manuscript evidence is slightly in favor of "our" rather than "your." "Our" is the reading of P[46], Aleph, C, D*. "Your" is found in B, D[bc].

15:49; Philippians 3:20,21; 1 John 3:1,2).[10]   The world cannot see the Christian's real life at present, just as it cannot see Christ.   But the day is coming when what is presently hidden will no longer be hidden.

B. General Exhortations About the Christian Life.   3:5-17

1. Vices to eliminate.[11]   3:5-11

a. Immoral behavior.   5-7

3:5 – *Therefore consider the members of your earthly body as dead to immorality, impurity, passion, evil desire, and greed, which amounts to idolatry.*

Therefore – Verses 1-4 have encouraged seeking and thinking about things above and avoiding thinking about things on the earth.   "Therefore" with which verse 5 opens indicates that the verses which follow are a logical conclusion from what was written in 3:1-4.   The asceticism advocated by the deceptive teachers dismally fails to check sensual indulgence (2:23).   Paul here outlines how Christians stop sensual indulgence.   The Christian does so by renouncing all old sinful behaviors and developing the virtues that are an expression of the new life.

---

[10] "The whole passage forms a complete and magnificent picture of the spiritual life in Christ -- the means of its beginning, the signs of its presence, and the hope of its close.   It may be compared with the fuller yet hardly completer picture of Romans 8" (Barry, *op. cit.*, p.49).

[11] Later in this chapter we shall have Virtues to Cultivate.   At this place, many contemporary commentaries write about "vice lists."   They call attention to a similar list in Ephesians 5:3-6.   Elsewhere in the letters of Paul they occur in the following passages: Romans 1:18-32; 1 Corinthians 5:9-11; Galatians 5:19-21; 1 Thessalonians 4:3-7; 1 Timothy 1:9,10; 2 Timothy 3:2-5. Disappointingly, often the commentaries leave the inference that there is nothing special about the lists we find in Paul's writings.   While it is true that similar lists of vices are of frequent occurrence in ancient literature, such lists did not just evolve as men grew more sophisticated.   The source behind the original lists are the commands and revelations of God (Romans 1:32).   The Old Testament prophets repeated lists of commands the Israelites constantly were breaking (e.g., Jeremiah 7:1-15; Ezekiel 18:1-32).   The Dead Sea Scrolls also have such lists (see Millar Burrows, *The Dead Sea Scrolls* [New York: Viking Press, 1955], p.375, 386, 387).   Because so many of the New Testament vice lists are alike, some scholars maintain that prior to the composition of any of the known Christian writings, there was a recognized body of ethical teaching imparted to converts at the time of baptism (see 1 Thessalonians 2:13, 4:2; 2 Thessalonians 2:15, 3:6).   But, when nothing more is said about where the list originated, we are left with the idea that this body of ethical teaching may have been nothing more than a human invention.   Now, while we may be assured that new converts were given ethical instructions, we may also be assured that the original preachers who taught those rules were inspired mouthpieces speaking for the Lord.

Consider the members of your earthly body as dead – What Paul says here in Colossians 3:5 is analogous to what he had written earlier in Romans 6:11-13, "Even so consider yourselves to be dead to sin, but alive to God in Christ Jesus. Therefore, do not let sin reign in your mortal body so that you obey its lusts, and do not go on presenting the members of your body to sin as instruments of unrighteousness; but present yourselves to God as those alive from the dead, and your members as instruments of righteousness to God." Since Paul has just spoken about controlling the thoughts (3:2) it is obvious that the imperative verb with which this verse begins, *nekrosate* ("mortify," KJV; put to death[12]), is not to be interpreted literally, any more than Jesus' words "cut off the right hand" and "pluck out the right eye" if they cause us to offend (Matthew 5:29,30) were to be taken literally. Christianity teaches self-control when it comes to the uses to which the members of the body are put, and self-control begins with a man's thoughts. In Romans 6:11 "consider yourselves as dead to sin" (*logizesthe ... nekrous*) is analogous with *nekrosate* here in Colossians 3:5, except that here the tense is aorist (calling urgently for a decisive action) while there the tense is present (indicating that such self-control is a continuing responsibility for the Christian). The Christian lives on two planes so long as he remains in this mortal body. In his spirit he already belongs to the age to come, but his body is still involved in this present age. Yes, he is a new man inside, but he still lives in a body that is subject to the temptations stirred up by the devil. So the exhortations to the new man to control the body he lives in are perfectly proper. The Christian deliberately determines what the eyes will look at and what the hands will touch; and the decision is to be in harmony with what Christ above and the Holy Spirit prompt (Romans 8:13), not according to the selfish and temporal desires of our bodies.

To immorality, impurity, passion, evil desire -- All the terms in this verse identify manifestations of selfishness. The first four are about seeking selfish gratification of sexual desire. The Greek term translated "immorality" or "fornication" (see Ephesians 5:3) is used in the Bible to refer to any sexual activity outside of marriage (and marriage is understood in the Bible to be permanent, monogamous, and heterosexual). Immoral sex, which takes what rightly belongs to another person's spouse, or potential future spouse, is an act of selfishness. "Impurity" (as in Ephesians 5:3) describes filthy thoughts of a sexual nature, and these, too, are primarily acts of selfishness. The next two words do not occur in

---

[12] The proper translation of *nekrosate* ("consider ... as dead" in NASB) is "put to death." *Nekrosate* is the first of a series of imperative verbs found here and in the following verses. The KJV word "mortify," though etymologically accurate, carries a different connotation today than it did in 1611.

the parallel passage in Ephesians 5. "Passion" (*pathos*) is a passive mental receptiveness to ideas or suggestions concerning immoral sexual activity stimulated from without. Whereas "immorality" and "impurity" referred to actions, this word speaks of inappropriate thoughts and selfish desires for such actions. The word "desire" (*epithumia*) speaks of an intense desire that actively seeks gratification, while the adjective "evil," in this context, speaks particularly of sexual desire.[13]

And greed, which amounts to idolatry – "Greed" is another form that selfishness can take. The Greek word for "greed" (*pleonexian*) is a compound form whose root meaning suggests a desire to have more. Since there is a "the" before "greed" in the Greek, it is likely this term suggests a category distinct from the sexual sins just enumerated. "Greed" is a ruthless desire to acquire material things or earthly honors, even to the disregard of the rights of others. "To call such greed 'idolatry' is not too strong. Self-seeking is the worship of self instead of the worship of God, the substitution of self for Christ, in one's affections."[14] It is sobering to contemplate the fact this command to "put to death" selfish practices is written to Christians; Christians may certainly experience selfish sexual desires and greed. But there is this encouragement, that such desires and passions can be mastered. Change can occur and those old sinful behaviors are things that should be allowed to occur "no longer" (Ephesians 4:14,17).

3:6 – *For it is on account of these things that the wrath of God will come,*

For it is on account of these things – "These things" are the five vices just listed in verse 5. Paul here introduces the first of two reasons why Christians should put to death such thoughts and behaviors.

That the wrath of God will come – While God is loving and forgiving, we dare not think that He is casual about sin. At Ephesians 2:2,3 and 5:6 it was explained that the "wrath of God" is His settled displeasure against sin which leads Him to punish those who did not fear His wrath enough to quit their sins. The Greek

---

[13] The word "evil" is added to "desire" because the Greek word "desire" (*epithumia*) is neutral – the context must determine if it is a good (e.g., Christ's "desire" to eat the Passover with His disciples, Luke 22:15) or a bad desire. "It is the evil desires that must be put to death, not just intense desires of any kind. Indeed, a Christian should have an ardent desire for good causes" (Shannon, *op. cit.*, p.435).

[14] Hendriksen, *op. cit.*, p.147.

reads, "is coming." It is what is sometimes called "a prophetic present tense" (cf. John 4:21; 14:3). Something is so certain that it can be spoken of as having already arrived. God's wrath at times is experienced in this life (Romans 1:18-32), as well as after the final judgment (Revelation 21:8). These five vices just listed (verse 5) "attract God's displeasure like a magnet attracts iron or like a high steeple on an isolated hill draws lightning."[15]

3:7 – *and in them you also once walked, when you were living in them.*

And in them you also once walked – "Them" gathers up all the sins listed in verse 5.[16] This verse gives a second reason why the sins listed in verse 5 are an impropriety in the life of the believer. They are a hangover from the old life.

When you were living in them – The two verbs in this verse, "walked" and "living" both describe behavior, a lifestyle. "When you were living in them" calls attention to how they lived in sin before they became Christians. "This is not the only place in the New Testament epistles where a catalogue of pagan vices is immediately followed by a reminder to the readers that not so long ago these things characterized their own lives (cf. 1 Corinthians 6:9-11; Romans 6:19-23; Titus 3:3; 1 Peter 4:1,2)."[17]

b. Hostile attitudes. 8a

3:8a – *But now you also, put them all aside: anger, wrath, malice,*

But now you also, put them all aside – "But now" marks an emphatic contrast. Now that they have become Christians, oh, what a change in their lives! To be sure, the Colossians were not perfect Christians; but relatively speaking, they had made a change and their lives were to show it. "Put aside" is an imperative verb;

---

[15] *Ibid.* The KJV has an additional phrase ("upon the sons of disobedience") at this place. The manuscript support for the words is weak and since Ephesians 5:6 reads like Colossians 3:6, it has been supposed that the words in the later manuscripts of Colossians are an interpolation from Ephesians.

[16] If the reading in the previous verse ("upon the sons of disobedience") were retained, this verse might be translated "among whom."

[17] E.K. Simpson and F.F. Bruce, *Commentary on the Epistles to the Ephesians and Colossians* in the NICNT, (Grand Rapids: Eerdmans, 1957), p.271.

this is a command.[18]   In a lively change of metaphor that carries the same idea as "put to death" (verse 5), Paul urges the readers to discard them as one discards a garment once worn that no longer fits.   Put them "all" aside, all the things already enumerated and the things about to be named, all of them without any exception.

Anger, wrath, malice – In case we are about to congratulate ourselves that we do not do any of the vices listed in verse 5, here comes another list Christians need to work on.   This list of vices speaks of kinds of behavior that disrupt the relationship between neighbors.   The first three hostile attitudes were also listed at Ephesians 4:31.   "Anger" is *orge*, indignation, irritation, exasperation, embitterment.   "Wrath" is *thumos*, selfish anger that boils over when someone does something wrong to us.   "Malice" is *kakia*, the spirit that prompts one to injure or hurt his neighbor.

c. Improper speech.   8b

3:8b - *(Put away)* slander, and *abusive speech from your mouth.*

Slander, *and* abusive speech from your mouth – "Slander" translates *blasphemia*, a word that denotes insulting and slanderous talk – here, against one's fellow man.   "Abusive speech" (*aischrologia*) means either abusive speech or obscene language.[19]   "Foul-mouthed abuse" was Lightfoot's suggested translation.[20]   "No pure heart can utter foul speech.   'Out of the abundance of the heart the mouth speaketh' (Matthew 12:34 ASV).   From the same fountain do not come forth both sweet and bitter waters (James 3:10,11).   See also James 1:26, 'bridle his tongue'."[21]   The tongue was not given for men to slander others or speak abusive things, or to speak lies.

---

[18] This is the second of four imperatives that help us outline this portion of the epistle.

[19] "This is another word from Paul that seems especially relevant in our day.   Nearly every movie and television program contains what might be described as filthy communication.   The language is used either to shock or to provide a twisted form of humor, neither of which is an acceptable use of God's precious gift of speech" (Shannon, *op. cit.*, p.436).

[20] Lightfoot, *op. cit.*, p.214.

[21] Frank H. Marshall, *Standard Adult Bible Teacher and Leader*, 1955 (Cincinnati; Standard, 1954), p.98.

d. Lying. 9a

3:9a -- *Do not lie to one another*

Do not lie to one another – This is the third of the imperatives that are highlighted in this section.   The Greek (a present imperative with *mē*) forbids the continuance of an action already going on.   "Stop lying!"   "One another" indicates that Paul is dealing with relationships within the Christian community.   Recall Ephesians 4:25 where the reason for not lying is that "we are members of one another."[22] "Christians are to be honest people.   Anyone who claims to be a follower of the One who is the truth (John 14:6) should find lying intolerable.   Lying is actually the speech of the devil (John 8:44)."[23]

e.   Remember who you are.   9b-11

3:9b – *since you laid aside the old self with its evil practices,*

Since you laid aside the old self with its evil practices – Two reasons to stop lying to one another are given in this clause and the next.[24]   In this first reason, repeating the idea written in Colossians 2:11,12, Paul reminds them of what happened at their baptism.   As it did in Colossians 2:11, the verb "laid aside" *(apekdusamenoi)* conveys the picture of divesting a garment.   What in verse 11 was called "the body of the flesh" is here called "the old self."   See Ephesians 4:22-24 for a fuller description of how the old self was put off at baptism.[25]   The "old self" is the unregenerate self.   The "old self" here describes each Christian of Colossae during the days when he or she was an idolater with all the vices that go with paganism.   The idea in the old self being laid aside is that the Christian

---

[22] Only in Colossians and Ephesians do we find Paul giving a general warning against lying.   What reason there was for this we cannot tell.   Findlay (*op. cit.*, p.150) suggests the reason may be found in the deceit of the false teachers.

[23] Shannon, *op. cit.*, p.436.

[24] The participles translated "laid aside" and "put on" are being treated as circumstantial participles.

[25] "Calling on Christ in baptism, we asked Him to cleanse us from the old self, putting to death our lives of rebellion and raising us to lives of submission to Him (Colossians 2:12,13).   What are we saying to Him, and what are we saying about ourselves, if we continue to live as if we had never asked Christ to make us new?" (Jon Weatherly, *Standard Lesson Commentary 2012-13* [Cincinnati: Standard, 2012], p.212.)

has had a life-changing experience wherein the old habits and characteristic actions were consciously repudiated and abandoned.[26]

3:10 – *and have put on the new self who is being renewed to a true knowledge according to the image of the One who created him*

And have put on the new self – This verse introduces the second reason why the Colossians should stop lying to one another (3:9). What Paul is saying is that not only is lying inconsistent with what it means to have risen with Christ to walk in newness of life, but also there are some positive virtues to be developed. Living as a Christian means more than just avoiding sin. It means acquiring a new, different perspective and lifestyle. Perhaps the use of *neos* ("new") rather than the usual *kainos* (Ephesians 4:24) pictures the conversion of the Colossians as being recent. The "new self" says that the convert's "spirit" is alive because of righteousness (Romans 8:10).

Who is being renewed to a true knowledge – "True knowledge" expresses the aim or goal of the renewal. The Greek word here translated "true knowledge" is *epignosis* and there well may be an intentional contrast with the knowledge (*gnosis*) held out to the Colossians by the false teachers, a knowledge which was distorted and imperfect when compared to the true knowledge available through Jesus Christ. The renewal by which one arrives at this "true knowledge" is the result of continual process ("being renewed" is *anakainoumenon*, a present tense, expressing a continuous process of renewal). Dealing with the same idea, Paul wrote to the Romans about being transformed by the renewing of their minds so that they may demonstrate God's perfect and acceptable will in their lives (Romans 12:1-3). He expressed an analogous idea in 2 Corinthians 4:16 when he wrote how "the inner man is being renewed day by day." In each believer this new self is a progressively developing mind-set and behavior. Both "new self" and "renewed" occur in the parallel passage at Ephesians 4:22-24. There we were told the renewing takes place in the spirit of the mind. It also speaks of the new self as being created like God in two aspects, holiness and righteousness. As Paul continues to write this letter to the Colossians, he will articulate the behavior that comes out of the renewed mind, the renewed self.

---

[26] "Paul does not claim that his converts have no faults; nor does he expect that each will be entirely without sin. But he does insist that each shall hate sin as his worst enemy, and make a heroic struggle to overcome the evil impulses that he now despises" (Marshall, *op. cit.*, p.99).

According to the image of the One who created him – While some insist that "image" refers to Adam being created in the image of God, and that God is the One who did the creating, "it is hard to resist the interpretation that image (if not also the creator) here refers to Christ (see 1 Corinthians 11:7; 2 Corinthians 3:18; 4:4; Hebrews 1:3; also John 12:45; 14:9)."[27]   The phrase then indicates that Christ is our exemplar.   When He arose from the dead He was no longer subject to the devil's temptation; instead the life He lives, He lives unto God (Romans 6:10,11).   When we rise from the baptismal waters to walk in newness of life, we, too, should be unreceptive to temptations from the devil, but instead live to please God.

3:11 – a renewal *in which there is no* distinction between *Greek and Jew, circumcised and uncircumcised, barbarian, Scythian, slave and freeman, but Christ is all, and in all.*

***A renewal* in which there is no *distinction between* Greek and Jew** – The same process of "renewal" (verse 10) occurs in all believers[28] – whatever, as the rest of the verse indicates, their ethnic or social or cultural situation.   Paul's "no distinction" may be a criticism of Gnostic exclusivism.   The word "Greek" stands for Gentiles as a whole, not just people from Greece.[29]   "Greek and Jew" says the renewal into the image of Christ recognizes no racial boundaries nor identity.   In Christ, all can experience the renewal into the image of Christ.

Circumcised and uncircumcised – A man may be circumcised or uncircumcised in the flesh.   The renewal process works on both the circumcised and uncircumcised.   No one is admitted to the renewal because he is circumcised; no one is excluded from it because he is uncircumcised.   Paul's argument here implies that the issue of circumcision formed one of the particular emphases made by the deceptive teachers at Colossae.

---

[27] Weed, *op. cit.*, p.87.

[28] A word of explanation for "a renewal" being printed in italics in the NASB is in order. The Greek simply reads "where" but the antecedent is the renewal which occurs after the old self has been put off, and the new self put on.   NASB has also inserted "distinction between" to help express the idea contained in the Greek.   Peake (*Expositor's Greek Testament*, p.540) explains that the Greek word *eni*, translated "there is" is an older form of *en* ("in") and has the significance of *enestin* ("is present in").

[29] The word "Greek" (*hellēn*), in such antithetical places where there is a contrast with "Jews," "embraces all nations not Jews that made the language, customs, and learning of the Greeks their own" (Thayer, *op. cit.*, p. 205).   In this sense the word is used in John 7:35, Acts 11:20 and 14:1.

Barbarian, Scythian – Because there is no "and" between these words like there is between the other pairs, some have thought these words may be intended as a climax. The term "barbarian" referred to anyone who did not speak Greek, no matter how cultured he or she might otherwise be. The Greek word used here imitated how foreigners sounded to Greek ears – as if they were saying "bar, bar, bar, bar." Thus we get the term barbarian. Perhaps this suggests that no language barrier keeps the renewal process from working. The name "Scythian" was applied to the savage and warlike nomads from the areas north and northeast of the Black and Caspian seas. 600 or more years before Christ hordes of these ferocious folk deluged the countries of the Fertile Crescent including Palestine. Josephus wrote, "The Scythians delight in murdering people and are little better than wild beasts."[30] "Herodotus (IV.75) described them as living in wagons, offering human sacrifices, scalping and sometimes flaying slain enemies, drinking their blood, and using their skulls for drinking-cups. When a king dies, one of his concubines is strangled and buried with him, and, at the close of a year, fifty of his attendants are strangled, disemboweled, mounted on dead horses, and left in a circle round his tomb. The Scythians passed through Palestine on their road to Egypt, c. 600 BC, and a trace of their invasion is supposed to have existed in the name Scythopolis, by which Bethshean was known in Christ's time. Their ancient invasion of Palestine is referred to under the name of Gog in Ezekiel 38,39. "[31] It is very likely to be inferred that among the Christians at Colossae were some descendants of the ancient Scythians, or perhaps recent immigrants into the area. Even though a man, before becoming a Christian, may have been as uncivilized and wild as a Scythian, that does not hinder the renewal process from working.

Slave and freeman – No one is excluded from the renewal process because he is a slave; no one is admitted because he is free. Slavery was a fact of life in the Biblical world. Few probably even considered the possibility of its nonexistence. Here Paul does not speak directly to the issue of slavery; he simply affirms that in Christ the slave and the free person are alike when it comes to the renewal process. Social distinctions or social caste present no hindrance. At Colossae, Onesimus and Philemon are examples of slave and free.

But Christ is all, and in all – In the original, "Christ" stands with great emphasis last in the clause. He is all that is needed, and in Him all persons have the same

---

[30] *Against Apion*, II. 269.

[31] Vincent, *op. cit.*, p. 914.

opportunities for renewal.[32]   Even when folk have become immersed believers (i.e., they have died and been raised with Christ, 2:12), such external distinctions may continue to exist between Greek and Jew, bond and free.   Nevertheless, renewal will occur, with no regard to those externals concerning, externals which the false teachers claimed to be important.   In Ephesians 1:23 we were told that Christ imparts His fullness to the church; He "fills all in all."

2.   Virtues to cultivate.   3:12-17

a.   A merciful spirit.   12

3:12 – *And so, as those who have been chosen of God, holy and beloved, put on a heart of compassion, kindness, humility, gentleness and patience;*

And so – "And so" ties what is about to be written with the fact that Christians have put on their new selves.   Verses 10-11 have told us that the renewal process works for all converts, whatever their ethnic, religious, or social backgrounds.   Renewal requires not only putting off old vices (verses 5-9), but it also requires that certain virtues are to be cultivated.

As those who have been chosen of God, holy and beloved – Paul bases his appeal to develop positive virtues upon three facts: Christians are chosen of God, are set apart for God, and are loved by God.   That Christians have been "chosen" reminds us of what Paul wrote in Ephesians 1:4,5.   Back in eternity when God was making His eternal plan, He chose or elected that those who were *in Christ* would be destined to glory.   Whether or not a man is in Christ is the man's own choice, not something determined by God like a robot is programmed.[33] Involved in the path to glory is the cultivation of the virtues about to be listed. "Holy", the same word as "saints" in Colossians 1:2, says the Christian is consecrated to God in thought and life.   He or she is set apart to sacred service. Such a consecration requires the development of the virtues.   "Beloved" says the

---

[32] The conjunction "and" (in the phrase "Christ (is) all *and* in all") shows that both parts of the phrase must be given recognition.

[33] Calvinistic writers have found some of their doctrine in this verse.   "Chosen" (or the word may also be translated "elect") is explained as being God's gracious determination that certain folk were to be saved.   Election back in eternity precedes sanctification in time, another act of God on those whom He chose to save.   The perfect passive participle "beloved" is interpreted to mean that God's election resulted from His divine love.   For a detailed study of this whole topic, see the author's "The Doctrine of Predestination" in *New Testament Epistles: Romans* (Moberly, MO: Scripture Exposition Books, 1996), pp. 544-571.

Christian is the object of God's special love.[34]   If they are loved by their heavenly Father, His children should love one another (verses 12-15).   Christians are to exhibit some of the nature of their heavenly Father.

Put on a heart of compassion – This is the fourth in a series of imperative verbs that have punctuated this section of Colossians.   "Put on" (an aorist imperative, to express a sense of urgency in obeying this command) is repeated from verse 10, and tells us these virtues about to be named do not just happen, they must be willfully and deliberately cultivated.[35]   A "heart of compassion" is the first of the virtues Paul identifies.[36]   A study of the synonyms "compassion" and "mercy" may help us grasp the meaning of this word translated "compassion."   "Mercy" (*eleos*) manifests itself chiefly in acts rather than words, while "compassion" (*oiktirmos*) is used rather of the inward feeling of compassion which abides in the heart.   A criminal might ask for *eleos, mercy,* from his judge; but hopeless suffering may be the object of *oiktirmos, compassion*.[37]   Some Biblical examples of compassion and what results from such an attitude of heart are to be found in Matthew 9:36, 14:14, and 18:27.

Kindness, humility, gentleness and patience – Perhaps there is a logical progression of thought in these virtues that are named following compassion. "Kindness" (*chrestotes*) is an attitude toward others that expresses itself by trying

---

[34] To the church, the true Israel, belongs the titles given to Old Testament Israel, such as elect, holy, beloved (cf. Romans 2:29, 9:6; Galatians 3:29, 6:16; Philippians 3:3; 1 Peter 2:9).   In Mosaic times, Israel was God's chosen people (Exodus 19:3-6).   (Actually, it was just an "Israel" within "Israel," Romans 9:6-8.)   "Replacement theology" is a pejorative term used by defenders of the dogma that the Jewish people always have been and always will be God's chosen people to cast aspersions on the affirmation that only those who are in Christ (whatever their ethnic background) are, in this new covenant age, God's chosen people.   Romans 11 plainly shows that unbelieving Israel has been cut off from the olive tree.   Jesus said the kingdom would be taken from Israel and given to people bringing forth fruits worthy of repentance (Matthew 21:43).

[35] Conscientious Christians, as they read this section, should ask themselves, "Which of these virtues am I deliberately working on this week?"

[36] When it is remembered that Colossians 3:2 talked about controlling one's thoughts, "heart" is a good choice to translate the Greek word *splanchna*, which refers to the upper viscera rather than the lower bowels.   It focuses attention on filling the thoughts and the mind with these virtues.

[37] George R. Berry, "New Testament Synonyms #30," *A New Greek-English Lexicon to the New Testament* (Chicago: Wilcox & Follett, 1948), p.128.

to do good to those others.[38]   Biblical examples of kindness are found in the good Samaritan (Luke 10:25-37) and in Barnabas (Acts 4:36,37, 15:37).   Kindness combines the ideas of goodness, kindliness, and graciousness.   God is kind (Romans 2:4) and Paul encourages His readers to imitate God in this respect. "Humility" (*tapeinophrosune*) is an inner attitude of the heart that does not think more highly of itself that one ought to think (Romans 12:3,6).[39]   Philippians 2:3 says "with humility of mind let each of you regard one another as more important than himself."   A Biblical example of humility might be the centurion who said, "I am not worthy for you to come under my roof" (Luke 7:6).   "Gentleness" (*praütes*) is the special mark of the man who has a delicate consideration for the rights and feelings of others.   It is the man who is willing to make concessions. Meekness is not weakness or spinelessness.   It is submissiveness under provocation, the willingness rather to suffer injury than to inflict it.   Moses, who was very meek, is an example (Numbers. 12:3).   Meekness was a characteristic of Christ (Matthew 11:29).   It is a fruit of the Spirit (Galatians 5:23), and a trait that brings a blessing (Matthew 5:5).   "Patience" (*makrothumia*), as explained at Colossians 1:11, denotes the self-restraint that enables one to bear injury and insult without resorting to hasty retaliation.   "Longsuffering indicates the willingness to wait as long as it takes for others to make the right response, just as God waited for us to respond to Him (Ephesians 4:32)."[40]   *Makrothumia* speaks of "the man, who, having to do with injurious persons, does not suffer himself easily to be provoked by them, or to blaze up in anger."[41]   It is an attribute of God (Romans 2:4) and a fruit of the Spirit (Galatians 5:22).   "What a longsuffering hero was Jeremiah during his lengthy period of prophetic activity."[42]

b. A forgiving spirit.   13

3:13 – *bearing with one another, and forgiving each other, whoever has a complaint against anyone; just as the Lord forgave you, so also should you.*

---

[38] See Trench, *op. cit.,* p.232-235.

[39] Though it is the same word used in Colossians 2:18,23 for the mock humility of the deceptive teachers, and though the pagans thought little of this quality (to them it was servility), Christianity has given this word a special new meaning.   There is a genuine humility that leads one to avoid asserting his or her own rights or privileges.

[40] Weatherly, *op. cit.,* p.214.

[41] Wuest, *op. cit.,* p.224.

[42] Hendriksen, *op. cit.,* p.157.

Bearing with one another – Two Greek participles (*anechomenoi*, "bearing with") and *charizomenoi* ("forgiving") give specific expression of what is involved in patience. A similar exhortation was given to the Ephesians (cf. Ephesians 4:2, "showing forbearance to one another in love"). The verb "bear with" deals with present offenses and calls for a willingness to bear with those whose faults or unpleasant traits in word or action irritate us. "One another" (*allēlōn*) is a reciprocal pronoun.[43]

And forgiving each other – The participle translated "forgiving" comes from the same verb (*charizomai*) that was used in Colossians 2:13. When it comes to past offenses, Paul encourages the same kind of gracious forgiveness that we have received from the Lord. It is the same word used of what the money lender did to the two debtors in Jesus' parable (Luke 7:42). The present tense participle emphasizes the idea that such gracious forgiveness is to be unceasing and even unwearying (compare "seventy times seven" in Matthew 18:22). In His Sermon on the Mount Jesus spoke about the need for forgiving others (Matthew 6:12,14). "Each other" (*heautois)* is an intensive personal pronoun that apparently is used as a reciprocal pronoun.

Whoever has a complaint against anyone – Legitimate complaints (*momphē*, cause for complaint, matter of complaint, reason to find fault[44]) will arise from time to time within the congregation. When they do, the readers are urged to be gracious toward the offender. Perhaps it could be said that both Philemon and Onesimus had a complaint against the other.

Just as the Lord forgave you, so also should you – This is the grand motive for forgiving our brothers. "Just as" (*kathōs*, "even as" [ASV]), means according as, in proportion to, in the degree that. We are to forgive in the same way Christ forgave us.[45]   If we refuse to forgive, we treat Christ's forgiveness of us with

---

[43] Reciprocal pronouns picture plural subjects being affected by an interchange of the action expressed by the verb. "They hit one another" means first one hit the other, then the other hit the one. So "bearing with one another" means you bear with me, and I bear with you.

[44] *Momphē* is found only here in the New Testament and in the LXX of the Old Testament. It is found regularly in the classics with the meaning of blame or reproach.

[45] The manuscript authority (P[46], A, B, D, G, and the Latin Bible) is in favor of "Lord" instead of "Christ" (KJV). But since the name "Lord" is specially applied to Christ in these epistles (see for example, Ephesians 4:5), there is no real difference. In the parallel passage in Ephesians 4:32, Paul bids his readers to be kind and tender-hearted one to another, "forgiving each other, just as God in Christ also has forgiven you."

contempt.   "It is cruel and cold hearted to refuse forgiveness to someone who has repented of wrongdoing.   To do so is to put that person out in the cold.   It is as inhumane to do that in our attitude as it would be to do so in a literal sense."[46]

c.   A loving spirit.   14

3:14 – *And beyond all these things* **put on** *love, which is the perfect bond of unity.*

And beyond all these things *put on* **love** – The verb "put on" is supplied from verse 12, and "these things" refers back to the virtues already named in verses 12 and 13.   *"Over all these"* (so the Greek, literally) continues the metaphor of putting on articles of clothing and this verse seems to convey the idea that love is put on top of all the other articles of clothing.   "Love is the outer garment which holds the others in their places."[47]   "Love" is thoughtfully doing what is spiritually best for the other person.   It is intelligent and purposeful self-giving. How love behaves is described in 1 Corinthians 13.   In Philippians 1:9, it was Paul's prayer that their love might abound more and more.

Which is the perfect bond of unity – This verse has first described the supreme importance of love, and now Paul describes why it must be put on, namely, because it is the bond that ties them all together.   When love for the other members of the congregation is the ruling motive, then the other virtues will not be difficult to come by.   The word here translated "perfect" was translated "complete" at Colossians 1:28.[48]   The person in whom love ties all the other virtues together is a mature Christian.   Barry may have rightly suggested that something the   false teachers emphasized   caused Paul to write this remarkable

---

[46] Knofel Staton, *Standard Lesson Commentary 1992-93* (Cincinnati, OH: Standard, 1992), p.397.

[47] Lightfoot, *op. cit.*, p.222.

[48] The KJV reads "bond of perfectness," which shows us the word *teleios* is in the genitive case.   How this genitive should be interpreted is a matter of long discussion in the commentaries. We judge it should be treated as a genitive of apposition, so that love becomes the bond in which "perfection" or "completeness" exists.

expression.[49]   The false teachers sought "perfection" in a knowledge that was the exclusive privilege of the few.   Paul explained that love, a virtue which is possible for all Christians and which ties together all the other Christian virtues, is the thing that results in real perfection.

d. A peaceful spirit.   15a

3:15 – *And let the peace of Christ rule in your hearts, to which indeed you were called in one body; and be thankful.*

And let the peace of Christ rule in your hearts – "Let" is not an option; the verb here is an imperative, another in the series of imperative verbs that punctuate this section of Colossians.   The true reading is "peace of Christ" rather than "peace of God" (KJV).   What is the "peace of Christ"?   In this commentator's judgment, this imperative is another in the series we have called virtues to be cultivated.   These virtues deal with our relationships with our brothers and sisters in Christ, so "peace" appears to mean peace or harmony among the members of the Christian community.   The following phrase, which is about being one body, also points to this as the correct idea.   It is called the "peace of Christ" because it is the kind of relationship He wants among Christians.   The Greek word translated "rule" is taken from the sports world of Paul's day.[50]   The word described the action of a judge, or umpire, in deciding the outcome of a competition.   "Hearts" in this place speaks of thoughts, attitudes of mind.   Thus, Paul is saying that thoughts about keeping the brotherly peace which Christ desires are to act as the arbiter governing all of our relationships in the church. The peace of Christ, not the rules and regulations of the deceptive teachers (2:18), is to be the controlling motive behind our actions and reactions with one another in the family of God.

To which indeed you were called in one body – The "peace of Christ" is the antecedent of "to which."   God calls men to become Christians through the gospel (2 Thessalonians 2:14).   When men respond to the invitation they become part of the one body, the church.[51]   Keeping the unity of the body is a strong argument for peace.   Paul says that we are called to peace.   We are not to treat

---

[49] Barry, *op. cit.*, p.53.

[50] *Brabeuo* ("rule") is the simple verb from which the compound *katabrabeuo* (translated "keep defrauding" or "giving judgment against you," NASB mg. at Colossians 2:8) is formed.

[51] See Ephesians 2:14-22 for a detailed treatment of the "one body."

being peacemakers as something optional.   Paul wrote to the Romans, "If possible, so far as it depends on you, be at peace with all men" (Romans 12:18). If Christians would give peace this kind of priority, we would go a long way toward being the one body the Lord desires His church to be.

e.   A grateful/thankful spirit.   15b-17

And be thankful – The present tense imperative *ginesthe* ("be") indicates that gratitude is to be a habit.   "Be" (or it could be translated "become") indicates that it is a habit that must be acquired.   "Learn to be grateful" (Knox).   Perhaps it speaks of being thankful for fellow members of the body, and especially for any service done by them.   Verse 17 will specifically refer to giving thanks to God. The same duty is commanded at Ephesians 5:4.   A failure to give God thanks (Romans 1:21) was a sin that caused folk who had at one time known God to go away from Him into idolatry.   "Certainly the refreshing change in our lives that results from removing the vices and embracing the virtues should make us grateful people indeed."[52]

3:16 – *Let the word of Christ richly dwell within you, with all wisdom teaching and admonishing one another with* **psalms** *and* **hymns** *and* **spiritual songs,** *singing with thankfulness in your hearts to God.*

Let the word of Christ richly dwell within you – "Let it dwell" (*enoikeito*) is a present imperative.   It is not an option.   It is a command.   The imperative verb is an appeal to the will.   Each reader will have to decide whether or not to obey. "The word of Christ" refers to the gospel which is a word about Christ (if "of Christ" is an objective genitive), or a word from Christ (if "of Christ" is a subjective genitive).   By the "word of Christ" here, Paul cannot mean the written volume of the New Testament as we understand it, for much of it had not yet been written.   What he meant here was the message of the gospel, spoken by Paul, Timothy, Epaphras, and others, which they had heard and were treasuring in their memories as the Word of Christ.   "You" is plural, likely meaning the congregation as a whole.[53]   How do the members let the word dwell in them

---

[52] Shannon, *op. cit.,* p.437.

[53] "Does 'in you' mean 'within you' (as individual Christians) or 'among you' (as a Christian community)?   Perhaps he would not have cared to be pinned down too firmly to either alternative, although if one of the two had to be accepted, the collective sense might be preferred in view of the context" (Bruce, *op. cit.,* p.237).

richly (in ample measure)? Each would pay careful attention when the word was spoken, would submit to its authority, and would attempt to translate its lessons into daily living.

With all wisdom teaching and admonishing one another – "One another" in Greek is a reflexive pronoun (*heautous*, "yourselves") which is likely used as a reciprocal pronoun ("one another").[54] The correct punctuation of the remainder of verse 16 is uncertain. (1) The KJV and ERV treat "in all wisdom" as being attached to what precedes, "Let the word of Christ dwell in you richly in all wisdom." Phillips reads, "Let Christ's teaching live in your hearts, making you rich in the true wisdom." So punctuated, the rest of the verse then gives two things the Christians are to do: one is to teach and admonish one another with psalms, hymns, and spiritual songs; the other is to sing with thankfulness in their hearts to God. (2) The RSV, NASB, and the Nestle text treat "with all wisdom" as modifying the words which follow, namely, "teaching and admonishing." The resulting thought is that under the influence of the word of Christ, Christians are to do two things: one is to teach and admonish one another,[55] making use of all the wisdom in the word of Christ; and the other is that they are to sing with gratitude in their hearts to God, using psalms, hymns, and spiritual songs. Whichever way we decide to punctuate the verse, we see the responsibility of every Christian to communicate the faith to one another. "Teaching one another" is something the saints (each and all of them – not just the leaders) are to do continuously (present tense participle). "Admonishing" (*noutheteō*) means "to warn, exhort, admonish." The word contains the ideas of encouragement, reproof, and blame, as well.[56]

---

[54] Reflexive pronouns "reflect" the action expressed by the verb back to its own subject. Reciprocal pronouns picture plural subjects being affected by an interchange of action expressed by the verb (e.g., "love one another" = I love you, you love me.) If *heautous* here is used as a reciprocal pronoun, perhaps it speaks of an assembly on the Lord's day, or a social gathering, or family worship, or at festive occasions. Observe that the immediately following context speaks of household groups. If it is used as a reflexive pronoun, what Paul wrote means Christians are to use the wisdom contained in the word of Christ to teach and admonish themselves.

[55] There was a very similar expression at 1:28, where essentially the same thought is expressed in an almost identical statement. The differences are: (1) in 1:28 it is what Paul and Timothy are doing; here in 3:16 it is what the Colossian believers are admonished to do; (2) in 1:28 the object is somewhat broader, "every man," while here in 3:16 it is mutual teaching and admonition among congregational members. The fact that, in the almost identical phrase in Colossians 1:28, the phrase "in all wisdom" modifies "teaching and admonishing," shows it likely is to be so construed here, as the NASB does it, and not attached to the preceding clause (as Lightfoot thought).

[56] Wuest, *op. cit.,* p.227.

With psalms *and* hymns *and* spiritual songs – The terms "psalms, hymns, and spiritual songs" were explained in the study of Ephesians 5:19.[57] As a careful comparison of Ephesians 5:19 with Colossians 3:16 reveals, where Ephesians describes something that was the result of "being filled with the Spirit," here in Colossians the result flows from "the word of Christ richly dwelling in" the believers. Neither passage should be explained without reference to the other, in this commentator's judgment. Our interpretation of this passage is once again influenced by how the words are punctuated. According to the KJV, Christians are to teach and admonish one another with "psalms and hymns and spiritual songs." According to the RSV, Christians are pictured as singing psalms and hymns and spiritual songs with thankfulness in their hearts to God.[58] One translation causes us to think of the singing that occurred in the public assembly, just as 1 Corinthians 14:15 speaks of hymns being sung to the congregation with a purpose of edifying. Ancients used verse and rhythm to help students learn lessons. Perhaps Paul is picturing songs full of Christological content being used as teaching tools in the public assembly.[59] The other translation causes us to think not only of the assembly on the Lord's Day, but also of everyday life whether at home or anywhere else. It has been the testimony of Christians from the earliest times that "Christ put a song in my heart." And it is, perhaps, no exaggeration to say that songs have taught more theology to new converts than textbooks. "There is an interesting, unique association between music and the development of Christian character. No other religion is so fully expressed in song as is the Christian faith. A happy heart springs forth almost spontaneously in song; and who has more reason to be happy than the Christian."[60]

---

[57] These three words for songs had distinctive meanings. "Psalm" indicated a song accompanied by the harp; "hymn" meant a religious song, but did not suggest accompaniment; and "ode" (here translated "song") was a broad term for a poem that was meant to be sung.

[58] The RSV treats the participles "teaching," "admonishing," and "singing" as circumstantial participles. That version reads "Let the word of Christ dwell in you richly, as you teach and admonish one another in all wisdom, and as you sing psalms and hymns and spiritual songs with thankfulness in your hearts to God."

[59] This commentator has been very hesitant to accept the contemporary scholarly dictum that a number of New Testament passages (e.g., Philippians 2:5-11; Ephesians 5:14) had their origin in an early Christian hymn. Such a handling of those passages not only leaves us with doubts as to the original source of the words, but also results in serious questions concerning the truthfulness of what the passages affirm. It is one thing to say the early church may have converted Christian teaching to hymns to be used as teaching tools, and another thing to say that such hymns were the source of what has come to be written in our Bibles.

[60] S. Edward Tesh, *Standard Lesson Commentary 1974-75* (Cincinnati, OH: Standard, 1974), p.416.

Singing with thankfulness in your hearts to God – Singing (*adontes*) may take place in the worship assembly/service or in any ordinary situation.   As the margin shows, the Greek for "with thankfulness" is literally "in grace" or "in His grace."[61] On the basis of 1 Corinthians 10:30, where the word *chariti* is translated "thankfulness," and in line with the immediate context (verses 15 and 17 each speak of being thankful), the most probable meaning here for *chariti* would seem to be thankfulness or a grateful attitude.   "In your hearts" may be connected with "thanksgiving," in which case it emphasizes all the things for which a Christian could be thankful.   Or "in your hearts" may be connected with "singing," in which case it could be taken to mean "singing with all your hearts," fervently, enthusiastically.   The KJV has "to the Lord" where the NASB reads "thankfulness to God."   In the parallel passage at Ephesians 5:19, Paul wrote of "singing and making melody with your heart to *the Lord*" (presumably meaning Christ).   Pliny said the Christians sang hymns to Christ as God.[62]   When we recall that the deceptive teachers denied that Jesus is God, it may well be that Paul meant keep on singing your psalms, hymns, and spiritual songs to Jesus.   He is God!

If we may use this passage and Ephesians 5:19 to give us some broad principles with respect to what may or may not be sung at the public assembly of believers on the Lord's Day, the following would be observed: (1) Do not neglect the Old Testament psalms, especially the Christological ones.   Many have been set to music.   (2) Hymns and songs of thanksgiving to God and Christ would be appropriate.   (3) Poems composed and set to music by church members, poems which teach great Scriptural truths, are appropriate also.

3:17 –   *And whatever you do in word or deed, do all in the name of the Lord Jesus, giving thanks through Him to God the Father.*

And whatever you do in word or deed – Here Paul gives us a kind of summary exhortation which covers every aspect in life.   "'Whatever you do' is a contrast to the many specific rules and regulations which the false teachers were trying to impose on the Colossians (2:16-23).   Paul simply enunciates a comprehensive principle, and permits believers to work it out for themselves in perfect freedom."[63]   "This does not apply to what we do in church only,   but to whatso-

---

[61] There is a manuscript variation showing two readings (*en te chariti* or *en chariti*) and which is most likely the original reading is not certain.

[62] Pliny, *Epistle* x.97.

[63] Hendriksen, *op. cit.*, p.164.

ever we do.   This means in our work places, in our homes, in our leisure time, in our reading, in our purchases, in our payment of our debts, in our commitments, in our fellowship – in whatever we do."[64]

Do **all in the name of the Lord Jesus** – The Christian life is not so much regulated as it is motivated.   Perhaps Goodspeed got "in the name of the Lord Jesus" right when he translated it to mean "as followers of the Lord Jesus."   This interpretation reflects the thought that to act in the name of a person is to act as his representative.   While the New Testament does contain certain imperative verbs addressed to the Christian, it does not contain a detailed code of rules for the Christian.   "What the New Testament does provide is those basic principles of Christian living which may be applied to all situations of life as they arise."[65] The words Paul just wrote enunciate one of those principles.[66]   "Lord Jesus" speaks of His preeminence in relation to the entire universe (just as did 1:3-23 and 3:11).

Giving thanks through Him to God the Father – This is one of the several emphases on thanksgiving in Colossians (Colossians 1:12, 2:7, 3:15, 4:2).   The prayers of thanksgiving were to be offered to God in His character as Father (see Colossians 1:2, 3, 12).[67]   The Colossians are directed to offer their thanksgivings through Jesus, rather than through angelic mediators whom the deceptive teachers were suggesting as mediators.   The Lord Jesus is the One by whom we have access to the Father (Romans 5:1,2; Ephesians 2:18, 3:12; Hebrews 10:19-22) and from whom we receive all the benefits of redemption (Romans 3:24-26; Ephesians 2:5-10; Colossians 1:14; Titus 3:4-7).   "As the Christian exercises his or her liberty, the believer should ask, 'Am I able to thank God the Father for having given me the opportunity to say or do this?'"[68]

---

[64] Knofel Staton, *Standard Lesson Commentary 1992-93* (Cincinnati, OH: Standard, 1992), p.398.

[65] Bruce, *op. cit.,* p.285.

[66] Paul's 1 Corinthian letter also contains a series of principles by which specific matters, which are neither commanded nor prohibited, may be decided.

[67] The KJV reads "to God and the Father" but the word "and" is not well supported in the manuscripts, perhaps being interpolated from Ephesians 5:20.

[68] Bruce, *op. cit.* p.286.

It is likely that the following verses give concrete examples of applying the principle just laid down in verse 17, examples of how life in Christ may be expressed in everyday affairs.

C. Special Exhortations. Family Relationships to be Strengthened. 3:18-4:1

Summary: The Christian home is a special place where "doing all in the name of the Lord Jesus" (verse 17) can be practiced by each Christian – husbands and wives, children and parents, servants and masters. The instructions here given are not in as much detail as found in the parallel passage in Ephesians 5:22 - 6:9.

What we have here is a kind of "table of household duties" or simply "house-table" (German, *haustafel*)[69] or "household instructions" (*haustafeln*). Such codes of conduct existed in many ancient cultures alongside public law. However, the critical notion "that the New Testament writers merely copied such tables and coated them with a thin veneer of Christianity – merely (!) adding "in Christ" – misses the point entirely. Between these pithy directives as presented in the New Testament and the maxims of the Stoics and other moral philosophers, there is, indeed, at times, a superficial resemblance, but there are several main differences."[70] "In contrast to Jewish and pagan teaching, Paul emphasizes the mutuality of rights and responsibilities. A second Christian distinctive is the motivation urged upon the reader. The Christian is motivated by his relationship to Christ, and his responsibility to God (e.g., 3:18,20,22-25)."[71] From the fact that similar lists occur elsewhere in Paul and Peter (see Ephesians 5:22-6:9; 1 Peter 2:18-3:7; 1 Timothy 2:8-15, 6:1-2; Titus 2:1-10), we may think such instruc-

---

[69] Ever since Martin Luther's German translation of the Bible (first completed edition, 1534), in which this section and its parallel in Ephesians 5:22-6:9 appeared under the caption, *"Die christliche Haustafel,"* these and similar passages (1 Peter 2:18-3:7) have been labeled by scholars as "Christian household codes."

[70] Hendriksen, *op. cit.*, p.167.

[71] E.E. Ellis, "Colossians" in the *Wycliffe Bible Commentary*, edited by Charles F. Pfeiffer and Everett F. Harrison (Chicago: Moody Press, 1962), p.1344.

tions were given to new converts by all Christian teachers, the heart of the instructions coming from the Lord Jesus Himself and His apostles.   Given their wording, they easily could have been learned by heart as they were given to new converts.

1. Wives and husbands.   3:18,19

3:18 *–Wives, be subject to your husbands, as is fitting in the Lord.*

Wives, be subject to your husbands – The mental picture is that this letter is being read in the public assembly, and the folk addressed are in the audience, listening.   This admonition ("be subject" is a middle voice verb in the Greek) calls for voluntary submission.   Wives are free and responsible agents who can make their own decisions while recognizing their own husband as the leader in the family.[72]   There is a divinely instituted hierarchy in the order of creation, and in this order the place of the wife comes next after that of her husband (1 Corinthians 11:3,7-9).

As is fitting in the Lord – Paul is giving this as the reason why Christian wives should be submissive to their husbands.   "In the Lord" means the Christian wife's relation to her husband is determined by her status "as a Christian," which is what the Greek prepositional phrase "in the Lord" means.   The verb translated "is fitting" is literally "was fitting;" it is an imperfect tense in the Greek and it implies that such submission has been fitting since the time of the wife's entrance upon the Christian life.[73]   Other passages in Scripture teach the same truth here being expressed (cf. Genesis 3:16; 1 Corinthians 14:34,35; Ephesians 5:22-24; 1 Timothy 2:11-15; Titus 2:5; 1 Peter 3:1-6).

3:19 – *Husbands, love your wives, and do not be embittered against them.*

Husbands, love your wives – Paul gives two ways the Christian husband may demonstrate he is doing all in the name of Jesus.   Stated positively, the husband is to love his wife.[74]   "Love" is *agapao*, which involves active and unceasing care

---

[72] While the better manuscripts here do not read "your *own* husbands," Ephesians 5:22 does, and 1 Corinthians 7:2 is the apostolic prohibition of polygamy.

[73] The imperfect tense does not necessarily contain a criticism as though the obligation had not been fulfilled by the wives at Colossae.

[74] The *Bible Translator's Handbook* warns "unless the translation is carefully worded, it may in some languages suggest that a husband should have more than one wife."   This would not be what Christianity teaches.

for her well-being, especially her spiritual well-being. The parallel passage in Ephesians 5:25-32 shows how Christ's love is an archetype of the husband's love for his wife.

And do not be embittered against them – Negatively, Paul tells husbands they cannot be doing all in the name of Jesus and at the same time be harsh or exasperated with their wives. To fulfill this command about no harsh treatment or cross tones will take self-control on the part of the husband. Out of the heart, whether there is bitterness or sweetness there, will come actions and attitudes toward the wife.

2. Children and their parents. 3:20,21

3:20 – *Children, be obedient to your parents in all things, for this is well-pleasing to the Lord.*

Children, be obedient to your parents in all things – Compared with Ephesians 6:1-4, there is greater brevity and simplicity here in Colossians concerning the topic of parents and children. Since the mental image is that this letter is being read in the public assembly, the children (both males and females) addressed are old enough to be responsible members of the congregation. "Parents" makes no distinction between father and mother; both are to receive obedience. This admonition is completely in harmony with Scripture elsewhere (e.g., Exodus 20:12; Proverbs 1:8; Matthew 15:4-6; Ephesians 6:1-3). "Be obedient" (*hupakouete*, a present tense meaning to habitually obey) is the one obligation Paul places upon children. The word implies a "readiness to hear and carry out orders; the child is to listen to and carry out the instructions of his or her parents,"[75] and to be submissive to discipline. "All things" states the principle, while "possible exceptional cases obviously come under the principle of obeying God rather than man."[76] "Disobedience to parents is one of the vices of paganism (Romans 1:30). It marks the ever-increasing wickedness of 'the last days' (2 Timothy 3:2)."[77]

---

[75] Vaughn, *op. cit.*, p.218.

[76] Meyer, *op. cit.*, p.369.

[77] Hendriksen, *op. cit.*, p.170.

For this is well-pleasing to the Lord – The oldest manuscripts read "in the Lord" and likely says that obedience is well-pleasing to God when the children do so because they are Christians ("in the Lord").[78] "Although in an extreme case a young person may have to choose Christ's will in opposition to that of non-Christian parents (cf. Luke 14:26), this course should be taken only after sober thought and Christian counseling."[79] Under the Law of Moses, disobedience to parents was looked at as also being disobedience to God (Exodus 20:12, 21:17; Leviticus 19:3, 20:9; Deuteronomy 5:16).

3:21 – *Fathers, do not exasperate your children, that they may not lose heart.*

Fathers, do not exasperate your children – The Greek construction (a present imperative with *mē*) prohibits the continuance of an action already going on. "Stop exasperating your children." The specific mention of "fathers" likely reflects the fact that the father is head of the household and thus has a special responsibility for training the children.[80] "Fathers should create an atmosphere which will make obedience an easy and natural matter, namely, the atmosphere of love and confidence."[81] Praise for well-doing is as much a part of discipline as is pointing out the wrong done. The verb translated "exasperate" is *erethizete*, meaning "stir up."[82] One can stir up for good (2 Corinthians 9:2) or for evil (as in this prohibition). The sense here is that Fathers "are not to challenge the resistance of their children by their unreasonable exercise of authority. Firm discipline may be necessary, but it must be administered in the right spirit. Par-

---

[78] It probably does not say that children must obey only when their parents are Christians ("in the Lord").

[79] Ellis, *ibid.*

[80] "The possibility that the word 'fathers' here has the meaning of 'parents' must be granted (see also Hebrews 11:23). However, the fact that in the preceding verse the more usual word for *parents* is used would rather seem to indicate that in the present passage 'fathers' means just that. Though the responsibility for the education of the children rests on both parents, and the father will consult mother, the probability is that the father is here regarded as the head of the family" (Hendriksen, *op. cit.*, p.172).

[81] Hendriksen, *op. cit.*, p.172.

[82] The manuscripts behind the KJV have *parogizete* ("provoke to anger") instead of *erethizete* ("embitter"), but it is an inferior reading, likely borrowed from Ephesians 6:4 where it is genuine. The Greek word *erethizo* is as old as Homer (*Iliad*, i.32; iv.5) who almost always uses it of provocation to combat.

ents should not give in to fault-finding, nor always be nagging their children."[83]
One of the striking features of these household instructions is their reciprocal
character. Both children and fathers have responsibilities. The same is true for
both husbands and wives, slaves and masters.

That they may not lose heart – This is the reason Paul gives for his counsel to
fathers. The Greek word (*athumeo*) has in it the idea of "losing heart" and
suggests going about in "a listless, moody, sullen frame of mind."[84] "Parents can
be so exacting, so demanding, or so severe that they create within their children
the feeling that it is impossible for them to please."[85] "The children lose heart,
thinking 'No matter what I do, it's always wrong.' There should be no nagging,
no constant 'Don't do this' and 'Don't do that' ... A good father spends time with
his children, teaches, entertains, and encourages them, and by his example as well
as by outright, verbal instruction, points them to Christ."[86]

3. Slaves and their masters.   3:22 - 4:1

3:22 – *Slaves, in all things obey those who are your masters on earth, not with
external service, as those who merely please men, but with sincerity of heart,
fearing the Lord.*

Slaves, in all things obey those who are your masters on earth – Since this
letter was to be publicly read to the congregation, we gather that both slaves and
slave owners were present among the assembled believers. They, too, were part
of ancient households, so we are continuing the household instructions, all of
which are intended as examples of how believers were to "do all in the name of
the Lord" (verse 17). The verb tense calls for habitual obedience. As was true
in Ephesians 5:5-9, here the instructions to slaves are given in much more detail
than are instructions to wives, husbands, parents, and children. "Both here and
in Ephesians the injunctions to slaves are more extended than those to masters,
and are accompanied by special encouragements. This is likely a reflection of

---

[83] Vaughn, *op. cit.,* p.219.

[84] Lightfoot, *op. cit.,* p.227.

[85] Vaughn, *ibid.*

[86] Hendriksen, *ibid.* Of course, there are times when "Don't" is the proper word, just as
there are times when "Do" is the proper word.

the social structure of those churches."[87]   Also, Paul's knowledge that Onesimus, the runaway and returning slave, would be present in the congregation when this letter was read out loud, may have suggested to him to write this peculiar emphasis on the right relation between the slave and his master.[88]   "When Paul instructs slaves to obey their masters 'in all things,' he probably means 'not only in matters pleasant and agreeable but also in matters unpleasant and disagreeable.' He cannot have meant, in *absolutely* all things."[89]   When men, slave or free, are given orders by one in authority that would require disobedience to God, the Christian's duty is to obey God (see Acts 5:29).

Not with external service, as those who merely please men – The word *ophthalmodouleias* ("external service," service performed when the master is watching, simply to catch his eye for selfish purposes[90]) is plural in the Greek, and "very aptly describes a slave's repeated acts, a long series of deceitful and imperfect service."[91]   The service of the Christian slave was to be as conscientiously and sincerely rendered in the master's absence as in his presence.[92]

But with sincerity of heart, fearing the Lord – "The Lord" is here the Lord Jesus Christ.[93]   "Sincerity of heart" translates *en haploteti kardias*, "a phrase that implies the absence of all base and self-seeking motives."[94]   Slaves render service to their earthly masters as has   been here commanded because they have

---

[87] Bruce, *op. cit.*, p.293.

[88] Instead of the usual word for a slave master (*despotes*), both here and in Ephesians 6:5 Paul uses the word *kurios* for "master."   The words translated by the NASB as "on earth" are the same words translated "according to the flesh" at Ephesians 6:5.

[89] Hendriksen, *op. cit.*, p.173.

[90] The word "external service" occurs only here and at Ephesians 6:6.   It may have been coined by Paul.

[91] W. Alexander, "Colossians" in *The Bible Commentary*, edited by F.C. Cook (New York: Charles Scribner's Sons, 1886), p.679.

[92] Recall that as we studied Ephesians we spoke of employees rather than slaves, in order to make 21st century application of these principles.

[93] Some manuscripts read "God" as does the KJV.

[94] Vaughn, *op. cit.*, p.220.

reverence for Christ, Who expects His followers to act in this way. Reverence for the Lord, not fear of an earthly master, should be the primary motive for service. The eyes of the Lord are always upon the Christian, even during an earthly master's absence.

3:23 – *Whatever you do, do your work heartily, as for the Lord rather than for men;*

Whatever you do, do your work heartily – Two different Greek words are translated "do" in the English text: "Whatever you do (*poieō*), do (*ergazomai*) it." The first "do" (*poieō*) refers to the mere doing of something, i.e., a reference to daily tasks the slave had to do. The second "do" is a more energetic word than the first word. *Ergazomai* means, "to labor, do work, to carry it out, do it diligently." It is the opposite of indolent or half-hearted. "Heartily" (literally "from the soul"[95]) means put your soul into the work, with honest dedication. Give every task the best that you have.

As for the Lord rather than for men – Do each task like you were doing it for Jesus, to please Him. Such an attitude will transform the most menial jobs and give dignity to all of their work. What outsiders will think of Christ and Christianity is directly related to the quality of the Christian slave's service. In spirit, people cease to be slaves when they begin to work for the Lord, and no longer are simply doing their work for their earthly masters only.

3:24 – *knowing that from the Lord you will receive the reward of the inheritance. It is the Lord Christ whom you serve.*

Knowing that from the Lord you will receive the reward of the inheritance – "From the Lord" stands first in the Greek for emphasis. "Inheritance" stands last in the Greek for secondary emphasis. The heavenly inheritance has already been introduced at Colossians 1:12. The language "inheritance" may come from the Old Testament promised land where Israelites were granted a portion or place on which to live. In this world slaves are seldom heirs; only a son could be an heir (Genesis 21:10; Romans 8:15-17; Galatians 4:7). The slave may get no earthly inheritance from his earthly master, but the participle "knowing" encourages the Christian slave to constantly keep this fact in mind, namely, that

---

[95] Paul has used both "heart" (verse 22) and "soul" (verse 23) to describe the inward motivation of the Christian slave. "Soul" implies more than heart. The Christian slave puts his heart and soul into his work, and he does it with "good will" (Ephesians 6:7).

the faithful 'slave' of Christ will receive a son's portion of the eternal inheritance. That is the reason he works heartily for the Lord.[96]   "Receive" which translates *apolempsesthe*, and "reward" which translates *antapodosin*, together combine the ideas of receiving what is due and receiving in full.   The inheritance is the reward.

It is the Lord Christ whom you serve – This clause serves as a succinct summary of the Christian duty of slaves who would work hard as for the Lord and not for men (verse 23).[97]   Paul wants the slaves who are Christians ever to remember that they are really serving the Lord Christ, not just an earthly master.   The expression "Lord Christ" is found only one other time in the New Testament, and that in a similar context contrasting earthly lords with the Lord (see Romans 16:18).   The Messiah Jesus, the Lord of heaven and earth, is the slave's employer.[98]   What a privilege and honor!

3:25 – *For he who does wrong will receive the consequences of the wrong which he has done, and that without partiality.*

For he who does wrong – "For" indicates a reason why the Christian slave should obey these instructions.   If he does not, he is doing wrong, and wrongdoers will be punished by the Lord.   "He" who does the wrong in this context is clearly the slave, but in Ephesians 6:9 similar language refers to the master.[99]   It would be doing wrong to give only eyeservice (verse 22) to the earthly master.

Will receive the consequences of the wrong which he has done – The Lord's judgment on disobedience is as certain as His reward for faithfulness.   "Receive" (*komizomai*, to carry off) speaks of what is true after the final judgment.   The habitual wrong doer will carry off some heavy consequences for his misdeeds.

---

[96] The Bible regularly indicates that judgment is according to works (habitually doing what the Lord says) – e.g., Matthew 7:20;   Romans 2:6-10;   2 Corinthians 5:10;   Revelation 20:12,13.

[97] In the KJV this clause begins with a "for," but the word is not found in the best manuscripts.   Its addition causes this clause to lose its summary force.

[98] Earlier in this passage (verse 22) *kurios* was used of the slave's earthly master.   Twice here in verse 24 the word *kurios* ("Lord") is used of Jesus the Messiah.

[99] If such a warning can refer both to slave and master, why can it not also refer to husbands and wives, and fathers and children?

And that without partiality – It is noteworthy that here the statement "without partiality" ("there is no respect of persons") is attached to the warning to slaves, whereas in Ephesians 6:9 it is attached to the warning to masters. Wrong, even though done by a slave, will be punished because there is no favoritism with the Lord.[100]

---

[100] "The entire passage about the duty of slaves (verses 22-25) may seem completely irrelevant in our day. It contains, however, an enduring principle. Christians, whatever their work, are, like slaves in Paul's day, to see it as a service rendered to the Lord. This is what motivates them to give honest, faithful, ungrudging work in return for the pay they receive. Moreover, it imparts a sense of dignity in work, regardless of how unimportant it may seem" (Vaughn, *op. cit.*, p.220).

4:1 – *Masters, grant to your slaves justice and fairness, knowing that you too have a Master in heaven.*

Masters, grant to your slaves justice and fairness – This verse brings to a close the household instructions which began at 3:18. It would therefore have been better to have made the chapter break after this verse, since it contains the master's responsibilities toward his slaves. Just as there were reciprocal responsibilities in the other household instructions, here are the master's responsibilities to his slaves. The mental image is that this letter is being read in the public assembly, so the masters being addressed are Christians. Slaves have been urged to follow a Christian work ethic as they serve their masters. Masters, too, have a Christian ethic to follow. The word translated "grant" (*parechō*) suggests deliberate care and personal involvement on the master's part. Masters are to grant their slaves what is just, be it food (Proverbs 31:15), or wages (James 5:4), or the amount of work expected, neither too much (Proverbs 12:10), nor too little (Proverbs 29:21). Masters are also to grant to their slaves "fairness." The word is *isotēta*, which literally means "equality." It likely refers to the fact that the Christian slave is to be treated by his master as a brother in Christ.[1]

Knowing that you too have a Master in heaven – In language nearly verbatim with Ephesians 6:9, Paul gives a reason why the Master should grant to slaves justice and fairness. This reminder that human masters must recognize they have a heavenly Master brings to mind Jesus' teaching in His Sermon on the Mount, "For in the way you judge, you will be judged; and by your standard of measure, it shall be measured to you" (Matthew 7:2). It is to the Lord that Christian masters are accountable for how they treat their slaves. If earthly masters expect justice and fairness when they stand before their heavenly Master in the final judgment, they should grant justice and fairness to the fellow men on earth. Here we have application of the Golden Rule (Matthew 7:12) to the master-slave relationship.

D. Final Words of Encouragement Concerning Religious Duties to be Faithfully Performed.   4:2-6

1. **Persistent prayer.   4:2-4**

---

[1] Vincent (*op. cit.*, p.917) made this comment: "Literally, *the equality*. Not equality of condition, but the brotherly equality growing out of the Christian relation, in which there is neither bond nor free." Even if the slave was not a Christian brother, that fact "was no justification for harsh or unjust treatment. A man who is genuinely Christian cannot exploit or take advantage of another man" (Guy Leavitt, *Adult Teacher's Commentary 1958* [Cincinnati: Standard, 1957], p.307).

4:2 – *Devote yourselves to prayer, keeping alert in it with* **an attitude of thanksgiving;**

Devote yourselves to prayer – Verses 2-4 are almost an exact parallel to Ephesians 6:18-20. *Proskartereite* ("devote," or "continue," KJV) in this passage implies persistence in prayer.[2]   Jesus taught His disciples to persevere in prayer and not to lose heart when one's petitions are not immediately answered (Luke 18:1-8).

Keeping alert in it with *an attitude of* **thanksgiving** – It is difficult to know precisely what "keeping alert" means. Perhaps what Paul has in mind is that, "while continuing in prayer, the worshiper will be alive/alert to such matters as: (a) his own needs and those of the family, church, country, world;   (b) the dangers that threaten the Christian community;   (c) the blessings received and promised; and   (d) the will of God."[3]   A soldier on sentry duty must deliberately keep alert. Perhaps the language suggests that prayer is not something that will occur automatically, but rather is something that will have to be undertaken deliberately, just as keeping awake on sentry duty requires deliberateness. The prayers of the Christian should be characterized by a spirit of thankfulness (see on Colossians 1:12). "Our enemy's activity should not make us forget what God has already given us.   When we pray with thanksgiving, we make requests with confidence, remembering how richly God has blessed us in the past."[4]

4:3 – *praying at the same time for us as well, that God may open up to us a door for the word, so that we may speak forth the mystery of Christ, for which I have also been imprisoned;*

Praying at the same time for us as well – Verse 3 is a continuation of the sentence which began with verse 2. It will conclude with verse 4. "At the same time" means that as the Colossians offer up prayers to God (verse 2) they should include the needs of Paul and his companions.[5]   In Ephesians 6:18,19, Paul asked for the readers' prayers not only for themselves but also for all the saints and for

---

[2] "Prayer" translates the general word for prayer, *proseuche*. See Trench, *Synonyms*, p.188.

[3] Hendriksen, *op. cit.*, p.179.

[4] Weatherly, *op. cit.*, p.219.

[5] "Us" certainly includes both Paul and Timothy (cp. Colossians 1:1), if not also Paul's other companions (Colossians 4:10,11) and even Epaphras (Colossians 4:12).

him (Ephesians 6:18).   Here, Paul's requests prayers for himself and his associates that all of them might have opportunities for witnessing.

That God may open up to us a door for the word – This *hina* clause gives the content of the prayer which He wants them to pray.   The apostle wants them to keep asking God to give him another opportunity (the metaphor of an open door) to proclaim the Christian message.   Philippians 1:12-14, which we judge was written after this letter to the Colossians asking for their prayers, indicates that this prayer for opportunities was answered in a positive way.

So that we may speak forth the mystery of Christ – When Paul wrote these words he was a prisoner in Rome.   When he spoke of an "open door," he was not asking that the doors be opened and he be released from his imprisonment.   No, he wanted that open door right here and now even while he was still being held as a prisoner!   Acts 28:30,31 shows us he did have opportunities to teach, with no one hindering him.   What Paul wants is opportunity to preach "the mystery of Christ;"[6] he wants opportunities to unfold God's eternal plan hidden in earlier ages, but now revealed in Christ.

For which I have also been imprisoned – Colossians 4:18 tells us Paul was in chains.   He was not being held as a prisoner because he was a criminal.   He was imprisoned because of preaching Christ Jesus as Lord, i.e., the gospel, especially to the Gentiles.   This had infuriated certain powerful Jewish leaders who, after having arrested him in a mob action, made false accusations against him before Roman authorities, accusations which resulted in his continuing imprisonment (Acts 21:17-28:30).

4:4 – *in order that I may make it clear in the way I ought to speak.*

In order that I may make it clear in the way I ought to speak – This specific request concerning their prayers for him is similar to the request in Ephesians 6:20.   Not only does he want them to pray for an open door (opportunities to preach) but he also wants them to pray that he may speak with all possible clarity. The "it" which he wishes to make clear is the "mystery of Christ" (verse 3), the mystery of redemption in Christ especially for the Gentiles.   Weed has suggested that behind this second request may have been Paul's particular concern with his coming defense before Roman judges, at which time, since so much might hang on the way he made his defense, it is his desire that he make it clear to the judges

---

[6] On "mystery," see Colossians 1:26,27, 2:2; and Ephesians 1:9 and 3:4,6.

the message he, as an ambassador of Christ, was bound to speak.[7] Or, perhaps, Paul is asking that he will be inspired to speak in a way that is equal to the greatness of the message.

2. Behavior toward non-Christians. 4:5,6

a. A winsome walk. 5

4:5 – *Conduct yourselves with wisdom toward outsiders, making the most of the opportunity.*

Conduct yourselves with wisdom toward outsiders – Paul has just asked for their prayers for his speaking when in the presence of non-Christians. Now he turns to his readers, in order to suggest that they are to behave in a similar manner when dealing with non-Christians. The verb translated "conduct yourselves" is *peripateō*, "to walk, to order one's behavior."[8] It is an imperative verb; this is a command. "Outsiders" is the technical term for persons outside the body of the church, outside of the kingdom of God or heaven.[9] Jesus Himself explained that habitually doing the will of God is necessary if one would enter the kingdom. He said, "Not everyone who says to Me, 'Lord, Lord,' will enter the kingdom of heaven, but he who does the will of My Father who is in heaven *will enter*" (Matthew 7:21). What is involved in "with wisdom" has been unfolded in detail in Ephesians 5:3-16. Do nothing that will disgrace Christianity in the eyes of the outsiders.[10] "Paul's words imply that believers are to be cautious and tactful so as to avoid needlessly antagonizing or alienating their pagan neighbors."[11] If Christians will make their lifestyles winsome and attractive, unbelievers may respond to the gospel and become insiders.

---

[7] Weed, *op. cit.,* p.99.

[8] See notes on "walk" at Colossians 1:10, 2:6, and 3:7.

[9] See 1 Corinthians 5:12,13; 1 Thessalonians 4:12; and 1 Timothy 3:7 for other passages where non-Christians are designated as "outsiders."

[10] "Outsiders judge Christianity, not from preaching, nor from books, nor from the conduct of its Founder and His apostles, but from what they see in the daily walk and conversation of the members of the church" (Albert Barnes, "Colossians" in *Barnes' Notes on the New Testament* [Grand Rapids: Baker, 1955], p.282).

[11] Vaughn, *op. cit.,* p.222.

Making the most of the opportunity – Paul here employs a figure of speech from the mercantile world. The Greek literally translated is *"buying up* the opportunity."[12] The picture is of a merchant who does not wait for an opportunity for making a profit to fall into his lap.[13] Instead, he eagerly looks for and goes after such opportunities. Likewise, the Christian looks for opportunities for making a good impression and witnessing to outsiders. Every Christian is encouraged, when he has his opportunity to witness, to use it to the full while the opportunity lasts.

b. Gracious speech. 6

4:6 – *Let your speech always be with grace, seasoned,* **as it were,** *with salt, so that you may know how you should respond to each person.*

Let your speech always be with grace – In this context, our translators have correctly supplied the imperative verb "let it be." Paul was concerned for his own speech (verse 4), and he was concerned for the speech of his readers as their opportunities to speak come and go. Paul is still continuing his exhortation about relations with non-Christians. Just what is meant by *en chariti* (translated "with grace") is not totally clear. Perhaps it means to use words that make God's grace known to the hearers. Perhaps it speaks of words that are not abusive, abrasive, or vindictive, but rather pleasant, attractive, winsome, courteous. "Note '*always*,' that is, gracious speech should be used both in addressing a group or in talking to a neighbor, both when conversing with an equal or when replying to someone in authority, to rich and poor alike, not only in proclaiming the message of salvation but also in discussing the weather."[14]

Seasoned, *as it were,* **with salt** – Like salt makes meat more savory, ancient Greek and Latin authors used "salt" as a metaphor to designate the wit and liveliness that gives zest and an agreeable flavor to one's words. "What you say and the way you say it should always cause people to be pleased and interested."[15] Perhaps what Paul penned in   Ephesians 4:29 is a good commentary: "Let no

---

[12] The Greek word translated "opportunity" is *kairos*, which essentially denotes a significant point or moment in time; in contrast, duration of time is the idea in the Greek word *chronos*.

[13] It may be appropriate to recall the parables of the hidden treasure and pearl of great price in Matthew 13.

[14] Hendriksen, *op. cit.*, p.183.

[15] Bratcher, *op. cit.*, p.101.

unwholesome word proceed from your mouth, but only such a word as is good for edification according to the need of the moment, so that it will give grace to those who hear."

So that you may know how you should respond to each person – "To each person" is *heni hekasto,* meaning each single person. The conversation of Christians must not only be "opportune as regards the time; it must also be appropriate as regards the person being addressed."[16]   Findlay has expressed the reasons why the Colossians needed to cultivate the kind of speech verse 6 has asked for.

> For their faith was assailed by persuasive sophistry (Colossians 2:4, 8, 23) and by brow-beating dogmatism (Colossians 2:16, 18, 20, 21).   They were, like St. Paul, "set for the defence of the gospel," placed in the van of the conflict against heresy.   They needed, therefore, "to have all their wits about them," so as to be able, as occasion required, to make answer to each of their opponents and questioners, that they might "contend" wisely as well as "earnestly for the faith." 1 Peter 3:15 is a commentary on this verse: the parallelism is the closer because that Epistle was addressed to Churches in Asia Minor, where the debates out of which Gnosticism arose were beginning to be rife; and because, likewise, "the hope that was in them" was a chief object of the attack made on the Colossian believers (Colossians 1:5, 23, 27; Colossians 2:18; Colossians 3:15).[17]

V. PERSONAL SECTION. 4:7-17

The body of the letter, in which Paul has met head-on the false teachers threatening the church at Colossae, has now been completed. He has given a masterful exposition of the preeminence of Jesus Christ. On the foundation he laid in chapter 1, Paul has denounced the false and pernicious "philosophy" being taught by some in the Lycus valley. In place of the taboos of that system, Paul has presented the lofty ethics and the Christian life the "new self" should live, even giving examples of how Christianity's teachings strengthen family relationships, and how Christians are to relate to those on the outside. Now in the final portion of the letter, he gives some information about the messengers who will carry this letter to Colossae, then a series of personal greetings from some of his associates, along with some instructions to exchange letters with the

---

[16] Lightfoot, *Colossians*, p.233.

[17] Findlay, *op. cit.*, pp. 210,211.

church at Laodicea, a word to Archippus, and then ending with a concluding signature, exhortation, and benediction.

A. The Mission of Tychicus and Onesimus.   4:7-9

4:7 – *As to all my affairs, Tychicus,* **our** *beloved brother and faithful servant and fellow bond-servant in the Lord, will bring you information.*

As to all my affairs, Tychicus – The reference to Tychicus in verses 7-8 presents an almost word for word similarity with Ephesians 6:21,22.[18]   Evidently, he was the bearer of both the letters to the Colossians and to the Ephesians.   For what we know concerning Tychicus see the comments at Ephesians 6:21.   "All my affairs" is a verbal report of what has been happening to Paul, and how he was doing.   The same expression occurs at Philippians 1:12.

Our **beloved brother and faithful servant and fellow bond-servant in the Lord** – These words of commendation of Tychicus (verses 7,8) and Onesimus (verse 9) are given to ensure their welcome by the Colossian church.   "Beloved brother" shows that Tychicus was a fellow Christian known and loved by the church at Colossae.[19]   "Faithful servant" (*pistos diakonos*) may identify him as a loyal servant of Christ, or it may refer to his relationship to Paul (he is, as Weymouth renders it, a "trusted assistant"), or Paul may have reference to his service to the churches.   If it has the same sense the word did when applied to Epaphras (Colossians 1:7), Paul is putting Tychicus on an equal footing with Epaphras; both men have the interests of the congregation in mind as they carry out Paul's wishes toward the congregation.   "Fellow bond-servant" speaks of Tychicus as a bond-servant of Christ,   just as was Epaphras (Colossians 1:7).[20]

---

[18] "Remembering that the two epistles were sent at the same time, and that Ephesus was a church far better known than Colossae, we cannot but regard this as supporting the idea that Ephesians was an encyclical letter" (Barry, *op. cit.*, p.58).

[19] The article "the" before "beloved brother" in the Greek indicates Tychicus is well known to the Colossians.

[20] This commentator has been hesitant, on the basis of the term "fellow bond-servant," to accord to certain individuals named in the New Testament the title of "apostolic assistant" or "apostolic delegate."   While recognizing the temporary offices of apostle and prophet in the early church (Ephesians 4:11), and the permanent offices of evangelist, elder (pastoring- teacher), and deacon in the church, he has been hesitant to accept the idea of an elaborate hierarchy of leadership this early in the history of the church.   Lightfoot *(op. cit.,* p.234) has called attention to the fact that in the post-apostolic church the term "fellow bond-servant" became the customary form of address from a bishop to a deacon.   He thinks that the use of the term here and in Colossians 1:7 is an interesting evidence of the birth and growth of language later used when such a hierarchy had developed.

The prefix "fellow" before "bond-servant" declares Paul's sense that he and they were united in the work of the Lord.

Will bring you information – Tychicus would convey information not contained in the letter he was carrying to Colossae about what has happened to Paul recently, and doubtless would interpret the letter to the recipients, answering any questions they might have.   It will be remembered that under the Roman empire there were no postal establishments for carrying private letters with regularity, so such letters had to be sent by private individuals.[21]   So letter carriers and word-of-mouth communication were important in the early church.

4:8 – *For I have sent him to you for this very purpose, that you may know* **about** *our circumstances and that he may encourage your hearts;*

For I have sent him to you for this very purpose – "I have sent" is an episto-lary aorist, which is best translated by an English present tense, "whom I am sending."   Tychicus carried this letter.   Perhaps the wording indicates that Tychicus had been given specific directions to include Colossae in his itinerary.   In the following clauses, Paul explains the purpose he had in mind for sending Tychicus to Colossae.

That you may know *about* our circumstances – Other possible readings here include "that he may know about your circumstances"[22] and "that I may know about your circumstances."[23]   The reading "that you may know about us" may have crept in from Ephesians 6:22.   If it is what Paul originally wrote to Colos-

---

[21] Alexander, *op. cit.,* p.682, gives ancient documentation about how private letters had to be sent by individuals.

[22] This is the reading found in P[46].   The reading "that you may know about our circumstances" (NASB) is the reading found in A, B, D* (corrected), and in some Old Latin manuscripts.   To have verse 8 read "that you may know about our circumstances" would make three verses in a row where Paul spoke of their knowing about his circumstances.   This may be evidence that one of the other readings is to be preferred here in verse 8.

[23] This is the reading found in Codex Claromontanus, the Latin Vulgate and Syriac versions, and in the Textus Receptus, and was the reading preferred by Tischendorf.   The difference between "he may know" (γνῷ) and "I may know" (γνῶ) is the presence or absence of an iota subscript in the Greek.

sae, it would indicate Paul was anxious to alleviate any anxiety the Colossians may have had about his welfare. If "that he may know about your circumstances" is what Paul originally wrote, it would indicate an apprehension on Paul's part that circumstances at Colossae may have changed between the time Epaphras left for Rome to consult with Paul and the time Tychicus arrives at Colossae with this letter. If "that I may know about your circumstances" is what Paul originally wrote, it implies that Tychicus is to report back to Paul concerning what he finds the circumstances of the church to be. Paul has earlier indicated his deep concern for the faithfulness of the Colossians (Colossians 2:1). Just as Paul had learned the state of the Thessalonians through Timothy (1 Thessalonians 3:6); of the state of the Corinthians through Titus (2 Corinthians 7:6,13); of the state of the Philippians through Epaphroditus (Philippians 4:18); so did Paul especially wish to learn about how things were with the church at Colossae.

And that he may encourage your hearts – This clause gives a second purpose for which Tychicus had been sent to Colossae. If the reading "that you may know about our circumstances" was original, then these words mean if the Colossians might tend to be discouraged when they hear of Paul's circumstances, Tychicus is to encourage them. If one of the other readings was original, then Tychicus' mission was that of impressing the apostle's teaching on the congregation in order to strengthen them. (See the notes about encouragement at Colossians 2:2.)

4:9 – *and with him Onesimus,* **our** *faithful and beloved brother, who is one of your* **number.** *They will inform you about the whole situation here.*

And with him Onesimus – Since it is connected with the verb "I have sent" (verse 8), what this clause means is that Onesimus is accompanying Tychicus. He is the same person named in the letter to Philemon.[24] Why Onesimus is also bound

---

[24] Onesimus, who is named in several of Paul's letters, has been suggested as the one who first made a collection of the Pauline corpus of letters (cf. John Knox, *Philemon Among the Letters of Paul* [Chicago, 1935], p.98ff). In this commentator's judgment, instead of Onesimus being the collector, Lewis A. Foster's suggestion is more likely correct, namely, that Luke is the one who made the first collection of Paul's letters (cf. Lewis A. Foster, *Seminary Review* XIV:2 [1963], pp.41-56).

for Colossae, we may learn in detail from the epistle to Philemon, verses 10-20.

***Our* faithful and beloved brother** – By calling Onesimus "our faithful and beloved brother" the apostle emphasizes before the entire congregation what he wrote in verse 16 of his personal letter to Philemon. Whatever Onesimus was when he ran away, the returning runaway slave is now a brother in Christ.

Who is one of your *number* – The Greek reads "one of you," with the "you" being plural. It means Onesimus was from their city, he was a fellow-Colossian. If "you" refers to the Christian readers of this letter, then here is an affirmation that Onesimus is now a fellow Christian. Hendriksen has offered the idea that this line was "meant to be a powerful support for the plea on Onesimus' behalf which Paul addressed to Philemon, the slave's master, who also was one of the members of that congregation."[25] The congregation is being enlisted to treat Onesimus as a fellow believer.

They will inform you about the whole situation here – "The whole situation here" is a wider expression than "my affairs (circumstances)" in Colossians 4:7. It can include not only what is happening to Paul (his circumstances in the progress of the judicial proceedings against him), but also what is happening to the church at Rome. By placing Onesimus alongside Tychicus as a reporter of Paul's situation, Paul is telling the church, as well as Philemon, that he now regards Onesimus as living up to his name, i.e., that he is profitable, helpful, reliable.[26]

B. Salutations from Paul's Companions.   4:10-14

> *Summary*:   In verses 10-14 six persons (three of Jewish birth and three of Gentile birth) join in sending greetings to the Colossian church.

4:10 – *Aristarchus, my fellow prisoner, sends you his greetings; and also Barnabas' cousin Mark (about whom you received instructions: if he comes to you, welcome him);*

---

[25] Hendriksen, *op. cit.*, p.185.

[26] The Greek word "Onesimus" means "profitable."

Aristarchus, my fellow prisoner, sends you his greetings – Aristarchus was a Jew by birth, one "from the circumcision" (Colossians 4:11).[27] He was from Thessalonica (Acts 20:4), and is first named as being dragged along with Gaius into the theater during the riot/tumult at Ephesus (Acts 19:29). A few months after the riot was over, Aristarchus is named as one of the messengers who accompanied Paul (Acts 20:4) on the journey to Jerusalem with the offering for the saints at Jerusalem. When, after two years imprisonment at Caesarea, Paul has appealed his case to Caesar and is being sent to Rome, Aristarchus is again named by Luke as "being with us" (Acts 27:2) as the long voyage to Rome is beginning.[28] Commentators have struggled to explain the meaning of "fellow prisoner."[29] In Philemon 23,24 it is Epaphras who is also called a "fellow prisoner." There is no evidence that either Aristarchus or Epaphras had actually been arrested and held in custody as was Paul.[30] These men may well have alternately volunteered to share Paul's imprisonment, assisting him in every possible way. "Sends you his greetings" is *aspazomai*, meaning to greet, to wish well.

And also Barnabas' cousin Mark – Mark, the one whom we recognize as the writer of the second Gospel, sends greetings both to the Colossians (this verse) and to Philemon (Philemon 24). It is indicated by Paul's inclusion of these per-

---

[27] Ideas included in the brief biological sketches here given of Aristarchus and Mark are adapted from Barry, *op. cit.*, p.58.

[28] Whether or not Aristarchus went all the way to Rome, or stayed in the company only as far as Myra, cannot be proved for certain. At any rate, he is with Paul (in Rome, we judge) at the time Paul writes to the Colossians. On the voyage to Rome, Lightfoot *(Epistle to the Philippians,* pp.11,35) was of the opinion that Aristarchus disembarked at Myra, went overland to Rome, and arrived there before Paul. This is how the Roman Christians (Lightfoot believed) knew of Paul's coming. A better conjecture would be to have Aristarchus or someone go on ahead of Paul from Puteoli to Rome and tell the brethren he is coming. This would account for brethren from Rome coming to meet Paul (Acts 28:14,15).

[29] The root meaning of *aichmalōtos* is "one caught with a spear"; hence, a war-captive, and then simply a captive or prisoner.

[30] "It is certainly not a little curious that in the epistle to Philemon (verses 23,24), sent at the same time, it is Epaphras who is called the 'fellow prisoner,' while Aristarchus is simply classed among the 'fellow workers.' This variation is interesting to us as one of the characteristic marks of independence and genuineness in the epistles; but it can only be accounted for by mere conjecture, such as that of their alternately sharing the apostle's captivity" (Barry, *ibid.*). This variation may point to taking "fellow prisoner" in a metaphorical way, the idea being that these men had been taken prisoner by Christ.

sonal greetings in the letters he is writing that Mark was associated with Paul in Rome at this time during Paul's first Roman imprisonment. Under what circumstances Mark had recently come to Rome at the time of Paul's first imprisonment, we are not told. The references to Mark before this moment in time present an interesting picture. It is likely the first allusion to Mark is found in Mark 14:51-52, on the supposition the incident there related is Mark's own personal recollection of being present when Jesus was arrested prior to His crucifixion. The first definite reference to Mark is Acts 12:12. 1 Peter 5:13 ("Mark, my son") likely means that some time after Jesus' death and resurrection Mark was one of Peter's converts. This reference to Mark in Colossians is the first notice of him since the day at the beginning of Paul's second missionary journey when Paul rejected him from a role as "helper," because on the previous journey he had "deserted" them at Perga, and had "not gone with them to the work" (Acts 15:38). At that time, Mark had gone with Barnabas to Cyprus, to work alongside Barnabas in the latter's home country. Now here in this verse we will read about a formal charge to the Colossian church to "welcome him" – making this a kind of "letter of commendation" (2 Corinthians 3:1). Perhaps it is implied that the Colossians had known about how Mark had incurred Paul's displeasure. If so, this commendation would tell them that since the time Mark had gone off with Barnabas, Mark has done so well that he had been restored to Paul's confidence. The apostle no longer regards him as a liability, but recommends him warmly. In the epistle to Philemon (verse 24), Mark is named as among Paul's "fellow workers." In Paul's last letter, written shortly before he died a martyr's death, there is a touch of peculiar pathos in the charge which he, left alone in prison with his old companion Luke, gives to Timothy to bring Mark and come to Rome (2 Timothy 4:11).[31] Mark is warmly commended to Timothy as now being "useful to me for service." Evidently Paul's old rebuke had done its work, and, if Mark did join Paul in the closing days of his life, he probably thanked him for nothing so much as for the loving sternness of days gone by.[32] After Paul's death, a 4th century AD tradition has it that Mark did evangelistic work in Alexandria, Egypt, and died there.

---

[31] At that time, during Paul's second Roman imprisonment and some four years or so after the writing of Colossians, Mark must have had a ministry somewhere close to Ephesus. This would make it easy for Timothy to comply with Paul's request to get Timothy and bring him along to Rome.

[32] Since early Christian literature (Eusebius, *H.E.* V.8) has Mark in Rome about AD 67 or 68 and serving as Peter's interpreter, it is likely Mark did come to Rome per Paul's request.

A note of clarification is needed concerning Mark's relationship to Barnabas. The Greek word translated "cousin" in the NASB is *anepsios*. A "cousin" is the child of an aunt or uncle. The KJV translation "sister's son" (or nephew) is a meaning the word *anepsios* did not have until after the close of the apostolic age. Since Mark was the son of the Mary in whose Jerusalem home the early church often met (Acts 12:12), if the KJV's translation "sister's son" is correct, that would make Barnabas and Mary brother and sister. If "cousin" is the better translation, Barnabas and Mark are relatives, but not as close as "nephew" would indicate.

(About whom you received instructions: if he comes to you, welcome him) – What these instructions were that concerned Mark,[33] and when they were issued, we do not know.[34] We do not know who issued the instructions to the church at Colossae – whether Barnabas or Peter or Paul. If Paul did not issue them, he knew about them. It seems that Mark has been given instructions to leave Rome and make a trip to Asia Minor, and his itinerary might or might not include Colossae. If he does visit the church there, he is to receive a whole-hearted welcome. This directive implies that the Colossians knew about the earlier misgivings Paul had about Mark, and without the directive might have been cool in their reception of Mark. Paul's words "welcome him" would tell the Colossians that Mark has been restored to Paul's confidence, and the Colossians were to have confidence in him as well.

4:11 – *and* also *Jesus who is called Justus; these are the only fellow-workers for the kingdom of God who are from the circumcision; and they have proved to be an encouragement to me.*

And *also* **Jesus who is called Justus** – "Jesus" is the way the Hebrew name "Joshua" was spelled in Greek.[35] Being a Jew, it is likely this man was called Joshua among Hebrew-speaking folk. "Called" gives the impression he was better known in the Gentile world by his Roman name, Justus, rather than by his

---

[33] The antecedent of "about whom" is Mark, not Barnabas, as the Greek grammar shows.

[34] Being a second person plural verb, "you received" is probably not to be treated as an epistolary aorist. If, as is most likely, it is an historical aorist, the instructions had already been received before this letter from Paul to Colossae arrived.

[35] "Jesus" (or "Joshua") was a very common name in the first century.

Hebrew name.[36]   Many Jews at that time had a Roman name in addition to their Jewish name.   Concerning this man, Jesus Justus, we know nothing beyond the mention of his name here and that he was with Paul at the time this Colossian letter was written.   His name does not even occur in Philemon 23,24, even though all the other names here given are mentioned there.[37]

These are the only fellow-workers for the kingdom of God who are from the circumcision – Acts 28:30ff shows that while Paul was in Rome during his first imprisonment, he spent two years proclaiming "the kingdom of God and telling the story of the Lord Jesus Christ."   It was during this first imprisonment that Paul writes this letter to the Colossians.   There is a sense of sadness when he says there are only three converts to Christianity whose ethnic background was Jewish who were working alongside him.[38]   The kingdom long predicted as coming by the Old Testament prophets, and then announced as being "at hand" by John the Baptist and Jesus during their ministries (Matthew 3:2 and Mark 1:15), had begun on the day of Pentecost (Acts 2).   What grieved Paul was that there should have been many from among the Jews who were Paul's fellow workers (his best helpers) for the kingdom.   Only three, how disappointing.   We have had the term "kingdom" at Colossians 1:13 and at Ephesians 5:5.   The phrase "kingdom of God" here means, in effect, "so as to promote the reign of God, in Christ, over man and in him, here and hereafter."[39]

---

[36] The Greek equivalent of the Latin "Justus" is *dikaios*, "just, righteous."   The Greek "righteous" and its Hebrew equivalent *zadok* were given to Jewish people who were careful to observe the Law of Moses.   The surname "Justus" was worn by other men besides the one named here (Acts 1:23; 18:7).   In fact, tradition tells us that James "the Lord's brother," was known as "the just."   We wonder how one who bore our Lord's name should also have come by a surname which was also one of Jesus' titles ("the Just One" or "the righteous One", Acts 22:14 and compare Luke 23:47 and 1 Peter 3:18).

[37] Theodor Zahn (*Introduction to the New Testament* [Grand Rapids: Kregel, 1953], Vol.1, p. 459) has well pointed out that the list of names found both in Colossians and Philemon, and especially the addition of the name of Jesus Justus, creates difficulties for those who would impugn the authenticity of either Colossians or Philemon.   If Philemon was authentic, and Colossians was not, why should a forger who was copying names from Philemon when creating the letter we call Colossians venture to add the name of an unknown person, and especially to give him the name Jesus, a name that so soon became sacred among Christians?   If Colossians was authentic and Philemon was not, why would the forger not have copied all the names into Philemon that he found in Colossians?

[38] For the term "fellow-workers" see notes at Philemon 1.

[39] Moule, *op. cit.*, p.264.

And they have proved to be an encouragement to me – The aorist tense "proved" may point to some particular recent crisis. "Encouragement" translates the Greek *paregoria,* a word used only here in the New Testament. From this Greek word comes our word "paregoric," which denotes relief from pain or grief. The Latin translators chose the word *solatium* ("solace") to translate this term. "The apostle's statement with reference to these three men as the only Jewish-Christian fellow workers who had been a comfort to him implies deep disappointment with other people of his own race."[40]   If we lay alongside this notice with one we read in Philippians 1:15,16, it would seem likely that the brethren who held aloof from Paul in "envy and strife" and whose conduct produced that sense of isolation of which Paul speaks so pathetically, were Jewish believers.   Paul keenly felt this alienation in Rome; perhaps, then, in these words there is intended another exhortation to the Colossians lest they too become alienated by taking up some alternative faith.

4:12 – Epaphras, who is one of your number, a bondslave of Jesus Christ, sends you his greetings, always laboring earnestly for you in his prayers, that you may stand perfect and fully assured in all the will of God.

Epaphras -- Following the greetings from three Jewish Christians, Paul now adds those from three Gentile Christians who were also Paul's fellow workers, namely, Epaphras, Luke, and Demas.   Much has been related about the men being named in these verses in the Detailed Introduction to Colossians.   In Colossians 1:7 Epaphras was identified as the founder of the church at Colossae.   Colossians 4:12,13 concern Epaphras' work as evangelist at Colossae, Laodicea, and Hierapolis.

Who is one of your number, a bondslave of Jesus Christ, sends you his greetings – "One of your number," as it did in Colossians 4:9, seems to mean that Epaphras was a Colossian by birth.   The fact that Epaphras is sending his greetings indicates that Epaphras will remain behind in Rome after Tychicus and Onesimus have left on their journey to Colossae.   He not only sends greetings to the church in this letter, but he also sends his greetings in Paul's letter to Philemon (Philemon 23).   Of course, all Christians are "slaves of Christ" (Ephesians 6:6), meaning they are obedient and submissive to Christ.   But there is a good possibility the title "bondslave" – since it is used of James (James 1;1), Jude (Jude 1:1),   Paul himself (Romans 1:1), and   Timothy (Philippians 1:1 and 2 Timothy

---

[40] Hendriksen, *op. cit.,* p.190.

2:24) – may be indicative of a special ability to speak by inspiration, similar to the Old Testament prophets whom God called "My servants the prophets" (e.g., Jeremiah 26:5).

Always laboring earnestly for you in his prayers – "Laboring" translates *agonizomenos* ("wrestling, striving in an athletic contest"; see 1:29 for the same word) and "earnestly" (or "fervently" in the KJV) is added to give the modern reader a sense of the intensity of Epaphras' prayers. One who agonizes in prayer is expressing deep concern for the ones being prayed for. The next phrase in this verse expresses one particular concern Epaphras had in mind. It was the danger of their wavering under the influence of the deceitful teaching at Colossae.

That you may stand perfect and fully assured in all the will of God – To state the things about which Epaphras had been earnestly praying brings Paul once more to the very problems which occasioned the writing of this letter (see 1:23,28, 2:7). The same word "stand" is repeated three times in the stirring appeal of Ephesians 6:11-14. When congregations are threatened by the attacks from false teachers, it is above all things needful that they should stand fast. "All the will of God" means the things God wills,[41] and probably should be taken with both participles ("stand" *and* "fully assured"). "Stand perfect (*teleioi*)" in the will of God refers to their spiritual maturity, so they are no longer children tossed to and fro by every wind of doctrine (cp. Ephesians 4:13,14). "Fully assured[42] in all the will of God" stands in contrast to the doubts and fears the deceitful teachers might raise with their bold pretensions that they had something more to offer than the Christianity already embraced by the Colossians. "Epaphras does not want these churches that are dear to his heart to be deluded by error. That is why he wrestles for them in prayer."[43]

---

[41] Other passages where the "will of God" speaks of the thing He wills, rather than the act of willing, are Luke 12:47; Ephesians 5:17; and 1 Thessalonians 5:18.

[42] The KJV reads "complete" because the Textus Receptus has a different word (*peplērōmenoi*) here than the one (*peplērophorēmenoi*) translated "fully assured" in the NASB. As a result, commentaries based on the KJV will have a different explanation for this last phrase of verse 12 than the notes offered above. "Fully assured" is a perfect tense participle, indicating past completed action with present continuing results.

[43] Hendriksen, *op. cit.*, p.191.

4:13 – *For I bear him witness that he has a deep concern for you and for those who are in Laodicea and Hierapolis.*

For I bear him witness – Paul, who had abundant opportunity to know, affirms that he can personally assure the Colossians that Epaphras has a continuing concern for the churches of the Lycus River valley.

That he has a deep concern for you – Epaphras is said to have "deep concern" (Greek, *polun ponon*, "distress, anxiety") for the Christians in Colossae. The key word *ponon* suggests heavy toil to the extent of pain.[44] It speaks of great emotional distress as he worried about their spiritual welfare.

And for those who are in Laodicea and Hierapolis – In the Detailed Introduction to Colossians, we learned that Laodicea[45] and Hierapolis[46] were cities near Colossae. This brief statement about Epaphras' anxiety for the churches in those cities indicates that they, too, were in danger of being infected by the same decep-

---

[44] Because of a manuscript variation, the KJV reads "great zeal" at this place rather than the better attested *polun ponon*, literally "much labor." The Greek has three synonyms for work or labor: *kopos* ("labor," 1 Corinthians 15:58; 2 Corinthians 6:5), which emphasizes the fatigue or weariness that comes from laboring; *mochthos* ("hard labor," 2 Corinthians 11:27; 1 Thessalonians 2:9), which emphasizes the pain and sore muscles hard labor can produce; and *ponos* ("heavy toil"), which at one time emphasized the effort that goes into work, but by New Testament times had come to speak of the pain (Revelation 21:4). From that, when the term was used figuratively, as here, it means anxiety or emotional distress.

[45] The church at Laodicea was one of the seven churches to whom Christ sent the book of Revelation (Revelation 1:11). In those years, a third of a century after Paul's time, Christ had some strong words of advice for the church there (Revelation 3:14-22).

[46] Hierapolis (that is, the holy city) was so named because of the multitude of its pagan temples. Ancient coins from the area bear the images of Apollo, of the Ephesian Artemis, of Aesculapius, and of Hygeia. The two last-mentioned idols were worshiped in Hierapolis on account of the hot medicinal springs which abounded there and lured sick folk from around the world to come seeking relief. This place is now called Pamukale, or the Cotton-Tower, on account of the white cliffs which lie round about it. The ruins of the town are so magnificent as to show that it was once one of the most splendid cities in the ancient world. Though this allusion in Colossians implies there was a church there, there is no other mention of it in the New Testament. From early Christian literature there was a thriving church there for years, and Papias was born there.

tive philosophy that threatened Colossae.[47]   Epaphras, who has just been given Paul's warm commendation, provides a superb model for the Christians in all three cities to follow.

4:14 – *Luke, the beloved physician, sends you his greetings, and* also *Demas.*

Luke, the beloved physician, sends you his greetings – The name "Luke" is Roman (the Latin *Loucas* is an abbreviation of *Lucanus*).   Since Luke is not included among those of the circumcision (verse 11), it is proper to infer from this passage that Luke was a Gentile – the only New Testament writer so identified.[48] This man is best known to us as the author of the third Gospel and of Acts of Apostles.[49]   As "we" and "us" in Acts 27,28 imply, Luke came to Rome at the same time Paul first did.[50]   It is very probable that the original Greek, which is even more emphatic, "Luke, the physician, the beloved one," tells us that not only was Luke considered to be a dear friend by Paul, but that Luke has also served as Paul's personal physician.[51]   Whatever miraculous healings apostles were able

---

[47] Another interpretation (suggested by E.F. Scott, *The Epistles of Paul to the Colossians, to Philemon and to the Ephesians*, p.90) would connect the "trouble" (*ponon*) to which Epaphras put himself with the earthquake which in the early AD 60's shook the Lycus valley (Tacitus, *Annals*, xiv.27).   According to Scott's theory, the idea behind this language "much labor" is that Epaphras has been laboring to provide financial help for the stricken inhabitants.   However, there is no precise and consistent testimony with reference either to the exact date nor the extent of the earthquake. The best indication is that the earthquake occurred after Colossians was written and delivered.

[48] From both Colossians and Philemon 24, we learn that Luke and Mark, who wrote the second Gospel, were together in Rome.   This fact has been used as one argument that Luke made use of Mark's Gospel as one of his sources (see the Synoptic Problem).   The chief problem with this literary dependence view is that Luke's Gospel was written 7 or 8 years before Mark's. According to early Christian literature, Mark wrote about the time Peter was martyred, AD 68. Luke's Gospel was written before Acts, and Acts is dated AD 63.

[49] There is no basis for questioning the ancient statement of Irenaeus (iii. 14, 1) that Luke the physician is also the writer of the third Gospel.

[50] While Luke's name is not mentioned in Philippians, it is mentioned in Colossians and Philemon.   This may be indicative that Philippians was written later than Colossians and Philemon.

[51] Only here are we told that Luke was a physician.   W.K. Hobart (*Medical Language of St. Luke* [Grand Rapids: Baker, 1954]) argued that this designation of Luke as a physician finds confirmation from the similarity of medical language in Luke-Acts with the language of the Greek medical writers.   While a case can be made that some of the language of Luke-Acts is what any well-educated person in the first century could command, the language found in Luke-Acts still matches what we would expect a trained physician to regularly speak and write.

to do, and whatever the benefit of the spiritual gift of healing, neither brought any discredit, in Paul's view, on the skill and knowledge of the trained physician.

And *also* Demas – At this point in time, as Paul writes from his first Roman imprisonment, Demas, who is commended as one of Paul's "fellow workers" (Philemon 24), one of Paul's assistants in the ministry, also wished to be remembered to the church at Colossae.[52]   Sadly, it is but a few years later (from Paul's second Roman imprisonment) that we have another allusion to Demas: "Demas, having loved this present world, has deserted me ... only Luke is with me" (2 Timothy 4:10,11).   Demas, once a fellow worker with Paul tragically will end up loving this world more than working for Christ.

C. The Charge to Exchange Epistles with Laodicea.   4:15-17

4:15 – *Greet the brethren who are in Laodicea and also Nympha and the church that is in her house.*

Greet the brethren who are in Laodicea – The Colossian Christians are instructed to convey Paul's greetings to their Christian brothers in the neighboring city of Laodicea.   The next verse explains the occasion on which such greetings could be extended, namely, at the time someone makes a trip to Laodicea in order to exchange letters with the brethren there.

And also Nympha and the church that is in her house – In light of the fact that the next verse speaks of "the church in Laodicea" whereas this verse speaks both of "the brethren" who are there and of a congregation that meets in Nympha's house, it would appear that there was more than one congregation of believers in the city.   One group of brethren in Laodicea are specially singled out.   May we suppose this group was especially vulnerable to the threat posed by the deceitful teachers who are active in the Lycus valley?

---

[52] Since there is a commendation in Philemon, the absence of any commendation here in Colossians (a letter written at nearly the same time as Philemon) should not be interpreted as indicating Paul was already beginning to have doubts about this man.

There is a manuscript variation here, some reading Nymphas and some Nympha, some reading "the church in his house" and some reading "the church in her house."[53] The word "church" means nothing more than an assembly of people. "The church in her/his house" tells us a congregation of believers was accustomed to meet in this home. In the New Testament the word "church" is used both in a local sense (we read of the "churches" of Achaia, or Galatia, or Macedonia) and in a universal sense (we read of the "church" throughout all Judea and Galilee and Samaria, Acts 9:31, NASB). There were, of course, no church buildings in apostolic times. In the New Testament, "church" always designates an assembly of believers, never the building in which they met. We may suppose that those who offered their homes as a meeting place were people of some means, so as to have a room large enough to accommodate an assembly of say 20 to 40 people.[54]

4:16 – *And when this letter is read among you, have it also read in the church of the Laodiceans; and you, for your part read my letter* that is coming *from Laodicea.*

And when this letter is read among you – This is but one of many verses in the New Testament which give us the picture of the apostolic writings being read aloud in the public assemblies of the Christians on the Lord's Day. 1 Thessalonians 5:27 contains specific instructions to have that letter read aloud among all the brethren. The blessing pronounced on the "reader" and "those who hear" at Revelation 1:3 speaks of that book being read aloud in the public assem-

---

[53] Depending on the position of the accent mark, the Greek name may be either masculine or feminine. Νυμφᾶν is the accusative form of the masculine Νυμφᾶς, "Nymphas". Νύμφαν is the accusative form of the feminine nominative Νύμφα, "Nympha"). The following clause also displays a variation with "in *her* house" being the more strongly supported reading as opposed to those manuscripts which read either "in his house" or "in their house."

[54] In the New Testament we are introduced to house churches: in Jerusalem there was a group meeting in the home of Mary, the mother of Mark (Acts 12:12) while other believers were elsewhere. Priscilla and Aquila were accustomed to use their home as a meeting place for the brethren in whatever town they happened to be living at the moment, whether it be Ephesus (1 Corinthians 16:19) or Rome (Romans 16:3-5). In Philippi, some Christians met in Lydia's house (Acts 16:40). In Corinth a group of believers met in Gaius' house (Romans 16:23). At Colossae, Philemon's home was used as a meeting place for the church (Philemon 2). "Church buildings set apart for Christian worship did not appear in the Roman empire before the 3rd century" (Alexander, *op. cit.*, p.683).

blies to which it was addressed. Even the final greetings "Grace be with you" in 1 Timothy and Titus, where "you" is plural, indicates the intention that those letters were to be read aloud in the public assembly. The writers of the letters recognized the authority of what they were writing, and that what they were writing held value for more than just those immediately addressed. "The definitive aid to the Colossians' spiritual growth is the guidance of Scripture. Paul writes letters to churches as a substitute for his own presence, a 'virtual' form of mentoring/discipling. But his letters are more than his own wise advice. Paul consciously writes from a position of authority, under God's inspiration, declaring to the church the meaning and implications of the good news of Jesus."[55]

Have it also read in the church of the Laodiceans – The expression translated "have it read" instructs the Colossians to take an active part in seeing to it that this letter is read to the church at Laodicea. Someone from Colossae will be delegated to deliver the letter to Laodicea. Laodicea was just a few miles down the river from Colossae, so the church there was evidently exposed to the same dangers from the deceptive philosophy and false teachers as was the church at Colossae. That is why it would be helpful for the Laodiceans to have the same strong Christian doctrine which Paul has written to the Colossians.

"In the direction to interchange epistles with the Laodicean church, we trace the way in which apostolic writings became more widely circulated, and recognized as authoritative in the church at large. The churches recognized and affirmed that authority, keeping the apostle's letters to read long beyond the situations that prompted them. They are copied for believers in other places to read. This process is the first step toward the collection of authoritative Christian documents we call the New Testament."[56] "Thus it was that they were 'canonized,' i.e., accepted as a part of the 'canon' or rule of divine truth."[57] Perhaps the Colossians first made a copy of the letter to send to the Laodiceans while keeping the original for themselves. With each church having her own copy of the letter, it could have been read over and over for a long time beyond the situation that prompted its first writing. Paul's instructions here for the exchange of letters may cast some light on the earliest impetus to collect the letters

---

[55] Weatherly, *op. cit.*, p.223.

[56] Barry, *op. cit.*, p.61. Whether or not books were read on a regular basis in the public assembly had a direct impact on the determination which placed books in the canonical or doubtful lists that were compiled by Eusebius and other early church writers.

[57] Barry, *ibid.*

of the apostle. 2 Peter 3:15,16, which was written before AD 68, the date of Peter's death, indicates that Paul's letters already were circulating and being collected.

And you, for your part read my letter *that is coming* **from Laodicea** – All the Greek says is "the from Laodicea" with the understood antecedent of the feminine article "the" being "epistle." It is implied that Paul has written a separate letter that is circulating and which will come to Colossae from Laodicea.[58] When it arrives, it, too, is to be read in the Sunday assembly of the believers. The question, "What was this 'letter ... from Laodicea'?" has given birth to a host of conjectures,[59] including these: (1) It is an epistle, written by Paul, which has been lost, since we do not have a letter entitled "To the Laodiceans" in our New Testament canon.[60] (2) In the second century AD, an apocryphal "Epistle to the Laodiceans" was composed to fill the gap, and is included in many of the Old Latin manuscripts before the time of Jerome, and is also found in many manuscripts of the Latin Vulgate.[61] (3) The correct suggestion (in this commentator's judgment) is that the letter intended is the one we call the epistle to the Ephesians.[62]

---

[58] It is a mistake to read the Greek as though it speaks of a letter written by Paul while he was in Laodicea. Though Galatians, 2 Timothy, 1 Thessalonians, 2 Thessalonians, and 2 Timothy have all been nominated, none fits this hypothesis.

[59] These conjectures can be examined in detail by reading Lightfoot's *Excursus* on this verse (*op. cit.*, p.274-300).

[60] On the question of lost apostolic letters, this commentator holds that while it is possible for an inspired letter to an individual to have become lost, it is not likely that an inspired letter to a church has been allowed to become lost.

[61] In the Detailed Introduction to Colossians, we have included a translation of *The Apocryphal Epistle to the Laodiceans.* It is little more than a tame compilation of phrases gathered from Paul's extant epistles. "For more than nine centuries this forged epistle hovered about the doors of the sacred Canon, without ever finding admission or being peremptorily excluded. At length the revival of learning dealt its death-blow to this and to so many other spurious pretensions" (Lightfoot, *op. cit.*, p.299).

[62] Such was the opinion of Marcion, AD 140, and is the conclusion promoted by Lightfoot. In the Detailed Introduction to Ephesians, we suggest that as Tychicus and Onesimus passed through Laodicea on their way to Colossae, they left the circular letter we call Ephesians, and that from thence it started its journey to the churches of Asia Minor until it eventually ended up at Ephesus.

4:17 – *And say to Archippus, "Take heed to the ministry which you have received in the Lord, that you may fulfill it."*

And say to Archippus – The last instruction Paul has for the Colossian Christians is an exhortation to them to speak a special word to Archippus. Archippus may have been the son of Philemon and Apphia, or at least a member of the household of this husband and wife who lived at Colossae, and in whose home a congregation of believers in Colossae was accustomed to gather for worship. We can only conjecture what were the particular circumstances that led Paul to give the Christians this admonition concerning Archippus. Perhaps the church was directed to give this charge to Archippus because they were the ones who ordained him to the ministry. The ordaining church does have a continuing responsibility toward the ones ordained. When encouragement is needed, it is given; when an exhortation to work harder at the ministry is needed, it is given.

"Take heed to the ministry which you have received in the Lord, that you may fulfill it" – From the designation "our fellow soldier" in Philemon 2, and from the statement here about his having a "ministry," it seems right to suppose that Archippus is an evangelist, a gospel preacher.[63] Philemon 2 may indicate he worked with the church at Colossae, and this passage may indicate he worked with the church at Laodicea. We could see him being the preacher in the absence of Epaphras who had come to Rome to get the apostle's special help for the churches of the Lycus valley. If, as we have suggested, "received" does not refer to his being ordained by the local congregation, then it might speak of having been ordained by Epaphras. Evangelists did look out for faithful men to whom they could entrust the passing on of the word of the Lord. "In the Lord" identifies Archippus' ministry as being one of which Jesus Himself approves. It seems doubtful that Paul is calling for a reprimand in the sense that Archippus is to be publicly rebuked for failing his duties. It seems more likely that Paul is directing the members of the congregation to give Archippus words of encouragement be-

---

[63] We do not know whether the "ministry" (*diakonia*) is to be understood in the narrower sense of the office of deacon (as at 1 Timothy 3:8), or to the work of an evangelist (as at 2 Timothy 4:5, "Do the work of an evangelist; make full proof of your ministry" [*diakonian*]), or to some individual business relating to the service of the church. Later church tradition makes him bishop of Laodicea. There is some evidence that evangelists were the ones who filled the position which early Christian literature designates as "bishops." Those individuals who are called "bishops" in post-apostolic times certainly exercised an oversight beyond the oversight that elders (plural) in the local congregation exercised.

cause what he has been doing in Epaphras' absence is exactly what should have been done. "Fulfill it" means 'Go right on doing the important work you are doing; we are with you and promise to help you in every way we can.' Of course, the Colossians can say this only if they are in complete agreement with what Paul has written in this letter, especially concerning the preeminence of Christ and the resulting opposition to the deceptive philosophy that was a threat to Christianity. If he continues his ministry in the Lord, and they support him wholeheartedly, it will help protect the congregations from the dangers the Christians face.

Conclusion. 4:18

> *Summary:*   This final verse contains an autograph, a salutation, an exhortation, and a benediction.

4:18 – *I, Paul, write this greeting with my own hand. Remember my imprisonment. Grace be with you.*

I, Paul, write this greeting with my own hand – At this place Paul has taken the pen to sign the letter and to add a few closing words. With the exception of Philemon (which appears to have been penned in full by Paul personally, Philemon 19) and Galatians (Galatians 6:11 seems to say Paul wrote that whole letter himself), most of Paul's letters were dictated (e.g., Romans 16:22; 1 Corinthians 16:21; 2 Thessalonians 3:17). Then, when the scribe had finished taking the dictation, Paul would take the pen in his own hand and add his own signature and a closing greeting.[64]

Remember my imprisonment – As he reached for the pen and papyrus, the chain, fastened on his left hand, would partially be in the way, and would be an immediate reminder of his imprisonment. That would explain this touching request, "Remember my imprisonment." This plea may be a special request for their prayers on his behalf, or it may be an appeal for their fidelity to the gospel which he preached and for which he was suffering. If it is an appeal for their prayers, that for which he seeks their prayers may be learned from Ephesians 3:13, 6:20; and from Philippians 1:13, 2:17.

---

[64] Such a handwritten note would guarantee the letter was an authentic product of the mind and heart of Paul, and it would discourage the spread of spurious letters (see 2 Thessalonians 2:1,2).

Grace be with you – The letter ends as it began,[65] with the simple but profound prayer, "Grace be with you," a prayer that they may continue to enjoy the favor of God, which they will do if they remain in Christ.[66]

---

[65] The KJV carries a closing "Amen," but the manuscript evidence for the omission of that word here is considerable. The KJV also carries a subscription reading "Written from Rome to the Colossians by Tychicus and Onesimus." This subscription, as is true of the ones found elsewhere in the KJV, are attributed to Euthalius, a fifth century church leader. It was not part of the original text, but is an inference drawn from Colossians 4:7-9.

[66] Some Pauline letters have spoken of "the grace of our Lord Jesus Christ" (cf. 1 Thessalonians 5:28; 2 Thessalonians 3:18; 1 Corinthians 16:23). On the meaning of "grace," see note on Ephesians 1:2.

Commentary On

Philemon

Concise Introduction To
PHILEMON

Not everything powerful comes in large packages. The epistle to Philemon is an example.

A slave named Onesimus had run away from his master, Philemon. Somehow that slave came into contact with Paul while Paul was a prisoner in Rome. Converted to Christianity (Philemon 10), the runaway became a friend of Paul and a helper to him. Paul wrote this letter to the slave's master, who also happened to be one of Paul's friends.

This letter was written to intercede with Philemon, who himself had been converted to the Christian faith by Paul (verses 19,20), to receive Onesimus back as a Christian brother (verses 15-17).

In Colossians 4:9, Onesimus is said to be from Colossae; as a consequence, it can be assumed that Philemon, Apphia, Archippus, and the church that meets in Philemon's house are all also in Colossae, but this is not explicitly said in the letter to Philemon.

Philemon is one of the Prison Epistles, most likely written around the same time as Ephesians, Philippians, and Colossians.

Knofel Staton wrote that the letter is meaningful to us in these ways:

1. *A model of reconciliation.* This letter calls for acceptance of another as a Christian brother, though class distinctions put a big gap between them.

2. *An intercessory letter.* This is a magnificent example of one Christian's intercession for another Christian, with no benefit coming to the intercessor.

3. *A counter-cultural letter.* There were millions of slaves in the Roman empire. The usual punishment for a runaway slave was harsh. What Paul requested went against the grain of the times. There are occasions when we Christians must take a stand against the customs of our times.

4. *A revolutionary letter.* We discover in this letter one of the powerful ways to change a social system. It is not by picking up arms, but by encouraging

the change to begin from the inside. Paul was asking Philemon to make some internal changes that would result in a different way of treating Onesimus. There are extraordinary possibilities in ordinary people. We are to encourage and utilize these potentialities. All people are created in the image of God, and that is how God expects us to treat them.

5. *A persuasive letter.* There are many principles of persuasiveness in this letter; but none call for being belligerent, mean, dictatorial, or inflexible. Any of us who seek to persuade others can learn lessons from the way Paul persuaded Philemon.[67]

PEOPLE LIKE US

It is generally true that we like people who are most like ourselves. Conversely, we tend not to build friendships as quickly with people who are not like us. Sometimes, if we are not careful, prejudices can develop toward those who are not like us.

The letter to Philemon encourages us to take a closer look at how we view people, and to see them as Jesus sees us. This letter is not a theological treatise; it is a very personal letter permeated with genuine emotion. It does not deal with issues in the abstract; it deals with them in the context of a very real set of circumstances being addressed to very real people.

Philemon, the slave owner, and Onesimus, the escaped but repentant slave, are asked to become models of the reconciliation possible through Jesus. This would be no easy task for either of them. In the world of the first century they were miles apart on the socio-economic scale: Philemon was an apparently well-to-do businessman; Onesimus, a humble slave. How they responded to Paul's appeal had the potential to provide an impressive testimony of the uniting power of the gospel.

There is an important lesson here for all of us. It is quite possible for us to believe that the gospel should go to everyone, even to people who are not like us, but at the same time refuse to accept such people into our own fellowship. Paul appealed to Philemon to display a willingness to break down social barriers in the name of Jesus. His appeal is addressed to us, too.

---

[67] Knofel Staton, *Standard Lesson Commentary 1992-93* (Cincinnati, OH: Standard Publishing Co., 1992), p.402.

In our study of Philemon we will see that there is more than just social change at stake; the importance of forgiveness is also a pivotal issue. This, too, is difficult. According to the standards of the day, Philemon would have been under no obligation to be kind to or to forgive his slave. But Paul knew of Philemon's Christian commitment and appealed to him to "go the second mile" with a person whom society would have said did not deserve such treatment. This appeal also is addressed to us.[68]

SLAVERY?

Some Bible students wish that Paul, and the New Testament in general, had more to say about the evils of slavery. Actually, it comments very little on the subject; perhaps the closest to a criticism of slavery comes in Paul's reference to "men-stealers" (i.e., slave-traders) in 1 Timothy 1:10 (KJV).

"Slavery was simply a part of first-century culture. No one would have given serious consideration to abandoning it, for they could not have conceived of an alternative. But Paul put into effect the transformation of the master-slave relationship by urging Philemon to treat the now-become-Christian Onesimus as a brother in Christ rather than as a slave. It seems that Paul did not try to change society as such, but to change individuals and to encourage them to apply Christian principles to every situation. In that way, society would be changed."[69]

Outline of Philemon

Epistolary Opening. 1:1-3

I.   Thanksgiving for Philemon's Faith and Love.   1:4-7

II.   An Appeal to Philemon on Behalf of Onesimus.   1:8-20

Final Greetings and Benediction.   1:21-25

---

[68] "People Like Us" is adapted from Michael Shannon, *Standard Lesson Commentary 1999-2000* (Cincinnati, OH: Standard Publishing Co, 1999), p.442.

[69] *Ibid.*

THE EPISTLE TO PHILEMON

EPISTOLARY OPENING.   1:1-3

1:1 – *Paul, a prisoner of Christ Jesus, and Timothy our brother, to Philemon our beloved* brother *and fellow worker,*

Paul – Following the usual format (signature, address, and greeting) for first century letters, the writer first signs the letter. However, when we compare the epistolary opening of Colossians 1:1-2 we observe that the words by which the writer identifies himself and the words that describe the recipient of the letter are significantly different. These differences suggest that Paul deliberately changed how he worded the opening of this letter so that his appeal for Onesimus will be favorably received.

A prisoner of Christ Jesus – Whereas in Ephesians 1:1 and Colossians 1:1 Paul styles himself "an apostle of Jesus Christ," thus identifying the authority with which he speaks, here he speaks more personally, calling attention to the fact that he is a "prisoner of Christ Jesus." Though Paul was in custody of Roman guards (Acts 28:16), he views his imprisonment as being directly related to the work he has been doing for Jesus Christ.[70] Paul will soon (verses 8,9) plainly state his courteous determination not to order Philemon what to do, but rather for love's sake to appeal to him. In harmony with that stated determination Paul uses words intended to appeal to the sympathy of Philemon.

And Timothy our brother – Timothy's name also occurs in two of the other epistles (Philippians 1:1; Colossians 1:1) which were written from the same first Roman imprisonment. Perhaps Timothy served as Paul's secretary as Paul dictated the letter. After Timothy's name is mentioned, both here and in Philippians 1:1, the plural is dropped so that this is Paul's own personal letter. "Our" here includes both Paul and Philemon and likely implies that Philemon was well acquainted with Timothy. The title *brother*, likely used in the sense that Timothy is a fellow Christian,[71] a brother in Christ, will also be given to Onesimus

---

[70] Cp. Ephesians 3:1, 4:1, 6:19-20; Philippians 1:13; Colossians 4:3. Perhaps Philemon, too, when he re-reads this letter (as we suppose he must have done several times) and reflects upon all Paul has written, will reflect on the profound idea that he also needs to be in bondage to Christ's will.

[71] The designation "brother" is used of Quartus (Romans 16:23); Sosthenes (1 Corinthians 1:1); and Apollos (1 Corinthians 16:12).

(verse 16). Since both men are now fellow brothers in Christ with Philemon, will Philemon get the message to treat Onesimus just he would treat Timothy?

To Philemon – Almost all that we know of Philemon is contained in this short letter. In the Detailed Introduction to Philemon it has been indicated he was an influential Christian in the city of Colossae (Colossians 4:9), in whose home in that city a congregation of Christians met. Philemon at an earlier time had been won to Christ by Paul (Philemon 19). He is a slave owner and one of his slaves, having run away, is now returning of his own free will. Paul's letter to Philemon pleads the runaway Onesimus' case to his former master.[72]

Our beloved *brother* and fellow worker – "Our" in this case includes both Paul and Timothy. What in particular is signified by the appellation "fellow worker" is not known, though it has something to do with the spread of the gospel. "Fellow-laborer" might be illustrated by Philemon placing his home at the disposal of the church for its meeting place. It might refer to Philemon using his wealth and influence for Christ. Exactly when all three had worked together is not known, but perhaps after his conversion he joined Paul and Timothy at Ephesus during Paul's three year-long Ephesian ministry (Acts 20:31) when "all ... Asia heard the word of the Lord" (Acts 19:10).

1:2 -- *and to Apphia our sister, and to Archippus our fellow-soldier, and to the church in your house:*

And to Apphia our sister – She is Paul and Timothy's "sister" in the Christian sense.[73] It tells us she had embraced the gospel, been immersed, and was a member of the body of Christ at Colossae. There seems little doubt that Apphia[74] was Philemon's wife, and if so likely would have been in charge of the household

---

[72] Included in the Detailed Introduction to Philemon is a typical "right of sanctuary" letter written by Pliny (about 40 years after Paul's letter to Philemon) on a similar subject.

[73] The KJV reads "to our beloved Apphia," but based on manuscript evidence the NASB does not carry the feminine adjective "beloved." Codices Aleph, A, D*, E*, and F read *adelphe* (sister) for *agapete* (beloved). The Latin Vulgate reads "beloved sister."

[74] Some of the older commentators raised the question whether or not her name might be the Roman name Appia. Lightfoot (*Saint Paul's Epistles to the Colossians and Philemon* [Grand Rapids: Zondervan, nd], p.306-308) has shown that Apphia (sometimes spelled Aphphia, and sometimes Aphia) occurs in many Phrygian inscriptions, so it is likely she was a native of the Lycus River valley, rather than from Rome.

slaves.   That this letter is addressed to her also seems to reflect the custom of the times which gave the wife the day-to-day responsibility for the slaves, so she is as much a party to the decision concerning what to do about Onesimus as was her husband.

And to Archippus our fellow-soldier – The traditional interpretation has been that Archippus is not only the son of Philemon and Apphia, but, in light of the designation "fellow-soldier," is also a preacher of the gospel,[75] working with the church that meets in Philemon's home.[76]   In this capacity he is being encouraged to lend his influence in the decision concerning what to do about Onesimus.   It is not clear whether "fellow-soldier" speaks of his present ministry, or whether "fellow-soldier" says that there was a previous time when Archippus and Paul had been comrades in arms, perhaps during the apostle's sojourn at Ephesus (AD 54-57).

And to the church in your house – "The church in your house" reflects the practice of individual Christians making their homes available as meeting places for the public assembly of the saints for worship (see Colossians 4:15; Romans 16:5; 1 Corinthians 16:19).   "Your" is singular, and most likely refers to Philemon, the main person addressed (verse 1), rather than to one of the three secondary addressees (see the three addressees separated by "and") named here in verse 2.[77]   Although this is a letter addressed primarily to an individual, if this letter to Philemon is read aloud in the public assembly, then Philemon would be watched by the congregation to see that he did the right thing by Onesimus.   The folk in the congregation would understand the importance of forgiveness and at the same time could exert some appropriate influence on Philemon should he fail to fulfill Paul's request.   "Perhaps it is to this part of the address, which directed the letter to a congregational circle, that we are indebted for the preservation of the

---

[75] Elsewhere in the New Testament the preachers Epaphroditus (Philippians 2:25) and Timothy (2 Timothy 2:3) are called either fellow-soldier or soldier of Christ.   That Archippus is a preacher agrees with the instructions in Colossians 4:17 that he is to "take heed to the ministry which you have received in the Lord, that you may ... fulfill it."

[76] In the Detailed Introduction Philemon, attention has been given to the alternative view of John Knox that this letter is actually addressed primarily to Archippus, the leader of the house church, and that he is Onesimus' slave owner, and that Philemon, who is then made the preacher at the church, is being enlisted to help persuade Archippus to take Onesimus back.   It was also noted there that Knox's hypothesis has not found acceptance among the students studying Philemon.

[77] It is because "Archippus" is the nearest antecedent to "your" that suggested to Knox his alternative theory.

document – the only one of the certainly very numerous private letters which the apostle wrote in the prosecution of his many-sided labors."[78]

1:3 – *Grace to you and peace from God our Father and the Lord Jesus Christ.*

Grace to you – Following his signature and the address of the letter, Paul next, in words identical to his greeting in six of his other epistles,[79] gives his greetings to Philemon and the other addressees (the "you" is plural). The words are Paul's prayer for Philemon and the others. To speak of grace is to remind them that God had infinite compassion on them when He forgave their sins. Will they have similar compassion on Onesimus?

And peace – Paul prays that the readers may continue to be recipients of and enjoy God's grace and peace. Folk are at peace with God when sins are forgiven and they are living in harmony with God's wishes for them.

From God our Father and the Lord Jesus Christ – The linking of "God our Father" and "the Lord Jesus Christ" as joint sources of grace and peace is possible only if it be recognized that Jesus is as much Deity as is God the Father. It seems to be implied that continuing to receive such grace and peace is contingent on Philemon honoring Paul's request.

I. THANKSGIVING FOR PHILEMON'S FAITH AND LOVE (1:4-7).

1:4 – *I thank my God always, making mention of you in my prayers,*

I thank my God always – After writing a greeting or salutation, it was the custom in first century letter writing to include an expression of thanksgiving. Paul follows this custom in every letter of his we have except the one to the Galatians. The singular personal pronoun "I" indicates that from this point on, we no longer

---

[78] H.A. Meyer, *Critical and Exegetical Handbook to the Epistles to the Philippians and Colossians and to Philemon* (Winona Lake, IN: Alpha Publications, 1980), p. 399. The letters from Paul to Timothy and Titus may seem like private letters, too, but the plural "you" in the benedictions' "Grace to you" of those letters indicates that the congregations to which those men preached were also in view.

[79] Romans 1:7; 1 Corinthians 1:3; 2 Corinthians 1:2; Galatians 1:3; Ephesians 1:2; Philippians 1:2.

have Paul and Timothy speaking to Philemon and the others.   It is Paul himself who now speaks heart to heart with Philemon.   Depending on how we punctuate this verse, "always" may express either the frequency of Paul's giving thanks,[80] or it may be indicative of how often in his prayers Paul mentions Philemon.   The thanksgivings in Paul's letters regularly introduce some subject that will be developed later in the letter.[81]   This one seems intended to establish a relationship between Paul and Philemon that will best facilitate a gracious reception of this letter.

Making mention of you in my prayers – Paul assures Philemon that although he has not seen Philemon for some time, nevertheless Paul remembers to pray for Philemon regularly.   If "in my (*epi*) prayers" has the meaning of "at the time of," it indicates that Paul still observed the formal times of prayer honored by the Jews. There are several delicate touches in this thanksgiving, all of them intended to show Philemon that to Paul he is someone special, and that Paul thinks of him often.   Philemon should not draw the conclusion that had it not been for a need for a letter on behalf of Onesimus, Paul would have not even had Philemon in his thoughts.   We have a similar statement about "making mention of you in my prayers" in Ephesians 1:6, and from such statements we gather that Paul prayed for churches and individuals by name.[82]

1:5 – *because I hear of your love, and of the faith which you have toward the Lord Jesus, and toward all the saints;*

Because – Here Paul tells *why* he gives thanks to God in his prayers.   He was thankful for Philemon's love and faith.   This language is not flattery; rather, Paul

---

[80] If we punctuate as does the NASB with a comma after "always," then Staton's comment is apropos.   "Paul never let the circumstances of his life interfere with his prayer time.   In the four letters Paul wrote during this Roman imprisonment, not once did he complain about his situation. Instead, his prayers were punctuated by thankfulness to God" (Knofel Staton, *Standard Lesson Commentary 1992-93* [Cincinnati, OH: Standard, 1992], p.402).

[81] E.g., see how the reference to Philemon's love (verse 5) prepares for the request in verse 9 which is "for love's sake"; also see how the mention of "fellowship" (verse 6) prepares for the request based on Philemon's regarding Paul as a "partner" (verse 17).

[82] Michael Shannon wrote a thought-provoking comment concerning many of our prayers as compared with Paul's prayers.   "So much of our prayer lives is devoted to our wants.   It appears that much of Paul's prayer life was devoted to others rather than to his own wants or needs" (M. Shannon, *Standard Lesson Commentary 1999-2000* [Cincinnati, OH: 1999], p.443).

calls attention to Philemon's Christian character, for on that he will base his appeal for Onesimus.

I hear of your love and of the faith which you have toward the Lord Jesus, and toward all saints – "I hear" is a present tense verb, 'I keep hearing.' Perhaps it was from both Onesimus and Epaphras (Colossians 1:7,8; 4:12) that Paul kept hearing about Philemon. Philemon was one subject of conversation between the folk in Rome who were with Paul. Interestingly, the name "Philemon" means loving. Paul here notes that he has been told that Philemon is living up to his name. The word order here (compared with what Paul wrote in the companion letter to the Colossians in which we read "your faith in the Christ Jesus and the love which you have for all the saints," Colossians 1:4) has caused commentators to theorize the reason behind the unexpected order at this place. Perhaps Paul is dictating his thoughts "in the sequence in which they occur to him, without paying regard to symmetrical arrangement. The first and prominent thought is Philemon's love. This suggests the mention of his faith, as the source from which it springs."[83]   Others have thought it better to see here a 'chiasmus' (ABBA pattern) in which Philemon's love is directed toward all God's people and his faith is in the Lord Jesus.[84]   One writer commenting on the Greek text and noting a difference in prepositions (it is "toward [*pros*] the Lord Jesus" but "toward [*eis*] the saints") has suggested that the change of prepositions reflects the fact that the risen and glorified Christ cannot be reached by bodily efforts, whereas the saints here on earth can actually be reached and ministered to personally.[85]   "God does not call us to have a relationship with Christ only, but also with other Christians. We contradict Christian teaching if we meet to express our faith in Christ while nursing animosity toward people sitting around us."[86]   By telling Philemon that he thanked God for Philemon's love and faith, Paul is further preparing Philemon to listen sympathetically to the request he is about to make on behalf of Onesimus.   Philemon's love is   directed to all the

---

[83] W.O. Oesterly, "The Epistle to Philemon" in *Expositor's Greek Testament* (Grand Rapids: Eerdmans, 1967), Vol.4, p.212.

[84] Alfred Barry, "The Epistle of Paul to Philemon" in *Ellicott's Commentary* (Grand Rapids: Zondervan, 1959), Vol.4, p.271.   Some later scribes making copies of Philemon have taken it upon themselves to change the word order, thus giving us "your faith toward the Lord Jesus and your love toward all the saints."

[85] S.J. Eales, "Philemon" in the *Pulpit Commentary* (Grand Rapids: Eerdmans, 1960), Vol.21, p.2.

[86] Staton, *ibid*.

saints, not just a favored few.   And now, numbered among those who are saints is none other than Onesimus.

1:6 – and I pray *that the fellowship of your faith may become effective through the knowledge of every good thing which is in you for Christ's sake.*

And I pray – The NASB has added these words in italics since the first word in the Greek is *hopōs* (translated "that"), a word that often follows a verb of praying to introduce the content of the prayer.

That the fellowship of your faith may become effective – Papyri use *energos* ("effective") of a mill in working order.[87]   If "fellowship of your faith" means a fellowship that faith prompts, then Paul prays that Philemon's faith ("your" is singular in the Greek) will be in a working order (cp. James 2:18, where one's faith is demonstrated by one's deeds, and James 2:26, where we are told faith is dead if it has no works).   While the general idea is clear, the exact meaning of each of the expressions in verse 6, and their connection to each other, has been declared to be "unusually difficult to understand."[88]   "Fellowship of your faith" evidently speaks of a liberal distribution to others as a result of his faith.[89]   Such a liberality will be needed in the case of Onesimus.   "Among other good things, forgiveness and a cordial welcome to a penitent runaway slave would show people that Christianity makes a difference, and so many of them would be more ready to accept it."[90]

Through the knowledge of every good thing – What is intended by "every good thing"?   Some manuscripts read "of every good work."   What does Paul have in mind as he speaks of the knowledge which Philemon and the others addressed in

---

[87] A.T. Robertson, "The Epistles of Paul (Philemon)," in *Word Pictures in the New Testament* (Nashville: Broadman Press, 1931), Vol. 4, p.465.

[88] Arthur A. Ruprecht, "Philemon" in *Expositor's Bible Commentary* (Grand Rapids: Zondervan, 1978), Vol. 11, p.459.

[89] The same word "fellowship" (also translated "participation") is used of an offering sent to help others at Romans 15:26; 2 Corinthians 8:4, 9:13; Philippians 1:5; 1 Timothy 6:18.   The KJV rendering "the communication of thy faith" has led commentators to write about how Paul wants Philemon to communicate or demonstrate his faith to other Christians so they can learn to partake of the fruits, to wit, by doing more good deeds.   In this commentator's judgment, such a handling introduces an idea into the passage which obscures the point actually being made.

[90] Staton, *op. cit.*, p.403.

verse 2 have? Does the Greek *en epignosis,* literally "in full knowledge of ...," say Philemon (and the others) already have a knowledge of every good thing, or is Paul praying that Philemon (and the others) will develop a knowledge of "every good thing" they might need to do?[91] Either way, the underlying idea is that knowing and doing such a "good thing" would result in a generous sharing of the effects of their faith in Onesimus' case.

Which is in you for Christ's sake – This "you"[92] is plural, apparently including all the folk named in verses 1 and 2, namely Philemon, Apphia, Archippus, and the church. "Which" refers back to "every good thing." "For Christ's sake" is literally "toward Christ Jesus." This language suggests a lesson Jesus once taught, that "to the extent that you did it to one of these brothers of Mine ... you did it to Me" (Matthew 25:40). If they treat the returning Onesimus kindly as this letter requests, it would be as though they were doing it to Jesus Himself.

1:7 – *For I have come to have much joy and comfort in your love, because the hearts of the saints have been refreshed through you, brother.*

For I have come to have much joy and comfort in your love – "For" indicates verse 7 is giving a reason for something just said. Does it tie with verse 5, so that this verse tells why Paul prays that Philemon's faith may be effective in every good work? Does this tie with what Paul wrote in verse 4, thus giving another reason why Paul thanks God for Philemon? The aorist tense verb, translated "I have come to have,"[93] captures and pictures the moment of joy which Paul experienced on the occasion when he first heard the good news about Philemon's love and his ministry to the saints, a love and ministry he is about to highlight in this verse. "I had much joy ..."[94] reminds us that Philemon's love has been repeat-

---

[91] A similar prayer is found in each of the Prison Epistles (see Ephesians 1:17; Philippians 1:9; Colossians 1:9.) "It describes the true order of Christian life, so fully and beautifully drawn out in Ephesians 3:17-19, beginning in faith, deepened by love, and so growing to knowledge" (Barry, *op. cit.,* p.52).

[92] "In you" has slightly better manuscript support than "in us," but the editors almost universally favor "in us." See B.M. Metzger, *A Textual Commentary on the Greek New Testament* (New York: United Bible Societies), p.657 for the argument.

[93] The KJV reads "we have great joy"; however, the preferable reading is (as in A, C, F, G, N) "I had much joy."

[94] There is a manuscript variation at this place, with *charin* ("grace") rather than *charan* ("joy"). If the reading *charin* were original it means thankfulness of spirit, gratitude, such as was expressed in verse 4.

edly alluded to in the opening verses of this letter. The word translated "comfort" ("consolation," KJV) can also be translated "encouragement." It literally means a calling alongside, often for the purpose of rendering some kind of assistance. Not only did Paul experience joy, he felt a sense of encouragement when he heard of how Philemon's love expressed itself in helping others. That is something Onesimus will need.

Because the hearts of the saints have been refreshed through you – The KJV reads "because the bowels of the saints are refreshed." The Greek word *splanchna*, translated "bowels" in the KJV, but "hearts" in the NASB, refers to the nobler viscera (heart, lungs, liver). See the same word used at Philippians 1:8 where the NASB has "affection." Used figuratively, the word expresses the depths of a person's feelings. "Refreshed" (*anapepautai,* cf. verse 20) is the very word the Lord used in His word of promise (Matthew 11:28), "Come to Me, all you who are weary and burdened, and I will give you rest" (*anapauō,* "I will refresh you"). When the saints (and these are not limited just to those in Philemon's household) needed relief and rest, Philemon came through with exactly the charitable help needed. Philemon, having been spiritually "refreshed" by Christ, could refresh others. It is obvious at this point that Paul is preparing Philemon for the favor he is about to ask. He is depending on Philemon's compassion to govern how he will treat his runaway slave.

Brother – This word appears last in the Greek sentence for emphasis. Paul will again use this affectionate word in verse 20. Indeed, in this place the title "brother" has a peculiar appropriateness. Not only does Paul count him as a brother, but all the saints who have been refreshed by him have been treated as if they were brothers in the family of Christ. Well, Philemon is about to find out that he has another new brother in Christ, one Onesimus.

II. AN APPEAL TO PHILEMON ON BEHALF OF ONESIMUS. 1:8-20

1:8 – *Therefore, though I have enough confidence in Christ to order you to do that which is proper,*

Therefore – "Therefore" ties the following request to Philemon's kind character recognized in verses 6 and 7.   What Paul is about to request is completely in line with Philemon's well-known disposition.

Though I have enough confidence in Christ to order you to do that which is proper – Paul reminds Philemon of his apostolic authority.   As an apostle, Paul had the "right" or "authority" (*paressia*, "confidence") to issue an order, and no doubt Philemon would have carried it out.   But as someone has observed, a person changed against his will is of the same opinion still, so Paul refrains from ordering how Philemon is to act in this matter.   The Greek word *aneko* (translated "proper") means something that is ethically suitable, something that fulfills a moral obligation.   "What is fitting/proper"[95] points to what is proper for Philemon, as a Christian, to do in the circumstances concerning Onesimus.   "Paul had no doubt about what was the right thing to do.   But it would not be so easy for Philemon to see how right it was.   He was the one who had lost a slave.   If he now would take that slave back without punishment, would other slaves be encouraged to run away?   How often do one's selfish interests cloud one's perception of right and wrong."[96]

1:9 – *yet for love's sake I rather appeal to you – since I am such a person as Paul, the aged, and now also a prisoner of Christ Jesus –*

Yet for love's sake I rather appeal to you – The sentence begun in verse 8 continues on here in verse 9.   Rather than command Philemon what to do, Paul wants to give him an opportunity to act as love would lead him to act.   To receive back and forgive Onesimus would be a praiseworthy expression of Philemon's love to both Onesimus and Paul.

Since I am such a person as Paul, the aged, and now also a prisoner of Christ Jesus – Although Paul may appeal to Philemon to grant his appeal for love' s sake, he is still willing to tug at Philemon's emotions, especially any love he might have for a senior saint – "Paul the aged" – and love for a person who is being persecuted for doing what is right – "a prisoner of Christ."   The latter expression

---

[95] "The KJV reads 'that which is convenient.'   The word 'convenient' does not have the connotation today it did in 1611.   Paul does not mean that Philemon should make a choice on the basis of what is easiest for him.   In the English of the King James translators 'convenient' meant what is fitting and appropriate" (Shannon, *op. cit.*, p.444).

[96] Staton, *op. cit.*, p.403.

is exactly the same expression found at Ephesians 3:1.[97]   Paul's description of himself as "aged" reflects the fact he is about as many years old as it is years AD. If this letter to Philemon was written about AD 62 or 63, then Paul is in his early sixties.[98]

1:10 – *I appeal to you for my child, whom I have begotten in my imprisonment, Onesimus,*

I appeal to you for my child – With the preceding verses as preparation, Paul now begins his appeal on behalf of Onesimus.   First, he will help Philemon to see Onesimus in a new light.   While temporarily withholding the name of Onesimus, Paul indicates by means of the words "my child" that he and Onesimus have a special relationship.   This same term of endearment is used of Titus (Titus 1:4) and Timothy (1 Timothy 1:2), and likely with the same meaning.   In the next phrase Paul goes on to show he is using "child" in a spiritual sense.   We wonder if Philemon would have been surprised to see the words "my child" attached to the name of Onesimus.

Whom I have begotten in my imprisonment – This figure of speech (compare "I have begotten you through the gospel," 1 Corinthians 4:15 KJV) indicates that Paul has been instrumental in converting Onesimus to faith in Christ.   This conversion is a fact that would have been new to Philemon.   Even while in prison Paul had many opportunities to present the gospel (Philippians 1:12,13).   It is clear from this verse that the runaway slave Onesimus has come to Rome and has somehow come to the house where Paul was held under house arrest (Acts 28:30). Faith comes by hearing the word of Christ (Romans 10:17), and this is what Paul shared with Onesimus, leading him to become a Christian as he obeyed the gospel.

Onesimus – Now for the first time Onesimus' name is mentioned.   In Greek, the word Onesimus is last in Philemon 10, evidently withheld deliberately until Phile-

---

[97] If Paul were a free man, he might have handled the case differently.   "Under more usual circumstances, a free man could have assumed custody of a runaway slave after he had given guarantees of his return to the public officials, and he could have suggested that the slave be formally assigned to him for a time.   This was not uncommon" (Ruprecht, *op. cit.,* p. 460).

[98] Instead of "the aged," a few manuscripts read "ambassador" (*presbeutes*) like the parallel in Ephesians 6:20 does ("I am an ambassador in chains").   *Presbutes* ("aged") and *presbeutes* ("ambassador") were often confused by scribes, as they first listened to the words being dictated before writing on the page, since both are pronounced nearly alike.   It is doubtful that Paul intended any tone of authority (such as "ambassador for Christ" would convey) in this letter to Philemon.

mon's mind had been prepared to think specifically about this runaway. All we know about Onesimus from the New Testament is what we can glean from this letter to Philemon and from Colossians 4:9. Commentators, who treat 4:9 as meaning that Onesimus was a native of Colossae, have speculated whether he was a slave born in Philemon's house of a slave-mother, or whether, while he was still a youth, he had been sold into slavery by his father, "a custom so common to the Phrygians (as to the Circassians in later times) as to have been noticed by Cicero."[99] Early Christian literature has been understood to show that Onesimus later became well-respected leader in the church.

> As he traveled to his execution in Rome, Ignatius (d. AD 115) was met by representatives of several churches who brought him refreshment and encouragement, and who took back letters from him to their churches. Among these visitors was Onesimus, from Ephesus, of whom Ignatius speaks most favorably throughout his letter to the Ephesian church. Although Onesimus is a fairly common slave name, very few other slaves named Onesimus would also have been as likely to rise to such a prominent leadership role in the church. If Onesimus were a teenager at the time he sought Paul's mediation, he would be in his 70s when he met Ignatius in AD 115 AD.[100]

1:11 -- *who formerly was useless to you, but now is useful both to you and to me.*

Who formerly was useless to you – Paul uses a soft word "useless" (unserviceable) to describe the loss Philemon suffered when Onesimus ran away (whether or not verse 18 indicates he stole something as he fled). This verse includes an interesting play on the meaning of words. "Onesimus" which meant "useful" or "profitable" was a common slave name. Though derived from a different root (*chrestos*), the other two main words in this verse have a similar meaning ("useless" translates *achrestos* and "useful" translates *euchrestos*). The name Philemon means "affectionate" or "one who is kind." If the slave was expected to live up to his name, then what about the master?

But now is useful both to you and to me – Onesimus had not lived up to his name when he ran away, but had become quite unprofitable to Philemon. But that changed when Onesimus became a Christian. "Now" indicates that his new birth had made Onesimus a different person. Paul's statement that Onesimus had

---

[99] Eales, *op. cit.*, p.3.

[100] David DeSilva, *An Introduction to the New Testament* (Downers Grove, IL: Inter-Varsity Press, 2004), p.676.

been useful "to me" is an affectionate picture of the new Christian Onesimus as ministering to Paul's needs while Paul continued to be a prisoner. In the words "useful to you," Paul is saying that Onesimus was ready to be useful to Philemon. However, his usefulness to Philemon depended on Philemon's willingness to use him as much as on Onesimus' willingness to be used. A Christian slave, welcomed warmly and treated as a brother, would be much more useful than a slave treated cruelly because he once had run away.

1:12 – *And I have sent him back to you in person, that is,* **sending** *my very heart,*

And I have sent him back to you in person – This explains how Onesimus could become useful to Philemon. "I have sent" is likely an epistolary aorist referring to something that is happening as Paul writes. The Greek word for "sent back" is a word used technically for referring a case to a higher court. Paul was turning the case over to Philemon for a verdict.

> Something should be said about the faith of Onesimus. He was doing something quite courageous by returning to Philemon – something that demonstrated the sincerity of his commitment to Christ. Onesimus could have remained a fugitive, but he chose to return instead. Paul said he was sending Onesimus (verse 13), but Paul was in no position to force him to return. While Paul may have urged him, we have to see this as a voluntary act on the part of Onesimus.[101]

"In person" may suggest that Onesimus himself was the bearer of this letter. From Colossians 4:7,9, it is clear that Onesimus accompanied this letter.[102]

---

[101] Shannon, *op. cit.*, p.444. If Onesimus initiated the return, then "this passage should not be adduced to prove that we ought to send back runaway slaves to their former masters against their own consent; or to justify the laws which require magistrates to do it; or to show that they who have escaped should be arrested and forcibly detained; or to justify any sort of influence over a runaway slave to induce him to return to his former master. There is not the least evidence that any of these things occurred in the case before us, and if this instance is ever appealed to, it should be to justify what Paul did – and nothing else. The passage shows that it is right to aid a servant of any kind to return to his master, if he desires it. It is right to give him a 'letter,' and to plead earnestly for his favorable reception if he has in any way wronged his master – for Paul did this" (Albert Barnes, "The Epistle of Paul to Philemon," in *Barnes' Notes on the New Testament* [Grand Rapids: Baker Book House, 1955], Vol. 8, p.302-303).

[102] The KJV has the command "receive him" immediately after "whom I have sent." The better manuscripts do not carry the word here, though it is found in verse 17. Commentators explaining the KJV would remark on how Philemon would not have had opportunity to think over Paul's request before seeing Onesimus. Instead, facing Onesimus, the slave owner would need to decide right then.

That is, *sending* my very heart – With these words Paul is telling Philemon how fond he was of Onesimus. We might say "he is as dear to me as my own soul." Implied is the idea that whatever Philemon did with Onesimus would be tantamount to doing it to Paul.

1:13 – *whom I wished to keep with me, that in your behalf he might minister to me in my imprisonment for the gospel;*

Whom I wished to keep with me – The "wished" is an imperfect tense in the Greek indicating continuing action over a period of time, "I was wishing." As he briefly describes what has happened before he wrote this appeal letter, Paul admits that he considered keeping Onesimus with him, so that Onesimus might minister unto him and help him in the proclamation of the gospel during his imprisonment. We cannot help but wonder whether Onesimus made a request to be allowed to remain with Paul, whether it was a growing friendship, or whether Onesimus' ready helpfulness was the thing that triggered Paul's unfulfilled wish to keep Onesimus close by.

That in your behalf he might minister to me in my imprisonment for the gospel – "Imprisonment for the gospel" means imprisonment being endured because he had been preaching the gospel (cp. verse 9). Paul does not speak of Onesimus slaving for him, but instead uses a word ("minister") that speaks of helpful assistance, such as one who was under house arrest would need. The present tense verb says "keep on ministering to me." Onesimus had been of considerable help to Paul the prisoner. This statement of Onesimus' continuous ministry also suggests to Philemon that Onesimus is now worthy to be trusted. The expression "in your behalf" is Paul's delicate way of stating his assumption (based on their previous associations, verse 10) that Philemon would have wished to help Paul in whatever way he could (especially ministry in the gospel) had it been possible.

1:14 – *but without your consent I did not want to do anything, that your goodness should not be as it were by compulsion, but of your own free will.*

But without your consent – The meaning of "consent" for *gnōmēs* (a word often translated as "opinion" or "judgment") is frequently attested in the papyri.[103] Paul thought about keeping Onesimus in Rome, reasoning that his good friend Philemon would gladly contribute the slave's service to the good work Paul was

---

[103] William F. Arndt and F. Wilbur Gingrich, *A Greek-English Lexicon of the New Testament* (Chicago, IL: University of Chicago Press, 1956), p. 162.

doing. But Paul would not do that without Philemon's knowledge or consent. "In his imprisonment Paul needed a helper, but his needs took second place to Philemon's rights. Retaining a slave could be done only with the owner's consent."[104]

I did not want to do anything – Paul's desire to not take advantage of Philemon overruled his wishes to continue to avail himself of Onesimus' needed assistance. One almost senses that subtly Paul is asking Philemon to return the slave so that he might continue helping the apostle's mission efforts (see also verses 18,20,21).

That your goodness should not be as it were by compulsion – Any benefit Paul would derive from the ministry of Onesimus is acknowledged as coming from Philemon, because (though a runaway) Onesimus was still Philemon's slave. Had Paul encouraged Onesimus to remain in Rome and never told Philemon where Onesimus was, or had Paul only sent a letter asking for Philemon's consent, it would have left every impression that Philemon, rather than doing something of his own free choice, was being constrained to make his slave available to Paul.

But of your own free will – "A gift given out of necessity is no gift at all, but 'God loves a cheerful giver' (2 Corinthians 9:7)."[105] Paul will give Philemon every opportunity to be a cheerful giver.

1:15 – *For perhaps he was for this reason parted* **from you** *for a while, that you should have him back forever,*

For perhaps he was for this reason parted *from you* **for a while** – With "for," Paul is about to suggest another reason for his decision to send Onesimus back, namely he was hoping Philemon might come to see the providence of God behind all that has happened. Had Paul not sent Onesimus back, he might have defeated the purpose for which Onesimus was allowed to be separated from Philemon for a time. Paul avoids using the expression "run away," but rather uses the word "parted." He writes "parted" in the passive voice, rather than middle, which suggests there was something more than Onesimus parting himself, but his departure was divinely ordered for good. "Sometimes it is hard to see anything good in a loss we have suffered; but Paul was looking at this situation through the eyes of Romans 8:28: 'We know that God works all things together for good to

---

[104] Staton, *op. cit.*, p.404.

[105] Shannon, *op. cit.*, p.445.

those who love Him'."[106]   "For a while" is literally "for an hour."   "There appears to be considerable probability in the conjecture that Paul here again refers to Roman Law.   A gentle hint is given that Onesimus is not to be considered a *fugitive* slave.   The jurisconsults define the fugitive as 'he who leaves his master with the intention of never returning'."[107]

That you should have him back forever – We think these words have a dual meaning.   Paul is promising Philemon that he would have a better slave than he had before, one who would serve well and faithfully as long as he lived.   But because of God's hand in the events leading to Onesimus' conversion, Paul also encourages Philemon to realize that he now has the prospect of having Onesimus' company in heaven forever.

1:16 – *no longer as a slave, but more than a slave, a beloved brother, especially to me, but how much more to you, both in the flesh and in the Lord.*

No longer as a slave – This is the first time in the letter Onesimus is called a slave.

But more than a slave, a beloved brother – Here is another new thought for Philemon to digest.   Onesimus, in the lowest social status in the Roman world – a slave with no rights – was now on a spiritual plane equal with his owner Philemon and with Paul the apostle.   Onesimus' new status (a "brother," and more, a "beloved brother") was because of his new relationship to Christ.   A verse in the song "O Holy Night" has caught the spirit behind what Paul wrote in this verse: "Truly He taught us to love one another, His law is love and His gospel is peace.   Chains shall He break, for the slave is our brother, and in His name all oppression shall cease."

Especially to me – "Especially" (*malista*) is an old superlative form which intensifies "beloved."   By this means Paul emphasizes how much he loves his Christian brother Onesimus.

But how much more to you – Paul may specially think of Onesimus as a beloved brother, but Philemon has more reason now to have a special place in his heart for his new brother in Christ, Onesimus.

Both in the flesh and in the Lord – Perhaps "in the flesh"   refers to the fact that

---

[106] Staton, *op. cit.*, p.405.

[107] William Alexander, "Philemon" in the *Bible Commentary*, edited by F.C. Cook (New York: Charles Scribner's Sons, 1904), p. 844.

Onesimus, by returning, is showing he felt a strong attachment to his master. Perhaps "in the flesh" is intended to signal that Onesimus and Philemon were both Gentiles, and therefore rightly termed brothers in the flesh. Philemon, who had been won to Christ by Paul (see verse 19), and Onesimus, who also had been won to Christ by Paul (verse 10), are thus both "in the Lord," and as such are fellow members of the body of Christ and therefore spiritual brothers. Relations in both planes ("in the flesh" and "in the Lord") must be carried on simultaneously. Such dual relationships can still complicate the economic and social relations of Christians.

> Our earthly relationships are heightened by our common sonship to the Heavenly Father through Jesus Christ. Our new relationship with one another cannot be restricted to just worshiping together on Sunday; it must flow into our work ethic with one another during the week. This does not mean there will no longer be employer or employee. Those distinctions will be there even between Christian brothers. But it means we are to use the principles of Christian ethics toward each other – fairness and kindness.[108]

1:17 – *If then you regard me a partner, accept him as* you would *me.*

If then you regard me a partner – The word translated "regard" is literally "to have" or "to hold." The word translated "partner" *(koinonos)* means to have something in common with someone else. Usually some word is attached to "partner" to explain the job or cause in which both parties are participating (cp. Romans 11:17, "partaker with them of the rich root of the olive tree," or 1 Peter 5:1, "partaker also of the glory that is to be revealed"). The only other place "partner" is used without explanatory words is in 2 Corinthians 8:23, where Titus is called Paul's "partner and fellow-worker." "Partner," standing by itself as it does here, must indicate some special bond of fellowship between Paul and Philemon. Here it embraces having common hopes, common principles, a common view of how brothers in Christ should view things. A "partner" is more than an intimate friend. To appeal to partnership in Christian fellowship is the strongest form of appeal possible for Paul to use.

Accept him as *you would* me – Only now does Paul spell out the real point of this letter to Philemon. All the preceding has led to Paul's request in this verse. Whatever Philemon would do to Paul, were it Paul standing there before him, he is being asked to do for Onesimus. "Accept" translates *proslambano*, a word that means to welcome, or receive kindly. Can we imagine the respect and honor

---

[108] Staton, *ibid.*

Philemon would have given Paul if he were his house guest? Can Philemon show that kind of warm welcome to Onesimus?

1:18 – *But if he has wronged you in any way, or owes you anything, charge that to my account;*

But if he has wronged you in any way – Paul now guards against any possible hindrances to Philemon's receiving Onesimus favorably. The wording of the conditional sentence in the Greek implies nothing about whether or not the "if" is true. It may or may not be true. Paul asks, "Suppose he has wronged you," evidently referring to the time when Onesimus ran away. Paul uses the general word "wronged" rather than indicating a specific crime. Philemon might well think that the failure on Onesimus' part to serve in his appointed tasks had resulted in a wrong.

Or owes you anything – We cannot be certain that the slave had stolen anything at the time he ran away,[109] but if anything were missing when a search of the house was made, the suspicion would be that the runaway was the guilty party. And in addition, Philemon might think of the loss of income that resulted from the departure of a highly skilled slave whose activities would add to the wealth of the slave's owner.

Charge that to my account – This language pictures an accountant who is keeping books. Paul is preparing to tell Philemon that he is willing to pay for whatever loss to Philemon there may have been. This wonderfully gracious offer to assume any financial obligations Onesimus might have is an altogether astonishing statement. This is real brotherhood between Paul and Onesimus. "Such an offer shows that Paul was willing to do more than just request favors of Philemon; he, too, was offering to make some sacrifices on behalf of Onesimus."[110]

1:19 – *I, Paul, am writing this with my own hand, I will repay it (lest I should mention to you that you owe to me even your own self as well).*

---

[109] A conditional sentence written with *ei* and the indicative in the protasis, and a present tense indicative in the conclusion, is known as a present general condition. Such a condition implies nothing concerning whether or not the "if" in the protasis is true.

[110] Shannon, *ibid.* "Roman law required that whoever gave hospitality to a runaway slave was liable to the slave's master for the value of each day's work lost. Paul's promise to stand guarantor (verse 19) may be no more than assurance to Philemon that he will make up the amount incurred by Onesimus' absence from work" (Ralph Martin, "Philemon," in *Zondervan Pictorial Encyclopedia of the Bible* [Grand Rapids: Zondervan, 1978]. Vol.4, p.754). See Oxy.Pap. 1422 for the redress before the law that slave owners could claim against any who sheltered slaves.

I, Paul, am writing this with my own hand – If Timothy's name at verse 1 indicates that Timothy was writing down the words in this letter as Paul was dictating it, then at this point Paul took the pen from Timothy and wrote with his own hand these words that he would pay whatever debt Onesimus owed to Philemon.[111]   Paul actually introduces here a regular bond couched in legal form. "As in our own society, handwritten statements of obligation carried great weight and legal validity."[112]

I will repay it – Paul here writes what amounts to a promissory note.   He uses *apotiso* ("I will repay"), a stronger form than the more usual *apodōsō* ("I will recompense"), for Paul is picturing himself like a parent who is obligating himself to pay the debt of his son.   Some have conjectured concerning where Paul would get the money, if Philemon should require repayment.   We remember that Paul, when he was a free man, often supported himself by working at his trade of tent maker.   He anticipates being free soon again, and if need be, he could work to earn it.   Too, the Philippian church had sent offerings to help Paul meet his obligations while a prisoner (Philippians 4:10-18).   Those monies were given to him freely; he might fairly spend them on his own "son in the faith" as much as on his own personal needs.

(Lest I should mention that you owe to me even your very own self as well) – In case Philemon was minded to total up the damages lost because of Onesimus, and send the bill to Paul, Paul here reminds Philemon that he owed Paul something.   Probably this verse means that Paul had brought Philemon to Christ, and therefore Philemon was indebted to Paul for his own self, his eternal life. Philemon could never repay Paul for that, and so he could hardly accept the payment that Paul offered.   How ungrateful would Philemon have showed himself if he had refused to grant the apostle's desire.

1:20 – *Yes, brother, let me benefit from you in the Lord; refresh my heart in Christ.*

Yes, brother, let me benefit from you in the Lord – "Yes" is the translation of a confirmatory Greek particle which serves to gather up the whole previous appeal on behalf of Onesimus.   The word "I" is emphatic in the Greek.   Paul puts him-

---

[111] Literally, "I did write it;" it is an "epistolary aorist" (cp. Colossians 4:8); "the tense commonly used in signatures" (Lightfoot, *op. cit.*, p.344).

[112] Ruprecht, *op. cit.*, p.462.

self forward as he pleads on behalf of Onesimus. "Let me benefit" (*onaimēn*), or "have help," is an optative verb in the Greek, a mood used to express a wish. The word is formed off the same root as was the name Onesimus, and the verb was often used with a special reference to the delight parents felt when being helped by their children. "In the Lord" perhaps means 'as you do what the Lord Jesus would have you to do.' Putting the whole clause together, Paul is saying "My child, you can do something for me. Would you, my brother, be as much of a benefit to me as I have found Onesimus to be. You will be if you do in this case what Jesus would want you to do." Philemon has been a blessing to others (verse 5). Now Paul asks a blessing for himself.

Refresh my heart in Christ – Perhaps, since Onesimus has been described as being the "heart" of Paul (verse 12), Paul is asking Philemon to bring joy to Onesimus. More likely, Paul seems to be asking Philemon to bring joy to Paul himself. He does so by echoing the vocabulary of verse 7, where he recounted how Philemon had refreshed the hearts of many. How, then, can Philemon do less than that for Paul? "Refresh" (*anapauson*) means to quiet, to relieve of anxiety. Both Onesimus and Paul felt strong emotions as they wondered just what Philemon might do. Those anxieties would be put at rest if Philemon does in this matter what is "in Christ,"[113] that is, agreeable to Christ's will in the matter.

FINAL GREETINGS AND BENEDICTION.   1:21-25

1:21 – *Having confidence in your obedience, I write to you, since I know that you will do even more than what I say.*

Having confidence in your obedience, I write to you – "I write" is an epistolary aorist. The word "obedience" calls for some careful thought. Paul has avoided giving any commands to Philemon (cf. verse 8), but he nevertheless seems to glide, as it were almost without being noticed, out of the tone of appeal as to an equal, into an expectation of obedience. But obedience unto whom? Rather than Paul picturing himself as an authority to be obeyed, should we not think of the Lord as being the one whom Philemon needs to obey. Paul was aware of such a submission to Christ earlier in Philemon's life, and having prayed for Philemon's deeper understanding of the Lord's will (verse 6), he confidently expects Philemon to continue his submission to Christ, even in this matter.

---

[113] The KJV reads "in the Lord," but the oldest manuscripts read, "in Christ." "In Christ" is the sphere in which Philemon's act of Christian love naturally ought to have its guidelines and parameters.

Since I know that you will do even more than what I say – "More than what I say" likely means more than "accept him" (verse 17), so it must mean giving Onesimus his freedom, and perhaps also returning him to Paul who greatly appreciated Onesimus' useful assistance (verse 13). "Paul has been criticized for not denouncing slavery in plain terms. But, when one considers the actual conditions in the Roman empire, he is a wise man who can suggest a better plan than the one pursued here for the ultimate overthrow of slavery."[114]

1:22 – *And at the same time also prepare me a lodging; for I hope that through your prayers I shall be given to you.*

And at the same time also prepare me a lodging – "At the same time" means along with your kindly reception of Onesimus. In case Philemon should think "Paul will never know what I did with Onesimus," Paul asks Philemon to prepare a guest room for Paul's use.[115] When Paul arrives as a guest, he will soon know what was done in Onesimus' case, and he expects that he will not be disappointed at what he learns.

For I hope that through your prayers I shall be given to you – Paul here announces his travel plans once his anticipated release from imprisonment is finalized.[116] He plans to come to Colossae, where he will need a place to stay, which he anticipates Philemon will provide. Some years earlier, Paul had written to the Romans of his desire to go to Spain (Romans 15:24, 28). In the intervening years, however, his plans had changed. He now intended to revisit the churches in Asia Minor and Macedonia. In case Philemon might think, "Paul will never come," Paul asks for Philemon's prayers for that very eventuality. Paul wants Philemon to pray that God would grant such a visit as a gracious gift (the meaning of the Greek *charisthesomai*, here translated "I shall be given"). It speaks of a favor from one in supreme authority. Paul pictures God's providence having a hand in what Caesar decides to do with Paul's case.

---

[114] Robertson, *op. cit.*, p.469.

[115] The word *xenia* translated "lodging" in the NASB can mean either "hospitality" or "guest room." No doubt such hospitality will be provided gladly by Philemon in his own house, but Paul, with his unfailing courtesy, does not specifically ask for this.

[116] The Greek *elpidzo* ("I hope") includes both hope and expectation. Colossians was sent at the same time as was Philemon. Paul's expectations expressed in Colossians 4:7-9 and here in Philemon both convey a certain hesitation about what the future holds for Paul. Paul's hope (here expressed) that he will be released from his imprisonment is not worded quite as strongly as is his anticipation of soon being released when he writes Philippians 1:25,26 and 2:24.

1:23 – *Epaphras, my fellow prisoner in Christ Jesus, greets you,*

Epaphras – In the Detailed Introduction to Colossians, we learn that Epaphras was a Colossian. He apparently was the evangelist who started the churches in Colossae, Hierapolis, and Laodicea, and who had recently come to Rome to enlist Paul's help in the fight against incipient Gnosticism that threatened the churches in the Lycus valley. He naturally sends his greetings to the folk back home.

My fellow prisoner in Christ Jesus – The meaning of "fellow prisoner" is not precisely clear. Epaphras, who came to Rome to seek Paul's help on a serious matter of Christian doctrine, is not named as a prisoner in Colossians 4:12. On the other hand, Aristarchus who was also in Rome with Paul is called a "fellow prisoner" (Colossians 4:10). The same word is used in reference to Andronicus and Junias (Romans 16:7). Was there a former time, unrecorded in Acts or the epistles, when these men had been imprisoned together because they preached the gospel of Christ Jesus? Or did both of these men, who were Paul's helpers, put themselves in the position of a prisoner by their association with Paul the actual prisoner? Or, did their close association with Paul excite the suspicion of the authorities and lead to their being temporarily imprisoned simply because they showed such an interest in Paul the prisoner? Since Paul was not strictly an *aichmalōtos* ("prisoner of war," see on Luke 4:18), the probabilities seem to favor a spiritual sense for the word.

Greets you – Epaphras was aware Paul was writing this letter to Philemon. It is implied that what Philemon will do with Onesimus is a matter of keen interest to Epaphras, too.

1:24 – as do *Mark, Aristarchus, Demas, Luke, my fellow workers.*

As do **Mark –** The same co-workers who send greetings to Philemon are also named in Colossians 4:10-14.[117] As Paul writes to Philemon, the same co-workers surround him as when he wrote the epistle to the Colossians. Both letters come from the same time-frame in Paul's life. John Mark was with Paul (Colossians 4:10), the same young man who failed Paul on the first missionary

---

[117] A sixth co-worker, Jesus Justus, is mentioned only in Colossians 4:11. We do not know why he is not named in the letter to Philemon. He may not have been known to Philemon, or he may have been absent when the letter to Philemon was written.

journey (Acts 12:12, 25; 15:36-41).   Paul had forgiven Mark and was grateful for his faithful ministry (see 2 Timothy 4:11).   Mark will write the Gospel of Mark about 5 years after Paul included his name as sending greetings to Philemon.

Aristarchus – Aristarchus was from Thessalonica.   He had accompanied Paul to Jerusalem at the close of Paul's third missionary journey when they took the offering to the saints at Jerusalem (Acts 19:29), and later he accompanied Paul on the trip to Rome (Acts 27:2).   He is still with Paul when Colossians and Philemon are written.

Demas – Demas is mentioned three times in Paul's letters: "Demas ... my fellow worker" (Philemon 24); "Demas" (Colossians 4:14); and "Demas, having loved this present world, has deserted me" (2 Timothy 4:10).

Luke – Luke, of course, was the beloved physician (Colossians 4:14) who accompanied Paul, ministered to him, and eventually wrote the Gospel of Luke and the Book of Acts.

My fellow workers – The same word was used of Philemon in verse 1.   It speaks of folk who are involved in the spread of the gospel of Christ.

1:25 – *The grace of the Lord Jesus Christ be with your spirit.*

The grace of the Lord Jesus Christ – This prayer is Paul's usual benediction in his letters.   See Galatians 6:18; Philippians 4:23; 2 Timothy 4:22.   Whether or not the readers experience the prayed-for grace likely depends on their response to what has been written earlier in the letter.

Be with your spirit – The plural "your" (*humon*) embraces to the whole group (Philemon, Apphia, Archippus, and the church in Philemon's house) included in the salutation (verses 1,2).   The wording of the phrase "be with your spirit" is somewhat unexpected, with the word "your" in the plural, and "spirit" in the singular.   There is envisioned some kind of composite unity between all the folk addressed.   Does Paul picture all of them being in whole-hearted agreement about accepting Onesimus and welcoming him into their fellowship?   Does Paul picture all of them being one in Christ (as described in see Colossians 2:2, 3:15; Ephesians 4:3ff; 1 Corinthians 3:16,17; 10:1, 12:12ff)?

Some ancient manuscripts close the letter with the word "Amen." Others close with a subscription which reads, "Written from Rome to Philemon, by Onesimus, a servant." Such subscriptions were added by scribes many years after the letters originally were written.[118] The words "by Onesimus" in the subscription indicate the scribe's belief that Onesimus carried the letter, not that he wrote it.

---

[118] All such subscriptions are of no authority, and in some cases (e.g., 1 Corinthians and Titus) are not always correct. The one here, drawn from information gleaned from the letter to Philemon itself, may be correct.

Commentary On

Philippians

Page 428

Concise Introduction To
PHILIPPIANS

The Christians at Philippi have been thirsty for news – any kind of news – from their beloved apostle Paul.

The church in the city of Philippi, located in the province of Macedonia, was the first church established by Paul in what we know as Europe. This took place during his second missionary journey. Acts 16 tells of Paul's vision of a man of Macedonia who pleaded with Paul to come there (verse 9). In Philippi the apostle's efforts resulted in the conversion of Lydia and her household, Paul and Silas' imprisonment after they cast a fortune-telling demon out of a servant girl, and finally the conversion of the prison keeper and his household. Thus began what became a strong and generous congregation.

From Philippi Paul had gone on to Thessalonica, where he had met with more rough treatment, and the church at Philippi had sent money to help him (Philippians 4:15,16). Later, when his journeys took him to Corinth, they again sent him an offering (2 Corinthians 11:9). Afterward, when Paul had occasion to travel between Greece and Asia Minor, Philippi provided a stopping place for him.

Now, a dozen years after those first meetings, Paul was imprisoned in Rome. Word reached Philippi that he was continuing his evangelistic labors, receiving visitors in the rented dwelling where he was permitted to stay, with soldiers probably chained to him. Gifts from Philippi helped with such expenses as rental payments. One substantial gift was delivered to Paul by Epaphroditus, who stayed for a time to help Paul in his work (Philippians 4:18, 2:25-30). During that time Epaphroditus fell seriously ill, and the news of that illness reached his friends back home, to their dismay. They also seem to have heard of a new and possibly threatening change in Paul's circumstance, namely, the time when his case would be finally decided and he will be either freed or executed.

To ease their anxieties, Paul wrote to the Philippians, sending the letter by Epaphroditus as he returned home. It is friendly, full of gratitude and warm greetings and instructions. It includes virtually no word of rebuke, but fervent exhortation that his friends live in harmony among themselves, loving one another as they have loved him. It breathes joyful confidence in Christ, and urges the same thankful joy upon its readers.

OUTLINE

I. INTRODUCTION. 1:1-11
   A. Signature, Address and Greeting. 1:1,2
   B. Thanksgiving. 1:3-8
   C. Paul's Prayer for the Philippians. 1:9-11

II. STATEMENT OF PAUL'S CONDITION AT ROME. 1:12-26
   A. His Joy that the Imprisonment Means the Gospel is Advanced. 1:12-14
   B. His Joy that the Imprisonment Means Christ is Proclaimed. 1:15-18a
   C. His Joy because of his Opportunities to Exalt Christ. 1:18b-26

III. A FIRST SERIES OF EXHORTATIONS/ADMONITIONS. 1:27 - 2:18
   A. Admonition to Stand Fast, United and Unafraid, Against Their Opponents. 1:27-30
   B. Admonition to Have the Right Attitude Toward Their Brethren. 2:1-13
      1. The fourfold incentive to a right attitude. 2:1
      2. The right attitudes are specifically described. 2:2-4
         a. Unity and harmony. 2
         b. Humble mindedness. 3
         c. Helpfulness. 4
      3. The Lord's example and pattern for the Christians to follow. 2:5-13
         a. Christ's example on the way through humiliation to exaltation. 2:5-11
         b. With God's help, the Christians may imitate this pattern. 2:12, 13
   C. Admonition to Continue to be Light Bearers in the World. 2:14-18

IV. INFORMATION ABOUT PAUL'S CO-LABORERS. 2:19-30
   A. Timothy and his Forthcoming Mission to Philippi. 2:19-24
   B. Epaphroditus and his Return to Philippi. 2:25-30

V. WORDS OF WARNING. 3:1-21
   A. Warning Against Judaizers. 3:1-3
   B. Paul Uses His Own Example as an Argument Against the Judaizers. 3:4-16
      1. I, Paul, the Pharisaic Jew, had things I thought were gain for me. 3:4-6
         a. I, not they (at least not in the same degree)
         b. What my parents gave me
            1) Circumcision ("circumcised the 8th day")
            2) Noble birth ("of the people of Israel, of the tribe of Benjamin, a Hebrew of Hebrews")

      c. What I, thru my own efforts, attained
         1) Recognition as a Pharisee ("as unto the Law, a Pharisee")
         2) Zeal ("as unto zeal, persecuting the church")
         3) Legal rectitude ("as unto legal righteousness, having become blameless")
   2. I, Paul, the Christian, have counted all such things as loss. 3:7, 8a
   3. I, Paul, the Christian, now count such things as rubbish. 3:8b-11
   4. I, Paul, the Christian runner, press on to the goal. 3:12-14
      a. His frame of mind (as he runs)
      b. His exertion
      c. His goal
      d. His reward
   5. Exhortation to the Philippians to have the same attitude Paul does. 3:15-16

C. Warning Against Copying the Example of Enemies of the Cross of Christ. 3:17-21

VI. A SECOND SERIES OF EXHORTATIONS/ADMONITIONS. 4:1-9
  A. To all, to Remain Firm. 4:1
  B. To Two Women, to Live in Harmony. 4:2
  C. To Syzygus, to Help These Women. 4:3
  D. To Cultivate those Positive Christian Virtues Which Produce the Peace of God. 4:4-7
  E. To Proper Meditation and Proper Actions. 4:8,9

VII. PAUL THANKS THEM FOR THE OFFERING. 4:10-20
  A. Thank-you Note Begun: Paul's Testimony About Learning the Secret of Contentment. 4:10-13
  B. An Expression of Appreciation for Their Partnership With Him Resumes and Completes this Thank-You Note. 4:14-18.
  C. Assurance of God's Loving Care, and Doxology. 4:19,20

VIII. CONCLUSION: CLOSING SALUTATIONS AND BENEDICTION. 4:21-23
  A. Greetings. 4:21,22
  B. Benediction. 4:23

Page 432

The Epistle to the Philippians

I. INTRODUCTION. 1:1-11

A. Signature, Address, and Greeting. 1:1,2

1:1 -- *Paul and Timothy, bond-servants of Christ Jesus, to all the saints in Christ Jesus who are in Philippi, including the overseers and deacons:*

Paul and Timothy – As was typical in letters written in the ancient world, Paul, the author, signs his name first. Timothy may have served as the secretary who wrote down the letter as Paul dictated it. That Paul usually dictated his letters appears clearly from Romans 16:22, and may be inferred from 1 Corinthians 16:21-24, Galatians 6:11, Colossians 4:18, and 2 Thessalonians 3:17.

Bond-servants of Christ Jesus – In many of his letters, Paul identifies himself as an apostle of Christ Jesus. Does he omit this designation here in his letter to the Philippians because it is intended to be a warm and personal letter? Is the designation "bond-servants" used in a non-technical sense to picture Paul and Timothy as being willing servants of their divine master, Christ Jesus?[1] If so, Paul is saying that he and Timothy are not acting in their own names, but as the agent of Christ Jesus. Or does the designation "bond-servant" carry a tone of official significance? In comments on Colossians 1:7 it has been noted that when Paul uses the term "bond-servant" of himself, he is claiming to be an inspired mouthpiece for God, (just as the Old Testament expression "My servants, the prophets" claimed inspiration for the prophets).[2] Paul did preach by inspiration, and Timothy also could be a preacher who preached by inspiration, for Timothy had a gift given by the laying on of an apostle's hands (2 Timothy 1:6).

To all the saints in Christ Jesus who are at Philippi – This line in the epistolary

---

[1] The term *douloi* ("bond-servants") is explained by Adolph Deissmann as a Hellenistic usage, based on the practice of a freed slave's becoming a devotee of the deity (Adolph Deissmann, *Light From the Ancient East* [Grand Rapids: Baker Book House, 1965], pp.323-330).

[2] If "bond-servants" here in Philippians is a parallel to Old Testament usage, then the meaning is that both Paul and Timothy are commissioned for a divine task. There is, in fact, some evidence that this word and its cognates have a special relationship to the ministry in Paul's writings (cf. 2:22; 2 Corinthians 4:5; Galatians 1:10-12; Romans 16:18).

opening identifies the ones to whom this letter was addressed. Paul uses the word "saint" as a general name for his converts, like "Christian."[3] Christians are saints, not because they are sinless (for none would qualify) but because they are dedicated to Christ. The saints to whom this letter is addressed are "in Christ Jesus" (that is, they have been baptized into His one body),[4] and they are living in Philippi, a city in Macedonia.[5] The word "all" occurs very frequently in this epistle. Perhaps here it is the expression of warm natural affection. All the Christians in Philippi were dear to him. Then again, perhaps the frequent repetition of "all" (1:1,3,4,7,8,25; 2:17; 4:19) reveals how much congregational unity was on Paul's mind, a preoccupation difficult to explain without presupposing real or threatened disunity (cf. 3:2ff, 4:2,3).

Including the overseers and deacons – Overseers[6] and deacons were congregational leaders and helpers – two kinds of local church officials. They are numbered among the "saints." We are glad these two classes are named in this letter for it shows indisputably they were in existence at an early stage in church history (see Acts 14:23), rather than being a later, post-apostolic development in church polity.[7] Since elders and deacons were two orders of officers in any local church, the question is asked, "Why are they included in the address of this let-

---

[3] The words "saint" and "holy" are translations of the same root word in Greek. See notes at Ephesians 1:1 on the word "holy" to be reminded of the word's meaning. It means set apart to sacred service.

[4] People dedicated to a pagan god could be called "saints" of that god. It was to those devoted to Christ that Paul was writing. "Christ" is the Greek translation of the Hebrew "Messiah." Jesus is the Messiah.

[5] Concerning the history of the church at Philippi, see the Detailed Introduction to Philippians at the close of this volume.

[6] A comparison of Acts 20:20,27 and Titus 1:5,7 shows that "overseers" (the Greek word is translated "bishops" in the ASV) and "elders" were two different names used interchangeably for the same leadership function/office in the local congregation. It should also be carefully noted that the word is plural. Each congregation in New Testament times had "elders" (plural). The plural is much at variance with a later development of a single bishop over a number of congregations.

[7] See J.B. Lightfoot's dissertation on "The Christian Ministry," in his volume on *Saint Paul's Epistle to the Philippians* (Grand Rapids: Zondervan, 1953), pp.181-269. The reference from Paul's first missionary journey as well as reference to elders at the Jerusalem Conference (Acts 15:2) indicates that before AD 51 elders were selected to oversee the local congregations. The reference, therefore, to "overseers" here in Philippians should not be marshaled as evidence of a late date for the writing of Philippians.

ter?" The best guess is that these leaders had taken the initiative in gathering and distributing the gifts sent to Paul by the Philippians, both now and on previous occasions.

1:2 – *Grace to you and peace from God our Father and the Lord Jesus Christ.*

Grace to you and peace – Ancient letters began with the author's signature, the address, and then a word of greeting to the recipients. Since Christian congregations included believers from both Greek and Jewish backgrounds, Paul offers greetings to both. Paul changed the conventional Greek greeting from "hail" (*charein*) to "grace" (*charis*), and poured a Christian meaning into the Jewish greeting of *shalom* ("peace"). And his Christian version of greeting is actually a prayer he offers for his readers.[8] He prays that God's loving-kindness ("grace") and spiritual wholeness, prosperity, and well-being ("peace") may be experienced by his readers.

From God our Father and the Lord Jesus Christ – The source of Paul's prayed-for blessings is both the Father and the Lord Jesus Christ. Both equally are the source of grace and peace that come to the Christians.[9] Paul's placing of Jesus on a level with God the Father in this verse is one of the evidences of Jesus' deity. So does the use of the designation "Lord" since *kurios* ("Lord") was the word the Septuagint translators used to translate the four letter sacred name YHWH.[10] "Lord" therefore has tremendous Christological implications (cf. Mark 12:35-37 and Acts 2:34,35 where Psalm 110 is applied to Jesus). "Christ" tells us Jesus is the long-promised Messiah.

B. Thanksgiving. 1:3-8

1:3 -- *I thank my God in all my remembrance of you,*

---

[8] The entire sentence has already become common in his letters, appearing verbatim in Romans, 1 Corinthians, 2 Corinthians, Galatians, and Ephesians, and with slight modifications in his other epistles.

[9] For an explanation of the imagery of the fatherhood of God see comments at Ephesians 4:6, 5:20, 6:23.

[10] The Hebrew word for "Lord" (*adonai*), which was used in the Old Testament both as a title and as a substitute for God's sacred name YHWH, was translated into the Septuagint as *kurios*. The early Christians used both the Aramaic equivalent (cf. *Maran* in 1 Corinthians 16:22) and the Greek term as titles for Jesus.

I thank my God – Continuing to follow conventional format of Greek letter-writing of his day, Paul next expresses a thanksgiving to God for the recipients of the letter.[11]   Paul's thanks are addressed to that glorious Being whom he calls "my God."   The pronoun "my" speaks not so much of possession as of personal relationship.   It reminds us of Acts 27:23, "God, to whom I belong, and whom I serve."   It reflects Paul's personal devotion to God.

In all my remembrance of you – The thanksgiving is prompted by the joyous memory Paul had of his Philippian friends.   "The Philippians stood by Paul and repeatedly sent him funds in his trouble and imprisonment.   He was thankful for their help, but most of all he was thankful for the Philippians themselves."[12]   All his memories of the Philippians are happy ones.[13]

1:4 – *always offering prayer with joy in my every prayer for you all,*

Always offering prayer with joy – "The words 'joy' and 'rejoice' occur no less than thirteen times in this short letter; they express what his own feeling is, and what he desires that theirs should be."[14]   The word "joy" means a lively emotion of happiness, gladness, pleasantness, being delighted.   "Paul says that his happy memories were reflected in his prayers for the Philippians.   Joy permeated his prayers even while he prayed for their needs."[15]   The reasons for Paul's joy will be stated in the following verses.   "Prayer" is *deēsis,* "supplication," a request to

---

[11] Nearly all of Paul's epistles (with the few exceptions readily accounted for, such as Galatians and Titus) have words of thanksgiving following the epistolary opening, but with this exception: Paul addresses his thanks to God, not to one of the pagan gods, as was the custom in non-Christian writings.

[12] S. Edward Tesh, *1973-74 Standard Adult Lesson Commentary* (Cincinnati, OH: Standard, 1973), p.403.

[13] "All my remembrance of you" is better than "every remembrance of you" (KJV).   *Pase* ("all") is used with *te mneia* ("remembrance") in the predicate position, and thus stresses totality.

[14] Alfred Barry, *The Epistle of Paul the Apostle to the Philippians* in Ellicott's Commentary (Grand Rapids: Zondervan, 1959), Vol.8, p.66.

[15] Homer Kent, "Philippians" in *The Expositor's Bible Commentary* (Grand Rapids: Zondervan, 1978), Vol.11, p.105.   "Verse 4 contains the first of five uses of *chara* ('joy') in Philippians (others are 1:25; 2:2,29; 4:1).   In addition, the verb *chairo* ('rejoice') appears seven times (1:18; 2:17,18,28; 3:1; 4:4 [twice]), and the compound *sunchairo* ('rejoice [with]') occurs twice (2:17,18).   Joy is clearly the prevailing atmosphere of the epistle" (*op. cit.*, p.107).

God on behalf of someone else and their needs.[16]   The particular topics of his petitions for them are revealed in verses 9-11.

In my every prayer for you all – "You all" indicates that Paul's petitions for the Philippians omitted none of them.   Even in Philippi there were definite spiritual needs.   There were imperfections (Philippians 1:9-11; 2:2,4,14,15; 4:2) and dangers (Philippians 3:2,18,19).   So Paul again and again ("always … in every supplication") beseeches the Lord that these needs may be supplied.

1:5 – *in view of your participation in the gospel from the first day until now.*

In view of your participation in the gospel – The immediate reason for his thanksgiving is now given here in verse 5; namely, the Philippians' sympathetic partnership with him as he goes about preaching the gospel.   They were partnering with him by providing their missionary offerings to support him as he traveled and preached (Philippians 4:15,16).   The same Greek word ("participation") is used for a missionary offering in Romans 15:26 and in 2 Corinthians 9:13, where it is translated "contribution."   The Greek word also is sometimes translated "fellowship" (as at Acts 2:42), which tells us that real fellowship means to contribute something of yourself to the lives of others.   The word "gospel" originally meant "a reward for bringing good news, but later it came to be used for good news itself, often the joyous news of victory in war."[17] The Philippian financial support of Paul made it possible for him to continue preaching the good news of Christ and the victory that has been won by Him for all mankind.

From the first day until now – Ten years before this letter was penned, Paul first came to Philippi (Acts 16:14,15).   And all through the years since, the Philippians had supported Paul financially.   Philippians 4:16 tells us they sent an offering to him just after he left Philippi and went on to Thessalonica.   2 Corinthians 11:9 tells of an offering sent to him while he was in Corinth.   Philip-

---

[16] See comments at Ephesians 6:18 concerning the Greek synonyms for prayer.

[17] I-Jin Loh and Eugene A. Nida, "Philippians" in *A Translator's Handbook on Paul's Letter to the Philippians* (Stuttgart: United Bible Societies, 1977), p.12.   See the extended footnote #61 concerning the "gospel" in the author's *New Testament Epistles: Romans* (Moberly, MO: Scripture Exposition Books, 1996), p. 16,17.   "In the New Testament it always means good news itself and refers to the salvation that God has made possible through the death and resurrection of Jesus Christ.   The word appears nine times in Philippians and is used in a variety of ways.   It is the message about Jesus Christ that is proclaimed (Philippians 1:5; 4:15), defended (1:7,16), promoted, spread, and advanced (4:3; 1:12; 2:22).   It is also the standard of Christian living and basis of faith (1:27)" (Loh, *ibid.*).

pians 4:10 tells of a more recent offering. The recent heroic mission of Epaphroditus, who had risked his very life in the interest of delivering another missionary offering to Paul, was, as it were, the climax of this glorious manifestation of "participation in the gospel from the first day until now."

1:6 -- For I am *confident of this very thing, that He who began a good work in you will perfect it until the day of Christ Jesus.*

For I am **confident of this very thing** – As we see it, verse 6 gives the reason why Paul can make supplications about the future of the Philippians, and make them with joy! God's help is available for the asking.[18] God could be counted on to be faithful.

That He who began a good work in you will perfect it – Verse 7 will go on to indicate that the "good work" Paul had in mind is their ability to share in the spread of the gospel.[19] God provides the means for his people to be generous; it is something He does all the time (see 2 Corinthians 9:9-11). God gave the means for the previous missionary offerings. What God started He will finish ("perfect it"). He has blessed the Philippians in the past. God will continue to bless the Philippians. That's why Paul makes his prayers with such confidence – he knows the character of God. Again, it should be emphasized that this is but one of the many Old and New Testament passages which teach that God has a providential hand in His world. He has not gone off somewhere, leaving His creation to fend for itself as best it can.

Until the day of Christ Jesus – What Paul promises here is that God will provide His people with the means to be generous until the second coming of Christ. "The day of Christ Jesus" is a phrase occurring with only slight variations six times in the New Testament (1 Corinthians 1:8, 5:5; 2 Corinthians 1:14; Philippians 1:6,10, 2:16). This expression is the New Testament equivalent (2 Peter 2:9, 3:12; 1 John 4:13-17; 1 Thessalonians 5:2-11) of the Old Testament "day of the Lord" (Isaiah 2:12; Ezekiel 7:6-8; Zephaniah 1:14-18). "This name is given to

---

[18] Since verse 5 gave the reason why he gave thanks to God, not a few commentators also think that verse 6 is giving a further reason for his thanksgiving.

[19] In this commentator's judgment, neither is "participation" (fellowship) in verse 5, nor "a good work" here in verse 6, a reference to the conversion of the Philippians, nor is it proper to treat "He ... will perfect it" as a promise of the perseverance of the saints. That is reading into the passage more than what Paul is making reference to, namely, their missionary offerings to him. Nor should the verb tense "began" be explained as a reference to the crisis of conversion.

the day because Christ as *Kurios* ["Lord"] is to be judge."[20]   Not until that day has arrived will that work of God be completed in which He enables Christians to be hearty participants in spreading the gospel.   It is something He does to the end of the age (2 Corinthians 9:9).[21]

1:7 -- *For it is only right for me to feel this way about you all, because I have you in my heart, since both in my imprisonment and in the defense and confirmation of the gospel, you all are partakers of grace with me.*

For it is only right for me to feel this way about you all – The NASB marginal reading tells us that the Greek reads "Just as it is right."   Paul has just expressed a joyous attitude about the Philippians (verses 3-6).   He now asserts that such an attitude is "just as" it should be when all things are considered.   "Right" (*dikaion*) is to be understood in the general moral sense of "proper," rather than the religious connotation of "righteous."   The word translated "feel" is a present tense infinitive and so refers not to just a specific act of thought on a single occasion, but to an habitual conviction or feeling.   "You all" here is another example of the apostle's studied inclusiveness (cf. 1:1).

Because I have you in my heart – Interestingly enough, the phrase in the Greek can also mean "because you hold me in your heart."[22]   However, the order of the words in the Greek as well as what he writes in verse 8 make it probable that Paul is speaking of his attitude for them.   Paul's attitude is what it is because he loves them.   By saying that he holds them in his heart (*kardia*), he is saying something more than that they had a place in his affections.   He regards them as being at the very center of his life.

Since ... you all are partakers of grace with me – Paul now tells why he loves them as he does.   "Grace" in this verse seems to be synonymous with the privilege described in Ephesians 3:8:   "To me, the very least of all saints, this

---

[20] H.A.A. Kennedy, "The Epistle to the Philippians" in *Expositor's Greek Testament* (Grand Rapids: Eerdmans, 1967), Vol. 3, p.419.

[21] These words are not to be taken as implying that Paul mistakenly expected the second coming during his lifetime.   But until and when that day occurs, God can be counted on to be faithful in His supplying the needs of His children.

[22] Most versions have treated *me* ("me") as the subject of the infinitive phrase *to echein me en te kardias humas*, thus giving the sense "I have you in my heart."   In contrast, the *humas* ("you") could be the subject of the infinitive, resulting in "you hold me in such affection" found in the NEB.

grace was given, to preach to the Gentiles the unfathomable riches of Christ."[23] "You all are partakers" indicates that all the Philippian Christians (not just a few of them) have been involved in the financial support of Paul's missionary work. Paul says that by their financial support of the preaching of the gospel, the Philippians had become sharers, joint sharers, partners in his work.

Both in my imprisonment and in the defense and confirmation of the gospel – As Paul writes this letter, he may be in chains (*desmois*), but he is still preaching the gospel. From his "own hired house" (Acts 28:30,31), though under guard, the Gentiles were hearing the gospel. The Philippians' recent offering (Philippians 2:25-30, 4:18) is helping Paul to continue his ministry. "Defense" is the translation of the Greek word *apologia*, meaning (not an admission that one is wrong, but) a proof that one is right.[24] *Bebaiōsis* ("confirmation") was a technical legal term for a legally valid statement, a confirming proof.[25] Since there is a single Greek article for both nouns, Paul is thinking of "defense" and "confirmation" as one event – a successful defense would be a confirmation. Commentators are divided on the question of whether or not this language points to a trial or formal hearing of his case. In opposition to William Hendriksen's view that a formal hearing has already been held,[26] this commentator's judgment is that Paul's accusers never came, so no such formal hearing was ever held. Pat E. Harrell in his commentary suggests Paul speaks here by way of anticipation. He has not yet made his defense, but the Philippians' support helps him to be ready for that defense and confirmation of the gospel should a day in court ever come.[27] Paul has so worded it that it is the gospel that is on trial more than he himself. His statement that the Philippians are "partakers" with him in the outcome of that case reflects the fact that the outcome would ultimately affect them all. Their financial support of Paul indicated they felt the same way; namely, that the gospel was important and worth fighting for.

---

[23] The reason we thus limit our definition of "grace" to "apostolic ministry" is because the rest of the verse puts some limits to the "joint participation" of which Paul is speaking.

[24] The second century "Apologies" for Christianity, e.g. by Justin and Tertullian, are proofs that Christianity is the right religion.

[25] Kent, *ibid*.

[26] William Hendriksen, "Exposition of Philippians" in the *New Testament Commentary Series* (Grand Rapids: Baker, 1962), p.57.

[27] Pat E. Harrell, *The Letter of Paul to the Philippians* (Austin, TX: R.B. Sweet, 1969), p.32.

1:8 -- *For God is my witness, how I long for you all with the affection of Christ Jesus.*

For God is my witness – Paul has just written "I have you in my heart" (verse 7). He now shows that this claim is no exaggeration. God, he says, will support his claim. Only God can read Paul's heart and see his real feelings.[28]

How I long for you all with the affection of Christ Jesus – Again we have the inclusive "you all." "With the affection of Christ Jesus" might mean 'my love for you is patterned after Christ's love for you' (cf. Philippians 2:5). It might mean 'I love you with the same heart-hunger Jesus felt for men,' or 'I yearn for your welfare with the same compassion as Christ does.'

C. Paul's Prayer for the Philippians.   1:9-11

1:9 – *And this I pray, that your love may abound still more and more in real knowledge and all discernment,*

And this I pray – Verses 3-8 have spoken of Paul's *thanksgiving* on their behalf. Now he identifies two things for which he *prays* for them. He asks that their love may (1) increase, and (2) be carefully regulated. "If we study carefully the opening thanksgivings and prayers of Paul's epistles, we may note that he always thanks God for what is strong in the church to which he writes, and prays God for the supply of that in which it is weak."[29]

That your love may abound still more and more – "That" (*hina*) introduces one topic included in his prayers for them. "This is the first appearance in this epistle (cf. 1:16, 2:1,2) of the great Christian word 'love' (*agape*)." *Agape* is an attitude that involves the will, and so can be commanded ("love your enemies," Matthew 5:43-48) and cultivated. It "has the general connotation of seeking the other person's good."[30] In this commentator's judgment, Paul has in mind the kind of love they have just shown in the offering they sent to him.   But Paul is

---

[28] Paul's words here are probably not an oath, but a simple statement of fact. There are, however, passages where "God is my witness" is a solemn oath (e.g., Romans 1:9; 2 Corinthians 1:23; 1 Thessalonians 2:5,10). These instances show in what sense Paul interpreted Jesus' command to "make no oath at all" (Matthew 5:34).

[29] Barry, *op. cit.*, p.67.

[30] Harrell, *op. cit.*, p.56. Such love is often described as doing what is spiritually best for the other person.

hardly asking for a bigger offering next time. Rather, he is praying that their financial involvement in mission work may increase by leaps and bounds, since there are other gospel preachers who need such support as they have been sending to Paul. Love, like other Christian graces, can grow.

In real knowledge and all discernment – These words put some limits on their love. Love must not be a raging flood, for raging floods do more destruction than good. Paul prays their love will abound more and more, and their generosity to missions must be within the bounds of good sense and discretion. Love should be regulated by knowledge and discernment, not blind impulse. "Knowledge" (*epignosis*) is a word Paul uses much,[31] and is always used by him in the sense of full knowledge of God's revealed truth. "Discernment" says their love should be judicious. Have they been sending offerings (like the one they sent to Paul) elsewhere, and were some of them "senseless"? We must be careful in our expressions of love. Some missionaries do not deserve to be supported!

1:10 -- *So that you may approve the things that are excellent, in order to be sincere and blameless until the day of Christ;*

So that you may approve the things that are excellent – The results of such a love, limited by knowledge and discernment, are now stated. One result is that they will have the capacity "to approve what is excellent." The Greek word *dokimazo,* translated "approve," was once used in reference to the assaying of metal and of the testing of coins for genuineness. By New Testament times it had pretty well lost its narrow frame of reference, but it did keep the nuance of an approval that comes from examination. Moffatt's translation "so that you may have a sense of what is vital" comes close to the idea. Using knowledge and discernment, Christians will know which missions to support and which not to. A person who possesses love but lacks knowledge and discernment may reveal a great deal of eagerness and enthusiasm. He may donate to all kinds of causes. His motives may be worthy and his intentions honorable. Yet he may be doing more harm than good. Such an individual may also at times be misled doctrinally. We need knowledge and discernment to keep us from becoming the dupes of slick-tongued adventurers and religious charlatans.

In order to be sincere and blameless until the day of Christ – Not only will abounding love regulated by knowledge and discernment result in giving to what is vital, but a second result is that this in turn will help them to pass under Christ's

---

[31] See Romans 1:28, 3:20, 10:2; Ephesians 1:17, 4:13; Colossians 1:9,10; 2:2, 3:10; 1 Timothy 2:4; 2 Timothy 2:25, 3:7.

eye with approval on the day of judgment.   It is Christ's second coming that is
called "the day of Christ" (see on verse 6).   One of the things that will be
examined in the final judgment is how we have spent our missionary dollars – to
whom they have been sent.   The examination will take place in bright sunlight
("sincere" translates *eilikrines*, judged in the light of the sun) so nothing is hidden.
It will check whether we have stumbled ourselves, and whether we have caused
others to stumble ("blameless").   Financial support sent to undeserving
missionaries leaves the giver with a flaw, a fault, something bad, at the judgment.
"Until" translates *eis* (not *achris* as in verse 6), and does not denote time only, but
implies preparation for the day.   On this day every believer must stand before his
Lord and give an account of his deeds (2 Corinthians 5:10).

1:11 -- *having been filled with the fruit of righteousness which* **comes** *through*
Jesus Christ, to the glory and praise of God.

Having been filled with the fruit of righteousness – Paul is still picturing the
judgment on the "day of Christ."   The conduct that will receive Christ's commendation at the judgment must have been characterized by "the fruit of
righteousness."[32]   Missionary offerings are one kind of such "fruit" (Philippians
4:17).[33]   "Righteousness" says the Philippians are doing what is right for their
fellow men as they partner with Paul in the defense and confirmation of the
gospel.[34]

Which *comes* **through Jesus Christ** – The Greek shows that it is the "fruit," and
not the "righteousness," that Paul speaks of as being mediated by Christ.   No
mere man is ever able to produce the fruit by his own unaided efforts.   Jesus has
a part in producing the fruit, for apart from Him the disciple can do nothing (John
15:5,8).

---

[32] The verb "having been filled" is a perfect tense verb in the Greek, indicating past
completed action with present continuing results.

[33] The best manuscripts read "fruit" (singular).   The image of a tree, heavily laden with
fruit, is one found often in the Old Testament (Amos 6:12; Proverbs 11:30; Hosea 10:12) and also in
the New (James 3:18; 2 Corinthians 9:10).

[34] Because the word translated "righteousness" is also translated "justification" in many
places, some commentators on Philippians think that justification by faith is the topic here alluded
to, and that the fruit results from salvation enjoyed and participated in by individual believers.   While
it is true that "righteousness" can speak of a right relationship with God, the word also is used of right
relationships with man, so that, in this commentator's judgment, Paul is writing about fruit that results
from doing what is right toward one's fellow man.

To the glory and praise of God – The picture Paul is drawing in these closing words of his prayer is of new converts who will be led to praise God because good fruit (an involvement in missions to win men to Christ, and lack of giving offense) is found in the Philippians' lives. This is in accord with Jesus' own teaching, "Let your light shine before men in such a way that they may see your good works and glorify your Father who is in heaven" (Matthew 5:16). "Glory" likely says that God will be made to look good; men will think well of Him.[35] "Praise" pictures God's majesty as being acknowledged as redeemed men offer Him homage both now and in eternity.

II. STATEMENT OF PAUL'S CONDITION AT ROME. 1:12-26

> *Summary*:   In these verses Paul informs his readers about his present situation (verses 12-17), and reflects on his hopes and expectations (verses 18-26).

A. His Joy that the Imprisonment Means the Gospel is Advanced. 1:12-14

1:12 -- *Now I want you to know, brethren, that my circumstances have turned out for the greater progress of the gospel,*

Now – In a sense, as he shares how things are with him, Paul is saying to the Philippians that their offering is already producing good results in Rome.

I want you to know, brethren – Perhaps Epaphroditus (Philippians 4:18) has told Paul of the Philippians' concern about his welfare. He begins his information about himself with an expression that indicates what is about to be written is of considerable interest or importance. "'My brothers' is Paul's favorite way of describing his fellow believers in the Christian community."[36]

That my circumstances – The ASV translated this as "what has happened to me."   We can fill in the things that have happened to him since he parted from

---

[35] Paul uses the word "glory" more than 75 times in his epistles. It is a word with many different, though related, meanings. Each time we come across the word, we must pick the one that fits the context of the passage we are studying. Hendriksen (*op. cit.*, p.62,63) has a long footnote which nicely introduces the different meanings.

[36] Loh, *op. cit.*, p.19.

them (Acts 20:6). Paul's ministry had been somewhat limited since he was seized by the Jews in the temple area of Jerusalem at the close of his third missionary journey (Acts 21:27-33). Following his arrest at Jerusalem, Paul spent two years captivity at Jerusalem and Caesarea. Then came the voyage toward Rome ending in shipwreck on the island of Malta. Then came upwards of two years imprisonment at Rome, awaiting a hearing before Caesar. He lived under guard in his rented house and carried on his ministry with all whom he could contact (Acts 28:30,31). The Philippians were greatly distressed at the news of Paul's imprisonment. What would happen to the cause of Christ now that their beloved apostle was in chains? "Perhaps they even worried that their offerings to Paul might be like 'feeding a dead horse'."[37] Paul wrote encouragingly that what might have appeared as a setback was in reality an important opportunity to spread the gospel.

Have turned out for the greater progress of the gospel – "The picture Paul paints, of course, is one of his imprisonment. The colors he selects to portray his own circumstances, however, are so subdued that only gradually does the viewer realize that it is not so much a self-portrait as it is a picture of the gospel's progress."[38] "Progress" translates *prokope*, "a verb used originally of a pioneer cutting his way through brushwood,"[39] going ahead into a new area to open it for settlers to follow. "Paul's imprisonment was not the end of his missionary activity. So far from shutting the door, it opened the door; so far from being a barrier, it opened the way to new spheres of work and activity, into which he would never have otherwise entered."[40] The result of his "circumstances" were different than might have been expected.[41] "The conditions surrounding his imprisonment and trial had brought his message to the favorable attention of many in Rome who would otherwise not have heard it; or hearing, would have given it

---

[37] Hendriksen, *op. cit.*, p.67.

[38] Harrell, *op. cit.*, p.60

[39] Alexander Souter, *A Pocket Lexicon to the New Testament* (Oxford: Clarendon Press, 1960), p.216.

[40] William Barclay, *The Letters to the Philippians, Colossians, and Thessalonians* in The Daily Study Bible Series (Philadelphia: Westminster Press, 1959), p.25.

[41] The NASB has used "greater" to translate the Greek *mallon*, which in this context (where the other part of the comparison is not stated) could well be translated "rather."

little attention."[42]   The progress of the gospel has been on two fronts: the praetorian guard and the local church.

1:13 -- *So that my imprisonment in* **the cause of** *Christ has become well-known throughout the whole praetorian guard and to everyone else,*

So that my imprisonment in *the cause of* **Christ has become well-known –** Paul's bonds were literal bonds, for he was constantly chained to a Roman soldier (Acts 28:30).   What has become well-known is that Paul was a prisoner, "not for crimes against society or for crimes against the state, but it was because of his relationship with Christ (the text is literally 'in Christ') that he was in bonds. The incarceration of Paul was related to the incarnation of Christ."[43]

Throughout the whole praetorian guard – First, it should be noted that there is no word for "guard" in the Greek.   Literally, the original reads "in all the praetorium."   The Greek word *praitōrion* is used in several different senses.[44] The NASB margin tells us the word can mean "the governor's palace," and when so used it would refer to the Roman military headquarters in any province. However, in this context, the term certainly refers to people, not a building; thus, the NASB's "whole praetorian guard" is a good translation,[45] and likely refers to

---

[42] Ed Hayden, *1957 Standard Lesson Commentary* (Cincinnati, OH: Standard, 1956), p.409.

[43] Harrell, *op. cit.*, p.61.

[44] In the Detailed Introduction to Philippians (at the end in this volume), it is shown that this word and how it is translated has been a key topic of discussion since it concerns the place of authorship for the Philippian letter, indeed, if not for all the Prison Epistles.

[45] "The expression 'praetorium' [here in Philippians] cannot refer to a building (as it often does in the Gospels), but must indicate some people, comparable with 'everyone else' at the close of verse 13.   Several Greek inscriptions use the word praetorium in a personal sense to designate the praetorian guard of the emperor in Rome (L. Heuzey and H. Daumet, *Mission Archaeologique* [1876], nos. 130f.; *Inscriptiones Graecae,* XIV [1890], no. 911; W. Dittenberger, *Orientis Graeci Inscriptiones,* II [1905], no.707).   This corresponds to a normal Latin literary usage (Pliny, *Nat.Hist*, xxv.6 [17]; Suetonius, *Nero* 9;   Tacitus, *Hist*. i.20).   During the first Christian centuries the praetorian guard was always garrisoned in Rome, although part of it would have provisionally accompanied the emperor abroad.   Inscriptions found at other places (as also those quoted above) have to do only with individuals who had earlier been members of the Roman bodyguard. Representatives of the theory that Philippians was written from Ephesus believe that inscriptions found on a road near this city prove that a praetorian detachment was garrisoned in Ephesus.   This is wrong, for the documents in question (*CIL* 6085 = 7135 and 7136) were made for a veteran who had been a member of the guard and who now served at this road as a rural policeman (*stationarius*). The praetorian guard itself had to be where the emperor was, and for the days of Paul this implies nothing but Rome."   B. Riecke, "Philippians, Ep. to the," *The New International Standard Bible Encyclopedia* (Grand Rapids: Eerdmans, 1979), Vol.3, p.839.

the soldiers who guarded Paul. The praetorian guard was comprised of 10,000 handpicked soldiers who served as the emperor's body guard. According to Acts 28, Paul was not imprisoned in the imperial guard's barracks (camp). Instead, he was under constant guard (Acts 28:16,30) in his own rented quarters. The praetorian soldier guarding him would stand watch and then be relieved by another soldier, and so on, around the clock. "'We are guarding a very remarkable prisoner,' they would say, 'and we are firmly convinced that his imprisonment is not for any crime he has committed but solely for his connection with Christ whom he proclaims'."[46]

And to everyone else – The Greek words so translated may be either masculine or neuter.[47] Presumably, since the next verse talks about people, this clause refers to other people in Rome in addition to the guards. His case, and even better, his cause, Christ's cause, had become the talk of the town. Immediately upon his arrival in Rome Paul addressed the chief of the Jews (Acts 28:17) and later a larger number (28:23), so the Jewish community in Rome was familiar with his situation. For two years he received all that came to him (28:30), so little by little, from Paul's visitors and Paul's guards, his case and his cause became known to the general public in the city of Rome.

1:14 -- *And that most of the brethren, trusting in the Lord because of my imprisonment, have far more courage to speak the word of God without fear.*

And that – This verse tells of a second way Paul's imprisonment in Rome has turned out to the greater progress of the gospel. The first was that Paul's relationship with Christ had become known to the praetorian guard and to every one else.

Most of the brethren – Previously, Paul called the Philippians "brethren." (see 1:12). Now Paul uses the term to identify Roman Christians. The church in Rome had been in existence for some years before Paul came (Romans 1:7-15). Just who the brethren were who are encouraged by Paul's conduct, we cannot say. Perhaps they are the ones from the provinces who came to the city after Claudius'

---

[46] Hendriksen, *op. cit.,* p.69.

[47] The KJV translators treated the Greek words as neuter when they rendered them as "in all other *places.*"

edict expired (see Acts 18:2).[48]   "Most" of the brethren (the majority) took courage; there were some exceptions, the language implies.

Trusting in the Lord – What do the words "in the Lord" modify?   (1) The KJV and ASV read "brethren in the Lord."   (2) It might read "bonds in the Lord."[49] (3) The RSV reads "made confident in the Lord" and the NASB reads "trusting in the Lord because of my imprisonment." Elsewhere (Philippians 2:24, 3:3,4; Galatians 5:10; 2 Thessalonians 3:4) Paul writes about "trusting in the Lord," and so we incline to this reading here.   Paul's example gives others courage.   After all, if the Lord is taking care of Paul, then the Lord will take care of them, too.   If Christ has not abandoned Paul the prisoner, then he will not abandon Paul's fellow Christians in Rome, either.

Because of my imprisonment – Paul's bonds were the occasion for the people in Rome to see the Lord at work in Paul's life.   The Lord had sustained Paul most wonderfully (Philippians 4:13), not only while in Rome, but also on the way to Rome as a prisoner (Acts 23:11, 27:23).   What the Lord had done for Paul, He could and would do for them.

Have far more courage to speak the word of God without fear – "Courage is contagious.   When, in coming to Rome, Paul saw the brethren, he thanked God and took courage (Acts 28:15).   Now because of him, they in turn thanked God and took courage."[50]   While Paul was using his contacts with his praetorian guards to maximum effect, Roman Christians were carrying the message where he could no longer go.   Yes, Paul was a prisoner, but he was still alive and proclaiming the message.   The Roman Christians see that they, too, could survive as well if they went on preaching.   Paul faced his situation with quiet courage.   They could do the same, and with greater freedom.   They might even do so more easily since there were now Christians in Caesar's household (Philippians 4:22).   Their new courage erupted in speech (the Greek is *lalein*, which implies a contrast with being silent).   The present tense indicates it was no momentary enthusiasm, but a continual speaking.   The "Word of God" is one of

---

[48] This note about the "ones from the provinces" assumes the folk named in Romans 16 were known to Paul out in the provinces before they came to Rome.

[49] However, the order of the words in the original (where "in the Lord" and "my bonds" are separated by the verb "being confident") pleads against this meaning.   Besides, the resulting interpretation, "trusting in my bonds in the Lord" makes little sense.

[50] Hayden, *op. cit.,* p.410.

several synonymous phrases Paul employs to denote the gospel of Christ.[51]   Not all the brethren lost their fear of what would happen to them if they were vocal Christians, but the majority have taken courage from Paul's example.   No longer are they afraid to speak out for Christ.

B. His Joy that the Imprisonment Means that Christ is Proclaimed. 1:15-18a

1:15 -- *Some, to be sure, are preaching Christ even from envy and strife, but some also from good will;*

Some, to be sure, are preaching Christ even from envy and strife – Verses 15a and 17 go together, and need to be read together to see that Paul speaks of two different groups of preachers who have different motives for preaching.   The motive of the first group was to cause Paul distress in his imprisonment.   The motive of the other group (verses 15b and 16) is described as having good will towards Paul.   The "some" (since there is a contrast to "most" in verse 14) are evidently Christian brethren, but a smaller segment of brethren than those alluded to in the previous verse.   "Preaching," which translates *kerusso,* a word that originally meant to perform the duty of a herald, is the standard New Testament word for the proclamation of the gospel.[52]   The two groups of men of whom Paul is thinking are all preaching Christ (see verses 15, 17, 18).   As far as one is able to gather from the text, none of the preachers is preaching false doctrine.   Who are the preachers whose motives are envy and rivalry, and who are trying to cause

---

[51] The best uncial manuscripts read here, "the Word of God," not just "the word" as the Byzantine text and P[46] have it.   Harrell (*op. cit.*, p. 63) identifies the synonymous phrases as "word of life" (2:16); "word of God" (1 Corinthians 14:36; 2 Corinthians 2:17, 4:2; Colossians 1:25); "word of Christ" (Colossians 3:16; 1 Timothy 6:3); and "word of the Lord" (1 Thessalonians 1:8, 4:15, 2 Thessalonians 3:1).   To this list we may add "the word of the cross" (1 Corinthians 1:18) and "the word of truth" (Ephesians 1:13).

[52] Bible students need to beware of the neo-liberals' distinction between *kerygma* and *didache*.   *Kerygma* is said to be the kernel of truth that lies behind most of our New Testament writings, while *didache* refers to the additions and accretions to the original kernel made by church people as the years passed.   Anything that is miraculous or super-natural in the record is said to be *didache*, and therefore not permanently valid or even true to fact.   Such a distinction is fatal to the validity of most of Christianity, and is therefore unacceptable.   Bible students also need to be aware that an attempt is made to distinguish between "preaching" (*kerusso*), which is affirmed to be evangelistic in thrust, and "teaching" (*didaskein*), which is affirmed to be instruction or teaching of believers.   In passages like 1 Corinthians 1:23, 9:27, 15:11, it may be that church preaching (instruction of believers) cannot be ruled out since the distinction between missionary preaching and church preaching cannot be clearly inferred.

Paul more distress?[53]   Perhaps these preachers "had been leaders in the church before Paul's coming and were stirred to envy by the fruitfulness of his ministry and the respect accorded to him by the brethren.   The gospel these leaders preached was straight and pure; hence Paul could approve of it.   But their motives were selfish.   Except for their jealousy to prod them, they would have shown little interest in winning the lost."[54]

But some also from good will – The second group of preachers in Rome (verses 15b, 16) consisted of those who were motivated by good will towards Paul.   The next verse will give us the essence of this good will.   This group of preachers had a strong affection for Paul and his work – they were not trying to gain back a former prestige for themselves.   These "some" are also a segment of the brethren alluded to in verse 14.   Perhaps this group of preachers were doing things which Paul as a prisoner could not do.

1:16 -- *The latter* **do it** *out of love, knowing that I am appointed for the defense of the gospel;*

The latter *do it* **out of love** – A word needs to be said about the verse order here. The KJV has verse 17 before verse 16, because some manuscripts have such an order.   Most newer Bible translations present the verses in the order we find them in the NASB.   The word "love" has been studied in the notes at Philippians 1:9.   The context here indicates Paul is the object of this love.   In contrast to the envy and rivalry that motivated the other group, this second group of preachers is motivated by love for him.[55]

Knowing that I am appointed for the defense of the gospel – The participle translated "knowing" likely has a causal connotation – they love Paul because they know why he is a prisoner in Rome.   "Defense" (as in Philippians 1:7 above)

---

[53] Not a few commentators suppose that the "dogs" warned about in Philippians 3 are the ones who are trying to cause Paul more grief.   "Strife" – dissension, party spirit – was one of their divisive characteristics (Philippians 3:3; Romans 2:28).   It is difficult to imagine Paul would commend such people for speaking "the word of God" (1:14) and then denounce them as "dogs," evil workers," and "false circumcision" (3:2).   These rival preachers in Rome are not to be identified with the Judaizers in Corinth who preached "another Jesus and a different gospel" (2 Corinthians 11:4) nor the Judaizers in Galatia who preached "a different gospel" (Galatians 1:6-9).

[54] Hayden, *ibid.*

[55] Of course, it could be said that the love of Christ naturally issued forth as love for His faithful servant, as well as in love for the lost to whom they were preaching.

means vindication of the gospel. What Paul has been preaching is right. "Appointed" (*keimai*) is a military term describing a soldier posted as a sentinel. "If we give the word a more metaphorical meaning, this verse says Paul had been 'put there' (*keimai*) not by his own miscalculations, nor by chance, but by the operation of God's providence. God had brought him to this place for the defense of the gospel."[56] Beneath the surface this language seems to imply that this second group of folk who recognized the nature of Paul's imprisonment had responded with a renewed effort to preach the gospel he represented. They stepped up their evangelistic work to ensure that the gospel did not fail to be proclaimed while he was imprisoned. That was a wonderful way to show their love for the apostle.

1:17 -- *the former proclaim Christ out of selfish ambition, rather than from pure motives, thinking to cause me distress in my imprisonment.*

The former proclaim Christ out of selfish ambition – "The former" takes up again the group of preachers first introduced in verse 15a. "Proclaim" is a translation of *katangellousin,* a compound word which reflects an intensification of effort on their part. The meaning of "proclaim" is substantially the same as "preaching" (*kerusso,* verse 15), that is, to proclaim the gospel with authority. Aristotle used the word *eritheia* ("selfish ambition") to denote "a selfish pursuit of political office by unfair means."[57] It came to denote one who was self-seeking; he was working for himself, rather than donating his services to someone else. They "proclaim Christ," so Paul found no fault with the content of their message. The problem was their motive for preaching.

Rather than from pure motives – This group's craving for honor and prestige crowded out any nobler motives for preaching. Those who were motivated in their preaching by such a selfish spirit might make followers of Christ, and the followers might be blessed, but there would be little credit due to the self-seeking preachers. They would have their reward if Paul suffered more discomfiture.

Thinking to cause me distress in my imprisonment – The present infinitive pictures what they hope is happening as Paul writes. Just how they supposed that

---

[56] Kent, *op. cit.*, p.111.

[57] William F. Arndt and Gingrich, F. Wilbur, *A Greek-English Lexicon of the New Testament* (Chicago: University of Chicago Press, 1957), p.309.

their increased evangelistic activity would add to Paul's "distress"[58] while he was imprisoned is not clear. Perhaps when he sees them free to move around and preach, this would make his chains more galling. Perhaps, since the Roman government was uneasy about the Jewish population in Rome, the growth of the Christian society might stir the jailers to increased severity, which might prevent Paul's continuing to freely receive visitors to whom he could preach unhindered. Verses 18-20 record Paul's confidence that this malignant policy would be disappointed.

1:18a -- ***What then?   Only that in every way, whether in pretense or in truth, Christ is proclaimed; and in this I rejoice.***

What then? – What was Paul's reaction?   "What does it matter?" is his question. Regardless of the preacher's motives, if Christ was being preached, Paul rejoiced. Paul will not allow himself to be troubled by those preachers whose motives were selfish ambition.   We admire this trait in Paul.

Only that in every way, whether in pretense or in truth, Christ is proclaimed – Paul graciously dismissed the elements of motive and personal likes and dislikes, and came to what he considered the only important facet of what was happening in Rome, namely, the preaching of Christ.   Since Paul affirms that "Christ is proclaimed," it is obvious that "truth" and "pretense" here relate not to the substance of their preaching but to the motives of the preachers.   "Pretense" speaks of those who know how to cover up their selfish ambition as they are preaching.   "Truth" speaks of those whose sole aim is actually the glorification of their Lord and Savior.   How is it possible that selfish individuals can render any service to the gospel?   Because the listeners do not know the bad motives of the selfish preachers.   All the listeners hear is good, solid preaching; they do not see the bad motives.   "Christ is proclaimed" would also carry a message to the Philippians that their missionary offerings to Paul have not been wasted.   They have borne fruit.

And in this I rejoice – The hopes of the selfishly ambitious preachers are disappointed.   Paul doesn't feel the "distress" they hoped to cause for him. Paul's joy at the fact that Christ is preached crowds out every other consideration.

---

[58] "*Thlipsis* ('distress') literally means *friction*. 'To rouse friction by one's chains' is a vivid way of portraying the consternation of a person who cannot rectify a situation because of some limitation which has been placed upon him" (Robert H. Mounce, "The Epistle to the Philippians" in *The Wycliffe Bible Commentary* [Chicago: Moody Press, 1962], p. 1322).

This is the first time this key-word "rejoice" occurs in this letter. "Rejoice" and "joy" will occur many more times (cf. 1:18b,25;   2:2,17,18,28,29;   3:1; 4:1,4,10).

C. His Joy Because of his Opportunities to Exalt Christ.   1:18b-26

1:18b -- *Yes, and I will rejoice,*

Yes, and I will rejoice – Perhaps we should treat the word "yes"[59] as the beginning of a new paragraph.[60]   Verse 19 begins with the particle "for," indicating it is connected to something just said, rather than beginning a whole new thought.   For this reason, a number of translations treat these words "Yes, and I will rejoice" as the beginning of a new paragraph.   One reason Paul rejoices (verse 18a) is that whatever the motive, the gospel is preached.   Now he tells us another reason why he shall continue to rejoice.

1:19 -- *For I know that this shall turn out to my deliverance through your prayers and the provision of the Spirit of Jesus Christ,*

For I know that this shall turn out for my deliverance – "For"[61] at the beginning of this verse shows that the verse gives the reason why Paul intends to continue to rejoice (verse 18b). "This" is apparently a reference to Paul's present imprisonment.[62]   "Know" is *oida*, a confident knowledge, the result of considering the evidence, not *ginosko*, a knowledge that comes by experience. He feels sure that the outcome of the present situation will be his "deliverance." *Soteria* is best taken as "deliverance" or release from this imprisonment.   The word "salvation" is one of the words regularly used to translate *soteria* as the mar-

---

[59] It is unexpected to see the Greek conjunction *alla* translated as "yes."   It apparently is what is called an emphatic use of *alla* with the sense of "certainly," "indeed," or "in fact."   (H.E. Dana and Mantey, Julius R., *Manual Grammar of the Greek NT* [New York: Macmillan, 1946], p.240-241).

[60] If this clause is taken with verse 18, it expresses a strong determination not to lapse into irritation at the deceptive conduct of those preachers whose motives were bad (and who were trying to add to Paul's distress).

[61] The better Greek manuscripts read *gar* ("for") rather than *de* ("and").

[62] Another interpretation found in some commentaries is that "this" refers to the preaching of Christ that verse 18 alluded to.   Such comments are based on the KJV which reads "and" rather than "for" at the beginning of verse 19.

ginal note indicates,[63] but such a sense here (namely, of primary or ultimate salvation from sin) is not indicated. We think Paul is anticipating his release from his present imprisonment, since in 1:25 and 2:24 he expresses confidence in his near-term release so that he will be able to see them.

Through your prayers and the provision of the Spirit of Jesus Christ – Paul pictures his deliverance as being accomplished by two means: one was the prayers of the Philippians on his behalf; the other was the assistance furnished by the Holy Spirit.[64] "Twice previously (1:4,9) Paul has indicated that he prayed for the Philippians. Now he assumes that they also pray for him, an assumption he frequently makes concerning his converts (cf. 2 Corinthians 1:11; Colossians 4:3; 1 Thessalonians 5:25)."[65] "Prayers" is again *deēsis* (see notes at 1:4), which denotes requests for a particular benefit.[66] "The Spirit of Jesus Christ" (or sometimes "the Spirit of Christ") is a name for the Holy Spirit found in a number of instances in the New Testament (e.g., Romans 8:9; 2 Corinthians 3:17; Galatians 4:6; 1 Peter 1:11). The word picture behind "provision" (*epichoregias*) is of generously supplying whatever was necessary to pay for a chorus and or drama presented in the theater. "Help" (NIV) might catch the idea, but "rich provision" would catch the idea even better. What "provision" might Paul be referring to? Several answers are suggested elsewhere in Scripture. Perhaps Paul is repeating the idea he wrote in Romans 8:26,27, that "when men with their prayers have supplied all that they can, the Spirit intercedes to improve upon their petitions and to supply blessings   more wonderful than we know how

---

[63] Since the word has several different meanings in the New Testament ("deliverance, preservation, safety, salvation" [Thayer, *op. cit.*, p.612]) the context must decide in each case which meaning to give *soteria*. Because of the statement he makes in verse 20, some Bible students conclude that Paul is using the word loosely; if he is released it will show in his life, or should he be executed he speaks of his own future salvation as he is brought home to be with Christ. Goodspeed translated Philippians 1:19, "All this will turn out for my highest welfare." Still others, on the basis of the Septuagint of Job 13:16, which Paul apparently quotes, maintain that Paul has reference to the ultimate vindication of his stand for Christ.

[64] In this commentator's judgment, the genitive "of the Spirit" is a subjective genitive, meaning the provision which the Spirit gives. It also seems right to treat "of Christ Jesus" as a subjective genitive, making Jesus the one who sends the Spirit (John 15:26).

[65] Harrell, *op. cit.*, p.68.

[66] If *soteria* is "deliverance" rather than salvation, then this is not a request that they pray for his future salvation. Verse 22 of Philemon shows that Paul is asking for prayers to be offered that he be delivered from the confinement of imprisonment.

to ask."[67]   Perhaps Paul wrote "the Spirit of Jesus Christ" rather than simply "the Holy Spirit" to call attention to Christ's promise that the Holy Spirit would give men on trial the wisdom to know how to speak and act (Luke 12:12).[68]   Certainly in an apostle's case, the Holy Spirit had the ability to plant thoughts in his mind, even before Paul began to speak.   This would fit "not be put to shame" (i.e., not be shamed into silence) of which he speaks in the next verse.

1:20 -- *according to my earnest expectation and hope, that I shall not be put to shame in anything, but* **that** *with all boldness, Christ shall even now, as always, be exalted in my body, whether by life or by death.*

According to my earnest expectation and hope – Verse 20 continues the sentence begun in verse 19 so that "according to ..." describes the expected results of the "provision of the Spirit."   "Earnest expectation" (*apokaradokia*) pictures a concentrated, intense look into the future, which turns its gaze away from everything else to fix it on the one object of its desire.   In the Greek text "earnest expectation" and "hope" are nouns that are grammatically joined so as to indicate that they are aspects of a single concept.   The one thing on which Paul focuses is explained in the phrases which follow.

That I shall not be put to shame in anything – The object of the apostle's expectation as he looked into the future is twofold: 1) I shall not be shamed into silence, and 2) Christ will be honored.

But *that* **with all boldness** – The basic idea in "boldness" (*parresia*) is that of "free" or "bold speech," "openness" or "courage in speech."   The supposition is that Paul has in view his coming testimony before his imperial judges.   When that day comes, if it does, it would not be easy to give a courageous witness in those circumstances.   Yet as Paul anticipates what he will say, any failure to stand firm in loyalty to Christ would, for Paul, be "shame" and a cowardly restraint.   That's why he looks for help from the Holy Spirit when he has opportunity to witness.

Christ shall even now, as always, be exalted in my body, whether by life or

---

[67] Hayden, *op. cit.,* p.411.

[68] If we were to treat "of Christ" as an objective genitive, making Christ the recipient of the Spirit's help, then we would have Paul reminding his readers that the very same Spirit who sustained Jesus in His trials is the one who was operative in Paul's case, and would sustain him during his trials (cp. Hebrews 9:14).

by death – Such free speech was a privilege the Roman empire granted to its free citizens and not to others. Paul is focused on using that occasion to glorify Christ whatever may be the verdict of the tribunal. "Even now" seems to imply that the time of crisis is very near. It is nearing time for a decision about his fate to be made. Paul's ambition was that Christ would be exalted during his trial just as Paul had "always" attempted to exalt Christ. Most likely the implied agent (the one who does the exalting of Christ) is none other than the Spirit (verse 19) who would help Paul be bold in speech, which in turn would cause men to think more of Christ. Through many changing circumstances Paul had held to a steady course in his life and preaching. He is determined that he will not change now. He will keep trying to cause men to think well of Christ. Attempts have been made to explain the language "in my body." Perhaps one of the more satisfactory attempts is the idea that a born-again Christian uses the members of his or her body as tools by which righteousness is accomplished (Romans 6:13). Paul is thus saying, 'I am going to see to it that my body is used in such a way – whether I live and am set free or whether I die by execution – that Christ is magnified in other people's estimation.'

> Since he became a Christian, Paul always used his body to do and say what would bring honor to Christ. He hoped and fully intended to keep on doing that. If he were freed, he would honor Christ with his teaching and missionary work as he had been doing. If he was not released shortly, or if he were put to death, he would honor Christ by teaching all who came to him or in his writings, and should it so be, by dying fearlessly instead of denying the faith.[69]

1:21 -- *For to me, to live is Christ, and to die is gain.*

For to me, to live is Christ – Being introduced by "for," this verse gives a reason for what Paul has just said. Having indicated that decision time is near, he discusses the subject at some length. He tells the Philippians that the sole aim in his life was to honor Christ and to work for Christ. If the decision is release ("to live"), he will continue to serve Christ. "To me" is in the emphatic position which implies a contrast with others. Just who is in Paul's mind as he draws the contrast is not certain. It might be "those to whom he has just been referring, and who, no doubt, are still very much in his mind; namely, the preachers 'who proclaim Christ out of selfish ambition.' *Paul*, then, in contrast with them, is not

---

[69] Orrin Root, *1979-80 Standard Adult Lesson Commentary* (Cincinnati: Standard, 1979), p.51. John A. Bengel (*Gnomon of the New Testament* [Edinburgh: T&T Clark, 1860], Vol.4, p.125) has noted that the apostles were not omniscient in respect to their own futures; they lived in faith and hope just as we do.

self-centered, but *Christ*-centered. He (Paul) is concerned with the honor and glory of his wonderful Redeemer."[70]

And to die is gain – Should the tribunal sentence Paul to be executed, physical death is not the end of a man's existence.[71] For the Christian, to be absent from the body is to be present with the Lord (2 Corinthians 5:6-8). But in our judgment, Paul is thinking of more than gain for himself. In a context where bringing honor to Christ is the subject, "gain" likely speaks of gain for Christ. Paul's physical death would end his work here on earth, but it would open up a whole new world of service. This is in harmony with Revelation 7:15 which tells us the redeemed "serve God day and night in His temple," and with Revelation 22:3 which tells us that the throne of God and of the Lamb will be in heaven, "and His bond-servants shall serve Him."

1:22 -- *But if* I am *to live* on *in the flesh, this* will mean *fruitful labor for me; and I do not know which to choose.*

But – In the NASB several words in italics have been inserted in this verse and the next to smooth out Paul's grammar.[72] Paul, in perplexity that stirred his emotions, was weighing the advantages of two possibilities – to continue to live on earth or to depart and be with the Lord – and was asking himself if the choice between these two were his, which would he choose. He doesn't know whether he would prefer to serve Christ here or to enter into His presence and serve Him in heaven.

If *I am* to live *on* in the flesh – The expression "to live in the flesh" means to go on living in this world, to continue living in his human body.

This *will mean* fruitful labor for me – "Labor" is a term frequently used by Paul to refer to his missionary labor (Romans 15:18; 2 Corinthians 10:11; Philippians 2:30); so is "fruitful" (Romans 1:13). If Paul is released, he will continue his

---

[70] Hendriksen, *op. cit.*, p.76.

[71] The two infinitive phrases "to live" and "to die" are present tense and aorist tense. The former stresses the progressive nature of living. The aorist simply looks at the fact of dying.

[72] A word-for-word translation in the order the words appear in Greek would be as follows: "But if to live in the flesh this *is* to me a fruit of work and what I shall choose I know not." There are three clauses in the Greek: (a) "if to live in the flesh," (b) "this to me a fruit of work," and (c) "I do not know which to choose." At issue is how far the "if-clause" runs, and where the conclusion clause begins.

work of spreading the gospel to unevangelized peoples.   This will result in fruit; that is, souls won to Christ through his further ministry.

And I do not know which to choose – We expect to read Paul's verbalization of what the result of the other alternative ("to die") would mean to him, but he breaks off the discussion without ever stating the alternative.   He leaves his readers to fill in the alternative mentally.   The Greek word translated "know" (*gnōridzō*) regularly has the meaning "to cause to know, to make known, or to tell."   Such a causal meaning would make good sense in the present passage.   Paul would be saying "I cannot tell you" which destiny I'd rather have.   This is why the KJV translators wrote "I wot not," where "wot" is an old English present indicative, of which the infinitive is "to wit" (i.e., to testify).

1:23 -- *But I am hard pressed from both* directions, *having the desire to depart and be with Christ, for* that *is very much better;*

But I am hard pressed from both *directions* – The word picture in "hard pressed" is of a traveler in a narrow, rocky defile, with a wall of rock on either side, leaving only two choices – go ahead or go back.   As Paul thought of his prospects, he sees only two prospects, though in his case either alternative was a good one.

Having the desire to depart and be with Christ – The word picture in "depart" (*analusai*) is of the loosening of tent pegs in order to take down a tent so that one may move on to another place, or the weighing anchor of a ship to release it from its mooring so it may be on its journey.[73]   It is a euphemism for "to die."   "The physical body (as in 2 Corinthians 5:1) is looked upon as a mere tent.   Each day is a march nearer home, and death is the last striking of the tent on arrival."[74] "And be with Christ" indicates that "the apostle knows that when his soul departs from this earthly life, it is immediately *with Christ* [in Paradise, Luke 23:43].   It does not 'go out of existence' until the day of the resurrection, nor does it 'go to sleep' (Psalm 16:11, 17:15; Matthew 8:11; Luke 16:25; John 17:24; 1 Corinthians 13:12,13;   2 Corinthians 5:8; Hebrews 12:23; Revelation 6:10, 20:4).   It at once

---

[73] M.R. Vincent, *Word Studies in the New Testament* (Wilmington, DE: Associated Publishers and Authors, 1972), p.875.

[74] Barry, *op. cit.,* p.258.

enjoys blessed fellowship with the Savior (Acts 7:59)."[75]   Paul tells us he had a desire and yearning to depart and be with Christ.   For Paul, there is "on one side an eager wish to get out of the pressures and discomforts and persecutions of this life and be at home in glory with Jesus.   This is a perfectly natural wish when one is old and suffering, if he is completely sure of the glorious life that is to come.   Who has not heard some old saint say sincerely, 'I wish the Lord would just take me home'."[76]

For *that* is very much better – Paul piles up three comparative adjectives as he tries to express how much better heaven is than life here on earth.   "The Greek phrase here (*pollo mallon kreisson*[77]) is very emphatic, and the apostle seems to labor for language which will fully convey his idea that heaven is 'better beyond all expression'."[78]   Passages such as Romans 8:18 ("...the present time are not worthy to be compared with the glory that is to be revealed to us"), 2 Corinthians 5:8 ("to be absent from the body and to be at home with the Lord"), 2 Timothy 4:7,8 ("in the future there is laid up for me the crown of righteousness which the Lord ... will award to me ... but also to all who have loved His appearing"), and Philippians 3:14 ("the prize of the upward call of God in Christ Jesus") explain why heaven is very far better.

1:24 -- *yet to remain on in the flesh is more necessary for your sake.*

Yet -- In the previous verse we have given one side of the circumstances that were pulling Paul in one direction.   Here we have the other side – namely, the need of the Philippians.

To remain on in the flesh is more necessary for your sake – An opportunity to minister to the believers in Philippi is   recognized as being more important than

---

[75] Hendriksen, *op. cit.*, p.78.   When the dead are described as "sleeping" (as Acts 7:60; 1 Corinthians 15:51,52;   1 Thessalonians 4:14,15), it is speaking of the body, not the soul.

[76] Root, *op. cit.*, p.52.

[77] "*Kreisson* is the comparative form of the adjective *kratus* ('more excellent'), which is commonly used as the comparative of *agathos* ('good'), plus the comparative adverb *mallon* ('to a greater extent"), and the dative adjective *pollo* ('much') used adverbially" (Kent, *op. cit.*, p.117).

[78] Albert Barnes, "Ephesians, Philippians, Colossians" in *Barnes's Notes on the New Testament* (Grand Rapids: Baker Book House, 1955), p.158.

his desire to depart and be with the Lord.   He will state what some of those needs were in the next verse as well as later in this very letter.

> The church had not existed for much longer than a decade.   Only yesterday some of its members had emerged from idolatry and immorality of heathendom. Though this was a wonderful church in many ways, it had its weaknesses, and it was confronted with real dangers (see Philippians 3:1-3, 3:19, 4:12). Accordingly, Paul was ready for the present, if it were God's will, to forego the enticing glories of heaven in order to be of help to the Philippians.[79]

1:25 -- *And convinced of this, I know that I shall remain and continue with you all for your progress and joy in the faith,*

And convinced of this – The "this" concerning which Paul was convinced is what he has just written in verse 24, namely, that his ministry was still needed by the brethren in Philippi.   We presume that it was through Epaphroditus, the messenger who came to Paul from Philippi (Philippians 2:25), that Paul became convinced of the need for his ministry there.

I know that I shall remain and continue with you all – There is a play on words in the original.   The Greek verb "remain on" in verse 24 was *epimenein*.   Now as he writes "I shall remain," Paul uses another form of the verb *meno*, and then he uses a third form for "continue" (*parameno*), which expresses the idea "I shall abide side by side with you."   Here, again, we have Paul's inclusive "you all" (cp. 1:1,4,7,8).[80]   The word translated "know" in this phrase is *oida*, the same verb he used in verse 19.   Here, as there, it is doubtful that this verb can be taken as meaning that Paul had miraculous or prophetic insight into the future course of his career.   As the verb *oida* referred more to personal conviction rather than prophetic insight when he spoke of not seeing the Ephesian elders again (Acts 20:25),[81] so we understand the meaning of the verb here in Philippians 1:25. What was the basis of Paul's conviction that he would be delivered from imprisonment and be able to visit Philippi?   Probably Paul's personal conviction

---

[79] Hendriksen, *op. cit.*, p.79.

[80] Hendriksen (*op. cit.*, p.79) believed that "This 'you all' probably includes more than the church at Philippi."

[81] 1 Timothy 1:3 and 2 Timothy 1:15,18, 4:20, written some years after the meeting with the Ephesian elders recorded in Acts 20, show that Paul's expectation of not seeing the Ephesians again proved to be mistaken.   Thus we say that "know" does not involve infallible prophetic insight.

arose from the circumstances.   The two years of waiting for his accusers to come is nearly over.   He is confident by now that they are not coming.   He just has to wait for the time to elapse and he will be set free.

For your progress and joy in the faith – What Paul expects to accomplish (after he is released) by his ministry among the readers is expressed in these words and also in the words that are in apposition to this clause in verse 27.   "Faith" here might refer to a body of doctrine, namely, the Christian faith.   It also might have reference to each individual Christian's personal faith.   Earlier in this letter, Paul spoke of the "progress of the gospel" in Rome in spite of his imprisonment (Philippians 1:12), in fact, largely because of it.   Now he uses the same word about the "progress" of the Philippians.   He pairs with it another significant word, "joy," a key-word in this epistle (see 1:4,18).   Paul pictures his continuing ministry among the Philippians as resulting in a continuing increase in faith and a greater delight in it.

1:26 -- *so that your proud confidence in me may abound in Christ Jesus through my coming to you again.*

So that your proud confidence in me – The sentence which was begun in verse 25 continues on here in verse 26.   When it is recognized that the Greek word used here is *kauchēma*[82] (not *chairo* and its derivatives, the word usually translated "joy" or "rejoicing" in Philippians), the KJV translation "your rejoicing in me" makes good sense here.   "Through many gifts and words of appreciation the Philippian saints had made evident their appreciation for Paul.   Their joy would be even more abundant because of his release from prison and his coming to be with them.   The Philippians would exclaim, 'Paul, we are very happy to have you with us once more'."[83]

May abound in Christ Jesus – The original reads, "in Christ Jesus in me."   The Philippians are pictured as rejoicing in what Christ has done in Paul's case.   The Philippians (if they followed Paul's request, 1:19) have been praying for his release.   Now Paul is describing their joy at answered prayers.   The Philippians are pictured as thanking Christ for bringing their dear friend to them again.

Through my coming to you again – Note the word "again."   Paul had visited Philippi at least three times before this letter was sent to Philippi: once on his sec-

---

[82] *Kauchema* is often translated "boast."

[83] Ed Hayden, *1988-89 Standard Adult Lesson Commentary* (Cincinnati, OH: Standard, 1988), p.270.

ond missionary journey (Acts 16:11-40) and twice during his third missionary journey, once on his way toward Corinth (2 Corinthians 8:1-5) and again on his way from Corinth toward Jerusalem (Acts 20:5,6). All the historical evidence points to the fact that Paul's expectation was fulfilled, and that, having been released, he actually visited the Philippians once more.

> First Timothy 1:3 speaks of a visit by Paul to Macedonia, which evidently took place after his first imprisonment in Rome. The joyous reunion with the Philippian Christians that most likely took place during this journey surely must have fulfilled Paul's expectation that the Philippians' joy in Christ would be increased by his presence with them. In turn his joy would be enhanced by being able to witness how the Philippians had grown in dedication to Christ. Apart from Jesus such joy, even in the midst of severe hardship, is not possible.[84]

III. A FIRST SERIES OF ADMONITIONS.   1:27-2:18

> *Summary*: In one of the grandest passages in all Paul's writings, "he now proceeds to give his readers some practical exhortations. Until he can personally minister to their faith, he must content himself with writing to them. Their standard of Christian consistency and efficiency must not be regulated by his personal presence or absence."[85]

A. Admonition to Stand Fast, United and Unafraid, Against Their Opponents.   1:27-30

1:27 - *Only conduct yourselves in a manner worthy of the gospel of Christ; so that whether I come and see you or remain absent, I may hear of you that you are standing firm in one spirit, with one mind striving together for the faith of the gospel;*

Only – Having discussed his own and the gospel's future, Paul now turns to discuss the future of the Philippians (1:27-2:18).   Paul says, "Only."   That is,

---

[84] Ed Hayden, *1999-2000 Standard Adult Lesson Commentary* (Cincinnati, OH: Standard, 1999), p.345.

[85] M.R. Vincent, *The Epistles to the Philippians and to Philemon* in the International Critical Commentary Series (Edinburgh: T&T Clarke, 1961), p.31.

whatever happens to him personally, whether he comes to see them, or remains absent, the important thing is for them to be sure to conduct themselves as believers, in a manner appropriate to the gospel of Christ.

Conduct yourselves in a manner worthy of the gospel of Christ – "Conduct yourselves" translates a Greek verb which means literally "behave as citizens."[86]

> Paul's words say literally, "Behave as citizens in a manner worthy ...." The language would resonate with his Philippian readers. Philippi was a special city, a colony of Rome; its people were Roman citizens, and were expected to conduct themselves accordingly. Here Paul reminded the Christians that they were a colony of Heaven, having citizenship there, and were expected to act like it (compare Philippians 3:20).[87]

"Gospel[88] of Christ" may be a subjective genitive (the gospel of which Christ is the author), or an objective genitive (the gospel which proclaims Christ). Since verse 28 has the gospel coming "from God," it seems the objective genitive interpretation is to be preferred here. "Gospel of Christ" is Paul's usual way of designating the message he and the other New Testament preachers proclaimed (cf. 1 Corinthians 9:12; 2 Corinthians 2:12; Galatians 1:7; 1 Thessalonians. 3:2). The idea that the Christian life is to be shaped by something of greater value than this world's standards is fairly common in Paul's letters (1 Thessalonians 2:12; Colossians 1:10; Ephesians 4:1). Verses 27-30 are one sentence in the Greek. These verses will go on to show that some conflict of antagonism or persecution threatened the Philippians at this time. Paul has in mind what the Philippians' reaction to that conflict would be. Paul is concerned over how they will conduct themselves during this time of difficulty.

So that whether I come and see you or remain absent, I may hear of you – The question of whether he would live or die (noted in Philippians 1:20-26) was not firmly answered. Paul expected to be released from his imprisonment and

---

[86] Customarily, when Paul speaks about conduct or behavior, he employs the Greek word *peripatein*, "to walk" (e.g., Philippians 3:17,18). Here, however, he uses a term (*politeuesthe*) which refers to one's conduct or behavior as a citizen.

[87] Hayden, *88-89*, p.270.

[88] See the notes at Philippians 1:5 for the meaning of "gospel." Hendriksen (*op. cit.*, p.81-85) has a helpful study entitled, "What is the Gospel?"

to visit Philippi again; but he might not be released from prison. However, he would still follow news of them with vital interest. The most important item of that news would concern their unity in contending for the revealed truth of the gospel (compare Jude 3). They were to have one controlling attitude and purpose. "Paul now goes on to give some specifications, some examples, of the right conduct he is urging. First, Christians stand firm; second, they should be united in one spirit and one mind; third, they should be energetic (striving together); fourth, they should be defending the faith against those who would oppose it and be extending the faith by preaching the gospel and winning others."[89]

That you are standing firm in one spirit – "Standing firm" is a military metaphor which would resonate with citizens of Philippi, many of whom were ex-soldiers.[90] Men who have been in a war know what it is to be able to stand when under attack, and how sometimes it is very hard to do so, especially when others run away. Paul wants the Philippian Christians to stand fast like the famous Macedonian phalanx did.[91] Were the Philippians facing persecution, or hostile attitudes from non-believers? Verse 28 will speak of opponents. Chapter 3 talks about the "dogs." For "in one spirit" the Twentieth Century New Testament translation has "animated by one spirit."[92] In light of Romans 8:5-9, Paul may be saying "I want to hear that you people are standing firm as your enlivened spirits prompt you to do."

With one mind striving together for the faith of the gospel – Not only are the Philippians to stand firm, but they are also to strive side-by-side (*sunethlesan*).[93]

---

[89] Root, *op. cit.*, p.53.

[90] Philippi was a military colony, its chief magistrates (Acts 16:20) were *praetors*, (Greek, *strategoi*), literally, "generals."

[91] We have a similar use of the military figure of standing one's ground against the hosts of evil in Ephesians 6:13-17.

[92] The commentaries debate whether or not "one spirit" should be translated as "Spirit" or "spirit" or "attitude." Vincent (*Philippians*, p.33) presents the arguments for "attitude" when he writes about a "disposition which is communicated in Christ to believers, filling their souls, and generating their holy qualities and works." If the phrase "one spirit" is parallel to "one soul" (and those words "one soul" immediately follow having no separate preposition in the Greek), then the sense of man's spirit is manifestly suggested. Remember that "soul" and "spirit" make up the inner life of man.

[93] The *sun* on the verb "striving together" does not mean they are striving or contending against Paul, but in fellowship with each other the Philippians are striving or contending for the gospel.

Since the previous metaphor was drawn from the military world, perhaps this too is still a military metaphor, of fellow soldiers standing side by side to repel the attack of an enemy. Or perhaps Paul has changed metaphors, drawing this one from the gladiatorial games where all the members of the team struggled equally hard to win the contest. Where the NASB reads "with one mind" the Greek reads "with one soul." Paul is saying that he wants all their desires and emotions concentrated on one object. He wants them all acting together in the one great work (cp. Acts 4:32). He wants to hear that there is an *esprit de corps*, or camaraderie, in the Philippian congregation that binds all the members together "for the faith of the gospel." This is the only time in the New Testament where this particular construction ("for the faith of the gospel") appears. "Faith" in this passage likely refers to a body of doctrine (the content of what is believed) just as is true also of the use of "faith" in Galatians 1:23; Ephesians 4:5; 1 Timothy 4:1, 5:8; and Jude 3,20.[94] "Of the gospel" means the "faith" which the gospel teaches. In view of the danger that outsiders would attempt to distort the truths taught in the gospel, this clause pictures the Philippians as actively and energetically promoting each other's understanding of the great doctrines of the Christian faith.

1:28 - *in no way alarmed by* your *opponents -- which is a sign of destruction for them, but of salvation for you, and that* too, *from God.*

In no way alarmed by *your* opponents – Continuing the examples of right conduct which began with verse 27, Paul now tells the Christians not to be scared or intimidated by those who oppose them. "Alarmed" (*pturomenoi*) is a picturesque word often used to describe the terror of a startled horse about to stampede.[95] The word "opponents" is used to "denote those who opposed the

---

[94] John C. Poirier, "The Meaning of Πίστις in Philippians 1:27," *The Expository Times* 123 no.7 (April 2012), p.334-337, has argued that in this place the lesser-known rendering of *pistis* as "stewardship" is to be preferred to the translation "faith" in the NASB. This suggestion changes the picture slightly, as it makes the Philippians to be striving together alongside of Paul (sharing in the *stewardship* of the gospel with which he was entrusted) rather than striving alongside each other to arrive at a common goal.

[95] Diodorus Siculus (xvii. 34,6), speaking of the chariot-horses of Darius at the battle of Issus, uses this word: "Frightened (*pturomenoi*) by reason of the multitude of the dead heaped round them, they shook off their reins." Plutarch (*Repub. Ger. Praec.*, p. 800) uses the word of a multitude of people that was scared like a shy and fickle animal.

Christian faith, including opponents of Jesus (Luke 13:17), as well as adversaries of the church, both Jewish and Gentile (1 Corinthians 16:9; 2 Thessalonians 2:4; 1 Timothy 5:14)."[96]   Who are the "opponents" being faced by the Philippian Christians?   If we let verse 30 explain (a verse which speaks of the "same conflict" they have seen Paul struggle against), we would identify the Philippians' opponents as being unbelievers, whether pagan or Jewish.   Paul's first trouble at Philippi was triggered by "Romans" who were involved in the occult (Acts 16:16-23) and who used government officials to punish Paul and Silas.   Likewise, Paul's current imprisonment, first at Caesarea and then at Rome, resulted from the Jews' antagonism toward him, and their use of Roman courts to punish him.[97]

Which – The Greek word so translated is the feminine pronoun *hētis*, and whose antecedent is "faith" (a feminine noun).[98]

Is a sign of destruction for them, but of salvation for you – "The faith of the gospel" is the thing that is a sign of destruction for the opponents.   "Sign" (*endeixis*) was an Attic law-term denoting proof obtained by an appeal to facts.[99] When the great propositions of the gospel are studied it soon becomes apparent that opponents of the gospel are bound for destruction.   "Destruction" (*apoleia*) speaks of eternal punishment in hell.   *Apoleia* is the regular New Testament term for eternal destruction and is so used in the Gospels (Matthew 7:13; John 17:12), Paul (Romans 9:22), and Peter (2 Peter 2:1,3).[100]   "Salvation" is future and eternal for the Christian, as contrasted with destruction for the opponents.   When

---

[96] Kent, *op. cit.*, p.120.

[97] Because the word "Judaizer" is often not carefully defined (were they Jewish Christians, or unbelieving Jews?), we are hesitant to call the Philippian opponents "Judaizers," especially since there is nothing in 1:28-30 that requires us to identify these opponents with the ones introduced in chapter 3.

[98] The relative pronoun "which" does not point back to the 'fearlessness' of the Philippians, for the term "no way alarmed" is masculine.

[99] Kennedy, *op. cit.*, p.431.   If the word speaks of an appeal to the facts, then Lightfoot's suggestion (*op. cit.*, p.106) that there is an allusion here to the sign of life or death given by the populace in the amphitheater when a gladiator was vanquished, by turning the thumbs up or down, is beside the point.

[100] "What is meant is not simple extinction of existence ... but an everlasting state of torment and death (Albrecht Oepke, *Apoleia*, *TDNT*, 1:397)" (Kent, *ibid.*).

the great propositions of the gospel are studied, one of the things emphasized is the glorious future in store for the followers of Christ.   While the opponents may not now see the "sign," Christians certainly can appeal to the facts of the gospel and see what their future holds.

And that *too*, from God – "That" (*touto*, neuter) refers grammatically neither to "salvation" nor to "sign" nor to "faith" (all of which are feminine nouns, and for which the feminine form of "that" would be required).   The only neuter word in the preceding verses is "gospel" (*euangeliou*).   The gospel, which has communicated their Christian doctrine, has come from God.

1:29 -- *For to you it has been granted for Christ's sake, not only to believe in Him, but also to suffer for His sake,*

For – "For" introduces a reason why it was said the "faith of the gospel" is a "sign" of salvation.

To you it has been granted – The word "granted" (*echaristhe*) speaks of "granting it as a privilege," a "favor," or as a "gracious gift."   As the verse will go on to elaborate, both the opportunity to become Christians and their opportunity to suffer for Christ were privileges granted to them by God.

For Christ's sake – Since the preposition ("in behalf of") appears twice in this verse, perhaps Paul originally intended simply to write "it has been granted on behalf of Christ to suffer."   But in mid-sentence he thinks to add the reason why they may have to suffer, namely, because they have become believers in Him.   God has granted what He has to the Philippians as a favor to Christ (*huper Christou*, "on behalf of Christ").

Not only to believe in Him – The opportunity to "believe in Him" was granted to the Philippians, when Paul, acting under the direction of the Holy Spirit, went to Philippi rather than to Bithynia or Asia (Acts 16:6-10).   The preacher first went to Philippi because God so directed him.[101]   "Believe in Him" here includes

---

[101] That God is represented as granting to the Philippians an opportunity to believe in Christ must not be read as though each individual's personal faith is a gift of God, as some denominational preachers word it.   "Faith comes by hearing the word of Christ" (Romans 10:17).   As is explained elsewhere in this volume on the Prison Epistles, not even Ephesians 2:8 says that faith is something given to certain individuals by God Himself.

obedience to Christ's commands.[102]   The Greek verb is in the present tense, and points to the continuousness of the action of faith.

But also to suffer for His sake – A second thing granted to the Philippians was to suffer on Christ's behalf (*huper autou*).   "If we question the propriety of referring to suffering as a privilege, a 'gracious gift' (*echaristhe*), we must remember that the New Testament regards suffering as God's means of achieving His gracious purposes both in His own Son (Hebrews 2:10) and in all believers (James 1:3,4; 1 Peter 1:6,7)."[103]   From the following verse, it appears as if the suffering which the Philippian Christians are experiencing is in the form of persecution because they are Christians.   Elsewhere we read that Christians who suffer for Christ could rejoice in their sufferings; e.g., Peter and John went on their way from the Council "rejoicing that they had been considered worthy to suffer shame for His name" (Acts 5:41) and "to the degree that you share the sufferings of Christ, keep on rejoicing" (1 Peter 4:13).   Such rejoicing requires the sufferer to recognize that he or she has been granted a "gracious gift."   Jesus said, "Blessed are those who have been persecuted for the sake of righteousness, for theirs is the kingdom of heaven" (Matthew 5:10).

1:30 -- *experiencing the same conflict which you saw in me, and now hear* **to be** *in me.*

Experiencing the same conflict which you saw in me – This verse serves to define what Paul meant when he wrote about opponents (verse 28) and about suffering for Christ's sake (verse 29).[104]   The present tense participle translated "experiencing" and the characterization "the same conflict which you saw in me" together indicate that the Philippians are at the present moment enduring similar persecution as that which occurred in their city during Paul's second missionary

---

[102] Leon Morris (*The Gospel According to John* in the NICNT [Grand Rapids: Wm. B. Eerdmans, 1971], p.335-337) has shown that *pisteuo* ("to believe") followed by a prepositional phrase (either *eis,* as here, or *en*) speaks of an obedient faith.   See also J. Gresham Machen, *New Testament Greek for Beginners* (New York: The Macmillan Company, 1923), p.85, for similar evidence.

[103] Kent, *op. cit.*, p.119.

[104] The Greek construction ("experiencing" is a participle in the nominative plural), if strictly taken, points back to the first clause in Philippians 1:27 ("that you are ... in no way alarmed by your opponents").   This makes the words following the dash in verse 28 of the NASB a sort of parenthesis.   If we treat the construction here as being broken grammar, then verse 30 gives the details explaining the last words of verse 29.

journey (Acts 16:19-40).   2 Corinthians 8:1,2 is a further indication of present persecution when it tells us that "a great ordeal of affliction" has been occurring recently to the churches of Macedonia.

> In Philippi, Paul had been "advertised" by a demon-possessed girl, had been slandered, mobbed, stripped, flogged, thrown into a dungeon, his feet locked in gruesome stocks.   The devil was behind all this.   Influenced by Satan, the masters of the slave-girl, the infuriated rabble, and many others had joined in inflicting on him this "shameful treatment" (Acts 16:16-24).   The Philippians had seen this conflict between the kingdom of light and the kingdom of darkness.[105]

And now hear *to be* in me – Though he was now far away in Rome, they had heard from others what he was undergoing there.   Messengers had gone back and forth between Philippi and Rome, and they carried news of Paul's imprisonment at the hands of the Romans.   Through this very letter (see 1:12-17, 4:14) also, and through Epaphroditus, they are hearing about Paul's bonds.   They are also hearing about those "opponents" who were causing distress for him in his bonds.

---

[105] Hendriksen, *op. cit.*, p.91.

B. Admonition to Have the Right Attitude Toward their Brethren. 2:1-13

1. The fourfold incentive to a right attitude. 2:1

2:1 -- *If therefore there is any encouragement in Christ, if there is any consolation of love, if there is any fellowship of the Spirit, if any affection and compassion,*

If therefore – The second in the series of admonitions, which began at Philippians 1:27, is introduced here, though "therefore" shows this admonition is closely connected with what precedes. In the previous admonition in the closing paragraph of chapter 1, Paul had expressed the ardent wish that he might hear that the Philippians "are standing firm in one spirit, with one mind striving together (side by side) for the faith of the gospel" (1:27). In this second admonition Paul will encourage the Philippians to "make my joy complete" (2:2)[1] by endeavoring to look out for the interests of others in the Christian community, rather than acting selfishly. Here in verse 1, Paul introduces this second admonition by means of a series of "if-clauses" in the Greek. The clauses are written in such a way as to assume that what is said in the premise (the "if-clause") is true.[2] Thus, the "if-clauses" are intended to establish some powerful motives or incentives for their doing what verses 2-4 suggest.

(If) there is any encouragement in Christ – If we translate *paraklesis* as "encouragement" (rather than "consolation" as did the Vulgate and KJV[3]), then Paul's first incentive is that Christians were responsible to heed the words of Jesus Christ, who certainly exhorted to unity of believers (John 17:20-23). Surely, that is an appeal to a strong motive.

---

[1] Verses 1-4 form one long sentence in the Greek. "Make my joy complete" (verse 2) is the only main verb in the Greek of this whole sentence.

[2] The word "if" is not intended to express doubt. The Greek construction of these "if-clauses" is what is known as first class conditional sentences. Such constructions assume that what is said in the premise (the "if-clause") is true. Though no verb occurs in these "if-clauses" in the Greek, our translators have rightly supplied "is" to complete the sense.

[3] The choice of "consolation" to translate *paraklesis* may have been found in the reference to persecution with which chapter 1 closed. When folk are persecuted, the highest aid they can get comes from Christ. He comforts the afflicted. Or those translators may have understood Paul as saying you can console me by doing what I ask in this admonition.

If there is any consolation of love – The word translated "consolation" is *paramuthion*, which means persuasive power, friendly persuasion. Paul does not define whose love he has in mind, and probably leaves it vague on purpose. Perhaps it is Paul's love for the Philippians ('If my love for you has any persuasive power'), or Christ's love for the Philippians ('If Christ's love for you means anything at all to you'), or their love for one another ('If your love for one another is in deed, not just in thought or words'). The second motive or incentive to which Paul appeals is love, an appeal based on the idea that love does move a person to action.

If there is any fellowship of the Spirit – We have had the word for "fellowship" at 1:5. It means participation or partnership in a common cause. The meaning of this third motive to which Paul appeals is greatly influenced by the answer to some technical matters: shall we use a capital "S" or small "s" to translate *pneuma*,[4] and is "of the Spirit" an objective or subjective genitive?[5] When all these questions have been answered, we suppose that Paul is saying something like this: 'Since you have experienced the life and blessings produced by the Holy Spirit, you surely are ready to listen to my plea for unity.'

If any affection and compassion – The fourth motive to which Paul appeals is an appeal to human kindness. There is a problem with the Greek grammar as the text currently stands in our manuscripts. The word translated "any" does not agree with either the word translated "affection"[6] or the word translated "compas-

---

[4] The same issues are involved here as were involved in 1:27 ("in one spirit"). Capital "S" makes it a reference to the Holy Spirit. Small "s" makes it a reference to the human spirit, or to an attitude.

[5] If we take it as an objective genitive, "fellowship of" (or participation in) would mean that all the Philippian Christians *sharing* the same Spirit (or "spirit") would be ample reason for a unified church. Capital "S" would say the indwelling Spirit was something that all the Philippian Christians had received. If we take it as a subjective genitive, it means that the Spirit created or wrought the fellowship. To so behave as to rupture the harmony created by the Spirit would be working in direct opposition to what the Spirit was trying to achieve.

[6] The Greek word *(splangchna)* here translated "affection" is the same word translated "heart" at Philemon 7. For an explanation of the word see the comments in this volume on Philemon 7.

sion," both of which are plural forms in the Greek.[7]   Regardless of the grammatical disagreement, the idea Paul has in mind is clear.   Again, Paul does not specify toward whom the "affection (tender mercies) and compassion" which he has in mind are directed.   Perhaps he is speaking of affection for one another in the Philippian church.   Perhaps we may picture him as saying, 'If you have any affection for me, then listen to my appeal.'   Could they resist such a plea?

2. The right attitudes are specifically described. 2:2-4

> As Paul appeals for right attitudes, he specifically asks that there be unity and harmony (verse 2), humble mindedness (verse 3), and helpfulness (verse 4).

a. Unity and harmony. 2

2:2 -- Make my joy complete, by being of the same mind, maintaining the same love, united in spirit, intent on one purpose.

Make my joy complete – There was joy in the heart of Paul as he thought about the Philippians (1:4).   But there was room for more joy.   The picture is of a cup, a partly full cup of joy.   It was not full to the brim.   It was not running over with bubbling joy.   Paul wants them to fill up his cup of joy.   As long as there were some right attitudes lacking, as long as there were problems in the congregation at Philippi, Paul's joy could not be full/complete.   The thing that will fill Paul's cup is not a speedy release from prison, but the spiritual progress of each and every one of the Philippian Christians.   He needed to know that those brethren in Philippi were working together in perfect harmony.

By being of the same mind – The marginal note "that you be" in the NASB indicates there is a *hina* ("that") in the Greek, which serves to introduce the content of this admonition which, if it were followed by the Philippian Christians, would result in making his joy complete.   "Being of the same mind" translates

---

[7] *Ei tina* (the neuter plural reading found in the Textus Receptus) would be correct Greek, rather than *ei tis* (the masculine singular reading found in all the uncials).   Did the amanuensis make the mistake, as he hurriedly wrote what Paul was dictating?   (This is the suggestion of Lightfoot, *op. cit.*, p. 108).   Did Paul, full of emotion as he was speaking, actually use bad grammar?   (This is the suggestion of B.C. Caffin, "Philippians" in *The Pulpit Commentary* [Grand Rapids: Eerdmans, 1962], p.58.)   Under any circumstance, the reading *ei tis* is a valuable testimony to the scrupulous fidelity of the early transcribers, who copied the text as they found it, even when it contained readings so manifestly difficult.

Greek words which mean "you think the same thing." What is involved in their thinking the same thing is elaborated in the following clauses.[8] "What Paul asks is not some faceless conformity, but a solid commitment to the same purpose and cause – a commitment sufficiently powerful to override the tendencies toward bickering and division."[9] "Paul did not expect total uniformity in the Philippians' preferences and opinions; but he did expect their mind-set, attitude, and commitment to be centered on Christ."[10]

Maintaining the same love – This is one item included in "being of the same mind." Love for each other – love being the fruit of the Spirit (Galatians 5:22) – is something that must be worked at to be maintained.

United in spirit – "United in spirit" is an attempt to translate a nominative plural noun *sumpsuchoi*, which literally means "joined in soul."[11] The KJV and ASV translated it as "of one accord." Our word "accord" comes from the Latin *ad + cor* and means "heart to heart," or two hearts beating as one. The picture suggested is of two hearts in perfect key, a symphony of feeling. The whole congregation of Christians is (in a sense) a choir, and must be kept in tune. If each one of us keeps his life in tune with God, it will not be impossible to get in tune with each other.

Intent on one purpose – Here is a second item included in "being of the same mind." The Greek behind "intent on one purpose" is literally "thinking the one

---

[8] The two circumstantial participles translated "maintaining" and "intent" modify the verb translated "being (of the same mind)."

[9] Hayden, *88-89*, p.276.

[10] Hayden, *99-2000*, p.354.

[11] Another technical matter must be decided here. There is no participle connected with *sumpsuchoi*. Should we mentally add a participle like we must do a bit later in verse 3 ("doing"), and make this an independent item? Or should we let the Greek participles in this verse decide the number of items included in "being of the same mind"? If we do this we likely should omit the comma, with the result that "united in spirit" no longer is an independent item in this list. "United in spirit" then would be part, either of the preceding item ("united in spirit maintaining the same love"), or part of the following item ("united in spirit intent on one purpose"). Comments offered above indicate this commentator's judgment that the latter is the better option.

(thing[12])."   Paul wants them to set their minds on "the one," that is on oneness, unity, harmony.   If we omit the comma after "spirit" and we join "united in spirit (soul)" with "intent on one purpose," we have this phrase saying that "thinking" is the thing that animates the soul.   In Paul's view of man, the inner attitude determines the outer life (Romans 8:5-8; 2 Corinthians 13:11).   Folk in the congregation are to so love and think that they work together to see there is no disharmony in the congregation.

b. Humble mindedness.   3

2:3 -- *Do nothing from selfishness or empty conceit, but with humility of mind let each of you regard one another as more important than himself;*

Do nothing from selfishness or empty conceit – Paul has just indicated in verse 2 that inner attitudes determine our conduct.   Now he is going to identify two negative attitudes, "selfishness" and "empty conceit", that will result in disruption and destruction of the desired unity and harmony Paul wants to see in the behavior of the Philippian Christians.[13]   "Selfishness" is a word Paul has used already (1:17) of some preachers in Rome who loved to trouble him because they were motivated by "envy and strife" (1:15).   Paul does not want to see such an attitude of selfish ambition in the church at Philippi.   The Greek word translated "empty conceit" is a combination of the two words which mean "hollow" and "opinion."[14] It is eagerly seeking honor or acclamation that does not rest on character or accomplishment but rather on an inflated opinion of one's own value or importance.   The man who is proud or a braggart, who has an air of "better than thou," has a hollow opinion of himself.   "Selfish ambition" is knocking the other person down; "empty conceit" is elevating or commending one's self over others.

But with humility of mind – The antidote to selfishness and conceit is humble mindedness.   The Greek word *tapeinophrosune* translated "humility of mind" is a term that is not found before it appears in the New Testament.   A related word,

---

[12] The Greek word "one" is neuter.   We must add a neuter noun (such as "purpose," NASB) to complete the meaning.

[13] Though the NASB reads "do nothing," there is no participle or verb in the Greek of this first clause of verse three.   All the Greek has is the word "nothing."   Either we must mentally supply a verb or participle (such as "contemplate," a word that speaks of an inner disposition), or we supply the participle "thinking" (*phronoutes*) from the end of the preceding verse.

[14] Mounce, *op. cit.*, p.1324.

tapeinos, which spoke of "cowardliness, groveling, rank self-abasement, submission because of fear," was used by the self-assertive Greeks to refer to an undesirable attitude. The appearance of the new word *tapeinophrosune* looks like the Bible writers coined a new word to describe the attitude that would best depict how a Christian thinks. "Humility of mind" has been described as "the position of one who has stooped down to lift another up."[15]

Let each one of you regard one another as more important than himself – Thoughtful consideration (the verb form translated "regard" means *esteem*) for others is what is being taught. It is calling on Christians to think of others, not necessarily as essentially superior, but as worthy of preferential treatment. This is a good definition of what "humility of mind" is. "If I think you are better than I am, and you think I am better than you are, how can there be strife between us? If you prefer to give honor to me, and I prefer to give honor to you, both of us are honored (Romans 12:10)."[16] "It is 'more blessed to give than to receive' tributes, credit, and words of encouragement as well as money and material goods."[17] "Each one" is plural in the better Greek manuscripts; thus, this is a rule for all Christian lives at all times. It is difficult to practice this Christian virtue, but such deference is a beautiful behavior; the absence of it is "pig manners," every one for himself.

c. Helpfulness. 4

2:4 -- *Do not* merely *look out for your own personal interests, but also for the interests of others.*

Do not *merely* look out for your own personal interests – As humility of mind (verse 3b) is the antithesis of "empty conceit," so consideration for others (verse 4) is the antithesis of selfish ambition. In this verse, Paul is not teaching that a man must pay no attention at all to his own interests,[18] but he is teaching that the Christian must not selfishly fix his eye upon his own personal interests to the exclusion of those of others. The Christian has no right to conduct his life by the law of the jungle.

---

[15] Hayden, *99-2000*, p.354.

[16] Root, *op. cit.*, p.59.

[17] Hayden, *ibid.*

[18] See notes below on the word "also." The NASB has rightly inserted "merely" lest the instruction be misunderstood.

But also for the interests of others – The word "also" should not be overlooked. Paul is not saying a person should not give any attention at all to his own affairs.[19] Rather, Paul is likely reproducing the Savior's teaching. Jesus taught that His followers should "love your neighbor as yourself" (Matthew 19:19), a command which receives added stress when the neighbor is a brother or sister in Christ (John 13:34; Galatians 5:10). It may be noted that even Jesus' command leaves room for a person to pay attention to his own interests – though not exclusively. Both times the word "interests" occurs in this verse the Greek has simply the neuter plural word "the," so we must supply a noun. "Interests" is a good choice, for the exhortation seems to be a broad, general term that speaks to us of "helpfulness" wherever it is needed.

> ### 3. The Lord's example and pattern for the Christians to follow. 2:5-13
>
> #### a. Christ's example on the way through humiliation to exaltation. 5-11

2:5 -- *Have this attitude in yourselves which was also in Christ Jesus,*

Have this attitude in yourselves – If our minds direct our behavior, and if the Lord's people are to exhibit Christlike behavior, they must begin with the mind – the basic attitude – exhibited by Jesus. For this reason, Paul's review of the gospel does not deal with the words Jesus spoke or the miracles He worked. It does not even speak directly of His resurrection. It speaks rather of the attitude with which Jesus approached His ministry. Specifically, what that attitude was will be unfolded in the verses following. The Greek translated "have this attitude" in the NASB is a present imperative which literally means "keep thinking this."[XX] The NASB margin indicates scholars have not agreed on the translation of *en humin* – whether it means "among you" or "in yourselves." If the translation "among you" is accepted, the verse speaks about their collective or group attitude. If, as is more likely correct,[20] the translation "in you" or "in your-

---

[19] "If a person were so foolish as to neglect his own interests altogether, he would soon become a burden to others. The Christian way is rather for each one to earn his own living if he can (2 Thessalonians 3:11,12), and to provide for his own family (1 Timothy 5:8). The word 'also' is a sign that Paul is saying a person should not consider his own interests *only*, but *also* the interests of others" (Root, *op. cit.*, p.60).

[XX] There is a manuscript variation as to the verb, whether it is *phroneistho* (a 3rd person singular, present passive imperative) as the Textus Receptus has, or whether it is *phroneite* (a 2nd person plural present active imperative) as the Nestle Text has it. Because of these variant readings, several different translations have been given to this verse.

[20] Caffin (*op. cit.*, p. 59) has this word, with which we agree: "The words, 'in Christ Jesus,'

selves" is accepted, the verse speaks of the personal attitudes of the individual Christians. This verse thus says that each Christian is responsible to seek and develop his own personal Christ-like attitude.

Which also was in Christ Jesus – The great example of the proper attitude is Christ Jesus. The attitude we Christians should have is the attitude Christ had, which was an attitude of self-renunciation with a view to helping others. That is the attitude each Christian is commanded to develop.

2:6 -- *Who, although He existed in the form of God, did not regard equality with God a thing to be grasped,*

Who – "With this verse begins what is perhaps the best known and, in many ways, the most significant passage in the letter."[21] The antecedent of "who" is "Christ Jesus," and "who" serves as the subject of what is said in both verses 6 and 7 which follow, one of which speaks of His pre-incarnate existence and the other of His human condition. Nearly every word in this passage has been the subject of fierce controversy, and because of this, there is an extended treatment at the end of the Detailed Introduction to Philippians that discusses the history of the controversies and the reasons for adopting some of the conclusions we do in the comments which follow.

"Although verses 5-11 contain one of the outstanding Christologies in the New Testament, they were written to illustrate the point of humility and selflessness."[22] Two assertions are made concerning Jesus the Messiah (Christ): He always existed in the form of God, and He did not regard that as something to be grasped or held on to no matter what.

The author of this commentary is reluctant to say (as do many modern commentaries) that with this verse Paul begins quoting a Christian hymn already in circulation amongst the churches.[23] Truly, there is a form and rhythm found in these verses, but 1 Corinthians 13 indicates Paul was quite capable of writing

---

show that the corresponding words, 'in you,' cannot mean 'among you,' but in yourselves, in your heart."

[21] Harrell, *op. cit.*, p.87.

[22] Kent, *op. cit.*, p.22.

[23] See the section in the Detailed Introduction to Philippians titled "The controversy over the interpretation of Philippians 2:5-11" beginning on p.724. A weighty and unsuitable result of the attempt by some to say the words of verses 6-11 are poetry and not theology, or that the source of the words is unknown, is that today's readers are left with a huge doubt about the Deity of Christ.

in a poetic style, and Ephesians 5:25-27 is evidence that Paul can make a sublime statement about Christ almost incidentally in order to illustrate a practical point.

Although He existed in the form of God – The circumstantial participle *huparchōn*, translated "existed", is a present tense participle which we would translate *"though existing* in the form of God." The present tense indicates Jesus' continuing condition, and Paul's choice of *huparchōn* (rather than the common Greek word for "being", which is *eimi*) describes what the pre-incarnate Christ always was in His "essential and unchangeable nature."[24] "Form" translates the Greek *morphe*. A quick study of Greek synonyms helps us grasp what Paul is saying about Jesus. In this passage we have both "form" (*morphe*) and "fashion" (*schema*). The term *morphe* denotes that the outward manifestation corresponds to the inner essence, in contrast to the noun *schema* (2:7), which refers simply to the outward appearance, which may be temporary. Barclay has a good illustration of the difference between *morphe* and *schema*.

> The essential *morphe* of any human being is manhood -- the fact of his manhood is constant, and never changes. But a person's *schema*, his outward form, will continually be changing. A baby, a child, a boy, a youth, a man of middle age, an old man -- always have the *morphe* of manhood, but the outward *schema* changes all the time ... Now the word Paul uses for Jesus being in the "form" of God is *morphe*: that is to say, Jesus is unalterably in the form of God; His essence, His unchangeable nature is divine. However His outward *schema* might alter, He remained in essence and in being divine.[25]

So, Paul begins by saying that Jesus always was and always is essentially, unalterably, and unchangeably God![26]

Did not regard equality with God a thing to be grasped – The Greek beneath "equality with God" is *isa theon*. *Isa* is an adverb (not the adjective *ison*, which would describe His being) and so describes His manner of existence; Jesus was living a manner equal with the manner in which God lives. The ASV's "being

---

[24] Loh, *op. cit.*, p.55. To try to express the nuance of this verb some translators have chosen to use the English word "subsisting" rather than "existing."

[25] William Barclay, "The Letters to the Philippians, Colossians, and Thessalonians" in *The Daily Study Bible Series* (Philadelphia: Westminster Press, 1959) p.44. Vincent (*op. cit.*, pp.78-90) has a helpful excursus on verses 6-11, especially the application *morphe* and *schema* to Jesus Christ.

[26] Again, it is to be emphasized that the participle *huparchōn* is a present tense, and it stands in sharp contrast with all the aorist tenses which follow it.

on an equality with God" was a good way to translate the Greek adverb.[27] "Grasped" translates *harpagmon*, a verb that can be translated either actively or passively.[28] We judge the passive meaning to be correct because the next verse, beginning with "but," implies a contrast to something just said. Jesus did not regard living in a manner of equality with God a thing He tenaciously had to hang on to (cling to) at all costs, but He emptied Himself. Jesus did not grasp or "cling to His prerogatives as God's equal" (Phillips translation). The Lord's willing descent from celestial glory to earthly servanthood is noted in 2 Corinthians 8:9, "For you know the grace of our Lord Jesus Christ, that though He was rich, yet for your sakes He became poor." The previous phrase here in verse 6 spoke of Jesus' equality of being with the Father. He always was and is the same divine person. Now this phrase tells us (if we may illustrate it thusly) that He was willing to give up His penthouse for a dwelling in the ghetto.

2:7 -- *But emptied Himself, taking the form of a bond-servant,* and *being made in the likeness of men,*

But emptied Himself -- In three swift clauses Paul describes what Jesus did instead of tenaciously clinging to a manner of living equal with God that was His by nature. "Emptied" translates the verb *kenoō*, a word which means, quite literally, "to empty," and is used of pouring something out of a container, until the container is empty.[29] He did not give up any of His Deity (the "form of God" in which He always exists[30]), but He did give up the independent exercise of some of the prerogatives of Deity when He became incarnate and temporarily subordinate to the Father (Matthew 28:18; John 12:49). It could be worded that Jesus gave up His glory when He became incarnate, since in Gethsemane Jesus prayed that the Father would glorify Him with "the glory which I ever had with

---

[27] This phrase should not be interpreted as though it denied essential equality of the Son with the Father, for that would make it contradict the first clause in this verse which has affirmed Christ's essential Deity.

[28] The KJV's "thought it not robbery to be equal with God" treated the verb in an active sense, with the idea being that Jesus did not think of asserting Himself so as to be equal with God.

[29] Barclay, *op. cit.*, p.45. This passage has provided the title given to studies of *Kenosis Christology*, i.e., theories which probe the nature of Christ's "emptying" Himself. (See discussion of this and related topics beginning on p.738 in the Detailed Introduction to Philippians.)

[30] The New Testament plainly shows that the incarnate Christ is no less than God Himself. Romans 9:5; Colossians 1:15,19; and Revelation 1:13-16, where Christ now looks like the ancient of days though He is in His "subordinate" state in the mediatorial kingdom.

Thee before the world was" (John 17:5).[31]   "Down from His glory, ever living story, my God and Savior came, and Jesus is His name."[32]   Since Philippians 2:6 has spoken of Jesus as not insisting on clinging to His existence in a manner equal to God, it is obvious this is what Jesus gave up.   This verb "emptied" is followed by two participles (*labon*, "taking"; and *genomenos*, "being made") which modify the verb "emptied" and effectively show what this emptying involved.   It must be remembered that Paul is illustrating the attitude of stooping down to look out for the interests of others (rather than merely for one's own interests).

Taking the form of a bond-servant – One of the things Jesus did when He emptied Himself at the time of His incarnation was to take the form of a bond-servant.[33]   This is the only time Jesus is called a "bond-slave" (*doulos*) in the New Testament, and He was a bond-slave of God, not of men.[34]   Worded another way, "bond-servant" speaks of His temporary subordination to the Father.   The word translated "form" (*morphe*) is the same word used in verse 6.   It speaks of inner essence, not just outward appearance.   Christ's actions as a bond-servant came from the inside; they were not just play acting.   The word "taking" (*labon*) does not imply an exchange, but rather an addition.   He always exists in the "form of God" (verse 6), so that was not relinquished; but He did take on something in addition to His inner essence of Deity.   "He took on the form of a bond-servant while He retained the form of God."[35]   As He emptied Himself to serve others, He laid aside glory and heavenly station, but He could not lay aside His divine being.

---

[31] Kent (*op. cit.,* p.124) aptly alludes to Mark Twain's novel *The Prince and the Pauper*, describing a son of Henry VIII who temporarily changed positions with a poor boy in London, as providing an illustration of what Jesus did as He emptied Himself of His living in a manner of equality with God.

[32] William E. Booth-Culbertson, "Down From His Glory" in *Rodeheaver's Gospel Solos and Duets,* Number 3 (Winona Lake, IN: Rodeheaver Hall-Mack Co., 1938), p.45.

[33] The participle translated "taking," an aorist tense, points to the same time He emptied Himself (also an aorist tense) as being the time when He took on the form of a bond-servant.

[34] Jesus was a "servant" (*diakonos*) of men (Matthew 20:28; Luke 22:27; Romans 15:8), and in some passages is called a "servant" (*pais,* 'Child') of God (cf. Matthew 12:18; Acts 3:13, 4:27,30 – passages which reflect the "Suffering Servant Poems" of Isaiah 42:1-4 and 52:13).   It was Christ Jesus who said, "I am in the midst of you as one that serves" (Luke 22:27).

[35] Hendriksen, *op. cit.,* p.109.

***And* being made in the likeness of men** – "Being made" (*genomenos*) could be translated, "being born in the likeness of men," for *ginomai* is sometimes so used.[36] "Likeness of men" indicates He became a member of the human race ("men" is plural). Inasmuch as angels are servants (Hebrews 1:7,14), Paul makes it clear when Christ became a bond-servant. It was when He took on the likeness of human beings. The Greek word "likeness" (*homoiōmati*) has a different connotation than *eikōn* ("image") does. It stresses similarity but leaves room for differences. He was a real man,[37] but He was more than a man. There were certain respects in which He was not absolutely like other men.[38] In the four Gospel accounts (Matthew 1:18,23, 3:17; Mark 1:11; Luke 1:32-35, 2:11, 3:22; John 1:1,14), from the very first Jesus is presented as both the Son of God and the Son of Man. He was the Son of God before He was the Son of Man. He *continued to be* the Son of God; by contrast, He *became* (*genomenos*) the Son of Man.

2:8 -- *And being found in appearance as a man, He humbled Himself by becoming obedient to the point of death, even death on a cross.*

And being found in appearance as a man – This first phrase in verse 8 looks at Jesus from the standpoint of how He appeared in the estimation of men.[39] As far as external "appearance" (*schemati*) was concerned, to other men He appeared to

---

[36] The difference between the two Greek words for "born" (*gennao* and *ginomai*) is this – *gennao* speaks of coming into being for the first time; *ginomai* speaks of a change from one kind of existence to another.

[37] The word "likeness" suggests similarity, but this does not mean that Christ's humanity is unreal (cf. Romans 8:3; Hebrews 2:7,14).

[38] For example, at times He had to ask for information just like other men have to ask (John 11:34), and at times He could read men's minds (John 2:24,25), which is a prerogative of Deity (Jeremiah 17:10).

[39] "*Heuretheis* ('found') is not a Hebraism, nor does it stand for *einai* ('to be'). *Einai* expresses the quality of a person or thing in itself; *heuretheis* expresses the quality as it is discovered and recognized" (Vincent, *op. cit.*, p. 60). There is a contrast between the closing phrase of verse 7 which describes what Jesus actually was, and the opening phrase of verse 8 which describes how He appeared to men.

be a mere man (*hos anthrōpos*).[40]   *Schema* (see the word explained in notes above at verse 6) refers to Jesus' outward physical features, His looks, clothing, and manner of action; it contrasts with *morphe* which describes His inner essence.

> Jesus appeared to the world just like any other man.   Joseph was considered His father (Matthew 13:55).   His divinity was not revealed in His personal appearance; there was no halo constantly about His head.   Like other men He could become hungry, exhausted (Matthew 4:2; John 4:6,7; Mark 4:38); His tear ducts worked (John 11:35).   And, as other men, He became subject to physical death, which in His case meant death on a cross.[41]

He humbled Himself by becoming obedient to the point of death – Christ's emptying of Himself did not stop with His becoming temporarily subordinate to the Father ("bond-servant"), nor with His becoming a human being ("being found in appearance as a man").   There was a further step in His humility (stooping down to help another).[42]   It was a tremendous comedown for Jesus to become a man, but that was only the start.   Jesus humbled Himself more than that.   Paul is giving Christ as an example of the kind of humility he is speaking about.

> It took humility of mind for the Word to become man at all.   Even if He had become the emperor of the world it would have been a very great comedown.   But Jesus went far beyond that in His humanity.   He became a baby in a manger, a carpenter in Nazareth, a wandering teacher in Galilee and Judea.   He became "despised and rejected of men; a man of sorrows and acquainted with grief" (Isaiah 53:3).   And then He went to the cross to suffer an ignominious death.   And Paul says, "Let this mind be in you."   If we have such a mind in us, surely we will have no difficulty with the small sacrifices we make day by day in order to be in harmony with our brothers as Paul urges in verses 2 and 3.[43]

Even death on a cross – It was no ordinary death that Christ went through because of humble mindedness.   Of all forms of death, crucifixion was the most

---

[40] On a few occasions the apostles saw His glory, glory as the only begotten God (John 1:14,18), but such occasions were the exception, not the rule, during Jesus' earthly ministry.

[41] Enos Dowling, *1962 Standard Lesson Commentary* (Cincinnati, OH: Standard, 1961), p.362.

[42] Though the KJV has an "and" in this phrase, there is no "and" between "humbled himself" and "becoming obedient" in the Greek.   The participle "becoming obedient" implies that the supreme act of self-humiliation consisted in the Lord's voluntary submission to death.

[43] Root, *op. cit.*, p.61.

torturing, the most full of shame, a death reserved by the Romans for slaves and the worst and most despised criminals in the empire, a death accursed in the eyes of the Jews (Deuteronomy 21:23). It is hard to imagine any greater humility than the humility that accepted such a terrible, torturing death for the sake of others.

2:9 -- *Therefore also God highly exalted Him, and bestowed on Him the name which is above every name,*

Therefore also – The word "therefore" is important. It translates *dio*, which means "as a consequence of His humiliation."[44] What happened in Jesus' case follows the general rule that Jesus Himself taught, "He who humbles himself shall be exalted" (Luke 14:11; see 1 Peter 5:6). "On at least three occasions Jesus made that statement. He advised against claiming the best seats at dinner parties (Luke 14:10,11); or parading one's own virtues in prayer (Luke 18:14); or taking the titles of honor in religion (Matthew 23:12). Here, in a sense larger than all of these, the same principle is demonstrated."[45]

God highly exalted Him – In the previous verses the emphasis was on what Christ did because of His humble mindedness. Now the emphasis is on God's response to Christ's attitude and actions. The aorist tense "highly exalted" points to the time of Christ's resurrection, ascension, and coronation. "Highly exalted" translates the compound Greek word *huperupsōsen* (from *hupsoō*, "exalt," and *huper*, "above") which might be translated "super exalted." Paul could have written "exalted," and that would have told us that Jesus was back to where He was before He became incarnate. Why did Paul add the comparative *huper* ("highly" or "above")? In what does His superior dignity consist? It cannot mean that Jesus was more God after His death than before. Before His incarnation, He was Deity in heaven; He was no less Deity while on earth (He never gave up His "existing in the form of God"), and He is no more Deity following the ascension (He still exists in the form of God). What does Jesus have now that He did not have before His incarnation? He has a glorified human body, for one thing. In heaven right now He is the glorified Son of Man (Acts 7:56). It will be as the "Son of Man" that He "comes in the clouds of heaven" (Daniel 7:13; Matthew 26:64), and has "authority to execute judgment" (John 5:27). As a consequence of Jesus being willing to humble Himself, God exalted

---

[44] Vincent, *Word Studies*, p. 880.

[45] Hayden, *88-89*, p.277.

Him.   When God exalts a man, how much more magnificent is the man's position than when he tries to exalt himself.   Philippians, are you listening?

And bestowed on Him the name which is above every name – The same word translated "granted" at Philippians 1:29 is here translated "bestowed."   It speaks of something God did graciously, wholeheartedly, in addition to highly exalting Jesus, at the same time He highly exalted Jesus.[46]   The better Greek manuscripts read "*the* name, " not just "*a* name" as some versions have it (see KJV), but since Paul does not tell us in plain words what the name is, there has been a great diversity of opinion on this point.[47]   Perhaps, as the next two verses might suggest, "Lord Jesus Christ" is the name in Paul's mind.   Or perhaps Paul meant that God gave to Jesus such honor and glory ("name") that every title by which He is known becomes a supreme term of honor and an occasion of praise.[48]

2:10 -- *that at the name of Jesus every knee should bow, of those who are in heaven, and on earth, and under the earth,*

That at the name of Jesus every knee should bow – "That" (*hina*) may express either the purpose of Christ's exaltation, or the result of His exaltation.   We might render it "so that."   We suppose Paul is telling us what God had in mind when He super-exalted Christ – He wanted all beings to bow in acknowledgment of who Jesus is (verse 10), and to confess that He is Lord (verse 11).   The words here in Philippians 2:10-11 are adapted from Isaiah 45:23, a passage quoted in Romans 14:11.   In Isaiah the words, "to Me every knee will bow," are the words of Jehovah.   That Paul can apply the words to Jesus Christ, as he does in Philippians and Romans, is a powerful testimony to the Deity of Jesus Christ. Since "in the name" is the phrase constantly used for worship of God (e.g., "So I

---

[46] "Bestowed" (*echarisato*) is an aorist tense just like the verb "highly exalted."   Both refer to the time of our Lord's resurrection, ascension, and coronation.

[47] Some of the opinions seem to miss the requirements of the text.   For example, some say "Jesus" is the name, but the context which has the giving of the name as something which occurred at the same time God exalted Him appears to rule out that option.   Again, some say "Lord" (*kurios*, which was the Greek word used in the LXX to translate the four letter sacred name, YHWH) seems to be ruled out by the fact that Jesus always was existing in the form of God.   He was Lord before He was exalted at the close of His earthly ministry (John 13:13).   He was Jehovah (YHWH) from all eternity (cp. Isaiah 6:1-10 with John 12:39-41, and Joel 2:32 with Romans 10:9-13).

[48] This proposed explanation reflects the fact that there are times when "name" is used in the Hebrew Scriptures for the majesty, glory, and dignity (as in the phrase, "Praise the *name* of the Lord").

will bless You as long as I live; I will lift up my hands in Your name," Psalm 63:4), what Paul is picturing is worship (submission) being given to Jesus.[49] Likewise, if "bow the knee" (i.e., to kneel) before Baal identified one as his worshiper (1 Kings 19:18; Romans 11:4), then bowing the knee at the name of Jesus indicates that the highly exalted Jesus is being worshiped. A difficult question to answer with certainty is whether this worship is something done during the present age,[50] or something done at the final judgment (as the words from Isaiah 45:23 are explained in Romans 14:11,12), or both.

Of those who are in heaven, and on earth, and under the earth – The three terms "in heaven," "on earth," and "under the earth" also occur in Revelation 5:13 and may have been an ancient way of designating the whole universe.[51] If so, Paul writes that the day will come when the whole universe acknowledges the universal power and authority of Jesus Christ. The KJV/ASV translated this passage as "of *things* in heaven, and *things* on earth ...," whereas the NASB reads "of those *who* are in heaven ...." The difference arises from the fact that the three Greek terms may be either masculine or neuter. If we treat the terms as neuter ("things"), as including all of creation, animate and inanimate, then the idea here taught is similar to what Paul wrote in Romans 8:19-22 about the whole creation being submissive to the Son of God. If we let the mention of "every knee" and "every tongue" (verse 11) lead us to think of personal beings, then the NASB, which takes the terms as masculine, results in the better translation.

---

[49] *En to onomati* is to be translated "in the name of" (as the ASV), and not "at the name of" (as the KJV/NASB). The Greek word "Jesus" (*Iesou*) can be either genitive or dative, allowing the phrase to be translated either as "at the name of Jesus" or "at the name Jesus." The former yields the idea of "at the name that belongs to Jesus" (i.e., the name given to Him at His exaltation).

[50] If the language speaks of the present age, it likely pictures conversion to Christ as well as Christians offering worship to Christ. If this worship is something done in the present time, unless it is recognized that Jesus is Deity, the adoration here claimed for Him would be idolatry, for it would be addressed to a creature rather than the Creator. In passing, the custom of genuflection (bowing the knee) at the name of Jesus, as is done in some churches, has arisen from a misinterpretation of this passage.

[51] The three terms Paul uses have been used by critics to lampoon what they say the Bible teaches, namely a "three tiered universe." The three tiers are said to be heaven above, earth in the middle, and Hell beneath the earth. See Gerhard F. Hasel, and Michael G. Hasel, "The Unique Cosmology of Genesis 1 Against Ancient Near Eastern and Egyptian Parallels," in *The Genesis Creation Account*, edited by Gerald A. Klingbeil (Berrien Springs, MI: Andrews University Press, 2015), p.13-21, who show that although many Biblical scholars have treated Biblical cosmology as though it reflects ancient mythology, a careful study of the Old Testament texts shows that a "three-storied universe" it is not a proper characterization of what the Scriptures actually say.

Attempts have been made to identify more precisely who are included in the three groups of beings. There is relative agreement on the first two. "Those in heaven" include "the cherubim and seraphim, yes all the ten thousand times ten thousand good angels, including archangels. Also, of course, all redeemed human beings who have departed from this earthly life are included (Ephesians 1:21, 3:10; 1 Peter 3:22; Revelation 4:8-11, 5:8-12, 6:9-11)."[52] Those "on earth" are people still living on earth when the second coming occurs (1 Corinthians 15:50-53; 1 Thessalonians 4:16,17), if the time depicted when every knee shall bow is the consummation. It is the third term that causes us pause. The term translated "under the earth" (*katachthonioi*) occurs only here in the New Testament, though it was a term used in Greek mythology of the subterranean regions where Hades and Persephone lived half of each year, along with the souls of the dead. While we doubt Paul has simply adopted a term from pagan mythology, it is possible Paul used a term familiar to his readers to identify some beings that we meet elsewhere in the Bible. "By the phrase 'under the earth' are we to understand that Christ continues to rule over those who have died physically? Paul writes in Romans 14:9: 'For to this end Christ both died, and rose, and revived, that he might be Lord both of the dead and the living'."[53] "Those who have not bowed the knee to Christ in their lifetime will acknowledge Him when the dead, small and great, stand before the Lord to be judged (Revelation 20:12-15)."[54] What Paul's words picture is a universal acknowledgment of who Jesus is as all beings kneel before Him. We are reminded of Revelation 5:13, "And every created thing which is in heaven and on the earth and under the earth and on the sea, and all things in them, I heard saying, 'To Him who sits on the throne, and to the Lamb, be blessing and honor and glory and dominion forever and ever'."

2:11 -- *And that every tongue should confess that Jesus Christ is Lord, to the glory of God the Father.*

And that every tongue should confess – With this verse Paul arrives at the climax for which he has been preparing. This is what God was expecting when

---

[52] Hendriksen, *op. cit.,* p.115.

[53] Dowling, *ibid.*

[54] Hayden, *1957*, p.435. Since behind the gods of paganism were demons, it has been argued whether or not the demons are in Paul's view when he speaks of "those under the earth." Will they, too, be forced to acknowledge Him at the final judgment? We do not know.

He bestowed on Jesus a name above every name.[55] "Confess" means simply to acknowledge the kingship of the newly crowned Lord. (The word *homologeō* means to confess, that is to say the same thing, and when we confess that Jesus Christ is Lord, we say the same thing about Jesus that God has said. The compound form *exhomologeō* found here intensifies the meaning. It is God's intent that every creature capable of utterance is to openly proclaim that Jesus Christ is Lord. This confession will occur at the time of the consummation and final judgment.[56]

That Jesus Christ is Lord – Now we are told what "the name which is above every name" (verse 9) actually is. It is "JESUS CHRIST IS LORD." Of the three words in this confession, "Lord" is emphatic by its position in the Greek sentence.[57] The combined terms "Jesus Christ" identifies the man Jesus of Nazareth with the promised Messiah (John 4:25), and includes all the tremendous significance which that term had for the Jews. The first gospel sermon declared that Jesus was "both Lord and Christ" (Acts 2:36) so the confession that "Jesus Christ is Lord" is not something new to those who have obeyed the gospel. When He comes on the clouds of heaven at the time of His second coming, "on His robe and on His thigh He has a name written, KING OF KINGS AND LORD OF LORDS" (Revelation 19:16).

To the glory of God the Father – Goodspeed translates, "And thus glorify God the Father." This phrase shows the ultimate result of worship given to Jesus and the confession that He is Lord. God is to be glorified! The glorification of Christ does not in any way limit the honor due to the Father. When folk give honor to Christ, God the Father is honored, too. We remember that this whole picture of Christ's humiliation and subsequent exaltation was intended by Paul to encourage his readers to develop and live by an attitude like the attitude which Jesus exhibited (2:5). The implication is that for believers such a life will result in God's glory, just as it did for Jesus.

---

[55] This note about what God was expecting reflects the better manuscript reading "should confess" (an aorist subjunctive, found in P[46], *Aleph*, B) over "will confess" (a future indicative, found in A, C, D, and the TR). The subjunctive has been adopted by Nestle 25th edition, while the indicative is preferred by the UBS.

[56] There is a confession of faith in Jesus made by folk who are in the process of becoming a Christian (Acts 8:37). However, the occasion of such initial confessions differs from the occasion being pictured here in Philippians 2. Thus, it looks like Barclay (*op. cit.,* p.49) is not correct when he wrote "these four words were the first creed that the Christian church ever had."

[57] See notes at Philippians 1:2 on the meaning of the word "Lord."

b. With God's help, the Christian may imitate this pattern. 12,13

2:12 -- *So then, my beloved, just as you have always obeyed, not as in my presence only, but now much more in my absence, work out your own salvation with fear and trembling.*

So then, my beloved – "So then" shows that the exhortation in verses 12 and 13 is an inference drawn from the example of Christ (Philippians 2:6-11). Verses 12 and 13 are one long sentence in the Greek. Verse 12 gives the exhortation while verse 13 gives an incentive to comply with the exhortation. By reminding the Philippians that he loves them ("my beloved"), Paul is saying that this exhortation and the following admonitions are spoken out of love.

Just as you have always obeyed – By and large, the members of the Philippian church have always "hearkened" (*hupekousate,* obeyed as the result of hearing) to the demands of God as expressed in the gospel.[58] What a high tribute Paul gave to his dear friends in Philippi. "You have always obeyed." Just as Jesus obeyed (see verse 8, where the same Greek word was used); so the Philippians have obeyed.

Not as in my presence only, but now much more in my absence – Once before in this letter (1:27), Paul had mentioned their need to be as diligent in his absence as they were when he was present with them. Between preachers, congregations may tend to stop doing any Christian activity; even the Sunday assemblies may experience a sort of lethargy. It is against such slackening that Paul here encourages the Philippians to "work out your own salvation."[59] Because Paul's own future was uncertain, the Philippians must plan to carry on without him.

Work out your own salvation – The Greek verb (*katergazesthe*) is a present tense imperative and could well be translated "keep on working it out." This synonym for "work" always has the idea "of bringing to completion, to a full and complete and perfect accomplishment and conclusion. It is as if Paul said, 'The

---

[58] The verb "obeyed" has no object, which raises the question, 'Obey whom or what?' "In other places where Paul speaks of obedience, it is obedience 'to a standard of teaching' (Romans 6:17); or 'to the gospel' (Romans 10:16; 2 Thessalonians 1:8), or 'to Paul himself' (2 Thessalonians 3:14)" (Harrell, *op. cit.*, p.96).

[59] The Greek shows that these words about his presence with them or his absence from them are to be joined with the verb which follows ("work out your own salvation") more than with the verb "obeyed" which preceded.

working out your salvation has already commenced.   Don't stop working halfway; do not be satisfied with a partial salvation.   Go on working until salvation is fully and finally completed in your case'."[60]   'Don't quit just because I am not there watching you,' Paul says.   (They are not to be like little children who obey only until their mother's back is turned.)   "Your" translates a reflexive pronoun *heautōn*, "your own."[61]   "Personal responsibility can hardly be expressed more clearly."[62]   "Salvation" here is analogous to Christ being exalted after His obedience.[63]   It doesn't read "work for" your salvation, but "work out" your salvation."   In this context, the Philippians have been praised for their habitual obedience, and have been asked to have the same love, to be of one mind, and in humility to serve one another.   This is how they work out their salvation.   Such activity is "faith" for faith is habitually doing what God says.

With fear and trembling – "With fear and trembling" is not a contradiction of the joyful spirit which Paul encourages the Philippians to have.   While the Christian rejoices in the Lord, the careful Christian at the same time nourishes a holy fear of God which in turn results in the person's habitual obedience to God's will.   In the Greek, the words "fear and trembling" precede the verb, for emphasis.   "Fear" (a wholesome dread of offending God) and "trembling" (a trembling anxiety to obey God at all times) are vital when it comes to working out one's salvation.   We need afresh, all of us, a sense of solemn responsibility to Almighty God.   "As it is put in the book of Hebrews, we try to 'serve God acceptably with reverence and godly fear: for our God is a consuming fire' (Hebrews 12:28,29)."[64]

---

[60] Barclay, *op. cit.*, p.51.

[61] It is not the reciprocal pronoun *allēlōn* which would mean "one another's."   The ASV reads "your own salvation."

[62] Harrell, *ibid.*

[63] We learned in notes at Philippians 1:19 that the Greek word translated "salvation" can have different meanings, depending on the context.   Commentators, who are attempting to make their comments on this verse harmonize with the doctrine of justification by faith only, may comment on the necessity of sanctification which follows justification, or they may try to make "salvation" mean "health" and then attempt to affirm the passage relates primarily to the community rather than to the individual (the words "work out" and the reflexive pronoun *heautōn* "yourselves" are plural) and that Paul is concerned for the "health" of the Christian community at Philippi.   (Cf. G.F. Hawthorne, "Philippians, Letter to the," in *Dictionary of Paul and His Letters* [Downers Grove, IL: InterVarsity Press, 1993], p.713).

[64] Root, *ibid.*

2:13 -- *for it is God who is at work in you, both to will and to work for* **His** *good pleasure.*

For it is God who is at work in you – For" shows that verse13 is a reason to comply with the exhortation just given in verse 12 to work out their salvation with fear and trembling. "God" is emphasized since the word appears first in the Greek word order. God is at work in your lives[65] – pay attention! "The emphasis lies on 'God' for two reasons. (1) In the matter of attaining salvation, they really have to deal *not* with Paul, but with God. (2) They must enter upon this momentous course not lightly, but 'with fear and trembling,' for if they miss the goal it means that they have deliberately rejected the purpose of God."[66] "At work" translates *energeo*; God Himself is energizing the Christians.

Both to will and to work – "To will" and "to work" identify the twofold result of God's energizing working in the Christian. "To will" is *to thelein*, "the willing." If we were to say that God plants thoughts in the minds of Christians, we would not be far from what Paul is here asserting.[67] By means of the prompting of His indwelling Spirit, God brings about "resolve" or "desire" in men's hearts.[68] "To work" indicates that after God plants the idea, and the Christian desires to do the "work" which God has suggested, God then gives the Christian help and strength to do the work. "The Holy Spirit living within them helps the Christian both to determine to do God's will and to carry it out with determination. The Holy Spirit does not overpower us so as to compel us either to will or to work. Each of us must choose ('work out your own salvation') to work with the Spirit or not work with Him."[69]

---

[65] *En humin* can mean either "in you," in the sense of "in your hearts," or it can mean "among you," meaning "in the Philippian church." Most likely we are to understand this as teaching that God works in the heart of each individual believer (as 1 Corinthians 12:6; 2 Corinthians 4:12; Ephesians 2:2; Colossians 1:24 all mean). Vincent, *op. cit.*, p.66.

[66] Kennedy, *op. cit.*, p.440.

[67] This verse is speaking of God's activity on the Christian; it does not speak of what is called in some theological systems "prevenient grace." If that idea is taught at all in the Word, its advocates will have to look elsewhere to find it.

[68] There are two Greek synonyms translated "will" or "wish." "Between *thelein* and *boulesthai*, the general distinction is that *thelein* expresses a determination or definite resolution of the will; while *boulesthai* expresses an inclination, disposition. or wish. The two are often, however, interchanged in the NT, and it is not always possible to force the distinction of meanings ... Here *thelein* speaks of a definite purpose or determination" (Vincent, *op. cit.*, p.66).

[69] Root, *ibid.*

For *His* good pleasure – The thrust of this clause is debated. Perhaps, since there is no word for "His" in the Greek, the passage says that "God is at work ... for good will." That is, He wants folk in the church to have "good will" toward each other.[70] Or, if the versions that insert "His" are correct, perhaps it says that God's prompting and helping activities are limited to areas that please and delight Him. If so, the promise of this verse is not a *carte blanche* statement of God's help. Rather, it says God leads believers "to will and to do" those things, relative to their ultimate salvation, which are in accordance with His own will, the things that please Him.[71]

C. Admonition to Continue to be Light Bearers in the World. 2:14-18

2:14 -- *Do all things without grumbling or disputing;*

Do all things – This is the third in the series of admonitions which began at Philippians 1:27. In the Greek, verses 14-16 form one complex sentence. Paul has just spoken about the necessity of obedience, and about working out one's salvation with fear and trembling (verse 12). Perhaps now he lists some of the specific elements involved in "working out one's salvation." The emphasis in this command falls on "all things," which actually is the first word of the verse in

---

[70] One might opt for this explanation without having to adopt for *soterian* (see notes above at 2:12) the meaning "health," rather than "salvation."

[71] Since the word translated "good pleasure" is the same word translated "good will" at Philippians 1:15, in verses 12 and 13 we have touched certain phrases and expressions which have caused commentators to write about God's sovereignty and man's free will. Some emphasize God's will and God's sovereignty to the degree that man's free will is almost obscured. Is this a correct view of God and His will? When all the passages are considered, it is the teaching of the Bible that God helps men work out their own salvation, yet without in any way destroying their own personal responsibility and self-activity. The whole picture, in outline form, is this:

- God takes the initiative in men's salvation (2 Thessalonians 2:13; 1 Timothy 2:4) by making it available.
- He works through human agency (1 Timothy 4:16) for mankind's salvation, offering them invitations through the gospel (2 Thessalonians 2:14).
- Then, if man responds by becoming a Christian, God will again go to work (Philippians 2:12-13).
- He makes us alive with Christ, raises us up with Christ, and seats us in heavenly places with Christ (Ephesians 2:5,6).
- If man of his own free will does not respond to God's initial invitation to become a Christian, then eternal salvation will be missed.
- If the Christian does not give due diligence, that salvation can be forfeited (Hebrews 2:3).

   A different view is presented by commentators who give precedence to God's sovereignty to the extent that if He wills something it is bound to happen. Now we begin to see the importance of the synonyms for God's will that footnote #68 above introduced.

the Greek text. "Most Christians are able to do some things without complaint. It is when we are exhorted to be doing 'all things' with a joyful spirit that the difficulty comes."[72]

Without grumbling or disputing – Obedience may be given grudgingly or voluntarily. It is the latter that Paul wants from the Philippians. Obedience must be cheerful and willing. "'Grumbling' (*gongusmoi*) is the word used in the LXX to describe the "murmurings" of the people against the leadership of Moses (cf. Exodus 17:3; Numbers 11:1, 16:41; 1 Corinthians 10:10)."[73] It has the connotation of discontent, rebellious conduct, outward actions resulting from rejection of authority. "Disputing" (*dialogismoi*, "questioning") is a common Pauline word (Romans 1:21, 14:1; 1 Corinthians 3:20; 1 Timothy 2:8) for the "questions" (like "why do I have to?") which often precede the hesitation which characterizes those who rebel to authority. By the use of these two words, Paul shows that submission to God's will must be inward as well as outward. Paul does not, in so many words, identify toward whom the grumbling and disputing are directed. Since both words are plural in the Greek, and since as the sentence continues (verse 15) he talks about being blameless and innocent, it looks like Paul has in mind mutual disagreements and disputes among the Philippians themselves.

2:15 -- *that you may prove yourselves to be blameless and innocent, children of God above reproach in the midst of a crooked and perverse generation, among whom you appear as lights in the world,*

That you may prove yourselves to be blameless and innocent – Paul now gives three reasons why he wants them to do all things (as they work out their own salvation) cheerfully and without disputing: 1) He desires the Philippians to be blameless and harmless;   2) He desires them to be of the greatest service to others (lights, holding forth the word of life);   3) He wants to be proud of them at the judgment. "Prove to be" translates the better attested *genesthe* ("become"), which calls for continual progress in working out their salvation. Unregenerate men are not "blameless and innocent," and Christians do not easily become such. It is something that has to be worked at. The words used here ("blameless," *amemptos, and* "innocent," *akeraios*) are not the same words used at Philippians 1:10 where the NASB has "sincere and blameless." The first word here speaks of external actions. By their actions they would give no occasion for others to accuse them of having done wrong. The second word ("innocent") speaks of in-

---

[72] Kent, *op. cit.*, p.129.

[73] Harrell, *op. cit.*, p.98.

ternal attitudes. They would not think of injuring anyone. This is what Jesus meant when he exhorted His followers to be as innocent as doves (Matthew 10:16).

Children of God above reproach – Apparently the verb *genesthe* ("become") is to be read with this phrase too, so that the whole thought is 'in order that you may become children of God above reproach.' A person becomes a "child of God" when he or she is born again (John 1:12,13). Since the Philippian Christians were already "children of God," it seems that becoming "blameless and innocent" is the area where they had growing to do. The word "without blemish" is, according to the best manuscripts, the same as that which is used in Ephesians 1:4, where we learned that it described sacrifices suitable to offer to God. This word *amomos*, "above reproach", thinks of the whole life and the whole man as an offering to God. It thinks of taking every part of our life, our work, our pleasure, our sport, our home life, our personal relationships, and making them all such that they can be taken and offered to God.

In the midst of a crooked and perverse generation – "Generation" may be used broadly to speak of a group of contemporaries. "Crooked" may describe the contemporaries as morally warped, while "perverse" describes them as spiritually twisted or distorted. This whole clause "children of God above reproach in the midst of a crooked and perverse generation" is a reminiscence, not a quotation, of Deuteronomy 32:5 (LXX), often called "The Song of Moses." Close parallels to this language are also found in Matthew 12:39 ("evil and adulterous generation"), 17:17 ("unbelieving and perverse generation"), and in Acts 2:40 ("perverse generation"). All of these passages were spoken about Jewish people. Now the question to be answered is to whom does Paul refer? Does Paul have in mind Jewish people in Philippi? Has he taken language originally spoken of the Jewish people and used it to characterize the Gentile peoples among whom the Philippians live? Or, most likely, should we understand that "crooked and perverse generation" simply describes the unconverted neighbors of the Philippians who are watching how the Christian lives? There are to be no obvious flaws in the Christian's witness. A church with a reputation for disharmony and internal conflict does not make a good impression on the world around them.

Among whom you appear as lights in the world – "Among whom" points to the very people just described in the previous phrase as a "crooked and perverse generation." "You" are the Philippian Christians. Since "lights" (*phōster*) is a word that is used of the stars (LXX at Genesis 1:16; Daniel 12:3; and Revelation 1:16,20, 21:11), the word *kosmos* here might better be translated "universe" rather than "world." Christians are pictured as being like the stars shining in the midnight sky. The verb *phainesthe,* translated "you appear", can be either indicative or imperative in the Greek,[74] and it may be translated either as "you appear" or "you shine."[75] The NASB treats it as an indicative, as stating a present fact. It is not that they are told to shine, but they are being reminded that they already do shine, and are to so live that their light shines out unhindered. This is why the Christian must be careful to be "above reproach." If the Christian's behavior is just like that of their unconverted neighbor, there is no way to help lighten the neighbor's darkness.

2:16 -- *Holding fast the word of life, so that in the day of Christ I may have cause to glory because I did not run in vain nor toil in vain.*

Holding fast the word of life – Since verses 14-16 form one long sentence in the Greek, all the things that have been encouraged in those verses (so that the Philippians are "above reproach") are related to being able to do what this phrase calls for. The phrase "word of life" is not used elsewhere by Paul, but similar expressions in John 6:68 and Acts 5:20 strongly indicate that what is signified is the gospel of Christ. It is called the "word of life" because it makes people alive, just as Ephesians 2:15 describes what happens when folk respond to the invitation to be in Christ. "Life" is somewhat akin to "salvation." The ASV translated *epechein* as "holding forth" rather than "holding fast" as does the NASB. The translation "holding forth" seems to be more suitable in a missionary context than is "holding fast."[76] "This verb (*epechein*) signifies 'extending to others' (food, drink, or the like ...)."[77] It pictures believers as holding out or offering the "word of life" to others for their acceptance. Since the word translated "holding forth" is a circumstantial participle, it indicates that the believers would function as "lights in the world" *"while* holding forth the word," or *"if* they hold forth the word," or *"by* holding forth the word." Believers, as "lights shining in the world"

---

[74] "Appear" is something the Philippian Christians are expected to continue doing (taking it as indicative), or something they are commanded to do (taking it as imperative).

[75] Arndt and Gingrich, *op. cit.,* p.859.

[76] The translation "holding fast" treats what the believers are doing as a contrast to the "crooked and perverse generation," but it also requires treating the preceding clause ("among whom you appear as lights in the world") as parenthetical. Lightfoot (*op. cit.,* p.118) defends this translation.

[77] J. Gwynn, "Philippians" in *The Bible Commentary* edited by F.C. Cook (New York: Charles Scribner's Sons, 1886), Vol. 3, p.613.

are constantly proclaiming their Maker and Redeemer to a world lost in sin. They perform this glorious missionary task by holding forth the word of life, the gospel of salvation, not only as preached but also as practiced.[78]

So that in the day of Christ I may have cause to glory – "The day of Christ" we learned at Philippians 1:6 is a reference to the judgment day, a day more commonly called "the day of the Lord" by Paul. Paul is saying that if the Philippians conduct themselves well in word and deed, when the final judgment occurs, and their lives are weighed in the balances, he will be able to point to them with pride as evidence that his ministry was fruitful. In 1 Thessalonians 2:19,20 Paul says a similar thing to the Thessalonian Christians.

Because I did not run in vain nor toil in vain – "Run" expresses Paul's energetic missionary activity.[79] "Toil" pictures laboring until one is weary and exhausted.[80] Paul worked long and hard hours at carrying out his commission to be the apostle to the Gentiles. The verbs "run" and "toil" are aorist tense, and Paul is pictured as, in the final judgment, looking back upon his finished course. If Paul's converts prove to be unfaithful, then all of his missionary labors will have been wasted (it was all for nothing, *kenos,* "vain"). But if the Philippians are ushered into heaven, that will prove his evangelistic work among them was not wasted.

2:17 -- *But even if I am being poured out as a drink offering upon the sacrifice and service of your faith, I rejoice, and share my joy with you all:*

---

[78] Harrell (*op. cit.*, p.99,100) has observed that the most significant thing about this passage, and its context, is somewhat obscured for modern readers. The subject under discussion is specific rather than general -- the apostle's instructions concern *the spread of the gospel.* Harrell corroborates his observation by making statements similar to these: There is a relationship between 'obedience' (verse 12) and the spread of the gospel. The ideas in verses 15 and 16 are related to the proclamation of the gospel. The word "harmless" was employed by Jesus (Matthew 10:16) as he sent forth the twelve to spread the gospel. The same usage ("innocent in what is evil") is seen in Paul's contrast of the Roman Christians and the heretical preachers (Romans 16:19). The suggestion that Paul is speaking of the spread of the gospel in this context is further seen by observing the significance of "lights" and related concepts in Scripture. See Jesus' affirmation "You are the light of the world" (Matthew 5:14-16), a text that pertains to the communication of the message to unbelievers. There can be little doubt then that in these verses about "lights in the world," Paul is exhorting the Philippians to be diligent in the spread of the gospel.

[79] Perhaps, as he writes about running, he has the metaphor of the athletic stadium in his mind, as in Galatians 2:2, when he expressed the same dread about the Galatians.

[80] Vincent, *op. cit.,* p.70.

But even – The prospect of standing before Christ with his missionary work all done reminded Paul that for him the end of his missionary work might be soon. Whether it be sooner or later, Paul's language in this verse indicates that he anticipates that a martyr's death likely is the probable way his ministry here on earth will be ended.

If I am being poured out as a drink offering – Paul changes metaphors again. Instead of the athletic stadium, now the picture behind his language is the sacrificial ritual. The word order[81] and the present passive indicative[82] verb all imply the very real possibility of a martyr's death. Paul had a special knack for speaking in language that people could understand. Again and again he took his illustrations from the ordinary affairs and activities of the people to whom he was speaking or writing. "Drink offering" is such an illustration. Both Jewish and Greek religious practices included the use of a cup of wine (a "libation") poured out ceremonially in connection with certain sacrifices being offered to deity. In Jewish ritual the libation was poured out beside the altar before the sacrificial animal was burned; in Greek ritual the libation was poured out on top of the sacrifice as the climax of the sacrifice.[83] In Paul's own mind, a "drink offering" is what his shed blood would be, were he to be martyred. Paul was perfectly willing to die for Christ. He counted it a privilege to make his life a sacrifice and an offering to God.

Upon the sacrifice and service of your faith – While the preposition *epi* may mean "upon" or "over" (as in a Greek or Roman sacrifice) or "in addition to" (like a Jewish sacrifice), "the fact that Paul is writing from Rome to a Gentile church seems to indicate that the metaphor is cast in the mold of heathen rather than Jewish sacrificial usage."[84] Since "the sacrifice and service" in the Greek employs only one article with two nouns, it probably is a hendiadys, meaning

---

[81] The Greek word order is *ei kai* (the "if" is assumed as a fact) rather than *kai ei* (which implies there is very little possibility the "if" will in fact happen).

[82] The verb *spendomai* is passive voice, indicating someone else would do this pouring out of his life blood. "The present tense verb *spendomai* must be understood as a vivid reference to the future. Paul is probably thinking of his present imprisonment as 'the beginning of the end' for himself, whether it be climaxed at the close of the present imprisonment or a few years later" (Hendriksen, *op. cit.*, p. 126). As it turned out, Paul was not executed until his second Roman imprisonment, which happened some years after the writing of this letter to the Philippians.

[83] Numbers 15:1-10; Homer, *Iliad*, 11:775; Josephus, *Ant.*, III.9.4.

[84] Vincent, *op. cit.*, p.72.

"sacrificial service."   Just how the faith of the Philippians can be conceived of as a "sacrifice" has proven difficult to explain.[85]   We understand that their "faith" is what motivates their behavior.   "Service" translates *leitourgia,* a word which looks at the sacrifice as being something a priest offers.   Since every Christian is a priest, and since the Philippian believers are being persecuted (see Philippians 1:29), perhaps we can think in the direction of the Christians being motivated by their faith to offer their bodies, if need be, as a sacrifice.   Stripped of its metaphorical language, Paul is saying that he views his possible martyrdom as a sacrifice to God just as he views their faithful sacrificial service as a suitable offering to make to God.

I rejoice and share my joy with you all – "I rejoice" (*chairo*), Paul could say, because their faith (which resulted from his ministry among them) is an accomplished fact, and because the thought of departing to be with Christ, which is very far better, gave him joy.   'I also share in the joy *(sungchairo)* which you experience in the new life you have received.'   If the Philippians remain faithful to Christ, Paul can rejoice even in the face of death.   Paul was glad on his own account that he had been the instrument of their salvation.

2:18 -- *And you too,* **I urge you,** *rejoice in the same way and share your joy with me.*

And you too, *I urge you,* **rejoice in the same way** – When the Philippians have a sacrificial service view of Paul's ministry, and of his death as a crowning libation to a life of sacrifice, they, too, can rejoice with him in what happens to him.   By adding "I urge you" in italics, the NASB has tried to show that the verbs in this verse are imperatives.

And share your joy with me – They must learn to rejoice like Paul is rejoicing about his situation, for to die a martyr's death is to win a martyr's crown.   Perhaps it was a passage like this which led some Roman Christians to form a chorus and sing a sacrificial hymn round the martyr Ignatius.[86]

---

[85] One popular explanation, comparing Romans 15:16 where sacrificial words are also used, considers Paul himself to be the ministering priest, and understands the metaphor as picturing a priest being slain at the altar, his blood being shed while he is presenting the Gentiles (who have come to be believers in Christ) as an offering to God.

[86] Vincent (*ibid.*) calls attention to this striking figure and cites Ign. *Rom.*ii. and also *Trall.* i. as his source.

IV. INFORMATION ABOUT PAUL'S CO-LABORERS. 2:19-30

Summary: Verses 19-30 form a section in which Paul discusses his co-workers in general and Timothy and Epaphroditus in particular. As soon as he knows the disposition of his case, Paul hoped to send Timothy to Philippi with two responsibilities: one, to give them the news, and two, to report back to Paul what he learns about the condition of the Philippian church. In the meantime he was sending Epaphroditus, their messenger to Paul in his distress, back to Philippi in order to ease the Philippians' concern and restore their cheerfulness.

A. Timothy and His Forthcoming Mission to Philippi. 2:19-24

2:19 -- *But I hope in the Lord Jesus to send Timothy to you shortly, so that I also may be encouraged when I learn of your condition.*

But I hope in the Lord Jesus to send Timothy to you shortly – Perhaps the "but" is intended to contrast what is a possibility (his martyrdom, verse 17) with what he actually hopes will happen (namely, that he will be set free and resume his missionary travels, verse 24). His "hope in the Lord" pictures Jesus as being the providential ruler of this world who would grant to Paul to do what Paul's hope was. For this important mission of imparting information to the Philippians and obtaining news about them, Paul has selected Timothy. Verse 23 indicates that "shortly" means "as soon as I see how things will go with me."

So that I may also be encouraged when I learn of your condition – The words of this phrase imply that after visiting Philippi, Timothy was to meet Paul somewhere and report to him on the state of the Philippian church. Paul does not indicate to the Philippians where that meeting was to take place. Where the meeting might take place surely would depend on the disposition of Paul's case. If he is not released, then Timothy would return to Rome to report. If Paul were released, then the meeting could take place in Asia Minor where Paul planned to journey upon his release (Philemon 22). 1 Timothy 1:3 indicates that there was a time when Timothy and Paul were together at Ephesus following his release from the first Roman imprisonment. Perhaps that is where the meeting took place. It has been some time since Epaphroditus had left Philippi and come to Rome; therefore, it has been some time since Paul had been informed of their condition. There is no specific statement about the content of the news Paul wishes to hear about their "condition" (literally, "the things concerning you"). However, the context suggests that what he desires to hear concerns the peace and harmony of the church.   The word "also" implies that the encouragement[87] will be a two-way thing.   The Philippians will be "cheered" by news about Paul – and Paul will be "cheered" by news about the Philippians.

2:20 -- *For I have no one* else *of kindred spirit who will genuinely be concerned for your welfare.*

For I have no one *else* of kindred spirit – Paul here gives a reason why he is sending Timothy in particular; namely, he has a unique fitness for the task.   'I have no one else who would feel so deep an interest in their welfare.'   If we recall that Timothy was there when the church at Philippi was planted (Acts 16), it seems that all we need say is that none of Paul's other current helpers are as familiar with or as interested in the Philippians as Timothy was.   Such familiarity was exactly the needed qualification for this mission.   "Likeminded" was the ASV translation of *isopsuchon,* "of kindred spirit."   The commentaries have debated to whom Timothy is being compared.   One suggestion is that Timothy is as likeminded about the Philippians as is Paul himself.   Timothy has traveled with Paul since AD 51 or 52 (it is now AD 63).   Timothy has had a good length of time to learn under Paul just what Paul's wishes and loves were.   Another suggestion, the one followed in these comments, is that the comparison is between Timothy and Paul's other current evangelistic helpers who might have been available to be sent on this mission.   None of them are as interested in the spiritual welfare of the Philippians as Timothy is.

Who will genuinely care for your welfare – "Genuinely" translates *gnesios* (lit., *born in wedlock*; thus "like a brother").   Timothy's previous association with the brethren at Philippi has resulted in an affection for them like they were family.   "Care" ("concern") is a strong word, sometimes translated "anxiety."   Timothy has the same absorbing anxiety for the Philippian church that Paul has.   The versions that have translated the Greek (which literally is "in the things concerning you") as "for your welfare" are perhaps not far wrong in their choice of words.

2:21 -- *For they all seek their own interests, not those of Christ Jesus.*

For they all seek after their own interests, not those of Christ Jesus – The language implies that in his mind Paul   has evaluated the men available to make

---

[87] *Eupsucheo* here translated "encouraged" occurs only here in the New Testament. Arndt and Gingrich (*op. cit.,* p.330) tell us the word was frequently used in grave-stone inscriptions as a final wish ("farewell," "have courage") for the departed.   Harrell (*op. cit.,* p.103) suggests that "the choice of the word here suggests that these exchanges of information would be the final communiques" between Paul and the Philippians.

the trip to Philippi that Timothy has been chosen to make. As he evaluated the men, and perhaps even had some making excuses when approached on this subject, he observes that in them there was a selfishness which made them unfit for the mission. At Philippians 1:15,17 it has already been shown that some gospel workers in Rome were inspired by less than noble motives. Now we learn that even among Paul's own helpers there were those whose motives were selfish. In comparison with Timothy, these other possible messengers had more interest in themselves and their own comforts than in "the things of Christ,"[88] namely, making the long trip to Philippi and then bringing back news concerning the welfare of the Philippian church to Paul. Attempts have been made to identify those who were judged unfit to make the journey because they were more concerned with furthering their own interests. If our judgement that Philippians was written at a later date than the other Prison Epistles is correct, then the workers named in those (e.g., Colossians 4:10-14; Philemon 23,24) may not have been at Paul's side at the time he wrote these words. Apart from Timothy there was no one he could count on at the moment.

2:22 -- *But ye know his proven worth that he served with me in the furtherance of the gospel like a child* serving *his father*.

But you know of his proven worth – The Philippians may not have known these other possible messengers, but they knew Timothy. The Philippians' knowledge (*ginosko*) of Timothy came from personal experience during his ministry in Philippi (Acts 16). He had proven (*dokimen*[89]) to be a man of good character and an able gospel worker.

That he served with me in the furtherance of the gospel like a child *serving his father* – The time of serving alluded to was when together they evangelized in the city of Philippi (Acts 16). Not only had the Philippians personally observed Timothy's worth, but Paul vouches for him on the basis of many years of personal experience. The italics indicate there is a broken sentence here. The

---

[88] There is in these verses in the Greek a repetition of the phrase "the things concerning" which is obscured in many of our English translations. It occurs in verses 19,20,21, and 23, and it is used to discuss Paul and Timothy's interest in the welfare of the Philippians, the possible messenger's interests in their own affairs and their neglect of the affairs of Christ, and then of Paul's own personal situation.

[89] See the comments on "approve" at Philippians 1:10 where the same root word occurs. The word translated "proven" was originally associated with the idea of "testing" in order to determine worth. When the testing proved positive the word has the meaning of "approved" or "proven."

Greek reads "as to a father a son with me he served in the gospel." It looks as though Paul started to say that as a child served a father, so Timothy served him. But instead of writing "he served me" he says "with me" as if to perpetuate the thought that both he and Timothy were servants of Christ (Philippians 1:1) rather than making himself the master and Timothy his servant. A child who serves with his father is working at the same task and trying to lighten the father's heavy load. In order that God's truth might be established in the hearts of men – including the Philippians – Timothy had been doing all in his power to lighten Paul's heavy load. "Timothy's service was a thoroughly dedicated, spontaneous, loving ministry in the interest of and for the promotion of the gospel."[90]

2:23 -- *Therefore I hope to send him immediately, as soon as I shall see how things* go *with me:*

Therefore I hope to send him immediately – "Therefore" summarizes the brief aside about Timothy's qualities which show he (the Greek sentence begins with *touton*, "this one") is the right person to send. "Immediately" (*exautes*) gives the impression that the delay until he should see how things turned out would not be a long one. "I hope to send" tells us that Timothy will not be traveling with Epaphroditus, the bearer of this letter, but rather that Paul wants Timothy to wait until there is more definite information about the outcome of Paul's case.

As soon as I see how things *go* with me – The two years of the first Roman imprisonment are nearly over. According to Roman jurisprudence, if a man's accusers did not appear to press charges, the accused was released. This is what Paul anticipates as happening (though, of course, there was a faint chance the Jews would yet arrive in Rome to press charges).[91] Once his case has been ended, the Philippians, far from being left in the dark, will be informed by no one less than beloved Timothy, who will carry the news to them without delay.

2:24 -- *and I trust in the Lord that I myself also shall be coming shortly.*

And I trust in the Lord that I myself also shall be coming shortly – Although granting that the decision might go either way, Paul was confident that his release

---

[90] Hendriksen, *op. cit.,* p.136. On the "gospel" see notes at Philippians 1:5,27.

[91] The "soon" in "as soon as I see" has been supplied by the translators. The oldest manuscripts here read *aphido* (remarkable for the aspirate *phi*) instead of *apido*. It is an aorist subjunctive from *aphorao* which means to "look away at something in the distance" (cp. its use at Hebrews 12:2).

was in prospect, and that he would fulfill his wish to visit the Philippians. "I trust" (*pepoitha*) means "I am confident" (the same Greek word was translated "confident" at Philippians 1:6.) "In the Lord" acknowledges that every thing Paul may do was to be consistent with, and submitted to, the will of the Lord. "If the Lord wills, we shall both live, and do this or that" (James 4:15 ASV). "Shortly" (*tacheos,* the same word used at Philippians 2:19, is a reasonably flexible term) could mean a few weeks, or a few months. What is clear is that Paul no longer thought of going on to Spain, as he once had planned after seeing Rome (Romans 15:28). His long imprisonment in Caesarea and Rome, plus the fact that the anticipated threat of the Gnostics (Acts 20:29ff) had now materialized, made it necessary for Paul to try to set things in order in the province of Asia. Philippi also tugged at his heart. Was the apostle released from his first Roman imprisonment? Did Paul soon follow Timothy to Philippi? The answer to these questions must be yes. The historical allusions found in Paul's letters to Timothy and Titus[92] can only be explained if Paul indeed was released and did travel back to Macedonia and Asia Minor.[93]

B. Epaphroditus and his Return to Philippi. 2:25-30

Summary: How soon Timothy or Paul himself may be able to visit them is uncertain, but he is sending Epaphroditus to them at once. The Philippians are told that Epaphroditus had fulfilled their commission to him (verse 25). The reasons for his return are stated (verses 26-28), and the manner in which he should be received when he arrives in Philippi is indicated (verses 29,30).

2:25 -- *But I thought it necessary to send to you Epaphroditus, my brother and fellow-worker and fellow-soldier, who is also your messenger and minister to my need,*

But I thought it necessary to send to you Epaphroditus – *Hēgēsamen* ("I thought") here and *epempsa* ("I sent") in 2:28 are epistolary aorists; they point to the time of reading the letter, and not to that of writing it. In ancient correspondence it was customary for the writer to adopt the reader's perspective.   In our

---

[92] From the historical allusions we have Paul visiting Miletus (2 Timothy 4:20), Crete (Titus 1:5), Ephesus (1 Timothy 1:3), Macedonia and so probably Philippi (1 Timothy 1:3), Troas (2 Timothy 4:13), and Nicopolis (Titus 3:12).

[93] See this argued in the Epilogue to the author's Acts Commentary, "The Last Labors and Letters of Paul," as well as in the introductory studies in his commentary on the epistles to Timothy and Titus.

language, viewing the situation from the point of view of the writer, the present tense "I count it necessary" and "I am sending" would be used. The epistolary aorist implies that Epaphroditus carried this letter back to Philippi, and the verses now about to be written explain why Paul thought it was necessary to send Epaphroditus back to Philippi and to do so immediately. Little is known about Epaphroditus. Putting together the information we have in Philippians (2:25-28, 4:18) about Epaphroditus, we come up with these facts: (1) He had been commissioned by the Philippian church to carry an offering to Paul, the prisoner, and to be his constant assistant and attendant. (2) While carrying out his mission, after being a while in Rome, he had become critically ill. (3) His friends in Philippi had heard about this illness and had become alarmed in turn. As more time passed, Epaphroditus learns about their anxiety back home. (4) God graciously restored Epaphroditus to health. (5) Epaphroditus then yearned to return to Philippi, in order to allay the fears of the brethren there with respect to his health. (6) Paul, in complete accord, sent him back to Philippi, requested a cordial "Welcome home!" for him, and in all probability made him the bearer of this letter.

My brother and fellow-worker and fellow-soldier – The Philippian church had sent Epaphroditus to Rome to stay with Paul and help him on their behalf; if Epaphroditus came back home, there might be those who would think he had failed to do what they wanted him to do for Paul. In order to silence any possible criticism or remove any possible disappointment, Paul first gives Epaphroditus a tremendous tribute as he uses three words to describe how he views their relationship with each other. He is "my brother," that is, he is a fellow Christian, a member of the same spiritual family, with God as their Father. Paul and Epaphroditus have a warm relationship toward each other. He is "my fellow-worker." Using a term borrowed from the workshop, Paul says that Epaphroditus has worked hard right alongside Paul in the labors of the gospel all the while Epaphroditus was in Rome. He is "my fellow-soldier," a word that pictures Paul and Epaphroditus as fighting side by side against the enemies of the gospel. Phillips translates it as "my comrade-in-arms." What they had done together was more than just work; it was a struggle, a battle.

Who is also your messenger and minister to my need – The previous three terms described Epaphroditus' relationship to Paul; these next two designations speak of Epaphroditus' relationship with the Philippian church. He was their "messenger" (*apostolos,* literally, "your apostle"). "Apostle" means "one sent on a mission."[94]   In the present case the assignment given to Epaphroditus by the Philippian church was "not only to bring to Paul the financial gift from the Philippian church (Philippians 4:16), but also to serve Paul in whichever way that service might be needed (see 'minister to my need'[95]), e.g., as his personal attendant and as his missionary assistant.   Hence, Epaphroditus had been sent both to bring a gift and to be a gift from the Philippians to Paul."[96]   Paul is saying, as it were, 'Epaphroditus has done what you sent him to do.   Bear in mind that he is returning to you, not as though he were failing to fulfill what you sent him to do, but because I myself consider it necessary to send him back to you.'

2:26 -- *because he was longing for you all and was distressed because you had heard that he was sick.*

Because he was longing for you all – Paul identifies three reasons why he thought it necessary to send Epaphroditus back to Philippi.   One concerns Epaphroditus himself, that his longing might be satisfied and his distress relieved (verses 26,27).   The second concerns the Philippians, that they may rejoice (verse 28a).   The third concerns Paul himself, that he may be less sorrowful (verse 28b). "He was longing" (*epipothōn ēn* – a present participle and the imperfect tense verb, "He was continually longing for you all") says that Epaphroditus was homesick.[97]   "His love for the church that had sent him becomes so overpowering that he yearns to see again the familiar faces of those whose sympathy is so real, and whose anxiety must be removed."[98]   There is nothing wrong or blameworthy if a missionary becomes homesick.

---

[94] In the pages of the New Testament we meet men who were apostles of Jesus (sent on a mission by Him) and men who were apostles of churches (sent on a mission by a local congregation).   Although the same word is applied to both groups, they differ in who gave them their commission.   Two examples of apostles (or "messengers") of churches are here and 2 Corinthians 8:23.

[95] "Minister" translates *leitourgon*; we had a similar word *leitourgia* in 2:17, where see notes. Readers should be aware that this passage, 2:17, and Romans 15:16 are appealed to by the Roman Catholic Church to justify a "priesthood."   (The word in Romans, *hierourgeo*, "ministering [as a priest] a sacrifice," is different).   A priest was a "go between"; this is what Epaphroditus has done between Philippi and Paul.   While the gift he brought is called a "sacrifice" at Philippians 4:18, and a "service" at Philippians 2:30, there is no evidence he is thought of as officiating at a sacrifice (versus the Catholic idea of a priest who officiates at the sacrifice of the mass).

[96] Hendriksen, *op. cit.,* pp.139,140.

[97] "The same verb was used of Paul's own feelings toward the Philippians in 1:8.   It is used of a newborn baby's longing for milk (1 Peter 2:2)" (Kent, *op. cit.*, p.135).

[98] Hendriksen, *op. cit.*, p.141.

And was distressed because you had heard that he was sick – The exact nature of Epaphroditus' sickness is not stated, though the next verse does give us some details about it. As indicated in the Detailed Introduction to Philippians, this verse implies that word of the Epaphroditus' illness had reached Philippi, and that a report of the Philippians' resulting alarm had been brought back to Rome. When Epaphroditus became aware of the alarm in Philippi over his health, he became very upset. The word *adēmonōn* ("distressed) is of uncertain derivation but it probably comes from *adēmos*, "away from home." The same word was used in Matthew 26:37 and Mark 14:33 to express the anguish Jesus experienced in Gethsemane (He was homesick for heaven). Was he worried that they might be thinking that he was a loafer, or had been more of a burden than a help to Paul? Was that the cause of his distress?

2:27 -- *For indeed he was sick to the point of death, but God had mercy on him, and not on him only but on me also, lest I should have sorrow upon sorrow.*

For indeed he was sick to the point of death – The initial *kai gar* ("for indeed") implies that the previous statement that Epaphroditus had become ill was really an understatement of the case,[99] since the man had nearly died. He had been gravely ill. Twice (verses 27,30) it is affirmed he was near to death. They had been correctly informed about him. Commentaries have speculated on the nature of his illness. Perhaps he caught the terrible Roman fever, epidemics of which often swept the city. Perhaps his illness was the result of over-exertion. Perhaps he simply suffered the kind of critical illness that is the common experience of all us humans.

But God had mercy on him – The illness was so severe that Epaphroditus would not have recovered had not God intervened and shown mercy. It would appear that Epaphroditus was restored to health, not because Paul worked a miracle of healing,[100] but rather because God had stepped in and restored Epaphroditus to health in answer to the prayers of Paul and many other Christians. God providentially does many amazing and wonderful things in answer to prayer. Such

---

[99] Lightfoot, *op. cit.,* p.123

[100] On a later occasion, Trophimus, one of Paul's helpers, was left at Miletus because he was sick (2 Timothy 4:20). Paul worked no miracle in his case, either. Paul may well have wanted to heal his friends by working a miracle, but it looks like the signs of an apostle (2 Corinthians 12:12) were only performed to credential the message or to show that the apostles were genuine messengers from God. Miracles were worked not at the will of the apostle, nor even to meet an apostle's own personal needs or wishes, but they were worked when God willed them to corroborate the truth the apostles were presenting.

healings in answer to prayer are the result of an exertion of divine power, but technically we do not call such healings "miracle."

And not on him only but also on me, lest I should have sorrow upon sorrow – The second of these double sorrows for Paul obviously would have been Epaphroditus' death, had that been the outcome of this critical illness. The first of the sorrows was grief already felt over his friend's illness when it looked like he was going to die. "God had mercy on both Epaphroditus and Paul! It is comforting to know that the heart of God is filled with mercy, that is, with loving-kindness and active pity."[101]

2:28 -- *Therefore I have sent him all the more eagerly in order that when you see him again you may rejoice and that I may be less concerned* **about you.**

Therefore I have sent him all the more eagerly in order that when you see him again you may rejoice – A second reason for sending Epaphroditus back to Philippi is here stated. Paul wants the Philippians to rejoice. Their joy had been clouded (verse 26) by news of Epaphroditus' illness. They would rejoice again when they see him in person alive and well.[102] "I have sent" is another epistolary aorist, and refers to Paul's present sending him along with this letter. "All the more eagerly" (a comparative adverb) says that Epaphroditus has been sent back sooner than otherwise would have been done. If it were not for the serious illness and the distress felt about it among the Philippians, Paul well might have welcomed his services longer, perhaps even until his case was decided in the courts. It was important that Epaphroditus accompany this letter to Philippi. The Philippians' distress over his sickness would give way to rejoicing. The distress that Epaphroditus felt would be relieved. The church would have a true explanation of what happened, and thus there would be a happy conclusion to the whole affair and all the parties in the matter would be satisfied.

And that I may be less concerned *about you* – This is a third reason why Paul has prompted Epaphroditus to return to Philippi. To know that it will bring joy to the Philippians will make Paul's own burden lighter. He had a concern over problems in the churches (2 Corinthians 11:28) and knowing that their distress had been eased would mean he had one less thing to be anxious about. Easing their

---

[101] Hendriksen, *op. cit.*, p. 142.

[102] It cannot be decided whether "again" goes with the verb "see" or with the verb "rejoice."

distress meant more to Paul than any benefit he might derive from Epaphroditus' ministry to him in prison.

2:29 -- *Therefore receive him in the Lord with all joy, and hold men like him in high regard;*

Therefore receive him in the Lord with all joy – "Therefore" means because of all these reasons just stated it is Paul's will that Epaphroditus return to Philippi. Paul is concerned with the kind of reception Epaphroditus would receive when he arrives home in Philippi. He tells the folk at Philippi the kind of welcome that would be appropriate for their messenger who had served with such distinction. As has already been stated in verse 25, the Philippian church not only delegated Epaphroditus to carry their offering to Paul, but they also intended him to stay in Rome and be Paul's personal servant and attendant. Paul tells the brethren at Philippi that Epaphroditus' early return to Philippi is not something with which they should find fault. 'He is not being disobedient to the commission you gave him when you sent him to Rome. Give him a cordial welcome. He deserves an appropriate homecoming.' If we allow Romans 16:2 (where similar language occurs) to guide our thinking, then what was true in Phoebe's case when she came to Rome, was to be the kind of welcome Epaphroditus gets when he arrives in Philippi. 'Treat him as you would if it were the Lord Himself visiting.'

And hold men like him in high regard – "Men like him" denotes that Epaphroditus was an eminent example of an entire class of loyal, valiant, and self-effacing ministers. 'He deserves more than a welcome. Honor him! Hold him in high regard for what he has done.' There must have been a need for Paul to write these directions about how he was to be received, for otherwise the church might have done neither. The plea for the proper esteem and treatment of soldiers of the cross is not without point today. The treatment Paul requests for Epaphroditus is still appropriate treatment in all similar cases.

2:30 -- *because he came close to death for the work of Christ, risking his life to complete what was deficient in your service to me.*

Because he came close to death for the work of Christ – In this verse Paul states the reasons why a warm welcome and special honor should be accorded to Epaphroditus. First, in his mission to Rome and while at Rome he had been carrying out the work of Christ, and it nearly cost him his life. The "work of

Christ"[103] in this context is the work for which Epaphroditus had been commissioned by the church, namely, the service he could render to Paul for the furtherance of the gospel.

Risking his life to complete what was deficient in your service to me – Paul here gives a second reason why Epaphroditus should be honored. He had been trying by his labors to do for Paul what the Philippians themselves would have done had they been present in Rome. The best supported reading here is *paraboleusamenos*, "risking his life," rather than *parabouleusamenos*, "not regarding his life" (KJV). "Risked his life" is from the gambler's vocabulary; "he gambled with his life."[104] Barry insists that the word means not merely having staked his life, but having staked it recklessly.[105] We doubt that the idea of recklessness is involved, but we do not doubt that Epaphroditus was in grave danger of some kind as a result of his trip to Rome and his presence in Rome, and that he took calculated risks that he might realize a gain for the cause of Christ. Whether there is reference to no more than the violent illness which brought him to the verge of death (as Hendriksen thinks[106]), or whether there is reference to some other danger that Epaphroditus decided to chance in order to carry out his commission from the church, we have no way of knowing. Barry believed he risked his life through over-exertion in the cause of serving Paul,[107] and this may be the idea. The English translation "to complete what was deficient in your service to me" carries a touch of reproach which is not implied in the original.[108] The Philippians are not being blamed! Their support of Paul went beyond what other churches did (Philippians 4:14-18). The only deficiency in their gracious interest was that they themselves could not be present with Paul in his imprison-

---

[103] The manuscript readings at this place vary between "Christ" (P[46], B, D, G, K) and "Lord" (Aleph, A, P), and simply "for the work's sake" (C). Already the simple expression "the work" was getting a technical meaning, like "the way" and "the name." It signified the cause of Christ, and Paul used it absolutely in Acts 15:38 about John Mark, who "had not gone with them to the work."

[104]   Vincent, *op. cit.*, p.77.

[105] Barry, *op. cit.*, p. 276.

[106] Hendriksen, *op. cit.*, p.144.

[107] Barry, *ibid.*

[108] Similar expressions in 1 Corinthians 16:17 and Colossians 1:24 do not imply reproach or criticism.

ment, in order to be able to help personally. Epaphroditus did that which their absence prevented them from doing. They could not come themselves in person and could only send their love by proxy. Epaphroditus, in their behalf, dared all and did a sacrificial service[109] on their behalf which Paul would never forget.

---

[109] "Service" translates *leitourgia*, for which see notes at 2:17 and 2:25.

V. WORDS OF WARNING.   3:1-21

A. Warning Against Judaizers.   3:1-3

3:1 -- *Finally, my brethren, rejoice in the Lord.   To write the same things* **again** *is no trouble to me, and it is a safeguard for you.*

Finally, my brethren – The Greek words *to loipon* translated "finally" had several uses in the ancient world.   Indeed, they could signal to an audience that the speaker or writer was nearing the end of a sermon/letter/subject, but this expression was also used to introduce a new subject.   The preceding topic is closed, and the speaker or writer passes to another.[1]   Paul here turns to what we have characterized as words of warning.

Rejoice in the Lord – If they will rejoice[2] in the Lord Jesus, the overtures of the false teachers (about which Paul is about to pen some warnings) will fall on deaf ears.   "On the assumption that the epistle is a unity, Paul's exhortation to rejoice in the Lord should be understood as belonging with what follows."[3]   If they will rejoice in the Lord, the following warning about the Judaizers will be heartily accepted, and the unity which Paul has been urging will be safeguarded.

To write the same things *again* – This sentence has puzzled the commentators no little.   To what does Paul refer that he says you are about to hear the same thing again?   Suggestions include, (1) a reiteration of the calls to rejoice;[4]   (2) a repetition of the exhortations to unity and against dissension, such as 2:2-4, 14-16;   (3) 'to write the same things to you that I have written to others;'   (4) a reiteration in writing of the things he had personally spoken by word of mouth when he was last in Philippi;   (5) a repetition of things written in a previous letter

---

[1] This beginning of chapter 3 introduces another of the critical problems of the letter.   Since "finally" is often used to indicate the conclusion of a letter/sermon, it has been argued that, originally, the letter to the Philippians ended here, and that the letter as we now have it is a composite of two separate letters.   See the Detailed Introduction to Philippians on "Integrity" where such an hypothesis is vigorously rejected.

[2] The word translated "rejoice" (*chairete*) can be translated "farewell."   In classical Greek the word is used as a salutation when folk meet ("greetings, rejoice"), and when they part ("farewell"), but the word does not appear with this latter sense in the New Testament, unless here.

[3] Kent, *op. cit.,* p.138.   In the Detailed Introduction to Philippians the matter of the unity of this epistle is explained.

[4] Hendriksen (*op. cit.,* p.147) seems to opt for this view.   "This is by no means the first time Paul has touched on the exalted theme of joy (see 1:4, 2:17,18, 2:28,29)."

now no longer extant.[5]   If Paul referred to previous warnings about opponents of Christianity generally, then 1:27-30 would be an earlier instance in this letter. We see no reason why Paul cannot here be repeating what he has both said to them orally when with them, and what he has written earlier in this same letter. Certainly, unity in a congregation could be imperiled by the Judaizers.

Is no trouble to me, and it is a safeguard for you – If students are not listening, it can be discouraging and irksome to repeat a lesson.   But when the speaker recognizes that the spiritual safety of the listeners is at stake, it is no trouble to go over and over again the great basic truths of the Christian faith.   "Safeguard" implies there is danger present, and it is a worthy goal to safeguard believers from being misled and ensnared in wrong doctrine.

3:2 -- *Beware of the dogs, beware of the evil workers, beware of the false circumcision;*

Beware ... beware ... beware – Like the blows of a gavel signaling for attention, three times Paul speaks this word of warning.   He offers these words so that the church at Philippi, by giving heed, may be safeguarded against spiritual and moral loss.   "Beware" (*blepete*) means to keep your eyes open for them, to constantly be on the guard against them.

Of the dogs ... of the evil workers ... of the false circumcision -- In verse 3b Paul gives a threefold description of *one* type of people, namely, God's true people.   Likewise, rather than finding in this verse three different classes of false teachers for whom the Philippians were to be on the lookout,[6] we think all three words describe *one* group of dangerous opponents of Christianity.   The opponents Paul is here warning against are Judaizers.[7]   The Judaizers in Galatians

---

[5] "The reference is probably to a former letter, or to former letters to the Philippians, which are lost" (Vincent, *op. cit.,* p. 91).   In the Detailed Introduction to Philippians we examine the arguments that Paul wrote more than one letter to the Philippians (including Polycarp's statement about Paul's "letters"), and conclude that the arguments are not convincing, especially in the absence of any trace of another epistle.

[6] A typical proposal advanced by those who attempt to show that these three titles refer to three different classes of false teachers identifies the dogs as being the heathen, the evil workers as being the false teachers introduced in Philippians 1:15, and the false circumcision as being the Judaizers.   Reasons for not identifying the Judaizers with the teachers referred to in 1:15-17 have been detailed at that place.

[7] "The words are a precise parallel to Paul's denunciations of Judaizing teachers in Galatians and 2 Corinthians.   Cf. Galatians 1:7; Galatians 1:9; Galatians 5:12; 2 Corinthians 11:13; 2 Corinthians 2:17" (Kennedy, *op. cit.,* p.448).

are deliberately characterized as being "false brethren who had sneaked in to spy out our liberty which we have in Christ Jesus, in order to bring us into bondage" (Galatians 2:4). They were not real Christians, but pretended to be when they sought admittance into local churches. While it may have been no trouble for Paul to repeat the warning, the fiery vehemence of his language certainly betrays emotional overtones.

- The Jews called the Gentiles "dogs," i.e., unclean,[8] mainly because of their disregard of the distinction between clean and unclean food.[9] Jesus used the term "dogs" in reference to opponents of God's truth (Matthew 7:6). "Chrysostom's hint that Paul means to retort the name upon the Judaizers, as now by their own willful apostasy occupying the place outside the spiritual Israel which once belonged to the despised Gentiles, is probably right."[10]

- Paul calls these men "workers" (*ergatas*). As indicated at Philippians 1:22 and 2:25, this word was an almost technical term for missionaries or itinerant preachers. The Judaizers whom Paul describes were very much like the Pharisees whom Jesus denounced (Matthew 23:15), whose energetic missionary activity involved "travel about on sea and land to make one proselyte." In 2 Corinthians 11:13 Paul called them "deceitful workers." Here he calls them "evil workers."[11] Their activity sprang from bad motives, and the results were that their converts were twice as liable to go to Hell after they were converted to Pharisaism as they had been before they were converted. The Judaizers, in their own self-righteous minds, would have been quite sure they were not evil workers. But Jesus had already exposed them. He indicated they preached their works of the Law to others but didn't practice it themselves. They bound heavy burdens on others, but did not lift a finger ease the burdens. By their traditions they voided the Law of Moses. They certainly were not workers of righteousness as they supposed in their own minds.

- Our English translations have struggled to find a word with the right nuance to translate the third term Paul uses to characterize the Judaizers. "Concision"

---

[8] "The noun *kuon* ('dog') used in a disparaging sense must be distinguished from *kunarion*, the diminutive form which denoted the 'house dog' [cp. 'little dogs,' Matthew 15:27] as distinct from the 'yard dog' or 'dog of the streets' (Michel, *Kunarion*, TDNT, 3:1104)" (Kent, *op. cit.*, p. 144).

[9] "There is a Rabbinic saying, "The nations of the world are like dogs" (Barclay, *op. cit.*, p.67).

[10] Barry, *op. cit.*, p.278.

[11] Paul's language may reflect Psalm 59:6,14 where persecuting Jews are compared to dogs, and Psalm 58:2 where they are described as workers of evil (doers of iniquity).

is the way the ASV did it; "false circumcision" is the NASB's attempt; "men who mutilate themselves" is how the TCNT renders it.   In verses 2 and 3 there is a sarcastic play on words (a paronomasia) in the Greek.[12]   In verse 3 we have *peritemnein* = circumcision.   In verse 2 we have *katatemnein* = cutting, mutilation of the flesh.   *Katatemnein* is the word used in the LXX (1 Kings 18:28) for worshipers of Baal who "cut themselves" during the contest with Elijah.   Elsewhere in the LXX the verb is used to denote the pagan practice of cutting the flesh during a frenzied religious ceremony (Leviticus 21:5; Isaiah 15:2).   The way Paul uses the word suggests the Judaizers are not much different from the pagans in this matter of cutting the flesh.[13]

3:3 - *For we are the* true *circumcision, who worship in the Spirit of God and glory in Christ Jesus and put no confidence in the flesh,*

For we are the *true* circumcision – "For" gives a reason why he can speak as he did in verse 2 about the Judaizers.   "We" is emphatic in the Greek.   Whether of Jewish or Gentile background, "we" who are Christians are the ones to whom the term "circumcision" (in all its meaning[14])   can be applied in this Christian age.[15]

---

[12] A paronomasia is a combination of like-sounding words, and Paul is fond of this kind of pun.

[13] Care must be exercised as we comment on what Paul has written.   Since the time of Abraham, circumcision had been the mark of God's chosen people (Genesis 12:9-14).   Circumcision was an ordinance of God.   For a man to be in covenant relationship, however, something far more was needed than a mark on the body.   There had to be a corresponding attitude of heart (Leviticus 26:41; Deuteronomy 10:16, 30:6; Jeremiah 6:10; Exodus 6:20).   As the years passed, the corresponding attitude of heart became lost to many Jews.   By Paul's time, the Jews proudly called themselves "the Circumcision"; scornfully they called others "the Uncircumcision" (Ephesians 2:11).   Christian preachers such as Paul had to attempt to correct the erroneous ideas about circumcision that prevailed in the first century AD.   In Romans 2:28,29, Paul has set forth the Biblical attitude about circumcision: "For he is not a Jew who is one outwardly; nor is circumcision that which is outward in the flesh.   But he is a Jew who is one inwardly; and circumcision is that which is of the heart, by the Spirit, not by the letter; and his praise is not from men, but from God."   Similar truths are emphasized in Ephesians 2:11 and Colossians 2:11.   Thus, what Paul writes is not directed toward Jews in general, but toward those who were Judaizers.

[14] The NASB has printed the word "true" in italics to show there is no corresponding word in the Greek.   But the addition of the word correctly catches the point Paul is making.   He makes a similar point elsewhere when he distinguished between the two circumcisions: one is merely outward -- of the flesh; the other is inward -- of the heart (Romans 2:28,29, 4:9; Galatians 2:9, 6:14ff; Ephesians 2:11; Colossians 2:11,12).   Cp. Acts 7:51 for Stephen's characterization of his Jewish accusers.

[15] It seems correct to see in the emphatic "we" an implication that the Judaizers about whom the Philippians are being warned were not Christians, something which was also true of the Judaizers who troubled the churches of Galatia (Galatians 2:4).

It is noteworthy that Paul found it necessary to explain numerous times that Christians do have a "circumcision" that expresses God's real intent behind the divinely given covenant sign. It looks like the Gentile Christians needed this ammunition to counter the Judaizers' presentation of the importance of that physical act. What Paul teaches here is entirely in harmony with what is taught elsewhere. In Colossians 2:11-13 Paul explains in what sense it may be said that Christians are the true circumcision. Since "neither is circumcision anything, nor uncircumcision, but a new creation" is everything (Galatians 6:15), it is evident that Paul is using the term figuratively when he uses it to speak of the Philippian Christians. As the verse continues, Paul explains the reasons why he can speak of the Philippian Christians as the "true circumcision."[16] They are the ones who, (1) worship God in the spirit, (2) glory (rejoice) in Christ Jesus, and (3) put no confidence in the flesh. These three phrases all show that something has happened to the man's heart.

Who worship in the Spirit of God – What Paul wrote and what Paul meant when he wrote this phrase is complicated by several matters. As we attempt to determine what Paul wrote we are faced with variations in the still-extant manuscripts. Some of these manuscripts read "who worship God in [the] spirit".[17] Others read "who worship in [by] the Spirit of God".[18]

The Chester Beatty papyrus P[46] omits "God", with the resulting translation being "who worship in spirit."[19] This translation is attractive because it results in something similar to Jesus' great declaration on the nature of worship, that we "worship in spirit and truth" (John 4:24). This also results in something similar to the parallel passage in Romans 1:9, where Paul writes "whom I serve (*latreuo*) in my spirit." It also matches beautifully with Paul's emphasis that true circumcision is something in the heart.

---

[16] Just as Paul characterized the Judaizers by three terms in the previous verse, so here in verse 3 he explains the true circumcision by three descriptive phrases.

[17] When translating the dative *pneumati*, a decision must be made whether to use a capital "S" ("Spirit") or a small "s" ("spirit").

[18] Manuscripts which read "worship God" have "God" in the dative case ($\theta\varepsilon\tilde{\omega}$). Manuscripts which read "of God" have "God" in the genitive case ($\theta\varepsilon o\tilde{\upsilon}$). The majority of the Uncial manuscripts have the genitive reading.

[19] It may be that this is the original reading, and the other texts containing the word "God" (whether $\theta\varepsilon\tilde{\omega}$, or $\theta\varepsilon o\tilde{\upsilon}$) are efforts by a scribe to explain the original reading.

Now we must take up the word translated "worship", which is *latreuontes* in the Greek. Two words are translated "worship" in the New Testament: *proskuneo*, which emphasizes submission to deity, and *latreuo*, which emphasizes service done for the deity. Here in Philippians, such service (e.g., missionary activities) is guided by the man's spirit which has been born again (John 3:6) and which gets directions from the Holy Spirit, especially through the Word (Romans 8:4-10). Since the Judaizers have not been born again (and such a person is dead in trespasses and sins, Ephesians 2:1), their service (missionary activities) cannot be anything but external.[20]

And glory in Christ Jesus – The second distinctive characteristic of the "true" circumcised is stated positively in these words – he is one who boasts or exults or rejoices in Jesus the Messiah. This is not something the Judaizers did. Most of the Judaizers had not even become Christians (they were "false brethren ..." per Galatians 2:4). The Pharisees were dogged opponents of Jesus during His earthly ministry and have been since. Paul loves the beautiful passage in Jeremiah 9:23,24, and in abbreviated form quotes it both in 1 Corinthians 1:31 and in 2 Corinthians 10:17, "But he who boasts, let him boast in the Lord." Christians boast in the Lord. What the Judaizers boast in will be enumerated in the following verses.

And put no confidence in the flesh – This is a third distinctive characteristic of the "true" circumcised. "Flesh" is used in the sense of something external to the heart, or inner man. The Pharisaic Judaizers often claimed, "We are descended from Abraham" (Matthew 3:9; Luke 3:8; John 8:33), to which Jesus responded if that is all that mattered, "God could raise up descendants to Abraham from rocks." The Pharisees were proud of their physical descent from Abraham, their physical circumcision, their physical, visible giving (Matthew 6:2-5), and their public praying to be seen of men (Matthew 6:2-5). What God is looking for is folk of whatever nationality who have the faith of Abraham (Romans 4:16; Galatians 3:26).

---

[20] "*Latrueontes* ... was used especially of the service rendered to God by Israelites as His peculiar people, as Acts 26:7; or *latreia*, Romans 9:4; Hebrews 10:1,6 ... A Jew would have been scandalized by the application of this term to Christian service. It is purposely chosen with reference to 'the circumcision'" (Vincent, *op. cit.*, p.93). If the ASV and NASB are correct in capitalizing "Spirit," this verse is still a sharp rebuke of the Judaizers for it would imply that they are not led by the Holy Spirit as they do their missionary activity.

B. Paul Uses His Own Example as an Argument Against the Judaizers. 3:4-16

1. I, Paul, the Pharisaic Jew, had things I thought were gain for me. 3:4-6

3:4 -- *Although I myself might have confidence even in the flesh. If anyone else has a mind to put confidence in the flesh, I far more:*

Although I myself might have confidence even in the flesh – "I myself" is emphatic and prepares us to think of a comparison. Paul compares himself with the Judaizers, with the idea being that when it comes to having "confidence in the flesh" he could do it better than they if he wished to.[21] When he was a Pharisee, he had all the "advantages" that the Judaizers boasted in, and he had them to a greater degree than the Judaizers. It cannot be claimed by the Judaizers that Paul's rejection of certain Jewish "advantages" was sour grapes simply because he did not possess them. If such fleshly advantages were important, Paul argued, he could show a record that would outweigh them all. As it were, Paul says, 'I've been where they are, and when I was, I was fighting against God and was violently opposed to what He was doing to save men.'

If anyone else has a mind to put confidence in the flesh, I far more – From here through the end of verse 6 Paul is using an *ad hominem* argument, similar to the one he used in 2 Corinthians 11:16-20.[22] The "anyone else" is the Judaizer referred to indefinitely in the second verse. "I far more" says that 'If we are going to compare fleshly pedigrees, I have an even stronger claim than the Judaizers do.' This introduction to his argument prepares us to interpret the seven credentials about to be listed as they would be seen in the eyes of a Pharisee. Paul first lists his inherited privileges. He then itemizes those things which were his own personal achievement.

---

[21] Vincent (*op. cit.*, p.95) affirms that *pepoithēsin* can mean either subjective "confidence" or "ground of confidence." See also BAG, p. 649. Having denied that believers have confidence in the flesh (verse 3), Paul would hardly be using the word in its subjective sense here.

[22] In the background of the passage in 2 Corinthians 11:16-20 is the factor that when others boasted of their position, the Corinthians listened to such arguments. Paul there says he was speaking foolishness (2 Corinthians 11:21) for a moment and indulges in such a boasting argument. So, here, Paul is to be understood as temporarily adopting the position taken by the Judaizers in order to refute their arguments.

3:5 -- *Circumcised the eighth day, of the nation of Israel, of the tribe of Benjamin, a Hebrew of Hebrews; as to the Law, a Pharisee;*

Circumcised the eighth day – Perhaps Paul begins his list with circumcision because it was the main point in a Judaizer's eyes. The Greek literally says, "in circumcision I am an eighth-day-er." This way of speaking was an idiomatic expression[23] that has been smoothly rendered by our translators. It had been the commandment of God to Abraham, "He that is 8 days old among you shall be circumcised" (Genesis 17:12). This commandment had been repeated as a permanent part of the Law of Israel (Leviticus 12:3). Zealous Jewish parents would see that this law was kept to the letter, as Paul's parents had done.[24] There may be an implication that "circumcised the eighth day" was something that could not be claimed by every Judaizer. "In all likelihood *some* of these were proselytes from the Gentile world, and as a result had been circumcised not on the eighth day but as adults."[25]

Of the nation of Israel – Paul's second inherited privilege is that he was a direct descendant from the patriarch Jacob, whose name was changed by God Himself to "Israel" (Genesis 32:28), and whose name became the sacred name of the Jews as God's covenant people (Romans 9:4; 2 Corinthians 11:22; Ephesians 2:12), and who received the same promises that were given to Abraham. To be descended from Jacob was a greater advantage than simply being descended from Abraham, since not all of Abraham's descendants were among the chosen people: children of Ishmael and Esau were excluded, as were some others.

Of the tribe of Benjamin – Why does Paul mention this, a fact he proudly called attention to on more than one occasion (Acts 13:21; Romans 11:1)? To be a Benjamite, for some reason, was recognized by Jewish people as being a special honor. Of all the tribes descended from Jacob, none was more Israelitish than Benjamin. Benjamin was the only son of Israel born in the land of promise (Gen-

---

[23] Similar idioms are found at John 11:39 (he "is a four-day-er") and Acts 28:13 (a "two day-er").

[24] "He was neither a proselyte, circumcised as an adult, nor an Ishmaelite, circumcised (as Josephus tells us, *Antiquities*, xii. i. §§ 2; see Genesis 17:25) at age thirteen, but a member of the covenant from infancy" (H. G. C. Moule, "Philippians" in *Cambridge Bible for Schools and Colleges* [Cambridge: At the University Press, 1889], p. 87).

[25] Hendriksen, *op. cit.*, p.156.

esis 35:16-20), and his mother was Rachel who was Jacob's most beloved wife (Genesis 35:17,18). Benjamin did not become apostate as did some of the other tribes. Following the Babylonian captivity, it was people from the tribes of Benjamin and Judah who formed the nucleus of Israel restored (Ezra 4:1). Both Mordecai and Esther came from Benjamin and had much to do with the deliverance of Israel. It would seem obvious that few of the Judaizers could make a claim to such distinguished heredity as Paul could.

A Hebrew of Hebrews – This claim seems to speak of something other than his racial descent already mentioned. Perhaps Acts 6:1 helps us understand the point being made here, for in that passage the distinction between "Hebrews" and "Hellenists" refers to a language difference. Almost always in the New Testament "Hebrew" (or a more accurate translation might be "Aramaic") is a reference to language (cf. Acts 21:40, 22:2).[26] Though he was reared in Tarsus, neither he nor his family were tainted with Hellenism as were many of his contemporaries. Not only did his parents speak Hebrew, but he grew up in a home where Hebrew customs were observed. He was made familiar with the Hebrew Scriptures, and he and his parents spoke the Hebrew language in their home. The Hebrew Jew, who retained, wherever born, the old tongue, education, and customs of his fathers, held himself superior to the Grecian or Hellenist, who tried to assimilate themselves to the language, thoughts, and habits of the folk around them, whose culture was tainted with Greek ideas.

As to the Law, a Pharisee – Thus far Paul has called attention to his inherited privileges. Now he proceeds to mention his personal attainments. While being a Sadducee was an hereditary position, one became a Pharisee (or a Zealot or an Essene) by choice. As had several generations of his ancestors (Acts 23:6), Paul had chosen to embrace the Pharisees' approach to the Law of Moses.[27] The Phar-

---

[26] "The Old Testament does not know the word 'Hebrew' with reference to language. In the Apocrypha and New Testament the term 'Hebrew' is used almost exclusively of the Aramaic vernacular" (Vincent, *op. cit.*, p.97).

[27] "Law" here is anarthrous in the Greek. The attempt of some scholars a century ago to distinguish between *nomos* and *ho nomos*, as though one spoke of Divine law in general while the other specially referred to the Mosaic Law, has proven to be incorrect. Others tried to show that one had emphasis on keeping the Law as a method of justification in opposition to faith. That, too, has also proven to be an unsustainable and arbitrary distinction. Paul uses the terms "Law" and "the Law" with no sharp distinction between them.

isees were the strictest sect of the Jews (Acts 22:3, 26:5).[28]   Before his conversion Paul was exceedingly zealous for the traditions taught by the Pharisees (Galatians 1:14).   In fact, it was the acceptance of certain sets of man-made religious rules that differentiated between Pharisees and other Jewish sects such as the Essenes. One wonders whether or not Paul chose to call attention to his own background among the Pharisees because the Judaizers (at least those in Galatia) were of the sect of the Pharisees, too (Acts 15:5).

3:6 -- *As to zeal, a persecutor of the church: as to the righteousness which is in the Law, found blameless.*

As to zeal, a persecutor of the church – The second point of Paul's self-commendation for his own personal achievements concerns his zeal as a persecutor of the church. "Zeal for God, for His house, and for His law, was the highest praise of an Old Testament saint (see Numbers 25:11,13; 1 Kings 19:10,14; Psalm 69:9)."[29]   Paul's persecution of the church is given as the evidence of his zeal.   Paul had been one of the most bitter opponents of the early Christians.   He had breathed out threatening and slaughter against the disciples of the Lord.   He traveled from city to city, putting in chains and committing to prisons both men and women (Acts 9:1,2, 22:1-5, 26:9-15; 1 Corinthians 15:9). Once Paul did to Christians exactly what the Judaizers were now doing to him. But here too, Paul had an "advantage" over the Judaizers.   He had been a persecutor, and many had died because of his zealousness.   Not many of the Judaizers could equal that!   All this, obviously, is contradictory to what Paul the Christian would do, but he is arguing *ad hominem*.

As to the righteousness which is in the Law, found blameless – This is the third area of personal achievement to which Paul calls attention as he lists the kind of things the Judaizers took pride in.   In this context, "righteousness ... in the Law" is righteousness as interpreted or understood by a Pharisaic Jew – what Paul was before his conversion to Christ.   He calls it "a righteousness of my own" in verse

---

[28] "There were not very many Pharisees: there were never more than about 6000 of them, but they were the spiritual athletes of Judaism.   Their very name means *the separate ones*.   They had separated themselves from all common life and from all common tasks in order to make it the one aim and duty of their lives to keep every smallest detail of the Law.   It was Paul's claim that not only was he a Jew who had retained his ancestral religion, but he had also devoted his whole life to the most rigorous and unbending observance of it.   No man knew better from personal experience what Jewish religion was at its highest and most demanding peak" (Barclay, *op. cit.*, p.74).

[29] Vincent, *op. cit.*, p.98.

9. Righteousness, as the Pharisees interpreted it, consisted largely in the know-how and proficiency in performing rituals just right, dipping the hands precisely the correct way before eating, et al.; that is, carefully observing what were known as "works of the Law" (Romans 3:20,28; Galatians 2:16).   These were man-made religious rules, not rules that God had commanded.   When Paul writes "found blameless," he is claiming for himself a careful observance of the works of the Law, something many of the Pharisaic Judaizers could not claim (for, according to Jesus, they bound rules on others which they did not practice themselves, Matthew 23:3,4)

2. I, Paul, the Christian, have counted all such things as loss.   3:7,8a

3:7 -- *But whatever things were gain to me, those things I have counted as loss for the sake of Christ.*

But whatever things were gain to me – In the two preceding verses, Paul enumerated seven things a Pharisee would call gain, or assets.[30]   "'Whatever' indicates the previous listing was not exhaustive but illustrative."[31]   The imperfect tense verb *ēn* ("were") depicts Paul's continuing attitude as a Pharisee regarding his heritage and personal achievements prior to his conversion.   "But" with which this verse begins prepares us to hear the startling reversal in Paul's attitude since the risen Lord appeared to him on the Damascus road to call him to be the apostle to the Gentiles.   A few days later in Damascus it was told him what to do to be saved.   There had been a reversal of all his values and priorities.

These things I have counted as loss for the sake of Christ – Philippians has been called "an epistle of decisions,"[32] since *hegeomai* ("to consider, to reckon, to count, to deem") occurs so often (2:3,6,25; 3:7,8).   The verb here ("I have counted") is in the perfect tense in the Greek.   It speaks of a past completed action with present continuing results.   The risen Christ had shown Paul that his Pharisaic zeal was badly misplaced.   Paul arrived at the same decision after carefully weighing the facts, and that decision still stands.   What he once thought

---

[30] The word translated "gain" is plural in the Greek.

[31] Kent, *op. cit.*, p.140.   The word *hatina*, translated "whatever," calls attention to a category of things.

[32] Harrell, *op. cit.*, p.118.

were gains (assets) had now amassed into one great loss.[33] "Loss" suggests the old "assets" were worse than useless; rather, they were a hindrance because they had to be unlearned. His zeal for Pharisaic Judaism made him reject the Christ, the gospel, and led to his persecution of those who had accepted Christ. "For the sake of Christ" needs explanation. As Paul describes how he weighed the facts that led to his decision, it became evident to him very quickly that if he were unwilling to renounce his Pharisaic values he would have to do without any relationship to Israel's long promised Messiah. That was too high a cost for him. To have a relationship with Christ was all that mattered, now.

3:8a -- *More than that, I count all things to be loss in view of the surpassing value of knowing Christ Jesus my Lord, for whom I have suffered the loss of all things,*

More than that – The sentence begins with the piling up of Greek particles, *alla men oun ge kai*, as Paul tries to give strong expression to the statements in verses 7 and 8. As thoughts crowd Paul's mind he apparently left out words as he dictated the letter. A literal rendering of the Greek particles would be "But, indeed, therefore, at least, even." If we were to attempt to supply the words that got left out it might read like this: 'But, indeed (that is not all), therefore (I affirm) at least (I could affirm more) even (this, that) I still do count all things to be loss in view of the all-surpassing value of knowing Christ Jesus my Lord.'

I count all things to be loss – The verb "count" in this clause is in the present tense. Nearly 30 years have passed since Jesus stopped Paul on the Damascus road. His changed views concerning the relative value of what a Pharisee considered to be "assets" versus seeing in Jesus the long-promised Messiah have not changed. Let no one think that his decision to see Pharisaism as a liability was a snap decision, as though taken in some impulsive and unguarded moment, as a decision he now regrets. "I am still counting ..." all things to be loss, yea more than a loss, a gigantic liability. By using *panta* ("all things") rather than *tauta* ("those things," verse 7), Paul's thought broadens from his Jewish advanta-

---

[33] The words "gain" and "loss" are words that come from the world of accounting and bookkeeping. The language suggests that when he was still an unconverted Pharisee, he used to mentally keep books. In one column he would add up his assets (all those Pharisaic Jewish distinctives he used to think so important), and in the other column add up his debts. Elsewhere (in commentaries on Romans and Galatians) we have shown that it is in error to treat "works of the Law" as being the same as what modern denominational theologians call "works of merit." Nevertheless, it appears to be true that "gains" in this Philippians passage does reflect a Pharisaic belief that progress toward righteousness did result from certain inherited privileges and pedigree as well as things which were one's own personal achievement. Nevertheless, verse 9 following will show that it was not God's righteousness the Pharisee achieved. '

ges just mentioned to include everything that might conceivably be a rival to what it means to recognize Jesus as the promised Messiah and to commit one's life to Him. Family, friends, and former associates had become strangers and enemies. Comforts of home had been exchanged for shipwreck and prison, and substantial wealth had been forfeited for the privilege of working with his own hands to support himself and his team of missionaries. "He had paid a high price, but 'when he had found one pearl of great price, [he] went and sold all that he had, and bought it' (Matthew 13:46)."[34]

In view of the surpassing value of knowing Christ Jesus my Lord – His attitude of willingly having suffered the loss of what he once valued has not changed at all. For Paul, knowledge of Jesus Messiah was not just something experienced years earlier. His experience with Jesus the Messiah is a delightful continuing relationship. The Greek word translated "surpassing value" (or "excellency," KJV) is *huperechon*, the neuter of the present participle of *huperecho*. By writing the neuter participle with an article, Paul makes the expression more forceful than if he had used the cognate noun *huperochē*. We might render it "all-surpassing greatness" and it is likely intended to be a sidelong glance at the supposed "assets" or advantages he once counted on. To know the Messiah and have a relationship with Him is a blessing so surpassing and transcendent that nothing else is worthy to be called good in comparison with that one highest good. As Chrysostom says here, "When the sun has appeared, it is loss to sit by a candle."[35]

3. I, Paul, the Christian, now count such things as rubbish. 3:8b-11

3:8b -- *And count them but rubbish in order that I may gain Christ,*

And count them but rubbish – His attitude of having willingly suffered this loss (earlier phrases in verse 8) has not changed at all. With another present tense verb, he says 'I continue to count those things I used to value as "assets" as being rubbish.' It is still debated just what this word *skubala* ("rubbish," "dung" [KJV]) implies. While this is striking language to a modern reader, it would have been shocking to a Judaizer. (1) Taking it to mean "refuse, garbage, dog's food," it would be very shocking. What the Judaizers prize so very highly, the apostle considers to be nothing but garbage, something that is fit only to be thrown to the dogs. This would make Paul very consistent in his use of figures of speech; he

[34] Tesh, *op. cit.*, p.411.

[35] Barry, *op. cit.*, p. 281.

had just a moment ago (see 3:2) called these dangerous enemies "dogs." (2) Taking the other meaning of the word ("dung," as in the KJV), Paul is meaning that he considers all the things which the Pharisees valued as not worth keeping any more than one would keep a pile of manure.

In order that I may gain Christ – This is a purpose clause connected with "I count them ..." and says it was his purpose to think thus of the old Pharisaic assets precisely in order that he might gain Christ. "I may gain" is the verbal form of the same word translated "gain" in verse 7. Paul still has the bookkeeping metaphor in mind, with its columns of profit and loss. The values of his former pattern had seemed at one time to be immensely profitable to him, but now they were nothing. The only important thing in the asset column was gaining Christ, i.e., recognizing and embracing Him as the promised Messiah. Verses 9-11 will explain why gaining Christ is something to be entered in the asset column of a man's life.[36]

3:9 -- *And may be found in Him, not having a righteousness of my own derived from* the *Law, but that which is through faith in Christ, the righteousness which comes from God on the basis of faith,*

And may be found in Him – Now Paul begins to unfold the benefits a person enjoys when he gains Christ. At Philippians 1:1 we learned the meaning "in Him (Christ)." Paul wants to be a member of His body, or (as pictured in another passage) a living branch of the true Vine. "Found" may mean the possible time frame Paul has in mind when this finding will be of great importance. Some think Paul has in mind that, at the time of his physical death, he wants to be found to be "in Christ." Some think Paul has in mind all the rest of his earthly life, and appeal to verses 9 and 10 for evidence. Still others, noting the sentence continues on through verse 11, think Paul has in mind the time of the final resurrection and the final judgment. When does Paul want to be found "in Christ"? Today, tomorrow, forever!

Not having a righteousness of my own derived from *the* **Law** – "Righteousness," that is, a right standing or acceptability with God, is a difficult term to define because of the wide range of ideas contained in the concept represented by this Greek word. The epistle to the Romans has much to say about righteousness (or "justification," the two different translations of the same word) and about how

---

[36] Following the NASB's division of the verses is unfortunate, for it makes verse 9 begin right in the middle of a subordinate clause, separating the two verbs ("may gain," and "be found") that are used following the same introductory conjunction ("in order that"). As a matter of fact, the thought in verses 9-11 is simply the expansion of the idea in our phrase, "that I may gain Christ."

God reckons a man as either righteous or unrighteous depending on the presence or absence of faithfulness to God's revealed will.

"My own" (*emen*) is a possessive adjective in the Greek, a form that is more emphatic than the possessive pronoun "my" (*mou*). It shows that the contrast about to be made in this verse between "a righteousness of my own" and "the righteousness of God" is a strong one. When Paul was a Pharisee, conscientiously observing "the works of the Law" (Pharisaic rules), he had a righteousness, but it was not the kind of righteousness that God has revealed He looks for in men. By contrasting "a righteousness of my own" with "the righteousness which comes from God" Paul is acknowledging that what made a man righteous in the eyes of a Pharisee was not what made a man righteous in the eyes of God. Pharisaic Judaism was "derived from the Law" but it was not by "faith" (habitually doing what God says).[37]

"Derived from *the* Law" must *not* be explained as being synonymous with conformity to the Law of Moses. Denominational writers, whose mantra is that salvation is by faith not works, have been accustomed to so explain this and similar language (such as "works of the Law" in Romans 3 and Galatians 2) as being the same as keeping the Law of Moses. However, Romans 2:13 shows that if one wished to be counted as righteous during the Mosaic Age, he had to be an habitual "doer of the Law" to be justified. We must not make comments on Philippians 3 that will contradict what is plainly stated in Romans 2.

But that which is through faith in Christ – The Greek reads "faith of Christ" (*dia pisteos Christou*, a genitive case) and in this clause may well refer to Christ's faithfulness to the mission on which God had sent Him into the world.[38] God's way of saving man – righteousness, justification – involves the sacrificial death of Jesus on Calvary (Romans 3:24,25).

The righteousness which *comes* from God on the basis of faith – The righteousness which Paul now enjoys, because he has gained Christ and has been found to be in Him, is a righteousness which has its source in God. In Romans

---

[37] Compare Matthew 15:2-9 and Mark 7:5-9 where Jesus made the same evaluation of Pharisaism, namely, that by emphasizing their traditions they actually voided the Law of Moses.

[38] The same genitive phrase occurs elsewhere in the epistles and a recent debate has centered on whether or not Christ is the object of the faith, or whether Christ is the subject who demonstrated faith. Though we opt for the latter at this place, it does not require that we always treat the genitive as being a subjective genitive. Vincent, for example (*op. cit.,* p. 102) has urged that in Mark 11:22; Romans 3:22; 2 Corinthians 10:5; Galatians 2:16, 3:22; 2 Thessalonians 2:13; and James 2:1, this genitive phrase means "faith *in* Christ."

1:16,17 Paul used "salvation" and "the righteousness of God" as interchangeable terms. How such "righteousness" has been provided by God is carefully explained in Romans 3:21-28, and what was there written matches beautifully with what Paul here writes as he says that the righteousness which comes from God is through the faithfulness of Christ (*dia pisteos christou*) and it requires faithfulness (*epi te pistei*) on the part of men.[39] The Greek in this clause reads "upon faith" (*epi te pistei*), and means based upon faith, or on the condition of faith. This is the phrase in this passage that identifies for us the condition upon which righteousness is imputed/reckoned by God to men. He looks for faithfulness to the revelation He has given to men. When He sees such faithfulness He then grants salvation to men. The strong contrast ("but," *alla*) between "the righteousness which *comes* from God" and "my own righteousness" plainly says that God does not grant salvation when what He sees are "works of *the* Law" – the man-made religious rules like those, for example, imposed on people by the Pharisees (see Romans 3:20,28, 5:1; Galatians 2:6, 3:11). When Paul the Pharisee relied on "a righteousness of my own," he was not emphasizing obedience to what God had revealed.

3:10 -- *That I may know Him, and the power of His resurrection, and the fellowship of His sufferings, being conformed unto His death;*

That I may know Him – Because Paul used an articular infinitive here, there are two ways this verse may be understood. (1) It may be a *purpose* clause expressing the intent or motive behind "knowing Christ Jesus" (verse 8). (2) It may be the *result* of having "the righteousness which comes from God on the basis of faith" (verse 9).[40] The Greeks had two words for "know" – *eidenai*, which means to have an external acquaintance with facts, or an intellectual conviction as to their reality; and *ginōskō*, the word used here, which means to know by personal experience. Paul's aim is not to know about Christ; it is Paul's aim personally to know Christ, i.e., to experience what Christ can do in his life.[41]

---

[39] The idea that God has been faithful to His covenant (something that is in fact true, Romans 3:3) is not likely the idea intended here when Paul wrote "on the basis of faith."

[40] Either of these ways is more satisfactory than the explanation of those who skip back to the words "I suffered the loss of all things." In this commentator's judgment, Paul is clearly no longer speaking about the time of his conversion, but is speaking of his present yearning to get to know Christ better and better right along.

[41] Some have appealed to this expression about "knowing" Christ to justify attempts to have a mystical experience of Christ such as ancient ascetics sought. This commentator rejects any such idea that Paul is encouraging mysticism or self-induced altered states of consciousness.

And the power of His resurrection – It is better to translate *kai* as "even" rather than "and," so that verses 10 and 11 offer an explanation of what it means to "know Him." Paul (1) wants to experience the power of Jesus' resurrection in this life; (2) he wants to participate in the fellowship of Jesus' sufferings; and (3) he wants to participate in the resurrection of the righteous. That's what it means to know (*ginōskō*) Him. The same power that raised Christ from the dead is available to the Christian (Ephesians 1:19ff). "Power" in Ephesians 3:11 seems equal to the Holy Spirit. Is it thus here, too? If so, it says that as the Holy Spirit helped raise Christ (Romans 8:11), the indwelling Holy Spirit helps Christians to live the Christian life. Pharisaic Judaism had offered Paul no such benefit as this. No wonder he says that knowing Christ is very far better.

And the fellowship of His sufferings, being conformed to His death – One participates (*koinonia*, fellowship) in Christ's sufferings by being conformed (a circumstantial participle) to His death. "One article is used with *dunamin* ("power") and *koinonian* ("fellowship") showing they are aspects of a single unity – in this case, facts of Paul's concept of what is involved in knowing Christ."[42] "Conformed" (*summorphizomenos,* from *summorphos*) is a present participle, implying a continual progress. It is not something that happened once, back at the time of baptism. Rather, it is something that happens continually after one has become a Christian. Since "being conformed to His death" is something that happens continually, it is not likely that Paul means he is desiring to die a martyr's death like Jesus died. More likely, Paul means laying down his life, day by day, laying aside self-interest for interest in Christ, just like Christ laid aside self-interest in His desire to be a blessing to others (2:5-11).

3:11 -- *In order that I may attain to the resurrection from the dead.*

In order that I may attain – The NASB ignores the Greek words *ei pōs* ("if somehow") that one finds translated in the KJV's "if by any means." The other three times *ei pōs* occurs in the New Testament (Acts 27:12; Romans 1:10, 11:14) there is some uncertainty about the matter stated. The verb "attain" (*katanteso*) means to arrive at the end of a journey; it presents the figure of a pilgrimage. It indicates a destination which is to be reached, some goal to be achieved. Once we have decided on the meaning of the rest of the verse, we may then give a plausible reason for the uncertainty Paul seems to express.

---

[42] Kent, *op. cit.,* p.145.

To the resurrection from the dead – This phrase expresses the outcome for which Paul the Christian now aims his life. While the language refers to the physical resurrection of dead bodies at the second coming of Christ, the way the Greek is worded (*ten exanastasin ten ek nekrōn*) appears only here in the New Testament. The Greek has the usual word for resurrection (*anastasin*) prefixed with a preposition *ek* (the spelling is changed to *ex* for the sake of euphony*)*, and then the *ek* is repeated in the following words. This unusual wording leaves us with a translation something like "the out-resurrection from the dead." The double use of the preposition *ek* plus the plural word *nekrōn* ("dead") strongly suggests a resurrection in which some dead ones are left behind. The Bible elsewhere speaks of "the resurrection of the righteous" (Luke 14:14), and perhaps teaches that the final resurrection will take place in two stages – the righteous first; and then, following the catastrophical renovation of the universe, the resurrection of the wicked.[43]

The uncertainty expressed in this verse does not reflect any doubt on Paul's part that there will be a final resurrection of dead bodies (cf. 1 Corinthians 15:22,23) or that the righteous will be invited to inherit the kingdom prepared since the foundation of the world (Matthew 25:34). However, just as elsewhere Paul warns others about a possible lapse from faith (1 Corinthians 10:12; Galatians 3:3, 5:4; Philippians 2:12), he here recognizes the same need for caution himself lest he become unfaithful (cp. 1 Corinthians 9:27) and so miss the resurrection of the righteous.[44] In passing, in reply to some who have accused Paul of being mistaken about the time of Christ's second coming, thinking it would occur within his lifetime, this passage is so worded that Paul pictures himself among those who would need to be raised from the dead when that glorious day dawns.

4. I, Paul, the Christian Runner, Press on to the Goal. 3:12-16

*3:12 -- **Not that I have already obtained** it, or am already become perfect: but I*

---

[43] This presentation of the resurrection in two stages is not intended to be an agreement with modern premillennialism's resurrection of the righteous 1000 years before the resurrection of the wicked. Nor is it intended to give support to the idea sometimes taught that the resurrection and Great White Throne judgment (spoken about in Revelation 20:11ff) involves the wicked only. The "sea" that gives up the dead which are in it (Revelation 20:13) is likely the "sea of glass" before God's throne (Revelation 4:6, 15:2) on which the souls of the righteous have, during the intermediate state, awaited the coming resurrection and judgment.

[44] *Anastasis* and "resurrection from the dead" is language that denotes physical resurrection, and not the rapture as proposed by John F. Walvoord, *Philippians: Triumph in Christ* (Chicago: Moody Press, 1971), p.88.

press on in order that I may lay hold of that for which also I was laid hold of by Christ Jesus.

Not that I have already obtained *it* – "Not that" guards against a possible misunderstanding of what he has already written. Yes, he already knows Christ Jesus as his Lord (verse 8), but there are still things to be looked forward to yet in the future. The aorist tense verb "obtained" points back to the Damascus road experience nearly thirty years before, when Jesus the Messiah appeared to him and called him to be an apostle to the Gentiles (Acts 26:16-18). The NASB has printed "it" in italics since the text does not make clear what it is to which Paul has not yet attained.[45] Paul has just been talking about attaining unto the resurrection of the righteous (verse11) and will also speak of the prize of the upward call of God in Christ Jesus (in verse 14). These future events together seem to be the goal to which he says he has not yet attained.[46]

Or am already become perfect – The Greek is a perfect passive form (*teteleiomai*) and the ASV correctly translated it "or am already made perfect." It is not by Paul's own actions that he may become "perfect," but by Christ's action (assuming "Christ" is the unstated subject of this passive voice verb). What then is meant by "made perfect"? *Teleios*, here translated as "perfect", has a variety of meanings, depending on the context. "Paul does not here refer to moral sinlessness; he meant completion or fulfillment of the purpose for which Christ had called him."[47] Christ who called him to be an apostle has not yet declared his mission "complete."

But I press on – The verb here (*diōkō*) is used of the chase and of the foot-race

---

[45] The verb translated "obtain" here is not the same one translated "attain" in verse 11. Here, *lambano* means to get, to receive, to win a prize, as in 1 Corinthians 9:24.

[46] The text does not make clear what it is that Paul has not yet attained. There is no object in Greek for the verb "obtained" here in verse 12. Commentators are divided as to what its object is. Some suggest it is all that is included in verses 8-11. Others interpret the object as being the prize referred to in verse 14. Yet others believe Paul is referring to his resurrection from the dead in verse 11.

Hidden behind many of the comments offered by the commentaries on this section of Philippians is the question of whether or not the thing Paul says he has not yet attained is spiritual and moral perfection. Some appeal to the language of 1 Corinthians 9:24-27 as being a parallel passage. But while some of the language in 1 Corinthians 9 is the same, the topic there is self-control which allows him to defer to a weak brother when it is needful. Is that the same as spiritual and moral perfection? It is this commentator's judgment that, as we comment on these verses, we should not talk about whether or not one may reach sinless perfection in this life.

[47] Tesh, *op. cit.*, p.413.

where out ahead on the track there is a finish line to be crossed. It is a present tense verb, denoting a constant pursuit of the goal, "I keep pressing on." Paul presses on in his Christian life (verse 10) and in his mission as apostle in order that he may attain unto the resurrection of the righteous and the prize to which verse 14 alludes. "To Paul, the Christian life was always a process of spiritual growth. One could never stop growing and rest on his past credits and reputation."[48]

In order that I may lay hold of that for which also I was laid hold of by Christ Jesus – Marshall's interlinear shows that the Greek words read "if indeed I may lay hold, in as much as (*eph hō*) also I was laid hold of by Christ Jesus."[49] In some English versions, the translators (such as the NASB) have added some words in an attempt to fill out the suppressed sense behind the words *eph hō*. Without adding words the sense is clear enough. Is Paul not speaking of his mission when he writes "I was laid hold of by Christ Jesus"? Not his conversion, but his call to the apostolic ministry (Acts 26:16-18) is the topic. The Lord Jesus had laid hold of Paul on the road to Damascus and had commissioned him to be the best possible representative for His kingdom. Paul here states his determination to pursue that purpose with a passion "lest he disappoint Jesus and fail Jesus and frustrate the dream and the purpose for which Jesus had grasped him."[50]

3:13 -- *Brethren, I do not regard myself as having laid hold of* it *yet; but one thing* I do: *forgetting what* lies *behind and reaching forward to what* lies *ahead,*

Brethren, I do not regard myself as having laid hold of *it* **yet** – Verses 13-14 repeat and unfold the thought of verse 12. Addressing the readers as "brethren," Paul shows this loving appeal to them is a matter which is of serious concern both to him and them. "Regard" is a verb that speaks of a conclusion which is reached only after a careful consideration of the facts. The perfect active "laid hold" implies that, having made the capture, Paul may sit at ease since he has made it. "Yet" translates *oupō* ("not yet"[51]) and says that though he has not presently laid hold of the prize, his ultimate goal is to do that. That Paul feels he must repeat

---

[48] Tesh, *ibid.*

[49] Alfred Marshall, *The Interlinear Greek-English New Testament* (London: Samuel Bagster and Sons, 1958), p.785.

[50] Barclay, *op. cit.*, p.82.

[51] The manuscripts vary between the negatives *ou* ("not," as the UBS printed text has it) and *oupō* ("not yet," as the Nestle printed texts read).

his point about "not yet" seems a clear hint that there were people at Philippi, such as the ones identified at 3:2, who prided themselves on having already laid hold of a prize.

But one thing *I do* – The broken sentence is forceful and dramatic – it literally says "But one thing!"[52] It speaks of concentration, of the single-mindedness of his purpose.   The successful runner in the race "practices persistent concentration on one, and only one, objective, namely, to press on toward the goal, and receive the prize.   He permits nothing to divert him from his course."[53]   Paul's one ambition was to reach the goal.

Forgetting what *lies* behind and reaching forward to what *lies* ahead – "Forgetting" is a present participle indicating a continuing process of not remembering.   In Jewish thinking when something is remembered it is allowed to dominate or determine present attitudes and actions.   What are the "things which are behind" which Paul must continually forget?   In verses 5-7 Paul has made reference to his Jewish heritage and how that was no longer important to him.   In verses 9-12 he has emphasized his Christian attainments.   Behind were years of fruitful apostolic labors.   He might have been satisfied to rest upon his past accomplishments.   But no.   Anticipating release from imprisonment, he will resume his apostolic ministry to which Christ has called him.   He'll reach out, he'll stretch out to do it.   Reaching or straining forward graphically portrays a runner in the homestretch of a race who draws upon all his remaining strength as he extends himself to the utmost, using every ounce of energy, to reach the goal.   Whereas the evil workers (3:2) who have come to Philippi have their attention focused on the past, and what they have already accomplished, Paul's attention is firmly fixed on the future.

3:14 -- *I press on toward the goal for the prize of the upward call of God in Christ Jesus.*

I press on toward the goal – The word translated "goal" (*skopon*) refers to the pole or finish line on which the runner fixes his look as he runs.   "I press on" (*diōkō*) is the same verb ("I am pressing on") and the same topic as when the verb was used in verse 12.   The goal is the successful completion of his mission as apostle.

---

[52] The Greek reads *hen de* with no verb.   Our translators have supplied *poiō* ("I do"), not *logizomai* ("I regard"), because *hen* ("one thing") refers to what follows, which is a matter of doing, not of reckoning or regarding.

[53] Hendriksen, *op. cit.*, p.172.

For the prize of the upward call of God in Christ Jesus – We make a careful distinction between the "goal" and the "prize." "For" translates *eis*, "unto." First the goal is reached, then comes the prize. While "goal" rivets attention on the race that is being run, "prize" centers the thought on the glory when the race is over and won. In the ancient stadia, at the end of the race, the winner received the prize. The successful runner was summoned from the floor of the stadium up to the king's seat in the stands, where the king presented the prize to the winner of the race. In the ancient races, the prize often was a crown-shaped wreath of leaves (1 Corinthians 9:24). The prize Paul wishes to receive is to hear King Jesus say "Come up here!" into His presence where he might receive his crown of righteousness (2 Timothy 4:7,8).[54] That is what will happen when the "out-resurrection from the dead" occurs. This commentator doubts the "upward call" has reference to the call or invitation to become a Christian, which would be a reference to entering the race.[55] Rather, if we allow the stadium figure to guide us, the "upward call" occurs when the race is complete. A case might be made that Paul, here in verse 14, has in mind what John describes in Revelation 11:12, where what likely is pictured is the rapture of the church which happens when a voice from heaven says, "Come up here!"

5. Exhortation to the Philippians to Have the Same Attitude Paul does. 3:15-16

3:15 -- *Let us therefore, as many as are perfect, have this attitude; and if in anything you have a different attitude, God will reveal that also to you;*

Let us therefore, as many as are perfect, have this attitude – The description of "us ... as many as are perfect" might better be translated as the NASB marginal note suggests, "as many as are mature." In verse 12 Paul denied that he had "already become perfect" (*teteleiōmai*), yet he here uses *teleioi* (a cognate noun) to refer to himself and others. The other times Paul uses the term *teleios* when referring to persons (1 Corinthians 2:6, 14:20; Ephesians 4:13; Colossians 1:28, 4:12), he does not mean sinless perfect, but rather is describing a certain level of spiritual growth and stability in contrast to babes in the faith. Implied in his use of this term may be the suggestion that, in his judgment, the Philippians are surely mature enough in the faith not to be swayed by the Judaizers. That being true,

---

[54] While Jesus is subordinate to the Father, only the Father knows the time of the second coming (Matthew 24:36). In harmony with this, Paul here has God using Christ Jesus to issue the upward call when the time for that call comes.

[55] Kent (*op. cit.,* p. 143) presents the view that the upward call is not a reference to what happens at Christ's return, but is a reference to God's calling men to salvation.

he encourages them to think in harmony with what he has just written. "Let us ... have this attitude" (*phronōmen*, a present subjunctive) is an exhortation addressed to the readers as well as to himself to continue to think like this. This what? If we would understand what "this attitude" is, we only need recall all he has said in verses 2-14. There Paul tells us that he has counted as rubbish all the fleshly things the Judaizers put confidence in. He recognized Jesus as the Messiah and Lord, and desired to be found in Him having a righteousness that comes from God (verse 9). He wanted to experience the power of the risen Lord at work in his own life. He was determined to press on toward the goal. He wanted to hear the upward call of God and attain to the "out-resurrection from the dead." He longs to see the same attitude embraced by the readers of this letter to the Philippians.

And if in anything you have a different attitude – "And if" (*kai ei*) regards the supposition as possible, but he has no reason at the moment to think any of the Philippian believers would have such a different attitude. "Different" translates the adverb *heterōs*, which implies any other attitude would be incorrect. "A different attitude" would be one different from the one Paul has just expressed in verses 2-14. Vincent tells us that the force of *phroneite*, translated as "a different attitude" in the NASB, should be carefully noted. "It has been shown (ch. 1:7) that *phronein* signifies the general disposition of mind rather than the specific act of thought. Paul is dealing not with differences of opinion, but rather with dispositions or thought patterns which underlie the spiritual life."[56]

God will reveal that also to you – "That ... also" says that like other things He has already revealed to you, He will reveal (uncover, unveil) what is faulty about your different attitude. "God reveals truths He wants men to know by the words of Paul and other teachings of Scripture."[57] 1 Corinthians 2:14-16 also indicates the indwelling Holy Spirit helps folk understand the teachings given by revelation and written down by inspiration.

3:16 -- *However, let us keep living by that same* standard *to which we have attained.*

---

[56] Vincent, *op. cit.*, p.114.

[57] Root, *op. cit.*, p.19. "It may be that Paul was referring to the prophets or inspired preachers who were in the church in those days. They received a message directly from God to deliver to the people. An example is Agabus (Acts 11:27,28; 21:10,11)" (Tesh, *op. cit.*, p.414).

However, ... by that same *standard* to which we have attained – "However" (*plen*, "nevertheless") indicates that in the meantime, until the correct attitude is learned, the Christian has a responsibility to live up to what he knows of the teaching of Christ and the will of God. "The condition for future enlightenment is to walk according to present light."[58] "That ... to which we have attained" refers to the gospel of Christ, which has in it a message so adapted to mankind that all may grasp the great "standard" (a word which the NASB translators have inserted). All the better manuscripts at this place have the article and an adjective (*tō autō*, "the same") and leave the reader mentally to supply some noun that agrees with "same." The KJV follows a different Greek text at this place. It reads *tō autō stoichein kanoni, tō autō phronein*, "let us walk by the same rule, let us mind the same thing." Perhaps the Textus Receptus here in Philippians has been influenced by Galatians 6:16, since the reading found here at 3:16 is not well-supported in the manuscripts. A "rule" (*kanoni*, "canon") is something that has been measured that in turn becomes the standard by which other things are measured. "Paul recognizes that Christians, though proceeding along the same path, may be at different stages of progress and should be faithful to as much of God's truth as they understand."[59]

Let us keep living – The word for "keep living" (*stoichein*) means to "walk in file," to "keep the step," "to keep in line with." It pictures soldiers marching, each in step and each in his place in the rank and file. The metaphor calls for Christians to maintain a consistent life in harmony with the understanding of God's truth they already have. The gist of Paul's exhortation is 'Let us not deviate from those principles and attitudes that have brought us safely to our present stage of Christian maturity.'

C. Warning Against Copying the Example of Enemies of the Cross of Christ. 3:17-21

3:17 -- *Brethren, join in following my example, and observe those who walk according to the pattern you have in us.*

Brethren, join in following my example – In the previous verse Paul had encouraged them to keep in step in the Christian walk. Now he gives them two models to follow: his own example, and the example of other faithful Christian

---

[58] Mounce, *op. cit.*, p.1328.

[59] Kent, *op. cit.*, p.143.

leaders whose conduct resembles Paul's. Calling his readers "brethren" suggests a reason for heeding this exhortation. If they are members of the same spiritual family, should not the behavior of each one remind others they really are brothers? The word translated "join" (*ginesthe*, translated "be" in the ASV) is a present imperative verb, while the word translated "example" is *summimētai*, "fellow imitators" or "co-imitators." The Philippian Christians already have been imitating Paul. The first phrase in this verse encourages them, all of them, to be united as they continue to copy his example.[60]

And observe those who walk according to the pattern you have in us – There were others besides Paul who would serve as good examples for them to imitate. "Observe" means "take note, look at, consider" – and do it in order to imitate them.[61] "Walk" (*peripateo*, walk about, walk around) is used metaphorically to describe conduct or behavior as folk moved hither and thither in the daily path of life. "Us" likely includes Luke, the long-time preacher at Philippi, as well as Timothy and Epaphroditus (see Philippians 2:19-30) who, besides Paul, were good examples or patterns whom the Philippians might imitate.[62] "It is easier to do right when we observe others doing it. For our own help we should take notice of the others who are doing right. The wrongdoers may be more noticeable, more spectacular; they may get the headlines and be prominent. But there are some people doing right. Look for them."[63]

---

[60] At first appearance, this might look like naked egotism and phenomenal self-conceit on Paul's part. It is not. Paul was highly conscious of his own conduct, knowing it served as an example for his converts (cf. 4:9; 1 Thessalonians 2:10). Elsewhere he tells us that his readers should "Be imitators of me, even as I also am of Christ" (1 Corinthians 11:1). Before pointing to himself as an example, he had reminded the Philippians of Christ as the chief example (Philippians 2:5-8). J.A. Bengel (*Gnomon of the New Testament* [Edinburgh: T & T Clark, 1860], vol.4, p.148) proposed that even here in Philippians 3:17 the unusual word Paul uses (*summimētai*) asks the readers to join together with him in imitating Christ, but his proposal has not been adopted by most commentators. Instead, there is nearly unanimous agreement that Paul was inviting his friends, not simply to listen to him, but also to imitate him.

[61] In Romans 16:17, where it is translated "keep your eye on," we have the same word here translated "observe," but there the observation is with the intention of avoiding the folk who caused dissensions and hindrances.

[62] *Tupon,* translated "pattern" or "type" (Romans 5:14, 6:17; 1 Corinthians 10:6,11; 1 Thessalonians 1:7) originally had reference to the visible impression left by a stylus on a wax writing tablet which was intended to be a guide in the teaching of writing. It speaks of a model or pattern to be copied. The translation "ensample" at this place in the KJV is "an Old French and Middle English derivative of the Latin *exemplum*" (Moule, *op. cit.*, p. 102).

[63] Orrin Root, *1985-86 Standard Lesson Commentary* (Cincinnati: Standard, 1985), p.20.

3:18 -- *For many walk, of whom I often told you, and now tell you even weeping,* **that they are** *the enemies of the cross of Christ,*

For many walk -- "For" tells us that verses 18 and 19 give us the reason for the admonition in verse 17; namely, there are too many horrible examples of behavior which a person might foolishly copy.[64]   Commentators have found it difficult to identify who the "many" were, since the following phrases which Paul used to describe the "many" are capable of being explained in such a way as to seemingly justify any one of several suggested identifications. As a result, a number of differing proposed identifications are found in the commentaries, including these:

(a) Perhaps the "enemies" warned about in these verses are the same folk warned about earlier in chapter 3.   (1) One such attempt is based on the idea that the three terms used in 3:3 refer to three different groups, with "dogs" being a reference to *the Gentiles*.   The characterizations of these enemies of the cross given in verse 19 could be interpreted as describing Gentiles in general. If Paul does have in view Gentiles in general, the fact that he weeps when he thinks and speaks about how they live is indicative of how his soul was vexed by the ungodly lifestyles he observed in the world around him.   (2) Another attempt treats the "enemies" warned about as being the same group of *Judaizers* who were denounced in 3:2-16. It is affirmed that since verse 17 is tied closely with verses 2-16, it is unlikely that verse 18 introduces a different group of enemies.   Attempts are made to show that the characterizations given in verse 19 can be applied to the Judaizers. They were enemies of the cross, and did set their minds on earthly things. Romans 16:18, which apparently has Judaizers in view, uses the same expression as found here in verse 19 when it states they "are slaves ... of their own appetites."[65]

(b) Other attempted identifications find these "enemies of the cross" to be a different group than those which 3:2-16 warned about.   (1) One attempt has proposed that *missionaries teaching incipient Gnosticism* are the enemies Paul here has in view.   Verse 19 is interpreted to refer to a libertine lifestyle such as is attributed to many Gnostics, both by Paul (2 Timothy 3:2-8; Titus 2:11,12) and by Peter (2 Peter 2:10-20, 3:3-7). A case could be made that Philippians, written about the same time as Ephesians and Colossians, could

---

[64] "Walk" is metaphorical for behavior, just as in verse 17.

[65] In the author's commentary on Romans, the phrase "slaves ... of their own appetites" is explained to refer not so much to pre-occupation with kosher food laws but rather to behavior "inspired by self-interest and [that] has self-satisfaction as its goal, rather than obedience to the Lord."

be expected to make some reference to these new enemies of the cross just as did those two other Prison Epistles.   However, what Paul writes in verse 18 causes us to hesitate to adopt this view, since we are hard put to identify when Paul previously had warned the Philippians about this new group of enemies of the cross.   (2) Another attempt interprets verse 19 as depicting a licentious or libertine lifestyle, and the suggestion is made that Paul is warning about *nominal Christians* who used their Christian liberty as a cloak for licentiousness.   We know from 1 Peter 2:16 ("Act as free men, and do not use your freedom as a covering for evil") and from Paul's language elsewhere (Romans 3:8, 6:1,15) that there were men who took Christian teaching and warped it until they could use what Christian preachers said as justification for loose living.   The term "libertines" is often used to describe such folk.

In summary, each of these suggested identifications has looked appealing at first sight, but none has won common acceptance.   Perhaps, we need to restudy what Paul wrote in the close of verse 19, to see if we can find a better way to identify the "enemies."   A careful study of the original Greek shows that the sentence begins (in verse 18) with a subject ("many") in the nominative plural, which when combined with the main verb results in the translation "many walk." Up until the last clause in verse 19 (where the sentence begun in verse 18 ends), the clauses, which summarize what Paul had often told them and is now telling them again about the "many," are written in the accusative and genitive cases. But when we come to the final clause of verse 19 ("the ones who are setting their minds on earthly things"), Paul again wrote a nominative plural.   All the intervening phrases which summarized Paul's warnings are true precisely because the "many" are earthly minded.   We would let verse 19 identify this group whose example is to be avoided as being those who are *"earthly minded"* or "worldly minded."   In this commentator's judgment the "many" of verse 18 includes more than the people introduced in 3:2-16.   Those folk may have been earthly minded, but they are not the only ones whose thoughts are here below rather than on heavenly things.

Of whom I often told you – The Greek verb is an imperfect tense which says, "I used to tell you."   "Often" translates *pollakis*, which means "many times."   We presume Paul is making reference to how he used to speak thus of the "enemies" when he was preaching at Philippi.

And now tell you even weeping – "Now" contrasts with "often" in the past time. Once more Paul repeats his warning, and his heart is filled with grief and pain for the enemies of Christ. He cares about their eternal destiny. He is not speaking from an attitude of animosity but from an attitude of grief and mourning as one would mourn the dead.[66]

***That they are* enemies of the cross of Christ** – This is the first of several summary statements by which Paul reminds the Philippians about what he has already told them and now is telling them again. That such folk are enemies of the cross is what made this group such an ominous example and threat to the church at Philippi. They live as enemies, surprisingly, of the cross of Christ. "Enemies of Christ" might be expected, or even "enemies of the gospel." But why "the cross"? It must be that folk whose minds are set on earthly things treat the redemption wrought at Calvary with hostile indifference. God thought the redemption of mankind was so important that He sent His Son to die for lost man. What God thinks important hardly crosses the minds of earthly minded persons.

3:19 -- *Whose end is destruction, whose god is* their *appetite, and* whose *glory is in their shame, who set their minds on earthly things.*

Whose end is destruction – This is the second of the summary statements concerning the people whose examples are to be avoided. At the close of their earthly lives, these enemies of the cross will end up being sentenced to hell. "Destruction" (*apoleia*) is the word used of what happens to men who refuse to believe and be saved (John 3:16). It is the regular word for eternal loss, the opposite of *soteria* ("salvation").[67] They will not hear an invitation to "come up here" (verse 14). This is intended as a strong incentive not to follow their example.

Whose god is *their* appetite – In this context, "god" seems to have the sense of what they value most. This figure of speech ("appetite" is "belly" in the Greek) pictures the earthly minded folk being motivated completely by self-satisfaction and self-interest. Their only real concern is what their own bodies desire. They

---

[66] The word translated "weeping" is *klaio*, a word used to describe those who mourn the dead. Thayer, *op. cit.*, p.347.

[67] There are two ultimate destinies at the end of human life: one is as *soteria* ("salvation"), the other is *apoleia* ("destruction," 1 Corinthians 1:18, 2 Corinthians 2:15-16). The latter word by no means denotes the annihilation of the wicked. See notes at Philippians 1:28 and at 2 Peter 3:6.

make little effort to keep their physical appetites under control.[68]   Christianity encourages its devotees to practice self-control (e.g., James 3:1-12).

And *whose* glory is in their shame – The word "glory" in this place carries the idea of boasting, so that the "enemies" are described as boasting about or holding in high esteem something about which they should be ashamed.[69]   That which they boast about is a disgrace.   But what was that something?   If the words Paul has spoken to the Philippians (verse 18) were similar to what he wrote in the first chapter of Romans, perhaps we have a Scriptural answer to this question concerning the thing about which earthly minded folk were boasting.   In Romans 1:21-25, Paul described folk who did not honor God or give Him thanks.   They professed themselves to be wise, but became fools.   They exchanged the truth of God for a lie and then worshiped and served the creature rather than the Creator. What followed was disgraceful behavior (Romans 1:26-31) and even giving hearty approval to those who so misbehaved (Romans 1:32).   We judge that "professing themselves to be wise" and "giving hearty approval" (to folk who practice things worthy of death) are specific examples of boasting about something that really is a disgrace.

Who set their minds on earthly things – Since verse 17 Paul has been pointing to the right example to be imitated by the Philippians.   With the words in this last clause of verse 19 (written to agree with the subject "many" of verse 18) Paul identifies the bad example of living which the Philippians are keep on avoiding. Just as we appealed to Paul's writings in Romans to illustrate the phrase "whose glory is in their shame," so we appeal to one of the Prison Epistles just recently written to help us flesh out what Paul is here writing to the Philippians.   In his letter to the Colossians Paul exhorted those Christians to set their minds on things

---

[68] This clause is a reason why many commentators have hesitated to identify the "enemies" of verse 19 with the Judaizers of verses 2-16.   Rather than trying to force the reference somehow to be to kosher food laws, it seems to point in a different direction.   Similar language is used at a later time in the New Testament to describe certain Gnostics who took opportunity at the love feasts to gorge themselves on the food being provided ("reveling in the love feasts," 2 Peter 2:13 NASB margin; and "these men are hidden reefs [stains] in your love-feasts," Jude 12).   Vincent (*op. cit.,* p.117) gives examples from ancient literature where similar language as that found here in verse 19 is used to describe gluttons.

[69] The NASB translators added "whose" in italics, thus making this phrase another characteristic of the enemies.   R.C.H. Lenski (*Interpretation of St. Paul's Epistles to the Galatians, to the Ephesians, and to the Philippians* [Columbus, OH: Wartburg Press, 1946], p.860) argued that this is not a new feature, since it is not introduced by *hōn* ("whose") as the other members are.   He argued that this clause continues the second characteristic, "'whose god the belly and (thus) their glory in their shame.'   The things their fleshly belly nature dictates to them, in obedience to which they see 'their glory,' are in reality nothing but their shame and disgrace."

above, not on things that are on earth (Colossians 3:2). He highlighted some disgraceful behaviors practiced by folk whose minds are set on things that are on the earth (Colossians 3:5-9), called attention to the change made in them when they became Christians (Colossians 3:10,11), and then enumerated how a person behaves whose mind is set on things above (Colossians 3:12-17). Jesus' rebuke of Peter, when he had attempted to correct his Master (Jesus said to Peter, "you are not setting your mind on God's interests, but man's," Matthew 16:23), is another illustration of how a person can get things badly wrong when he sets his mind on earthly things. The Bible has many passages which address the importance of what a man constantly thinks about. "As a man thinks in his heart, so is he" (Proverbs 23:7). The parable of the rich fool (Luke 12:16-21) pictures vividly a mind set on things of earth and the outcome of such a life. Jesus said, "Out of the heart come evil thoughts, murders, adulteries, fornications, thefts, false witness, slanders. These are the things which defile the man ..." (Matthew 15:19,20). When people mind earthly things, that thinking is the root of their sin and degraded living. The word "earthly" is regularly used in Scripture in contrast to "heavenly" (cf. John 3:12; 1 Corinthians 15:40; 2 Corinthians 5:1; Colossians 3:1-4), and so here it prepares us for the contrast highlighted in the verses that follow.

3:20 -- *For our citizenship is in heaven, from which also we eagerly wait for a Savior, the Lord Jesus Christ,*

For our citizenship is in heaven – "For" indicates this verse is a positive reason to imitate Paul's good example (the emphatic "our" picks up the "us" of verse 17) rather than the horribly negative example (introduced by "for" in verse 18) of those who set their minds on earthly things.[70] The word "citizenship"[71] would

---

[70] Whenever a word is emphatic it calls attention to an implied contrast. In this place we should notice the twofold contrast between the "many" and "we" and the contrast between "earthly" and "heaven" in verses 19-20.

[71] We are faced with a technical problem concerning the meaning of the noun *politeuma*, translated "citizenship" in the NASB text, and "commonwealth" in the NASB margin. A cognate noun *politeia* is found at Acts 22:28 where it is translated "citizenship," and at Ephesians 2:12 where it is translated "commonwealth." The cognate verb (cf. 1:27) meant the conduct or behavior of a citizen or member of a group, and the rendering of the KJV ("conversation") here in Philippians 3:20 was founded on the original sense of that word which is "conduct or behavior in one's dealings with society." "Commonwealth" is a group of citizens united by common interests; in this place, those common interests involve imitating the behavior example of Paul and his helpers (verse 17). "Citizenship" carries the idea of status with all the rights and duties incumbent on a resident of a city or a country. If we accept this translation for *politeuma*, the rest of verse 20 gives one of the duties of the citizen of heaven.

have struck a familiar chord to the Philippians who were proud of their status as Roman citizens (Acts 16:12,21). Even though Rome was a far-off city, their pride in Roman citizenship was shown by speaking the language of Rome (Latin), by wearing Roman dress, observing Roman customs, keeping Roman holidays and ceremonies, and worshiping the emperor as their savior. "Our citizenship is in heaven" ('in the heavens'[72]) makes a spiritual application of this apt metaphor to Christians. To have citizenship in the "Jerusalem which is above" (Galatians 4:26, KJV) is already a present privilege.[73] Christians are "fellow-citizens with the saints, and are of God's household" (Ephesians 2:19). In whatever place they live, Christians are a little colony of heaven (just as Philippi was a colony of Rome).[74] Instead of living like mere earthlings, should not Christians live like heaven's citizens are expected to live, speak heaven's language, wear heaven's dress, observe heaven's customs, and worship the Savior whose home heaven is? Folk who are citizens of heaven must have heavenly interests. They must seek first His kingdom and His righteousness (Matthew 6:33). They cannot have their minds fixed simply on earthly things. Paul now goes on to show that an eager expectation of the Savior's return will do much to protect believers from setting their minds on earthly things.

From which also we eagerly wait for a Savior, the Lord Jesus Christ – The Greek pronoun translated "from whence" is singular, literally "out of which (place)." Perhaps the Greek construction is treated as an adverbial one, in which case the noun "heavens" (though plural) is regarded as a singular place. Perhaps the singular "from whence" refers back to *politeuma*, in which case the word translated "citizenship" is treated as if it denoted a city. Whichever way we take it, the idea is clear. The verb translated "eagerly wait" (*apekdechomai*) includes both the ideas of eager waiting and longing for Him to come. A man who is watching and waiting for the Lord's return will live a different lifestyle than the person whose mind is set on earthly things. In our heavenly hometown lives the

---

[72] The Greek translated "in heaven" is plural (*en ouranois*) and is the same terminology found in Colossians 1:5 and 2:10. We are reminded of the phrase "in the heavenly *places*" (*en tois ouraniois*, Ephesians 1:3, 2:6, 3:10).

[73] The verb translated "is" is *huparchei* (not a form of the verb *eimi*, "to be"), and is an emphatic way to affirm something as already existing. Though Christians are living temporarily as "strangers and exiles" (Hebrews 11:13; 1 Peter 2:11) in this or that city or country down here on earth, actually they are already citizens of heavenly Jerusalem. Christians "are *now* members of the heavenly commonwealth, and live and act under its laws" (Vincent, *op. cit.,* p.119).

[74] W. Carl Ketcherside's commentary on Philippians is titled *A Colony of Heaven* (St. Louis: Mission Messenger, 1980).

Savior,[75] the Lord Jesus Christ (note all three words[76]). One of these days He is coming to take us home. We do not want to be ashamed when He comes. We want to be living as good citizens of heaven. It is in the capacity of "Savior" that Christians eagerly wait for Him – the same capacity in which they have already received and known Him (cp. Ephesians 5:23, "He is the Savior of the body [the church]"). Jesus is Savior of both soul and body. As the following verse shows, it is the body that will be saved when King Jesus comes to earth again.

3:21 -- *Who will transform the body of our humble state into conformity with the body of His glory, by the exertion of the power that He has even to subject all things unto himself.*

Who will transform the body of our humble state into conformity with the body of His glory – In this verse Paul explains one special thing Jesus the Savior will do for citizens of the Kingdom when He comes from Heaven. The "body of our humble state" is the weak mortal body humans now live in.[77] "The physical body is subject to many humiliations: sin, pain, weakness, injury, sickness, and finally death and decay."[78] "The body of His glory" is the glorified body Jesus now has since His resurrection.

The change will happen at the second coming. Paul here uses language that pictures the event from the standpoint of those who are alive at the time of Christ's return. The Jews who did believe in resurrection looked merely for the

---

[75] The use of the word "Savior," used by Paul in his first recorded sermon (Acts 13:23), is found after that in Paul's writings only in the Prison Epistles (Ephesians 5:23; Philippians 3:20), and frequently in the Pastoral Epistles (1 Timothy 1:1, 2:3, 4:10; 2 Timothy 1:10; Titus 2:10,13, 3:4,6). Half of those times it is used of God the Father, and half of the time it is used of Jesus. Perhaps the metaphor of citizenship is being continued. Was the Roman emperor sometimes referred to as "savior"? Well Christians, too, have a "Savior" in their capital city, and He is a Savior worthy of that appellation, for He far excels the emperor. The imperial title "savior" implied nothing more than helper, and few of the emperors gave much help to the masses, at that. Our Savior, the Lord Jesus Christ, is the divine helper of all believers, and He gives help both in time and at the second coming.

[76] See notes at Philippians 1:2 and 2:9,11.

[77] Barclay (*op. cit.,* p.87) tells us that the KJV here may leave a wrong idea when it speaks about "our *vile* body," especially since in contemporary speech "vile" would mean that the body is an utterly evil and horrible thing. However, when the KJV was translated in the 16th century, "vile" still retained the meaning of its derivation from the Latin word *vilis,* which in fact means nothing worse than "cheap, valueless."

[78] Hayden, *op. cit.,* p.419.

restoration of the present body.   That was not the right idea of what will happen at all.   Paul here speaks of our present body being "transformed" *(metaschē-matizo)* so as to be "in conformity" *(summorphon)* with the glorified body Jesus now has.[79]   In 2 Corinthians 3:18 we learn that, if we are Christians, the process of transformation of our spirits from glory unto glory is already begun.   Paul now tells us that this conformity of the Christian to Christ is ultimately to extend to the body.[80]   John describes the change that shall occur at the second coming in these words, "When He appears, we shall be like Him" (1 John 3:2).   Paul himself uses the words, "We shall bear the image of the heavenly" (1 Corinthians 15:49), and we shall be "conformed to the image of [the Father's] Son" (Romans 8:29).   1 Corinthians 15:35-49 gives us details about the resurrection body which are only hinted at here in Philippians.[81]

By the exertion of the power that He has even to subject all things to Himself – This stupendous claim Paul makes about the transformation of the body may cause some to ask, 'What about those martyrs who were devoured by lions? What about those who were burned alive.   What about those who were buried at sea, and their corpses eaten by sharks?   Yes, what about millions of others, particles of whose dead and decaying bodies are in various stages of disintegration?   How is what you claim about transformation possible?'   Paul's answer to this question is that it will all be accomplished by the superhuman "power" *(energeia)* which permits Jesus to subject all things to Himself!   "He who was the companion and helper of God in creation was able to command the things of creation when He walked the earth.   He certainly is able to exercise power to change our physical body from that which is corruptible to that which is spiritual and glorious and incorruptible.   It is within His power to do this."[82]   He is able to subdue all things unto Himself.

---

[79] On the difference between "fashion" (*schēma*, outward appearance) and "form" (*morphē*, inner essence), see notes at Philippians 2:7,8.   The difference helps us to see the meaning here, too.   Christ transforms the outward, earthly body; the new glorified body will reflect the inner status of the redeemed just as Christ's glorified body reflects His status.

[80] The ideas introduced at 3:10-11, especially about the "out-resurrection from among the dead," are here unfolded.

[81] One significant contrast in the 1 Corinthians passage is between the "physical" body we now wear and the "spiritual" body we shall wear then.   "Physical" (*psuchichos*) says this earthly body is exactly suited for a soul to animate; "spiritual" (*pneumatikos*) says the glorified body is one exactly suited for a spirit to animate.

[82] Hayden, *ibid.*

VI. A SECOND SERIES OF EXHORTATIONS.   4:1-9

A. To All, To Remain Firm.   4:1

4:1 -- *Therefore, my beloved brethren whom I long* to see, *my joy and crown, so stand firm in the Lord, my beloved.*

Therefore – The following exhortations are based on what has just been written. "Therefore" equals "because you are citizens of heaven" and "because our Savior" is coming again, and because He "will transform the body of our humble estate into conformity with the body of His glory" (3:20,21), you are to conduct yourselves in the ways I am about to enumerate.[1]

My beloved brethren whom I long *to see* – On several occasions in this letter, Paul has called the Philippians "brethren." Now in this verse he uses a series of six endearing terms to express his deep affection for them. Repeating a word he used in 1:8, he tells them again that he longs to be with them. Expressed in this word is "a hint of the pain caused by his separation from them."[2] He seems scarcely able to find words adequate to express his love for the Philippians, so he continues ...

My joy and crown – They are his present joy (the reports he has heard about their present spiritual growth have made him happy) and their presence with Christ would be his future crown when Christ comes to reward His servants.[3] Paul here uses the same words "joy and crown" that he used of Christians who lived in Thessalonica, "What is our hope and joy and crown of rejoicing? Are not ye in the presence of our Lord Jesus Christ at his coming? Ye are our glory and our joy" (1 Thessalonians 2:19,20, KJV). That passage also indicates this crown is received at the second coming of Christ.

---

[1] "Just as at the conclusion of the description of the 'depth of the riches both of the wisdom and knowledge of God' (in Romans 11:33), and just as at the glorious climax of the doctrine of the resurrection (in 1 Corinthians 15:50-57), so here, Paul makes the vision of the future glory to be an inspiring force, giving life to the sober, practical duties of the present time" (Barry, *op. cit.*, p.290).

[2] Vincent, *op. cit.*, p.129.

[3] There are two Greek words translated "crown:" one is *diadēma*, which signifies a royal crown; the other (the one used here) is *stephanos*, which is a wreath-shaped crown such as was given to victors in an athletic contest (1 Corinthians 9:25) or to honored guests in a banquet hall (see *Athen.* xv, p.685; Aristoph. *Ach.* 636;   Plat. *Symp.* 212).

So stand firm in the Lord, my beloved – "So" may gather up the ideas of Paul's example (3:17), living as is fitting for citizens of heaven (3:20), as well as 'so that you may continue to be my joy and crown' (4:1). "Stand firm" is a present imperative meaning always remain steadfast and true. The word Paul uses for "stand firm" is the word which would be used for a soldier standing fast in the shock of battle, with the enemy surging down upon him. It is the same word he used in 1:27 ("stand firm in one spirit"). In Ephesians 6:11,13,14, Paul has given the command to "stand" to soldiers of Christ. When others run away, it is hard to stand one's ground. Rather than listening to the Judaizers or the earthly minded who were warned about in chapter 3, the Philippian Christians are to stand fast in the Lord. Although it is not always certain what the phrase "in the Lord" means, here it seems to mean "as you have been taught" or "stay in the body of Christ." Verses 2-9 will give specific examples where standing firm is needed. Paul repeats "beloved" to show that his instructions are rooted in the best of all possible motives, because he loves them and wants the best for them.

B. To Two Women, To Live in Harmony.   4:2

4:2 -- *I urge Euodia and I urge Syntyche to live in harmony in the Lord.*

I urge – The verb is *parakaleo,* to beg, to encourage, to exhort, to call alongside. Paul tenderly pleads with each (note he repeats the verb as he addresses each woman); he calls each to his side. Each woman is given an equal responsibility to make an attempt to live in harmony with the other.

Euodia ... Syntyche – The feminine pronouns *autais* ("these") and *haitines* ("who") in verse 3 show that Euodia and Syntyche are the names of two women.[4] We have no further knowledge of these two women other than is indicated in this and the following verse.[5]   Hendriksen makes the following listing of things we

---

[4] The KJV spelling of "Euodias," as though the term *Euodian* were masculine, is incorrect. This mistranslation, in turn, led to the conjecture they were husband and wife – perhaps even the Philippian jailer and his wife (cf. Acts 16:25-34). H.A.W. Meyer, *Critical and Exegetical Handbook to the Epistles to the Philippians and Colossians and to Philemon* (Winona Lake, IN: Alpha Publications, 1980), p. 160, tells that Theodore of Mopsuestia "quotes the opinion that the two were husband and wife."

[5] Many strange attempts have been made to find symbolism in these names. For example, Baur and the Tubingen school offered the suggestion that Euodia and Syntyche are symbolic of Gentile and Jewish Christianity. "The names are common in the inscriptions and there is no warrant for allegorizing them to represent parties in the church." (Kent, *op. cit.,* p.150).

can safely affirm about Euodia and Syntyche.[6]   (1) They were, at the time of the writing of Philippians, and had been for some time, members of the church at Philippi.   For the large part played by women in the first days of the gospel at Philippi, see Acts 16:13-18,40.   (2) When the church was founded and/or at a later visit of Paul to Philippi, they had been the apostle's fellow workers, and as such had co-operated harmoniously and enthusiastically with each other and with Paul and his companions (verse 3).   (3) A deplorable disagreement had arisen between them, which called forth this apostolic admonition.   (4) We do not know the cause of the strained relations between these two, but their quarrel was something that was having a negative effect on the congregation.

To live in harmony in the Lord – "In harmony" translates the same Greek that at Philippians 2:2 was "being of the same mind."   There may be an indication of the cause for the strained relations between these two women in verses 4-6, or it may be that all that can be said is that it looks like a clash of personalities. Whatever the cause, it looks like both women held positions in their dispute that were out of harmony with what Jesus would have them do.   Since both are "in the Lord," Paul calls on each to be determined to end the strained relations.   If they expected to be one in Christ in heaven, they had best be so here and now.

C. To Syzygus, to Help These Women.   4:3

4:3 -- *Indeed, true comrade, I ask you also to help these women who have shared my struggle* in the cause of *the gospel, together with Clement also, and the rest of my fellow-workers, whose names are in the book of life.*

Indeed, true comrade, I ask you also – At this point Paul seeks to enlist the aid of a third party to help in bringing these women together.   The Greek word translated "indeed" is *nai* ("Yea," or "Yes"[7]) which implies that Paul's request is not an absolute command, but is something that is genuinely needed.   "I am asking" (*erotaō*, a request made of an equal) reminds us that this letter was to be read out loud at the public assembly on the Lord's day.   Whoever this third party is, he would first hear this request as the letter was read.   The whole congregation would know he was to make an effort to reconcile the women.   In the title to this paragraph it is indicated that this third party bore the name Syzygus.   The Greek

---

[6] Hendriksen, *op. cit.*, p.190.

[7] There is a manuscript variation here, some having "and" (*kai*), and some having "yea" (*nai*).   The latter is the better attested reading.

translated "true comrade" is *gnēsei suzuge*. Either one (or neither one, for that matter) could be a proper name. If the man's name is Syzygus, then the word "true" (genuine) means "live up to your name – a joiner together." If the man's name is Gnesius, then "comrade" is an adjective describing his position and activities in the gospel. If neither is the man's name, we are left to conjecture who it is that is addressed.[8]

To help these women – This obviously means help Euodia and Syntyche to reconcile their differences. Sometimes folk want to reconcile their differences but find it difficult to be the first one to make a start. That is when a third party can step in, speak the first word and become a peacemaker. The work of peacemaker has a high reward (Matthew 5:9), and is like the work of God in Christ (Ephesians 2:14).

> It is significant to see that when there was a quarrel in the Church at Philippi, Paul mobilized the whole resources of the Church to mend it. Paul thought no effort too great to maintain the peace of the Church. A quarreling Church is not a Church at all, for a quarreling Church is a Church from which Christ has been shut out, and to which He cannot gain access. No man can be at peace with God and at variance with his fellow-men.[9]

Who have shared my struggle in *the cause of* **the gospel** – Here Paul gives a reason why Syzygus should help the women toward their reconciliation. "Shared my struggle (see this word *sunethlesan* at 1:27) in the gospel" says there was a time, perhaps during the time Paul was in Philippi on his second missionary journey, when women were his first hearers at Philippi (Acts 16:13-15), when these women worked alongside Paul to advance the cause of the gospel. Exactly what these women did, and on what occasion, is not made clear. Perhaps they ministered in some fashion similar to Lydia who opened her home to Paul and his helpers. Perhaps they took the gospel message Paul preached and taught it to others. If these two women once labored together with Paul, by settling their dif-

---

[8] Numerous are the conjectures which have attempted to identify the person referred to. The guess made by Clement of Alexandria that it was Paul's wife is shown to be wrong by the fact that the adjective ("true") is masculine. A more believable guess is that the reference is to Silas, who was Paul's fellow worker on the second missionary journey (Acts 15:40). Since Timothy was with Paul when this letter was written (Philippians 1:1), it is not likely he is the "true comrade," nor is it Epaphroditus who carried this letter to Philippi, though both of these have been nominated. Those who suggest it could be Luke are right that Luke was present when Philippi was first evangelized, but it looks like Luke was in Rome, not Philippi, when the Prison Epistles were written (Colossians 4:14; Philemon 24).

[9] Barclay, *op. cit.*, p.91

ferences they could again work side by side in the cause of the gospel. It is implied that their present discord was not helping the cause of the gospel.

Together with Clement also – This clause may be connected either with the verb "help" or with the verb "shared my struggle." If the former, then Clement is asked to combine his efforts with those of Syzygus in helping the women to be reconciled. If the latter, which is most likely in view of how this verse continues, then the verse speaks of how the two women offered help to Clement just as they had to Paul. In our judgment this latter is the better idea, not only because the verb "shared my struggle" is nearest to "with Clement," but also because the other reading would have Paul giving this conditional commission to an indefinite number of folk rather than to one person. This is the only reference to the man in the New Testament,[10] so all we know about Clement from the New Testament must be deduced from this verse. "Philippi was probably the scene of the labors referred to, since Paul speaks of them as familiarly known. Clement appears to have been a Philippian Christian who assisted in the foundation of the church at Philippi. This is suggested by 'the rest of my fellow workers'."[11]

And the rest of my fellow-workers – Paul had more fellow-workers in the gospel when he was at Philippi than just Clement whom he has just named. Since he has named some fellow-workers, is he simply using this means of getting himself out of the difficult position of hurting feelings by failing to name all his associates? Whatever be the case, the idea is the two women have helped numerous gospel workers. That is the reason Syzygus should heed Paul's request and help these women work out a reconciliation.

Whose names are in the book of life – Those other fellow workers may not be named in this letter, but their names are already recorded in a more important

---

[10] From the time of Origen (*In Joann.* 1.29) downwards, this Clement has been identified with Clement of Rome, the writer of the oldest extant piece of early Christian literature, namely I Clement. As is the case with many of the early church traditions, this one may or may not be true. The attempt to identify him with Clement of Rome, which originated with Origen, is generally abandoned. See Lightfoot, *op. cit.*, p.168ff; and George Salmon's article "Clemens Romanus" in Smith and Wace, *Dictionary of Christian Biography* (London: J. Murray, 1877-87).

[11] Vincent, *op. cit.*, p.132.

book than this letter, namely, the book of life.[12]   Since Paul nowhere else mentions this book, the fact that a few sentences earlier he had spoken of the "citizenship ... in heaven" (3:20) may have suggested the reference he makes to it here.   As ancient cities maintained a register of their citizens (cf. Isaiah 4:3; Ezekiel 13:9; Daniel 10:20), so there is a list maintained of the names of citizens of heaven (Luke 10:20; Hebrews 12:23; Revelation 13:8, 17:8, 20:12,15, 21:27, 22:19), here called "the book of life."   When a person becomes a Christian, God adds his or her name to the book of life.   If a person becomes unfaithful, Scripture warns that person's name is blotted out of the book (Revelation 3:5; Exodus 32:33).[13]   If a person is faithful until death, his or her name is forever fixed in the book of life.

D. To Cultivate those Positive Christian Virtues Which Produce the Peace of God.   4:4-7

4:4 -- *Rejoice in the Lord always; again I will say, Rejoice!*

Rejoice in the Lord always – Verses 4,5, and 6 each begin with an imperative verb, and all the imperatives in verses 4-7 are plural in form.[14]   These plurals raise the question: to whom are these words especially addressed?   To the whole church, or to the two women in particular?

- Just as Paul addressed both women in verse 2, so it is possible to picture his addressing both women here in verses 4-7.   As he does so, "Paul points to those things which form the temper of Christian citizenship (a series of Christian virtues) – joy in Christ – forbearance like His – [the nearness of the Lord] – prayer which lays all on God – thankfulness to God – the peace of God."[15]   If the women will concentrate on and practice what Paul writes, their strained relationship and dissension will be ended.   If the words are addressed

---

[12] The relative "whose" certainly refers to "my fellow-workers," but it may also refer to all those named in verses 2 and 3, including the two women Euodia and Syntyche.   There is no verb in the Greek but our translators have correctly supplied "are" rather than "may be."

[13] The passages that refer to the book of life do not involve the doctrine of an unconditional, irreversible predestination, or the phrase "to blot out of my book" could not be used.

[14] The NASB treats verses 4-7 as a single paragraph.   We have chosen to follow this lead as we have composed the title we have given to this paragraph.   Another way to outline the material would be to give each imperative a separate paragraph title, e.g., to rejoice in the Lord, to be big-hearted, and to pray instead of worry.

[15] Gwynn, *op. cit.,* p.632. [This commentator has substituted "the nearness of the Lord" for the actual words Gwynn wrote at this place.]

to Euodia and Syntyche in particular, it looks like rejoicing in the Lord may be an antidote to rejoicing over something selfishly desired by each, which in turn, it seems to be implied, had led to their disharmony.

- At the same time, as this letter is being publicly read to the assembled congregation of Christians, certainly there are lessons not only for the women but also for all the assembled brethren (as suggested by 4:1). Each person listening as the letter is read would be reminded of positive Christian virtues to be cultivated. In "rejoice in the Lord!" we again have the keynote of this epistle (see 1:4,18, 2:17,18, 3:1). Joy in the Lord is a virtue which can be and should be cultivated.[16] If this exhortation is addressed to all the brethren, then the thought broadens to suggest a person who is in Christ has much to be joyful about. However dark and dreary the present circumstances, in the Lord a Christian can "always" find something to rejoice about.

Again I will say, rejoice! – The call to rejoice in the Lord is so urgent that Paul repeats it again. Perhaps this is the first step that Euodia and Syntyche must take if they are to be reconciled. The word "rejoice" rings out ten times in these four short chapters of the letter to the Philippians. Root understood this exhortation to be addressed to all the readers, and calls attention to the fact that Paul (who asked his readers to follow his example, 3:17) is asking them to do the very thing that he himself is doing.

> Paul the prisoner was writing to Philippians who were being persecuted (Philippians 1:29), but he wrote a joyous letter. He rejoiced that the gospel was being preached (verse 18). He looked forward to the Philippians rejoicing when he would see them again (verse 26). He expected to rejoice at Christ's coming because he then would see the results of all his work (2:16). If his life was to be sacrificed in the course of his service, he rejoiced in that and he called the Philippians to rejoice with him (verses 17,18). He sent Epaphroditus to bring rejoicing to his brethren (verse 28). He called his fellow Christians to rejoice in the Lord, for this is one of the marks of the people of God (3:1,3).[17]

If rejoicing in the Lord is practiced, it will guard the readers from attacks by folk who put confidence in the flesh and whose   minds are set on earthly things (3:2-

---

[16] That joy can be commanded indicates it is something that can be cultivated. 1 Peter 1:6 speaks of rejoicing even though for a while we suffer grief in all kinds of trials. "In the Lord" may mean in His presence (see verse 5) or in communion with Him.

[17] Root, *op. cit.*, p.74.

19). It will help folk who have personality clashes to be reconciled. It will help folk who are being persecuted to remain faithful through the ordeal. It will aid a man who is facing certain death to set his mind on things above.

4:5 -- *Let your forbearing* spirit *be known to all men.   The Lord is near.*

Let your forbearing *spirit* be known to all men – The word translated "forbearing *spirit*" is *epieikes*, which is a hard word for which to find an English equivalent.   The article on *epieikes* in TDNT offers these possible English meanings: "forbearance, yieldedness, geniality, kindliness, gentleness, sweet reasonableness, considerateness, charitableness, mildness, magnanimity, generosity."[18]   Of these "sweet reasonableness" (a readiness to listen to reason, the willingness to yield one's personal rights for another's benefit) seems to come closest to the virtue Paul wants his readers to cultivate. Is this an appeal to the two women? If it is, it directs them to stop being rigorous and obstinate in their stand for what each thinks is her just due. There is no joy in such narrow selfishness; there is joy in generosity and gentleness. Paul urges that their sweet reasonableness be so conspicuous that even people outside the church will be able to see it. If this is an appeal to the whole congregation, then we see that Christians are to be known even to outsiders for their beautiful disposition. It is a reminder that the world is watching how Christians live, and a reminder that inconsistent living becomes an excuse for outsiders to belittle Christianity.

The Lord is near – If we connect this sentence with what was said earlier in verse 5, then this sentence is added as a motive or an encouragement to let their forbearing spirit be obvious to all men.[19]   "Lord," as at Philippians 2:11, is likely a reference to Jesus.[20]   But what is meant by "near" (or "at hand" as the margin reads)?   It is not a mistaken affirmation by Paul that the second coming of Jesus

---

[18] H. Preisker, *"epieikes"* in *Theological Dictionary of the New Testament*, edited by Gerhard Kittel (Grand Rapids: Wm. B. Eerdmans, 1965), Vol.2, p.588-590.

[19] There is some question concerning the connection of this sentence with the rest of the context. Does it go with what precedes (a motive to be big-hearted), or what follows (a motive to stop being anxious), or is it appropriate to treat it as giving a motive or an encouragement both for what precedes and what follows? A good case could be made for taking it both ways.

[20] Those who take this sentence with the following verse, where God specifically is named, think "Lord" here is a reference to God the Father.

was near.[21]   Rather, it is a statement (like Matthew 28:20, "Lo, I am with you always") that says the Lord is close beside each of us, watching us.   It serves as a gentle prod to the readers to conduct themselves accordingly.   It may also remind us that Jesus Himself is an example to us in this matter of big-heartedness. Elsewhere, Paul writes, "Now I Paul myself urge you by the meekness and gentleness of Christ ..." (2 Corinthians 10:1).

4:6 -- *Be anxious for nothing, but in everything by prayer and supplication with thanksgiving let your requests be made known to God.*

Be anxious for nothing – Here is introduced a third Christian virtue to be cultivated, namely, to take to God in prayer those matters that might cause anxiety rather than just giving way to anxiety.   "Stop being anxious about anything" is another way to render the passage since the Greek prohibits the continuance of an action already going on.[22]   The words Paul uses here are almost a repetition of Jesus' command in His Sermon on the Mount (Matthew 6:25-34).   Martha has left us a memorable example of such anxiety (Luke 10:40) and how anxiety can strain relationships.   If Paul's words are directed toward Euodia and Syntyche, we are left to wonder whether they give us a clue concerning the cause of the conflict between those two women.   Did those two women have a conflict over where each thought they should be, just as Martha had an issue over where she thought both she and her sister should be?   If, on the other hand, verses 4-7 are addressed to the whole congregation at Philippi, Orrin Root's comments about handling anxiety are apropos.   "When we don't have enough money to pay this month's bills, when the body is sick, when baby's temperature rises to 104, or when a dear friend turns against you, we do not let anxiety paralyze us into inaction.   We pray to our Father, we tell Him all about our needs, and we don't forget to thank Him for what He has already done for us."[23]

But ... by prayer and supplication with thanksgiving – The point of the rest of this verse is that prayer is the antidote for worry and anxiety.   Chrysostom defined

---

[21] Psalm 119:151 (LXX 118:151, where the Greek is the same as here in Philippians 4:5), which reads "You are near, O LORD," speaks of the Lord's presence, not His coming.

[22] When the word *merimnao* occurs, the context must determine whether the "concern" is good or bad.   It may be a distracting care, an undue concern, fretfulness (as in Matthew 6:25-34) or it may be a kindly concern, a genuine interest in the welfare of others (as at Philippians 2:20).

[23] Root, *1985-86 Standard Lesson Commentary*, p.21.

proseuche ("prayer") as prayer to obtain good, and he defined *deēsis* ("supplication") as prayer to avoid evil.[24] "Thanksgiving" (*eucharistias*) says all our prayers are to be made with a spirit of gratitude, acknowledging past favors, present blessings, and firmly-grounded assurance for the future. "To pray in any other spirit is to clip the wings of prayer."[25]

In everything ... let your requests be made known to God – The word picture in "to God" is that you are talking to Him face to face. "Requests" (*aitēmata*) are prayers for a definite, specific object or need or thing. "Let your requests be made known" is a third person imperative construction. It is a command. "Made known," the same word used at verse 5, means to declare or speak your requests to God as if He did not already know what your needs are (Matthew 6:8). Be specific in your requests. What blessing do you need?[26] Is this command addressed to Euodia and Syntyche in particular? Is Paul telling them to present their needs to God and make some definite requests of Him, rather than following the improper ways they have been trying to handle their disharmony with each other? If this command is addressed to the whole congregation, Paul is saying, "In each emergency, little or great, as it arises, pray; cultivate the habit of referring all things, great or small, to God in prayer."[27] "'In everything' does not mean we are to be thankful *for* everything. We are not thankful because we are sick, or because we lose a job or a home or a loved one. But even in such tragedies there are other things to be thankful for. We are to see them and keep on giving thanks."[28]

4:7 -- *And the peace of God, which surpasses all comprehension, shall guard your hearts and your minds in Christ Jesus.*

---

[24] For the precise distinctions among these terms for prayer, see Richard C. Trench *Synonyms of the Greek New Testament* (Grand Rapids: Eerdmans, 1966), pp.188-192; Geo. Ricker Berry, "New Testament Synonyms," in *A New Greek-English Lexicon to the New Testament* (Chicago: Wilcox and Follett, 1948), p.120; and comments at Ephesians 6:18.

[25] Hayden, *op. cit.,* p.426.

[26] Making specific requests helps us to know and to be thankful when our prayer is answered.

[27] Caffin, *op. cit.,* p.156.

[28] Knofel Staton, *1992-93 Standard Lesson Commentary* (Cincinnati: Standard Publishing, 1992), p.371.

And the peace of God – "And" shows this verse is intended to express the consequence either of answered prayer (verse 6) or the consequence of cultivating the three virtues named in verses 4-6. "The peace of God" is an expression that occurs only here in the New Testament. It evidently speaks about a peace which comes from God (a genitive of origin), a peace He gives to a person's mind.[29] If verses 4-7 are addressed in particular to Euodia and Syntyche, verse 7 is a promise that by cultivating the virtues Paul has enumerated they will find their clash ended and they again can be living in harmony. If verse 7 goes only with verse 6, then verse 7 is a promise that follows a request made with thanksgiving; God's peace will replace the anxiety. "God's peace is the opposite of being torn apart by anxiety and going to pieces."[30]

Which surpasses all comprehension – The Greek word *nous*, translated "comprehension," has several possible meanings. (1) It can refer to intellectual activity as one plans and thinks about how to solve or master a problem. If we opt for this meaning, the verse says that God's peace will produce a higher satisfaction than all our careful planning and clever ideas that arise from self-assertion. (2) If it refers to comprehension or understanding, it says that God's peace is as unfathomable as is the love of Christ (Ephesians 3:19). It goes far beyond all that a man might imagine His peace to be.

Shall guard your hearts and your minds in Christ Jesus – This clause explains what the peace of God does to men's hearts and minds. "Guard" is a military word (cf. 2 Corinthians 11:32, "guarding") the Philippians would identify with since they were used to the sight of Roman sentinels standing guard. In many passages "heart" is a reference to thoughts, but since here we have both "hearts" and "minds" being guarded, perhaps we should treat "hearts" in this place as speaking of the emotions (like fear and apprehension) while "minds" would then be more the intellectual side of man. "In Christ" is the sphere where such peace is available. God's divine peace is assigned as guardian only to those who are in fellowship with Christ Jesus. It is a solemn reminder to Paul's readers that outside of the closest possible union with Christ there is no protection, no safekeeping by God's peace. If Euodia and Syntyche continue to be at odds with each other, they will deprive themselves of God's peace. If any of Paul's readers continue to indulge in anxiety instead of with thanksgiving making their requests

---

[29] In the salutations and benedictions of Paul's letters he often prays for "peace" for his readers. It is a word that embraces spiritual well-being.

[30] Staton, *ibid.*

known to God, they too will be without the peace of God that could guard their hearts and minds.[31]

E. To Proper Meditation and Proper Actions. 4:8,9

4:8 -- *Finally, brethren, whatever is true, whatever is honorable, whatever is right, whatever is pure, whatever is lovely, whatever is of good repute, if there is any excellence and if anything worthy of praise, let your mind dwell on these things.*

Finally, brethren – The paragraph structure in the NASB suggests there is a new topic being introduced here in verses 8 and 9, a topic unrelated to what has been written in verses 4-7. "Brethren" indicates the following exhortation is intended for all the Christians at Philippi, not just Euodia and Syntyche. "Finally" indicates that this is going to be the last exhortation in this series of exhortations which began at 4:1. We do not come to the verb in this sentence ("let your mind dwell on these things") until we reach the end of the verse in the Greek.[32]

Whatever is true – "Whatever" introduces six of the following topics, while the last two are introduced by "if ... any." The way each of the topics is introduced causes us to pause a moment on each of the words written -- true, honorable, right, etc. "'True' (*alēthē*) has the sense of valid, reliable, and honest – the opposite of false."[33] Chapter 3 called attention to some things that are not true. Do not spend time thinking about those things. What God has said is true (Romans 3:4).

---

[31] "Quite literally, anxiety troubles the heart. The arteries narrow, the blood pressure goes up, the heart works harder, the possibility of blockage increases. God's peace avoids this stress. God wants us to enjoy living, not just endure it. But this promise is no less precious when we take hearts to mean our emotions. Too often we are upset over trivial things, distracted, torn in our feelings and thinking. Such things are better committed to the Lord in thankful prayer" (Staton, *op. cit.*, p.372).

[32] Because Paul tells us these are things we are to habitually think about, we are hesitant to speak of this as being a list of virtues to be cultivated. The items might better be characterized as being wholesome topics to think about. At Colossians 3:5 we discussed the matter of lists of virtues and vices being common among pagan moralists, and whether or not Paul is simply copying this or that *Manual of Discipline* (of some Essenic sect), or this or that (perhaps a Stoic list) pagan list. Whether or not it is right to call this list virtues, there is no reason even to suppose Paul is simply copying some pagan list, since all the terms are found in the Greek versions of the Old Testament (LXX or Symmachus), and most of them appear elsewhere in the New Testament.

[33] Kent, *op. cit.*, p.152.

Jesus is the truth ("I am the truth," He said [John 14:6]).   "A man should always set his thoughts on the things on which he can rely, the things which will not fail him, or let him down."[34]

Whatever is honorable – *Semna* is a difficult word to translate.   Used of church leaders, it is the quality ("dignity") which makes them worthy of respect (1 Timothy 3:8,11; Titus 2:2).   The ASV margin has "worthy of reverence." "Honorable" is not a bad choice of English words.   In an age noted for its flippancy and lack of intellectual seriousness, and for its frivolity, whatever things are "venerable" surely merit earnest consideration.

Whatever is right – "'Right' (*dikaia*) refers to what is upright or just, conformable to God's standards and thus worthy of His approval."[35]   Believers are to "gratefully meditate on God's righteous acts (Revelation 15:3), appreciate righteousness in others, and should plan righteous words and deeds."[36]

Whatever is pure – The word used here (*hagnos*) is not common in the New Testament.   *Hagnos* describes that which is morally pure, that which is undefiled. "When it is used ceremonially, it describes that which has been so cleansed that it is fit to be brought into the presence of God, and used in the service of God. This world is full of things which are sordid and shabby and soiled and smutty. When a man gets his mind into such a state, it soils everything of which he thinks. The Christian's mind is set on the things which are pure; his thoughts to be are so clean that they can stand even the scrutiny of God."[37]

Whatever is lovely – "'Lovely' (*prosphile*) occurs only here in the New Testament.   It appears in the LXX (Esther 5:1) and Josephus (*Antiq.* I.18.12; XVII.6.22) and relates to what is pleasing, agreeable, attractive, or winsome."[38] That which, when it is seen by others, calls forth love.

---

[34] Barclay, *op. cit.*, p.97.

[35] Kent, *ibid.*

[36] Hendriksen, *op. cit.,* p.198.

[37] Barclay, *op. cit.*, p.98.

[38] Kent, *ibid.*

Whatever is of good repute – This is the only occurrence of this adjective *euphēma* in the New Testament. It is derived from two words, one of which means "to speak" and the other which means "well." It is not easy to find a good English equivalent. "It might not be going too far to say that it describes 'the things which are fit for God to hear.' There are ugly words, and false words, and impure words, and far too many of them, in this world. On the lips of the Christian, and in the mind of the Christian, there will be only words which are fit for God to hear."[39]

If there is ... – Up until now the topics of meditation have been introduced by "whatever." Now, the last two are introduced by "if there is." Scholars have speculated on why the change of introductory expression. Hendriksen suggested these last two are summaries of the first six, so that the first three deal with virtue ("excellence") while the last three deal with praise.[40] Harrell suggested the change of introductory words may "indicate that the apostle intends the final two qualities to be summary concepts which include whatever else should be on the list."[41] Kent offered the view that this change of introductory words is "a rhetorical device that forces the reader to exercise his own discernment and choose what is 'excellent' and 'praiseworthy'."[42]

Any excellence – The only other writer in the New Testament who uses this word *aretē* is Peter (1 Peter 2:9; 2 Peter 1:3,5). In Peter's writings the word has the meaning of a "desire to do right." The KJV used the word "virtue" to translate this Greek word. Thayer offers "(1) a virtuous course of thought, feeling, and action" and "(2) any particular moral excellence, as modesty, purity" for *aretē*.[43] The word *aretē* "was one of the great classical words. In classical thought it described every kind of excellence. It could describe the excellence of the ground in a field, the excellence of a tool for its purpose, the physical excellence of an animal, the excellence of the courage of a soldier, and the virtue of a man."[44]

---

[39] Barclay, *op. cit.,* p.99.

[40] Hendriksen, *op. cit.,* p.199.

[41] Harrell, *op. cit.,* p.140.

[42] Kent, *ibid.*

[43] Thayer, *op. cit.,* p.78.

[44] Barclay, *ibid.*

Paul seems to be saying that anything at all that is a matter of moral and spiritual excellence is a matter worthy for the Christian to ponder.

And if anything worthy of praise – "Praise" translates *epainos*, a word also used at Philippians 1:11. It speaks of the approval that comes to a man who practices virtue. It may be those things for which praise from God is given that are to be pondered. It may be those good things for which praise from good men is elicited that are the things to be pondered.

Let your mind dwell on these things – The margin reads, literally, "ponder these things." This is the verb of the sentence, and is the last word in the sentence, and so appears to be emphatic. *Think about it!* The verb is a present imperative. Paul is telling the Philippians to be constantly thinking about the excellent and praiseworthy things he has just enumerated in verse 8. The Christian can control what goes through his mind. Long ago Solomon wrote of man, "As he thinketh in his heart, so is he" (Proverbs 23:7 ASV). Thoughts which fill the mind soon result in corresponding actions. The topics just listed are the proper topic of meditation for the Christian. It is not a sterile contemplation that Paul asks for. We are caused to think of Romans 12:2, "be transformed by the renewing of your mind."

> Perhaps an illustration from the world of music will help. The "pitch" for a piano tuner is taken from a tuning fork. The tuning fork for the Christian is whatever rings true (judged by the Biblical standard of morality -- judged by God's righteousness itself). There are ever new and changing questions that have to be tested by the Christian's spiritual tuning fork. Just as the piano must be kept in tune -- so must our sensitive spiritual natures be kept clean and sweet.[45]

4:9 -- *The things you have learned and received and heard and seen in me, practice these things; and the God of peace shall be with you.*

The things you have learned and received and heard and seen in me – All four verbs in this clause in the Greek are aorist tenses, and refer to the time when Paul was among them. The first two verbs describe how, while he was in Philippi, he instructed them by word of mouth. "Learned" pictures the Philippians as being pupils. "Received" pictures the teaching as being done by word of mouth. "Received" is the regular word for receiving a "tradition." What Paul taught he had learned from Christ (Galatians 1:12); the Philippians

---

[45] Source unidentified.

learned from Paul what Christ had taught him. Before there were written New Testament Scriptures, the truths and ethics taught by Christ had to be learned as teachers handed them over to their pupils.[46] The last two verbs remind the Philippians that while he was in Philippi, they saw in Paul a living example, a pattern of the Christian life both in his everyday speech and in his conduct. As the "in me" indicates, for the second time in this letter (cf. 3:17), Paul points to himself as the example for the Philippians to copy. He certainly was aware not only of careful living but also of his apostolic authority and message as he writes these words.[47]

Practice these things – Paul concludes this exhortation with a call to action. Using a present tense imperative verb, he writes, "Practice these things!" Practice them as a habit.[48] Put them into practice and keep on doing them. In his Sermon on the Mount and in His parables, Jesus called on His hearers to put into practice the truths they had heard. Such doers, He said, were like wise men who built their house on the rock (Matthew 7:24). They were like good ground who brought forth an abundant crop (Matthew 13:23; Luke 8:15). It becomes clear that both the truths of Christianity which Paul taught as well as the thinking or meditation about which Paul spoke in verse 8 were all intended to influence the behavior of the Philippians.

And the God of peace shall be with you – This exhortation closes with a wonderful promise to those who constantly practice their Christianity. "God of peace" is one of Paul's favorite titles for God (Romans 16:20; 1 Corinthians 14:33; 1 Thessalonians 5:23; Hebrews 13:20). Paul likely is using "peace" in the sense the term often is used in Scripture (e.g., Psalm 72:7, 85:10; Micah 5:5), namely, a way of referring to the Messianic salvation of which God is the source and provi-

---

[46] It is deceitful handling of the passage for Barclay to say "This stands for the personal interpretation of the gospel and of its truth which Paul brought to them." It is not true that each of the inspired apostles and prophets of the New Testament took what they received from Jesus and deliberately shaped and changed it according to their own experience and their own thinking!

[47] "'In me' sets Paul's teaching apart from that of the heathen philosophers. They could and did urge their followers to give their attention to the highest principles, as Paul did in verse 8, but they could not offer any visible example of their ideals, as he could" (Hayden, *op. cit.*, p.426).

[48] The verb translated "practice" is *prasso*, not *poieo*. Trench *(Syn.*, pp.361-364) explains the connotation. *Poieo* ("do" or "make") pictures the end of the act, the idea of accomplishing something, while *prasso* ("practice") pictures continually or repeatedly being busy about the means by which the object is to be attained.

der.[49]   God has many gifts and qualities, but His provision of salvation is one shared by every one who becomes one of His adopted children.   Think of it, that is the God who will be with us.   James 4:5 has a very similar promise: "Draw near to God and He will draw near to you."   What a boon to have God present as a constant Helper and Friend!

VII. PAUL   THANKS   THEM   FOR   THE   OFFERING.   4:10-20

A. Thank-you Note Begun: Paul's Testimony About Learning the Secret of Contentment.   4:10-13

4:10 -- *But I rejoiced in the Lord greatly, that now at last you have revived your concern for me; indeed, you were concerned* before, *but you lacked opportunity.*

But – Having concluded his teaching and exhortation, as Paul prepares to close this letter, he again (cf. Philippians 1:3-5) expresses his thanks to them for the missionary offering they sent to him.   Epaphroditus had carried an offering from Philippi to Paul (4:18) and this letter "to the Philippians" is a thank you note from the missionary to his financial supporters.

I rejoiced in the Lord greatly – The adverb "greatly" is in the emphatic position in the Greek.   Instead of writing a simple "thank you for the offering", with grace and dignity Paul acknowledges the offering received by attempting to express the depth of his rejoicing when it arrived.   The aorist tense "rejoiced" seems to look back at the moment when Epaphroditus unexpectedly arrived with the offering and with it a reminder that his beloved friends in Philippi had not forgotten him. "In the Lord" ties together all the details that went into the offering.   The Philippians were in the Lord, Paul was in the Lord, their desire to be financially involved in Paul's missionary work was also prompted by the Lord, and Epaphroditus' safe arrival was also attributable to the providence of the Lord.

That now at last you have revived your concern for me – The figure of speech in the verb "revived" is that of the plant that grows and flowers again in spring after having lain dormant through the winter.   Bengel supposed that the metaphor

---

[49] The peace which God provides results from reconciliation with Him and with others who become Christians.   It is the theme of the gospel (Acts 10:36) which is also known as "the gospel of peace" (Ephesians 2:17, 6:15; Romans 10:15).   Christ is "the Lord of peace" (2 Thessalonians 3:16), and bestows peace (John 14:27, 16:33).

was derived from the season; that the Philippians had sent this offering in the spring, and that Paul was writing this letter in the spring when plants were beginning to bloom again.[50]   A problem involved in the interpretation of this verse is whether this verb "revived" is to be taken as transitive or intransitive.   If we take it as intransitive, then it is the Philippians who have been revived.   If we take it as transitive, then the word says that the Philippians caused their concern for Paul's welfare to bloom afresh.   How this verb is interpreted has a bearing on the meaning of "you lacked opportunity," which follows in the next clause of this verse.   The Philippians had supplied Paul's needs on former occasions (see 2 Corinthians 11:9; Philippians 4:16).   After a lapse of some time, the Christians in Philippi had sent Epaphroditus, a member of the congregation, to deliver the things they had contributed (Philippians 4:18).   Paul is not being critical when he writes "now at last."   As he goes on to explain, the Philippians just had not had opportunity to support him financially for a while.   Paul is full of joy that they are still willing to back his ministry financially.   He is telling them how sweet it was to be remembered again by his old friends in his hour of trial.[51]

---

[50] J. A. Bengel, "On the Epistle to the Philippians," in *Gnomon of the New Testament* (Edinburgh: T. & T. Clark, 1860), Vol. 4, p.154.

[51]Perhaps a summary of Paul's attitudes toward accepting financial support from the people to whom he was ministering at the present time and from the people he won to Christ may be helpful here, to show that he has not been inconsistent when it comes to accepting financial support for his mission work.   When entering a new field, Paul often worked at his trade of tentmaking to provide money for himself and the other missionaries traveling with him (Acts 18:3, 20:33-35; 1 Thessalonians 2:9; 2 Thessalonians 3:7-10).   By supporting himself, by working with his own hands, he limited the opportunity sought by those who were ready to impute wrong motives to him.   As he states in his letter to Titus, Paul has always been careful lest he give any occasion for being thought of as being in the class of empty talkers and deceivers who were teaching just for the money (Titus 1:10,11).   Nevertheless, at Thessalonica, someone had accused Paul of thus hiding his covetous intentions (1 Thessalonians 2:5 ASV), a slander he flatly repudiates.   Someone at Corinth had raised insinuations about Paul's motives.   In response, in 1 Corinthians 9:6-18 Paul indicates that preachers have a right to receive financial support from the folk to whom they are preaching, and he also indicates that he had deliberately decided not to make use of that right.   In 1 Corinthians 9:19-23 Paul explains why he chose to offer the gospel without charge: he was exercising one of his rights in the realm of Christian liberty so that he might win more converts to Christ.   Even so, Paul did not escape criticism from enemies of the gospel.   They accused him of robbing other churches (2 Corinthians 11:7,8) so he could preach at Corinth "without charge."   He was accused of using Titus to raise money for himself under pretense of getting money for the poor saints at Jerusalem (2 Corinthians 12:16-18).   With such false charges so easy to make, no wonder Paul was extra careful lest he give his detractors any opportunity to say he was just in the ministry for the money.   While he did not take wages from folk to whom he was currently preaching, when he went to work in a new field, he did welcome financial support from already established churches (2 Corinthians 11:8; Philippians 4:10-20).

Indeed, you were concerned *before*, but you lacked opportunity – Paul pauses to make it clear that his words "now at last" were not intended as a criticism of them. Using imperfect tense verbs ("concerned" and "lacked") he says he knows they were concerned all along, and all the while they were concerned they were lacking opportunity. Paul wanted his readers to know he was not complaining, as though they had neglected him. Perhaps the lack of opportunity was tied in with Paul's own circumstances which have been highly irregular in recent years – imprisonment, shipwreck, etc. 'Where is he, and where could we send the money?'[52] Perhaps the lack of opportunity to raise money was the result of their own circumstances, for the Macedonian Christians were experiencing deep poverty (2 Corinthians 8:1,2).[53]

4:11 -- *Not that I speak from want; for I have learned to be content in whatever circumstances I am.*

Not that I speak from want -- Paul has said, "I rejoiced ... *greatly*." Those words, too, were easily subject to possible misinterpretation. He does not mean to imply he was complaining about being hard pressed financially (which he had been). They should not interpret his words to mean that it was the relief of this need that primarily gave him great joy, for he goes on to tell them he had schooled himself to accept and be content whatever his financial situation. Nor does he wish to leave the impression that "I rejoiced ... greatly" means he is hinting for future favors. It is so easy to say "thank you" in a tone of voice that says, 'I hope you will give me something special like this again.'

For I have learned to be content in whatever circumstances I am – The marginal note tells us that the word translated "content" literally means "self-sufficient." It has the sense of being independent and meeting his own needs rather than depending on others to meet his needs.[54] It is significant that Paul had

---

[52] How did the Philippians learn of Paul's whereabouts? Did they first learn about Paul's imprisonment and about his transfer to Rome from Aristarchus, at the time Paul was on the way to Rome by ship? See comments on Acts 27:2 in the author's *New Testament History: Acts, in loc.*

[53] If "revived" is transitive, their lack of opportunity is bound up in Paul's imprisonment and travels, not in their lack of desire or ability. If "revived" is intransitive, their lack of opportunity was the result of financial straits which are now somewhat abated.

[54] The Greek word *autarkes* ("content") was a great word in Stoic philosophy for the ideal wise man. To the Stoic the word described a person who accepted apathetically whatever came. The Stoic taught that a person had within himself all the resources necessary for impassively coping with life. The word passed from Stoic philosophers into popular speech by Paul's time. Paul uses the word to say he has learned to cope, but his is not an apathetic coping. He goes on to say he has learned to depend on Christ's strength as he experiences the varying circumstances of life. The word *autarkes* also occurs at 2 Corinthians 9:8 and at 1 Timothy 6:6 where Paul says that "godliness actually is a means of great gain, when accompanied by contentment."

to "learn" this virtue. "Learned" (*emathon*) signifies having learned by experience. From 2 Corinthians 11:26,27 we ascertain that Paul had had plenty of experiences during which he learned the lesson. Contentment (self-sufficiency) was something Paul had to learn during the years he was making journeys to spread the gospel. His external circumstances, especially in the area of finances, fluctuated greatly. In the verses following, with such words as "humble means" and "prosperity," "filled" and "going hungry," "abundance" and "suffering need," he will go on to describe the kind of circumstances he has in mind.

4:12 -- *I know how to get along with humble means, and I also know how to live in prosperity; in any and every circumstance I have learned the secret of being filled and going hungry, both of having abundance and suffering need.*

I know how to get along with humble means, and I also know how to live in prosperity – In the Greek there is an "and" (left untranslated in the NASB) which shows that in this verse Paul is explaining what he meant by "content." "I know" (in place of "I have learned" in the previous verse) gives the result of his learning experiences. He has learned the lesson of how to be "content." "Humble means" speaks about living in poverty. "Prosperity" speaks about being affluent or having plenty. In times when funds were short, Paul had found a way to provide some sort of sustenance for himself and his friends, without becoming a burden upon others, either by way of dependence or complaint (Acts 20:34; 1 Corinthians 4:11,12; 2 Corinthians 11:9,27). "Prosperity" says there were times when folk had been generous to him. "We are not told much about his times of plenty, but he was one of several prophets and teachers at Antioch (Acts 13:1). Certainly he was not hungry when he was a guest in Lydia's house (Acts 16:14,15). Perhaps he earned a good living when he made tents with Aquila and Priscilla (Acts 18:1-3)."[55] It is hard to learn to be content (self-sufficient) when living in poverty, but to carry oneself properly in the midst of plenty is no easy matter either (Proverbs 30:8; Mark 10:23-25). That, too, has to be learned.

In any and every circumstance I have learned the secret – There are lean years and fat years; the pendulum swings back and forth. The word translated "learned

---

[55] Root, *79-80*, p.77.

the secret" is the verb used of initiation ceremonies in the Greek mystery religions.[56]   It is a vivid way of saying that he has been thoroughly initiated into life situations where "contentment" was required.   "Any (Greek, *en panti*) circumstance" refers to particular situations, while "every (Greek, *en pasin*) circumstance" takes all the situations as a whole.   It is not an easy matter to go from one extreme (plenty or poverty) to the other (poverty or plenty).

Of being filled and going hungry, both of having abundance and suffering need – Paul first describes the contrasting circumstances in terms of food.   The word "filled" (*chortazesthai*) was often used of animals who had plenty of fodder or grass, so as to be fattening up.   Here it speaks of having plenty to eat.   "Hungry" gives the word picture of animals who have no grass at all.   Then using the contrasting terms "abundance and ... need," he returns again to the terminology of finance.   "Suffering need" says there were times when he had "fallen behind," a common expression of one who is in debt financially.   Paul used a middle voice verb to tell about his "suffering need," a construction that indicates how he felt the pressure of being behind in his finances.[57]   Such a feeling of pressure is intensified when you can see others who have things that are considered necessities while you are having to do without as you struggle to get out of debt.

4:13 -- *I can do all things through Him who strengthens me.*

I can do all things – There is a beautiful gradation in the verbs Paul used as he spoke of his learning to be "content" – "I have learned; I know; I am instructed; I can."   The verb *ischuo*, translated "I can do," is a synonym for power, a synonym that calls attention to an inner power put forth or exerted.   It is a not a power that is inherent, but as the verse goes on to say, it is a power given to him.   In this context, doing "all things" does not mean escaping from confinement, walking on water, or flying to the moon.   In the context Paul is still talking about being independent and meeting his own needs rather than depending on other human beings to meet his needs.

---

[56] Paul's use of such terms (such as initiated, mystery, and knowledge) as are found commonly in the mystery religions should not be pressed to prove some hypothesis that Paul's doctrines were copied from the mystery religions.   Such a claim, once popularly made, has been soundly refuted.   See Gresham Machen, *The Origin of Paul's Religion* (Grand Rapids: Eerdmans, 1925).

[57] Other examples of a middle voice verb being used to express one's personal feelings are Luke 15:14 ("he began to be in need"); Romans 3:23 ("fall short"); and 2 Corinthians 11:3 ("am afraid").

Through Him who strengthens me – Though the KJV reads "through Christ," the best manuscripts omit "Christ" and read instead "in the one who" or "in him who." The NASB has capitalized "Him" based on the conviction that Paul surely has reference to Christ since in 2 Corinthians 12:9,10 he wrote something similar, saying that the power of Christ dwelt in him, and that he was made strong when he found himself in weaknesses and difficulties. "'The Lord stood with me, and strengthened me,' Paul wrote at a time when human friends had left him and he seemed helpless (2 Timothy 4:17). It was Christ who encouraged him in storm and shipwreck and angry sea (Acts 23:11). It was Christ who put a song in his heart in the darkness of the Philippian prison."[58] "Strengthens" translates another synonym for power (*endunamounti*). This one tells the source of power which comes to be manifested in *ischuo* ("I can do all things"). The emphasis of this verse is upon "Him who strengthens me" and not upon "I." With these words Paul has completed his clarification of his statement "now at last" (verse 10); He was not criticizing the Philippians nor was he desperately seeking a future gift from them. He now proceeds to help them guard against a possible misunderstanding of the phrase "I have learned to be content" (verse 11).

B. An Expression of Appreciation for Their Partnership with Him Resumes and Completes this Thank-You Note. 4:14-18.

4:14 -- *Nevertheless, you have done well to share* **with me** *in my affliction.*

Nevertheless – As Paul resumes his thank-you, the adversative *plēn* ("yet, nevertheless") cautions the readers against drawing the conclusion that, because he had learned to be independent of outside help, he did not need their gift or that he was unappreciative of it. The best thanks he can give them is to recognize and commend the moral and spiritual significance of what they have done. He does this (1) by telling them it relieved him of his need (verses 14-16); (2) by pointing out how their offering had enriched them (verses 17,19); and (3) by emphasizing that their offering was an acceptable sacrifice, well-pleasing to God (verse 18).

You have done well to share *with me* **in my affliction** – He was definitely pleased with their gift. "You have done well (*kalos*)" says it was a noble thing, a beautiful thing. "To share" is a form of the verb for partnership or fellowship, and indicates that their partnership (Philippians 1:5) was still operating beautifully. "Affliction," the regular word for "tribulation" or "suffering," tells us how Paul looked at his time of imprisonment. Paul knew he was a prisoner

---

[58] Root, *op. cit.*, p.78.

because he had been preaching the gospel to the Gentiles. What Paul greatly appreciated was that the Philippians understood this and therefore did not abandon him just because he was imprisoned. By sending this offering to him, they were showing they were still partners with him in the cause of Christ. That was a cause for joy to him.

4:15 -- *And you yourselves also know, Philippians, that at the first preaching of the gospel, after I departed from Macedonia, no church shared with me in the matter of giving and receiving but you alone;*

And you yourselves also know, Philippians – In verses 15 and 16, Paul praises them for being partners with him by financially supporting his mission work since their earliest days as a church. The spelling *Philippesioi* ("Philippians") is the Latin way the name is spelled. Did they use the Latin spelling because they were a Roman colony and delighted in things Roman? The word is in the vocative case in the Greek; if there is any emphasis on the word (it stands first in the sentence), it likely "expresses earnestness and affectionate remembrance"[59] rather than an implied comparison with some other church. "You ... know" is to be taken as an indicative, not an imperative mood.

That at the first preaching of the gospel – Beginning with "that" the rest of the verse is a statement of what the Philippians and Paul knew.[60] In "first preaching of the gospel," Paul is looking back at his early preaching in Macedonia, about 10 or 11 years ago (Acts 16:12-40).[61]

After I departed from Macedonia – Paul's second missionary journey took him from Philippi to Thessalonica and then to Berea, which towns were all in Macedonia. From Berea he went on to Athens and Corinth (in Achaia), and from thence to Jerusalem and back to Antioch of Syria, from whence the journey had started (see Acts 16-18). The Greek adverb *hote* could be translated "when I departed," and would refer to an offering the Philippians sent to Paul as he was about to depart from Berea (Acts 17:14).[62] The Greek can be translated "after I

---

[59] Vincent, *op. cit.*, p.147.

[60] *Hoti* ("that") introduces an example of indirect discourse after a verb of "knowing."

[61] Compare the notes at 1:5 on "partnership in the gospel from the first day until now."

[62] Hendriksen (*op. cit.*, p.207) suggests that his "friends in Philippi had heard about Paul's troubles in Thessalonica and had immediately rushed to his aid in a material way." This verse (translated "when I departed") would then imply that the messenger with the Philippians' offering just caught up with Paul as he was leaving Berea (Macedonia) for Athens (Achaia).

departed" (as the NASB does), and would refer to what we know from 2 Corinthians 11:9, that the Philippians sent an offering to Paul while he was in Corinth.[63]

No church shared with me in the matter of giving and receiving but you alone – Paul states something well-known to both the Philippians and to himself. When the Philippian church was in its infancy, having just been established, at that very time they and they alone in their region became involved in supporting Paul as he went about preaching the gospel.[64] From the very start of the church, the Philippians had entered into the matter of missionary work by financially supporting Paul.[65] "Shared" (the Greek verb is *koinōneō*) indicates the Philippians had entered into partnership with Paul.[66] "Giving and receiving" says the Philippians were the givers and Paul was the receiver.[67] While "giving and receiving" is technical language from the business world, similar to "debits" and "credits" (or "expenditures" and "receipts"), it seems obvious that Paul is speaking figuratively. "Paul surely did not keep books on the gifts of his friends, nor did he list anything in the debit column."[68]

4:16 -- *for even in Thessalonica you sent* **a gift** *more than once for my needs.*

---

[63] From Acts 18:5 we learn that Silas and Timothy came from Macedonia and joined Paul when he had gone on from Athens to Corinth, where he was supporting himself by working with Aquila and Priscilla in their tentmaking business (Acts 18:1-3). Then Acts 18:5 tells us that after Silas and Timothy came Paul devoted himself completely to the word. There is every indication that Silas and Timothy were the ones who brought the offering from Philippi to which 4:15 makes reference.

[64] Paul does not mean that no other church ever sent him a missionary offering, for on later occasions other churches did come to his aid (cf. 2 Corinthians 11:8). Here he is zeroing in on the time that can be designated as "the first preaching of the gospel."

[65] Herein is a good lesson for church planters, namely, to teach the newly established congregation to get involved in missions.

[66] Here, likely, is a good text for the concept of direct support missions, and perhaps of a "living-link missionary" -- where the church enters into an agreement to send so much money on a regular basis to the missionary while he is on the field.

[67] Chrysostom, long ago, interpreted these words differently. Making reference to 1 Corinthians 9:11 as a parallel passage, he pictured the Philippians as giving worldly things to Paul in return for receiving spiritual things from him. However, the following verse here in Philippians explains what the Philippians gave and Paul received.

[68] Kent, *op. cit.,* p.157.

For – The Greek is *hoti* and likely is another case of indirect discourse after the introductory "you know" in verse 15, thus making this clause explicative of the preceding assertion. So understood, verse 16 becomes another example of their partnership with him.

For even in Thessalonica – Not only after he left Macedonia, but even before that time, when he had just passed from Philippi to Thessalonica, they sent offerings to him. What we learn here in Philippians supplements what we learn elsewhere about Paul's financial situation. After leaving Philippi, according to the book of Acts (17:1-9), the next city where Paul stopped to evangelize was Thessalonica. Although there is no mention in Acts of the source of Paul's funds while there, in his correspondence with the Thessalonian church he indicated that he had preached to them without charge (1 Thessalonians 2:5; 2 Thessalonians 3:8). Part of the reason he could preach without charge (those verses tell us) was because he worked with his own hands to earn his living. Now we learn that part of the reason he could preach without charge was because of the assistance from Philippi.[69]

You sent *a gift* more than once for my needs – In 1 Thessalonians 2:9 and 2 Thessalonians 3:8, Paul affirms that he labored with his own hands "night and day" to earn his living while he was in Thessalonica. We must conclude from what he writes here in his letter to the Philippians that their offerings supplemented, but did not supersede, his own resources. Small congregations should not bemoan the fact that what they have to send to the missionary is small. It will supplement his other resources, and may be just what is needed at the time it is received. "My needs" refers to his then present need while in Thessalonica. The Philippians had helped supply his needs "more than once."[70]

4:17 -- *Not that I seek for the gift itself, but I seek for the profit which increases to your account.*

---

[69] There is another way what we learn here in Philippians, as well as in Paul's letters to the church at Thessalonica, supplements what we learn from Acts. It has to do with how long Paul stayed in Thessalonica. Acts 17:2 tells us Paul stayed some weeks in Thessalonica, for he preached in the synagogue on three different Sabbaths. However, if he were there long enough to receive several offerings from Philippi (as this verse indicates), it looks as though he spent some months there. (Cp. W.J. Conybeare and J.S. Howson, *Life and Epistles of Saint Paul* [Hartford, CT: S.S. Scranton Company, 1910], pp.284-286.)

[70] The Greek translated "more than once" is literally "both once and twice." Leon Morris, "*Kai Hapax kai Dis*," *NovTest*. 1:3 [July, 1956], pp.205-208, has argued that this expression is general and does not express an exact number.

Not that I seek for the gift itself – The earlier anxiety lest they misunderstand what he is saying surfaces here again. "Not that" (*ouch hoti*) introduces a denial of a false conclusion that might be reached by the readers. "The gift" is a general term for any gift, not just the gift they had recently sent. The verb translated "I seek" is a present tense indicating an habitual attitude on Paul's part. His long thank-you note must not be taken as a hint that they should hurry more gifts his way. Paul's readers must not suppose that his primary concern was for their money. He goes on to affirm that it was not the gift but the giver that was the object of Paul's primary concern.

But I seek for the profit which increases to your account – He repeats the present tense verb with which he began this verse in order to emphasize what his real attitude is. The margin tells us that the Greek word translated "profit" is literally "fruit." Perhaps "fruit" corresponds with the picture (Philippians 4:10) of a tree reviving in spring and producing leaves and fruit. He used a similar figure at Philippians 1:11 when he spoke of the "fruit of righteousness." Or perhaps Paul is still drawing his metaphorical language from the world of accounting. The words "giving and receiving" (4.15) were accounting words. Now perhaps we learn that there is "interest" added to the Philippians' account. "Elsewhere Paul quotes Jesus to the effect that 'it is more blessed to give than to receive' (Acts 20:35). It is their blessing and not his that he seeks."[71] What is the interest or fruit that Paul has in view? Perhaps it is God's blessings in this life (Proverbs 11:25; 2 Corinthians 9:8-11; Philippians 4:19). Perhaps it speaks of a higher degree of glory in heaven following the judgment, similar to "lay[ing] up for yourselves treasures in heaven" (Matthew 6:20). In Romans, when seeking an offering from them to finance a proposed missionary tour to Spain, Paul also speaks of "fruit" being credited to them (Romans 1:13). See also Romans 15:28 where a benevolent offering is called "fruit." Whatever the "profit" is, the participle "increases" is a word that signifies a large abundance.

4:18 -- *But I have received everything in full, and have an abundance; I am amply supplied, having received from Epaphroditus what you have sent, a fragrant aroma, an acceptable sacrifice, well-pleasing to God.*

But I have received everything in full, and have an abundance – "But" translates the conjunction *de*, the mild adversative. Perhaps the connection is this – 'Though it is not the gift I am seeking from you, I have received it.' "I have an abundance" tells the Philippians that not only was his need supplied but that the

---

71 Harrell, *op. cit.*, p.147.

gift has more than taken care of his needs.   The metaphorical language from the world of finance continues.   The Greek *apecho panta* ("I have received everything") was the first century way to mark bills as "paid in full" and is equivalent to Paul's giving them a receipt for what they sent.[72]

I am amply supplied – Paul is saying that he needs no more for the present, so bountifully have the Philippians supplied his needs.   This introduces an explanation in the phrase which follows of what it is that he has received and how he now has abundance.

Having received from Epaphroditus what you have sent – At 2:25-30 we were introduced to Epaphroditus and his trip from Philippi to Rome.   This clause explains why Paul is amply supplied.   "From" (*para*) emphasizes the idea that Epaphroditus was the carrier of the gift from the Philippians to Paul.   "What you have sent" (literally "the things from you") tells us that what the Philippians sent may have included more than money, things such as reading materials and clothing.   (Cp. 2 Timothy 4:13 where, on a later occasion, Paul asks for the last two items to be brought to him).

A fragrant aroma, an acceptable sacrifice, well-pleasing to God – Paul has spoken about their missionary offering as it related to him (it amply supplied his needs), and then about how it related to the givers themselves (profit added to their account).   Now he takes up what God thought of their offering.   To express what God thought of their offering Paul changes metaphors.   He had employed the language of the business world up to now.   Now he uses the language of the religious world, the language of burnt offerings and sacrifices.   The expression "a fragrant aroma" (or "an odor of a sweet smell," ASV) was common in the Old Testament (see Genesis 8:21; Exodus 29:18; Ezekiel 20:41) to describe a sacrifice which was acceptable to God.   Whether or not the offering was one that smelled sweet to God, or one that made Him sick, depended on the attitude of the worshiper as he came bringing the sacrifice (see notes at Ephesians 5:2).   The worshiper's heart had to be right.   The Philippians are pictured as not just sending a gift to Paul but rather as giving their offering to God with the intention of furthering the Lord's work by helping His servant.   Giving their offering to God is what made their deed so grand.   Since the word "sacrifice" was used of free will offerings given out of gratitude, to call what the Philippians' have sent to Paul an "acceptable sacrifice" indicates that of their own free will they collected

---

[72] A. Deissmann, *op. cit.,* p.111-112,166,331 gives pictures from the ancient ostraca and papyri showing the use of *apecho panta* meaning "paid in full."

the offering for Paul, and that their giving of the offering was a result of their thanksgiving to God for the blessings He had given them.   With "well-pleasing to God" we may compare Hebrews 13:16, "Do not neglect doing good and sharing, for with such sacrifices God is pleased."   To tell the Philippians that God was well-pleased with what they had done was the highest praise Paul could have bestowed on the givers.

C. Assurance of God's Loving Care, and Doxology.   4:19,20

4:19 -- *And my God shall supply all your needs according to His riches in glory in Christ Jesus.*

And my God shall supply all your needs – The Philippians have helped supply Paul's need.   Now, Paul promises, "God shall supply … your needs."   This promise includes something other than the "profit" added to their account (verse 17).   "My God," that is, 'the One who means so very much to me,' will Himself be the One who will supply your needs now that you have made an offering to Him (verse 18).   "In words that countless Christians have relied on as one of the great Scripture promises, Paul now reminds his benefactors that 'his' God will do what he himself is in no position to do; namely, reimburse his benefactors."[73] The word "supply" is the same word translated "amply supplied" in the previous verse.   Because you have given, God shall fill your cup to the brim and overflow it in return, was Paul's promise.   We give first, and then God gives to us.   It is a promise that still is true.[74]   This is how God would, in a practical way, express His approval of their offering.

According to His riches in glory in Christ Jesus – "According to His riches" means on a scale commensurate with His wealth.[75]   "In Christ Jesus" says such rewards are given by God to His saints, to those in union with Christ.   "In glory" can mean either in a glorious manner or in glory hereafter.   In the light of 2 Corinthians 9:6-15 we treat this verse as a promise of God's special providence – something He does regularly for believers.   2 Corinthians 9:9 quotes Psalm 112:9 to emphasize that God's righteousness, His doing what is right, is something that endures forever.

---

[73] Kent, *op. cit.*, p.157.

[74] See Proverbs 11:25, 19:17, and 2 Corinthians 9:7-11. If we would like to have more money to manage, we must first show God that we are good managers.

[75] At Ephesians 1:7 we have "the riches of His grace," and at 3:16 we have the expression the "riches of His glory."   "Riches" is a way of saying that lavishness, generosity is involved.

4:20 -- *Now to our God and Father* **be** *the glory for ever and ever.   Amen.*

Now to our God and Father – As Paul reflects on God's marvelous care as He supplies the needs of His children (verse 19), it is little wonder that he breaks out into this doxology.[76] The change of pronouns – from "*my* God" (verse 19) to "*our* God" – should be noticed.   Paul is now picturing in his mind's eye both himself and the Philippians as united in two ways: united in the way they have received and will continue to receive help from God; and united in their praise to God for all His benefits.   The Greek construction translated "God and Father" indicates that only one person is meant, One who is both God and Father.[77]   God is the Father of all believers and it is the thought of God's fatherly care that gives rise to the doxology.

Be **the glory forever and ever** – "Be" is printed in italics indicating there is no verb in the Greek.   The NASB translators (rightly it seems) have chosen to supply an imperative verb "let it be!"   Paul is directing all God's redeemed children to do their utmost to give praises unto their God.   "*The* glory" (there is an article in the Greek) calls for God to be given the praise He deserves.[78]   Not only in this time does Paul wish for praises to be addressed to God.   He wants praises to be given to God on through eternity.   "Forever and ever" is literally "unto the ages of the ages."   Eternity to come does not consist of ages of years, but ages of ages, that is, countless ages.   If praises are given to Him in eternity, even as praises are given to Him now, it seems as though we will be able to remember even then what He did for us now.

Amen – "Amen" is an Aramaic word, spelled with Greek letters.   The word was often used in worship services, and was the means by which the worshipers expressed their hearty assent to what was said or done (see 1 Chronicles 16:36 and Nehemiah 8:6).   Here Paul is expressing his hearty consent to what he has just written by inspiration.

---

[76] Such doxologies are common in Paul's writings -- Romans16:27; Galatians 1:5; Ephesians 3:21; 1 Timothy 1:17; 2 Timothy 4:18.

[77] Sharp's rule of grammar (cf. Dana and Mantey, *op. cit.,* p.150, paragraph iii) tells us that "when two nouns in the same case are connected by the Greek word 'and,' and the first one is preceded by the article 'the' and the second is not preceded by the article, the second noun refers to the same person or thing to which the first noun refers, and is a further description of it."

[78] See notes at Philippians 1:11 for some of the ideas contained in the word "glory."

VIII. *CONCLUSION*:   CLOSING SALUTATIONS AND BENEDICTION.   4:21-23

4:21 -- *Greet every saint in Christ Jesus.   The brethren who are with me greet you.*

Greet every saint in Christ Jesus – Probably the greeting was done by means of the holy kiss.   The verb "greet" is plural.   Not just the one who reads the letter, but all the listeners are to greet every other saint.[79]   To greet each saint individually was an expression of personal affection.   It is entirely possible that Paul wrote these last three verses with his own hand (cp. Galatians 6:11; Colossians 4:18; 2 Thessalonians 3:17).   Such a thing was the customary way of closing letters in ancient times, namely, for the one who dictated the letter to add his own closing line, after the secretary had copied the rest of the letter.   At Philippians 1:1 Paul addressed this letter to "all the saints in Christ Jesus."   As was explained there, a "saint" is someone set apart or dedicated to Christ.   "In Christ Jesus" may be a description of whose "saints" are being talked about, or it may explain how the greeting was to be done; namely, greet them as Christ would greet them.   Of course, such a salutation would go a long way toward aiding the unity which has been one of the burdens of this letter.

The brethren who are with me greet you – The "brethren" are likely Paul's fellow-workers in Rome, since they are distinguished from the Christians who are living in Rome and who are mentioned in the next verse.   They have heard or seen that Paul is sending this letter to the Philippians, and have asked that their greetings, too, be extended.[80]   How many of those who were named in Colossians 4:10-15 and Philemon 23,24 were still with Paul at the time he penned this letter, we do not know.

4:22 -- *All the saints greet you, especially those of Caesar's household.*

---

[79] Since the letter specifically included the overseers and deacons (Philippians 1:1) in its address, a case could be made that they are the ones who are instructed to greet every saint.

[80] It will be recalled that at Philippians 2:20,21, Paul has said he had no one else of kindred spirit whom he might send to Philippi.   When Paul indicates that "the brethren" who are with him are sending greetings, some have found a discrepancy or an inconsistency with what was there affirmed about Timothy.   Our comments at 2:21,22 have been so worded that no discrepancy need be discovered here.

All the saints greet you – By "brethren" in the preceding verse, Paul obviously meant his inner circle of fellow-workers, so "all the saints" must refer to members of the Roman church. They are aware that Paul is sending this thank-you letter to Philippi and have asked him to include greetings from them. There is an implication that the saints in Rome were rejoicing over what the Philippians have done as they sent the evidence of their partnership with the apostle.

Especially those of Caesar's household – It is not clear to us why, of all the Christians who were members of the church in Rome, Paul lays special stress on the Christians belonging to Nero's household.[81]   The expression "Caesar's household" is Greek terminology for the Latin *domus* or *familia Caesaris*.[82] They might be slaves or freemen or even freedmen.   Included in such a "household" would be civil servants, officials on the emperor's staff who held posts of considerable importance in the day-to-day affairs of government. Others might be domestic servants.   The praetorian guard would be included.[83] People could become members of Caesar's household in a number of ways.   If some nobleman were found guilty of plotting against Caesar, he was executed, and upon his death all his slaves became part of Caesar's household.[84]   If slaves of a nobleman who lived in the provinces were willed to the emperor, then upon

---

[81] In the Detailed Introduction to Philippians found at the close of this volume, attention has been directed both to this expression "saints ... of Caesar's household" and to the expression "the whole praetorian guard" at Philippians 1:13 as being evidence this epistle was composed while Paul was a prisoner in Rome.

[82] Josephus (*Ant.* 17.5.8) uses the Greek expression "household of Caesar" in the same way.   Nero would have been the emperor when Philippians was written.

[83] Lightfoot in a detached essay on "Caesar's household" (*op. cit.*, p.171-177) sets forth the information that the names of many of the folk (Ampliatus, Urbanus, Apelles, Tryphaena, Tryphosa, Patrobas, Philologus) to whom greetings were sent in Paul's letter to the Romans (Romans 16:9-15) are also found in sepulchral inscriptions belonging to members of the *"domus Augusta,"* or the imperial household.   The article on *oikia* in Arndt and Gingrich (*op. cit.*, p.560) lists sources where further investigation of "household" may be pursued.   This article also shows that, according to prevailing usage, the emperor's "household" does not refer to members of the emperor's family or his relatives.   Seneca, who was Nero's tutor and later advisor, would have been a member of Nero's "household."   The evidence that he may have been a Christian can be seen in Lightfoot's essay on "St. Paul and Seneca" (*op. cit.*, p.270-328).

[84] See notes in this writer's commentary *New Testament Epistles: Romans*, concerning the households of Aristobulus and of Narcissus who are named in Romans 16:10,11.   It appears to be very probable that both Aristobulus' and Narcissus' "households" were in fact the slave-establishments, the former being that of the son of Herod the Great, and the latter being that of the favorite of Claudius, both of which have been transferred to the possession of the emperor.

the death of the nobleman, the slaves would be transferred to Rome, but still retain their family identity as "the household of ...." Since it seems clear that the folk named in Romans 16:5-15 must have been known to Paul before they moved to Rome, we may surmise they came to Rome from provinces in the east. It seems more than likely that some of them came from Philippi, or at least were known to the Christians at Philippi. This would account for Paul's "especially" calling attention to them. Whoever these members of Caesar's household were, it is of interest to see how far the influence of the gospel has been felt in the Roman world.

4:23 -- *The grace of the Lord Jesus Christ be with your spirit.*

The grace of the Lord Jesus Christ be with your spirit – As he usually does, Paul closes this letter with a prayer of benediction, and this is one of his favorite benedictions (see Galatians 6:18; Philemon 25).[85] The "grace of the Lord Jesus Christ" means grace which He bestows. This prayer by Paul for the readers says "I pray that the Lord Jesus Christ may continue to show you grace," or "... show you his great kindness," or "... be so kind to you." "Your" is plural in the Greek. All the folk listening as this letter is read publicly to the assembled congregation would hear this benediction as addressed personally to each one of them. "The Philippians had sent their gifts to Paul. Paul had only one gift to send to them – his blessing. But what greater gift can we give to any man than to remember him in our prayers,"[86] and call down God's blessings on him! The regenerated spirit is the contact point between God and his child, the place where the grace of the Lord Jesus Christ enters the life of the believer. The grace given by the Lord Jesus Christ is received in "the spirit" of man for this very purpose, that the whole man ("body, soul, and spirit") may be preserved blameless to "the coming of our Lord Jesus Christ" (1 Thessalonians 5:23).

Some manuscripts conclude with an "Amen" (KJV). Most likely it was not present in the original but was added by copyists in accordance with liturgical practice. Unless we opt for the hypothesis that it was added by later copyists, it would be difficult to account for its omission in many early manuscripts.

---

[85] Instead of "be with your spirit," the KJV reads "be with you all." However, the better supported reading (P^{46}, Aleph, H, L, D, Vulg., Syriac) is "be with your spirit."

[86] Barclay, *op. cit.*, p.107.

A subscription is carried in the manuscripts in the Textus Receptus tradition. It reads, "It was written to the Philippians from Rome by Epaphroditus." "By Epaphroditus" means it was carried by Epaphroditus, not written by him.

Paul's prayer of benediction to the Philippians is this commentator's prayer for those who have been reading this commentary. "The grace of the Lord Jesus Christ be with your spirit."

Page 576

Detailed Introductions

to the

Prison Epistles

Detailed Introduction to Ephesians

A. HISTORICAL ALLUSIONS

1. **Historical allusions at the beginning of the epistle, 1:1ff:**

    a. 1:1 – "Paul." The letter begins with the author's signature, as was the custom of the ancients when writing letters.

    b. 1:1 – In the NASB, the destination is given, in part, as "To the saints which are at Ephesus."

        1) However, "at Ephesus" (*en Epheso*) is missing from some manuscripts, a marginal note in the NASB tells us. Those manuscripts are:

            a) Codex Sinaiticus (Aleph), though absent from the original copy, the words have been added by a later corrector.
            b) Codex Vaticanus (B), where the words "in Ephesus" have been added in the margin by a corrector. The corrector is designated as B^2 and is thought to date from nearly the same time as B (the original).
            c) P^{46} (Chester Beatty Papyrus) is the earliest extant manuscript of Paul's letters. It comes from the first or second century, while Sinaiticus and Vaticanus are from the fourth century. P^{46} has the title "To the Ephesians" though verse 1 does not have the words "at Ephesus" in the text.
            d) Codex Beza (D), a fifth century manuscript, has a space left where some manuscripts have "in Ephesus."
            e) 67^2 – a reputable twelfth century minuscule. "In Ephesus" was in the manuscript originally, but a corrector has marked them as an interpolation.
            f) 1739 – a tenth century manuscript.

        2) "At Ephesus" is found in all the other extant manuscripts.

    The committee that produced today's standard critical text of the Greek New Testament was evenly split on the question of the authenticity of "at Ephesus." They left the words in the text on account of the vast number of manuscripts that carry the words, but bracketed the words on account of the quality of the witnesses which do not include the words.[1]

3) Various suggestions have been given in an attempt to explain the omission of "at Ephesus" in some of the very best manuscripts:

a) Perhaps several copies of this letter were made by Paul, and the name was filled in as the letter was being delivered. (This does not appear probable. If several copies were made, why could not the destination have been filled in by Paul while at Rome, rather than waiting for the messenger to fill in the various destinations?)

b) Perhaps the scribe who wrote codex Beza had several manuscripts before him, comparing them as he copied – some with and some without "at Ephesus" – and he purposely left the destination blank, intending to do more research on the problem.

c) Perhaps the letter was originally written with "in Ephesus" in the text, and someone later cut it out. (Compare Marcion's excision of the words "in Rome" at Romans 1:7).

d) The most probable explanation is that there was only one letter written by Paul, and the destination was left blank. The one who delivered the letter and read it aloud in the church supplied the name of the people to whom he was reading the letter.[2]

4) More will be said about the "destination" later.

a) It is not easy to decide whether the words "at Ephesus" were in the original text and omitted from later copies, or whether they were inserted in the later copies where the original did not have them.

b) This much is sure: three of the oldest Uncials and one of the best of the Papyrus manuscripts do not carry "at Ephesus". This must be satisfactorily explained.

---

[1] Bruce Metzger, *Textual Commentary on the Greek New Testament* [Stuttgart: United Bible Societies, 1971], p.101.

[2] The Greek "to the saints who are ..." would expect a prepositional phrase following identifying the place where the saints were.

c. 1:2 – The usual Pauline greeting

1) There was a form usually followed in letters in Hellenistic times.

   a) The signature first – "Paul"
   b) Destination given – "To the saints ..."
   c) Greeting – "Grace to you and peace" ... i.e., "Hello"
   d) Other portions of a Hellenistic letter included:
       - Thanks to the gods for the welfare of the recipient
       - The body of the letter
       - A personal note added by the hand of the one who dictated
         the letter (after the scribe finished it to this point)

2) In the epistle of James we have the precise Hellenistic opening for
    a letter.

   a) Comparing James and Ephesians, you can see the difference.
       James has "James ... to the 12 tribes ... Greetings." Paul has
       "Paul ... to the saints ... Grace and peace."[3] Paul does not use
       the conventional greeting. Instead, with slight modification,
       in which he substitutes the Christian word "grace" (*charis*
       ["grace"]) for the Greek *chairein* ["greetings"]), he combines
       both the Greek and the Hebrew (*shalom*, peace) forms of
       greeting.
   b) This is done, it appears, for two reasons. First, there were
       people of both Greek and Hebrew backgrounds in the
       churches. Second, the terms "grace" and "peace" now have
       a new meaning, a Christian meaning, and are most appropri-
       ate. Grace is unmerited favor (to you), a prayer for their
       salvation. Peace is also a prayer that the readers may have
       peace with God and peace with man.

d. 1:3 – The usual thanksgiving

1) After the greeting, in almost every epistle, Paul has a word of
    thanksgiving.[4]

---

[3] Compare the greeting in the other letters of Paul, and it will be seen how Paul customarily opens his letters this same way.

[4] There is a thanksgiving in every letter but Galatians, where he is so stirred up by the apostasy that he leaves out the thanksgiving.

2) Paul, perhaps using good psychology, tries to offer a good word for every church to which he writes. A word of praise where it is genuine would make the readers more inclined to read and heed what he writes.

e. From this letter's beginning, what have we learned about the time of writing? If it is addressed to Ephesus, then this letter was written after the founding of the Ephesian church. That occurred during Paul's third missionary journey, AD 54-58. If the letter is a circular letter addressed to churches in the Roman province of Asia Minor, we must assign a date to the letter after there were churches established in that area. This, too, seems to point to a time no earlier than Paul's third missionary journey, during which "all who lived in Asia heard the word of the Lord" (Acts 19:10).

f. Is anyone with Paul when he writes?[5] When we compare Colossians 1:1 and Philemon 1, we learn that, when those letters were written, Timothy was with Paul. If Ephesians were sent out at the same time that Colossians and Philemon were, we would expect to find Timothy's name in Ephesians 1:1. How should its absence be explained?

2. Historical allusions at the conclusion of the letter, 6:20ff

a. 6:20 – Paul calls himself an "ambassador in chains." Paul was a prisoner when this letter is written. See also 3:1,13 and 4:1.

b. 6:20,21 – The only person whose name appears in Ephesians is "Tychicus." Elsewhere we learn that Tychicus is carrying the letters "to the Ephesians" and "to the Colossians" (4:7-9), and is accompanied by Onesimus, who likely carried the letter to Philemon. The closing verses of Colossians mention 10 people. Philemon names 10. Why is Ephesians different?

c. In the KJV there is a subscription which reads, "Written from Rome unto the Ephesians by Tychicus." Such subscriptions were not in the autographed copy, but were added later when copies of the autograph were being made. Sometimes the subscriptions are right, sometimes

---

[5] By observing who is with Paul when he writes a letter, we can look into the Book of Acts for times during Paul's ministry when those same folk are with Paul. This helps us date the letters.

the subscriptions are wrong.   This one tells that Ephesians was written from Rome and "by Tychicus" indicates that it was carried for delivery by Tychicus.   Is this correct?

3.   Observations

In the early years of Paul's missionary work, he was almost totally occupied with evangelizing areas that had not heard the gospel and with establishing and maintaining new congregations of believers.   To the churches where he was well-known, if he wrote at all, his letters were limited to that which was critical for the congregation at the moment. Those letters also contained personal comments and greetings.   Toward the close of his missionary journeys as recorded in Acts, Paul did write a letter to a church where he had not visited.   In this letter to Rome he introduced himself, explained the great central doctrines which he taught, and sought their financial support for a proposed missionary tour to Spain.

After his letter to Rome, Paul's situation changed.   He was arrested at Jerusalem and imprisoned for two long years at Caesarea, and then for two more in Rome.   If messengers came from some congregation, he could still hear about how the church was doing, and he could write a letter to them.   A visitor or messenger coming to Paul from the church occasioned the writing of both Colossians and Philippians.

The years in prison gave Paul opportunity to reflect on the whole Christian mission as it had developed and as to its future.   The time could not be far distant when he and the other apostles would no longer be there to write letters and send personal messages for the guidance of the churches. Something was needed to help ensure that the work Paul and the other apostles had begun would be carried on as the Lord wanted it to be, even after their deaths.

This need, we perceive, is what prompted Paul to write the letter we call "Ephesians."   In it, Paul sets forth the distilled essence of all the best of his other letters.   Doctrines presented elsewhere in bits and pieces to meet urgent needs are here developed into a harmonious pattern.   The urgent plea in 1 Corinthians for unity within the local congregation is broadened in Ephesians to an appeal to maintain the unity of the Spirit in all the congregations in which the letter is read.   A theology of unity among believers is here elevated to a theology for all time.   The instruction to the Thessalonians about the Lord's   return is seen in Ephesians to be but part of the strategy of God's eternal purpose as He provides salvation for lost men. The old racial prejudices between Jews and Gentiles that threatened the fabric of the congregations of Antioch and Galatia are here resolved in Christ who is our peace and has made both Jewish and Gentile believers into one new body. If men are "in Christ" all is well both now and for eternity. What Paul wants the readers of this letter to do is to realize the spiritual blessings they have and then let this realization be the motive that helps them live for Christ in the midst of a dark world.

B. DESTINATION: *To whom is the epistle written?*

1. The title appended to the book at an early date also has "To the Ephesians." When men added the title, the wording of the addition indicates a belief the letter was addressed to the church at Ephesus. It was a tradition in early Christian literature to speak of this epistle as addressed to the Ephesians.[6] Typical would be Tertullian who wrote, "The apostle, too, writing to the Ephesians, says that God 'had proposed for Himself, at the dispensation of the fulfillment of times, to recall to the head' (that is, to the beginning) 'things universal in Christ, which are above the heavens and above the earth in Him'" (cp. Ephesians 1:9,10).[7] Any conclusion about the original destination of this letter must account for this early Christian tradition.

2. The question of destination is even more closely connected with the opening words of the epistle, "To the saints who are at Ephesus, and who are faithful in Christ Jesus." However, as we have already seen, the words "at Ephesus" are missing from some of the oldest and best manuscripts of this letter (P[46], Aleph, B).[8] With the words "at Ephesus" omitted, the phrase giving the destination could be translated "to the saints, the ones who are also (*kai* = "also") faithful in Christ Jesus." This would have the letter addressed to any believers in Christ Jesus; that is, to any assembly of believers to whom Tychicus personally delivered the letter.

---

[6] See Irenaeus. *Adv. Haer.*, v.2.31; Clemens Alex, *Strom.*, iv.8; *Paedag.*, i.5.

[7] Tertullian, "On Monogamy," chap.v.

[8] Lightfoot believed that whenever Aleph, Vaticanus, and 67[2] concurred in supporting a Pauline reading, the original text was invariably reflected. J.B. Lightfoot, *Biblical Essays* (London: Macmillan, 1893), p.380.

3. Some early Christian writings have been regarded as giving evidence that the words "at Ephesus" were missing in manuscripts available to those writers.

   a. Ignatius (AD 115) is often adduced as evidence that "at Ephesus" was missing in the manuscript he had. In one place he wrote, "Paul ... in every epistle makes mention of *you* in Christ Jesus ...."[9] In this commentator's judgment, these words are too obscure to be of much value. How can we be sure when he says "every epistle" that there is an allusion to Ephesians. If we admit that Ephesians is included in "every epistle," would Ignatius' words prove that "at Ephesus" was missing any more than they would or would not prove that "who are faithful" was missing?

   b. Tertullian (AD 200), as noted above, in one place has the apostle Paul writing "to the Ephesians." In another place he wrote, "I pass by here another epistle which *we* have inscribed to the Ephesians, but the heretics to the Laodiceans."[10] Again he writes, "According to the true testimony of the church, we suppose the epistle to have been sent to the Ephesians. But Marcion sometimes inclined to alter the title, as if he had made a very diligent inquiry into the matter. Yet the title is of no importance since the apostle wrote to all men when he wrote to some."[11] Note, Tertullian does not indicate that Marcion changed the *text* (i.e., the wording at Ephesians 1:1); instead, Tertullian finds fault with Marcion for changing the *title* (i.e., the title "To the Ephesians" prefixed to the letter). Evidently Marcion read Paul's request that the Colossians and the Laodiceans should exchange letters (Colossians 4:16), and drew the conclusion that the letter "from Laodicea" referred to the letter we call "Ephesians." He thus altered the *title* (not the text) from "To the Ephesians" into "To the Laodiceans," for which, some 50 years later, Tertullian took him to task.[12]

---

[9] Ignatius, *Ad Eph*, chap.xii.

[10] Tertullian, *Adv. Marc.* v.11.

[11] Tertullian, *Adv. Marc.* v.17.

[12] A few details concerning how *titles* came to be added to the letters now in our New Testaments will help our understanding at this point. In ancient days letters were written on rolls of papyrus. When they were finished, they were tied with thread, and, if they were specially private or important, the knots of the thread were then sealed with wax. But it was seldom that any address

Tertullian elsewhere[13] criticized Marcion for changing the *text* of various of Paul's epistles, so Tertullian knew the distinction between *title* and *text*.

It can be rightly deduced that Marcion's text must have had "at Ephesus" missing, or he could not have altered the title. In fact, it can be inferred that Tertullian also was aware that there were manuscripts in existence which had "in Ephesus" missing at 1:1, for if Tertullian had the phrase in his text, he would surely have used that fact against Marcion's alteration of the title.

c. Origen's commentary on Ephesians (AD 210) shows that the manuscript on which Origen was commenting did not have the words "at Ephesus" (1:1), though Origen himself regarded the letter as addressed to the Ephesians.[14]

d. Basil the Great, bishop of Caesarea (writing about AD 350), indicated that ancient copies of Ephesians which he had examined did not contain the words "at Ephesus" at Ephesians 1:1. He wrote, "And writing to the Ephesians as truly united by knowledge to *Him who is*, he called them in a peculiar sense *those who are*, saying, 'To the saints *who are*, and the faithful in Christ Jesus.' For so those before us have transmitted it, and we have found it in the ancient copies."[15] Basil's opening line is indicative that the letter was generally known in his day as having been written "to the Ephesians." But his comments reflect the fact that "at Ephesus" was not to be discovered in any of the "ancient copies" that were before him. And note, he wrote this c. AD 350, and he speaks of manuscripts which were then ancient.

---

was written on them, for the very simple reason that, for the ordinary individual, there was no postal system in the ancient world. There was a government post, but it was only available for official and imperial correspondence, and was not available for the ordinary person and for his letters. Letters in those days were delivered by hand; they were given to someone to deliver personally, and therefore no address on the outside was necessary. So the titles of the New Testament letters were not part of the original letters at all. They were inserted afterward when the letters were collected (and stored in presses) for convenience and ease of identification of the rolled-up scroll.

[13] Tertullian, *Adv. Marc.* v.18.

[14] See J.A. Cramer's *Catenae Graecorum Patrum (Chain of Greek Fathers) in Novum Testamentum,* 1844. Accessed at http://literalchristianlibrary.wikifoundary.com.

[15] *Adv. Eunomium* 2.19.

He could not be speaking of Codex Sinaiticus or Vaticanus, which would have been only about 25 years old at that time.

e. Jerome (AD 387), in his commentary on Ephesians 1:1 wrote, "Some are of the opinion from what was said to Moses, 'Thou shalt say to the children of Israel, *He who is* has sent me' (Exodus 3:14), that the saints and faithful at Ephesus were also designated by a term denoting *essence*, so that from *Him who is,* they are called *those who are*. This is an over-refined speculation. Others suppose that he wrote simply not to *those who are*, but to *those who are* saints and faithful *at Ephesus*." When Jerome repeats what the opinion of "some" was, he was undoubtedly referring to Origen's comments on Ephesians 2:1. Jerome's language implies that two readings existed in his day, viz., "Those who are," and "Those who are *at Ephesus.*"

All these things lead plainly to one conclusion – that while there was a clear tradition declaring that the letter was "to the Ephesians," yet there was a blank in the oldest manuscripts after the words "which are." These two factors are important and must be accounted for. But there are more factors to be taken into account as we attempt to determine the original destination of this letter we know as "Ephesians."

4. There are features in the letter itself that are claimed as being incompatible with a strictly Ephesian destination.

    a. There is an absence of special allusion to individual members in the church, and a lack of various personal salutations. There is a general invocation of "peace be to the brethren" (6:23), but no mention of any individual by name, save Tychicus (6:21). There is not even an allusion to the "elders" whom, with so much affection, he had addressed at Miletus (Acts 20), and to whom he had given so solemn a charge.[16]

    b. Paul speaks of the persons to whom this epistle is addressed as if he had little or no personal knowledge of them. How could such a thing be true if this letter were addressed to the church at Ephesus? In

---

[16] On the other hand, it must be remembered that it is not the apostle's *invariable* practice to insert personal salutations to members of the congregation to which he addressed in writing. No individuals are saluted by name in either of the Thessalonian letters, or in Galatians.

Ephesians 1:15 he wrote, "having *heard of the faith* in the Lord Jesus which exists among you, and your love for all the saints." Paul had been three years among the Ephesians. He spent more time at Ephesus than at any other recorded mission point. How then can he write in such a manner as implies he merely has *heard* of their faith and love?[17] In Ephesians 3:2,3, he wrote, "if indeed you have heard of the stewardship of God's grace which was given to me for you." On the assumption this letter is addressed only to Ephesus, this verse is hard to explain. Did Christians at Ephesus know about Paul's commission to preach to the Gentiles only by hearsay? At Ephesians 4:21, the Greek translated "if indeed" speaks of an assumption that Paul believes to be true. If the letter is addressed to Ephesus, where Paul himself had taught them about Jesus Christ, would he not know what they had heard?

c.   A lack of historical references in the epistle is also said to be an argument against a strictly Ephesian destination. Only two facts are noticed in the letter: (1) Paul's imprisonment, and (2) Tychicus has been sent. Timothy was well-known to the Ephesians. Timothy was with Paul at the time this letter was written (Colossians 1:1). A case could be made that the omission of his name here is inconsistent with the opinion that the letter was intended solely for the church at Ephesus.

d.   The church in Ephesus was composed not only of Gentiles but also of Jewish Christians (Acts 19:8-10,17), whereas this epistle is directed particularly to Gentile believers (2:11,19; 3:1; 4:17,22). It is maintained that on the hypothesis that Ephesians was a circular letter the address to Gentile believers in particular is more easily explained.

e.   The opening of Ephesians (Ephesians 1:3ff) strongly reminds us in form, though not in substance, of the opening of the general epistle of Peter (1 Peter 1:3-7) to these churches not only in Asia Minor but other nearby provinces (1 Peter 1:1). This suggests that Ephesians, too, is a general epistle.

---

[17] Defenders of an Ephesus only destination answer that Paul is not making reference to their first hearing of the gospel, but alludes instead to how things have progressed in the years since Paul was last personally in their town. He is still hearing good reports about them. It is also pointed out that in his epistle to Philemon, who was one of his own converts, Paul uses this very expression, "I *hear* of your love and ... faith."

5. Taking these various facts into consideration, three possible destinations have been suggested.

    a. It has been suggested that the letter was originally addressed *"to the Laodiceans."* Evidence for this view is found in the special allusion made in Colossians 4:16, where we read about Paul's "letter that is coming from Laodicea." In addition to Colossians 4:16, there are the letters which were included in Marcion's *Apostolicon*:

Galatians	–	293 lines in the book
Corinthians	–	1460 lines in the books
Romans	–	920 lines in the book
Thessalonians	–	299 lines in the books
Laodiceans	–	312 lines in the book
Colossians	–	208 lines in the book
Philippians	–	208 lines in the book
Philemon	–	38 lines in the book

    What is striking about this list of names? We are familiar with all the books by name except Laodiceans. The book we call Ephesians is not listed, yet the letter to the Ephesians contains 312 lines. Evidently, what Marcion called "Laodiceans," we call "Ephesians." Was Marcion using a title for the letter that was already familiar to the churches, or was he introducing a novel idea?[18]

    If we were to accept this suggestion that the letter was originally addressed to Laodicea, we are obliged to explain how the letter lost its original address to Laodicea and came to be connected with Ephesus. Two suggestions have been made. (1) The church at Ephesus came to know that the church at Laodicea possessed a very wonderful letter from Paul. We could rightly suppose that the Christians at Ephesus sent to Laodicea asking for a copy of the letter. We might also suppose that this letter at Laodicea had no destination specified in verse 1, but rather had a blank space there, as some of our earliest manuscripts have a blank there. Laodicea was in a district notorious for earth-quakes, and it may well have been that all of Laodicea's archives were destroyed, and that, therefore, when churches needed or wanted a copy of "Laodiceans, " they were obliged to go to Ephesus to make a copy, for that would be where the

---

[18] It would be well to review what Tertullian (alluded to above) wrote against Marcion on this matter.

only copy survived. (2) The second suggested explanation was propounded by Harnack. First, he noted that in her later days, the church in Laodicea fell from grace. In Revelation 3:14-22, there is a letter from Jesus to the church in Laodicea which makes sad reading. In that letter the church in Laodicea is sadly and unsparingly condemned by the exalted Christ. Harnack thought it possible that after Revelation was written, folk would not go to Laodicea to get copies of Christian books. Instead, people would go to Ephesus, so the name of Ephesus became attached to the letter, since it had no other name within the text.

However, there is also evidence against this suggestion that Laodicea was the destination: (1) The liberties taken by Marcion with the canon and the canonical books show that little weight is to be attached to him. (2) There is not a single manuscript that reads "at Laodicea" in Ephesians 1:1. (3) If this letter were sent to Laodicea at the same time that Colossians was sent, and carried by the same messenger (Tychicus), it is hard to understand why the Laodicean brethren would be greeted in Colossians, and no greetings at all appear in the letter supposedly addressed particularly to them.

b. A second suggestion is that the letter was addressed *to the church at Ephesus*.[19] Proponents of this view are confident that: (1) Since it is possible to explain of the lack of historical allusions and salutations, these do not prove that others than the Ephesians were addressed. The Ephesians were not strangers to Paul when he wrote to them. Their conditions, their trials, their dangers were known to him; but he had been absent from them for the space of about six years. He had only heard of their steadfastness and faith during those six years. Only in those epistles written a short time after Paul left the churches do we find personal salutations. The time element is a possible reason for the difference in Ephesians. Might it not be quite possible that Paul may have kept individual relations in the background in this one letter, though he did not do so generally, so that the exalted teaching about the body of Christ might be the only thing seen? (2) The fact that the early church fathers, generally, speak of the letter as

---

[19] R.C.H. Lenski, *Interpretation of St. Paul's Epistles to the Galatians, Ephesians, Philippians* (Columbus, OH: Wartburg Press, 1946), p.331-336, strongly defends this position. C.E. Arnold, "Ephesians, Letter to the," in *DPL*, p.244, tells us that Hans Conzlemann, "Der Brief an die Epheser," in *Die Briefe an die Galter, Epheser, Philipper, Kolosser, Thessalonicher und Philemon* (Gottingen: Vandenhoeck and Ruprecht, 1976, pp. 86-124); J. Gnilka, *Der Epheserbrief* (HTKNT X/2 Frieburg: Herder, 1971), and A. Lindemann, *Der Epheserbrief* (Zurich: Theologischer Verlag, 1985) also defend the view that the letter was addressed specifically to the church at Ephesus.

written "to the Ephesians," suggests that the original destination was the church at Ephesus. (3) The reading "at Ephesus" is sufficiently supported at Ephesians 1:1 to be regarded as having been in the original autograph.[20] (4) The letter has been called "The Epistle to the Ephesians" since the middle of the second century when the title was likely first affixed.[21]

Objections to the view that the letter was originally sent specifically to Ephesus include the fact that it is not easy to explain why the best extant manuscripts of Ephesians at 1:1 do not carry "at Ephesus" if the letter was addressed to the Ephesians. The other objections which have been brought against the view that this epistle was really addressed to the Ephesians are summed up by Conybeare and Howson: (1) Why are there no personal greetings to a congregation he knew so well? (2) Would Paul have described the Ephesians as a church whose conversion he knew only by report (Ephesians 1:15)? (3) Would he speak to them as only knowing himself (the founder of their church) to be an apostle by hearsay (Ephesians 3:4)? (4) Would he describe the Ephesians as so exclusively as "Gentiles (Ephesians 2:11, 4:17), and so recently converted" (Ephesians 5:8, 1:13, 2:13)? (5) Would Paul write to Ephesus as if someone other than himself was the one who planted the church (Ephesians 2:20, 3:5)?[22]

c. The most probable of the three suggestions concerning the destination is that the letter originally was an *encyclical letter*, intended for the churches in the province of Asia Minor. Supporters of this view insist that it best accounts for the features in the letter itself that seem

---

[20] The reading "at Ephesus" is found in A, D, E, F, G, K, L, and all the ancient versions (e.g., the Latin, the Syriac). These translations must have been made from Greek manuscripts older than most of those we now have. "At Ephesus" is the *only* reading in *all* the ancient versions. "This may be one place to part company with those manuscripts (P[46], Vaticanus, Sinaiticus [which have "at Ephesus" missing]) and affirm the accuracy of the widely attested alternative tradition, that is, 'at Ephesus' was the original reading" (Arnold, *op. cit.*, p.244).

[21] Irenaeus (*Adv. Haer.* v.2.36) cites Ephesians 5:30 as being found in the Epistle to the Ephesians. Clement of Alexandria (*Strom.* iv.65) cites Ephesians 5:21-25 in the same way. Tertullian (*Adv. Marcion* v.11.17) also knew the letter as having been sent to Ephesus.

[22] W.J. Conybeare and J.S. Howson, *The Life and Epistles of St. Paul* (Hartford, CT: The S.S. Scranton Company, 1901), pp.762ff.

to be incompatible with a strictly Ephesian destination. With the omission of the words "at Ephesus" at 1:1, the letter is addressed to "saints who are faithful in Christ Jesus." Such folk could be found in any number of towns. That it was addressed to saints who lived in Asia is compatible with the fact that Tychicus (who carried the letter, Ephesians 6:21,22) was traveling to this area (Colossians 4:7-9). If Ephesians is a circular letter, it would explain why Paul does not include any greetings of a personal nature. What is written in 1:15 and 3:2,3 about the source of Paul's knowledge of the people being addressed fits the hypothesis of a circular letter addressed in many instances to churches with whom Paul was not personally familiar. This suggestion would also explain why Timothy is not mentioned as being with Paul since Timothy was not known to many of the churches in which the letter would be read.

The circular letter hypothesis helps explain the references in Colossians 4:15,16, where the Laodiceans were greeted, and also the instructions to the Colossians to get the letter that is coming from Laodicea. Why should folk at Colossae read the "epistle from Laodicea"? If it dealt with the peculiar needs of that sister church, this instruction would be inexplicable. But, if it were what "Ephesians" is – general in character and dealing with a truth not identical with the main truth of the Colossian epistle, but supplementary to it – then the direction to get the epistle from Laodicea is intelligible at once. The language "the letter that is coming from Laodicea" is wholly supportive of the suggestion that a letter circulating among the Asian churches, and we believe that letter which was circulating throughout the churches is our Ephesians.

Perhaps the strongest objection to Ephesians being a circular letter is this question: How would the letter come to have "at Ephesus" at Ephesians 1:1 if it were originally an encyclical with "at Ephesus" missing? The answer to this question requires us to reconstruct how all the Prison Epistles were first delivered to their intended readers. Three of the Prison Epistles (Ephesians, Colossians, and Philemon) are carried by Tychicus and Onesimus (a runaway slave who, after being converted to Christ by Paul, is returning to his owner). They are traveling together from Rome to Colossae.[23]   The first thing to be done would be to get Onesimus to Colossae before soldiers or slave catchers captured him.   If the ship on which Tychicus and Onesimus sailed landed at Miletus, they would have bypassed Ephesus, thus having no opportunity to deliver the Ephesian letter.   Traveling inland along the Meander River valley toward Colossae, they would come to the place where the Lycus River flowed into the Meander. Going up this valley, they would pass through Laodicea before coming to Colossae.   As they passed through Laodicea, they left the circular letter with the church there, and gave them instructions to send it on to the church at Colossae.[24]   Tychicus and Onesimus would have hurried on to Colossae, delivering the letters to the church at Colossae and to Philemon.   Seven of the churches of Asia named in Revelation 2-3 are listed in the order of their situation on the Roman postal road – Ephesus, Smyrna, Pergamum, Thyatira, Sardis, Philadelphia, and Laodicea.   Once the letter we call "Ephesians" was delivered to Colossae, Tychicus could take it and, following the circle of cities on the postal road, would finally arrive at Ephesus, where the letter, we suppose, was retained.   When the books composing the New Testament were collected into a volume, it would so happen that the autograph copy of the circular letter would be found in Ephesus, and thus designated as "Ephesians."   This is how, we suppose, the *title* "To the Ephesians" would come to be attached to the letter, since it was from Ephesus that copies would reach Christians generally.

A second objection to Ephesians being a circular letter is the matter of how the words "at Ephesus" came to be included in the text at Ephesians 1:1, if the words were not there in the autograph.   Two options present themselves.   One option is the suggestion that when the letter was written, a blank space was left where the destination would usually be specified.   As Tychicus carried the letter from place to place and read it aloud in the congregational meeting, he would ver-

---

[23] See the discussion in the Detailed Introduction to Colossians, "How were the prison epistles sent out?"

[24] It is more than likely, before sending the original on to Colossae, that the church at Laodicea made a copy of the letter for later use in their public assemblies.

bally supply the local place name where Paul had left a blank.[25] Since several important manuscripts lack not only the place name but also the preposition *en* ("in" or "at") as well. The other option is to treat the words "at Ephesus" as an interpolation made by some scribe who was making a copy of Paul's autograph letter which he found housed with the church in Ephesus.

6. When all the evidence is weighed, it would appear that the letter's original text was addressed in a very general way "to the saints who are also faithful in Christ Jesus." This would make the letter suitable for any Christian congregation whether in Asia or in other provinces, especially where Paul was not personally known.

C. AUTHORSHIP AND ATTESTATION

1. The importance of the study of authorship

Though thirteen letters in the New Testament have Paul's signature on them, the number of contemporary scholars denying the Pauline authorship of many of these letters is increasing. It is now rather common to read that some "Paulinist" (a lover of Paul) wrote this or that letter and signed Paul's name to it.[26] It is even claimed that such pseudonymity was an accepted phenomenon in the early church.

---

[25] "It is possible that originally there was a blank space for the bearer of the circular letter to insert the name of the particular community, but as yet, no parallel to this has been found in ancient Greek literature." (Joseph A. Grassi, "Ephesians" in the *Jerome Biblical Commentary* [Englewood Cliffs, NJ: Prentice Hall, 1968], p. 341). A. Skevington Wood, "Ephesians" in *Expositor's Bible Commentary* (Grand Rapids: Zondervan, 1978), Vol.11, p.11-12, lists objections to the idea Ephesians was a circular with a blank space where the address "at Ephesus" now occurs in our versions.

[26] Rather typical of the present-day denial of the Pauline authorship of Ephesians are these quotes: "Everything points instead to a later follower of Paul who used Colossians as the basis for his own reinterpretation of the Pauline gospel" (A.T. Lincoln, *Ephesians*, WBC 42 [Dallas: Word, 1990], p.lxvii). "The theology of Ephesians makes the Pauline composition of the letter completely impossible" (W.G. Kummel, *Introduction to the New Testament*, rev. ed., [Nashville: Abingdon, 1975], p.360). Or again, the author of Ephesians was "a well-known disciple and companion of Paul who published this letter under the apostle's aegis either during the apostle's final imprisonment or (more probably) after his death" (R.P. Martin, *Ephesians, Colossians, and Philemon*, Interpretation Commentaries [Louisville: John Knox, 1992], p.4).

Before passively accepting such claims, it would be well to consider some of the consequences inherent in the denial of the Pauline authorship. If Paul did not write Ephesians, it is a forgery. A forgery is a form of a lie. If Ephesians contains a lie as to who wrote it, it cannot be inspired of God, for God cannot lie (Titus 1:2). If Ephesians is not inspired of God, it is only human wisdom, and it just as likely to contain untruths as any other book written by human wisdom alone. A denial of the Pauline authorship opens the door for doubts about the apostolicity of the letter, its authoritativeness, and its truthfulness in what it affirms. This is a steep price to pay for denying the Pauline authorship. If in fact Paul did not write Ephesians, then all the autobiographical statements in the letter must immediately be branded as lies. Included are these:

1:1   – The book was not written by an apostle of Jesus Christ.

1:15-17– The claim of prayer for the church by Paul is a lie.

1:18   – Paul never prayed that the eyes of their heart might be enlightened.

3:1,2   – The addressees would have never heard of any stewardship given by God to Paul for their benefit.

3:4   – The addressees would have no way of knowing Paul's insight into the mystery of Christ.

3:7   – Paul indeed may have been made a minister of the gospel, but how can we know the same thing is true of the fictive author of this letter (if it is a forgery in Paul's name)?

3:14ff   – The prayer attributed to Paul would be a figment of the imagination.

4:1   – That Paul made any such entreaty as here specified would be seriously called into question.

4:17   – How could anyone affirm that Paul ever made such an affirmation as this verse claims?

5:32   – We would have no way to know whether the mystery about Christ and the church is actually a Pauline doctrine.

6:21,22–   We would have no solid evidence that it was Paul who sent Tychicus, since these are words put into Paul's mouth by the fictive author of this letter.

Now we begin to see the importance of studying authorship. Such a study will demonstrate that we are not required to surrender the apostolic authorship of Ephesians, nor need we be influenced to join in the skepticism about the supernatural source and authority of the books of the New Testament.

Detailed Introduction to Ephesians

2. Internal and external evidence concerning the authorship of Ephesians

a. *Internal evidence* for the Pauline authorship of Ephesians includes: (1) The author twice signs his name, "Paul" (1:1, 3:1); (2) The autobiographical information in Ephesians matches what we know about Paul from Acts, including his imprisonment (4:1) and the fact that he was the apostle to the Gentiles (3:1); (3) The frequent personal references to himself and his activities are incorporated into the body of his argument (cf. 3:3ff, 7-13; 4:1,17; 5:32; 6:19-22); (4) The portrait of Paul's apostolic ministry in Ephesians 3:2-13 is very like what we find in Romans 15:14-21 and Colossians 1:23-2:5.

b. The *external evidence* attesting to the Pauline authorship of Ephesians is unbroken and unassailable.[27] This external evidence consists of allusions, quotations, and canonical listings.

Allusions show that the letter existed and was used as authoritative, but do not name the book or the author. Such allusions include:

1) Clement of Rome (AD 96)

Scholars versed in early Christian literature acknowledge that Clement knew and used Ephesians. I Clement 46 includes the language "the one God, one Christ, one spirit of grace ... one calling" (cp. Ephesians 4:4-6).

1 Cl. 2.1 = Eph. 5:31	36.2 = Eph. 1:18
46.6 = Eph. 4:4-6	59.3 = Eph. 1:18

2) Ignatius (AD 115)

As noted above in the discussion of destination, whether *Ad Eph.* chap.xii is an allusion to Ephesians 1:1 is disputed. Alford says:

Ad Eph 1:1 = Eph. 5:1	*Ad Eph* 9:1 = Eph. 2:20-22
	Ad Smyrna 1:2 = Eph. 1:23, 2:16

---

[27] Aart van Roon, *The Authenticity of Ephesians* (Leiden: Brill, 1975) is a good defense of the Pauline authorship of Ephesians. Werner G. Kummell, who denies the Pauline authorship on internal grounds (p.360), admits that the Pauline authorship of Ephesians "is extraordinarily well attested in the early church" (*op. cit.*, p.357). Any commentator who would deny the Pauline authorship of Ephesians on internal arguments (and these are what contemporary denials are based on) certainly is obligated to give an adequate explanation why the external evidence for the Pauline authorship is believed to be false.

3) Polycarp (AD115)

"And it is expressed in these scriptures, 'Be ye angry and sin not';
and 'Let not the sun go down upon your wrath'" (*Ep. ad. Ppns.*
12.1) is an allusion to Ephesians 4:26. Other allusions include:

Ad Phil 1:3 = Eph. 2:5,8,9	1.2 = Eph. 4:2ff
	5:1= Eph. 5:25

4) Didache (AD 120)

Didache iv.9-11 = Eph. 6:5,9.	6.14 = Eph. 3:17
16.8-10 = Eph. 3:21,22, 17	6.11 = Eph. 2:10; 4.22

5) The Epistle of Barnabas (AD 130)

6.11 = Eph. 2:10	16:8-10 = Eph. 3:21,22
6.14 = Eph. 3:17	

Annotated quotations in early Christian literature are references that not
only quote a verse, but also make direct mention of the book by name, or
directly mention of the author's name. Annotated quotations include:

1) Irenaeus (AD 180)

"Even as the blessed Paul says in his epistle to the Ephesians, that
we are members of his body, of his flesh, and of his bones"
(Ephesians 5:30). (*Adv. Haeres 5.2.3*)

Adv. Haer. 1.8.5 = Eph. 5:13
5.14.3 = Eph. 1:7; 2:13,15

The letter Irenaeus references is ascribed to the apostle Paul and
is treated as authoritative.

2) Clement of Alexandria (AD 190)

"Wherefore [Paul] writes also in the epistle to the Ephesians, 'Be
ye subject one to another in the fear of God'" (Ephesians 5:21).
(*Stromata* iv.8)

Clement also writes, "Writing to the Ephesians, [Paul] has most clearly unfolded that which is sought for, in this manner, 'Till we all come into the unity of the faith and the knowledge of the Son of God, unto a perfect man, unto the measure of the stature of the fullness ...'" (Ephesians 4:13,14). (*Paedag.* 1.5)

3) Tertullian (AD 200)

See the material under "Destination" above.

4) B.F. Westcott (*Canon of the New Testament*) has shown that the epistle was quoted by the heretical and Gnostic writers – Ophites, Basilides, Valentinus, and others.

The Gnostic Valentinus refers to Ephesians 3:14-18 as *he graphe* (the Scripture).[28]

The Nag Hammadi Gnostic writings (from as early as the second century AD) have documents which quote verses from Ephesians as being the words of the great apostle Paul. For instance, Ephesians 6:12 is quoted in the *Hypostasis of the Archons* as from "the great apostle" (II.86.20-25). The same verse is cited in the *Exegesis of the Soul* (II.6.131) as the words of Paul.[29]

When a book appears in the *canonical listings*, it is a sign that a position of special authority and value was attributed to the book. As noted above, Marcion (AD 140) has the letter in his canon. He did not question the authenticity, but thought it was meant for other readers than the Ephesians; he called it "Laodiceans." The Muratorian Canon (AD 170) names *ad Ephesos* as *secunda* (line 51) among the epistles to seven churches written by Paul. Eusebius reports that the "fourteen epistles" of Paul (which must include Ephesians) are "manifest and clear" so far as their genuineness is concerned, and he classifies them among the "divine writings" that all confess (*homologoumena*) belong in the New Testament canon.[30] Ephesians is found in all the ancient versions, which is further

---

[28] Clement of Alexandria, *Stromata* vi.34.

[29] Arnold, "Ephesians" in *DPL*, p.241.

[30] Eusebius, *H.E.* iii.3.4-7.

evidence that it was held without doubt among the acknowledged books belonging in the Canon. It is very reassuring to find that Ephesians is one of the best attested of Paul's letters.[31]

3. A concise overview of higher criticism's denial of the Pauline authorship of Ephesians

This epistle has been regarded as written by Paul until the consensus was challenged at the turn of the 19th century.

At the turn of the 19th century, the rise of rationalistic criticism of the Bible led many to begin questioning the Pauline authorship of Ephesians on internal grounds. One of the first to question the Pauline authorship was W.M.L. de Wette (c. AD 1830). The early critics, using the manuscript evidence available at that time, had no reason to be suspicious of the text in the Textus Receptus that read "in Ephesus," nor the title "The Epistle to the Ephesians." But those two references gave rise to doubts about the letter's genuineness. It was deemed incredible that Paul could have written such an impersonal letter, devoid of personal references to people with whom he had labored three years. It was judged fallacious that Paul should write to the Ephesians in terms of only hearsay ("if indeed you have heard of the stewardship of God's grace which was given to me" [3:2] or "I too, having heard of your faith in the Lord Jesus" [1:15]). The critics then began to look for other evidences the letter might not be Pauline. They singled out the close relationship of Ephesians to Colossians, the long sentences in Ephesians, the peculiar phrase "His holy apostles and prophets" (3:5, cf. 2:20), and put forward vocabulary studies that seemed to produce many "non-Pauline" words in Ephesians.[32]

---

[31] A solid presentation of Pauline authorship of Ephesians has been made by D. Guthrie *(New Testament Introduction,* pp.490-508), by E.F. Harrison, and W.L. Lane, in their introductions to the New Testament. Peter T. O'Brien also concludes in favor of the Pauline authorship.

[32] DeWette concluded the epistle is a wordy expansion of Colossians and not to be attributed even indirectly to Paul (W.M.L. de Wette, *Einleitung in das Neue Testament* (Leipsig: Messner und Lünemann, 1826). Alford answers DeWette's objections to the Pauline authorship *(Alford's Greek Testament,* v.3, p.40-42). Meyer *(Einl.* p. 20 ff.) and Davidson also treat DeWette's objections in full *(Introduction to New Testament.* vol. ii. pp. 352–60). Baur in his *Paulus, der Apostel Jesu Christi,* pp. 417–57, also denied the Pauline authorship of both Ephesians and Colossians because he believed he found in the letters ideas and diction of Gnostic and Montanistic times. It was the outspoken denial of authenticity by F.C. Baur and his followers which has had the greatest influence on the subsequent course of scholarship.

Two of the most massive attacks on the Pauline authorship of Ephesians were made by Edgar J. Goodspeed in America and C. Leslie Mitton in England.[33] In fact, the number of scholars who believe that Paul did not write Ephesians is perhaps increasing.[34] Typical of what one reads in contemporary introductions to Ephesians are the conclusions of Ralph Martin, who argued that "a well-known disciple and companion of Paul [namely Luke] published this letter under the apostle's aegis either during Paul's final imprisonment or (more probably) after his death." He did so by gathering (from Romans, Corinthians, and Colossians) a compendium of Paul's teaching on the theme of Christ-in-His-church, to which body of teaching he added a number of liturgical elements (prayers, hymns, and confessions of faith) drawn from the worshiping life of the apostolic communities with which he himself was familiar. The purpose of the epistle was to show the nature of the church and the Christian life to those who came to Christ from a pagan heritage and environment, and to remind the Gentile Christians that Paul's

---

[33] Edgar J. Goodspeed authored two books which denied the Pauline authorship of Ephesians – *The Meaning of Ephesians* (Chicago: University of Chicago Press, 1933) and *An Introduction to the New Testament* (Chicago: University of Chicago Press, 1937). He offered twenty-one reasons why Paul (in his opinion) could not have written Ephesians. Donald Guthrie, "The Epistle to the Ephesians" in *Introduction to the New Testament* (Downer's Grove: InterVarsity, 1990 revised edition) has a rebuttal of many of the reasons Goodspeed proposed. C. Leslie Mitton also had two influential works – *The Epistle to the Ephesians* (Oxford: Clarendon Press, 1951), and "The Authorship of the Epistle to the Ephesians," *Exp.T* 67 (1955-56), p. 195-198. Mitton listed 12 objections to the Pauline authorship of Ephesians. Six of these principal objections are briefly listed by Danker, "Ephesians" in the *New ISBE* (Grand Rapids: Eerdmans, 1979), Vol.2, p.109,110.

[34] R.E. Brown (*An Introduction to the New Testament* [Doubleday, 1997], p.620) suggests that 80 percent of the recent commentaries on Ephesians deny the Pauline authorship. Among books published in the last half of the 20th century may be mentioned the following: Hans Conzlemann, *Der Brief an die Epheser in Die kleineren Briefe des Apostels Paulus* (Gottingen: Vandenhoeck and Ruprecht, 1962); James L. Price, *Interpreting the New Testament* (New York: Holt, Rinehart, and Winston, 1961); Howard Clark Kee and Franklin W. Young, *Understanding the New Testament* (Englewood Cliffs: Prentice Hall, Inc., 1957); John A. Allan, *The Epistle to the Ephesians* (London: SCM Press, 1959); Charles Masson, *L'Epitre de Saint Paul aux Ephesiens* (Paris: Delachaux et Niestle, 1953); George Johnston, "Ephesians, " in *The Interpreter's Bible Dictionary* (Nashville: Abingdon Press, 1962); Richard Heard, *An Introduction to the New Testament* (London: Adam and Charles Black, 1950); Francis W. Beare, "Ephesians" in *The Interpreter's Bible* (Nashville: Abingdon Press, 1953). W.G. Kummel wrote, "The theology of Eph. makes the Pauline composition of the letter completely impossible," *Introduction to the NT* (rev. ed., Nashville: Abingdon, 1975), p.360. A.T. Lincoln, having decided that Ephesians is literarily dependent on Colossians, regards Ephesians' use of Colossians as the primary reason to reject Pauline authorship for Ephesians. "Everything points ... to a later follower of Paul who used Colossians as the basis for his own reinterpretation of the Pauline gospel" (*Ephesians* in WBC 42, Dallas: Word, 1990, p. lxvii).

theology of salvation-history never disowned the Jewish background out of which the (now predominantly) Gentile church came.[35]

Once the Pauline authorship has been abandoned, scholarly debate turns to different concerns. One issue is now to decide whether Ephesians represents a later development of Christian thinking and ecclesiology, and whether these features of the letter place its composition in a period after Paul's lifetime and in the period of "early catholicism."[36] Scholars are more and more affirming that Ephesians contains a body of developed doctrine which places it in a period of time after Paul's death, and in a time when the church was growing in self-consciousness as an institutional organization.

Lest beginning Bible students be overwhelmed by contemporary arguments put forth against the Pauline authorship of Ephesians, it seems appropriate to present briefly some of the arguments used by scholars who have questioned the genuineness of Ephesians: *(1) Differences in language and style.* The number of *hapax legomena* (words that occur only once) are counted, with the result that 41 Greek words are found in Ephesians not found elsewhere in Paul's writings, and 36 Greek words are not found elsewhere in the New Testament. Nineteen other words are common only to Ephesians and Colossians. In addition to the *hapax legomena*, it is affirmed that in Ephesians certain vocabulary words are used with totally different meanings than when Paul used them. For example, the word "mystery" is said to be used in Ephesians 1:9 and 3:9 with a different meaning than it has in Colossians 1:26, 2:2, 4:3. Other words alleged to be used with different meanings are "dispensation" *(oikonomia)*, "reconciliation" *(apokatalasso)*, and "fullness" *(pleroma)*. Concerning style, there are many long sentences including numerous relative pronouns (e.g., 1:3-14; 1:15-23; 2:1-10; 3:1-6; 4:11-16) and participles (2:14-16; 4:18-19). Adjectives tend to be piled

---

[35] Ralph P. Martin, "Ephesians" in the *Broadman Bible Commentary* (Nashville: Broadman, 1971), p.126; and Martin, Ralph P., "An Epistle in Search of a Life-Setting," *ExpT* 79 (July 1968), p.296-320.

[36] "Early catholicism" is a term used by some New Testament scholars to designate the development they perceive in Christian thought and institutional organization which happened in the church after the death of the apostles. Congregational government went from local autonomy to Diocesian bishops whose hierarchical authority extended over numerous congregations in a given geographical area. Some scholars, who deny the apostolic authorship of the Pastoral Epistles, Ephesians, Colossians, and 2 Peter, believe they can find traces of this so-called early catholicism in those letters.

up, especially with reference to the attributes of God (1:19, 2:7).[37] *(2) The similarity of Ephesians to Colossians and to other Pauline letters.* Of the 155 verses in Ephesians, over one third are parallel to Colossians both in content and in order. The parallels found in Ephesians to other Pauline epistles besides Colossians bring the total of parallel material to over 85 percent of the verses in Ephesians. To some scholars, that's too much virtual "copying" for Paul to have been the author of Ephesians.[38] *(3) Alleged differences in doctrinal emphasis and content.* The emphasis in Ephesians is principally on the risen and exalted Christ, whereas in Paul's writings the emphasis was on Christ's death. In Ephesians, there is little reference to the second coming, a topic so prominent in Paul's writings. The picture given in Ephesians is that of a church growing and progressing in history, rather than of one waiting for the imminent return of Christ (e.g., 2:21-22; 4:12,13). The emphasis in Paul's letters is often on the local church, whereas in Ephesians the emphasis is on the universal body of Christ, over which Christ is the head. Argument has been made from 2:20 and 3:5 that the writer of Ephesians was a second-generation Christian looking back to the time when the church first received the good news and now reveres the memory of the founders.

What beginning Bible students need to be told is that there are important considerations that serve to counterbalance the impression made by these internal arguments against the Pauline authorship. *(1) It is solely on arguments drawn from internal evidence that the Pauline authorship is denied.* When new manuscript discoveries showed the possibility the letter was not originally addressed solely to the church at Ephesus, the primary evidence the critics had used to decide against its genuineness was no longer valid. That is when the critics turned to arguments based on vocabulary, style, and alleged internal inconsistencies. It appears there was a negative bias against the Pauline authorship that led many writers to search for arguments to support their negative views. *(2) Differences in language and style.* The number of *hapax legomena* in the New Testament must be compared to the number in other Pauline epistles of similar length. Galatians has 33, Philippians has 41, Colossians has 38. Indeed, 36 words occur in Ephesians and in no other Pauline epistle (the total is

---

[37] Erasmus (*Annotationes in Novum Testamentum*, 1519) was the first to note these features: long, ponderous sentences; many relative clauses; abstract nouns in profusion; the use of parallel phrases and clauses in close apposition (4:12ff); the piling up of synonyms (1:11, 1:19, 2:15, 4:23, 6:10) connected together by the use of the genitive case (1:19). (Ralph P. Martin, "Ephesians" in the *Broadman Bible Commentary* [Nashville: Broadman, 1971], p.127.)

[38] Greater details about the similarities between Ephesians, Colossians, and other Pauline epistles are given below under "Critical Problems."

44 if the Pastorals are not considered Pauline).   But most of these are concentrated in the specialized sections on the church as the bride of Christ (5:25-33) and the description of Christian armor (6:13-17).   There are 18 words not found elsewhere in the New Testament except in Paul's writings.   The word "mystery" is consistently used with its meaning of something not clearly revealed in Old Testament times, but now is.   What is also true is that several doctrines (not just one) now revealed by the apostles were a mystery in Old Testament times.[39]   *(3) The similarity of Ephesians to Colossians and other Pauline letters.* What we find in Ephesians and Colossians is similar to what we find in Romans and Galatians.   Both Romans and Galatians deal with justification apart from "works of the Law," precisely because two audiences needed similar teaching; one is not copied from the other.   Why not also suggest that Ephesians and Colossians likewise deal with one topic because the various readers needed this teaching?   Paul can write two letters covering substantially the same material. *(4) Alleged differences in doctrinal emphasis and content.*   Far from being a reminiscence of a previous generation of leaders, 2:22 and 3:5 are a presentation of apostolic authority by an apostle himself.   The term "holy" in 3:5 must not be confused with modern connotations.   Modern theologians believe doctrinal differences arose as part of an evolutionary change in the early church's theology, that theological concepts grew as the years passed.   This is very different from the belief that the apostles delivered a revelation from God.   We are very slow to affirm that Ephesians represents a more mature development of Pauline thought and theology, as though it were all something he thought up on his own and was unaided by the Holy Spirit.[40]

4. ***Conclusion*:   The internal and external evidence points to Paul as the author of this epistle**.

A summary of our study of the authorship of Ephesians is contained in these few words: For eighteen centuries, the internal and external evidence for the authorship of Ephesians (evidence stronger than for most any other book in the New Testament) led scholars to affirm the Pauline authorship of Ephesians. However, over the last two hundred or so years, some scholars, using arguments drawn solely from internal evidence,   have voiced a denial of the Pauline author-

---

[39] The commentary calls attention to the different truths that are called a "mystery."   In addition, attention will be given to the various words in Ephesians which the critics have argued are used with different meanings than the meaning Paul gave to the words.

[40] F.F. Bruce, "St. Paul in Rome 4:   The Epistle to the Ephesians," *BJRL* 49:2 (1967), p.303ff, has argued that ideas which are stated in outline in the earlier epistles are merely unfolded/developed and continued in Ephesians.

ship.   In this commentator's judgment, the presentation of those internal arguments alleged to disprove the Pauline authorship has not been even-handed.

All the ancient manuscripts and versions agree in stating Paul wrote the epistle.   All the Christian writers of the early centuries agree to the Pauline authorship of this letter. How could any man living in the 19th, 20th, or 21st centuries be better qualified to judge what Paul could have written in the 1st century than the Christian scholars who lived in the centuries near to the time of Paul?   Contemporary writers have failed completely to explain on what factual basis the historical evidence of the early centuries should now be branded as totally in error.   Until such evidence is produced, the proper thing to do is to continue to defend the Pauline authorship of Ephesians.

D. TIME AND PLACE OF WRITING

To a great extent, a decision about the date of composition depends, of course, on the view taken of the Pauline authorship of the letter. Treat it as written by some Paulinist, and dating the letter becomes pure speculation[41] and there is no way to know from where it was written.   Treat it as written by Paul while he was a prisoner (Ephesians 3:1, 4:1, 6:20), and the date that may be assigned to the writing is determined by the decision as to the place of writing. The traditional view is that the letter was written at Rome during Paul's first imprisonment there.[42]   The dates for the Paul's first Roman imprisonment are AD 61-63.

Acts 28:30 tells us Paul stayed two full years in his own rented quarters during his first imprisonment in Rome.   Roman jurisprudence had it that if a man's accusers did not come within 2 years, the case was dismissed, and the prisoner was free to go.   Philemon and Colossians, written at the same time and carried by the same messenger as was Ephesians (Ephesians 6:21,22; Colossians 4:7-9), show that Paul expected a soon release from prison (Philemon 22). Hence, these letters must have been written toward the close of that two-year imprisonment, i.e., AD 62 or 63.

---

[41] Until the discovery of P52 (the Ryland's Papyrus fragment of John's Gospel, dated at AD 125), higher critics (denying the Johannine authorship of the Gospel) proposed a mid-second century date for the 4th Gospel.   Many who denied the Pauline authorship of Ephesians would say (because of its high Christology, a Christology like that in John's Gospel) that Ephesians was written about the same time as the 4th Gospel was.   Now that it is possible to date John's Gospel late in the first century, it is not uncommon to find higher critics assigning a similar date to Ephesians (which they affirm is pseudonymous, not Pauline).

[42] See above, in the General Introductory Studies to these Prison Epistles.

E. OCCASION AND PURPOSE OF WRITING

A study of the historical allusions in Ephesians provides us with no stated occasion or purpose for the writing of Ephesians such as one finds in the other Prison Epistles. For example, Colossians was written in response to the disturbing news which Epaphras has brought to Paul, and its purpose was to combat some exceedingly dangerous religious ideas which were a deadly threat to the churches in the Lycus valley. Then there is the need to have the runaway slave Onesimus returned to Philemon. He had been befriended by Paul and had been led to become a Christian by Paul. The letter to Philemon is an appeal to Philemon on Onesimus' behalf. The letter to the Philippians is a thank-you letter for a missionary offering the Philippians have sent to Paul.

Since the historical allusions in Ephesians give us little help when we try to pinpoint Paul's purpose for writing, to ascertain his possible purpose we must attempt to tie together two things – Paul's overriding concerns at the time this letter was written, and the theme that pervades this whole letter. That theme is this: How the readers could contribute to a glorious church, a church that has no spot or wrinkle because the members are working to preserve the unity of the faith and are diligently practicing Christian morality, thus helping to ensure that the church would carry out God's mission for her in the world.

Paul spent his life teaching Gentiles that they could be Christians without also having to become Jewish proselytes. This was exceptionally displeasing to Jews generally, for they conceived the Mosaic Law to be binding upon all; the Jews were bitterly prejudiced against uncircumcised Gentiles who presumed to call themselves disciples of the Jewish Messiah. While Paul taught Gentile Christians to stand like a rock for their liberty in Christ, as he did in Galatians and Romans, yet he did not want them to be prejudiced against their Jewish fellow-Christians, but to regard them as brothers in Christ. Paul did not want to see two churches, a Jewish church and a Gentile church, but *one church*, with Jewish and Gentile believers one in Christ. His gesture in behalf of unity to the *Jewish* elements in the church was the great offering of money which he and his helpers carried from Gentile churches, at the close of his third missionary journey, to the poor saints in Jerusalem (Acts 21). His hope was that this demonstration of Christian love might cause Jewish Christians to feel more kindly toward their Gentile brethren. His gesture in behalf of unity to the *Gentile* elements in the church would be this epistle, written to congregations made up largely of Gentile converts, a letter in which he would exalt the oneness, universality, and unspeakable grandeur of the body of Christ, and would remind them of their privileges and responsibilities. Let them constantly endeavor to maintain the unity of the Spirit in the bond of peace (Ephesians 4:3).

F. OTHER CRITICAL ISSUES

1. **The similarity between Ephesians and Colossians has proven a problem to many.**

   a. There are many verses that are similar in the two books.

      1) Compare:

Colossians	1:10	Ephesians	4:1
	1:13		1:6
	1:18		1:22, 23
	1:16		1:10
	1:22		2:15, 16, 1:4, 5:27
	1:23		3:7
	1:24		3:1
	2:11		2:11
	2:13		2:1
	3:16		5:19, 20
	3:18		5:22ff

      2) The striking similarities are expressed in a number of ways by those who are commenting on them.

         –   It could be worded that there are only *four* passages in Colossians, except a few verses in chapter 1, not parallel-ed in Ephesians – 2:1-9, 2:16-22, 3:1-4, and 4:9-18.
         –   It could be worded that Ephesians contains *five* passages not parallel to anything in Colossians – 1:3-14, 3:14-21, 4:4-6, 5:22-33, and 6:13-17.[43]
         –   It could be worded that the fact that 83 words are found both in Colossians and Ephesians and only in those letters points to a special literary relationship between the two (i.e., one must be copied from the other). Moulton notes that in Colossians the margin of the ERV has seventy-two references to Ephesians but only eighty-eight to all of the

---

[43] See Julicher's *Introduction to the Literature of the New Testament*, p. 375ff.

other Pauline Epistles. Goodspeed wrote that "three-fifths of Colossians is reflected in Ephesians."[44]

3) Exactly opposite conclusions have been drawn from these similarities: One conclusion is that Ephesians is nothing but a "verbose enlargement" of Colossians.[45] The other conclusion is that Colossians is merely an abridged copy of Ephesians (which tacitly denies the inspiration of Colossians).

b. Before too much weight is given to the analogous expressions and sentiments, it should be noted that Ephesians and Colossians also exhibit dissimilarities which give each letter a character of its own.

1) There is a polemic tendency in Colossians (against the heresy). Ephesians does not have such a controversial aspect.

2) The doctrinal matters peculiar to Ephesians are remarkable:
   a) The statement of salvation by grace, chapter 2
   b) The prayer for the Ephesians, chapter 3
   c) The Christian panoply, chapter 6

3) A careful study shows repeatedly and unmistakably that these differences are not accidental; they arise from a fundamental distinction between the leading ideas in the two epistles. Ephesians is an exposition of the church as the body of Christ. Colossians is an exposition of the sole headship and true Deity of Christ.

c. *Conclusion of the matter*: For Paul to write similarly to two different audiences is not unheard of, especially if their circumstances required a similar communication. It has been shown that the two letters were written about the same time in Paul's life. They were addressed to the same geographical region. Assuming what has been documented – namely, that Ephesians was a circular letter intended for a number of congregations – the Ephesians letter deals with matters all the churches needed to consider. Colossians, written to a specific church

---

[44] Goodspeed, *Key to Ephesians*, p.8.

[45] Such a statement of course denies the inspiration of Ephesians. Arnold ("Ephesians," *DPL*, p.242) tells us that most scholars who see Ephesians as pseudonymous contend that it depends heavily on Colossians as its primary literary source (e.g., Lincoln, Schnackenburg, Lindemann, Mitton, et al.).

with specific problems, makes application of some of the key ideas included in the circular letter to give the Colossians directions concerning those specific problems.

2. **The relationship of Ephesians to the other Pauline epistles.**

a. Here is how the case is worded by those who would deny the Pauline authorship of Ephesians: It has been alleged that Ephesians reads like a "mosaic," implying that it is "shot through" with expressions from earlier Christian writings.[46] Goodspeed believed he found that out of 618 phrases into which Ephesians may be divided, 550 have unmistakable parallels in the other Pauline letters either in "word or substance." Although Mitton concedes that Goodspeed overstated the case, he still found 250 phrases in Ephesians that have parallels in other Pauline writings – an amount far in excess of a genuine Pauline epistle, he thought.

b. Barker has attempted to provide us with some balance in this matter.

To arrive at the totals of verbatim parallels between Ephesians and the other Pauline letters which Goodspeed and Mitton use, they include: "six parallels consisting of a single word, twenty eight phrases of two words, eighteen of three, and twelve of four. Of the twelve parallels counted which consist of more than five words, seven occur in Colossians, two are citations from the OT, two more are formulae benedictions, and one consists of a standard Pauline introduction formula."

"Neither Goodspeed nor Mitton exercised care to discover in their test book, Philippians, parallels to other Pauline epistles. ... If one counts the number of words in Ephesians that occur in phrases that have exact verbal correspondence with other Pauline writings, the total amount will be 148. If one makes a similar count of Philippians, the corresponding total will be 129. Considering the difference in length between the two books, the results are negligible. Moreover, if one subtracts the Colossians parallels from both books, Philippians is left with 123 instances of verbatim likenesses compared to 115 in Ephesians."

---

[46] See Ernst Kasemann, p.289.

Barker concludes by saying, "The evidence indicates that although there is a remarkable relation between Ephesians and Colossians, there is nothing at all unusual concerning the relation of Ephesians to the other Pauline epistles."[47]

3. Concerning the relation between Ephesians and 1 Peter

Bible students have observed resemblances and similarities between Ephesians and 1 Peter,[48] especially when the following verses are compared.

Ephesians 1:3	1 Peter 1:3
Ephesians 6:14	1 Peter 1:13
Ephesians 1:4	1 Peter 1:20
Ephesians 1:20, 21	1 Peter 3:22

Further, the injunctions to slaves, husbands, and wives in 1 Peter and in Ephesians are quite similar. The verses are enough alike that some scholars have argued for literary dependence, some attempting to show that Peter is a copy of Ephesians, or others that Ephesians is a copy of Peter.

We think it likely that Peter has seen copies of these Pauline letters. In 2 Peter 3:15,16 we have evidence that Paul's letters have already been collected, and even Peter's readers are acquainted with them, just as he is. Why should not apostles study the writings of other apostles as Daniel had studied the writings of other prophets (Daniel 9:2)? Even though it is likely Peter has seen Paul's letters, we are not making a case for literary dependence, nor are we using such alleged dependence to try to make a case for the denial of apostolic authorship either of Peter or Ephesians. But we are affirming this: since both Paul and Peter were apostles of Jesus, we could expect both to present the same Christian doctrine. Why could not the Holy Spirit have inspired both men to write similar things, whether or not Peter had ever seen Paul's letters?

---

[47] G.W. Barker, "Ephesians, Letter of Paul to the," *Zondervan Pictorial Encyclopedia of the Bible*, edited by Merrill C. Tenney (Grand Rapids: Zondervan, 1978), Vol.2, p.318.

[48] For further details on this critical matter, see Abbott's notes in *International Critical Commentary*, p.xxiv-xxix.

4. Which letter (Colossians or Ephesians) was written first?

"As to the order in which the two epistles were written, it cannot well be ascertained."[49]   Since we are not trying to establish a case for literary dependence (i.e., is Colossians an abbreviation of Ephesians, or is Ephesians an expansion of Colossians?), we would not pay much attention to this question, save for the delightful attempts at reconstructing how the Prison Epistles came to be written, each depending somewhat on which letter is thought to have been written first.

a. Arguments that Colossians was written first -- and reconstructions based on that hypothesis:

Following are some of the arguments used[50] to show that Colossians was written first: (1) When comparison is made of Ephesians 6:21 with Colossians 4:7, we find in the Ephesians verse the conjunction "*also*" which is not found in the Colossian verse.   Ephesians reads, "That you *also* may know my affairs, how I am doing, Tychicus ...."   It is inferred from the word "also" that Colossians had already been written, and so they knew of Paul's affairs (at least in Paul's mind they did, for, it is affirmed, Tychicus had already told them of his affairs).   When next he writes Ephesians, he thinks "you *also* may know my affairs."   (2) The epistles to Philemon and Colossians must have been written about the same time because Onesimus, who carried the former to his old master, went with Tychicus (who was carrying Colossians) from Rome to Colossae.   Since we learn from Ephesians 6:21,22 that Tychicus was the bearer of the letter called "Ephesians," that letter must have been written very shortly, perhaps a few days (it is argued), after that to the Colossians.   (3) Since Colossians was called forth to meet a specific situation in Colossae, it is sometimes asserted that Colossians was written first because the similar ideas found in Ephesians are always expressed in an "unmistakable fullness of language" as compared to the compact brevity of Colossians.

---

[49] See Samuel Davidson, *New Testament Introduction* (London: Samuel Bagster and Sons, 1849), Vol. 2, p. 346ff.

[50] That Colossians was written first is maintained by L. Cappellus, J.J. Lange, DeWette, Neander, Harless, Olshausen, Steiger, Wiggers, Meyer, Wieseler, and others including Alford, Ellicott, Davidson, Weed, Bruce, and Barclay.   Apparently also Lewis Foster held that Colossians was written first, for this was the order of epistles studied in Foster's New Testament Introduction class at the Cincinnati Bible Seminary -- Colossians, Philemon, Ephesians, Philippians.

Reconstructions of how the Prison Epistles came to be written – based on the priority of Colossians – are similar to Barclay's note (here reproduced) on the "Quintessence of Paul."

> If Ephesians is an encyclical letter, and we believe that it is, Ephesians is Paul's supreme letter. We have seen that Ephesians and Colossians are very close to each other. We believe that what happened was that Paul wrote Colossians to deal with a definite situation and a definite outbreak of heresy. In so writing, he was led to use this great expression of the all-sufficiency of Christ. He said to himself, "This is something that I must get across to all men;" so he took the matter he had used in Colossians; he removed all the local and temporary and the controversial aspects of it; and he wrote a new letter to tell all men of the all-sufficient Christ. Ephesians, as we see it, is the one letter Paul sent to all the eastern Churches to tell them that the destined unity of all men and of all things could never be found except in Christ, and to tell them of the supreme task of the Church -- the task of being Christ's instrument and body in the task of world-wide and universal reconciliation of man to man, and of man to God. That is why indeed Ephesians is the Queen of the Epistles.[51]

b. **Arguments that Ephesians was written first** – and reconstructions based on that hypothesis:

Following are some of the arguments used[52] to show Ephesians was written first: (1) The words "you also" in Ephesians 6:21 refer to all the congregations to whom this circular letter was delivered. It says exactly nothing about information people might receive in some other epistle about Paul's situation. (2) Paul has not included Timothy's name after his own in Ephesians 1:1, as he does in the epistles he wrote (Colossians 1:1 and Philippians 1:1 and 2:19) when that faithful friend was at his side. Prior to Paul's first Roman imprisonment, Timothy is last mentioned in Acts in 20:4, as a helper carrying the offering to Jerusalem. The argument is that Ephesians must have been written before Timothy arrived in Rome.   Having completed some errand, Timothy arrives in

---

[51] William Barclay, "The Quintessence of Paul" in "The Letters to the Galatians and Ephesians: in the *Daily Study Bible* (Philadelphia: Westminster, 1958), p.83. The expression "The Quintessence of Paulinism" was the title of a lecture by A.S. Peake, *BJRL* 4 (1917-18), pp.285-311. Henry Alford, "Prolegomena". The Epistle to the Colossians" in *Alford's Greek Testament* (London: Rivingtons, 1871), vol.3, p.41,42 also has a reconstruction of the apostle's meditations and desires in the light of the priority of Colossians. It is troubling to this commentator to find that reconstructions based on the priority of Colossians tend to make Ephesians merely the human product of the mind of Paul, rather than also being the product of revelation and inspiration. The unacceptable result of this is that Ephesians tends to be ignored as being of little importance to Christian thought and practice.

[52] That Ephesians was written first was the opinion of Theodoret, Usher, Lightfoot, Burton, Braune (Lange's Commentary).

Rome, and Colossians (Colossians 1:1) and Philippians (Philippians 1:1) were written. It has even been suggested that Timothy and Epaphras arrived in Rome together just after Ephesians had been written.[53]   (3) There is expressed in Ephesians no anticipation of being soon released from his imprisonment such as one finds in Philemon 22 and Philippians 1:12-14, and 4:22. So the argument is made that Paul's circumstances when Ephesians was written were different from when Philemon and Philippians were written at a later time.[54]   (4) The simple fact that Tychicus carries both Ephesians and Colossians is no proof that Ephesians was written after Colossians. What is wrong with the idea that Ephesians was already written before Colossians – could they not still both be carried by Tychicus?   (5) Another argument is derived from the second chapter of Colossians, where the worshiping of angels and other matters are introduced that were not included in Ephesians; whence it is concluded that after writing Ephesians, Paul received information which he did not possess when he wrote that circular letter.

A reconstruction of how the Prison Epistles came to be written – based on the priority of Ephesians – would look like this: Paul's third missionary journey (Acts 18:1-21:17) ended with the delivery of the offering to the saints in Jerusalem -- an attempt to show the Jewish Christians that Gentile Christians loved them and to win love and respect of the Jewish believers for their Gentile brothers. The offering was well received (Acts 21:17). However, before this visit to Jerusalem was completed, Paul was falsely accused by Jewish unbelievers who stirred up a mob, and which would have killed Paul had he not been rescued by Roman soldiers and put in protective custody. Political intrigue and corruption resulted in Paul's being kept in custody for two years at Caesarea. Appeal of his case to

---

[53] Elsewhere in this Detailed Introduction to Ephesians we have offered the suggestion that it is because Ephesians is a circular letter, going to churches where Timothy was not known, that his name is not included at Ephesians 1:1. Davidson (*op. cit.*, p. 347) argues that the absence of the name in Ephesians is no argument at all that Timothy was not present with Paul. After all, there are amazingly few historical references in Ephesians. Onesimus, who accompanied Tychicus, is even omitted from Ephesians (cp. Ephesians 5:21,22 and Colossians 4:7-9). All individual and personal allusions are lacking in the Ephesian letter; therefore, Timothy's name is quite consistently suppressed.

[54] There are several weaknesses in this argument. One is that there is no expressed anticipation of release apparent in the epistle to the Colossians, which was written and sent at the same time Philemon was. That Ephesians and Colossians were written with little time between their composition is required by the fact that both were carried to their destinations at the same time by same messenger. The other weakness is that Philippians may well have been written from a later time in Paul's imprisonment (as indicated by the word "shortly" in Philippians 2:24, "I trust ... that I myself also shall be coming shortly") than were the other three, and this fact would have no bearing on the order of writing for Ephesians and Colossians.

Caesar led to a voyage to Rome, and then to Paul's being under house arrest in Rome as he waited for his trial.

As the months of waiting passed, Paul had little contact with any of the already-established churches. What will happen to those congregations when he and the other apostles and prophets are no longer present in the world, and how will the churches be encouraged to be congregations which will bring honor to Jesus? What they needed to guide them is a carefully composed presentation on the general theme of the glorious church, and especially about God's plan and purpose for the church that Jewish and Gentile believers be one body in Christ.[55] Taking advantage of his house arrest, Paul set about to write a positive exposition of the Christian world view – a succinct summary of key teachings he has presented since he received revelations from Jesus and began preaching the gospel. Paul has just finished writing Ephesians, and was about to send it, when Epaphras arrives from Colossae with news about the church there and the heresy that was beginning to trouble it. Paul immediately writes the Colossian epistle, making application of the universal truths (enunciated in Ephesians) to the special necessities of the Colossian church.[56] Onesimus, at this time, recently having become a Christian, decides to return to his old master and seek forgiveness, so a letter is hurriedly penned to Philemon, and this too is carried by Tychicus and Onesimus as they journey toward Asia with the three letters – Ephesians, Colossians, and Philemon.

G. EPHESIANS IN THE HANDS OF CONTEMPORARY INTERPRETERS

Every time the current popular philosophy changes, a whole new set of commentaries soon appears, in which it is attempted to show that the Bible matches current popular philosophy, and that current popular emphases have much to offer when it comes to the interpretation of Bible passages. Early in the 20th century, Kant's existentialism led to Neo-orthodoxy. Then Heideggar's exi-

---

[55] This language about Ephesians being a "carefully composed presentation" does not rule out Paul's receiving ideas by revelation and writing them down by inspiration. We must not forget that his job as an apostle was to unfold the mystery that God had commissioned the apostles to make known to the world.

[56] We think that Paul would hardly delay sending a letter to Colossae in order to take time to compose Ephesians. But he could write Colossians quickly, including the statement about Tychicus which had already been written at the close of Ephesians, for now Tychicus would have two letters to deliver. So, while which letter was written first is a matter of conjecture, this commentator leans to the idea of the priority of Ephesians.

stentialism led to Neo-liberalism. As the 21ˢᵗ century begins, post-modernism is leading to a number of new approaches to the study of the Scriptures.

1. Genre

We have no problem with identifying the particular form or "genre" of any piece of literature – since such identification plays a significant role in the interpretation of that literature. For example, when we have a newspaper in hand, we tend to treat a news article differently than we do a piece that is labeled as an editorial. We treat cartoons on the editorial page differently than we do pictures in the sports section. If we are watching a movie, a documentary and a western are not given the same credibility. If we have a book in hand, it helps us to know if it is fiction or nonfiction. Genres (what "kind" or "sort" is it?) are categories based on some set of stylistic criteria. Who benefits from such categorization of things? Audiences, most certainly.

Emphasis on the identification of genre flourished when humanism was the popular philosophy. Then the attempt to identify what genre Ephesians is became a standard part of Biblical studies. Predictably, when certain genres were advocated for Ephesians, along with that came the mental impression on the readers that the material was not true or authoritative.

We are accustomed to speak of "the epistle to the Ephesians," thus identifying the genre as being that of a first-century letter. A challenge to this genre is found in the details contained within the writing itself. Bible critics believed they could identify a number of items – such as hymns, creedal confessions, stereotyped liturgical formulas – that did not fit in the genre of a typical letter of antiquity. Consequently, it is not unusual to find it now proposed by some that the work is a theological tract,[57] or by others as a wisdom discourse,[58] or a written homily.[59] If proponents of these different genres also deny the Paul-

---

[57] E. Kasemann ("Epheserbrief" in *Religion in Geschichte und Gegenwart*, 2:517-520) described it as a "theological tract" merely dressed up like a letter. So did R.H. Fuller, *A Critical Introduction to the New Testament* (London: Duckworth, 1966), p.66.

[58] H. Schlier, *Der Brief an die Epheser* (Dusseldorf: Patmos, 1957) p.21, called it a "wisdom discourse," focusing on the role of Christ as personified wisdom.

[59] Moffatt (*Introduction to the Literature of the New Testament*, p.373ff) treated it as a homily rather than a letter. A.T. Lincoln ("Ephesians" *WBC*, 42, p.xxxix) characterizes it as "the written equivalent of a sermon or homily." "The Homily Called Ephesians" is the title of Ben Witherington's commentary on Ephesians in his book *The Letters to Philemon, the Colossians and the Ephesians: A Socio-Rhetorical Commentary on the Captivity Epistles* (Grand Rapids: Eerdmans, 2007).

ine authorship of the work, those two factors certainly dissuade us (the audience) from attaching any idea to "Ephesians" that it might be a word from the Lord. This is lamentable.

Because Ephesians retains many conventions of the Pauline letter form, it is probably best explained as an actual letter,[60] which was intended to be read aloud to assembled congregations of Christians, just as the letters to the Romans, Corinthians, and Galatians were.

2. Life-Setting

Both Neo-orthodox and Neo-liberal scholars attempted to show that there are three levels of material in the New Testament writings. The first level included what Jesus actually said and did, of which we know very little. The second level was supposed to be what the apostles actually said and did, after they had modified and adapted what Jesus taught. We also know very little of this level, it was claimed. The third level, which supposedly we have in the books of our New Testaments, is what the early church said and did after the apostles had all died, and after the church had modified and adapted what the apostles had told them. It became very popular to search for clues in our New Testament books for the life-setting in the early church that led to their keeping and editing the material that had come to them in the way it now appears in our Bibles.

What is the supposed life-setting (*Sitz im Leben*) for Ephesians? Of course, one's view on the authenticity of the letter has a significant impact on how this question is answered. Those who deny that Paul wrote this letter have not been able to agree on the life-setting.[61] Goodspeed, Knox, and Mitton argued that Ephesians was a general letter written toward the end of the first century as an introduction to the collected letters of Paul. N.A. Dahl supposed Ephesians was a tract written for the newly baptized Gentile Christians to remind them of the implications of their faith and baptism. The opening prayer sounds like a benediction given before a baptismal service; chapter 2 is practically a baptismal homily; and chapters 4-6 include catechetical instructions particularly pertinent

---

[60] Arnold, *op. cit.*, p.240.

[61] See R.P. Martin, "An Epistle in Search of a Life-Setting," *ExpT* LXXIX (1968), p.297. Martin has a later article titled "Reconciliation and Unity in Ephesians" published in *Review and Expositor* 93 (1996), p.203-235. We have already summarized Martin's views in a paragraph above.

for the newly baptized.[62]   R. Schnackenburg described Ephesians as a first-century letter, rather than a tract or a sermon.   He sees it as "a theologically-based, pastorally-oriented" pseudonymous letter written to a circle of churches in Asia Minor around AD 90 addressing two contemporary and pressing concerns: the internal unity of each of the congregations and the need for a distinctively Christian lifestyle in a pagan environment.[63]   Lincoln, who supposes the letter is written after the death of Paul, reconstructs the situation on this fashion: the readers have lost the apostle as a unifying source of authority and so are lacking a sense of community cohesion.   The pseudonymous letter was written to fill the void.[64]

3. A proliferation of new methods and approaches

During the latter half of the twentieth century, "a growing number of New Testament scholars have chafed under what has been perceived to be the restrictive and inadequate paradigm of the historical-critical methodology."[65] Some would jettison the historical-critical method altogether in favor of structuralism, while others sought to build upon the historical-critical method by developing ways to move beyond the restrictions and inadequacies.   After such disciplines became popular in the state colleges and universities about the middle of the 20th century, Biblical studies have been influenced by an influx of methodologies which were borrowed from sociology, cultural anthropology, rhetoric (ancient and modern), modern linguistics, political science, women's studies, and literary criticism.   Briefly we introduce three of these attempts.

a. Rhetorical Criticism

Since James Muilenburg, in his 1968 SBL Presidential address, urged Bible scholars to move beyond form criticism to what he called "rhetorical criticism,"

---

[62] N.A. Dahl, "Gentiles, Christians, and Israelites in the Epistle to the Ephesians" *HTR* 79 (1986), p.38.

[63] R. Schnackenburg, *The Epistle to the Ephesians* (Edinburgh: T&T Clark, 1991), p.22-35

[64] A.T. Lincoln, *Ephesians,* Vol. 42 in *WBC* (Dallas, TX: Word, 1990), p.lxxxv-lxxxvii.

[65] M.R. Mulholland, "Sociological Criticism," in Black and Dockery's *New Testament Criticism and Interpretation* (Grand Rapids: Zondervan, 1991), p.299.

a flood of works has appeared.[66] Nevertheless, "the application of rhetorical criticism to New Testament documents is still in its infancy stage, so very little has yet been written on Ephesians from this perspective. A noteworthy beginning is A.T. Lincoln's commentary on Ephesians ('Ephesians,' *WBC* 42, Dallas: Word, 1990), which attempts to observe the rhetorical purpose of the flow of thought throughout the letter. He concludes that the writer combines the epideictic and the deliberative rhetorical genres (Lincoln, xli-xlii)."[67]

In the ancient Greco-Roman world, rhetoric was the art of persuading audiences by persuasive public speaking. Aristotle's *The Art of Rhetoric* (4th century BC) was the first definitive exposition of rhetoric in the ancient world. Romans like Cicero (c. 87 BC), Caecilius (c. AD 92), and Quintillian (c. AD 96) also contributed to the refinement and dissemination of rhetoric throughout the Roman world. Early in the 1900s the study of classical rhetoricians such as Aristotle and Cicero enjoyed a resurgence of interest, particularly within American universities. These studies have shown that, according to Aristotle, a discourse which is designed to persuade usually begins with an *exordium*, an introduction which serves to elicit the sympathy of the audience; possibly a *narratio*, a narrative section which serves as a statement of facts; and these are often associated with a *digressio*, a digression which is thematically linked to the proposition(s) of the central argument. Then follows the *partitio*, or summary of the argument/proof, before the *probatio*, the argument proper. Then follows a *peroratio*, a summary of the main themes, often with an *exhortatio*, a concluding exhortation. Roman teachers of rhetoric, like Quintillian, Cicero, and Caecilius, built upon and modified Aristotle's earlier work. For example, Cicero viewed the production of rhetoric (that is, the construction of a persuasive speech) as involving five elements: firstly *invention* (choosing a topic); secondly *arrangement* (how the parts are ordered); thirdly *style* (figures of speech, etc.); fourthly *memory* (memorizing the elements of the speech); and fifthly *delivery* (the actual giving of the speech before a live audience). Cicero insisted that the speaker (known as the 'rhetor') should progress through these five activities in order when preparing a speech, and when delivered, only if all five elements were deliberately included, would a speech be coherent and as persuasive as the circumstances might permit.

---

[66] *Rhetorical Criticism and the Bible*, ed. by Stanley E Porter and Dennis L. Stamps (London: Sheffield Academic Press, 2002), can serve as a helpful introduction to this area of study.

[67] C.E. Arnold, "Ephesians, Letter to the," in *Dictionary of Paul and His Letters* (Downers Grove, IL: InterVarsity, 1993), p.239-240.

Three kinds of rhetoric are described: forensic, deliberative, and epideictic. "*Forensic* speech defends or accuses someone regarding past actions; *deliberative* speech exhorts or dissuades the audience regarding future actions; *epideictic* discourse affirms communal values by praise or blame in order to affect a present evaluation. These three rhetorical genres seek different kinds of response from the audience. Forensic: Is it just? Deliberative: Is it expedient? Epideictic: Is it praiseworthy?"[68]

Many commentators today argue that Paul used the rhetorical style of his day, and that it is helpful for us as we try to interpret Paul's writings to be acquainted with ancient rhetoric. However, Ephesians has proven difficult to classify.[69] In addition to this fact, there are other reasons to be hesitant about using rhetorical criticism in an attempt to interpret Paul's letters. First, if rhetorical criticism is viewed as a tool which enables a New Testament interpreter to detect authorial intent in the original text through the analysis of classical patterns of persuasion and argumentation, then perhaps it would be useful. But as post-modernism influences the critics, rhetorical criticism is no longer interested in authorial intent. Rather the emphasis has now become to discover the meaning in the text as received by any reader, or to deconstruct the text into the oppositions or ambiguities that in post-modern thought are regarded as always already present in any attempt to control language. This whole process leaves us with no inspired word from the Lord. Second, Paul himself insisted that his preaching was not marked by the use of persuasive rhetoric (1 Corinthians 1:17-2:3), and his speeches in Acts do not reflect the categories of Greco-Roman rhetoric. Should we expect, then, to find his letters consciously displaying such rhetoric? Rhetoric was a recognized tool for public speaking, not letter writing. Third, O'Brien points out that the early church fathers, *who were trained in*

---

[68] G.W. Hansen, "Rhetorical Criticism," in *Dictionary of Paul and His Letters* (Downers Grove, IL: InterVarsity, 1993), p.822,23.

[69] The letter has a long theological section (chapters 1-3), and then a long section of exhortation (chapters 4-6). Some have attempted to show that the letter to the Ephesians is an epideictic piece of rhetoric. Indeed, chapters 1-3 might be treated as praise, praise to God for the deeds he has done through Jesus Christ on behalf of humanity, as explicitly demonstrated in the church. But what about chapters 4-6? "In Ephesians ... the praise is much less specific and the appeals are much more extensive than in typical 'letters of praise' (*epainetikai*; S.K. Stowers, *Letter Writing in Greco-Roman Antiquity* [Philadelphia: 1986], p.77-85). Moreover, the writers of epideictic letters ordinarily understood themselves as either inferior or equal to those whom they addressed (Stowers, 1986, p.79) – which is by no means the case in Ephesians, where much is made of Paul's unique status and role (chap. 3)" (Victor P. Furnish, "Ephesians" in *ABD*. II. p.536).

rhetoric, did not interpret Paul in light of rhetorical theory.[70]   Why then should we think this is going to be a helpful tool?   "The notion that 'this method better than any other holds the hermeneutical key that will unlock the true meaning of the apostles writings' is seriously flawed."[71]

b. Social-Science Criticism

Social-scientific criticism, which has roots in form criticism's search for the "life-setting," is an exegetical method that attempts to explore the original social and cultural setting of a text through clues embedded in the text, and by constructing models that simplify and systematize the data for comparative purposes.   Emphasis in this method is less on the individual author and more on the social community within which the author lived and communicated, because meaning (in a post-modern worldview) is understood as a socially-constructed phenomenon.   Models of social phenomena in the Mediterranean world – such as kinship and family, honor and shame, patronage and clientage, social status, the evil eye, purity and pollution, food and table fellowship, ritual, gender and sexuality, haves and have-nots – are emphasized.[72]

Social-scientific criticism as a method of Bible study began taking shape roughly at the same time as the interest in rhetorical analysis was growing, and for the same reason – namely, the growing dissatisfaction with the then-current methods of Biblical studies, such as form and redaction criticism and Bultmann's demythologization, all of which failed as a means of understanding the phenomena of early Christianity.   Sociology as an academic discipline had begun being taught in the universities about 1890. Within a hundred years from this beginning, scholars such as John Elliott, Gerd Theissen, John Gager, Wayne Meeks, Abraham Malherbe, Bruce Malina, and others began using sociological models in an attempt to describe

---

[70] Peter T. O'Brien, *The Letter to the Ephesians* in the Pillar New Testament Commentary series (Grand Rapids: Eerdmans, 1999).

[71] J.A.D. Weima, "Rhetorical Criticism" in *Handbook of Classical Rhetoric*, edited by Stanley Porter (Leiden: Brill, 1997), p.468.

[72] David A. DeSilva, *Honor, Patronage, Kinship & Purity: Unlocking New Testament Culture* (Downers Grove: InterVarsity, 2000).

the social world of the Bible.[73]   In 1979, Elliott and Malina began a working relationship, in which was planted the seed that would later sprout as the Context Group, the name chosen in 1990 for a group of international scholars, who emerged from earlier associations in the Society of Biblical Literature and the Catholic Biblical Association, and who are committed to the use of the social sciences in Biblical interpretation.[74]

Elliott and Malina offer three common sociological conclusions to illustrate the results obtained using this method in Biblical studies: (1) Ancient Mediterranean cultures were honor/shame cultures.   Ethics were based largely on peer pressure, on whether the person brought honor or shame to the group.   (2) These cultures had a perception of "limited good" – that one can gain only if another person loses.   (3) Early Christian groups had characteristics of marginalized sects, and their theological views were shaped by their social situation.   Stephen Barton critiques Elliott: "It appears rather one-sided to represent conversion and subsequent Christian instruction as the product of underlying social forces of marginalization, when it appears more

---

[73] In 1979 John Elliot presented a paper to the Catholic Biblical Association of America surveying the growing scholarly interest in social-scientific interpretation of the Bible. He noted, in particular, the work of Gerd Theissen entitled *Sociology of Early Palestinian Christianity* (translated by John Bowden [Philadelphia: Fortress Press, 1978]). After surveying the literature up to that point Elliott proposed a method he termed "sociological exegesis." He demonstrated this methodology in his 1981 publication of *A Home for the Homeless: A Sociological Exegesis of 1 Peter, Its Situation and Strategy* (Philadelphia: Fortress Press, 1981). This work has been followed by a virtual tidal wave of works seeking to interpret the Bible from a social-scientific model. The most prolific writers in this new movement have been Bruce Malina, Jerome Neyrey, and John Pilch. Elliott himself published *What is Social-Scientific Criticism?* (Minneapolis: Fortress Press, 1993). Bruce Malina and John Pilch produced a book titled *Social-Science Commentary on the Deutero-Pauline Letters* (Philadelphia: Fortress Press, 2013). This commentary on the text of what the authors affirm are Deutero-Pauline letters provides a contextual approach to the study of Colossians, Ephesians, and 2 Thessalonians that is thoroughly grounded in the original audience's ancient socio-cultural setting.   According to the publisher's blurb, this volume provides essential "reading scenarios" on specific cultural phenomena in these letters, including forgery, normative conflict, *paideia* (training), and household codes. The "reading scenarios" sections present the perspective of the original audience drawn from anthropological studies of the Mediterranean social system, offering clues for filling in the unspoken or implicit elements of the writing as a Mediterranean reader would certainly have done.   This volume also presents what the authors call "the transformation of the memory of Paul" in early Christianity that, in the authors' reconstruction of things, reflects the concerns and interest of the Pauline communities after Paul's death which, supposedly, in turn led to the production of these "deutero-Pauline letters."

[74] In 1991 The Context Group published *The Social World of Luke-Acts: Models for Interpretation*, edited by Jerome H. Neyrey (Peabody, MA: Hendrickson, 1991). In 2008 the Group published *The Social World of the New Testament: Insights and Models* (Peabody, MA: Hendrickson, 2008), edited by Neryey and Eric C. Stewart.

likely that the marginalization of the Christians is the result of their conversion and distinctive lifestyle."[75]

Other critiques of social-science criticism have been articulated.[76] (1) Sociology, like other sciences, tends to favor naturalistic explanations even if they contradict the text. (2) Some commentators have tended to discard Biblical teachings on the basis that it had a specific function in its original setting, while our cultural situation is very different. (3) The models used by social-science critics are not universally accepted. Sociological models based on modern third-world cultures may not apply so easily to ancient Mediterranean cultures, and yet this is how the models are constructed. (4) The underlying presupposition that the New Testament documents were the products of the early church (rather than being attributed to the apostles themselves) is flawed. Susan Garrett has observed, "One cannot take it for granted that documents were always *products* of communities."[77] (5) The discipline of sociology (to explain why people cannot get along with one another) began late in the 19th century after the Biblical doctrine of sin had been rejected. How astounding that it has now become a tool to explain the Bible.

c. Socio-Rhetorical Criticism

The merger of rhetorical criticism (previously called "narrative criticism" or narratology) and social scientific criticism under the label socio-rhetorical criticism traces its roots to a 1975 article by Vernon K. Robbins entitled "The We-Passages in Acts and Ancient Sea Voyages."[78] In that article Robbins argued the "we" passages in Acts reflect a well-known cultural phenomenon

---

[75] Stephen Barton, "Social Setting of Early Non-Pauline Christianity," in *Dictionary of the Later New Testament* (Downers Grove, IL: InterVarsity, 1997), p.1107.

[76] Helpful articles and important critiques are in Susan Garrett, "Sociology of Early Christianity," in Volume 6 of the *Anchor Bible Dictionary*, edited by David Noel Freedman (New York: Bantam Doubleday Dell Publishing Group, 1992); in M.R. Mulholland's chapter on "Sociological Criticism" in David Black and David Dockery's *New Testament Criticism & Interpretation* (Grand Rapids: Zondervan, 1991), p.297-316; and in James Dvorak, "John H. Elliott's Social-scientific Criticism" *TRINJ* 28NS (2007), p.251-278.

[77] Garrett, *op. cit.*, vol. 6, p.94.

[78] Vernon K. Robbins, "The We-Passages in Acts and Ancient Sea Voyages," in *Perspectives on Luke-Acts*, ed. C.H. Talbert (Edinburgh: T&T Clark, 1978), p.215-42.

in Mediterranean literature, a phenomenon that represented a cultural interweaving of stories of sea voyages dating back to Homer's *Odyssey*. Robbins followed this article with a subsequent book applying socio-rhetorical analysis to the Gospel of Mark.[79] In 1996 Robbins outlined a method of socio-rhetorical analysis entitled *Exploring the Texture of Texts: A Guide to Socio-Rhetorical Interpretation,* a work which remains the standard introduction to the field.[80] Over the past 20 years, Ben Witherington, while all the time refining the method, has produced a series of what are called socio-rhetorical commentaries on New Testament writings, including the Gospel of Mark, the Book of Acts, and some of the Pauline epistles including one on Philippians[81] and one on *The Letters to Philemon, the Colossians and the Ephesians: A Socio-Rhetorical Commentary on the Captivity Epistles* (Grand Rapids: Eerdmans, 2007).

In this latter volume, all three letters are examined in light of what Witherington calls "Asiatic rhetoric" coupled with studies of the social world. There were several forms of rhetoric in the first centuries BC and AD, with two of the chief ones known as Atticist and Asiatic rhetoric, with Asiatic being more wordy and ornamented.[82] Taking examples from Cicero, whose sentences were

---

[79] Vernon K. Robbins, *Jesus the Teacher: A Socio-Rhetorical Interpretation of Mark* (Philadelphia: Fortress Press, 1992).

[80] Vernon K. Robbins, *Exploring the Texture of Texts: A Guide to Socio-Rhetorical Interpretation* (Valley Forge: Trinity Press, 1996). Robbins maintains a web site where one can find a glossary of socio-rhetorical terms. It can be accessed at http://www.religion.emory.edu/faculty/robbins/SRI/defns/s_defns.cfm.

[81] Ben Witherington III, *Paul's Letter to the Philippians: A Socio-Rhetorical Commentary* (Grand Rapids: Eerdmans, 2011).

[82] Cicero, in his work, *Brutus*, claimed that there are two standards of style: "Atticist" and "Asiatic" (Patricia Bizzell and Bruce Herzberg, *The Rhetorical Tradition: Readings from Classical Times to the Present* [Boston: Bedford, 2000], p.284). "The *Asiatic style,* that is, the style in which little else is required other than high-sounding words and sonorous periods, made its appearance among the Greeks in the first century before Christ. It is represented by the declamations of Dion Chrysostomus, Aristides, Themistius, and Libanius; productions which conclusively show that it is possible to use language skillfully without conveying any important ideas." (Evangelinus Apostolides Sophocles and Joseph Henry Thayer, *Greek Lexicon of the Roman and Byzantine Periods* [Cambridge, MA: Harvard Univ. Press, 1914].) In his *Roman Lives,* Plutarch notes the popularity of Asiatic rhetoric (usually a more flowery and bombastic form of rhetorical delivery than its Attic counterpart) where he says of Mark Antony: "He adopted the so-called Asiatic style of speaking, which was flourishing with particular vigor just then and which bore a considerable resemblance to his life, in that it was a kind of showy whinnying, filled with vain prancing and capricious ambition."

often long and complex, characterized by attention to balance, rhythm, and rhetorical effect, Witherington attempts to make a case for its use in each of these three letters.   Ephesians especially, Witherington affirms, is filled with examples, since it is written in a style that is characterized by "a flow of colorful words, often involving redundancy ... alliteration, assonance, and digressions" (p.5), "long lugubrious sentences" and "the absence of conjunctions, so that the sentences keep flowing in the torrent of eloquence" (p.18).   According to Witherington, Ephesians is an example of epideictic rhetoric. [83]   In his view, it is not a true letter but a circular epideictic homily with only the basic epistolary elements.   The title of his comments on Ephesians is "the Homily called Ephesians."[84]

Critiques of social-science criticism have been voiced.   The above-stated objections concerning both rhetorical and social science criticism are valid here. There is an over confidence about the extent to which rhetorical criticism can explain the structure and content of these Pauline letters.   One wonders why earlier writers have not made the connection between the Prison Epistles and Asiatic rhetoric, since Asiatic rhetoric had such a long history prior to the New Testament.   While Witherington uses his analysis of Asiatic rhetoric as a strong underpinning for Pauline authorship of all three epistles,[85] one wonders how he would answer those who point to the different rhetorical and writing styles found in Romans, 1 Thessalonians, and Galatians, all of which are letters which were written to groups in different parts of the Roman empire and whose rhetoric is not identified as "Asiatic."   It does not look like the kind of rhetoric identified in any of these letters has any bearing on the question of their authorship.   Would not such apparent inconsistencies be avoided if we heeded Paul's own statement about not using persuasive rhetoric (1 Corinthians 2:1)?   Furthermore, as did the rhetorical critics' outlines, so the socio-rhetorical interpreters' outlines for the epistles seem forced in places, for they force Paul into their chosen rhetorical arrangement imposed upon the letters, rather than letting the letters form their own outline.

---

[83] Witherington's judgment that Ephesians is best read as epideictic rhetoric does not match the arguments by Lincoln that Ephesians should be read as a hybrid of epideictic (chapters 1-3) and deliberative (chapters 4-6) rhetoric.   This disagreement is symptomatic of the difficulties of applying the categories of Greco-Roman macro-rhetoric with any precision to the phenomena of Paul's letters.

[84] Witherington defines a homily as a word of exhortation with a three-part rhetorical structure similar to the *narratio, probatio, and peroratio* of speeches delivered by orators.

[85] Witherington, *Philemon, Colossians and Ephesians*, pp.2-3, 11-19, 25, 30, 239, 252, 355.

To this commentator, each of these newer attempts to solve some problems inherent in the historical-critical method has failed, precisely because the meaning of the text as intended *by the author* (an inspired apostle of Christ) is abandoned. Instead, the meaning of the text is sought *in the audience's response* to the writings.

The proliferation of interpretive methods in recent years has produced considerable fragmentation of New Testament Studies. It leaves the would-be interpreter with the feeling he is in a department store where numerous choices of hermeneutical methods are offered. There is also the feeling that, while one may choose from the wide variety available, there is a strong probability that whichever one is chosen will soon be discarded as unsatisfactory.

Charles Cosgrove nicely summarized the situation as the 21st century began.

> Looking back, three things stand out as epochal shifts that have set the course of New Testament studies for years to come. First, the history of the discipline during this century reflects the shift from modernity to postmodernity or, better, from modernity to the beginning of "modernity on endless trial" in biblical studies (to borrow a phrase from Leszek Kowlakoski). Second, it is the story of the secularization of the field. Less than ever before does the church determine the questions that New Testament scholars ask. Third, it is the story of globalization; the emergence of the global Information Age, which makes possible unprecedented forms of communication, cooperation, and solidarity at the same time that diversity and the sheer enormity of the new global house of study make it nearly impossible to do anything but "local theology." All three of these trends mark the end of cultural Christendom for biblical studies. We should not underestimate this revolution. Nor should we imagine that all its surprises have already been sprung.[86]

H. CONTENTS

In content, Ephesians is a very general epistle when compared with a letter like Colossians. Perhaps the last letter Paul wrote before he sat down to write Ephesians was Romans. That, too, as to content, has been classified as a general epistle. Some say that, in Ephesians, Paul takes up where he left

---

[86] Charles Cosgrove, "A History of New Testament Studies in the 20th Century." *Review and Expositor*, 96 (1999), p.379-80.

off in Romans, and writes about the same general problem. In Romans, he looks to the past, and the relationship of the Gentiles and Jews to God and the church. In Ephesians he looks forward, to what that relationship can be.

In one sentence, the contents of Ephesians are "The Church is the body of Christ." Whereas in Colossians, Paul emphasizes the uniqueness and the adequacy of the cosmic Christ (Colossians 1:15-17), Paul turns in Ephesians to write about the cosmic significance of the church, the body of Christ, through which Christ is proclaimed. Ephesians has more to say about the church than any other New Testament epistle. It has been called "the letter about the church."

Appropriately, Wilbur Fields titled his commentary on this letter "The Glorious Church: A Study of Ephesians."[87] He begins his book with these words, "The church is the most precious institution on earth today. Ephesians has more to say about the church than any other New Testament letter. We need to picture the church in our minds as the glorious church described in Ephesians." Then he asks his readers to "consider the glorious church described in Ephesians."

1. *Christ loves her*, 5:25. Men may despise and belittle her, but Jesus Christ loves her.
2. *The church shall be presented to Christ,* 5:27. What will the people who are not in the church do then?
3. *God's wisdom is demonstrated by the church,* 3:10. If you are not in the church, God sent Christ to die all in vain, as far as you are concerned. You make God's mercy to appear to be foolishness.
4. *God is glorified in the church,* 3:20-21. Out in the world you cannot glorify Him.
5. *There is one body, one church,* 4:4. Because of the divisions among those who believe in Christ, the world does not believe that God sent Him, John 17:20-21. Pray to God that men will abandon their loyalty to denominations and sects and be members only of that glorious church to which God adds all saved people, Acts 2:47.
6. *Christ is the Head of the church*, 1:11, 5:23. Our opinion of the church will be just as high as our opinion of Christ.

---

[87] Wilbur Fields, *The Glorious Church: A Study of Ephesians* in the Bible Study Textbook series (Joplin, Mo: College Press, 1960).

7. *The church is the fullness of Christ*, 1:22-23.   If we love Christ, we shall love the church, for it is filled by Christ.
8. *Christ is the Savior of the body*, 5:23.   All saved people are members of the church.   You cannot be saved and not be a member of the Lord's church.
9. *She shall be holy and without blemish*, 5:27.   No man can excuse himself by saying, "There are too many hypocrites."
10. *The church is the beloved bride of Christ,* 5:31-32.   Don't you want to be married to Jesus?   And what will the Lord do to those who hate and hurt His bride?[88]

---

[88] *Ibid.*, p.11,12.

Detailed Introduction to Colossians

A. HISTORICAL ALLUSIONS

1. Historical allusions at the beginning of the Epistle, 1:1ff

a. 1:1 – This letter is signed by Paul, who calls himself an apostle of Jesus Christ. Timothy is with Paul, and perhaps penned the letter as Paul dictated it.   Timothy was probably known at Colossae.

b. 1:2 – Destination – "To the saints and faithful brethren ... who are at Colossae." "Grace to you and peace from God our Father," a typical epistolary greeting, appears here in verse 2.

c. 1:3ff – The usual Pauline thanksgiving

Colossians is structured like a normal Hellenistic letter: signature, address, greeting, thanksgiving and prayer, body, exhortation, epistolary closing.

d. 1:4-7 – The wording "since we heard of your faith" and "the gospel ... has come to you" seems to imply that Paul has never been to Colossae. 2:1 seems to indicate the same thing.

e. 1:7 – "You learned *it* from Epaphras" – Evidently it was Epaphras who by preaching the gospel planted the church at Colossae.

Epaphras is called a fellow prisoner of Paul's in Philemon 23. Here it is "fellow bond-servant." These are expressions that need further study. In what sense are Epaphras and the apostle Paul on an equal plane ("fellow-"), either as prisoners or as bond-servants?

– Epaphras is called "a faithful servant (*diakonos*) of Christ." "Servant of Christ" says Epaphras "had acted not so much under the authority of Paul but under the authority of Paul's Lord."[1] The genitive "of Christ" following the designation "servant" designates the person for whom the ministering or serving is done. Christ is the one whom Epaphras serves faithfully.

---

[1] Curtis Vaughan, "Colossians," in *Expositor's Bible Commentary* (Grand Rapids: Zondervan, 1978), Vol.11, p. 176.

- The Greek *diakonos* is sometimes translated "deacon," sometimes "servant," sometimes "minister." *"Deacons"* is found in Philippians 1:1 and 1 Timothy 3:8,12 (each of which speak of an office in the local church). *"Servant(s)"* is found in Matthew 20:26, 22:13, 23:11; Mark 9:35, 10:43; John 2:5,9, 12:26; Romans 15:8, 16:1 (Phoebe); 1 Corinthians 3:5; 2 Corinthians 3:6, 6:4, 11:15,23; Colossians 1:7; 1 Timothy 4:6. *"Minister(s)"* is found in the NASB at Romans 13:4; Galatians 2:17; Ephesians 3:7, 6:21; and Colossians 1:23,25, 4:7; in the KJV *"minister(s)"* is found at Matthew 20:26; Mark 10:43; Romans 13:4, 15:8; 1 Corinthians 3:5; 2 Corinthians 3:6, 6:4, 11:15,23; Galatians 2:17; Ephesians 3:7, 6:21; Colossians 1:7,23,25, 4:7; 1 Thessalonians 3:2; and 1 Timothy 4:6. In some of these passages the evangelist/ preacher is the one who is styled as a "minister" or a "servant."

- The imprecise use of "minister" (servant) raises issues of church polity. Epaphras is called "a minister" (servant) in Colossians 1:7; so is Tychicus in Colossians 4:7. In what sense is the term used? It could be that Epaphras and Tychicus are called "ministers" (as are others) because they had a particular task/ function with the local congregation. On the other hand, Epaphras evidently held a special connection with the church at Colossae: he appears to have been responsible for their first hearing of Christ; and now, at the time Colossians is being written, he is at Rome reporting to Paul about the brethren at Colossae. Is Epaphras an evangelist? Is this his office in the church? Was there an office of "minister" in the church? Or are the terms "minister" and "evangelist" but two different designations for the same office/function? Other verses may help us decide. Timothy was an evangelist (2 Timothy 4:5) and is also called a "minister" (1 Timothy 4:6). Philip the deacon later in life is also called Philip the evangelist (Acts 21:8). Epaphras has certainly done the work of an evangelist, spreading the gospel and establishing a church in Colossae. We struggle trying to use Bible names for Bible things. Can an evangelist/preacher be called "a minister"? Yes, for that seems to be done here. Should an evangelist be called "*the* minister of a church"? Evidently not, nor should the evangelist do all the "ministering." The elders should be taught and encouraged to do their work, as also the deacons.

    – 1:7 also says that Epaphras was serving in Colossae "on our behalf."[2]

    "A faithful servant on our behalf" perhaps indicates Paul had sent Epaphras to evangelize at Colossae and in the Lycus valley. It is not a proof text for apostolic succession.

f.   1:8 – Epaphras has reported to Paul concerning the state of the Colossian church.

    Epaphras came to Rome to see Paul because he needed Paul's help. Some new religio/philosophical ideas were being taught in Colossae. Perhaps folk weren't listening to Epaphras when he warned against them, and so he seeks the help of an apostle. Perhaps the people will listen to Paul.

g.   1:15-20 – A series of profound assertions regarding the uniqueness and preeminence of Jesus Christ.

h.   1:24-29 – Paul tells some of his present circumstances.

2. Historical allusions at the conclusion of the Epistle, 4:7-18

a.   4:7 – Tychicus is with Paul when this letter was written, as is Onesimus (4:9). Tychicus will carry the letter to Colossae. "I have sent," verse 8, is generally understood to be an epistolary aorist. Tychicus will report to the church about the condition of Paul. In fact, he carries three letters – Colossians, Philemon, and Ephesians. Cp. Colossians 4:7,8 and Ephesians 6:21,22.

b.   4:9 – Onesimus was a runaway slave who belonged to Philemon. This verse implies that Philemon evidently lived in Colossae. Tychicus and Onesimus were to fill in the details about Paul's imprisonment when they arrived at Colossae.

c.   4:10-14 – Names several of Paul's young preacher boys, and indicates what each of their current assignments were.

---

[2] A manuscript variation reads "your behalf," (see "for you" in the KJV).

"Aristarchus, my fellow-prisoner."   See the Detailed Introduction to Philippians for further information about Aristarchus.

"Mark" has been sent out on an evangelistic tour by Paul, a journey which may eventually see him visiting Colossae.   This is the same John Mark who left Paul's missionary party during the first missionary journey (Acts 13:13), and who, according to this verse, has now been reconciled to Paul.   Later, he will write the second gospel. Concerning him, Paul writes to the Colossians "about whom you received instructions" and "if he comes to you, welcome him."

"Jesus Justus."   A Jewish Christian.   Nothing more is known of him.

"Epaphras," was a native of Colossae, and now is in Rome.   Per 1:7,8 he brought news of the conditions at Colossae to Paul.   He evidently is a circuit preacher, working the congregations of Colossae, Laodicea, and Hierapolis.[3]   It has been supposed that "Epaphras" is a shortened form of "Epaphroditus," and it well may be, but he is not to be confused with the messenger of the Philippian church who had the same name (Philippians 4:18).

"Luke, the beloved physician."   The author of Luke and Acts, and a companion on Paul's second, third, and journey-to-Rome tours. (The "we-passages" in Acts indicate Luke's presence.)   Hobart has written a book showing that the language of Luke is the vocabulary of a physician.[4]

"Demas."   Later (by the time of the second Roman imprisonment) this man will forsake Paul, loving the present world more than the rewards offered by the gospel (2 Timothy 4:10).

d.   4:15 – "Nympha." This name may be either feminine or masculine. According to the KJV, Nymphas was a male.   According to the RSV,

---

[3] On the relative location of the three cities, see the map in "General Introduction to the Prison Epistles."

[4] William K. Hobart, *The Medical Language Of St. Luke: A Proof from Internal Evidence that "The Gospel According to St. Luke" and "The Acts of the Apostles" Were Written By the Same Writer and That Man was a Medical Man* (1882).   Reprint: Kessinger Publishing, 2010.

Nympha was a female. There was a church meeting in the house of Nympha/Nymphas, which was in Laodicea.

e. 4:16 – This epistle was to be read to the church at Colossae, and then sent to be read (out loud in a worship service) to the church at Laodicea. The Colossian brethren are exhorted to read "my letter *that is coming* from Laodicea." What letter is this?

f. 4:17 – "Archippus." Evidently this man is an evangelist, and he took over the work of Epaphras in the three churches of Colossae, Laodicea, and Hierapolis while Epaphras was making his trip to Rome and back.

Compare the opening of Philemon (verses 1,2), where Archippus is also named. Two opinions are given concerning him.

1. Some suggest he was a circuit rider between the three cities, and that he had a room in Philemon's house, where he stayed when in Colossae.

2. Others suggest Apphia is Philemon's wife, and that Archippus is their son, and the circuit evangelist of the churches in the absence of Epaphras.

g. 4:18 – Paul signs the letter in his own handwriting. The previous verses have been dictated, but this salutation is written by Paul himself. "Remember my imprisonment (bonds)" indicates Paul was in prison when this letter was written. The request to be remembered by the Colossians likely asks for their remembrance as they prayed.

h. Subscription (KJV) – "Written from Rome to the Colossians by Tychicus and Onesimus." Is this correct?

B. THE CITY OF COLOSSAE AND THE FOUNDING OF THE CHURCH THERE

1. The city of Colossae[5]

---

[5] In Section 1 of his introduction to this epistle, the position and history of Colossae are admirably described by J.B. Lightfoot, *St. Paul's Epistles to the Colossians and to Philemon* (Grand Rapids: Zondervan, nd).

a. Colossae was a small town situated on the southern bank of the Lycus River in the interior of the Roman province of Asia, an area located in the western end of the country we know as Turkey,[6] about 100 miles east of Ephesus.   Its nearest neighbors were Laodicea (10 miles away to the west) and Hierapolis (13 miles away to the west), which stood on opposite sides of the river, and both those towns also had congregations of believers (Colossians 2:1, 4:13).

The site of ancient Colossae viewed from the north.   Originally at a junction of the main overland trade route from Ephesus and Sardis to the Euphrates, the city lost its commercial role to Laodicea when the road to Pergamum was moved to the west.[7]   The mountain three miles to the south of the site is Mt. Cadmus (8,013 ft. high).

---

[6] In Hellenistic times, Colossae was located on the western border of the province of Phrygia.

[7] See this picture in color in *Encountering the New Testament*, by Walter Elwell and Robert Yarbrough (Grand Rapids: Baker, 1998), p. 320-21.   It is found in black and white in the article on "Colossians" in the New ISBE (Grand Rapids: Eerdmans, 1979), Vol.1, p. 733, and attributed to W. S. LaSor.

Colossae lay in the valley of the Lycus River near the spot where the river disappears into an underground chasm, out of which it soon emerges again to empty itself into the Meander River.[8]

b. In ancient times (4th & 5th centuries BC), Colossae was the most important city in the area.   In the time of the Persian king Xerxes (481 BC) it was described as populous, large, and wealthy.[9]   The great prosperity of this region was chiefly due to its manufacture of woolen textiles.   The neighboring uplands afforded excellent pasture for sheep, and the streams of the Lycus valley were peculiarly favorable to the dyer's art.   Both Colossae and Laodicea were actively engaged in the trade in wool and dyed textiles, of which Colossae had formerly been a chief center, giving its name (*colossinus*) to a valued purple dye.[10]

c. Before the Romans came to dominate Anatolia (the western and central portion of the land we call Turkey), Colossae was one city in the ancient empire known as Phrygia.

About 521 BC, the Persians under Darius conquered this area.   Then Alexander the Great conquered the Persians, and the area fell under Greek control.   In the chaotic period after Alexander's death, northern Phrygia was overrun by Celts, and as the years passed this area came to be known as northern Galatia.   In 188 BC, the southern remnant of Phrygia came under the control of the kings of Pergamum whose kingdom covered much of the western portion of Anatolia. The last king of Pergamum (Attalus III) bequeathed his kingdom to Rome in 133 BC.   Having conquered much of the rest of Anatolia, the Romans, for administrative purposes, redrew the boundary lines of the countries.   The north eastern part of ancient Phrygia became

---

[8] There is an Eastern Orthodox legend (not older than the 4th century AD) respecting the origin of the chasm.   The archangel Michael, during a flood of the Lycus, caused the river to flow underground, thus causing the flood to abate.   See Andrew Lloyd Bennett, "Archaeology From Art: Investigating Colossae and the Miracle of the Archangel Michael at Kona." *Near East Archaeological Society Bulletin* 50 (2005), p.15-26.   Herodotus (d. 425 BC) already had described the river as sinking into the underground chasm (vii.30), so the later legend is questionable.

[9] Xenophon, *Anabasis,* i.2.6; Herodotus, *Histories*, vii.30.

[10] G.G. Findlay, "The Epistle to the Colossians" in the *Pulpit Commentary*, edited by H.D.M. Spence and Joseph S. Exell (Grand Rapids: Eerdmans, 1962), Vol. 20, p.i.

part of the huge new Roman province of Galatia, and the western part of Phrygia (in which Colossae, Laodicea and Hierapolis were located) became part of the Roman province of Asia.

d. Because of the influence of the Roman empire, Laodicea and Hierapolis became considerable cities, and Colossae declined in importance until it was only a "small town" in the first century AD.[11] The Romans changed the road system, and this led to a decline in the social and commercial importance of Colossae. Laodicea grew and became the chief city of the immediate district. Hierapolis was also helped to grow because it became a health resort famous for its hot springs and medicinal baths.[12]

e. A regional earthquake hit the Lycus River valley in the mid AD 60s, and all three cities suffered extensive damage.[13] Laodicea was so wealthy that she was rebuilt without the help of state or foreign aid, though other cities in the valley relied on aid from Rome to rebuild.[14]

Coins and inscriptions from the 2nd and 3rd centuries AD exist, showing the gods and goddesses worshiped at Colossae.[15] By about the 4th century AD, the ancient site of Colossae was deserted and a new town (whose ancient name was Chonae, and its modern name Honaz) was built nearby.

---

[11] Strabo, *Geography*, xii.8.13.   Strabo died in AD 24.

[12] Strabo, *op. cit.*, xiii.4.14.

[13] Tacitus (*Annals* xiv.27) dated the quake in the *7th year of Nero* (Nero was Emperor of Rome from AD 54-68, putting the earthquake around AD 61). Eusebius (*Chron. Olymp.* 210.4) dated an earthquake which destroyed Colossae, Laodicea, and Hierapolis in the 10th year of Nero (AD 64). Orosius (vii.7,12) also placed the earthquake after the burning of Rome in AD 64. The date of the earthquake has been used as evidence for the dating of Colossians. Paul did not refer to this catastrophic event; thus, some scholars believe Paul had either not yet heard the news, while others believe that his letters to Colossians and Philemon predated the quake.

[14] Tacitus, *ibid.*

[15] Edwin Freed, *The New Testament: A Critical Introduction* (Belmont, CA: Wadsworth Pub. Co., 1991), p.302.

There have been no excavations at Colossae,[16] but the site has been identified since 1835 when a traveler named W.J. Hamilton identified the city ruins. These included some marble stones from buildings, fragments of columns, "a hollow cave of a theatre, of which several seats were still *in situ*," and some graves in the cemetery.[17]

f. The population of Colossae

In the apostolic age its population consisted of indigenous Phrygians and Greek settlers, together with a fair proportion of the Jewish colonists who resided in Phrygia from the time of Antiochus the Great (223-187 BC) onwards.[18] "Calculations made on the basis of temple taxes sent to Jerusalem indicate that there were approximately 11,000 adult Jewish males in the district of Laodicea a century prior to Paul."[19]

g. Pagan religion in Colossae centered around the cult of Cybele, the mother goddess, whose worship involved fertility rites, and also ascetic practices and ritual mutilation.[20] The design on coins struck in Colossae suggests the existence of cults of Isis, Serapis, Mithras, Demeter, Helios (the sun), Selene (the moon), the Ephesian Artemis,

---

[16] Flinders University of Australia is currently preparing for an excavation. (http://www.bibleplaces.com/colossae.htm)

[17] William John Hamilton, *Researches in Asia Minor, Pontus and Armenia: With Some Account of Their Antiquities and Geology* (London: J. Murray, 1842), Vol. 1, p.508.

[18] Josephus *(Antiquities*, xii. 3.4) tells us that 2000 Jewish families were settled in the area under an edict of Antiochus III (2nd century BC). These Jewish residents were imported not from Palestine but from Mesopotamia and Babylon.

[19] Michael R. Weed, "The Letters of Paul to the Ephesians, the Colossians, and Philemon" in the *Living Word Commentary* series (Austin, TX: R. B. Sweet, 1971), p.28. The subject of the great numbers of Jews in Asia Minor is treated by E. Schürer in an article on the "Diaspora" in *Hastings' Dictionary of the Bible* (New York: Charles Scribner's Sons, 1909), Vol. 5, pp.93–95. See also William Ramsay, *Letters to the Seven Churches* (Grand Rapids: Baker, 1963), ch. XII. pp.142–157, ch. XXIX. pp.420–422.

[20] David DeSilva, *An Introduction to the New Testament* (Downers Grove, IL: IVP Academic, 2004), p.690.

and Men, a native Phrygian divinity.[21]   Egyptian and Eastern religions, the mystery religions, and the philosophies of the Stoics, Epicureans, and others were influential.[22]

2. The founding of the church at Colossae

The church of Colossae, unlike the churches of Ephesus and Philippi, is not mentioned in the Book of Acts.   Although we have no specific historical record of the establishment of the church at Colossae, there are possible hints in the letter to the Colossians and also in the companion letter to Philemon.   The Christians in Colossae were involved with at least two "house churches" (see Colossians 4:15 and 4:9 with Philemon 2), and evidently neither was started by Paul himself, nor had Colossae ever been personally visited by Paul (Colossians 1:4 and 2:1[23]). It appears from Colossians 1:7 that Epaphras, a native Colossian (Colossians 4:12), having planted the church at Colossae, was still to some extent involved with it, as well as with the neighboring churches of Laodicea and Hierapolis (Colossians 4:12,13).   From the beginning, Epaphras labored at the evangelization of the Lycus valley at Paul's direction (Colossians 1:7, "on our behalf"). Since Colossae was in the Roman province of Asia, whose capital was Ephesus, we can, therefore, hardly be wrong in referring the introduction of Christianity to Colossae to the time of Paul's three years' stay at Ephesus during his third missionary journey, at which time we are expressly told that "all who lived in Asia heard the word of the Lord, both Jews and Greeks" (Acts 19:10).

Several allusions in Colossians indicate that a number of the Colossian Christians were of Gentile background.   Colossians 1:21 pictures them as formerly alienated from God and hostile to Him, engaged in evil deeds. Colossians 1:27 speaks of Paul's mission to the Gentiles as something God willed. Colossians 2:13 pictures them before their conversion as being Gentiles ("uncircumcised') and spiritually dead because of their own sins.

---

[21] Sherman E. Johnson, "Laodicea and Its Neighbors" in *The Biblical Archaeologist Reader 2*, ed. D.N. Freedman and E.F. Campbell Jr. (Garden City, NY: Doubleday, 1964), p.357.

[22] Weed, *op. cit.*, p.27.

[23] The usual interpretation of Colossians 2:1 ("on your behalf and for those who are at Laodicea, and for all those who have not personally seen my face") is that Paul never had visited the towns of Colossae, Hierapolis, and Laodicea.

Concerning the founding of the Colossian church, a few commentators have argued that Paul did indeed start the church in that town. Davidson listed the arguments used to advocate the Pauline origin of the Colossian church, though he himself did not believe in the Pauline origin.[24] Included were these arguments:

[1] It appears from Acts that Paul traveled twice through Phrygia (Acts 16:6, 18:23) and thus it is probable that, in one or the other of the journeys, he visited the principal cities, such as Colossae and Laodicea.

> *Rebuttal*: That Paul traveled twice through Phrygia does not demonstrate that he visited Colossae and Laodicea. In his first journey through the area (during his second missionary journey), he passed from Cilicia and Derbe to Lystra, thence to the northeastern part of Phrygia (through Phrygian-Galatia[25]) to Mysia and Troas. This route lay north and east of Laodicea, Hierapolis and Colossae. In his second trip through the area (during his third missionary journey), Acts 18:23 has Paul passing through the region that is both Phrygian and Galatian.[26] As he began this journey, he would be visiting the churches of Derbe, Lystra, Iconium, and Pisidian Antioch. Next Luke has him passing through some "highlands" ("Paul, having passed through the upper country," Acts 19:1). There were two routes by which one might journey from Pisidian Antioch to Ephesus. One was through the *low* country, along the Lycus and Meander River valleys, passing through Colossae, Hierapolis, and Laodicea. The other route was called the *upper* route because it took the traveler across the high tablelands of the interior of Asia Minor. Taking the northern route through the highlands, Paul would have approached Ephesus from around the north side of Mt. Messogis, a long range of mountains between the Meander and Cayster rivers.

[2] Again, those attempting to show that Paul established the Colossian church argue that the Colossian epistle exhibits proofs of the intimacy and affection existing between the writer and the Colossian believers.

---

[24] Samuel Davidson, *An Introduction to the New Testament* (London: Samuel Bagster and Sons, 1849), Vol.2, p.397-400.

[25] It should be remembered that when the Romans came to control this huge area, they redrew the boundary lines between the then existing countries and ethnic groups.

[26] The Greek expression "Phrygian and Galatian region" contains two nouns connected by "and" with only the first having the article "the" – a construction which allows both terms to refer to the same thing (see "Sharp's rule of grammar" in H.E. Dana and J.R. Mantey, *A Manual Grammar of the Greek New Testament* (New York: Macmillan, 1927), p.147). It speaks of the region that was both Phrygian and Galatian.

Rebuttal: Indeed, Paul seems to have a correct knowledge of their state of being. He is confident that they have been grounded and well instructed in the faith of the Gospel. He speaks of their love for him, and gives them such exhortations as imply personal acquaintance (1:6,8,23, 2:5-7,20-23, 4:3,4,7-9). The salutations in Colossians 4:10 suppose the Colossians to have been well acquainted with Paul's fellow-travelers and fellow-laborers. It is also admitted that Paul speaks of the Colossians in such a manner as to show his anxiety for their state, his knowledge of their circumstances, his familiarity with their belief, and with the progress they had made in divine things. But his personal presence in Colossae is not thereby required. He could have been informed regarding all these by Epaphras (Colossians 1:7,8).

[3] It is alleged that the Colossians were endowed with spiritual gifts (3:16), which they could not have received from any other than an apostle.

Rebuttal: Colossians 3:16, "wisdom," in no way implies the possession of spiritual gifts.

[4] It is argued that in 1:21-25, Paul does, in effect, say that he himself had dispensed the gospel to the Colossians.

Rebuttal: When Paul does allude to the fact that he himself was responsible for the first preaching of the gospel in a place, he clearly and specifically states that fact. For example, see 1 Thessalonians 2:1-2,13, and 14 where Paul says "you received from us the word of God's message ... and became imitators of the churches of God in Christ Jesus that are in Judea." Or, again, see 1 Corinthians 3:10, 4:14 where Paul plainly alludes to the fact he planted the church at Corinth. What then is the point of 1:21-25? When one reads Colossians 1:21-29 together with Colossians 2:1-7, it becomes obvious that in this whole section Paul is explaining why he can assume authority to write to them though they have never seen his face. He is fulfilling his commission as an apostle of Jesus Christ to the Gentiles. Paul knows that the gospel Epaphras has preached to them is the same gospel Paul himself had been commissioned to preach. He gives his imprimatur to what Epaphras preached, and he wants them to continue to walk in the faith they had already embraced (Colossians 2:6,7).

[5] Colossians 2:1,2 is interpreted to mean that the Colossians and Laodiceans had seen Paul's face, but that there were some elsewhere who had not seen his face.

Rebuttal: It seems best to interpret these verses on the supposition that the last clause of verse 1 explains the two preceding, and points to the fact that the Colossians and Laodiceans had not seen Paul's face.

[6)] Finally, it is asserted that the epistle to Philemon affords evidence that Paul had been among the Colossians, since Philemon was a Christian and his home was at Colossae.

Rebuttal: Philemon 19 does imply that Philemon had been converted to Christianity by Paul, but this does not prove that Paul must have been to Colossae where Philemon lived.   Could not Philemon have been in Ephesus when he heard Paul, and then gone back home as a Christian and begun the church that met in his home?

We will abide by our conclusion that Paul had never been at Colossae, that Epaphras founded the church there and, having recently come to Rome, has informed Paul about the Christians in Ephesus.   The picture he gave Paul is of a congregation obedient to the gospel (Colossians 2:6).   Paul gave thanks to God for them (Colossians 1:4-6) and expresses his joy for their Christian lives and the stability of their faith in Christ (Colossians 2:5).

There are indications in the New Testament and in early Christian literature concerning the subsequent history of the churches in the Lycus valley.[27]   If Paul carried out his plans as indicated in Philemon 22, Paul did visit the Lycus valley after his release from his first Roman imprisonment.   Mark, the Gospel writer, visited and ministered in this area before AD 68 (1 Peter 1:1 and 5:13; 2 Timothy 4:11 has Mark near to Ephesus where Timothy is when 2 Timothy was addressed to him).   Philip, either the apostle Philip or the evangelist Philip, settled in this area after the destruction of Jerusalem in AD 70.[28]   John the Apostle lived in Ephesus, and about AD 96 addressed the book of Revelation to "the seven churches that are in Asia" (Revelation. 1:4), and later in the book included a separate short letter to Laodicea   (Revelation 3:14-21).   The home of the early

---

[27] Lightfoot, *op. cit.*, pp.40-72, gives a detailed summary of available information from early Christian literature.

[28] Footnote #6 on Eusebius, *H.E.* III.31 shows us that the ancient writers confounded Philip the evangelist and Philip the apostle as they reported about the deaths of the notable leaders.   The editor of *The Nicene and Post Nicene Fathers* (Grand Rapids: Eerdmans, 1952) series opts for Philip the evangelist as the one living at Hierapolis late in the first century.   Lightfoot (*op. cit.*, p.46) argues it was Philip the apostle.

Christian writer Papias was in the area.[29]   About AD 200, churches in the Lycus valley were involved in the quartodeciman controversy, and in the controversy against Montanism.[30]   Both Hierapolis and Laodicea were represented at various of the councils and synods in the 4th and 5th centuries.

C. AUTHORSHIP AND ATTESTATION

It would be well to review what was written in the Detailed Introduction to Ephesians about the importance of the matter of the authorship of these letters. As was true there, so here.   Such a study will demonstrate that we are not required to surrender the apostolic authorship of Colossians, nor need we be influenced to join in the skepticism about the supernatural source and authority of the books of the New Testament.

1. Internal Evidence

Three times the writer identifies himself as Paul (Colossians 1:1,23, 4:18). There is much that harmonizes with what we know about Paul and his writings. The high Christology in this letter is what we have come to expect from Paul.[31] The two-fold emphasis (doctrinal and hortatory) found in the letter to the Colossians is similar to what one finds in many of Paul's letters.   The long sentences, such as Colossians1:9-20 and 2:8-12, are like Paul's style in his other epistles, e.g., Romans 1:1-7, 2:5-10,14-16, 3:23-26; Galatians 2:3-5,6-9; and Philippians 3:8-11.

2. External evidence

The external evidence for Colossians is not equal to that of some other Pauline epistles.

---

[29] Eusebius, *H.E.* III.39.

[30] Eusebius, *H.E.* IV.27, who cites the works of Claudius Apollinaris, bishop of Hierapolis.

[31] An idea that some have affirmed in recent centuries, namely, that John's Christology is higher than, say, that of Paul or Peter who both wrote earlier than John, is not to be maintained.   Is Paul's Christology, or John's, distinctive from that of other New Testament writers?   No.   The apostles of Jesus presented a consistent doctrine about the Christ.   Later in these notes we shall address the claim by some critics that the Christology in Colossians is more cosmic than is found elsewhere in Paul's writings.

a. The relation of Colossians to Philemon

Both the letters to Philemon and to the Colossians are signed by Paul. While some critics, beginning in the nineteenth century, have disputed the idea that Paul wrote Colossians, it is the consensus of those same scholarly critics that Philemon is incontestably Pauline. If one is Pauline, why is not the other also granted to be Pauline? Both of these letters were sent to the same town and in all likelihood conveyed at the same time by the same messenger. Both contain the names of Timothy, Onesimus, Archippus, Epaphras, Mark, Aristarchus, Demas, and Luke. Consistently, can one be treated as incontestably Pauline and the other denied to Paul? If Philemon is Pauline, does not the relation of Colossians to Philemon point to the Pauline authorship of Colossians, also?

b. Allusions[32]

1) "Steadfast in faith," found in Colossians 1:23, is alluded to by Ignatius (AD 115)[33] and by Polycarp (AD 115).[34] Ignatius' language "visible and invisible" and "the heavens"[35] may be an allusion to Colossians 1:16.

2) The *Epistle of Barnabas* xii.7 (AD 130) has the phrase "in Him are all things and unto Him are all things," which may be an allusion to Colossians 1:16.

3) Justin Martyr (AD 150) has an allusion to Colossians 1:15-17. In his *Dialogue with Trypho* he wrote "Christ is the first-born of all things made; the first-born of God, and before all creatures."[36] He

---

[32] An *allusion* is a reference that shows the passage or book being quoted exists.   Ideas from the book are quoted, or paraphrased, without citing the author or the source.

[33] *Ad Eph*. x.3.

[34] *Ad Phil*. x.1.

[35] *Ad Smyr*. vi.1.

[36] *Dial c. Tryph*. chap.100.   (See also chaps.84, 85.2, 138.2)

also says that God "ordered all things through Him."[37]   There is an allusion to Colossians 2:11 when he wrote "circumcised with the circumcision of Christ through baptism, having put off the old Adam ... and put on Christ."[38]

4) Theophilus of Antioch (AD 180) has "He begot His emanated Word, the first-born of every creature,"[39] which is an allusion to Colossians 1:15.   Theophilus also quotes "set your mind on things above,"[40] which appears to be an allusion to Colossians 3:2.

c. **Annotated quotations**[41]

1) Irenaeus (AD 180) is the first to name Paul as the author.   "And again in the epistle to the Colossians [Paul] says, 'Luke the beloved physician greets you'."[42]   Compare Colossians 4:14. Colossians 1:21 is quoted by Irenaeus, "the apostle in the epistle to the Colossians says, 'And though you were formerly alienated, and enemies to His knowledge by evil works, yet now you have been reconciled in the body of His flesh, through His death, to present yourselves holy and chaste, and without fault in His sight'."[43]   In fact, Hendriksen notes that "not a single chapter of Colossians remains unquoted or not referred to in the works of Irenaeus. Now when Irenaeus ascribes Colossians to Paul, this testimony should carry considerable weight."[44]

---

[37] *Apol.* i.46, ii.6

[38] *Quest. Et Respons. Ad Orthod.*   Question 102.

[39] *Ad Autol.* ii.22.

[40] *Ad Autol.* ii.17.

[41] In *annotated quotations*, unlike allusions, we find the author and/or the source definitely named.

[42] *Advers. Haeres.* iii.14.1.

[43] *Advers. Haeres.* v.14.2

[44] William Hendriksen, "Colossians and Ephesians," in *New Testament Commentary* (Grand Rapids: Baker, 1964), p.36.

2) Clement of Alexandria (AD 190) several times speaks of the Pauline authorship of Colossians. "And in the epistle to the Colossians, [Paul] writes 'Admonishing every man, and teaching every man in all wisdom, that we may present every man perfect in Christ'." (See Colossians 1:28).[45] Colossians 2:8 is cited at *Strom*. vi.8, and Colossians 1:9 is cited at *Strom*. v.10.

3) Origen (AD 210) quotes 2:18,19 as from Paul to the Colossians.[46]

4) Tertullian (AD 200) attributes Colossians to Paul. "From which things the apostle restraining us, expressly cautions against philosophy, when he writes to the Colossians, 'Beware lest any man spoil you through philosophy and vain deceit, after the tradition of men, contrary to the foresight of the Holy Spirit'." (Colossians 2:8).[47]

In Tertullian's writings against Marcion there are a number of passages where Colossians is attributed to Paul.[48]

d. Canonical Lists

1) Colossians is included in the Chester Beatty Papyrus P[46] that is a collection of Paul's letters.

2) Marcion (AD 140) included Colossians among the ten epistles he accepted as Pauline.[49]

3) *The Muratorian Fragment*, a survey of New Testament books written about AD 170, definitely names Paul as the author of Colossians.[50]

---

[45] *Stromata* i.1

[46] *Contra Cels.* v.8.

[47] *De Praescript. Advers. Haer.*, chap.vii.

[48] See *Adv. Marc.* v.19.

[49] *Ibid.*

[50] Hendriksen, *ibid.*

4) Eusebius (AD 325) placed Colossians among the *homolo-goumena* (books everyone received as Scripture).

5) Colossians is included in all the versions beginning with the Old Latin in the second century and the Peshito Syriac (a revision of the Old Syriac made in the 5th century).

e. "The external evidence for the Pauline authorship is therefore strong. Never until these later days of arbitrary criticism has the genuineness of the epistle been questioned."[51]

3. The Pauline authorship of Colossians has been questioned/rejected mainly on internal grounds.

a. The Pauline authorship was first rejected by 19th century writers.

A book by E.T. Mayerhoff, published posthumously by his brother, was the first to contest the genuineness of the Pauline authorship.[52] Mayerhoff argued from: (1) vocabulary and style, which he thought differed from other Pauline writings, (2) the appearance, to Mayerhoff, that Colossians was a condensation of Ephesians (which Mayerhoff did accept as genuine), and (3) alleged references to a disputation with Cerinthus (a 2nd century Gnostic). A few years after Mayerhoff's work appeared, W.M.L. DeWette reversed this argument, defending the authenticity of Colossians and rejecting Ephesians as the work of a later writer who drew on the former epistle.[53] F.C. Baur and the Tübingen school denied the Pauline authorship based on the belief that Colossians reflected acquaintance with 2nd century Gnosticism and therefore could not have been written by Paul.[54] Ewald

---

[51] Alfred Barry, "The Epistle to the Colossians" in the *Layman's Handy Commentary Series* (Grand Rapids: Zondervan, 1957 reprint), p.4.

[52] Ernst Theodor Mayerhoff, *Der Brief an de Kolosser, mit vornehmlicher Berücksichtigung der drei Pastoralbriefe, kritisch geprüft* (Berlin: Hermann Schultze, 1838). A summary of Mayerhoff's arguments has been given by John Eadie, *The Epistle of St. Paul to the Colossians*, (Grand Rapids: Zondervan, 1957), p.xxiv-xxx.

[53] W.M.L. DeWette, *Kurzgefasstes exegetisches Handbuch zum Neuen Testament-Aufl.2,4: Kurze Erklärung der Briefe an die Colosser, an Philemon, an die Ephesier und Philipper* (Leipzig: Weidmann, 1847).

[54] F.C. Baur, *Paulus, der Apostel Jesu Christi* (Stuttgart: Becher & Müller, 1845), pp. 417-457.

advanced the opinion that the epistle was written by Timothy after receiving from Paul special instructions with regard to the contents.[55]   In 1872, H.J. Holtzmann advanced the theory that there was a shorter Pauline Colossians written at the same time as Philemon, and that numerous verses were interpolated by the same hypothetical 2nd century Gnostic writer of our Ephesians, converting that shorter but genuine Pauline epistle into Colossians in its present form.[56]   Holtzmann put Ephesians and Colossians in parallel columns, and whatever was found in Colossians that is also Ephesians must be (he alleged) an interpolation, not originally written in Colossians by Paul.   As a result, for example, for Holtzmann, of chapter 3 of Colossians, only verses 3,12,13,17 were regarded as original.   All the rest, he affirmed, was interpolated by a later hand.   In an 1885 series of articles on Holtzmann's hypothesis, Hermann Von Soden modified Holtzmann's theory by reducing the amount of interpolations.[57]   He later recognized the whole epistle as Pauline with the exception of 1:16b,17, which he thinks may be a gloss because it disturbs the symmetry.[58]

b.   The Pauline authorship continued to be rejected by some 20th century writers.

In 1950, Charles Masson tried to revive Holtzmann's theory of interpolations.   Masson's hypothesis was that there originally was a short version of Colossians which was a genuine Pauline letter, to which the unknown author of Ephesians added additional material, and published both letters under Paul's name.[59]   In 1950, P.N. Harrison hypothesized that Colossians, as we have it now, is an expansion by the author of Ephesians of a genuine letter which had accompa-

---

[55] Heinrich Ewald, *Die Sendschreiben des Apostels Paulus* (Gottingen: Dieterichs, 1857), p.xii, 466ff.

[56] H.J. Holtzmann, *Kritik der Epheser- and Kolosserbriefe* (Leipzig: Engelmann, 1872).

[57] *Jahrbücher für Protestantische Theologie*, 11 (1885), pp.320ff, 497ff, 672ff.

[58] A.S. Peake, *The Epistle to the Colossians*, in Expositor's Greek Testament (Grand Rapids: Eerdmans, 1967), p.488.

[59] Charles Masson, *L'Epitre de Saint Paul aux Colossians* (Neuchâtel: Delachaux & Niestlé, 1950), p.86.   Masson proposed that the original shorter "Colossians" lacked 1:5-6,9-29; 2:1-5,7,10,11b,12b,13-15,17-19,22-23; 3:1-2,5-11,13b-17,22b-24; 4:3c,4,8b,12b,13,16.

nied our Philemon.[60]   Harrison's interpolation theory is closely akin to Holtzmann's except Harrison limits the non-Pauline interpolated material to 1:15-24, 2:4,8-23, the passages where all the alleged non-Pauline characteristics occur. He supposed the original Colossians dates to Paul's Ephesian ministry, with the interpolations being added forty or fifty years later.[61]   In 1951, F.C. Synge revived Mayerhoff's original suggestion that Ephesians is a genuine Pauline letter while Colossians is but a poor imitation.   Synge hypothesized that Colossians was produced by some writer who borrowed material from Ephesians while also drawing some personal names from Philemon.[62]   E.P. Sanders concluded in a 1966 journal article that materials drawn from three or more of Paul's genuine letters by a "secondary imitator" have been conflated in Colossians 1:15-16, 1:20-22a, 2:12-13, 3:5-11.[63]   Gunther Bornkamm,[64] Joachim Gnilka,[65] Victor Furnish,[66] Eduard Lohse,[67] Petr Pokorny,[68] and Raymond Brown[69] all have concluded that Colossians is not only pseudonymous but also post-Pauline, written about AD 70 or 80.

---

[60] P.N. Harrison, 'Onesimus and Philemon' in *Anglican Theological Review*, vol. XXXII (Oct. 1950), p.272.

[61] *Op. cit.*, p.273.

[62] F.C. Synge, *Philippians and Colossians* (London: SCM, 1951), pp.51-57.

[63] E.P. Sanders, "Literary Dependence in Colossians," *JBL* 85 (1966) p.40.

[64] Gunther Bornkamm (Die Hoffnung im Kolosserbrief, in vol.2 of *Geschichte und Glaube* (*Gesammelte Aufsätze,* vol.4;   Munich: Kaiser, 1971), p.206-213.

[65] Joachim Gnilka, *Der Kollosserbrief* in Herders theologischer Kommentar zum Neuen Testament 10/1 (Freiburg: Herder, 1980), p.19-26.

[66] Victor Furnish, "Colossians, Epistle to the," in *Abingdon Bible Dictionary* (New York: Doubleday, 1992), Vol.1, p.1094.

[67] Eduard Lohse, *Colossians and Philemon* in the Hermeneia series (Philadelphia: Fortress, 1971), p.177-183.   See also Eduard Lohse, "Pauline Theology in the Letter to the Colossians," *NTS* 15 (1969), p.217-18.

[68] Petr Pokorny, *Colossians.   A Commentary*, tr. By Sigfried Schatzmann (Peabody, MA: Hendrickson, 1991), p.10-19.

[69] Raymond Brown, *An Introduction to the New Testament* (New Haven, CT: Yale University Press, 1997), pp.610-615, appeals to five internal arguments for spuriousness: vocabulary, style, theology, the dispute with false teachers, and the characters and situation.

c. A summary of the arguments marshaled against a Pauline authorship.

Despite the external evidence and the self-claims of the text, Colossians has been counted among the "disputed" Pauline letters for the following reasons:

(1) *Similarity to Ephesians.* W.G. Kümmel stated that out of 155 verses in Ephesians, 73 have some verbal parallel with Colossians.[70] That is sufficient similarity for some to find evidence that one or the other of the letters was the result of copying. Many hypotheses have been advanced in an attempt to explain these undoubted resemblances. For example, scholars have advanced hypotheses about which letter was written first. If Colossians was first, who is responsible for Ephesians? If Ephesians was first, who is responsible for Colossians? And in either case, what was the motive behind the imitation of the genuine one? Did someone abbreviate a longer original, or did someone interpolate materials into a shorter original? And who might the someone have been?

(2) *The type of heresy opposed in the letter.* The heresy combated in Colossians was identified with 2nd century Gnosticism. If it is true that Colossians was written to deal with a 2nd century heresy, it makes the writing of Colossians too late to have been by Paul.

(3) *Vocabulary and style.* Some earlier arguments against the Pauline authorship appealed to the vocabulary found in Colossians, both the presence of words not found elsewhere in Paul's writings (*hapax legomena*[71]) and the absence of many of Paul's favorite terms terms[72] (e.g., righteousness, revelation, prove, obedience, salvation, fellowship, law, and believe) found in the "capital epistles" (*Hauptbriefe*[73]). Recent writers have focused attention on the letter's style, as distinct from its vocabulary.[74] Sentences in Colossians (e.g., 1:3-8, 2:6-15) are

---

[70] Paul Feine, Johannes Behm, and Werner G. Kümmel, *Introduction to the New Testament*, 14th rev. ed. Tr. A. J. Mattill, Jr. (Nashville: Abingdon, 1966), p.253.

[71] Words that occur only once in the New Testament are called *hapax legomena*, "things uttered once." Sometimes words that occur only once in Paul's writings are called *"hapax legomena* in Paul." More than fifty words in Colossians are not found elsewhere in Paul's writings. This number jumps to eighty-seven words if the Pastoral Epistles are treated as being non-Pauline.

[72] "Paulinisms" is the technical term used to refer to such favorite words.

[73] The German term, meaning "principal (or main) letters," is used to cover 1 and 2 Corinthians, Galatians, and Romans, which most critics admit are Pauline.

[74] One very influential book concerning style is W. Bujard, *Stilanalystische Untershungen zum Kolosserbrief als Beitrag zur Methodik von Sprachvergleichen* (Gottingen: Vandenhoeck and Ruprecht, 1973).

said to be significantly longer and more complex than in many of Paul's letters. The claim is made that there is an unusual number of genitival combinations, e.g., "the reward of the inheritance" (3:24), "putting off the body of ... flesh" (2:11), "the increase of God" (2:19), and "the hope of glory" (1:27). Participial constructions and relative clauses are employed much more frequently, as are an unusual number of instances of the prepositional phrase with *en* (thirteen in 1:9-23, and fifteen in 2:9-15).

(4) *Theology.* A number of the critics have concluded the letter is full of non-Pauline ideas, especially in the areas of Christology and ecclesiology, all of which are supposed to suggest that the letter comes from a later time period than Paul. It has been alleged that the high Christology of the epistle, especially Colossians 1:15-20 and 2:9,10, is unlike the recognized Pauline statements of 1 Corinthians 8:6 and Romans 8:31-39. Supposedly, this passage rather reflects a date nearer the middle of the 2nd century. It is alleged that the Christology of the epistle (viz., "in Him all the fullness of Deity dwells in bodily form") is too much like the Logos doctrine of John (which critics date in the 2nd century), and therefore must come from a later time than Paul. The emphasis on the influence that Christ's death had over angels and demons in the unseen world (2:15) is said to be different from the effect His death had on individual salvation, such as Romans and Galatians emphasize. Alleged differences in ecclesiology focus on the idea that Christ is head of the body, the church (1:18), and on the allegation that the Colossian letter comes from the post-apostolic era of "early catholicism" (*Frühkatholizismus*) because Epaphras (4:12) is (Marxsen believed[75]) treated as a successor to Paul, and so represents apostolic succession.

(5) *Pseudonymity embraced.* Having concluded that the internal evidence rules out the Pauline authorship of Colossians, critics have gone to work to try to identify the hypothetical author or authors who forged Paul's name on the letter. Timothy, Epaphras, and a Pauline school centered in Ephesus have all been suggested as the possible pseudonymous writer.

4. The Pauline authorship has been stoutly defended.

a. 20th century advocates of the Pauline authorship

---

[75] W. Marxsen, *Einleitung in das Neue Testament* (Guetersloh, Germany: Mohn and Co., 1963), p.160. See footnote #36 in the Detailed Introduction to Ephesians for further information about "early catholicism."

As soon as critics offered their hypotheses to deny the Pauline authorship, their arguments were answered. Alfred Barry (1903) strongly refuted both Holtzmann's theory and Baur's theory in his paragraph on "The Genuineness of the Epistle."[76] So did T.K. Abbott,[77] H.A.W. Meyer,[78] Andrew Zenos,[79] and John Eadie,[80] all of whose works are still available for study. The evidences and arguments supporting the historic view of the Pauline authorship of Colossians have continued to be clearly set forth by Henry C. Thiessen,[81] William Hendriksen,[82] Donald Guthrie,[83] E. Percy,[84] P.T. O'Brien,[85] and Douglas J. Moo, who points out, "The letter's claim to be written by Paul is no casual matter. It is a claim built into the warp and woof of the letter, elaborated with detail after detail."[86]

---

[76] Alfred Barry, "The Epistle to the Colossians" in *Ellicott's Commentary on the Whole Bible* (Grand Rapids: Zondervan, 1959 reprint), Vol.8, p.92,93.

[77] T.K. Abbott, "The Epistles to the Ephesians and the Colossians" in the *International Critical Commentary* (Edinburgh: T&T Clark, 1956 reprint), p.l-lix.

[78] H.A.W. Meyer, *Critical and Exegetical Handbook to the Epistles to the Philippians and Colossians and to Philemon* (Winona Lake, IN: Alpha Publications, 1979 reprint), p.199-205.

[79] Andrew C. Zenos, "Colossians, Epistle to the," in *The Popular and Critical Bible Encyclopedia and Scriptural Dictionary* (Chicago: Howard-Severance Co., 1911), Vol.1, p.442.

[80] John Eadie, *Commentary on the Epistle of Paul to the Colossians* (Grand Rapids: Zondervan, 1957 reprint), p. xxii-xxx.

[81] Henry C. Thiessen, *Introduction to the New Testament* (Grand Rapids: Eerdmans, 1954), p.229-231.

[82] William Hendriksen, "Exposition of Colossians and Philemon" in *New Testament Commentary* (Grand Rapids: Baker, 1964), p.19-37.

[83] Donald Guthrie, *New Testament Introduction: The Pauline Epistles* (Chicago: Inter-Varsity Press, 1968), p.167-171.

[84] The Pauline authorship is stoutly defended by E. Percy, "Zu den Problemen des Kolosser und Epheserbriefes," *ZNW* 43 (1950Ы1), p.178-194.   See also his *Die Probleme der Kolosser- und Epheserbriefe* (Lund: C. W. K. Gleerup, 1946)

[85] P.T. O'Brien, *Colossians, Philemon* in Word Biblical Commentary 44 (Waco, TX: Word, 1982), p.xli-xlix, and his "Colossians" in *Dictionary of Paul and His Letters*, ed. By Gerald F. Hawthorne and Ralph P. Martin (Downers Grove, IL: Inter-Varsity, 1993), p.150-152.

[86] Douglas J. Moo, *Pillar New Testament Commentary: The Letters to the Colossians and to Philemon* (Grand Rapids: Eerdmans, 2008), p.28-29.

Eduard Schweizer[87] and James D.G. Dunn[88] have adopted Ewald's argument that Colossians was composed at Paul's direction by Timothy.

b. Summary of the answers to the arguments of the negative critics

Substantive answers have been proffered to the various reasons the Pauline authorship has been disputed. (These answers are listed in the same order given above):

(1) *Similarity to Ephesians.* The most natural conclusion would be that all the similarities between Colossians and Ephesians are due to the same author writing and dispatching these epistles at one and the same time, but sending them to different places. Since a number of passages can be identified which seem to prove the priority of Ephesians and an equal number which would seem to be just as conclusive that Colossians was the earlier, the question of which letter was written first still has not been solved with certainty. Due to the fact that proponents of an interpolation theory have not been able to identify exactly which verses are or are not interpolations, it may be affirmed that the relationship of Colossians and Ephesians is not correctly presented when it is said Ephesians is an elaboration of the nucleus of Colossians by a later writer, or that Colossians is an abridgement of Ephesians by some later writer.[89]

(2) *Type of heresy.* It is no longer widely held, as early critics did, that the heresy opposed in Colossians is to be identified with the fully developed Gnostic systems of the 2nd century. Instead, as will be shown subsequently in these introductory studies, there is increasing recognition that the type of heresy the epistle to the Colossians attacks is not the developed Gnosticism of the 2nd century AD, but an incipient Gnosticism which had already emerged in Judaism prior to the time of Christ. "The Dead Sea Scrolls have unveiled developments within Judaism con-

---

[87] Eduard Schweizer, *The Letter to the Colossians: A Commentary*, tr. By A. Chester (Minneapolis: Augsburg, 1982), p.21-24.

[88] James D.G. Dunn, *The Epistles to the Colossians and to Philemon*, in NIGNT (Grand Rapids: Eerdmans, 1996), p.38. See also James D.G. Dunn, "Pseudepigraphy" in the *Dictionary of the Later New Testament and Its Developments,* ed. Ralph Martin and Peter H. Davids (Downers Grove, IL: Inter-Varsity, 1997), p. 982.

[89] Are we to believe that the original Pauline Colossians was known only to the interpolator who rescued it from oblivion, only to consign it to oblivion again? Are we to believe that the early Christians allowed a genuine letter from Paul to become completely lost without trace or mention, for the sake of two forgeries by an unknown non-Pauline hand from a later date? The whole thesis has too many unacceptable ramifications to be accepted. Six further objections to the interpolation theory may be seen in G. Johnson, "Colossians" in *Interpreter's Dictionary Of Bible* (Nashville: Abingdon, 2000), p.659.

firming suspicions that it contained a speculative element which would well account for the existence of the type of phenomenon which the writer of Colossians opposes."[90]

(3) *Vocabulary and style.* The *hapax legomena* arguments that have been used against the authenticity of Colossians cannot stand up to serious examination. Percy has shown that the totals of such *hapax legomena* in Philippians, a genuinely Pauline letter of comparable length, are not much different from Colossians – 76 words used in Philippians are found in no other Pauline letter and 36 of these are present nowhere else in the New Testament, and this does not lead critics to reject the Pauline authorship of that letter.[91] Furthermore, most of the 34 *hapax legomena* in Colossians are located in Colossians 1:9-25 and in 2:4-23, which is most natural in view of the fact that Paul is therein engaged in refutation of heretical concerns not dealt with in any earlier letters. When it comes to the claim that Paul's favorite words are missing from Colossians, it should not be overlooked that there is also a lack of such words in the letters admitted by the critics to be Paul's. "Righteousness" occurs only once in 1 Corinthians or Galatians, and not at all in 1 Thessalonians. The verb "justify" does not occur in 1 Thessalonians, Philippians, or in 2 Corinthians. Likewise, "salvation" does not appear in Galatians or in 1 Corinthians. Regarding the matter of style, long sentences written by Paul are found at Romans 1:1-7 (93 words in the original); Romans 2:5-10 (87 words); Philippians 1:3-7 (88 words); Philippians 3:8-11 (78 words). Romans 1-2 contain a number of synonyms, as does Philippians 1; and genitives abound in 1 Corinthians, Romans, and Philippians. It is not necessary to deny the Pauline authorship of Colossians when it has many of the same vocabulary and style features as letters admitted to be Pauline.

(4) *Theology.* On the topic of the high Christology alleged to be only in Colossians, we deny the evolutionary hypothesis that the doctrine about Christ's Deity grew as time passed. Granting the similarity of John and Paul concerning who Jesus is, it remains to be shown why two apostles should not have the same view of the person of Christ. Why should not all the writers in the early church have the same exalted view of the person and work of Christ? Further, there is no need treat Colossians 1:15-29 and 2:8 as being a peculiar presentation of who Jesus is, as unlike anything else Paul wrote. Romans 9:5 calls Jesus God. Philippians 2:5-9 presents a profound statement of Jesus' pre-existence, Deity, and incarnation. So do 1 Timothy 3:16 and Titus 2:13. The doctrine of the cos-

---

[90] Weed, *op. cit.,* p.29.

[91] Percy, *op. cit.,* p.17.

mic significance of Christ's mission to earth is not new (cf. Romans 8:19-22; 1 Corinthians 1:24, 2:6-10, 8:6); rather, it may be said that what was implied here and there in some of Paul's earlier epistles is unfolded more fully in Colossians as a foil to what the false teachers at Colossae were advocating. The Christology in Colossians fits well with what Paul wrote in Philippians 2:6-11. Regarding ecclesiology, the church is already compared to the body in 1 Corinthians 12:12-27 and Romans 12:4,5. A correct reading of Colossians 4:12 does not support the doctrine of apostolic succession, or that Colossians originated in the post-apostolic period called "early catholicism."[92]

(5) *The idea of pseudonymity is to be rejected* for a number of reasons. *First*, in spite of critic's assurances to the contrary, there is no certain evidence that the earliest Christians recognized pseudonymous writings among the Biblical books. E.E. Ellis has correctly called attention to the exclusion from the canon on pseudonymous works such as *1 Enoch, 4 Ezra,* or the apostolic pseudepigrapha such as the *Epistles of Paul and Seneca* or the *Apocalypse of Peter*. Ellis also has correctly judged that the reason they were excluded was precisely because the names of the authors assigned to the works were the false appropriation of names that were intended to carry the weight of authority.[93] *Second*, it is difficult to envisage a scenario where 4:7-17 can be explained if Colossians is post-Pauline. *Third*, what was true for Ephesians if it is deemed pseudonymous is also true here; namely, that there is a steep price to pay for pseudonymity. The data that may be discovered in the letter concerning its destination, the occasion of its composition in the mission to Rome of Epaphras (1:7b-8), who is himself pictured as a Colossian and the putative founder of the congregation (1:5b-7; 4:12-13), may all be deemed to be make-believe. Make-believe also is the mission of Tychicus and Onesimus who are going to tell the Colossians all about Paul's present circumstances and bring them words of encouragement (4:7-9). So, too, are the first-person personal references (1:23-25, 1:29-2:5, and 4:3). All these little touches must be judged to have been slipped in by the forger in an attempt to give this letter a believable setting within Paul's lifetime. *Fourth*, the whole theory (itself the child of redaction criticism) that there even was a post-Pauline school which attempted to keep Paul's teachings alive by producing writings in his name is based on circular reasoning. Lohse and Dunn have both flatly stated that once certain letters have been identified as being post-Pauline, the existence

---

[92] For a recent challenge to the concept of early catholicism cf. I.H. Marshall, "Early Catholicism in the New Testament," *New Dimensions in New Testament Study,* ed. R.N. Longenecker and M.C. Tenney (Grand Rapids: Zondervan Publishers, 1974), 217-231; and L. Morris, "Luke and Early Catholicism," *WThJ* 35 (1973), p.121-136.

[93] E.E. Ellis, "Pseudonymity and Canonicity of New Testament Documents" in *Worship, Theology and Ministry in the Early Church: Essays in Honor of Ralph P. Martin,* ed. M. Wilkens and T. Paige; *JSNTSup* 87 (Sheffield: JSOT Press, 1992), p.218-19.

of those letters then is construed as a testimony that such a school existed.[94] Accept the letters that bear his signature as being Pauline, and there is no evidence such a school ever existed. The statement of Paul's commission to preach the gospel (Colossians 1:23-2:5) is the same language we find in 2 Corinthians 10-13 where Paul defends his apostolic authority. It is a great mistake to use (as Kasemann has done with Colossians[95]) a genuine apostolic claim as a proof of a post-Pauline school who made up such a position. The role of an apostle of Jesus in Colossians is precisely the same as that pictured in 2 Corinthians 10-13 where Paul defends his apostolic authority. An apostle's authority was not limited to just the churches he planted, but transcended the particulars of time and place and encompassed the world. Indeed, Paul does not go where other apostles have evangelized, but he (like Peter) exercised authority over all the congregations, even those planted by other apostles and evangelists.

5. There is no irrefutable reason to question the Pauline authorship of Colossians.

Our long presentation of the authorship question reflects that it is a major battleground issue among introductory studies to Colossians. What has been shown is that denials of the Pauline authorship are based on arguments from alleged *internal* evidence, and often by folk who are trying to make the Bible agreeable with the popular philosophy current in the critic's time frame.

External evidence may be summarized as follows: "There is no shred of evidence that the Pauline authorship of the whole or any part of this epistle was ever disputed until the nineteenth century. It has formed a part of the Pauline Corpus as far back as can be traced. Evidence of such character cannot lightly be swept aside."[96] The links (same signature, same people who send greetings, Onesimus named in both) between Colossians and Philemon (which is granted to be genuinely Pauline) are further support in favor of the Pauline authorship of Colossians. Douglas J. Moo's conclusion concerning internal evidence bears

---

[94] "The rise of deutero-Pauline writings presupposes ... a school tradition" (Lohse, *Colossians,* p.181 note 12). Dunn's theorizing about who may have comprised such an alleged post-Pauline school begins with a reference to the letters allegedly written by this school (James D.G. Dunn, "Pauline Legacy and School," in *Dictionary of the Later New Testament and Its Development,* ed. Ralph p. Martin and Peter H. Davids [Downers Grove, IL: InterVarsity, 1997], p.888).

[95] Ernst Kasemann, *Essays on New Testament Themes,* tr. W. J. Montague (London: SCM, 1964), p.166,167.

[96] Guthrie, *op. cit.,* p.170.

repeating: "The letter's claim to be written by Paul is no casual matter. It is a claim built into the warp and woof of the letter, elaborated with detail after detail."[97]

D. THE COLOSSIAN CRISIS

The letter itself suggests Paul's reason for composing it. Disquieting information about a new danger to the young churches was brought to Rome by Epaphras (1:7,8, 4:12,13). As Paul writes to confront this danger, he describes it as being a "philosophy" (2:8). He was using the word "philosophy" as it was used in the 1st century, as referring to an elaborate system of "contemporary religious beliefs."[1]

Just what this elaborate system was is the other major issue of dispute in Colossian studies. Even a name for the danger has proven elusive. Lightfoot called it "the Colossian heresy."[2] Some have attempted to identify it as Essenism,[3] or Jewish *Merkebah* mysticism.[4] But none of these account for all the

---

[97] Moo, *ibid.*

[1] The Jewish philosopher Philo (10 B.C.-A.D. 50) wrote of "the philosophy of Moses" (*De Mutatione Nominum* 39). He also referred to Judaism as the "philosophy of our ancestors" and as "Judaic philosophy" (*Legatio ad Gaium* 23 and 33). Similarly, Josephus wrote of the three Jewish sects as "three philosophies," i.e., three schools of philosophy (*Antiquities* XVIII.1.2).

[2] Lightfoot, *op. cit.*, p.73. Care must be taken here: (1) A heresy is a false teaching that challenges or contradicts the established faith. To call the false teaching at Colossae a "heresy" rightly carries with it the implication that the teachings of the apostles already presented a unified body of doctrine, "the faith once for all delivered to the saints" (Jude 3). Post-modernism has led some 21st century scholars to affirm that there were competing Christianities in the 1st century world, with the 2nd century finally beginning to see a unanimity of accepted Christian doctrine. Of course, if this were true (which we deny), to talk of "heresy" when there was no settled "faith" would be anachronistic. (2) To call it the "*Colossian* heresy" may leave the erroneous idea the heresy was a matter of interest 2000 years ago, but of no interest today. Nothing could be further from the truth. Ideas similar to the ones taught by the errorists at Colossae are being propagated by many teachers in the 21st century – many of whom claim no relationship to Christianity, but some of whom do. These ideas are as wrong in the 21st century as they were in the 1st century.

[3] Lightfoot, "The Colossian Heresy," *op. cit.*, pp.73-113, considered the Colossian heresy to be a form of Gnostic Judaism.

[4] F.F. Bruce, "The Colossian Heresy" in *BibSac* 141 (July-Sept. 1984), p.201-204.

terms used in Colossians 2. Not a few contemporary writers speak of "incipient Gnosticism" or "religious syncretism"[5] since ideas drawn from several religious belief systems had been melded into an elaborate religious system by folk living in the Lycus valley.

Epaphras' and Paul's concerns indicate that some church members were beginning to be impressed by the false teachings. When ideas drawn from Christianity began to be assimilated into the philosophy, the more dangerous it became to the faith and stability of the Christians (2:5).

1. Allusions to the teachings and practices of the system

The nature of the troublesome problem at Colossae can only be inferred from the contents of the epistle. It would appear from Paul's emphasis on Christology in this letter (1:15-23, 2:9-15) that the philosophy circulating at Colossae called into question the preeminence of Christ. In addition, Paul makes specific statements (2:8-23) that seem to be confronting particular deceptive teachings. Scholars have examined these counter-arguments in an attempt to identify the philosophy's characteristics. However, some of the terms Paul uses in these verses are subject to different interpretations,[6] and this in turn has rendered uncertain our attempts to establish the identity of the thing being opposed.

Some things that have be gleaned from an overview of key verses include:

a. 2:1 – The mention of Laodicea indicates that the Colossian heresy was a danger there, also.

b. 2:2 – Paul wants men everywhere to know the "mystery" of God. Is there something about the heresy that he is setting in the right light with this explanation? Are its doctrines regarded as secret "mysteries" available only to a few elite "mature ones" (1:27,28)?

---

[5] Freed, *op. cit.*, p.303. See also Clinton Arnold, *The Colossian Syncretism - The Interface Between Christianity and Folk Belief at Colossae* (Grand Rapids: Baker, 1996).

[6] Five terms in particular have been the subject of intense study: *stoicheia*, "elementary principles" (2:8,20); *threskeia tōn angelōn*, "worship of angels" (2:18); *tapeinophrosunē*, "humility" (2:18,23); *embateuo*, "intruding" (2:18); and *ethelothrēskeia*, "self-made religion" (2:23).

c. 2:3 – The emphasis in the letter on "wisdom" (1:9,28; 2:3,23; 3:16; 4:5) and "knowledge" (1:6,9-10; 2:2-3; 3:10) and "insight" (1:9; 2:2) suggests the deceptive teachers claimed access to ancient "wisdom" and "knowledge."

d. 2:4 – Suggests the Christians were being pressured to conform to the religious beliefs and practices of their Jewish and pagan neighbors. 2:8 warns the readers lest they be taken captive (carried off as spoil). The plunder turns out to be the Christians if they become victims of the deceptive teachers.

e. 2:8 – "Philosophy and empty deception," "according to the tradition of men," "according to the elementary principles of the world," and "not according to Christ" are all descriptions of the religious system Paul is combating. The three "according to" phrases are intended to describe the source of the false teaching. First, it is designated as being "according to the traditions of men," which means it was a human invention that ran counter to Biblical truths, and especially to the essential truths of their Christian faith. "Empty deception" warns that it sounds very plausible, but it is a clever trick to mislead folk. Second, when Paul says the teachings are "according to the elementary principles (Greek, *stoicheia*) of the world," he seems to be saying that demons were the source of the deceptive religious system against which this letter warns.[7] The term *stoicheia,* translated "elementary principles," has a broad range of meanings. It can refer to "elementary instruction" (like abc's), or to the "physical elements" (earth, air, fire, and water, the elementary building blocks of the universe in ancient understanding), or "spirit beings" believed to rule over the elements ("elemental spirits," RSV).[8] In this commentator's judgment, the last is the correct understanding of Colossians. "Not according to Christ" indicates the philosophy is not at all what Jesus taught, and furthermore, it would not be possible to mix belief and unbelief. Verse 8 is the first of three warnings in Colossians 2 about the dangers of this philosophy.

f. 2:9-15 – What is the point of stopping in the midst of the discussion to tell us that all the "fullness" dwells in Christ?   And that He is the

---

[7] Compare "doctrines of demons" at 1 Timothy 4:1.

[8] Arnold, *op. cit.,* has an entire chapter (chapter 6, p.158ff) on the subject of the *stoicheia.* His conclusion is that the reference here in Colossians is to elemental spirits. This refers to what we call animism, the belief in local spirits or deities thought to have authority over an area.

"head of all principality and power" (verse 10)?   It is implied in these verses that Christ's exalted status over all creation, including the hostile powers, was being undermined by the deceptive teachings and teachers at Colossae.   They must have had a peculiar explanation of "fullness" (Greek, *plērōma*).   That seems to be the reason for calling attention to the fact that all the "fullness of Deity" dwells in Christ, and that He is the "head over all rule and authority" (verse 10).   It seems that the deceptive teachers were undermining Christ's exalted position over rulers and authorities, "rulers and authorities" (verse 15) being different ranks of angels in the false philosophy.[9]   Paul has picked up terms used by the false teachers and shows that Christians (those who have been buried with Him in baptism, verse 12) have nothing to fear from the elemental spirits, because they were overcome at the cross.   In fact, even the Old Testament – the writings used by some of the deceptive teachers to document their beliefs – had been nailed to the cross.   That a new covenant has been given in its place seems intended to be a rebuttal to some ideas included in the deceptive philosophy.

g. 2:16,17 – Paul's second warning begins with "therefore," which shows that this warning grows out of what Paul has just said about Christ's complete preeminence, and the fact that He removed the Law and triumphed over the rulers and authorities.   When Paul says "Let no one judge you," we conclude he is making a general reference to any of the devotees of the philosophy, rather than to an individual leader among them, and it looks like those devotees were condemning the Christians for not observing obsolete Mosaic rules (or their own additions to the Mosaic regulations) concerning eating and drinking[10] and observing special days on the religious calendar followed by the

---

[9] "The heresy implied there were spirit-powers who controlled the natural world and were to be revered as mediators between God and His creation.   Both the person and work of Christ were underrated by this system of angelic mediators, and His sole office as Lord of creation and all-sufficient Redeemer of the Church was seriously imperiled." (Ralph P. Martin, "Colossians, The Epistle to," in *Zondervan Pictorial Encyclopedia of the Bible*, ed. by Merrill C. Tenney (Grand Rapids: Zondervan, 1978), Vol.1, p.915.)

[10] The word translated "food" is not *brōma* ("food") but *brōsis*, "the act of eating," and the word translated "drink" is not *poma* ("drink") but *posis*, "the act of drinking."   The Essenes had rigorous restrictions regarding both eating and drinking.   The fact that these restrictions extended beyond traditional Jewish food laws may serve to indicate that the underlying concern, with them as well as with the deceptive teachers at Colossae, was a dualism that treated the physical world as evil.

devotees.[11]   There is a good possibility the things highlighted in this verse were treated as a means of reaching "fullness" (verse 10).   That would explain why Paul indicates they have already been made "full" ("complete," verse 10), and why he insists that the Mosaic materials pointed to Christ (verse 17).[12]

h.   2:18-22 – Paul's third warning identifies some of the major beliefs and practices found in the elaborate religious system which he is condemning.   "Let no one keep defrauding you of your prize" comes from a rare Greek word which denotes to act as a referee or judge in an athletic contest.   With this athletic metaphor, where the umpire or referee gives an unfair judgment which robbed the victor of his prize, Paul cautions his readers about the dangers of mystical experiences which are self-induced by means of sensory deprivation.

This warning contains several of the most puzzling expressions found in the whole letter to the Colossians.   The *first* of these, found in verses 18 and 23, is translated "delighting in self-abasement" in the NASB,[13] or "delights in false humility" in the TEV and NIV.[14]

The *second* of these is translated as "the worship of angels."   It is not exactly clear how this should be understood.   Are the angels to be understood as the worshipers (Greek: a subjective genitive) or as the objects of worship (Greek: an objective genitive)?   Both interpretations have been explored, with ancient sources being searched for examples.   Since "worship" is *threskeia*, which denotes the external practice of religion, perhaps there were actual ceremonies

---

[11] "Sabbath days" seems to point to a Jewish calendar, as also would the demand of the would-be judges that the new moon and the annual festivals of Passover, Pentecost, and Tabernacles be observed. All these were commanded in the Law of Moses, but we who follow Jesus are not obligated to keep these holidays.   The Essenes at Qumran attached great importance to calendrical questions as 4QMMT has indicated, but the Essenes apparently differed from the Pharisees in their calculation of sacred seasons (perhaps following the calendar enjoined in the Book of Jubilees). We may suppose something similar was being called for in Colossae.

[12] "The Law was our tutor to lead us to Christ" and "now that faith has come we are no longer under the tutor" (Galatians 3:24,25).

[13] There is a marginal note in the NASB showing that the Greek word translated "self-abasement" is actually the word elsewhere translated "humility."

[14] The NEB takes the whole phrase to mean "people who go in for self-mortification."

in which angels as a class (the Greek reads "worship of *the* angels") were worshiped.[15]   There is a close connection between the "false humility" and the "worship of angels."[16]   Later Gnostics taught that God was too high and men were too insignificant to approach God directly, so they sought to contact deity through the mediation of angels (aeons).   As a precursor to this later view, the Colossian devotees of the deceptive philosophy could be pictured as insisting that their worship of the angels rather than the supreme God was an expression of humility on their part.   In order that the angels might be obliged to pay attention to men, the men worshiped them.

"Taking his stand on *visions* he has seen" is the *third* of the puzzling expressions in this paragraph.   The person who would defraud the Colossian Christians is further described with another participle (*embateuōn*) which modifies "let no one ...."   According to Thayer's Lexicon, the participle can mean "to go on in detail about what he has seen."[17]   There is evidence that the word was used of the initiatory rites of the mystery cults, which rites were designed to lead the initiate to have visions and mystical experiences.[18]   If that is how the term is used here, Paul is scornfully quoting the very language used by the would-be referees to describe their self-induced visions.   They spoke of "entering in (being initiated) into the things which they saw."

"Inflated without cause by his fleshly mind" is a *fourth* descriptive phrase characterizing the ones who were not to be allowed to act as umpires against the Christians.   As a result of experiencing visions, the umpire's fleshly mind is said to be "puffed up."   They thought themselves superior to those who had not had such visions.   Verse 19 then states the self-appointed umpire makes his mistakes because he

---

[15] Angel worship did develop in Gnosticism of the 2nd century (the schools of Cerinthus and Valentinus).

[16] In Greek the word for "false humility" and the expression for "worship of angels" are governed by the same preposition.

[17] Joseph H. Thayer, *A Greek-English Lexicon of the New Testament* (New York: American Book Co., 1889), p.206.

[18] Arnold (*op. cit.*, p.104ff) devotes an entire chapter to analyzing how this word was used in local mystery cults near Colossae.

has no vital contact with Christ, who is the head of the church (Ephesians 1:22,23).

In Colossians 2:20 Paul uses the term *stoicheia* again, reminding the Colossians that the "elemental spirits" no longer are a threat to those who have died with Christ (which is what their baptism was all about, verse 12). Therefore, the ascetic regulations alluded to in verse 21 ("Do not handle, do not taste, do not touch"!), which are in accordance with the commandments and teachings of men (verse 22), were no longer needed to ward off the *stoicheia* and their pernicious influences (as animistic religionists once believed).

i. 2:23 – Paul closes his warning about the "philosophy" with several pointed statements. First, there is a statement which explains why needless rules and regulations are accepted by so many people: they seem reasonable, they appear to be wise. But they are not God's wisdom. Paul castigates it as a self-imposed or self-made religion; God never commanded it. He again speaks about the false humility (the same word as used in verse 18) and then about the "severe treatment of the body" (which we have called sensory deprivation). Paul's final appraisal is that asceticism is a dismal failure. Such rules are ineffective when it comes to attempting to control the body so as to avoid fleshly indulgence.

2. Brief introduction to 2nd and 3rd century Gnosticism

For many years what we knew about 2nd and 3rd century Gnosticism was what we could deduce from the Christian writers such as Justin Martyr,[19] Irenaeus,[20] Tertullian,[21] and Hippolytus,[22] who all wrote refutations of it. Now, our knowledge of Gnosticism has been greatly increased because of the discovery of 13 papyrus manuscripts in Egypt in 1945. Known as the Nag Hammadi Library, these manuscripts were part of a Gnostic library. Translation work on the find was slow. Two of these manuscripts, the *Jung Codex* and the *Gospel of*

---

[19] *On the Resurrection*, and *Syntagma*.

[20] *Against Heresies*.

[21] *Against Marcion*.

[22] *Against Valentinus*.

Thomas, show that the early Christian writers' description of Gnosticism was exactly right. Another recently found Gnostic work is the *Gospel of Judas,* found at El Minya, Egypt, in the 1970s.

There was more than one system or school of Gnostics, but the following elements are found in most of the systems.

1. *Gnosticism was syncretistic.* Ideas were gathered from Jewish sources, from Greek philosophy, and from Eastern religions. After Christianity was introduced into the world, ideas from it were assimilated, too. As a result, Tertullian regarded Gnosticism as the product of the combination of Greek philosophy and Christianity.[23]

2. *Gnostics claimed to have superior wisdom which was hidden from others* who had never been initiated into the system. The word "Gnosticism" comes from a Greek root which means "to know." Such secret knowledge the select few Gnostics had access to was made the condition of salvation,[24] and was considered to be superior to faith. The general emphasis among the Gnostics was 'Join our group and we will teach you the things you really need to know in order to have salvation.' Gnostics taught that one could not learn what men needed "to know" either in the church or in the gospel of Christ. 'There is something more men need to know, and if you will just join us, we'll teach you so that you will have the "knowledge" that Christianity fails to give you.' The Gnostic movement was a secret organization. Men, vainly puffed up, thought it was something to be invited to become a Gnostic.

3. *Most Gnostic systems were dualistic.* In theology, "dualism" (from the Latin "duo" meaning "two") refers to the ancient doctrine that there are two independent divine beings or eternal principles, one good and the other evil.[25] In Greek philosophy, "dualism" was the idea which treated spirit as good and all matter as evil. Dualism resulted in a number of speculations concerning the relationship of God to the created universe, how creation occurred, and how communication (if any) could be carried on in either direction between God and men.

---

[23] *On Prescription Against Heretics* 7.

[24] Care must be exercised here since "salvation" to a Gnostic does not mean what "salvation" does to a Christian who has been nurtured on Biblical truths. For the Gnostic, it is salvation from ignorance, not salvation from sins. As an adherent of a Gnostic school, you would learn its teachings about the spiritual world and learn to reject the physical world of the Demiurge. You would especially learn to reject the God of the Bible.

[25] Zoroastrianism, the ancient religion of Babylon, was dualistic. The two gods were Ahura Mazda (the god of light) and Angra Mainyu (the god of darkness).

4. *To Gnostics, the Supreme Being (God) is an impersonal being or force.* The triune, personal God whom we meet in the Bible is not to be confused with the impersonal being that was thought to be the Supreme Being in Gnostic theology. In fact, the God of the Bible was pictured by Gnostics as being the bad God, while the impersonal wholly-other Supreme Being of Gnosticism was the good God. Gnostics used the term "fullness" (*plērōma*) when speaking of the wholly other Supreme Being. In some Gnostic systems, the word "fullness" in a Greek philosophical sense refers to the totality of virtues, attributes and energies of the Supreme Being, in contrast to "emptyness" (*kenōma*)[26] or incompleteness (*hysterēma*)[27] or deficiency (*hēttēma*). In other Gnostic systems (e.g., Valentinianism), "fullness" (*plērōma*) was used for the totality of all the thirty emanations from God.[28] The Supreme Being was outside the *plērōma*. Thus, for Cerinthus, *plērōma* expressed the fullness of the Divine Life out of which the Divine Christ descended upon the man Jesus at his baptism, and into which He returned.[29]

5. *How can creation be explained?* How could a good God create an evil world? Gnostics held that the Supreme Being did not create the world directly. Instead, some lesser beings (angels, spirits, aeons) emanated from the "fullness" (*plērōma*) of the Supreme Being, and from those lesser beings (in different and descending degrees of imperfection) emanated some lesser beings, until finally one of them called the Demiurge (or great workman), an evil aeon, created the world. Gnostic lore was full of "endless genealogies" (1 Timothy 1:3,4) in an attempt to account for all these emanations. In Gnostic teaching the Demiurge and the God of the Bible are the same beings. Thus, all of nature, being matter, is evil and a mistake made by the Demiurge who was ignorant of the Supreme Being.[30] This is how Gnostics attempted to maintain the essential separation of matter and spirit, matter being intrinsically evil and the source from which all evil has arisen.

---

[26] Irenaeus, *Adv. Haer.* I. iv. 1

[27] Irenaeus, *Adv. Haer.* I. xvi. 3; Hippolytus vi. 31.

[28] *The Gospel of Truth,* I:41. "All emanations from the Father are *plērōmas.*" James M. Robinson, ed., *The Nag Hamadi Library in English* (San Francisco: HarperSanFrancisco, 1988), p.50.

[29] Irenaeus, *Adv. Haer.* I. xxvi. 1, III. xi. 1, xvi. 1.

[30] The Gnostic doctrine completely ignores the fact that what God created was very good (Genesis 1:31), and then because of sin was subjected to futility/vanity (Romans 8:20). God didn't create it the way it is now.

6. *Gnosticism embraced an elaborate system of elemental spirits*. Many of these ideas were assimilated from Greek mythology. On the subject of cosmogony, Diogenes Laertius spoke of the Pythagorean teaching (c. 500 BC and onwards) that the upper air contains the sun, moon, and stars, which are inhabited by spirits who control human destiny. The atmosphere is filled with spirit-powers who are to be venerated, and the soul must be kept purified (through ascetic practices, including ritual washings, abstaining from meat, and avoiding pollution) if it is to pass through the spheres to the divine regions after death.[31] In the Gnostic *Book of Enoch* 82:10 ff., the stars have their angels; each of the four seasons has its angel; each of the 12 months of the year has its angel; and each of the 360 days of the year (the full extent of the year at that time) had its angel.

7. *Gnostics encouraged mystical experiences or visions*. The Hellenistic world as well as the Roman empire was filled with mystery cults. They were called mystery religions because they were secretive, often shrouded in a body of rituals not to be revealed to the uninitiated. The Eleusinian mysteries celebrated yearly at Eleusis near Athens in Greece antedated the coming of Christ by 1500 years. It eventually spread to the borders of the Roman empire. The cult of the Syrian goddess Cybele (or the Great Mother) was perhaps the most popular of all these religions. However, other cults also appealed to a great number of Romans, such as the cult of the mother-goddess Isis and her son Osiris from Egypt, the cult of Dionysius from Greece, and the cult of Mithra from Persia (which was known before 500 BC). Some were introduced to the Mediterranean world by the soldiers of Alexander the Great as they returned from the wars. Some were popular with soldiers of Rome. Traders, merchants, slaves, and deportees from foreign countries helped spread the mystery religions. So, it is not surprising to find a syncretistic Gnosticism embracing such mystical elements which were already popular with the masses. Many of these ancient religions had ways of inducing visions and mystical experiences. Some were the result of inducement by hallucinogenic drugs, some by ascetic practices, or other sensory deprivation. The mystical visions (altered states of consciousness) were explained as being an experience of the divine. When ideas from Judaism were included in the Gnostic syncretism, appeal could be made to genuine visions given by God to the prophets and others, along with a false claim that the visions that were self-induced were no different than those that one can read about in the Old Testament. Did not Ezekiel have a vision of God, and did not the visions given to the prophets result in revelations being given? That would tend to make more believable the false claim that Jesus gave Thomas secret revelations not given to the other apostles (such is claimed in the Gnostic *Gospel of Thomas*), or that Jesus gave revelations

---

[31] Diogenes Laertius, *Lives* 8:24-33.

concerning visions to Mary Magdalene (such as claimed in the Gnostic *Gospel of Mary*).

8. *When it came ethics and matters of daily living, Greek dualism resulted in one or the other of two extremes among the Gnostics.* Some Gnostics practiced a rigid *asceticism*. Since, according to their dualistic philosophy, matter was evil, they tried to entirely avoid contact with matter, or reduce the contact to a minimum. In practice, Essenism taught that one should live on a spare diet of vegetables only, abstain from marriage, and even avoid anointing the body with olive oil, so necessary in hot climates. The material part of man was to be subdued and mortified that the spirit might be set free and rise to its proper level. Other Gnostics, going to the opposite extreme, taught that *libertinism* was the way to live. Unrestrained indulgence of any fleshly desires was permitted since (as they wrongly believed) what the body did made no difference to, nor could it hurt, the spirit.

9. *Dualism also caused Gnostic doctrine about Jesus to branch off in different directions.* Gnostics taught that the emanation known as Christ was not equal with the Supreme Being, but was a being of much lesser status, being aeons and aeons beneath God the father. In Gnostic thinking, the earthly Jesus and the aeon Christ are not to be identified. Docetic Gnostics said that when the aeon Christ was on earth, he just seemed to have a human body. The visible Christ did not actually have a fleshly body, they said. The people only thought they saw Christ. He did not actually exist in human form.[32] Adoptionist Gnostics said the divine Christ came upon the human Jesus at his baptism and left before the human Jesus was crucified. One of Jesus' sayings from the cross (in slightly reworded form, "my power, my power, why have you forsaken me?") is said to be evidence that the divine Christ had abandoned Jesus.[33]

---

[32] It was also taught that Christ did not actually die on the cross. One explanation of the cross was that Simon the Cyrene, who picked up cross, was the one crucified, when the soldiers became confused because of the mob circling about. While Simon was killed, Christ stood by and watched! It was against this Docetic doctrine that 2 John 1:7 famously objects when it states, "Many deceivers, who do not acknowledge Jesus Christ as coming in the flesh, have gone out into the world. Any such person is the deceiver and the antichrist" (NIV).

[33] Gnostics taught that Calvary and the blood of Jesus have no salvific effects; instead, a man must save himself by immersing himself in the Gnostic religion. Gnostics taught that "Jesus" and the "Christ" are two different things. Some Gnostics said that by learning from past ascended masters, Jesus became the Christ. They taught that we, too, can all become "Christs" who in turn are "divine" enough to be leaders and helpers for other souls passing through this world on their way to becoming Christs. This becoming a "Christ" is what the Gnostics called "salvation."

10. *Gnosticism taught reincarnation.* Gnostics divided humanity into three groups: (a) The carnal (*hylics*), who are hopelessly lost because they were all material with no spirit. (b) The soulish (*psychics*), who were part soul (matter) and part spirit, and who usually were identified as those who were in the church. They could be saved if they followed the Gnostic path. The best of the *psychics* had to be reincarnated 33 times, and each time they needed to embrace Gnosticism before they could gain enough knowledge (*gnosis*) to be admitted to the 7th heaven, thus ending the cycle of reincarnation. (c) The spiritual (*pneumatics*), usually the Gnostic teachers themselves, received something from the *plērōma* when they were born, and so would be saved automatically, irrespective of how they lived while on earth. This division of humanity into three groups was a clever way to explain how Gnostic teaching could actually come from Jesus when the message conflicted with that taught by Jesus' apostolic companions. If the Church consisted of people *(psychics)* who needed a different message than typical Gnostic beliefs, then you could say that Jesus kept the apostles around for that purpose. In the meantime, he passed his true knowledge on in secret to Mary Magdalene, Lazarus, or some other person.

11. *Gnostics believed in seven heavens* (though some had 365, one for every day in the year). Each level of heaven had an aeon who was ruler over that level of the heavens – that is, one aeon was in charge of, or was a sort of guard at, the entrance into each of the heavens.

---- S U P R E M E   G O D ----

7th Heaven	Aeon Guard	
6th Heaven	Aeon Guard	*All this maze*
5th Heaven	Aeon Guard	*of heavens and*
4th Heaven	Aeon Guard	*Aeons was called*
3rd Heaven	Aeon Guard	*Plērōma, "fullness".*
2nd Heaven	Aeon Guard	
1st Heaven	Aeon Guard	**Compare Colossians 2:9**

----   E A R T H   ----

At death, according to Gnosticism, the deceased started up toward the 7th heaven, the ultimate goal, toward the presence of the Supreme Being. If you lived a good life on earth, you might slip past three or perhaps four of the heavens, and their aeon guards. But then, you would be caught; and if you did not have a Soter (a savior who knew the password), you would be dragged back down to earth to live another life, and to start the process all over.   The special knowledge (*gnosis*) in which they took pride let you know the Savior and the passwords to get you by the aeon guards and into the 7th heaven.   The special passwords and special knowledge were a "mystery" to those not initiated into the Gnostic sect.

3.   Compatibility with Incipient Gnosticism

The affinities between the philosophy at Colossae (point #1 above) and what grew to became 2nd & 3rd century Gnosticism (point #2 above) strongly suggest that what we are witnessing in the religious philosophy at Colossae was the beginning of one of numerous forms of Gnosticism that later flourished and plagued the church.[34]

Some have questioned whether Gnostic ideas were prevalent as early as the mid-1st century AD.[35]   There is evidence in the New Testament of at least a rudimentary or embryonic Gnosticism before the end of the 1st century.[36]   In his address to the elders from Ephesus (Acts 20:29,30), Paul predicted the soon arrival of a new threat to Christianity that would capture some of the very men to whom he was giving this warning.   That new threat we identify as incipient Gnosticism.   In Paul's letters written in the mid AD 60s we have allusions to ideas which would become constituent elements of Gnosticism.   2 Timothy 2:18 calls attention to the error of those who   argued that the resurrection was already

---

[34] Gnosticism never was a single monolithic system.   Edwin Yamauchi ("The Gnostics and History," *JETS* 14/1 [Winter 1971], p.29) lists the names of eight famous Gnostic leaders known to us from early Christian literature and none of their systems were exactly alike.

[35] The earliest origins of Gnosticism are obscure and still disputed.   For this reason, some scholars prefer to speak of "gnosis" when referring to 1st century ideas that later developed into Gnosticism and to reserve the term "Gnosticism" for the synthesis of these ideas into a coherent movement in the 2nd century.

[36] Rudolf Bultmann argued for what he called a pre-Christian Gnosticism that, he averred, greatly influenced the writings we call the books of the New Testament.   When it is shown there were streams of Gnostic ideas in the 1st century, we are not giving aid and comfort to Bultmann's conclusions about the pervasive influence of such pre-Christian Gnostic ideas on Christian doctrine. On the contrary, the apostles and prophets who wrote the New Testament spoke for Jesus Christ, not for the Gnostics.   The original apostolic Christianity is based on the teachings of Jesus Christ. It is very likely that even the idea of a dying-rising savior God was borrowed by later Gnostics from Christianity, rather than the other way around.   (See Edwin Yamauchi, *Pre-Christian Gnosticism: A Survey of the Proposed Evidence* [Grand Rapids: Eerdmans, 1973].)

past.   We also have references to those who espoused an ascetic attitude toward marriage, an attitude based upon what seems to be a negative outlook upon the physical creation (1 Timothy 4:3-4).   These folk about whom Paul is writing seem to boast in a falsely named "gnosis" (1 Timothy 6:20).   2 Peter warns about the coming of scoffers, and by the time Jude was written (c. AD 75) Jude could say that what Peter had predicted had happened (Jude 17-19).   We treat both 2 Peter and Jude as being anti-Gnostic in emphasis, for those folk were present and were a danger to the church.   In John's writings, which were written before the end of the 1st century, there are warnings about Gnostic ideas.   In the Gospel of John (John 1:14, 19:34, 20:27), in 1 John (1:1-3, 4:1-3), and in 2 John (1:7), there are rebuttals to those who held a Docetic view of Jesus.   In 1 John 2:22 there is a clear reference to those who held that Jesus and the Christ were two different beings, an idea that became part of the belief system of many Gnostics.   We also have the evidence of Ignatius of Antioch, who, in his letter to the Smyrnaens, combated Docetic views of Christ at the beginning of the 2nd century.   So it would not be anachronistic to suggest that the Colossian philosophy stands in the stream of ideas that eventually came together to form the Gnosticism combated by the early church fathers.

Although the precise origins of each of the major Gnostic ideas are a matter of scholarly debate, it is now generally stated that the religious syncretism at Colossae, like many of the later forms of Gnosticism, was a combination of ideas from several sources, including Judaism, Greek philosophy, and Eastern religious mysticism.   When one thinks about the first of these sources, it must be remembered that Judaism was not monolithic.   In 1st century Judaism there were several distinct major sects – Pharisees, Herodians, Sadducees, Essenes, and Zealots.   Post-exilic Judaism was so vulnerable to syncretism that it has been said one should not speak of Judaism but of Judaisms.   The Judaism at Colossae seems to have been a native Phrygian variety since the orthodoxy of the Phrygian Jews was suspect in the eyes of their Palestinian and Mesopotamian brethren. The Judaism in the Lycus valley was not the Pharisaic form of Judaism against which the churches of Galatia had to be put on their guard at an earlier date (Acts 15 and Galatians 2), but was a variety of Judaism that had some features similar to the views held by the Essenes at Qumran.[37]

---

[37] There are also practices found in Qumran literature that have no parallel in the deceptive philosophy about which Colossians warns.   The elaborate washings (including Miqva'ot) and the reverence of the Sun at Qumran are unparalleled in Colossians.   Perhaps the emphasis on asceticism at Colossae has the same roots as did the quasi-monastic mode of living at Qumran. The point is that the distinctive Essene beliefs and practices at Qumran as well as the Phrygian kind of Judaism are examples of the religious syncretism that was invading the Jewish world in the 1st century.

That the deceptive religious system at Colossae had some beliefs and rites traceable to Judaism should not be thought surprising, for we have already noted how a large Jewish population came to be settled in the region of the Lycus valley. The emphasis on circumcision and the demand that sacred times be observed – festivals, new moon, and Sabbath (2:11-16) – reflect the religious background of many of the folk who lived in and around Colossae.   So it begins to look like the Gnostic ideas already in the Lycus valley culture before the end of the 1st century had begun to take root and flourish in the Jewish community living there.   It is no wonder that a growing number of scholars are looking more and more to Judaism as the incubator of many Gnostic doctrines.

For those ideas found in Gnosticism which cannot be traced to 1st century Judaism, most can be traced to the fusion of religious beliefs and cultures that arose first as a result of Persian conquests which helped spread eastern mysticism into the Mediterranean world and then later the conquests of Alexander the Great which led to the spread of Hellenism.   These ideas all antedated Christianity.

Zoroastianism, the religion of ancient Persia, was brought to the Mediterranean world by the soldiers of Alexander the Great, 300 BC, and by Jewish folk who were resettled from Babylon to areas in the Mediterranean world. That religion was spread by word of mouth, by tradition.   Colossians 2:8 calls attention to the fact that the philosophy at Colossae was "according to the traditions of men."[38]   Zoroastrian scriptures were called the *Avesta* ("tradition"). The *Avesta* circulated orally for centuries.   Commentaries on the Avesta were composed in the 9th century AD and are known as the *Zend*.   The debate continues concerning how much Jewish folk were influenced by these Eastern ideas.   For example, dualism was found both in Zoroastrianism (Ahura Mazda was the good god, and Angra Mainyu was the evil god) and Greek philosophy. The Essenes had a dualism in their writings.   In the *War Scroll* from Qumran, the spiritual forces were classified into the good and the bad, the angels of light and the angels of darkness, each headed by a supreme angel, named Michael and Beliel respectively.   We do not know the source of these ideas at Qumran, whether they arose from Zoroastrianism or Hellenism.

In Gnosticism, an aeon named Sophia (wisdom), some 28 generations or emanations down from the Supreme Being, was the one whose actions led to the creation of matter.   While some have proposed that the demiurge idea (a debased

---

[38] Edwin M. Yamauchi, "Did Persian Zoroastrianism Influence Judaism," *Artifax*, Winter 2013, p.13-17.

deity who created the universe) is suggested by Plato's *Timaeus*, others have debated whether this particular cosmological myth originated in Zoroastrianism[39] or in sectarian Judaism.[40]

If the study shifts to angels and spirits, Judaism, Hellenism, and Zoroastrianism all have angels and demons. The *Book of Jubilees* claims that, on the first day of creation, God created various orders of angels: of the Presence, of the winds, of the clouds, of cold, of heat, of hail, of thunder. The *Book of Enoch* (eleven copies of which were found among the Dead Sea Scrolls) has an elaborate angelology very similar to Gnosticism's angelology. There were Jewish communities whose reverence for angels bordered on worship. Kraabel has shown that Anatolian Judaism, as evidenced by the Sabathikos Inscription, participated in Lydian-Phrygian piety which was characterized by "angel worship."[41] Philo identified the "angels" of Judaism with the "demons" of Greek mythology.[42] Plutarch also spoke of demons, spiritual beings whose abode is in the air, that is, in the realm between the gods and men.[43] It is from Zoroastrianism that many of the modern characterizations of demons are derived. The Jews did pick up astrology from Babylon as evidenced by the zodiacs that decorate floors in some of the most ancient synagogues. Such astrology has spirit beings who inhabit the planets and who control events on earth.

Greek philosophy likely provided Gnosticism with its anthropology, in which man's soul/spirit was said to be a divine spark temporarily imprisoned in the tomb called the physical body, a view prefigured by Plato (*Phaedo*) and the songs and poetry of Orpheus.

---

[39] R.M. Grant, *Gnosticism and Early Christianity* (New York: Harper and Row, rev. ed. 1966). Edwin M Yamauchi, "The Descent of Ishtar, the Fall of Sophia, and the Jewish Roots of Gnosticism," *Tyndale Bulletin*, 29 (1978), p.143-175.

[40] Judaism knew of the descent of pre-existent wisdom (Sirach 24; 1 Enoch 42:1-2). The hypothesis of a Jewish origin for the Fall of Sophia has been most persuasively advanced by G.W. MacRae, "The Jewish Background of the Gnostic Sophia Myth," *NovT* 12 (April 1970), p.86-101. He thought the fall of Eve (Genesis 3) and the fall of the celestial beings (Genesis 6) might form the background of the Gnostic cosmological myth. Birger Pearson, *Gnosticism, Judaism and Egyptian Christianity* (Minneapolis: Fortress Press, 1990) also argues for a Jewish source for the cosmological myth in 2nd century Gnosticism.

[41] A. Thomas Kraabel, *Judaism in Western Asia Minor under the Roman Empire* (Harvard ThD Thesis, 1968), p. 145. Steven Fine, ed., *Sacred Realm: The Emergence of the Synagogue in the Ancient World* (New York: Oxford University Press, 1996), p. 65.

[42] Philo, *Gig.* 263 6-7 (Loeb).

[43] Plutarch, *De defectu oraculorum* 416C.

When the topic turns to mysticism, visions, and entering a higher spiritual experience, that idea too might have had either Persian (Mithraism) or Hellenistic (Eleusinian mysteries) origins.[44]   Both these religions were called mystery religions because they were secretive, often shrouded in a body of rituals not to be revealed to the uninitiated.   To achieve immortality and union with the god required a period of preparation in which the initiate followed the religion's precepts in an effort to become pure.   Once this period was over, the initiate performed a ritual, usually one of great emotional intensity, with the result that he or she would experience a vision and be said to be in union with the god.   The Dead Sea Scrolls bear evidence that the mystical tradition of union with the divine was a part of the religious life at Qumran.   The text called *Songs of the Sabbath Sacrifice* gives clear evidence of Jewish mysticism.   Fragments of *First Enoch*, which is considered the oldest text of Jewish mysticism, were also found with the Scrolls.

The idea of reincarnation may have come either from Hellenism or from the Eastern religions, where Hindus, Buddhists and Jains made this doctrine the foundation of their philosophy.   Among the ancient Greeks, the Greek Pre-Socratics (philosophers from Miletus and Ephesus) discussed reincarnation. Pythagoras, Socrates, and Plato may be numbered among those who made reincarnation an integral part of their teachings.   In the *Republic* Plato makes Socrates tell how Er, the son of Armenius, miraculously returned to life on the twelfth day after death and recounted the secrets of the other world.   After death, he said, he went with others to the place of Judgment and saw the souls returning from heaven, and proceeded with them to a place where they chose new lives, human and animal.   He saw the soul of Orpheus changing into a swan, Thamyras becoming a nightingale, musical birds choosing to be men, the soul of Atalanta choosing the honors of an athlete.   Men were seen passing into animals and wild and tame animals changing into each other.   At the end of his life, Socrates said, "I am confident that there truly is such a thing as living again, and that the living spring from the dead."   Pythagoras claimed he could remember his past lives, and Plato presented detailed accounts of reincarnation in his major works.   Though it is not a Biblical doctrine, the idea of reincarnation came to be embraced by some

---

[44] We have not attempted to show that mysticism in Gnosticism had a Jewish origin, namely, in Merkebah mysticism which did flourish in Jewish circles.   The reason is that our information about Merkebah mysticism comes from the Talmud and may date not earlier than the end of the 1st century AD.   At best, this would be evidence that mysticism was practiced in some Jewish circles.   See Gershom Scholem, *Major Trends in Jewish Mysticism* (Tel Aviv: Schocken Publishing House, 1941).

Jewish sects. The 1st century Jewish historian Flavius Josephus wrote that the Pharisees, the Jewish sect that founded rabbinic Judaism, believed in reincarnation. He writes that the Pharisees believed the souls of evil men are punished after death. The souls of good men are "removed into other bodies"[45] and they will "have power to revive and live again."[46] Josephus records that the Essenes of the Dead Sea Scrolls lived "the same kind of life" as the followers of Pythagoras, the Greek philosopher who taught reincarnation.[47] The Carpocratians and the Ophites believed in the transmigration of imperfect souls. In the *Hermetica,* a Graeco-Egyptian series of writings on cosmology and spirituality attributed to Hermes Trismegistus, the doctrine of reincarnation is also central.[48]

Whether the emphasis on asceticism (Colossians 2:16-23) at Colossae came from Jews or from the pagans is not certainly known. Pagans had dietary rules (some were vegetarians, Romans 14:2,3); Jews did, too. The Jewish sect known as the Essenes had strict prohibitions with respect to meat and wine – even oil. Such items were not to be touched, let alone tasted.[49] Perhaps the Jews in the Lycus valley had similar restrictions, or perhaps their ascetic views were simply part of the pervading culture of the age. Anatolian Jews were concerned with "proper food." Decrees preserved in Josephus indicate the government made it its responsibility to guarantee proper food to the Jews in Asia Minor.[50] Self-imposed asceticism provided a feeling of superior spirituality. It gave the impression that the successful ascetic had managed to rise above fleshly desires and was now in a separate category.

This brief study of the beginnings of Gnostic ideas has shown that both Gentiles and Jews were capable of assimilating into their religion ideas that were floating around in the culture of the time. There is every reason to believe that the Colossian philosophy was Judaistic Gnosticism in its infant form. The Gnos-

---

[45] Jos. *Wars*, II.8.14

[46] Jos. *Ant.* XVIII.1.3

[47] Jos. *Wars,* II.8.11

[48] The dating of the Hermetic literature is uncertain and may come from after the middle AD 60's.

[49] Jos. *Wars* II.8.3,11

[50] Jos. *Ant.* XIV.10.24

ticism of Colossae was vague and undeveloped, in its infant stages, not like that found in the 2nd century. But what today's readers need to take into account is that many of the same dangerous ideas are prevalent in the 21st century. They are as threatening to the Christian's spiritual health today as they were in the 1st century. The antidotes given in Colossians are still the spiritual medicine that will keep today's Christian healthy.

4. The Christology of Colossians

Colossians sets forth the dignity of Christ as head of the church. His headship is set forth first positively (1:18-20), then polemically, in a warning against error (2:8,16,18). Robertson has said that Colossians is Paul's "full length portrait of Christ."[51]

He is God's Son,   1:14
He is the object of the Christian's faith,   1:4
He is the redeemer,   1:14
He is the image of the invisible God,   1:15
The firstborn (Lord) of all creation,   1:15
In Him all things were created,   1:16
He is before all things, and in Him all things hold together,   1:17
In Him, through Him, and for Him, all things have been created,   1:16
He is the beginning, the firstborn from the dead,   1:18
He is head of the church,   1:18
All the fullness of grace dwells in Him,   1:19
He has made peace through the blood of His cross,   1:20
He is the reconciler of the universe,   1:20
He has reconciled us to God through His fleshly body,   1:22
In Him all the fullness of Deity dwells in bodily form,   2:9
He is the head over all rule and authority,   2:10
All the treasures of God's wisdom and knowledge lie hidden in Him,   2:3
He is the standard by which all religious teaching is to be measured,   2:8
He is the reality of the truth foreshadowed by the regulations and rituals of
    the old covenant,   2:17
Following His resurrection He is enthroned at the right hand of God,   3:1
One day He will be gloriously manifested,   3:3,4

---

[51] A.T. Robertson, *Paul and the Intellectuals* [Nashville: Broadman, 1959], p.12.

Paul makes an unambiguous reply to the mistaken emphases found in the Colossian heresy:

> Paul's answer to this 'tradition of men' is to set against it the one trustworthy tradition, the true doctrine of Christ. Christ, he says, is the very image of God, the One who embodies the plenitude of the divine essence, in which these elemental spirits have no share at all. And those who are members of Christ realize their fullness in Him; they need not seek, and they cannot find perfection anywhere else. It is in Christ that all wisdom and knowledge are concentrated and made available to His people – not just to an elite, but to all. Christ is the one Mediator between God and man, not in the sense of one who occupies the lines of communication between them and can transmit messages passing from one side to the other, but in the sense that He combines Godhead and manhood in His single person and so brings God and man together. Christ is the one through whom and for whom all things are created, including the principalities and powers to which the Colossians were being tempted to pay tribute. But why would those who are united with the Creator of those principalities and powers think it necessary to appease them? Above all, Christ by His death is revealed as the conqueror of these principalities and powers. On the cross He fought and won the decisive battle against them. Not only did He repel their attack upon Himself and turn the cross into His triumphal chariot before which they were driven as His vanquished foes, but by that victory He liberated His people also from their power. Why then should those who through faith-union with Christ had shared His death and resurrection go on serving those beings whom He had so completely conquered? Far from being a form of advanced wisdom, this false system that they were being urged to accept, with its taboos, bore all the marks of immaturity.[52]

E. TIME AND PLACE OF WRITING

Colossians was obviously written during an imprisonment of Paul (4:10,18), but the epistle itself contains no indication as to the place of the imprisonment. In the General Introduction to the Prison Epistles we have studied the various conjectures concerning the place of writing – whether Caesarea, Ephesus, or the traditional view, Rome – and have opted for Rome as the place of writing.[53]

---

[52] F.F. Bruce, "Colossians," *New International Standard Bible Encyclopedia* (Grand Rapids: Eerdmans, 1979,) Vol.1, p.734.

[53] For Colossians, the place of writing is not of first importance, as it makes little difference to the exegesis whether it was sent from Rome or Caesarea or Ephesus.

The indications of time and place for this letter are strikingly similar to those found in Ephesians and Philippians. In each of the letters, Paul indicates he is writing from prison (Colossians 4:10,18; cp. Ephesians 3:1,13; 4:1; 6:19,20; Philippians 1:12-20; Philemon 9,10,13). Like Ephesians, Colossians was carried by Tychicus, who is given the same official commendation in both letters (Colossians 4:7,8; Ephesians 6:21,22). The persons named in Colossians 4:7-14 are all, except the last, named in the close of Philemon (verses 23,24). The greetings from Paul's fellow workers indicates they had direct access to him, and this is consistent with Paul's first Roman imprisonment (Acts 28:30).

All these indications point to a time toward the close of Paul's first Roman imprisonment as being the time of writing. We date Paul's first Roman imprisonment AD 61-63. The date we give this book is the same as that for Ephesians and Philemon – AD 62.[54]

F. OCCASION AND PURPOSE OF WRITING

The arrival of Epaphras (1:8, 4:12) in Rome, with news respecting the affairs of the Christians at Colossae, was the immediate occasion of Paul's writing. Most of Epaphras' news about the church at Colossae (and the nearby sister churches) was favorable, but there was one disquieting feature: at Colossae, there was a strong inclination on the part of some Christians to entertain a deceptive teaching which (although they did not suspect it) would inevitably subvert the pure gospel which they had accepted only a few years before. That deceptive teaching at Colossae was a threat to the well-being of the church, and Paul's letter to the Colossians is his vigorous reaction to the danger.[55]

---

[54] In the Detailed Introduction to Ephesians, we opted for the view that Ephesians was written before Colossians.

[55] The issues Paul dealt with in Colossians sound very contemporary. Do the heavenly bodies have any influence over our lives? The millions of people who consult their horoscopes and astrological data each day in the daily newspapers would say, "Yes!" Is there any relationship between diet and spiritual living? Does God speak to us in mystical experiences? Are such experiences to be sought? Do the Eastern religions have something to offer the evangelical Christian? We need this important letter today just as they needed it in AD 62 when Paul wrote it. On the present-day meaning to be drawn from Paul's use of 1st century astrology and mythology, see F.F. Bruce, "St Paul in Rome 3: The Epistle to the Colossians," *BJRL* 48:2 (1966), p.284, and Jung Young Lee, "Interpreting the Demonic Powers in Pauline Thought," *Novum Testamentum* 12 (Jan. 1970), p.54-69.

Perhaps one other factor is included in the occasion of writing. Onesimus is returning to Colossae, accompanied by Tychicus, which gave opportunity to send the letter. The two also carried the letters we call Ephesians (Ephesians 6:21,22) and Philemon (Philemon 1:1).[56]

G. CRITICAL MATTERS

1. The Epistle from Laodicea

At Colossians 4:16, Paul writes, "When this letter is read among you, have it also read in the church of the Laodiceans; and you, for your part, read my letter *that is coming* from Laodicea." The first part of the verse is clear. The direction was given, doubtless, because the churches were just a few miles apart, likely had the same evangelist (Archippus), and would be exposed to the same deceptive doctrine. However, what is meant by the latter part of the verse, about the "epistle *that is coming* from Laodicea," is not as clear.

A brief examination of the opinions on the subject seems necessary:

[1] It has been supposed that the reference is to a letter sent from the Laodiceans to Paul, proposing to him some questions which they desired him to answer. It is further supposed that Paul now wishes the Colossians to procure that letter in order that they might more fully understand the drift of this letter which he now is sending to Colossae.

Objections to this opinion: (a) The language, rather than implying a letter *from* Laodicea, obviously speaks of a letter written by Paul and *sent to* Laodicea. The churches are being instructed to make an exchange of letters from Paul, and one church is to read that which the other has in its possession. (b) If the letter had been addressed to Paul, it was doubtless in his possession. If he wished the church at Colossae to read it, nothing would be more natural or obvious than to send it by Tychicus, along with the letter which he now sent. (c) If a letter had been sent to him by the

---

[56] Some redaction critics have proposed a different life-setting. Recall that redaction critics find three levels of material in our New Testaments – what Jesus said and did, what the apostles said and did, and what the early church believed and did. Käsemann, having rejected the Pauline authorship of Colossians, proposed that a post-Pauline author took over the hymn now found in Colossians 1:15-20 and other traditional materials in order to combat heresy in the sub-apostolic age. Redaction criticism results in a denial of the Christian faith and therefore is to be rejected as a method of Bible study.

Laodiceans, proposing certain questions, why did Paul send the answer to the church at Colossae, and not to the church at Laodicea? The church at Laodicea would have been the one entitled to a reply. (d) It is not necessary to require that such an epistle must be in our possession and that it must be read in order to understand this Colossian letter. Colossians is not more difficult of interpretation than the other Pauline epistles.

[2] It has been supposed the epistle referenced was one written by Paul to Timothy (i.e., 1 Timothy), and that Paul was staying at Laodicea when he wrote that letter. Support for this opinion is found in the KJV's subscription to 1 Timothy, "The first to Timothy was written from Laodicea ...."

Objections to this opinion: (a) Evidence that 1 Timothy was written this early (viz., AD 62) is virtually non-existent. In fact, it is the judgment of this commentator that 1 Timothy is to be dated at a time subsequent to the first Roman imprisonment out of which the Prison Epistles came. (b) There is nothing in 1 Timothy which would throw any important light on the Colossian letter. (c) The subscriptions to the letters, as found in the KJV, are of little authority and are often erroneous.

[3] It has been supposed by some that Paul refers to some letter which had been sent to the Laodiceans, which we do not now have in the New Testament, a letter which is now lost.

Objection to this opinion: It does not seem reasonable that any inspired letter, addressed to a church, would have been allowed to become lost.

[4] There is an extant letter known as "St. Paul's Epistle to the Laodiceans." It is generally agreed this letter is spurious, being nothing but a collection of sayings from Paul's other epistles. It reads as follows:

"Paul, an apostle, not of men, neither by men, but by Jesus Christ, to the brethren in Laodicea. Grace be to you, and peace, from God the Father and our Lord Jesus Christ. I give thanks to my God always, in my prayers, that you are mindful of me and are persevering in good works, waiting for the promise in the day of judgment.

And let not the vain speeches of some who would conceal the truth disturb you to turn you away from the truth of the gospel which has been preached to you. Now God grant that all they who are of me may be borne forward to the perfection of the truth of the Gospel, to perform those excellent good works which become the salvation of eternal life.

And now my bonds are manifest, in which bonds I am in Christ, and at the present time; but I rejoice, for I know that this shall be for the furtherance of my salvation, which is through your prayer and the supply of the Holy Spirit, whether by life or by death. For me to live is Christ, and to die is joy.

But our Lord Himself shall grant you His mercy with us, that possessing love you may be of the same mind and think the same thing. On this account, brethren, as you have heard of the appearing of the Lord, so think and do in the fear of God, and it shall be eternal life to you, for it is God who works in you.

Do all things without murmurings and disputings. And for the remainder, brethren, rejoice in the Lord Jesus Christ, and see that ye keep yourselves from all base gain of covetousness. Let all your requests be made known with boldness unto God, and be firm in the mind of Christ.

And finally, brethren, whatsoever things are true, whatsoever things are honest, whatsoever things are holy, whatsoever things are just, whatsoever things are lovely, these things do. And what you have heard and received, keep in your hearts, and it shall give you peace.

Salute all the brethren with an holy kiss. All the saints salute you. The grace of our Lord Jesus Christ be with your spirit. Amen. Cause that this epistle be read to the church of the Colossians, and do you also read the epistle from Colossae."

We agree with those who hold that this is not an epistle the apostle Paul would have written; it is a mere forgery.

[5] Some say that our "Philemon" is the "Epistle from Laodicea" of Colossians 4:16. See this discussed in the Detailed Introduction to Philemon.

[6] Many have supposed, and rightly we believe, that the "Epistle from Laodicea," to which Paul makes reference we now have under another name, "Ephesians." This is the view arrived at in our Detailed Introduction to Ephesians. According to this supposition, "Ephesians" was originally an encyclical letter which started at Laodicea and ended up at Ephesus.

2. Early Christian Hymns copied?

It is often said in modern critical commentaries that the words found in Colossians 1:15-17 are taken from some (imaginary) early Christian hymn.[57] The

---

[57] R.P. Martin, "An Early Christian Hymn: Col. 1:15-20," *EQ* XXXVI.4 (1964), p.195-205.

cautions voiced regarding a similar claim that Philippians 2:5-11 is an early Christian hymn apply here as well. Coffman (at Colossians 1:15[58]) has a suitable reply to such a hypothetical reconstruction:

> Now, admittedly, this is a very carefully thought-out paragraph, or sentence, of 137 words, and the organization of it is obvious; but for another Pauline paragraph manifesting these same qualities see Paul's long salutation in Romans and the analysis and discussion of it in my commentary on Romans, Romans 1:8ff.[59] We reject out of hand the allegation that this marvelous paragraph is some kind of hymn or liturgical chant used in worship services in the early church.[60] Such a view is not supported by any evidence whatever except the imagination of scholars; and it is based upon several very tenuous and unsure premises. (1) That Paul would need to reach into the current hymnology of his day for accurate expression of the nature and essence of the being of Christ Jesus; (2) That the great Christology of this passage had 'developed' in the early church. On the contrary, far from having developed any such exalted conception of Christ, those early churches were in danger of being carried away into the worship [veneration] of angels, etc. If the brethren at Colossae were singing these words already when Paul wrote them, there would have been no temptation to Gnosticism, and no need for Paul to have written them. Of course, what some have in mind, through making a hymn out of this passage, is to make it easier for them to deny that Paul wrote it, or that it is indeed authoritative Scripture.[61] This remarkable paragraph has every mark of Pauline authorship, being a similar careful work, comparable to Rom. 1:1-7. As G. Campbell Morgan expressed it:
>
> > It is here that Paul set forth the glories of the person of the Redeemer in a passage that is unique for its revealing beauty. He summarized the whole truth concerning the glories of the person of Christ in his declaration that "it was the good pleasure of the Father that in Him should all the fullness dwell."

---

[58] James B. Coffman, *Commentary on Galatians, Ephesians, Philippians, Colossians* (Austin, TX: Firm Foundation Publishing House, 1977), p.358,359.

[59] Addenda by GLR: It is the high Christology of the passage that makes it objectionable to some contemporary writers. Hebrews, too, is Pauline, and it has a very high Christological content. As to the structure of this passage, there is no scholarly consensus as to the number and content of the stanzas.

[60] Addenda by GLR: It might lend itself to such a usage once it had been written, but to say that its *origin* is shrouded somewhere in the mists of unrecorded church history is unacceptable.

[61] Addenda by GLR: It also makes it easier for critics to insist that the idea of who Jesus was grew by evolutionary processes from a Palestinian peasant to a Greek God, and that it took a century for such a high view of Jesus to have begun to be believed.

3. How were these letters (the Prison Epistles) sent out?

Onesimus, a runaway slave from Colossae, had come to Rome. There, he had found Paul, or had been brought to Paul. Onesimus, now a Christian, has asked Paul to plead on his behalf ("seeking sanctuary," that is called) with Philemon. Philemon was probably wealthy. He owned a home that was big enough for a church to meet in it. Perhaps Onesimus had been sent to Ephesus on business; and instead of going back home, he bought a ticket to Rome.

Onesimus was converted by Paul. Paul then urges Onesimus to go back to Philemon. But what if Onesimus were arrested and dragged back to Philemon? Slaves who ran away and were caught were punished severely, often killed. But Paul, sending Onesimus back, writes to Philemon, "Receive him as a brother."

Tychicus was sent with Onesimus, and this afforded Paul an opportunity to send these letters. According to Ephesians 6:21, Tychicus also carried Ephesians along with Colossians and Philemon.

The first thing to be done is to take Onesimus home. Because he was accompanying Onesimus, and because of the danger of Onesimus' being captured (who would believe Onesimus' story that he actually was returning home, if he were captured and returned by soldiers or slave catchers?), Tychicus would likely want to take him home first. Colossians 4:9 indicates that Colossae is home for Onesimus and Philemon. If Tychicus and Onesimus landed at Miletus, they would bypass Ephesus (thus not stopping to deliver the Ephesian letter). Traveling inland along the Meander River valley they would come to the place where the Lycus River flowed into the Meander. Going up this valley, they would pass through Laodicea before coming to Colossae. As they passed through Laodicea, Tychicus left the letter we call "Ephesians" before going on to deliver Onesimus and the letters to Philemon and the Colossians.

Detailed Introduction to Philemon

A. HISTORICAL ALLUSIONS

1:1 – The writers of ancient letters signed their names first. This one bears Paul's name as the author.

The writer identifies himself as "a prisoner of Christ Jesus."

Many of Paul's letters begin with his typical words of authority (cp. Romans 1:1; 1 Corinthians 1:1; 2 Corinthians 1:1; Galatians 1:1). Was there a good reason why Paul does not call himself an apostle or a bondslave as he further identifies himself?

From what imprisonment does Paul write this letter? Do we get any help for deciding this question later in the letter? The traditional view is that this letter comes from Paul's first Roman imprisonment. Is there any reason to abandon this ancient view?

"And Timothy our brother" indicates that Timothy was with Paul when the letter is written.

Why is his name included here in verse 1? For many of the Pauline epistles, the historical allusions in the letters can be laid alongside what can be read in the Book of Acts. Does Timothy's association with Paul give us any help dating this letter to Philemon? Verse 4 has Paul speaking in the first person ("I"). Could it be that Timothy served as the secretary who penned the actual letter as Paul dictated it?

"To Philemon, our beloved brother and fellow-worker."

Following the signature, ancient letters gave the name of the intended recipient of the letter.

What can we learn about Philemon from this letter and elsewhere? Colossians 4:9 seems to indicate that Philemon lived in Colossae. It is nowhere actually said that Philemon was a Colossian, but this is inferred from the fact that Onesimus, his slave, is a Colossian (4:9).

The rest of the letter indicates Philemon was a Christian slave owner whose slave Onesimus, for some reason, had run away. "Beloved" indicates Paul felt a close personal friendship with Philemon.

When and where had Philemon worked closely together with Paul in the spread of the gospel, as the appellation "fellow-worker" suggests (cp. Colossians 4:11)?

1:2 – "And to Apphia and ... to Archippus." Who are these people?

Apphia is quite possibly Philemon's wife. So tradition has it.

Archippus, according to Colossians 4:17, held a ministry which he had received from the Lord. We would call him a preacher or evangelist. In Colossians 4:15, he is connected with the church in Laodicea; here in Philemon he is connected with Philemon and Apphia. What do we make of these bits of information? Was he, perhaps, a circuit riding preacher for the churches in Laodicea, Hierapolis, and Colossae, working in these churches during the absence of Epaphras who has made a trip to Rome to see Paul (Colossians 1:7,8)? Was he perhaps staying at Philemon's home when in Colossae? Was he perhaps the son of Philemon and Apphia, and also the evangelist of the churches, especially during the absence of Epaphras?[1]

Why did Paul include Archippus in the address of this letter? By addressing the letter to the three, was Paul trying to make sure that Philemon will accept Onesimus well, since even the preacher in the town must read the letter?

"To the church that is in your house." The pronoun "your" is singular, and the traditional view is that it refers to Philemon. A church met in Philemon's home. Philemon is evidently a wealthy man, wealthy enough to own slaves and to have a home large enough to accommodate the public assembly of the church. By including the church among those addressed, Paul indicates the letter was originally intended to be read to the congrega-

---

[1] We are just speculating, of course, about Archippus' places of ministry. While it is possible that Archippus was a circuit rider, we must remember that Nympha (or Nymphas), too, was a church leader at Laodicea (Colossians 4:15). This person's name is spelled Nympha (feminine. NASB) or Nymphas (masculine, KJV). If masculine, was Nymphas the preacher for the church that met in his home, or was he the one who made his home available for the congregation's meetings? If feminine, did the church meet in her home? Was there more than one congregation in Laodicea, with the one meeting in Nympha's home getting special mention in Colossians 4:15? We have no way of being certain about the answers to these questions.

tion. It is thus a personal letter, but not a private letter. It deals with an issue that involves the entire Christian community, not just one person.

1:3 – Following the signature and address, ancient letters usually included a word of greeting. The wording of the greeting here is the usual words of greeting found in Paul's letters.

1:4-7 – The next thing included in ancient letters was a word of thanksgiving.

The thanksgivings in Paul's letters often introduce what he is going to talk about in the letter; his thanksgivings tend to lay the foundation for the rest of the letter. Here Paul gives thanks to God for the love and faith of Philemon, a love and faith that encompasses all the saints of God.

By using the expression the "fellowship of your faith" (verse 6) Paul is indicating he wants Philemon to put his faith to work. But doing what?

1:8,9 – Paul begins his appeal for Onesimus.

Paul begins by saying, 'I could order you (verse 8) to accept him (verse 17), but rather, I appeal to you for love's sake (verse 9).'

Why should Paul appeal to his imprisonment again, and why call attention to his age? How old was Paul?

1:10 – Paul's appeal on behalf of Onesimus.

From verses 15 and 16 we learn that Onesimus is a runaway slave. We have questions concerning why Onesimus ran away. Was it because Philemon was a bad, harsh master? Evidently not, for verse 7 shows Philemon's reputation for love, generosity, and kindness, something evidently made known to Paul by Epaphras or Onesimus. We suppose the reason lies in the fact that Philemon created an opportunity (perhaps by sending Onesimus on an errand to Ephesus); and Onesimus, discontented with his lot, left.

By reading between the lines, Philemon will learn several things about Onesimus from this sentence. He will learn that Onesimus ended up in Rome, and has somehow come in contact with Paul and has been converted by Paul ("begotten in my imprisonment," verse 10). How did Onesimus get to Paul? Onesimus could have known Paul personally and sought him out. Perhaps Onesimus accidentally met Epaphras on the street. Onesimus is recognized as a runaway slave, but instead of reporting him, Epaphras took Onesimus to Paul, where Onesimus was taught and converted. Or perhaps some of Paul's fellow workers in Rome may have come upon Onesimus, not knowing him personally, but because of his need brought him to Paul, who then learned of the connection to Philemon.

1:11 – Describes the profound difference conversion has made in Onesimus' life. The KJV reads that he once was "unprofitable" to Philemon, but now is "profitable" to both Paul and Philemon. There is a play on words here in the Greek. "Onesimus" in Greek means "helpful" or "useful" or "profitable"; it was a fairly common name for a slave in the Roman world.

> Why might he be described as "useless" to Philemon? Perhaps it is because one would get no slaving out of a runaway slave. Since skilled slaves cost a great deal of money to purchase, perhaps nothing more need be supposed than that Philemon, having considerable money invested in this slave, now anticipated a loss of his investment. It may be reading too much into the word "useless" to infer from it that when he ran away, Onesimus had taken jewels or silver.

1:12 – "I have sent him back" translates a Greek construction called an "epistolary aorist." This means Paul is sending Onesimus back to Philemon at the same time that he sends this letter to Philemon.

> What did Roman law require a person in Paul's situation to do about a runaway like Onesimus? Did Paul have any option except to send him back? What punishment did Roman law allow the slave owner to inflict on a caught fugitive slave? Was the punishment lesser if the slave returned voluntarily, rather than being forcibly returned by slave catchers?

1:13,14 – Paul says, 'I would have liked to keep him here with me, to wait on me in your place, while I am in prison for the gospel.'

> However, Onesimus is being sent back by Paul, because Paul did not wish to go against Philemon's will, or do something with Philemon's property without his consent. It would not have done any good to force good on Philemon. Philemon had to do the Christian thing according to his own free will.

1:15 – Paul is saying, 'Perhaps it was in the plan of God that you lose him for a while, that you might have him for eternity.' To Paul, is all that has transpired with Onesimus and Philemon a good illustration of how God works all things together for good to them who love Him (Romans 8:28)?

1:16-22 – In our mind's eye, we can see Philemon in a room which has many doors through which he might escape. With a few deft statements, Paul closes each one of the doors, leaving Philemon no real choice but to do what Paul asks him to do in the case of Onesimus.

> Onesimus returns. Philemon may think, 'He is a runaway slave; I'll punish him to set an example.' Paul closes that door – "Receive him as a brother. Welcome him as a beloved brother in Christ" (verse 16).

> In case Philemon thinks, 'Well, there are different kinds of brothers,' Paul closes that door –"Receive him as you would me. Welcome him as you would me" (verse 17). In effect Paul asks Philemon not to inflict any of the usual punishments that a runaway slave might expect.

> Perhaps Philemon might think, 'But he owes me ....' If a slave were missing, Philemon would look around to see if any of his possessions were gone. And if anything was missing, it would be blamed on Onesimus, even if Onesimus had not taken it. In that case Philemon may be thinking, 'I shall take it out on his hide,' – Paul now closes that door. "Charge that to my account" (verse 18) and "I, Paul, am writing this with my own hand" (verse 19). This is just like signing his name on the IOU. It is a legally binding commitment to cover any debts Onesimus may have.

> And in case Philemon starts adding up the debt to charge Paul, Paul closes that door. "Philemon, remember you owe me a great deal. Remember that you are a Christian because of my preaching" (verse 19). It is likely that Philemon was converted by Paul, probably while Paul was at Ephesus during his third missionary journey (Acts 19:10). (Remember, we doubt that Paul had visited Colossae previous to these letters.)

1:20,21 – "Refresh my heart in Christ." "I am confident that you will do even more than what I ask," says Paul.[2] Paul has a powerful, yet tender, approach through psychology in the words of this letter. His appeal implicitly says, 'Let me hear that you did the Christian thing.' "More than I

---

[2] Some of the readings offered for verses 14-21 are this commentator's own translation.

ask" means more than the "accept him" for which Paul has already asked in verse 17. The word emancipation seems to be in the background of Paul's thoughts, but is never quite spoken.

1:22 – Paul closes another door to Philemon. Just in case Philemon thinks, 'Paul will never know what I do to Onesimus – so I'll go ahead and punish him,' Paul says, "Prepare a lodging for me, for I'll soon be in Colossae to visit with you." This is not like Paul to demand living accommodations. He is just closing another door. When Paul stepped into the door of Philemon's home, what would be the first words he would ask? "Where's the guest room?" No, the first question Paul would ask is, "Where is Onesimus?"

> One other door is closed. Just in case Philemon should think, 'This Paul surely is meddling in my business. I hope he never comes,' Paul closes that door. He says, "You pray that I may be restored to you."

1:23-25 – The epilogue to the letter.

"Epaphras" sends greetings to Philemon.[3]

Paul's fellow-workers (Mark, Aristarchus, Demas, and Luke) also send their greetings to Philemon. The same workers are named in Colossians 4:10-14, which leads us to the conclusion that the letters to Philemon and to the church at Colossae were written and sent at the same time.

The familiar Pauline benediction closes this letter to Philemon.

The KJV carries a subscription, "Written from Rome to Philemon, by Onesimus, a faithful servant." Where did the subscriptions attached to Paul's letters in the KJV come from? The subscriptions cannot be traced further back than the 5th century AD, and are ascribed as being written by a church leader named Euthalius, who arrived at his conclusions by interpreting the historical allusions within each letter. Some he got right, and some he did not. In the subscriptions, the "by ...." line means the letter was carried by the person named, in this case Onesimus. Is this correct? The traditional view has been that Onesimus and Tychicus (see Colossians 4:7 and 9) traveled together from Rome and carried letters to Colossae, to Philemon, and to "the Ephesians" (Ephesians 6:21ff).

---

[3] See the Detailed Introduction to Colossians where this man Epaphras is further identified.

B. WHY IS THIS EPISTLE INCLUDED IN THE NEW TESTAMENT?

1. It seems like a small private transaction. Should such be included in our Scriptures? If it is a personal letter, why put it in the Bible where it will be read by everyone and used as a rule of faith and practice?

   That it was addressed to the church (as well as to Philemon, Apphia, and Archippus) may provide a clue concerning how it came to be preserved and ultimately included in the canon.

2. Perhaps the effect of the letter is a reason it has been preserved. What was the effect of this letter?

   It can hardly be doubted that Onesimus, after having been commended to Philemon in such terms, was restored to his favor, and was set at liberty.

   There is a tradition (*Can. Apost.* 73) that Onesimus was emancipated by his owner, Philemon, and (*Constit. Apost.* 7. 136) that he was ordained by Paul as bishop of the church at Berea in Macedonia, and afterward suffered martyrdom at Rome.

   There is also the information given in Ignatius' epistle *To the Ephesians* (1:6) that a young man named Onesimus was the bishop of the church at Ephesus in AD 115. But the age of the bishop and the time of the Ephesian letter make it certain that the Onesimus mentioned by Ignatius and the one here in Philemon are not to be identified.

3. Several strong lessons in this letter have been emphasized as being good reasons for its inclusion in the canon.

   (a) It gives a first-class example of Christ's commandment to "Love one another." It is much like the book of Ruth. Ruth gives a picture of life in the time of the Judges. Philemon gives an example of life during Paul's day.
   (b) It shows a Christian's responsibility to his brother. When folk are converted to Christ, old things are passed away, all things become new. The resulting brotherhood makes a profound change in how folk treat others who are now brothers in Christ. If we may suppose that Onesimus and Philemon were men of different race (something that is not at all certain), the letter to Philemon points in the direction of what race relations are to be among Christians.

(c) It shows a Christian's responsibility to live as his Lord wants him to live.

4. We judge that the Holy Spirit's real reason for including this letter in the New Testament canon lies in precisely what the letter says about a Christian's attitude toward slavery.

Slavery existed in Old Testament times, and certain Mosaic rules addressed the issue (cf. Exodus 21:1-27, 22:1-3; Leviticus 25:39-46; Deuteronomy 15:13-15, 23:15). Slavery – some forced upon others, and some entered into voluntarily to pay off debts – was also an important social issue in the first century.

A huge percentage of the population in the Roman world was slave. Barclay puts the number of slaves in the empire at 60 million.[4] Roman armies made captives of conquered foreign peoples and brought the skilled ones to Rome where they were forced to become slaves.

In the Roman world, the treatment of and attitude toward many slaves was less than human. Roman law, more cruel than Athenian, imposed practically no limits on the power of the master over his slave.

> Under Roman law the slave was a chattel. Varro classified slaves among implements, which he classified as *vocalia*, articulate speaking implements, such as slaves; *semivocalia*, having a voice but not articulating, such as oxen; *muta,* dumb, such as wagons. The attitude of the law toward the slave was expressed in the formula *servile caput nullum jus habet*: the slave has no right. The master's power was unlimited. He might mutilate, torture, or kill the slave at his pleasure. Pollio, in the time of Augustus, ordered a slave to be thrown into a pond of voracious lampreys. Augustus interfered, but afterward ordered a slave of his own to be crucified on the mast of a ship for eating a favorite quail. Juvenal describes a profligate woman ordering a slave to be crucified. Someone remonstrates. She replies: "So then a slave is a man, is he! 'He has done nothing,' you say. Granted. I command it. Let my pleasure stand for a reason" (vi., 219). Martial records an instance of a master cutting out a slave's tongue. The old Roman legislation imposed death for killing a plough-ox; but the murderer of a slave was not called to account. Tracking fugitive slaves was a trade. Recovered slaves were branded on the forehead, condemned to double labor, and sometimes thrown to the beasts in the amphitheater. The

---

[4] William Barclay, "Introduction to the Letter to Philemon" in the *Daily Study Bible Series* (Philadelphia: Westminster Press, 1960,), p.310.

slave population was enormous. Some proprietors had as many as twenty thousand.[5]

In AD 61, only a year or two before the letter to Philemon was written, and probably during Paul's two-year imprisonment in Rome, as told by Lightfoot, "a terrible tragedy had been enacted under the sanction of law."

> Pedanius Secundus, a senator, had been slain by one of his slaves in a fit of anger and jealousy. The law demanded that in such cases all the slaves under the same roof at the time should be put to death. On the present occasion, 400 persons were condemned to suffer by this inhuman law. The populace, however, interposed to rescue them; and a tumult ensued. The Senate accordingly took the matter into deliberation. Among the speakers, C. Cassius strongly advocated the enforcement of the law. "The dispositions of slaves," he argued, "were regarded with suspicion by our ancestors, even when they were born on the same estate or in the same houses and learnt to feel an affection for their masters from the first. Now however, when we have several nations among our slaves, with various rites, with foreign religions or none at all, it is not possible to keep down such a rabble except by fear." These sentiments prevailed, and the law was put in force. The roads had to be lined with Roman soldiers as the prisoners were led to execution, to prevent a further outbreak of the people.[6]

The Roman attitudes toward slaves, which made slaves less than human, was a grievous social evil that needed to be eradicated. Christianity introduced the fundamental principles that eventually led to changes in men's attitudes. Paul knew and appreciated slavery's actual abuses and evil possibilities, and he addressed those issues by laying down principles by which both Christian slaves and Christian masters were expected by the Lord to live. Philemon is one book in the New Testament that deals very specifically with the problem of slavery. Paul recognizes two worlds. In the realm of the spirit, Philemon and Onesimus, since both are now Christians, are equal (Galatians 3:26-28; Colossians 3:10,11; Philemon 16). In the realm of the flesh, they are different. Paul leaves the matter of Onesimus' slavery to Philemon's judgment, a decision, however, that is to be made after taking the will of the Lord into account

---

[5] M.R. Vincent, "Philemon" in *Word Studies in the New Testament* (Wilmington, DE: Associated Publishers and Authors, 1972), p.921.

[6] J.B. Lightfoot, *Saint Paul's Epistles to the Colossians and Philemon* (Grand Rapids: Zondervan, nd), p. 321.

("do more than what I say"). In his letter to the Colossians, Paul tells the slaves not to enter into rebellion in attempt to throw off their slavery (Colossians 3:22ff). In his first letter to the Corinthians, Paul urged that men should abide in that outward condition which they held before becoming a Christian (1 Corinthians 7:20-24); after all, when a person has become a Christian, the slave is the Lord's freedman, just as the free man, when he becomes a Christian, is the Lord's bondslave. Christian slave masters were to treat their slaves with love and fairness (Ephesians 6:9; Colossians 4:1). 1 Timothy 6:1,2 has instructions to Christian slaves to treat their masters as worthy of all honor so that the name of God and our doctrine not be spoken against, and if their masters were Christians, they were to serve all the more knowing they were benefitting a fellow-Christian by their work for their master. Titus 2:9,10 reads, "Urge bondslaves to be subject to their own masters in everything; to be well-pleasing, not argumentative, not pilfering, but showing all good faith that they may adorn the doctrine of God our Savior in every respect."

History has shown that when Christian principles are allowed to leaven society, abusive and inhumane slavery ends. Early Christian literature shows how one expression of Christian benevolence was the use of funds to purchase the freedom of slaves.[7] In fact, it is only in Christian countries where slavery has been curtailed and then finally eradicated.

C. AUTHORSHIP AND ATTESTATION

1. Internal evidence for Pauline authorship

The writer calls himself Paul three times (verses 1,9,19). The thought, sentiment, and expression are thoroughly Pauline, and his return of Onesimus to his master, and his pointed appeal to the slave master Philemon, are in perfect harmony with what Paul wrote elsewhere on the topic of slaves and masters.[8]

Some objections have been raised to the Pauline authorship, though purely on subjective grounds.

(1) There are only ten words which are not found in Paul's other writings. To argue from these, as some have, that they disprove the Pauline authorship is

---

[7] 1 Clement 55:2; Hermas, *Mandates* VIII:10; Ignatius, *To Polycarp* 4.

[8] See Ephesians 6:5-9; Colossians 3:22-4:1; 1 Timothy 6:1,2.

to assume the absurd principle that a writer, after having produced two or three compositions, must in the future confine himself to an unvarying circle of words, whatever be the subject he may discuss.

(2) It has also been objected that the entire story of Onesimus is just that, a romantic story, originating in a desire to veil a truly Christian idea in an appropriate dress. But contemporary secular history has examples of letters similar to that which gave occasion for the writing of this letter.[9] Those letters were not just romantic stories.

(3) An idea was held in some of the early centuries that the subject matter of the epistle is too low to be Holy Spirit inspired. Jerome, writing of such, writes, "They will have it either that the Epistle addressed to Philemon is not Paul's, or that, even if it be his, it has nothing in it tending to our edification; and that by many of the ancients it was rejected, since it was written for the purpose merely of commendation, not of instruction."[10] But this kind of criticism did not prevail against the common acceptance of its authenticity.

(4) In the higher criticism of modern times, the book has been generally accepted as Pauline. One exception to this was F.C. Baur, who claimed that the letter was "historical romance" written in the second century to instruct the church in handling the slavery question.[11]

We find no valid objection to the Pauline authorship from internal grounds.

2. External evidence for the Pauline authorship

Since the epistle is very short and of a personal nature, we would not expect many notices of it in the early literature. Nevertheless, what we find consistently points to the Pauline authorship.

Allusions – Ignatius (AD 115) may have a reflection of Philemon 20 in his Ephesians 2 and in Magnesians 12. Tertullian (AD 200) asserted that Marcion received Philemon into his canon. "This epistle alone has had advantage from its

---

[9] Compare, for example, the letter written by Pliny the younger, included in notes below.

[10] Jerome, *Epistle to Philemon*, vol. 7, p.742, ed. Vallarsii, 1737.

[11] F.C. Baur, *Paulus*, Vol.II, p.88ff. It is because of the close connection between Colossians and Philemon that Baur was forced to date Philemon in the second century, for he had already denied the genuineness of Colossians and dated it in the second century. This treatment of Philemon has been called one of Baur's worst blunders (B. Weiss).

brevity, for by this it has escaped the falsifying hands of Marcion.   Nevertheless, I wonder, that when he receives one epistle to one man, he should reject two to Timothy and one to Titus, which treat of the government of the church."[12] Epiphanius (c. AD 375) likewise noted that Marcion included Philemon in his canon.[13]

Annotated quotations – Origen (AD 210) is the earliest Christian writer whose works are still extant who quotes Philemon and ascribes it to Paul. "'Which Paul being aware of, in the epistle to Philemon said to Philemon about Onesimus" (and then proceeds to quote verse 14).[14] "As Paul says to Philemon" (and then quotes verse 7).[15] "Concerning Paul it was said to Philemon" (and then quotes verse 9)."[16]   Eusebius (AD 325) included the epistle in the *homologoumena*, the books accepted as canonical by all the churches.[17]   Jerome (AD 400) commented on the epistle to Philemon, and alludes to some who either rejected its canonicity, or made objections to it.   But he answers the objections by affirming that it had been always received by all the churches in the world.[18]

Canonical listings – That the epistle to Philemon was included in the canon by both Marcion and Eusebius has already been noted.   The epistle is included in the Muratorian canon (AD170) as well as being included in the Old Latin and Old Syriac versions of the New Testament.

Since it is true that Philemon has been included in the collected epistles of Paul from the moment the first collections were made, there is no reason to be hesitant about its Pauline authorship.

---

[12] Tertullian, *Adv. Marcion.* 5.42

[13] Epiphanius, *Adv. Haeres.* 42.9.

[14] Origen, *Homil. In Jerem.* 19

[15] Origen, *Comment.in Matth.* Tract. 34

[16] *Ibid.*, Tract. 33

[17] Eusebius, *H.E.* III.25

[18] Jerome, *Comment in Epis. Ad Philemon* Proem. Ed. Benedict, Vol.4, p.442.

D. DATE AND DESTINATION

1. Date and place of writing

The time of writing this letter coincides with the time of the composition of Colossians, Ephesians, and Philippians.   The epistle to Philemon is closely linked with the epistle to the Colossians.   Both were carried by the same bearer, Onesimus (with whom, however, Tychicus is joined in the epistle to the Colossians, Colossians 4:7,9).   The persons who send greetings in both Philemon (Philemon 23,24) and Colossians (Colossians 4:10-14) are the same, except one, Jesus called Justus (Colossians 4:11).   In both letters alike Archippus is addressed (Philemon 2; Colossians 4:17).   Paul and Timothy are named in the epistolary opening of both letters.   In both, Paul alludes to the fact he is a prisoner at the time he is writing (Philemon 9; Colossians 4:18).   Hence, it follows that the letters to Philemon and to the Colossians were written at the same time, which was also about the same time as the epistle to the Ephesians was written.

Concerning the time and place of writing, see the Detailed Introductory Studies to these other epistles, where the decision was reached that all come from Paul's first imprisonment in Rome, which is dated AD 61-63.   Thus, we assign a date of about AD 62 for the writing of Philemon, Colossians, and Ephesians.

While the evidence says the letters to Philemon and the Colossians were written from the same place at nearly the same time, the order in which these prison epistles were written has proven to be a hard question to answer.   Some have proposed the idea that Colossians was written prior to Philemon, since in Philemon Paul asks that a guest room be prepared as he hopes soon to be visiting Philemon (Philemon 22).   On the other hand, when writing to the Colossians, Paul says "Pray for us also, that God may open us a door for the word" (Colossians 4:3), as though he expected to be a while longer in Rome.   Still others have suggested that once Epaphras arrived in Rome (Colossians 1:7,8), with news which resulted in a letter being prepared for the church at Colossae, this must have also been the time it was decided to send Onesimus back to Philemon.   It is supposed that Epaphras recognized Onesimus and that this led to discussions between Paul and Onesimus and Epaphras concerning the pros and cons of what to do concerning Onesimus.   Thus, it has been conjectured, the letter to Philemon concerning Onesimus was composed after the one to the church at Colossae.

2. Destination

The traditional view has been that the letter was written to Philemon, whose home was in Colossae.   According to the letter, Philemon had a runaway slave named Onesimus (Philemon 10). Colossians implies that Onesimus is from the city of Colossae (Colossians 4:9), and if that is true, it follows that his owner/slave-master, Philemon, also was from Colossae.

Some scholars have debated the traditional view, opting for Laodicea as being the town in which Philemon lived. Karl G. Wieseler taught that Philemon was a Laodicean, and he even identified the letter to Philemon as being "the epistle from Laodicea" alluded to in Colossians 4:16.[19] Wieseler's views have been adopted, with certain modifications, by Goodspeed and Knox. Goodspeed has Philemon, Apphia, Archippus, and "the church in your house" (Philemon 1,2) all located in Laodicea,[20] and further suggested that the letter we call Philemon is the "letter from Laodicea" (Colossians 4:16[21]) on the ground that the letter referred to in this way would not have been lost. Goodspeed also has Paul intimating to Philemon (Onesimus' slave owner) that he would like to have Onesimus back to assist him.[22] He identified the Onesimus named in this letter to Philemon with the Onesimus whom Ignatius later has as the bishop of Ephesus, and argued Onesimus was the one responsible for putting together the Pauline corpus.[23]

John Knox's reconstruction of the background for this letter claimed that Archippus, who lived at Colossae, was the owner of the slave and the ultimate recipient of the letter.[24] It is Archippus who is addressed in verses 4 to 24 of the letter, and the "ministry" (Colossians 4:17) which Archippus is admonished to complete refers, Knox suggested, to the way he was to receive and handle Onesimus. It was Paul's deeper purpose, Knox believed, in writing this letter, not just to secure Onesimus' freedom, but also to secure the services of Onesimus

---

[19] Karl Geo. Wieseler, *Chronologie des Apost. Zeital.* (Gottingen: Vandenhoeck und Ruprecht, 1848).

[20] Edgar J. Goodspeed, *An Introduction to the New Testament* (Chicago: University of Chicago Press, 1937), p.112.

[21] Goodspeed (*The Key to Ephesians* [Chicago: University of Chicago Press, 1956], p.iv-xvi) argued that there is little likelihood that there would have been a third letter written at the same time as Colossians and Philemon, so our Philemon must be the "letter from Laodicea." To support this claim, however, it must be shown that Philemon was fundamentally a letter to the church and not to an individual, and it is doubtful that verse 2 should be understood in this fashion.

[22] Goodspeed, *Introduction*, p. 120. Goodspeed (p.123) acknowledged indebtedness to John Knox for some of his conclusions.

[23] Goodspeed, *op. cit.*, p.123. Lewis A. Foster advanced a better hypothesis, in this commentator's judgment. He proposed that Luke, the author of the Gospel and Acts, was the one responsible for the collection of Paul's letters. *Seminary Review* XIV.2 (Winter 1968), p.41-56.

[24] John Knox, *Philemon Among the Letters of Paul*, revised edition [Chicago: University of Chicago Press, 1935; revised edition, Nashville: Abingdon, 1959], p.91-108.

for himself.[25]   He imagined that Philemon was a prominent leader of the churches in the Lycus valley, with probable residence in Laodicea, and that the letter was delivered to Philemon first so that he would use his influence to ensure that Archippus released Onesimus from slavery and would send him to assist Paul. Knox, as did Goodspeed, equated Philemon with "the letter from Laodicea" which Paul wanted read in the church at Colossae (Colossians 4:16).   Knox based his reconstruction on the belief that the restored Onesimus is the same person who is later named as bishop of Ephesus.[26]   In fact, Knox, too, makes Onesimus responsible for collecting Paul's letters, thus suggesting a possible reason why this brief letter to Philemon was preserved and included in the collection.   Knox also hypothesized that Ephesians was composed to be a cover letter for the group of Pauline letters once they had been collected.

Knox's proposed reconstruction of the situation has not won a following. In reply to that reconstruction:

- it seems most likely that Philemon, the first person addressed in the letter, is the intended recipient.   It would be strange to find the real addressee mentioned third in the opening of the letter.
- It is best to understand that Philemon lived at Colossae.   In Colossians 4:9, Onesimus is identified as "one of your number."   If he came from Colossae, then more than likely his owner lived there.[27]
- The part of Knox's reconstruction which is the most open to question is the identification of this letter with the one mentioned in Colossians 4:16.   The "letter that is coming from Laodicea" is better identified as being the letter we now know as "to the Ephesians."
- Luke is perhaps the better choice for the one who collected Paul's letters. The inclusion of this letter in the canon testifies to the recognition of its value in the early church, and probably also to Philemon's compliance with Paul's request to do more than he asked, but it may be saying more than we can know to attribute its inclusion simply to Onesimus' influence.

---

[25] John Knox, "Philemon" in the *Interpreter's Bible* (Nashville: Abingdon, 1955), Vol.11, p.557. P.N. Harrison, "Onesimus and Philemon," *Anglican Theological Review*, XXXII (1950), p.268-84, shared the traditional opinion that the master of Onesimus was not Archippus but Philemon, but agreed with Knox concerning the deeper purpose of the letter as being an unspoken request for Onesimus to be sent back, whether as slave or free, as a helper for Paul.

[26] Ignatius, *To the Ephesians*, 1:3, 1:2, 6:2.

[27] All that can be inferred with any confidence from Colossians 4:9 is that Onesimus was connected with Colossae before he ran away. It must be observed that we do not know the circumstances behind Onesimus being a slave. Was he born to slave parents? Was he sold into slavery by his parents to pay a debt? Was he captured in some foreign land by Roman soldiers and sold into slavery to Philemon?

- Was it truly Paul's intention that Philemon should emancipate Onesimus, sending Onesimus back as a free man to minister to Paul's needs? Several lines of reasoning within the letter argue against this conclusion, and such a conclusion is probably more than the letter implies. "I know that you will do even more than what I ask" (Philemon 21) refers back to "accept him" (Philemon 17); it is doubtful that there is an unspoken request about sending him back to assist Paul. The imperatives in the epistle (verses 17,18,20,22) are all concerned with a *reconciliation* between Philemon and Onesimus, not to any benefit Paul might derive from the relationship. The "ministry" which Archippus is to fulfill (Colossians 4:17) would seem to imply more than simply a willingness on his part, as Knox reconstructed it, to relinquish his slave, for it is difficult to conceive of this kind of "ministry" as a trust "received" from the Lord. A better explanation of Colossians 4:17 is that Archippus is the evangelist for the churches of the Lycus River valley in the absence of Epaphras. This is the "ministry" he is to fulfill.

E. OCCASION AND PURPOSE OF WRITING

1. Occasion

Onesimus, a native of Colossae, the slave of Philemon, had fled to Rome, and there was converted to Christ by Paul.[28] Paul apparently persuaded Onesimus to voluntarily return to his owner's house. The report of Philemon's kind and loving character (Philemon 5,6) may have contributed both to the belief that Philemon would be amenable to treating a penitent slave with kindness rather than the harshness that Roman law allowed, and that Onesimus was to act in the belief that Philemon's Christianity would rule what happened upon the fugitive's return.

An occasion arose which afforded an opportunity for Onesimus to return to Philemon. Epaphras, a preacher at Colossae, has come to Rome to seek Paul's help concerning certain dangerous doctrines that were beginning to threaten the church at Colossae. To strengthen the church against these false teachings, Paul wrote a letter to the church which was sent by Tychicus (Colossians 4:7-8). At the same time Tychicus made the journey bearing the letter, Onesimus could travel with him back to Colossae. Having persuaded Onesimus to return to his master, Paul furnished him with this letter to recommend him, as no longer merely a servant, but a brother also, and to secure a favorable reception by Philemon.

---

[28] See comments on Colossians 4:9 plus the discussion in the Detailed Introduction to Colossians elsewhere in this commentary on the Prison Epistles.

2. Purpose

As commentators try to reconstruct the background of Philemon, a number of questions are asked. (1) Why did Onesimus decide to leave Philemon's house? Did he run away and become a fugitive slave? Or was he sent by Philemon to help Paul in prison?[29] Was he not running away at all, but was he rather seeking a third party (an "advocate") who might negotiate a return to the owner's house under improved conditions?[30] Was Onesimus not a slave, but an apprentice?[31] (2) How did Onesimus come into contact with Paul (who was under house arrest, Acts 28:30)? Did he search for Paul? Did one of Paul's fellow workers who knew Onesimus meet him by chance on the streets of Rome and take him to Paul? (3) Did Onesimus seek asylum ("right of sanctuary") with Paul, rather than seeking asylum in a temple (such as the one dedicated to Artemis in Ephesus) or at a statue of the emperor, in order to beg the priests or attendants to work out a sale of the slave to a more humane owner? Was seeking asylum the farthest thing from Onesimus' mind when he first came into contact with Paul? (4) If Onesimus were a fugitive slave, was Paul obligated by Roman laws regarding slavery to return Onesimus to his owner?[32] Did such laws apply only to Roman citizens, and what is the possibility that Philemon, a Phrygian, might not even be a Roman citizen?[33] (5) What role should Paul's direct advice (1 Corinthians 7:21) to Christians who were slaves play in interpreting this letter to Philemon? Possible answers that may be given to these questions are included in the verse-by-verse comments on pertinent passages in these Prison Epistles.

Sara Winter has proposed a reconstruction of the background that differs from that of Knox. She has modified Knox's views, as the title of her article indicates, by applying sociological and literary critical methods to the interpretation of the text.[34]

---

[29] Sara C. Winter, "Paul's Letter to Philemon," *NTS* 33 (1987), p.1-15.

[30] While slaves who sought an advocate were not classified as "fugitives" (Proculus, *Dig.* 21.1.17.4), it is difficult to image that Onesimus would have to go as far as Rome to find an advocate.

[31] Albert Barnes, *Barnes' Notes on Thessalonians to Philemon* (Grand Rapids: Baker Book House, 1955), p.ccxci-ccxcvi.

[32] Roman law indicated action could be taken against any who harbored a runaway slave (Oxy P. 1422, 1643).

[33] J.D.M. Derrett, "The Functions of the Epistle to Philemon," *ZNW* 79 (1988), p.73.

[34] Sara C. Winter, "Methodological Observations on a New Interpretation of Paul's Letter to Philemon," *Union Seminary Quarterly Review* 33:3 (Jan 1984), p.203-212.

In a footnote, Winter tells how a suspicion that Apphia was not the wife of Philemon (or at least that her marital status was unimportant to the matter of the letter) triggered a desire to present what might be a better explanation for the background of the letter than the traditional explanation. In the article, Winter proposed the following four points concerning the occasion and interpretation of the letter: (1) Archippus is the wealthy patron who owns the house in which the house church is located and to whom the request concerning Onesimus is directed. Philemon and Apphia are church workers. They are named first because the matter of Onesimus concerns the church. (2) The verb "I have sent him back" (verse 12) prompts the conclusion that the recipients of the letter knew that Onesimus was with Paul, as opposed to the traditional view that Onesimus accompanied the letter as it is delivered. What Paul is supposed to be saying, Winters indicates, is not that Onesimus has been sent, but that "I have sent his case to a higher court."[35] The thanksgiving, she proposed, informs them of Onesimus' arrival and the good (verse 6) he has brought the prisoners. The Colossae congregation (the church in Archippus' house) apparently sent Onesimus to aid Paul in prison (just as the Philippians had sent Epaphroditus). (3) Verses 8-14 take the form of a legal petition. Onesimus is the object of Paul's request; Paul petitions the recipient Archippus to permit Onesimus to remain with him in the service of the gospel (verse 13). (4) Onesimus is no longer to be considered as a slave within the Christian community (verses 15-17). Paul offers to settle any debts Onesimus may have incurred while serving in Archippus' household (verses 18-19), and requests that Onesimus be manumitted so that his social and legal status will be changed according to Roman law (verse 21).

Winter's reconstruction is open to several challenges.

- Does not the phrase in verse 13, which in the Greek begins with "whom," specifically say Paul has sent Onesimus back? If Onesimus is not staying with Paul after the letter is sent, this cannot be a petition to let Onesimus remain with him.
- The "your" in verse 6 refers to the recipient of the letter, not to "them" (plural) as Winter's reconstruction has it.

---

[35] Sara C. Winter ("Paul's Letter to Philemon," *NTS* 33:1 [January 1987], p.7) has examined Philemon for parallels to legal forms and language used in Paul's day, and believes that these are significant analogies which help to explain certain phrases in the letter. Paul's appeal to Philemon 10 (*parakalo ... peri*) for example, is like a formula used in legal petitions. *Anapempo* in Philemon 12 ("I am sending him ... back to you ...") is a legal term better understood as referring Onesimus' case "to the proper authority." The idea of partnership (*koinonia*) between Paul and Philemon, notes Winter, has more of the elements of a "consensual association," a *societas* in which partnership was legal binding. She concludes that Paul's plea to Philemon is that Onesimus be received into this *societas* as an equal partner.

- Is the reason Winter must interpret "accept him as you would me" (Philemon 17) as being figurative language precisely because that command, taken literally, would undermine her main thesis as to the purpose of the letter?
- Why does Winter avoid offering an explanation of the "fulfill your ministry" statement (Colossians 4:17) to Archippus?
- Would the church have sent a non-Christian slave to minister to Paul?
- What happens to this reconstruction when the sociological and literary critical methods of interpretation she relies upon are replaced by some newer method based on the then current popular philosophy?

In conclusion, the position taken in this commentary concerning Paul's purpose for writing this letter is in harmony with traditional view. This letter is an example of the kind of appeal that might be made on behalf of a runaway slave who is returning voluntarily to the master from whom he fled. "Paul writes this brief letter chiefly to move the relationship between Philemon and Onesimus to a new level, one in which they will relate to each other no longer as master and slave but as brothers in the Lord. This requires a great step of obedience and magnanimity on Philemon's part, who is being asked to give away his rights by the world's standards so that he can live out what is right in the new family of God."[36] It will also require great faith and courage on Onesimus' part since he is placing his future, if not his life, into the hands of Philemon, who will have to choose how to respond to Paul's letter of appeal. Will he choose harsh punishment or forgiveness? There was no way Onesimus or Paul could be sure of the outcome.

F. CRITICAL MATTERS

1. "Right of Sanctuary"

In the ancient world, if a slave ran away and became repentant, the slave could go to an influential man and ask that man to plead his case to his former master. There is still in existence such a letter written by Pliny the younger in which he writes a letter on behalf of a slave seeking sanctuary.

C. Plinius to his friend Sabinianus, Greeting.

A freedman of yours, whom you said you were angry with, came to me, and prostrating himself at my feet, as if at your own, clung to them. He wept much, and begged much; much of the time, too, he was silent; in short, he gave me a

---

[36] David DeSilva, *An Introduction to the New Testament* (Downers Grove, IL: InterVarsity Press, 2004), p.670.

confidence of his penitence. I believe him to be truly a reformed character, because he is sensible that he has done wrong. You are angry, I know; and you have reason to be angry, this also I know: but mercy wins the highest praise just when there is the most righteous cause for anger. You loved the man, and, I hope, will continue to love him: meanwhile it is enough that you should allow yourself to yield to his prayers. You may be angry again, if he deserves it; and in this you will be the more readily pardoned if you yield now.

Concede something to his youth, something to his tears, something to your own indulgent disposition. Do not torture him, lest you torture yourself at the same time, for it IS torture to you, when one of your gentle temper is angry. I am afraid lest I should appear not to ask, but to compel, if I should add my prayers to his. Yet I will add them the more fully and unreservedly, because I scolded the man himself with sharpness and severity; for I threatened him straitly that I would never ask you again. This I said to him, for it was necessary to alarm him but I do not use the same language to you. For perchance I shall ask again, and be successful again, only let my request be such, as it becomes me to prefer and you to grant. Farewell.[37]

From this letter we can learn to expect certain emphases in such a letter, including an appeal to the usefulness of the slave, an appeal to the worth of the man (as every man is worth something), and a statement that the man is sorry and won't do it again. Pliny even tugs at the slave master's emotions by describing the pitiful sight of the slave as he came seeking sanctuary. Paul does all these things, plus an inclusion of the fact that Onesimus (who has recently become a Christian) now can be expected to be dedicated to the responsibilities that were his.

2. Is the letter to Philemon an allegory to the work of Christ?

Man is a runaway slave from God, so the allegory goes. Jesus came to bring men back to God. "If man has wronged Thee, charge that to my account," says Jesus to His Father (as Paul did to Philemon). Jesus pleads that there be no punishment for the returned runaway slave. "Treat him as you would me," Jesus is supposed to be saying.

It is this commentator's judgment that we need not treat Philemon as an allegory if our only reason for so doing is to explain why this short letter came to be included in the canon.

---

[37] Pliny, *Ep*. ix.21,24, written ca. AD 108.

3. Location in the Canon

Why does Philemon follow Titus (a letter in the fourth group of Pauline epistles), when it is one of the third group of Prison Epistles? Why is it not included along with Ephesians-Philippians-Colossians? The answer is this: in the Western canon of New Testament books, Paul's epistles are arranged first according to destination (to churches first, and then those addressed to individuals), and then according to length. Philemon is the shortest of the personal books, so the order we find is 1 & 2 Timothy, Titus, and lastly, Philemon.

G. OUTLINE

Epistolary Opening.   Salutation to Philemon and his house, 1-3

I. Thanksgiving for Philemon's love and faith,   4-7
II. A Plea/Request on behalf of Onesimus,   8-22

Final Greetings and Benediction,   23-25

Detailed Introduction to Philippians[1]

For the letters in the New Testament, it is mandatory to begin any detailed study of the letter with a search for any historical allusions within the epistle which would give us clues concerning authorship, destination, date of writing, place of writing, and the purpose for writing.

A. HISTORICAL ALLUSIONS

1. Historical Allusions at the beginning of the letter, 1:1ff

Letters in the ancient world began with the signature of the author, a statement of destination for the letter, and a word of greeting to the recipient of the letter. When we examine Philippians looking for those customary things, this is what we see: (1) The signature on this letter is "Paul" (1:1). Timothy is also named, which not only means that Timothy was with Paul at the time the letter was written, but may also mean that he was the penman who wrote as Paul dictated the contents of the letter. (2) The destination is "to all the saints in Christ Jesus who are in Philippi" to which is added the words "including the overseers and deacons." "Overseers and deacons" were congregational leaders in the early church, but we wonder why they were singled out for special mention here. (3) In 1:2 we have Paul's words of greeting, and the wording as it appears in this letter also appears in his letters to the Corinthians, the Galatians, the Romans, and "to the Ephesians." Paul's words of greeting in a slightly modified form are found in 1 & 2 Thessalonians, Colossians, 1 & 2 Timothy, Titus, and Philemon.

Following the usual epistolary opening, ancient letters often included a word of thanksgiving. Philippians 1:3-11 are Paul's words of thanksgiving. In his other letters, Paul often uses his words of thanksgiving to give a preview of what the rest of the letter is about. Is that true for Philippians? Perhaps it is. In verse 5 Paul makes reference to their "participation" in the gospel from the first day until now. In 2 Corinthians 8:4 the word "participation" had to do with an offering of money being sent to the saints at Jerusalem. We wonder if "participation" here in Philippians has something to do with a gift of money. In 1:7 the author speaks of "my imprisonment" (NASB), or "in my bonds" (ASV). This indicates Paul is a prisoner at the time he writes this letter to Philippi. We are reminded of similar language in Ephesians, Colossians, and Philemon. We

---

[1] The spelling of "Philippians" is the Latin spelling of the word, just as it is the Latin spelling that occurs at Philippians 4:15.

wonder, is it the same imprisonment alluded to in those letters? In 1:9 he prays that their love may abound still more and more. What does he have in mind? How is their love to be expressed? In more and greater offerings to Christian missions? He also prays the Philippians will exercise knowledge and discernment as they express their love. To what do these words point? In 1:10 Paul indicates he wants the Philippians to discern things that are excellent so that they will be blameless when the day of Christ comes. The day of Christ is evidently the final judgment. What does the idea of being blameless at the final judgment have to do with how they express their love? 1:11 speaks of "the fruit of righteousness." In Romans 1:13 Paul indicated he wanted to give the Christians at Rome an opportunity to produce some "fruit." Later, as he is explaining that he wants them to support his coming mission to Spain (Romans 15:28), Paul again uses the word "fruit". Is Paul speaking about the Philippians' offering to missions when in 1:11 he indicates he wants their lives filled with "fruit"?

More historical allusions occur in Philippians 1:12-14. In verse 12, Paul writes about how the things which have happened to him "have turned out for the greater progress of the gospel." We ask "what things?" In verse 13 he says that as a result of his imprisonment the "whole praetorian guard" has been influenced. Where would one find members of the praetorian guard? An answer to this question helps us determine where Paul was when he wrote this letter.[2] Not only has the whole praetorian guard learned that Paul's imprisonment was "in the cause of Christ," but verse 14 indicates that his imprisonment has encouraged many nearby preachers to speak the word of God without fear. It looks like they had been reticent to speak out before, but no longer. But then immediately verse 18 causes us to ask how the preaching of some gospel preachers might cause Paul distress in his imprisonment.

Philippians 1:19 indicates that the prayers of the Philippians and the provision of the Spirit of Christ could result in Paul's "deliverance." The marginal note tells us the word can also mean "salvation." Is Paul speaking of a soon-release from imprisonment, or about eternal salvation? Since verse 26 speaks of Paul's hope of visiting Philippi again, it looks like release from imprisonment is what is intended by "deliverance." While we know about the power of prayer and the Spirit, do we know anything about Roman jurisprudence that might allow Paul to express such a hope? In turn, does that knowledge help give any hint about the time when this letter was written?

---

[2] This now sounds like he is a prisoner in Rome. In the General Introductory Studies to this third group of Paul's letters, we concluded that the language "the whole praetorian guard" sounds like Paul is a prisoner in Rome. A summary of the key points presented there is also found below under "Place of Writing."

2. Historical allusions at the conclusion of the letter, 4:1ff

In Philippians 4:2 we learn that two women in the church, Euodia and Syntyche, were at odds with each other. May we suppose that Paul's appeals, both to the women and to a person he calls upon as a "true comrade" to help the women be reconciled, should be included in a summary of reasons why the letter was written? A number of questions come to mind. How widespread was the division or dissension? Who is the "true comrade"? The Greek word translated "comrade" is *suzuge* which might be a proper name, "Syzygus." Proper names in the ancient world had meanings, and since this word can be translated as "yokefellow" (ASV), one view is that this man is being asked to live up to his name as he tries to get the two women reconciled and yoked back together in their service for the gospel. Clement of Alexandria suggested the person addressed is the wife of Paul, but the fact that the word is masculine appears to be against this idea. Another suggestion is that this person is the husband of either Euodia or Syntyche, but would a person so related to one of the disputants be in a position to be a peacemaker? Another suggestion is that Paul is addressing Lydia (his first convert in Philippi), for otherwise she is not alluded to in the letter. The omission of her name from Philippians is not necessarily remarkable. She was from the town of Thyatira, and not a native of Philippi, so it is not at all to be expected that she necessarily would be found here in Philippi 10 years after her conversion. Besides, the fact that "true comrade" is masculine seems to be against the idea that Lydia is the one intended. Because the letter is addressed to the "overseers and deacons," some understand the person addressed here to be the chief elder of the church. It is very likely an anachronism to think that such a position as chief elder existed this early in church history. Yet another attempt to identify the "true comrade" has proposed that it is none other than Epaphroditus who, though the bearer of this letter, is here charged with the work of reconciliation. Still other suggestions have included Peter, Barnabas, Luke, Silas (Acts 16:19-40), or the jailer (so thought Theophylact). All that is known about the "true comrade" is that it was someone whom Paul regarded as associated with himself in the work of the gospel, one who had worked with the women and with Clement, and one who was so prominent at Philippi that it would be understood who was referred to without more particularly designating him. Perhaps, then, could Paul's *gnēsie syzygos* have been Luke in Philippi? Not if the date of writing is AD 62 or 63 since Luke is with Paul in Rome at that time (Colossians 4:14).

One reason Paul gives to encourage the true comrade to work with the women is that they have been long time helpers "in the cause of the gospel." Not only have they helped Paul in the past, but they helped Clement and other fellow-workers (4:3).

The name "Clement" raises some interesting questions. Is this person to be identified with the man we know as Clement of Rome, whose letter to the Corinthians known as 1 Clement, and written about AD 96, we still have extant? It would not be impossible for the Clement named in Philippians to be the Clement of Rome; however, Clement was a rather common name, so not too much argument can be made from the name itself.

In Philippians 4:9 the exhortation to practice "the things you have learned and received and heard and seen in me" indicates Paul has lived and worked among the readers. Later in this Detailed Introduction to Philippians we shall call attention to what we know from the Book of Acts about the founding and history of the church in Philippi. Paul was involved in that. This bit of information helps establish some rough parameters as we try to determine a possible date of writing.

In Philippians 4:10-18 Paul alludes to the missionary offerings the Philippians had sent to him. Several questions come to mind as we read these verses looking for historical allusions. What does verse 10 mean when he writes "you have revived your concern for me; indeed, you were concerned before, but you lacked opportunity"? In verse 14, where our version reads "you have done well to share with me in my affliction," the words "share with me" translate the same word that was translated "participation" back in 1:5. In fact, the word occurs again in 4:15 ("shared with me"), where it becomes obvious that Paul is speaking about a missionary offering the Philippians have sent. When Paul indicates in verse 15 that no church sent offerings to him when he first left Macedonia, except the Philippians, he gives us another clue to be included when we try to determine the date of writing. We also are caused to think about Paul's habit of refusing to take pay for his work from those to whom he was presently preaching (1 Corinthians 9:14-18). As a rule, rather than taking pay from those in the town where he was working, Paul supported himself by working at his trade as a tentmaker. He did this because there were so many enemies and false teachers who would make wrong use of his example or put a wrong construction on it. Paul was seeing to it that no one could accuse him of being in the ministry merely for the money. Paul is not being inconsistent when he later accepted support from churches in towns where he is no longer preaching. In harmony with his willingness to accept support from converts after he left their town, we learn from 4:16 that twice while Paul was at Thessalonica, the Philippians sent offerings to him. And when he was in Corinth, they also sent an offering to him (2 Corinthians 11:9). When we come to Philippians 4:18 we have information that helps us determine the occasion and purpose of this letter. We are told that Epaphroditus (a man about whom we hope to learn more as we study Philippians) recently has brought another offering to Paul.   This letter to the Philippians is a "thank you" note for that recent offering which the Philippians had sent.   Now, too, we understand the phraseology we encountered in Philippians 4:10.   There had been some time between offerings received from Philippi, and for this recent one Paul is expressing his gratitude in as many ways as he can.   Why, even God was pleased, he tells them, with their offering to their missionary.

Philippians 4:21-23 are closing words of greeting and salutation.   "Greet every saint in Christ Jesus" (verse 21) likely says that every saint in Philippi has had a part in providing the offering; so when this letter is read publicly to the congregation, they are to take turns congratulating each other for their part in the offering.   In verse 21 we have "the brethren who are with me greet you" and in verse 22 we have "all the saints greet you ...."   What is the difference between "brethren" and "saints"?   Could the "brethren" be Paul's helpers (his 'preacher boys') who are with him when he writes?   The "saints" are the Christians in the town where Paul is, and who know he is writing this letter to Philippi.   The Philippians are thus assured that their generosity toward Paul the missionary is appreciated both by Paul's helpers and by the Christians in the town where Paul is.   In fact, in verse 22 he specifically mentions "those of Caesar's household."   Christians in the royal palace of Caesar indicates the place of writing is Rome.   Thus, the historical allusions thus tell us that Paul is in Rome when he wrote this letter to the Philippians.

In the KJV there is a subscription to the letter which reads "It was written to the Philippians from Rome by Epaphroditus."   Is this correct?   The subscriptions were not part of the autographed letter, but were added to the letter when scribes were making copies of it.   Some of the subscriptions found in the KJV are correct, and some are not.   This one may be correct.   The wording "by Epaphroditus" does not mean that it was written by Epaphroditus, but that the letter was carried to Philippi by Epaphroditus.

3.   Other allusions in the epistle

Occasionally in Paul's letters, one finds historical allusions in the body of the letter.   There are several in Philippians.

In 2:19, Paul tells the Philippians he hopes to send Timothy to them shortly.   Then in 2:24, Paul tells them he plans to come to see them shortly, after he sees how things will go for him in Rome.   Does this imply a trial?   Does this indicate that the two-year limit is almost up, and that he now feels that his accusers won't come, and therefore he anticipates being set free according to the Roman jurisprudence of the time?

In 2:25-28, Paul tells the Philippians he has sent Epaphroditus back to Philippi. The infinitive "send" is likely an epistolary aorist, which would lead to the plausible conclusion that Epaphroditus was the one who carried this letter from Paul to Philippi. In these same verses we learn more about Epaphroditus. After coming to Paul with the offering, Epaphroditus had become sick and nearly died. The Philippians had heard about this critical illness and were concerned, and the news of the church's concern for the man who had borne their missionary offering had reached back to Paul in Rome. Now, by the grace of God, Paul tells us, Epaphroditus had recovered, and is being sent back to Philippi, to relieve the people of their concern. This sequence – the time needed for information about Paul's whereabouts to get to Philippi, the time for a messenger to get to Rome with their offering, plus the time needed for news about Epaphroditus' sickness to travel from Rome to Philippi, and then for information about the Philippians' concern for him to travel back again to Rome – has been used as a clue to the time of writing of the letter to the Philippians.

In Philippians 3:4-12 we have details about the life history of the author. The items cited about his being a persecutor of the church (verse 6) and about his being "laid hold of by Christ Jesus" (verse 12), which likely refers to what happened to Paul on the Damascus road (Acts 26:16-18), especially fit what we know of Paul, and are internal clues as to the Pauline authorship of this letter.

B. HISTORY OF PHILIPPI AND THE PHILIPPIAN CHURCH

1. The location of Philippi

Luke calls Philippi "a leading city of the district of Macedonia" (Acts 16:12).[3] The famous Roman road, the Via Egnatia, which connected Rome in the west with her conquered lands in Asia to the east, passed through Philippi. About 10 miles to the southeast of Philippi, the Via Egnatia passed through Neapolis, which served, in effect, as Philippi's seaport. To the westward of

---

[3] "District" reflects the fact that in 168 BC Macedonia was divided into four administrative districts by the Romans. The word translated "leading" is *prōtē* ("first, chief"). This cannot mean that Philippi was the capital of the province, for Thessalonica held that distinction. Nor does it mean that Philippi was the capital of its district, for Amphipolis served that function. Evidence from a later period shows that *prōtē* was an honorary title given certain cities, and this perhaps explains Luke's use of the term (F.J. Foakes-Jackson and Kirsopp Lake, eds., *The Beginnings of Christianity: Part I, The Acts of the Apostles* [Grand Rapids: Baker Book House, 1965], Vol. IV, p. 188). This volume by Foakes-Jackson and Lake, pages 187-191, is a good source for information about Philippi.

Philippi, the Via Egnatia connected with Thessalonica and eventually the western coast of Macedonia. The ruins of Philippi have been unearthed by archaeologists. The route of the Via Egnatia ran from northwest to southeast through the city, and passed between the forum of the city on the south side of the road and the foot of Mount Orbelos (now called Mt. Lekani) on the north. The ruins of a magnificent theater are still to be seen on the side of that mountain. Acts 16:13 tells us that Paul and Silas went "outside the gate to a riverside, where we were supposing there would be a place of prayer."[4] A mile west of the city are the ruins of a Roman arch near the River Gangites. Such an arch usually symbolized the city limits of a Roman settlement. Philippi held a very strategic position, both commercially and militarily, because of its location on the natural land route from Europe to Asia. Its strategic advantages were equally favorable to the spreading of the gospel.

2. History of Philippi

Soon after gold was discovered nearby, Philip of Macedon, himself just having come to power in 359 BC, established a military garrison on a site known as "Krenides" (*krēnidēs*, "wells" or "springs," presumably so called because of the presence of a good water supply[5]) in order to take control of the neighboring gold mines. He renamed several small communities in the area after himself, giving them the plural name "Philippi."[6] The gold from the area financed his army in their effort the unify Greece. The gold also helped finance the armies of Alexander the Great, who was the son of Philip. By the time both leaders had died, the gold had been depleted.

When Alexander the Great died, his kingdom eventually was divided among several of his strong generals who in turn fought wars (the Wars of the Diadochoi) against each other as each tried to become ruler of all of Alexander's empire. By

---

[4] The word translated "place of prayer" at Acts 16:13 is *proseuche*. "The term may simply refer to a designated meeting place in the open air. Josephus (*Ant*. XIV.10.23-24), however, records several decrees giving Jews in the Eastern Mediterranean the right to build edifices for their religious observances, using the same term [*proseuche*]" (David DeSilva, *Introduction to the New Testament* [Downers Grove, IL: InterVarsity Press, 2004], p.643).

[5] Diodorus Siculus xvi.4.8

[6] Philip II, of Macedonia, ruled from 359-336 BC. See "Philip of Macedon," *National Geographic* (July 1978), p.55-77.

301 BC (after the Battle of Ipsus) the powers in the Mediterranean world were Ptolemy I Soter who ruled Egypt, Cassander who ruled Greece, Lysimachus who ruled Macedonia and northern Asia Minor, and Seleucus I Nicator who ruled central Asia Minor, Syria, and all of what was once Mesopotamia and Persia. In the years immediately following, Macedonia was the prize which several of these men and their descendants fought over.

In the second century BC, when it became evident that Egypt and the Ptolemies could be conquered, Macedonia under Philip V and the Seleucids under Antiochus III formed an alliance to conquer and divide Egypt among themselves. Rome was invited to intervene, and the Romans defeated Philip V. They also drove the Seleucids out of Greece and out of Asia Minor. Following Philip V's death (179 BC), his son, Perseus of Macedon, attempted to restore Macedonian influence. In 168 BC, Roman legions smashed his Macedonian phalanx at the Battle of Pydna, and in an effort to ensure peace in the area, Rome divided Macedonia into four districts (or client republics).

A Roman civil war followed the assassination of Julius Caesar in 45 BC. Philippi was aligned with the forces of Brutus and Cassius (who had helped assassinate Caesar) against the Second Triumvirate (Octavian, Antony, and Lepidus). It was just west of Philippi that in 42 BC the two decisive battles were fought between these two forces. The partisans of the Republic were defeated by Octavian and Antony. In honor of their victory, Octavian and Antony made the city of Philippi a Roman colony[7] and swelled its population by settling there veterans from their army who had served their time. Philippi is surrounded by vast farmlands, much of which was given as land grants to the veterans of the Roman armies. About ten years later, following the Battle of Actium in 31 BC, in which Octavian (known in the New Testament as Caesar Augustus) defeated Antony, the status of Philippi was raised. Octavian became sole ruler of the Roman empire. The city's population was increased by partisans of Antony who were expelled from Rome. Many of the Philippians alive when this letter was written would have been descended from those veterans and partisans. The colony was reorganized and now its citizens enjoyed the privilege of Roman citizenship. Being made a Roman colony and being granted Roman citizenship provided the inhabitants of Philippi with numerous advantages, including being

---

[7] A "colony" was a place of military significance. There is a north-south range of mountains in Macedonia that divides Europe from Asia. Just at Philippi that range dips down into a pass, and therefore Philippi commanded the road from Europe to Asia, for through that pass the road must go.

self-governed,[8] immunity from paying tribute to Caesar, and, since being governed by Roman law, treated as if they actually lived in Italy.[9]   Pride in Roman citizenship was shown by speaking Latin, the language of Rome, by wearing Roman dress, by observing Roman customs, and by keeping Roman holidays and ceremonies.   This is how life in the city was at the time Paul entered it and planted a church there.

3. History of the Philippian church in the apostolic age

In about AD 51 or 52, in response to the Macedonian call (Acts 16:6-10), Paul and his companions had crossed the Aegean Sea from Troas to Neapolis and followed the renowned Egnatian Way some ten miles up and over the coastal range to the city of Philippi.   The conversions of Lydia and the Philippian jailer and his household (Acts 16:14-33) were the beginning of the church there. Lydia's house became the meeting place for the brethren who formed the nucleus of the church.

The change from "we" (Acts 16:11-13) to "they" (Acts 16:40) when Paul and his helpers left Philippi and headed toward Thessalonica indicates Luke (the author of Acts) stayed behind to be the preacher for the infant congregation.   He must have been a good preacher, for Paul says that he was famous for the gospel (2 Corinthians 8:18-20).   He will serve as their evangelist for about 5 years, until the "we-passages" begin again at Acts 20:6, as Paul and a number of messengers from the churches pass through Philippi on their way to Jerusalem with an offering for the poor saints there.

It is from 2 Corinthians and from Paul's letter to the Philippians that we learn of the Philippian church's interest in supporting Paul as their missionary. While Paul was in Thessalonica shortly after leaving Philippi (Acts 17:1-9), the church in Philippi twice at least had sent gifts for his needs (Philippians 4:15,16). When Paul went on to Corinth, the Philippians sent another offering (2 Corinthians 11:9).   2 Corinthians 11:8 implies that other congregations besides Philippi were involved in supporting Paul's mission work.

---

[8] This self-rule by the *duumviri*, or by the magistrates, as they were more popularly called (cf. Acts 16:20), was a matter of considerable pride ("we are Romans") -- a pride reflected in Paul's letter by two allusions to their colonial government (cf. Philippians 1:27, 3:20).   At 3:20, Paul in effect tells the Philippian Christians "You are a colony of heaven," which is a greater honor than being a Roman colony.

[9] Foakes-Jackson and Lake, *op. cit.*, pp.187-190.

Indications are that Paul visited Philippi in AD 57 on his way from Ephesus through Macedonia to Greece while on his third missionary circuit (Acts 19:21,22 and 1 Corinthians 16:5). The common tradition dates the Second Epistle to the Corinthians from Philippi on that occasion.

Toward the close of his third missionary journey, Paul leaned heavily upon the church in Philippi as money was being raised for the poor saints in Jerusalem from the churches in Galatia, Asia, Macedonia, and Achaia. The churches of Achaia were quick to promise and slow to pay (2 Corinthians 8:11). Paul used their prompt pledges to stir the Macedonian churches to activity (2 Corinthians 9:2). He then spurred the Achaian churches on to actual participation by the liberality and prompt giving of the Macedonian churches (2 Corinthians 8:1-15, 9:1-5). Clearly, the church at Philippi, poor and generous, long had the habit of giving; it set the pace for the other Macedonian churches and for the Achaian churches as well.

About a half-dozen years later, when the Philippians learned Paul was a prisoner in Rome, they sent another gift. The last instance of their "fellowship," after an interval when they "lacked opportunity" (Philippians 4:10), was when they sent Epaphroditus to Rome with their offering (Philippians 4:18). That Paul can say he was "amply supplied" (4:18) seems to suggest they have fairly outdone themselves this time.

As he wrote to the Philippians, Paul indicated that he hoped soon to visit the brethren at Philippi again (Philippians 2:24). At a period subsequent to this epistle to the Philippians, and after his first Roman imprisonment, we learn from 1 Timothy 1:3 that Paul went into Macedonia and so, no doubt, fulfilled his hope of revisiting this well-loved church.

4. Post-apostolic history of the church and the town

Ignatius, bishop of Antioch (d. AD 115), stopped in Philippi early in the second century on his way to Rome (where he would eventually be condemned as a Christian and thrown to the wild beasts).[10] The Philippian Christians treated Ignatius kindly and wrote a letter of sympathy to his home church in Antioch.

---

[10] Alexander Roberts and James Donaldson, eds., "The Martyrdom of Ignatius" in *The Ante-Nicene Fathers* (Grand Rapids: Eerdmans, 1953), Vol.1, p.127.

From Rhegium, Ignatius wrote a letter back to the Philippians.[11]   After the Philippians received it, they wrote a letter to Polycarp, bishop of Smyrna, asking him to send them copies of any letters of Ignatius which he might have.   Polycarp complied with their request and also wrote the church a letter of his own, full of comfort and cheer.   In this letter, Polycarp also censured a presbyter, Valens, and his wife for avarice, although the church at Philippi seemed to be doing well. The letter from Polycarp to them, mainly practical and hortatory, implies, with but slight reservation, that the Philippian Christianity was still strong and vigorous, and that the Christians there had a constant and grateful memory of Paul the apostle.[12]

After that, we have a few records of bishops of Philippi, whose names are appended to the decisions of the councils held at Sardica (AD 344.), Ephesus (AD 431), and Chalcedon (AD 451).[13]   Ruins of church buildings in Philippi, dating from the 3rd to 6th centuries, attest to a vigorous Christianity in that place. Catastrophic earthquakes in the early 7th century AD, together with invasions by Slavs and Bulgars, brought the city into a state of decline.   After the Turkish conquest (AD 1387) the city and its fortifications were abandoned and fell into ruin.

C. AUTHORSHIP AND ATTESTATION

1.   Internal evidence as to authorship

The writer signs his name as "Paul" (1:1).   The historical allusions like his imprisonment (1:7), the autobiographical details (3:4-6), and the preaching in Macedonia (4:15) all fit Paul.   The language, style, and structure are Paul's.   For the most part, Paul's letters (and Philippians is no exception) followed the ancient Greek letter form, but with appropriate Christian modifications.   The epistolary opening names the author, gives the address, and includes a greeting.   His letters then typically offer a prayer for the readers, emphasizing their spiritual welfare and often including an introduction to the topics to be covered in the letter.   Then

---

[11] Roberts and Donaldson, "Epistle of Ignatius to the Philippians" in *The Ante-Nicene Fathers*, Vol.1, p.116-119.

[12] Roberts and Donaldson, "The Epistle of Polycarp to the Philippians" in *The Ante-Nicene Fathers*, Vol.1, p.33-36.

[13] M.N. Tod, "Philippi" in *The International Standard Bible Encyclopedia*, edited by James Orr (Grand Rapids: Eerdmans, 1949), Vol.4, p.237.

Paul proceeds to the main body of the letter, which may contain several topics. Paul's letters differ from Greek letter form when Paul regularly includes words of Christian exhortation, sometimes interspersed in the body of the letter, and sometimes as a separate practical section following the main body's emphasis on doctrinal matters. Ancient letters closed with some final greetings and a final wish, which in Paul's case becomes a prayer of benediction which asks for blessings from God to the readers.[14]

2. External attestation to the Pauline authorship and canonical authority of Philippians.

a. Allusions

1) Clement of Rome (AD 96) has reflections of Philippians 4:15 (ch.47), 1:27 (ch.21), 1:10 and 2:15 (ch.2), and 2:5 (ch.16).

2) Ignatius (AD 115) has reminiscences of 2:3, 2:17, 3:15 in *Rom* ii, and *Philad*. viii.

3) Polycarp (AD 115), addressing a letter to the Philippians, includes expressions taken from Paul's letter to the Philippians. In chapters ii, ix, and xi he has allusions to 1:27, 2:10, 2:16, 3:18, and 4:10. (He also has annotated quotations, see below.)

4) Shepherd of Hermas (AD 140) has language like 4:3 (*Vis.* i.3) and 4:15 (*Mand.* v.2).

5) The Didache (AD 140) has reflections of 1:8 (*Levi* 4), 3:21 (*Benj.* 10), 2:6-8 (*Zab.* 9), and 2:15 (*Levi* 14).

6) The Epistle to Diognetus (c. AD 150) in ch.5 has language resembling 3:20.

7) Justin Martyr (AD 150) in *De Resurr.* 7 has an allusion to 3:20.

---

[14] "... [I]t seems proper to say that the apostle Paul uses the basic form of the secular Greek letter to accomplish his purpose related to the demands of the Christian mission activity and yet is not limited to that form." Ronald Russell, 1982, "Pauline Letter Structure in Philippians," *Journal of the Evangelical Theological Society* 25.3 (Sept.), p.306.

8) Melito of Sardis (d. AD 180) in *Frag.* 6 has a reflection of 2:6.

9) Theophilus of Antioch (d. AD 183) in *ad Autolycum* alludes to 1:10, 3:19, and 4:8.

10) *The Epistle of the Churches of Vienne and Lyons* (AD 177) has a reflection of 2:6-8.[15]

b. Annotated Quotations

1) Polycarp (AD 115)

"For neither I, nor any one like me, can reach the wisdom of the blessed and renowned Paul ... who when absent wrote to you letters; into which if ye look, you will be able to edify yourselves in the faith which has been given you."[16]

"But I have neither perceived nor heard any such thing in you, among whom the blessed Paul labored, who are named in the beginning of his epistle, for he boasts of you in all the churches which then alone knew the Lord."[17]

2) Irenaeus (AD 180)

Irenaeus quotes from every chapter and calls the letter Paul's. One example is, "As Paul also says to the Philippians: 'I am full, having received of Epaphroditus the things which were sent from you, an odour of a sweet smell, a sacrifice acceptable, well-pleasing to God'."[18]

---

[15] A sentence from this Epistle is preserved for us by Eusebius, *H.E.* v.2.

[16] Polycarp, *Ep. Ad. Philippians,* iii, in Ante-Nicene Fathers, edited by Alexander Roberts and James Donaldson (Grand Rapids: Eerdmans, 1953), Vol.1, pp.33-37.

[17] Polycarp, *Ep. Ad. Philippians, xi.* Later in these Detailed Introduction notes it will be necessary to call attention to the fact that Polycarp wrote both "letters" (plural) and "epistle" (singular).

[18] Irenaeus, *Advers. Haeres.,* iv.18.4.

3) Clement of Alexandria (AD 190)

"When Paul confesses of himself, 'Not as though I had already attained, either were already perfect ....'" (Philippians 3:11,12).[19]

In *Stromata* iv.3, he quotes Philippians 2:20. In iv.5, he quotes 1:13. In iv.13, he quotes 1:20,30.

4) Tertullian (AD 200)

Tertullian, who was active at the close of the second century, possessed a thorough knowledge of Philippians. Among the references in his writings are the following passages:

"When (the apostle) mentions the several motives of those who were preaching the gospel, how that some, 'waxing confident by his bonds, were more fearless in speaking the word,' while others 'preached Christ even out of envy and strife, and again others out of good will' many also 'out of love,' and certain 'out of contention,' and some 'in rivalry to himself ....' " (cf. Philippians 1:14-17).[20]

"It is in expectation of this for himself that the apostle writes to the Philippians: 'If by any means,' says he, 'I might attain to the resurrection of the dead. Not as though I had already attained, or were already perfect' ... but for all that he goes on to say: 'I however, follow on, if so be I may apprehend that for which I also am apprehended of Christ.' Nay more: 'Brethren,' (he adds), 'I count not myself to have apprehended: but this one thing (I do), forgetting those things which are behind, and reaching forth into those things which are before, I press toward the mark for the prize of blamelessness, whereby I may attain it;' meaning the resurrection of the dead in its proper time." (cf. Philippians 3:11-14)[21]

---

[19] Clement of Alexandria, *Paedag*. i.6.

[20] *Against Marcion*, v.20.

[21] *On the Res. of the Flesh*. xxiii.

c. Canonical lists

Marcion's *Apostolicon* (AD 150) carries the book. It is included in all the ancient catalogues from the Muratorian Canon (AD 170) downwards, and is included in all ancient versions, beginning with the Syriac (AD 175) and the Old Latin (AD 200). Philippians is placed among the undoubted Epistles of Paul by Eusebius (AD 325)[22] and is in Athanasius' list of canonical books (AD 367).[23]

3. Since the mid 1800's, some critics have tried to deny the Pauline authorship.

In accordance with German and French traditions of literary criticism, for a brief moment, a few negative critics came up with their usual internal arguments alleged to disprove the Pauline authorship of Philippians. F.C. Baur (1845) was the first to assail the letter. As he attempted to make the New Testament letters fit into Hegel's dialectic, he tried to demonstrate that the letter was a pious fraud from about AD 95, designed to reconcile the "Petrine" and "Pauline" factions of the church. He suggested that these parties were symbolically represented by Euodia and Syntyche (4:2).

Critics alleged that there are anachronisms in the letter which argue against a Pauline authorship.

(1) For example, critics pointed to the reference to "overseers and deacons" in Philippians 1:1, and attempted to argue that such offices were not yet established during Paul's life. Such a claim is shown to be groundless when there is a reference to elders (bishops) in Acts 14:23 (which tells of an event that would be dated about AD 48), in Acts 20:17 (an event dated about AD 58), in 1 Thessalonians 5:17 (dated as early as AD 51), and in 1 Timothy 3:2 and 3:8 (dated about AD 65 or 66). If Philippians is dated in the early AD 60's, it can hardly be

---

[22] Eusebius, *H.E.* iii.3.5.

[23] Athanasius, "39th Festal Letter" in the *Nicene and Post-Nicene Fathers*, 2nd series, edited by Philip Schaff and Henry Wace (Buffalo, NY: Christian Literature Publishing Co., 1892), Vol.4, p.550-55.

said the reference to bishops and deacons is an anachronism.[24]   This letter deals with the reception of a missionary offering from the church; a believable hypothesis explaining why bishops and deacons are mentioned in the greeting of the Philippians letter is that they have taken the lead in the collection and distribution of the congregation's funds.

(2) Another alleged anachronism, once used to show Philippians is non-Pauline, was based on the presumption that Gnostic ideas and vocabulary are found in Philippians. Gnosticism was a heresy that flourished in the 2nd and 3rd centuries AD, and words such as "knowledge" (1:9), "initiated" ("learned the secret," 4:12), and "become perfect" (3:12) found in Philippians are commonly found in Gnostic writings. This alleged anachronism had some impact as long as the assumption held true that Gnosticism did not have an impact upon Christianity until a time much later than Paul.   However, recent studies, especially since the discovery of the Gnostic documents at Nag Hammadi in Egypt, have shown that Jewish Gnosticism was already flourishing among the Essenes and others before the mid-1st century AD.   Even if it is admitted that the few words found in Philippians are indeed common with Gnosticism, those vocabulary words can no longer be called an anachronism that somehow argues against the Pauline authorship.   In fact, it is now regularly agreed that several New Testament books were written to combat incipient Gnosticism, among them Colossians, 2 Timothy, 2 Peter, and Jude.

More recent attacks have centered on the high Christology of the Kenotic passage, Philippians 2:6-11.   Critics have pontificated that Paul would not write of the pre-existence of Christ like this passage does.   Such a claim ignores that in 2 Corinthians 8:9 the pre-existence of Christ is the thought underneath the language that "though He was rich, yet for your sake He became poor."[25]

---

[24] The dictum that the reference to "bishops and deacons" is proof against the Pauline authorship is only acceptable if certain other conclusions are accurate. First, of course, is the presupposition that in the apostolic age the evolutionary concept of church polity is correct. Second, the Pauline authorship of the Pastoral Epistles must be rejected. Finally, the Book of Acts, which shows a similar church polity (Acts 14:21-23, 20:28), must be judged as unreliable. This is too steep a price to pay for attempting to show that Paul could not have written Philippians 1:1.

[25] Below, in the section titled "Critical Issues," an in-depth study will be made of the Kenotic passage to examine and critique the idea now being advanced that the passage does not teach Christ's pre-existence nor His Deity. In addition, in that same section on "Critical Issues" it will be necessary to study carefully the critical effort to show that Philippians is not one epistle, but a composite of two or more letters. Either of these matters could be used as an argument against the Pauline authorship of the letter as a whole, or of the particular passage in question.

4. **Most modern scholars no longer attempt to deny the Pauline authorship of Philippians.**

Denial of authenticity made from internal evidence simply cannot stand up to the external evidence for the Pauline authorship of Philippians. What is now being done instead by contemporary critics is to challenge and deny the traditional conservative theological conclusions, with the result being that the modern Bible student is left with precious little on which to build one's faith. Therefore, in those places in the letter to the Philippians where the foundations of the faith are most attacked, the comments offered are intended to provide the reader with reasons for embracing a strong faith in the Lord Jesus Christ.

D. PLACE OF WRITING

In the General Introduction to the Prison Epistles, earlier in this volume, the possibilities suggested for the place of writing have been covered in detail. There it has been shown that Rome has long been the traditional view as the place where Paul was when he wrote the Prison Epistles. It was also pointed out that in recent times other places, such as Ephesus or Caesarea, have been put forth as possible places of writing. At that place, it was shown the arguments against both Ephesus and Caesarea (e.g., the soon-release Paul anticipates in Philippians) virtually demands Rome as being the proper choice when choosing the place from which Paul wrote this letter. The references in Philippians to the "praetorian guard" (1:13) and "Caesar's household" (4:22) are strong indications that the traditional view – namely, that Philippians was written from Rome – was and is the correct view.

E. DATE OF WRITING

Determining the place of writing does much to settle the question of the date of writing.[26] In our "New Testament Chronology" we have dated the first Roman imprisonment as being from AD 61-63.[27]

---

[26] This statement assumes the integrity of Philippians, which will be discussed later in this Detailed Introduction to Philippians. Of course, if Philippians is a composite, as some now claim, of two or three fragments of Pauline letters, the possibility of more than one place and date of origin would have to be considered.

[27] See Gareth L. Reese, *New Testament History: Acts* (Moberly, MO: Scripture Exposition Books, 2002), pp.xviii-xxi. If we were to adopt the Ephesian origin, the date of composition would be about AD 54, since we date Paul's great Ephesian ministry from AD 51-54.

Earlier in this volume, in the General Introduction to the Prison Epistles, we have explored the order in which the Prison Epistles likely were written. There, we concluded that Philippians came from late in Paul's first Roman imprisonment.[28] The date we suggest, therefore, is AD 62 or 63.

F. OCCASION OF WRITING

"Occasion" seeks to answer why the letter was written at one particular time as opposed to another. One reconstruction suggests that Paul is answering a letter sent to him by the Philippians. This scenario also posits that part of the contents of that letter are found in Paul's reply; namely, that the Philippians feared that Paul was not satisfied in regard to the gift sent him (too small), or was displeased by the delay (since the Philippians sent regular remittances to him). It is true that Philippians is most letter-like. Paul does not appear to be developing a theme as he does in Romans, Ephesians, and Galatians. Nor is he correcting grave errors as he does in 1 Corinthians, Galatians, and Colossians. But the supposition that this letter-like form of Philippians is due to the fact that he is answering a letter received from Philippi is more than the evidence will support.

A more plausible reconstruction of the occasion is based on the fact that the imminent return of Epaphroditus to Philippi gave Paul an opportunity to send this letter. This is the immediate occasion for the writing of Philippians. Paul's first Roman imprisonment lasted from AD 61-63, which was about ten years after he had founded the church in Philippi, and about three or four years after he had last visited there. Apparently, Paul had not heard from them for some time (4:10), and may have been wondering if they had forgotten him, or if, per chance, some false teacher had come along and stolen the church away from him, as had so often happened to Paul's churches. Then Epaphroditus arrived from far away Philippi with an offering of money.   Paul was deeply touched, and profoundly

---

[28] Jim Reiher, "Could Philippians have been written from the Second Roman Imprisonment?" *Evangelical Quarterly*. Vol. LXXXIV. No. 3 (July 2012), p.213-233. This article summarizes the other theories as to the place of writing and offers examples from selected scholars who adhere to different theories. Then it presents an alternative option for consideration, namely, the second Roman imprisonment (AD 67-68). This view is not sustainable. The Prison Epistles, in which Paul anticipates release from imprisonment, do not match the second Roman imprisonment. 2 Timothy, written from that second Roman imprisonment, show that Paul knows he will be executed rather than being freed.

grateful, for he was in sore need of funds. Epaphroditus nearly lost his life in this ministry to Paul. When Epaphroditus recovered, Paul sent him back with this beautiful letter (2:25-30, 4:18), which includes his thanks for their gift.

G. CRITICAL ISSUES

The section title "Critical Issues" reflects the fact that there are areas where Bible critics have raised questions that in many cases tend to undercut and unsettle the basic tenets of the historic Christian faith. What is actually going on is scholars are applying modern methods of interpretation to Paul's letter, methods such as literary criticism, form-criticism, textlinguistics, and socio-rhetorical criticism, all of which are attempts to make the Bible match what is the currently popular philosophy in hopes of making the Bible more acceptable to the masses.

1. The integrity or the unity of the epistle

Is Philippians as we have it one letter or is it a composite of fragments from two or three letters woven together by a later editor?

Several bits of evidence are appealed to by critics who speculate that Philippians as we have it is a composite. (1) The fact that "finally" occurs twice in the letter, at 3:1 and 4:8. This is said to indicate that both of these places were once conclusions of separate letters. (2) Personnel are discussed at 2:19-30, whereas normally we find such discussion reserved for the close of Paul's letters. (3) It is claimed that the tone of chapter 3 is quite different from what precedes it. (4) It is claimed that Paul would hardly wait until the end of the letter (4:10-20) to say thank you to the Philippians. (5) An early Christian writer, Polycarp, spoke of Paul's letters (plural) to the Philippians, not letter (singular).[29] (6) In some passages the writer speaks of his imprisonment, and in others he does not.

Typical of the attempts to isolate the different units in the alleged composite is Joseph Fitzmyer's presentation. He identifies the parts as Letter A, Letter B, and Letter C.

> *Letter A:* 1:1-2; 4:10-20 – A note in which Paul thanked the Philippians for their aid.
>
> *Letter B:* 1:3-3:1; 4:4-9,21-23 – The letter in which Paul explained his personal situation, gave news of Epaphroditus and Timothy, and sent his instructions to the community.

---

[29] See the citation of Polycarp above under "Authorship and Attestation."

Letter C: 3:2-4:3 – A short note to warn the Philippians about the Judaizers.[30]

Most of those who partition Philippians claim to be able to find in it the whole of one and parts of two letters.   John Reumann used the presence and absence of references to imprisonment as he attempted to identify the three supposed original parts.

(A) Paul's thank you letter, 4:10-20 – Written about AD 54, with no indication of imprisonment

(B) 1:1-3:1 and probably parts of 4:1-9, 21-23 – Written in late AD 54 or early A.D. 55 from a prison in Ephesus

(C) 3:2-21 and possibly parts of 4:1-9 – Written in late AD 55, and contains no indication of imprisonment

Reumann believes that in AD 90-100 these parts were combined to form the one letter we now call Philippians.[31]

A number of commentaries published late in the 20th and early in the 21st centuries proposed similar compilations of material into our present Philippians.[32] In a 1984 study on Philippians, Wolfgang Schenk attempted to develop new support for a compilation hypothesis by attempting to use what he identifies as "textlinguistic" methodology.[33]

---

[30] Joseph A. Fitzmyer, "Philippians" in *Jerome Biblical Commentary* (Englewood Cliffs, NJ: Prentice Hall, 1968), p.248.

[31] John Reumann, *Philippians: A New Translation with Introduction and Commentary* in the Anchor Yale Bible Commentaries (New Haven, CT: Yale University Press, 2008), p.3.

[32] Willi Marxsen, *Introduction to the New Testament,* trans. G. Buswell (Philadelphia: Fortress, 1968), p.61-62. Norman Perrin, *New Testament, an Introduction* (New York: Harcourt Brace Jovanovich, 1974), p.105-106. (Perrin gives no indication of where he thinks 4:21-23 belongs.) F.W. Beare, *Commentary on the Epistle to the Philippians,* 2nd ed., Black's New Testament Commentaries (London: Adam & Charles Black, 1969), p.1-5. Walter Schmithals, *Paul and the Gnostics,* trans. J.E. Steely (Nashville: Abingdon, 1972), p.78-81. G. Bornkamm, "Der Philipperbrief als paulinische Briefsammlung," *Neotestamentica et Patristica*, Supplement to Novum Testamentum 6 (Leiden: E.J. Brill, 1962), p.192-202. B.D. Rahtjen, "Three Letters of Paul to the Philippians," *New Testament Studies* 6 (1959-60), p.167-173.

[33] Wolfgang Schenk, *Die Philipperbriefe des Paulus,* Stuttgart: W. Kohlhammer, 1984.   His presentation was strongly critiqued by Veronica Koperski, "Textlinguistics and the Integrity of Philippians: A Critique of Wolfgang Schenk's Arguments for a Compilation Hypothesis," *Ephemerides theologicae Lovanienses*, 68 (Dec. 1992), p.331-367.   Schenk replied to Koperski in "Der Philipperbriefe oder die Philipperbriefe des Paulus?   Eine Antwort an V. Koperski," *ETL* [70:1] (Jan. 1984), p.122-131.

In 1985, D.E. Garland published an influential study of the integrity of Philippians in which he answered the arguments of the critics who proposed to dissect and rearrange the parts the letter.[34] Moises Silva pointed to Garland's article as "the most important contribution in this field" and concluded with the accolade that Garland's article "has, in my opinion, changed the complexion of the contemporary debate."[35]

The case for the integrity of Philippians includes these points.

(1) As is true with arguments for an alleged composite nature of 2 Corinthians, scholars can offer no explanation of the hypothetical redactor's method or logic or motive for making the letter we know as Philippians.

(2) The negative critics, hopelessly contradictory in their attempts to fix the dividing lines of each supposed fragment, destroy each other's arguments and leave the case for the integrity of the epistle standing.

(3) In the ancient manuscripts, the only form of Philippians is as one letter. There is no evidence in the manuscript tradition for the alleged parts ever circulating independently of the whole. No manuscript ever found has a doxology for the alleged first part, or a greeting and address for the alleged second or third parts. The oldest textual evidence of the Pauline corpus, the Chester Beatty Papyrus P[46], has Philippians intact. Indeed, this manuscript recently has been dated by one scholar as belonging to the first century.[36] If that date is true, it allows little time for a supposed redactor of fragments to do his work and then have the new composite be recognized as canonical, all before a copy of it was included in the Pauline corpus.

(4) Paul certainly alludes to the Philippians' gift in Philippians 1:5-7, so it is inaccurate to affirm that Paul waited until the end of his letter before including any expression of thanks.

(5) "Finally" at Philippians 3:1 does not need to be interpreted as evidence we are nearing the end of the letter. The word "finally" can be understood in the sense of "in addition."[37] In fact, its use in the midst of Philippians as a

---

[34] D.E. Garland, *The Composition and Unity of Philippians: Some Neglected Literary Factors*, in NT 27 (1985), p.141-173.

[35] Moises Silva, "Philippians" in the *Wycliffe Exegetical Commentary* (Chicago: Moody, 1988), p.14-16

[36] Y.K. Kim, "Palaeographical Dating of P[46] to the Later First Century, *Biblica* 69 (1988), p.248-257.

[37] William F. Arndt and F. Wilbur Gingrich, *A Greek-English Lexicon of the New Testament* (Chicago: University of Chicago Press, 1956), p.481.

Detailed Introduction to Philippians

transition to a new topic is paralleled by Paul's usage elsewhere (1 Thessalonians 4:1).

(6) A statement in Polycarp's letter to the Philippians (*Ad Phil.* xi.3), which uses the singular "epistle" in referring to Paul's writing to Philippi, seems to neutralize any argument that could be based on the plural "letters" in that very same letter (*Ad Phil.* iii).[38]

(7) The fact that each time popular philosophy changes a new study of Scripture is thought necessary, tends to make us wary, both of the methods utilized (such as literary criticism and redaction criticism) and of the conclusions to which those studies lead.

The statement made by A. Plummer in 1919 is still true. He wrote concerning Philippians, "There is no reasonable doubt that all four chapters were written as parts of one and the same letter, and in the order in which we have them."[39]

2. The controversy over the interpretation of Philippians 2:5-11

The meaning of this paragraph has been the subject of debate since the Christological controversies raged among the early church fathers. Beginning in the late 19th century and continuing through the 20th and into the 21st centuries, a mass of books and articles has been produced.[1] The purpose of this short intro-

---

[38] Greek idiom commonly permits the use of the plural "letters" (*epistolai*) with a singular meaning. Cf. J.B. Lightfoot, *St. Paul's Epistle to the Philippians* (Grand Rapids: Zondervan, 1953 reprint), p.140-141.

[39] A. Plummer, *A Commentary on St. Paul's Epistle to the Philippians* (London: Robert Scott Roxburghe House, 1919), p.xii. Three recent major commentaries on Philippians have decided in favor of the integrity of the letter. They are G.F. Hawthorne, *Philippians* in the Word Biblical Commentary 43 (Waco, TX, 1983); M. Silva, *Philippians* in the Wycliffe Exegetical Commentary (Chicago: Moody, 1988); and P.T. O'Brien, *The Epistle to the Philippians: A Commentary on the Greek Text* in the New International Greek Testament Commentary (Grand Rapids, MI: Eerdmans 1991).

[1] A.B. Bruce, in 1876, wrote that the diversity of opinion on these six verses was "enough to fill the student with despair, and afflict him with intellectual paralysis" (A.B. Bruce, *The Humiliation of Christ* [New York: A.C. Armstrong, 2nd ed. 1899], p.8). Writing about a century later, R.P. Martin, *Carmen Christi: Philippians II. 5-11 in Recent Interpretation and in the Setting of Early Christian Worship* (Cambridge: University Press, 1967) had a bibliography of about 500 items. A revised edition of Martin's book, published by Eerdmans in 1983, included a Supplementary Bibliography of an additional 45 items. Gerald F. Hawthorne, "Philippians" in *Word Biblical Commentary* (Waco, TX: Word Books, 1983), p.71-75, has a listing of over 150 books and articles. He calls attention to the listing of books and articles written since Martin's book found in Robert B. Strimple, "Philippians 2:5-11 in Recent Studies: Some Exegetical Conclusions in *WTJ* 41 (1979), p.247-268.

duction to this controversy is to point out some rocks and shoals to be avoided as one tries to navigate through the intricate arguments and discussions which are to be found in the commentaries.

The chief point to be kept in mind is that behind much of the contemporary interpretations is an attempt to make what the Bible says match whatever current philosophy is popular. As a result, every time popular philosophy changes, a new method of Bible interpretation must be introduced. Of course, making the Bible match the current popular philosophy certainly changes what one thinks the text says. When rationalism was the prevailing philosophy, miracles were thought impossible and Jesus could not be the divine Son of God. Any passage of Scripture that might so present Him had to be explained away. Hegel's dialectic philosophy and the theory of biological evolution entered the picture. To keep up with this, the 19th century saw the rapid development of a new method of Bible study called biblical criticism, or higher criticism. Literary critics searched for sources for the materials in the Bible, a search that tacitly ignored and denied any Holy Spirit inspiration for the Scriptures. Instead, the Scriptures were reconstructed to picture a naturalistic, non-supernatural picture of Jesus of Nazareth. When the 20th century dawned, a new philosophy known as existentialism was flourishing and the adoption of this philosophy resulted in the introduction of form-critical and redaction critical principles into the study of the Scriptures. In Heidegger's form of existentialism, nothing supernatural can be accepted. So when these critics turned to the study of Paul's epistle to the Philippians, they centered their attention on Philippians 2:5-11, since that passage had traditionally been understood to present the Person of Jesus as being a divine being. When the form and redaction critics had finished with their work, we no longer have a supernatural Jesus. What we have instead is the hypothesis of the development of Christology so that the human Jesus eventually became believed by pious folk to be Deity. Now, in the 21st century, postmodernism has become the prevailing philosophy and new methods of study, such as linguistic analysis, social-science criticism, textlinguistics, and rhetorical criticism, have begun to be applied to this critical passage. These current studies result in spending all our time searching out the original literary form or structure, the authorship, the alleged life-setting, the alleged original meaning, and the alleged redaction of the passage by Paul. The result of these studies is that Jesus has been dethroned from His glory, and postmodernism's mantra that "all truth is relative" means that doctrinal norms must be construed much more loosely than once was the case. It has also become common to assert that there were competing Christianities at the beginning, and this pluralistic view has weakened Christian claims to having the truth of God for the well-being of the world.

Recognizing that hidden philosophical biases have undergirded much of the scholarly writing will help us understand how so many divergent ideas could come to be written, all of them different and yet all of them professing to explain the passage.

a. What title shall we use to designate these verses?

As the discussion concerning the import of this part of Philippians has progressed, it has been found convenient to attempt to have a kind of shorthand term with which to identify it. However, scholars cannot agree on what term to use when calling attention to the verses in Philippians 2:5-11. At one time it was called "the Kenotic passage."[2] If using the title "Kenotic" automatically suggests, as it once did, that Jesus gave up some or all the attributes of deity when He became incarnate, it is a title that is not satisfactory.

During the past 100 years, it became commonplace in scholarship to call Philippians 2:6-11 "the Christ-hymn."[3] This designation also has baggage for it conjures up an image of lyrics inserted by Paul into the middle of the letter to the Philippians, and thus can be prejudicial against the veracity of what is claimed for Jesus in these verses.

John Reumann rejects the label "hymn" and prefers the classification of "encomium," a rhetorical term for praise or blame.[4]

It has been called a "psalm."[5] "Psalm," however, brings to mind the poetry included in the Old Testament book called "Psalms," yet the structure of Philippians 2:5-11 is not like those poems.

---

[2] This title became popular during the Christological controversy of the late 1800s concerning what attributes of deity Christ divested (Greek, *ekenōsen*) when He became incarnate.

[3] Ralph P. Martin's title *"Carmen Christi"* is not quite right, for if, indeed, it is a hymn, it is not a hymn *to* Christ, but a hymn *about* Christ. M. Bochmuehl, *The Epistle to the Philippians* in NNTC (Peabody, MA: Hendrickson, 1998), p.116,117 argues forcefully against calling this passage a "Christ-hymn."

[4] John Reumann, *Philippians: A New Translation with Introduction and Commentary* in Anchor Yale Bible Commentaries (New Haven, CT: Yale University Press, 2008), p.333,339.

[5] Ernst Lohmeyer liked to call the passage a "psalm." See Colin Brown, "Ernst Lohmeyer's *Kyrios Jesus*" in *Where Christology Began: Essays on Philippians 2*, Ralph Martin and Brian Dodd, eds. (Louisville, KY: Westminster John Knox Press, 1998), p.17-19.

The passage has been called a "pericope,"[6] that is, a section of Scripture suitable for reading in public worship.

It has been identified as exalted prose.[7] While this designation is likely correct, the language is not convenient shorthand to refer to the passage.

b. The form and structure of Philippians 2:6-11 in modern research

Johannes Weiss (1899) was the first to call attention to what he called the poetic, rhythmic nature of these verses.[8] G.H. Talbert stated that "the first person to isolate the passage and call it a hymn was Arthur S. Way in the first edition of his translation of the epistles (1901)."[9] When the passage is called a hymn, the scholars have in mind an ancient Greek or Hebrew poetical format. However, the critics have reached no agreement in their attempts to determine the strophes in the "hymn." (1) In 1928, Ernst Lohmeyer used form criticism to isolate verses 6-11 and called it a pre-Pauline Christological hymn, presenting an analysis of the passage in two strophes,[10] each consisting of three three-line stanzas. He saw two matching strophes (6-8 and 9-11), but to get these matching strophes Lohmeyer had to omit the phrase "even death on a cross" (verse 8d) and assert that the phrase was a Pauline addition to a pre-Pauline hymn.[XX] Lohmeyer's proposal about the structure of the passage has encouraged others to attempt to determine the structure. (2) Joachim Jeremías proposed three strophes of four lines each, though at the cost of removing parts of verses 8, 10 and 11. He regarded them as Pauline additions to the hypothetical original hymn.[11] (3) Ralph

---

[6] J.A. Sanders, "Dissenting Deities and Phil. 2:6-11," *Journal of Biblical Literature,* LXXXVIII (1969), p.279.

[7] Gordon D. Fee, "Philippians 2:5-11: Hymn or Exalted Pauline Prose," *Bulletin for Biblical Research* 2 (1992), p.29-46.

[8] B. Eckman, "A Quantitative Metrical Analysis of the Philippians' Hymn," *NTS* 26 (1980), p.258.

[9] G.H. Talbert, "The Problem of Pre-Existence in Phil. 2:6-11," *Journal of Biblical Literature,* LXXXVI (1967), p.141-142

[10] Lohmeyer used the German *Strophe,* which can mean "stanza," "verse," or "strophe," each of which words has a slightly different connotation. He used "strophe" to distinguish his line arrangement from the arrangement of verses as found in the Biblical text.

[XX] E. Lohmeyer, *Kyrios Jesus: Eine Untersuchung zu Phil. 2:5-11* (Heidelberg: Winter, 1928), p.4ff.

[11] J. Jeremias, in an article in *Studia Paulina,* ed. by J. N. Sevenster and W. C. van Unnik (Harlem: E.F. Bohn, 1953), p.152-154; *idem.,* "Zu Phil. 2:7: Εαυτόν Εκενωσεν," *NovT,* 6 (1963), p.186-87.

P. Martin developed a suggestion made by Rudolf Bultmann in which he rearranged the lines of the hypothetical "hymn" to give six couplets of two lines each, which he thought would have been suitable for antiphonal chanting in a worship setting.[12]   His resulting translation of the lines leaves us with little idea of who Christ is.[13]   (4) Charles H. Talbert used the criteria of parallel expressions and chiastic devices in the "hymn" to offer a division of the "hymn" into four strophes of three lines each.[14]   He also removed the phrase "death on a cross" from his arrangement of the lines and strophes.   (5) Jean-Francois Collange proposed an outline that has 4 strophes with four lines each.[15]   His analysis treats verse 11c as a doxological response, and makes verse divisions in the middle of verses where no verse divisions appear warranted.   (6) So pervasive has the idea become that this passage is an ancient hymn that the lines are displayed as such in the 26th and 27th editions of Nestle's Greek Testament.   (7) R.H. Gundry, calling attention to the finite verbs and participial phrases in the Greek, has proposed a chiastic structure for the verses.[16]

If it is so obvious the lines were an ancient hymn, it seems we should not have such disagreement concerning what lines should be included, and how they should be arranged into strophes.   It causes us to be hesitant to join the chorus of scholars who call this passage an ancient hymn.

c.   The authorship of Philippians 2:6-11

For the last 100 years it has been affirmed in many scholarly circles that the verses are a hymn whose authorship and provenance are unknown.   This is a critical issue, going to the heart of the doctrine of inspiration and of the original meaning of the verses.

---

[12] Ralph P. Martin, *Carmen Christi: Philippians 2:5-11 in Recent Interpretation and in the Setting of Early Christian Worship* (Cambridge: University Press, 1967), p.36.

[13] See I. Howard Marshall's review of "The Christ Hymn in Philippians 2:5-11" in the *Tyndale Bulletin,* 19 (Jan. 1968), p.104-127.

[14] Talbert, *ibid.*

[15] Jean-Francois Collange, *The Epistle of St. Paul to the Philippians,* tr. A. W. Heathcote (London: Epworth Press, 1979), p.83-86.

[16] R.H. Gundry, "Style and Substance in 'The Myth of God Incarnate' according to Philippians 2:6-11," in S.E. Porter and M.D. Goulder, eds., *Crossing the Boundaries: Essays in Honour of Michael D. Goulder* BIS 8 (Leiden: Brill, 1994), p.272-274.   Gregory Fewster in "The Philippians 'Christ Hymn':   Trends in Critical Scholarship," *Currents in Biblical Research* 13/2 (2015), p.197, points out the segments of Gundry's proposed chiasm are not balanced, and therefore "it becomes difficult to see how the chiasm can hold together at this point."

A variety of suggestions has been set forth concerning how Philippians 2:6-11 originally came to be composed.

(1)   One view affirms the verses were borrowed by Paul from *an earlier Christian source.*[17]   However, scholars opting for this view have not been able to agree concerning that supposed earlier Christian source.

(2)   Another view has Paul borrowing the verses from *an earlier non-Christian source* and adding a few phrases himself to give it a Christian significance.[18]   It should be emphasized here that opting for the non-Pauline authorship of the verses in their entirety is not a benign decision,[19] and that some notable exceptions to the idea of a pre-Pauline source have been published.[20]

(3)   A third view tried to show that verses 6-11 are not Pauline but are *a later interpolation.*[21]   Textual evidence in the Greek manuscripts of Philippians does not support the view that the passage is a later addition.

(4)   A fourth view suggests that *Paul composed the verses at a time previous to the writing of Philippians* and then inserted them into the letter as he dictated it.[22]

(5)   The view advocated in this commentary is that the verses were *composed by Paul himself as he wrote this letter to the Philippians.*   Paul, the apostle of Jesus,

---

[17] Ernst Lohmeyer, *Der Brief an die Philipper* ... 13th ed. (Gottingen: Vandenhoeck & Ruprecht, 1964), pp.8,90,91. Since Lohmeyer's *Kyrios Jesus* (1928), these verses generally have been taken as a non-Pauline hymn.

[18] Below, in this Detailed Introduction to Philippians, the plethora of views about the possible non-Christian source will be itemized.

[19] C.K. Barrett (*From First Adam to Last* [London: A. and G. Black, 1962], p.70-72]) indicated the possibility that the pre-Pauline form of the hymn contained no reference to the pre-existence and Deity of Christ and that Paul himself inserted the phrase "existing in the form of God" and likely other material.   In contemporary scholarly criticism, the pre-Pauline words had no reference to Christ, nor to His incarnation, nor to His death, nor to His exaltation.

[20] Seyoon Kim, *The Origin of Paul's Gospel* (Grand Rapids: Eerdmans, 1982), p.147-149; D.A. Carson, Douglas J. Moo, and Leon Morris, *An Introduction to the New Testament* (Leicester: Apollos Books, 1992), p.318-319; Gordon D. Fee, *Paul's Letter to the Philippians* (Grand Rapids: Eerdmans, 1995), p.40-46.

[21] R.W. Hawkins, *The Recovery of the Historical Paul* (New York: Vanderbilt University, 1943), p.251-252.; Giza Vermes, *The Changing Faces of Jesus* (New York: Penguin, 2000), p.86.

[22] F.F. Scott, "The Epistle to the Philippians," *The Interpreter's Bible* (New York: Abingdon Press, 1955) Vol. 11, pp. 46,47.   Martin Dibelius, in the third edition of his commentary on Philippians (*An die Thessalinicher, an die Philipper* [Tubingen: Mohr Siebeck, 1937], p.72ff), has Paul as the author but originally composed by him independently of Philippians.

under the influence of Holy Spirit's inspiration, could and did write in an exalted lyrical style in such passages as Romans 8:35-39, 11:33-36, and 1 Corinthians 13 and 15.[23]

d. The search for a source of the alleged ancient hymn

Lohmeyer's work was influential in that it introduced the history of religions (*religionsgeschichte*) approach to Biblical interpretation to the passage in Philippians 2:6-11.[24] His example and the starting hypothesis that Paul was not the original author released scholars to go off in search of the source of the "ancient hymn." The underlying question was (not what ancient history served as its basis, but) what ancient myth served as its basis? Consequently, the scholars have come back with a multitude of suggestions, all of which are intended to validate the supposition that the doctrine about Jesus being Deity was an idea which developed incrementally in the early church.

(1) Some came back with an imaginary *early Christian source*. Postmodernism's pluralism has speculated that different Christologies must have been floating around in the early days of the church, and that our Bible represents the view that drove all the other (perhaps equally valid) views out of existence. The accusation is often made that Paul was the one who changed primitive Christianity into the form we now know it. In a reconstruction that would fit into such an imagined framework, Joseph A. Fitzmyer proposed an Aramaic reconstruction of the original hymn such as he supposed was used by the Aramaic-speaking Palestinian church. Fitzmyer has Paul adding the phrase "even death

---

[23] Two solid works advocating the Pauline authorship need to be read by folk who would question the Pauline authorship either on the basis of vocabulary (either the presence of un-Pauline vocabulary or the absence of Pauline vocabulary) or because of a balanced rhythmic structure. One is J.M. Furness, "The Authorship of Phil 2:6-11," *ExpT* 70 (1959), p.240-43. The other solid defense of the Pauline authorship is David Alan Black, "The Authorship of Philippians 2:6-11: Some Literary-critical Observations," *Criswell Theological Review* 2:2 (1988), p.269-289.

[24] Over a century ago, the history of religions (*Religionsgeschichte*) school of Biblical interpretation emphasized the degree to which Biblical ideas were the product of the cultural milieu. A driving idea in this approach to Scripture is that there is a Jewish and/or Hellenistic and/or Gnostic background to the mythological motifs found in the New Testament. (Anything supernatural in the Scriptures was classed as "mythological.") It was the history of religions research that gave birth to the interpretive method called form criticism.

on a cross" to the original hymn, thereby changing the theology.[25]   Using a slightly different scenario, Stephen (as he is presented in Acts 7), or perhaps one of Stephen's followers, was proposed by Ralph Martin as a possible candidate for the authorship of Philippians 2:6-11.[26]   F.W. Beare, who was Bultmannian in his theology, proposed that the verses were originally the work of a disciple of Paul.[27]

(2) A host of *non-Christian sources* have also been nominated.   Lohmeyer, searching for a mythological source, thought he had located it in Jewish apocalyptic ideas which were rooted in Iranian mythology about a pre-existent heavenly being (an angel) who became incarnate and then exalted.   He then affirmed that while the poem did not originally speak of Christ's earthly ministry, it was the stem from which the Christologies of Paul, John, and the epistle to the Hebrews had sprouted.[28]   Gnosticism has been searched for the possible source. Käsemann tried to finger Hellenistic Gnosticism,[29] while Sanders pointed to Jewish Gnosticism.[30]   Dieter Georgi thought he found the source in Hellenistic Jewish Wisdom literature.[31]   In addition, passages in the Old Testament have been mined looking for the source.   Some have suggested the Old Testament

---

[25] Joseph A. Fitzmyer, "The Aramaic Background of Phil 2:6-11," *CBQ* 50 (1988), p.470-83.   Otfried Hofius, *Der Christushymnus Philipper 2:6-11*, WUNT 17 (Tübingen: Mohr Siebeck, 1976), p.3-12, had argued the phrase was an integral part of the original hymn.

[26] Martin, *Carmen Christi*, p.xxxii, 304-5, 312, 318.

[27] F.W. Beare, *The Epistle to the Philippians* (New York: Harper & Brothers Publishers, 1959), p.30.

[28] Lohmeyer, *Kyrios Jesus*, p.23, 68f.   Ernst Käsemann ("A Critical Analysis of Philippians 2:5-11," English translation by Alice F. Carse, in *Journal for Theology and the Church* 5 [New York: Harper & Row, 1968], p.56) objected to Lohmeyer's appeal to a mythological source as being a dissolution of soteriology into cosmology and metaphysics and as being "theologically intolerable" and "from a Christian point of view" inadequate, falling short of Paul's justification of the ungodly by faith.

[29] Käsemann, *op. cit.*, p.62,66,72.

[30] J.A. Sanders, "Dissenting Deities and Phil. 2:6-11," *Journal of Biblical Literature*, LXXXVIII (1969), p.278-90.

[31] D. Georgi, "Der vorpaulinische Hymnus Phil.ii.6-11" in *Zeit und Geschichte* (R. Bultmann *Festschrift*), ed. E. Dinkler (Tübingen: J.C.B. Mohr, 1964) p.263-293.

Servant of Jehovah passages,[32] and some the Genesis account of Adam.[33]

If we take the Scriptures at face value, and not try to trace everything miraculous to a mythological source, we might find the true answer to the origin of what is written in 2:6-11 in the history recorded in John 13:3-17. There we see Jesus (who is God, John 1:1,14) in the form of a servant washing the disciples' feet. He knew that the Father had given everything into His hands, and that He had come from the Father and was going back to the Father. Before John's account is finished, Jesus has suffered death on a cross, and having risen has been glorified. It is the same picture of Jesus that Paul presents here in Philippians 2. He could write what he did because that is what really happened.

e. The real issue modern interpreters are facing is the obviously high Christology of the verses.

The real issue for the critics is that, on its face, this passage provides in a concise statement what Homer Kent calls "a sublime summary of Christology, from pre-existence to His exaltation."[34]   Many contemporary critics just cannot

---

[32] H. Wheeler Robinson, *The Cross in the Old Testament* (London: SCM Press, 1955), p.103-105. Eduard Schweizer ("Discipleship and Belief in Jesus as Lord from Jesus to the Hellenistic Church," *NTS* II/2 [1955], p.88) suggested the source for the hymn needs to be set in the wider context of the suffering righteous men in Judaism, rather than simply the Suffering Servant.

[33] James D. G. Dunn, *Christology in the Making: An Inquiry into the Origins of the Doctrine of the Incarnation* (London: SCM Press, 1980, 2nd ed., 1989), p.114-121.   N.T. Wright (*The Climax of the Covenant* [Edinburgh: T&T Clark, 1991], p.91-94) has also treated Philippians 2:6-11 as an example of Paul's Adam Christology, though he carefully distinguishes his views from Dunn's. Wright treats verse 6 as referring to Christ's pre-existence; Dunn concluded the passage has nothing to do with Christ's pre-existence.   Marvin R. Vincent already in 1897 (*A Critical and Exegetical Commentary on the Epistles of Philippians and Philemon*, ICC [New York: Scribners]) expressed clear reasons to reject this idea set forth as long ago as 1848 (Ernesti).   "As to the antithesis of the two Adams. It seems forced at the best, but is there any real antithesis?   According to the narrative in Genesis 3, Satan declared that the eating of the fruit would confer a knowledge which would make the eaters as gods, knowing good and evil; and the woman saw that the tree was to be desired to make one wise.   Nothing is said of a desire to be equal with God in the absolute and general sense. The temptation and the desire turned on forbidden knowledge.   The words 'as gods' are defined and limited by the words 'knowing good and evil'; and it is nowhere asserted or hinted in Scripture that Adam desired equality with God in the comprehensive sense of that expression" (p.86).   While Paul does make use of an Adam/Christ parallel in Romans 5 and 1 Corinthians 15, T. Francis Glasson ("Two Notes on the Philippians Hymn (II.6-11)," *New Testament Studies,* 21 [1974-1975], p.138) cautions us not to obtrude the Adam/Christ parallel "into passages where it is not relevant."

[34] Homer Kent, "Philippians" in *Expositor's Bible Commentary*, edited by Frank E. Gaebelein (Grand Rapids: Zondervan, 1978), p.100.

bring themselves to accept such a high view of Jesus, so some "explanation" must be found that will allow them to personally reject what readers for years have understood to be here written. Form and redaction critics have a working hypothesis that there are three levels of material in our New Testament Scriptures.[35] But this passage in Philippians has proven not to be an easy fit into such a scenario. It seems to speak loudly and clearly about the Deity of Jesus long before, according to the critics' timeline, church folk were supposed to be beginning to elevate Jesus in their thinking to a position of Deity.

Once it became clear that attacks on the Pauline authorship, and the search for a possible mythological source, were not going to yield the results the scholars were seeking, scholars began scrutinizing almost every word in the passage to see if they could find an avenue by which the high Christology of the passage plausibly could be denied.

These are some examples (they are so numerous as to be nearly mind-numbing) of the kind of interpretations proposed over the past century or so in an effort to expunge any idea of Jesus' Deity from the Philippians 2 passage. To provide some order to these examples, we have used the versification of the NASB, and we'll approach the verses phrase-by-phrase.

v.5a – "Have this attitude in yourselves" (Greek, *touto phroneite en humin*). This phrase is important to the meaning of all that follows. According to the traditional interpretation, verse 5 identifies the attitude individual Christians are to exhibit if they are to carry out the exhortation given in 2:3,4 about the humility of mind which excludes any selfishness or empty conceit and instead looks out first for the interests of others. The demonstrative pronoun "this" (*touto*) usually

---

[35] The first level included what Jesus said and did, of which we know very little, because the New Testament writings are said to be *geschichte* (German for 'interpretations' of what happened), not *historie* (German for what actually did happen). The second level is what the apostles taught and did as they interpreted Jesus to their hearers. We know very little of what they actually said and did. Most of the content in our New Testament books (the third level) is said to reflect what the early church believed after both the apostles had changed and adapted what Jesus had said, and after the writers of the New Testament books had changed and adapted what had been handed to them by the apostles. The apostles and then the writers allegedly made the changes and adaptions in order to meet the life situation being addressed when the apostle spoke or when the book was finally written. Such a thesis, of course, results in the thrust of scholarly studies now being to try to determine what the earlier levels actually included and taught. Let it be asked, Where is there convincing evidence of three such levels of material – save in the scholars' constructs of how things must have been? Recall that the constructs themselves result from applying the current popular philosophy to the study of Scripture.

points back to something already said.   Verse 4 has just spoken about looking out for the interests of others rather than your own personal interests.   It appears that verse 5 is intended to say Jesus did exactly that; verses 6-8 go on to explain how.[36] *Phroneite* (translated "attitude") speaks of a mind-set, something constantly to be thinking about.   It is a present imperative, calling for continuous action.   *En humin* may be translated as "in yourselves" or "among you" (cf. NASB mg.)   The plural verb *phroneite* does not lend itself well to a group ("among you") interpretation of verse 5b et al.   The command asks each individual reader to have the same mind-set being described in these verses.

v.5b – "Which was also in Christ Jesus" (Greek, *ho kai en Christō Iesou*). "Which"[37] picks up the idea introduced by "this," namely, "do not *merely* look out for your own personal interests, but also for the interests of others" (verse 4). The words "in Christ Jesus" (2:5) have been a battle ground in this long-running debate about the meaning of Philippians 2:5-11.

- Lohmeyer tried to treat this second phrase in verse 5 as the title of the following "ancient hymn" which he thought he had identified.[38]

- Others have tried to say the words mean "in the Christian community," as indeed the words "in Christ" often mean.   In this passage, can "in Christ Jesus" mean "in the Christian community," so that this passage no longer talks about some attitude Jesus Himself might have had?   No.   Morna Hooker has noted that we find here not the usual Pauline expression, "in Christ" but "in Christ Jesus."   She suggests this slight change in wording is perhaps significant   as a warning not to assume too   quickly that the

---

[36] Lohmeyer (*Kyrios Jesus*, p.12), having argued that *touto* in the construction here has retrospective reference, tried to make the first part of the verse a complete sentence (i.e., "Have this attitude in yourselves!") with the imperative intended to reinforce the commands already given in verses 3 and 4.   His theory about a pre-Pauline hymn being inserted at this point required him to break up verse 5 as he did.

[37] The papyrus and uncial manuscripts had no accent marks or breathing marks.   Our Greek texts print "*ho*" as a neuter relative pronoun (with both a rough breathing mark and a grave accent stand over it) meaning "which" or "what," rather than as the neuter article "the" (which in Greek has only a rough breathing mark, but no accent mark).   The only difference between a neuter relative pronoun and a neuter article is in whether or not a grave accent mark is added.

[38] Lohmeyer (*op. cit.*, p.13), having decided the following verses were an ancient hymn, tried to show that this second clause in verse 5 was the ancient way of introducing work which one wished to quote.   For example, at Luke 20:37, a passage from Exodus 3:6 is referred to (in the Greek) as "in the bush," and in Romans 11:2 the words "in Elijah" were used to cite a passage from 1 Kings 19:10.   So Lohmeyer tried to make a case that the words "what [was] in Christ Jesus" were actually the way an ancient poem titled "Christ Jesus" would have been cited.

phrase here is the Pauline "code word" for union with Christ.[39]   Thus we look for the following words to unfold how Jesus looked out for the interests of others more than He looked out for His own interests.

v.6a — "Who although he existed in the form of God" (Greek, *hos en morphē theou huparchōn*).   The relative pronoun "who" refers back to the antecedent, Christ Jesus.[40]   It certainly looks as though verses 6-8 are intended to depict the attitude Jesus Himself had.   *Huparchōn* ("existed") is a present tense participle, a form which indicates continuous action.   The KJV at this place has "who being in the form of God," but the English word "being" is not quite strong enough to catch the connotation of *huparchō*, a word which means to "subsist" or to "exist (really)."   If the NASB had translated the participle as "although existing," it would have caught the nuance very well.

The participle *huparchō* is present tense, and whoever reads the text carefully "must take account of the fact that the present participle here in verse 6 stands in temporal contrast with the aorist participle *labōn* ("taking") in verse 7, thus indicating that before this person described by *huparchōn* took the form of a slave (2:7), He already was existing in the form of God."[41]   When Jesus took the form of a slave, He still was existing in the form of God.

"Form" (*morphē*) has been understood from classical times as referring to an inner essence more than to outward form (which was *schēma*).   "Lightfoot, in his admirable essay (*Philippians*, p.127) examined the use of the Greek words *morphē* and *schēma* with a completeness which leaves little or nothing to be desired."[42]   *Schēma* is the outward shape or fashion; *morphē* suggests the inner essence.   The *morphē* (inner essence) of a human stays the same, but the *schēma*

---

[39] Morna D. Hooker, "Philippians 2:6-11," *Jesus und Paulus: Festschrift für Werner Georg Kümmel zum 70* (Göttingen: Vandenhoeck & Ruprecht, 1975), p.154.

[40] Lohmeyer thought that *hos* ("who") did not belong to the original song itself, and so, with no manuscript evidence whatever to support his action, substituted the definite article *ho*, giving the translation "the one existing in the form of God."   However, J.C. O'Neill ("The Source of the Christology in Colossians," *NTS* 26 [1980], p.90.) has shown that in similar contexts *hos* stands for "he it was who."

[41] Gerald F. Hawthorne, "In the Form of God and Equal with God" in *Where Christology Began*, Ralph P. Martin and Brian J. Dodd, eds. (Louisville, KY: Westminster John Knox Press, 1998), p.97.

[42] Edwin H. Gifford, "The Incarnation: Philippians 2:5-11" in *The Incarnation of Christ*, Henry Wace, ed. (London: Longmans, Green and Co., 1911; reprinted Minneapolis, MN: Klock & Klock Christian Publishers, 1981), p.15.

may change (e.g., from baby to adult to old age). In fact, it is not possible to have the "form" (inner essence) of God without being God,[43] so it should be no surprise that the word "form" has been a battle ground. For example, attempts have been made to prove that the time pictured in verse 6 is not Jesus' pre-existence, but His existence here on earth. Two avenues have been pursued in order to arrive at this conclusion. (1) It has been proposed that *morphē theou* speaks of a body like Adam's since Scripture says Adam was made in the "image (*eikōn*) of God" (Genesis 1:27, 9:6). Numerous attempts have been made to show that *morphē* and *eikōn* are interchangeable terms.[44] If true, then Philippians 2:6a would not be speaking of Jesus' pre-existence as God, but of His human body after His incarnation. But this effort has not been convincing because *morphē* is the inner essence; it is *schema* that denotes the body, the outward appearance. (2) In the LXX and in the New Testament, the word *doxa* ("glory") was used to describe the visible form of God by which His majesty was made manifest to humanity (e.g., Romans 1:23; 1 Corinthians 11:7; 2 Corinthians 3:18). So some authors have proposed that *morphē* and *doxa* are interchangeable terms and therefore *morphē* must speak not of His Deity but of His exalted status or position. The effort, too, is mistaken since *doxa* speaks of outward appearance, whereas *morphē* speaks of inner essence.

v.6b – "Did not regard equality with God a thing to be grasped" (Greek, *ouch harpagmon hēgēsato to einai isa theō*). Lightfoot long ago demonstrated that the construction of this entire phrase was an idiom meaning "a prize to be clutched and retained at all hazards."[45] Glasson has therefore noted, "If the phrase as a whole carries a recognized meaning, it is a mistake to isolate one word, *harpagmos*, and discuss its significance."[46] Yet such wording isolations are rife.

---

[43] "It can be said ... that no one could be described as being *en morphē theou* who was not indeed God Himself. Thus the passage does provide an implicit proof that Christ pre-existed in objective equality with God." R.E. Wilson, "He Emptied Himself," *JETS* 19 (1976), p.279-281.

[44] See e.g., Martin, *op. cit.*, p.108,109. See also Jerome Murphy-O'Connor, "Christological Anthropology in Phil II,6-11," *RB* 83 (1976), p.25ff.

[45] J.B. Lightfoot, *Saint Paul's Epistle to the Philippians* (London: Macmillan & Company, 1913, reprinted Grand Rapids: Zondervan, 1953), p.111. R.W. Hoover ("The *Harpagmos* Enigma: A Philological Solution," *HTR* 56 [1971], p.95-119) has strongly argued the whole phrase is an idiom.

[46] T. Francis Glasson, "Two Notes on The Philippians Hymn (2:6-11)," *NTS* 21 (1974), p.133. Glasson goes on to write (p.134), "We use many idiomatic phrases in everyday speech and no one would think of pressing the literal meaning or looking at single words in isolation. We speak of 'exploring every avenue', which means the same as 'leaving no stone unturned'. How mistaken it would be to dwell on the word 'avenue' and to inquire if this were an avenue of trees or of skyscrapers. 'Jumping at an opportunity' has completely lost any connection with acrobatics. Again, single words are often used in a metaphorical way. We say a statesman embarked on a certain policy or course of action. Now embarking literally means to go on board a ship; but the idiomatic expression has nothing to do whatever with seafaring."

(a) How to translate *harpagmon* has been a battlefield.[47]   Interpretations have varied between:

(1)   The view of the Latin church, called *res rapta* (something already possessed having been obtained by violence).   The KJV and the Douay version (which read "thought it not robbery to be equal with God") adopted the Latin view, and seem to imply that, until He snatched it, there was a time when Jesus was not on an equality with God.[48]

(2)   The view of the Greek fathers, properly called *res retinenda* (something already possessed but not necessarily to be held on to at all costs).   J.B. Phillips reflected the view of the Greek fathers with the reading "did not cling to his prerogatives as God's equal."

(3)   A more modern idea, called *res rapienda* (something not yet possessed but could be if one wished).   The NEB has adopted view #3 with the reading "did not think to snatch at equality with God."[49]

English translations of verse 6 have reflected the ongoing debate.   Several modern translations (NASB, NIV, RSV) have adopted an ambiguous view when they offer the translation "did not count equality with God a thing to be grasped."

(b) What *isa theō* ("equality with God") means has been a battle ground.   Some have treated this expression as though it were synonymous with *morphē theou*, but this is not right.[50]   *Isa* is an adverb and so describes His manner of existence

---

[47] As commentators have tried to explain what *harpagmon* means, the Latin terms (*res rapta, res rapienda,* etc.) have not been carefully and consistently defined, and this creates confusion for English readers who are trying to understand what is being claimed as the meaning of *harpagmon*.

[48] Lightfoot (*op. cit.,* p.134) rightly objected to this translation since the meaning it implies is a *non sequitur*.   "It takes no account of the clauses which immediately precede and follow," clauses which concern Christ's humility.

[49] The increased popularity of the view that sees verse 6a as speaking of a merely human Jesus has resulted in an increase in the popularity of taking 6b in what has been called the *res rapienda* sense, i.e., that it speaks of Christ refusing to consider equality with God as something to be snatched at.   This interpretation, in turn, sets forth in some modern commentators' minds an implied contrast with the first Adam who did aspire to equality with God.

[50] The KJV translation "to be equal with God" which treats the phrase as being synonymous with *morphē theou* can be misleading.   Existence "in a manner equal to God" is not the same as being "in the form of God."   The mode of existence may change, but not God's essential nature.

(i.e., living a manner equal with the manner in which God lives); it is not the adjective *ison*, which would describe His being.   The choice of words in the ASV and NASB, "equality with God," does a better job of catching the nuance of the Greek adverb.[51]   "Equality with God" would seem to be explained by Jesus' words "the glory which I ever had with You before the world was created" (John 17:4), and by "for you know the grace of our Lord Jesus Christ, that though He was rich, yet for your sakes He became poor" (2 Corinthians 8:9).

(c) Even what is being negated by the location of "not" (*ouch*) in the Greek has been a topic of debate.   In Greek word order, the negative particle "not" usually immediately precedes the word it negates.   In the Greek, *ouch* precedes *harpagmon*.   But in this case, because the whole expression is an idiom, *ouch* is properly viewed as negating the verb "regard," just as our English translation has it.   The passage is clearly explained in Lightfoot's paraphrase: "Be humble as Christ was humble: He, though existing before the worlds in the form of God, did not treat His equality with God as a prize, a treasure to be greedily clutched and ostentatiously displayed: on the contrary He resigned the glories of heaven."[52]

v.7a - "But emptied Himself" (Greek, *alla heauton ekenōsen*).   "Emptied" (*ekenōsen*) has long been a battlefield.   Of what did Jesus empty Himself?

(a) Some scholars started with the premise that Christ emptied Himself of "the form of Deity."   In the late 19th century scholars in Germany and England had a running debate concerning which attributes of Deity Jesus might have given up when He emptied Himself.[53]   Critics of this "Kenotic Christology," as it came to be called, replied that such a view   is not in harmony with the continuing action

---

[51] Jerome Murphy-O'Connor's treatment of *einai isa theō* as the 'right to be *treated* as if he were god" is certainly mistaken.   Murphy-O'Connor went on to affirm that Jesus had this right, not because He actually was God, but because He was a sinless human being (Jerome Murphy-O'Connor, "Christological Anthropology in Phil. II.6-11," *RB* 88 (1976), p.39,40.)   James D. G. Dunn, *op. cit.*, p.120ff also adopted this interpretation.

[52] Lightfoot, *ibid.*   Clearly, verse 6 has stated that Jesus was not only existing in the form of God, but He was also equal with God.

[53] Karl Barth (*Church Dogmatics: The Doctrine of Reconciliation* [Edinburgh: T & T Clark, 1956], Vol. 4, Part 1, p.180) was not the first to allege that "*kenosis* consists in a renunciation of His being in the form of God ...."   Before that, the Lutheran theologian Gottfried Thomasius (*Christi Person und Werk* [Erlangen: T. Bläsing, 1856,57) argued that God has two kinds of attributes, internal (power, truthfulness, holiness, love, joy) and external (omnipotence, omniscience, omnipresence).   Jesus, the eternal Son, "set aside" the external attributes but revealed those internal attributes while incarnate.   In Him we see the love of the Father and in Him we see God's "heart" made visible.   A.M. Fairbairn carefully worked out this idea in his *The Place of Christ in Modern Theology* (New York: Charles Scribner's Sons, 1894).

indicated by "existing in the form of God" (verse 6a). If Jesus gave up any attributes of Deity, he would no longer have been "existing in the form of God." Another view (based on the premise that it was "the form of God" that was emptied) was the so-called "Krypsis Christology." "Krypsis" is a Greek word that means to hide or conceal. There certainly were times during His earthly ministry when Jesus displayed divine attributes.[54] However, there were times when Jesus was on earth that He did not display attributes of Deity.[55] That is, He had and retained the attributes, but He concealed them under the vesture of human flesh; He chose at times not to display them. It may not be right to say that the attributes were *concealed*. It might be better simply to say that since He was also human (Hebrews 2:14,17), He did not *use* divine attributes except on those occasions when men would doubt He was Deity if He did not exercise those attributes. In fact, if the Son of God had divested Himself of "the form (*morphē*) of God" at His incarnation, He would thereby have ceased to be God. This Jesus did not do, for Jesus Himself claimed to be God while He was here on earth (John 5:17,18, 8:58, 13:13).

(b) Scholars who think the Suffering Servant Poems of Isaiah are being reworked by Paul have suggested that "emptied Himself" is a translation of "He poured out Himself to death" from Isaiah 53:12.[56] This interpretation makes Philippians 2:6-8 a reference to Calvary rather than focusing on His incarnation. Stephen Fowl has objected to this interpretation, and his arguments have seemed to carry the day.[57]

(c) It looks as though it has to be His mode of existence – here called "equality with God" – that was the thing which Jesus voluntarily relinquished in order to become incarnate. Perhaps it can also be said that, when He emptied Himself, He gave up the independent exercise of the prerogatives of Deity (John 8:28, 12:49,50, 14:10). "Down from His glory, ever living story, my God and Savior came, and Jesus was His name ... The Great creator became my Savior, and all God's fulness dwelleth in Him" (Susan Hawthorne).

---

[54] His reading of men's minds (John 2:25), giving sight to the man born blind (John 9:1-33), stilling the tempest (Mark 4:39), and the feeding of the 5000 (Mark 6:39-44) are examples of divine attributes being displayed by Jesus.

[55] God cannot be tempted (James 1:13), but Jesus could be (Matthew 4:1). God is all knowing, but at times Jesus had to ask questions (John 11:34). Christ did not know the time of the end (Mark 13:32).

[56] Robinson, *ibid.*

[57] Stephen Fowl, *The Story of Christ in the Ethics of Paul,* JSNTSup 36 (Sheffield, JSOT Press, 1990), p. 61-64.

v.7b - "taking the form of a bond-servant" (Greek, *morphēn doulou labōn*). "Taking" in this clause is an aorist participle. So is "being made" in the next clause. These aorist tense participles have been explained in two different ways – as an action that preceded the main verb "emptied,"[58] or as an action simultaneous with the main verb "emptied."[59]

The KJV translators at this place added the word "and" both before this phrase and before the one immediately following. That addition leads to a mistaken understanding of what Paul wrote. Paul didn't write "He emptied Himself *and* took" nor did He write "*and* was made," as though those two actions were something in addition to emptying Himself. Paul used circumstantial participles to indicate how or in what way Jesus emptied himself of his mode of existence on an equality with God. The Greek could well be translated, "but emptied Himself, by taking the form of a servant, by being made in the likeness of men." The second phrase unfolds the meaning of the first, and the third unfolds the meaning of the second.[60] "If you ask how Christ emptied Himself, the apostle answers *by taking the form of a servant*. If you ask again, how Christ took the form of a servant, the answer follows immediately, *being made in the likeness of men*."[61]

Notice, Paul did not write that Jesus emptied Himself of *morphē theou*, nor does it say He exchanged one form for another. Paul does say that while "existing in the form of God" Jesus "took the form (*morphē*, inner essence) of a bond-servant." The Christological interpretation is that at the time of the incarnation, when Christ took the inner essence of a bond-servant, He wholly submitted His will, His affections, and His desires, to the will of the Heavenly

---

[58] C.F.D. Moule *An Idiom Book of New Testament Greek*, second edition [Cambridge: University Press, 1959], p.100) is often appealed to for corroboration of this interpretation. He indicated that he has found "in the New Testament no exception to the rule that an aorist participle denotes an action prior to that of the main verb, with the possible exception of two passages in Acts." Interpreters who are cool toward the idea of Jesus being Deity and pre-existent will then claim that the emptying took place during Jesus' life here on earth, and that the emptying followed His "taking the form of a bond-servant" and "being made (or born) in the likeness of men."

[59] Gifford, *op. cit.*, p.38 has correctly argued that the aorist tense participles here picture action simultaneous with the action of the aorist tense verb *ekenosen* ("emptied").

[60] When this sequence of ideas is noted, it becomes obvious that Käsemann's hypothesis (cited by Martin, *op. cit.*, p.179), that "taking the form of a servant" indicated Jesus' acceptance of humanity's bondage to elemental spirits of the universe, is mistaken and foreign to what Paul wrote.

[61] "The Primitive and Apostolic Tradition of the Doctrine concerning the Divinity of our Saviour Jesus Christ" vi.21, in *The Works of George Bull*, collected and revised by Edward Burton (Oxford: At the Clarendon Pr., 1827), p.349. (Italics are his.)

Father.[62]   He added the one form without giving up the other.   He didn't have to divest Himself of the *morphē theou*.   He could become subordinate to the Father and still be God.   Jesus wasn't just play acting.   His inner essence was that of a bond-servant.[63]   He was wholeheartedly doing something for someone else; He was not just looking out for His own personal interests (see Philippians 2:4).

v.7c – "*And* being made in the likeness of men" (Greek, *en homoiōmati anthrōpōn genomenos*).   There is no word "and" in the Greek.   The addition of this word in the NASB causes us to miss the point, that "being made in the likeness of men" is an explanation of how Jesus took the form of a servant.

Since *genomenos* could be translated as "being born" (as it is in Galatians 4:4), an attempt has been made to show that this expression "born in the likeness of men" is a reference to Jesus being descended from Adam.[64]   It is true that Jesus was descended from Adam (as the genealogy in Luke 3:23-38 shows), but it is doubtful this is Paul's emphasis here in Philippians.   Had Paul wished to speak of Jesus's birth, *gennao* would have been the more proper verb (as at Romans 9:11 and Galatians 4:23,29).

"Being made" is a better choice for *genomenos*, which also occurs in verse 8, since it would be unusual to assign different meanings to the same word used twice in such close proximity.   "The plural 'men' is used because Christ's humanity represented that which is by nature common to all men."[65]   "Likeness" (*homoiōmati*) says Jesus was similar to us humans ("men" is plural), but not absolutely like us.   The Greek word "likeness" (*homoiōmati*) has a different connotation from *eikōn* ("image").   "Likeness" stresses similarity but leaves room

---

[62] In the garden of Gethsemane Jesus prayed, "Not as I will, but as You will ..." (Matthew 26:39).   Numerous writers have supposed that Paul's language here ("bond-servant") is intended to call to mind the Isaianic Suffering Servant Poems.   Caution must be urged, since the word regularly translated "servant" in the LXX of Isaiah is *pais*, not *doulos*.

[63] The fact that "bond-servant" translates *doulou*, a word that means "slave," led to numerous articles about the meaning of this word when the writers were in the midst of the nineteenth century effort to end human slavery.   Some used the passage to defend the existence of slavery; others argued that Jesus was not a slave of men but of God so the passage had no bearing on the issue of human slavery.   See Gifford, *op. cit.*, p.38,39.

[64] C.H. Talbert ("The Problem of Pre-existence in Philippians 2:6-11," *JBL* 86 (1967), p.150) suggested that "in the likeness of men" is intended to treat Christ as being a "son of Adam" just as it was said of Seth that he was "in his (Adam's) own likeness (Heb. *demuth*)" (Genesis 5:3).

[65] Gifford, *op. cit.*, p.44.

for differences. Jesus was a real man,[66] but He was more than a man.[67] While the pre-existent Jesus, existing in *morphē theou* ("form of God"), could live in a mode of "equality with God," when Jesus emptied Himself by taking the *morphēn doulou* ("form of a bond-servant"), the mode of existence was now "in the likeness of men."

v.8a – "And being found in appearance as a man" (Greek, *kai schēmati heuretheis hōs anthrōpos*). "And" seems to introduce a break. "Being found" says that "after He had assumed the conditions of humanity, and men's attention was drawn to Him, they found Him like a man."[68] When His contemporaries looked at the human Jesus, His outward appearance (*schēma*) was like that of other men.[69] Howard Marshall notes: "It is impossible to make sense of numerous phrases in verses 6-8 if they are understood solely against the background of the earthly life of Jesus." To drive home his point, he asks what would be the force of the aorist participle in verse 7c, *genomenos*, "being made in the likeness of men," and what would be the meaning of verse 8a, "being found in appearance as a man"?[70]

---

[66] The word "likeness" suggests similarity, but this does not mean that Christ's humanity was unreal as the Gnostics tried to argue. (See Tertullian's citation of Marcion's use of this passage in *Adv. Marcionem*, v.20). Romans 8:3 and Hebrews 2:7,14 indicate that Jesus' human body was just like other men's bodies.

[67] Martin (*op. cit.,* p.197ff) dealt with the possible meanings of *homoiōma* (he offered [1] identity or equivalence, and [2] similarity or resemblance), and then based on the assumption the passage says nothing about the inner relationship of the "natures" of Christ he offered three possible explanations of the passage: (1) that Jesus was born into the world in exactly the same way as that in which all men are born (a statement that, in the hands of some writers, is a tacit denial of the virgin birth); (2) that Philippians 2:7 is intended to say something more ambiguous than Romans 8:3 says ("God sent his own Son in the likeness of flesh of sin"); and (3) Philippians 2:7 is worded the way apocalyptic writers who were hesitant about portraying something transcendent by any earthly expression would write. It is a shorthand way of referring to "one like the Son of Man" (Daniel 7:13; Ezekiel 1:26). The starting assumption is the real problem behind these proposed solutions to what "likeness" might mean.

[68] M.R. Vincent, *Word Studies in the New Testament* (Wilmington, DE: Associated Publishers and Authors, 1972), p.880.

[69] "Appearance" *(schēmati)* had to do with "external bearing" as in distinction from "form" *(morphē)* which has to do with that which is "essential and permanent" (William F. Moulton and George Milligan, *The Vocabulary of the Greek Testament* [Grand Rapids: Eerdmans, nd], p.619).

[70] I. Howard Marshall, "The Christ-Hymn in Philippians 2:5-11. A Review Article," *Tyndale Bulletin*, 19 (1968), p.116.

v.8b - "He humbled Himself by becoming obedient to the point of death" (Greek, *etapeinōsen heatou genomenos hupēkoos mechri thanatou*). The verb *tapeinoō* means to make low, to humble, and its corresponding adjective *tapeinōs* means low-lying, that which is even or level with the ground. Christ is pictured, we might say, as allowing Himself to be treated as dirt under men's feet. The reflexive pronoun "Himself" in "He humbled Himself" reflects the voluntary nature of His action. Paul is illustrating how far Jesus went as He was looking out for the interests of others (verse 5). Not only was Jesus looking out for the interests of others when He emptied Himself (verse 7), but "He humbled Himself" is another example of His putting the interests of others ahead of His own.[71] He was still existing in the form of God when He did this. "He learned obedience from the things which He suffered" (Hebrews 5:8). "The Greek ... makes it plain that the Lord did not *obey death but obeyed the Father* so utterly as even to die.[72]

v.8c - "even death on a cross" (Greek, *thanatou de staurou*). In the *schēma* of a man Jesus could experience physical death. And He did. Not just any death, but cruel and humiliating crucifixion is what He stooped to endure. "'Even' *(de)* brings into prominence the special quintessence of this death. This was no ordinary death, but one of intense shame and suffering (cf. Deuteronomy 21:23; Galatians 3:13)."[73] The mind of Christ which believers are to exercise is only fully seen when we consider the entire span of Christ's existence, from His pre-existence in heaven to His death on a cross.

Per Lohmeyer, this is a verse added by Paul to the existing hymn he has appropriated. Lohmeyer's presentation, and that of those who have followed his lead, leaves us empty. He treats verses 6 and 7 as all being mythological. It is all what folk *thought* happened, but there is no evidence any of it ever did – save the death on the cross. When this fact is recognized, one loses interest in studying such analyses as Lohmeyer's any further.

v.9a- "Therefore also God highly exalted Him" (Greek, *dio kai ho theos auton huperupsōsen*). "Wherefore also" *(dio kai)* introduces the fact that *in consequence of* Christ's voluntarily emptying Himself and humbling Himself, He has been exalted by the Father. Here, quite clearly, "God" is a reference to God

---

[71] A.B. Bruce in a previous generation took the idea from this verse and made it the title of his book *The Humiliation of Christ.* Contemporary efforts that attempt to show that "He emptied Himself" and "He humbled Himself" both have reference to what happened at Calvary are mistaken.

[72] H.C.G. Moule, *Philippian Studies* (Glasgow: Pickering and Inglis Ltd., 1898), p.94.

[73] C.M. Horne, "'Let This Mind be in You.' An Exposition of Phil. 2:5-11." *Bulletin of the Evangelical Theological Society* (1960), p.41.

the Father, in distinction to the Son. While verses 6-8 spoke of what Jesus did, verses 9-11 speak of what God has done. Despite this, verses 9-11 have still proven to be a battleground.

(a) One issue has been whether "therefore" indicates purpose or result. Was what God did when He exalted Christ earned (Catholic writers find merit in what Christ did), or was it granted as a gift? "Bestowed" in verse 9b certainly indicates Christ's exaltation was granted as a gift.

(b) Another issue revolves around claims that verses 9-11 don't fit the emphasis of the context. The question is asked why these verses were included.

(1) One answer has been an affirmation that verses 9-11 are intended to show that verses 6-8 speak not of Jesus' Deity and pre-existence, but only of His earthly life and since. The word "therefore" was mistakenly made to mean that Paul intended verses 9-11 to be parallel with verses 6-8. By putting an interpretation on verses 9-11 which makes them refer only to Jesus' earthly life and since, it could then be argued that verses 6-8 (being parallel) had no reference to His deity or pre-existence.

(2) When this idea did not prove acceptable, other more recent scholars have turned to Rhetorical Criticism to try to find an answer to this question of the purpose of verses 9-11, but without much success.[74]

(c) The meaning of "highly exalted" has also entered into the debate about what the passage says about Jesus. "Highly exalted" *(huperupsōsen)* is an aorist indicative verb. Since it follows a reference to Christ's crucifixion, this verb seems to point to the resurrection and ascension of our Lord as the next great historical event in the life of our Lord.[75]

---

[74] Larry J. Kreitzer ("'When He at Last is First'; Philippians 2:9-11 and the 'Exaltation of the Lord,'" in *Where Christology Began: Essays on Philippians 2*, Ralph P. Martin and Brian J. Dodd, eds., [Louisville, KY: Westminster John Knox Press, 1998], p.114-118) lists efforts by Charles J. Robbins ("Rhetorical Structure in Philippians 2:6-11," *CBQ* 42 [1980], p.73-82); Duane F. Watson ("A Rhetorical Analysis of Philippians and its Implications for the Unity Question," *NTS* 30 [1988], p.57-88); Claudio Basevi and Juan Chapa ("Philippians 2:6-11: The Rhetorical Function of a Pauline 'Hymn'," in *Rhetoric and the New Testament: Essays from the 1992 Heidelberg Conference*, ed. by S.E. Porter and T.H. Olbrecht, JSNTSup 90 [Sheffield: Sheffield Academic Press, 1993], p.338-56); and L. Gregory Bloomquist (*The Function of Suffering in Philippians*, JSNTSup 78 [Sheffield; Sheffield Academic Press, 1993], p.97-118). He laments that these authors do not find the same emphasis on eschatology in these verses that he thinks is there.

[75] If it is true, as many have speculated, that Paul here is quoting a mythological story originally included in some pre-Pauline hymn, but is applying it to Jesus, a case could be made for the often-stated misrepresentation that Paul was responsible for changing Christianity into some-thing different than what was taught before He became involved. Of course, if Paul is only quoting a myth, and brashly suggesting that what the myth affirmed was true in Jesus' case, then we cannot

But what is it that Paul is asserting happened on that occasion? *Huperupsōsen* is a compound verb made up of *huper* ("above") and *hupsoō* ("to exalt above"). Ordinarily, the prepositional prefix *huper* intensifies the verb; hence, we could translate it "super-exalted." But, scholars ask, what can the preposition *huper* mean? One who started out as human conceivably could be exalted to a higher position than he had, but can one who at all times exists in the form (*morphē*, inner essence) of God be super-highly exalted? Is He now greater than God?

So scholars have debated the force of the prefix *huper*. Perhaps it has a comparative force, meaning Christ was exalted to a position He did not have before. Perhaps it has a superlative connotation, meaning that "God exalted Him to the highest station"[76] without any suggestion that He was raised to a higher position than He had in His pre-existent state. Or perhaps "highly exalted" refers to the fact that Jesus has something now (a glorified human body) which He did not have before His incarnation. If this last explanation satisfies the meaning of "highly exalted," then this verse cannot be used to prove that the whole passage antecedent to this verse deals with Jesus' humanity, and not His Deity or pre-existence, as many have tried to prove.

(d) Morna Hooker demonstrated that the points emphasized in 2:6-11 very nicely tie together verses both before and after that pericope. Verses 6-8 support what Paul wrote in 1:27-2:4, and verses 9-11 support what Paul will write in 3:20,21.[77]

v.9b – "And bestowed on Him the name which is above every name" (Greek, *kai echarisato autō to onoma to huper pan onoma*). "And" (*kai*) suggests this is something in addition to His being "highly exalted." *Echarisato*, translated "bestowed," indicates that what was done by God was a gracious gift. There are many conflicting ideas concerning what "the name" (there is a "the" in the Greek) that is "above every name" is. Arguments have been advanced that the name is

---

affirm that anything Philippians 2:6-11 records, other than Jesus' death, ever actually happened, and we will be forced, as many have been, to try to find other evidence for the alleged development of Christology in the early days of the church. That is too high a price to pay for embracing the thesis that these verses had a mythological origin.

[76] Beare, *Philippians*, p.85. (Cp. the usage of the same verb in Psalm 97:9 [96:9, LXX], where God is "highly exalted" above all other gods.)

[77] Morna Hooker, *From Adam to Christ: Essays on Paul* (Cambridge: Cambridge University Press, 1990), p.88-102.

"Jesus,"[78] "Jesus Christ,"[79] "Lord" (in the sense the word is equivalent of "Jehovah" in the Old Testament[80]), the "new name" of Revelation 3:12, "Son" (the name which Hebrews 1:4ff says He inherited), and "Lord Jesus Christ" (the name which seems to be suggested by verse 11a here in Philippians 2).

v.10a – "That at the name of Jesus every knee should bow" (Greek, *hina en tō onomati Iesou pan gonu kampsē*).   "That" (*hina*) introduces a clause which tells the purpose of His exaltation and of His being given the name that is above every name.   God wanted every knee to bow to Him.

(a) Scholars have debated concerning the time when this bowing of the knees takes place.   Is it now during the whole church age, or is at a future time (at or after the judgment)?   If it is now during the church age, is this the first passage where the worship of Jesus by the church is described?[81] The way the question is worded, one must be careful lest it just be taken for granted that Jesus is just now, perhaps for the first time, being thought of as a Deity to be worshiped.   "Worship" is a translation of the words for 'submission' (*proskuneo*) and 'service' (*latreuo*), and the church certainly was in submission to Jesus before Philippians was written.   If it is something that happens in the future, how does this passage match what

---

[78] Henry Alford ("Philippians" in *Alford's Greek Testament* [London: Rivingtons, 1871], Vol.3, p.169) called attention to Acts 9:5 ("I am Jesus whom you are persecuting") as being Jesus' own answer to what "the name" is.   However, He had been given this name before Calvary and before He ever was exalted (Matthew 1:21).

[79] H.A.W. Meyer, *Critical and Exegetical Handbook to the Epistles to the Philippians and Colossians, and Philemon* (Winona Lake, IN: Alpha Publications, 1980 reprint of the 1906 edition), p.81;   M.R. Vincent. "Philippians" in *ICC*, p.62.

[80] H.A.A. Kennedy, "The Epistle to the Philippians" in *Expositor's Greek Testament*, W. Robertson Nicholl, ed. (Grand Rapids: Eerdmans, 1967), p. 439.   *Kurios* ("Lord") was the Greek word used in the LXX to translate the Hebrew sacred name YHWH.   The problem with this suggestion for "the name" is that if Jesus was always existing in the form of God, He already in essence was YHWH.   That is not something He gained after His earthly ministry.   Instead of going to the Old Testament for the source of the name "Lord," in 1921 William Bousset (*Kyrios Christos*, English translation by John E. Steely [Nashville: Abingdon, 1970], chap.3) called attention to the way the pagans divinized their heroes, calling them "Lord."   He supposed this was what was happening to Jesus here in this passage in Philippians 2.   However, if we accept the historicity of John's account, Jesus Himself claimed to be "Lord" (John 13:13) long before Philippians was written.

[81] See Richard J. Bauckham, "The Worship of Jesus in Philippians 2:9-11" in *Where Christology Began*, Ralph P. Martin and Brian J. Dodd, eds. (Louisville, KY: Westminster, John Knox Press, 1998), p.128-139.

Scripture elsewhere says about the future?[82]   It may be a mistake to offer only an either/or option when answering the question about the timing. Both in this world and in the world to come folk are pictured as bowing the knee to and confessing Jesus Christ.

(b) Scholars have debated what the word "bow the knee" means.   Are folk to genuflect when they hear the name of Jesus, or is this action indication of submission to Jesus?[83]

(c) Scholars who have adopted the idea that verses 6-11 are an ancient hymn have also debated whether the words here in the first part of verse 10 were part of the original hymn or were later added to it by Paul himself.

(d) For those who believe that in verse 10 Paul added words to a pre-existing hymn, it is common to observe that the language here in the first part of verse 10 is similar to Isaiah 45:23.   As a result, a number of scholars have tried to show that an Old Testament theocentric passage has been reinterpreted Christologically by Paul.   Whereas the Old Testament passage was a declaration that the sovereignty of God would one day be acknowledged and proclaimed throughout the world, Paul has reworked the Old Testament passage in order to introduce the idea of Christ's Lordship into the Christology of the church.[84]   This handling of Isaiah is wrongheaded.   If Jesus has always existed in the form of God, Paul's possible use of Isaiah would not be the introduction of a new idea, but rather is simply an unfolding of a truth idea already contained in the Old Testament passage.

---

[82] If one opts for this bowing of the knee as being in future, care must be exercised lest it should be claimed that this passage in Philippians 2 was one of the early attempts to explain the alleged delay or postponement of the *parousia*.   Since Käsemann's time (first in his essays, and then more recently in his massive commentary on Romans) many scholars have followed his lead and have affirmed that as the years of the first century passed, there was a change in doctrine about the time of the second coming.   No longer was the second coming expected within the lifetimes of the first generation of Christians.   In harmony with this, Philippians 2 was supposed to infer that Paul had changed his mind about an imminent *parousia*, and now was teaching that the bowing of the knees to Jesus was something off in the distant future.   Two presuppositions lie behind this reconstruction which posits a change in eschatology.   One begins with the alleged priority of Mark's Gospel and supposedly finds a different eschatology in the later books of Matthew, Luke, and, especially, in John.   The other presupposition is that the earlier Pauline letters show a different eschatology than the later Pauline letters.   (In fact, the so-called deutero-Pauline letters are affirmed to be someone else's eschatology, not Paul's.)   See Paul J. Achtemeier, "An Apocalyptic Shift in Early Christian Tradition: Reflections on Some Canonical Evidence," *CBQ* 45 (1983), p.231-48; Richard Longenecker, "The Nature of Paul's Early Eschatology," *NTS* 31 (1985), p.85-95.

[83] Martin, (*op. cit.*, p.264.265) has a long footnote on how the expression "bow the knee" has been interpreted.

[84] See Kreitzer, *op. cit.*, p.119,120.

v.10b – "Of those who are in heaven, and on earth, and under the earth" (Greek, *epouraniōn kai epigeiōn kai katachthoniōn*).   The three terms "in heaven," "on earth," and "under the earth" also occur in Revelation 5:13 and may have been an ancient way of designating the whole universe.   If it was an idiomatic expression, then what was stated above (verse 6) is also true here: "If the phrase as a whole carries a recognized meaning, it is a mistake to isolate one word ... and discuss its significance."

Yet that very thing has been done and continues to be done.   In the comments offered on this verse in the commentary section of this book, we have indicated the questions Bible students have struggled with: are the terms masculine or neuter, and who precisely are included in the three groups

(a) The KJV/ASV treated the terms as neuter, translating "*things* in heaven and *things* on earth."   If we let the mention of "every knee" (verse 10) and "every tongue" (verse 11) lead us to think of personal beings, then the NASB, which takes the terms as masculine, results in the better translation.

(b) Various interpretations of the three groups have been put forth.

> (1) Clement of Alexandria thought they referred to angels in heaven, men on earth, and the departed dead in Sheol.[85]

> (2) Chrysostom identified the three as being angels in heaven, men on earth, demons under the earth.[86]

> (3) Cullmann and Käsemann interpret all three terms to refer to hostile spirits (i.e., demons) whom the ancients used to believe had control over the inhabitants in heaven, on earth, and in the underworld.   These writers and those who follow their lead suppose Philippians 2:10,11 is intended to show these invisible spirits are now subjected to Christ.[87]   While the spirits are subject to Christ (Daniel 7:27; Colossians 1:15), it is a stretch to think Paul simply made up the idea by reworking an ancient myth.

---

[85] Clement of Alexandria, "Fragments from the Latin Translation of Cassiodorus" in *ANF*, Alexander Roberts and James Donaldson, eds.   (Grand Rapids: Eerdmans, 1951), Vol. 2, p. 575. Alford (*op. cit.,* p.169), (Kennedy, *op. cit.*, p.439), and Otfried Hofius (*op. cit.*, p.53,54), and Gordon Fee (*op. cit.*, p.224,225) make the same identification.

[86] John Chrysostom, *Homilies*, on Philippians, *in loc.*   Lohmeyer, *Kyrios Jesus*, p.59 opts for the same identification.

[87] Oscar Cullmann, *The Earliest Christian Confessions*, J.K.S. Reid, tr. (London: Lutterworth Press, 1949), p.59-62; Käsemann, *Critical Analysis*, p.87ff.   See also Ignatius, *Ad Trall.* IX.

Once form and redaction critics have determined to their own satisfaction that Paul is reworking Isaiah 45:23 at this place, they are then bothered by the fact that this phrase is not in Isaiah. "Why did Paul add it?" is the question asked by redaction critics. A popular answer is that He has inserted a pagan myth about the battles that occurred in the underworld between the gods in order to introduce some supposed cosmic ramifications which were involved in Jesus' being super exalted. Instead of suggesting that Paul has made up a story, why not treat what he has written as a depiction of what actually happened? Compare what Peter wrote, that Jesus Christ "is at God's right hand, having gone into heaven, angels, authorities and powers being made subject to Him" (1 Peter 3:22 ASV).

v.11a - "And that every tongue should confess that Jesus Christ is Lord" (Greek, *kai pasa glōssa exomologēsētai hoti kurios Iesous Christos*). Readers of the commentaries will find a number of questions raised about this seemingly straightforward statement.

(a) For example, scholars who have identified verses 6-11 as an ancient hymn have raised the question whether this verse is an addition by Paul to the original hymn, or whether it was part of the original hymn. Those scholars who have chosen the view that verse 10a was an adaptation by Paul of Isaiah 45:23 will go on to affirm that verse 11a is another place where he has taken the Old Testament Jehovah passage and reworded so as to refer to Jesus. Since the LXX has the verb *omeitai* ("swear allegiance") at Isaiah 45:23, whereas Philippians 2:11 has *exomologēsētai*, scholars who think Paul is reworking Isaiah 45 find Paul's change of terms significant, saying "it could be argued that the shift is an indication of the liturgical nature of the hymn – that it served as a confession of faith."[88]

(b) Another question revolves around the significance of *exomologēsētai*. That verb is from *homologeō*, which means to speak the same thing *(homos,* 'same' and *legō,* 'to speak'), to assent, to agree with. It is a compound verb where the prefixed preposition *ek* intensifies the verb, giving the sense, "to openly declare in agreement with."[89] There is a manuscript variation at this place, some having an aorist subjunctive form, *exomologēsētai*, and some having a future indicative form, *exomologēsetai*. The textual evidence is rather evenly divided, and either form would picture a confession sometime in the future after Christ was exalted. The only difference is that the future tense might picture a continuous confession while the aorist subjunctive would picture a one-time confession.

---

[88] Kreitzer, *op. cit.*, p. 120.

[89] Horne, *op. cit.*, p.42.

(c) Another question debated concerns the timing as to when this confession is made? Is it during the church age or at the judgment? Whatever decision has been made concerning the timing of "bowing the knee" will affect the decision concerning when the confession is made. Social science criticism has seen in the proclamation that Jesus is "Lord" an explicit rejection of Roman imperial propaganda which tended to dictate that "Caesar is Lord."[90]

v.11b – "to the glory of God the Father" (Greek, *eis doxan theou patros*). A straightforward reading of this phrase would lead us to think of the purpose God had in mind for exalting Jesus was so that every knee shall bow and every tongue confess that Jesus Christ is Lord. God is pictured as getting praise for what He has done in and through Jesus. This was God's whole purpose in working out our salvation. One thinks of the ever-widening circles of praise to God as pictured in 2 Corinthians 4:15, both now and in eternity. If it doesn't occur before the end of this age, there will come a time in the future when God will receive the honor He deserves for the salvation He has provided.

How surprising it is then, to find that this last phrase in verse 11 has caused great consternation among the scholars. It has been said, "It seems hard to justify the presence of the extra line 'to the glory of God'."[91] If Jesus has been highly exalted, it is asked, shouldn't He be the One Who is glorified? Does Paul envision Jesus stepping aside to allow God the Father to receive the praise? Rather than the exalted Lord stepping aside, what Paul is saying is the exaltation of Christ does not in any way limit the honor due to the Father. Rather, when folk give honor to Christ, God the Father is honored, too.

As we conclude this survey of the issues facing interpreters of Philippians 2:5-11, in this commentator's judgment it is safe to say that the efforts to rid the passage of any traces of Deity for Jesus Christ have failed. If they had been successful, would not the efforts to find a plausible alternative meaning for the passage have ceased? As we have read the attempts to explain this passage using form or redaction or other modern methodologies based on ever-changing underlying philosophical viewpoints, we have seen that the real problem is not what the verses themselves say. The real problem is what so far has proven to be impossible – namely, an attempt to make Philippians fit into a preconceived pattern of how (in the scholars' minds) things just must have been.

---

[90] P. Oakes, *Philippians: From People to Letter* (SNTSMS 110) (Cambridge: Cambridge University Press, 2001), p.129-174.

[91] Martin, *op. cit.*, p.272ff.

f.   Was the concept that Jesus is God an idea that developed slowly?

When religious liberalism flourished, radical historical criticism was the tool scholars used.   It involved the abandonment of the doctrine of the inspiration of the Scriptures.   Rather than the Scriptures being the word of God to men, the Scriptures are treated as having been produced by fallible human beings. Scripture was therefore subject to the intrusion of error and wrong ideas.

The currently popular theory that three levels of material are embedded in our New Testament writings has already been introduced.[92]   Allegedly, each level reflects a different conception of Jesus' Godhood that flourished during the course of the 1st century AD.   Since the task of removing all ideas of Jesus' Deity from Philippians 2 has proven impossible, many Biblical scholars are now attempting to assign this passage to one of the alleged stages of development of the idea that Jesus is God.

Titles of books and articles which have appeared since the 1960s make clear the scholars' beliefs that Christology developed.   A few examples will suffice. Ernst Käsemann's article "The Beginnings of Christian Theology," first published in 1960, was reprinted in his *New Testament Questions for Today* (Philadelphia: Fortress Press, 1969), p.82-107.   The title of Maurice Casey's book, *From Jewish Prophet to Gentile God: The Origins and Development of New Testament Christology* (Cambridge: James Clark & Co., 1991), clearly states the thesis of his book.   James D.G. Dunn has a book titled *Christology in the Making: A New Testament Inquiry into the Origins of the Doctrine of the Incarnation* (London: SCM Press, 1980; 2nd edition, Grand Rapids: Eerdmans, 1996).   Dunn's proposal that Philippians reflects an Adam-Christology is situated in his larger assertion that such an Adam-Christology was "widely current in the Christianity of the 40s and 50s," the Philippians' hymn being one of the fullest expressions of this attitude (p.114).   Ralph Martin and Brian Dodd have edited a book entitled *Where Christology Began: Essays on Philippians 2* (Louisville, KY: Westminster John Knox Press, 1998).   This book makes clear that the scholars whose works are reviewed are hopelessly divided about where and when certain ideas in the alleged third level of material actually made their appearance.

If we reject this method of Scripture interpretation which presupposes such levels of material, and instead take the verses of Scripture at face value, we find throughout Scripture a consistent testimony to the Deity of Jesus.   The doctrine of the Deity of Jesus is *not* an idea that developed   over a period of time in the

---

[92] See footnote #35 above.

early church.   Before there ever was a church, the Old Testament prophecies have Jesus being both human and Deity, as His discussion with the religious leaders on the great day of questions indicated (Matthew 22:41-46).   The Old Testament pictures Him as a physical descendant of Adam, yet also speaks of Him as being "Immanuel" = God with us (Isaiah 7:14).   Romans 1:3,4 describes Jesus both as "descendant of David" and "Son of God."   Earlier in this study, we called attention to the fact that Jesus Himself claimed to be equal with God (John 5:17,18, 8:58, 13:13).   Instead of positing some Adam-Christology in the AD 40s and 50s, why not acknowledge the views about Jesus held by the refugees from Saul's persecution: in the AD 40's in Antioch, they preached that Jesus is Lord (Acts 11:20).   The high Christology of Philippians 2:6-11 is exactly the same as the high Christology of Philippians 3:7-11, especially where Paul refers to "the surpassing value of knowing Christ Jesus as my Lord."[93]   What then is the conclusion to which these statements lead?   It is this: reject the idea that the Scriptures are all of human origin and therefore merely someone's faulty beliefs about what may or may not have happened.   Treat them, instead, as being pure holy truth – and the picture of who Jesus was and is will be seen to be consistent from Genesis 1 to Revelation 22.[94]

Beware of articles written from the standpoint of a slowly developing Christology.   While some *hearers* may have been slow to grasp the fact of Jesus' Deity, God's *mouthpieces* spoke with one voice.   The Old Testament Messianic prophets, Jesus Himself, and all His apostles, from the very first, presented the Messiah as being both God and man.   What the apostles and early church thought about Jesus being the Son of God "developed in the context of the self-witness of Jesus who knew Himself to be the Son of God."[95]   Peter's testimony stated the fact that the apostles did not follow cunningly devised myths when they made known to us the powerful coming of our Lord Jesus Christ (2 Peter 1:16).   It is a serious error to treat Philippians as the reworking of some ancient myth.

---

[93] Veronica Koperski, *The Knowledge of Christ Jesus My Lord: The High Christology of Philippians 3:7-11*, CBET 16 (Kampen: Kok Pharos, 1996).

[94] For a full presentation of the doctrine that the New Testament is witness to the divine nature of Jesus the Son of God, see Vincent Taylor, *The Person of Christ in New Testament Teaching,* Macmillan, London (1958); and I. Howard Marshall, "The Development of Christology in the Early Church," *Tyndale Bulletin* 18 (1967), pp.77-93.   Marshall highlights the fact that since Jesus was crucified in AD 30 and Paul wrote about the "Lord Jesus Christ" in his first letter about AD 51 to the Thessalonians, not enough time has elapsed for an alleged myth about His Deity to have developed.

[95] Marshall, *op. cit.,* p.93.

g. The place and purpose of these verses in the letter to the Philippians

The Bible student, reading for the first time many of the recent commentaries on Philippians 2:5-6 ("Have this attitude in yourselves which was also in Christ Jesus, who although existing in the form of God ..."), will be surprised by the vigorous denial of what is called the "ethical interpretation" of these verses.   Barth,[1] Käsemann,[2] R.P. Martin,[3] and J.A. Sanders,[4] all tell us that there is no basis for such an interpretation.   To understand what these authors are saying, several things must be remembered:

(1) By calling verses 6–11 a pre-Pauline hymn, those verses have been separated from verse 5, with the result that it can be said that what is written in verse 5 has no bearing on the original purpose of verses 6-11.

(2) "Ethical example" was a title given by Käsemann and others to a theological position of 19th century religious liberalism which found nothing more than an ethical example in the Philippians passage.   To religious liberalism, the passage actually gave no *historical* information about Jesus.   (Thus, when some authors reject the "ethical example" interpretation, they are only talking about jettisoning old liberalism's view, not necessarily denying that this passage as a whole does in fact say something about Jesus and does call for following Jesus' example.)

(3) Hooker identified the theological bias behind some denials that Jesus is treated as an example for Christians to follow.   "It is only the dogma that the Jesus of History and the Christ of Faith belong in separate compartments that leads to the belief that the appeal to a Christian character appropriate to those who are in Christ is not linked to the pattern as seen in Jesus Himself."[5]

Once scholars had questioned or denied Pauline authorship of verses 6-11, they then attempted to reproduce the hypothetical original form of the passage. Since the verses were believed to have had a separate existence other than how they are used in the letter to the Philippians, it became a scholarly pursuit to invent hypotheses concerning what that original use might have been before Paul alleg-

---

[1]   Karl Barth, *Erklärung des Philipperbriefes* (Zurich: Zollikon, 1928), p.53-62.

[2] Ernst Käsemann, "A Critical Analysis of Philippians 2:5-11," English translation by Alice F. Carse, *Journal for Theology and the Church* 5 (New York: Harper & Row, 1968), p.84.

[3] Martin, *Carmen Christi*, p.71,72.

[4] J.A. Sanders, "Dissenting Deities and Phil. 2:6-11," *Journal of Biblical Literature*, LXXXVIII (1969), p.280.

[5] Hooker, "Philippians 2:6-11," p.154.

edly adapted it. Lohmeyer offered the view that the original use of the hymn was at the celebration of the Lord's Supper, since both the hymn (verses 10,11) and the Lord's Supper ("you proclaim the Lord's death until He comes," 1 Corinthians 11:26) have an eschatological emphasis.[6] Käsemann offered the view that verses 6-11 were once used at baptismal services.[7] Jacob Jervell likewise has suggested that the hymn was baptismal, since in baptism believers are conformed to the image of their Lord as depicted in the hymn.[8] This understanding of the hymn is independent of Jervell's further theory (p.247ff) that the hymn holds together two diverse Christologies in verses 6-8 and 9-11. Martin's view was that the original hymn contained neither an ethical example nor a theological treatise about Christ, but was "a piece of *Heilsgeschichte*." Its background, he wrote, should be sought possibly "in some Greek-speaking Christian community whose biblical traditions had been modified by Hellenistic Judaism."[9] What quickly becomes painfully obvious is that once the verses have been divorced from Paul's letter, we have no way of knowing what the alleged original hymn meant or where it came from. Furthermore, the interpretations offered for the passage become mere guesswork and tend to produce whatever preconceived idea the interpreter brings to the passage.[10]

Some have tried to use this passage in Philippians to help reconstruct a picture of what worship was like in Christian congregations in apostolic times. Part of the problem Martin and others face is the fact that our knowledge of Christian hymnody is rather limited. Colossians 3:16 and Ephesians 5:19 speak of "psalms, and hymns, and spiritual songs" but we are not at all certain those verses picture something happening in the Sunday assembly. 1 Corinthians 14:26 indicates that individual believers came prepared to sing a psalm when the church assembled. James 5:13 directs folk who are cheerful to sing praises, but again it is not at all certain this was in a congregational setting. It is half a cen-

---

[6] Lohmeyer, *Kyrios Jesus*, p.65ff.

[7] See Ernst Käsemann, "A Primitive Christian Baptismal Liturgy" in *Essays on New Testament Themes* (London: SCM Press, 1964), p.149-58.

[8] Jacob Jervell, *Imago Dei: Gen. 1.26f. Im Spätjudentum, in der Gnosis un in den paulinischen Briefen* (Gottingen: Vandenhoeck & Ruprecht, 1960), p.206.

[9] Martin, *op. cit.*, p.83,84. "Salvation myth" might catch the significance of the German *Heilsgeschichte*. "Myth" means the things recounted didn't really happen; they were just made-up stories.

[10] For example, interpreters who see an anti-imperial motif to the New Testament writings will impose that idea onto Philippians. For example, see F.M. Heen, "Phil 2:6-11 and Resistance to Local Timocratic Rule: *Isa theō* and the Cult of the Emperor in the East" in *Paul and the Roman Imperial Order*, R.A. Horsley, ed., (Harrisburg, PA: Trinity Press International, 2004), p.126,127.

tury later that Pliny tells us about the practice of early Christians when assembled to "sing praises to Jesus as unto God."[11]   With such a lack of evidence, it should not be thought surprising that attempts are made to show Philippians 2:6-11 is a possible example of such a hymn to Christ, nor should it be surprising that other high Christological passages (Colossians 1:15-20; 1 Timothy 3:16; Hebrews 1:3a-4; and even John 1:1-14) are treated the same way.

How much better to treat Philippians 2:5-11 as part of Paul's letter and to find the purpose of those verses to be precisely what verse 5 suggests – namely, to present Jesus as the grand example of an attitude by which Christians should live.   This takes away the guesswork about the place and purpose of these verses.

h. The views taken in this commentary

(1) The straightforward, face value reading of Philippians 2:5-11 is accepted. Paul exhorts the Philippians to humility and unselfishness in 2:1-4, and then seems to reinforce this by appealing to the example of Christ Himself. As Paul highlights Jesus' willingness to look out for the interests of others, he calls attention to Jesus' pre-existent Godhood, His historical manhood, His consequent exaltation, and to the fact that God would be honored if the whole creation confessed that Jesus Christ is Lord.   Presumably Paul completes his appeal to the example of Christ by calling attention to His vindication, perhaps implying a promise of future reward for Christians who follow His example.

(2) There are reasons to be very cautious about claiming that verses 6-11 in Philippians 2 were an early pagan or Christian hymn inserted by Paul at this place in his letter.

(3) The interpretive methods used by form and redaction criticism which presuppose three levels of material in our New Testament writings are rejected. Rejected also is Neo-orthodoxy's attempt to distinguish between the Jesus of History and the Christ of Faith, and then attempting to divide up New Testament passages to seemingly corroborate such a dichotomy.

(4) Current popular philosophy changes with disquieting regularity. Changing one's theology each time to match these popular philosophy changes has proven to be a mortal danger to Christian beliefs and ethics; it creates wrong presuppositions with which to begin studying Scripture.   100+ years of attempts

---

[11] Pliny, *Epistle to Trajan*, X.97.

to concoct an explanation for these verses from Philippians so that they match current popular philosophy have failed. That should be long enough to convince us it cannot be done and should not be attempted. One begins to think that God was way ahead of the scholars when the Holy Spirit helped Paul to write this timeless passage.

(5) Rejected also is the dictum of pluralism that there were competing Christianities in the years immediately following the death and resurrection of Jesus. The apostles of Jesus spoke with one voice as they were moved by the Holy Spirit. To be sure, there were folk like the Judaizers and the Gnostics who made an attempt to change what the apostles taught, but right Christian doctrine and life reflected the truths the apostles taught.

(6) With solid reasons for believing in the inspiration of the New Testament apostles and prophets, the developmental view of Christology is flatly rejected. The Christology of Philippians is no different than the Christology in the four Gospels and elsewhere in the New Testament. Jesus was human and divine. There was no reason for Paul to deviate from this. There was no reason for Paul to develop this. There was no reason for the early church to add to this.

3. The meaning of *pistis christou* in Philippians 3:9

In verse 9 of chapter 3 Paul tells his readers that it is his desire to be found in Christ, "not having a righteousness of my own derived from *the* Law, but that which is *dia pisteos christou*, the righteousness which *comes* from God on the basis of faith." There are six other passages in Paul's writings where the construction *pistis christou* occurs (Romans 1:17; 3:22, 26; Galatians 2:16 [twice], 20; 3:22). Much of the current debate concerning the meaning of this phrase has centered on its use in the Galatians and Roman passages. Just recently have scholars begun to focus also on Philippians 3:9.

A paragraph or two to give the background of this critical issue will be helpful toward understanding what is being argued. For years now, there have been two running debates: (1) One concerning the nature of faith,[1] and whether or not it is a meritorious work, and (2) One concerning whether or not the Greek

---

[1] Scholars in the Lutheran camp defend one view, and non-Lutheran scholars have presented the other.

pistis christou which has "Christ" in the genitive case should be translated as "faith in Christ" (objective genitive) or "faith of Christ" (subjective genitive).[2]

Regarding the nature of faith debate, when *man's* faith is the subject these issues are involved: Is faith a gift from God, or is faith a response that a hearer of the gospel can exercise? Is faith mental assent, or is faith a change of life? (For example, Luther held that faith, which brings union with Christ, imparts to man divine attributes.[3]) Is faith something that must be given form, whether by our love for God (Luther) or by our love for fellow man, such as might be evidenced by deeds of charity (the Roman Catholic view)? This latter question reflects a running debate concerning the meaning of "faith working through love" in Galatians 5:6. Defenders of each of these views have seen their position being threatened by arguments for the objective or subjective genitive view of *pistis christou*.

If, when *man's* faith is the subject, we allow such verses as Romans 3:12; Galatians 5:6,7; and Hebrews 10:36-38 to guide us, we will define "faith" as habitually doing what God says (i.e., faithfulness).[4] With such a Biblical definition for faith, there is no need to feel threatened by a decision concerning whether *pistis christou* is an objective or a subjective genitive. Additionally, Romans 10:17 tells us that in this Christian age faith comes by hearing the word of Christ.

The objective genitive interpretation of *pistis christou* (i.e., faith *in* Christ) has been the traditional view. However, for about 200 years now, there has been an increasing call for interpreters to treat at least some of the occurrences of *pistis christou* as being a subjective genitive, thus emphasizing that Christ Himself was faithful to God when He was here on earth.

With the exception of the Syriac version, which treated the expression as a subjective genitive, the early church writers treated *pistis christou* as an objective

---

[2] Most modern translations of the English Bible translate the phrase as "faith *in* Christ." The King James Version was not consistent, translating it in some places as "faith of Christ," but at least once as "faith in Jesus" (Romans 3:25). NET and ESV render *pistis Iēsou Christou* at Romans 3:21,22 as "the faithfulness of Jesus Christ." Paul Pollard ("The 'Faith of Christ' in Current Discussion," *Concordia Journal* 23/3 [July 1997], p.213-228 has a very helpful history of the various stages of the controversy. Some of the ideas included in this brief study were suggested by Pollard.

[3] Tuomo Mannermaa, "The Doctrine of Justification and Christology: *The Christ Present in Faith*," *Concordia Theological Quarterly* 64/3 (July 2000), p.216.

[4] See also the special study #16 entitled "The Faith that Saves" in Gareth L. Reese, *New Testament History: Acts* (Moberly, MO: Scripture Exposition Books, 2002), p.598-610, where it is documented that faith includes knowledge, assent, confidence, and obedience.

genitive.[5]   From about 1795 to 1891 there were a few writers who tried to make a case for the subjective genitive reading.[6]   Not many followed their lead until a new phase of the debate sprang up in the 1950s and 1960s.[7]   When the debate called "the New Perspective on Paul" began in the late 1970's, proponents of the New Perspective were accused of not believing that faith is a gift from God.   This issue was then argued anew, and so were the objective vs. subjective genitive interpretations.   Reading *pistis christou* as "the faith of Christ" (subjective) allowed opponents of the New Perspective to argue that verses which were being given an objective reading, and which were then interpreted to mean that faith is something a man must exercise, were wrong because *pistis christou* had been mis-

---

[5] Roy Harrisville, "*Pistis Christou*: Witness of the Fathers," *NovT* 36 (1994), p.233-241. "When Roy Harrisville searched the *Thesaurus Linguae Graecae* for forms of the *pistis christou* construction in the writings of the early church fathers, he found that the Fathers understood *pistis christou* as objective in every case in which they clearly indicated the sense of the genitive" (Debbie Hunn, "Debating the Faithfulness of Jesus Christ in Twentieth-Century Scholarship" in *The Faith of Jesus Christ: Exegetical, Biblical and Theological Studies,* ed. By Michael F. Bird and Preston M. Sprinkle [Peabody, MA: Hendrickson, 2009], p.15.) "According to the Peshitta Version, the Syrian Church understood the construction as a subjective genitive ... It renders Galatians 2:16 in the following way: "Therefore we know that man is not justified from the works of the law, but by the faith of Jesus the Messiah ...." (George Howard, "Notes and Observation on 'The Faith of Christ'," *Harvard Theological Review*, 60/4 [Oct 1967], p.400.

[6] James Macknight treated some passages as being subjective genitive, e.g., Philippians 3:9, Romans 3:26 (*A New Literal Translation from the Original Greek of All the Apostolic Epistles*, London: Longman, Hurst, 1795); J.P. Lange and F.F. Fay, *The Epistle of Paul to the Romans* (New York: Charles Scribner's Sons, 1869), p.129; and Johannes Haussleiter, "Der Glaube Jesu Christi und der christliche Glaube," *NKZ* (1891), p.109-145, 205-230. Several of Haussleiter's arguments occur in almost every contemporary study, including: (1) a tautology results in Romans 3:22 if *pistis Iēsou Christou* is taken as an objective genitive; and (2) *ek pisteōs Iēsou* in Romans 3:26 is parallel to *ek pisteōs Abraam* in Romans 4:16.

[7] C.F.D. Moule ("Reply to Torrance," *Exp.Tim* 68 [1957], p.111-114) made the point that to treat all the passages as a subjective genitive tended to reduce the emphasis on the necessity of a human response of faith when the gospel is heard. E.R. Goodenough ("Paul and the Hellenization of Christianity," *Religions in Antiquity: Essays in Memory of Erwin Ramsdell Goodenough*, ed. by Jacob Neusner [Leiden: E.J. Brill Co., 1968], p.23-68) made the argument that since *pistis christou* is usually placed in contrast to "the works of the Law," it is Jesus' faith, not faith in Jesus, that is the alternative to justification by Law. This commentator has argued in his commentaries on Romans and Galatians that it is a mistake to treat "works of the Law" as synonymous with obeying the Law of Moses. Such an interpretation, it is there pointed out, makes Romans 3:20,28 contradict Romans 2:13b, and therefore it cannot be right. Since the publication of the Dead Sea Scrolls, "works of the Law" is now known to mean man-made religious rules based on the Law, rules such as the Pharisees (with their "traditions of the elders"), Sadducees, and Essenes all made. George Howard (*op. cit.,* p.459-465) added a new element when he suggested that "the faith of Christ" is what validates the covenant God made with Abraham whereby all the nations of the earth would be blessed. Now, it is true that Christ's death validates the covenant, but is *pistis christou* the expression to prove it? Would not the argument in Hebrews 9:15 about the need of the death of the covenant victim be a better Biblical text to use?

read as an objective genitive. Increasing support for the subjective genitive interpretation followed the publication of Richard B. Hays' book, *The Faith of Jesus Christ.*[8] However, Morna Hooker[9] and James D.G. Dunn[10] have defended the objective genitive interpretation. Stanley Porter concluded his paper with these words, "when Paul used the phrase *pistis christou* he was indicating that Christ was the proper object of faith."[11] The linguistic analyses of Hooker, Dunn, and Porter must be refuted if one wishes to argue for the subjective genitive in all the verses where it occurs.

It is very likely that some are proponents of the subjective genitive because it bolsters what otherwise might be a weak interpretive case.

- In the Jesus of History v. the Christ of Faith debate, the subjective genitive helps the argument that Paul is treating the Jesus event as history rather than interpreting an event.

- Some writers adopt the subjective genitive reading in order to bolster their argument that Scripture does not present men's faith as being a meritorious work.

- The debate between objective and subjective genitive is significant soteriologically, for it deals with how a man is saved. Does God do it all, or is there man's part to salvation?

Certainly, the idea of Jesus' faithfulness is clearly taught in the New Testament. In Hebrew 2:17, Jesus is presented as a "faithful high priest in the things pertaining to God." In Hebrews 3:2 we are told Jesus "was faithful to Him Who appointed Him." In Revelation 3:14 Jesus is called a "faithful and true Wit-

---

[8] Richard B. Hays book has gone through two editions. The first one, *The Faith of Jesus Christ: An Investigation of the Narrative Substructure of Galatians 3:1-4:11*, SBLDS 56 (Chico, CA: Scholars Press) was published in 1983. The second edition, *The Faith of Jesus Christ: The Narrative Substructure of Galatians 3:1-4:11* (Grand Rapids: Eerdmans) was published in 2002.

[9] Morna Hooker, "Πιστις Χριστου," *NTS* 35 (1989), p.321-342.

[10] James D.G. Dunn, "Once More, Πιστις Χριστου," *SBL 1991 Seminary Papers*, ed. David J. Lull (Atlanta: Scholars Press, 1991), p.714-729.

[11] Stanley Porter, "*Pistis* with a Preposition and Genitive Modifier: Lexical, Semantic, and Syntactic Considerations in the *pistis Christou* Discussion" in Bird and Sprinkle, *op. cit.,* p.543.

ness." So to read *pistis christou* in the subjective sense, as "the faith *of* Christ," in some of the New Testament passages would not be introducing a new idea. That is, the subjective genitive is in fact a possible reading. However, at each occurrence, we must still decide whether or not it is the correct reading.

The conclusion is this: Perhaps in a few verses (and Philippians 3:9 may be one of them[12]) *pistis christou* should be taken as a subjective genitive, as speaking of Christ's faithfulness. But to treat the genitive phrase in *every* case as being Christ's faith would result in a near total elimination from Paul's letters of Who the Christian is to believe in. Romans 10:14, Philippians 1:29, and 1 Timothy 1:16 – all of which read "believe in Him" – would be all we have left in Paul's writings.

4. Paul's opponents in chapter 3

"One of the most hotly debated issues in the contemporary study of Philippians is that of the nature and identity of the opponents to whom Paul alludes in his letter."[1] Gordon Fee tells us that "the secondary literature on this issue is second only to the huge output on 2:6-11."[2] A number of issues have been debated. What designation might we give to the opponents introduced in these chapters? Are the opponents in chapter 1 and those in chapter 3 the same or are they different groups of opponents? While the opponents in chapter 1 are Christians (though some have wrong motives for their preaching), are the opponents of chapter 3 Christians or non-Christians? Another issue is whether the opponents of chapter 3 were active in the city of Philippi, thus posing an actual threat for the Philippians, or were they active elsewhere, traveling from place to place and so were only potentially dangerous to the Philippians?[3] Sharply debated also is the question of whether Paul discusses one or two (or even three) groups in 3:2-19.

---

[12] Paul Foster makes the case for the subjective reading in Philippians 3:9, in *"Pistis Christou* Terminology in Philippians and Ephesians," chapter 6 in Bird and Sprinkle, *op. cit.*, p.107,108.

[1] Peter T O'Brien, *The Epistle to the Philippians* (Grand Rapids, MI: Eerdmans, 1991), p.26-27.

[2] Gordon D. Fee, *Paul's Letter to the Philippians* in the New International Commentary on the New Testament (Grand Rapids, MI: Eerdmans, 1995), p.7.

[3] If they were not already in Philippi, the urgency of Paul's warning in chapter 3 suggests the danger was real and that they soon would be in Philippi.

In his commentary on Philippians, Gordon Fee pointed out that as many as 18 different suggestions have been made for the identity of the "opponents."[4] Readers of commentaries thus have to do some careful sorting and comparing of what they are reading with what the Scriptures say.

The intent of this Introduction is to give an overview of some of the main suggestions, before sharing the view that is presented in this commentary.

(1) Some writers present the view that a single group of opponents is depicted in the letter.[5] But there is a division observable among these writers – i.e., did this single group consist of Jewish Christians,[6] unconverted Jews,[7] Gentile God-fearers trying to encourage Gentile converts to Christianity to join them in keeping the Law, some group of Gnostics, or Cynics?[8]

---

[4] Fee, *ibid.* See John J. Günther, *St. Paul's Opponents and Their Background: A Study of Apocalyptic and Jewish Sectarian Teachings* (NovTSup 35; Leiden: Brill, 1973), p.2, for a list of seventeen options that are usually discussed for identifying those Paul opposes in Philippians 3.

[5] So, e.g., Chris Mearns, "The Identity of Paul's Opponents at Philippi," *NTS* 33/2 (1987), p.194-204. Herbert W. Bateman IV ("Were the Opponents at Philippi Necessarily Jewish?" *BibSac* 155 [January-March 1998], p.39-61) identifies 1:15-17, 27-28 and 3:2-19 as all describing the same opponents.

[6] The idea that Jewish Christians may have been trying to influence the Philippian Christians to become like them perhaps goes back to F.C. Baur, whose reconstruction of Christian origins posited a struggle between a Petrine/Jewish Christianity and a Pauline/Gentile Christianity. Baur's attempted reconstruction reflects an Hegelian dialectic philosophy being imposed on the Biblical records. There is little Biblical evidence that the alleged Jewish Christians, supposedly led by Peter and James, were in any way connected with the Judaizers who troubled Gentile Christian congregations in Galatia, Corinth, and Rome.

[7] The Judaizers who troubled the churches of Galatia were Pharisees who pretended to have become Christians (cp. Acts 15:5 with Galatians 2:4).

[8] As attempts are made to identify the Philippian opponents, a question being asked is this: How would a predominantly Gentile church in a city like Philippi, with little or no Jewish presence, have understood Paul's epithets in Philippians 3:2? Stated another way, how would a people surrounded by pagan examples of dogs, evil workers, and mutilators of the flesh have understood Paul's appellations? Would they think of a group with which they had little experience (namely, militant Jewish missionaries), or would they think of Greco-Roman cults and religions with which they did have experience? In at least two articles, Mark Nanos has proposed that the terms "dogs, evil workers, mutilators" can very plausibly be used to refer to such groups as the Cynics or worshipers of Cybele, among others. However, to make a case for Cynics or worshipers of Cybele as being the opponents Paul warns about, Nanos offers a surprising way to explain how Paul's autobiographical sketch (Philippians 3:5-14) fits into the argument of Philippians as a whole. Nanos proposes that Paul has continued to live as a Jewish Christian, has encouraged his newly planted congregations to do likewise, and the warnings in Philippians are intended to counter the local Greco-Roman behavioral norms that were in conflict with the values of Judaism. (See Mark Nanos, "Paul's Reversal of Jews Calling Gentiles 'Dogs' [Philippians 3:2]: 1600 Years of an Ideological Tale Wagging an Exegetical Dog?" *BibInt* 17 [2009]: 448-482; *idem.*, "'Judaizers'? 'Pagan' Cults? Cynics?: Reconceptualizing the Concerns of Paul's Audience from the Polemics in Philippians 3:2,

(2) Frequently two groups of opponents are identified, with those in chapter 1 distinguished from those denounced in chapter 3.[9] Dueling hypotheses concerning the one group identified in chapter 3 include: they were Gnostic missionaries with libertinistic tendencies;[10] or Jewish missionaries (e.g., the Pharisees who traveled land and sea to make a proselyte, Matthew 23:15) who were promoting Judaism;[11] or Jewish Gnostics;[12] or "divine man" missionaries alleged to be identical with those who are attacked in 2 Corinthians; [13] or Jewish Christians who were promoting a perfectionist doctrine of the Law and a libertine lifestyle;[14] or imperial cult members who were objecting to the fact the Christians at Philippi had withdrawn from their cult.[15]

18-19" in *The People Beside Paul: the Philippian Assembly and History From Below*, ed. By Joseph A. Marchal, [Williston, VT: SBL Press, 2015], p.183-22.)

[9] So, *e.g.*, Karl Barth, *The Epistle to the Philippians*, trans. by J.W. Leitch (Richmond, VA: John Knox Press, 1962), p.37,67; J.B. Polhill, "Twin Obstacles in the Christian Path: Philippians 3," *RevExp* 77 (1980), p.359-371; G.F. Hawthorne, "Philippians, Letter to the" in the *Dictionary of Paul and his Letters,* eds. G.F. Hawthorne, R.P. Martin (Downers Grove, IL: Inter-Varsity Press, 1993), p.711.   A similar perspective is held by David E. Garland, "The Composition and Unity of Philippians," *NovT* 27/2 (April 1985), p.141-173.   He has one group being warned about in chapter 3.

[10] Walther Schmithals, "Die Irrlehrer des Philipperbriefes, " *ZthK* 54 (1957), p.297-341.

[11] A.F.J. Klijn, "Paul's Opponents in Philippians III," *NovT,* VII (1964), p.278-284.

[12] Bo Reicke, *Diakonie, Festfreude und Zelos* (Uppsala, 1951), p.302.

[13] Robert Jewett, ("Conflicting Movements in the Early Church as Reflected in Philippians," *NovT* 12 [1970], p.368,369) calls attention to some articles in the late 1950s and early 1960s by Siegfried Schulz, Dieter Georgi, and Gerhard Friedrich which proposed that Paul's opponents at Corinth were "divine-man" missionaries.   "They called attention to the divine-man concept in the Hellenistic world, which assumed a correspondence between the missionary and the god he served; they felt it was essential that a valid apostle be a living demonstration of such transcendence.   They placed a high value on ecstatic visions, miracle working, rhetorical capacity for inspired proclamation, a domineering personal demeanor, proven worthiness through congregational letters of recommendation, a valid claim for congregation financial support, and a transcendent, even transfigured style of life.   Thus they attacked Paul for his bodily weakness (2 Cor. 10:10, 11:30 ff., 12:7-10, 13:4), his unfortunate experiences of suffering and persecution (2 Cor. 4:8-12, 11: 23-33), his poor speaking ability (2 Cor. 10:10, 11:6), his lack of esoteric knowledge, visions, and ecstacy (2 Cor. 3:3-17, 12:1-5; 5:13, 12:4), his unassuming demeanor (2 Cor. 11:20-21) and his habit of self-support (2 Cor. 11:7-11)."

[14] Helmut Köster, "The Purpose of the Polemic of a Pauline Fragment,'" *NTS* 8 (1961-62), p.331.

[15] Raymond Brewer, "The Meaning of Πολυτευεσθε in Philippians 1:27," *JBL* 73/2 (Jun 1954), p.76-83.   After summarizing how an idea of behaving as a citizen ties together the passages in Philippians, on page 83 he summarizes his article with these words, "Paul seems to have employed these words to say, 'Continue to discharge your obligations as citizens and residents of Philippi faithfully and as a Christian should; but do not yield to the patriotic pressure to give to Nero that which belongs to Christ alone'."

(3) Often three groups are detected, one being the "other preachers" in chapter one, and two different groups in chapter 3.[16]

(4) If the opponents in 1:28 are differentiated from three separate groups identified in 3:2-19, that makes a total of four separate groups.[17]

(5) As many as five groups are possible: the partisan proclaimers of Christ who were active in the city of Paul's imprisonment (1:14-18), the adversaries destined for destruction who were located in Philippi (1:28), the dogs and evil workers (3:2-4), the "perfectionists" who had a righteousness of their own (3:9-16), and the enemies of the cross of Christ (3:18,19).

As was the case with the so-called "Christ hymn" in chapter 2 of Philippians, such also is the case when trying to identify Paul's "opponents." That is, not a few proffered interpretations have been triggered by an underlying popular philosophy or a certain new method of interpreting Scripture. In addition, when each of the hypotheses is examined closely, it will be seen that the attempted identification of Paul's opponents may treat one portion of the evidence well, only to have difficulty with the other portions of the evidence in the letter.

Reasons are given at each place in the commentary for the conclusions presented. Briefly, these are the positions taken in the commentary:

(a) In 3:2-16, *Judaizers* are the group warned about. This choice rests on Paul's autobiographical statement where he claims to have been once like the folk the Philippian Christians are now to be on their guard against.

(b) The choice to treat the "enemies of the cross" (3:18,19) as a separate group from those warned about in 3:2-16 rests on the difficulty of explaining all

---

[16] J.B. Polhill (*op. cit.*, p.360) tells us this is a position often associated with Bernard Weiss (1859), who saw the three groups respectively as Gentiles, false Christian teachers, and Jews. This threefold enumeration is not as tidy as it at first may appear. John Reumann (*Philippians: A New Translation with Introduction and Commentary* in the Anchor Yale Bible Commentaries [New Haven: Yale University Press, 2008]) on p.203,204 lists ten different hypotheses concerning the identity of the "other preachers" in 1:14-18, and (on p.469) lists nine different proposals attempting to identify the group in 3:2ff. Robert Jewett, *op. cit.*, p.390 and Gordon Fee, *op. cit.*, p.374 argue for two different groups in chapter three, but do not agree when it comes to identifying the two groups.

[17] J. Hugh Michael, *The Epistle to the Philippians* in Moffatt New Testament Commentary series (New York: Hodder & Stoughton, 1929), p.69,133,172.

the negative characteristics given in verse 19 if we assume the Judaizers are still the objects of Paul's warnings.

(c) In Philippians 1:14-18, the people who opposed Paul in Rome were *fellow Christians*. Paul calls them "brothers" (1:14). Though they preached Christ, they did so for the purpose of causing Paul more suffering while he was in prison.

(d) In the allusions at Philippians 1:27-30, those who were opposing the Philippians may well be *local citizens and Roman government officials*. Such opponents would be akin to those who persecuted Paul during his first visit to Philippi, after he was falsely accused to the city authorities by owners of a slave girl out of whom Paul had cast a demon (Acts 16:19-40). It is not easy to make a case that either group in chapter 3 is to be identified with those persecutors who are alluded to in 1:27-30.

5. Purpose/Genre

Based upon the ideas emphasized in the letter, it could be said that Paul had multiple purposes for writing.

1. Paul is giving *a report to the Philippians concerning his circumstances* and how the gospel is progressing both inside and outside the prison in Rome.

2. The letter is *a "thank-you note" for a missionary offering* sent by the Philippians to Paul, plus encouragement to continue their support for genuine Christian teachers and missionaries. Three times – 1:3-11, 2:19-30, 4:10-20 – Paul expresses his appreciation for the love and kindness of the Philippian church as expressed in the offering he has recently received by the hand of Epaphroditus.[1]

3. Running through the letter is a thread we might call *"an appeal for unity."* It is from this appeal for unity that the Kenotic passage (2:1-11) arises. There is an appeal to the women (4:2) for unity. The false teachers who were seeking to allure the Philippians (3:2) were a serious threat to unity.

---

[1] Hesitation about the purpose of Philippians being a thank-you letter has been expressed for these reasons: (1) Why was his thanks delayed until the very end of the letter? (2) Why did Paul allow some months to pass before even acknowledging their gift to him? Such a delay in sending them his thanks cannot be due to lack of opportunity, since news had already reached the Philippians that Epaphroditus had fallen ill. In reply to the first objection, it is obvious that Paul's thanks were not delayed until the end of the letter. In reply to the second objection, Paul may well have sent a spoken word of thanks earlier, but here is his formal, written expression of thanks.

4. *There is an emphasis on Christ.* "The names Jesus Christ, Christ Jesus, Lord Jesus Christ, Lord Jesus, Jesus, Christ, Lord, and Savior occur 51 times in the 104 verses of this epistle."[2]

5. "The immediate purpose was to send *a note of commendation and explanation* along with Epaphroditus so as to head off any criticism that Epaphroditus was returning prematurely from his charge. This, in turn, allowed Paul the opportunity to assure the church of his grateful appreciation for their gift ...."[3]

Contemporary writers, interpreting the letter from a social-science criticism, or a linguistics, or a rhetorical criticism standpoint, all have offered various explanations of the purpose/genre of this letter. For example:

- David Alan Black saw Philippians as an example of *deliberative rhetoric.* He wrote, "I will argue that Philippians is an integral composition whose primary rhetorical function is deliberative, that is, the bulk of the letter is directed toward solving the issue of disunity arising from the exigence reflected most clearly in 4:2-3. 'Unity for the sake of the gospel' provides the overarching framework and motif within which the other themes and concerns are introduced and elucidated."[4]

- Ernst Lohmeyer in his 1929 commentary on Philippians introduced the view that Philippians presents a *theology of martyrdom.* Philippians was written against the background of a developing martyr theology in the church. Our word martyr comes from the Greek word meaning witness *(martus).* In the Pauline church the highest kind of witness which one might give was in terms of being willing to die for Christ. This theme of martyrdom winds its way throughout the New Testament and reaches a pinnacle in Revelation 6:9 where the martyrs are before God's throne in heaven.[5]

- Ben Witherington and Gordon Fee have identified Philippians as being a *letter of friendship.*[6] Examining Philippians within the context of ancient letter

---

[2] Kent, *op. cit.*, p.99.

[3] Robert H. Mounce, "The Epistle to the Philippians" in *Wycliffe Bible Commentary*, ed. by Charles F. Pfeiffer and Everett F. Harrison (Chicago: Moody, 1962), p.1319.

[4] David Alan Black, "The Discourse Structure of Philippians: A Study in Textlinguistics," *NovT* 37:1 (January 1995), p.16.

[5] See James. L. Blevins, "Introduction to Philippians" in *Review and Expositor*, 77/3 (Summer 1980), p.317-318.

[6] Witherington did this in his *Friendship and Finances in Philippi* (Valley Forge, PA: Trinity Press International, 1994), and then he rejected the idea in his later work *Paul's Letter to the Philip-*

writing, Fee concludes that the epistle contains all of the elements of a "letter of friendship" combined with elements of a "letter of moral exhortation,"[7] thus giving it a unique place in the Pauline corpus. As a letter of friendship, Philippians makes up for the mutual absence of both parties, reflecting goodwill, deep affection, reciprocity, and mutual benefit. In addition, it demonstrates the "agonistic" character of friendship as involving mutual enemies. That is, the enemies of one's friend become, in turn, one's own enemies. Philippians also reflects the custom of moral instruction through letters within the context of friendship.[8]

- Charles Cousar concludes that "Philippians is a *community-building letter* in which the apostle seeks to mold the thinking of his readers in a distinctively Christian way."[9]

- Peter Oakes approaches the letter to the Philippians with a *reader-response interpretation*.[10] Two imaginary Philippian Christians, Jason and Penelope, one suffering a great deal, and the other not very much, are pictured as reading Paul's letter, and each receives a very different message. Taking his cue from 2 Corinthians 8:1-5 and Philippians 1:27-30, Oakes argues the Christians at Philippi are under the duress of economic suffering from their unconverted neighbors, likely because they have ceased to honor the gods and were persuading others to do the same. Oakes agrees there is a call for unity running through the letter, but he affirms that this emphasis on unity does not take into account all of the material in the letter. He identifies the other important theme as being suffering. In chapter 2 Paul is offering his own suffering and that of Christ as example and encouragement toward unity. Oakes treats 2:6-11 as a Pauline composition for the occasion, based on previous formulations of the story of Christ. He tries to tie 2:9-11 with the context by suggesting that it deals with the granting of authority to Christ and would have been heard by the readers not as opposition to the cult of the emperor but as opposition to imperial politics. Christ is being proclaimed as a new ruler – one who, in keeping with ancient traditions of good leadership,

---

pians: A Socio-Rhetorical Commentary (Grand Rapids: Eerdmans, 2011).

[7] Fee, *op. cit.*, p.2.

[8] *Ibid.*, p.10.

[9] Charles B. Cousar, *Philippians and Philemon: A Commentary* in the New Testament Library Series (Louisville: Westminster John Knox, 2009), p.17.

[10] Peter Oakes, *Philippians: From People to Letter* (Cambridge: Cambridge University Press, 2001).

is worthy of his throne not because he sought his own glory, but because he set an example of heroism in the face of suffering. (Since Oakes does not write much about chapters 3 and 4 of Philippians, his assertion that the theme of suffering covers more of the material of the letter than does the theme of unity is questionable.)

- Mary Fairchild has proposed that the purpose of Philippians is to show that "joy in the Christian life is all a matter of perspective. True joy is not based on circumstances. The key to lasting contentment is found through a relationship with Jesus Christ." Whatever one's circumstances may be, there is joy in suffering, in believing, in serving, and in giving. "This is the divine perspective Paul wanted to communicate in his letter to the Philippians."[11]

Since Philippians is a thank you letter for a missionary offering, this epistle could be studied for ideas and suggestions concerning missions and the support of missions. A sample of the ideas that may be found includes:

- We may look forward to hearing from those missionaries whom we support. It may be by a letter such as Philippians, or a monthly newsletter or e-mail, or it may be a personal visit from the missionary (as 2:24 suggests).

- 1:5 and 4:15,16 suggest that one of the first things to teach a newly planted congregation is the blessing of being involved in mission work. The Philippians' participated in the gospel from their first days, and sent offerings to Paul very soon after he helped start the church at Philippi.

- 1:6 informs us that God, who makes it possible to give to missions the first time, will keep on helping his children do good work until the second coming of the Lord Jesus.

- 4:19 gives an apostolic promise that after we have given, God will supply all our needs and do it generously.

- 1:7 and 4:14 instruct Christians to not cease providing support should the missionary be falsely imprisoned, as was Paul.

- 1:7 pictures each and every member of the Philippian congregation being involved in this missionary enterprise. This is a worthy goal: to have each and every member praying for and supporting a missionary.

---

[11] http://christianity.about.com/od/newtestamentbooks/a/Philippians.htm, accessed July 25, 2016.

- Just as Paul prayed the mission giving of the Philippians would increase (1:9), so may we pray a similar prayer for our brethren. However, such giving should not be like a raging torrent, but should be guided by careful discernment about what is good and excellent as opposed to that which is not (1:9).

- Knowledge of what our missionary is doing on the field (1:9) can be gained by visits to the field and then reporting back to the supporting church or churches, just as Epaphroditus is pictured as doing in 2:25-30.

- 1:10 soberly warns that it is possible the Lord may find fault with some of our offerings, or lack thereof, on the day of judgment. It behooves us all to seek to be blameless in His sight.

- 1:19 helps us to see that prayers offered for our missionaries will result in God providentially intervening in their lives.

- While we are offering prayers and providing support for our missionaries, we are to conduct ourselves in a manner worthy of the gospel of Christ (1:27). There is joy in serving Jesus and in supporting those who are heralding Christ Jesus' blessings.

H. OUTLINE

See the outline printed in the "Concise Introduction to Philippians."

THE PRISON EPISTLES INDEX

Abraham - 67,759

Absent in body - 308,463,589,715

Absent from the body - 457,459

Abusive speech - 170,186,347,376

Access to God - 102,103,121,122,137, 323,362

Achaia - 391,565,712

Acts, book of, *passim* 4,13,19,389,581,621,636,681,706, 718

Acts of Paul - 9

Acts of Titus -

Adam - 72,79,113,119,121,172,218, 219,220,292, 318,319,350,642, 732,736,741

    First - 729,737

Adam Christology - 732,751,752

Adamic nature - 168

Adoption - 31,39,41,44,45,46,55,80,89,141, 169,183,222,256,280

Adoptionist - 316,664

Aeons - 282,287,290,296,300,310,314,316,317, 330, 335,659,662,664,665,668

Aesculapius - 388

Affection(s) - 44,228,231,274,340,341,345,411,414, 434,439,441,450,470,471,472,499,543, 572,586, 638,689,740,766

Affliction(s) - 10,297,298,469,564,706

    See also: Paul, imprisonment: suffering

Agabus - 532

Against Heresies - 271 ,660

Against Marcion - 588,643,660,716

Against Montanus - 640

Against Valentinus - 660

Aged, Paul the - 2,412,413

Age(s) - 20,32,52,53,54,77,113,118,120,132, 156,239,299,300,324,374,439,571

    apostolic - 384,635

    of accountability - 76,293

    Mosaic - 524

    present - 70,71,301,344,485,671, 746,750,757

    sub-apostolic - 672

    to come - 70,71,84,85,342,344

Ahura Mazda - 661

Alexander the Great - 633,663,668,709

Aliens - 96,104

Alive, made, in Christ - 64,75,80,81,82-86,89, 92,126, 163,318,320-323,344,349,491, 494

Altered states of consciousness - 263,329, 331,332,525, 658,659,663

Ananias - 298

Andronicus - 149,424

Angels - 47,53,70,71,73,101,108,120,238, 275,280,281,286,300,314,317,325,326, 329,333,481,486,648,657,658,662,663, 668,669,731,748,749

    fallen - 71,238,239,290,324

    hierarchy - 286,317,657

    present at the creation - 325

    worship of - 262,263,325,329,330, 338,611, 655,658,659,669,678

    See also: Colossians, Colossian crisis.

Anger, angry - 96,135,138,170,173,174,178, 179,181,226,227,279,346,347,366,596, 699,700

Angra Mainu - 661

Anthropomorphism - 185

Antioch

    Pisidia - 637,642,667,712,715

    Syria - 105,562,565,583,752

Antiochus III – 635,710

Antony, Mark - 621,710

Anxious, anxiety - 19,65,230,251,307,380, 388,422,489,499,503,504,506,550,551, 553,554,568, 638

Apocalypse of Elijah - 197

Apocalypse of Peter - 652

Apocrypha - 8,9,197,307,393,518

Apostle(s), apostleship - 37,51,64,65,102,105, 110-114,117,119,139,143,145,146,148, 149-151,202,206,215,221,250,251,268, 270,272,279,298,300,303,311,322,364, 456,484,503,505,558,598,602,608,612, 618,620,653, 666,752

    foundation of the - 105

    of Christ - 37,149,403,594, 653, 756

    of churches - 37,149,503

    the signs of - 505

    temporary office – 378

Apostolic authority - 25,37,412,558,602,653

Apostolic Constitutions - 687

Apostolic delegate - 254,378

Apostolic succession - 273,629,648,652

Apostolic teaching - 380,640,651

Appetite(s) - 535,537,538

Apphia - 399,404,405,401,425,631,682,687, 694,698

Approve the things that are excellent - 442, 631,641, 675,682,687,693,694-698, 704

Aristarchus - 4,19,23,381,382,424,425,561, 630,641,686

Aristobulus - 573

Aristotle - 451,616

Arius, Arian(s) - 40,63

Ark of the covenant - 144

Armor of God (panoply) - 34,234,235-247, 281,324,602

Aroma, fragrant -183-185,568,569

Artemis - 10,106,150,389,635,697

Article, Greek - 53,56,82,86,106,131,151,189,215,312, 324,340,378,393,440,496,522,526,533,5 71,637,735

    absence of - 125

    of previous reference - 82,86,324

Ascetic, asceticism - 263,275,334,335,337- 339,342,525, 635,660,663,664,667,671

Asia (Roman province) - 5,10,12-14,18,19, 24,25,30,51,122,158,241,254,261,377, 384,393,404,423,429,467,498,502,581, 587,590-593,613,615,632,634-637,639, 669,671,708-712

Athletic metaphor - 329,495,658

Atonement - 93,112,185

Attitude - 78,79,85,93,134,135,142,169,170, 173,180-182, 203,205-207,225,229,231- 234,265,277,279,311,326,332,346,347, 353-357,361,369,373,430,431,439-441, 464,470,471-477,480,483,487,493,513, 520,522,529, 531-533,537,560,568,569, 667,688,689,733-735,753

Augustine - 80,199,221

Augustus, Caesar - 322,688,710

Authorities

    angelic - 119,120,285,286,749

    civil - 207,225,251,252,374,424,764

    demonic - 145,324,325,330,657

Authority

    angels - 70

    apostolic - 25,37,112,162,392,403, 412, 558,602,638,653,681

    Christ's - 72,73,139,206,211,261, 283,292, 313,315,483,485

    hierarchical - 600

    of the word of Christ - 358,392

    parental - 224,227,228,366

Baptism - 58,66,86,170,178,214,282,320,339, 343,348, 526,614,642,660,754

    buried in -140,318,319,334,657

    immersion - 140,214,319,339

    infant - 319

    into Christ - 45,103

    of suffering - 140

    of the Holy Spirit - 140,146

    one - 32,139-141

    See also: Buried with Christ; Dying with Christ; Raised with Christ.

Baptismal aorists - 166,167,280,282,341

Baptismal formula - 216

Baptismal homily - 614

Barbarian - 350,351

Barnabas - 149,354,381-384,705

Barnabas, Epistle of - 641

Battle - 34,145,153,235,236,240,241,247,503, 544,673,749

    of Actium - 710

    of Ipsus - 465,710

    of Pydna - 710

    with Satan - 245

Behavior - 54,67,77,90,133,134,163,177,184, 189,198,203,209,224,263,264,321,327, 331,335, 343-347,375,463, 474-476,494, 534-539,558,762

Believe, believed - 43,45,56-59,67,68,87,126, 139,140,158, 268,269,309,467,468,537, 624,647,760

Belshazzar - 238

Benediction - 35,132,255-257,264,378,395, 406,422,425,431,553,572,574,575,607, 686,701,714,724

Benjamin, tribe of - 430,517,518

Bethshean - 351

Bishop(s) - 73,151,152,379,394,434,585,600, 640,687,694, 695,712,713,717,718

    See also: Elders

Bitterness - 173,174,178,179,365

Blameless, blamelessness - 41-44,214,216, 217,294,431,442,443,492,493,519,520, 574,704,716,767

Blessing(s) - 38,59,66,67,94,113,116,123, 139,141,206,262,267,274,300,373,391, 422,435,455,471,486,522,552,568,570, 574,714,767

    Spiritual - 31,39-60,123,176,187, 257,583

Blood - 184,237,351,496

    of bulls and goats - 184

of Christ - 47-49,53,95,96,219,324,
328,664
of the cross - 291,292,672
Boast, boasting - 87-89,461,515,516,538,
667,715
Body, bodies
Christ's - 147,294
See also: Christ, bodily form
exalted in my - 455
human - 160-162,181,245,288,333,
334,343,456, 458,541,664
of Christ, *see*: Church, body of
Christ
of doctrine - 139,155,185,189,311,
343,461,465, 600
of the flesh - 318,319
of sin - 319
one new - 31,32,91,95,100,116,137,
206,357, 434,583,612
resurrection - 46,59,69,84,139,170,
178,216, 222,289,342,527
severe treatment of - 337,660
Body, soul, and spirit - 64,76,126,574
Boldness - 15,121,251-253,455,456,677
Bond
of peace - 32,133,136,137,162, 605
of unity - 137,356
Bonds (imprisonment) - 1,5,12,100,232,352,
446,448,469, 631,676,703,716
Bond-servant(s) - 271,272,378,379,433,457,
479-481,484, 627,740-742
Bondslave - 386,480,681,690
Book of Enoch - 197,652,663,669,670
Book of life - 545,547,548
Breastplate of righteousness - 34,237,241-244
Brother(s)
in Christ - 4,62,100,104,173,185,
190,193,222,230, 253-
256,265,266,309,355,357,372,
378,380,381,399,401,403,404,
410,411,415,418,421,444,476,
502,503,604,611,679,681,685,
687,698,699,764
of Christ - 149,385,390
weak brethren - 327,528
Brutus and Cassius - 621,710
Buddhism - 670
Buried
in baptism - 140,318,319
with Christ - 140,318,319,334,
335,657
Burnt offering - 569
By nature - 79,80

Caesar, Julius - 710
Caesarea - 3-7,15-20,57,150,382,445,466,
502,582,585, 612,673,719
Caesar's household - 6,7,13,18,23,448,572-
574,707,719
Calendar: sacred - 328,657,658
Call, calling - 30,66,67,72,116,133,134,137-
139,142,172, 280,288,357,408,595
to apostleship, Paul's - 37,110,111,
115,253,298, 528,529
upward, in Christ Jesus - 459,528,
530-532
Callous - 164
Canon - 533
Marcionite - 10-12,589,597,643,
691,692,717
Muratorian - 597,643,692,717
New Testament - 150,392,393,597,
687,688,701
Old Testament - 247
Captive - 109,312,656,688
Captivity, led captive - 144,145
Catholicism -
Early - 600,648,652
Roman - 88,221,298,504,619,744,
757
Cerinthus - 310,330,644,659,662
Certificate of debt - 321,322
Chains - 2,6,109,236,252,253,265,374,396,
413,440,445, 452,519,581
Chester Beatty Papyri - 59,514,578,643,723
Children - 224-228,422
and parents - 34,207,224,264,363-
367
in the faith - 33,156,157,387
of God - 39,45,61,63,68,91,100,
104,124,172,178,183,222,282,
353,439,492,493,559.571,767
of Israel - 586
of light - 185,190-193
of wrath - 79,80
Chose, chosen - 31,39,41-47,56,88,94,118,
149,298,352, 353,513,517
Christ, Jesus Christ:
agent in creation - 119,287,542
agent in reconciliation - 70,99-101,
104,275,288-294, 324,642,672
all-sufficient - 610,657
ascended on high - 144-148,342
baptism of - 282,310,662,664
Beloved - 31,38,31,46,47.281,282
bodily form -736,742
blood of: *see*: Blood, of Christ

Christ, Jesus Christ: (*continued*)
cornerstone - 105,106
cosmic - 624
creator - 119,542
crucifixion - 82,101,319,383,483,
    664,743,744, 752
death of - 48,51,98,100,101,103,
    147,235,294,298,319,323,324,
    341,383,437,482,483,526,601,
    642,648,673,729,732,739,743,
    754,759
deity - 39,72,119,139,147,155,189,
    216,279,290,310,315,316,406,
    435,477,479,483-485,606,648,
    651,672,718,725,726,729,730,
    733,736, 738-740,744,746,750-
    752
descent - 146,147,479
earthly ministry - 147,482,484,515,
    731,739,746
emptied Himself - 479,480,738-740,
    742,743
equality with God - 256,477-480,
    736,737-742
exalted, exaltation - 69,70-73,75,84,
    289,315,324,340,430,476,483,
    484,485,487,589,601,657,729,
    733,736,743-746,749,750,755
example - 182,184,208,222,224,
    276,430,476,477,482,488,534,
    551,753,755
existed in the form of God – 285,
    477,478,735,747
faithful high priest - 759,760
fills all in all - 73,218,352
firstborn of creation - 284,285,672
firstborn from the dead - 288,289,
    672
fullness of deity - 315,678
gave gifts to men - 133,142-148
glorification - 42,69,74,147,219,
    257,265,279,283,316,342,408,
    483,541,732,745
glory of - 73,279,316,480,482
head of the church - 4,30,39,71-76,
    210,262,288,601,624,648,660,
    672
hope of glory - 300,301
humiliation - 430,476,483,487,724,
    743
image of God - 283,284,288,672,
    673

incarnate, incarnation - 40,46,90,
    101,118,147,167,280,289-
    291,316,446,479,480,483,652,
    726,729,736,738,739,745,751
indwelling - 128
Lord of the universe - 288,370,658
Lord, lordship -32,38-40,60-63,73,
    111,120,121,133,139,145,162,
    184,189-193,198, 200,204,205,
    224,228,233,235,256,268,276,
    288,309,310,317,355,362,366-
    370,406-408,435,439,448,484,
    487,501,522,548-550,564,
    574,657,746,747,749,764
love(s) - 32,125,129,130,184,210,
    212,213,218,256,441,553,624
made in the likeness of men - 479,
    481,740-742
man of sorrows - 482
mediatorial role - 70,102,206,330,
    333,479,673
meekness - 354,551
Messiah -
mystery of God - 32,104,109,111,
    112,114, 305,306,373,593
nearness - 548,550
obedience - 482,489,743
person and work - 4,53,651,657
preeminence - 262,283,284,340,
    657
pre-existence - 284,652,718,729,
    732,733,736, 740-745,755
raised with - 89,352
resurrected, raised from the dead -
    73,82,90,102,138,147,234,279,
    288,289,319,320,342,383,437,
    483,525,526,541,672,744,756
sacrifice - 38,70,97,103,183-185,
    213,298,323, 329
seated at Father's right hand - 69,
    70-74,146, 257,339-342,672,
    749
second coming of - 40,53,71,84,
    139,170,178,216,240,289,342,
    438,439,443,486,487,527,541-
    543,551,601,767
Son of Man - 481,483,742
sufferings - 82,103,184,213,298,
    325,468, 482, 525,526,732,743
supreme - 71
temptations of - 247,248
triumph of - 145,324-326,657

Christ-hymn,   *see*: Hymn to Christ
Christian liberty,   *see*: Liberty, Christian
Christology - 265,283,289,479,603,640,648,
    651,652,655,672,678,718,725,732,735,
    738,745,747,751,752,756
        Adam-Christology - 751,752
        Krypsis Christology - 739
Church:
        body of Christ - 4,30,34,57,62,73,
            74,91,115,129, 140,152-154,
            181,211,218,219, 234,288,297,
            357,419,606,624,654
        bride of Christ - 216,217,219,221,
            222,602,625
        buildings - 391,713
        dwelling of God - 107
        God's building - 30,102,104-107,
            125
        holy temple - 106
        household of God – 30,104,234,
            299,540
        in the house - 390,391,404,405,
            636,682,694,698.
        See also: House church.
        leadership of - 141,152,153,158,
            160,207,254,378,414,434,450,
            555,602,639,703
        persecution of,   *see*: Persecution
        presented in all her glory - 216,217
        temple of God - 31,103-107
        unity of - 133-144,155,357,434,471,
            472,474,510,582,615,764-766
        universality of - 32,72,108,601,605
Circumcision - 91-93,350,382,384,389,430,
    513,517,668
        false - 450,511,513
        true - 317,318,513-515,642
Citizens, citizenship - 30,94,104,463
        Heavenly - 84,341,539,540,543,548
        in the kingdom of God - 93,104,541
        of Philippi - 464,540,710,763,764
        Roman - 456,463,540,697,711
Clamor - 179
Cleanse, cleansed, cleansing - 53,214-217,
    319,555
        ceremonial - 319
        from sin - 96
Clement
        companion of Paul - 545,547,705,
            706
        of Alexandria - 546,590,596,643,
            705,716,748
        of Rome - 12,208,547,595,706,714

Coarse jesting - 186,187
Codes: household - 363,619
Codex Manuscripts
        Alexandrinus - 59
        Vaticanus - 59,280,578,583,586,590
        Sinaiticus - 578,586,590
Collection of Paul's letters - 380,643,694,695
Colonies, Roman - 463,464,540,565,710,711
Colossae, *passim*
        city of - 631,632
        church in - 19,25,261,273,295,376,
            380,592, 628,631,636,693
        earthquake destroyed - 634
        false teaching at - 158,265,272,286,
            301,310,327, 337,350,654,657
        map showing location - 14
        where Philemon lived - 13,253,270,
            272,391,682
    See also: Colossians, Colossian crisis
Colossians, Epistle to
        analysis
        authorship - 1,19,25,640-654
        Colossian crisis - 654-673
        Concise Introduction to - 261-264
        critical matters - 675-679
        date and place - 673,674
        Detailed Introduction to - 627-679
        relation of epistle to Ephesians -
            605-607,609-612
        relation to Philemon - 641
        style - 640,644-648,650-652
        subscript - 396
Comfort -149,176,254,255,410,411,713
Commandment, first, with promise - 225,226
Commonwealth of Israel - 93,95
Compassion - 170,181,352,353,406,411,470,
    471
Complete in Christ - 301,302,305,315-320,
    326
Concern
        for all the churches - 62,304
        for others - 22,61,181,305,327,380,
            387, 388,463,498,499,506,559-
            561,706
Conduct: Christian - 32,65,77,90,133,163,
    170,186,193, 198,234,275,375,443,462-
    464,474,495,534,543, 558,767
Confession
        of faith - 216,487,599,749
        of Jesus Christ as Lord - 155,484,
            486,487,748,749,755
        of sin - 194

Confidence -
121,411,412,422,438,448,461,502,513,
516,549,716
    in the flesh - 513-516,549
Conforming to Christ -525,526
Consciousness - 58
    altered states of - 331,332,335,
526,663
    prophetic - 113
Consolation - 255,411,470,471
Consummation - 53,72,148,324,486,487
Content, contentment - 431,559-564,767
Conversation - 539
Conversion - 68,79,80,89,98,111,127,167-
170,173,191,202,222,269,280,295,321,
349,404,413,418,429,430,485,519,525,
590,619,636,684,705,711
Corinth - 5,11,308,391,429,438,450,462,
560,565, 566,638,706,711,761,762
Courage - 1,17,116,123,135,251-253,447-
449,455,699
Course of this world -76,77
Covenant(s) - 80,94,95,517
    ark of the - 144
    blood of the - 48
    of promise - 93,94
    Mosaic (old) - 99,319,328,672
    new - 98,99,319,328,353,657
    seal of the - 93,319,514
    strangers to
    with Abraham - 99,759
    with David - 94
Covetousness - 187,188,677
Creation - 53,118,284,288,292,325,485,672
    Gnostic ideas of - 285,657,662,668
    gospel proclaimed in all - 295,296
    new, *see*: New creation
    of the universe
    of the world - 46,89
    restored - 53,72,291
Creation-Ruination-recreation theory - 43
Creed(s) - 487
    Nicene - 284
Cross - 38,70,87,95,98,100,101,129,145,147,
184,214, 221,239,283,291,292,298,321-
324,431, 481-483,657,664,673,728,730,
732,743
    blood of the - 672
    enemies of the - 533,535-537,763,
764
    sayings from the - 664
    word of the – 449

Cybele - 635,663,761
Cynics - 761,762

Darkness-light - 199,282
Darkness - 190-192,281,564,661
    angels of - 668
    deeds of - 193-198
    domain of - 281,469
    forces of - 237,238
    powers of - 238,281
    Prince of - 194,248
    spiritual - 238,281
    world rulers of - 238,281
David - 72,92,113,123,124,144,752
    covenant with, *see*: Covenant with
David
    Psalms of - 204
David's throne - 70,146
Day, days
    evil - 199,200,239-241,245-250
    last – 265
    long on the earth
    of Christ Jesus - 438,443,494,495,
704
    of judgment - 187,294,443,495
    of redemption - 48,176,178
    of the Lord - 438,495,676
Deacon(s) - 116,254,272,378,379,394,433,
434,572,628,703,705,717,718
Dead - 76,323,343,344,459,486,542,748
    arise from the - 196,197
    first-born from the - 288,289,672
    in trespasses and sins - 75,77,79,81,
89,163, 235,279,320,515
    raised from the - 68,69,73,75,82,83,
145,235,318-320,526
    resurrection from the - 527,528,531,
532,542
    resurrection of the - 527,716
    souls of the - 486
    spiritually, *see*: Death, spiritual
    to sin - 170,344
Dead Sea Scrolls - 328,343,651,669,670,671,
759
Death - 69,72,344,345,347,458,505,507,573,
574,663,670,671,688,710
    baptism into - 319
    body of - 318
    deliverance from - 31

Death – (*continued*)
 entered the world - 292
 eternal - 76,184
 of Christ, *see*: Christ Jesus, death of
 Paul's, *see*: Paul, death - 24,383,
  455-457,497,523,593,599,600,
  615,619,719
 physical - 97,184,292,294,320,482,
  541,743
 spiritual - 31,76,79,80-83,126,163,
  320,321,636
 to the enmity - 100,101
Deceitful
 lusts - 168
 scheming - 156-159,236
 teachers - 270,271,387,391
 workers - 512
Decrees - 99,334,335
 against us - 322
 Roman government - 671,709
 submit to - 335
Deities, pagan - 201,435,659,670
Deity - 106,315,330,481,498,515,
 See also: Christ, deity
Deliverance - 31,47,59,91,330,453,454,704
 of Israel - 518
Demas - 4,386,389,390,424,425,630,641,686
Demeter - 635
Demiurge - 285,661,662,668
Desire(s) - 345,732
 evil - 343,344
 of the flesh - 537,664
 of the mind - 79,80
 to depart and be with Christ - 458-
  460
Destruction - 246,465,466,537,763
Devil - 48,53,58,77-80,119,158,165,168,174,
 175,194,236-240,244-248,281,291,338,
 344,348, 350,469
 god of this world - 77
 See also: Satan
Diaspora – 635
Didache - 596,714
Different gospel - 450
Diogenes Laertius - 663
Diognetus, epistle to - 714
Discernment - 65,441,442,704,768
Discipline - 227,228,308,309,313,365,366
 ascetic - 338
Disobedience - 80,245,370
 acts of - 76
 children of - 191
 sons of - 76,78,79,189,190,346

to God - 366,368
 to parents - 224,227,365,366
Dispensation - 52,275,298,583,600
Disputing - 491,492,677
Dissipation - 201,202
Divine-man missionaries - 763
Docetism - 294,664,667
Doctrine(s) - 30,42,44,55,82,99,126,157,171,
 263,269,286,297,315,465,582,602,652,
 655,690,752
 apostles' - 155
 body of - 139,140,155,295,311,461,
  465,600,654
 Catholic - 221
 Charismatic - 202
 Christian - 305,392,424,467,608,
  654,666,756
 deceptive - 265,270
 Docetic - 664
 every wind of - 156-158,387
 false - 155,157,449
 Gnostic - 291,294,296,662,664,668
 of apostolic succession - 662
 of Christ - 127
 of demons - 656
 of divine election - 42
 of double predestination - 42,44
 of justification by faith only - 489
 of original sin - 80
 of perseverance of the saints - 295
 of reincarnation, *see*: Reincarnation
 of salvation by grace - 83
 of Scripture - 70
 of sinless perfection - 155
 of subsequence - 58,202
 of the merit of the saints – 298
 of unconditional eternal security -
  83,179
 of universalism – 291
 speculative (Gnostic) - 277
Dogs, beware of the - 459,464,511,512,523,
 535,762,764
Dominion(s) - 70,71,285,286
 Christ's - 73,486
 given to Adam - 72
 of Satan - 282
Door for the word - 373,374,693
Double predestination, *see*: Doctrine of
 double predestination
Doxology - 32,130,132,431,570,571,723,728
Drink offering - 495,496
Drunk with wine - 201,202

Dualism - 268,285,335,657,661,664,668
Dying with Christ - 334,335,660
    See also: Baptism.

Early Catholicism, *see*: Catholicism, Early
Early Christian literature - 1,66,79,215,254,
    307,383,388,389,394,414,547,583,595,
    596,639,661,666,690
Early Church Fathers -
    129,325,589,617,639,667,712,713,724,
    737,758
Earthly
        masters - 231,232,368-370,372
        mindedness - 536-538,544
Earthquakes in the Lycus valley - 369,389,
    634
Edification - 149,176,177,187,377,691
Egypt, miracles in, *see*: Miracles in Egypt
Elder(s) - 151,152,378,394,434,628,705,717
        Ephesian - 9,122,150,460,586,666
        Jerusalem - 322,434
        Jewish - 759
        traditions of the - 314
Elect, the - 53,87,111,294
Election - 42,43,239,352
    See also: Doctrine of election
Elemental spirits - 314,315,330,335,656,657,
    660, 663,673,741
Elementary principles - 312,314,334,335,337,
    655,656
Eliphaz - 178
Emancipation - 686,687
Emotion(s) - 51,173,221,368,388,400,412,
    422,436,457,465,472,512,553,670,700
        God's - 55,67
Empty deception - 263,312,313,337,656
Encouragement - 30,85,198,204,250,254,345,
    359,367, 380,384,386,394,411,414,499,
    550
        in Christ - 470
        words of - 228,272,372,475,652
Enemies
        of the cross - 431,533,535-537,763,
        764
        of the gospel - 503,560
Enmity - 97,98,100-102,106,136,256
        with God – 292
Enoch, Book of, *see*: *Book of Enoch*
Envy - 386, 449,450,474,716

Epaphras - 24,150,261,262,267-273,275,295,
    296,301-304,309-311,328,358,373,378,
    380,382,386-389,394,395,408,424,404,
    611,612,627-631,636,638,639,641,648,
    652,654,655,674,682-684,686,693
Epaphroditus - 3,4,15,22,23,273,380,405,429,
    430,438, 444,460,469,498,501-509,534,
    546,549,559,560,568,565,575,698,705,
    706-708, 712,715,720-722, 765,768
Ephesians
        authorship - 593-603
        and Colossians - 605-607,609-612
        and the Pauline corpus -670,608
        and 1 Peter - 608
        Concise Introduction to - 29-35
        contents - 623-625
        critical issues - 605-
        Detailed Introduction to - 578-625
        destination - 583-593
        historical allusions - 578-583
        in the hands of contemporary
            interpreters - 612-623
        occasion and purpose - 604,605
        outline -31-35
        subscript - 257
        time and place of writing - 21,603,
            604
Epiphanius - 692
Epistle from Laodicea - 675,677,694,695
Epistle to the Laodiceans - 393,676
Epistles of Paul and Seneca - 652
Epistolary aorist - 111,254,384,415,421,422,
    502,503, 506,629,684,708
Equality with God - 256,477-480,732,736-
    738,740,742,752
Equipping of the saints - 145,152,153,157
Equality with God - 732,736-738,740,742
Er, the son of Armenius - 670
Eschatology - 2,745,748
Essenes - 313,327,328,336,518,519,657,658,
    667,668, 671,718,760
Esther - 518
Eternity - 42-44,51,54,55,85,89,120,122,132,
    246,341, 352,444,484,571,583,685,751
Ethics - 155,263,339,377,619,664
        Christian - 193,419,558,756
Euodia - 544-554,705,717
Eusebius - 298,383,392,597,634,639,640,644,
    692, 715,717
Evangelism - 383,429,451,452,495

Evangelist(s) - 17,18,145,148,150-153,159,
    254,272,328,378,386,394,424,628,631,
    639,653,675,682,696,711
Eve - 218
Evil(s) - 33,53,65,68,95,172,180,185,189,217,
    233,237,239,250,291,292,318,338,341,
    345,366,493,495,536,552,657,661,664,
    732
        aeon - 662
        age – 77
        angels - 120,324
        authority - 78
        day(s) - 199,200,239-241,245,247,
            250
        deeds - 194,281,293,294,636
        demiurge - 285
        desire - 343-345
        eye - 618
        feelings - 180
        hosts of - 464
        impulses - 349
        influence - 78,157
        men - 671
        of slavery - 401
        one - 174,201,245,246,248,249
        powers - 78,315,325
        practices - 348
        social - 689
        speaking - 180
        spirits - 239,315,324
        thoughts - 539
        tricks - 236
        workers - 450,511,512,530,762,763
        world - 662
Evil-merodach - 230
Example
        Christ's, see: Christ, example
        ethical - 754,755
        good - 145,200,539
        of Abraham - 340
        of Job - 279
        Paul's - 516,533,534,539,544,549,
            558
Exhortation(s) - 32-35,133,134,149,162,168,
    172,177, 183,198,233-235,248,255,263,
    264,310,343,344,355,359,361,363,376,
    378,386,394,395,428,430,431,462,476,
    488,490,510,531-534,543,549,554,558,
    616, 617,627,638,706,714,733,766
Exodus from Egypt - 146
Eyeservice - 230,370

Fairness - 372,419,690
Faith - 33,61,62,82,87,90,99,127,153,157,255,
    261,267,301,318,406,460,466,489,587,
    614,654,658,690,699,719,757-759
        a gift from God? - 87,467,757,758
        access through - 121,122
        body of doctrine - 139,155,295,310,
            311,461,465

        Christian - 47,61,133,360,399,461,
            465,511, 656,672,675,721
        comes by hearing - 57,105,167,215,
            320,413,467
        confession of - see: Confession, of
            faith
        fellowship of - 409,683
        household of – 142
        in the Lord Jesus - 60,61,122,171,
            268,282,308,408,413,524,598,
            673,756
        justified by - 292,443,489,523,524,
            731
        obedient - 57,309,468
        of Abraham - 515
        of Christ (pistis Christou) – 756-760
        of the gospel - 462,464,465,467,
            470,629
        one - 32,139,140
        Philemon's - 406-410,683,701
        sacrifice and service of - 496,497
        saved through - 85,86,88,90
        shield of - 34,245
        steadfastness in - 293,641
        the, once for all delivered - 51,65,
            654
        unity of the - 153-155,161,597,604
        word of - 215
        working through love - 657
        works of - 88
Faithful, faithfulness - 86,122,179,192,232,
    241,370,372, 380,525,533,757,759
        brother, brethren - 266,380,381,627
        in Christ Jesus - 29,37,38,583-586,
            591,593
        Jews - 95,104,280,292
        minister - 253,254
        sayings - 90
        servant - 232,271,272,378,450,627,
            629,683
        unto death – 548

False teachers - 157,265,269,270,272,275, 281,286,296, 301,304-306,312,315-318,329,331,336,349,361,510,657
   at Colossae, *see*: Colossae, false teaching at
   at Laodicea - 392
   at Philippi - 764
Family of God - 56,104,124,357,699
   See also: Household of God
Far off - 95,101,102,113
Fatherhood of God - 141,435
Fathers - 227,366,367,370
   See also: Early Church Fathers, Patriarchs
Fear(s) - 1,34,121,173,369,387,447-449,503, 553,704
   and trembling - 229,230,488-491
   of Christ - 207,208,275,367,368
   of God - 208,345,596,677
   of the spirits - 245,281,657
Fellow bond-servant - 271,272,378,627
Fellow-Christians - 266,268,308,381,403,604, 690,764
Fellow-citizens - 30,104,540
Fellow-heirs - 45,115,116,301
Fellow-imitators - 534
Fellow-members - 115,116,301,358,419
Fellow-partakers - 115,116,301
Fellow-prisoners - 11,272,381,382,424,627, 630
Fellow-soldier - 243,248,394,404,405,465, 502,503
Fellow-worker - 61,383-386,390,403,404,419, 424,425,502,545-548,572,638,674,681-686,706
Fellowship - 100,115,153,163,185,334,362, 400, 407,409,419,425,437,438,465,712
   of His sufferings - 525,526
   of the Spirit - 470,471
   of the mystery - 118
   with Christ - 191,224,553
   with God - 53
Festival(s) - 326-328,658,668
Filthiness - 186
First Adam
   See: Adam, first
First Enoch, see *Book of Enoch*
First fruits - 289
Firstborn of all creation, *see*: Christ, firstborn of creation
Flaming missiles - 245,246

Flesh - 91,93,218,219,229,297,317,320,368, 418,513,761
   and blood - 237
   body of the - 317,318,648
   Christ's - 97-100,184,294,316,596, 642,664
   confidence in - 513-516,549
   cutting the - 513
   desires of - 338,664,671
   live on in the - 457,459
   lusts of - 79,80,338
   two shall become one - 220-222
Fleshly
   indulgence - 337,338,660
   mind - 332,659
Food laws -
Food or drink - 326,327
Footwear of the gospel
Forbearance - 134-136,355,550
Forces: elemental *(stoicheia)*, *see*: Elemental spirits
Forgiveness - 138,180,182,409,699
   of sins - 38,41,47-50,83,85,86,114-117,141,214,221,282,283,294, 298,320-324
   of one another - 174,181,183,355, 356,401, 405,612
Form - 542,745
   of a bond-servant - 479,480,740-742
   of God - 283,285,477-479,483,484, 735-739, 746,753
Form criticism - 615,618,721,725,727,730, 733,748,750,755
Former manner of life - 167
Fornication - 344,539
Foundation - 295,309
   doctrinal - 262,283
   of apostles and prophets - 105,150
   of the world - 42-44,90,214,527
Free will - 46,43-45,82,87,404,416,491,570, 684
Freedom - 4,18,49,251,423,694
   from festival regulations
   from food regulations
   See also: Liberty, Christian.
Freeman - 9,133,350,351,413,421,536, 573,690, 696
Freedmen - 18,19,229,573,690,699
Friendship - 272,400,416,682,765,766

Fruit(s) - 192,201,270,409,568
    bearing - 276,277
    comes through Christ - 443
    of the light - 191,281
    of righteousness - 443,568,704,767
    of the Spirit - 192,274,354,473
    worthy of repentance - 353
Fruitful labor - 457,495,530
Fruitfulness - 277,450
Full armor: see: Armor of God
Fullness (plērōma) - 74,130,284,289,316,600,
    656,657,662,665
    of Christ - 74,130,155,156,160,181,
        284,289-292,656
    of deity - 315-317,648,672
    of God - 129,130,316
    of times - 41,52,300
    See also: Christ: fullness of God
    See also: Church: fullness of Christ.
Future, see: Eschatology

Gain/loss metaphor - 430,516,520,521,562
Gaining Christ - 522,523
Galatians
Garbage, see: Refuse
Garden of Eden
Generation(s) - 668
        all, forever and ever - 131,132
        crooked and perverse - 492-494
        past ages and - 299,300
Generosity - 50,81,143,176,183,192,442,550,
    570,683,707
Gentiles - 56,57,76,77,80,88,91-94,102,113-
    118,162,168, 252,299-301,321,350,419,
    512,535,590
Gentleness - 134-136,170,339,352-354,550,
    551
Gift
        Christ's - 142,143
        of God - 85,87
        of God's grace - 116
        of the Holy Spirit - 57-59,127
Gifts - 429
        diversity of - 142
        given to the church - 33,144-148
        sent to Paul - 435,461,504,564-568,
            574,711,720
        spiritual, see: Spiritual gifts
    See also: Ministries.

Giving and receiving - 565,566,568
Glorification - 86,342
    Christ's - see: Christ Jesus,
        glorification
Glory - 47,89,123,131,216,300,342,443,444,
    494, 513,515,537,541,568,571,736,750
    Christ in you, the hope of - 300,301,
        648
    Father of - 63
    of His inheritance in the saints - 66,
        67
    praise of His - 41,46,55,56,59,60,63
    riches of His - 125,127,278,570
    to be revealed - 419,459
    See also: Christ Jesus, glory of;
    See also: God, glory of; Shekinah
Gluttony - 538
Gnostic, Gnosticism - 275,276,309,664,666,
    730,731
        adoptionism,   see: Adoptionist
        angel worship, see: Angels, worship
            of
        anti-Gnostic thrusts - 280,281,283,
            288,290, 300,322,538
        asceticism,   see: Asceticism
        Cerinthus,   see: Cerinthus
        deceivers - 189
            See also: Deceitful teachers
        disparaged Christ - 288,310,315,664
        dualistic ideas,   see: Dualism
        demonically inspired – 282
        denial of personal sin - 302
        denial of resurrection - 289,296
        denial of second coming - 289
        Docetism,   see: Docetism
        emanations, see: Aeons; Demiurge
        endless genealogies - 300,662
        Hellenistic - 731
        incipient - 51,270,424,535,651,655,
            666
        Judaism,   see: Judaism, Gnostic
        libertine lifestyle - 536,664
        matter is evil - 291,662
        mystical experiences - 663
        "Mystery,"   see: Mystery, Gnostic
            use of the term
        New Testament books against - 65,
            158,282,306, 667,718
        no emphasis on love of the brother -
            62,268
        origins of - 668-671,718
        plērōma,   see: Fulness (plērōma)

Gnostic, Gnosticism – (*continued*)
    pre-Christian - 666
    reincarnation, *see*: Reincarnation
    second-century - 271,644,645,650,
       651,659,660-666
    seven heavens - 665
    Supreme Being - 662
    teaching about Calvary (non-
       salvific) - 292,294, 664
    teaching about God - 271,330,662
    Valentinus, *see*: Valentinus
    writings – 307
    See also: *Book of Enoch*; *Gospel of*
      Judas; *Gospel of Mary*; *Gospel of*
      Thomas; *Jung Codex*; Nag
      Hammadi Gnostic Library
Goal – 188
    history moved to its - 148,287
    of the Law - 328
    of the ministry of the saints - 154-
      156
    press on to the - 431,527-532
Gog - 351
Gold mines in Macedonia - 709
Golden rule - 34,232,372
God - *passim*
    Almighty - 103,489
    anger of - 174
    armor of, *see*: Armor of God
    attributes of - 50,86,89,171,354,600
    cannot be tempted - 739
    character
    children of, *see*: Children of God
    Creator - 118-120,171,220,286
    eternal - 285
    eternal purpose (plan) - 43,44,54,83,
      89,120,121,252,374,583
    family of, *see*: Family of God
    the Father - 30,38,39,141,206,255,
      256,362,486
    the Father all-glorious,
    the Father of Jesus Christ - 39,40,
      257,267
    our Father - 124,266,267,406,435,
      571,627
    foreknowledge - 43,280
    form of, *see*: Form of God
    glory of - 56,62,63,125,126,279
    grace of, *see*: Grace of God
    holiness, *see*: Holiness of God
    household of, *see*: Household of
      God
    insight - 50

invisible - 283,284,672
is my witness - 441
kingdom of, *see*: Kingdom of God
knowledge - 64,543,672,739
likeness of - 170
living - 94,140,155
love of - 32,44,81,129,256,282
manages history - 110
mercy of - 81,505
might of - 67,68,234,235,278,
    279,302, 303
one - 32,141,190
pleasure – 491
power of - 31,60,67-71,117,145,
    278,320
presence - 555
providence, *see*: Providence
purpose of, *see*: God, Eternal
    purpose
right hand of - 70,72,339,340,672,
    749
righteousness, *see*: Righteousness
    of God
sacred name - 435,484
sovereignty - 54,491,747
strength - 67,68,234,235
throne of, *see*: Throne of God
will of - 37,46,50,51,54,55,200,230,
    231,265,274,275,300,349,375,
    387,491,524
wisdom of - 32,50,119,120,129,300,
    302,307,624,672
word of, *see*: Word of God
working of - 320-323,490,491,677
workmanship - 89
wrath of - 80,189,190,345,346
God of this world, *see*: Devil, god of this
  world
God is my witness
God-fearers - 761
Godhead - 39,141,142,145,188,216,276,284,
  657
Gods and goddesses - 38,94,141,194,195,291,
  434,486, 580,634,661,668,745,749,766
Good will - 183,231,369,449,450,491,716
Good works - 89-91,271,276-278,409,438,
  444,676
Goodness - 191,192,194,354,416,417
Gospel, *passim*
    advancement of
    defense and confirmation of - 1,439,
      440,450,451

Gospel (*continued*)
    faith of the - 465,466,470
    furtherance of the - 123,500,508
    hope of the - 295,296
    minister of the - 117,296,297,594
    mystery of the - 251-253
    of Christ - 17,270,299,358,425,462,
        463,494
    of peace - 244,245,559
    of salvation - 56,269,495
    participation in the - 437,438,703
    preaching the - 17,57,105,116,150,
        270,296,416,424,464,565,653
    proclamation of the - 449,495
    progress of the - 445,447,461,704,
        764
    the message of truth - 57,157,171,
        243,676
    word of the - 67,262,269-271
    word of the Lord - 247
Gospel of Judas - 661
Gospel of Mary - 664
Gospel of Thomas - 660,663
Gospel of Truth - 662
Grace, *passim*
    an attribute of God - 82,83,86
    and peace - 38,406,435,580,627
    be with you - 392,395,396
    freely bestowed on us - 47
    given to Paul - 117,303
    lavished on us - 49
    given to each of us - 143
    glory of His – 46
    growth in - 334
    of God - 22,271
    of our Lord Jesus Christ - 396,
        425,574,738
    partakers of - 439
    prevenient - 143,490
    riches of His - 49,84-85,570
    saved by - 81,83,86,90,606
    second work of - 126
    throne of - 121
Gratitude - 187,280,310,358,359,411,552,569,
    707
    See also: Thankfulness.
Greco-Roman culture - 213,616,617,761
Greed - 164,165,185,186,343,345,738
Greeting(s) - 38,572,703
    from Paul - 37,262,265,267,395,
        403,406,422,424, 430,433,435,
        510,580,627

    from Paul's companions - 3,11,23,
        377,381,382,386,389,572,573,
        589,653,693
Grumbling - 491,492
Guest room (for Paul) - 12,423,686,693

Hades -145,147,486
Hapax legomena - 600,601,647,651
Haustafel, see: Codes, household
Healing - 91,390,505
Heart(s) - 32,67,134,178,181,201,230,293,305
    322,369,439, 471,553
    attitude of the - 354,513
    believes in the - 139
    Christ may dwell in your – 127
    circumcision of the - 318,513
    comfort your - 254,255
    encourage your - 379,380
    eyes of your - 64,66,126,594
    guard your - 552,553
    hardness of - 163,164
    lose - 109,122,248,366,367,373
    make melody with your - 203-205,
        361
    of compassion - 181,352,353
    of God - 43,506,738
    of the earth - 147
    of the saints - 410,411
    refresh my - 421
    rule in your - 357
    sincerity of - 229,230,367
    singleness of - 34,230
    thankfulness in your - 358-361
    thinks in his - 539,557
Heavenly - 539
    bodies - 674
    city - 340
    Father - 44,183,353,419,741
    home - 269
    Jerusalem - 95,540
    Master - 372
    places - 39,42,69-71,83-85,95,119,
        120,237,239,257,269,285,292,
        491,540
    tabernacle – 53

Heavens - 139,643
    atmospheric - 239
    birds of the - 147
    creation of the - 89,120,285
    far above all the – 147
    seven - 316,317,667
    starry - 42,239
    things in - 52,53
    three, *see*: Third heaven
Hebraism - 79,80,81,188,190,191,483
Hebrew of Hebrews - 430,517,518
Helios - 635
Helmet of salvation - 34,246,247
Heresy, Colossian, *see*: Colossians, Colossian
   crisis
Heritage - 31,41,54,55,59
Hierapolis - 13,272,304,386,388,424,630-634,
   636-640,682
Hinduism - 670
Holiness - 43,170,171,187,214,217,349
    of God - 316,738
    Spirit of - 169
Holy Spirit - *passim*, 64,103,169,249,455,526
    anointing of the - 64
    be filled with - 33
    do not grieve - 178,179
    fellowship of the - 471
    filling of the - 64,198,201,202,
      207,223
    gift of the - 57,319
    indwelling of the - 59,126,131,188,
      278,526
    inspired by the - 114,247,251,608,
      691,725
    names of the - 65,454
    personality of - 59,178
    pledge - 188
    quench the - 128,178
    of promise - 31,41,56,58,103
    praying in the - 249
    resist the - 178
    seal, *see*: Seal, sealed
    temple of the, *see*: Temple of the
      Holy Spirit
    unity of the - 137
    working of the - 41,203,274
Homily - 613,622
   See also: Baptismal homily
Hope - 23,66,269,423,455,543
    in Christ - 41,55,56
    in the Lord - 498
    laid up in heaven - 66,269
    learned from the gospel - 262,267

    no, in the world - 93,94
    of eternal life - 93
    of glory - 300,301,648
    of heaven - 262,301
    of His calling - 66,137
    of the gospel - 295
    of salvation - 247
    one - 32,138,139
    theology of, *see*: Theology of hope
House church - 391,405,636,698
Household
    codes, *see*: Codes, household.
    Caesar's - 6,7,13,18,23,448,
      572-574,707,719
    Nero's - 573
    Archippus' - 698
    Lydia's - 429
    of Aristobulus - 573
    of God, *see*: Church, household of
      God
    of faith, see: Faith, household of
    of Narcissus - 573
    of the Philippian jailer - 429,711
    Philemon's – 411
Humble
    means - 562
    mindedness - 430,472,474,483
Humiliation, *see*: Christ, humiliation of
Humility - 134-136,170,330,339,352-354,477,
   655,733,755
    Christ's - 482,483,737
    false - 658-660
    mock - 354
    of mind - 474,475
Husband(s) - 34,207-225,233,264,363-367,
   370,394,405,544, 608,705
Hygeia - 388
Hymn, hymns, hymnody - 477,497,599,613,
   678,754
Hymn to Christ - 477,675,677,678,726,727-
   736,742,743, 747,749,751-755

Idolater, idolatry - 186-188,312,343-345,348,
   460,485
Idol's temple - 194
Ignatius - 414,497,584,595,641,667,687,690,
   691,694,712-714,748
Ignorance - 163,164,166,661

Image
    of Christ - 171,349,350
    of God - 283,284,288,290,400,673
    of invisible God - 283,284,672
    of the heavenly - 542
Imitation, imitators
    Christian example - 154,534,538,
        539
    of Christ - 217,430,534
    of God - 33,183,354
    of the church of God - 638
Immortal, immortality - 296,670
Imperative(s), *see*: Indicative and imperative
    forms
Impurity - 164,165,185,188,343-345
In Christ, *passim*
    babes - 156
    believe - 57,68
    complete - 301,302
    created - 89
    faithful in - 29,37,38,583,585,591
    new life - 207,235,363
    our position - 132,134
    redemption - 48,374
    saint(s) - 433,572,703,707
    sum up all things - 51,52
    united in - 31,39,75,95
    See also: Gentiles; Jews and Gentiles.
    See also: in the Lord
Indicative and imperative forms -
    107,131,188,494
Inheritance
    God's - 54,66,67
    in the kingdom of God - 187-189
    our - 41,59,115,262,280
    reserved in heaven - 341
    reward of the - 369,648
    See also: Heritage
Initiation, mystery religions - 320,332,563
Inner man - 32,125-127,169,235,278,349,515
Inspiration - 113,150,275,387,532,612,729,
    756
    denial of the, of Scriptures - 144,
        725,750
    denial of the, of the Prison Epistles -
        25,606
    of Paul - 117,144,251,392,571,610,
        730
    of the apostles - 64,114,149,300
    of the prophets - 113,149,433
Instruction of the Lord - 227,228
Integrity
Intimacy - 221

Iranian mystery religion, *see*: Mystery religion,
    Iranian.
Irenaeus - 271,389,583,590,596,642,660,662,
    715
Isis - 635,663
Israel
    believing - 111
    children of - 586
    commonwealth of - 93,95
    court of (temple) - 97
    house of - 125
    Jacob - 92,517
    land of nation of - 517
    people - 54,69,92-94,97,227,343,
        353,430,518
    spiritual - 512
    true - 353
    unbelieving - 353

Jains - 670
James
    Lord's brother - 149,385,761
    Epistle of - 580
Jealousy, *see*: Envy
Jerome - 188,192,197,208,239,393,596,691,
    692
Jerusalem, *passim*
    church at - 152
    destruction (AD 70) - 296,639
    dividing barrier wall - 97
    heavenly, *see*: Heavenly Jerusalem
    Paul, prisoner in - 16,445,582
    saints in - 5,15,254,382,425,560,
        604,712
    temple at, *see*: Temple at Jerusalem
    temple taxes sent to - 635
Jerusalem Conference - 327,434
Jesus Christ, *see*: Christ, Jesus Christ
"Jesus of History" v. Christ of Faith" debate -
    753,755,759
Jesus Justus - 4,385,424,630
Jewish Wisdom Literature - 731
Job - 178,279
John (apostle) - 62,65,69,114,310,311,468,
    531,542,639,648,651
    Christology of - 289,640,651,731
    epistles of - 270,667
    Gospel of - 603,667,747

John (Baptist) - 335,385
John Mark, *see*: Mark
Joints and ligaments - 160,164,332-334
Josephus - 97,226,244,282,313,351,496,517,
    555,573,635, 654,671,709
Joy - 194,422,461,510,549,550,738,766,767
        in Christ - 4,462,548
        in the faith - 460,461
        offering prayers with - 436
        Paul's - 61,62,308,410,411,430,444,
            449,453,470, 472,496,543,560,
            639
        Philippians' - 497,506,507
Judaism - 314,319,330,521,526,651,654,663,
    667-669,762
        Anatolian - 669
        first century – 667
        Gnostic - 654,731,762
        Hellenistic - 754
        mystical ideas in - 332
        post-exilic - 667
        rabbinic - 671
    See also: Essenes;   Pharisees
Judaizers - 37,430,450,466,510-522,531,532,
    535,534,544, 722,756,761,764
Judas (a New Testament prophet) - 149
Jude - 150,386
    Epistle of - 667,718
Judea - 265,391,482,638
Judgment - 60,233,370,483,492,568,746,749
        according to deeds - 91,370
        day of - 187,294,443,676,767
        day of Christ - 495
        great white throne - 527
        final - 189,232,346,370,372,
            485-487,495,523,704
        sheep and goat - 90
Jung Codex - 660
Junias - 149,424
Justice - 5,192,372
Justification, justified - 214,443,524
    by faith, *see*: Faith, justified by

Kerygma and didache - 449
Kind, kindness - 41,45,45,50,51,81-87,116,
    180,181,203,322,339,352-354,401,414,
    471,550,683,696

Kingdom - 93,144,540
    gospel of the - 91
    mediatorial - 479
    mysteries of the - 300
    of Christ - 187-189,281,282
    of darkness - 469
    of God - 104,189,216,282,340,384,
        385
    of heaven - 84,282,375,468
    of light - 469
    of Pergamum - 633
    of Persia - 238
    Prepared from the foundation of the
        earth - 527
    taken away from Israel - 353
    word of the - 201
Knee
    bend the - 123
    bow the - 123,485,747,749
    every, should bow - 484,486,746,
        750
Kneeling in prayer - 123
Knowing Christ - 521,522,525,526,752
Knowledge - 64,130,271,453,673
    true - 305,306,349
    false - 275
    full - 65,275,442
    Gnostic emphasis on - 65,307,357,
        661, 665,666, 718
    of every good thing - 409,410
    of God - 64,65,276,277,442,543
    of God's will - 274,275,278
    of Him - 65
    of the Son of God - 33,154,155,
        159,597
    real - 441,442
    spiritual - 31,60,66
Krenides - 709
Krypsis Christology, *see*: Christology, Krypsis
    Christology

Labor - 175,176,302,369,385,386,388,457,567
Laodicea - 13,14,19,264,272,304,378,386,388,
    390-394,424,584,588-591,630-634,636-
    640,679,682, 694
        Epistle from, *see*: Epistle from
            Laodicea
Latin Versions - 124,221,280,290,355,379,
    393,404,590,644,717

Law
  a shadow of things to come - 328
  abolished, abrogated - 101,321,322,
      328,657
  end of the - 99
  of commandments - 97,98
  of Moses - 44,88,93,97,98,115,270,
      314,322,325,366,385,513,517,
      518,524,604,658,763
  our tutor to lead us to Christ - 658
  righteousness which is in the - 519,
      523,524,756
  Roman - 45,232,418,420,684,688,
      689,696-698
  under, to Christ - 338
  works of, *see*: Works of Law
Leadership - 143,152,254,378414,434
Letter from Laodicea, *see*: Epistle from
  Laodicea
Letters
  collection of the Pauline - 608,614,
      643,694,695
  form of ancient - 256,267,403,433,
      435,572,580, 584,681,683,703
  groups of Paul's - 1,2,261
  of commendation - 762
  of friendship - 766
  of praise - 617
  phrases in capital - 243,244
Liberalism, religious - 750,753
Libertines - 536,763
Liberty
  Christian - 362,536,560,604
  Paul set at - 1,687
  spy out our - 512
  See also: Freedom.
Lie, lying - 33,165,171-173,177,243,263,347,
  348,538,594
Life - 104,288,341,342,494,562
  book of, *see*: Book of life
  Christian - 58,66,83,159,165,180,
      234,263,277,343,362,377,463,
      526,533,558,599,766
  eternal - 47,93,138,421,676
  future - 94,139
  holy - 33,162
  manner of - 167
  new - 34,82,171,172,175,177,207,
      235,320,339, 497
  of God - 163,164
  or death - 455,456,676
  purity of - 33,185
  risking his - 507,508

spiritual - 82,89,155,278,341,342,
      532
  to come - 94,459
  word of, *see*: Word of life
Light(s) -102,191,195,279
  bearers - 491,492
  bring to - 118
  children of, *see*: Children of light
  Father of - 63
  fruit of the - 191
  inheritance of the saints in - 280
  unapproachable - 63
  you appear as, in the world - 493,494
  you are, in the Lord - 190
  See also: Darkness- light.
Liturgy - 99
Lower parts of the earth - 146,147
Love - 32,61,134,160,184,228,255,256,273,
  407,412,442, 450,476,555
  Christ's, of the church - 212,213,
      222, 624
  consolation of - 470,471
  for the brethren - 62,305,472
  God's, *see*: God, love of
  holy and blameless in - 43,44
  husbands are to, their wives - 210,
      212,217, 222,364
  put on - 356
  rooted and grounded in - 127
  speaking the truth in - 158
  walk in - 33,183
  your, for all the saints - 60,61,
      268,269,408,587
  your, may abound more and more -
      441,704
Love feast(s) - 538
Luke - 3,15,19,23,150,382,389,424,425,546,
  599,705,708, 747
  physician - 389,630,642
  possible collector of Paul's letters -
      380,694,695
  Gospel of - 15,389
Lust(s) - 165,186,245
  of deceit - 167,168
  of the flesh - 79,338,344
  of the mind, *see*: Desires of the mind
LXX, *see*: Septuagint
Lycus River valley - 12,13,16,304,314,336,
  377,388,389,391,404,424,592,604,629,6
  32-640,668,679,695
Lydia - 391,429,546,562,705,711
Lystra - 94,637

Macedonia - 4,17,266,391,429,462,502,565,
    687,708-710
        churches of - 391,423,469,712
Macedonian call - 429,711
Malice - 170,179,180,346,347
Man
        new - 97,99,100,138,168-172,175,
            176,180,187, 321,344
        old - 162,168-172,175,179,183
Marcion - 12,19,393,579,584,585,588,587,
    597,643,691, 692,717,742
Marcion's *Apostolicon* - 588,717
Manual of Discipline - 554
Mark - 4,15,150,381-384,391,424,425,508,
    630,639,641,686
        one of Peter's converts - 383
        Mark, Gospel of - 389,425,621
        alleged priority of - 747
Marriage - 165,185,212,213,215,220,222,344
        abstaining from - 664
        mixed - 208
        sacrament - 221
Martyrdom - 497,498,687,765
Masoretic text - 144,173
Master(s) - 34,207,225,230,232,253,264,367,
    399,414,415, 469,609,612,690,695,699
        according to the flesh - 229
        power of, over his slave - 688,689
        slave - 2,17,25,229,233,367-372,
            419,420
Maturity - 533
        spiritual - 33,153-156,302,387
Meekness - 135,354,551
Melody - 203,205,361
Men-pleasers - 231
Mercy - 353
        God's, *see*: God, mercy of
Messenger (Grk. "apostle") - 503,711
Messenger
        letter carrier - 3,377
        news carrier - 469,582
        offering carrier - 382,460,498,502,
            565,589,603, 611,708
Messiah, *see*: Christ
Metaphors - 9,104-107,167,192,199,210,280,
    310,311,324,347,356,382,451,496,497,
    534,559,737
        adoption - 45
        athletic - 329,465,495,658
        bookkeeping - 523,568,569
        citizenship - 540,541

military - 236,244-247,305,309,324,
    464,465,533
mixed - 128,157
open door - 374
triumphal procession - 325
Michael (archangel) - 633,668
Miletus - 19,502,505,586,592,670,679
Mind - 66,164,247,293,357,554
        darkened - 194
        desires of the - 79,80
        fleshly - 329,332,659
        futility of the - 162
        guard your - 552,553
        hardened - 164
        hostile in - 293
        humility of - 354,472,474,475,483
        lowliness of - 330
        one - 462-465,489
        renewing of the - 349,557
        same – 472,473
        set your - 169,263,332,340,535-538,
            642
        spirit of the - 167-169
Mind-set - 349,473,734
Minister - 116,150,152,153,272,295,296,298,
    383,416, 628,696
        a good, of Jesus Christ - 150
        faithful - 253,254
        of the gospel - 117,297,594
        to my needs - 503-504
Ministry - 109,143,153,154,263,394,445,460,
    497,500,546, 682
        fulfill your - 360,696,698
        Paul's Ephesian - 8,404,595,646,719
        take heed to your - 394,405
        work of - 153
Miracles - 117,149,279,476,505,725,762
        in Egypt - 69
        at Red Sea - 67
Mithras, Mithraism - 635,670
Monergism - 82
Money - 15,23,60,176,341,355,421,429,475,
    551,560,561,566-570,604,684,703,706,
    712
Montanism, Montanus - 598,640
Moral excellence - 556
Morality - 557,604
Mordecai - 518
Mosaic Age, *see* Ages, Mosaic
Moses - 354,493,586
        Song of - 493
        See also: Law of Moses

Mount Athos - 335
Mount Cadmus - 632
Mount Messogis - 637
Mount of Olives - 145
Mount Orbelos - 709
Mount Sinai - 145,146
Muratorian canon, *see*: Canon, Muratorian
Mutilation - 513,635,688,761
Mystery - 47,52,119,133,306,600
    administration of the - 118
    can be known - 32,111
    concerns Gentiles' equal privileges -
        32,114, 115,300
    explained by apostles and prophets -
        149,612
    first marriage contained a - 212,220-
        222
    Gnostic use of the term - 666
    hidden in ages past - 299,300,602
    of Christ - 32,109,112,306,373,374,
        594
    of His will - 39,41,50,88
    of the church universal - 32,108
    of the gospel - 251-253
    made known by revelation - 109,114
    made known to Paul - 32,110
    true knowledge of God's - 306
    unknown in previous ages - 32,113
  See also: Christ, the mystery of God.
Mystery religions - 302,331,332,636,663
    Eleusinian - 194,670
    initiation into - 306,563,659
    Iranian
Mysticism - 127,329,333,525,670
    Eastern religious - 218,314,667
    Jewish - 670
    Merkabah - 655,670

Nag Hammadi Gnostic Library - 597,660,662,
    718
Name(s) - 484
    above every name - 283,483,484,
        487,745
    are in the book of life - 545-547
    believe in the, of His Son - 269
    Christ's - 118,134
    every, that is named - 70,71
    in(to) the name of - 114,140,361,
        362,367,485
    Sacred - 139,435,484,746

Nebuchadnezzar - 238
Needs - 154,208,251,551
    God will supply all your - 570,767
    the, of the churches - 25
    Paul's - 22,415,560,563,696,711
    pray for specific - 251,436
    spiritual - 131
Neo-liberalism - 449,613,614
Neo-orthodoxy - 612,614,755
Nero - 5,225,252,446,573,634,763
New birth - 57,64,126,171,191,414
New covenant - 98,99,319,328,353,657
New creation - 31,69,75,89-91,100,288,514
New life, *see*: Life, new
New man, *see*: Man, new
New moon - 326,327,658,668
New Perspective on Paul - 758
New self - 167-170,349,350,377
Newness
    of life - 82,83,289,319,321,322,339,
        349
    of spirit - 169
Nicean creed, *see*: Creeds, Nicean
Nicephoris Callisti - 9
Noah - 185
Nympha - 390,391,630,631,682

Oath - 441
Obed-Edom - 144
Obedience, obedient - 34,39,40,59,83,90,422,
    467,488,491, 492,647,757
    children to parents - 224-226,365
    Christ's, *see*: Christ, obedience
    faith - 57,309,468
    habitual - 489
    slaves to masters - 229-231,367
    to Christ - 386
    to the gospel - 639
Octavian - 710
Offering - 409,437,704
    drink, *see*: Drink offering
    for Jerusalem - 4,5,15,254,382,610,
        703
    from Philippi - 14,22,421,429,431,
        438,442-445, 503,507,559,566-
        570,604,706,707,712,720,764,
        767
    to God - 44,183-185,493,497
  See also: Gift

Old Covenant - 328,672
Old Latin version - 280,290,379,393,644,692, 717
Old self - 167,168,170,318,319,348,350
Old Testament - 48,69,88,96,111-115,118, 144-146,185,190,197,221,222,226,241, 243,244,275,328,353,369,433,435,438, 443,485,518,519,569,657,663,731,732, 746,747,749
    food laws - 327
    Greek versions of - 144,554
    prophets - 58,113,114,120,247,303, 343,385,387, 751,752
    Psalms - 204,361
    saints - 38
    Scriptures - 144,196,306
    times - 50,52,54,69,94,100,111,114, 252,272,280,292,299-301,325, 602,688
    types and shadows - 57
On Prescription Against Heretics – 661
On the Resurrection - 660,716
Onesimus, *passim*
    a faithful and beloved brother - 380
    collected Paul's letters? - 380
    converted by Paul - 2,24,413
    early church tradition concerning - 687
    runaway slave - 12,368,399
Opponents
    of the Philippians - 430,462,465, 466-469,511, 512,760-764
    Paul's - 331
Oral tradition - 310,557,658
Ordinances - 97-99,322,326,513
Origen - 71,192,205,547,585,586,643,692
Original sin, *see*: Doctrine, of original sin
Osiris - 663
Outsiders - 198,369,375,376,465,550
Overseers - 151,152,207,433,434,572,703, 705,717
    See also: Bishops

Paganism - 348,365,486
Pamukale - 388
Panoply of God, *see*: Armor of God
Papyrus - 395,579,584,660,734
    See also: Chester Beatty Papyri; Rylands Papyrus

Parabolani - 508
Parents - 34,165,207,220,224-229,264,363, 365-367,422, 430,517,518,695
Parousia - 342,747
    See also: Christ, second coming of
Participation in the gospel - 437,438,703,767
Partnership in the gospel - 437,565
Passion - 165,245,343-345
Pastor(s) - 145,148,151-153,378
Patience - 134,136,170,228,278,279,339,352-355
Patriarchal Age - 52,300
Patriarch - 517
Paul, *passim*
    the aged - 2,412
    ambassador in chains - 2,236,374, 581
    apostle - 30
    of Christ Jesus - 37,108,109
    apostle to the Gentiles - 117,118
    appeal to Caesar - 5
    autograph - 395,421,631
    Christology, *see*: Christology
    companions - 381-387
    concern for all the churches - 62
    death - 600
    desire to visit Spain – 12
    empowered - 117,303
    example, *see*: Example, Paul's
    first recorded sermon - 541
    fought with wild beasts - 9
    having a righteousness from God - 525
    Hebrew of Hebrews - 518
    imprisonment(s) - 2,4-7,9,10-12,21, 204,302
    See also: Prisoner
    minister of the gospel, *see*: Minister of the gospel
    ministry – 445
    and Onesimus, *see*: Onesimus
    and Philemon, *see*: Philemon
    persecutor of the church - 117,519
    Pharisee - 431,518
    prayer(s) - 31,38,60,62-66,108,123-130,262,267, 274,407,441
    preached from Jerusalem to Illyricum - 270
    presses on toward the goal - 529-531
    prisoner in Rome - 22,382,383, 399, 413,429, 444,447,549,603,674
    prisoner of Jesus Christ - 2,109, 133,403,446

Paul (*continued*)
  refusing to take pay - 706
  repudiation of asceticism - 338
  Roman citizen - 265
  suffering(s) - 1,32,108,122,297,298
  of the tribe of Benjamin - 517
  tribulations of - 122,123,298
  use of the Old Testament - 144,226,
    227
  See also: Apostle; Colossians, authorship;
    Ephesians, authorship; Philemon
    (Letter to), authorship; Philippians,
    authorship
Paulinism - 610,647
Peace - 30,38,95,97,100-102,266,291,546,557,
  558,580,672
  be to the brethren - 255,586
  bond of - 32,133,136,162,605
  Christ is our - 96
  from God - 267,406,435
  gospel of - 244,559
  of Christ - 357
  of God - 431,548,552,553
  offerings - 185
  with God - 245,292,546
Pentecost - 16,54-57,102,113,114,117,146,
  221,328,385,658
Perfect, perfection - 114,124,153,155,216,
  302,346,356,357,386,387,527,528,531,
  597,643,716,718
Pergamum - 631,633
Persecution - 135,463,470,512,708,752
  of the church - 117,431,519
  of Paul - 122,297,412,459,468,
    762,764
  of the Philippians - 464,468,497,549
Persephone - 486
Perseverance - 248,250
  See also: Doctrine, of perseverance of the
    saints
Persians - 633,668,670
Personality, corporate
Persuasive argument - 307
Peter, Apostle
  death - 383
Petition - 248-250,373,437,455,698
Pharisees - 55,88,98,220,313,327,328,336,
  337,512,515,518-520,525,658,667,671,
  759,761,762
Philemon (letter to) - 1,588
  authorship and attestation - 690-692
  Concise Introduction to - 399-401
  critical matters - 699-701

date and destination writing - 21,
  692-696
Detailed Introduction to - 681-701
historical allusions - 681-687
occasion and purpose - 4,696-699
outline - 701
place of writing - 19
relation to Colossians - 641
subscription - 425,686
why included in the canon - 687-690
Philemon (person), *passim*
  church in his house - 405
  his faith - 407-409,683
  his love for others - 407,408,410,683
  his wife - 405,631,682
  resident of Colossae - 13,681,693
  slave owner - 25,253,414,417,681,
    690
Philip (the apostle) - 639
Philip (the evangelist) - 17,18,140,149,150,
  166,272,628,639
Philip of Macedon - 709
Philippi (city)
Philippians
  authenticity - 717-719
  authorship and attestation - 713-717,
    728-730
  Concise Introduction to - 429-431
  controversy over Philippians 2:5-11
    - 724-756
  critical issues - 721-768
  Detailed Introduction to - 703-768
  historical allusions - 703-708
  history of Philippi - 708-711
  history of the Philippian church -
    711-713
  date of writing - 434,719,729
  integrity - 721-724
  occasion -720
  outline - 430,431
  place of writing - 7,13,19,22,604,719
  purpose/genre - 14,764-767
  subscription – 575
Philo - 226,238,654,669
Philosophy - 119,270,377,392,395,558,643,
  656,657,659, 660,667
  Colossian - 263,281,283,285,312-
    322,337,655,671
  current popular - 20,612,613,653,
    698,721,724, 725,733,755
  first-century religious belief - 313,
    613,654,666
  Hegel's dialectic - 725

Philosophy (*continued*)
    sources of Colossian - 312-315, 336,661
    Stoic - 561,562,636
    See also: Dualism
Phrygia - 314,332,404,414,632-637,669,697
Piety - 669
Plato - 314,670
Plato's *Republic* - 670
Plato's *Timaeus* - 669
Pliny, the elder - 446
Pliny, the younger - 203-205,361,404,691, 699,700,755
Pluralism, religious - 730,756
Poetry - 205,477,670,726
Polycarp - 511,596,641,690,713-715,721,724
Polygamy - 217,364
Poverty - 561-563
Power(s) - 70,71,76-78,108,235,237,238,240, 246,302,317, 657,749
    miraculous - 58
    of darkness, *see*: Darkness, powers of
    of evil, *see*: Evil, powers of
    of God, *see*: God, power of
    of His resurrection - 525,526
    of sin - 60,168
    strengthened with, in the inner man - 125,126,278
    that works within us - 130,131
    See also: Principalities and powers
Praetorian guard - 2,6,7,16,23,446-448,573, 704,719
Praetorium - 6,13,16,446
Praise - 40,46,131,248,341,484,513,570,617, 726
    of His glory - 41,55,56,59
    to God - 31,39,56,67,130,132,204, 257,443,571, 750
    sing - 754,755
    worthy of - 554,557
Pray, prayer(s) - 129,237,248,251,274,373, 386,407,453, 552,575,599,767
    answers to - 127,131,505
    exhortation to - 35,248
    for Paul - 1,2,18,22,23
    for wisdom - 279
    in the Spirit - 248-250
    intercessory, *see*: Intercessory prayer
    Model - 182,248
    of thanksgiving - 262,267,551
    Paul's, *see*: Paul, prayers of
    persistent - 264,372

    place of - 709
    posture in - 49
    to God - 124,126,206
    without ceasing – 248
    See also: Petitions
Preach, preacher, preaching - 17,32,73,102, 110,117,152,153,166,267,272,273,298, 301,394,405,433,449,450,488,629,630, 682,704,711
    apostolic - 69,119,306,340
    financial support for - 560
    the gospel, *see*: Gospel, preaching the
    motives for - 451-453,760
    the mystery - 116,374
    See also: Evangelist
Predestination - 43,54,55,352,548
    to adoption as sons - 31,41,44-46, 183,256
    double - 42,44
Pre-incarnate existence of Christ, *see*: Christ, Pre-existence
Premillennialism - 527
Presbyter(s) - 713
Prince
    of darkness, *see*: Darkness, prince of
    of the kingdom of Persia - 238
    of the powers of the air - 76-78
Principalities and powers - 281,286,317,673
    See also: Angels
Principles of the world - 312,314,334,335,337, 655,656
    See also: Elementary principles
Prisoner - 5,7,48,61
    See also: Fellow-prisoner; Paul, prisoner of Christ; Paul, prisoner in Rome
Prize - 329,459,528-531,658,716,736,738
Procession, triumphal, *see*: Triumph
Profit - 567-570
Progress - 445
    in spiritual growth - 154
    in the Christian faith - 61,460,461
    of Christianity - 23
    of the gospel, *see*: Gospel, progress of the
Promise - 59,113,553,554,558,570,712
    commandment with a - 225,226
    covenants of, *see*: Covenants of promise
    Holy Spirit of, *see*: Holy Spirit, of promise
    in Christ Jesus - 115,116
    of eternal life - 138

Promised Land - 280,369,517
Prophet(s) - 532
    My servants, the - 272,387,433
    New Testament - 51,105,111,113,
       114,145,148-150,153,159,221,
       300,378,558,562,598,666
    Old Testament - 89,99,113-115,120,
       145,247,292,303,343,385,608,
       663,752
    spirits of the - 251
Prose - 727
Proselytes - 157,512,517,604,762
Prosperity - 249,435,562,633
Providence - 55,68,95,142,232,417,424,438,
    451,498,505, 559,570,767
Province(s) - 10,13,254,261,429,446-448,502,
    573,574,581, 587,590,593,632,634,708
Provision of the Spirit of Christ - 454,455,704
Psalms - 203-205,358-361,726,754
Pseudepigrapha - 307,650,652
Pseudonymous, pseudonymity - 25,593,603,
    606,615,647, 648
    rejected - 652
Pure motives - 451
Purgatory - 88
Put off-put on - 33,162,167,168,183,348,
    350,642
Pydna, Macedonian defeat at - 710
Pythagoras, Pythagoreans - 663,670,671

Qumran - 328,658,667,668,670
Quotations from the Old Testament - 69,95,
    101,113,114,144,172,173,175,184,196,
    197,218,225,226,243,244,248,325,454,
    484,515,570,734

Rabbinic views - 78,92,144,146,238,512,671
Race, *see*: Athletic metaphor
Raised with Christ - 89,352
    See also: Baptism.
Realized eschatology, *see*: Eschatology, real-
    ized

Reconcile, reconciliation - 31,70,95,99,399,
    600,642
    cosmic - 292,293,324
    horizontal
    personal - 179,545-549,610,696,705
    to God - 59,91,95,100,101,121,137,
       275,288-291, 294,321,672
Redactor - 723
Redaction criticism - 618,652,675,724,725,
    733,748,750,755
Redemption - 31,41,43,48-50,86,90,91,111,
    118-120,252,274-276,282,283,307,362,
    374,537
    day of - 178
    eternal - 324
    of God's own possession - 59
    through His blood - 47
Refuse - 522
Regeneration - 83
    washing of - 214
    See also: New birth
Regulations - 98,322,337,357,657,660, 672
Reincarnation - 269,280,296,665,670,671
Rejoice, rejoicing - 56,130,308,309,436,452,
    453,461,496,506,549,561,573,676, 677
    crown of - 543
    in my sufferings - 297,468
    in the Lord - 4,489,510,514,548,559
    in tribulations - 255
Religious syncretism - 655,667
Renewal, renewed - 350-352
    in the spirit of your minds - 167-170
    of your mind - 557
    to a true knowledge - 349
Replacement theology - 353
Res rapienda - 737
Res rapta - 737
Res retinenda - 737
Resurrection   -
    89,296,458,523,527,541,543,667
    bodies, *see*: Bodies, resurrection
    Christ's, *see*: Christ, resurrection
    from among the dead, *see*: Dead,
       resurrection from the
    of the righteous - 526-528
    of the wicked - 527
Revelation - 112,113,251,300,305,315,343,
    525,532,610, 612,647,663
    from God - 162,313,602
    general - 76
    given to Paul - 32,109-114
    of the mystery – 119

Revelation (*continued*)
    special - 76
    spirit of - 62,65
    without a written – 80
Revelation, Book of - 69,340,639
    seven churches of - 29
Reward(s) - 228,232,269,369,370,432,544, 547,571,649,756
Rhetoric - 615,616,617,622,726
    ancient - 617
    Asiatic - 621,622
    classical - 616
    deliberative - 617,618,765
    epidiectic - 617,622
    forensic - 617
    Roman - 616
Rhetorical criticism - 615-617,620,622,725, 744,765
Riches - 66,300,543
    of Christ - 117,118,299,440
    of God - 74,570
    of His glory - 125,126,278
    of His grace - 47,49,50,84,85,570
Right hand of God - 69,70,72,73,84,146, 257,339,340, 342,672,749
Right of sanctuary - 24,25,404,697,699,700
Righteousness - 82,120,126,170,171,187,191, 192,307,320,323,344,349,443,456,468, 513,540,647,651,704
    breastplate of, *see*: Breastplate of righteousness
    crown of - 459,531
    God's - 570
    from God - 523-525
    fruit of, *see*: Fruit of righteousness
    Jesus, king of - 137
    which is in the Law - 519,520, 523,756
    See also: Breastplate of righteousness, Fruit of righteousness
Risking his life, *see*: Life, risking his
Roman Catholicism, *see*: Catholicism, Roman
Romans, Epistle to - 1,2,5,11,75,423,523,588, 602,622,623
Roman empire - 270,296,379,391,399,423, 456,622,634, 663,710
Roman emperor - 225,541
Rule - 70,672
    let Christ, in your hearts - 357
Rulers and authorities - 119,120,237,238,285, 286,316,317, 324-326,330,657
Rylands Papyrus (John fragment) - 603

Sabathikos Inscription - 669
Sabbath day - 326-329, 567,658,668
Sacrifice - 100,184,185,351,420,482,495-497, 504,568,569, 715
    without blemish - 44
    See also: Christ, sacrifice
Saint(s) - 35,51,60-62,67,114,125,128-130, 185,186,216,298-300,316,341,352,359, 570,683,703
    at Colossae - 266,268,269,627
    at Ephesus - 29,37,38,578,580,583-586
    at Philippi - 433,434,461,707
    at Rome - 573,707
    equipping of the - 33,145,152-158, 160
    fellow-citizens with the - 30,104,540
    greet every, in Christ - 572
    hearts of the - 410,411
    inheritance of the, in light - 280,281
    love toward all - 407,408,587
    Old Testament - 38,519
    perseverance of the – 438
    petition for all the - 248-250
    poor, at Jerusalem - 5,15,254,382, 425,560,604, 611,703,711
    very least of all - 117,439
Salt, speech seasoned with - 376
Salvation - 38,46,58,80,82,83,134,188,247, 262,437,453,465-467,525,537,647,704
    blessings of - 43
    by grace, *see*: Grace, saved by
    call to, God's - 134
    conditional - 88
    God's power exerted in - 67
    Gnostic ideas of - 661,664
    a gift - 87,89
    God's part and man's part in - 87,759
    gospel of your, *see*: Gospel of salvation
    helmet of, *see*: Helmet of salvation
    in/through Christ - 39,102,291,316, 750
    not a result of works - 88,90,524
    of the Gentiles - 115,301
    plan of - 73,188
    provided by God - 82,86,559,583
    work out, with fear and trembling - 488-492
Sanctified, sanctification - 120,213-216,276, 302,352,489
    by faith in Me - 115,282
    See also: Holiness

Sarcastic play on words - 513
Satan - 145,163,174,238,240,245,250,282, 469,732
   See also: Devil
Schemes of the devil - 158,236
Scheming, deceitful, *see*: Deceitful scheming
Scythian(s) - 350,351
Scythopolis - 351
Seal, sealed - 202
      ancient letters were, with wax - 584
      for the day of redemption - 178,179
      of the old covenant - 93
      with Holy Spirit - 31,41,56-58,64
Second advent, *see*: Christ, Second coming of
Selene - 635
Self-abasement - 329,330,338,475,658
Self-assertion - 135,179,475
Self-interest - 526,535
Self-made religion - 337,655,660
Self-sufficient - 561,562
Selfish ambition - 451,452,456,474,475
Selflessness - 477
Sensuality - 164,165
Septuagint (LXX) - 85,144,145,172-175,201, 220,225,237,238,241,247,279,290,293, 324,355,435,454,484,492,493,513,551, 554,555,736,741,745,746,749
Serapis - 635
Sermon on the Mount - 355,372,551,558
Servant(s) - 415
      of Christ -271-273,297,378,627
      of Elisha - 238
      of the Lord - 732
   See also: Bond-servant
Severe treatment of the body - 335,337-339, 660
Shadow of things to come - 57,328,329
Shame - 121,165,168,195,326,455,468,483, 537,537,618, 619,743
Second work of grace - 126
Sharp's rule of grammar - 151,189,206,312, 571,637
Shepherd of Hermas - 596,714
Shekinah - 63
Shield of faith - 34,245
Sick - 22,91,152,153,288,388,504,505,541, 551,552,569,708
Silas - 149,150,204,429,466,546,566,705,709
Silly talk - 186
Silvanus - 150
Sin offering - 294,324
Sincere - 442,443,492
Sinful nature - 58,79,318

Singing - 46,143,203-206,276,358-361,497, 754,755
Sin(s) - 52,76,94,100,134,163,164,168,178- 180,185,188,189,215,292,293,320,346, 539,620,662
      Adam's - 72,292,320
      atonement for, *see*: Atonement
      body of, *see*: Body of sins
      bonds of - 320
      cleansed from - 96
      dead in, *see*: Dead in trespasses and sins
      dead to, *see*: Dead to sin
      do not - 173,596
      do not let, reign - 344
      elders who - 152
      entered the world - 291,292
      forgiveness of, *see*: Forgiveness of sins
      freed from - 103,292,319
      God's displeasure with - 80,345
      guilty of - 79
      joking about - 187
      lost in - 495
      offering, *see*: Sin offering
      original, *see*: Doctrine, of original sin
      physical universe affected by - 53
      practice of - 80,190
      propitiation for - 323
      punishment for - 164
      sacrifice for - 323
      salvation from - 83,454,661
      separation from - 33,192
      slaves of - 48,49,79,88,318-320
      unforgiven - 323
   See also: Trespasses and sins.
Singleness of heart - 34,230
Sitz im Leben - 600,614,675,725
Slander - 170,179,180,347,539,560
Slave(s), slavery - 18,34,225,229,230,233, 234,367-372,400,401,483,573,663,679, 688,690,741
      branded - 19
      catchers - 17,19,592,679
      vs. free - 232,350,351
      freeing of - 48,231,433,690
      in Old Testament times - 688
      and masters - 34,207,229,264,367, 690
      names - 414,684
      no longer as a - 418
      of Jesus Christ - 34,230,231,386

Slave(s), slavery (*continued*)
  of sin, *see*: Sin, slaves of
  of their own appetites - 535
  Roman laws concerning - 688.689
  runaway - 12,261,381,399,413-415,
    420,679
  See also: Onesimus;   Masters, slave;
  Right of Sanctuary
Socio-rhetorical criticism - 620-622,721
Socrates - 670
Son of Man, *see*: Christ, Son of Man
Songs of the Sabbath Sacrifice - 670
Sons of disobedience,   *see*: Disobedience,
  sons of
Sophia - 50,275,307,668,669
Sorrow - 153,178,181,505,506
Speaking the truth - 158,159
Speech - 616,617,676
  abusive - 170,347
  bold - 455,456
  clean in - 33,176
  filthiness of - 186
  foul - 347
  gracious - 264,376
  improper - 263,347
  purity of - 33,185,186
  unwholesome - 177
  with grace - 187,198,376
Spirit
  forbearing - 550
  human - 64,65,76,81-83,126,127,
    137,163,167-169,178,202,216,
    249,273,318,320,321,339,349,
    471,514,515,542,574,669
  I am with you in - 308
  kindred - 499,572
  now working in sons of disobedience
    - 78
  of the mind - 169,349
  of wisdom - 62,63
  standing firm in one - 464,544
  the Lord be with your - 425,574,677
  united in - 472,473
  worship God in the - 514
  See also: Holy Spirit; Inner man
Spiritism - 88,245,281,315,317,656,663
  See also: Animism; Elemental spirits;
    Evil spirits
Spiritual blessing(s), *see*: Blessing, Spiritual
Spiritual gifts - 143,149,272,390,638
Spiritual growth - 154156,392,529,531,543
Spiritual songs - 203-205, 358-361,754
Spiritual wisdom, *see*: Wisdom, spiritual

Stature - 33,130,154-156,160,181,597
Steadfastness - 61,278,279,293,295,589
Stealing - 175,176,312
Steward, stewardship - 52,299,465
  from God - 298,299
  of God's grace - 109,110,587,598
Stoicism - 363,554,561,562,636
Stranger(s) - 30,37,93,94,96,104,163,290,522,
  540,589
Strife - 386,449,450,474,716
Struggle - 237-239,241,245,247,290,304,305,
  349,466,545-547
Subjection, submission - 34,58,71,73,198,207-
  212,223-225,227,229,231,233,334,335,
  364,365,422,485,492,515, 746
Substance belongs to Christ - 328
Suffering - 353,468,526,732
  need - 562,563
  whole creation is - 292
  See also: Christ, sufferings;   Paul,
    suffering
Suffering Servant Poems - 480,732,732,739,
  741,766
Supreme Being (Gnostic) - 296,662,664,665,
  668
Sword of the Spirit - 34,246-248
Synagogue - 146,567,669
Syntyche - 544,546,548,549-554,705,717
Syriac Versions - 144,379,574,590,644,692,
  717,757
Syzygus - 431,545-547,705

Tacitus - 389,446,634
Teachers - 145,148-152,558,562,764
  deceitful, *see*: Deceitful teachers
  false, *see*: False teachers
  Gnostic - 269,282,308,665
  Jewish - 16
  Judaizing - 512
Teachings of men - 336,337,660
Temple
  at Jerusalem - 5,97,107,445
  idol's, *see*: Idol's temple
  in heaven - 457
  of Aretmis - 697
  of god, *see*: Church, temple of God
  of the Holy Spirit - 318
  pagan - 388
  taxes - 635
  the church - 31,103,105-107

Temptation(s) - 58,248,249,344,350,732
    See also: Christ, temptations of
Tender-hearted - 180,181,339,355
Tertullian   -   204,440,583-585,588,590,597,
    643,660,661,691,716,742
Textus Receptus - 66,119,379,387,472,533,
    575
Thanks, thankfulness
        in the name of Lord - 206,361
        to God - 31,39,62,117,132,206,267,
            361,436,570,683
    See also: Gratitude
Thanksgiving, introductory - 436,580
        in Colossians - 262,267,627
        in Ephesians - 31,39,580
        in Philemon - 406,683,701
        in Philippians - 430,435,703
Theology of hope - 67
Theophilus of Antioch - 642,715
Thessalonians, Epistles to
Thessalonica - 4,22,23,382,425,429,437,523,
    560,565-567,706,708,709,711
Things
        above - 169,263,339,340,642
        all, become visible - 195,196
        approve the, that are excellent - 442
        done in secret - 194,195
        giving thanks for all - 206
        He might fill all - 147,148
        I can do all - 563
        in heaven - 53,285,291,292,485,748
        let your mind dwell on these - 557
        on earth - 53,169,285,291,341,485,
            748
        put all, in subjection - 71
        sum up all, in Christ - 41,51,53
        under the earth
        vain - 94
Third heaven - 42,147,239
Three levels of material in the New Testament,
    alleged – 614,675,733,751
Throne(s) - 71,82,285,286
        Christ's – 82,84
        David's - 70,146
        in heaven - 69,71,84,340,765
        Nero's - 252
        of God - 286,332,340,457,765
        of grace - 121
Time(s)
        fulness of - 41,52
        pray at all - 248-250
        use of - 198-201

Timothy - 21,148,150,254,265,266,272,358,
    383,403,405,433,498-501,566,587,591,
    610,611,639,703
Timothy, Epistles to - 1,65,502,676,720
Titus - 150,152,254,272,419,560
Titus, Epistle to - 1,90,392,406,436,502,692
Tradition(s)
        early church - 7,9,10,15,383,385,
            547,583,681,695,698,712
        Jewish - 262,314,512,519,524,657
        of men - 312-314,337,643,656,668,
            673,759
        oral, *see*: Oral tradition
        Zoroastrian - 313,668
Transformation - 191,217,247,349,401,541-
    543,557
Trespasses and sins - 47,49,75-77,79,82,89,
    126,163,235,320,324,515
Trickery of men - 156-159
Triumph - 324-326
Trinity, *see*: Godhead
Trophimus - 505
Trust - 23,86,291,299,309,447,448,501,502,
    611,696
Truth - 76,111,149,159,172,270,310,452,612
        all, is relative - 725
        apostles led into all -114
        deviate from - 49,76
        fruit of light - 191,192
        girdle of - 34,241,242
        God's - 64
        holiness of the - 170
        is in Jesus - 166,167
        Jesus taught - 76
        message of, *see*: Gospel, message
            of truth
        sanctify them in the - 215
        speaking the, in love - 158,172
        tell the - 33,171,243
        walking in the - 159
Tubingen School - 544
Tychicus - 3,4,16,19,24,25,29,30,35,150,253-
    255,257,261,264,378-381,386,393,396,
    581-583,586,589,591,592,594,609,611,
    612,628,629,631,652,674-676,679,686,
    687,693,696
Types and shadows - 57

Uncircumcision - 91,92,140,320,321,350,513, 514,604,636
Understanding - 50,65,111-113,120,130,163, 166,200,201,209,249,274-276,305-307, 422,465,533,553
Underworld - 748,749
Unfathomable riches of Christ - 117,118, 299,440
Unfruitful deeds of darkness - 193,194, 196,197
Unity - 99,136,141,255,430,474,511,604,766
    bond of - 137,305,356
    congregational - 434,511,582
    exhortation to - 134
    of Philippians,   see: Philippians, integrity
    of all believers - 31,75,471
    of the faith, see: Faith, unity of
    of the Spirit, see: Holy Spirit, unity of the
    plea for - 471,472,572,582,764
    preserving the - 33,136,137,142,604
  See also: Church, unity of.
Universe - 43,53,111,148,171,184,262,282-288,290,362,485,493,527,661,669,671, 740,748
Universalism - 53,291
Upward call of God - 459,528,530-532
Useful, usefulness - 176,383,414,415,423,684, 700

Vain
    deceit - 643
    I did not run in - 494
    things – 94
    toil in - 494,495
Valentinianism - 330,597,659
  See also: Gnosticism
Vices - 165,189,191,195,345-348,358
    catalogs of - 185,343,554
    to eliminate - 263,343
Vienne and Lyons, Epistle to - 298,715
Virtues - 133,135,181,182,192,195,353,356, 357,475,483,557
    catalogs of - 180,554
    to cultivate - 172,180,263,343,349, 352,357,431,548-554,561
Visions - 69,298,332,429,663
    self-induced - 263,329,331,332,335, 659,663,670,762

Vocabulary
    arguments based on - 601,644,647, 648,651,730

Walk - 77,89,90,134,276,309,310,346,533-536
    according to the course of this world - 76
    as children of light - 190-193
    as Gentiles do - 162-164,168
    be careful how you - 198
    in a manner worthy of the Lord - 276
    in love - 33,183
    in newness of life - 82,289,319, 322,339,341,349
    in truth, see: Walking in the truth
    in wisdom - 33,198
    let us, by the same rule - 533
    winsome - 375
    worthy of the calling - 133,134,142, 172
Wall - 105
    dividing - 96,97
Walls, broken, see: Jews and Gentiles; Reconciliation: horizontal; Slave v. free.
Washing
    ceremonial - 215,319,663,667
    of regeneration - 214
    of water - 213-217
Weakness - 240,354,564
    Paul's bodily - 762
    Holy Spirit helps our - 249
    human - 184,541
Western Text - 70,273
Wickedness - 365
    spiritual forces of - 237,239
Will - 55
    both to, and to work - 490,491
    counsel of His - 37,41,54,55
    freedom of the, see: Free will
    good - 34,37,180,183,230,231,369, 449,450,491,716
    ill - 178-180
    kind intention of His - 44-46
    mystery of His - 50,51,88
    of God - 31,41,51,53,230,231,265, 274-276,300,325,375,386,387, 460,489,491,492,524,636,741
    of the Lord - 33,133,198,200,201, 224,422,502,690

Wind of doctrine - 156-158, 387
Wisdom - 120,271,301,302,359,375,643,656, 715
    appearance of - 337,338
    Christian - 33,198,279
    Jesus grew in - 156
    of God, *see*: God, wisdom of
    of men - 275
    spirit of - 62-65
    spiritual - 274,275
    treasures of - 306,307
    See also: Jewish Wisdom Literature; Sophia
Wisdom discourse - 613
Wives and husbands - 34,207-213,217,220, 223,264,363-365,608
Women - 209,431,519,544,545-550,705,764
Word - 361
    of Christ - 57,203,295,320,358-360, 413,449,467,757
    of confession - 216
    of life - 492-495
    of God - 1,138,155,188,192,193, 196,215,246-248,273,298,299, 447-450,704,751
    of the Lord - 394,404,581,636
    of truth - 262,269,270,313
    unwholesome- 176-178,377
Work ethic - 176,372,419
Workmanship, God's - 87,89,171
Works
    of darkness, *see*: Darkness, deeds of
    of faith, *see*: Faith, works of
    of the Law - 88,512,520,521,524, 525,602,758
    of merit - 521
    of supererogation - 88
World - 95,119,183,186,270,296,317,342,480, 494,555
    ancient - 13,37,92,175,306,388,400, 433,510,585,616,699,703,705
    conduct in the - 32,133,234
    creation of the - 46,119,285,286, 662,738
    death entered the - 291
    elementary principles of the - *see*: Elementary principles
    end of the - 240
    evangelization of the - 299
    foundation of the - 42-44,90,214,527
    God loved the - 43,45
    god of this, *see*: Devil, god of this world

    heavenly - 108
    Hellenistic - 663,762
    light bearers in the - *see*: Light bearers
    living in the - 334,335,457
    Mediterranean - 296,618,663,668, 710
    pagan - 138
    present - 190,226,390,425,630,748
    reconciling the - 324
    Roman - 418,574,616,684,686,688
    sin entered the - 291
    spiritual - 285,661
    the course of this - 76,77
    to come - 190,229,748
    unregenerate - 77
    unseen - 314,648
    without God in the - 93,94,293
World forces, world rulers (*kosmokratores*) - 237,238,246,281
Worship - 73,103,141,185,195,237,330,337, 338,485,513,515,569,658
    assemble for - 93,233,361,394,405
    Christian - 391,485,487,678,722, 728,746,754
    in the Spirit, *see*: Spirit, worship in the
    of angels - 262,286,325,329,330, 611,658,659,669,678
    of God - 485,514
    of idols or heathen gods - 195,326, 388,634,635,761
    the emperor - 540
Worthy
    of the calling - 133,172
    of the gospel - 193,462,463,767
    of the Lord - 276,278
Wrath - 80,170,179,346,347,596
    children of, *see*: Children of wrath
    of God, *see*: God, wrath of
Wrinkle - 216,604

Xerxes - 633

Zechariah - 101
Zend Avesta - 313,668
Zoroastrianism - 281,282,313,661,668,669

OTHER BOOKS BY GARETH L. REESE

New Testament History: *Acts* (097-176-5235)

New Testament Epistles: *Romans* (097-176-5200)

New Testament Epistles: *1 Corinthians* (097-176-5251)

New Testament Epistles: *2 Corinthians and Galatians* (097-176-5278)

New Testament Epistles: *1 & 2 Thessalonians* (099-845-186X)

New Testament Epistles: *1 & 2 Timothy and Titus* (097-176-5227)

New Testament Epistles: *Hebrews* (097-176-5219)

New Testament Epistles: *1 & 2 Peter and Jude* (097-176-5243)

New Testament Epistles: *James & 1,2,3 John* (097-176-526X)

Order from:
Scripture Exposition Books
803 McKinsey Place
Moberly, MO, 65270
www.glreese@cccb.edu

www.ingramcontent.com/pod-product-compliance
Lightning Source LLC
Chambersburg PA
CBHW061957090426
42811CB00006B/964